ENGLISH RECUSANT LITERATURE
1558–1640

Selected and Edited by
D. M. ROGERS

Volume 311

THOMAS STAPLETON
A Counterblast
1567

THOMAS STAPLETON

A Counterblast to M. Hornes Vayne
Blast against M. Fekenham

1567

The Scolar Press
1976

ISBN o 85967 323 5

Published and printed in Great Britain by
The Scolar Press Limited, 59-61 East Parade,
Ilkley, Yorkshire and
39 Great Russell Street,
London WC1

NOTE

Reproduced (original size) from a copy in Cambridge University Library, by permission of the Syndics.

References: Allison and Rogers 796; STC 23231.

A COUNTERBLAST TO
M. HORNES VAYNE

BLASTE AGAINST M.
Fekenham. Wherein is set
forthe:

A ful Reply to M. Hornes Anfwer, and to euery part ther-
of made, againſt the Declaration of my L. Abbat of
Weſtminſter, M. Fekenham, touching, The
Othe of the Supremacy.

By peruſing vvhereof ſhall appeare, beſides the holy Scriptures, as it vvere a
Chronicle of the Continual Practiſe of Chriſtes Churche in al ages and
Countries, frō the time ef Conſtantin the Great, vntil our daies:
Prouing the Popes and Biſhops Supremacy in Eccleſiaſti-
cal cauſes: and Diſprouing the Princes Supremacy
in the ſame Cauſes.

By Thomas Stapleton Student in Diuinitie.

Athanaſ. in Epiſt. ad ſolita. vitā agentes. pag. 459.

When was it heard from the creation of the worlde, that the
Iudgement of the Churche ſhould take his authoritie from the
Emperour? Or when was that taken for any iudgement?

Ambr. lib. 5. epiſt. 32.

In good footh, if we call to minde either the whole courſe of
Holy Scripture, or the practiſe of the auncient times paſſed, who
is it that can deny, but that in matter of faith, in matter, I ſaie, of
faith, Biſhops are wont to iudge ouer Chriſtian Emperours, not
Emperours ouer Biſhops?

LOVANII,
Apud Joannem Foulerum,
An. 1567. Cum Priuil.

Regiæ Maiestatis Gratia Speciali Concessum est Thomæ Stapletono Anglo, librum inscriptum, A Counterblaste to M. Hornes Vaine Blaste &c. per aliquem Typographorum admissorum tutò & liberè imprimendum curare, & publicè distrahere, nullo prohibente. Datum Bruxellis. 27. Maij Anno. 1 5 6 7.

Subsig.

Pratz.

TO M. ROBERT HORNE,

THOMAS STAPLETON WISHETH
Grace from God, and true repentance of
al Herefies.

F the natural *wifedome and forefight,*
M. Horne, defcribed of our Sauiour in
the Gofpel by a parable, had bene in you,
at what tyme you firſt fet penne to pa-
per, to treate of the Othe of Supremacy:
you would not, I fuppofe, fo rafhly haue attempted an en-
terprife of fuch importance. The Parable faith. VVho   Luc. 14.
is it amonge you, that minding to build a Caftle,
fitteth not doune firſt and reckoneth vvith him
felf the charges requifit thereunto, to fee if he be
able to bring it to paffe, left that hauing layed the
foundation, and then not able to make an ende, al
that fee him, begin to laugh him to fcorne, faying, beholde: this man beganne to builde, but he
hath not bene able to make an ende? *The matter*
you haue taken in hande to proue, is of fuch and fo greate
importaunce, as no matter more nowe in Controuerfie.

It is the Caftle of your profeſſion. The keye of your
doctrine. The principal forte of all your Religion. It is
the piller of your Authority. The fountaine of your Iu-
rifdiction. The Ankerholde of all your proceedinges.
                    * ij   *VVithout*

THE PREFACE

Without the right of this Supreme Gouernement by you here defended, your cauſe is betrayed, your doctrine diſſolueth, your whole Religion goeth to wracke. The wante of this Right ſhaketh your Authoritye, ſtoppeth your Iuriſdiction, and is the vtter ſhipwracke of all your Procedings.

Againe, it toucheth (you ſay) the prerogatiue of the Prince. It is the only matter which Catholikes ſtand in, by parliamēt enacted, by booke Othe required, vpō greate penalty refuſed. Other matters in cōtrouerſy whatſoeuer, are not ſo preſſed.

Thirdly, you haue takē vpon you to perſuade ſo great a matter, firſt to a right lerned and reuerēt Father, in priuat cōferēce: and next to al the realme of Englād, by publiſhing this your Anſwer, as you cal it. The weightier the matter is, and the more confidently you haue taken it vpō you, the more is it looked for, and reaſon would, that you did it ſubſtantially, lernedly, ād truly: and before you had entred to ſo great a worke, to haue made your reckoning, how you might bring it to perfection.

But now what haue you don? Haue you not ſo wrought, that all your faire building being cleane ouerthrowen, mē beginne (as the Ghoſpell ſaieth) to laughe you to ſcorne, ſaying: Beholde, this man beganne a great matter, but beinge not able to finiſhe it, he is fayne to breake of?

You will ſay: Theſe be but woordes of courſe, and a

ccrtaine

certain triumphe before the Victory. Haue I not groūded this work of myne vpō the foundatiō of holy Scriptures? Haue I not posted it vp with the mighty stronge pillers, of the most learned Fathers? Haue I not furnished it with a ioyly variety of Stories deducted from al the most Christian Emperours, Kinges and Princes of more then these. xij. hundred yeares? Haue I not sensed it with inuicible rampars of most holy Councels both general and national? And last of al, haue I not remoued all such scruples and stayes of conscience, as though it were, brambles and briers out of the waye, to make the passage to so fayre a Forte, pleasant, easy, and commodious?

You haue in dede M. Horne, in owtwarde shewe, and countenance sette a gay glorious and glistering face vppon the matter : A face I say, of holy Scriptures, of Fathers, of the Canon, the Ciuill, and the lawe of the Realme, of manye Emperours, Kinges and Princes (for proufe of a continuall practise of the like Supremacye nowe by Othe to the Q. Highnes attributed) in the auncient Churches of England, Fraunce, Germany, Spayne, Italy, Grece, Armenia, Moscouia, Æthyopia: But all is but a Face in dede, and a naked shewe, without Substāce of Truth and matter.

It is like, to the Aples and grapes and other fruits of the countrey of Sodome and Gomorre, which growing to a full rypenes and quantitye in sight, seeme to the eye very faire and pleasant : but when a man cometh to plucke

Aug. de ci
uit. Dei li.
21. cap. 5.
Iul. Soli=
nus ca. 48.
Cornel.
Tacit. li. 8.
Aegesipp.
lib. 4.

* iij *of them*

THE PREFACE

of them and to taſt, he ſhal finde them vnnaturall and pe=
ſtilente, and to ſmoder and ſmoke away, and to reſolue
into aſhes. Such is the effect of your whole booke: It bea=
reth a countenance of truth, of reaſon, of learning. But
coming to the trial and examination of it, I finde a peſti=
lent ranke of moſt ſhamefull Vntruths, an vnſauery and
vaine kinde of reaſoning, and laſt of al, the whole to re=
ſolue into groſſe Ignorance. For proufe hereof, I wil ſhort=
ly lay forth, an abridgement of your whole demeanour.

M. Horns
Grāmer.

And wherewith ſhal I better begin, thē with the begi=
ning and foundatiō of al ſciēces, and that is, with grāmer
it ſelf? Whereof I neuer heard or read in any man, bea=
ring the vocation that you pretēde, either more groſſe ig=
norance, or which is more likely and much worſe, more
ſhameful and malicious corruptiō. You Engliſh Conue=
nit: which is, it is mete and conuenient, into,

Aunſwer Fol. 42.
col. 1.
Replie Fol. 180.
col. 1.
Aunſwer Fol. 53.
col. 2.
Replie Fol. 217.
Aunſwer Fol. 79.
col. 1.
Replie Fol. 311.
col. 2.
Aunſwer Fol 83
col 1.
Reply Fol. 350.
col. 2.

it ought: which is the Engliſh of oportet, not
of, conuenit. You Engliſh Recenſendam, to
be examined and confirmed, where it ſigni=
fieth ōly, to be read or reherſed. Item where
your Author hath Priuilegia irrogare, that
is, To geue priuileges, you translate it quyte
contrarye: To take avvaye Priuileges.
Againe in the ſame Author, pro quauis cauſa:
which is, for euery cauſe: you trāſlate it, for any
cauſe, as if it were, pro qualibet or quacūq;
cauſa. Al which foule ſhiftes of howe much im=
portance

portaunce they were, I referre you to the leaues of this booke, here noted vnto you in the margin, together with the leaues of your own booke. Many like gay grāmaticall practises might yet be shewed. Yea in your late Visitation at Oxforde, exercised by your Chauncelour and sonne in Lawe (as beside al lawe you cal him, hauing maried your bastard, not your lawful daughter) in al the copies of articles that your said Chauncelour proposed to be subscribed, are these woordes: Regina supremus Gubernator Ecclesiæ Anglicanæ : for Suprema gubernatrix: And so remaineth that clause to this houre vnreformed. So that, if it were nothing, but for false Latin, a scholer might honestly refuse to subscribe to such an Article.

An. 1566.
Comp. Anglic. Mar. 18.
See more of this in this Replye, fol. 480. b.

   Nowe what shal I say of your logike and exact kind of reasoning? As there is nothing in a writer more requisit, that meaneth truly, so the more you haue broken the rules therof, the more is your shame, and the lesse ought the credit of your whole Booke to be. I neede not descend to the particulars, your perpetuall maner of writing being suche, as your whole discourse seemeth nothing els but a mishapen lumpe of lewde and loose argumentes. For this being the matter which you haue taken iu hande to proue by the examples of other Princes, and by the practise of Councells, that the Laye Magistrates are Supreme Gouernours in all Ecclesiastical causes, this vniuersall proposition being that which should be concluded, your premisses

M. Horns Logike.

mißes

*miſſes are allwaies mere particulars: your proufes proᵈ
cede euer of ſome one fact or matter Eccleſiaſtical, but
neuer of all: And yet thoſe matters that you bring, being
partly no Eccleſiaſtical matters at all, partly vntruly
fathered vppon the laye Magiſtrate. So that, as euer you
faile in truth of matter, ſo you neuer make good forme of
argument. And you can tell your ſelfe: (they be your*

Anſvver.
fol. 108. a.

owne wordes) that younge Logicians knovve, this
is an euil conſequent, that concludeth vpon one
or diuerſe particulars affirmatiuely an vniuerſal.
*This euil conſequent M. Horn, is the only conſequét that
you make in all your booke, where you play the Opponents*

Anſvver.
fol. 4. fol.
100. fol.
105.

*parte. For the which I referre you and the Reader to the
three firſt bookes of this Reply. VVith the like good lo=
gique you lay forthe falſe definitions and falſe diuiſions
of your owne Inuention.*

M. Horns
Rhetorik

*As for your Rhetorike, you worke your matters ſo
handſomly and ſo perſuaſiuely, that there is not almoſt a=
ny one Scripture, any ſtory, any Councel, any Father, any
Author ỹ you alleage, which maketh not directly againſt
your purpoſe, and beareth withal an expreſſe and euidét
teſtimony for the Popes Supremacy, not only otherwher,
but euen in the very ſame place and allegation that you
alleage and grounde your ſelfe vpon. And this chaunceth
not once or twiſe, but in a maner cuſtomably, as by per=
uſing this Reply, you ſhal ſoone perceyue. And therefore
I wil not ſpecially note it here vnto you, as a rare or ſeldome*

dome thinge. Neither will I thanke you for bringing to our handes so good stuffe to proue our principall purpose by, but say herein vnto you, as S. Augustin sayd in the like case of the Donatistes, alleaging the workes of Optatus, by the which they were euer confounded, and the Catho= likes cause maruailously furdered. Nec tamé ipsis, sed Deo potius hinc agimus gratias: vt enim illa om= nia vel loquendo, vel legendo pro causa nostra promerent, atque propalarent, veritas eos tor= sit, non charitas inuitauit. *Neither doe we yet thanke them for their so doing, but rather God. For that they should bring forth and vtter either by talke, or by allea= ging, al those thinges for our matter, the Truth forced them, not any Charity inuited thē. And truly so M. Horn, that by your own Authors you are euer confounded, the Truthe of our cause forceth you, as not being able to al= leage any Author that maketh not for vs, not any good wil to our cause or to vs moued you.*

Aug. cont. Dona. post Collation. cap. 34.

Againe what a newe Cicero, or Demosthenes are you, that laye forth to M. Fekenham, as a good and a persua= sible motiue, to enduce him to take the Othe of the Princes Primacy, the former erroneous doinges of certayne Re= uerend Fathers, whereof they haue so farre repented, that for refusal of this Othe thei haue suffred depriuation, and haue and doe suffer imprisonment, and are ready besides, by Gods assistance, patiently to suffer, whatsoeuer Gods prouidence hath gratiously prouided for them? Where=

**

vnto

vnto both they and other haue good caufe much the more to be encouraged, cōfidering that after al this ftruggling and wraftling againft the Truth by you ād your felowes M. Iewel and the reft, the Truth is daily more and more opened, illuftred, and confirmed . And your contrary do= ctrine is or ought to be difgraced and brought in vtter difcredit, with fuch as doe but indifferently weigh the moft wretched and miferable handling of the holy Fa= thers and Councelles before by M. Iewel, as al Englande knoweth, and nowe by you Maifter Horne, which are not much inferior to him in that pointe of legerdemayne. For as in his moft lying Reply againft D. Harding, fo in this your Anfwer to M. Fekenhams treatife, there is neither Scripture, nor Coūcel, nor doctour, nor any thing els that cometh through your hands, which you doe not miferably mangle, corrupte, and peruerte: and that by a number of difhoneft and fhameful fhifts: which particularly to fpe= cifie would be to long and tedioufe.

But to fay fomwhat for an example, the principall parte of all your fhifting ftandeth in a certaine merue= loufe kind of a newe and a falfe Arithmetike, fomtime by Addition, fometime by diminution and Detraction.

Thus to make your matter of the Princes Supreme go= uernement in al ecclefiaftical caufes more probable, you interlace twife thefe woordes (as one that had the cure and authoritie ouer all)*and againe, in the fame leaf*(as one that had authoritie ouer them)*which* *you find*

M. Horns miferable peruertig of his au= thours.

By addi= tion.

1. Anfwer fo. 20. b. Reply fo. 88. b.

you finde not in your Authours.

Thus you shuffle in this pretye sillable (All) *to Socrates, and againe to Theodoretus.*

So you springle in these woordes (by his su- preame authoritie) *to your narration out of the saied Theodoretus. And by and by to your nar- ration out of Sozomenus, these woordes* (and the Bishops could not remoue him.)

So you adde to Liberatus this woorde (de- pose:) *And to the Actes of the Chalcedon Coū- cell, these woordes,* (vvhich othervvise must be deposed.) *And to the Actes of the sixt Ge- nerall Councell these woordes* (to examine and confirme.)

You thrust into the narration of Antoninus *and* Marius, *that which they say not: and to the narration of* Quintinus Heduus *fyue ful lines, that are not in your author touching* Pope Iohn *the.* 22. *and many other like things otherwhere.*

And yet I can not tel, whether your peruersity be more in your false multiplication, or in your false diminution. In framing the state of the que- stion by the statutes of the realme, you leaue out the beginninge and the ende of the Statute. You leaue out of Ma- *cians oration.* ij. *or.* iij. *woordes, that make moste againste you. You pare awaye from the sentence that your selfe*

** ij   *reherseth*

2.
Ansvver fo. 22. a.
Reply. fo. 98. b.

3.
Ansvver fol. 24. b.
Reply. fol. 107. b.

4.
Ansvver fol. 16. a.
Replie fol. 115 b.

5.
Ansvver Fol. 26 b
Replie Fol. 116. b

6.
Ansvver fo 30. a.
Replie Fol. 118. b

7.
Ansvver Fol. 32. b
Reply. Fol. 144. a

8.
Ansvver fol. 53. b.
Replie. fo. 216. b.

9.
Ausvver fol. 81. a
Replie fol. 334. a

10.
Ansvver fol. 89 b
Replie fol. 378. b

By *Diminution.*

1.
Ansvver fol 19. b
Replie fol. 83. a

2.
Ansvver fol. 33. a
Reply fo. 147. a

3.
Anſvver
Fol. 36.
Replie
Fol. 162.

reherſeth out of the fourthe Romaine councel, the tayle of it immediatly following your own words: that is, Totam cauſam Dei iudicio reſeruantes, quite ouerthrowing your newe ſupremacy.

4.
Anſvver
fo. 37. b.
Replie
Fol. 167. a

In like maner from the narration of the ambaſſadry of Pope Iohn, you conceale the neceſſary circumſtances of the ſame: as you doe frō many other narrations, the which being truely ſet in, doe vtterly deſtroye al your vntrue aſſertions. After this ſorte to theſe woordes of Iuſtinian the

5.
Anſvver
Fo. 42. a.
Reply. fo.
Fol. 179 b

Emperour (theſe things vve haue determined) you choppe in of your owne (by ſentence) and withal choppe awaye that which immediatly followeth, ſanctorū Patrum Canones ſequuti.

In this maner whereas throughout your booke, one of your great matters to proue Emperours and Kinges ſu

6.
Anſvver
fol 74.
& ſo 78. a
Replie. fo.
Fol. 282. d.
&. 306. a.

preme heades of the Churche, is the inueſturing of biſhops (which yet neuertheleſſe is but an impertinent matter) you tell vs ſtil of this inueſturing, and make a great buſie nedeleſſe ſturre about it, but y̌ the ſaid Emperor or Kīg, as for example Charlemaine, Otho the firſt, and other receyued that priuilege from the See of Rome, and againe that other Emperours and Kinges, as for example, themperour Henry the. 5. in Germany, and in England King Henry the firſt, yelded afterwarde, and gaue ouer the ſaid inueſturing, which things appere aſwel by other Authors, as by your owne that your ſelfe alleageth, you paſſe them ouer with great ſilence. For yf you had tolde theſe

and

and such like stories of the inuesturing of Bisshops true=
ly and fully, then had your newe supremacy bene quite di=
stroyed.

For the saied cause, whereas you telle, vs that Philip
the Frenche kinge swore the Pope to certaine conditions,
you altogether dissemble, what those conditions were.

For the same cause, you leaue out of your Author Io.
Anth. Delphinus in the middle of the sentēce, a line or two:
Least that yf you had sincerely sette in those woordes,
they would haue ouerthrowen your fonde, folishe and he=
retical paradoxe, that the Authoritye to excommunicate
appertayneth neither to Bishop, nor Priest.

Wel, to sette a side (least we be to tediouse) all other
places of like corruption (which plentifuly abunde euery
where in your aunswere) we will only touche, of a greate
number, two or thre, apperteining to our own domesticall
stories.

You will proue to vs, that King Henry the first was
supreme head of the Churche of England and why trowe
you? Forsoth because the spiritual condescended, in a
Councel at London, that the Kings officiers should pu=
nish Priestes for whoredome. Is not this I praye you an
importante and a mighty argumente, to proue the Kings
supremacye by, which rather directly proueth the clear=
gies supremacye, of whome the Kinge had this authori=
tye? And yet such are your accustomable arguments, as
may sone appere to the reader. But this is not the thinge

** ij   we now

7.
Ansvver
fo. 80 b.
Reply fo.
330.a.

8.
Ansvver
fo. 106. a.
Reply. fo.
448.a.

9.
Anſvver
fol. 77.a
Replie
fo. 299.a

*we nowe ſeeke for : but to knowe , what kinde of whore-
dome it was, that the Prieſts ſhould be puniſſhed for . Lo
this, though you alleage. 7. marginal authors , durſte you
not ones touche . For yf you had, you had withall proued
your own whoredome, ād ſuch as is much worſe then was
theirs.*

10.
Anſvver
fol. 39.b
Replie
fo. 380.a

*Againe you labour to proue by Browghton a temporal
Lawier , that by the Lawe of the realme, the King was
then taken for ſupreme head of the Church ,* for that all
are vnder the King , and the Kinge is vnder God
only , *but you moſt ſhamefully diſſemble, that the ſaid
Browghton ſpeaketh but of the Kings authority in temporal things: and that in the place by your ſelf alleaged, he
ſaith,* that as Emperours and Kings are the chiefe
rulers for temporal things: ſo for ſpiritual things
the Pope, is the chief ruler, and vnder him, Arch-
biſshops, Biſshops and other.

*But of al other Lyes, this that we ſhal nowe ſhewe is
one moſt Capitayne, and notable. Of al ſtories by you moſt
miſerably and wretchedly pinched, pared , and diſmembred , the ſtorie of our firſt and noble Chriſtiā King Lucius, is moſt ſhamefully contaminated, depraued, and deformed . The conſent of al ſtories as wel Domeſticall
as externall , yea as wel of Catholikes as of heretikes (as
farre as I can yet by diligente ſearche, poſsibly finde) is,
that the ſaied Kinge Lucius was chriſtened by the helpe,
aduice , and inſtruction of Pope Eleutherius . But you
M. Horne*

*M. Horne beare such a spitefull and malitiouse hart to
the Pope, and to the See of Rome, that contrarye to
the narration of all other, yea of your owne dere bro=
ther Bale (the cheife antiquarye of Englishe Prote=
stantes) you auouche, that he and his subiectes were
baptized, and that he reformed the Heathnishe reli=
gion, and did other thinges, that you reherse out of Po=*
lidore, vvithout any Authoritie, knovvledge
or confent of the Pope. *And yet befide all other,
your owne authour Polidorus, fayeth, that he was chri=
ftened, and the prophane worshippinge of the falfe
Gods was banyshed, and other thinges done by the ad=
monition, helpe, and aduice of the faid Pope Eleu=
therius Ambaffadours. And therefore you reherfing
Polidorus woordes of the faide Kinge Lucius mofte
falfly and lewdely, doe cutte awaye from Polidorus his
fentence (by your felfe recyted) all that euer Polido=
rus writeth of Pope Eleutherius and his Legats.*

 *I trufte Maifter Horne, that, when any indiffe=
rente Reader hath well confidered, thefe and fuche
other like partes, that euery where you playe in this
your Aunfwere, and withall, the cancred and malicioufe
harte that you beare to the Apoftolicall See of Rome,
which moft euidently burfteth out in the handling of
the forefayde ftory of Lucius, he fhall fynde good caufe
to take yowe as you are, falfe and malicioufe, and not to*
truft

II.
Anfvver
fol.93.b
Keplie
fol.397.

Anſwer
fol. 47. a.
& fol. 55.

truſt the reporte of ſuch a partial writer, yea of ſuch an evident falſary. But it is no newes for a man of your coate, to be partial in Popes matters, or to cal the Pope himſelf the childe of perdition, or to terme his lawful doings, Horrible practiſes, *as you doe.*

Anſwer
fol. 101. b.
Reply.
fol. 435. a.
& 436. b.

But to avouche him to be a more periculous ene∗ my to Chriſt, then the Turke, *and that* Popery is much more idolatrous, then Turkery, *I thinke you are the firſt Engliſh proteſtant, that ever wrote ſo Turkiſhly. Such Turkiſh trechery might better haue bene borne in the laviſhing language of your hotte ſpur= red Miniſters in pulpit, then in the adviſed writing of a prelate of the Garter in printe. With the like diſcretiõ you cal bleſſed S. Auguſtin, of whome we Engliſhmen firſt receyued our Chriſtendome, in contempt and deri∗*

Anſwer
fol. 58. &
59.

ſion, the Popes Apoſtle, *maligning in him the name of the Apoſtle of Englande, and calling him beſide, together with the bleſſed Apoſtle of Germany and Martyr, Bo= nifacius,* blinde guides and blinde buſſardes. *But who ſo bolde as blinde bayarde? or who can ſee leſſe in o= ther men, then ſuch as can ſee nothing in them ſelues? And what doe you els herein, but like a furious Aiax, thinking to deface the Pope, fall a whipping and rayling at his ſhepe, (ſuch ſhepe, I ſay as Chriſt committed to Pe= ter, whoſe ſucceſſour the Pope is) as Aiax in his fury whipped the ſhepe of Vliſſes, thinking he had whipped Vliſſes himſelfe? But as the fury of Aiax reached not to*
Vliſſes

Vlyſſes perſon, but onely encreaſed his owne miſery and madnes: ſo your Turkiſh talke M. Horne, blemiſheth not the See Apoſtolike, or hurteth it the valewe of one ruſhe, but only expreſſeth the Turkiſh ſprit that lurketh within you. Therefore bluſter and blowe, fume and frete, raue ād raile, as lowdely as lewdely, as beſtly as boldly, do what you can you muſt heare, as the Donatiſts hearde of S. Auguſtine: Ipſa eſt Sedes, quam ſuperbæ non vincũt inferorum portæ. *That See of Peter, is the See, which the proude gates of hel doe not ouercome. The more you kick againſt that Rock, the more your break your ſhinne.*

You bluſter not ſo boyſterouſly againſt the Pope, as you lie moſt lewdely vpon the right Reuerent, and lerned Father M. Fekenham, whoſe perſon you impugne, for lacke of iuſte matter, with moſt ſlaunderous Reproches. As where you ſay of him, that the Catholikes had euer a feare of his reuolting, *that,* he ſemed in a maner reſolued and ſatiſſied in this matter, *that,* his doinges ſhould be a preparation of rebellion to the Quenes Maieſties perſon, *and that,* he vviſsheth the Pope ſhould reigne in her place, *that he* maketh his belly his God, that he promiſed to recãte in Kinge Edvvardes daies, *and laſt of all,* that he chaunged in Religion. ix. times, yea. xix. times. *Theſe be ſuch ſlaunderous Reproches M. Horne, and the perſon whome you burden them withall, ſo farre from all ſuſpicion of any ſuch foule matter, among all ſuch as theſe*

***

many

Auguſt. in Pſal. cont. partē Donᵃ. Tom. 7.

Anſvver fol. 2. a.

Fol. 7. & fol. 104. fol. 3. b.

Fol. 6. a.

Fol. 7. b. Fol. 128. a.

many yeres haue knowen him and his behauiour, that yf
you were fued hereof vpon an Aɛtion of the cafe, as you
well deferue no leffe, cōfidering of what vocatiō and true
deferued reputation he is, whome thus vilainouflye you
flaunder, you woulde I feare be driuen at the left, to doe
that at Paules Croffe, which about Waltham matters
(you knowe the eſt your felfe) the Regeſtre of Hamp-
fhiere was driuē at that place to doe. So fhould the goſpell

Mr th. 7

be fulfilled, Looke vvith vvhat meafure you haue
meafured *to other,* vvith the fame it fhal be meafured again to you. *And fo fhould* Lex talionis *in*
you wel and worthely take place. As it doth by Gods pui-
dence fal out vpō you, in that you tel your Reader in great

Reply fo. 52.

fadnes, that M. Fek. is a great Donatiſt. For by that occa-
fiō you fhal find your felf and your felowes M. Horn moſt
rightly and truly proued Donatiſts: and M. F. to be as far
frō that lewde feɛt, as you are frō a true Catholike.

But of al your other flaunderous lyes heaped moſte
wrongefully vpon M. F. this one which to omit the reſt, I
wil onelye now note, is moſt ridiculous. You bluſter excee-
dingly, and are in a vehemēt rage with Maiſter Feken-

Anſvver
fol. 128.
col. 1. &
129 col. 1.
Replie.
Fol. 517.

ham. You fay that if his friends vvould but a litle examine his falfe dealing vvith the Fathers, thei
vvould no longer beleue him, but fufpeɛt him as
a deepe diſſembler, or rather abhorre him as an
open flaūderer and belier of the Aunciēt Fathers.
And to exemplifie this greuous accufation, you tel him in
that

that place, that he manifeſtlie māgleth, altereth, peruerteth, and corrupteth a ſaying of S. Auguſtin.
A man would here ſuppoſe M.Horn, that you had ſome
great and iuſte occaſion, thus greuouſly to charge ſuch a
man as M.Fekenham is, and that in printe, where all the
worlde may reade it and conſider it. What is the place
then? Thus it is. M. Fekenham alleageth S. *Auguſtine*
ſaying thus. Iſtis cede, & mihi cedes: *yelde to theſe, ād*
you ſhall yelde to me. You ſay S. *Auguſtine hath no ſuche*
wordes, but thus. Iſtis cede, & me non cædes. *Yelde*
to theſe, and thou ſhalt not ſtrike or whippe me. Nowe
put the caſe, it were as you ſay. Doth this Alteration or
chaunge deſerue ſuch a greuous Accuſation? You confeſſe
your ſelfe in the ſame place, and doe ſay to M.Fekenham:
And yet this corrupting of the ſentence maketh
it ſerue no vvhit the more for your purpoſe. *And*
is then M.Fekenham to be abhorred of his frendes
for an opē ſlaunderer and belier of the Auncient
Fathers, *whē he ſo altereth them, that yet they make no=*
thing for him? Who ſeeth not, that in caſe. M. Fekenham
had altered the wordes of S. *Auguſtin, yet ſeing he got no=*
thing by the exchaunge, nor vſed them to any guile or de-
ceyuing of his Reader, he litle deſerued ſuch a greuous
Accuſation.

Fol. 517.
& ſequēt.

   But nowe ſo it is, as I haue in this Replie more am=
plye declared, that the woordes by Maiſter Fekenham
alleaged, are the true wordes of S. *Auguſtin according to*
             *** ij   *foure*

foure feueral prints that I haue fene: two of Paris, one of Bafil, an other of Lyōs. And the words as you would haue them read Maifter Horne, are in none of thofe printes at all in the text of S. Auguftine. Onely in the later print of Paris. An. 1555. thofe wordes by you auouched ftand in the margin as a diuers reading, and the woordes by M. Fekenham avouched ftande in the text, as they doe in all other printes befide, for the true text of S. Auguftin. And who feeth not nowe, that all this was but a quarel picked, without defert? And you M. Horne to haue fhewed your felfe a moft ridiculous wrangler?

But Gods name be bliffed. The dealing of Catholike writers is fo vpright, that fuch fmal occafiōs muft be picked, and vpō fuch trifles your Rhetorike muft be beftow-ed: els againft their dealing you haue nothing to fay.

With the like felicity your brother Iewel in his late Sermon the. 15. of Iune laft at Paules Croffe, layed ful ftoutely and confidently to D. Hardings charge, for al-leaging the Decades of Sabellicus: faying with great bra-uery, but with exceding foly, that Sabellicus neuer vvrote Decades, but only Aeneades: Wheras yet al that euer haue fene Sabellicus, do know, that he wrote of his Rapfodia, Æneades: and of Venice matters, De-cades: which booke with the very page of the booke D. Harding truly alleaged. Whereby it is euident, that M. Iewel either is extreme recheleffe and vtterly careleffe what he preacheth or printeth, or at the leafte is at a full pointe

point to lie on, as he hath begunne, whatſoeuer come of it.
Of the which minde alſo it ſemeth your ſelf are M. Horn.
For (to omitte other ſpecialities, as of ^a *framing argu=*
ments vpon M. Fekenhams diſcourſe, which he neuer fra=
med, nor the diſcourſe beareth, of ^b *your contradictions,*
whereby you ſhewe the vnſtablemeſſe of your own iudge-
ment, with ſuch like) your Aunſwer is ſo fraighted and
ſtuffed with falſhoods, your Vntruthes doe ſo ſwarme and
muſter all a long your book, that for the quantity of your
Treatiſe, you are comparable to M. Iewel.

    Your Vntruthes amounte to the number of ſix hun-
dred foureſcore and odde. They be ſo notorious and ſo ma-
ny, that it pitieth me in your behalfe, to remember them.
But the places be euident and crie Corruption, and maye
by no ſhift be denied.

    If my curioſyty in noting them diſpleaſe you, let the
vttering of the firſt diſpleaſe your ſelf, and then you will
the leſſe be diſpleaſed with me. You knowe, M. Iewel hath
ledde vs this daunce. Be not angry M. Horne, if we follow
the round. Moderat your penne better. Report your Au-
thours more ſincerelye. Tranſlate your allegations more
truly. Laye downe the whole ſentences without concea-
ling of ſuch matter as ouerthroweth your purpoſe: Say no
more then you finde in the Stories. Slaunder not your
betters. Deale more aduiſedly and vprightly. So ſhal your
Vntruthes be the fewer an other time. But ſo wil your
cauſe, I aſſure you M. Horne, come forthe ſtarke naked,

a Fol. 127
120. & 123.
Reply
451. a.
b Anſwer
fo. 96. 97.
105. et 107
Reply.
411. b. 416
a. 447. a.
451. b.

✱✱✱ iij   *feble,*

feble, and miserable. The beauty and force of your Cause consisteth and depēdeth altogether of lyes and vntruthes.

If you ioyne obstinacy to folie, as Maister Iewell doth, so shamefully in opē Sermon iustifying him selfe, but not clering him selfe of any one of so many hundred Vntruths iustlye and rightly layed to his charge: then as I saied before, I may iustly say, that you are at a point to lie, whatsoeuer come of it. Like as a protestant of late dayes being pressed of a Catholike for extreme lying, and not being hable to clere him selfe, saied plainely and bluntlye:

Quamdiu potero, clades adferā, Latebunt quamdiu poterunt. Valebunt apud vulgus ista mendacia. *Well. I wil deface them(meaning the Catholikes) and doe some mischiefe to them as longe as I am able. My lies shall lie hidde, as longe as maye be. And at the leste the common people shall fall in a lyking with them.*

If you be at this pointe, then knowing where to haue you, we knowe also what to make of you, aud for suche to esteme you. A false Prophet, and a lying Master, *such as S. Peter spake of,* bringing in vvicked and damnable sectes. *God geue them grace, which are deceiued by you, so well to knowe you, as we that doe examine your writinges, haue good Cause to knowe you.*

This your Aunswer M. Horne (as I vnderstand) you haue presented to diuers of the Quenes Maiest. most Honorable Councell, intending thereby not onely to discredit

---

Vide Remundum Rusum, in Duplicatione cōt. Patronū Molinæi. Fol. 76.

2. Pet. 2.

credit Maiſter Fekenham , and to increaſe his trouble,
but alſo to bring into diſpleaſure , all other the Queenes
Highnes Catholike ſubiectes : of which full many , one-
lye for conſcience ſake , haue refuſed ; and doe yet refuſe
the Othe that you here moſte ignorantlye defende. For
this purpoſe alſo at the verye ende of your booke, you re-
ferre as it were the whole matter to the moſt Honorables
ſaying.

To Conclude, by the premiſſes it maie appeare to the Honorable as by a taſte , vvhat ſinceritie there is in you. *Thus much you ſay for diſcre-*
diting of M. Fekenham.

You adde a greuous Accuſatiõ againſt al the Catholik
ſubiects of England, ſaying. And laſtlie your quarreling by ſpreading this booke, vvas and is to impugne and barke againſt the Q. Maieſt. Lavvful
and due Authoritie, vvhich you and your complices dailie labour to ſubuert : vvhich matter I
refer to be further cõſidered by the graue vviſe-
dom of the moſt Honorable. *And w this poiſoned ãd*
cãcred Reproch you end your whole book: geuĩg your Rea
der to vnderſtãd ỹ the very end ãd ſcope of your book was
to ingraffe in ỹ Noble hartes of the moſt Honorables a
great miſliking ãd heauie diſpleaſure, not only of and a-
gainſt M. Fek. already in trouble, but alſo of and againſt
the whole number of Catholikes: who haue alwaies conti=
newed and ſhewed them ſelues the Quenes Maieſt . moſte
loyal

*loyal and obediēt subiects, and haue deserued no such Re-
proche at your handes M. Horne.*

*You haue therefore M. Horn, in this Reply, a iust and
a ful defence, partly* * *againſt your moſt slanderous accu-
sation, but chiefly and eſpecially of the whole Cauſe and
Queſtion in Controuerſy. As you did to M. Fekenhams
Treatiſe, ſo I to your Aunſwer haue replied through out. I
haue not omitted any one parte or parcel of your whole
book. As I haue here printed againe the whole, to encreaſe
of charges, ſo haue I anſwered the whole, to edifying of
the Reader.*

*** See the
3. Chapter
of the . 1.
booke.**

*If by this Reply you find your ſelf ſatisfied, and are cō-
tent to yelde to the Truth, ſo euidently and abundantly o-
pened vnto you, than both I and al other Catholikes will
both better truſt you, and geue God thankes for you.*

*But if after the peruſing of this Reply, you ſhal think
you are not fully and in euery point confuted: I wiſhe that
the moſt Honorable, to whom ſo cōfidently you commend
your own doings, woulde commaunde you, to proue it ſo to
the worlde by a ful Reioyndre. A ful Reioyndre I ſay, and
perfect, to al and euery part of this Reply, as I haue here
replied to al and euery part of your Anſwer: not omitting
any one example, of Councel, Prince, or Countrie by you
alleged. And that you put in my whole Anſwer, not omitting any one line or ſentence, either of the text, or of the
margent.*

*If the Truth be on your ſide, you haue no cauſe to ſtick
hereat.*

hereat. You wil feme to wante no learning. Abylytieto beare the charges we are fure you want not.

Goe thorough therefore as you haue begun, with this faire building of yours, if you thinke your foundatiõ good, or the caufe which you ground vpon fure. Goe through I fay, that it may appere you haue geuē M. F. good caufe to remoue his fcruples, and to be perfuaded at your handes.

Els if you now draw backe, and think by filēce to drown the matter, firft for your faire peecè of worke, fo fhamefully brokē of, men wil laugh you to fkorne, as the ghofpel by the parable told you: Then al mē may knowe, that your great vauntes of your Walthã talke and reafoning, are but wordes of courfe to faue your poore honour, I fhoulde fay, honefty. Thirdly, that M. Fekenhãs fcruples are moft lerned ãd inuincible reafons. And laft of al, that the Othe which you fo earneftly perfuade him to take, can of nomã be taken without manifeft Periury. Whereof enfeweth, ý you moft horribly offend Gods Diuine Maiefty, which doe burden mens confciences with fuch euident periury. The worfte that I wifhe you M. Horne, is, that you retracte your haynous herefies, and proue a true Chriftiã. And thus for this tyme I take my leaue of you.

Vale & Refipifce.

Thomas Stapleton.

Τὸ ἀληθὲς ὡς ἀληθῶς ἀληθὲν.

****   THE

THE PREFACE

TO THE READER.

T had bene much to be wiſſhed (gentle Reader)that the right reuerent and learned Father my L. Abbat of Weſtminſter, M. Feckenham, whom M. Hornes Booke moſte toucheth, might him ſelfe (as he is moſt able, and as I ſuppoſe, as wel willing)haue anſwered it alſo . But ſeing his ſtate is ſuche , that he preſently can not doe it, I being by ſome of my frendes requeſted to trauaile in the matter, was at the firſt not very willing thereto : as for diuerſe other cauſes , namely for that in very dede I was ful purpoſed, hauing ſo largely prouoked ſuche ſharpe aduerſaries, eſpecially M. Iewel, for a ſeaſon to reſte,and to ſtande at my own defence,if any would charge me: ſo chiefly for theſe two cauſes.

Firſt,for that many things in this booke pertaine to certaine priuat doinges betwixt M .Feckenham and M . Horne , of the which I had no ſkil.Secodely,for that a number of ſuch priuate matters touching the ſtate of the Realme occurred , as to them without farder aduiſe, I could not throughly ſhape any anſwer. Howbeit afterward it ſo happened,that by ſuche as I haue good cauſe to credit, there came to my knowledge ſuch Inſtructions, as well for the one as for the other,that I was the better willing to employ ſome ſtudy and paines in this behalfe. Not for that I thinke my ſelf better able thē other,but for that I would not it ſhould ſeme,that there lacked any good wil in me,either to ſatisfie the honeſt deſire of my frēdes,or to helpe and relieue ſuche,as by ſuch kinde of bookes are already pitefully inueigled and deceiued:or to ſtay other yet ſtanding , that this booke be

not

not at any time, for lacke of good aduertifement, a ftombling ftocke vnto them.

I haue therefore by fuch helpes, as is aboue faied, added my poore labour thereto, and with fome diligence in the refte, fhaped to the whole booke, a whole and a full Reply. Wherein I rather feare, I haue faied to much, then to litle. But I thought good in a matter of fuche Importance, to be rather tedious to make al perfitte, then fhorte and compendious, to leaue ought vnperfecte. Before then that thou fhalt enter (good Reader) into the Replie it felfe, it fhal be well, to take fome aduertife-ment, with a certaine vewe by a fhorte and fummary compre-henfion, of the whole matter. Whereby bothe to the Cõtrouerfy in hande thou fhalt come better inftructed : and, what in the whole worke is to be looked for, thou fhalt be aduertifed.

M. Hornes Anfwer, as he calleth it, refteth in two partes: In the firft and chiefeft he plaieth the Opponent, laying forthe out of the holy Scriptures bothe olde and newe, out of Councelles bothe Generall and Nationall, out of Hiftories and Chronicles of all Countres, running his race from Conftantine the greate, downe to Maximilian greate grãdfather to the Emperour that nowe liueth, taking by the way the kinges of Fraũce, of Spaine, and of our owne Countre of England fince the Conquefte, all that euer he could find by his own ftudy and helpe of his frends, partly for proufe of the like gouuernement of Princes in Ec-clefiaftical caufes, as the Othe attributeth nowe to the Crowne of Englande, partly alfo for difproufe of the Popes Supremacy, which the Othe alfo principally intendeth to exclude. In the fecond and later parte he plaieth the defendant, taking vpon him to anfwer and to fatisfie, certaine of M. Feckenhams Ar-gumentes and fcruples of confcience, whereby he is moued not to take the Othe. Howe wel he hath plaied bothe his partes, the

perufall

perufal of this Reply wil declare. The doings of eche part , vpon what occafion they rofe, thou fhalt vnderftād in our Anfwer to M. Hornes Preface.

For the more lightfome and clere Intelligence of the whole that is and fhall be faied to and fro, I haue diuided the whole Proceffe into foure bookes : keping the fame order and courfe, that Maifter Hornes Aunfwere did leade me vnto. To the firft parte of the Aunfwere , wherein he layeth forthe his proufes for defence of the Othe , I Replie in three Bookes. Comprifing in the firfte booke, his Obiections out of Holy Scripture : In the Second, his Obiections out of the firft fix hundred yeres. In the third, his Obiections out of the later 900. yeares, vntil our owne dayes . Eche booke I haue diuided into feuerall Chapters, as occafion ferued . In the feconde and third bookes, where we enter the courfe of tymes , I haue noted at the toppe of eache page , in one fide the yeare of the Lorde , on the other fide , the name of the Pope, Prince , or Councell , or other Principal matter in that place debated : to thentent (Gentle Reader) that at the firft fight euen by turning of a leafe thou mighteft knowe, both where thou arte, and what is a doing : both the Age and tyme (which exceedingly lighteneth the matter) and alfo the Pope, Prince or Councel of that tyme. In thefe three bookes, what I haue particularly done, yf thou lyft fhortly to fee , at the ende of the thirde booke thou fhalt find a briefe Recapitulation of the whole.

To the fecond part of M. Hornes Anfwer , I haue replied in the fourth Booke. By perufing wherof it fhal wel appeare , both what ftrong and inuincible Argumentes M. Fekenham right lernedly propofed, as moft iufte caufes of his fayed Refufall : and alfo what feely fhifts and miferable efcapes M. Horne hath deuifed, to maintayn that obftinatly , which he ons conceyued erronioufly.

niou∫ly. E∫pecially this thou ∫halt find in ∫uch places of the fourth book, where thou ∫ee∫t ouer the Head of the leaues in this letter, The Othe:The Othe:

Now good Reader, as thou tendre∫t thy own Saluatiõ, and ho-pe∫t to be à ∫aued ∫oule, in the ioyful and euerla∫ting bli∫∫e of Heu-uẽ, ∫o cõ∫ider and weigh wel with thy ∫elfe , the importance of this matter in hand. Fir∫t Religiõ without Authority, is no Re-ligion : For no true Religion (∫aith S. Augu∫tine) can by any meanes be receiued without ∫ome weighty force of autho-rity. *Then if this Religiõ, whereby thou hope∫t to be ∫aued, haue no Authority to ground it ∫elf vpon, what hope of Saluation re-mayning in this Religiõ can∫t thou cõceyue? If it haue any Au-thority, it hath the Authority of the Prince, by who∫e Supreme Gouernement it is enacted, erected and forced vpõ thee . Other Authoritye it hath none . If then that Supreme Gouernement be not dewe to the Laye Prince , but to the Spiritual Magi-∫trate, and to one chiefe Magi∫trate among the whole Spiritua-lty, thou ∫ee∫t thy Religiõ is but a bare name of Religion and no Religion in dede.*

Again, if this Supreme Gouernmẽt be not rightly attributed to the Laye Magi∫trate, in what ∫tate are they, which by booke othe do ∫weare that it ought ∫o to be, yea and that in their Con-∫ciẽce they are ∫o per∫uaded? Is not Periury, and e∫pecially a wil-ful Continuance in the ∫ame, a mo∫t horrible and dãnable crime in the ∫ight of God? And doth not Gods vengeaunce watche o-uer them, which ∫lepe in Periury? I wil be a Quicke witne∫∫e to Periured per∫ons., *∫aith God by the Prophet Malachie.*

Nowe if that Supreme Gouernement may dewly and rightly appertayne to our Liege Soueraigre , or be any Principall parte of a Princes Royall power , as Mai∫ter Horne ∫toutelye, but fondely anoucheth, or of his dutifull ∫eruice to God, which neuer

Aug. de v-til. credẽdi cap. 9.

Malac. 3. Ero te∫tis velox.

**** iij   Prince

THE PREFACE.

Prince in the Realme of England before the dayes of king Hēry the. 8. vſed or claimed, which neuer Emperour, Kinge, or Prince what ſoeuer without the Realme of Englande, yet to this preſent howre had, or attempted to haue, which the chiefe

Replie Fol. 22. & Fol. 508.

Maſters of the Religion nowe Authoriſed in Englande doe miſlike, reproue, and condemne, namely Martin Luther, Iohn Caluin, Philip Melanchthon, and the Magdeburgenſes, as in place conuenient I haue ſhewed: which alſo in no time or Age ſence Princes were firſt chriſtened, in no land or Coūtrie, in no Councel General or National, was euer witneſſed practiſed, or allowed: laſt of al, which directly fighteth with Chriſtes Commiſſion, geuen to the Apoſtles, and their Succeſſours in the Goſpell, and ſtandeth direct cōtrary to an Article of our Crede, if ſuch Supreme Gouuernement, I ſay, may be laweful and good, then is the Othe lawefull, and may with good Conſcience be taken.

But if theſe be ſuche Abſurdities, as euery mā of any meane conſideration ſeeth and abhorreth : then may not the Othe of any man that hath a Conſcience be taken, neither can this Supreme Gouernement be poſsibly defended for good and laweful. That al theſe Abſurdites and many yet more, which to auoide prolixitie I here omitte, do hereof depende, this Reply, gentle Reader, abundantly proueth.

The Primacy of the Biſhop of Rome, againſte the which the Othe directly tendeth, (as M. Horne auoucheth) is euidently here proued, not only in our dere Countrie of Englande, as well before the Conqueſt as ſythens, but alſo in all other Chriſtened Countres, not only of all the Weſt Churche, as of Italy, Spaine, Fraunce, Germany and the reſte, but of the Eaſt Churche alſo, yea amonge the Aethyopians and Armenians. And that by the witneſſes of ſuch Authours, as M. Horne him ſelfe hath builded his proufes vpon for the contrary.

The

TO THE READER.

The practise of the . 8 . first General Councelles, and of many National Councelles beside, in Spaine, Fraunce, and Germanye, hath pronounced euidently for the Popes and Bishoppes Supremacy, and nothing for the Princes in matters Ecclesiasticall. It is now thy parte, Christē Reader, not to shutte thy eyes, against the Truthe, so clerely shining before thy face.

Against the which Truthe, bicause M. Hornes whole Answer, is but as it were a Vayne Blaste, the Confutation of that Answer, to auoide confusion of Replies, whereof so many and diuers haue of late come forthe, I haue termed for distinctiō sake, a Counterblaste.

And nowe, gentle Reader, most earnestly I beseche thee, of all other Articles, that be this day ouer all Christendō controuersious, through the great temerite of selfe willed heretiks raised vp, most diligently to labour and trauaile in this of the Supremacy: As being suche, that to say the Truthe, in effecte al other depende vpon.

Of Protestantes some be Lutherans, some Zwinglians, some Anabaptistes, some Trinitaries, and some be of other sectes. But as they all being otherwise at mutuall and mortall enemitie emonge themselues, conspire against the Primacy of the See Apostolike: so a good Resolution ones had in this pointe, staieth and setleth the Conscience, as with a sure and stronge Anker, from the insurgies and tempestes of the foresaide rablemēt, and of all other sectes, and schismes.

Contrary wise, they that be ones circumuented and deceaued in this Article, are caried and tossed, with the raging whaues and flouddes of euery errour and heresy, without staie or settling, euen in their owne errours.

I reporte me to the Grecians, who forsaking the vnitie of the Romaine Churche, and being first Arrians, defying the
Pope

THE PREFACE

Sozo.lib.
3.cap.8.
Socrat.li.
2 cap.15.

Pope, as it may appeare by the letters of Eusebius the greate Arrian and his felowes to Iulius then Pope, fell after to be Macedonians, Nestorians, Eutychians, Monothelites, Iconomaches, with diuers other greate Heresies, eche Heresy breeding great numbers of sectes, and all conspiring against the See Apostolike, vntil at the last proceding from heresy to heresie (diuers Recōciliations with the Romaine See comming betwene, which staied a longe time Gods highe vengeaunce that ensewed) they fel to Turkish Captiuitie, in which (ô lamentable case) they remayne to this day.

Opta.li.2.

I reporte me to the Africans, who falling from the vnitie of the Romaine See, first in the Donatistes despising the Iudgemente of Pope Melchiades in the very first springe of their heresy (where then it might haue bene stopped, if they had geuen eare to their chiefe Pastour) then falling to be Pelagians, and soone after Arrians, by the conqueste of the

Victor de persequut. Vandal.

Wandalles, became in time Infidelles, as to this daie they continue.

In parua Confessio. de cœna Domini.

I reporte me laste of all, to these Heresies of the Northe, the Bohemians fyrste, and nowe Luther, and his scholers. Whiche wythin fewe yeares, their Maister yet liuing and flourisshing, wente so farre from hym, that he pronounced them in open writyng, Heretiques, and Archeheretiques. And yet they nowe (I meane the Sacramentaries) whome Luther so defyed, beare the greatest swaye of all other sectes.

Staphylus in Apolo. part. 3.

What the ende of these Heresies wyll be (except we abandonne them in tyme) Hungarie and Lifelande maye be a lesson vnto vs: whiche by Luthers heresye, are bothe fallen awaye, as from the Romaine Churche, so from the Romaine Empire, the one into the Turkes handes, the other into the Moscouites.

But

TO THE READER.

But to leaue forayne Countres for triall, what it is to sepa-rat our selues from the See Apostolike, our owne domesticall af-fayres maye serue vs for a sufficient example.

At what time kinge Henry the 8. first banished the Po-pes Authoritie out of Englande, as the kinge and the Parlia-ment thought, (though erroneously) that this doing imported no schisme nor herefy, so they thought likewise, in suche sorte to prouide, that the people shoulde not fall into the other er-rours of the newe Lutheran or Sacramentary religion, which then the kinge and the Parliament no lesse abhorred, then they did Turkery. But what was the issewe, all the worlde knoweth, and England, the more pitie, greuously feeleth.

For immediatly bookes came so thicke abrode, as well of the Lutheran, as of the Zwinglian sette, and the people fell so fast to a contentation and liking with them, that the king was fayne to make diuers streight lawes, and Actes of Par-liament for the repressing of herefy, yea and to forbidde the Actes and Monu-mentes fol. 553. *common people the reading of the Bible. And he sate in his owne person in iudgement, vpon Lamberte the Sacramen-tary. Neither the Lutherans and Zwinglians onely swar-med in the realme, but the Anabaptistes also, twelue of the sayed Anabaptistes being burned aboute one tyme.*

Nowe thoughe king Henrye altered no matter of fayth, sa-uing this Primacie onely, but kepte constantlye the Catholike fayth otherwise, and though suppressing the Abbeys, he would not suffer religiouse men, that had vowed chastitye, to marie: yet after hys death, and in the minoritye of hys sonne kinge Edwarde, all the lawes that he had made towching matters of religion (sauing against the supremacie) were repelled and abolished. And a new religion was through out the realme set forthe.

* * * * *

To the

To the which though the Religion nowe vſed be much con-
farmable, yet is there in many thinges muche diueiſitie. As
among other, for the mariage of Prieſtes: for the which they
had ſome colour in king Edwardes daies by Acte of Parliament. Nowe they haue both the Church lawe, and the lawe of
the Realme againſt them, and which more is, the verie lawe
of God, that ſaieth, Vouete & reddite. Make your vowe, and
perfourme it. And S. Paule ſaieth, Habentes damnationem,
quia primam fidem irritam fecerunt. Incurring damnation,
becauſe they haue broken their firſt promiſe.

Againe, in the firſt yeare of our gratious Queene, the Acte
of Parliament, for making and conſecrating of Biſſhoppes, made
the .28. of kinge Henrye was reuiued. And yet the Biſſhoppes
were ordered not accordinge to the acte, but according to an
acte made in kinge Edwarde his dayes, and repelled by Quene
Marye and not reuiued the ſayde firſt yeare. And yf they will
ſay, that that defecte is nowe ſupplied, let them yet remember
that they are but parliament and no Churche Biſſhoppes, and
ſo no Catholike Biſſhoppes, as being ordered in ſuch manner and
faſſhion, as no Catholike Church euer vſed.

But thys is moſt to be conſidered and to be lamented of all
thinges, that wheras no Acte of Parliament can geue anye ſufficient warrant, to diſcharge a man from the Catholike faythe,
and wheras yt was aswel in king Henries dayes by Acte of Parliament, as euer before, through out all Churches of Chriſtendome, ſithens, we were chriſtened, taken for playne and open
hereſie, to denie the reall preſence of Chriſtes bodye in the Sacramente of the aulter (for maynteining of the which hereſie
there is no acte of Parliamēt God be thancked, neither of king
Edwardes tyme, nor in the tyme of our graciouſe ſoueraygne
Ladie and Quene that nowe is) yet doe theſe men teache and
preache

Pſalm.75

i. Tim.5.

preache and by writing defend and maynteine the saied greate and abhominable heresie, with many other, for the which they can shewe no warrante of anye temporall or spirituall lawe, that euer hath bene made in Englande.

All this haue I spoken to shewe it is most true, that I haue saied, that there will neuer be redresse of errour and heresie, or any staie, where men are once gone from the vnitie of the See Apostolike, which is the welspring and fountaine of all vni tie in the Catholike faith.

And touching this question of the Supremacie, that we haue in hand, if we wel consider it, we shall find, that we doe not agree, either with the other Protestantes, or with our selues. or in this pointe, that we make the Prince the supreme head of the Churche, we neither agree with Luther him selfe, or his scholers, which denie this primacie: nor with Caluin and his scholers the Sacramentaries. Caluin saieth: They were blasphemers, that called King Henrie head of the Church: One of his scholers, Iacobus Acontius, in a booke dedicated to the Queenes Mai. blameth openly the ciuil magistrate, that maketh him selfe the Iudge of controuersies, or by the aduise of other commaundeth this doctrine to be published, that to be suppressed.

Nowe some of Caluins scholers, and our owne countriemen haue taken forth such a lesson, that they haue auouched in their bookes printed and publisshed to the world, that a woman can neither be head of the Church, nor of any Realme at all.

Againe, manie of the Protestants though they will not, the Pope should haue the chiefe gouernement (because they like not his true doctrine) yet they thinke it meete and conuenient, that there be some one person ecclesiasticall, that maie haue this supreme gouernement for matters of the Church.

***** ij   *It is*

No countrey in Christendome acknovv¬ ledgeth the prince for su¬ preame head be¬ side En¬ glande.
Lutherus. Contra Art. Loua¬ uienses. Tom.2. Magdeb. in præfat. Cent.7. Caluinus. in Osee. 1. et Amos.7 Iacob. Acontius Stratagē. Satanæ. lib.3. See the leafe.15. Andreas Modre. de Ecclesia lib.2.c.10.

THE PREFACE.

It is also to be considered, that the wordes of the Othe nowe tendered, for the mainteining of the Princes Supremacie, are other , then they were in King Henries , or King Edwardes daies : with a certaine addition of greatest importance , and such as to a ciuil Prince, specially to the person of a woman can in no wise be with any conuenient sense applied : I meane of these wordes, Supreme Gouernour aswell in all spirituall or ecclesiasticall thinges or causes , as temporall . *Such large and ample wordes were in neither of the foresaied Kings times put into the Othe. And yet had they bene more tolerable in their persons (for that men be capable of spiritual gouernmēt frō the which a woman is expresly by nature , and by scripture excluded)then they are nowe.These wordes are such,I saie,as can not with any colourable pretext be excused.*

Neither is it inough to saie (as the Iniunctions doe) that the Quenes Maiestie entendeth not to take more vpon her, then King Henrie her father , or King Edward her brother did, what so euer that were ,more or lesse : but it must be also considered , what she or her Successours may take vpon her or them by the largenes of these wordes (for an Iniunction can not limit an Acte of Parliament :) and whether there be any either Scripture or other good doctrine ecclesiastical, sufficient to satisfie their consciences , that refuse especially this Othe. Which doth not only, as it did before,exclude the Apostolical See , and all Generall Councelles also , as (though not in plaine wordes, yet in effect)in excluding the ecclesiastical Authoritie of al foren persons and Prelates: but doth further adioyne the foresaied newe addition lesse probable,and lesse tolerable , then was any other parte of the former Othe.

And therefore certaine Protestants of some name andreputation being tendred this Othe by commission ,haue refused it.

it. *Yea and how well trow you, is this supreme Gouuernement liked of those Ministers, which withstand the Quenes iniunctions touching the order of semely Apparell, &c?*

Thus ye perceyue, that as we are gone from the constante and setled doctrine of the Church, touching this primacy, so we agree not, no not among our selues, either in other pointes, or in thys very Article of the Supremacy. Neither shal we euer fynd anie cause of good and sufficiente contentation, or constancye in doctrine, vntill we returne thither, from whence we first departed, that is, to the See Apostolike. Which of al other people our Nation hath euer most reuerenced and honoured, and ought of al other most so to doe: As from whence both the Britaines and Saxons receiued first the Christian faith. This returne God of his mercie graunt vs, when it shall be his blessed pleasure: Amen.

In Louaine, the last of September. An.15 67.

Thomas Stapleton.

¶ An Aduertifement to the Lerned Reader.

TOuching certain Authors alleaged in this Reply, about matters of our own Countre, it is to be vnderftanded. that of certayne writen Copies not yet printed which we haue vfed, as of Henricus Huntingtonenfis, and Gulielmus Neubrigenfis, or Noueoburgenfis,, or Neoburgenfis many thinges are in the faid Copies, which feme not to be writen of thē, but of Some others. As in the Copie of Henricus Huntingtonenfis, certayne thinges are founde, which feme not to be writen of him, but to haue bene gathered out of his workes, and to haue bene writen by fome other: whom we coniecture to be Simeon Dunelmenfis. Alfo in the Copie of our Neubrigenfis many thinges are added both at the beginning and at the ende, which feme not to haue ben writen by Neubrigenfis him felf, but by fome other. And that which is added at the beginning, was writen as we vnderftand nowe of one Alphredus Beuerlacenfis, who liued vnder king Steuen: The additions which do followe, who wrote we yet knowe not, except it were Roger Houeden. This I warne thee of, gentle Reader, to thentent that if hereafter the forefaid Copies come forth in printe (as this very yere Neubrigenfis did) and that the printed Copies haue more or leffe then we reporte out of the writen Copies, thou may not fufpect any falfhood or forgery in vs, but vnderftanding the cafe as we haue faied, maieft take our dealing to be, as it is, true and fincere. Therefore hauing conferred the printed Neubrigenfis, with the writen Copie, and finding fome difference: as ofte as that which I alleage out of Neubrigenfis, is in the printed Copie, fo ofte I haue noted in the Margent, the booke and Chapter of that Copie. And when that I alleage, is in the writen, not printed Copie, I note in the Margent: Neubrig. M.S. for: Manufcriptus.

Againe in quoting the leaues of the Tomes of Councells, I haue alwaies in maner folowed the former Copies printed at Collen in three Tomes: Anno. 1551. Only towarde the ende of this booke I haue folowed the laft edition of this prefent yere, quoting the leaues according to that Edition, and then for perfpicuites fake I haue added in the Margent. Edit. Poftr.   Vale.

·Ω φίλησα προθύμως Τὰ δ'ύναῖα.

AN ANSVVERE TO
THE PREFACE.
THE PREFACE OF
M. HORNE.

It is novve an vvhole yeare paſt, ſince I heard of a book ſecretly ſcattered abroad by M. Fekenham emong his friends: And in Aprill laſt, I came by a Copie therof. Vvhen I had read the booke, and perceiued both the matter and the maner of the mans doings therin: I ſavv his proofes ſo ſlender: and his maner of dealing ſo ſhameles: that I ſtood in doubt vvhat to do, vvhether to diſcouer the man by vvriting, or to ſhake him of vvith ſilence. If i had not ſeene a further meaning in his ſetting forth and publiſhing the book (.1.) the he durſt plainely vtter, for then his cunning could by any meanes anſvveare vnto: or then, that I vvith a good conſcience mought haue neglected: I vvoulde haue paſt it ouer vvith ſilence, as a peece of rvoorke not vvorthy of anſvvre. But ſeing the (.2.) chiefe end and principal purpoſe inteded, as may be iuſtly gathered in publiſhing the booke, vvas, to ingraſte in the mindes of the ſubiectes, a miſliking of the Queenes Maieſtie, as though ſhee vſurped a povver and authoritie in Eccleſiaſticall matters, vvhereto ſhee hath no right: to ſlaunder the vvhole Realme, as though it vvere ſtranged and directly againſt the Catholike Churche, renouncing and refuſing to haue Communion therevvith: And vnder my name to deface the myniſters of Chriſtes Churche: I could not chooſe, oneles I vvould vvilfully neglect my duety to her Maieſtie, ſhevv my ſelfe ouermuche vnkinde vnto my natiue Countrie, and altogeather become careles of the Churche Myniſterie, but take penne in hand, and ſhape him a ful and plaine anſvvere, vvithout any curioſitie.

T. Stapleton.

 T is to be knowen (gentle Reader as I aſſuredly vnderſtand) that the Reuerent Father, my L. Abbat of Weſtmynſter; M. Fekenham being priſoner in the Tower, and ſuppoſing that the othe of the ſupremacie then paſſed in the Parliament holden at Weſtmynſter in the fifte yere of the Queenes Maieſties

A   ieſties

iefties raigne, fhould foorthwith (as it was probable)be tendred him and others, gathered as it were in a fhedule , certain reafons and caufes, why he thought he could not with
fafe confcience, receiue the faid othe. Minding to offer the
faid fhedule. to the Commiffioners, if any came. The faied
fhedule M. Fekenham deliuered to M. Horne at Walthã a
manour place of the Bifhop of Winchefter in Hamfhier, he
being at that time there the faid M Horns prifoner, by the
committie of the Queene her highnes honourable Councel : and that vpon this occafion.

In M. Fekenhams abode at Waltham, there was daylie.
conference in matters of Religion, namely of the principall
pointes of this Treatife, betwene him and M Horne, as himfelfe confeffeth. In the which fpace, he required M Fekenham, fundry and diuers times, that he woulde by writing,
open vnto him the ftaies of his confcience , touchinge the
othe of the Queenes highnes Supremacie being the whole
matter and caufe of his trouble, with no fmal promifes, that
he fhould fufteine no kinde of harme or iniurie therby: And
in fine, if there came no furder fruit or benefitte therof vnto him, the whole matter fhould be fafly folded vppe , and
left in the fame eftate where they beganne. Wherevpon
M. Fekenham. thinking verely all things by him promifed,
to be as truely meant as fpoken, made deliueraunce to M.
Horne of a fmall Treatife, deuifed by him before his comming foorth of the Tower, entituled: *The Anfwere made
by M. Iohn Fekenham, Prieft and Prifoner in the Tower, to the
Queenes highnes Commiffioners , touching the othe of the Supremacie.* With this declaration alfo , made vnto the faid
Mafter Horne , that vpon the paffing of the faid ftatute, he
thought to haue deliuered the faid Treatife, to the Commiffioners.

The caufe
vvhy M.
Fekenhã
deliue-
red his li-
tle Trea-
tife to M.
Horne.

fioners (if any came) as the ſtaie of his conſcience, concerning the refuſall of the foreſaid othe : And foraſmuche as
they came not, he being as before is ſaid, vrged and preſſed by the ſaid M. Horne to open vnto him by writing, the
cauſes forcing him to breathe, and ſtaie vpon the taking of
the foreſaid othe, made deliuerance of the very ſame Treatiſe deuiſed in the Tower, with the foreſaid Title and declaration. Which Treatiſe being afterwarde encreaſed as
wel by M. Hornes Anſwers, as by M. Fekenhams Replies
thervnto made : after his return back againe to the Tower,
he ſent one copie to the right honorable the L.Erle of Leceſter and one other to Syr William Cicil Knight. and Secretarie vnto the Queenes highnes, (with the ſame title that
the printed book conteineth)both of them being deliuered
by M. Lieutenant of the Tower. This ſhedule or litle Treatiſe M. Horne calleth a booke, yea and that made with the *Fol.* 1.
helpe of the reſt : that he might ſeme after two yeares and *pag.* 2.
more to haue done a worthy and a notable aƈte, in anſwering ſix poore leaues (for thereabout in M Hornes booke
amounteth the quantitie of M. Fekenhams Treatiſe) and to
haue made a great conqueſte vpon M. Fekenham and his
fellowes : woorthie for this great martiall prowes to be,
if al other thinges faile, a Prelate of the Garter. This his　Vvhy M.
Treatiſe was he forced to deliuer to the right Honorables,　F.cauſed
as before for his neceſſary purgation concerninge ſuche　the ſame
falſe accuſations and ſlaunders, as Maiſter Horne had　to be de-
made and raiſed vppon him, as ſhall heereafter in more　liuered to
conueniente place be ſpecified. VVherefore this beeing　the Coū-
done as ye haue heard ſo plainly, ſo ſimply and vpon ſuch　cell.
cauſe ſheweth that M. Fekenham had no ſuch meaning, as
M. Horne here falſly ſurmiſeth. As one, who hadde his

　　　　　　　A ij　　　　　princi-

principall and chiefe regard, how to fatiffie his owne, and not other mennes confciences, howe to faue him felfe from flaunders and vntrue accufations, and not to woorke with other men by perfwafion. VVherefore this is an vntrue and a falfe furmife of M. Horne : as are the other two here alfo, in faying that M Fekenhã meant otherwife, then he durft plainly vtter, or by his cũning could aunfwer vnto.

M. Horne. The 2. Diuifion.

Vvherein I follovv the order of M. Fekenhams booke : I make the proofes according to his requeft : and befides my proofes foorth of the Scriptures, the auncient Doctours, the Generall Councels and Nationall : I make proofe by the continual practife of the Church (.3) in like gouernment as the Queenes Maieftie taketh vpon her, and that by fuch Authors, for a great fort of them, as are the more to be credited in this matter, for that they vvere moft earneft fautors of the Romifh fea, infected as the times vvere, vvith much fuperftitiõ, and did attribute vnto the fee of Rome, and fo to the vvhole Clergie fo much authoritie in Churche matters, as they mighte, and muche more then they ought to haue done.

The third vntruth. you neuer proue the like gouernemente Namely in al Eclefiafti-cal things and caufes,

Stapleton.

I wil not charge M Horne, that his meaning is to ingraffe in the mindes of the fubiectes, a mifliking of the Queenes Maieftie, as though fhee vfurped a power and autoritie in Ecclefiafticall maters, whereto fhee hath no right, as he chargeth M. Fekenham withal: vnleffe perchance he were of Councell with the holy brotherhode of Geneua for the Booke, whereof we fhall hereafter fpeake that fpoyleth the Queenes Maiefty of al her authority as wel têporal as fpiritual and vnleffe he hath in opẽ fermõ at VVinchefter main-teined, cõtrary to the Queenes ecclefiaftical iniunctions, fuch as would not reform their difordered apparel and that, after he had put his hand as one of the Queenes cõmiffioners, to the redreffe of the faied diforder . And vnleffe he hath and doth

doth maítein many things befíde, yea and cótrary to the la ́
wes and orders of the realm late fet forth cócerning maters
ecclefiafticall, as it is wel knowé and to be proued he hath
don as wel in the defending of the Minifter of *Durley* near
the Manour of Bifihops Walthā refuſing the faied order, as
otherwiſe. But this may I boldy fay, and I doubt nothinge
to proue it, that in al his boke, there is not as much as one
worde of fcripture, one Doctour, one councell generall or
prouincial not the practife of any one countrey throwgh
owte the worlde counted Catholike, that maketh for fuch
kinde of regiment, as M. Horne avoucheth, nor any one
manner of proufe that hath any weight or pythe in the
worlde to perſwade. I wil not fay M. Fekenham but any o-
ther of much leſſe witte, learning and experience. I fay M.
Horne commeth not ones nighe the principall matter and
queſtion, wherein M Fekenhā would and of right ought to
be refolued. I fay further in cafe we remoue and fequefter
al other proufes on oure fyde, that M. Horn fhal by the very
fame fathers, councels, and other authorities by him felfe
producted fo be ouerthrowen in the chief and capital queftion (vnto the which he cometh not nighe as a man might
fay, by one thowfande myles) that his owne company may
haue iufte caufe to feare leaſt this noble blafte fo valiantly
and fkilfully blowen owte of M. Hornes trompet fhall en-
gender in the harts of all indifferent and difcrete Readers,
much caufe to miftrufte, more thē they did before the whol
matter, that M. Horne hath taken in hande to iuftifie.

Wherefore as it is mete in al matters fo is it here alfo có-
ueniét and neceſſary to haue before thyne eyes, good Reader, the ſtate and principal queſtion controuerſed betwene
the parties ſtanding in variance: And then diligently to fee,

A iij   how

how the proufes are of eche party applied, for the confirming of their affertions.

The prin-
cipal que-
ftions cō-
cerning
Ecclefia-
ftical regi-
ment,
vvhich
M. Horn
doth not
ons tou-
che.

There are therfore in this caufe many things to be confidered.   Firfte that Chrifte lefte one to rule his whole
Churche in his fteade from tyme to tyme vnto the ende of
the worlde. Secondly that this one was Saint Peter the
Apoftle, and now are the Bifhoppes of Rome his fucceffours. Thirdly that albeit the Bifhop of Rome, had no fuch
vniuerfal gouernment ouer the whole, yet that he is and
euer was, the patriarche of Englande and of the whole
wefte Church, and fo hath as muche to doe here as any o-
ther patriarche in his patriarkfhippe. Then that all were it,
that he had nothing to intermedle with vs nor as Pope, nor
as patriarche, yet can not this fupremacy of a ciuil prince be
iuftified: whereof he is not capable efpeciallye a woman,
but it muft remayne in fome fpiritual man.   Befide this the
Catholikes fay that as there was neuer any fuche prefidēte
heretofore in the Catholike Churche: fo at this prefent
there is no fuch (except in England) neither emonge the
Lutherans, the Zwinglians, the Swenckfeldians or Anabaptiftes, nor any other fecte that at this daye raygneth or ra-
geth in the worlde.   None of thefe I faye agnife their cyuil prince, as fupreame gouernour in al caufes fpiritual and
temporal: Laft of al I fay and M. Fekēnham wil alfo faye
that euen M. Horne him felfe in this his anfwere retreyteth
fo farre backe from this affertion of fupreame gouernment
in all caufes fpirituall and temporall, whiche is the ftate
and keye of the whole queftion, that he plucketh from the
prince the chief and principal matters and caufes ecclefiafticall, as we fhall here after plainely fhewe by his owne
woordes.

No fuch
regiment
as M.
Horne
defēdeth
among al
the fectes
fauing ir
England.

M. Horne
himfelfe
denieth
this fupre-
macie in
al caufes
ecclefia-
ftical.

The

The premisses then being true and of owre syde abundantly proued, and better to be proued, as occasion shall serue, as nothing can effectually be brought against them, so M Horne, as ye shal euidently perceiue in the processe, stragleth quyte from al these points, besetting himselfe, all his study and endeuor to proue that which neither greatly hyndereth oure cause, nor much bettereth his: and for the which neither maister Fekenham nor any other Catholike will greatly contende with him: whiche is when all is done, *that Princes may medle and deale with causes ecclesiasticall.* Which as it is in some meaning true, so dothe yt nothing reache home to the pointe most to haue bene debated vpon. And so is much labour vaynely and idlelye employed, with tediouse and infynite talke and bablinge, all from the purpose, and owte of the matter, whiche ought speciallye to haue bene iustifyed. And therefore this is but an impudente facing and bragging to say, that he hath proued the like regiment that we deny, by the Fathers, by the Councels and by the continual practise of the Churche.

Now it is worthy to see the iolye pollicy of this man, and howe euen and correspondent it is to his fellowe protestants. M Iewel restrayneth the Catholikes to .*600*. yeres as it were by an extraordinary and newe founde prescription of his owne, embarringe al Later proufes. Yet he him selfe, in the meane tyme runneth at large, almoste one thowsande yeares Later, shrynkinge hither and thyther, taking tagge and ragge, heretike and Catholik, for the fortifying of his false assertions. This wise trade this man kepeth also, and to resolue M.Fekenham, and setle his conscience, he specially stayeth him self vpon *Platina, Nauclerus, Abbas Vr-*

The vneuen dealing of the protestants.

bas Vrſpergenſis,Sabellicus,AEneas pius,Volaterranus, Fabian,
Polichronicon,Petrus Bertrandus,Benno the Cardinal, *Durã-*
dus,P.AEmilius,Martinus pœnitentiarius,Polidorus Virgilius.
And ſuch lyke as he him ſelf declareth otherwhere and in
this place alſo confeſſeth. Nowe all be it the Catholiques refuſe no Catholique writer,nor in this matter haue
cauſe ſo to doe. yet in a matter of ſuch importance ,which
beſide the loſſe of al téporal relief and beſyde bodily death
importeth alſo euerlaſting damnation to the Catholikes,(if
the caſe ſtande , as M. Horne and his fellowes beare vs in
hande ,reaſon would he ſhould haue fetched the ſubſtance
of his proufes much higher,yea within the *600.* yeres whervnto they ſtrayne and binde vs. The which the Catholikes
haue already performed againſt M. Iewel , not in the ſubſtance of the matter onely,but euen in the iuſtifying of the
preciſe wordes,wherein M.Iewel hathe framed to himſelf
by a fooliſh wylynes, or wylye foolyſhnes, the ſtate of the
queſtion I meane for the wordes of *head of the Church,* and
vniuerſall Buſhop.

And what if M Fekenham nowe Syr would reuel with
yow with lyke rhetorike,and require of yow to proue by
the fathers writing within the ſayde. *600* . yeares theſe expreſſe words:*Supreame heade,or gouernour in all cauſes ſpiri-*
*tual and temporal,*to haue bene geuen and attributed to any,
ciuil Magiſtrate ? Againe that the temporal men without,
yea and againſt the conſent of the whole clergy, altered the
ſtate of religiõ called and vſed for Catholik throughout the
whole corps of Chriſtendome one thouſande yeares before
with ſuch other articles, as concerne the regiment Eccleſiaſticall that ye. in this your booke defende ? Ye haue not,
no nor ye can not, proue any ſuch matter either by expres
woordes,

A chal-
lenge to
M.Horn.

wordes or by any good induction or confequēt in the firſt
and former Fathers. And yet fomwhat were it , if the Later
Fathers might helpe yow.

But what an impudent face , as harde as any horne or
ſtone haue ye befide your mere foly , to make the worlde
belieue, that the authours aforefayde allowed fuch kinde of
regiment of ciuill Princes as the Catholikes now denye.
Whiche affertion is fo certainely and notorioufly falfe, that
M. Horne him felf can not, nor doth not deny, but that his
owne authours , were *moſte earneſt fautours of the See of*
Rome . And howe then maye it ones be thoughte by a-
ny wife man that they ſhoulde allowe the doings of fuche
that forfake and abandon al maner of authority of that See,
further then is the cōmen authority of al other Biſſhops, yea
and make the Biſſhop of that See to whome the fayde authors attribute fo large and ample authoritye and prerogatiue as may be , and whome they agnife as fupreame iudge
in matters of faith, a very Antichriſte. Thefe things be incredible, thefe things (as the prouerbe is) hange together
like germans lipps: and fo ſhal ye, good Readers, fee the matter moſt euidently fal owte . And therefore, M. Horne,
where you haue of late openlye fittinge at a table in London (as I am credibly informed) bragged, that ye haue quyte
cōfuted the Papiſts with their own papiſtical Doctors, how
true this is, I truſt it ſhall by this anfwere plainely appeare.

M. Horne.   The 3. Diuifion .

Their iudgements and fentences ſhal appeare in reading by the forme of
letter: for leauing foorth the Latine to auoide tedioufnes , 4. I haue putte into
Engliſh the Authours mindes and fentences, and caufed them , for the moſte
parte, to be Printed in Latine letters, that the Engliſh reader may knovv and
decerne the Authours fayings from mine.

If this that I haue done, vvorke that effect in the Engliſhe Reader, vvhich

B   he ought

M Horns
tale incre
dible,

M. Horns
late
bragge.

The 4
vntruthe
For he
vvrongs
fully al-
legeth
both the
vvordes
and mea-
ning of
his Au-
thours.

he ought to seeke, and I d. wishe, I haue wonne that I wrought for: but otherwise, let men say and iudge what they liste, I haue discharged my consci: ence and shewed the trueth. Anno Domini. 15 65. Feb 25.

Rob. Wynchester.

Stapleton.

A great vntruth. For M. Horne doth not faithfully, but most corruptly and falsly alleage the authours wordes, and vseth his owne in steade of theirs: and to suche as he truely reheireth, he geueth an vnmete and an improbable sense of his own making, as we shal particularly notifye, when the case re-quireth.

THE

THE FIRST BOOKE, CONTEI-
NING MANY PRIVAT DOINGES OF

M. Fekenham, the State of the Que tió answer to
M. Hornes oppositions out of holy scriptures
both olde and newe, with a declara-
tion, who are the right Do-
natists, Protestants
or Papistes.

M. Fekenham.

The declaration of such scruples and staies of consci-
ence, touching the Othe of Supremacy, as M. Iohn Feken-
ham by writing did deliuer vnto the L. Bishop of Win-
chester, with his resolutions made thereunto.

M. Horne.

The property of him that meaneth to declare rightly any matter done, is to set forth the trueth vvithout malice to obserue the due circumstances of the matter, persones, and times: and to vse simple plainesse vvithout guileful ambiguities (.5.) Ibis Title is so replenished vvith vntrue report, and ambiguous sleightes, vvithout the note of any necessary circumstance, that there is not almost one true vvorde therein: vvhereby you geue at the first a taste to the indifferent reader, vvhat he must looke for in the sequele.

You pretende, and vvould haue your frendes to thincke, that the first fovver chiefe pointes set foorth in your booke, vvere deuised by you, put in vvriting, and so deliured vnto me, as the matter and grounde vvherupon, the conferéce to be had betvvixt me and you should stande: And that I made thereunto none other but such resolutions, as it hath pleased you (.6.) vntruly to report. In the first parte, you conueigh an vntrueth vnder a coulorable and ambiguous meaning, in these vvoordes, as M. Iohn Fekenhã by vvriting did deliuer vnto the L. B. of VVincheſter. In thother part (.7.) you make an vntrue report vvithout ary colour at all, I doe graunt and vvill not deny, that you deliured to me a booke: vvhich, I thãke God, I haue to shevv, vvhere-

B ij   by

The ʃvn-
truthe in
vvrong-
fully char
ging M.
Fekeham
for the
Title of
his trea-
tiſe.
The 6. vn
truthe,
the reso-
lutiõs are
truly rea
ported, as
ſhal ap-
peare.
The 7 vn-
truthe
Slaunde-
rous.

by to difproue you. The fame vvil declare the time vvhen, the place vvhere, the occafion vvherefore, the perfonnes to vvhome the booke vvas vvritē, and vvhat is the matter in generall therein conteyned : VVhereunto muft be added , at vvhat time the fame vvas deliuered vnto me, vpon vvhat occafiō, and to vvhat ende. Al vvhich circumftances you omitte in your booke publifhed, leaft you fhoulde haue bevvrayed your felfe, and haue appeared in your ovvne likeneffe.

Stapleton

The Firſt Chapter concerning the Title of M. Fekenhams declaration.

 *H I S* was an happy happe for M. Horne, that it happed M. Fekenhā with the omitting of fuche flender circumftances to minifter to him matter of fuch triflynge talke, wherein otherwife M. Horne fhould haue had nothing to haue fayde. For here is he very exacte and precife in circumftances to be kepte , with al dewe obferuation, in a by matter , which whether it be true or falfe doth nothing either preiudicate or touche the principal queftiō, that is, whether the refolutiōs were made before Mäifter Fekenham deliuered vp his matter in writing, or after. For this being true, that thefe refolutiōs were made to take away the fcruples and ftayes of M. Fekenhams confcience, whiche fcruples rofe and prycked his confciéce by and throughe fuch reafons and caufes firft vttered by talke and after by writing alleaged : wherein, I pray yow, hath M. Fekenham offended you M. Horne, fo greuouflye, that therfore he fhould be noted of fo *vntrue reporte , that there is not almoft one true worde in the title of his treatife*: that he fhould be noted *of ambiguoufe fleights* , yea and of malice to in prefixinge the fayed tytle to his Treatife ? And that he fhould *conueigh vntrueth vnder coulorable and ambi-*

ambiguouſe meaning , as not obſeruing the circumſtance of
time, place, and perſon. What inconuenience is it , I praie
you, though M. Fekenham wrote in the Tower, that whiche he deliuered to M Horne at Waltham: What inconuenience followeth, I praye you , if he minded firſt to deliuer the ſame to his examiners in the Tower, or els where,
as occaſion ſhould ſerue: Is this ſufficient to diſproue him,
to condemne him, to ſlaunder him of ſurmiſed vntruth: It
is rather to be thought of ſuch as are not malitiouſe., to be
plaine dealing: not to diſſemble with you , but euen as he
had penned the writing before, ſo without any alteration to
deliuer it. Who neuertheleſſe, afterward hauing occaſiō
to exhibit and preſent the ſame writing to others, did ſim-
plie without guile or deceipt, ſignifie it to be deliuered vnto you at Waltham. And was it not ſo: Denie it , if
you can. Euerie Childe, by this may ſee how fonde and
fooliſh this your cauil is. But what is all this to the matter
and thing now in hand? It is, as your ſelfe confeſſe , but a
circumſtance. But M. Horne now himſelfe keepeth ſo little his owne rules and precepts of circumſtance that beſide
the miſerable and wretched peruerting and deprauing of his
owne authors he doth ſo often and ſo malitiouſly omit and
concele the due circumſtances of things by him reported
(neceſſary for the full illuſtration and opening of the whole
and entiere matter) that concerning this fault which he vniuſtly and triflingly obiecteth to M. Fekenham, he may moſt
iuſtly haue the prick and price, as they ſay.

But now that I remember, and aduiſe my ſelfe a litle better, I ſuppoſe I can not altogether excuſe M. Fekenham for
this title, but muſt race out therof foure words, and in ſteed
of *Lord Buſſhop of Wincheſter*, ſet in M. Robert Horne: M.

A iij   Fekenham

Hovv vvel M. Horne keepeth his ovvn rule of circum-ſtances.

In vvhat point the title of M. Fek. Treatiſe may be counted faulty.

Fekenham diſſembling and winking at the common error, whereby in the eſtimation of many, ye are both called and taken for the Biſhoppe of Wincheſter : whereas in deede ye are but an vſurper, and an intruder, as called thereto by no lawfull and ordinary vocation, nor canonicall conſecration, of his great modeſtie and ciuilitie, willing the leſſe to exaſperate yowe and others, thowghe he well knewe ye were no right byſſhop, yet after the vſuall ſort calleth and termeth yow Lorde Byſſhop of Wincheſter. But I muſt be ſo bolde by your leaue, as plainelye and bluntelye to goe to worke with yowe (as I haue done before with M. Grindall and M. Iewel yowr pewefellowes) and to remoue from you this glorious glittering Pecoks taile, and to call a figge a figge, and a horne a horne: and to ſaye (and that moſte truely) that ye are no Lorde Byſhoppe of Wincheſter, nor els where, but onely M. Robert Horne. For albeit the Prince may make a Lorde at her gratious pleaſire whome ſhee liketh, yet can ſhee not make you Lorde Biſſhoppe of Wincheſter, conſidering yee are not Lorde but in reſpecte of ſome Baronage and temporalties belonging and annexed to the See of Wincheſter. But you vſurping the See, as you are no Biſhoppe, ſo for the conſideration aſforeſaid, yee are no Lorde, nor Prelate of the Garter. For yee can be no Prelate of the Garter, being no Prelate at al: that being a prerogatiue appropriate to the Prelate and Biſhoppe of Wincheſter. Now that you are no true Biſſhoppe, it is euident by that your vocation is direct contrarie to the Canons and Conſtitutions of the Catholik Churche, and to the vniuerſall cuſtome and manner heretofore vſed and practiſed not onely in Englande, but in all other Catholique Countries and Churches, deliuered to vs from

hande

M. Horne no Biſh nor Pre, late of the Gar, ter.

hande to hande, from age to age, euen from the firfte graf=
fing and planting of the faith, efpecially in England.   For
the whiche I referre mee, to all autentique and aunciente
recordes, as well of Englande as of other Nations, concer=
ning the ordinarie fuccefsion of Byfhoppes, namelye in
the forefayed See of Winchefter.   For there was not,
no not one in that See, that did not acknoweledge the
Supremacye of the See of Rome, and that was not con=
firmed by the fame, vntil the late time of Maifter Poynet:
who otherwife alfo was but an vfurper, the true Byfhop
then liuing, and by no lawfull and Ecclefiafticall order
remoued or depriued.   Yee are therefore the firfte Bif=
fhoppe of this fewte and race, and fo confequentlye, no
Byfhoppe at all: as not able to fhewe, to whome yee did
ordinarilie fuccede, or anye good and accuftomable eyther vocation, or confecration.   Whiché point being ne=
ceffarilie required in a Bifhoppe, and in your Apoftles Lu=
ther and Caluin, and other lacking, (as I haue otherwhere
fufficientlye proued, though you by deepe filence thinke
it more wifedome vtterlie to diffemble, then ones to an=
fwere) they being therewith preffed, were fo mefhed and
bewrapped therein, that they coulde not in this worlde
wytte what to faye thereto, anfwering this and that, they
wift nere what, nor at what point to holde them. Yea Beza
was faine in the laft affemblie at Poify, with filence to có=
feffe the inuincible truth.

   But let it fo be, that your vocation was good and found
yet haue you difabled your felf to occupie that roome, and
either ought not to be admitted, or forthwith ought ye to be
remoued, for that ye are yoked (or as ye pretende) maried:
and as wel for the maintenáce therof, as of many other abho
                                                        minable

M. Horn
the firfte
B. of his
race in
the See of
Vvinche=
fter.
In the
Fortreffe
of our
firft faith
annexed
to Ven.
Bede.par.
2.cap.1.3.
& .8.
The Pro=
teftantes
vvóder=
fully tro=
bled a=
bout the
queftió of
the con=
tinual fuc
cefsion of
Bifhops,

minable errors (in case you stand obstinately in them) no
doubt an Heretike. That ye liue in pretensed Matrimonie
with your Madge al the worlde knoweth, colouring your
fleshly pleasures vnder the name of an honorable Sacramēt,
by this your incest wretchedly prophaned and vilained
Ye keep now your said Madge, in the face of al the worlde
without shame, whiche in King Henries daies ye kepte in
hucker mucker and lusky lanes as many other did of your
sort: especially M. Cranmer that occupied the See of Cāter-
burie: who caried about with him his prety conie in a chest
full of holes, that his nobs might take the ayer.

Lecherie
turned
into the
name of
vvedlock

You wil perchance stande in defence of your pretensed
mariage, and also of your other heresies, and say they are
no heresies at all, and turne lecherie into wedlock as some
of your sorte haue of late daies turned, vppon good fridaie,
a Pigge into a Pike, putting the said pigge in the water and
saying: goe in pigge, and come out pike. But then I referre
you to the olde Canons of the Fathers, to the writinges especially of S. Augustine, of Epiphanius, of Philaster and
other, that among other heresies, recite some of those that
you openly and your fellowes maintaine. Yf ye will reiect

M. Horn
and his
fellovves
accōpted
heretikes
by the
Apologie
of Eng
land.

Apologia
Lati. iii. 3.
pag 33.

the poore Catholiques, S. Augustine and Epiphanius also,
yet I trust you will not be againft your owne famouse A-
pologie, whiche saith that Epiphanius nombreth fourscore
Heresies(of the which it is one, for a man after the order of
Priesthode to marie)and S. Augustine a greater nomber and
so concludeth you and the residue to be heretikes. If ye wil
denie ye mainteine any of those heresies, your preachings,
your teachings and writings beare full and open testimony
againft you. What then haue you to iustifie your cause?
You wil happely forsake and abandon S. Augustines autho-

ritie

ritie withal the olde Canons and Councels, and flye vnder the defence of your brickle bulwarke of Actes of Parliament.

O poore and sely helpe : o miserable shift that our faith should hang vppon an acte of Parliamente, contrary as wel to all actes of Parliament euer holden in Englande before, as to the Canons and Fathers of the Catholike Churche. A strange and a wonderfull matter , to heare in a Christian common welth, that matters of faith are Parliament cases. That ciuill and prophane matters , be conuerted into holie and Ecclesiasticall matters.   Yea and that woorse is, that Laie men that are of the folde onely, not shepheards at all, and therefore bounde to learne of their Catholique Bisshoppes and Pastours , may alter the whole Catholique Religion, maugre the heades of all the Bishoppes and the whole Conuocation.   This is to trouble all things : this is , as it were , to confounde togeather heauen and earth.

But yet let vs see the prouidence of God : These men, that relinquishing the Church, would hang only vpō a Parliament, are quite forsaken, yea euen there where they looked for their best helpe.   For I praye you, what warrant is there by acte of Parliament to denie the Real presence of Christes bodie in the holie Euchariftia?   Is it not for anye Parliament as well herefie nowe, as it was in Quene Maries, King Henries, or anye other Kinges dayes?   What can be shewed to the contrarie?   Doth not Luther your first Apostle and his schollers, defie you therefore, as detestable Heretiques?   Nowe concerning Transubstantiation and adoration, is it not well knowen, thinke you, that in King Edwardes dayes, there was a preaty legerdemaine played , and a leafe putt in at the printing, which

Marginal notes:
Religion altered in Englond agaist the vil of the vvhole Clergie.

M. Horn can not defend and mainteine his herefies nor him=selfe to be a Bishop by anie lavve of the Real. me.
See the Apologie of Sta philus Fol 81.

C   was

was neuer propofed in the Parliamente? What Parliamente haue your Preachers to denye free will, and the
necefsitie of baptizing children? Againe I pray you, is
there any Acte to confirme your vnlawful mariage? Doth
not in this point the Canonicall Lawe ftande in force, as
well nowe as in King Henries daies? And fo doth it not
followe, that yee are no true Bifhoppe? Befide, is it not
notorioufe, that yee and your Colleages, were not ordeined no not according to the prefcripte, I wil not fay of the
Churche, but euen of the verye ftatutes? Howe then
can yee challenge to your felfe the name of the Lord Biffhoppe of Winchefter? Whereof bothe the Municipall
and Ecclefiafticall Lawe dothe woorthelye fpoyle you?
Wherefore as I fayed, let vs dafhe out thefe wordes, and
then no reafonable man fhall haue any great caufe to quarell againft the Title of M. Fekenhams Treatife.

The. 2. Diuifion. M. Horne.

The booke by you deliuered vnto mee, touching the Othe, was writen in
the Tovver of London (as you your felfe confeffed, and the true title therof, doth
plainly teftifie) in the time of the Parliamēt holden Anno quinto *of the Q.*
Maiefiie. Ianua. 12. *at which time you litle thought to haue foiourned with*
me the winter follovving, and much leffe meant, to deliuer me the fcruples and
ftaies of your cōfcience in writing, to be refolued at my hands. And although
you would haue it feeme, by that you haue publifhed abroade, that the caufe
why you wrot, was to be refolued at my hande : yet the trueth is (as you your
felfe reported) that you and your Tovver fellovves, hearing that the Statute
moued for the affuraunce of the Queenes royall povver, would paffe and be
eftablifhed, did conceiue that immediately after the fame Seffion, Commif-
fioners fhoulde be fente vnto you, to exact the Othe. VVhereuppon you
to be in fome readines, to withftande and refufe the duetie of a good fub-
iecte, (.s.) not without helpe of the refte (as may be gathered) deuifed the
matter conteyned in the booke, committed the fame to writing, and pur-
pofed to haue deliuered it for your anfvvere touching the Othe of the Supre-
macie.

The. 8. vn-
truth, flā-
deroufe,

macy to the Comissioners, if they had come. This may appere by theTitle of that booke that you first deliuered to me, which is worde for worde as follovveth.

The answere made by M. Iohn Fekenham Priest, and prisoner in the Tower, to the Quenes highnes Commissioners, touching the Oth of the Suprem a cie.

In this Title there is no mencion of scruples and stayes deliuered to the Bisshoppe of VVinchester, but of aunsweare to the Queenes Commissioners. I am not once named in the iitle, ne yet in the booke deliuered to mee: neither is there one worde as spoken to me: although in the booke set abroad, you turne all as spoken to me. In your booke published are found these kinds of speaches: *To the L. Bishop of VVinchester. VVhen your L. shalbe able &c. I shall ioyne this issue vvith your L. &c. But it is farre otherwvise in your booke deliuered to me, namely. To the Queenes highnes comissioners. VVhen ye the Queenes highnes comissioners shalbe hable &c. I shal ioine this issue vvith you, that vvhen any one of you, the Queenes hignes comissioners, &c. From October, at what time you were sent to me, vnto the end of Ianuarie, there was daily conference betwvixt vs in matters of Religion, but chiefly touching the foure pointes, which you terme scruples and stayes of conscience, and that by worde of mouth, and not by any writing. In all which points, ye vvere (.9.) so answered, that ye had nothing to obiect, but seemed resolued, and in a maner fully satisfied. VVhervpon, I made aftervvard relation (of (.10.) good meaning tovvards you) to certain honorable persons of the good hope i had conceiued of your conformity. At whiche time, a certaine friend of yours standing by, and hearing what I had declared then to the honorable in your comendacion, did shortly after (.11. reporte the same vnto you, which as it seemed, you did so much mislike (doubting that your confederates should vnderstand of your reuolt (12) which they euer feared, hauing experience of your shrinking fro them at (.12.) VVestminster in the coference there, the first yere of the Q. Maiestie) that after that time I founde you alvvaies much more repugnat, and cotrary to that wherin ye before times seemed in maner throughly resolued: And also to goe from that you before agreed vnto. By reason vvhereof, vvhen in debating betwvixt vs, you vsinge manye shiftes, amongst other, did continuallie quarell in Sophistication of vvordes, I did vvill you, to the ende vve might certainlye goe forvvarde in

the

C iij

*These vvere in deede the vvoorste kindes of speaches In all that booke of M Feck. The 9.vn truth. M. Fekenha vvas neuer so ansvvered. the 10.vn truth. Incredible. The.11. vntruth. There vvas no suche reporte made. The.12. vntruth. sladerous The.13. vntruth. notoriously sladerous.

the pointes materiall, that you vvoulde vvryte your Positions or Assertions, in fourme of Propositions: vvhiche I coulde not cause you to doe
in anye vvise, but yee vvoulde still stande vncertainelye in graunting
and deniyng at your pleasure: yea, althoughe I for the better agreemente
to be had, did dravve suche in fourme of Assertion, and gaue them in
vvritting vnto you, as I gathered of your ovvne mouthe to be your opinion: yet vvoulde yee in no vvise stande too, and reste in any one certainelye, but vsed still your accustomed vvrangling and wādring at large.
Vvhiche your behauiour so muche misliked mee, that I coulde not but earnestly
charge you vvith inconstancie, in that yee woulde sometimes denie, that
yee before had graunted: and also graunte, that yee before denyed.   Then
being so muche pressed herevvith, and perceiuing that your frovvarde quarelling vvith the plaine vvoordes of the Statute, coulde no lenger couer
your euill meaning, at the length you did require, that I vvoulde put in
vvriting the vvoordes of the Othe, vvith the sence or interpretation added thereunto, as you considering thereuppon, might deuise the fourme of
your Propositions, vvhereuppon we might afterwarde debate.   By this it
may appeare, bothe how vntrue it is, that you hitherto had deliuered vnto mee any suche scruples of yours in writing, as you pretende in the Title
(for then I needed not to haue sought any Propositions of your Assertions)
and also how vntrue that is, that the interpretation of the Othe whiche I
wrote at your requeste, before I euer sawe anye writing of yours, was to
answere your scruples and staies deliuered to mee in writing.

The Seconde Chapiter: declaring by the way, the order of the late disputations at Westmynster.

HERE is no matter effectual, but that may seme
already by our former answere sufficiently discharged: sauing that it serueth to accumulate
and increase the heap of M. Horns vntruths, as
that this shedule should be made *not without the helpe of the
rest.* How proue you that M. Horn? *As it may be gathered, ye*
say,

ſay. yea,but why haue you ſo ſone forgottē your late leſſō?
Where be your circumſtances that enforced yow ſo to gather. why were they not according to your owne rule ſpecified? Againe ye ſay,M.Fekenham *was ſo anſwered at your
hands,that he had nothing to obiecte but ſemed to be reſolued,
and in a maner ſatisfied.* Syr,we cal vpon yow yet ons againe
to remember your former rule, with the which ye ſo ſtrait-
ly and vaynly charged M.Fekenham.But yet here ye ſeame
to be ſomwhat better aduiſed, mollifying the matter with
theſe wordes *in a maner ſatisfied :* other wiſe yt had paſſed
al good maner and honeſty to, ſo vntruly to make that reporte the cōtrary being ſo wel knowen , that he neuer yelded vnto you in any one pointe of religiō, neither in courte
nor yet in manour,nor elſe where .

 Then haue we an heape of other vntruthes packed vp
together: As that M.Horne ſhould *haue a good meaning towards M. Fekenham,* making of him within ſix lines after an
vntrue and a ſlanderouſe report *as to reuolte* from the relligion by him receiued and profeſſed at baptiſme , to reuolte
from the fayth of Chriſtes Catholike Churche , to reuolte
from al the moſt bleſſed Sacraments, and from the vnity of
the ſaide Churche,and thereby to become as ſtarke a ſchiſmatike and an heretike as M . Horne him ſelfe ys. Was this
M Horne , your good and frendly meaninge towards M.
Fekenham? He thāketh yow for nawght he will none of it:
he hath eſpyed yow: ye proferre him to muche wronge Of
like ſorte is your other ſaying of M Fekenhams frende that
ſhould ſtande by, when yow made relation of the hope ye
had of M.Fekenhams conformity,and that M.Fekenhā vpō
your reporte to him by his,frend ſhould be more repugnant
then he was before. This ſeemeth to be made of your owne

head,to furnifhe your own forged tale withal: Which if it had bene true, why did yow not according to your owne rule fet forthe the truthe thereof, obferuing the dewe cir＊cumftances of the matter,perfon,tyme,and place ? But this incomparably paffeth and farre excedeth al your other for-fayde vntruthes,that ye fay M.Fekenham fhould fo fhrinke from *his cōfederats*(as yow terme them more malicioufly thē truely*)in the conferēce made at Weftminfter, that they fhould euer fince conceiue a feare of his conftancy in religion.*

I befeach yow good Syr,in what one point of religion, did he fhrinke from his company in that cōference at Weft-minfter?Was the matter wherin he diffented from them any other than this; That,whereas both they and he alfo hadde agreed vppon a booke towching the queftions then in cōtrouerfie betwene yow and thē, the right honorable Lord keaper of the great feale,commaunded them in the Quene her highnes name to beginne and to reade their booke firft, which they refufed to doe,and yet he for his parte thought it not good to difobey the Quenes highnes commaunde＊mente therein and thervppon offered himfelfe to beginne the difputation,and the Lord keper would not permit him fo to doe,what an offence I befeache yow hath M. Feken-ham cōmitted herein, fo great as worthy a dafhe with your penne?What fhrynkinge in religiō cal yow this, when in the defence thereof he did fo openly proferre him felf to put forthe the firft argumente?

The booke that was fet forth of the fayd conference for the difgracing and deprefsing of the Catholiks, dothe yet geue fome commendation to M. Fekenham for the caufe aboue fayde and nothing towcheth him with any fufpicion of inconftancy,or mambring in religion,as ye moft vniuft-ly doe ly doe:This is your own fyne and fingular inuention.

And now here ons againe we muſt plucke yow by the hornes,and cal yow home to your owne rule,and demaũde of yow:Sir how know yow that his Towre fellowes haue conceiued ſuch a feare of him? What proufe are ye now able to make thereof? Ye haue ſpoken the words:ye haue writen them:ye haue ſet them forth in printe to the vewe and fight of the worlde. And that I trowe of a very good meaninge towardes M.Fekenhã. Yea forſothe. Who ſeeth it not,and withal what an honorable prelate yow are thus to ſtuff and farſe your booke, with an heape of ſuch ouer-ſights and open vntruthes?

I might now paſſe forth to the reſidewe of M.Hornes book,ſauing that the mẽtiõ of the conferẽce at Weſtmynſter and the book thereof made,occaſioneth me a litle to ſpeake thereof,for that I perceiue many are ſlaundered therby, ſur-miſyng the Catholiks gaue ouer,for that they were not able to defende and mainteyne their ſide: But theſe mẽ ſhal vn-derſtãde, that the very cauſe was, that they might not be ſuffred to reply to their aduerſaries,but were commaunded ſtraite to a new queſtion the firſt vndetermined,and nothíg by them anſwered by reaſon their replication was cut of.

I ſpeake nothing of the vneuen dealing and handling of the matter,as that the Catholiks being in poſſeſsion of the truth frõ time to time in the Churche continued and obſer-ued were yet notwithſtanding diſuantaged and put to the proufwith much more iniury,then if a man that had an hũ-dred years and more quietly enioyed his Lãds,ſhould ſodély be diſturbed ãd diſpoſſeſſed thereof,vnleſſe he could proue his poſſeſsiõ,to hĩ that had no right or intereſt to claime the ſame.Which I ſay not,for that the catholiks had not,or did

Concer/ning the conferẽce at VVeſt mynſter in the firſt yere of the Quenes Maieſties Reigne.

not:

not fhewe fufficient euidence, but for the maner of the ordering and dealing therein, the Catholiks being very much
ftraited for fhortnes of tyme: befide that it was a fruytleffe
and a fuperfluofe enterprife: For in fo manygreat and weighty matters . as now ftande in controuerfie and debate , to
what ende and purpofe was yt to debate vppon thefe 3.
matters only , whether the feruice may be in the mother
tong : whether any one realme may alter and chaunge the
rites and ceremonies in the Churche and make newe: whether the maffe be a facrifice propitiatory. feing that the firft,
and the fecód queftion, be no queftions of faith, and the. 3. dependeth vpon the queftions of tranffubftantiation , and the
real prefence; which ought firft to haue bene difcuffed: and
then this, as acceffory thereunto?

Againe, what prefidente or example can be fhewed of
fuch kinde of difputation to be made before the Laye men
as Iudges? Suerly howe daungeroufe this matter is , befide
manyfolde recordes of Antiquity , the miferable examples
of our tyme doe fufficiently teftifie : efpecially at Monfter
in Germany. Where by thefe meanes the Lutherans thruft
oute the Catholiks, and where euen by the very fame trade,
ere the yeare wente abowte , the Lutherans them felues
were thruft owte by the Anabaptiftes . And then within a
while after followed the pytiful tragedy plaied there by the
fayd Anabaptifts the worthy fruit of fuch difputatiós. Now
albeit thefe difputatiós were nothing neadful at al, and much
leffe for that in the parliamét time, when this cóference was
had, the whol clergy (whofe iudgemét fhould haue bene in
this cafe of chieffeft importáce)vniformly agreed, afwel vpó
the real preféce as tráfubftantiatió ãd the facrifice alfo, with
the fupremacy of the Pope, and made their húble petitió(as
became

The ques
ftiós dif-
orderly
put out.

At Mó-
fter by
reafon of
Difputa-
tions, in
one yere
the Lu-
therans
thruft out
the Catho
liks, the
Anabap-
tifts the
Lutherás
Sleiden
lib. 10.
The cler-
gies fute
to the
parliamét

became their vocatiō)that the aūciēt relligion might not be
altered in the parliamēt,although they could neuer obtaine
that their petition might there be read, yet if they woulde
nedes haue gonne forward with their diſputations , reaſon
had ben,that they ſhould haue begonne with the chief and
principal points,and not with the dependant and acceſſo-
ry mēbers,or matters nothing touching faith:and withal to
haue ſuffred the Catholiks , to haue replied to their aduerſaries,whiche they could not be ſuffered to doe,leaſt their
aduerſaries weaknes ſhuld (as it would haue done in dede,
and now daily doth,God be praiſed) euidently and openly
haue bene diſciphered and diſcloſed. Wherin whether the
Catholiks were indifferently dealt withall, I reporte me to
all indifferent men. Surely among all other things concerning the ſupremacy of the prince in cauſes Eccleſiaſtical, the denial wherof is more extreamely puniſhed by the
law,then any other matter of religion now in controuerſy,
ther would haue ben much more mature deliberatiō, eſpecially conſidering that aboue.x.hundred yeares paſt,in diſputations of matters of faith,whereto the Catholikes were
prouoked in *Aphrica*,the ſaid Catholikes required, that at
the ſaid diſputations ſhould be preſente the Legates of the
See of Rome,as the chief and principal See of Chriſtēdom.
But let vs now returne to M.Horne.

*The Ca-
tholikes
not ſuf-
fred to
replie.*

*The Ca-
tholikes
required
in Aphri-
ca the
Popes le-
gate to be
preſent in
diſputati-
ons with
the Ariās.
Vict.lib.2.
de perſeq.
Vandal.*

M.Horne.   The.3. Diuiſion.pag.3.a.

*After this in February follovving, certaine perſons of vvorſhip reſorted to
my houſe,partly to ſee me, and partly to heare ſomevvhat betvvixt me and
you. And after that vve had reaſoned in certaine pointes touching Religion,
vvherein ye ſeemed openly to haue little matter to ſtande in , but rather did
yelde to the moſte inſubſtance that I had ſaied : neuer the leſſe being after
vvithdravven in ſome of their companies , although yee did ſeeme openlye to
conſent and agree vvith me in that I had ſaid : Yet (ſaid you)the* matter

D   it ſelfe

ít felfe is grounded here *(pointing to your breaſt)that ſhall neuer goe out.* VVhiche being tolde me, I did vehemently then challenge you for your double dealing and colourable behauiour : ſaying , that I thought you did not that you did,of any conſcience at al:and therefore compted it but loſt labour further to trauaile vvith ſuch a one as had neither conſcience nor conſtancy. But you ,to ſhevv that ye did al of conſcience, ſhevved me both vvhat yee had ſuffred for the ſame in diuers manners,and alſo hovv the ſame vvas grounded in you long before. For prouſe vvhereof , ye offred to ſhevve me a booke of yours,that ye had deuiſed in the Tovver,and the ſame ſhortly after did deliuer vnto me,not as your ſcruples and dcubtes to be reſolued at my hande vvherein ye ſeemed in our conference before had (.14.) reſolued : but only to declare,that the matter had bene long before ſetled in you , and this vvas the only and mere occaſion of the deliuery of the ſaid booke vnto me, entituled as is before declared, and not othervviſe.

But as you haue caſt a miſt before the eyes of the readers,vnder the ſpeach of a deliuery in vvriting, z vithout noting of any circumſtance that might make the matter cleere, vvherein you ſhevve your ſelf to haue no good meaning : euen ſo haue you ſet foorth reſolutions of your ovvne deuiſe vnder my name, becauſe you are aſhamed to vtter mine, vvhervnto you yelded, and vvere not able to anſvvere.

The .14. Vntruth. That M. Fekenhã ſhoulde geue vp his Ireatiſe in vvriting after he vvas reſolued by M. Horn.

Stapleton.

How vnlike a tale this is,that M. Fekenhã ſhould either be reſolued by M. Horn,or being reſolued, ſhould thē geue vp his matter in writing for none other cauſe thē M. Horn reporteth,I durſt make any indifferent man iudge,yea a nūber of M. Hornes own ſect;there is no apparance,there is no colour in this matter. And therefore I wil be ſo bold,as to adde this to his other vntruthes : wherevnto I might ſet an other more notable ſtraight waies enſuing, that M. Fekenham ſhould ſet forth reſolutions of his owne deuiſe vnder M. Hornes name,ſauing that I leaue it to a place more appropriate,where the matter ſhal be more conueniently and more fully diſcuſſed.

In the anſvvere to the reſolutiõs,the 440,leaf.

The

The 4. Diuision. Pag. 3, b.   M. Fekenham.

For asmuch as one chief purpose and intent of this Othe is, for a more saulfgard to be had of the Quenes royal person, and of her highnes most quiet and prosperous reigne: I doe here presently therfore offer my selfe to receiue corporal Othe vpon the Euangelistes, that I doe verely think and am so persuaded in my conscience, that the Queenes highnes is thonly suprem gouernour of this realme, and of al other her highnes Dominiōs and Countries according as thexpresse words are in the beginning of the said Othe. And further I shall presently sweare, that her highnes hath vnder God, the soueraignty and rule ouer al manner of persons borne within these her highnes realmes of what estate (either Ecclesiastical or Temporal) so euer thei be.

M. Horne.

Hovv so euer by vvords you vvoulde seme to tendre her Maiesties saulsty, quietnes, and prosperous reigne, your (.15.) dedes declare your meaning to be cleane contrary. VVhat saulsty meane you to her person, vvhen you bereue the same of a principal parte of the royal povver? vvhat quietnesse seeke you to her persoune, vvhen one chiefe purpose and entent of your book published, is to stay and bring her subiects to an heretical misliking of her royal povver, vvhich is a preparation to rebellion against her person? Hovv much prosperity you vvish to her Maiesties reigne appeareth, vvhen that vvith (.15.) diepe sighes and grones you looke daily for a chaunge thereof, and (.17.) tharche Heretique of Rome, your (.18.) God in earthe, to (.19.) reigne in her place.

The third Chapter declaring the rebellion of Protestāts against their princes in diuerse Countres abrode, and the seditious vvritīgs of Englishh Protestāts at Geneua and otherwhere.

D ij   There

haue tēporal iurisdiction as the Quenes Ma: hath,

Side notes:

The 15. vntruethe vilainous and slaunderous.

M. Feken hã by all his dedes hath alls vvaies shevved himselfe a most obedient subiect.

The 16. vntruthe Diuelish and spri tish.

The 17. 18. and 19 vntruths blasphe mous hor rible and vilainous For nei ther is the pope any heretike, neither do Catho liks make him their God: Nei ther wish tt ei hi to reigne in the Que nes place, that is, to

Here haue bene many Kings in this realme before our time, that haue reigned vertuouſlye,
quietly, proſperouſlye, moſt honorably, and
moſt victoriouſlye, which neuer dreamed of
this kinde of ſupremacy: and yet men of ſuche
knowledge that they coulde ſone eſpye, wherein their authority was impaired, and of ſuch cowrage and ſtowtenes
that they woulde not ſuffer at the Popes hands, or at any o-
ther, any thing done derogatory to their Royal powre. And
albeit the Catholiks wiſhe to the Quenes maieſty, as quiet,
as proſperouſe, as longe, and as honorable an empire to the
honour of God, as euer had prince in the worlde, and are as
wel affected to her highnes, as euer were good ſubiects to
their noble princes aforeſayde: yet cã they not finde in their
harts to take the Othe: not for any ſuch ſyniſter affection as
M. Horne moſte maliciouſly aſcribeth vnto them, but onely for conſcience ſake, grounded vppon the Canons and
lawes of the holy Churche, and the continual practiſe of al
Chriſten and Catholike realmes, finally vppon holy Scripture, namely that ſaying of S. Peter. *Oportet obedire Deo, magis quàm hominibus.* God muſt be obeyed more then mé: So
farre from al rebellion againſt her highnes perſon, and from
ſuche ſighthes and grones, as Maſter Horne moſt wickedly
ſurmiſeth (wherein he ſheweth by the way his owne and
other his complices affection towarde the princes not affected in religion as they be) that they dayly moſt hartely
praye for her highnes preſeruation: So farre of I ſaye, that
as they haue already for God and his Catholike faith, ſuffered them ſelfe to be ſpoiled of all worldly eſtate, contente
alſo yf God ſhall ſo appointe, to be ſpoyled alſo of theire
lyfe, ſo is there none of them, whereof diuerſe haue
faith.

Act. 5.

faithfully and fruitfullie ſerued their Prince and Countrie, that is not willinge for the preſeruation of the Prince and his countrie, to imploye, if the caſe ſo require, witte, body, and life alſo. And for my part, I pray God hartily the tryall woulde ones come.

But this is an olde practiſe, firſt of the Painimes, and Ie-wes, then of the heretikes, falſly to obiect to the Chriſtians and Catholiques, priuie conſpiracies and ſedition, the more to exaſperate the Princes againſt them. And when truthe faileth, then with the Princes authoritie and lawes to feare them. Surely, this man bloweth his horne a wrong, with charging the Catholiques with ſedition, which is the verie badge and peculiar fruit of all their Euangelicall broode.

I let paſſe the Donatiſts, and their horrible tragedies: I let paſſe the Boheames with their blinde Captaine both in Bo-die and ſoule, *Ziſcha* (a meete Captaine for ſuche a caitife companie) with their deteſtable vprores, ſeditiō, and migh-tie armie againſt their Prince and Countrie: I let paſſe how cruellie they handeled the Catholiques, caſting. *12.* of their chiefe Doctours and Preachers, into a kill of hotte burning lyme : and how pitifully they murdered a noble Catholike Knight : firſt burning his feete, then his legges, then his knees, then his thyes, to force him to cōſent to their wic-ked doctrine, which when he couragiouſly and valiauntlye refuſed, they conſumed with fier the reſidue of his bodie. I let paſſe the traiterous poyſoninge of that noble yonge Prince Ladiſlaus the King of Boheme and Hungarie, at the time of his mariage in Praga, by the meanes of Georgius Pogebratius a great Huſſyte, for that the ſaied Ladiſlaus at his firſte entrie into his Towne of Praga, gaue but heauie lookes to the Huſsian Miniſters, but lighting of his Horſe

Act.24. Vid de per ſeq. Vand.
An olde practiſe of infi-dels, Ie-Vves, and heretiks.
Sedition the pecu-liar fruite of hereſy.

Vide vvald doct. fidei. tom 2. Doctrina-li, & Do-cumento.

Aene. Pius in Præfat. De orig. Bohemia, Naucle-rus gene-rat. 49. pag. 483.

D iij   embra-

embraced moſte louinglie the Catholique Prieſtes, ſaiyng:
Hos Dei Miniſtros agnoſco. Theſe I acknowledge for the Mi-
niniſters of God. And to come nearer to our owne
home, I let paſſe the great conſpiracies of Syr Roger Acton
and Syr Iohn Oldecaſtle with their complices againſt King
Henrie the fift.

Polidore.
lib. 2 2.
Hiſt. Ang.

    I referre me onely (to be ſhorte) to the tragicall enor-
mities yet freſhe in remembraunce , of Luthers Schollers
in Germanie, in Dennemarke , in Swethelande, and in our
Countrie in the time of Queene Marie : of the Caluiniſtes
in Fraunce, in Scotland, and preſentlie in theſe low Countries , of Brabant, Hollande, Flanders , and Lukelande :
Laſt of all, of the Anabaptiſtes in the Citie of Mounſter
in Weſtphalia. For theſe three noble Sectes iſſued of
that poyſoned roote of Luther and his ſtrompette Cate,
haue eche of them according to their hability, geuen forth
ſuche euidente argumentes of their obedience (forſothe)
to their Soueraines , that all the forenamed Countries, do
well not onely remember the ſame, but feele yet preſently
the ſmarte thereof.

    In Germanie the Lutherans bothe the commons vn-
der Thomas Muntzer their Captaine againſte their Nobles, and the Nobles them ſelues againſte their Emperour,
notoriouſlie rebelled, and that vnder pretence of Religion. The murder in one ſommer of fiftie thouſande men

Sleidan.
lib 4.in
fine.
Idē.li. 17.
&. 19.

of the communaltie at the leaſte (as Sleidan reporteth)
and the famous captiuitie of the Duke of Saxonie and the
Lantgraue of Heſſe vnder Charles the fift (the late moſt
renouned Emperour) who bothe ſtode in fielde againſte
him , will neuer ſuffer thoſe bloudie practiſes to be forgotten. The inſurrection of the people in Dennemarke
againſt

againfte their Nobles, and of the Nobles in Swethelande againfte their Prince (as witneffeth that learned Councellour of the late mofte Catholique Emperour Ferdinandus, Fridericus Staphylus) are knowen to all the worlde with the fuccefle thereof. The open rebellion of Syr Thomas Wiat in the raigne of Quene Marie (couering his herefie with a Spanifh cloke) Charing Croffe and Tower hill will neuer forgette. *In Apolog. hart.3.*

In Fraunce the Zwinglians not only by traiterous force bereauing the Prince of Piemont of his Towne of Geneua, and fixing there euer fince the wicked Tabernacle of their loytering herefies, but alfo euen vnder the King that nowe liueth (as with my eyes I haue my felfe there beholded) firft by vnlawfull affemblies againft open Proclamations, and after by open rebellion withoute meafure of bloudfhedde, by taking vppe of the Kings rentes in Gafconie and the Prouince, by poffefsing by violence his principal townes, Rhone, Orleans, Lions and fuche other, by murdering moft traiterouflie his General Captaine the noble Duke of Guife, haue fhewed their godly obedience to their Soueraigne Princes.

For the better and more large deciphering of all thefe tragicall feates wrought by the Caluiniftes in the Realme of Fraunce, I referre you, Maifter Horne, to an Oration made of this matter expreffelye, and pronounced here in Louaine, and tranflated eloquently and printed in our Englifhe tongue. What loyall fubiectes the Caluiniftes in Scotland, haue fhewed them felues towarde their Queene and Soueraigne, Knokes and his band, the flight of the Nobles, ad the murdering alfo of her moft dere Secretary, eue within her graces hearing, with other bloudy practifes, yet

hot

hot and freſh,beareth open witneſſe before al the worlde.
It is euident,that beſide and againſt the Princes authority,
your Religion (M. Horne) hath taken place there.

    To come to the outragious enormities of the low Coun-
tries here,what tongue can expreſſe, what penne can de-
ciphre ſufficiently the extremity thereof? Theſe men liuing vnder a moſt Catholique, moſte clement , and moſte
mighty Prince, (the loyaltie of their profeſsion is ſuche)
they neither reuerence his Religion, nor conſider his clemencie, nor feare his power: but contrary to his open edictes and proclamations , abuſing his rare clemencie in remitting vnto them the rigour of the Inquiſition , proceede
daylie to ouerturne the Relligion by him defended , to
prouoke his iuſte indignation , and to contemne his Princely power. For, a graunte beinge made of the mollification thereof for a ſeaſon, vntill the Kings pleaſure were
farder knowen : at the humble ſuite of certaine Gentlemē,
put vp to the Ladie Regent the.5.of April,in the yere.1566.

which graunt alſo was expreſſely made, vpō conditiō that
nothing ſhould be innouated in matters of Religion in the
meane while,theſe men yet,hauing an inche graūted them,
tooke an elle,and the rodde being caſt aſide , fel ſtreight to
more vnthriftineſſe then before. For ſone after flocked
downe into theſe lowe Countries, a number of rennegate
preachers, ſome out of Geneua and Fraunce , ſome out of
Germanie, ſome Sacramentaries,ſome Lutherās,and ſome
Anabaptiſts.Who lacking not their vpholders and ſtaies fel
to open preaching, firſt in Flaunders,and then next in Antwerp,the.24.of Iune of the ſaid yeare.1566. After at Tournay,and Valencēnes,in Holland and Brabant,in al Townes
wel nere,except onely this noble Vniuerſitie of Louaine :
which

which (God only be praised therefore) hath continued in al
these garboiles, troubles, and disorders, not only free from
all spoiles of their Churches and Chappelles, yea and of all
Monasteries round about, as few townes beside haue done,
namely Bruxels, Bruges, Lyle, Mounts in Henaut, Arras,
Douay, and no towne els of importance (as farre as I can
remember) but also hath remained free from all schismatical
sermons in or about the towne. Whiche of no great towne
in all Brabant and Flanders beside can be said.   God onely
be praised therefore, for whose only glory I write it. For as
this towne and vniuersitie, was aboue al other townes in al
this Land moste spyted and threatened of these rebellious
Protestantes (by reason of the Doctours and Inquisitours
here, whose rigour they pretended as a cause of their malice) so was it by Gods singular mercy, from their speciall
malice, moste singularly preserued.   To him onely be the
glorie and honour thereof. Els mans policie was no lesse,
and the power of resistance was greater in other townes
then in this. But God, I trust, hath shewed his singular mercie vppon this place, to stoppe the gaping Rauens mouthes, *Pulchrum*
the hereticall broode as well of this lande as otherwhere, *est coruos*
which thirsted after the bloud of the learned Doctours, and *deludere*
Catholique Students of this place.   *hiantes.*

To returne to our matter, the sermons beginning at Antwerpe, (without the towne walles) at the first fewe, at the
second, and thirde preachings and so foorth, greate numbers assembled. The more halfe alwayes as gafers on, and
harkeners for newes, then zealous Gospellers as they call
them selues. The number then bothe of the audience and
preachers increasing, a proclamation came from the court,
and was published in Antwerp the. vj. of Iulie, that none of

towne fhould repaire to fuche forraine preachings vppon
a paine . This was fo well obeyed , that to the Kinges
owne Proclamation, printed and faftened vpon the South
doore of S.Maries Church in Antwerpe, it was in the very paper of the Proclamation vnderwriten by a brother of
your Gofpell M. Horne, *Syrs: To morow ye fhall haue a Sermon at fuche a place and time.* As who woulde faye: a figge
for this Edicte , and as the traiteroufe brethern in Ant-

*An vn-
manerlie
talke
meet for
fo clenly
a Gofpel.

werp haue not fticked openlie to faye: * *Schyte op die Con-
ning* , We will haue the woorde, what fo euer oure Kinge
faie or commaunde to the contrarye . How thinke you
M. Horne ? Doe thefe men acknowledge their Prince
Supreame Gouernour in all Spirituall caufes ? But lette
vs goe on. To let paffe the continuance of their preachings without the walles, whiche dured aboute fix or feuen wekes, the Prince of Orenge gouernor of the towne,
labouring in the meane feafon a greate while but in vaine,
to caufe them to furceafe from their affemblies , vntill the
Kinges pleafure with the accorde of the Generall States

*Recueil de
chofes ad
uenues en
Anuers.
An.1566.*

were knowen, they not admitting any fuche delaie or expectation (as them felues in a frenche Pamphlet by them
publifhed in printe , without the name of the Author or
place of the printing, doe confeffe, forefeeing (as thei faid)
that no good would come thereof, and therefore obeying
the Magiftrat as much as them lifted) found the meanes to
bring their affemblies into the town it felf, fo farre without
the Kings or the Regents authoritye, as if they had had no
King at al out of the land, nor Regent in the land. But the
meanes which they found to bring this feate to paffe , was
fingular and notable.

Wheras the.*19.*of Auguft the Prince of Orenge departed
from

frõ Antwerp to Bruxels to the court, that being then in the
Octaues of the Afsũptiõ of our Lady, a fpecial folemnitie in
the chief Church of Antwerp town, the brethren both for
the Gouernors abfence emboldened, and in defpite of that
folénity more enkendeled, the.xx.of Auguft beig Tuefday
toward euenĩg, at the Antemne time betwene v.and.vj.of
the clock, began firft by certain boyes to play their Pageãt,
mocking and ftriking by way of derifion, the Image of our
Lady thẽ efpecially vifited and honored for the honorable
memorial of her glorious Afsũptiõ. At this light behauiour
of the boies fom ftirre being made, as wel by the Catholiks
then in the Church, as by the factiõ of the Caluinifts there
alfo thẽ afsẽbled, the Catholikes fearing a greater incõuenience, began to depart the Churche, and the brethren at the
rumour therof increafed very much. Herevpõ incontinẽt-
ly the Margraue of the towne, the chief Officer in the Gouernours abfence, being fone aduertifed by the Catholikes
of fome tumult like to arife, drew in al haft to the Church.
But the brethren by this time were become Lordes of
the Church, and had fhut the dores againft the Margraue.
Notwithftãding at length the Margraue going from doore
to dore gat in, and approching to the affemblie of the Caluinifts, willed and cõmãuded thẽ in the Kings name whofe
Officer he was, to depart the Church, and not to interrupt
Gods feruice as they had begun. Thei anfwered, thei came
alfo to do God feruice, and to fing a few Pfalmes ĩn his honor, that being a place moft cõueniẽt therfore. Many wordes pafsing betwen the Margraue and them, their number
being great and increafing ftil, the Margraue departed the
Church, nothing preuailing neither by faire wordes nor by
foule. The Magiftrate being thus reiected (as vnhable in

By vvhat
meanes
the nevv
prechĩgs
entered
firft the
tovvne
of Ant-
vverp.

E ij　　　deede

deede to withſtande the faction of the Rebelles., as it appeared well euen that night) the holy brotherhode went to their druggery. Firſt they ſong Pſalmes, pretending that only to be the cauſe of their meeting there at that time. At their Pſalmodie ruſhed in great numbers of people, ſome to ſee and be gone againe, ſome to remaine and accompanie them. I was my ſelf preſent at the beginning of this Tragedy (coming by chaunce to the towne that afternone) and I ſaw after the Margraue was gone out of the Churche, and their Pſalmodie begonne, not paſt (I verely ſuppoſe) threeſcore perſons aſſembled. Mary there ruſhed in continually greate numbers of ſuch as taried ſtill with them. All this was before ſix of the clock. From that time foreward, their melodie ſone ended, they proceeded to ſacrilege , to breaking of Images, to throwing downe of Aulters, of Organes, and of all kind of Tabernacles , as well in that Churche , as in all other Churches , Monaſteries and Chappelles of Antwerpe, to ſtealing of Chalices, to ſpoiling of Copes, to breaking vppe of ſeates, to robbing of the Churche Wardens boxes as well for the Churche as for the poore. And heerein , I will reporte that whiche I ſawe with myne eyes. In Sainte Iames Churche, the ſpoyle there being not ſo outragiouſe, as in other Churches, al the ſettles, benches and ſeates , made aboute the Churche pillers and Aulters for folke to ſitte and kneele in, were in maner left whole, one onelye excepted , placed at the weſt ende of the Churche, in the which were diuers little ſcobbes and boxes of gatherings for the poore. Theſe ſcobbes lo, onlye, were broken vp , and the contents viſited : for to them was their chiefe deuotion : All the reſte remained whole, and vnſpoyled.

To

To be fhorte,al that night(which to him that had bene prefent thereat,as I then was, might well feme *Nox Siciliana*)
the Zelous brotherhood fo folowed the chafe , that they
lefte not one Churche in Antwerpe greate or fmal, where
they hunted not vp good game , and caryed away flefhe
good ftore. Chalices,patens and cruets of golde and of fil-
uer,copes and veftiments of filke and of veluet,fyne linnen
and courfe,none came amiffe:They tooke al in good parte,
and tooke no more then they founde.What fhal I fpeake of
the very libraries fpoiled and burned , namely of the grey
fryers,and of the Abbye of S.Michael? To defcribe particularly the horrible and outragious facrileges of that night,an
eternal documet of the ghofpellike zele, of this facred brotherhood,woulde require a ful treatife of it felfe. Only this
much I haue fhorthly touched,that you may fee ãd palpably
feele M.Horne, if any common fenfe remaine in you,what
obedient fubiects your brethern are,which with in.*24*.my-
les of their Princes Courte,which contrary to the expreffe
admonition of the Magiftrat then prefent , contrary to all
law, reafon, right , or confcience, vnder pretence forfothe
of your ghofpels zele(the zele truly of Chriftes ghofpell,
was neuer fuch) feared not in great numbers to committe
fuch open robbery,thefte,felony,facrilege,and treafon.But
let vs procede.

This Noble Strategeme was a way to bringe their preachinges within the towne walles:for now they had I trow,
well deferued of the towne , and were right worthy of all
fauour and libertye . Therefore the Thurfdaye after,they
preached openly in our lady Churche, and the Saterday in
in the Burge Churche , and required to haue places in al the
Churches to preache. But at the firft two, and then fowre,

          E iij   and

and at laſt all the Catholiks Churches being forebidden thē, they obtayned yet certain places in the new towne to build them new Churches:which they did with great ſpede.The Caluiniſts builded foure,and the Lutherans two.This much grounde they gotte,by one nightes worke.

But was it poſsible, that ſuch a beaſtly beginning, ſhould haue eyther long cōtinuance,or any good ending? We ſhal ſee by the iſſue. In this moneth of Auguſt not in Antwerp only,but in Gant,Ypres,Valencene and diuers other towns in Flādres,Hartoghēbuſke,Lyre,and other in Brabant, in di uerſe towns alſo of Hollād,in ſome in Zelād, and through-out wel nere al theſe low coūtres,Churches wer robbed ād ſpoiled , though in few ſo outragiouſly or ſo vniuerſally as in the town of Antwerp.The ſtorme of this ſodayne ſpoiles being ſomwhat aſſwaged ād ſtopped by policy ād ſpedy reſi-ſtāce,yet the new preachigs took place about al towns: ōly Louain as I haue ſaid excepted. this beig the ōly maidē toun of any importance in al Brabāt and Flandres,for being free both within and many a myle aboute,no leſſe from al ſchiſ-matical preachings,then frō all ſacrilegious ſpoiles. God on-ly,as I haue ſaid,be praiſed therefore.But to procede,ſoone after theſe ſacrileges,thei fel to opē rebelliō.For whē al wēt not foreward as it liked the Miniſtres, by their perſuaſions, townes began to rebelle, and to ſhut their gates againſt the Kings ſouldiars,which to haue iuſtice don vpō Churchrob-bers, and to ſtay farder enormities the Prince cōmaūded to be admitted. Such were Tournay,Valencens,Hartoghen-buſke,ād Haſſels in Lukelād. But Tournay being ſoone re-couered,and the proteſtātical rebelles ſubdewed Valēcens held out euē to the battery ofthe wals: before which time all Catholiks being driuē out of the toune that opēly would ſhew thē ſelues for ſuch,al monaſteries being ouerthrowen,

the

the churches being turned into barns or ſtorehouſes for their
corne,the brethern of Antwerp enuying at the ioly liberty
and audacity of the Valéceners, attépted diuers times to ob-
tayn the like in their town alſo. Witneſſes hereof,the tumult
made about the grey fryers Church the *19.* of Septéber,the
Prince of Orége being preſent ſkãt able to ſtay it. The ſpoyl
renewed in S . Maries Church in the moneth of Nouébre,
whereof ſix the next day were hãged by the Conte Hoch-
ſtrat thé the Prince of Orenge his deputy. The burning of a
great part of the grey fryers Church and cloiſter in the firſt
Sõday of Lét. And laſt of al the opé,manifeſt,and notorious
rebelliõ made by the caluiniſts in Antwerp,the *13.*of March
laſt whé thei poſſeſſed the artillery of the town,plãted their
ordinãce in the great Maire,a ſtrete ſo called, ſtoode there
in armes againſt their Price,required opély the kayes of the
gates,ãd of the town houſe,the baniſhmét of al religious perſons ãd prieſts,ãd brefly as the cry thé wét about the ſtretes,
des Coopmãs goet,en Papé bloet the goods of the Marchãts ãd
the blood of the Prieſts. Theſe I ſay are manifeſt,clere ãd eui
dent witneſſes that the Caluiniſtes of Antwerp attépted no
leſſe rebelliõ,thé the town of Valécens praćtiſed in dede. But
of this Notorious attépt and of the whole maner, ende and
beginning thereof toward the end of this book I ſhall more
largely ſpeak, to the which place I remitte the Reader.

Now what a great and ſodayn ouerthrowe God hath geué to al theſe trayterous attépts of ghoſpellíg proteſtãts,and
how they haue wrought therein their own deſtrućtiõ (for
had they not attépted the dominiõ it ſelf,their hereſies (we
feare) would longer haue ben winkéd at , and perhaps not
repreſſed at al) how firſt the caluiniſts in Antwerp were by
mayne force of the Catholiks,(the Lutherás ioyning in that
feate

feate with thé, côstrayned to lay downe their weapons, and to crye, *Viue le Roy*, God faue the king, how fone after vpon palmefonday the towne of Valencenes was taken by the kings Captaynes, how ftraight after Eafter the preachers were driuen to departe Antwerpe, and al other townes and Cyties of thefe lowe Countries, how their newe Churches are made a pray to the kings fouldyars, briefely how al is re-ftored to the olde face and coûtenáce as nighe as in fo fhort a time may be, how wonderfully, mercifullye, and miracu-loufly God hath wrought herein, neither my rude penne is able worthely to expreffe it, nether my fmal experience can fufficiently report it. I leaue it therefore to a better time and occafion, of fome other more exactly and worthely to be chronicled.

This is lo M. Horne, the obedience of the Caluiniftes in thefe low coûtres here, as we hear daily with our eares and fee with our eyes. And truly experiéce hath to wel fhewed, that Proteftáts obey, vntil they haue power to refifte. Whé their faction is the ftronger fyde, as they refifte bothe Pre-lats and Popes, fo they laye at bothe Kinges and Keyfars. And to this the law of their Gofpel enforceth them, as their own Minifters perfuade them. So by the perfuafió of Theo-dore Beza (Caluins holy fucceffour now at Geneua) the vil-layne Poltrot flewe the Duke of Guife, his Princes Capitain General. By the Authority of Hermannus a knowen renna-gate now in Englande, and a famous preacher here, as be-fore in Italy for open baudery no lefle infamous, the towne of Haffels in Lukelande rebelled. By the encouragement and fetting on of the Miniftres (who for the time were the chiefe Magiftrats there) the towne of Tournay for a feafon alfo rebelled, and fent out ayde to the rebelles of Valécens,

who

who fped according to their defertes, being to the number **In Flã-**
of ij.M. or there aboute intercepted by the kings fouldyars **ders.**
and flayne within the twelue dayes at Chriftmas lafte. And
it is wel knowen, namely by the firft execution made after
the taking of Valencenes, aboute witfontyde lafte that the
Minifters themfelues were the chiefe Authours of the lõge
and obftynat rebellion of that towne. Such fupreme gouuerment of the Prince ouer caufes Ecclefiaftical your dere
brethern here (M. Horne) the Caluiniftes doe acknowledge
and practife. Which that it renewe not to a farder rebelliõ,
we for the peace of Gods Churche, and for our owne fafty
doe pray, and you for fauing your poore honefty, had nede
to praye. Except your harte alfo be with them (M. Horne)
though your penne condemne them.

Nowe for the purgation of the Catholiks, againft whom **The Ca-**
this man fo falfly and malicioufly bloweth his horne, yt may **tholikes**
feame a good and a conueniente proufe, of their quietnes **no fedi-**
tious fub-
and obedience, that al this. 8. years and more there hath not **iects,**
ben in the realme, no not one that I can heare of, that hath
bene conuicted, of any difloyalty, for worde or dead, concerning the Princes ciuil regiment : which they all wifhe
were as large and ample, and as honorable as euer was our
noble countreymans the greate Conftantines. And albeit
I knowe *quòd non fit tutum fcribere contra eos, qui poffunt*
præfcribere, Yet for matters of confcience and relligion
(wherein onely we ftande) we poore Catholikes mofte. **VVhye**
the catho-
humblye vppon our knees defire her highnes, that we may **liks fhuld**
with mofte lowlye fubmifsion craue and require, to be **be borne**
vvithal.
borne withall, yf we can not vppon the fodayn, and withoute fure and fubftantial groundes abandon that faith, that
we were baptized in, and (as we are affured) al our aunce-
         F   tours,

tours, and al her Maiesties own most noble progenitors, yea her owne most noble father King Henry the eight, yea that faith, which he in a clerkly booke hath most pythely defended, and therby atchieued to him and his, and transported as by hereditary succefsion, the worthy title and style yet remayning in her highnes, of the *defendour of the faith*. Other disobedience then in these matters, (yf there be any thing in vs worthy that name) wherein as I haue said our first and principal obedience must wayt vpon God, and his Catholik Church, I trust her highnes hath not, nor shal not find in any true Catholick.

The Quecnes title Defender of the faith.

Let vs nowe turne on the other syde, and consider the fruits of M. Horn his euangelical bretherne and their obedience, that by woordes woulde seame to recognise the Quenes Maiesty as supreame gouernour in al causes ecclestical. Who are those then, I praye yow M. Horne, that repine at the Quenes maiesties iniunctiös and ordinances, for the decente and comly apparrel mete for such as occupie the roome of the clergy? Whence came those. 16. Ministres to Paris, and what Ministres were they, but roundecappe Ministres of England, fleying the realme for disobedience? Who wrote and printed a booke at Rhone against the Queenes Maiesties expresse cömaundment of priestly apparel? Was it not Minister Barthelet, that publifhed before the infamous libel against the vniuersall Churche of God, bothe that nowe is and euer hath bene? As fonde nowe and peuifh against his owne congregation, as he was wicked before and blasphemous against the whole Churche of God? Who are they that haue preached withe a chayne of golde abowte their neckes in steade of a typpet? Who are those that preache euen in her highnes presence, that

The obedience of the Euägelicall brethren in causes Ecclesiastical.

the

the Crucifixe her grace hathe in her chappelle is the Idoll
withe the red face? Who are thofe I pray yow, that write:
Sint fanè & ipfi magiftratus membra & partes, & ciues Eccle-
fiæ Dei: imo vt ex toto corde fint, omnes precari decet. Flagrent
quoque ipfi zelo pietatis: fed non fint Capita Ecclefiæ, quia ipfis
non competit ifte primatus. Let the magiftrates alfo be members and partes, and cytizens of the Churche of God, yea
and that they may be fo, it behoueth vs al with al our harte
to pray, let them be feruente in the godly zeale of religion,
but they may not be heads of the Churche in no cafe: for
this Supremacy doth not appertayne to them.

(margin: Magdeb. pref. cēt. 7)
(margin: The Lu-theraā in Germany deny this fupremacie.)

    Thefe are no Papiftes, I trowe Maifter Horne, but youre
owne deare brethern of Magdeburge, in their newe ftorie
ecclefiaftical: by the which they would haue al the worlde
directed, yea in that ftory, whereof one parcel Illiricus and
his fellowes haue dedicated to the Quenes Maiefty: that
beare the worlde hand, they are the true and zeloufe fchollers of Luther.

(margin: Cent. 4.)

    In cafe ye thinke their teftimony not to haue weight
enowgh, then herke to your and their Apoftle Luther, who
writeth, *that it is not the office of Kings and princes to côfirme,*
no not the true doctrine, but to be fubiecte and ferue the fame.
Perhaps ye wil refufe and reiecte bothe the Magdeburgen-
fes and Luther to, as your mortal enemies, (yow being a fa-
cramentarye) and fuch as take yow and your fellowes for
ftark heretiks. A hard and a ftraunge cafe, that now Luther
câ take no place amóge a nóber of the euágelical brethern.
What fay yow then to *Andreas Modreuius?* Surely one of
the beft lerned of al your fect. How lyke yow then him that
faieth, *there ought to be fome one to be taken for the chiefe and*
Supreame head in the whole Churche in al caufes ecclefiaftical.

(margin: Côtra ar-tic. Lou. Tom. 2.)
(margin: Andreas Modreui-us de Ec-clefia lib. 2. c. 10.)

              F ij   Wel

Wel,I fuppofe you wil challenge him to as a Lutherane. Yf it mufte neades be fo, I truft M.Caluin your greateft Apoftle fhal beare fome fway with yow. I know ye are not ignorante that *he calleth thofe blafphemers, that did call kinge Henry the eight Supreme heade of the Churche of Englande:* and handleth the kinge hĩ felfe with fuch vilany , and with fo fpitefull woords,as he neuer handled the Pope more fpitefully,and al for this title of Supremacy , which is the key of this your noble booke . Can ye now blame the Catholikes M . Horne,yf they deny this fupremacy, which the heads of your owne religion, afwel Lutherans, as Zwinglias doe deny and refufe ?

The Zvvinglians deny this fuprema cy. Caluin c. 7. Amos .

O what a ftraunge kinde of religion is this in Englande , that not onely the Catholikes , but the very patriarches of the new euangelical brotherhod doe reiecte and condemne ? Perchaunce ye wil faye . Wel,for al this there is no Englifhe man of this opinion . Mary that were wonderfull , that if as we be fequeftred and as it were fhut vp from other countres by the great Ocean fea that doth enuyrõ vs, fo we fhould be fhut vp from the doctrine as wel of the Catholiks,as alfo the Proteftants of other cõtreis:and that with vs the Lutherans and Zwinglias fhould finde no frendes to accompany them , in this as wel , as in other points.But contente your felf M.Horne, and thinke you if ye do not alredy, that either your felf,or many other of your brethern like the quenes fupremacy neuer a deale in hart,what fo euer ye pretẽd and diffemble in words.Think ye that Caluin is fo flenderly frended in Englãd;his bookes being in fuch high price and eftimatiõ there?No,no,it is not fo to be thought.The cõtrary is to wel knowẽ:efpecially the thing being not only opẽly preached , by one of your moft

A nevve fecte in England contrary to al the vvorlde befide,as vvel papiftes as prote ftants. They may be called , λαικοκίφαλοι: Laicocephali:as ye vvold fay. Lay heads,or Laichead makers .

feruent

feruét brethren there in England, euen fince the Queenes
maiefties reigne : but alfo before openly and fharply writen againft , by your brethren of Geneua. Efpecially one
Anthonie Gilbie. Whofe wordes I wil as wel for my difcharge in this matter, fomewhat at large recite , as alfo to
fhew his iudgement, of the whole Religion as well vnder
King Henrie, as King Edward, and fo confequently of the
faid Religion vnder our gracious Quene Elizabeth, nowe
vfed and reuiued : that all the worlde may fee that to be
true, that I faid of the Supremacie , as alfo that the feruent
brethren, be not yet come to any fixe or ftable Religion,
and that they take this to be but fimple as yet, ãd vnperfit.

In the time (faith he) *of King Henrie the eight , when by* Antonie
Tindall, Frith, Bilney, and other his faithfull feruauntes, God Gilbie in
called England to dreffe his vineyarde, many promifed ful faire, his admo
whome I coulde name, but what fruite followed? Nothing but nition to
bitter grapes, yea bryers and brambles , the wormewood of a- England
uarice, the gall of crueltie, the poyfon of filthie fornication flo- lãd to call
wing from head to fote, the contempt of God, and open defence them to
of the cake Idole, by open proclamation to be read in the Chur- repétáce.
ches in fteede of Gods Scriptures. Thus was there no reforma- at Geneua
*tion, but a deformation, in the time of the * Tyrant and leche-* by Iohn
roufe monfter. The bore I graunt was bufie , wrooting and 1558.p.69.
digging in the earth, and all his pigges that followed him , but *See how
they fought onely for the pleafant fruites , that they winded religiofly
with their long fnoutes : and for their owne bellies fake, they teftantes
wrooted vp many weeds : but they turned the ground fo, min- fpeake of
gling good and badde togeather, fweet and fower, medecine and their
poyfon, they made, I faye, fuche confufion of Religion and La- Princes,
wes, that no good thing could growe, but by great miracle, vn-
der fuche Gardeners. And no maruaile, if it be rightlye confi-
F iij dered.

*dered. For this Bore raged againſt God, againſt the Diuell,
againſt Chriſte, and againſt Antichriſte, as the fome that he
caſte out againſte Luther, the racing out of the name of the
Pope. And yet allowing his lawes, and his murder of many Chriſtian fouldiars, and of many Papiſts, doe declare and euidentlie teſtifie vnto vs, eſpecially the burning of Barnes, Ierome,
and Garrette their faithfull preachers of the truthe, and hanging the ſame daye for maintenaunce of the Pope, Poel, Abel,
and Fetherſtone, dothe clearelie painte his beaſtlines, that he
cared for no Religion. This monſterous bore for all this, muſt
needes be called the Heade of the Churche in paine of treaſon,
diſplacing Chriſte our onely head, who ought alone to haue this
title. Wherefore in this pointe, O Englande, ye were no better then the Romiſhe Antichriſte, who by the ſame title
maketh him ſelfe a God, and ſitteth in mens conſciences, bani-
ſheth the woorde of God, as did your King Henrie, whome ye
ſo magnifie. For in his beſte time nothing was hearde but
the Kings Booke, the Kings Procedings, the Kings Homilies,
in the Churches, where Gods woorde onelie ſhould haue ben
preached. So made you your King a God, beleuing nothing
but that he allowed. I will not for ſhame name how he turned
to his wonte : I will not write your other wickedneſſe of thoſe
times, your murders without meaſure, adulteries and inceſtes
of your King, and his Lordes, and Commones. &c.*

Loe Maiſter Horne, howe well your Proteſtante
fellowe of the beſte race, euen from Geneua, lyketh this
Supremacie by plaine woordes, ſaiynge : that this title
whiche you ſo ſtoutlye in all this your booke auouche,
diſplaceth Chriſte, who owghte and that onely to enioye
it. And whereas ye moſte vntruely ſaye heere, that we
make the Pope our God in carth: Maiſter Gilbie ſaieth, that
you

you make your Prince a God, in attributing to her this wrong title, wherinChrist wil haue no copartener:Surely, we make no God of the Pope, and sometimes perhappes, no good man neyther.   And yet we reuerence him for his office and authoritie, that Christe so amplie and hono-rablie gaue him for preseruation of vnitie and quietnes in his Church. Your wisedome with like truth also appeareth in that you call the Pope *the Archeretike of Rome*, naming no man. And so your woordes so liberallie and wantonly cast out, doe as wel comprehend S.Peter, S.Clement,and other holy Martyrs, and Bishops there, as anye other.   I promise you a wel blowen blast and hansomly handeled. With like finenesse you call him Archeretike, that is the supreme Iudge ouer all Heretikes and heresies too, and that hath already iudged you and your Patriarches for Ar-cheritikes. Iwisse as well might the fellon at the barre in Westmynster hall to saue his life, if it mighte be, call the Iudge the strongest theef of all : and doubtles (had he a Prince on his side)his plea were as good as youres is: Now where ye say, *we would haue the Pope to raigne here in the Quenes place,* procedeth fro your lik truth ad wisedom. For albeit the Popes autority was euer chief for matters eccle-astical,yet was there neuer any so much a noddie,to say ad beleue the Pope raigned here:The Pope and the King beig euer two distinct persons, farre different the one from the other,in seueral functions and administrations:and yet wel concurrant and coincident togeather without anye immi-nution of the one or the others authoritie.

Wel,ye wil perhap say, that albeit M. Gilbie misliketh this title in the Prince,yet he liketh wel the religio, especi-ally such as now is, and such as was in King Edwards daies
which

which is all one.   Herken then I pray you, what his cen-
fure and iudgement is therof. *I will name* (faith he) *no par-*
ticular thinges because I reuerence thofe dayes (meaninge of
King Edwarde) fauing only the killing of both the Kings vn-
cles and the prifonment of Hoper for Popes garmentes. God
graunt you al repentant hartes. For no order or ftate did anye
parte of his duetie in thofe daies : but to fpeak of the beft,wher-
of you vfe to boaft , your Religion was but an Englifh Mattins
patched foorth of the Popes Porteffe: many things were in your
great booke fuperftitious and foolifh.   All were driuen to a
prefcript feruice like the Papifts, that they fhould think their
dueties difcharged, if the number were fayed , of Pfalmes and
Chapters.   Finallye, their coulde no difcipline be brought into
the Churche, nor correction of manners.

I truft nowe, M. Horne, that you will fomewhat the
more beare with the Catholikes,if they can not wel beare
the feruice and title which your companions fo yll liketh.
Yet becaufe ye are fo harde maifter to M. Fekenham and
his fellowes,to haue their doing *a preparation to rebellion a-*
gainft the Quenes perfon, for defeding Ecclefiaftical authority,which nothig toucheth her perfon or croun(as without the which it hath moft honorably continued and flori-
fhed many hudred yeres,and fhal by Gods grace continew
full well and full long againe, when it fhall pleafe God) let
this title and iurifdiction Ecclefiafticall goe,which al good
Princes haue euer forgon as nothing to them apertaining.
Let vs come to the very temporall authoritie,and lette vs.
confider who make any *preparation of rebellion,*the Catholikes or the Proteftants.

Who are they, I pray you, that haue fet foorth deuifes .
of their owne for the fuccefsion of the crowne withoute
the

Ibidem.
Fol.79.
Gilbies
iudge-
met con
cerninge
the reli-
gion that
novv is.

the Princes knowledge ?   Surely no Catholikes , but the very Proteſtants them ſelues.   Who blewe the firſt blaſt of the trompet I pray you ?   Who are thoſe that haue ſet foorth in open printed bookes in the Engliſh tongue, that neither Queene Marie, nor this our gracious Queene were lawfull inheritours of the Croune ?   And finally that it is againſte the Lawe of God and nature , that anye woman ſhoulde inherite anye principalitie or Kingdome ?   No Catholique I warrante you , but your holye brethren, ſo feruente in the woorde of the Lorde.   Yea amonge other M. Iohn Knoxe the new Apoſtle of Scotlande : *It is not birth onely* (ſaith he) *or propinquitie of bloud that maketh a King lawfully to reigne aboue the people profeſſing Ieſus Chriſt, and his eternal veritie, but in his election muſte the ordinãce which God hathe eſtabliſhed in the election of inferiour Iudges, be obſerued.*   Loe this Apoſtle excludeth al ſucceſsion as well of men, as women : and will haue the Kingdome to goe by election, that in caſe there be founde any Prince that fanſieth not this newe Apoſtle , that then he may be lawfullye depoſed , and a newe brother in his roome placed.   *And therefore I feare not* (ſaith he) *to affirme, that it had been the dutie of the Nobilitie, Iudges, Rulers, and people of Englande, not onelie to haue reſiſted, and againſt ſtanded Marie that Ieſabell, whome they call their Queene , but alſo to haue punniſhed her to deathe , with all the ſorte of her Idolatrous Prieſtes, togeather with all ſuche as ſhoulde haue aſſiſted her.*

Ye ſhall nowe heare the verdit of an other good man : a zealous brother of Caluins ſchole.   *I knowe* (ſaieth he) *ye will ſaie, the Croune is not entailed to the heires Males onelie , but appertaineth as well to the daughters .   And*

G   *therefore*

Iohn Knokes in his appellation and his exortatiõ to the nobilitie of Scotland Fol. 77. imprited at Geneua An. 1558. In his appellation to the Nobility the 36, leafe.

Chriſtopher Goodmã how Suaperiours

ought to
be obeied
and im
printe d
at Gene
ua by
Iohn
Crifpin.
1558.c.5.
fol.54.
therefore by the lawes of the Realme yee coulde not otherwife
doe. But if it be true, yet miferabie is the anfweare of fuche,
as hadde fo longe time profeffed the Gofpell, and the liuely
word of God: If it had bene made of Paganes and Heathens
whiche knewe not God by his woorde, it mighte better haue
bene borne withall: but amonge them that bare the name of
Gods people, with whome his lawes fhoulde haue chiefe au
thoritie, this anfweare is not tolerable.   And afterwarde.
If fhee had bene no baftarde, but the Kinges daughter as law
fullie begotten as was her Sifter that godlie Ladie and meeke
lambe, voide of all Spanifhe pride and ftraunge bloude, yet
in the ficknes and at the deathe of our lawfull Prince of Godlye memorie Kinge Edwarde the fixte, that fhoulde not haue
bene your firfte counfell or queftion : who fhoulde be your
Queene, but firfte and principallye, who had bene mofte me-
teft amonge your brethren, to haue hadde the gouernemente
ouer you, and the whole gouernemente of the Realme to rule
them carefullye in the feare of God.

     After this he fheweth his minde more expreffelye.

Cap 8.
fol.96.
A woman (faieth he) to reigne, Gods lawe forbiddeth, and
nature abhorreth, whofe reigne was neuer counted lawefull,
by the woorde of God, but an expreffe figne of Gods wrathe:
and a notable plague for the finnes of the people : As was the
raigne of Iefabell, and vngodlie Athalia : efpeciall inftru-
mentes of Sathan, and whippes to his people of Ifraell. I
M.Sands
dooe here omitte a Sermon made by one of your Prelates,
that bothe Queene Marie and our gracioufe Queene Elizabeth were baftardes.   And they faye that your felfe
(Maifter Horne) did the fame at Durham. Howe lyke
yee this, Maifter Horne? Is this a preparation of rebellion againfte the Queenes perfon, or no?   Yee will per-
                                                chaunce

chaunce to extenuate the matter , faye it is the priuate
doinge of one or two, difanulled by the refte.   Nay Syr,
yee fhall not fo fcape : I faye this was the commen confente and iudgemente of all your holie brethren of Geneua , as well Englifhe as other , yea of Maifter Caluin
him felfe, as it may be gathered by Maifter Whitingham
his Preface, to the fayed booke of Maifter Goodman. M. Vvhi-
tingam
in the
Preface.
Maifter Chriftopher Goodman (*fayeth he*) *conferred his*
Articles and chiefe Propofitions with the befte learned in
thefe parties, who approued them, he confented to enlarge the
fayd Sermõ, and fo to print it as a token of his duetie and good
affection toward the Church of Gcd. And thẽ if it were thought
good to the iudgement of the godlie, to tranflate the fame into
other lãguages, that the profit therof might be more vniuerfal.
    Lo good M. Horne, a fermon made at Geneua to al the
Englifh brethren, not only to depriue the Quene of her title of the Supremacy in caufes Ecclefiafticall, but euen in
temporal too, and from al gouernmẽt: the matter being có-
municated befide to the beft learned there.   And then M.
Caluin and M. Beza too, I trowe, gaue their verdiċt to this
noble and clerkly worke. And fo it feemeth to importe the
confent of al the gehennical(I fhould haue faid) the Geneuical Church. And who are thofe now that rule al the roft
in England but this good brotherhod? Men no doubt well
worthy, for whofe fakes the Catholiks fhold be thus hardly
hãdeled and to whome the Q. Maiefty is (who doubteth)
depelye bounde, and they worthie to be fo well cherifhed
at her hands, as they are. Thefe good brethren by their new
broched Diuinitie haue found a prety deuife, at their pleafure not onelye to depofe the Queenes Maieftye and the
Quene of Scotland : but alfo the greateft parte of all other

Princes, fuch I meane as be women, or haue holden their gouernment by their difcent from women. As did in our Countrie fince the conqueft Henrie the fecond, the fonne of Maude th'Emprefſe, daughter to King Henrie the firſte. As did Phillipp, Charles the late Emperours Father, holde Burgundie, and Charles him felfe the Kingdom of Spaine. I here omit now Petronilla the Prince of the Arragones, Maude of Mantua, bothe Iones of Naples, Margaret of Norwey, and other women Princes els where, as in Nauarre, and in Loraine. But what fpeake I of women only, when Knoxe, as I haue fhewed, will haue all Realmes to goe by election, and not by fuccefsion? So that now whereas the Catholiques, yea the ftarkeft Papift of all (as thefe men terme them) can be well contente, yea with all their hartes to affirme, that the Quenes Maieftie may enioye not onely this Realme, but euen the whole Empire, and wifhe no leffe (if it pleafed God) to her highnes, and finde no fault, but onely with that title, that is not competent for her highnes, and without the which fhee may reigne as nobly, as amply, as honorably, as euer did Prince in England, or els where, which neuer affected any fuch title: thefe men, who pretēd to the world, to profeſſe a wōderful fincere obferuatiō toward God and their Prince, do not only fpoile her of that title, but of al her right and intereſt to England, Fraunce, Ireland, or els where : making her incapable of al manner ciuile regiment. Which I truft the Quenes Maieftie ones wel confidering, wil gracioufly beare with the Catholiks that do not enuy her the one or the other title : but only defire that their confciences may not be ftreyned for the one of them. Whiche they vppon great groūds, and as they verely think, without any impairing of

ringe of her worldlye eſtate can not by othe aſſuredlye as
vouche:which thing thei truſte they may doe,without any
iuſte ſuſpition of ſeditiõ or rebelliõ. Wherewith M.Horne
moſte vniuſtly chargeth them:the ſayd note and blame moſt
iuſtly(for the cauſes by me reherſed) redounding vpon his
owne good brethern.

Which thing as he can not truely lay to any Catholike:
ſo of al men leaſt to maiſter Fekẽham. Whereof I truſt,cer-
tayn right honorables , as the Lorde Erle of Leceſter , the
Lord Erle of Bedforde,yea the Quenes Maieſtye her ſelfe
wil defende and purge him againſt M.Horns moſt falſe ac-
cuſation.Of whoſe doings in Quene Maries daies, the ſaid
right honorables with the right honorable my Lord Erle
of Warwyke can,and wil(I truſte) alſo reporte being then
priſoners , and he by the Quenes appointmente ſente vnto
them.M. Secretary Cycil alſo cã teſtifie of his doings towching Sir Iohn Cheke knight,whoſe life, lãds,and goods by
his trauail and humble ſuyte were ſaued . His hope is,that
the Quenes highnes his ſoueraygne good Lady wil thus
much reporte of him , how in the beginning of her highnes
troble , her highnes then being impriſoned in the courte at
Weſtmynſter , and before her committy to the towre , his
good happe was to preache a ſermon before Quene Mary,
and her honorable counſayle in the Courte, where he moued her Highnes and them alſo to mercy,and to haue cõſi-
deration of the Quenes highnes that now is , then in trouble and newly entred in priſon . What diſpleaſure he ſuſteyned therefore,I doe here omitte to expreſſe. But this I
certaynlye knowe , that he hath reported , and hath moſt
humb!y thanked almighty God and her highnes : that her
highnes hadde the ſame in remembraunce, at the firſte and

laſte

A moſte
true de-
fence for
M. Fekẽ-
ham.

firſt and laſte talke,that euer he had with her,in her palace
at Weſtmyſter not longe before her highnes Coronation:
I truſt theſe are ſufficient perſonnages for M . Fekenhams
purgation and diſcharge againſt your falſe accuſation. Wel
I beſeache almighty God,that Maiſter Fekenham may now
at the lengthe after ſeuen yeares impriſonmente , be made
partaker of ſuch deedes and doings,as he then ſhewed vnto
other men: And now let vs procede on, to the reſidewe of
your booke.

The. 5. Diuiſion.   M. Horne.

*If I knevv you not right vvel, I ſhould maruail,that you ſhame not to af-
firme,ſaying: I doe here preſently therefore offer my ſelfe to receyue a corporal Othe:and further I ſhal preſently ſweare &c.*
Seing that you neuer made to me any motion of ſuch an offer, neither did I at
any time require you to take any Othe.

*You thinke and are ſo perſuaded in conſcience(if a man may truſt you)
that the Quenes highnes is the only ſupreme gouernour of this Realm , and of
al her dominiõs and countries,and hath vnder God,the ſoueraignty and rule
ouer al manner of perſones,borne vvithin her dominions of vvhat eſtate either
Eccleſiaſtical or Temporal ſo euer they be . VVhereunto I adde this conſequent
vvhich doth neceſſarily follovv , Ergo : Your holy father the Pope is not (as
you think in your conſcience)the ſupreme gouernour ouer her highnes dominions,nor hath the ſoueraignty or rule vnder God ouer any perſonnes borne
vvithin the ſame.*

*The Quenes maieſty muſt needs herein take you but for a diſſembling flat-
terer,in that you vvil ſeeme ſomtime in general ſpeach, to attribute vnto her
the onely Supremacy vnder God,ouer her dominions and ſubiectes vvhich you
meane not,for vvithin a vvhile after in plaine vvordes you deny the ſame. And
your holy Father vvil geue you his curſe , for that being his ſvvorne Aduocate, at the firſt entry into the plea , you geue from him the vvhole title of
his vniuſt claime,to vvit,the ſupreme gouernaunce ouer the Quenes highnes
dominions and people. You muſt novv therefore make ſome ſhifte,and cal to
remembraunce one ſleight or other by ſome diſtinctiõ,vvhereby to auoide your*
holy

holy Fathers curſe, that you may continue vnder his bleſſing. You vvill expounde your meaning by reſtreyning the ſupreme gouernment of the Queenes
maieſty onely in cauſes Temporal, and not in cauſes or things Eccleſiaſticall.
But this diſtinction commeth to late, and vril doe you no eaſe, for that in both
theſe kindes of cauſe: you haue already graunted vnto her the only ſupreme
gouernmet: and that as you veri'y think perſuaded in conſcience: vvheruppon
you offer to receiue a corporal Othe vpon the Euangeliſtes. And this your
graunt paſſed frō you by theſe vvords: Ouer al maner perſones borne
vvithin her dominions of vvhat eſtate either Eccleſiaſtical or
Temporal ſo euer they be: In this that you graunt vnto her highnes
thonly ſupreme rule ouer the Lay and Eccleſiaſtical perſonnes: you haue alſo
concluded therevvith in all cauſes both Eccleſiaſtical and Temporal, vvhich is
plainly and firmely proued by this argument follovving.

A ſupreme gouernour or ruler is one, vvho hath to ouerſee, guyde, care,
prouide, order and directe the things vnder his gouernmeut and rule, to that
ende, and in (.20.) thoſe actions vvhich are appointed and doe properly belonge to the ſubiect or thing gouerned. So that in euery gouernment and rule
there are thre things neceſſarely cōcurrāt: the Gouernor, the Subiect, or mattier gouerned, and the obiect or mattier vvherabout and vvherein the gouernement is occupied and doth conſiſte. But the Quenes highnes, by your ovvne
conſeſſion, is the only ſupreme gouernour ouer al manner perſones Eccleſiaſtical borne vvithin her dominions: Ergo: Her highnes thonely ſupreme gouernour ouer ſuch perſones hath to ouerſee, guyde, care, prouide, order, and directe them to that ende and in thoſe actiōs vvhich are appointed and dee (21.)
properly belonge to Eccleſiaſtical perſones. And ſo by good conſequent you haue
renounced al foreine gouernment. For this excluſiue, Onely, doth ſhut out all
other from ſupreme gouernment ouer Eccleſiaſtical perſonnes: and alſo yee
doe (22.) affirme the Quenes maieſty to be ſupreme gouernour in thoſe actions vvhich are appointed, and that doe properly belong to Eccleſiaſtical perſones, vvhich are no other but things or cauſes Eccleſiaſtical.

The 4. Chapter: how princes be ſupreme gouernours ouer
al eccleſiaſtical perſons (their ſubiects) and yet not
in al Eccleſiaſtical matters.

Here

The 10.
vntruthe
For not
in actiōs
belongig
properly
to the
things go
uerned,
but belō-
ging pro-
perly to
the gouer
nour and
to his end
The 21.
vntruthe
prouedto
be ſo by
M. Horn
him ſelfe,
as it ſhall
ſtraight
appere.
The 22.
vntruthe
M. Feke-
ham affir
med no
ſuch thig

Ere is firſt a worſhipfull reaſon, and cauſe to marueyle at M.Fekenham, that he ſhoulde by writing preſently offer him ſelfe to receiue an othe, becauſe, he neuer made mention of anie ſuche Othe before, neither any ſuche was at anye tyme of him required. Surelye, this is as greate a cauſe to wonder at, as to ſee a goſe goe barefote. But nowe will hee playe the worthye Logician and M. Fekenham, wil he nil he, ſhalbe driuen by fyne force of a Logical definition to graunte the Quene to be ſupreme head in al cauſes eccleſiaſticall, for that he graunteth her to be ſupreame heade of al perſons bothe eccleſiaſtical and temporal. Becauſe(ſaieth he)the ſupreame gouernour or ruler is he, that ordereth and directeth al actions belonging and appointed to the ſubiects: ād therby inferreth, that the Quēnes Maieſty is ſupreame and onely gouernour euen in thoſe actions that belonge to eccleſiaſtical perſons, which are cauſes eccleſiaſticall. But as good ſkil as this man hath in Logike, (which is correſpondent to his diuinity) he hath browght vs foorth a faulty and a vicioule definition. For a Supreame gouernour is he, that hath the chief gouermente of the thig gouerned, not in thoſe Actions that may any way properly belonge to the Subiect or thing gouerned(as M. Horn ſaith) but in thoſe Actions that belonge to the ende, whereunto the gouernour tendeth. Which may wel be, althowgh he haue not the chief gouerment in al the actions of the thing gouerned: but in ſuche actions as properly appertayne to him as a ſubiecte to that gouernour. For in one man many rulers may and doe dayly concurre, whiche in ſome ſenſe may euery one be called his Supreame gouernours. As yf he be a ſeruant, the maiſter: and if he be a ſon in that reſpect

the

The defi
nitiō of a
Supreme
Gouer-
nour.

the Father : and yf his father and maifter dwel in a city, the
Maior alfo, is his Fathers and maifters , and fo his cheif gouernour to, for things concerning the ciuil gouernment of
the city. And of al thefe the prince chief and fupreame gouernour, as they be fubiects. Otherwife the prince doth not
intermedle with the fathers office, in duetifulnes dewe vnto him by his fon, nor with the maifter, for that gouerment,
he hath vppon his feruante: no more then with the fchole-
mayfter for the gouerment of his fchollers, and their actios,
or the maifter of the fhip for the actions and doings of the
mariners, otherwife then any of thefe offende the pofitiue
Lawes of the realme: and fo hath the prince to do with him
as his fubiecte, or when he fhal haue nede to vfe them for
the commen welth, wherein as fubiects and members of the
faid comen welth they muft to hi obey. Much like it is with
the Spiritual me, which be alfo mebers of the fayde comen
welth, ad therfor in that refpect fubiect to the price ad his
lawes: and fo is it true, that the price is fupream gouernour,
of al perfons afwel fpiritual as teporal : but that therfore he
fhould alfo be Supreame gouernour in al theiractions , wil
no more follow the of the actions of them before reherfed:

How the
prince is
the Su-
preame
head and
gouer-
nour of
al perfos.

Yea much leffe. For the better vnderftanding whereof it
is to be knowe, that before the comming of Chrift, Kinges
wer there many, but Chriftian Kinges none. Many comen
welthes wer there, but no Chrifte come welth, nor yet godly como welth properly to fpeke, fauig amog the Iewes, but
ciuil and politik. The end and final refpect of the which ciuil
comme welth was and is, vnder the regimet of fome one, or
moe perfons to whom the multitude comitteh the felf to be
ordered and ruled by, to preferue thefelues from al inward
and outwarde iniuries, oppreffions and enimies: and further

H   to proto prouide not only for their faftie ād quietnes, but for their welth and abundance , and profperoufe maintenance alfo. To this ende tendeth and reacheth , and no further the ciuile gouernment : and to the preferuation, tuition and furtherance of this end, chiefly ferueth the Prince, as the principal and moft honorable perfon of the whole ftate, which thing is common as wel to the heatheniſh , as to the Chriſtian gouernment. But ouer and befide, yea and aboue this, is there an other gouernement inftituted and ordeined by Chriſt, in a fpiritual and a myftical bodie, of fuch as he graciouſly calleth to be of his kingdom, which is the kingdom of the faithful, and fo confequently of heauen, whereunto Chriftian faith doth conduct vs. In the which fpiritual bodie, commonly called Chriftes Catholike Churche, there are other heades and rulers then ciuill Princes : as Vicars, Perfons, Biſhops, Archebiſhops, Patriarches, and ouer them al the Pope. Whofe gouernement chieflye ferueth for the furtherance and encreafe of this fpiritual Kingdome, as the ciuil Princes do for the temporal. Now as the foule of man incomparably paſſeth the bodie : fo doth this kingdom the other, and the rulers of thefe, the rulers of the other : And as the bodie is fubiect to the foule, fo is the ciuill kingdome to the fpiritual. To the which kingdom as wel Princes as other are engraffed by baptifme, and become fubiects to the fame by fpiritual generation, as we become fubiects to our Princes, by courfe and order of natiuitie whiche is a terreftrial generation. Further now, as euery man is naturallye bound, to defend, maintain, encreafe, adorne, and amplifie, his natural countrie : fo is euery man bounde , and muche more to employ himfelfe to his pofsibilitie, toward the tuition, and defence, furtherance and amplificatiō of this fpiritual

The ende of the fpiritual gouernmēt.

tual

tual kingdome, and moſt of al Princes them ſelues, as ſuche
which haue receiued of God more large helpe and faculty
toward the ſame, by reaſon of their great authority and téporal ſworde, to ioyne the ſame, as the caſe requireth with
the ſpiritual ſword. And ſo al good Princes do ād haue don,
aiding and aſsiſting the Church decrees, made for the re-
preſsion of vice and errors, and for the maintenance of vertue and true religion, not as ſupreame Gouernours them
ſelues in all cauſes ſpirituall and temporall : but as faithfull
Aduocates in aiding and aſsiſting the ſpiritual power : that
it may the ſoner and more effectually take place. For this
ſupreame gouernement can he not haue, onleſſe he were
him ſelfe a ſpirituall man, no more then can a man be a maſter of a ſhippe that neuer was mariner : a Maior that neuer was Citizen. His principall gouernemente reaſteth
in ciuill matters, and in that reſpecte, as I haue ſayed, he
is ſupreame Gouernour of all perſons in his Realme, but
not of al their actions, but in ſuche ſenſe as I haue ſpecified, and leaſt of all of the actions of Spirituall men, eſpecially of thoſe that are moſt appropriate to them, which
can not be, onleſſe he were him ſelfe a Spiritual mā. Wherfore we haue here two Vntruths: the one in an vntrue definitiō, the other in ſaiyng that the Prince is the ſupreme go
uernour in al cauſes ſpiritual, yea euē in thoſe that be moſt
peculiarly belonging to ſpiritual men, beſide a plaine cōtradiction of M. Horne directly ouerthrowing his own aſſertion here. *The Biſhoply rule and gouernement of Gods Churche*
(ſaith M. Horne) *conſiſteth in theſe three points : to feed the
Church with Gods woord, to miniſter Chriſtes Sacramēts, ād to
bind and loſe. To gouern the Church* ſaith he, *after this ſort, belōgeth to the oly office of Biſhops ād Church miniſters, ād not to*

VVhy
Princes
are moſt
boundt.
aide the
ſpirtual
povver.

Fol. 96. 57

H　ij　　　　　　　　*Kings*

Kings, Quenes, and Princes. The lyke he hath afterwarde.
Now then thefe being by his owne confefsion the actions
that properly belóg to ecclefiaftical perfons, and the prices
by his faid cófefsió hauing nothing to do therwith:how is it
thē true that the prince is the only fupreme head ād gouernor in caufes ecclefiaftical, ye in thofe that do properly belóg to perfons ecclefiaftical ? Or by what colour may it be
defended,that this faying is not plain contradictory and repugnante,to this Later faying which we haue alleaged,and
whereof we fhall fpeake more largelye when we come to
the faid place?Thus ye fee, M.Horne walketh like a barefoted man vpon thornes,not knowing where to tread.

The.6. Diuifion. Pag.5 a *M.Fekenham.*

*And of my part I fhal fweare to obferue and perfourme
my obediēce and fubiectió with no leffe loyalty and faithfulnes vnto her highnes, thē I did before vnto Quene Mary, her highnes Syfter of famous memory, vnto whome I
was a fworne Chaplaine and moft bounden .*

M.Horne.

*Like an (.23.)vnfaithful fubiect contrary to your Othe made to King Hē-
ry, and continued al the reigne of King Edvvarde , you helpt to fpoile Quene
Mary of famous memory of a (24.) principal parte of her royall povver,
righte and dignity.vvhich fhe at the beginning of her reigne had,enioyed,and
put in vre. the fame obedience and fubiection,vvith the like loyalty and faithfulnes,yee vvil fvveare to obferue and perfourme to Quene Elizabeth:but fhe
thāketh you for naught,fhe vvil none of it,fhe hath efpied you,and thinketh,
yee profer her to much vvronge.*

Stapleton.

M.Horn would haue a mā ons bemired,to wallow there
ftil.Neither is it fin to break an vnlawful othe,but rather to
cōtinew in the fame,as wickedKing Herod did: Now if Mᵗ.
Horne

Marginal notes (left):

M. Horn
contrary
to him
felf.

The 2?.
vntruthe
fläderous
For M.Fe
kenhā fo
did, not
as an vn-
faithful
fubiect:
but as a
repentāt
Catholik.
The 24.
vntruth
Thisis.
no parte
at al of
the Prin-
ces royal
povver

Horne can ones by any meanes proue this gouernemente to be a principall parte , or any parte at all of the Queenes royal power,I dare vndertake that not only M.Fekenham, but many mo,that now refuse,shal most gladly take the said Othe.He wer surely no good subiect,that would wish her highnes any wrong: neither can the maintenāce of the Catholik faith wherof shee beareth the title of a Defendor, be coūted any iniury to her highnes.Nether is it to be thought but if there had ben any wrong or iniury herein done to the Croune,some Christiā Prince or other in the world would haue ere this, ones in this thousand yeares and more, espied it, and reformed it too.

M. Fekenham; The. 7. Diuision. Pag. 5 a.

And touching the reste of the Othe , whereunto I am required presently to sweare, viz. That I doe vtterlie testifie and declare in my conscience , that the Queenes highnes is the only supreame Gouernour of this Realme, as well in al Spirituall or Ecclesiastical things or causes, as Temporal: I shal then of my parte be in like readines, to receiue the same, when your L. shalbe able to make declaration vnto me,how and by what meanes, I may swere thereunto, without committing of a very plaine and manifest periurie: which of my part to be committed , it is damnable sinne, and against the expresse woord of God writen, Leuit. Cap 9. Non periurabis in nomine meo, nec pollues nomen Dei tui. And of your parte to prouoke mee or require the same, it is no lesse damnable offence. S. Augustine in witnes thereof saith: Ille qui ho-

H iij   minem

minem prouocat ad iuratione̅ , &c. He who doth prouoke an other man to swere, and knoweth that he shal forswere him selfe, he is worse then a murderer : because the murderer sleeth but the body, and he sleeth the soule, and that not one soule, but two, as the soule of him whom he prouoketh to periurie, and his owne soule also by ministring the occasion therof. And the points of this Othe whereunto I can not presently swere without most plaine and manifest periurie, are these foure following.

M. Horne.

Mutato nomine, de te fabula narratur.

As in that whiche goeth before, you couertlie vttered manie vntruthes, althoughe sometime yee stu̅mble on the trueth againste youre will : so in the rest you fal to plaine and manifest vntruths : least men shuld not perceiue what you are. You were neuer required by me to svvere, and therfore this is an impudent kind of dealing, to saie: vvherunto I am presently required to swere, &c. I had none authoritie nor co̅missio̅ to require the Othe of you, neither might I tender it vnto you without peril to mie selfe: you being co̅mitted vnto me by the most honorable Cou̅cel, without whose order I could attempt no suche matter. You haue alreadie shevved in plaine matter, although not in plainnesse of speache, and that as you thinke, and are persvvaded in co̅science, that her highnes is the supreme gouernour , so well in causes Ecclesiastical as temporal. For hauing supremacie ouer the Ecclesiastical person, the same being not othervvise person Ecclesiastical, but in respect of Ecclesiastical functions, things and causes annexed and proprelie belo̅ging to Ecclesiastical persons : shee hath the Supremacie ouer the person in Ecclesiastical functions, things and causes. these being the only matter or obiect wherabout or wherein the rule ouer an Ecclesiasticall persone is occupied and doth be consiste.

This seemeth to be your glorie amongst your friendes, that you make mee an offer, to receiue this parte of the Othe, when I shall be able to declare by what meanes you maie svvere without committing plain and manifeste
periurie:

periurie : * Mine abilitie herein ſhal appeare in mine anſvvere to your foure
points : God make you as readie to perform for duties ſake, as ye wil ſeme
readie to offer, wherbie to purchaſe to your ſelfe a glorious eſtimation. But
wherfore did you not make this offer vnto me, either by woord or writing al
the time of your aboad with mee ? You plaie novve after your returne into
(. 25.) your holde, as you did after the Parliament before you came oute of
the Tovver to me. VVhen you ſavve the end of the Parliament , and vnder-
ſtood right well that the Othe was not like to be tendred vnto yeu, than ſent
you copies of the booke deuiſed for the aunſvvere touching the Othe, abroad
to your friendes, to declare your conſtancie and readines, to refuſe the Othe,
wherebie thei might be the rather enduced , to continue their good opinion
conceiued of you, and alſo paie your charges weekelie in the Tovver ſent vnto you (. 25.) euerie Saturdaie by your ſeruaunt, who wrote and deliuered
the copies abroade, as you tolde me your ſelfe . Nowe you are returned a-
gaine into the Tower, and perceiuing that your friends (as you gaue thē iuſt
cauſe) haue ſome (. 27.) miſtruſt of your reuolte and wauering inconſtan-
cie, whereby your eſtimation and fame, with their ſeruice to your God the
bellie is decaied, you haue deuiſed to ſet abroade the ſelfe ſame booke a-
gaine that you did before, and to the ſelfe ſame ende , altering or chaunging nothing at all, ſauing that you haue getten it a nevve name and Title,
and ſeeme as in this place, as though yee ſpake to mee by theſe woordes :
when your L. &c. VVhen as in very deed, there was neuer any ſuche
woorde ſpoken or writen to mee : and in the booke you deliuered to mee,
Your ſpeache is directed to the Commiſſioners, and not to me in theſe words,
VVhen ye the Quenes highnes cōmiſſioners ſhalbe able, &c.

* If your
abilitie be
no better
then here
apeareth,
it is none
at all.
The. 25.
vntruth.
The To-
vver is
not M.
Fekenhās
hold: For
it holdeth
him, not
he it.
The. 26.
vntruth.
The
Quenes
highnes
vvordes
in the
Tovver,
can teſti-
fie the
contrary.
27. A
heape of
ſlaunde-
rous and
railing
vntruths.

The fifth Chapter of other priuate doings betwene M. Fekenham and M. Horne.

Et ones againe M. Horne taketh in hande M.
Fekenhās grāut which may wel be grāuted, ād
by his great cūning and ſkilfulnes, wil thereof
inferre as before, that, that may not be graunted. But nowe he ſpitteth in his hande and taketh faſter
hold

holde, as he thinketh, and feing the lightnes of his former
reafon, would now geue greater weight to it with a newe
fetch, but yet as light and as weake as the other, and em-
ploying manifeft contradiction as before, and to be anfwered as before.   For albeit a man is not called an Ecclefiafticall perfon, but in refpecte of fome Churche caufe and
function, which we freely graunt to M. Horne, yet is he
neuer a whit the nearer of his purpofe, vnleffe he cã proue
that there were alfo no other refpecte, why he fhoulde be
vnder the Prince, but for caufes Ecclefiaftical.   For as we
haue faid, he is a fubiect alfo as other laie men are, and a
member befide of the ciuil common welth, in confideration whereof the Prince hath to doe with him, and not pro-
perlie as he is a Spirituall man, though bothe refpectes be
cõcurrant in one perfon and he be named of the worthyer.
As if M.Robert Horne were a laie man and a Painter the
Queene properlye hathe not to dooe with him as a Painter (vnlefle it were for fome lawe or order concerninge
Painters) but as Robert Horne her highnes fubiecte, and
borne vnder her obeifance.   So fhould the Queene haue
alfo to doe with you, yea in cafe yee were the true Bifhop
of Winchefter, but not proprely as Bifhop, or for your Bifhoply function, for the whiche ye are immediatlye vnder
your Archebifhop and the Pope, but confidering you as a
fubiect otherwife, or as Bifhop either touching your temporalties and no farder.   For the which the true Bifhops
alfo doe to their Prince their Homage. But what fhould I
further reafon with this man, which (as I haue faied) hathe
remoued the Prince from all fuperioritie concerninge the
mere Bifhoply or Prieftly function, and fo with a notable
contradiction hath full worfhipfully cõcluded againft him
felfe, and eafed his Aduerfarie of any further proufe, and

eafed

Hovve a
fpirituall
man is
vnder-
neath the
Prince ãd
hovv he
is not,

eafed M. Fekenham alfo for taking any othe, that the Quęne is fupreame head in al caufes temporal and fpiritual?

Here remayneth now for the refidew nothing greatlye to be anfwered, but only to fhew how M. Horn doth accumulate a huge heap of vntruths, as in notíg in M. Fekêhã an impudent kind of dealing: for writing: *Whereunto I am prefently required to fweare:* which may be truely verefied, feing as M. Horne him felf confeffeth yt was fo writê in that copy that fhould haue bene deliuered to the commifsioners at fuch tyme as they fhould haue prefently tendred M. Fekenham the othe: and in the fame forme and fafíhion delyuered to M. Horne: and nothing altred in the later copy but that this worde *commifsioners* is turned into *the Lorde bifhop of Winchester:* neither doth M. Fekenham faye *Whereunto I am required prefently to fweare of your L.* as he faieth afterward: *When your L. fhal be able &c.* And therefore there is no maner of impudency or vntruthe in the matter at all: how fo euer yt be, this matter is nothing apperteyning to the ftate of the principal queftió, and of fmal importaunce, nothing deferuing to be noted as an impudêt dealíg, but rather this kind of fpeach agreeth with M. Horns dealing here folowíg, who fpeaketh of M. Fekenhã, without any regarde fo loofely and lewdely as to faye, *he maketh his belly his God, that his frêds miftrufted his reuolting and wauering incôftâcy, that he fent foorth copies of the book* (as M. Horn termeth the fhedule) *when he fawe the othe fhould not be tendred him,* and fuch lyke. Where are nowe in this your falfe tale, the dewe circũftãces that ye nedeleffely required of M. Fekenhã moft neceffarie here to haue bene obferued of yow? Suerly the reft is as true, as that ye write of his feruante, and of his char-ges wekely defrayde by his frêds, and brought in by his fer-

I   uante

uate which is (as farre as I can vnderſtande) ſtark falſe. Why
doe ye not I pray you in theſe and your other blinde fonde,
foliſhe, and falſe gheſſes and ſurmiſes make your tale more
apparâte and cowlorable, clothing it with ſome côuenient
and dew circumſtances, that ye do ſo much harpe vppon a-
gainſt M. Fekenham?

Ye be now again blindly and lewdly harping vpô his re-
volte, to ſlaunder and deface him. Ye ſay he ſent out his copies when he vnderſtode right wel, that the othe was not
like to be tendered him. How proue ye it good Sir? He and
other Catholiks made their certain accompte that after the
end of the parliament, the othe ſhould haue ben offred thê:
what was the cauſe it was not exaĉted, I certainly know
not : were it for the great plague that immediatly reigned
and raged at London (I pray God it were no plague to puniſh the ſtraunge procedings in that parliament againſt his
holy Church, and to put vs in remembraunce of a greater
plague imminête and hanging ouer vs, in this or in an other
world onleſſe we repent) or were it, by ſpecial order, goodnes, and mercy of the Quenes Maieſty, I can not tel. But
this well I wote, no gramercy to you ſir, who ſo ſore thir-
ſted and lôged for the catholiks bloud. And therfore as ſone
as Gods plague ceaſed, thought to haue your ſelf plaged the
Catholiks, exaĉtig the Othe of M. Doĉtour Bonner, Biſhop
of Lôdon. But lo here now began your, and your fellowes
the proteſtant biſhops wonderful plague and ſcourge, that
throwgh your own ſeking and calling this man to the othe,
the matter ſo meruelouſly fel out, that ye and your felowes,
as ye were no church biſhops whoſe authority ye had forſaken and defied : ſo you were alſo no parliament biſhops.
Vpô the which (a pitiful caſe) your ſtate, your honour, your

After Gods plague M. Horne beganne his plage.

worſhip

worſhip,and biſhoply authority , yea faith and al now reſ-
tethe and dependeth.   A merueloufe prouidence of God,
that while ye could not be contente to ſpoile the true biſſhops of their wordly eſtate and honor,but muſt nedes haue
their poore lyfe and al,you your ſelf were founde to be no
biſhops,no not by the very ſtatutes of the realme. But lette
theſe thinges now paſſe,and herken we to Maiſter Hornes
blaſte.

The 8. Diuiſion.   Pag. 6. b.   M. Fekenham.

*Firſt is,that I muſt by a booke Othe vtterlyc teſtifie,
that the Queenes highnes is the onely ſupreme gouernour
of this realme,and that aſwell in all Spirituall or Eccleſiaſticall thinges or cauſes , as Temporall. But to teſtifie any thinge vppon a booke Othe, no man may poſſiblye
therein auoide periury,except he doe firſt know the thing
which he doth teſtifie , and whereof he beareth witneſſe
and geueth teſtimonye. And touching this knowledge,
that the Queenes maieſty,is the onely ſupreme gouernour
aſwell in Spirituall or Eccleſiaſtical cauſes as in Teporal,
beſides that I haue no ſuch knowledge,I know no way nor
meane whereby I ſhoulde haue any knowledge thereof.
And therefore of my part to teſtifie the ſame vppon a
booke Othe , beinge without (as I am in deede) al knowledge , I cannot without committinge of plaine and manifeſt periury. And herein I ſhal ioyne this iſſue with your
L. that whē your L. ſhalbe able,either by ſuch order of gouernment,as our Sauiour Chriſte left behinde him in his*

I ij   *Goſpell*

Gospel and new testament, either by the writing of such learned Doctours both Olde and new, which haue from age to age witnessed the order of Ecclesiastical gouern-mente in Christes Churche, either by the general Coun-cels, wherein the righte order of Ecclesiastical gouerne-ment in Christes Church, hath beene most faithfully de-clared and shewed from time to time: or elles by the conti-nual practise of the like Ecclesiasticall gouernment, in some one Church or part of all Christendom. Whan your Lordshippe shal be able by any of these fower meanes, to make proufe vnto me, that any Emperour, or Empresse, King, or Quene, may claym or take vpon thē any such go-uernmēt, in spiritual or ecclesiastical causes, I shal herein yelde, and with most humble thankes reken my selfe well satisfied, and shal take vppon me the knowledge thereof, and be ready to testifie the same vppon a booke Othe.

M. Horne.

The reason or argument that moueth you, not to testifie vpon a book Othe the Q. Supremacy in causes ecclesiastical, is this: No man may testifie by Othe that thing vvhereof he is ignorant and knovvet b nothīg, vvithout committīg periury. But you neither knovv that the Q. highnes is the onely supreme go-uernour asvvel in causes Ecclesiasticall, as Temporall: neither yet knovv you any vvay or meane vvhereby to haue any knovvledge thereof   Therefore to testifie the same vppon a booke Othe, you can not vvithout committing of plaine and manifest periury.

For ansvveare to the Minor or seconde Proposition of this argument: Although I might plainly deny, that you are vvithout all knovvledge, and vtterly ignoraunt both of the matter and the vvay or meane, hovv to come by knovvledge therof, and so put you to your prouf, vvherein I knovv, you must

needes

needes faile: yet vvil I not ſo anſvveare by plain negatiue, but by diſtinctiō or diuiſiō of ignorāce, And ſo for your better excuſe, declare in vvhat ſort you are ignoraut and vvithout al knovvledge. There are three kinds of ignorātes, the one of ſimplicity, the other of vvilfulnes, and the thirde of malice. Of the firſt ſort you cānot be, for you haue had longe time good oportunity, much occaſiō, and many vvaies vvhereby to come to the knovvledge hereof. Yea, you haue knovvē and profeſt openly by deede and vvorde the knovvledge hereof many yeers together. For you did (28.) knovv, acknovvledge, and confeſſe, this ſupreme authority in cauſes Eccleſiaſtical to be in King Hēry the eight and his heyres, vvhā your Abbay of Eueſhā, by cōmō cōſent of you and the other Mōks there vnder your couent ſeale vvas of your ovvn good vvilles vvithout compulſion ſurrendred into his handes, and you, by his authority, reſourmed, forſooke your * foliſhe vovve, and many (.29.) horrible errours, and ſuperſtitions of Monkery, and became a ſecular Prieſt, and Chaplaine to D. Bell, and aftervvarde to D. Bonner, and ſo duringe the life of King Henry the eight, did agniſe, profeſſe and teach opēly in your ſermōs the kings Supremacy in cauſes Eccleſiaſtical. This knovvledge remained ſtedfaſtly in you al the time of kinge Edvvard alſo. For although you vvere in the Tovver in his time, that vvas not for any doubt you made of his Supremacy, ſor that you ſtil agniſed: but for other points of religiō (.30.) touchig the miniſtratiō of the Sacramēts, vvhervnto you alſo agreed at the laſt, & promiſed to profeſſe & preach the ſame in opē auditory vvherſoeuer you ſhould be apointed (.31.) VVherupō a right vvorſhipful gentleman procured your deliuerāce forth of the Tovver, and ſo vvere you at liberty, neuer mēcioning any dout in this matter: but agniſing the Prices ſupremacy in cauſes eccleſiaſtical. VVherfore I may ſafly ſay, that the ignorāce and vvāt of knovvledge vvhich you pretend in your Minor Propoſitiō, is not of Siplicity, and therſore muſt nedes be of vvilfulnes, or malice, or mixt of both. The vvay and meanevvherby to haue this ignorāuce remoued, you aſſigne vvith this iſſue, that vvhē I proue vnto you, by any of the fovver meanes, that any Emperour, or empreſſe, King or Quene may take vpō thē any ſuch gouernmēt in ſpiritual or eccleſiaſtical cauſes, thē you vvil yeelde, take vpō you the knovvledge thereof, and be ready to teſtiſie the ſame by booke Othe. Truely, I haue often and many times proued this ſame that you require, and by the ſelf ſame meanes in ſuch ſort vnto you, that you had (.32.) nothing to ſaye to the contrarie. And yet neuertheleſſe you continue ſtil in your vvilfull and

I   iij   maliſious

The 32.
vntruth:
mere flaū
derous, as
may vvel
appere by
this your
booke.
Sapien. 1.

*malicious ignorance, vvhich cauſeth me to feare that this ſentence of the holy
ghoſt vvilbe verified in you:* In maleuolam animam non introibit ſa-
pientia, *Yet I vvil ones again proue after your deſire, euen as it vvere by putting you in remembraunce of thoſe things vvhich by occaſions in conferenſe, I
often and many times reported vnto you, vvhereof I knovv you are not ſimply ignoraunt.*

The 6. Chapter , defending M. Fekenham and others of Wilful and malitious ignorance for not taking the Othe.

OW are M.Fekenham and M.Horne come to
cople and ioyne together in the principal matter. M.Fekenham firſt ſaieth, he neither knoweth this kid of ſupremacy that M. Horn auowcheth, nor yet any way how to achiue or obtain to any ſuch knowledge. M.Horne ſaith he might well
put M.Fekenham to his prouf that he is not ignorāt. But by
the way, I trow of ſome meritoriouſe ſupererogation , or
as one fearing no ieberdy, he aduentureth the prouf himſelf
that M.Fekenham is not ignorant of this ſupremacy , and

The gētle
and louīg
harte of
M.Horn.

further to binde M.Fekenham the deaper to him for his exceding kindnes, wil ſhew for M. Fekenhams better excuſe
(o gentle and louing hart)that M.Fekenham is not ignorāt
of ſimplicity, but of wilfulnes and plain malice.

Tho. aqui.
de malo
quaſt. 3.

As touching this threfolde ignorance, by M . Horne alleaged out of the bookes of S. Thomas , as I wil not ſtycke
with him for that diſtinction, ſo onleſſe he can proue by S.
Thomas or otherwiſe that the ignorāce of this ſurmiſed ſupremacy, includeth wilfulnes or malice in M.Fekenham or
any ſuch like parſon, the diſtinction may be true , but the
cauſe neuer a deale furthered. Suerly yf ther were any ignorance in this point, it were ſuch as S . Thomas and other
cal inʃ

cal inuincicle ignorance, by no ftudy or diligence able to be put away, and therfore pardonable. But now the very authour brought forth by M. Horn fo fully and effectually difchargeth M. Fekenham of al thre, and chargeth M. Horne with the worfte of them three, that is wilfulnes and malice, as he fhal winne fmal worfhip, by alleaging of S. Thomas. For S. Thomas faieth plainly, that we are obliged and bound vpon paine of euerlafting damnation, to belieue that the Pope is the only fupreme head of the whole Church. And leafte M. Horne may reiecte his authority (which he can not wel doe vfing yt himfelf) as a late Latin writer, and to much affectioned to the Pope, S. Thomas proueth his affertion by Cyrill and Maximus two notable and auncient writers amonge the Grecians. Wherfore it foloweth, that neither M. Fekenham nor M. Horn, nor any other Chriftiã man can know the contrary : being fuch an euident and a daungeroufe fallhod, as importeth eternal damnation.

In Opufc, contra errores Græcorum. Oftēditur etiã, quòd fubeffe Romano Põtifici fit de neceßitate falutis.

Nay, faith M. Horn, how can M. Fekenhã pretende ignorance herein, when afwel in King Henry, as King Edward his dayes, he fet forth in his open fermons this fupremacy? And fo doe yow now, good M. Horne, and yet none more ignorant, and farder from knowledge than yow. For notwithftãding al your great brags and this your clerkly booke, ye knowe not nor euer fhall knowe, but that the Pope is the fupreame head of the Churche. Wel ye may (as ye doe) moft falfly, and to your poore wretched fowle, as well in this as in other pointes, moft daungerouflye, belieue the cõtrary, but knowe it you can not onleffe it were true. For *knowledge is only of true things,* and as the philofopher faith: *fcire eft per caufas cognofcere.* And ye doe no more knowe it, then the other matter that ye here alfo affirme

No man cã know an vntruthe.

ofM.

of M.Fekenhã,that he promised to professe and preache in
open auditory in King Edwards dayes,certaine points,tou-
ching the ministration of the Sacraments , contrary to his
former opinion : And vpon such promise was discharged
out of the towre:which yet ye know not to be true , for it
is starke false.And I pray yow how fortuned it,that his promisse so made to recante was neuer required of him,being
the onely thing that was sowght for at his handes?

The cause of his imprisonment then , as I vnderstande by
such as wel knoweth the whole matter , was not abowte
the ministration of the Sacraments,but towching the matter of Iustification,by onely faith and the fast of Lent: lyke
as it doth appere in the Archbishoppe of Caunterburies recordes,he being therfore in a solempne sessiõ holdẽ at Lã-
beth hal conuented before M . Cranmer , then Archebisshop of Caunterbury , and other commissioners appointed
for that matter.By the examination of the which recordes,
yow shal be conuinced of your vntruthe and errour therein,as in al the rest,I dowbt not by Gods helpe .

And touching the right worshipful gentleman ye meane
of,that is Sir Philip Hobbey, which did as ye saye,vpon M.
Fekenhams promise and submission procure his deliueraũce
out of the towre : As it is very true he did so : So it is false
and vntrue,that he did the same vppon any promise of recantation or of preaching in open auditory,before made of
his parte.But the verye intente of the borowing of M . Fekenhã for a tyme out of the towre,lyke as he saide him self,
was,that he should dispute,reason,and haue cõferẽce, with
certaine learned men touching matters of religion then in
controuersie:And according therunto,the first day of disputation, was betwixte thẽ and him, at the right honorable
my

The cause of M. Fekenhams imprison ment in K. Edvvardes dayes.

my Lord erle of Bedfords houſe then lodged ouer the gate Diſputations had
vvith M.
Fekenhā. at the Sauoy. The ſeconde daie was at the houſe of Syr
William Cicill Knight, Secretarie to the Quenes highnes,
at Weſtminſter in the canon rewe. The third daie was at
the white Friers, in the houſe of Syr Iohn Cheke Knight.
In al the which conferences and diſputations with manie
learned men, he was, the truth to confeſſe, muche made of,
and moſt gently vſed. And this diſputation ſo begunne at
London, did finiſhe in Worceſter ſhiere, where, he was
borne and had alſo a Benefice, by the meane whereof, and
by the ſpecial appointmēt of Syr Phillipp Hobbie, he came
before M. Hooper, then taken as Biſhoppe of Worceſter:
where he charginge M. Fekenham in the Kinges highnes
name to anſwere him, he kept foure ſeueral and ſolempne
diſputations with him, beginning in his viſitatiō at Parſhor,
and ſo finiſhed the ſame in the Cathedral Church at Worceſter. Where amongs many other, he founde M. Iewell,
who was one of his apponents. The ſaid M. Hoper was
ſo anſwered by M. Fekenham, that there was good cauſe
why he ſhould be ſatiſſied, and M. Fekēham diſmiſſed from
his trouble. As he had cauſe alſo to be ſatiſſied by the anſweres of M. Henrie Iolife Deane of Briſtow, and M. Ro- Vide diſ-
puta: ve-
nerabiliū
ſacerdotū,
& Ant-
uerp. im-
preſſ. 1564 bert Iohnſon: as may appeare by their anſweres now extant in print. But the finall end of all the foreſaid diſputations with M. Fekenhā, was that by the foreſaid Syr Phillipp Hobbey he was ſent backe againe to the Tower, and
there remained priſoner vntill the firſte yeare of Queene
Marie. And here nowe may you perceiue and ſee, M.
Horne, how ye are ouertaken, and with how many good
witneſſes in your vntruthe, concerning M. Fekenhams di-
miſsing out of the Tower.

A rable

A rablement of your vntruthes here I wil not, nor time will ferue to difcuffe : as that Monafteries were furrendered with the Monks goodwil, whiche for the mofte parte might fing *volens nolo:* that their vowes were foolifhe, and that they had many horrible errors. Marie one thing you fay, that M. Fekenham, I thinke, will not denie, that he fet foorth this Supremacy, in his open fermons, in King Henries daies : which was not vpon knowledge (as you without all good knowledge doe gather) for knoweledge can not matche with vntruth : but vpon very ignorance, and lacke of true knowledge and due confideratiõ of the matter, being not fo wel knowẽ to the beft learned of the Realme then, as it is now, to euery mã being but of mean learning. For this good, lo at the leaft, herefy worketh in the church, that it maketh the truth to be more certainly knowen, ãd more firmly and ftedfaftly afterward kept. *So* (as S.

Auguft.in Pfal.54. fuper ver. fum : Di. uifi funt pra ira. &c.

Auftine faith) *the matter of the B. Trinitie was neuer wel difcuffed, vntil Arriãs barked againft it : The Sacramẽt of penãce was neuer throughly hãdled, vntil the Nouatiãs began to withftand it. Neither the caufe of Baptifm was wel difcuffed vntill the rebaptifing Donatifts arofe and troubled the Church.* And euẽ fo this matter of the Popes Supremacy, ãd of the Princes, was at the firft euẽ to very learned mẽ a ftrãge matter, but is now to meanly learned, a well knowen and beaten matter. Syr Thomas More, whofe incõparable vertue ãd learning, al the Chriftian world hath in high eftimatiõ, and whofe witte Erafmus iudged to haue ben fuch as England nor had, neither fhal haue, the like: ãd who for this quarrel which we now haue in hãd fuffred death, for the preferua tiõ of the vnitie of Chriftes Church, which was neuer, nor fhalbe preferued, but vnder this one head ; as good a man,

and

ad as great a clerk, and as bleſſed a Martyr as he was, albeit he euer wel thought of this Primacy, and that it was at the leaſt wiſe inſtituted by the corps of Chriſtédome for great vrgét cauſes for auoiding of ſchiſmes: yet that this primacy was immediatly inſtitute of God (which thing al Catholiks now, ſpecially ſuch as haue trauailed in theſe late cótrouerſes do beleue) he did not mani yeres beleue, vntil (as he writeth himſelf) he read in the mater thoſe things that the Kigs highnes had write in his moſt famous booke againſt the hereſies of MartinLuther: amóg other things he writeth thus.
Surely after that I had read his graces boke therin, and ſo many other things as I haue ſene in that point by the continuance of this ſeué yeres ſins ãd more, I haue foúd in effeſt the ſubſtáce of al the holy Doſtors, froe S. Ignatius Diſciple of S. Iohn vnto our own daies both Latins ãd Grekes, ſo cóſonãt and agreïg in that point, and the thing by ſuch general Gouncels ſo confirmed alſo, that in good faith I neuer neither read nor heard anye thinge of ſuche effeſte on the other ſide, that euer coulde lead mee to thinke that my conſcience were well diſcharged, but rather in right great peril, if I ſhould follow the other ſide, and denie the primacie to be prouided by God.

It is the leſſe meruail therfore, if at the firſt, for lacke of mature and depe conſideration, many good & wel learned men otherwiſe, being not reſolued whether this Primacie were immediatly inſtituted by God, and ſo thíkíng the leſſe dãger to relét to the Kings title, eſpecially ſo terrible a law enaſted againſt the deniers of the ſame, wer ãd amóg them alſo Maiſter Fekenham, caried away with the violence of this cómon ſtorm and tempeſt·And at the firſt many of the cóuocation grãted to agniſe the Kings ſupremacy, but *quatenus de iure diuino,* that is, as far as thei might by Gods law.

K ij   which

See Syr Thomas More in a letter vvriten to Syr Thomas Cromwel fol. 1416. & 1417. Syr Tho. Mores firſt opinió of the Popes primacy:

The Popes primacy inſtituted by God.

Though the Primacie vvere not ordeined of God, yet could it not be reiected by anie one Realme.

Which is now knowen clearly to stand against it. And although the Popes Primacie were not grounded directly vpon Gods worde, but ordeined of the Churche, yet coulde it not be abrogated, by the priuate consente of any one or fewe Realmes : no more then the Citie of Londō can iustlye abrogate an act of Parliament. But whereas ye insult vpon M. Fekenham, for that he was ones entangled and wrapped in this common error, and would thereof enforce vpon him a knowledge of the said error, and woulde haue him perseuere in the same : and ones againe to fall quite ouer the eares into the dirtie dong of filthie schisme and heresie, ye worke with him both vnskilfully and vngodlye. And if good counsaile might finde any place in your harde stony hart, I would pray to God to mollifie it, and that ye would with M. Fekenham hartilie repēt, and for this your great offence, schisme, and heresie, as I doubt not he doth and hath done, followe S. Peter, who after he had denyed

Luc. 22.

Chrift : *Exiuit & fleuit amarè,* Went out and wepte ful bitterlie. For surely whereas ye imagine that ye haue in your cōference proued the matter to M. Fekenhā, so that he had nothing to saye to the contrarye, it is nothing but a lowde lewde lye vppon him : and that easelye appeareth, seeinge that after all this your long trauaile, wherein yee haue to the moste vttered all your skill, ye are so farre from full

M. Fekēha more cōfirmed then he vvas before, euen by M. Hornes booke.

answering his scruples and staies, that they seeme plainlye to be vnaunswerable, and you your selfe quite ouerborne and ouerthrowen, and that by your owne arguments and inductions, as we shal hereafter euidently declare. So that nowe M. Fekenham may seeme to haue good cause much more then before, to rest in the sayed stayes and scruples. I may not here let passe M. Horne that you cal this saiyng:

In

In maleuolam animam non introibit sapientia, a sentence of Sap.1. the holy Ghost. That it is no lesse, we gladly confesse it. But how dare you so pronounce of that saiyng, being written in the booke of wisedome? That booke, you wot wel, your brethren of Geneua accompt for no Canonical Scripture at al, suche as onelye are the sentences of the holye Ghoste (to speake absolutely and proprely) but in the notes before that booke, and certaine other which they cal *A- pocrypha*, doe call them onely, *bookes proceedinge of godlye men, not otherwise of force, but as they agree With the Cano- nicall Scriptures, or rather are grounded thereon.* In whiche sence not onely those bookes, but the writings also of the Fathers, yea and of al other men, may be by your sentence, *the sentence of the holy Ghoste.* And Brentius likewise in his *Prolegomenis*, agreeth with the Geneuian notes against M. Horne. Thus these fellowes iarre alwayes amonge them selues, and in all their doctrines, fal into such points of discorde, that in place of vniforme tuninge, they ruffle vs vppe a blacke Sanctus, as the Prouerbe is: *Quo teneam vultus mutantem Prothea nodo?*

In the Geneuiã Bibles printed at Geneua An. 1562.

Vide Ho- sium cõtr. Brent. *li.5*

The. 9. Diuision. Pag 8. a. M. Horne.

You require a proufe hereof, that an Emperoure or Empresse, King or Queene, maie claime or take vppon them anie suche gouernment (meaning as the Queenes Maieste our Soueraigne doth novv chalenge and take vpon her) in Spirituall or Ecclesiasticall causes. (.33.) For ansvveare I say, thei ought to take vppon them suche gouernment, therefore thei maie lausullie doe it. The former part is found true by the whole discourse of the holie Scriptures both of the olde and nevv Testament: by the testimonie of the Doctours in Christes Church: by the Generall Councels: and by the practise of Christes Catholique Churche throughout al Christendome.

The. 33. vntruth. imploy- ing a cõ- tradictiõ to your former ansvvere made to M. Fek, as I shall appere.

K iiij The

The. 7. Chapter opening a plaine Contradiction of M. Hornes.

Aifter Fekenham, as well at his abode with you, as fins his returne to the Tower, at fuch time as he enioyed the free liberty thereof, hath as I certaíly vnderftãd, declared to fom of his friends, that in your conference with him for a refolute anfwere to al the faid fcruples expreffed in al the foure points, *ye did much lament, that the right mea-*

The firft *ning of the Othe , had not bene in ceafon opened and declared*
anfvvere
of M. *vnto him. When the only lack of the right vnderftanding ther-*
Horne to *of, hath ben the caufe of fuch ftaies. Wheras the Quenes Ma.*
M. Fe- *meaning in that Oth is farre otherwife, then the expreffe words*
kenham, *are, as they lye* verbatim : *like as it dothe well appeare by her highnes interpretation made therof in her iniunctions.* Of the whiche matter we fhall be occafioned to entreate more at large herafter. But now after two yeres breathing ye frame an other anfwere quite iarring from the firft, affirming that

M. Horns the Queene *muft take vpon her fuch kind of regiment*, with-
fecõd an out any mollifiyng or reftraint. And this ye will, as ye fay,
fvvere
cõtrarye auouch by Scriptures, Fathers, Coũcels, ãd the cõtinual pra-
to the ctife of the Church. Both your faied anfweres being fo cõ-
firft. trary one to the other, what certaine and fure knowledge may M. Fekenham, by right reafon take and gather thereof to his cõtentation and fatiffaction of his mind in thefe mat-ters, when by fuch diuerfitie of anfweres, what other thing els may he iuftly thinke , then thus with him felfe ? That if you after fo manye and fo faire promifes, failed to open the very trueth vnto him, in your firfte aunfweare : what better affurance fhould he conceiue, of your truth in this your fecond anfwere? For if by difsimulation the truthe of

the

the matter was couertly hidde frō him in the firſt anſwere, what better truth may he boldly look for in this your ſecōd anſwere:thei being not both one, but variable and diuerſe? S. Gregory Nazianzene ſaith:*Verũ quod eſt,vnũ eſt:mendatiũ autē eſt multiplex.* The thig,ſaith he,which is true,is alwaies one,ād like vnto it ſelf,wheras the lye,the cloked and coū-terfait thing is in it ſelfe variable and diuers. By t he which rule here geuē,by ſo learned & graue a Father:I am here in the begining put to knowledge by the varietie of your an-ſweres,that thei cānot be both true.But if the one be true, the other muſt be falſe:and therof ſuch a diſtruſt iuſtly ga-thered,that I may conclude none of them both to be true, but both of them to be deceiuable and falſe.For the proufe and trial of this my cōcluſion,I refer me to your ſcriptures, Fathers,Councels,practiſe of the Churche,that ye woulde ſeme to reſt vpon:wherby neuertheles you your ſelf ſhall take a ſhameful foile and fall. Wherefore goe on a Gods name and bring foorth your euidences.

The. 10. Diuiſion. Pag. 8. a.

The holy Scriptures deſcribing the condicions , and propreties in a King, amongeſt other doth commaund, that he haue by him the booke of the lavv, (.34.)(.35.)and doe diligentlie occupie him ſelfe in reading therof,to the end he maie therby learne to ſeare the Lord his God (that is, to haue the ſeare of God planted within him ſelfe in his ovvne harte)to keepe al the wordes,and to accompliſh in deed al the ordinaunces,or ' as the olde tranſlation hath it al the ceremonies by God cōmaunded(that is)to gouerne in ſuch ſorte (.36.) That he cauſe by his princely authority,his ſubiects alſo to be-come Iſraelites.To witte, men that ſee, knovv,and vnderſtand the vvill of God. Redreſſing the peruerſues of ſuch as ſvverue from Gods ordinances or ceremonies. VVherupon it is, that God doth commaund the Magiſtrate,that he make(37)diligēt examinatiō of the doctrine taught by any,and that he do ſharply puniſh both the teachers of falſe and ſuperſti-tious religion, with the folovvers,and alſo remoue quite out of the waye all maner of euill.

K iiij   Goe

Truth is ſimple ād vniform.

The. 34. and.35. vntruths in falſe trāſlatig, and leaſ uing out a part of the ſen-tēce ma-teriall.

The.36. vntruth.

Te gloſſ. ordinar. hathe no ſuche thing.

The.37. Vntruth. The place of the Deute-ronomy flatly be-lyed.

*The. 9. Chapter, concerning the Kings duetie ex-
preſſed in the Deuteronomie.*

GOE on I ſaie in Gods name, M. Horne, and
proſequute your plea ſtoutlie : God ſend you
good ſpeed. And ſo he dothe, euen ſuche as
ye, and the honeſtie of your cauſe deſerue.
And at the very firſt entrie of your plea cauſeth you, and your clerkly and honeſt dealing, forthwith to
your high commendation ſo to appeare, that euen the firſt
authoritie that ye handle of all the holy Scripture plainlye
diſcouereth you, and cauſeth you to be eſpied : and openeth as well your fidelity, as the weakenes of your whole
cauſe: the which euen with your owne firſt blaſt is quite
ouerblowen.   Your infidelity appeareth in the curtalling
of your text, and leauing out the wordes, that immediatly
goe before, thoſe that ye alleage : beſide your vnſkilfulnes
(if it be not done rather of peruerſitie and malice) concurrant with your infidelitie .   Your vnſkilfulnes whiche is
the leaſt matter, ſtandeth in that ye ſaye the King is commaunded to haue by him the booke of the Lawe .   Your
texte ſaith not ſo Syr, but *Deſcribet ſibi Deuteronomium legis huius in volumine.* He ſhal write out this ſecond Lawe
in a booke : As Edmund Beck, a man of your ſecte, truely
hath tranſlated. Wel, let the King read in Gods name, not
onelye that booke , but all the whole Bible beſide : It is a
worthy and a commendable ſtudy for him. But let him beware, that this ſweete honie be not turned into poyſon to
him, and leaſt vnder this pleaſant baite of Gods worde, he
be ſodainly choked with the topicall and peſtiferouſe tranſlation: wherewith ye haue rather peruerted, then tranſlated the Bible printed at Geneua, and in other places : and
with

M.Hor-
nes vn-
ſkilfulnes

Deut. 17.

In the
greate
Bible de-
dicated to
King Ed
ward the
6. prin-
ted, 1549.

with your falſe daungerouſe damnable gloſes, where with you haue corrupted and watered the ſame , and made it as it were of pleaſante wine moſt ſowre vineger. The onely remedy and help to eſchewe and auoyde this daunger is,to take this booke and other holy writings faithfully tranſla-ted at the prieſts hands,as they from tyme to tyme haue re-ceiued them , and after ſuch order as your own texte ap-pointeth, ſaying : *When he is ſette vpon the ſeate of his king-dome,he ſhal write him out this ſeconde Law in a booke,taking a copy of the Prieſts , of the Leuiticall tribe.* Which later woordes ye haue, becauſe they make directly againſt you, quite leaſte out. And then immediatly foloweth howe he ſhal buſely read the ſayde booke and ſo forth . If this order had of Late yeares ben kept,and that Princes and other had taken the Bible as it is, and euer hath ben, of the prieſtes of the Catholike Church(orderly and lawfully ſucceding one the other,as the Leuits did)reade,tawght, and expounded, as wel in Greke and Hebrewe , as in Latin , theſe errours and hereſies ſhould neuer haue taken ſo deape a roote , as they haue now cawght.

Neither is this place onely meant,that the King ſhould take the bare lettre,but rather the expoſition withal of the ſaid Prieſts.For what were the King the better or any man elſe,for the bare lettre,if he had not alſo as ordinary a waye for his direction,in the vnderſtanding , as he had prouided him,for to receiue a true and an incorrupted copy?Where of we may ſee the practiſe in al ages in the Catholik Chur-che : whereof this place is the very ſhadowe and figure. For as the Proteſtantes them ſelues are forced by plaine wordes to confeſſe,that they know not the true worde or booke of God , but by the Churche : which from tyme to

Both, the boks of ſcripture and the xpoſition muſt be taken at the prieſts hands.

L   tyme

tyme delyuered theſe bokes:euen ſo by al reaſon and learning,they ſhould alſo côfeſſe,that the Church can no more
be deceiued in deliuering the ſenſe of the ſaide word , then
in deliuering the worde it ſelf . Which ſeing they will not
confeſſe (for then were we forthwith at a point and ende
with al their errours and hereſies) they muſt nedes continew in the ſame. And ſo while euery man in the expoſitiô
of ſcriptures foloweth his own head be it neuer ſo worldly wiſe or circumſpect,yet his own propre and peculiar,ſe·
parated from the common aduiſe and iudgement of the
whole Church:errours and hereſies haue and doe daylie
grow,and wil neuer ceaſe more and more to encreaſe and
multiply,onleſſe we take forth the leſſô I haue ſhewed you,
into this huge and infinite nôber , where with the world is
now moſt miſerably ouerwhelmed. Whereof the beſt remedy were,the exact obſeruation of this place,that ye haue
ſo wilily and ſleightly ſlipte ouer.

But moſt of al an other ſentence in the very ſaid chapter,
and euen the next to this ye alleage , that the King as ſone
as he is choſen, *ſhal beſtow his ſtudy vpon the reading of the
Deuteronomy.*Where Moyſes ſaieth,that in doubtful cauſes
the people ſhoulde haue their recourſe to the ſaid prieſtes ,
and to the iudge for the tyme beinge , meaning the highe
prieſte, of whome they ſhoulde learne the truthe : and
are commaunded to doe accordinglye , euen vnder payne
of death.Which place wel weighed and côſidered,ſerueth
to declare that I haue ſaid,that the King and others ſhould
receiue not only the letter which (as S . Paule ſaieth)doth
kil,but the true and ſincere meaning withal: wherein ſtandeth the life of the letter, as the life of mã with in his body,
yea the eternal lyfe(wherof by folowing lewde lying expo-
ſitions

An other
ſentence
in the ſaid
chapter
by M.
Horn al-
leaged
that ouer
throvv-
eth all
his boaſt

ſitions of holy write, we are ſpoiled) at the prieſts handes.
All which thinges ſerue directly for the primacy of them
and not of Princes. Nowe therefore goe on M. Horne,
and beinge at your firſt encountringe ouerblowen and diſ-
comfyted euen with your owne blaſte, thinke well whether it is lykely that ye ſhall hereafter bringe againſte your
aduerſary any thig, wherby he ſhould, as ye haue falſly ſlaūdered him, in a maner yelde, and be reſolued on your ſyde.

For as for the next place, it enforceth no ſupremacy. We
frely graunte you, that princes may ſharply puniſhe teachers of falſe and ſuperſtitiouſe religion and idolatry (being
thereof by the Prieſtes inſtructed) which is the matter of
your texte. But then take head to your ſelfe, Maiſter
Horne. For I ſaye to you, that ye, and your fellowes teache
falſe and ſuperſtitiouſe religion, many and deteſtable hereſies, and ſo withal plaine Idolatry. For hereſie is called a
very Idol, aſwel by ſcripture, as in the expoſition of the holy and learned fathers. And the are ye no ſimple Idolatour,
but one that mainteyneth a nomber of hereſies : with no
leſſe offence towardes God, than was the offence of the
Iewes that your place ſpeaketh of, when they ſette vppe
afterwarde, their idolls. And ſo haue ye geuen ſentence
againſt your ſelfe and haue tolde the Magiſtrate his office. Neither thinck you that ye may illude your puniſhment, by the cowlour of the late ſtatutes of the realme,
which though in manye thinges, ſerue for your worde-
lye indemnitye : yet that ye may kepe your Madge and
biſhoprike withall, and maye not be puniſhed for the obſtinate defence of ſuche fylthye mariage, and eſpeciallye
for the denyinge of the reall preſence in the bleſſed Sacramente of the aulter, and for many other things that your

Deut. 13.

Hereſie is
Idolatry.
Vinc. Lyr.
aduerſus
prophan.
nouit.
Hieron.
Zach. c. 13
Eſai c. 2.
& 8.
Augu. de
vera reli-
gion. c. 38.

forte daily write and preach, I trowe it wil be hard for you to bring forth any acte of parliamente, or any other conuenient and sufficient plea . And as I graunt this authority to punishe, to the ciuil prince: so (that this inferreth a superiority in al causes aswel ecclesiastical as temporal) I flatly deny: and most of al that ye haue proued your assertion , that princes ought to take vpon them such pretensed regiment, whereof the very place by you induced, sheweth as I haue said, the plain contrary. Now that you bring out of *Glosa or dinaria* , that the Prince is commaūded *by his Princely authority, to cause his subiects to become Israëlites* , it may perhaps be in some ordinary Glose of Geneua his Notes , Bales, or some such like, but as for the olde ordinary Latin Glose, I am right sure (M. Horn) it hath no suche thinge. This therefore may wel stande for an other vntruthe. As also that which immediatly you alleage out of Deuteron. *13.* For in al that chapter or any other of that booke, there is no such worde to be founde as you talke of . And thus with a ful messe of Notorious vntruthes, you haue furnished the first seruice brought yet to the table, cōcernig the pricipal matter. How be it perhaps though this be very course, yet you haue fyne dishes and daynty cates coming after. Let vs then procede.

The 11. Diuision. Pag. 8. b   M. Horne.

> *The beste and most Godly Princes that euer gouerned Gods people, did perceiue and rightly vnderstande this to be Gods vvil , that they ought to haue an especiall* ✻ *regarde and care for the ordering and setting soorth of Gods true Religion, and therefore vsed great diligence vvith feruent zeale to perfourme and accomplishe the same. Moyses vvas the supreme gouernour ouer Gods people (and vvas (.38.) not chiefe Priest or Bishop, for that vvas Aaron) vvhose authority, zeale, and care in appointing and ordering Religion amongest Gods people, prescribing to al the people, yea to Aaron and the Leuits, vvhat, and after vvhat sorte, they should execute their functions, correc*

✻ Regarde and chief rule: *Care and Supremgouernmēt are in diuerse thiges.*

The 38. vntruth.

Exo. MOY

ting

ting and chaſtening the tranſgreſſours, is manifeſtly ſet foorthe in his booke
called the Pentateuche.

The 9. Chapter: concerning the example of Moyſes.

 Aiſter Horne willing to ſeame orderly to procede, firſt bringeth in, what ſcripture commaū-
deth Princes to doe, and then what they did.
But as his ſcripture towching the commaundemēt by him alleaged nothing reacheth home
to his pretenſed purpoſe, but rather infringeth and plainely
marreth the ſame as I haue ſaide, and fully ſtandeth on our
ſyde: So I dowbte nothing yt wil fare with his examples, as
of Moyſes, Ioſue, Dauid, Salomon, Ioſaphat, Ezechias, Ioſias, and that they al come to ſhort, and are to weake to iuſtifie his aſſertion. But here am I ſhrewdly encombred, and
in a great doubte what to doe. For I coulde make a ſhorte
but a true anſwere, that theſe examples are fully anſwered
alredy, by M. Doctour Harding, and M. Dorman: and referre thee thither to thyne and myne eaſe (gentle reader)
and to the ſparing, not onely of penne, ynk, and paper, but
of the tyme alſo, whiche of al things is moſt preciouſe. But
then I feare me, woulde ſteppe forth, yf not M. Horne (a
good ſimple plain man in his dealings) yet ſome other iolye,
fyne, freſhe, pregnant, wytty fellowe, yea and bringe me to
the ſtraits which way ſo euer I did tread. Yf I ſhuld as I ſaid,
ſende the reader to them, then ſhould I heare, a foole, a
dolte, an aſſe that can ſay nothing of his own. Then ſhoulde
the cauſe be ſlaundered alſo, as ſo poore and weake, that it
could beare no large and ample treatiſe, yea with all, that
their anſweres were ſuch, as I was aſſhamed of them, and

L iij   there-

therefore wilylye and wiſelye forbeared them, with manye ſuche other triumphant trieflinge toyes. Againe yf I
ſhoulde repete or inculcate their anſweres, then woulde
Maiſter Nowell or ſome other ruſhe in vppon me with
his ruſlynge rhetorike that he vſeth againſte Maiſter Dorman and Maiſter Doctour Hardinge withe a preciſe accompte and calculation what either Maiſter Dorman or
Maiſter Doctour Hardinge borowed of Hoſius : or either
of them two of the other . And what I haue nowe
borowed of them bothe, or of either of them . And I
ſhoulde be likewiſe inſulted vppon, and our cauſe, as feble
and very weake, ſlaundered alſo . But on the one ſyde
leaſte any of the good bretherne ſhoulde ſurmiſe vppon
my ſilence anye ſuche diſtruſte, I will compendiouſly as
the matter ſhall require abridge their anſweres : and that
Maiſter Horne ſhall thinke that our ſtuff is not al ſpente, I
ſhall on the other ſyde for a ſurpluſſage, adioyne ſome o-
ther thinges to owre opponent accommodate . So that I
truſte either anſwere ſhalbe ſufficient to atchieue our purpoſe againſte Maiſter Horne . Then for Moyſes I ſaye
with Maiſter Doctour Hardinge, and Saint Auguſtyne,
that he was a prieſte aſwell as a Prince, I ſay the ſame with
Maiſter Dorman, with Philo Iudeus, with Saint Hierom,
and with Saint Hieroms Maiſter Gregorie Nazianzene.
And ſo conſequently Maiſter Horne, that Moyſes example ſerueth not your turne (onleſſe ye will kinge Henry
the eight, and his ſonne king Edward, yea and our gracious
Quene to be a prieſt to) but rather quite ouerturneth your
aſſertion. And thinke you Maiſter Horne, that the Quenes
authority doth iumpe agree, with the authority of Moyſes in cauſes eccleſiaſtical? Then maye ſhe preach to the
people

Pſalm. 98
Hieron in
Iouinianũ
lib. 1.
Greg Na-
zian. in
oration.de
Moyſe &
Aaron. &
in orat. ha
bita in
praſentia
fratris Ba
ſilij, &c.
Philo Iu-
deus de
vita Moyſi
lib. 3.
Exod 14
Ibidem .
Exod. 29.
& 35.

people as Moyſes did. Thē may ſhe offer ſacrifices as Moy- ſes.
ſes did. Then may ſhe côſecrate Prieſts, as Moyſes did côſecrate Aaron and others. Then may it be ſaid of the impoſi- *Deut*.34
tion of her hands as was ſaid of Moyſes. *Ioſua the ſon of Nun*
was ful of the ſprite of wiſedom: for Moyſes hadde put his hand
vpon him. It muſt nedes therfore follow, that Moyſes was a
prieſt, and that a high prieſt, which ye here ful peuiſhly deny. I ſay now further with M. Dorman, that put the caſe,
Moyſes were no prieſt, yet this example frameth not ſo
ſmothely and cloſely to your purpoſe as ye wene. For Moy
ſes was a prophet, and that ſuch a prophet, as the like was
not agayne.

Geue me nowe Maiſter Horn Princes Prophetes, geue
me Princes, and Lawe makers by ſpeciall order and appointmente ordeyned of God, to whoſe woordes God certainly woulde haue geuen as greate authority, as he wolde
and commaunded to be geuen to Moyſes: and then perchaunce I will ſay, that ye ſaye ſomewhat well to the purpoſe.

Agayne Moyſes was ſuche a ſpeciall Prophet, and ſo
ſingularlye choſen of God to be heard and obeyed in all
thinges, that he is in the holy ſcripture euidentlye compared to Chriſt him ſelfe: compared, I ſay, euen in the office of teaching and inſtructing. Moyſes in the Deuteronom foretelling the Iewes of a Meſsias to come, ſaieth:
The Lorde thy God wil rayſe thee vp a Prophet from among thy Deut. 18.
own nation and of thy brethern ſuch a one as my ſelf, him thou
ſhalt heare.

And this ſo ſpoken of Moyſes in the olde Lawe, is in the
new teſtamēt auouched ād repeted, firſt by S. Peter the chief Act. 3. et 7
Apoſtle, and next by S. Stephen the firſt Martir, and applied
                                                    to Chriſt.

to Chrift. If the Chrift muft fo be heard and obeied of vs, as
was Moyfes of the Iewes, no doubt as Chrift is a Kinge, a
Prophet, a Prieft and a Bifhop to vs, fo was Moyfes to the
a Prince, a Prophet, a Prieft and a Bifhop. As Chrift is of vs
to be heard and obeyed as wel in al matters Ecclefiafticall
as Temporal (for no temporal Lawe can haue force againft
the Law of Chrift amonge Chriften men) fo was Moyfes
to be heard and obeyed of the Iewes in matters and caufes
as well temporall as fpirituall. For why? The Scripture is

A&.7.

plaine. *Tanquam meipfum audietis*. You fhall heare that Prophet euen as my felfe. Shew vs M. Horne any Prince in the
new teftament fo conditioned and endewed, and then make
your argument on Gods name. Verely any Prince that now
is (namely in Ecclefiafticall gouernment) compared with
Moyfes is as the poet faieth, *Impar congreffus Achilli, Troilus*.

**Me muft
iudge by
Lavv and
not by
examples**

And the lawier faieth, *Legibus, non exemplis iudicatur*. We
muft iudge according to the precife rule of the Law, and
not by examples: Extraordinary doings enforce no ordinary prefcriptio or rule. The ordinary rule of Priefts iudgmets
without whies and whates, and fuch other triflinge importune inftances, as ye are wont to make againft it, by the law
of Moyfes and by your owne chapter before alleaged in
dowbtful cafes, muft abfolutelye vppon paine of deathe be
obeyed. By this rule of the Law you muft meafure al the
examples following, of Kings and Princes vnder this Law.
You muft fquare your examples, to the rule and not the
rule to the examples, onleffe ye will make of the Lawe
of God *Lefbiam regulam*, and both vnfkilfully and vnorderly worke therewith. And this one anfwere might wel ferue
for al the Kings doings now followig: Sauing I wil particularly difcede to euery one, and for euery one faye fomwhat.

Here

Here I wish to encounter with M. Nowel for his shifts
that he maketh to maintain the matter by Moyſes and the
reſidue, but becauſe it is M. Dormans ſpecial and peculiar
matter, I will leaue it vnto him, and be alſo in the reſidue,
as briefe as I maye.

M. Horne. The. 12 Diuiſion. Pag. 8. b.

*After the death of Moſes , the people as yet not entred and ſettled in the
promiſed land, the charge of chief gouernment ouer Gods people both in cauſes temporall and (.39.) Eccleſiaſticall, was committed to Ioſue , and not to
Eleaſar, for to him belonged (.40.) onelie the miniſtration of the things belonging to the Prieſtlie office. And to Ioſue the Prince belonged the ouerſight
both ouer the prieſts and people, to gouerne, guide, order, appoint and direct
eche eſtate, in all things that appertained to eche of their callings. Of the one
ye ſeme to haue no doubt at all: the other is as plaine. For at the appointmēt
of Ioſue, the Prieſts remoued the Arke of couenant and placed the ſame. He
did interprete vnto the people the ſpirituall meaninge of the tvvelue ſtones,
which ther had taken by Gods commaundement forth of Iordan, to be as Sacra
ments or ſignes. He circumciſed the children of Iſrael at the ſeconde time of
the great and ſolempne Circumciſion. He calleth the Prieſtes, commaundeth
ſome of them to take vppe the Lords Arke : other ſeuen of them to blovv ſeuē
trompets before the Arke, and appointeth to them the order of proceding. He
builded an Aulter vnto the Lord God of Iſrael, according to the Lavv of God:
he ſacrificeth theron, burnt ſacrifices and burnte offerings : He wrote there
vpon the ſtones, the Deuteronomie of Moſes : He read all the bleſſings and
curſings as thei are ſet forth in the booke of the Lavve: And he read al what
ſo euer Moſes had commaunded before al the congregation of Iſrael, &c. Laſt
of al Ioſue, to ſhevv that cauſes of Religion did ſpeciallie belong to his charge
and care, maketh a long and a vehement Oration vnto the Iſraelits, wherin he exhorteth them to cleaue vnto the Lorde with a ſure faith, a conſtant
hope and a perfect loue, obeiyng and ſeruing him with ſuch ſeruice as he hath
appointed in his Lavve. And doth zelouſie and with great threates diſwade
them from al kind of idolatrie and falſe Religion.*

The.39.
vntruth.
Ioſue had
not the
Supreme
gouerne-
ment in
cauſes
Eccleſia-
ſtical, but
Eleaza-
rus had it
The. 40,
vntruth.
For be-
ſide : In
all things
to be don
of Ioſue,
Eleazar
ſhoulde
inſtruct
him.
Ioſue. 3. 4
5 6. 8. 23.
24.

M   *The*

The. 10. Chapter concerning the example of Iosue.
Stapleton .

Iosue
no Su-
preme
Gouer
nour in al
Ecclesia-
sticall
causes.
Num.27

M.Nowel
put to his
shifts by
M.Dor-
man,

Num.27.

Iosue.3 4.
5. 6.8.13.
24.

THE Apologie allegeth as wel the example of
Moses, as of Iosue his doings with the residue
by M. Horne here alleaged. M. D. Harding
sheweth that allegatio to import no chief rule
in spiritual matters, as in deed it doth not.   Which chiefe
rule, did rest in the Prieste Eleazarus, at whose voice and
worde Iosue was commaunded, *to goe foorth, and come in,* a
place deaply dissembled by the Author of the Apologie.
For the auoiding whereof M.Nowell is put to many shifts:
first to glose, that this place concerning Eleazarus, may be
restrained for going and comming to and froe the warres.
whiche as it is true, so immediatlye before, it is generallye
writen, *Pro hoc si quid agendum erit, Eleazar sacerdos consulet
Dominum* For him (meaning Iosue) Eleazar shal ask counsel of God when any thing is to be done. In which words
we see euidently, that Iosue what so euer he did, touching
the gouerning of the people in Ecclesiasticall matters, he
did nothing of him self, but was in al such maters instructed
of Eleazarus the high Priest: whose part therfore it was alwaies to *ask counsel of God, when Iosue had any thing to doe.*
And though this place shuld be restrained to warfare only,
yet the authoritie geuen before by expresse wordes of the
law, to the high Prieste, whose iudgement is comaunded in
great doubts to be sought ad also followed, doth neuer the
lesse take place. And thervpo foloweth that al the testimonies of holy Scripture, brought forth by M.Nowel, and before him by M. Horne, can not, as they do not in deed, induce supremacie in causes Ecclesiastical. But th'execution
of the high Priests or lawes comademet, which in deed we

graunt

graũt to appertain to the Prince.And here I wil not quarel
with M.Nowel,either for quoting.*33.34.*for.*23.24.* and not
reformed,as he doth with M.Dorman for as ſmal a matter,
as for the miſquoting of S.Cyprian:or for treading M.Hor-
nes ſteppes,and borowing his allegations,which not with-
ſtandmg is a great obſeruation with him as a worthy mat-
ter(ye may be aſlured)againſt M.Dorman and M. D.Har-
ding.This is but a childiſh and boyiſh rhetorike,not ſo conuenient,Iwiſſe,for M.Nowel the ſcholemaiſter, as for the
boyes his ſchollers, whoſe propretye is to accuſe their fellowes of borowing,and to borow them ſelues like truants.
But for the doing of Ioſue,I wil further note,that then the
Prieſts toke vp the Arke of couenãt,ãd went before the people. Ioſue.13.
But I pray you M.Horne, howe was this obſerued of late
yeres, whẽ the lay men durſt aduẽture to take the guiding
of the Arke,and goe before the Prieſtes, and not ſuffer the
Prieſts to goe before thẽ? And durſt alter the ſtate of Chriſtiã religiõ,againſt the wil ãd minde of the Biſhops and the
whole Clergy then at their cõuocation aſsẽbled? Well, let
this paſſe for this preſent. I ſay no further for Ioſue his doings, ſauing that otherwiſe alſo they are not to be drawen
into an ordinarie rule, for that the Spirite of God was cer- Num.17.
tainelye in him : and for that he had parte of Moſes glory,
and the people commaunded to heare him. And thoſe
things that he did (wherof M. Nowell and Maiſter Horne
woulde inferre a Soueraigntie in cauſes Spirituall) he did
them by the expreſſe commaundemente of God. And
from ſuche Princes to all Princes indifferentlie to gather
the like præeminence in al points, were no ſure and ſound
gathering and collection.

Els if you wil haue your examples to proue and cõfirme,

Iosue.

Fol 23.
& 24.

then as Iosue circumcided, so let the Prince baptise, and as Iosue sacrificed vpon an Aulter, so let the Prince in Cope and Surplesse celebrate your holy Communion. Whiche two things as peculiar offices of Bishops and Priestes, M. Nowel excludeth flatly al Princes from, yea and saith, they oughte to be *vntouched of Prince or other person*. Thus againe either ye iumble and iarre one from an other, or els your Argument falleth downe right. Choose whiche of both ye will.

2 Sam 5.
The. 41.
vntruth.
Dauid
vvas not
Supreme
gouernor
in al man
ner cau-
ses, but
suffred
the Le-
uites in
Churche
matters
to liue
vnder
the rule
of their
high
Priest.
1. Par. 13.
15 16.
Dauid in
all these
matters,
determi-
ned no
doctrine,

M, Horne. The. 13. Diuision. Pag. 9. a.

Dauid vvhom God appointed to be the pastour (that is, the King ouer Isra el) to feed his people, did vnderstand that to this pastoral office of a King, did belong of duetie, not onelie a charge to prouide that the people might be gouerned vvith iustice, and liue in ciuil honestie, peace, and tranquillitie, publique and priuate: but also to haue a speciall regarde and care to see them fedde vvith true doctrine, and to be fostered vp in the Religion appointed by God him selfe in his lavve. And therefore immedratlie after he vvas vvith some quietnes setled in his royall seat, the first thing that he began to reforme and restore to the right order, as a thing that appertained especially to his princelie charge and care, vvas Gods religion and seruice, vvhich had ben decayed and neglected long before in the time of King Saul. For the better perfourmance vvhereof, as the Supreme gouernour ouer al the estates both of the laitie and of the Clergie (.41.) in all maner of causes: after consultation had vvith his chiefe Counsailers, he calleth the Priestes and Leuites, and commaundeth, appointeth, and directeth them in all manner of things and causes, appertaining to their ecclesiasticall functions and offices. He prepareth a semelie place for the Arke in his ovvne Citie. He goeth vvith great solemnitie to fetch the Arke of the Lord. He comaundeth Sad c id Abiathar the Priests, and the chief amog the Leuites, to sanctifie them selues vvith their brethren, and than to carie the Arke vppon their shoulders vnto the place apointed He comptrolleth the that the Arke was not caried before on their shoulders according to the lavv: and therfore laieth to their charge the breach that vvas made by the death of Vsa. He comadeth also the chief of the

Leuites

Leuits,to apoint amõg their brethrẽ, Muſiciãs to play on diuers kinds of inſtru- nor alte-
mẽts,and to make melody vvith ioyſulnes. He ſacrificeth burnt ãd peace offe- red any
rings, He bleſſed the people in the name of the Lord, He appointeth certain religion
of the Leuites to miniſter continually before the Arke of the Lord,to reherſe againſt the
his great benefits, to the honour and praiſe of the Lord god of Iſraell. And Prieſtes
for that preſent time he made a pſalme of gods praiſe, and appointed aſaph vvilles of
ad his brethren to praiſe god thervvith, He ordained the prieſts, Leuites, ſin- his ovvn
gers;and porters,and in ſome he apointed and ordered al the officers and offi- Supreme
ces,required to be in the houſe of the Lord, for the ſetting ſoorth of his ſeruice authori-
and religion. tye:

The. II. Chapter concerning the example of Dauid.

BOTH M. Dorman and M. Doctor Harding Da-
affirme that the proceedings of King Dauid uid.
are nothing preiudiciall to the Eccleſiaſticall
authoritie : in redreſsing of diſorders before
committed, or doing ſuche things as are here
reherſed. No more, then the reformatiõ of Religion made
by Quene Marie, as M. D. Harding noteth,which ye wot
wel, imployeth in her no ſuch ſupremacie.   Beſide that,
it is to be conſidered, as M. D. Harding toucheth,that he
paſſed other Princes herein,becauſe he had the gift of prophecie.   So that neither thoſe thinges that the Apologie
ſheweth of Dauid, or thoſe that yee and M. Nowell adde
thereunto, for the fortification of the ſaid ſuperioritie , can
by any meanes induce it. The ſcripture in the ſayed place
by you and M. Nowel alleaged,ſaith that Dauid did worke
iuxta omnia quæ ſcripta ſunt in lege Domini: according to all
things writen in the lawe of God.   Whereunto I adde a 1 Par.16.
notable ſaying of the ſcripture, in the ſaid booke by you alleaged, concerning Dauids doings by you brought foorth
touching the Prieſtes and Leuites : *vt ingrediantur domum*

*Dei iuxta ritum suum sub manu Aaron Patris eorum, sicut præ-
ceperat Dominus deus Israël.* Kinge Dauids appointmente
was, that the Leuites and Prieſtes ſhoulde enter in to the
houſe of God, there to ſerue vnder the gouernment. Of
whom, I pray you? Not of King Dauid, but vnder the Spiritual gouernmēt of their ſpiritual father Aaron ād his ſucceſſours. The gouernour of them then, was Eleazarus.
Where we haue to note: firſt, that Dauid appointed here to
the Leuites nothing of him ſelf: but *ſicut præceperat Dominus
Deus Iſraël:* as the Lord God of Iſrael had before apointed.
Secondlye, that King Dauid did make appointment vnto
them, of no ſtrange or new order to be taken in Religion,
but that they ſhould ſerue God in the Tēple, *iuxta ritū ſuū:*
after their owne vſage, cuſtome and maner, before time v-
ſed. Thirdly and laſt, King Dauids appointment was, that
they ſhould ſerue in the houſe of God *ſub manu Aaron patris
eorum,* as vnder the ſpirituall gouernmente of their Father
Aaron, and his ſucceſſours the high Prieſts. The whiche
wordes of the ſcripture doe ſo wel and clearly expres, that
King Dauid did not take vpon him any ſpirituall gouernement in the houſe of God (namely ſuch as you attributè to
the Quenes Ma. to alter Religion. &c.) that I can not but
very much muſe and maruel, why ye ſhoulde alleage King
Dauid, for any example or proufe in this matter. But moſt
of al, that ye dare alleage the death of Oza. Whiche is ſo
directly againſt our lay men, that haue not onely put their
hands, to ſuſteine and ſtaye the fal of the Arke (as Oza did,
for which attempt notwithſtanding he was puniſhed with
preſent deathe) but haue alſo of their owne priuate authoritie altered and chaunged the great and weightie pointes
of Chriſtes Catholike Religion : and in a māner haue quite
tranſ-

tranfformed and ouerthrowen the fame , and fo haue as a
man may fay, broken the very Arke it felf al to fitters. Let
them not dout, but that (except thei hartely repēt) they fhal
be plagued woorfe then Oza was, if not in this worlde, yet
more horribly in the world to come.   As for that you alleage of Dauid, that he made Pfalmes, ordeined Priefts, Leuites, fingers, and porters &c. thinke you, he did al this and
the reft of his owne authority, becaufe he was King of the
people? So you would your Reader to beleue. But the holy
Ghoft telleth vs plainly that Dauid did all this, *becaufe God* 2.Par.29.
had fo commaunded by the hands of his Prophets.   And thus
you fee, that by the declaration of the Prophetes , Gods
Minifters then, as Prieftes are now , the King did all thofe
Ecclefiafticall matters, and not by his Princely authoritie.
Againe the like you might haue alleaged of Carolus Mag- *Naucler.*
nus: *that he correɕed moſt diligently the order of reading and* *Generat.*
finging in the Church, that he brought firſt into Fraunce Cantŭ *29.pag 51*
Gregorianŭ, the order of finging left by S. Gregorie at Rome, ăd *& .52.*
appoynted fingers therefore, and when they did not wel placed *Krantz.*
other in their romes, and many other fuch like maters of the *lib.2.c 9.*
Church, wherin that godly Emperor much bufied himfelf, *Iuo Car-*
and yet exercifed no fupreme gouernmēt ouer the clergy, *not.lib.5.*
but was of al other Princes, mofte farre from it : as it maye *Nec vlte-*
eafely appeare to him that wil read in the Decrees, *Diſt.19.* *rius liceat*
In memoriam. where he protefteth obediēce to the See of *retractari*
Rome, *yea though an importable charge fhould be laied vppon* *per appel-*
him by that holy See. Alfo in the Decrees. xj. q. j. which Iuo *lationis*
alfo alleageth, where he renueth out of the Code of The- *negotium,*
odofius a law binding al his fubieɕs, *of al nations, Prouinces,* *quod epi-t*
and Countries of what fo euer qualitie or condition they were, *fcoporum*
and in all maner caufes , if the defendante require an Eccle- *iudicio re-*
fiafticall *ciditur.*

*fiafticall iudgement, it be not lawfull from the Biſhops ſentence
to appeale any higher.* And ſurely no Prince more recogniſed their duetifull obedience to the Spirituall Magiſtrate,
in ſpirituall cauſes, then ſuch as were moſt ready and carefull to aide, furder, and to their power directe all Spirituall
matters. Al this therefore proueth wel, that Godly Princes doe furder and ſette foorth Gods Religion, by meanes
ſemely to their vocation. But here is no manner inekling,
that Princes doe or did euer beare the ſupreme gouernmēt
in all Eccleſiaſtical matters, to decide and determine, to alter and change, to ſette vppe and plucke doune what Religion liked them, by their Princelye authoritie and mere
Soueraigntie.

The. 42.
vntruth.
For Salomon of
his ovvn
authoritie (as
your argument
runneth)
depoſed
not Abiathar: but
executed
only the
ſentence,
pronoūced before by
Samuell
Gods miniſter.
The. 43.
vntruth.
Thoſe
vvordes
are not in
the ſcripture alleged,

M. Horne. The. 14. Diuiſion. Pag. 9. 4.

*Salomon (.42.) depoſed Abiathar the high Prieſte, and placed Sadoc in
his roome And he builded the Temple, placed the Arke in the place appointed
for the ſame. Hallovved or dedicated the Temple, offred ſacrifices, bleſſed
the people, directed the Prieſtes, Leuites, and other Churche officers in their
functions, according to the order before taken by his Father Dauid. And
neither the Prieſtes nor Leuites, ſwerued in anie thing (.43.)
pertaining to their office) from that, that the King commaunded them.*

The. 12. Chapter concerning the example of King Salomon.

HE weight of this obiectiō reſteth in the depoſition of Abiathar the high Prieſt. Which
thing M. Dorman and M. D. Harding ſay imployeth no more ſuperioritie, then if a man
ſhoulde ſaye Q. Marie depoſed M. Cranmer, and yet was
not ſhee the chiefe, but an acceſſorie inſtrumente for the
furthe-

furtherance of thexecution. But Lord how M. Nowel here
besturreth him self? He fumeth and freateth with M. Dorman, who shal coole him wel inowghe I dowbt not. In the
meane while, I wil aske M. Horne and M. Nowel to, one
question. M. Horne saieth a litle before, that *Iosue sacrificed
burnte sacrifices and burnte offeringes, that King Dauid sacrificed burnte and peace offerings, that Salomon offered sacrifices.*
Were trow ye Iosue, Dauid, and Salomon priests? If so, thē
how bring you their examples to proue any thing for kings
and Quenes that are no priestes ? If not, then this phrase is
verefied, in that they caused the priests (to whome the matter perteyned) to offer sacrifices. And so whereas M. Horn
saieth of Iosue, that he sacrificed burnte sacrifices whiche
is agreable to the Latin: *Obtulit holocausta,* M. Nowel saieth Novvel
he commaunded sacrifice to be offered. And why then I praye fol. 166.
you M. Nowel, may not this phrase also be taken after the col. 1.
said sorte, that Salomon deposed Abiathar, in procuring him
by some ordinary way to be deposed for his treason? As M.
Crāmer might haue ben, though he were both deposed and
burnt for his heresy. But now M. Horn, that Salomō was but M. Horne
a minister and an executour herein, the very words imme- ouerthro
diatly folowing (the which becaufe they ferue plain against vven cō-
your purpose, you craftely dissembled) doe testifie. Which cerning
are these. *And so Salomon put away Abiathar, from beinge* the depo
priest vnto the Lorde, to fulfill the words of the Lorde Whiche sition of
he spoke ouer the house of Hely in Silo. And thus was Salomō Abiathar
but the minister and executour of Gods sentence published by the ve
before by Samuel the Leuite. Beside that the deposing of ry next
Abiathar doth not imploye that Salomō was the chief ruler line of his
in all causes Ecclesiastical, which is the butte that ye muste ovvne
shote at, and thē must ye prouide an other bow, for this wil text guile
                                                      fully by
                                                      him omit-
                                                      ted.
                                                     3. Reg. c. 2

                              N   not

Salo-
mon.
The 44.
vntruth.
The Scri-
pture ter-
meth not
any such
Princely
Authori-
ty.
2 Par. 17.
Gloss. ord.
* Not by
his ovvn
lavves e-
nacting a
religion,
vvhich
preachers
should
svveare
vnto.
2. Par. 19.
* feathe
Priestes
iudged,
not the
King.
The 4 5.
vntruth.
Thereap-
pereth
not in
Scripture
any such
prescrip-
tion made
vnto the
chiefe
Priestes
2. Par. 20

not shote home.   Where you say farder that *neither the Priests nor Leuites swerued in any thing (perteyning to their office) from that the King commaunded them* you haue swerued very lewdly frō the text of holy Scripture, and haue added to it those words (*perteyning to their office*) more then is expressed in the Scriptures , and haue printed them in a distinct letter, as the expresse wordes of the Scripture. With such homly shiftes an euil cause must be furdered .

M. Horne.   The 15. Diuision. Pag. 10. a.

Iosaphat hath no smal commendation in the Scriptures, for that he so studiously vsed his (.44.) princely authority in the reformation of Religion, and matters apperteyning, therunto. He remoued at the first beginning of his reigne al maner of false Religiō, and what so euer might becauie of offece to the faithful. *He sent forth through his kingdom visitours, both of his Princes, and also of the Priests and Leuits, vvith the book of the Lavv of the Lord. to the end they should instruct, and teache the people, and resourme all maner abuses in ecclesiastical causes accordig to that book. After a vvhyle he made a progresse in his ovvn person throughout al his countrey, and* * *by his preachers reduced ād brought again his people from superstitiō, ād false religiō vnto the Lord the God of their fathers. He appointed in euery tovvn throughout his kingdom, as it vvere Iustices of the peace, such as feared the Lord , and abhorred false religiō to decide cōtrouersies in ciuil causes: and in like sort be appointed and ordeined the high Priests vvith other Priests, Leuits, and of the chief rulers amōg the Israelits, to be at Hierusalem to decide, and* * *iudge cōtrouersies of great vveight, that should arise about matters of religiō and the Lavv. He did cōmaunde and prescribe (4 5.) vnto the chief Priests and Leuits, vvhat sourme and order they should obserue in the ecclesiasticall causes and controuersies of religion, that vvere not so difficult and vveighty . And vvhen any tokē of Gods displeasure appeared, either by vvarres or other calamity, he gaue order to his subiects for commō praier, and enioyned to thē publike faste, vvith earnest preaching of repentaunce, and seeking after the vvil of the Lord to obey and folovve the same.*

The

*The 13. Chapter concerning the example of King
Iosaphat.*

YOV alleage for the supreame gouernement of
King Iosaphat in spiritual matters(as the Apology doth)the *2*. of Paralip. the *17*. Chapter.
And as M. D. Harding and M. Dorman haue
written,so say I,that ye are they , which fre-
quent priuate hylles,aulters,and darke groues,that the Scripture speaketh of.Wherein you haue sette vp your Idolls,
that is,your abhominable heresies . We also confesse,that
there is nothing writen in holy Scripture of Iosaphat touching his Care and diligence aboute the directing of ecclesiastical matters,but that godly Christiã Princes may at this
day doe the same,doing it in such sorte as Iosaphat did.That
is:to refourm religiõ by the Priests,not to enacte a new reli
giõ which the priests of force shal sweare vnto.Ité to suffer
the Priests to iudge in cõtrouersies of religion, not to make
the decisiõ of such things,a parliamét matter.Ité not to prescribe a new forme and order in ecclesiastical causes,but to
see that accordig to the lawes of the Church before made,
the religiõ be set forth, as Iosaphat procured the obseruatiõ
of the olde religiõ appointed in the law of Moyses. Briefly
that he doe al this as an Aduocat,defendour,and Son of the
Churche,with the Authority and aduise of the Clergy (so
Iosaphat furdered religiõ not otherwise:)not as a Supreme
absolute Gouernour, cõtrary to the vniforme cõsent of the
whole Clergy in full cõuocation,yea and of al the Bisshops
at once. Thus the example of Iosaphat fitteth wel Christiã
Princes.But it is a world to see,how wretchedly and sham-
fully Maister Horne hath handled in this place the Holye
Scriptures. First, promysing very sadly in his preface,

to caufe his *Authours fentences for the parte to be printed
in Latin letters*, here courfing ouer three feuerall chapters
of the *2.* of Paralip. he fetteth not downe any one parte or
worde of the whole text in any Latin or diftinct lettre, but
handleth the Scriptures, as pleafeth him, falfe tranflating, mā-
gling them, and belying them beyonde al fhame. He telleth
vs of *the Kings vifitours, of a progreffe made in his own perfon,
throughout all his contrey, and of Iuftices of the peace:* whereas
the texts alleaged haue no fuch wordes at al. Verely fuch a
tale he telleth vs, that his ridiculous dealing herein (were
it not in Gods caufe, where the indignity of his demeanour
is to be detefted) were worthely to be laughed at. But from
fonde counterfeytig, he procedeth to flatte lying. For where
he faieth that Iofaphat *commaunded and prefcribed vnto the
chief Prieftes, what fourme and order they fhoulde obferue in
the Ecclefiaftical caufes and controuerfies of religion &c.* This
is a lewde ād a horrible lye, flatly belying Gods holy word,
thē which, in one that goeth for a bifhop, what can be don
more abhominable? No No, M. Horne, it was for greate
caufes, that thus wickedly you concealed the text of holy
Scriptures, which you knew, being faithfully fette down in
your booke, had vtterly confounded you, and your whole
matter now in hande.

　　For thus lo, faieth and reporteth the holy Scripture of
King Iofaphat, touching his dealing with perfons rather
then with matters ecclefiaftical. *In Ierufalem alfo Iofaphat
appointed Leuites and Priefts, and the chief of the families of
Ifraël, that they fhould iudge the iudgement and caufe of God to
the inhabitants thereof.* How Iofaphat appointed the Leuites and prieftes to thefe Ecclefiaftical functiōs, it fhal appeare in the next Chapter by the example of Ezechias. Let
vs now

2.Par.19
8.

vs now forth with the Scripture. *And Iofaphat commaunded
them faying:Thus you fhall doe in the feare of the Lorde faithfully and with a perfect harte.* But howe ? Did Iofaphat here
*prefcribe to the Prieftes any fourme or order which they fhould
obferue in controuerfies of Religion,* as M . Horne faieth he
did , to make folcke wene that Religion proceded then by
waye of Commifsion from the Prince onely ? Nothinge
lefle.For thus it foloweth immediatly in the text .   *Euery*
*caufe that fhall come vnto you , of your brethern dwelling in
their Cyties,betwene kinred and kinred, wherefoeuer there is
any queftion of the law,of the comaundement, of ceremonies,of
Iuftificatiõs , fhewe vnto thẽ, that they fyn not againft God &c.*
Here is no fourme or order prefcribed, to obferue in controuerfies of Religion:but here is a generall commaundement of the King to the Priefts and Leuits,that they fhould
doe now their duty and vocatiõ faithfully and perfectly, as
they had don before in the dayes of Afa and Abias his Father and grandfather:like as many good and godly Princes
among the Chriftians alfo haue charged their biffhops, and
clergy to fee diligently vnto their flockes and charges.And
therefore Iofaphat charging here in this wife the Prieftes
and Leuites,doth it not with threates of his high difpleafure,or by force of any his own Iniunctions,but only faith:
So then doing,you fhal not finne or offende. The which very
maner of fpeache , Chriftian Emperours and Kinges haue
eftefones vfed in the lyke cafe , as we fhall hereafter in the
thirde booke by examples declare. But to make a fhort end
of this matter euen out of this very Chapter , if you hadde
M.Horne,layed forth,but the very next fentence and faying of King Iofaphat , immediatly folowinge , you fhoulde
haue fene there,fo plain a feparation and diftinction of the
                              N iij   fpiritual

*In his quæ
ad Deum
pertinent,
præfidebit.*

*Exod. 4.
& 18.*

M. Horn
confoun-
ded by his
ovvne
book and
Chapter.

fpiritual and fecular power(which in this place you labour
to confounde)as a man can not wifhe any plainer or more
effectual.For thus faith king Iofaphat.*Amarias the prieſt ãd
your biſhop ſhal haue the gouernment of ſuch things, as appertayne to God. And Zabadias ſhal be ouer ſuch works as appertayne to the Kings office.*Lo the Kings office,and diuine mat‹
ters are of diftinct functiõs. Ouer Gods matters is the prieſt,
not as the Kings commiſsioner , but as the prieſtes alwaies
were after the exãple of Moyſes:But ouer the Kings works
is the Kings Officier.And marke wel M. Horne this point.
*Zabadias is ſet ouer ſuch works as belong to the Kings office.*But
fuch works,are no maner things pertayning to the Seruice
of God.For ouer them Amarias the prieſt is prefident.Ergo
the Kings office confifteth not aboute things pertayning to
God,but is a diftinct functiõ concerning the cõmon weale.
Ergo if the King intermedle in Gods matters,eſpecially if he
take vpon him the fupreme gouernmẽt thereof , euen ouer
the prieſts themfelues to whom that charge is committed,
he paffeth the bondes of his office , he breaketh the order
appointed by God,and is become an open enemy to Gods
holy ordinance . This place therefore , you depely diſſembled ãd omitted M.Horne,left you ſhould haue difcouered
your own nakedneſſe, and haue brought to light the vtter
cõfufion of you and your wretched doctrine.Except for a
fhift,you wil preſſe vs with the moſt wretched and trayterous tranflatiõ of this place in your common englifh bibles,
printed in the yere *1562.*Which for *præfidebit,*fhal gouerne,
doe turne,*is amonge you* . For your newe Geneuian bibles,
which you take (I doubte not) for the more corrected,doe
tranflate with vs : *ſhalbe chief ouer you* .

M Horne

M. Horne. The 16. Diuision. Pag. 10.b.

Ezechias the king of Iuda, hath this testimony of the holy Ghost , that the like gouernour had not been, neither should bee after him amõgest the kings of Iuda. For he cleaued vnto the Lord, and suerued not from the preceptes vvhich the Lord gaue by Moyses And to expresse, that the office, rule, and go-uernment of a godly king consisteth, and is occupied according to Gods ordi-naunce and precept , first of al in matters of Religion , and causes Ecclesiasti-cal, the holy Ghost doth commende this king for his diligent care in resourmig religion. He toke quite avvay (saith the holy ghost)al maner of Idolatry , su-perstition, and false religion, yea, euen in the first yere of his reigne , and the first moneth he opened the doores of Gods house: He calleth as it vvere to a Sy-node the Priestes, and Leuits, he maketh vnto them a long and pithy oration, declaring the horrible disorders and abuses that hath been in religion , the causes, and vvhat euils folovved to the vvhole realme thereupõ: He declareth his ful determinatiou to restore and resourme religiõ according to Gods vvil. He commaundeth them therfore, that they laying aside al errours, ignoraũce, and negligence, do the partes of faithful ministers.

4. Reg. 18.

2, Par. 29.

The Priestes and Leuits assembled together, did sanctifie themselues , and did purge the house of the Lorde from al vncleanes of false religion , at the commaundement of the King (. 46.) concerning things of the Lord. That don, they came vnto the King, and made to him an accompt and report vvhat they had don. The King assembleth the chief rulers of the City, goeth to the Temple, he commaundeth the Priests and Leuits, to make obla-tion and sacrifice for vvhole Israel. He appcinteth the Leuits after their order in the house of the Lorde, to their musicall instruments, and of the Priestes to play on Shalmes, according as Dauid had disposed the order (47.) by the coũ-sell of the Prophetes . He and the Prince commaundeth the Leuites to praise the Lorde vvith that Psalme that Dauid made for the like purpose . He ap-pointed a very solempne keaping and ministring of the Passeouer, vvhere-unto he exhorteth al the Israelites, and to tourne from their Idolatrye and false religion vnto the Lorde God of Israel. He made solempne prayer for the people. The king vvith comfortable vvoordes encouraged the Leuites that vvere zelous , and hadde right iudgement of the Lorde, to offre sacrifices of thankes geuing, and to prayse the Lorde the God of their Fathers , and assig-ned the Priestes and Leuites to minister , and geue thankes , accordinge to their

The 46. vntruth. Those vvordes (concer-ning thigs of the Lord) are no vvor-des of the text , but falsly ad-ded to ho-ly Scrip-ture.

The 47, vntruth. Holy Scripture falsified, ad may-med, as it shal ap-pere.
2. Par. 30,

THE FIRST BOOKE

*their offices in their courſes and tournes. And for the better continuance of
Gods true Religion, he cauſed a ſufficient and liberall prouiſion to bee made
from the people, for the Prieſts and Leuits, that they might vvholy, cheerfully,
and conſtantly, ſerue the Lorde in their vocation. Theſe doinges of the Kinge
Ezechias touching matters of Religion, and the reformation thereof, ſaieth
the holy ghoſt, vvas his acceptable ſeruice of the Lord, dutiful both to God and
his people.*

The 14. Chapter concerning the doinges of
Ezechias.

Ere is nothing brought in by you, or before
by the Apology (as M. Dorman, and M. Doctour Harding doe wel anſwere) that forceth
the ſurmiſed ſouerainty in King Ezechias, but
that his powre and authority, was ready and
ſeruiceable (as it ought to be in al Princes) for the executiõ
of things ſpiritual before determined, and not by him as ſupreame head newly eſtabliſhed: So in the place by you cited it is writen that he did, *that which was good before the
Lorde according to all things that Dauid his Father had done.*
So that as Dauid did al ſuch matters, becauſe the Prophets
of God had ſo declared they ſhould be done, ſo is Ezechias
folowing his Father Dauid vnderſtanded to haue done, not
enactig any religiõ of his own, but ſettig forthe that, which
Gods Miniſters had publiſhed. Likewiſe in your other
place, *according to the Kings and Gods cõmaundemẽt.* So other
where, he did that which was good ãd right *before his Lord
God, and he ſowght God, with al his harte, after the Lawe and
commaundemente, in al the works of the howſe of God.* And as
your ſelfe ſhewe, he appointed the Leuits *according as Dauid had diſpoſed the order:* And you adde *by the councel of the
Prophets,*

4. Reg. 18.
2. Par. 29
2. Par. 31.
2. Par. 29.

Prophetes, as though Dauid had firfte done it by the aduife or counfell only ofthe Prophetes, and by his owne autho-ritie. But the Scripture faith : Ezechias did thus *according as Dauid had difpofed, becaufe it was the commaundement of God by the hande of his.Prophetes* . So that in al that Eze-chias or before Iofaphat did, they did but as Dauid had don before : That is, they executed Gods commaundement de-clared by the Prophetes. This is farre from enactinge a newe Religion by force of Supreme Authoritie, contrarie to the commaundement of God declared by the Biflhops and Prieftes, the onely Minifters of God now in fpirituall matters, as Prophetes were then in the like.

M. Horne, *The.* 17. *Diuifion.* *pag.* 11 *a.*

Iofias had the like care for religion, and vfed in the fame fort his princely authority, in reforming al abufes (48) *in al maner caufes Ecclefiaftical Thefe Godly Kings claimed and toke vpon them the fupreme gouernment ouer the Ecclefiafticall perfons of all degrees, and did rule, gouerne, and direct them in all their functions, and* (.49.) *in all manner caufes belonging to Religion, and receiued this witnes of their doings, to witte, that they did acceptable feruice, and nothing but that which was right in Gods fight. Therefore it followveth well by good confequent, that Kings or Queenes may claime and take vpon them fuch gouernment in things or caufes Ecclefiafticall. For that is right, faith the holy Ghoft: they fhould than doe vvrong if they did it not.*

The. 48. vntruth. Boldly af uouched, but no vvay proued. The 49. vntruth. as before, but fom-vvhat more im-pudent.

The. 15. *Chapter of the doings of Iofias, with a con-clufion of all the former examples.*

Stapleton.

K I N G Iofias trauailed ful godly in fuppreffing Idolatrie by his Kingly authority. What then? So doe good Catholike Princes alfo, to plucke doune the Idols that ye and your brethrē haue of late fette vppe : and yet none of them, take them felues

Iofias

O   for

for fupreme heads in all caufes Spirituall. And ye haue hitherto brought nothing effectuall to proue that the Kings of Ifraell did fo : wherefore your conclufion, *that they did rule, gouerne, and direct the Ecclefiafticall perfons in all their functions, and in all maner caufes of religion*, is an open and a notorious lye : and the contrarye is by vs aucuched and fufficiently proued by the authority of the old Teftament, wherevppon ye haue hitherto refted and fetled yourfelfe.

It is here declared, that M. Horne cometh nothing nigh the principal queftion.

But now that ye in all your exáples drawe nothing nigh the marke, but runne at rádon, and fhoot al at rouers, is moft euident to him that hath before his eye, the verye ftate of the queftion : whiche muft be efpecially euer regarded of fuch as minde not to loofly and altogether vnfruitfully imploye their laboure, and loofe both their owne and their Readers labour. I pray you then good M. Horne bring foorth that King that did not agnife one fupreme head and chiefe iudge in all caufes Ecclefiafticall among the Iewes, I meane the high Prieft, wherein lieth all our chiefe queftion. Ye haue not yet done it, nor neuer fhal doe it. And if ye could fhew any, it were not worth the fhewing. For ye fhould not fhewe it in any good King, as being an open breache of Gods lawe geauen to him by Moyfes : as thefe your doings are an open breach of Chrift and his churches lawe, geuen to vs in the new Teftament.

2.

Againe what prefident haue ye fhewed of anye good King among the Iewes, that with his laitie, altered and abandoned, the vfuall religion a thoufande yeares and vpward cuftomablie from age to age receiued and embraced: and that, the High Prieft and the whole Clergie refifting and gainfaiyng all fuch alterations ? If ye haue not fhewed this, ye haue ftraied farre from the marke.

Wha

What euidence haue ye brought forth to fhewe that in 3.
the olde Law any King exacted of the Clergie *in verbo fa-*
cer.loty,that they fhuld make none Ecclefiaftical law without his confent, as King Henrie did of the Clergie of England? And fo to make the Ciuil Magiftrate the Supreame
iudge for the finall determination of caufes Ecclefiafticall?

What can ye bring forth out of the olde Teftamente to 4.
aide and relieue your doinges, who haue abandoned not
onely the Pope, but Generall Councels alfo : and that by
plaine acte of Parliament? I faye this partlye for a certaine
claufe of the Acte of Parliament , that *for the determina-* Generall
tion of anye thinge to be adiudged to be herefie , reafteth only Coucels
in the authoritie of the Canonicall Scriptures , and in the firft abando-
foure General Councels , and other Councels general ,Wher- n e dout
in any thing is declared herefie by expreffe wordes of fcripture. of England by
By whiche rule it will be hard to conuince many froward acte of
obftinate heretikes to be heretikes : yea of fuch as euen by Parliament.
the faied fower firft, and many other Councels general are
condemned for heretikes. Partly, and moft of al,I faye it,
for an other claufe in the acte of Parliament, enacting *that*
no forraigne Prince Spirituall or temporal fhall haue any au-
thoritie or Superioritie in this realme , in any Spirituall caufe.
And then I pray you, if any Generall Councell be made to
reforme our mifbelief, if we wil not receiue it , who fhall
force vs? And fo ye fee we be at libertie, to receiue or not
receiue any general Councel.And yet might the Pope reforme vs wel inough for any thing before reherfed(for the
Popes authority ecclefiaftical is no more forraigne to this
realme,then the Catholike faith is forraigne)fauing that he
is by expreffe wordes of the ftatute otherwife excluded.

O ij   Now

5.   Now what can ye fhewe that mere laie men fhould enioye ecclefiaftical liuings, as vfually they doe among you?

6.   What good inductiō can ye bring from the doinges of the Kinges of the olde Lawe to iuftifie, that Princes nowe may make Bifhoppes by letters patents, and that for fuche and fo long time as fhould pleafe them, as either for terme of yeares, moneths, weekes, or daies? What good motiue cā

7.   ye gather by their regiment, that they did vifit Bifhops and Prieftes, and by their lawes reftrained them to exercife any iurifdiction ouer their flockes, to vifite their flocks, to refourme them, to order or correcte them without their efpeciall authoritie and commifsion therevnto? Yea to

Note. reftraine them by an inhibition from preaching, whiche ye confefle to be the peculiar function of the Clergie, exem-

8. pted from all fuperioritie of the Prince? What? Thinke ye that yee can perfwade vs alfo, that Bifhops and Prieftes paied their firft fruits and tenthes to their Princes, yea and that both in one yeare, as they did for a while in Kinge

Gen.47. Henrie his dayes? Verelye Iofeph would not fuffer the very heathen Prieftes (which onely had the bare names of Priefts) to paye either tithes or fines to Pharao their Prince. Yea rather he found them in time of famine vpon the common ftore.

9.   Are ye able (fuppofe ye) to name vs any one King, that wrote him felfe Supreame head of the Iewifh Church, and that in all caufes as well Spirituall as Temporall: and that caufed an Othe to the Prieftes and people (the Nobilitie onelye exempted) to be tendred, that they in confcience did fo beleue? and that in a woman Prince too, yea and that vnder paine of premunire and plaine treafon too?

   O M. Horne, your manifolde vntruthes are difciphired

and

and vnbuckled, ye are eſpied, ye are eſpied, I ſay, well e-
nough, that ye come not by a thouſande yardes and more
nigh the marke.   Your bowe is to weake, your armes to
feable, to ſhoot with any your cōmendation at this marke:
yea if ye were as good an archer, as were that famous Robin Hood, or Litle Iohn.   Wel ſhift your bowe, or at the
leaſt wiſe your ſtring. Let the olde Teſtament goe, and procede to your other proufes, wherein we will nowe ſee if
ye can ſhoote any ſtreighter. For hitherto ye haue ſhotten
al awrye, and as a man may ſaye, like a blinde man.   See
now to your ſelfe from henſeforth that ye open your eies,
and that ye haue a good eye and a good aime to the marke
we haue ſet before you. If not, be ye aſſured we wil make
no curteſie eftſones to put you in remembrance.   For hitherto ye haue nothing proued that Princes ought, which
ye promiſed to proue, or that they may take vppon them
ſuch gouernment, as I haue laid before you, and ſuch as ye
muſt in euery parte iuſtifie, if either ye will M. Fekenham
ſhal take the Othe, or that ye entende to proue your ſelfe a
true man of your worde.

M. Horne. Ihe, 18. Diuiſion.   pag. 11. b.

You ſuppoſe, that ye haue eſcaped the force of all theſe and ſuch like god-
ly Kings (which dee marueilouſly ſhake your holde) and that they may not
be alleaged againſt you, neither any teſtimonie out of the olde teſtament, for
that ye haue reſtrained the proufe for your contentation, to ſuch order of go-
uernment as Chriſt hath aſsigned in the Ghoſpel, to be in the time of the nevv
teſtament, wherein you haue ſought a ſubtil ſhifte.   For whiles ye ſeeke to
cloke your errour vnder the ſhadovve of Chriſtes Ghoſpel, you bevvray your
ſecrete hereſies, turning your ſelf naked to be ſene of al men, and your cauſe
notvvithſtanding, left in the ſtate it vvas before, nothing holpen by this
your poore ſhift of reſtraint.   So that vvhere your friendes tooke you be-
fore but onely for a Papiſt: novv haue you ſhevved your ſelfe to them plainly

O   iij   *herein*

The.50.
vntruth.
Moſte
ſlaunde-
rous. M.
Horne
him ſelfe
and his
fellovves
are in ma
ny pnits
Donati-
ſtes, as
ſhal ap-
peare.
The 51.
vntruth.
Anſwere
the For-
treſſe M.
Horne,
annexed
to S.
Bede, if
you dare
to defend
this moſt
ſenſible
and moſt
groſſe
lye.
Auguſt.
Epiſt.48.
& 50.
Lib.2.
cont.lit.
Pet.ca.92
Lib 2.
can.Ep.2.
Gaud.ca.
26.

herein to be a (.50.) Donatiſt alſo. VVhen the Donatiſts troubled the peace
of Chriſtes Catholique Church, and diuided them ſelues from the vnity therof, as novv you doe: The godlie Fathers trauailed to confute their hereſies by
the Scriptures, both of the olde and nevve teſtament: and alſo craued aide
and aßiſtaunce of the Magiſtrates and Rulers to reforme them, to reduce
them to the vnitie of the Churche, and to repreſſe their hereſies, vvith their
authoritie and godlie lavves made for that purpoſe, to vvhome it belonged of
duetie, and vvhoſe eſpecial ſeruice to Chriſt is, to ſee, care, and prouide, that
their ſubiectes be gouerned, defended, and mainteined in the true and ſincere
religion of Chriſt, vvithout al errours, ſuperſtitions and hereſies, as S. Auguſtine proueth at large in his Epiſtle againſt Vincentius a Rogatiſt, in his, Epiſtle to Bonifacius, and in his booke againſt Petilian, and Gaudentius letters.
Againſt this Catholique Doctrine, your aunceſtours the Donatiſtes, ariſe vp
and defend them ſelues vvith this colour or pretence, that they be of the Catholique faith. and that their church is the Catholiqne church: (VVhich ſhift
for their defence againſt Gods truth. the Popiſh ſectaries doe vſe in this our
time, being (.51.) no more of the one, or of the other, then vvere the Donatiſts and ſuch like, of vvhom they learned to couer their horrible hereſies
vnder the ſame ſaire cloke.) that the ſecular Princes haue not to meddle in
matters of religion or cauſes Eccleſiaſtiall. That God committed not the teaching of his people to Kings, but to Prophetes. Chriſt ſent not ſouldiours but
fiſhers, to bring in and further his religion, that there is no example of ſuch
order, found in the Goſpell or nevv Teſtament. vvherbr it may appeare, that
to ſecular Princes it belongeth to haue care in matters of religion. And that
(as it ſemeth by that S Auguſtine by preuention obiecteth againſt them) they
ſubtilly refuſed all proufes or examples auouched out of the Olde teſtamente
(as ye craftely doe alſo, in binding me onelie to the Nevv teſtament) vvhich
S Auguſtine calleth: an odious and vvicked guile of the Donatiſts.
Let your friends novv, vvhome ye vvill ſeeme to pleaſe ſo much, vvhen you
beguile them moſt of all. vveigh vvith aduiſement, vvhat vvas the erronious opinion touching the authoritie of Princes in cauſes Eccleſiaſical of the
Donatiſts (as it is here rightly gathered foorth of S. Auguſtine) and let them
conſider vviſely theſe foule ſhiftes they make for their defence: And then
compare your opinion and guilefull defences thereof to theirs, and they muſt
needs clappe you on the backe, and ſaye to you Patriſas, (if there be any vpright

right iudgement in them) deming you so like your graundsier Donatus, as though he had spitte you out of his ovvne mouth.

The. 16. Chapter declaring in howe many pointes Protestants are Donatists: and by the way of M. Foxes Martyrs.

Stapleton.

ITHERTO, good Reader, M. Horne although vntruely, yet hath he somwhat order-like proceeded. But in that which followeth vntill we come to the. 20. leafe, beside moste impudent and shamelesse lyes, wherwith he would deface M. Fekenham, he prosequuteth his matter so confusely and vnorderly, leaping in and out, I can not tel howe, nor whither: that I verely thinke that his wits were not his owne, being perchance encombred with some his domestical affaires at home, that he could not gather them together, or that he the lesse passed, what an hodge potche he made of his doings, thinking which is like, that his fellowes Protestantes woulde take all things in good gree, knowing that poore M. Fekenham was shut vp close inough, from al answering. And thinking that no Catholique els woulde take vppon him to answere to his lewde booke. I had thought M. Horne, that from the olde Testament, ye woulde haue gone to the newe Testament: and woulde haue laboured to haue established your matters therby. Belike the world goeth very hard with you in that behalfe, that ye doe not so: sauing that here and there ye iumble in a testimonie or two, I can not tell how, but howe vnhandsomly and from the purpose, yea against your owne selfe, that I wot well, and ye shall anon heare of it also.

M. Horns disorderly Treatise.

In the

In the meane while it is worth the labour well to confider the excellent pregnant witte and greate skill of this
man, who hath in the former Treatife of M. Fekenham espied out (which furely the wifeft, and beft learned of all
the worlde I trowe, befide M. Horne, would neuer haue
efpied, fuch a fpecial grace the man hath geuen him of his
maifter the Deuill of mere malice, ioyned with like follie)
that M. Fekenham is an Heretike, and a Donatift. But yet
M. Fekenham is fomewhat beholding to him, that he faith
M. Fekenham hath *bewrayed his fecrete herefies.* Wherein
he faith for the one part moft truely. For if there be any
herefie at all in this matter furmifed vppon him, as certainly there is none, it is fo fecrete and priuie, that Argus hi n-
felfe, with al his eyes fhall neuer efpye it : no nor M. Horne
him felfe, let him prie neuer fo narrowly : whereas on the
other fide, M. Horn and his fellowes, and his Maifters Luthers and Caluins herefies, are no fecrete nor fimple herefies, but fo manifolde and fo open, that they haue no waye
or fhift to faue their good name and honeftie, blotted and
blemifhed for euer (without repentance) for the obftinate
maintenance of the fame. Where of many were, many hu̅-
dred yeares fince, condemned, partly by the holy Fathers,
partly by General Councels. You fay M. Fekenham hath
*fecrete herefies, and that Donatus is his great grandfir, and the
Donatifts the Catholikes auncetours:* but how truly, you fhal
vnderftad anon. In the meane while good Syr, may it pleafe
you fauourably to heare you and your maifters honorable
pedegre, and of their worthy feates and prowes. You haue
heard of them before perhaps, and that by mee. But fuche
things as may edifie the Catholike, ad can neuer be anfwered by the Heretike, *Decies repetita placebunt.*

M Horns
and his
fellovves
aucetors.

Howe

Howe say you then to the great heretik Aerius the Arrian, that said there was no difference betwene priest and
Bishop, betwene him that fasted and that did not faste, and
that the sacrifice for the deade was fruitlesse? How say you
to Iouinian, that denied virginity to haue any excellencye
aboue matrimony, or any special rewarde at Gods handes?
To the Arrians that denied the miracles done at the saintes
tobes to be true miracles, and that the martyrs ca not caste
out the diuels and relieue the that be possessed? To the Bo-
gomyles that said the deuils sate at the saints tobes and did
wonders there, to illude and deceiue the people, to cause
the people to worship them? To Berengarius condemned
in diuers councels, first for denying of the real presence in
the sacrament of the aulter, and then for denying the tran-
substantiatio? To the Paulicians, that saied these wordes of
Christe, *Take, eate, this is my body*, are not to be vnderstanded of his bodye, or the breade and wine vsed at the cele-
bration of our Lordes maundy, but of the holy scriptures,
which the Priests should take at Christes hand, and deliuer
and distribute to the people? To Claudius and Vigilantius,
that denied the inuocation of Saintes, and inueyed against
the blessed reliques, and the vse of Lights and other ceremonies in the Church? To the Massalians and other heretiks, saying that concupiscence as a sinne remayneth in vs
after holy baptisme? And because ye shal not say I suppresse,
conceile, or obscure, the chief and most notable persons of
your auncetry: how say you to the Emperours Philippicus,
Leo, Constantinus, condened with their adheretes by the. 7.
general councel at Nice, that vilayned by defacing, breaking
and burnig, the Images of al the holy hallowes of Christ, ad
Christes to? To whome for your more honour and glorye

P   I ad-

*August. et
Epipha. de
haref.*

*Hier. con.
Iouinian.
Ambro. li.
o. epi. 18
Ambros.
serm. 91.
Euth. in
Panopl.
tit. 33.*

*Euth. Zi-
gab. in Pa
nop. tit. 21
Hiero. cot.
Vig. Ionas
episcopus
Aurelian.
cot. Clau-
dium.
Euth. in
Panop. tit.
22.
August. li.
1. cont. 2.
epis. Pela.
ad Bonif.
cap. 13.
Cyril. li. 6.
cot. Iulia.*

I adioyne the Emperour Iulianus the Apoftata. Who as ye
doe in your books and pulpits, cried out vpon the Chriftiãs.
O ye wretched men, that worfhip the wood of the croffe, fet:
ting vp the figure of it vppon your forehed and dores: you there-
fore that are of the wifefte forte are worthy to be hated, and the
refidewe to be pityed, that treading after your fteppes come to
fuch a kinde of wretchednes. To the Pelagians, affirming that
children not baptized fhalbe faued? And yet are your maifters in this point worfe then the Pelagians, as wel for that
fome of them haue faid, that fome Infants thowgh vnbaptized fhalbe damned, and fome other though vnbaptized fhal
be faued: And fome of them efpecially Caluin and other
Sacramentaries fay, that they fhal come without Baptifme
to the Kingdom of heauen : which the Pelagians durfte
not fay, but that they fhould haue the life euerlafting, putting a difference, but peuifhly, betwixte thofe two . And if
ye thinke the race of your worthye generation is not fetched highe inoughe, we will mounte higher, and as high as
maye be, euen to Simon Magus him felfe. Of whome Marcion and Manicheus, and after long and honorable fuccef-
fion your Patriarches Luter and Caluin haue learned their
goodly doctrine againft free will. Yea to touche the verye
foundatiõ and wel fpring of this your new gofpel, which altogether is grounded vpõ iuftificatiõ without good works,
in that alfo ye drawe very nigh to the faid Simon Magus.

I forbeare at this time to fpeake of the refidewe of your
noble progenitours, hauing in other places (as I noted before) fpoken largely of the fame. This fhall fuffice, at thys
prefent, to make open to all the world, that they are no petit or fecrete herefies that ye and your fellowes mainteine.
Come foorthe once, and cleare your felfe of this onelye
obiection

Cyril lib.6
contra
Iulianũ.
Aug.lib.2
cõtr.2.epi.
Pelag.c.4.
Caluin in
his Infti-
tutions,
cap.18. in
fine: Ar-
gẽtorati
Impreff.
An.1545

Epiph. &
Philaft. de
baref.

Clemens
li.3. recog.
Iræneus.
li 1.ca.20.

In the
difcourfe
annexed
to Sta-
philus.
fol. 161. &
fequent.

obiection, if yow can, being so often preſſed therewith. If you maintaine olde condēned hereſies, what are yow leſſe then heretiks your ſelues? If yow maintaine them not, or if they be not olde hereſies which you maintaine, clere your ſelf if you be able. I aſſure you M. Horn, you and al your felowes wil neuer be able to auoide this one onely obiectiō. And therfore you and al your fellowes muſt nedes remaine ſtark hereticks, and for ſuch to be abhorred and abādonned (except you repēt) of al good Chriſtiās. Now as I haue pro- ued yow and your companions open and notable heretiks, ſo ſhal I ſtraite way purge M. Fekenham to be no Donatiſt, or any heretik otherwiſe, for any thing yet by you layde to his charge. But now Maiſter Horne beware your ſelf, leaſte this vniuſte accuſation againſt Maiſter Fekenham and the Catholikes whome ye cōpare to the Donatiſtes cauſeleſſe, moſte iuſtly and truely redounde vpon your and your fel- lowes heades. Beware I ſay. For I ſuppoſe I will laye more pregnante matter in this behalfe to your and their charge, then ye haue or poſſible can doe to Maiſter Fekenham or any other Catholike, whereof I dare make any indifferent Reader iudge. If I ſhould dilate and amplifie this matter at large, yt would riſe to a pretty volume: but I will purpoſely abridge yt, and giue the Reader as it were but a taſte.

They were al called firſt Donatiſtes: but as the firſt fell from the Churche Catholike: ſo fell they alſo afterwarde from their' owne Churche and maiſter, into an horrible di- uiſion, of the Maximianiſtes, Circumcellions, Rogatiſtes, Circenſes and others. A lyuelye paterne of the ſectes ſprōg from your Apoſtle Luther, as in their pedegree in the Apo- logy of Staphylus euery man may ſee.

The Donatiſtes would ſomtyme crake and bragge of

Margin notes:

Prote ſtants be Do natiſts

1. The diſſentiō of the Do- natiſts. *Auguſt. de hæreſ. & in Pſal. 36 & lib. 4. contra Creſc. c. 6.*

2. *Aug. lib. 2 contra Iu- lian. & lib 3. contra Creſco. c. 66. & lib 2. contra aduerſ. Leg. c 12.*

their multitude , and bring it as an argument that the truth
was on their fide,as doth your Apologie. Which being reftrayned by the Emperours Lawes, and dayly diminifhing,
then they cried , the truthe refteth with the fewe elected
and chofen parfons:then cried they:*O lytle flocke feare not, as
ye did, when ye were as yet but in corners, rotten barnes, and
Lufkye lanes.*

The Donatiftes when they could not iuftifie their own
doctrine, nor difproue the Catholiks doctrine , leauing the
doctrine, fel to rayling, againft the vitioufe lyfe of the Catholiks. In this point, who be Donatifts, I referre me to Luthers and Caluins books, efpecially to M. Iewel, and to your
owne Apologie.

4.
Aug. lib. 1.
euang.
quæst. 4.
cap. 38.
The Do-
natifts re-
fufe the
knovven
churcn.

The Donatiftes refufed the open knowen Catholicke
Churche, and fayde the Church remayned onely in thofe
that were of their fide in certayne corners of Afrike . And
fing not ye the like longe, preferring your Geneua and Wittenberge, before the whole Catholike Church befide?

5.
Vide Aug.
in breuicu
lo Collat.
diei 3. &
in lib. poft
Coll. ca. 31
See M.
Davves
in his 13
booke.

The Donatiftes corrupted the Fathers books wonderfully, and were fo impudent in alleaging them, that in their
publike conference at Carthage, they prefied much vppon
Optatus wordes , and layde him forth as an author making
for them, who yet wrote exprefiely againft them, and in all
his writings condemned them . Is not this I pray yow the
vfuall practife of your Apoftles Luther and Caluin, of M.
Iewel, and your own to, in this booke ? as I trufte we haue
and fhal make it moft euidet. And here let M. Dawes beare
you company to, in the crafty and falfe handling of his own
deare brothers Sleydans ftory, where he leaueth out Alexander Farnefius oration to the Emperour, wherein he fheweth the Proteftants diffenfions.

The

The Donatiſts to get ſome credite to their doctrine pretended many falſe viſions and miracles, and they thowght
that God ſpake to Donatus from heauen: And doth not M.
Foxe in his donghil of ſtinckinge martyrs pretely followe
them therein trowe you? Hathe not the lyke practiſe bene
attempted of late in Hūgary, to authoriſe the new ghoſpell
by pretēding to reſtore lyfe to an holy brother feyning him
ſelf to be dead, and by the great prouidence of God, found
to be dead in dede? Did not your Apoſtle Luther boaſt
himſelf of his viſions and reuelations? Which how cœleſti-
all they were doth ſone appere, for that hī ſelf writeth, that
the deuil appered vnto him in the night, and diſputed with
him againſt priuate maſſe: by whoſe mightye and weightye
reaſons Luther being ouerthrowen yelded, and incontinently wrote againſt priuate maſſe as ye cal it.

6.

*Auguſt. in
Ioannem
Tractat.13
An.'558.*

*in l. theut.
ad Senatū
Germa.
In lib. de
miſſ. An-
gul.*

Did not the Donatiſts preferre, and more exſteme one
national erronio) councel in Aphrica, then the great and
general coūcel at Nice? kepe not ye alſo this trade preferring your forged Conuocation libell before the Generall
Councel of Trident?

7.

Thei pre-
ferre a na
tionall
councel
before the
general.

The Donatiſts ſaid that al the world was in an apoſtaſie
at the cōming of their apoſtle Donatus: And is not Luther
the ſame man to yow, that Donatus was to them? doth not
one of your greateſt clerks there with you now write, that
Wyclyff begatte Huſſe, Huſſe begotte Luther and thē addeth a
ſhameful blaſphemous note, *this is the ſeconde Natiuitye of
Chriſte?*

*Aug.lib.2
de baptiſ.
cap.9.*

8.

*Auguſt. de
agone
Chriſti
c.29.*

The Donatiſts being charged and preſſed by the Catho
liks to ſhewe the beginning and continuance of their doctrine, and the ordinary ſucceſsiō of their Biſſhops, were ſo
encombred, that they could neuer make any conuenieente

The Au-
thour of
the har-
borovve.

9.

anſwere.

Prote
ftants
be

Opt. lib. 2.
Parte. 2
cap. 1. fol.
94.
Aug. lib. 2
cont. Pe-
til. ca. 92.
Optatus
lib. 2.
In his
Replie a-
gainſt M.
D. Har-
ding.

Optatus.
lib. 2. 6.
& 7.
The Do-
natiſtes
crueltie
to the
Catholiks
Optatus.
Lib. 6.

Aug. con-
tra Dona.
poſt Col-
lat. c. 31.

anſwer. And are not ye I pray you, with your felowes proteſtāt biſhops, faſt, in the ſame myre? If not, anſwer then to
my thirde demaunde in the Fortreſſe annexed to S. Bede.

The Donatiſts fynding faulte with Conſtantine, Theodoſius, and other Catholik princes, ranne for ſuccour to Iulianus the renegate and highly commended him. And doth
not M. Iewel, I pray you, take for his preſident againſt the
Popes primacy Conſtantius the Arrian, againſt Images
Philippicus, Leo, Cōſtantinus and ſuch like deteſtable heretiks by general councels condemned? Do not your ſelf play
the like parte in the Emperour Emanuel, as ye cal him, and
in other as we ſhal hereafter declare?

Now who are, I pray you, Donatiſts, *for the defacing and
ouerthrowing of Aulters , for vilaining the holy Chriſme, and
the holy Sacrament of the aulter ? Which they caſt vnto dogs:
Which ſtraitwaies by the ordinance of God, fell vpon them, and
being therin Gods miniſters, made them fele the ſmart of their
impietie.* It were a tragical narration, to open the great and
incredible crueltie that the Donatiſts vſed toward the Catholiks, and eſpecially their horrible rauiſhment of religious
Nonnes. And yet were they nothing ſo outragious, as your
Hugonots haue bene of late in France , and the beggarly
Guets here in Flandres, namely about Tournaye.

The Donatiſts ſaid of the Catholiks : *Illi portant, multorū
Imperatorum ſacra . Nos ſola portamus euangelia .* They bring
vs many of the Emperours letters, we bring the only ghoſpels. And is not this the voyce of all Proteſtantes whatſoeuer? Only Scripture, only the goſpel, only the word of God?
And for the firſt parte, what is more common in the mouthes of the Germayn Lutherans, of the French Caluiniſtes,
and now of the flemmiſh Guets, then this complaint, that
we preſſe them with the Emperours Diets, with the Kings
procla-

proclamations,and with the Princes placarts?To the which
they obey as much as the Donatiſts,when they haue power to reſiſte.

Wel,we wil nowe leaue of al other conference and cõ-
pariſons,and tarry a litle in one more.The Donatiſts though
they were moſt wicked Murtherers of others and of them
ſelues alſo , killing them ſelues moſte wretchedly without
any other outward violence don to them : yet were they
takẽ of their confederats for Martyrs.Of whome thus writeth S.Auguſtin.*Viuebant vt Latrones , moriebantur vt Cir-
cumcelliones,honorabantur vt Martyres.* They liued like robbers by the high way,they died like Circumcellions (meaning thei ſlew them ſelues)they were honored as Martyrs.
And now where lerned M. Foxe the trade to make his holy
canoniſation,in his deueliſh dirty donghil of his fowle heretical ãd trayterous Martyrs, but of thoſe ãd ſuch like ſchole-
maiſters? As of the Montaniſts, that worſhipped one Alexander for a worſhipful martyr,thowgh he ſuffred for no matter of religiõ,but for my ſcheuous murther.And of the Maniches,that kepte the day wherein their maiſter Manes was
put to death,more ſolemply,then Eaſter day.

Haue ye not thẽ in M.Foxe, Siꝛ Iohn Oldcaſtle,and Syr
Roger Acton canoniſed for holy martyrs,though they died
for high treaſon?yea their names al to be painted,daſhed,ãd
floriſhed in the kalender with read letters, I thinke becauſe
we ſhoulde kepe their daye a double feaſte ?   Whoſe and
their confederates condemnation for conſpiringe againſte
the Kinge , the nobilitye , and their countreye , appereth
aſwell by acte of parliament then made , as by the full
teſtimony of all our Engliſh Cronicles.Is not dame Elleanour Cobhã a ſtowte confeſſour in this madde martyrloge?
whoſe

The Do♦
natiſtes
counted
Martyrs.
Auguſt.
epiſt.68.

M.Foxes
ſtinking
Martyrs.
Euſeb.li.5
cap.18.
Niceph.
li.6.c.32.
Aug.con.
epiſt.Ma-
ni.ca.8.
Syr Iohn
Oldcaſtel
Syr Ro♦
ger Act♦
on.
Anno.2.
Henrici.5
cap.5.
Polidor.
Harding.
Fabian.
Haul.
Cooper.
Eleanour
Cobham.

Sir Roger Onely. Magaret Iordeman. The vvitch of Aey.

whofe banifhment was not for religion, but for confpiringe King Henry the fixts death by wytchrafte and forcery, by the help and afsiftance of M.Roger Bolinbroke, and Margaret Iordeman, commonly called the Witche of Aey? The which two were openly executed for the fame. But nowe is it worth the hearing to know, how handfomly M. Foxe hath conceyued his matters: wherein he plaieth in dede the wily Foxe and fpringleth with his falfe wily tayle, his fylthy ftale not into the doggs, but into his readers eies. And as the Foxe, as fome hūters fay, when he is fore driuen, wil craftely mount from the earth and kepe himfelf a while vpon the eather of a hedge, only to caufe the howndes that drawe after him to leefe the fente of the tracte : euen fo for all the worlde hath our Foxe plaied with his reader. But I truft I fhal trace him, and fmel him out wel inoughe.

Firft then, though M.Foxes authority be very large and ample in this his canonifation, and fuch as neuer any Pope durfte take vpon him, yea and though he hath authority to make martyrs, yet I dowbte whether he hath authority to make Knights to : for this Sir Roger Onley is neither a Sir,

See Harding, Fabia, Hall Cooper, grafton, the addition of Polichronicon,

but of M. Foxes making, nor Onley neither : But M.Roger Bolinbroke only: put to death for the treafon before fpecified, as not onely his owne authours Fabian and Harding, whome he doth alleage for the ftory of Dame Elleanour, but al other alfo doe teftifie. Truthe it is that Harding writing in Englifh meeter and fpeaking of this M. Bolinbroke endeth one of his ftaues with this worde *Only*, which is there to fignifie no name, but to better and fweate the meeter, and is as much to fay, as chiefly and principally, meaning that Maifter Roger was the principal worker in this nigromancy.   The meeters of Harding are thefe.

He

He waxed then ſtrange eche day vnto the King,
For cauſe ſhe was foreiudged for ſorcery,
For enchantments that ſhe was in working
Againſt the Church and the King curſedly,
By helpe of one M. Roger, only.

Harding.
in Hen.6
c.2¡2.

Whiche laſt woorde, ſome ignorant or Proteſtant Printer
hath made Oonly. And then hath M.Fox added a Syr, and
a Martyr too, and adorned him with no common inke, to
ſet foorth and beutify his Martyr withal. And ſo of M.Ro-
ger Bolinbroke, ſorcerer and traitour, by a cunning Metamorphoſis he hath made, Syr Roger Onlye Knight and
Martyr.

Wel, wil ye yet ſee further the craftie dubling of a Fox,
walking on the eather of the hedge? Conſider then that,
for Margaret Iordaman that notable witch (leaſt if he had
named her and M.Bolinbroke by their own names, he had
marred al the roſt) he placeth an other woman, that by his
owne rule died fortie yeares after. And yet can he not hit
vpon her name neither, but is faine to call her, in ſteed of
Ione Bowghton, the mother of the Ladie Yong, who in
deed is one of his ſtinking hereticall and foolifh Martyrs.
For fhe craked ful ſtoutly that there was no fier, that could
conſume or hurt her. I could here name a rablemente of
like holy Martyrs, as Richard Hune, that hong him ſelfe:
King, Debnam, and Marſh, hanged for ſacrilege. Beſide a
number of ſuch notorioufe and deteſtable heretiques, that
M. Foxe him ſelfe wil not I trowe, as great an heretike as
he is, denie them to be heretiks. As Peter a Germain being
an Anabaptiſt: as Anthonie Perſon an Heretike of the
ſecte of the Paulicians, of whom we haue ſpoken. As D.
Weſalian, that denied the holy Ghoſt to procede from the

See M.
Foxes
Martyr,
the 371.
leafe.
Alanus
Copus.
dialog.6.
cap. 16.
Hune
Debnam.
King.
Marſh.

D. VVeſ
ſalian.

Q   Father

Father and the fonne. And to conclude this matter, of the notable heretike Cowbridge, burnte at Oxford. Who expounded thefe wordes of Chrift, *Take eate this is my bodie that fhalbe betrayed for you.*thus: Take, eate, this is my body, in the which the peple fhalbe deceiued. Who alfo affirmed that the name of Chrift was a foule name, and therfore raced it out of his bookes, wherfoeuer he foūd it. And would reade for Iefu Chrift: Iefu, Iefu, faiyng that Chrift was the deceiuer of the world, and that al were damned in hel, that beleued in the name of Chrift. We wil now with this blef-fed Martyr of M. Foxes canonifation ende this talke with the whole conference, leauing it to the indifferent Reader to confider whether the Catholiques, or the Proteftantes, drawe nearer to the Donatifts.

Let vs then procede foorth, and confider vppon what good motiues, ye charge M. Fekenham to be a Donatifte, which are, to fay the truth, none other but falfhod and fol-lie. But, as ye furmife, the one is, *becaufe he craftelye and by a fubtill fhift refufeth the proufes of the olde Teftamente, as the Donatifts did.* The other, *becaufe he with the faid Donatifts fhoulde auouche, that fecular Princes haue not to meddle in matters of Religion, or caufes Ecclefiaficall : nor to punifhe anye man for fuche caufes.* Surely for your firfte motiue fo fine and fubtile a blafte of an horne, a man fhal not light-lye find againe among al the horners in England I fuppofe. But yet by your leaue Syr, your horne hath a foule flawe. When M. Fekenham offereth to yeld, *if ye can proue this res giment either by the order that Chrift left behinde him in the new Teftament, either by the Doctours, either by Councels, or els by the cōtinual practife of any one Church,* think you M. Horne that this is not a large and an ample offer? I wil not fay, that
this

this is a fubtyle fhift, but rather a very blind, bytle blonte fhifte of yours, to charge him with any refufall of the olde Teftament, either openly or couertly. There is not fo much as anye coniecture apparente, to gather this vppon, yea the olde Teftamente is not by this offerre, as ye blindlye and blontly gheaffe, excluded, but verely included. For if the new Teftament, which reherfeth many things out of the olde, haue any thing out of the olde Teftamente, that make for this regimente : yf any Doctour, olde or newe, yf any Councell haue any thinge oute of the olde Tefta-ment that ferue for this regimente, then is Maifter Feken-ham concluded, yea by his owne graunte. For fo the Do-ctour or Councel hath yt, he is fatisfied accordinge to his demaunde. Whereby it foloweth, that he doth not refufe, but rather alowe and affirme the proufes of the olde Tefta-mente. And furely wife men vfe not greatly to fhew that, that maketh againft them, but moft for them. Wherefore it is incredible, that Maifter Fekenham fhoulde ons imagyn any fuche fyftynge or fhyftynge as ye dreame of, hauinge wonne his purpofe againfte you euen by the verye olde Teftamente as we haue declared. And therfore it is fpo-ken but in your dreame, when ye fay, *ye haue thereby with meruelouſe force ſhaken M. Fekenhams holde* which fuerlye is fo forcible, as wil not beate down a very paper wal. And meruayle were it, yf ye fhoulde fo batter his holde, when that thefe your great cannons come not nigh his holde by one thowfande myles.

Againe this accufation is incredible. For M. Fekenham him felfe is fo farre of from this fufpition, that he himfelfe, bringeth in againft you many and good teftimonies of the old Law. (as fol. 109. and 123.) by the force whereof only he

may be

may be thought to haue ſhaken and ouerthrowen to, your rotten weake holde vnderpropped with your great Sampſons poſtes as mighty as bulruſhes. But I perceiue by your good Logike, your Law, and like Diuinity, ſiléce maketh a denial, and becauſe M. Fekenham maketh no mention in this place of the matter to be proued by the old Teſtamét, therfore he ſubtillie refuſeth the proufes thereof. But yee ſhould rather me thinketh induce the contrary, and that he conſenteth to you for the olde Teſtament : *Quia qui tacet, conſentire videtur:* (as the olde ſaiyng is) For he that holdeth his peace, ſeemeth to conſent : and ſo ye might haue better forced vppon him that all was yours, preſuppoſing that ye had proued the matter by the olde Teſtament.

But you will needes driue your reaſon an other waye. Let vs ſee then, what we Catholiques can ſaye to you for your Apologie by the like drifte. You and your Colleages, ſeing your ſelues charged with many hereſies, to wipe away that blotte if it be poſsible, and for your better purgation, take vpon you, to ſhew your whole, ful, and entier belief. And therevpon you recite the Articles of the common Crede. But now good Syr, I aſke you a queſtió: What if by chaunce you had omitted any one of them, would ye gladly be meaſured by this rule, yee meaſure M. Fekenham by ? Would ye be content, that the Catholiques ſhould lay to your charge, that ye ſubtilly refuſe that article, that you haue forſlowen to reherſe? If ye would not, thé muſt I ſay to you with Chriſte : *Quod tibi non vis fieri, alteri non facias.* Do you not to an other, that ye would not haue don to your ſelfe. If you ſay, that ye are content to ſtande to the very ſame lawe, as if ye be a reaſonable and a conſtant man you muſt needes ſay : Loe then good Syr, you haue

con-

concluded your felfe and all your companions plaine here: tiques, for the refufal of the Article, *Conceiued of the holye Ghoft*, whiche ye omitte in the rehearfall of your Creede, which Article I am affured, ye find not there. Then further, feing that the Archeheretique Eutiches, and before him Appollinarius in the recitinge of the common Creede ranne in a maner the fame race, you following them at the heeles, as faft as may be, pretermitting alfo thefe wordes : *Incarnatus eft de Spiritu fanctc*:here might we euen by your owne rule and exaumple, crye oute vppon you all as A-pollinarians and Eutichians, and that with more colou-rable matter, then you haue, eyther to make Maifter Fe-kenham a Donatifte, or that your Apologie hath to make the worthie and learned Cardinall Hofius a Zuenckfeldi-an. Wherein your Rethorique is all togeather as good, as is this yours here againft Maifter Fekenham. Neither doe we greatly paffe, howe the Donatiftes in this pointe demeaned them felues, and whether they openly or priui-lie fhonned proufes brought and deduced out of the olde Teftament. In deed the Manichees denied the authori-tie of the bookes of the old Law and Teftament : whiche I reade not of the Donatifts. Yea in the very fame boke and chapter by you alleaged, Petilian him felf, taketh his proufe againft the Catholikes out of the olde Teftament, whiche you know could ferue him in litle ftede, if he him felfe did reiect fuch kind of euidences. This now fhall fuffice for this branche, to purge M. Fekenham that he is no Donatift, or Heretique otherwife.

Concerning the other, befide your falfhood, your great follie doth alfo fhew it feffe too, as well as in the other, to imagin him to be a Donatift, and to think or fay as you fay

The Apologie of England in reciting the commō Crede leaueth out thefe vvoords Conceiued of the holy Ghoft. Tom. 1. Concil. pa.752. M. Horne and his fellovves by M. Horn his rule are Apollinarians, and Eutichians.

Lib. 2. contr. Petil. ca. 92.

they

they did,*that ciuile magiftrates haue not to do with religiō, nor may not punifh the trãfgreffours of the fame.*M.Fekenhã faith no fuch thing,ãd I fuppofe h e thinketh no fuch thing: and furder I dare be as bold to fay,that there is nøt fo much as a light cõiecture to be grõuded therof by any of M. Fekenhãs words,onleffe M. Horne become fodenly fo fubtil,that he thinketh no differéce to fay:the Prince fhuld not punifh an honeft true mã,in ftede of a theef, ãd to fay he fhuld not punifh a theef. Or to fay,there is no difference betwixt al-things ãd nothing. For though M.Fekenhã ãd al other Ca-tholiks do deny the ciuile Princes fupreme gouernmẽt in al caufes ecclefiafticall,yet doth not M. Fekenhã or any Ca-tholike deny but that ciuil Princes may deale in fome mat-ters ecclefiaftical as aduocates and defendours ofthe chur-che,namely in punifhing of heretikes by fharp lawes, vnto the which lawes, heretikes are by the Church firft geuẽ vp and deliuered by open excõmunication and condemnatiõ.

As for S.Auguftines teftimonies they nothing touch M. Fekenham, and therefore we will fay nothing to them,but kepe our accuftomable tale with you , and befide all other fcore vp as an vntruth that ye fay here alfo,that the Papifts are no parte of the Catholique Churche , no more then the Donatiftes.

* you fhoulde haue faid Protef-ftantes. vvho in fo many pointes (as hathe ben fhe vved re-femble the Do-natifts.

M. Horne.   The. 19. Diuifion.pag. 12. b.

But for that S. Auguftines iudgemẽt and mine in this controuerfie is all one,as your opinion herein differeth nothing at al from the Donatifts: I vvil vfe no other confirmation of my proufes alleaged out of the olde teftament, for the reproufe of your guilful reftraint, then Chriftes Catholique Church, vttered by that Catholique Doctour S. Auguftine , againft all the fectes of Donatiftes,vvhether they be Gaudentians, Petilians, Rogatifts, * Papifts, or any other petit fectes fprõg out of his loines vvhat name fo euer they haue.
S. Auftine againft Gaudẽtius, his fecond Epiftle affirmeth, faiyng:I haue

(faitʰ

(*saith he*)already heretofore made it manifeſt, that it apertained to the kings charge, that the Niniuites ſhoulde pacifye Gods wrath, which the Prophet had denoúced vnto thé. The kings which are of ChriſtesChurch, do iudge moſt rightly, that it appertaineth vnto their cure that you (Donatiſts) rebel not without puniſhmét agaíſt the ſame, &c. God doth inſpire into kígs that they ſhould procure the cómaundement of the Lorde, to be performed or kept in their kingdom. For they to whom it is ſaid: and now ye kings vnderſtand, be ye learned ye Iudges of the earth, ſerue the Lord in feare: do perceiue that their autoriti ought ſo to ſerue thelord, that ſuch as wil not obei his wil ſhould be puniſhed of that autority, &c. *Yea ſaith the ſame S. Aug.* Let the kings of the erth ſerue Chriſt, eué in making lawes for Chriſt. *meaning for the furtherance of Chriſtes religió.* How then doth kings (*ſaith S. Aug. to Boniſacius, againſt the Donatiſts*) ſerue the Lord with reueréce, but in forbiddingand puniſhing with a religious ſeuerity, ſuch things as are don againſt the Lords commaúdements? For a king ſerueth one way in that he is a man, an other way, in reſpeƈt that he is a king. Becauſe in reſpeƈte that he is but a má, he ſerueth the Lord in liuing faithfully: but in that he is alſo a king, he ſerueth in making lawes of cóuenient force to cómaúd iuſt things, ád to forbid the cótrary, &c. In this therfore kings ſerue the Lord, whé they do thoſe things to ſerue him, which thei could not do were thei not kings. &c. But after that this begá to be fulfilled which is writé: and al the kings of the earth ſhal worſnip him, al the nations ſhal ſerue him, what má being in his right wittes, may ſay to Kings: Care not you in your Kingdomes, who defédeth or oppugneth the Church of your Lord? Let it not appertaine, or be any part of your care, who is religious in your kingdome, or a wicked deprauer of Religion.

Lib.2.
cap.26.

Epiſt. 48

Epiſt. 50.

This was the iudgemét of S. Aug. or rather of Chriſtes Catholike Church, vttered by him againſt the Donatiſts, touching the ſeruice, authority, power, ád care, that Kings haue or ought to haue in cauſes ſpiritual or eccleſiaſtical, the which is alſo the iudgemét of Chriſtes catholik church, now in theſe dais maintei ned teined and defended, by the true miniſters of the ſame Catholique Churche, againſt al Popiſh Donatiſts : vvith the force of Gods holy vvoorde, bothe of the old and nevv Teſtament , euen as S. auguſtine did before. VVho to proue and confirme this his aſſertiō to be true againſt the Donatiſts, did auouch many moe examples, then I haue cited out of the old Teſtament : as of the King

Epiſt.48. *of Niniue, of Darius, Nabuchodonozor, and others : affirming that the hiſtories and other teſtimonies, cited out of the old Teſtament, are partely figures, and partly prophecies, of the povver, duety , and ſeruice that Kings ſhoulde ovve and perfourme in like ſort, to the furtherance of Chriſtes Religion in the time of the nevv Teſtament. The Donatiſts in the defence of their hereſie, reſtrained S. Auguſtine, to the exāple and teſtimony, of ſuch like order of Princes Seruice in matters of Religion, to be found in the Scriptures of the nevve Teſtament : meaning that it could not be found in any order that Chriſt lefte behind him, as you alſo fantaſied vvhē you vvrote the ſame in your boke folovving, yea, going euen cheke by cheke vvith thē. But S. Auſtine maketh anſvvere to you al for him and me both : VVho, rehearſing the actes of the godly Kings of the old Teſtament, taketh this for a thing not to be denied, to vvit,*

Epiſt.48 That the auncient actes of the godly kings mentioned in the Prophetical bokes, were figures of the like facts to be don by the godly Princes in the time of the new Teſtament.

And although there vvas not in the time of the Apoſtles, nor long time after, any Kings or Princes, that put the ſame ordinance of Chriſt in practiſe, al

Epiſt.50. *being infidels for the moſt part:* Yet the ſeruice of kings was figured (*as S. Auguſtine ſaith*) in Nabuchodonozor and others , to be put

Epiſt.48. in practiſe, whē this of.71.Pſalm ſhould be fulfilled: and al the kings of the earth ſhal worſhip Chriſt, and all nations ſhall ſerue him, &c. As yet in the Apoſtles time, this prophecy (*ſaith he*) was not fulfilled: and now ye Kings vnderſtand, be learned ye that iudge the earth, and ſerue the Lorde in feare with reuerence. VVhen the Chriſtian Emperours and Princes (*ſaith*

Lib.2.
cont.lit. *this Catholique Father*) ſhal heare that Nabuchodonozor, after he
Petil.c.92 had ſeene the marueilouſe power of almighty God, in ſauing
Dan. 3. the three yong men, from the violence of the fire , walking therin without hurte, was ſo aſtonied at the miracle , that he him ſelfe beinge before this but a cruell Idolatour , beganne

forth-

forthwith vpon this wonderous fight, to vnderftand and ferue
the Lorde with reuerent feare: Doo not they vnderftande, that
thefe thinges, are therefore writen and recited in the Chriftian affemblies, that thefe fhould be exáples to themfelues of
faith in God, to the furtherance of Religion? Thefe Chriftian
rulers, therefore minding according to the admonition of the
Pfalme, to vnderftand, to be learned, and to ferue the Lord with
reuerent feare, do very attentiuely giue eare, and marke what
Nabuchodonozor after faid: for he, faieth the Prophet, made a
decree or ftatute, for al the people that were vnder his obeif-
face: that who fo euer fhould after the publicatió therof, fpeak
any blafphemy againft the almighty, they fhould fuffer death,
ád their goods be cófinate. Now if the Chriftian Emperours, ád
Kings, do know, that Nabuchodonozor made this decree agáift
the blafphemers of God, furely they caft in their mídes, what
they are boúde to decree in their kigdoms, to wit, that the felf
fame God, and his Sacraméts, be not lightly fet by and cótem-
ned. *Thus farre S. Auguftin: By vvhofe iudgement, * being alfo the iudge-*
ment of the catholik Church, it is manifeft, that the order, rule, and gouern-
ment, in Ecclefiaftical caufes, practifed by the Kinges of the olde Teftament,
being figures and prophecies, of the lyke gouernment, and feruice, to be in the
Kinges vnder the nevv Teftament, is the order of gouernment, that Chrift left
behinde him in the Ghofpel and nevv Teftament: and fo directly confuteth your
(.52.)erroneous opinion.

× Note,
that new
S. Augu-
ftins iud
gemét is
alfo the
iudgemét
of the Ca
tholike
Chuiche.
The 5?.
vntruthe
M. Feke
hã hol-
deth no
fuch opi-
nion.

Stap'eton.

Lo, nowe haue we moe teftimonies of S. Auguftine to
proue that, for the which he hath alleaged many things out
of S. Auguftin alredy, and the which no man denieth. For
what els proueth al this out of S. Auguftine, both now and
before alleaged, but that Chriften Princes ought to make
lawes and cóftitutions (euen as M. Horne him felf expoundeth it fol. 12.b.) *for the furtherance of Chriftes Religion?* This
thing no Catholike denieth. And for my parte M. Horne,
that you may not thinke I haue now ben firft fo aduifed vp-

R

pon

pon fight of your booke, I haue forced that argument with many Exãples of Godly Emperours and Princes in my dedicatory Epiftle to the Quenes Maiefty, before the tranflated hiftory of venerable Bede. Briefly al S. Auguftins words force nothing els but that Chriftē Princes may make lawes to punifh heretikes (for that in dede was the very occafion why S. Auguftin wrote al this) and ought to fortifie the decrees of the Priefts with the execución of the fecular power, when obftinat heretickes wil not otherwife obey. Thus it ferueth our turne very wel. But nowe that Maifter Horne may not vtterly leefe all his labour herein, lette vs fee, howe thefe matters doe truely and trimly ferue againft his deare brethern, and M. Foxes holy Martyrs to. We faye with S. Auguftin, that Princes may punifhe wicked depra-

Li. 2. cõt. Petilianũ cap. 92. & Epift. 48. 50.

uers of religion. And we further fay, that ye are thofe. We fay with faint Auguftine, *that Chriftian Princes may make a decree yea of death: as did Nabuchodonofor againft the blafphemers of God, and carefully prouide, that God and his facramēts be not lightly cõtēned.* We fay ye are as great blafphemers, as euer Chriftes Church had: we fay ye be they, that haue contēned Chriftes Sacramentes, making of feuē two, and vfing

Princes ãd church lavves made a= gainft the proteftãs

thofe two after fuch forte, that the olde prouerbe may (the more pitye) in a maner take place, as good neuer a whit, as neuer the better. We fay further that not onely the generall Councell of Trente, but that the whole Churche hath condemned your opinions, by general and national Councelles manye hundred yeares fynce. And that Chriftian Emperours, Chriftian Princes, as well in other countries, as in Englande, efpeciallye the noble and worthye Kinge Henrye the fyfte, haue made many fharpe lawes, yea of death againft herefies. We do not, nor neuer did difalowe

thefe

thefe their doinges, as repugnante either to the olde or
new Teftamente. Why then cal you for this refpecte the
Catholykes, Popifhe Donatiftes? But will ye know Maifter Horne, who be in this point in very dede the Dol-
tifhe Deuelifhe Donatifts? Hearken on well, and ye fhall
heare.

    The Donatiftes as S. Auguftyne reporteth, fayde: *It was
free, to belieue, or not to belieue, and that faith fhoulde not be
forced.* Was not this I pray you the cōmō fong of the Lute-
rans in Germany, and Englande at their beginning? Was
not this your Apoftles Luthers opinion, that no man fhould
be compelled to the faith? And as there are many diffenfions, diuifions, fchifmes betwixte you the Sacramentaries,
and the Lutherans: fo are you diuided alfo in this pointe.
For your M. Caluin writeth, that a mā may laufully and by
Gods law be put to death for herefie, as he practifed himfelf
alfo, burning Seruetus the Arrian at Geneua. But al Luthers
fchollers in Germany are not fo forward. Yea fome of your
holy martyrs auouche, that the King cā make no law to punifh any maner of crime by death, ād that al fuch lawes are
contrary to the Gofpel. This was the opiniō of Sir Thomas
Hytton prieft, and yet is he a bleffed martyr in M. Foxe his
holy Kaléder, ād we muft kepe his feaft the x. of March by
M. Foxe. Yet in a book of praiers fet foorth by the brotherhod anon vpon his death, he is appointed to the .23. of February, and fo either M. Foxe or they miffe the marke. Except the one day be of his Martyrdom, and the other of his
Tranflatiō. And whereas M. Fox faith, that there remaineth
nothing of the faide Sir Thomas in writinge but onely his
name, (which is a lye, and more to by a fyllable) and that
I heare faye he is bufye to fette forthe a frefhe in printe

R ij   yet

VVho be
the true
Donatifts
for fayig
princes
may not
punifhe
tranfgref,
fours in
caufes of
religion.
Epifto. 50.
*Bonifacio
Comiti.
Fontanus
li 1, in hi-
ftor. no.
temp.
Vide epift.
Aug. 48.
in edit. Ba
fil. & an-
notationē
margina-
lē ibidem.*
Sir Thoꝛ
mas Hit-
ton prieft
M. Foxes
martyr.
A great
Lye of
M. Foxe.

yet ons againe, his huge monſtruous martyrloge, I wil doe
ſo much for him, as miniſter him plenty of good ſtuffe I
warrante you, to ſet forthe and adorne at his next edition,

S. Thoꝰ
mas Morę
in his prę
faceę to
Tyndal
the 144.
leafe, &c.

this worthy chãpiõ withal. I do therfore remit M. Foxe, to
Sir Thomas Mores books. There lo is matter inough for M.
Fox, ãd to much to: for euẽ by your own cõfeſsiõ he is no ſecret but an opẽ dãnable heretik, ãd a Donatiſt: ãd ſo I trowe
no martyr, but yet good inowgh, ãd as good as the reſidew
of this worthy Kalẽder. But now hath M. Foxe a far greater buſines in hande, for he muſt ſcrape out S. Iohn Old-

S. Iohn
Oldcaſtle
knight of
the ſame
opinion
vvith S.
Thomas
Hytton
prieſt.

caſtel knight, being not onely a traytour, but a deteſtable
Donatiſte alſo. Nowe al the weight reſteth to proue this
ſubſtancially to you and to M. Foxe, and to ſtoppe al your
frowarde quarrelings and accuſtomable eluſions agaiſt our
proufes. Wel, I wil bringe you (as I thinke) a ſubſtancial and
and an ineuitable proufe, that is M. Foxe him ſelfe, and no
worſe man. For lo thus he writethe of this worthy cnam-
pion, and that euen in his owne huge martyrologe, who
doubteth but to the great exalting and amplification of his
noble work, and of his noble holy Martyr: *The tenth article,*

Foxe in
his En-
gliſh mar
tyrol. the
139. leafe.
Col. 1.
M. Fekẽ-
hã pur-
ged by
M. Horn
himſelfe
of that he
layeth to
him.

ſaieth M. Foxe, *that manſlawghter either by warre, or by any*
pretended law of Iuſtice, for any tẽporal cauſe, or ſpiritual reue-
lation is expreſſely contrary to the new Teſtament, which is the
law of graceful of mercy. This worthy article, with a. 11. other
of lyke ſewte and ſorte, in a booke of reformatiõ (beilke very lyke to Captayn Keets tree of reformatiõ in Norfolke)
was exhibited in open parliament, yf we belieue M. Foxe.

Nowe you ſee M. Horn, where and vpõ whome ye may
truely vtter ãd beſtowe al this nedeleſſe treatiſe of yours a-
gainſt M. Fekenhã. And therefore we may now procede to
the remnãte of your book, ſauig that this in no wiſe muſt be

ouer-

ouerhipped, that euē by your own words here ye purge M.
Fekenhā, from this cryme, ye layde vnto him euen now, for
refuſing proufes taken out of the olde teſtamente. For yf, as
ye ſay, *the order and gouernr   nt that Chriſt leſte behinde in*
the Goſpel and new teſtament, is the order, rule, and gouernmēt
in Eccleſiaſtical cauſes practiſed by the Kings of the olde Teſta-
ment, then wil it follow, that M. Fekenham yelding to the
gouernment of the new, doth not exclude, but rather comprehende the gouernment of the olde Teſtament alſo, both
being eſpecially, as ye ſay, al one.

M. Horne. The 20. Diuiſion. Pag. 14.a.

Novv I vvil conclude on this ſorte, that vvhich I affirmed: namely that
Kings, and Princes, ought to take vpō the gouernmēt in Eccleſiaſtical cauſes.

Vvhat gouernement, orde, and dutifulnes, ſo euer belonging to any, God
hath figured and promiſed before hande by his Prophetes, in the holy Scriptu-
res of the old Teſtamēt, to be performed by Chriſt, ād thoſe of his kingdome:
that is the gouernmēt, order, ād dutifulnes, ſet forth, ād required in the Goſ-
pel, or nevv teſtamēt. But that faithful Emperours, Kings, and Rulers, ought
*of duty, as belonging to their office, to claime and take vppon them * the*
gouernement, authority, povver, care, and ſeruice, of God their Lorde, in
*matters of Religion, or * cauſes Eccleſiaſtical, vvas an order and dutifulnes*
for them : prefigured and fore promiſed of God by his Prophets, in the Scrip
tures of the olde Teſtament, as (.53.) S. Auguſtine hath ſufficiently vvitneſ-
ſed: Ergo. Chriſtian Emperours, Kings, and Rulers, ovve of duty, as belon-
ging to their office, to claime, and take vpon them, the gouernment, autho-
rity, povver, care, and ſeruice of their Lord, + in matters of Religion: or Spiri-
tual, or Eccleſiaſtical cauſes, is the gouernment, order, and dutifulnes, ſette
foorth, and required, in the Goſpel or nevv Teſtament.

This that hath been already ſaid, might ſatisfie any man that erreth of
ſimple ignoraunce. But for that your vvilfulnes is ſuche, that you (.54.) de-
light only in vvrangling againſt the truthe, appeare it to you neuer ſo plaine,
and that no vveight of good proufes, can preſſe you, you are ſo ſlippery, I vvil
loade you vvith heapes, euē of ſuch proufes, as ye vvil ſeeme deſirous to haue.

R iij   The

Rom. 1.
* Not
ſuch Su-
preme go
uernmēt
as the
Othe pre
ſcribeth.
* Not in
al cauſes
eccleſia-
ſtical.
The 53.
vntruth.
S. Augu-
ſtin hath
vvitneſ-
ſed no
ſuch lar-
ge and Su
preme go
uernmēr,
as you at-
tribute
povve to
princes.
* You cō-
clude not
in al thigs
ād cauſes,
and ther-
fore you
conclude
nothing
agaiſt vs,
The 54.
vntruth.
Slaunde-
rours.

THE FIRST BOOKE

The holy Ghoſt deſcribïg by the Prophet Eſay, vvhat ſhalbe the ſtate oſChriſts Church in the time of the nevv teſtamēt, yea novv in theſe our daies (for this

2.Cor.6. *our time is the time that the Prophet ſpeaketh of, as S. Paul vvitneſſeth to the Corinthiãs)addeth many comfortable promiſes, and amongeſt other maketh*

Eſa 49. *this to Chriſtes Catholike Churche, to vvitte, Kings ſhalbe Nouriſhing Fathers, and Quenes ſhalbe thy nources. Nouriſhing Fathers ſaith the gloſe en-*

Lyra in
Eſa.c. 49. *terlined,* In lacte verbi , In the mylke of the word, *meaning Gods* vvorde. *Lyra addeth :* This prophecy is manifeſtly fulfilled in many Kinges and Quenes, who receiuing the Catholike Faith, did feede the poore faithful ones , &c. And this reuerence to be done by Kings (*ſaith Lyra*) was fulfilled in the time of Conſtátine and other Chriſtian Kings. Certainly, *Conſtātin the Emperour,*

Al this of
Conſtan-
tine is
graunted
and ma-
keth no-
thing for
you.
Euſe. li.3.
de vita
Conſtāt.
Lib 2. *ſhevved himſelf to vnderſtand his ovvn ducty of nouriſhing Chriſtes Church appointed by God in his Prophecy: for he like a good, tender, and faithfull Nource father, did keep, defend, maintein, vphold, and feed the poore faithful ones of Chriſt: he bare the being as it vvere almoſt vveried and forhayed vvith the great perſecutions of Goddes enemies, and maruelouſly ſhaken vvith the controuerſies and contentions amongeſt themſelues, euen as a nource Father in his ovvn boſome: he procured that they ſhould be ſedde vvith the ſvveete milke of Gods vvorde.* Yea, he him ſelfe with his publike procla-*

The 55.
vntruth.
They
vvere
Idols, not
Images,
that
Conſtan-
tin for-
badde his
ſubiects
to ſet vp.
Li>4.de
vit.Cōſt.
Lib.1. mations, did exhorte and allure his ſubiectes to the Chriſtian Faith. *As Euſebius doth reporte in many places, vvriting the life of Conſtátine,* He cauſed the Idolatrous religion to be ſuppreſſed, and vtterly baniſhed, and the true knowledge and Religion of Chriſt, to be brought in and planted amõg his people. He made many holſome lawes, and Godly cõſtitutions, wherewith he reſtrayned the people with threates, foibiddinge them the Sacrificing to Idols: to ſeeke after the Deueliſh ãd ſuperſtitious ſothſaiyngs: to ſet vp (55.) Images: that they ſhoulde not make any priuie Sacrifices: and to be brief, he reformed al maner of abuſes, about Gods ſeruice, ãd prouided that the Church ſhould be ſedde with Gods worde. *Yea, his diligent care in furthering and ſetting foorth the true knovvledge of Chriſte, vvherevvith he ſedde the people, vvas ſo vvatcheful, that Euſebius doth affirme him to be appointed of God,* as it vvere the common or Vniuerſal Biſhop : *And ſo Con-*

ſtantine

ftantine tooke himſelf to be: and therefore ſaid to the Biſſhoppes aſſembled to-
gether vvith him at a feaſt, that God had appointed him to be a Biſhoppe.
But of this moſte honorable Biſhop and nourſhing father, more ſhalbe ſaide
hereafter, as of other alſo ſuch like.

The .17. Chapter opening the weakeneſſe of M. Hornes Con-
cluſion, and of other his proufes out of holy Scripture.
Stapleton.

Ow ye may conclude, that there is ſome regiment that Princes may take vpon thē in cauſes
eccleſiaſtical: but if ye meane of ſuch regimēt
as ye pretend, you make your recknyng without your hoſte as a man may ſay: and conclude
before ye haue brought forth any prouf, that they ought or
may take vpon them ſuch gouernment. For though I graūt
you al your examples ye haue alleaged, and that the doings
of the olde Teſtament were figures of the new, and the
ſaying of Eſaye, that Kings ſhoulde be Nowriſhinge Fathers
to the Church: and al things elſe that ye here alleage, yet al
wil not reache home, no not Conſtantines the great his
example. Who being an Ethnike became a Chriſtian, and
to the vttermoſt of his power, ſet forth Chriſtes religion in
al the Empire. what then? your concluſion of ſupreame regiment, wil not neceſſarily folow thereof. And when Euſebius calleth him, *as it were, a common or vniuerſal biſhop*, I
ſuppoſe ye meane not, that he was a biſſhop in dede. For
your ſelf cōfeſſe, that princes and Biſſhops offices are far diſtincted and diſſeuered, and that the one ought not to break
in to the office of the other. And if ye did ſo meane, Euſebius himſelf would ſone confounde yow, if ye reherſe Conſtantines whole ſentence, that he ſpake to the Biſſhopes.

M. Horne
doth cors
tal Euſe-
bius ſea-
tence.

For

THE FIRST BOOKE

For thus he faith to the bifhops. *Vos quidem eorum quæ intus sunt in Ecclesia agenda, ego verò eorum quæ extra sunt Episco-*

Euse.lib.4 de vita Constant. *pus à Deo sum constitutus.* You are bifhops faith he, of thofe things that are to be don within the Churche: I am bifhop of outwarde thinges. Which anfwere of his may fatisfie any reafonable man, for all that ye bring in here of Conftantine, or al that ye fhall afterward bring in: which declareth him no fupreme iudge or chief determinour of caufes Ecclefiaftical, but rather the contrary: and that he was the ouerfeer in ciuile matters. And the moft that may be enferred therof, is that he had the procuration and execution of Church maters: which I am affured al Catholiks wil graut.

But now whereas ye charge M. Fekenham partly with fubtil, partly with fowle fhiftes: this is in you furely, no fub-tyle but a blonte and a fowle fhamelefle fhifte, to fhifte the Idols into the Image of Chrifte and his faints : and whereas Conftantine put doune the paynims Idols, to make the fim-ple belieue, that the reformation which he made, was fuch as your reformation or ratner deformation is . For to leaue

Euseb lib. 3. de vita Constant. other things, to fay that Conftantine *forbadde to set vp Images*, is an open and a fhamelefle lye: for he fet vp the Croffe of Chrifte, that is fo owtragioufly and blafphemoufly vy-layned by you euery where, in the fteade of the idolles , he decked and adorned the Churches euery where with holy

Nice. con. act. 2. P.4. 429. Col-2. Images, the remembraunce of Chriftes incarnation, and for the worfhip of his faints, therby to fette forth the truth , and the worfhip of God, and to conuert al nations from Idola-trie and deuelifhe deceite.

M. Horne. The Diuision 21. Pag. 15.

Our sauiour Chrift meante not to forbidde or deftroy , touchinge the rule, feruice, and chardge of Princes in Church caufes, that vvhich vvas figured in

the

the lavve, or prophecied by the Prophetes. For he came to fulfil or ac- Mat.5.
complifh the lavve and the Prophetes , *by remouing the fhadovve*
and figure, and eftablifhing the body and fubftance to be feene, and to appere
clearly vvithout any mift or darke couer : yea, as the povver and authoritie
of Princes vvas appointed in the Lavv and Prophets, as it is proued, to ftretch
it felfe, not only to ciuile caufes, but alfo to the ouerfight, maintenance, fet-
ting foorth, and furtherance of Religion and matters Ecclefiaftical : Euen fo Mat.22.
Chrift our Sauiour (.56) confirmed this their authoritie , commaunding all The.56.
men to attribute and geue vnto Cæfar that vvhich belongeth vnto him : ad- vntruth.
monifhing notvvithftanding al Princes and people , that Cæfars authority is This pla
not infinit, or vvithout limits (for fuch authority belongeth only to the King ce of S.
of al Kings) but bounded and circumfcribed vvithin the boundes affigned in Matth.
Gods vvorde, and fo vvill I my vvordes to be vnderftanded, vvhen fo euer maketh
I fpeake of the povver of Princes. nothing

for the

Stapleton. Princes

fupreme

gouerne
M. Horne goeth yet nedeleffely foreward to proue that ment in
Chrift did not deftroy the rule of Princes in Churche cau- Ecclefia
fes, figured in the olde Lawe, and now at length catcheth fticall
he one teftimonie out of the new Teftament to proue his things.
faiyng : which is, *Geue vnto Cæfar, that belongeth vnto him.* Matth.22
Which place nothing at al ferueth his turne, but rather deftroyeth, I will not fay any figure of the old Teftament, but
M. Hornes foolifh figuratiue Diuinitie. For it is fo farre of
(that of this place M. Horne may make any ground, for the
Ecclefiafticall authoritye of Princes) that it doth not as
much as inferre, that we ought to pay fo much as tribute to
our Princes, but only that we may paie it. For the queftion was framed of the captious Iewes , not whether they
ought, but whether they might lawfully paie any tribute
to Cæfar . Whiche was then an externall and an infidell
Prince. For if M. Horne will fay thofe woordes importe
a precife necefsitie, he fhall haue muche a doe to excufe

S   the

the Italians, Frenchmen, Spaniardes, and our Nation, which
many hundred yeares haue paid no tribute to Cæſar. But
I pray you M. Horne, why haue you defalked and curtai-
led Chriſtes aunſwere ? Why haue you not ſet forth his
whole and entier ſentence : *Geue to Cæſar that belongeth to*
Cæſar, and to God that belongeth to God ? which later clauſe
I am aſſured, doth much more take away a ſupreme regiment in al cauſes Eccleſiaſtical, then neceſſarily by force of
any wordes binde vs to paie, yea any tribute to our Prince.
And wil ye ſee how it happeneth, that Hoſius a great learned and a godly Biſhoppe of Spaine, as M. Horne him ſelfe
calleth him, euen by this verye place proueth againſt the
Emperour Conſtantius, and telleth it him to his face, that
he had nothing to doe with matters Eccleſiaſticall? Whoſe
woordes we ſhall haue an occaſion hereafter to rehearſe.
Yea S. Ambroſe alſo vſeth the ſame authoritie to repreſſe
the like vſurped authoritie of Valentinian the yonger.
This ill happe hath M. Horne euen with his firſt authoritie of the new Teſtament, extraordinarie, and impertinent-
lie I can not tell howe chopped in , to cauſe the leaues of
his boke, and his lies, to make the more mouſter and ſhew.
But nowe, whereas this place ſerueth nothing for any authoritie Eccleſiaſticall in the Prince, and leaſt of all for his
preeminent and peerleſſe authoritie *in all cauſes Eccleſiaſti-*
call, as M. Horne fanſieth, Yet leaſt any man (being borne
doune with the great weight of ſo mightie a proufe) ſhould
thinke the Princes power infinite , M. Horne to amende
this inconuenience, of his greate gentlenes, thought good
to preuent this miſchief, and to admoniſh the Reader therof : and that his meaning is not by this place to geaue him
an *infinite authoritie, or without limites, but* ſuch onely as is

bounded

The pla-
ce of Mat.
21. ma-
keth ra-
ther quite
againſt
M. Horn.
Fol. 20.

Amb li.5.
Ep.32.

bounded and circumſcribed within the boundes of Gods worde: and leaſt ye ſhould miſtake him, he would himſelf ſo to be vnderſtanded. Which is for al this ſolemnitie, but a fooliſh and a friuolous admonitiō, without any cauſe or groūd: ād groūded only vpō M. Horns fantiſtical imaginatiō, and not vpon Chriſt, as he ſurmiſeth. Who willeth *that to be geauen to Cæſar that is Caſars, and to God that is Gods:* but determineth and expreſſeth nothing, that is to be geuen to Cæſar, but only paiement of money. And yet if we conſider, as I haue ſaied, what was the queſtion demaunded, it doth not determine that neither: though the thing it ſelfe be moſte true. Howe be it this admonition ſerueth Maiſter Horne and his brethren for manye and neceſſarye purpoſes, to rule and maiſter their Princes by, at their pleaſure: that as often as their doings like them not, they may freely diſobey, and ſay it is not Gods word, wherof the interpretation they referre to them ſelues. And ſo farre it ſerueth ſome of them, and the moſte zealouſe of them, that nowe their Prince, though *Supreme gouernour and iudge in al cauſes Eccleſiaſtical,* may not by *Gods worde,* appointe them as much as a Surpleſſe or Cope to be worne in the Churche, or Prieſtlike and decent apparell to be worne of thē otherwiſe. Yea ſome of them, of whom we haue already ſpoken, haue found a way, and that *by Gods woorde,* to depoſe the Quenes Maieſty from al manner of iuriſdiction as well temporal as ſpiritual: and that *by Gods holy worde.* Whereof theſe men make a very Welſhemans hoſe, to ſay the truth, and amonge other, M. Horne him ſelfe, for all his ſolemne admonition. For we plainly ſay, that this kind of ſupremacie, is directly againſt Gods holy worde.

M. Horne. *The. 22. Diuiſion. pag. 15. b.*

And

And this to be Christes order and meaning, that the Kings of the Nations

The.57.
vntruth.

*should be the supreme gouernours ouer their people, not only in temporal, but
also in Spirituall or Ecclesiasticall causes (.57.) the blessed Apostles Peter*

The apo-
stles ne-
uer de-
clared a-
ny suche
matter.
1.Pet.2.
Rom.13.

*and Paule, doe plainly declare. The supremacie of Princes they set foorth,
vvhen they commaund euery soule (that is, euery man, vvhether he be, as
Chrysostome saith, an Apostle, Euangelist, Prophete, Prieste, Monke, or
of vvhat so euer calling he be) to be subiect and obey the higher povvers, as
Kings, and their Lieutenants, or gouernours vnder them. And they declare
that this supreme gouernement is occupied and exercised in, or aboute the
praysing, furthering, and aduauncing of vertue or vertuous actions, and cōtrary vvise in correcting, slaiyng, ād repressing al maner of vice or vicious a-*

Epist.125.

*ctiōs, vvhich are the propre obiect or matter herof. Thus doth Basilius take the
meaning of the Apostles, saiyng :* This semeth to me to be the office
of a Prince, to aide vertue, and to impugne vice. *Neither S.
Paule, neither the best learned among the aunciente Fathers, did restreine
this povver of Princes, onely to vertues and vices, bidden or forbidden, in
the second table of Gods commaundementes, vvherein are conteined the duties one man ovveth to an other: But also did plainely declare them selues to
meane, that the authority of Princes ought to stretche it selfe to the maintenaunce, praise and furtheraunce of the vertues of the firste table, and the
suppression of the contrary, vvherein onely consisteth the true Religion, and
spirituall Seruice, that is due from man to God. S. Paule in his Epistle to*

1.Tim.2.

*Timothe, teacheth the Ephesians, that Kings and Rulers are constituted of
God, for these two purposes: that their people may liue a peaceable life, thou-
rough their gouernmente and ministerie both in godlines, vvhich is (as S.*

The.58.
vntruth.
S.Aug.
misseun-
derstan-
ded.
Lib 14.
De Trin.
cap.1
Lib.5. de
Ciuit.dei
cap.24.

*(.58.) Augustine interpreth it) the true and chiefe or propre vvorshippe of
God : and also in honestie or semelinesse : in vvhich tvvo vvoordes (Godlines and Honestie) he conteined vvhat so euer is cōmaunded either in the first
or second Table. S. Augustine also sheweth this to be his minde, vvhen de-
scribing the true vertues, vvhich shall cause princes to be blessed, novve in
Hope, and aftervvard in deed, addeth this as one especiall condicion, required
by reason of their chardge and callinge. If that (saith he)* they make
their power which they haue a seruaunt vnto Gods Maiestie,
to enlarge most wide his worshippe, Seruice, or Religion.
To this purpose also, serue all those testimonies, vvhiche I haue cited before

out of S. Aug. againſt the Donatiſts : vvho in his booke, De. 12. abuſio- *Grad. 6.*
num gradibus, teacheth that *a Prince or Ruler muſt labour to be had in* *Rom. 13.*
avve of his ſubiectes, for the ſeueritie againſt the traunſgreſſours of Goddes *Lib 2.*
Lavve. Not meaning only the tranſgreſſours of the ſeconde table in tempo- *cap. 83.*
rall matters : But alſo againſt the offendours of the firſt table in (.59.) Spi- *The. 59.*
rituall or Eccleſiaſticall cauſes or matters. VVhich his meaning he decla- *vntruth.*
reth plainely in an other place, vvhere he auoucheth the ſaiyng of S. Paule : *S. Aug.*
The Prince beareth not the ſworde in vaine, *to proue therevvith* *meaneth*
againſt Petilian the Donatiſt, that the povver or authority of Princes, vvhich *not to*
the Apoſtle ſpeaketh of in that ſentence, is geuen vnto them to make ſharpe *teach ſuch*
Lavves, to further true Religion, and to ſuppreſſe Hereſies and Schiſmes: and *gouerne-*
therefore in the ſame place, he calleth the Catholique Churche , that hathe *ment of*
ſuch *Princes to gouerne to this effect:* A Church made ſtrong, whole, *Princes*
or faſtened together with Catholique princes : *meaning that the* *in Eccle-*
Church is vveake, rent, and parted in ſonder , vvhere Catholique Gouer- *ſiaſticall*
nours are not, to maintaine the vnitie thereof in Churche matters, by their *matters,*
authoritie and povver. *as you*

Gaudentius *the Donatiſt, found him ſelfe agreeued that Emperors ſhuld* *teach, but*
entremeddle, and vſe their povver in matters of religion: affirming, that this *onely to*
vvas to reſtreine men of that freedome that God had ſet men in. That this *puniſh*
vvas a great iniurie to God, if he (meaning his religion) ſhould be defended *heretikes*
by men. And that this *vvas nothing els , but to eſteeme God to be one, that* *by lawes,*
is not able to reuenge the miuries done'againſt him ſelfe. S. Auguſtine doth *& by the*
anſvvere and refute his obiections, vvith the authoritie of S. Pauls ſaiyng to *ſame to*
the Romaines : Let euery ſoule be ſubiect to the higher powers, *maintein*
&c. For he is Gods miniſter, to take vengeance on him that *the Ca-*
doth euill : *interpreting the minde of the Apoſtle to be, that the authori-* *tholique*
tie and povver of Princes, hath to deale in Eccleſiaſtical cauſes, ſo (60)vvel *faith de-*
as in Temporal. And therfore ſaith to Gaudentius, and to you al: Blotte out *creed of*
theſe ſaiyngs (of S. Paule. 13. Rom.) if you can, or if you can *the Cler-*
not, then ſet naught by them, as ye doe. Reteine a moſt wic- *gie, not*
ked meaning of al theſe ſaiyngs (of the Apoſtle) leaſte you *by the*
looſe your freedome in iudging : or els truely for that as men, *Ciuile*
ye are aſhamed to doe before men , crie out if you dare : Let *Magiſtrat*
murtherers be puniſhed, let adulterers be puniſhed, lette all *lib. 2. cõt*
2 Epiſt.
Gaud. c. 11
The. 60.
vntruth.
S. Augu-
ſtine ne-
uer wrot
ſo.

VVhere is there in al this M. Horne, that the Princes hath to deale in Ecclesiasticall causes, so vvel as in temporall?

other faults, be they neuer so heinous or ful of mischief be punished (by the Magistrate) we wil that only wicked faultes against religiō be exēpt from punishmēt by the lawes of kings or rulers.&c. Herken to the Apostles, and thou shalt haue a great aduantage that the kingly power cannot hurt thee, doe wel, and so shalt thou haue praise of the same power,&c. That thing that ye doe, is not only not good, but it is a great euill, to witte, to cut in sunder the vnity and peace of Christ, to rebelle against the promises of the Gospel, and to beare the Christian armes or badges, as in a ciuil warre, against the true and highe King of the Christians.

The. 18. chapter declaring how Princes haue to gouerne in ca-
ses of the first Table: answering to certain places out
of the Canonicall Epistles of the
Apostles.

Stapleton.

ERE is nothinge M. Horne, that importeth youre surmised Supremacye. The effecte of your processe is, *Princes haue authoritie to mainteine, praise and further the vertues of the first table, and to suppresse the contrary, wherein onely cōsisteth the true Religiō and spiritual Seruice that is due frō mā to God.* And that he hath authority herein, *not only in the vertues cr vices bidden, or forbiddē in the second table of Gods cōmaundements, wherin are conteined the dueties one man oweth to an other.* This is grāted M. Horn, both of the *Catholiks, and of the soberer sort of Protestants (for Caroloftadius, Pelargus, Struthius, with the whole rable of th' Anabaptists deny it) that Princes haue authority both to further the obseruation, and to punish the breach of Gods cōmaundements as wel in the first table as in the second, that is, as well in such

Hosius. lib. 2. & Soto cont. Brentiū. Melanch. in lo.com. Cap. de magistr. Ciuilib.

actions

actions as concerne our dutie to God him felf, as in the dutie of one man to an other. But al this is (as not onely the
Catholike writers, but Melāchthon him felf and Caluin, do
expoūd) *quod ad externam difciplinam attinet*, as much as ap *Melanch.*
perteineth to external difcipline : and the Magiftrate is the *vt fuprà,*
keper and defender of both tables (faith Melanchthon) but
againe he addeth: *quod ad externos mores attinet*, as muche
as belongeth to external maners, behauiour , and demeanour. For in the firft table are cōteined many offences and
breaches, of the which the Prince can not iudge, and much
leffe are by him punifhable. As are all fuche crimes, whiche
proprely belong to the Court of Confcience. To wit, mifbelief in God, miftruft in his mercy, contempt of his commaundements, prefumption of our felues, incredulitie, and
fuch like : which al are offences againft the firft table, that
is, againft the loue we owe to God. Cōtrarywife , true belief, confidence in God, the feare of God, and fuch like, are
the vertues of the firft table.   And of thefe Melanchthon
truely faith: *Hæc funt vera opera primæ tabulæ,* Thefe are the *In Apolo-*
true workes of the firft table. The punifhing , correcting, *logia Cō-*
or iudging of thefe appertaine nothing to the authority of *feß. Art.*
the Prince, or to any his lawes : but only are iudged, cor- *18.*
rected and punifhed by the fpiritual fworde of excommunication, of binding of finnes, and embarring the vfe of the
holy Sacraments, by the order and authoritie of the Prieft
only and fpiritual Magiftrate. Which thing is euident not
only by the confefsion, doctrine, and continuall practife of
the Catholique Churche, but alfo by the very writinges of
fuch as haue departed out of the Churche , and will feeme
moft to extolle the authoritie of Princes, yea of your felfe
M. Horne, as we fhall fee hereafter.

Againe

Againe whereas, the chiefe vertue of the firſt table is to beleue in God, to knowe him, and to haue the true faithe of him and in him , in externall regimente (as to puniſhe open blaſphemy, to make lawes againſt heretiques, to honour and mainteine the true ſeruice of God) Princes eſpecially Chriſtians, ought to further, aide, and mainteine the ſame : But to iudge of it , and to determine , whiche is the true faith in God, how and after what maner he ought to be ſerued, what doctrine ought to be publiſhed in that behalfe, the Prince hath no authoritie or power at all. Therefore Melanchthŏ, who in his Cŏmon places, wil haue Princes to looke vnto the true doctrine , to correct the Churches (when Biſhops faile of their duetie) yea and to conſider the doctrine it ſelfe: yet afterward he ſo writeth of this matter, that either he recanteth as better aduiſed, or els writeth plaine contrary to him ſelfe. For thus he ſaieth of the Ciuile Magiſtrates : *Non condant dogmata in Ecclesia, nec inſtituant cultus: vt fecit Nabuchodonozor. Et recens in ſcripto, cui titulus eſt Interim, poteſtas politica extra metas egreſſa eſt. Sicut Imperatori Conſtătio dixit Epiſcopus Leŏtius.* ἑτερα δ' ἱκ ͡ʒεῖν ͡ʃαχϑεῖς ἑτέροις ἐπιχειρεῖς. *Nŏ ſunt cŏfundĕdæ functiones &c.* Let thĕ make no doctrines in the Church: neither appoint any worſhipping of God, as did Nabuchodonoſor. And euen of late in that writing which is entituled, the Interim, the Ciuile power hath paſſed her bounds and limites. As ones Biſhop Leontius ſaid to Conſtantius the Emperour : Thou being ſet to gouerne in one matter, takeſt vpon thee an other matter. The functions (of both magiſtrates) are not to be confounded.

In theſe woordes you ſee M. Horne, Melanchthon taketh away all authoritie from Princes in iudging or determining

In locis com. vbi ſupra.

In examine ordinădorum.

Suidas in Leontio.

mining of doctrine: and wil not haue the functions of both
Magistrates Spiritual and temporal to be confounded. Yea
M. Nowel himselfe with a great stomach biddeth vs shew,
where they deny, that godly and learned Priestes might accor-
ding to Gods woorde iudge of the sincerity of doctrine . As
though when the Prince and his successours are made supreme gouernours without any limitation, it fal not often
out, that the bishop, be he neuer so lerned or godly , shall
not ones be admitted to iudge of true doctrine, except the
doctrine pleafe the Prince : As though there had not ben a
statute made, declaring and enacting the Quenes Ma . yea
and her highnes successours (without exception or limitation of godly and vngodly, and yet I trowe no bishops)
to be the Supreme Gouernour in all thinges and caufes as
well spiritual as temporal. As though you M. Horne, had
not writen, that in bothe the tables, the Prince hath authority, *to erect and correct, to farther, and restrayne, to allow and*
punishe the vertues and vices thereto appertayning. As
though the gouernour in al caufes, is not also a iudge in all
caufes. Or as though it were not commonly so taken and
vnderstanded of a thoufand in Englande which haue taken that Othe to their great damnation, but if they repēt.
You therefore M. Horne, which talke so confufely and generally of the Princes Authority in both tables , doe yet
say nothing nor proue nothing this general and abfolute
Authority in al thinges and caufes , as iustely without exception the Othe expresseth . And therefore you bring in
dede nothig to proue your principal purpofe, to the which
al your proufes should be directed.

Againe where you alleage S. Augustin , that the worde
Godlynes mētioned in S. Paule to Timothe shoulde meane,

T   *the*

the true,chief, or proper worſhip *of God* (as though Princes
hauing charg therof, ſhould alſo haue authority to appoint
ſuch worſhip,when yet S.Paule ſpeaketh there of no ſuch
or of any authority at al in Princes, but onely that by their
peaſible gouernmēt we might with the more quiet attēd to
Gods ſeruice)you doe herein vntruly report S.Auguſtine,
or at the leſte miſſetake him.   For the woorde (godlines)
which S. Auguſtine will haue ſo to meane , is that which
the Greeks call ϑεοσίβεια, Gods ſeruice or religiō, as himſelf
there expreſſeth:but the word of the Apoſtle to Timothee,
is ἀϋσίβεια,godlynes . So aptly and truly you alleage your
doctors.But wil you know M.Horn,why th'Apoſtles both
S.Peter ād S.Paul ſo earneſtly taught at that time obediéce
to Prices?This was the cauſe.In the beginnīg of the church
ſom Chriſtiās were of this opiniō : that, for that they were
Chriſtē mē , they were exēpted from the lawes of the Infidel Princes:and were not bound to pay thē any tribut,or
otherwiſe to obey thē . To repreſſe and reforme this wrōg
iudgmēt of theirs,the Apoſtles Peter and Paule by you named,diligētly employed thē ſelues. Whoſe ſayings can not
imply your pretenſed gouernmēt:onleſſe yow wil ſay,that
Nero the wycked and heathenniſh Emperour was in his
tyme the ſupreme head of al the church of Chriſt,through-
out the empire,aſwel in cauſes ſpiritual as tēporal.And yet
in tēporal and ciuil matters I graunt you , we ought to be
ſubiect, not only to Chriſtiās, but euē to infidels alſo,being
our princes:without any exceptiō,of Apoſtle,euangeliſte,
prophet,prieſt or monk, as ye alleage out of S. Chryſoſtō.
As contrarywiſe the Chriſtian prince him ſelf,is for eccleſiaſtical and ſpiritual cauſes , ſubiect to his ſpiritual ruler.
Which Chryſoſtom hiſelf,of al mē doth beſt declare. *Alij*
ſunt

Auguſt.
lib.14.
cap. 1. De
Trinit.
1. Tim. 2.

1.Pet. 2.
Rom. 13.

Prieſtes
hod is a
boue a
kingdom

sunt termini &c . The bounds of a kingdome, and of priesthood (saith Chrysostō) *are not al one: This kingdom passeth the other:This king is not knowē,by visible things, neither hath his estimatiō,either for precious stones he glistereth withal, or for his gay goldē,glistering apparel. The other king hath the ordering of those worldly things:the authority of priesthod cometh frō heauē:What so euer thou shalt bind vpō earth,shalbe bound in heauē. To the king those things that are here in the worlde are cōmitted,but to me celestial things are cōmitted: Whē I say to me,I vnderstāde to a priest. And anon after he saith: Regi corpora &c.The bodies are cōmitted to the King, the sowles to the Priest:the King pardoneth the faults of the body,the priest pardoneth the faultes of the sowle . The Kinge forcethe , the priest exhorteth:the one by necessity, the other by giuing counsel: the one hath visible armour,the other spiritual. He warreth against the barbarous,I war against the Deuil.This principality is the greater. And therfore the King doth put his head vnder the priestes hands,and euery where in the old scripture priestes did anoynt the Kings.* Among al other bokes of the said Chrysostom,his book *de Sacerdotio* is freighted,with a nōber of lyke and more notable sentēces for the priests superiority aboue the Prince.Now thē M.Horn,I frame you such an argumēt.The Priest is the Prices superiour in some causes ecclesiastical, *Ergo* the Price is not the Priests superiour in al causes ecclesiastical.The Antecedēt is clerly prued out of the words of Chrysost.before alleged.Thus.The Priest is superiour to the price in remissiō of syns by Chrysostō:but remissiō of sins is a cause ecclesiastical or spiritual. *Ergo* the Priest is the Prices superiour in some cause ecclesiastical or spiritual.Which beig most true,what thig cā you cōclud of al ye haue or shal say to win your purpose,or that

T ij   ye here

Chrysost. homil. 4. de eo quod scriptū Esa.

Euidētly proued by S. Chrysost. the Price not to be the Superiour in causes ecclesiastis call.

ye here prefently fay ? *that the Prince hath the care afwell of the firft, as of the feconde table of the commaundements : and* I. Tim. 2. *that S. Paule willethe vs to pray for the Princes, that we may lyue a peaceable life, in godlines ãd honefty.* In the which place he fpeaketh of the heathennifhe princes, as appereth by that which foloweth, to pray for them that they may be côuerted to the faith: Or of al ye bring in out of S. Auguftin either againft the Donatifts (whereof we haue alredy faid inough) or *that Princes muft make their power a feruãte to Gods Maiefty to enlarge his worfhip, feruice and religion.* Nowe as all this frameth full yllfauoredly to conclude your principle: fo I fay that if S. Auguftine were aliue, he might truely and would fay vnto you, as he fayd vnto Gaudentius: and as your felf alleage againft your felfe and your bretherne. *That thing that ye doe, is not only not good, but it is a great euil: to witte, to cutte in fonder the vnity and peace of Chrift, to rebell againft the promifes of the ghofpell : or to beare the Chriftiã armes or badges, as in a ciuil warre, againft the true and the high King of the Chriftians :* he would fay, yf he were aliue vnto you, that as the Donatiftes, *did not deny Chrift the head, but Chrift the body, that is his Catholike Churche*, fo doe you. He would fay, that as *the Donatiftes fecte was condemned by Conftantin, Honorius, and other Emperours, the high Kings of the Chriftians:* fo are your herefies condemned not only by the Catholik Church, but alfo by the worthy and mofte renowned King Henry the fifte: and other Kings, as wel in England as elfe where : alfo by the high Kings of the Chriftiãs, that is themperours as well of our tyme, as many hundred yeares fince. And therefore ye are they, *that cutte in fonder the vnity ãd peace of Chriftes Church, and rebell againft the promifes of the Gofpel.*

S. Augu-
ftin reẽr
ned vpõ
M. Horn
and his
felovves
Lib 2. côt.
2. epiftol.
Gaudentij
cap. 11.

M. Horne

M. Horne. The 23. Diuision. Pag.17.a.

*Chryfoftom fhevveth this reafon,vvhy S. Paule doth attribute this title of a minifter vvorthely vnto the Kings,or ciuil Magiftrates:*becaufe that through fraying of the wicked men , and commending the good,he prepareth the mindes of many to be made more appliable to the doctrine of the word.

Eufebius alluding to the fentence of S.Paule,vvhere he calleth the ciuill Magiftrate , Goddes minifter,and vnderftanding that Miniftery of the ciuil Magiftrate to be about Religion,and Ecclefiafticall caufes,fo (.61.) vvell as Temporal,doth cal Conftantine the Emperour : The great light , and moft fhril preacher,or fetter foorth of true godlines:The one and only God(*faieth he*)hath appointed Conftantine to be his minifter,and the teacher of Godlines to al countreis.And this fame Coftantin,like a faithful and good minifter:did throughly fet foorth this : and he did confeffe him felf manifeftly to be the feruaunt and minifter of the high King. He preached with his imperial decrees or proclamations his God, euen to the boundes of the whole worlde. Yea *Conftantine himfelfe affirmeth , as Eufebius reporteth:*That by his miniftery he did put away and ouerthrowe al the euilles that preffed the worlde, *meanig al fuperftition, Idolatry, and falfe Religion .* In fo much (*faith this Godly Emperour*)that therewithal I both called again mankide,taught by my miniftery,to the Religion of the moft holy Law (*meaning the vvorde of God*)and alfo caufed,that the moft bleffed faith fhould encreafe and growe vnder a better gouernour(*meaning than had beene before*)for (*faith he*)I would not be vnthankeful to neglect namely the beft miniftery,which is the thankes I owe (*vnto God*)of duety.

This moft Chriftian Emperour did rightly confider,as he had bene truelye taught of the moft Chriftian Bifhops of that tyme,that as the Princes haue in charge the miniftery and gouernment in (.62.) all manner caufes either Temporal or Spiritual: euen fo , the chiefeft or befte parte of their Seruice or Miniftery to confift in the vvel ordering of Church matters,and their diligĕt rule and care therein , to be the mofte thankefull, acceptable,and duetifull Seruice that they can dee or ovve vnto God.

The 61. vntruth. Eufebius neuer vnderftood any fuch Miniftery of the Ciuil Magiftrat. *Lib. 1. De vit.Conft. Lib.2. De vit.Conft.*

The 62. vntruth. Impudĕt ad fhame leffe. Cõcluded, but no vvhyt proued.

T iij The

THE FIRST BOOKE

The.19.Chapter . Anſwering to the ſayinges of Euſebius and Nicephorus touching Conſtantin and Emanuel Emperours.

Stapleton.

See you not M . Horne come as yet nere the matter. I ſee not yet, that Conſtantin changed Religion, plucked down aultars, depoſed biſ-ſhops, &c. But that he was diligent in defen-ding the old and former faith of the Chriſtiãs. If S.Paul cal the ciuil magiſtrat a miniſter, becauſe through feare he côſtraineth the wicked to embrace the godly do-ctrin, as by your ſaying S.Chryſoſtom côſtrueth it, we are wel côtent therewith. And withal, that the beſt miniſtery and ſeruice of the great Conſtantin reſted in the ſettinge forth of Chriſtes true religion : and that he preached the ſame with his Imperiall decrees and proclamations , as ye oute of Euſebius recyte . Neither this that ye here al-leage out of place, nor al the reſidewe which ye reherſe of this Conſtantin (with whoſe doings ye furniſhe hereafter ſix ful leaues) can importe this ſuperiority, as we ſhal there more at large ſpecifie . In the meane ſeaſon , I ſay it is a ſtark and moſt impudêt lye, that ye ſay without any prouf, Côſtantin was taught of the biſhops, that Princes haue the gouernment in al maner cauſes, either têporal or ſpirituall. You conclude after your maner, facingly and deſperatlye without any prouſe or halfe prouſe in the worlde.

M. Horne. The Diuiſion 24. Pag. 17. b,

For this (.63.) cauſe alſo Nicephorus *in his Preface before his Eccle-ſiaſtical hiſtory, doth compare (.6 4.)* Emanuel Paleologus *the Empe-rour, to Conſtantin, for that he did ſo neerly imitate his duetifulnes in ru-ling, procuring, and reforming religiõ to the pureneſſe thereof:* VVhich a-mong al vertues, belôging to an Emperor, is moſt ſeemely for

the

the imperial dignity, and doth expresse it most truely, *as Nice-* *phorus saieth: vvho maketh protestatiō, that he saith nothing in the commen-* *datiō of this Emperour, for fauour or to flatter, but as it vvas true in deede* *in him. And so reherseth his (. 65)noble vertues exercised in discharge of his* *imperial duety tovvards God in Church matters , saying to the Emperour,* who hath glorified God more, and shewed more feruét zele towards hī in pure religiō, without feyning, thā thou hast don? who hath with such feruét zeale sought after the most sincere faith much endaungered, or clésed again the holy Table? whē thou sawest our true religion brought into perill with newe deuises brought in by cōterfaict and naughty doctrines , thou diddest defende it most painfully and wisely . Thou diddest shew thy selfe, to be the mighty supreme , and very holy an-chour and stay in so horrible wauering and errour , in matters beginning to fainte, and to perish as it were with shipwrak. Thou art the guid of the profession of our faith. Thou hast re-stored the Catholik and Vniuersal Churche , being troubled with new matters or opinions, to the old state. Thou hast ba-nished frō the Church al vnlawful and impure doctrin. Thou hast clésed again with the vvord of trueth, the téple frō chop-pers and chaungers of the diuin doctrin, and frō heretical de-prauers thereof. Thou hast been set on fier vvith a godly zeale for the diuine Table. Thou hast established the doctrin : thou hast made Cōstitutions for the same. Thou hast entréched the true religion vvith mighty defenses. That vvhich vvas pulled dovvne , thou hast made vp againe, and haste made the same vvhole and sound again, vvith a conueniét knitting togeather of al the partes and mébers (*to be shorte, thou haste, saith Nicephorus* *to the Emperour*) established true Religion and godlines vvith spiritual buttresses , namely the doctrine and rules of the aū-cient Fathers.

Stapleton.

Where ye say, *for this cause also &c.* This is no cause at all : but it is vntrue, as of the other Emperour Cōstantinus: and much more vntrue , as ye shall good reader straight way

vnder-

The 65. vntruth. For this Emperor vvas a stark here-tike.

The (66.) Princes suprema-cy in re-payringe Religion decayed. The 66. vntruthe fond and foolish as shal ap-peare.

vnderstande . But firste we will dissipate and discusse the myste that M . Horne hath caste before thyne eies : and wherein him self walketh either ignorantly, or maliciously, or both. Ye shal then vnderstande , that among many other errours and heresies wherwith the Grecians were infected and poysoned, they helde, cōtrary to the Catholike faith, that the holy ghost did not procede , from the father and the sonne, but from the father onely. In which heresie

The Grecians at the Coũcel of Lions, ac-knovv-ledged the Popes Primacy
Blōd. dec. 2. lib. 8.
Ioan. Bap. Egn. Rom. Prin. li. 2.
Nice. Gregor. li. 4. & 5.
Pachime-rus lib. 5.
Fyue notable lies concer-ning Images in the booke of homilies.
1.
2.

they dwelt many an hundred yeare. At the length abowte 300 . yeares paste the Emperour of Grece called Michael Paleologus came to the generall Councell kepte at Lions. Where the Grecians with the Latin Church accorded, aswel in that point, as for the Popes supremacy, both in other matters, and cōcerning the deuoluing of matters frō Grece to Rome by way of appeale . This Michael being dead the Grecians reuolted to their olde heresie against the holy ghost: and for the malicioufe spyte they had , against the Catholike faith , their Bisshops would not suffer him to be buried.

The author of the homely against Idolatry, as it is entituled , calleth this Emperour wrongfully *Theodorum Lasca-rim*, and saieth most ignorantly and falsly, that he was depriued of his Empire, because in the Councel of Lions he relented, and set vp images in Grece. Whereas he was not put frō his Empire, but from his royal burial , as I haue said, neither any word was moued in the said councell of Images, nor any Images of newe by him were set vppe, which had custombly continued in the Greeke Churche manye hundred yeares before: and so reuerently afterwarde continued euen till Constantinople was taken by the great Turke. And yet this good antiquarye and chronographer

wil

will nedes haue the Grecians, about a.700. yeares together with a moſt notorious lie, to haue bene Iconomaches, that is, Image breakers. Much other fooliſh blaſphemouſe babling is conteined in that Homilie. Yea many other ſhamelesſe lies are there, to diſgrace, deface, and deſtroy, the Image of Chriſt and his Saints : eſpecially one. Whereas he ſaith, that the Emperour Valens and Theodoſius made a Proclamation, that no man ſhoulde painte or kerue the Croſſe of Chriſt. And thereupon gaily and iolilye triumpheth vpon the Catholiques. Whereas the Proclamation neither is, nor was, to reſtreine all vſe of the Croſſe , but that it ſhould not be painted or kerued vppon the ground. Which theſe good Emperours, not Valens (for he was the valiaunt Capitaine and defendour of the Arrians) but Valentinianus and Theodoſius, did of a great godly reuerence they had to the Croſſe enact. And yet, as groſſe, as foule, and as lowd liyng a fetche as this is, M.Iewel walketh euē in the very ſame ſteppes, putting Valens, for Valentinian : and alleaging this Edict, as generall againſt al Images of the Croſſe. And yet theſe Homilies (the holy learned Homilies of the olde Fathers , namely of Venerable Bede , our learned Countrie man , whoſe Homilies were read in our Countrie, in the Church Seruice, aboue. 800. yeares paſt, as alſo in Fraunce and other where, reiected) are reade in M. Hornes and other his brethrens Dioceſſe: and are with M. Horne very good ſtuffe : as good perdie, as M.Hornes owne booke : and as clerkly, and faithfully handeled, as ye ſhall ſee plainly by the very ſelfe matter we haue in hande. Andronicus the elder, ſonne to this Michaell, whome M. Horne calleth ignorantly Emanuel. (for this Emanuel was not the ſonne of this Andronicus but of Caloioānes, ſonne

Li.1. Cod. Iuſtiniani tit.8, alias 11. M.Iewell alſo hath tvvo of the ſame fiue. In his Replie to the Article of Images. Nicephor. Greg.li.6. Three notable vntruths of M. Horne, in this one ſtorie. Volateran. li.23 Sabell. & Blondus. Lib.8. dec.2.

V   to

to Andronicus the yóger,to whó our Andronicus was grã-
father)after his fathers death fũmoned a coũcel of the Greci
ãs,wherin he and they annulled ãd reuoked that his Father
had don at the Coũcel at Liós , namely cõcerning the proceding of the holy Ghofte. And for the which Nicephorus
M.Hornes Author,beig alfo caried away with the cõmon
errour,as with an huge raging tẽpeft, doth fo highly auãce
this Andronicus.And fo withal ye fee vpõ how good a mã,
and vpõ how good a caufe M.Horne buildeth his new fupremacy to pluck doune the Popes old fupremacy. For the
infringing wherof the wicked working of wretched heretiks is with him,here and els where,as we fhal in place cõuenient fhew,a goodlye and godlye prefidente, as it is alfo
with M.Iewel for to mainteine the very fame quarrel,as I
haue at large in my Returne againft his fourth Article declared.

    But nowe M. Horne , what if thefe hereticaíi doinges
do nothing relieue your caufe,nor neceffarilye induce the
chief Superiority in al caufes,and perchãce in no caufe Ecclefiaftical,cõcerning the final difcufsing ãd determination
of the fame?Verely without any perchãce,it is moft plainly
and certainly true it doth not.For euen in this fchifmatical

O vvhat
a craftie
Coper ãd
fmothe
ioyner is
M.Horn?

Coũcel,and heretical Synagog, the Bifhops plaid the chief
part,and they gaue the final though a wrong and a wicked
iudgemẽt. Who alfo fhewed their fuperiority,though vngodly vpon this mans Father,in that they would not fuffer
him to be interred Pricelike:the felues much more worthy
to haue ben caft after their deceafe, to the dogs and ráués,
vpõ a dirty donghil.What honor haue ye gotte, for al your
crafty cooping or cũning ãd fmoth ioyning, for al your cõ-
bining,ãd as I may fay incorporating a nũber of Nicephorus

                                   fenten-

ſentences together, of the whiche yet ſome are one, ſome *Vide Præ-*
are two leaues a ſunder, and the firſt placed after the ſecond *fationem.*
and the ſecond before the firſte, and yet not whole ſenten- *Nicephor*
ces neither, but pieces and patches of ſentences, here and *in hiſto .*
there culled oute, and by you verye ſmoothlye ioyned *ſuam ec-*
in one continuall narration, in ſuch ſort that a man would *cleſiaſticā.*
thinke that the whole lay orderly in Nicephorus, and were
not ſo artificially by you or your delegates patched vppe,
what honor, haue you, I ſay, wóne by this, or by the whole
thing it ſelf? Litle or nothing, furthering your cauſe, ād yet
otherwiſe plaine ſchiſmatical and heretical. For the which
your hanſome holy dealing, the author of the foreſaid Homilie, and you, yea and M. Iewel too, are worthy exceding
thanks. But M. Horne wil not ſo leeſe his lóg allegatió out
of Nicephorus. He hath placed a Note in his Margin, ſufficiét (I trow) to cóclude his principall purpoſe. And that is
this. *The Princes Supremacy in repairing religion decayed.* This
is in deed a ioly marginal note. But where findeth M. Horn
the ſame in his text? Forſoth of this, that Nicephorꝰ calleth
th'Emperor, *the mighty ſupreme, ād very holy Anchor, ād ſtay*
in ſo horrible wauering, &c. Of the word *Supreme ancher,* he
cócludeth a *Supremacy.* But ô more thē childiſh folly! could
that crafty Cooper of this allegatió, informe you no better
M. Horn? Was he no better ſene in Grāmer, or in the pro-
feſsió of a ſcholemaiſter, then thus ſowly ād fondly to miſſe
the true interpretatió of the latine word? For what other is
ſuprema anchora in good engliſh, thē the laſt ancher, the laſt
refuge, the extreme holde and ſtaye to reſte vppon? As
ſuprema verba, doe ſignifye the laſt woordes of a man in
his laſt will: as *Summa dies,* the laſt daye, *Supremum iu-*
dicium, the laſt iudgemēt, with a nūber of the like phraſes,

V ij ſo

ſo *Suprema Anchora*, is the laſt Anchour, ſigniſiyng the laſt holde and ſtaie, as in the perill of tempeſt, the laſt refuge is to caſt Ancher. In ſuch a ſenſe, Nicephorus called his Emperour *the laſt, the mightie, and the holy Anchour or ſtaie in ſo horrible wauering and errour:* ſigniſiyng that now by him they were ſtaied fro the ſtorme of ſchiſme, as from a ſtorm in the ſea, by caſting the Ancher, the ſhippe is ſtayed. But by the Metaphore of an Anchour, to conclude a Supremacie : is as wiſe, as by the Metaphore of a Cowe to coclude a ſadle. For as well doth a ſaddle fitte a Cowe, as the qualitie of an Anchor reſemble a Supremacie. But by ſuche beggarly ſhiftes a barren cauſe muſt be vpholded. Firſt al is ſaid by the way of Amplification to extolle the Emperour (as in the ſame ſentence he calleth him the ſixth Element, reaching aboue Ariſtotles fift body, ouer the foure elemets with ſuch like). Then all is but a Metaphore, which were it true, proueth not nor concludeth, but expreſſeth and lighteneth a truth. Thirdly the Metaphore is ill tranſlated, and laſt of all, worſe applied.

Firma-
mentum
ſextum &
ſempiter-
num.

Now whereas in the beginning of your matter, the ſubſtance of your proufes hereafter ſtanding in ſtories, ye haue demeaned your ſelfe, ſo clerkly and ſkilfully here, the Reader may hereof haue a taſt : and by the way of preuention and anticipation, haue alſo a certaine preiudicial vnderſtäding, what he ſhal looke for at your handes in the reſidue. Wherefore God be thanked, that at the beginning hath ſo deciphired you, whereby we may ſo much the more, yea the bolder without any feare of all your antiquitie hereafter to be ſhewed, cherefully procede on.

M. Horne. The. 25. Diuiſion. pag. 18. 4.

Theſe and ſuch like Chriſtian Emperours, are not thus much commended
of th

of the Ecclesiasticall vvriters, for their notable doings in the maintenaunce and furtheraunce of Religion, as for doings not necessarilie appertaining to their office or calling: but for that they vvere exaumples, spectacles, and glasses for others, vvherein to beholde vvhat they are bound vnto by the vvorde of God, and vvhat their subiectes may looke for at their handes, as matter of charge and duety, both to God and his people. VVhich S. Paule doth plainly expresse, vvhere he exhorteth the Christians to make earnest and continual praier for Kings, and for such as are in authoritie, to this ende and purpose, that by their rule, ministerie, and seruice, not only peace and tranquilitie, but also godlines and religion, should be (.67.) furthered and continued among men: attributing the furtherance and continuance of religion, and godlines, to the Magistrates, as an especial fruite and effect of their duety and seruice to God and his people. Chrysostome expounding this place of the Apostle, doth interprete his meaning to be vnderstanded, of the outvvard peace and tranquilitie furthered, mainteined, and defended by the Magistrates, but chieflye of the invvarde peace of the minde and conscience, vvhich can not be atteined vvithout pure religion, as contrary vvise, godlines can not be had vvithout peace and tranquility of mind and conscience. *This vvould be noted vvith good aduisement, that S. Paul him selfe shevveth plainly prosperitie, amongst Gods people, and true religion, to be the benefites and fruits in general, that by Gods ordinance springeth from the rule and gouernmēt of Kings and Magistrates, vnto the vveale of the people. The vvhich tvvo, although diuers in them selues, yet are so combined and knitte together, and as it vvere incorporated in this one office of the Magistrate, that the nourishing of the one, is the feeding of the other, the decay of the one, destroyeth or (at the least) deadlye vveakeneth them both. So that one can not be in perfect and good estate vvithout the other. The vvhich knot and fastening together of religion, and prosperitie in common vveales, the most Christian and godly Emperours Theodosius and Valentinianus, did vvisely (.68.) see, as it appeareth by this that they vvrote vnto Cyrill, saiying: The suertie of our common weale, dependeth vpon Gods Religion, and there is great kinred and societie betwixte these tweine, for they cleaue together, and the one groweth with the increase of the other, in such sorte, that true Religion holpen with the indeuour of Iustice, and the

V iij   common

1. Tim. 2.
The. 67.
vntruth.
No suche
vvordes
in S. Paul
* This
vVouldd
be noted,
hovv ye
racke S.
Paule. He
nameth
not Relisgiō at all.
He doth
not attribute religion to
the rule
and gouernmēt
of the ciuile Magistrate,
but peace
and tranquilitie
onely in
godlines.
The. 68.
vntruth:
Thei saw
no suche
confounding of
the tvvo
functiōs
spirituall
and temporal as
you imagine.
Ciril. Ep.
17. li. 4

common weale holpen of them both, florifheth. Seing therefore, that we are conftituted of God to be the kinge, and are
the knitting together or iointure of Godlines and profperitie
in the fubiects, we kepe the focietie of thefe tweine, neuer to
be fundred: and fo farre forth as by our forefight, we procure
peace vnto our fubiects, we minifter vnto the augmenting of
the common weale: but as we might fay, being feruaunts to
our fubiects in al things, that they may liue godly, and be of a
religious conuerfation as it becommeth godly ones, we gar-
nifh the common weale with honour, hauing care as it is cō-
uenient for them both (for it can not be, that diligently prouiding for the one, we fhould not care, in like forte alfo for the
other) But we trauaile earneftly in this thing aboue the reaft,
that the Ecclefiafticall ftate may remaine fure, bothe in fuche
fort, as is feemely for Gods honour, and fitte for our times, that
it may continue in tranquilitie by common confent without
variaunce, that it may be quiete through agreemente in Ecclefiafticall matters, that the godlye Religion may be preferued vnreprouable, and that the lyfe of fuch as are chofen into
the Clergy, and the greate Priefthood maye be clere from all
faulte.

Stapleton.

And fhal we now M. Horne, your antecedent matter
being fo naught, greatly feare, the confequent and conclufion ye will hereof inferre? Nay pardie.   For lo ftraite
waye, euen in the firfte line, ye bewray either your great
ignoraunce, or your like malice. Not for calling this Emperour as ye did before Emanuell (let that goe as a veniall
finne) but for calling him *Chriftian Emperour*, and willing
him to be *an example, a fpectacle, a glaffe for others*, as *one
that* (as yee fayed before) *refourmed Relligion to the
pureneffe thereof:* which faying in fuche a perfonage as ye
counter-

counterfaite, cannot be but a deadly and a mortall finne.
Surely M.Fox of al men is depely beholding vnto you: for
if this be pure religion, the may he be the bolder, after your
folemne fentence once geauen, bearing the ftate of one of
the chief Prelates in the realme: and of a Prelate of the garter withal : to kepe ftill his holy daye, that he hath dedicated to the memorie of his bleffed Martyr, M. D. Wefalian,
of whom we fpake before. And yet I wene it wil proue no
great feftiual daie, for that he was an heretike otherwife alfo. Well I leaue this at your leafure , better to be debated
vpon betwene you and M.Fox. In the meane while to returne to the matter of your dealing, wherof I fpake : yf ye
knew not the ftate and truth of your Emperours doings, ye
are a very poore fely Clerke, farre from the knowledge of
the late reuerend fathers, Bifhop White, and Bifhop Gardiner : and how mete to occupie fuch a roome , I leaue it to
others their difcrete and vpright iudgemēts. And now Sir,
if this be pure religion, as ye fay , then haue ye one herefie
more, then any of your fellowes, as farre as I knowe, hath:
onleffe perhappes M. Foxe wil not fuffer you to walke all
poft alone. And then that I may a litle rolle in your railing
rhetorike, wherein ye vniuftly rore out againft M. Fekenham, may I not for much better caufe and grounde, faye to
you, then ye did to him, to make him a Donatift: M. Horne
let your friends now weigh with aduifemēt, what was the
erronious opinion of the Grecians againft the holy Ghofte:
and let them cōpare your opiniō and guilful defences therof to theirs. And they muft nedes clap you on the back, and
fay to you *Patrifas* (if there be any vpright iudgmēt in thē)
Deming you fo like your great graunfiers the Grecians, as
though they had fpitte you out of their mouth,

The great
ignorāce
or malice
of M.
Horne.

M. Hor-
nes rhe-
torik vp-
on him-
felfe re-
turned.

Now

Now for your conclusion, that you bring in vppon this Emperours and Conftantines example, it is nedeleffe and farre from the matter. Whereby by the place of S.Paule, before rehearfed, and nowe eftfone by you refumed, by Chryfoftome in his expofitions of the faied place, and by Cyrillus you would haue vs ferioufly admonifhed, that pro fperitie of the common welth and true religion, fpringeth from the good regiment of Magiftrates, whiche we denie not, and that the decaye of religion deftroyeth or deadlye weakeneth the other: which is alfo true, as the vtter ruine of the Empire of Grece proceding from the manifolde herefies, efpecially that, whereof we haue difcourfed, doth to wel and to plainly teftifie. And therefore I would wifh you and M. Foxe, with others, but you two aboue all others, with good aduifemente to note, that as the wicked Iewes that crucified Chrift about the holy time of Eafter, were at the very fame time, or thereabout, befieged of the Romans, and fhortly after brought to fuch defolation, and to fuche miferable wretched ftate, as in a manner is incredible, fauing that befide the forefeing and forefaiyng therof by Chrift, there is extant at this daie a true and faithfull reporte: Euen fo, your dearlings the Grecians, whofe errour, but not alone, but accompanied with fome other, that you at this daie ftoutly defend, yet efpecially refted in this herefie againft the holy Ghoft, that ye terme with an vncleane ad an impure mouth, pure religio, were in their chief city of Cöftätinople, in the time of Cöftantinus fon to Iohn, nephew to Andronicus your Emanuels father, euen about Whitfontide (at whiche time the Catholique Churche in true and fincere faith concerning the holy Ghoft, kepeth a folemne feftiuall daie of the holy Ghofte) fodenly by the wicked

1 Tim. 2.
Chryfoft.
ibidem.
Cyrill, li. 1
Epift. 17.
Tom. 4.

A good aduertifement for M. Horne to confider the caufe of the deftruction of Conftantinople.
Iofephus de bello Iud. & Hegefippus.
In the yeare of our Lord 1453.

wicked Turksbeſieged, and ſhortly after the city and the whole Greke empire came into the Turks hands and poſſeſsion. Wherein God ſeameth as before to the Iewes, ſo afterwarde to the Grecians, as yt were with pointing and notyfying yt with his finger to ſhewe and to notifie to all the worlde, the cauſe of the finall deſtruction, as well of the one,as of the other people.But what ſpeke I of Grece? we nede not ronne to ſo fare yeares or contries. The caſe toucheth vs much nearer:The realme of Boheame, and of late yeares of France and Scotlande, the noble contrey of Germany,with ſome other that I neade not name, be to to lyuely and pregnant examples,of this your true,but neadleſſe and impertinente admonition. For the whiche notwithſtandinge ſeeinge ye deale ſo freelye and liberallye, I thowght good alſo to returne you an other: I ſuppoſe not neadleſſe or impertinente for you, and ſuch other as doe prayſe and commende ſo highly this Andronicus doinges.

And nowe might I here breake of from this and goe further forth,ſauing that I can not ſuffer you,to bleare the readers eies, as thowgh the Emperours Theodoſius, and Valentinianus ſayings or doings ſhoulde ſerue any thinge for your pretenſed primacy: *We* (ſaith Valentinian to the Emperour Theodoſius) *owght to defende the faithe which we receiued of our auncetours withe all competente deuotion: and in this our tyme preſerue vnblemiſshed the worthy reuerence dewe to the bleſſed Apoſtle Peter. So, that the moſt bleſſed biſshop of the cyty of Rome, to whome antiquity,hath geuen the principality of prieſthod aboue all other, may (O moſt bleſſed father and honorable Emperour) haue place and liberty,to geue iudgement in ſuch matters as concerneth faith and prieſts.And for this cauſe the biſshop of Conſtã*

X   tinople

Hereſies the deſtructions of common vveales.

The popes ſupremacy proued by the Emperor Valentinian alleged by M. Horn. Tom.1 cõcil fo. 731 col.1.

*tinople,hath according to the folemne order of councells, by his lybel appealed vnto hi.*And this is writé M. Horne to Theodofius him felf, by a commó letter of Valentinian, and the **Dist. fol.** Empreffes Placidia and Eudoxia. Which Placidia writeth **731. co. 2.** alfo a particular letter to her faid fonne Theodofius , and altogether in the fame fenfe. Harken good M .. Horne, and geue good aduertifment : I walke not, and wander as ye doe, here alleaging this Emperour , in an obfcure generality, whereof can not be enforced any certàyne particularity of the principal Queftion : I goe to worke with you plainly , trewlye and particularlye : I fhewe you by your own Emperour and by playn words, the Popes fupremacy and the practife withal of appeales fró Conftantinople to Rome: that it is the leffe to be marueled at , yf Michael in the forfayde coúcel at Lions códefcéded to the fame . And your Andronicus with his Grecians the leffe to be borne withal for breaking and reuoking the faid Emperours good and lawful doings. Neither is it to be thought, that Theodofius thowght otherwife of this primacy. But becaufe ye hereafter wring and wreft him to ferue your turne , I will fet him ouer to that as a more commodioufe place to debate his doings therein.

M. Horne. The. 26. Diuifion. Pag. 19. a.

The 69. vntruth. Such like gouernimér you haue not, nor euer fhal be able to proue. *Hitherto I haue proued plainly by the holy Scriptures , and by fome fuche Doctours, as fró age to age haue vvitneffed,th' order of ecclefiaftical gouernmér in the Church of Chrift: yea by the confeffiòn, teftimony , and example of fome of the moft godly Emperours thefelues,that fuch (69.) like gouernment in Church caufes,as the Queenes maiefty taketh vpó her,doth of duty belóg vnto the ciuil Magiftrates and Rulers,and therfore they may,yea,they ought to claim and take vpon them the fame. Novv remayneth that I proue this fame by the continual practife of the like gouernment in fome one parte of Chriftendom,and by the general counfayles, vvherein (as ye affirme) the right*

right order of Ecclesiasticall gouernment in Christ his Church, hath been most faithfully declared and shevved from tyme to tyme ♦

Stapleton.

Hitherto you haue not brought any one thing to the substantial prouf of your purpose worth a good strawe: neither scripture, nor Doctour, nor Emperour . Among your fowre emperours by you named ye haue iugled in one that was a stark heretik, but as subtily, as ye thought ye had hādledthe matter, ye haue not so craftely coueyed your galles, but that ye are espied. Yet for one thing are ye here to be comended, that now ye would seame to frame as a certain fixed state of the matter to be debated vpō, ād to the which ye would seme to direct your proufs, that ye wil bring. And therin you deale with vs better, thē hitherto ye haue done seaming to seke by dark generalities, as it were corners, to luske and lurke in. Neither yet here walke ye so plainly ād truely as ye woulde seme: but in great darknes with a scose of dymme light, that the readers should not haue the clere vew and sight of the right way ye should walke in, whom with this your dark sconse ye leade farre awrie . For thus you frame vs the state of the Question.

M. Horne. The 27 ♦ Diuision. Pag. 19. b.

The gouernment that the Queenes maiesty taketh most iustly vppon her in Ecclesiastical causes, is the guiding, caring, prouiding, ordering, directing, and ayding, the Ecclesiastical state vvithin her dominions, to the furtheraunce, maintenaunce, and setting foorth of true religion, vnity, and quietnes of Christes Church, ouerseyng, visitig, refourming, restrayning, amending, ād correcting, al maner persons, vvith al maner errours, superstitiōs, Heresies, Schismes, abuses, offences, contempts, and enormities, in or about Christes Religiō vvhatsoeuer. This same authority, rule, and gouernmēt, vvas practised in the Catholik Church, by the most Christiā Kings and Emperours, approued, cōsirmed, and cōmended by the best counsailes, both general and national.

The

The . 20 . Chapter: Declaring the ſtate of the Queſtion be-
twene M. Horne and Fekenhā,touching the Othe.
Stapleton.

Ere is a ſtate framed of you(M . Horne) but
farre ſquare from the Queſtion in hande . For
the Queſtion is not nowe betwene M. Fekēham and you , whether the Prince may viſit,
refourme , and correcte all maner of perſons,
for al maner of hereſies and ſchiſmes,and offences in Chriſtian Religion , which perchaunce in ſome ſenſe might
ſomewhat be borne withal, if ye meane by this viſitation
and reformation the outward execution of the Churche
lawes and decrees,confirmed by the ciuill magiſtrate , ro-
borated with his edictes , and executed with his ſworde.
For in ſuch ſorte many Emperours and Princes ,·haue fortified , and ſtrenghthened the decrees of biſhops made in
Councels both general and national,as we ſhal in the proceſſe ſee. And this in Chriſtian Princes is not denied , but
commended. But the Queſtion is here now, whether the
Prince or lay Magiſtrat,may of him ſelfe , and of his owne
princely Authority , without any higher Eccleſiaſticall
power in the Churche,within or without the Realme viſit,refourme and correct,and haue al maner of gouernmēt
and Authority in al things and cauſes eccleſiaſtical, or no.
As whether the Prince may by his own ſupreme Authority,depoſe and ſet vp biſhops and Prieſts,make Iniunctions
of doctrine,preſcribe order of Gods ſeruice, enact matters
of religion,approue and diſproue Articles of the faith, take
order for adminiſtration of Sacraments,commaunde or put
to ſilence preachers , determine doctrine , excommunicat
and

The ſtate
of the
Queſtion

and abfolue with fuch like, which all are caufes ecclefiaftical,and al apperteyning not to the inferiour minifterye,
(which you graunt to Prieftes and biffhops onely) but to
the fupreme iurifdiction and gouernment,which you doe
annexe to the Prince onely . This I fay,is the ftate of the
Queftion,now prefent.For the prefent Queftion betwene
you and M. Fekenham is grounded vppon the Othe com-
prifed in the Statute:which Statute emplieth and concludeth al thefe particulars.

For concealing whereof, you haue M . Horne in the
framing of your ground according to the Statute, omitted
cleane the ij.claufes of the Statute , folowing. The one at
the beginning,where the Statute faith . *That no forayn per-*
fon fhall haue any maner of Authority in any fpirituall caufe
*within the Realme.*Ey which wordes is flatly excluded all
the Authority of the whole body of the Catholike Church
without the Realme : As in a place more conuenient, toward the end of the laft book,it fhal by Gods grace be euidently proued . The other claufe you omitte at the ende
of the faid Satute,which is this .   *That all maner Superio-*
rities,that haue or maye lawfully be exercifed, for the vifitatiõ
of perfons Ecclefiafticall , and correcting al maner of errours,
herefies,and offences, fhall be for euer vnited to the Crowne
of the Realme of Englande . Wherein is employed,that yf
(which God forbidde) a Turke, or any heretike whatfoeuer fhoulde come to the Crowne of Englande , by vertu of this Statute and of the Othe , al maner fuperioritye
in vifiting and correcting Ecclefiaftical perfones in al maner matters,fhould be vnited to him . Yea and euery fubiecte fhould fweare, that in his confcience he beleueth fo .
This kinde of regiment therefore fo large and ample I am

M. Horns
diffem,
blingfalf
hod.

right wel affured,ye haue not proued,nor euer fhal be able to proue in the auncient Church , while ye liue . When I fay,this kinde of regiment, I walke not in confufe,and general words as ye doe,but I reftrayne my felf to the forefaid particulars now reherfed,and to that platte forme,that I haue already drawen to your hand, and vnto the which Maifter Fekenham muft pray you to referre and apply your euidences . Otherwife , as he hath , fo may he or any man els , the chiefe pointes of all being as yet on your fide vnproued , ftill refufe the Othe. For the which doinges neither you , nor any man elfe , can iuftly be greued with him.

A reafo=
nable de=
fence of
the Catho
likes for
refufing
the OtheAs neither with vs M.Horne ought you or any mã els be greued for declaring the Truth in this point , as yf we were difcõtéted fubiects,or repyning againft the obediéce we owe to our Gracious Prince and our Countre.For befide that we ought abfolutely more obey God then man, and preferre the Truth (which our Sauiour himfelf protefted to be,encouraging al the faithful to profeffe the Truth, and geuing them to wit,that in defending that,they defended Chrift himfelf)before al other worldly refpects whatfoeuer,befide al this I fay, whofoeuer wil but indifferently confider the matter,fhal fee,that M.Horne himfelfe, in fpecifying here at large the Quenes Mai.gouernement,by the Statute intended , doth no leffe in effect abridge the fame , by diffembling filence , then the Catholikes doe by open and plain contradiction.For whereas the Statute and the Othe(to the which all muft fwere) expreffeth *A fupreme gouernment in al thinges and caufes* , without exception, Maifter Horne taking vpon him to fpecifie the particulars of this general decree , and amplyfying that litle

which

which he geueth to the Quenes Maiefty, with copy of
wordes, ful ftatutelyke, he leaueth yet out, and by that
leauing out, taketh from the meaning of the Statute the
principal caufe ecclefiafticall, and moft neceffary, mete,
and conuenient for a Supreme Gouernour Ecclefiafticall.
What is that, you afke. Forfoth: Iudgement, determining and approuing of doctrine, which is true and good,
and which is otherwife. For what is more neceffary in
the Churche, then that the Supreme gouernour thereof,
fhould haue power in al doubtes and controuerfies to decide the Truthe, and to make ende of queftioning? This
in the Statute by Maifter Hornes filence is not compri-
fed. And yet who doubteth, that of al thinges and caufes Ecclefiaftical, this is abfolutelye the chiefeft? Yea
and who feeth not, that by the vertue of this Statute, the
Quenes Maiefty hath iudged, determined, and enacted a
new Religiõ contrary to the iudgement of all the Biffhops
and clergy (in the Conuocation reprefented) of her
highnes dominions? Yea and that by vertue of the fame
Authority, in the laft paliament the booke of Articles prefented and put vp there by the confent of the whole conuocation of the newe pretended clergy of the Realme,
and (one or ij. only excepted)of al the pretended Biffhops
alfo, was yet reiected and not fuffred to paffe?

 Agayne, preachinge the woorde, adminiftration
of the Sacramentes, binding and loofing, are they not
thinges and caufes mere Spirituall and Ecclefiafticall?
And howe then are they here by you omitted, Maifter
Horne? Or howe make you the Supreme gouernment
in al caufes to reft in the Quenes Maiefty, yf thefe caufes
haue no place there?

Which

THE FIRST BOOKE

Which is nowe better (I appeale to al good confciences)
plainly to maintayne the Truthe , then diffemblinglye to
vpholde a fallhood? Plainly to refufe the Othe fo
generallye conceyued , then generally to
fweare to it, beinge not generallye
meaned? But now let vs fee
how M . Horne wil di-
rect his proufes
to the fcope
appoin,
ted.

THE

THE SECOND BOOKE, DIS-
PROVING THE PRETENSED PRA-
ctise of Ecclesiastical gouernement in Em-
perours and Princes of the first.600.
yeares after Christ.

M. Horne. The. 28. Diuision. *pag.* 19. *b.*

Constantinus (of vvhose careful gouernmēt in Church causes, I haue spo-
ken somevvhat before) tooke vpon him, and did exercise the (.70.) supreme
rule and gouernement in repressing al maner Idolatrie and false Relligion,
in refourming and promoting the true religion, and in restreining and correcting al maner errours, (chismes, heresics,and other enormities,in or about
religion, and vvas moued herevnto of duety, euen by Gods vvorde,as he him
self reporteth in a vehemēt prayer, that he maketh vnto God, saiyng: I haue
takē vpō me and haue brought to passe helthful things (*meaning*
reformation of Religion.) being perswaded (*therevnto*) by thy word.
And publishing to all Churches,after the Councel at Nice,vvhat vvas there
done : he professeth that in his iudgement, the chiefest end and purpose of his
Imperial gouernement, ought to be the preseruation of true religiō,and god-
ly quietnes in al Churches. I haue iudged (*faith this godlye Emperoure*)
this ought before all other thinges to be the ende or purpose,
(wherevnto I should addresse my power and authority in gouernement)that the vnitie of faith,pure loue, and agreemēt of
religiō towardes the almighty God,might be kept, and mainteined amōgest al Congregations of the Catholique Churche.

The.70.
vntruth.
Constan-
tine in re
presing
Idolatry.
&c. exer-
cised no
Supreme
gouernes
ment in
Ecclesia-
stical mat
ters.
Eufe li.2
&. 3. De
vita Con-
stant.

The first Chapter. Of Constantine the Greate,and of his diuers
dealing in matters Ecclesiasticall.
Stapleton.

OW M. Horne beginneth to walke, though
not more truly,yet more orderly then before.
Now wil he bring inuincible proufs,taken frō
the Councels General and National, from the
Emperoures, from Kings, and finaliye from the continuall

Y   practise

A briefe
rehearſall
of M.
Hornes
diſcourſe
in his
prouf s
againſt.
M.Feck.

practiſe of Chriſtendome. In deede he beginneth here
with Conſtantinus the Emperoure, and runneth on from
Emperour to Emperour, with a continuall race, euen to
the late Maximilian, Graundfather and next predeceſſour
to Charles the fiſt. Then haue we about a ten Kings of
Spaine, and about twelue of France, and as many of England alſo : and that ſins the Conqueſte : with diuers other
Kings and Princes : yea he hath in his ſide, as he ſaith, Moſcouia, Græcia, Armenia, and Aethiopia. As for Councels, what Generall, what Prouinciall, he hathe made a
great mouſter of them, and hath them all redy to ſerue him
as he braggeth, at the leaſt one halfe hundred. Beſide all
theſe, he is armed and fenced euen with the Popes Canon
lawes, and with a number of Popes them ſelues. For the
reſidue of his Authors, they are in great plentie. But I can
not tell for what pollicy, whereas they driue the Catholiks
to ſix hundred yeares, and pinne vppe their proufes within
thoſe boundes, this man by ſome ſpeciall prerogatiue, by
like, and for ſome deepe conſideration vnknowen to mee,
and perchaunce to him ſelf too, buildeth moſte vpon thoſe
that were after the ſix hundred yeares, yea a greate number of them by one ſix hundred yeares later. And with
theſe proufes he cōmeth now continually forth on, whole
70. leaues. But now alas how ſhall poore M. Fekenham
abide the brunt of ſuch a ſtrong and a mighty force ? It ſemeth he muſt nedes be borne quite ouer. And ſurely ſo he
ſhould be, if they could ones hitte him. But thanked be

God ther is one hūdred miles betwen him ād their ſtrokes:
And as farre doth M. Horne ſtraggle from the very matter
he taketh in hand to proue. Wherfore, good Reader, I pray
the haue good eye and regard to the thing that ought to be
proued

proued by M. Horne and then fhalt thou plainely fee that
M. Fekenhã is out of al danger of this terrible armye, as that
commeth nothing nigh to him by many a faire mile. Let
vs now in Gods name beginne with Conftantine who cõmeth firft to hãd, whofe doings, good Reader, by M. Horne
here alleaged, for thy more eafe, and for the better vnderftanding of M. Hornes whole drift, I wil orderly digeft, and
fhortly difpofe by certaine Articles.

The. dif*
cufsing
of Con*
ftantines
doings.

The firft then is (for afwere to this prefent point) that Cõ-
ftãtine repreffed idolatry, ãd falfe fuperftitiõ of the Painims:
but this proueth no principality fuch as our plat fourme requireth. And of this we haue alfo faid fomwhat before.

1.

M. Horne,   The. 29. Diuifion.   fol. 20. a.

*He did not only abolifh al fuperftitions and falfe religions, vvhich had ben
amongft the Gentils, but alfo he repreffed (.71.) by his authority, lavves, and
decrees, al fuch herefies as fprong vp amõgft the Chriftiãs, fharply reprouing
and correcting, the authors or mainteinours of heretical doctrines, as the No-
natiãs, Valentinians, Paulianes, and Cataphrigians, as Eufebius faith of him.
And Theodoretus doth recite a part of an Epiftle, that Cõftantine vvrote vnto
the Nicomedians, vvherin the Emperor hath this faying: If we haue chaft
bifhops of right opiniõ, of curteous behauiour, we reioice. But
if any be enflamed rafhly and vnaduifedly, to cõtinue the memory and cõmendation of thofe peftilẽt Herefies, his foolhar-
dy prefumptiõ, fhal forthwith be corrected and kept vnder by
my correctiõ, which am Gods minifter. Conftantinus alfo gaue In-
iunctiõs to the chief minifter of the churches, that thei fhuld
make fpecial fupplicatiõ to God for him. He enioyneth al his
fubiects, that they fhould kepe holy certaine daies dedicated
to Chrift, and the Saturday. He gaue a lawe vnto the rulers of
the Nations, that they fhould celebrate the Sõday in like fort
after the appointment of the Emperour. And fo the daies dedicated to the memory of Martyrs ãd other feftiual times, &c.
And' al fuch things (faith Eufebius) were done according to the
ordinaunce of the Emperour.*

The. 71.
vntruth.
Conftan*
tine re*
preffed
not here*
fies by
his Su*
preme au
thorityc,
but by a
Superior
authoriti
of Bif*
fhops, cõ*
demning
before
fuch he*
refies.
Euf. li.3.
De vita
Cõftant.
Li.1.c.19.
Lib. 4. De
vit Cõft.

Y ij   He

*He commaunded Euſebius the Biſhop, to draw certaine Inſtructions and
leſſons, as it vvere domilies, forth of the holy Scriptures, that they might
be reade in the Churches. VVhich vvas done incontinente, according to the
Emperours commaundement.*

Stapleton.

Conſtantine, ſaith M. Horne, by his lawes repreſſed
the Nouatians, Valentinians, and other heretikes. And ſo
woulde he repreſſe you and your hereſies too, if he were
now liuing (as no Biſhops) *continuing the memory and commendation of peſtilent hereſies,* that I maye truely vſe your
owne phraſe : neither for al that ſhould he be any ſupreme
head of the Church. If Conſtantine, of his owne authoritie had firſt of all men, the matter of thoſe heretiques ſtanding in controuerſie, determined the ſame, and pronoūced
them as a Iudge, to be heretikes, then had ye ſaid ſomwhat
to the purpoſe. But now he found them by the Biſhops ād
the Church declared (before he was borne) for heretikes :
So therefore he toke them, and ſo therfore he made ſharpe

M. Horns
proufis re
turned
againſt
him.

lawes againſt them. So that this place proueth onely Conſtantine to haue put in executiō the decree of the Biſhops :
and ſo it ſerueth very well againſt you for the Supremacie
of the Biſhops in ſuch matters.

As doth the next alſo for the holy daies ye alleage dedi∗
cated to Chriſt, as Sonday and other : For theſe holy daies
the Emperour did not firſt ordeine , but they were ordey∗
ned to his hand of the Church , before he was Chriſtened.
Namely the Sōday, as it may appere by the Coūcel of Nice

Cap. vlt.

it ſelf. And he like a good Prince was careful by his Emperial authority, to cōfirme the ſame, that the people drawen
frō worldly buſines, to the deſire of heauenly things, might
fruitfully obſerue thē. So that not ōly the Sōday, for the honour

nour of Chriſtes Reſurrection, but alſo many other dayes
were dedicated to the memory of the Martyrs of whom ye
ſpeake, before Conſtantines time, as appeareth well by S·
Cyprian, Tertullian, and Origen And thinke ye if Conſtan-
ſtantine were now aliue, that he woulde well beare to ſee
the auciēt Martyrs feſtiual daies aboliſhed? or that his eares
would not glow for ſhame to heare, that it were a ſuperſtitious thing, to pray for al Chriſten ſoules, his own ſoule being praied for as ſone as he was deade, by the good and deuout people? which (as Euſebius writeth) did therein to him
an acceptable ſeruice: Alſo to heare, that it were plaine Idolatrie, to pray to any Sainte in heauen, him ſelfe building a
noble and a ſumptuous Church in the honour of the Apoſtles, thinking therby to doe a thing that ſhould be profitable and holſome for his ſoule : Vt precibus, quæ eo loci ad honorē Apoſtoloru̅ futuræ eſſent, dignus haberetur. That he might
be made (ſaith Euſebius) a worthy partaker of ſuch prayers
as ſhuld be there made for the honor of the ſaid Apoſtles?

But Sir, I pray you, let me demaund of you a queſtion. If
Conſtantine were ſo godly a Prince as ye make him to be,
how chanced it, he co̅mau̅ded to kepe holy the ſatterday ?
Whē and where I pray ye, throughout all Chriſtēdom can
you ſhew by al that euer you haue read, that it was kept an
ordinary holiday? I am ſure it was neuer ſo kept. And great
maruel it is to mee, that the ſatturday, being euen in the very Apoſtles time, and by them tranſlated into the Sōday, in
the honour of Chriſtes glorious reſurrection, and leaſt we
ſhould ſeme to be Iewiſh, and Cōſtantine him ſelf, being ſo
earneſt againſt them that kept the Eaſter day after the olde
faſhion of the Iewes, ſhould ſo ſodenly become him ſelf ſo
Iewiſh. This might haue ben a fitte cōſtitution to be made

Y iij   of

great.

Euſeb. li. 4
ca. 15.
Cyp. li. 3.
ep. 6. &
li. 4. ep. 5.
Tert. de
coron mi-
lit.
Orig. in il
lud Mat.
vox in
Rama.
Praying
for the
dead and
to Saints
vva in
Conſtan-
tines
time.
Euſe. li. 4.
De vita
Conſtant.
cap. 71.
Euſeb. lib.
eodem.
cap. 60.

Of the
Ievve of
Tevvkeſ‧
burie
See Fabiã
the. 43.
yeare of
Henrie
the third.

of ſome of the Iewes, that to preciſely and ſuperſtitiouſlie
alſo kept that day: as the Iew did in Englãd, at Tewkiſbury.
Who falling vpon the Satturday (as Fabian writeth) into a pri‧
uy, would not for reuerẽce of his ſaboth day, be plucked out. Wher‧
of hearing the Earle of Glouceſter, and thinking to do as much
reuerence to the Sõday, kept him there till the mõday at which
ceaſon he was found dead. It had ben, I ſay, a fitte ordinãce to
haue ben made of ſome Iew, very vnfit for ſo good ãd ver‧
tuous a Prince as was Cõſtantine. Yet notwithſtãding I am
the better cõtent to paſſe this ouer, and find no great faulte
with you, but with Muſculus, whoſe tranſlation beſide his
notable falſe corruptiõ, is but very ſecõdary. But foraſmuch
as the cõmon copies of the Greke, ſeme not very ſincere in
this place, I wil not very much charge you neither. And yet
I can not altogether diſcharge him, or you, if ye thinke ſo
ignorãtly and groſly as ye haue writen, that Cõſtantine cõ‧
maunded the Satturday to be holdẽ as an holiday. And be‧
cauſe I am entered into this matter, I ſhal ſhewe thee mine
aduiſe, good Reader, and that I ſuppoſe, for τὰς ſhoulde be
readen ταῖς, adding one Iota, and ſo may there be made a
good ſenſe thus: *Wherfore he admoniſhed all that were vn‧*
der the Romain Empire, that they ſhuld vpõ ſuch daies as were
dedicated to our Sauiour, reſt and kepe them holy, as the Satur‧
day was wont to be kept holy. In remembrãce as it ſemeth me,
of thoſe thigs that our ſauiour did vpõ thoſe dais. Wel let vs go
now to the next, ãd that is, that Cõſtantine cõmaũded Ho‧
melies to be drawẽ out. So did Charles the maine too, and
yet no man toke him, for ſupreme head therin. And would
God that your homly homelies, had none other nor worſe
doctrine, than thoſe that the ſaied Charles procured to be
made: Or the Homelies of our country man the venerable
Bede

Euſeb. De
vita Coſt.
lib. 4. c. 18
δ᾽ιο τοῖς
ὑπὸ τ̃ν
ῥωμαι‧
ῶν ἀρχὴν
πολιτευο‧
μένοις ἄ‧
πασι ϭχο
λὴν ἄγειν
ταῖς ἐπω
νύμοις τ̃
ϭωτῆρος
ἡμέρας
ἐνουθέτει
ὁμοίωςδὲ
κ̀ι τὰς τοῦ
ϭαββάτϭ
τιμᾶν. &c

Bede made a litle before Charles his time, ãd yet extãt, ãd in the Catholik church authorifed. I pray God your Homelies may be made ones conformable to the doctrine of their Homelies.   *The. 30. Diuifion. Fol. 21. b.*

VVhen the Emperour heard of the great fchifme moued betvvixt Arius ãd Alexãder the Bifhop of Alexandria, vvhervvith the Churche vvas pitiouflie tormẽted, ãd as it vvere rẽt in fonder, be(.72.) toke vpõ him, as one that had the care ãd authority ouer al, to fend Hofius a great learned and godly Bifhop of Spaine, to take order, and to appeace the cõtẽtion, vvriting to Alexãder and to Arius a graue and alfo a fharp letter, charging Alexander vvith vanity, Arius vvith vvãt of circũfpection, fhevving them both, that it vvas vnfemely for the one to moue fuche a queftion, and for the other to anfvvere therin, and vndifcreetly done of them both. And therfore cõmaunded them to ceafe of frõ fuch contentious difputatiõs, to agree betvvixt them felues, and to lay afide frõ thenceforth fuch vain, and trifling queftiõs. He pacified alfo the fchifm at Antioch begun about the chofing of their Bifhop, to vvhom for that purpofe he fent honorable Embaffadors vvith his letters to a great nũber of Bifhops that thã vvere at Antioch about that bufines, and to the people, exhorting thẽ to quietnes, and teaching thẽ (faith Eufebius) to ftudy after godlines, in a decẽt maner, declaring vnto the bifhops, as(73) one that had autority ouer them, euen in fuch maters, vvhat things apperteined and vvere femely for thẽ to do in fuch cafes, and noteth vnto them a directiõ, vvhich they fhould folovv. And after he had (faith Eufebius) geuẽ fuch things in cõmaundement vnto the Bifhops or chief minifters of the Churches, he exhorted them that they would do al things to the praife and furtherance of Gods word.   *Stapleton*

Here are two things: The one that Cõftantine fendeth his letters to Arius and the B. of Alexãdria, to pacify ãd appeafe the cõtention begun with Arius. The other that he labored to pacify an other fchifm at Antioch, about the chofing of the B. of Antioch. Neither of thefe draw any thing nigh to the new primacy ye would eftablifh. And fuch letters might any other good zealous mã haue fent to thẽ, beig ɲo Emperour. And as for elections in thofe dayes, not only

the

The. 72. vntruth, ioyned vith follye Suprem gouernmẽt in al caufes folovveth verye courfelye of fendig letters to appeafe contention.
Socrat. li. 1. cap. 7. Sozom. li. 1. c. 16. Euf. li. 3. de vita Cõftant. The 73. vntrath. This fact fhevveth no autthoririe ouer the Bifhops in maters Ecclefiaficall.

THE SECOND BOOKE

the Emperour, but the people alſo had ſome intereſt therin. Wherefore here is no colour of your ſupremacie. And therefore to helpe foreward the matter, and to vnderſhore and vnderproppe your ruinouſe building withall, ye interlace of your owne authoritie theſe wordes (*as one that had the care and authoritie ouer all*) which your author Socrates hath not, and likewiſe (*as one that had authoritie ouer them*) which Euſebius hath not.

And here by the way, I woulde aſke of you, for eache matter a queſtion. If theſe of Alexander and Arius, were vaine and triefling queſtions, as ye alleage, why doe ye call Arius his errour, *an horrible hereſie*? And why ſay yee their diſſention was about *a neceſſary article of the Faith*? I moue it for this, that hereby we may vnderſtād, as wel the great neceſsitie of Generall Councels, as the Supreme gouernment of cauſes Eccleſiaſticall, to haue remained in the Biſhops there aſſembled. For Conſtantine that tooke not at the beginning, theſe queſtions to be of ſo great importāce, after the determination of the Councel, tooke Arius to be a very obſtinate heretique: and his hereſie to be an horrible hereſie, as ye cal it. Concerning the ſecond, as we graunt the Prince had to doe with election, and yet not proprely with election, but with the allowinge and approbation of Spirituall mens election: ſo I demaund of you, what intereſt the people hath in either election or approbation nowe in England? Againe I demaund, whether in the auncient Church the Prince might (as he may in England) not onely nominate a perſon to be elected of the Deane ād Chapter, but if they doe not elect within certaine daies, miſerablye to wrappe them in a premunire? I make moſt ſure accōpt ye ſhal neuer be able, to ſhew this. See then that euen in

your

Pag. 22. col. 2.

VVhy Conſtantine cal leth thoſe matters triefiing queſtions which aſtervvard he tooke for hereſie.

A Nevv ſtraunge manner of electiō novv in England.

your election, which is beside and out of our chiefe matter, ye are quyte out from the like regiment ye pretende to proue.

M. Horne. The.31. Diuision. Pag.21.b.

This supreme (.74.) authority of the Emperour in Church causes is moste linely expressed by S. Augustine and Eusebius, vvhere they make mention of the horrible Scisme stirred by the Donatists, against Cecilianus Bishoppe of Carthage: vvhose election and ordering to be Bishop of Carthage, Donatus and others of his companions misliked, and therfore made a Schisme in that Church. The question in controuersie vvas, vvhether Cecilianus being ordered Bishop, hauing the imposition of hands by Felix, vvere lavvfully consecrated and ordered or not. This controuersie made a lamentable trouble amongest the Churches in Aphrike. at the length, the Donatists accused Cecilian vnto the Emperour: desired the Emperour to appointe some Delegates to iudge of this cötrouersy. And for that al the Churchs in Aphrike vvere bided, either to the one partly, or the other, and for that Fraüce vvas free frö this cötention, they require iudges to be appointed by his authority from amongest the Frenche Bishoppes. The Emperour much grieued, that the Churche vvas thus torne in sundre vvith this schisme, doth appoint Melciades *Bißhop of Rome, and* Marcus *to be his (.75.) delegates and commissaries in this controuersy, vvith certaine other Bishoppes of Fraunce,* Melciades *colleages or felovv Bishops, vvhom the Emperour had cömaunded to be there vvith thê for that purpose. These commissioners vvith certaine other Bishoppes according to the Emperours commaundement mette at Rome, and after due examination had, doe condemne the Donatists, and pronounce Cecilianus cause to be good. From this sentence of the bishop of Rome, and other bishoppes his colleages being the Emperours delegates, the Donatists appeale vnto the Emperour, not onely accusing Cecilianus, but also* Melciades *the bishop of Rome, and other Cömissaries. VVherefore the Emperour causeth a Synode to be had at* Arelatum, *committing the cause to the bishop thereof, and other bishoppes assembled there by his commaundement, to be herde and discussed. VVhereüto he calleth* Crestus *the bishop of Syracuse a City in Sicilie by his letters. VVherein he declareth in (.76.) plain termes, that it belongeth*

Z   *to his*

The 74. vntruth. No such supreme authority is either by S. Augstin or Eusebius expressed as that appeare. Aug epist. 50. et 48 Euseb. lib. 10. cap. 5. The 75. vntruth. Eusebius hath no such vvoords of delegates or cömissaries, but alleageth for his so doinge: σεβασμιωτατον νόμον, the most holy law that is, the lavve

of the Church, vvhich had ordayned bishops to be iudges in Churche matters. The 76. Vntruth. Constantin in those letters hath no such thing either in plaine termes or obscure. Only he expresseth a desire to haue the contention ended,

Aug u.epi-ſtol.166.

Augu.epi- ſtol.162.

Epiſt 156.

This he did . But this he re- pented af- ter.

to his imperial cure , to ſee theſe controuerſies in Church cauſes to be deter- mined and ended . *Donatus* and his companions , being condemned alſo by theſe biſhops, in the Synode at Arelatum , and *Cecilianus* cleered , doe a- gain appeale vnto the Emperour from their ſentence, beſeching him to take the hearing and diſcuſſing of the cōtrouerſie. VVho calleth both the parties to- gether before himſelf at *Millayn*, and after he had herde the vvhole matter, and vvhat vvas to be ſaid on both ſides, * he gaue final ſentēce vvith *Cecilia- nus* , condemning the Donatiſts. VVho after al theſe things thus done , as S. *Auguſtin* ſaith, made a very ſharpe Lavv againſt the Donatiſtes, the vvhich alſo his Sonnes after him commaunded to be obſerued.

The . 2. Chapter of Conſtantines dealing in the appeales and ſuytes of the Donatiſtes .

Stapleton.

Of Con- ſtantines iudgemēt in the cauſe of Cecilian.

OF al that M. Horn bringeth of Conſtantines doings, or of any others this place ſemeth moſt cōformable, (not to that wherein we ioyn iſſue with him: which are a nomber of pointes, as I haue declared: in the proufe whereof in caſe M. Horn be defectyue in any one, M. Fe- kenham is at liberty from receiuinge the pretenſed othe:) but to that one point onely, that not the Biſhop or Pope himſelf, but the ciuil magiſtrate is, ſupreme iudge in cauſes eccleſiaſtical. And yet yf M. Horn could effectually proue this, he ſhould quyte him ſelf lyke a clerke . In dede your maiſter M. Caluin, M. Iewel, and others runneth to this ex- ample as to a ſtrong hold, which I trow neuertheleſſe wil

Artic. 4. fol. 105.& ſequent.

proue anon as ſtronge as a rotten rede . As alſo to any in- different Reader it may ſufficiently appeare , that hath or wil reade our Return vpon M. Iewels lying Reply, where this whole matter is anſwered at ful. Yet let vs ones againe lay forth the matter.

Con-

Conftantine,fay you,in a matter ecclefiaftical deuolued
to him by an appele *appointed as his Delegate the Pope him
felfe* , yea after the Popes fentence he appointed ,. vppon a
new appeale certain other Bifhhops.The appellants being
alfo agreued with this fentence,craued ayde at Conftanti-
tins own hands,who gaue the final fentence againft them.
Suerly thefe were froward quarreling men , what fo euer
they were.But what maner of men were they M. Horne?
Forfothe as ye truely fay, *the Donatifts* ,the moft peruerfe
and obftinate heretiks that euer the Churche fuffred.Is this
then,thinke you, a fure grounde to build your fupremacy
vpon? Suerly as fure,and as fownd,as was your Emperour
Emanuel,as ye call him. Befide this,where is the longe tedioufe fong, ye fonge of late againft M.Fekeham to proue
him a Donatifte? Ye fee here the Donatifts them felues a-
gainft the authority of temporal princes in Churche matters,which before ye denied:and fo may M.Fekenhã clere
himfelf, that he is no Donatifte . Ye had done wel, yf ye
had eafed your reader and your felf moft of all , with an
hãdfome worde or two interlaced,for the auoiding of this
contradiction . Wel belyke it was by fome voluntarie ob-
liuiõ forflone. I wil therfore take the paynes to fupplie this
defect of yours.I fay therfore that both is true.For when it
ferued their purpofe,and as lõg as they had any hope of any
relefe for their wicked herefies , they ranne to the Emperors, yea to Iulian the Apoftata, fetting him forth with no
fmal cõmendations , for ayde and helpe . And fo did they
now. But afterward when both this Conftantin and other
Emperors made fharp lawes againft thẽ,thẽ the world was
chaunged,then fang they a new fonge:*that it was not fitte
or feamely for the princes to bufie thẽfelues in Church matters.*

(marginal notes:) M.Horne buildeth his fupremacy vpon the doings of Donatifts — M.F.purged by M.Horne him felfe to be no Donatift. — The maruelous inconftãcy of the Donatifts

Yea ſo impudent and inconſtant they were, that thowghe
themſelues firſt browght the matter againſt Cecilian to
the Emperours audience,yet did they blame innocent Cecilian for their own faƈt,as a breaker of the Eccleſiaſticall
order.And are not your maiſters and côpanions I beſeache
you the true ſchollers of the Donatiſts in this behalfe, as I
haue before ſhewed ? And who are they , tell me by your
truth,that after ſentence geuen againſt them by the Pope,
by prouincial and general councels,yea by the Emperours
them ſelues,doe perſiſte and endure in their wicked hereſies,and that more wilfully then euer did the obſtinat Donatiſts?Are they not of your own whole and holy generation?Wel ſeing we haue now deliuered you from contra-
diƈtion,we may procede to the matter it ſelfe.

Ye ſay Conſtantine gaue ſentence euen after the Pope.
Yea but we ſay again(ſuppoſing this example true)that one
ſwallowe brigeth not the ſpring tyme with him.The preſident of one Emperor(for ye proue not the like in al your
book of any other)cá not enforce a general rule,nor make
a continual praƈtiſe of the Church : which is your ſpeciall
ſcope euer by you to be regarded.And ye ſhould haue regarded here(yf ye haue any regarde at al) the circumſtances of the matter.The Donatiſts were waxen very thycke
and great in Aphrik,yea to the nomber almoſt of.300. biſ-
ſhops.Their bands,their faƈtion were ſo great,their cruelty
vpô the Catholiks was ſo enormouſe,their obſtinat deſpe-
ratiô was ſuch,fearing no má, nor no puniſhmét, yea moſt
wickedly murtherig their own ſelues in great multitudes,
that the godly and wiſe prince Conſtantin,to mollifie their
fury,and by gentlenes and yelding to them to winne them,
fared with thé, as many good princes fare and beare with
the

The cir-
cûſtances
of Con-
ſtantines
iudgemét
in Ceciliás
cauſe
vvcighed

the people being in their rage, graunting them many thigs, greate
otherwife not to be graunted, for the fhonning of a greater
myfcheif: And euen fo did this good prince condefcende
to the Donatifts, partly cōmittig this caufe after the Popes
Sentence to other bifhops, partly taking it into his owne
hands: (both which was more then he ought to haue don,
as we fhal anon fee.) For al this he did not as one that toke
him felf (as ye dreame, and as (the more pity) appeales goe
in our cōtrey at the Arches and other where) for the lawful and ordinary iudge in caufes Ecclefiaftical. Which thig
wifely and godly confidering Melchiades the Pope with
other bifhops, to recouer the Donatifts, and to take away
al maner of quarelings from thē, and to reftore the Church
to her former vnity, fo miferably and pitifully by them ren-
ted and torne a fonder, did patiently beare with Conftan-
tyne: As a wife man would doe with the Mariners, yf in a
great huge tempefte, they goe fomwhat out of their common courfe, to faue their fhip, themfelues and al the other.
And as in the polytyke body: fo in the fpirituall body: the
magiftrats relent and winke at many things in fuch hurlye
burlye: and the lawes and canons, which otherwife fhould
take their force, be for fuch a tyme, nothing or fleightlye
exacted.

VVhy fomtime both ciuil lavves ād Ecclefia- ftical are vvinked and def- fembled at Nice Cōc. Can. 8.

For example, the canons of Nice forbidde, *that at one
tyme two bifshoppes fhoulde be with lyke authority in one fee:*
Now to go no further then our own Melchiades, and your
Donatifts: After the faid Melchiades had condemned the
Donatifts, he offered thē, yf they would repent and incor-
porate thē felues again to the vnity of the Catholik Chuch
from the which, by a fhameful fchifme they had difmem-
bred them felues, not onely his letters that they call com-

Z iij   munica-

Aug.epiſt.
50.et 162

municatorye , by the which they ſhoulde be counted
through out the worlde Catholikes : but alſo , whereas
by reaſon of this horrible diuiſion , in many places , were
in one ſee two biſſhops , the one a Catholike , the other a
Donatiſte, that he ſhould be confirmed , that was firſt ordeyned: and that the other ſhould be prouided of an other
biſſhoprike.And here by the way you ſee Melchiades and
not Conſtantines ſupremacy.

A notable
ſtory con
cerning
the Aphri
can biſ-
ſhops.
Auguſt.de
geſtis cū
Emerito.

Yea,which is more notable the caſe ſtanding in Aphrik,
that as I ſaid in many places two biſſhops ſate in one ſee together,of thre hundred Catholik Biſſhoppes aſſembled in a
Councel in the ſayde Aphrike , they were all,ſauing two,
(and yet thoſe two relented afterwarde too) contente to
geue ouer their biſſhopricks , to the ſaide Donatiſts , yf
they would return to the Church.And yet the Nicene canons were to the contrarye.Nowe I pray you M.Horne,
yf ye had bene then as Melchiades was, what would your
wiſedome haue done ? would you haue ſtepped forth and
haue ſaid to Conſtantine , that he vſurped an other mans
office?that he had nothing to doe in thoſe matters?and that
the matter being ons heard by him, it could not be deuolued into any other cowrte? and ſo not onely haue exaſpe-
rated the indurate and obſtinat Donatiſts,but alſo the good
and godly prince,lately conuerted to the faith,and by this
admonition thowgh trewe , yet out of ceaſon haſard all?

Nay, Nay, ye wil ſay,for al this Melchiades was but a
mere delegate to Conſtantin , who lawfully and orderlye
proceded in this caſe as owre prince doth now in like:and
that this is but my pretty ſhifte , and ye will put me to my
proufes . But I hadde thowght you your ſelfe would haue
proued hī a mere delegate, (ſeing you ſpeak it ſo perépto-
relye)

rely)and that nothing was don here extraordinarily. But I
fee wel you wil allwaies obiect as your brethern doe, not
caring what hath bene anfwered to the obiection already,
like as fimple logicioners in fcholes, when their argument
is preuented, haue no fhifte to inuente an other, or to
reply vpon the former folution, but doe fadly repete the
fame.To you therefore M. Horne,as before to M. Iewel,
I anfwer.The places by your felf alleaged and quoted doe
confounde you,and that in two places, brought out of S.
Auguftine. For firft in one of the epiftles that ye alleage,
S.Auguftyne doth reproue and rebuke the Donatifts, for
that they brought the matter to the Emperours confiftory:*and* faith *they fhould haue firft of all brought the matter to*
the bifshops beyonde the feas(he meaneth fpecially the Pope)
and faith further *that Conftantin himfelf, did more orderlye,*
when he refufed to heare the matter. Then in an other
epiftle alfo by you cited, he fayeth, *that the principalitye*
of the Apoftolike Chaire hath euermore bene in force in the
Roman Church. And now further concerning this appellation, he faith *that there was no neade why that the matter*
fhould haue bene heard again, after iudgemente geuen by Mel-
chiades. But yet Conftantine procured the matter to be
heard again at Arles,*relenting*(faieth S. Auguftin)*to the Do-*
natifts obftinacy,ād laborīg by al meanes to reftrain their great
*outragious impudency.*Now concerning Conftantin,that he
euē for the cōfideratiōs aforefaid,heard their caufe himfelf:
S.Auguftin faith,of him,*that he minded to afke pardō there-*
*of of the holy bifhops.*Wherby moft euidently appereth,that
al this his doing was extraordinary, and not to be drawen
into an vfuall example : or to be preiudiciall to the Ecclefiafticall power, and muche lyke to the fufferance of

It is pro-
ued by
tvvo pla-
ces alleae
ged by
M. Horn
that Cō-
ftantine
vvas no
lavvful
Iudge in
Cecilians
caufe.
Augu epi-
ftol.48.
Augu.epi-
ftol.162.

*A fanctis
antiftiti-
bus poftea
veniam
petiturus.*

Quene

Quene Mary, who for a tyme ſuffred her ſelf to be writen
and called the ſupreme head, thowgh ſhe miſliked the title,
and at the day of her Coronation openly reproued the
preacher for calling her ſo. And our gracioule Quene now
vſeth not that tytle by thoſe preciſe words. And I woulde
fayne know of you M. Horne, yf ye be ſo cunning, why
the name onely is ſhifted, the thing remayning one and the
verye ſelf ſame as before. Thanks now be geuen vnto God,
that hath ſo mercifullye wrowght with vs, that he hath
cauſed you, in the cheifeſt matter that ſeemeth of your ſide
in al your booke, by your owne author, your owne places
voluntarily by you, and for you layde forthe, to deſtroye
your own doctrine, and vtterly to ouerthrowe your ſelfe.
Perchaunce you are now angrie with your ſelfe, for this
miſhappe and ouerſight, and wil not ſtyck ſhortly (as ſome
of you beginne alredy pretely) to reiecte euen S. Auguſtin
himſelf, as a ſuſpect man, and partial in Church and biſhoply matters, him ſelf being a biſhop alſo. This rhetoryke I
feare me wil one day burſte out againſt him, and other as
good and as auncient as he: as it buddeth hanſomly alredy.
And yf it chaunce ſo to doe, we wil prouide for our ſelues:
and in this point, furniſhe our ſelues, with ſuch a witneſſe
as I thinke for ſhame you dare not deny, and yet for very
ſhame his teſtimony againſt you, ye may not abyde. That is
Conſtantine him ſelfe: who ſayd to the Donatiſtes, and ſo
withal to you their ſchollers in this point for this their ap-

Opta. li. 1.
M Horns
primacy
condem-
ned by
Côſtátine
hiu ſelf.
pellation. *O rabida furoris audatia: ſicut in cauſis gentilium
ſolet, appellationem interpoſuerunt.* O furioſe and madde
boldnes they appeale vnto me, as they were panyms and
and heathens. Howe lyke yow this M. Horne? Where is
now your like regiment, when Conſtantine himſelfe, for
this

this your defperat raging appeales, maketh you not muche better than a Pagan and an Heathen? Who fhal *clappe you on the backe now, and fay Patrifas*? Who is he now that is *fo like the Donatifts, as though he had fpit him out of his mouth?* What would he haue faid, and howe would he haue cried out if he liued now, or rather how woulde he haue pitied Britanie his owne natiue Countrie (as our Chronicles reporte) for this kinde of regiment, befide all other to many caufes of pitie and forowe, to beholde?

Now for a furpluffage M. Horne, to end this your greateft matter withal, fo oft, fo facingly, and fo fondly alleaged of all your brethren, I muft tell you, ye put not the cafe altogether right : Ye abufe your Readers. The principal matter was not, whether Cecilian was laufully cõfecrated, this was but a coincident, and a matter dependant. The princi-pal matter was, whether *Felix* (of whome Cecilian was in dede ordeined) were a *traitour*, as they then called fuch as in the time of perfequution, deliuered to the handes of the Infidels, the holy Bible to be burnt. This was *Queftio facti, non iuris* : as the Lawyers fay. And fuch as a laye man may heare wel inough. The other was coincident and acceffo-rie. And in fuch cafes the Lawyers fay, that a lay man may at leaftwife incidently heare and determine a caufe Eccle-fiafticall. Thefe and many other things mo, that might here be faid, doe mollifie and extenuate Conftantines faulte , if there were anye : and howe fo euer it be, this is ones fure, that your owne authorities doe quite ouerbeare you , and proue the Popes Primacie.

M. Horne. The. 32. Diuifion. pag. 21, b.

Athanafius alfo that mofte godly Bifhoppe, being ouer muche wronged in the Councell at Tyre, did flee and appeale from the iudgemente of that

A A *Synode*

Marginal notes:

The Great

Hovv like M. Horne is to the Dona-tifts. M. Horne in the. 12. folio.

Traditor.

Alciat. l. nõ plures Cod. de fa-crof. eccle-fiis.

The 77.
vntruth.
This was
no ap-
peale
of Atha-
nasius,as
shall ap-
peare.
Socr.li.t
cap 34
Theod li.
2 cap 28
The -3.
vntruth.
That
vvas no
Synod at
all, but
Negotiũ
Impera-
toriũm,
An impe
riall or
Courtlye
triall, as
Athana
sius cal
leth it
The.79
vntruth.
No suche
vvordes
in Atha
nasius.
Athanaf.
Apol 2.
fo'.91,
& 93.

(.77.) *Synod vnto Constantine the Emperour, declaring vnto him his griefes, beseeching him to take the hearing of the matter before him selfe : vvhiche the Emperour assented vnto, vvritinge vnto the Synode assembled at Tyre, commaunding them vvithout delaie to come vnto his Courte,* and there to declare before mee (*saith this most Christian Emperour*) vvhome ye shall not denie to be Gods sincere minister, how sincerely and rightly ye haue iudged in your Synod. VVhen this Synod vvas assembled at Tyre, the Catholique Bishops of Egypt, vvrote vnto the honorable Flauius Dionysius vvhom the Emperour had made his Lieutenaunte, to see all things vvell ordered in that Councell, and did desire him, that he vvould reserue the examination and (78)iudgemēt to the Emperor him self: yea they doe adiure him that he doe not meddle vvith their matter, but referre the iudgement thereof to the Empefour, who they knewe well, would iudge rightly according (.79.) to the right order of the Churche.

The third Chapter : Of Constantines Dealing in the cause of Athanasius.

Stapleton.

THIS obiection of Athanasius his appeale(as you call it) to Constantine, is a common obiection to all your brethren, and hath ben vsed namely of M. Iewell in his lying Replie in the fourth Article more then ones. For the which(if I listed to follow the fond vain of M. Nowel) I might call you M. Horne, a seely borower of your fellowes Argumēts,&c. But to leaue that peuish toy to boies, of whom M. Nowel in the time of his Scholemaistershippe may wel seme to haue learned it, ād to answere briefly the whole mater, first I refer you to my former āswer made to M. Iew. in my Returne, &c. in the fourth Article. And now for a surplussage, I say with Athanasius himself (who knew this whole mater better I trow, then you or M. Iewel) that this which you call a *Councell and a Synod at Tyre ,* from the
iudges

iudgement of which *Synod you* say *Athanasius appealed* non *to Constantine,* referring the whole matter to his hearinge, this, I say, was no Synod or Councell at all. For of this very assemblie of the Arrian Bishops at Tyre, where they accused Athanasius before the honourable Flauius Dionysius, the Emperours Lieutenaunt there, of grieuouse crimes, as of killing Arsenius, who then yet liued, and of a facte of his Priest Macharius, for ouerthrowinge of an Aulter, and breakig of a Chalice, of this assembly, I say, thus doth a holy Synod of Catholique Bishops and Priestes gathered together at Alexandria, out of Egypt, Thebais, Lybia, and Pentapolis, pronounce and affirme, as Athanasius in his secod Apologie (the booke by your selfe here alleged) recordeth. *Praeclari Eusebiani, quo veritatem scriptáque sua obliterent,* Athanas. in Apol. 2 *nomen Synodi suis actis praetexunt, quum res ipsa negotium Imperatorium, non Synodale haberi debeat. Quippe vbi Comes praesideat, & milites Episcopos suo satellitio cingant; & Imperatoria edicta quos ipsi volunt coire compellant.* These ioly Eusebians (these were Arrians) to the intent they may blotte out the truth, and their owne writings, doe pretéd to their owne doings the name of a Synode, whereas the matter it selfe ought to be counted an Imperiall mater, not the matter of any Councell or Synod. Loe Maister Horne, you with the Arrians, wil haue this to be a Synod: but we with the Catholique Bishhoppes of Egypt, Thebais, Lybia, and Pentapolis, and with Athanasius him selfe, denye flattelye it was any Synod at all, but onely *Negocium Imperatorium,* a matter Imperiall, a ciuile matter, a laie or temporal controuersie. I truste we with the Catholique Bishhoppes, and namely with Athanasius, shal haue more credit herein, then you M. Horne, and Maister Iewell, with the Arrians.

But

But why doe thofe Catholike Bifhops deny this matter to
be any Synodall or Councell matter? *Quippe vbi. &c.*
As in which matter (fay they)*the Countie*, the Emperours
Lieutenaunt, *was prefident, and fouldiours clofed the Biffhops
round about, and the Emperours proclamations compelled fuch
to mete as them lifted.*Behold M. Horne, for this very caufe
that the Emperour and his Lieutenaunt bore the chief rule,
therefore I fay, did thofe Catholike Bifhops accompte this
matter to be no Synod at al.   See I pray you M. Horne :
Homo homini quantum intereft, ftulto intelligens. See howe
farre fquare and extreme different your opinion is from the
iudgement of the Catholike Fathers and Bifihops fo many

*Aboue
12.hūdret
yeares.

* hundred yeares paft. You M. Horne and your fellowes,
will haue al Synods and Councels to be called, ordered, directed, gouerned, confirmed, approued and wholy gouer-

M. Horne
clean cō
trary to
the Catho
like Bif-
fhops of
the Pri-
mitiue
Churche

ned of the Price and his officers. And without the Princes
authority, cōmifsion, order, directiō, cōfirmation, and royal
affent, you wil haue no Synodes or Councelles of Bifhops
to auaile, or to haue force. Contrarywife, thefe Catholike
Bifhops in the Eaft Church, do for this very caufe reproue
and reiect the Affembly of certaine Bifhops, for no Synode
at al, becaufe al was there done by the authoritie, order, direction, and power of the Princes Lieutenaunt. And they
doe make a plaine diftinction betwene *Negotium Imperiale*,
and *Synodale*, betwene an Imperiall matter, and a Synodall
matter: as who fhoulde faye, If the Emperour beare all the
ftroke, it is no Synod, nor fo to be called.

Therefore thefe Catholique Fathers fay againe, in the
fame place within few lines after : *Si velut Epifcopi fefe Iu-*

Athana-
fius ibidē.

*dices volebāt effe, quid opus erat vel Comite, vel militibus, aut
edictis ad coeundum imperialibus ?* If thefe fellowes would
be

be them felues Iudges as Bifhops, what neded them to haue
either the Countie, or the fouldiars, or any Imperial Edicts
to make them affemble? As who would fay : In the Bifhoply iudgement, in the Synode of bifhops, it is not meete eyther to be fummoned by the Prince, or to haue his Lieutenaunt prefent, or to haue his gard of Souldiars. Thefe matters become the temporal Court, and the Ciuile Confifto-
rie, where by force of fubiection, lawes do procede. They
become not the Synods of Bifhoppes, where with quiet of
minde, with godly deliberation, freely and franckly, without feare or partialitie, Gods matters ought to be treated,
difcuffed, and concluded.

　Therefore againe thefe Catholik Fathers doe fay of this
Arrian Conuenticle at Tyrus: *Qua fronte talem conuent um,* Athana-
fius ibid.
Synodum appellare audent, cui Comes præfedit ? With what
face dare they call fuch an affemblye, by the name of a Synode, ouer the which the County was prefident? And yet
will yow M. Horne, that the ciuill Magiftrate fhall be the
prefident and Supreme gouernour, in and ouer al Synodes?
Maye not a man nowe clappe yow on the backe, and faye,
Patrifas, Arrianifas? And that yow are as like to the curfed
Arrians, as if Arrius him felf had fpet you out of his mouth?
Thofe Fathers cry yet againe vnto you and fay: *Quæ fpecies* Ibidem.
ibi Synodi, vbi vel cades, vel exiliũ, fi Cæfari placuiffet, cõftitue-
bitur? What face of any Synod was there, where at the
Emperours pleafure, either death or banifhmēt was decreed? This cõuenticle therefore at Tyrus was no Synod. Neither could therfore Athanafius appeale from any Synod to
the Emperoure. But that which Athanafius then did, and
which yow vntruely call an Appeale from the Synod, was
only a cõplaint to the godly Emperour Conftātine, againfte
　　　　　　　AA　iiij　　　　　　the

the vniufte violences of the honourable (as you call him)
Flauius Dionyfius: wherein alfo thofe Catholique Fathers
aboue mentioned, fhall witnefle with mee againft you.

For thus they write: *Quum nihil culpæ in comminiftro noftro Athanafio reperirent, Coméfque fumma vi imminens plu-
ra contra Athanafium moliretur, Epifcopus comitis violenti-
am fugiens, ad religiofifsimum Imperatorem afcendit, deprecãs
& iniquitatem hominis & aduerfariorum calumnias, peftulãf-
que vt legitima Epifcoporum Synodus indiceretur, aut ipfe au-
diret fuam defenfionem.* Wheras they could find no fault
in our fellowe Priefte Athanafius, and the Countye by
force and violence wrought many things againft Athanafius, the Bifhoppe declining the violence of the Countie,
went vp to the moft religious Emperor, complaining both
of the iniurious dealing of the Lieutenant, and of the flanders of his Aduerfaries, and requiring that a laufull Synode
of Bifhops might be called, or els that th'Emperour would
heare him to fpeake for him felfe. By thefe woordes we
see, that Athanafius appealed not from any Synodicall fentence of bifhops to the Emperour, as a Superiour Iudge in
Synodicall matters, but from the violence and iniuries of
the Lieutenaunt, to his Lord and Maifter, the Emperoure
him felf for to haue iuftice and audiéce, not in any mater of
Religion or controuerfie of the faith, but in a matter of fe-
lony laid to his charge, as the murder of a man, and an outrage committed by one of his Prieftes in a Churche. For
the which his aduerfaries fought his death. And yet when
they came before the Emperour, they chaunged their action, and pleaded no more vpon the murder, which was foũd
to be fo euident a lye (Arfenius being brought forth aliue,
before the benche, when they accufed Athanafius of his
death)

VVhat
maner of
Appeale
Athana-
fius made
to Con-
ftantine
the Em-
perour.

death neither vpō theChalice brokē,that being alſo a very
ridiculous ād a plain forged mater,but tney pleaded a newe
actiō of ſtoppig the paſſage of corne frō Alexādria to Conſtātinople,ād accuſed hī as an enemie to the Imperial court
and City.For proufwherof,the Arriās brought in falſe witneſſes, and periures. But yet the Emperour(as they write) *Athanaſ.*
moued with pitie,*ſatis habebat pro morte exilium irrogare:* *Apol.2.*
thought it enough in ſtede of death,tò baniſh him.Whiche *pag.364.*
he did at the importune ſuite and clamoures of the Arrian *Socrates*
biſhoppes,*forquietnes and vnities ſake in the church.*   But *lib.1.c.27*
Theodor.
afterward in his death bed the Emperour repentinge him, *li.1.ca.32*
commaunded Athanaſius to be reſtored to his Biſhoprickè a-
gaine,though Euſebius the Arrianthen preſent,laboured much
*to the contrary.*In al this, there was no Eccleſiaſtical or ſpiritual matter,but mere Ciuile matters in hand.

Neither was it any Eccleſiatical matter,that *the Catho-*
like Biſhops of Egypt (as you alleage.M. Horne.)*deſired and*
adiured Flauius Dionyſius the foreſaied Countie to reſerue the
examination and iudgement of, to the Emperour him ſelf. But
the matter was ſuche as we haue before rehearſed, matters
and actions mere Ciuile. Namely they adiured that iniurious and partiall Magiſtrate , the foreſayed Countie , not
to proceede farder againſt their Patriarche,then ſo grieuo-
ſlie attainted, but to referre the whole matter to the moſt
Religious Emperoure , where they doubted not to finde
more fauoure.   *Apud quem* (ſay they) *licebit & iura Ec-*
cleſie, & noſtra proponere.   Before whome we maye put *Vide Apol.*
foorth bothe the rightes of the Churche, and our owne. *2.Athan.*
Meaninge that by his clemencye , they mighte be ſuffe- *fol.427.*
Impreſſ.
red to procede in that matter among them ſelues orderly *Baſil. An.*
as the righte of the Churche and of the Canons required: *1564.*

not (as

not (as M. Horne falfely tranflateth it) *that the Emperour
Would iudge according to the right order of the Church.* There
are no fuch wordes in the letters of the Catholike Bifhops
of Aegipt alleaged by M. Horne. Otherwife,to feke any
iudgement of Churche matters, at the Emperours handes,
be you bolde M. Horne,no man knewe better then Athanafius him felfe,that he could not doe it. For it is Athanafius,M. Horne, that being reftored,as I haue faid,by Conftantines laft wil and Teftament,and after againe the fecód
time banifhed vnder the Arrian Emperour Conftantius,by
the meanes alfo of thofe Arrian Bifhops, appealed to Pope
Iulius, as his competent and ordinarye Iudge, and was by
him reftored to his Bifhoprike , together with many other
Bifhops of the Eaft, Paulus of Conftantinople, Afclepas of
Gaza, Marcellus of Ancyra, Lucius of Adrianople , with
many other, appealing then likewife to Pope Iulius. It is
Athanafius that faith : *When was it heard from the creation
of the worlde, that the iudgement of the Church fhoulde take
his authoritie from the Emperour?* And what coulde that
learned Father faye more directlye againfte you and your
whole booke M. Horne? Verely either that moft learned and auncient Father, whom the moft famous Fathers
of al Chriftendome haue alwaies from time to time reuerenced and honoured as a moft glorious light and a fingular piller of Gods Church, eitherthat mofte excellent Bif-
fhop, I fay, in whofe praife euen out of the teftimonies only of the beft writers a iuft Treatife might be gathered, did
fouly erre and miffe of the truth:either you M. Horne,and
your fellowes are in a great errour,and do defend an exceding abfurditie,damnable both to you and all that followe
you, forfwearing your felues by booke Othe , when yee

Sozom.
lib.3.c.8.
Tripart.
li.4.c.15.
Athanaf.
Apol.2.
Athanaf.
in epift.ad
folitar.vi-
agentes.
pag.459.

Athana-
fius and
M.Horne
of a clean
contrary
iudge-
ment.

fweare

swere, that in conscience you beleue, which you ought
not ones so much as to thinke. For see yet what this Notable Bishop pronounceth against you. It is Athanasius that
saieth it. *If this be the iudgement of bishops, what hath the* *Athana-*
Emperour to doe with it? Els if Cæsars threates conclude these *sius vbi*
matters, to what purpose haue men the Names of Bishoppes? *supra: pa-*
Contrarywise say you, M. Horne. It is *a principal part of the* *gina eadē*
Princes royall power, to haue the supreme gouernement in *Fol. 3 b.*
al maner causes Ecclesiastical or Spiritual.

O Barbarous heresye from the creation of the worlde
neuer heard of before. O Antichristian presumption. I say,
Antichristian presumption: I lerne of that most constant
bishop Athanasius so to say. For it is he that saieth these
woordes. *What hath Constantius omitted, that is not the* *Athanasi-*
parte of an Antichrist? Or what can he, when he cometh, doe *us in epist.*
more? Or howe shall not Antichrist at his coming finde a *vt supra*
ready way prepared for him of this Emperour to deceiue men? *pag. 470.*
For nowe againe in stede of the Ecclesiastical iudgement, he ap-
pointeth his palace to be the benche for Ecclesiasticall causes to
be hearde at. Seq, earum litium summum principem et Au-
thorem facit. And he maketh himself the Supreme gouernour and chief doer of those controuersies: he speaketh of
ecclesiastical. Now M. Horne, not our Gracious Soueraigne, of her owne desire taketh vppon her such gouernment: but you most miserable clawebackes, and wretched *In decer-*
flatterers do force her Grace to take that Title, the taking *nendo prī-*
and practising whereof by the assured verdyt of this most *cipē se fa-*
lerned Father, is a plaine Antichristian presumption. For *cere episco*
loe what he saieth yet agayne in the same page. *Who is it,* *porum: &*
that seing the Emperour to make him selfe the Prince of bis *præsidere*
shops in decreeing of matters, and to be president ouer Eccle- *Iudicijs ec*
B B *siasticall* *clesiasticis*

clesiasticall iudgements may not worthely say, that this Emperour is the very abhomination of the desolation, which was
foretolde by Daniel?See and beholde M. Horn, what a most
horrible absurdity you labour in your booke to persuade:
See to what an extreme inconuenience you force mens
consciences, when you tendre them the Othe, comprising
the same and more, which here Athanasius accompteth
the practise of Antichrist. Se last of all what traytours you
are to God and your Prince, which haue persuaded her
most Gracious highnes to take vpon her such kinde of gouernment which is a preparation to Antichrist, and resem-
bleth the abhomination of desolation foretolde by Daniel.
And thus much your own Author Athanasius. You see
how wel he speaketh for you.

Now that you alleage out of Socrates that Constantin
Socrat. li.
2. Cap. 28.
threatened Athanasius *he should be brought, whether he
would or no,*it auaunceth nothing the Authority of Constantine in Ecclesiasticall matters. For so much manye a
Prince doth to him, that lawfully called to a Councel will
not come, at the Churches commaundement. Wherein
he is rather a Ministerial then a principall doer. Neither
doth the place by you alleaged out of Socrates, proue that
Constantine examined and iudged the doings of the whole
Councell, but onely whether they had proceded against
Athanasius of enmity, or malice:And as Socrates there wri
Socrat. li.
2. cap. 34.
teth,*Constantin sayde, the suyte of Athanasius was, that in
his presence he might (being driuen thereto by necessyty) complaine of such iniuries as he had suffred.* And it appereth by
Theodoretus by you alleaged in the said first booke, that
the determination and definition of these matters rested
in the Bishops, the execution in the Prince.For the labour
of Con-

of Conſtantine with Athanaſius then was , onelye that he
woulde appeare before a Synode of Biſhoppes , which
had accuſed him diuerſlye before the Emperour , and of
thoſe Biſhoppes be tryed . Which the Emperour did , as
Theodoret writeth, ϖισϑεὶς ὡς ἱερεῦσι. Beleuing the accu- *Theod. lib.*
ſers of Athanaſius as Prieſtes , and thinkinge their accuſa- *1.cap. 28.*
tions to be true . ϖαυ̃ʼ ἅπασι γ̀ ἢϑυόει̃ʼα τυρευόμενα. For he
was vtterly ignorant of their deceytes and craftly dealinges , ſaieth Theodoret. Thus he iudged not him ſelfe o-
uer Athanaſius, but only procured,that to kepe peace in the
Churche , the biſhops might aſſemble together , and trye
their own matter among them ſelues.

M. Horne. The.33, Diuiſion. Pag.22,a.

There were no Churche mattiers, or Eccleſiaſtical cauſes , wherein the The 80.
continual practiſe of the Churche of Chriſte, in this Emperours tyme, yea and vntruth:
many hundreth yeeres after, did not attribute the (.80.)ſupreme rule, order, boldly as
and authority vnto Emperours and Kinges, vpon whome(.81.)al Churche uouched,
mattiers did depende, as witneſſeth Socrates , who ſheweth this reaſon of but no
that he doth thoroughout his Eccleſiaſticall Hiſtory mention ſo much the vvaye
Emperours.Becauſe that of the Emperors(ſaith he) after they be- The 81.
ganne to be Chriſtians,the Churche matters doe depende, yea vntruth.
the greateſt Councels haue bene, and are called together, ac- Socrates
cording to their appointment. *Euſebius commendeth the great boun-* belied, as
tiſulnes of Conſtantine towvardes all eſtates , But, (*ſaith he*) this Em- ſhal ap
perour had a ſingular care ouer Goddes Churche , for as one *In proæm.*
appointed of God to be a common or vniuerſail Biſhop , he *lib.5.*
called Synodes or conuocations of Goddes miniſters toge- *Lib. 1. De*
ther into one place, that thereby he might appeace the conté- *vit. Conſt.*
tious ſtriuinges that were amonge them in ſundry places . He
diſdayned not to be preſent with thé in their Synodes, and to
fit in the middeſt of thé, as it had been a meaner perſonage, có-
mending

mǝnding and approuing thoſe that bente them ſelues of good
meaning to godly vnity, and ſhewed him ſelfto miſlike on
the other ſide,and to ſet naught by ſuch , as were of contrary
diſpoſition.

Stapleton.

The general aſſertion that M.Horne here auoucheth,
that in Conſtantynes tyme , the continuall practiſe of the
Churche attributed in al Eccleſiaſtical cauſes the ſupreme
rule to Emperours , is but a great vntruthe boldly auouched , but no maner of way yet proued , as hath bene declared, nor hereafter to be proued , as it ſhall by Gods
grace appeare. Againe that he ſaieth : *All Churche matters did depende of the Emperours,* and for witneſſe thereof
alleageth Socrates, is an other no leſſe vntruthe alſo. For
this prety ſyllable, *All*, is altogether M. Hornes , and not
Socrates , pretely by him ſhifted in,to helpe forwarde a
naughty matter . The very text alleaged by M . Horne,
hath not that worde,nor ſpeaketh not ſo generally . But it
is no rare matter with men of M.Hornes brotherhood,to
ouerreache their Authours , and therefore the leſſe to be
wondered at,though not the leſſe to be borne with. And
to this place of Socrates I haue before anſwered in my
Returne againſt M . Iewel . That which foloweth out of
Euſebius , proueth M . Hornes purpoſe neuer a deale.
Except M . Horne thinke ſome waight to lye in thoſe
words,where the Emperour is called *a Common or Vniuerſall Biſhop*:as though we ſhoulde gather thereby, that the
Emperour was then , as the Pope is nowe , and hath allwaies bene.Except theſe woordes helpe M . Hornes primacy , nothing is there that wil helpe it, reade and conſider

*Socrates
ĩ proœmio
lib 5.*

*Art. 4.
Fol. 139.*

fider the place who lifteth. But as for thefe woordes what
fenfe they beare, no man better then Conftantine him
felfe by the report of the fame Eufebius alfo, can tell vs.
Conftantin in dede was called of Eufebius *as a comm̄õ bif-*
*fhop,*that is, as a common ouerfeer, by reafon of his pafsing
zele and fingular diligence in furdering Gods true Religion. But that he exercifed therein no fuch fupreme go -
uernement as M.Horne fancyeth, neither made him felfe
bifſhop of bifſhoppes, but ftayed him felfe within the limites and boundes of his owne Iurifdiction, it appeareth
manifeftly by thefe his woordes fpoken to a great number
of bifſhoppes, as Eufebius recordeth it in his own hearing
to haue bene faid. *I am alfo*, faith the Emperour,*a bifhop.*
Ἀλλὰ ὑμεῖς μὲν τῶ ἔισω τῆ ἐκκηλσίας, ἐγὼ δὲ τῶ ἔκ τ Θ. ὑπὸ
Θεοῦ καθιςάμεν Θ.,ἐπίσκοπ Θ. ἄν ἔιην. *But you are bifshoppes*
(or ouerfeers) of thofe thinges that are within the Churche.
But I being by God fette ouer thofe thinges that are without
the Church,am alfo as it were a bifshop,or ouerfeer. Marke
wel thefe words M. Horne. Your allegation auoucheth
not the Emperor abfolutely to be a bifſhop: but οἷα τίς κοινὸς
ἐπίσκοπ Θ. ἐκ Θεοῦ καθιςάμενος. *Appointed of God as a certain*
*cōmō bifshop.*that is, refembling for his great zeale to Gods
Church, the very office and perfon of a bifſhop. But here
the Emperour diftinctly expreffeth the true bifſhops office
and vocation to be different from his own office and calling. He confeffeth, I fay, expreffely, that the bifſhoppes are
appointed of God to be the Rulers, ouerfeers and directers
of thofe things that are within the Church, that is, that doe
concerne the gouernment of fpiritual caufes, and matters
mere ecclefiaftical. But him felfe he acknowledgeth to be
ordayned of God ouer thofe things that are without the

BB iij   Church,

διὰ τίς κοι-
νὸς ἐπί-
σκοπος.
Lib.1.ca.
37.de vita
Conſtant.

Lib.4.ca
24.de vit.
Conſtant.

Churche , as of wordly and ciuil matters ouer the which
he being the Emperour was the ſupreme gouernour , and
in that reſpect he thought he might after a ſorte call him
ſelf alſo a biſhop, which ſoundeth, an Ouerſeer, Ruler, and
Guyder of ſuch things as are to his charge committed. And
verily after the paterne and example of this Noble firſt
Chriſtian Emperour, firſt I ſay that opély profeſſed and defended the ſame, it may wel be thought, the words ſpoken
to Chriſtian Princes at their Coronatiō time, haue ben cōceiued and vſed. The which alſo , that the Reader may ſee
how diſtinct ād differét in dede the vocatiōs are of Prices
and Biſſhops, and yet how in ſome ſorte thei both are biſſhops, that is Ouerſeers of Gods people, as Cōſtantine profeſſed hī ſelf to be, I wil here inſert the very words vſually
reherſed to Princes at their coronatiō time by the biſhops
annointing them. Theſe are the words. *Accipe Coronā regni*
tui, quæ licet ab indignis, epiſcoporum tamē manibus, capiti tuo
imponitur, In nomine Patris, & Filÿ, & Spiritus Sancti: Quam
ſanctitatis gloriā, & honorē, & opus fortitudinis intelligas ſig-
nificare, & per hanc te participē miniſterÿ noſtri non ignores.
Ita vt ſicut nos in interioribus Paſtores, rectoreſq, animarum
intelligimur, ita & tu contra omnes aduerſitates, eccleſiæ Chri-
ſti defenſor aſsiſtas , regniģ, tibi à Deo dati : &c . Take the
Crowne of your kingdom, which is put vpon your heade
by the handes of biſſhops, though vnworthy , in the name
of the Father, the Sonne, and the Holy Ghoſt. The which
Crown you muſt vnderſtand, doth ſignify the glory ād honour of Godlynes, and the worke of Fortitude: By this alſo vnderſtād, that you are partakener of our Miniſtery . So
that, as we are knowē to be the paſtours and gouerners of
mens ſoules in matters internal , ſo you alſo ſhoulde aſsiſte

Vide Pon-
tificale im-
preſſum Ve-
netiis An.
1520.

25 2

as a defendour of the Church of Chriſt, and of the kingdom
geué to you by God, againſt al aduerſites. You ſee here M.
Horne, that as in the words of king Ioſaphat in the old law,
and of Cōſtantin the firſt Chriſtiā Emperour, ſo to this day
in the Coronatiō of al Chriſtē Princes there is made a plain
diſtinctiō betwene the Empeꝛours or Princes Oſſice, and
the Office, charge and cōmiſsion of a biſhop, cōmiſsiō I ſay
cōmitted to him not of the Prince, but of God. And dare
you then to cōfound thē? Or dare you for ſhame M. Horne
make the world beleue, that Cōſtantin bore himſelfe for a
Supreme Gouernour in al cauſes eccleſiaſtical or ſpiritual,
when he him ſelf in plain woordes confeſſeth, that of ſpiritual or Eccleſiaſtical matters the biſhops are of God (not
of him) appointed the Rulers and ouerſeers, but he hath of
God cōmitted vnto him the Charge and rule of thoſe matters that are out of the Church, that are in dede no Church
matters, but matters of policy, matters of ciuil gouerment,
matters of this world, and cōcerning this preſent life only?

The 82.
vntruth.
That vvil
neuer ap-
peare in
the order
of this
Councel.
The 83.
vntruth.
Not M.
Fekenhā
but M.
Hornes
opiniō is
cleerelye
condem-
ned by
the agree
ment of
theſe 318.
Fathers.

M. Horne. The 34. Diuiſion. Pag. 21. a.

The Eccleſiaſtical hiſtories make mention of many Synodes or councelles,
called or aſſembled at the appointment and order of this Emperour. But the
moſt famous and notable, vvas the Nicene Councel: about the vvhich, con-
ſider and marke, vvhat vvas the occaſion, by vvhoſe authority it vvas ſum-
moned and called together, and vvhat vvas the doings of the Emperour
from the beginning vnto the diſſolution thereof: and yee ſhal ſee plainely as
in a Glaſſe, that by the order and practiſe of the Catholik Church, notified in
the order of this general Councel, the (.82) ſupreme gouernment in Eccle-
ſiaſtical cauſes, is in the Emperor and and ciuil Magiſtrates, and your (83.)
opinion condemned by the vniforme agreement of. 318. of the moſt Catholik
Biſhops in the vvorlde, commending, and allovving for moſt godly, vvhat ſo
euer the Emperour did in, or about this councel. The occaſion of this famous
and moſt godly councell, vvas the great diſſention kindled, partly about a
neceſſarie Article of our beliefe, partly about a ceremony of the Churche.

Arius

Arrius incensed vvith ambitious enuie, against Alexander his bishop at A-
lexandria, vvho disputed in one of his lessons or treatises, more subtily of the
diuinity than aduisedly, as the Emperour layeth to his chardge, quarreled
Sophistically against him, and mainteined an horrible Heresie. Besides this,
the Churches vvere also diuided amongest them selues, about the order or ceremony of keeping the Easterday. The Emperour sent Hosius vvith his letters,
as I say, before, into the Easte parties to appeace the furious dissentiō about
both these matters, and to reconcile the parties dissentiug . But vvhen this
duetiful seruice of the Emperour, tooke not that effect vvhich he vvished and
hoped for, then as Sozomenus vvriteth, he summoned a councel to be holden
at Nice in Bythinia, and vvrote to al the chief Ministers of the Churches eue
ry vvhere, (.84.) commaunding thē that they should not fayle to bee there
at the day appointed. The selfe same also doth Theodoretus affirme, both tou
ching the occasion, and also the summons made by the Emperour . Eusebius
also vvriting the life of Constantine, shevveth vvith vvhat carefulnes , the
godly Emperour endeuoured to quenche these fiers. And vvhen the Emperour
(saieth Eusebius) savve that he preuailed nothing by sending of Hosius vvith
his letters, Considering this matter with him self, said, that this
warre against the obscure enemy troubling the Church, must
be vanquished by an other (meaning him selfe.) Therefore, as the
capitaines of Goddes army, towards his voayge , he gathered
together a Synode œcumenical, and he called the Bishops together by his honorable letters, and that they should hasten
them selues from euery place. These things, touching the occasion and
calling of this general counsaile by the Emperour, are affirmed to be true
also, by Nicephorus the Ecclesiastical historian . Yea , the vvhole counsaile
in their letters, to the Churches in Aegipt, and the East partes , doe testifie
the same Synode, to be called by the Emperour, saying: The great and holy Synode, was gathered together at Nice, by the grace of God,
and the most religious Emperour Constantine, &c.

Lib.1.c.17
The 84.
vntruth
There ap
peareth
in Sozo-
mene no
such im-
perial cō-
maunde-
ment, but
only that
he called
them to
mete at a
day.
Lib.1 c.7.
Lib. 3. De
vit. Const.
Lib.8, c.14
Theod, lib.
1, cap. 9.

The. 4. Chapter: Of Constantin the Emperour his dealing in the Nicene Councel, and with Arius after the Councell.

Staple-

Stapleton.

MAifter Horne here entreth to a greate matter, and maketh large promifes both to proue his principall purpofe effectually, and to confounde M. Fekēham manifeftly. But he wil I trowe, when he hath al fayed, be as farre from them both, as if he had helde his peace. Firft to proue a Supreme gouernment in Conftantin, he telleth vs that Conftantine fummoned the great Councel at Nice in Bithynia: but if he had fet in out of Ruffinus, *Ex Sacerdotū Sententia*: by the wil, minde, and confent of the Priefts, that is, of the bifhops: then had he marred all his matter: and therefore wilily he lefte it out. If he had added alfo out of Theodoret (whome he alleageth to proue that the Empe- rour fummoned this Coūcel) why and wherefore the Em- perour would be prefent at the Councel him felf, this ima- gined Primacy that Maifter Horne fo depely dreameth of, would haue appeared a very dreame in dede. *The Emperor Was prefent* (faith Theodoret) *bothe defirous to beholde the Number of the Bifhops, and alfo coueting to procure vnyty a- mong them.* Thefe and fuch like caufes doe the Ecclefia- ftical hiftories alleage. But for any fupreme gouernment that the Emperour fhould practife there, as namelye that his Royall affent was neceffary to confirme the Coūcell, or that without it Arius had not bene cōdemned, and that he iudged the herefie or any fuch matter, as you now M. Horne doe attribute to the Prince, hauing your whole re- ligion only by the Princes Authority enacted and confir- med, for any fuch matter I fay, neither in this Councel nor in any other doe the Auncient hiftories recorde fo much as one word. Your new Religion M. Horne, hath fet vp a new kinde of gouernment fuch as al the Chriftian worlde

Ruf. lib. 1. cap. 1. hift. ecclefiaft.

Theodore- tus lib. 1. ca. 7. hift. ecclefiaft.

C C　　　neuer

neuer knewe nor hearde of before.

Nowe that you ſay , *the occaſion of this famous and moſt godly Councel was the diſſenſion partly about a neceſſary Article of our beliefe , partly about a ceremony of the Churche,* which ceremony you ſay after, was, *of keeping the Eaſter-daye* yf it be ſo as you ſay (as it is moſt truely) what ſaye you to your owne Apologie that ſaieth , that the vſuall keeping of Eaſter daye is , *a matter of ſmall weight,* and to your greate Antiquary Bale, that ſaieth *it is but a ceremony of Hypocrites?* Suerly Conſtantin made a greater accompte of this vniforme obſeruation then ſo, ſeeing that it was the ſeconde chiefe cauſe that cauſed him to ſummon this *famous , and moſt godly Councell* as your ſelfe calleth it. Seing alſo that he maketh them not much better then Iewes that priuately in his time kept Eaſter daye otherwiſe, then Rome, Afrik, Italy, Aegypte, Spaigne, Fraunce, Grece, Brittanny , and many other greate countries that he him ſelfe reakoneth vppe . And here by the way falleth out in M. Iewel a lye or two, ſaying that our Countre. 700. yeres together kept their Paſchal daye with the Grecians otherwiſe then we doe nowe . Ye ſee I haue abridged. 300. yeares and a halfe at the leſt . For Conſtantin wrote theſe wordes ſtraight after the Nicene Councell ended, which was kept in the yere of our Lorde. 328.

In Centu. De ſcript. eccleſiaſt.

Euſeb. li. 3 cap. 18. de vit. Conſt.

M. Horne. The. 35. Diuiſion. Pag. 23. a.

The Biſhoppes (*as I ſaid before*) vvhen they thought them ſelues, or their Churche iniuried by others, vvere vvont to appeale and flie vnto the Emperour, as the (. 85.) ſupreme gouernour in al matters, and cauſes Temporall, or Spirituall , the vvhiche appeareth moſte playne, to be the practiſe of the Churche, by theſe Biſhops called vnto the Nicene counſaill. For vvhen they came to Nice , ſuppoſing them ſelues to haue nevve good oportunity , beyng nighe

The 85. vntruth, euer auouched, but neuer proued.

nighe vnto the Emperour, to reuenge their * priuate quarelles, and to haue redreſſe at the Emperours handes, of ſuche iniuries as they thought thẽ ſelues to ſuſteyne at others by ſhops handes, eche of them gaue vnto the Emperour, a Libell of accuſations, ſignifying vvhat vvronges he had ſuſteyned of his fellovve Biſhopes, and prayed ayde and redreſſe by his iudgemẽt. The Emperour forſeyng that theſe pryuate quarelings, if they vvere not by ſome policy, and vvyſe deuiſe ſequeſtred, and layd aſide, vvould muche hynder the common cauſe, tooke deliberatiõ, appointing a day, againſt the vvhich they ſhuld be in a readines, and commaunded them to prepare and bring vnto him all their libelles and quarelling accuſations, one againſt another: (Mark by the vvay, the craft and practiſe of Sathan, to ſlay and ouerthrovv good purpoſes, that euen the godly fathers and Biſhoppes, vvanted not their great infirmities, preferring their ovvn priuate trifles, before the vveighty cauſes of Gods Churche. And the vviſdome, zeale, and humblenes, of his moſte Chriſtian Emperour, vvho ſo litle eſtemed his ovvn honour, and authority, that he vvold rather ſeeme to be inferiour, or for the time no more than equal vvith his ſubiectes, to the ende, he might by his humbling of him ſelfe, aduance and exalt Gods glory, to the edifying and quietnes of his Churche.) The day came (vvhiche vvas the day before the firſt Seſſion ſhould be in the councel, as Socrates ſaith) the Biſhoppes did not ſleape their ovvne matters, but had their billes in a readines, and deliuered them vnto the Emperour. This vigilant nourſefather vnto Gods Churche, had cared and deuiſed ſo diligently for the common çauſe, as the Biſhoppes had done for their priuate quarelles: and therefore, vvhen he had receiued their Libelles, verye (.86.) politiquelye, ſaieth: (bicauſe he vvoulde irritate none of them for that tyme,) That the day of general iudgement ſhoulde be a fitte time for theſe accuſations, and Chriſt the Iudge, then vvould iudge al men: As for me (.87.) it is not leaſull to take vpon me (.88.) the iugement of (.89.) ſuche Prieſtes, accuſed, and accuſing one an other. Vvhereunto, neuertheles, he added this priuy nippe, to pynche them vvithal. For of al other thinges ((ſaith he) this is leaſt ſeemely, that Biſhoppes ſhoulde ſhevve themſelues ſuche, as ought to be iudged of others. And ſo cauſed the Libelles to be caſt into the fire, giuing them an earneſt exhortation to peace and quietneſſe.

* Being priuat quarels, theicould be no eccleſiaſtical matters touching religion, vvhich is euer commõ. Sozom.li. 1.cap.17. Li.1,ca.8.

The 86. vntruth. He did it religiouſly, not politiquely. The 87.88 and 89. vntruths, Sozomenes text in three places falſified. Sozom.li. 1.cap.17. Theod.lib. 1 cap.7.

Stapleton.

It is a worlde to fee the fingular logicke, and depe reafoning of M.Horne, that can of fuch flender premiffes inferre fuch mighty conclufions. *For the Emperour to be the*
Supreme Gouernour in all matters or caufes temporall or fpiri-
tuall, it appereth moft plain(faieth he) *to be the practife of the*
Church by thefe Bifshops called vnto the Nicene Councel. Anfwere firft M.Horne. How could this pofsiblye be a practife of the Churche, that neuer before was vfed in the
Churche ? Except you wil fay, that euen heathen princes
may be your Supreme gouernours in al caufes Ecclefiaftical. You knowe before this Conftantine there was neuer
Chriftian Emperour, to whome bifhoppes might put vp
their complaintes as to their Supreme gouernour, onelye
Philip excepted. Who is neuer read, euer to haue medled
with the left matter or caufe Ecclefiafticall, but liued rather like a clofe Chriftian, being afearde to difpleafe the
Romain Legions, who then were in maner al heathens, and
who(as the worlde then wente) bore al the ftroke in electing of the Emperour, and in the continuance alfo of him.
Eufeb.lib. Contrarywife, that he was fubiect to the Bifhops, it appe-
6.cap.27. reth wel by the doing of Pope Fabian, fhutting him out at
an Eafter tyme, from the number of cõmunicants, becaufe
he fticked to confeffe his finnes, as other Chriftians did.
Anfwere therefore firft to this, howe you auouche that for
a practife which was or coulde neuer be vfed ? Wel lette
this goe for an other vntruthe.

Now let vs heare howe ioylely you wil proue, that the
318.Fathers of the Nicene Councel, doe condemne M.Fe-
kenhams opinion, which before you promifed to doe. The
caufe is to your feeming, that certain Bifhops accufed one
the

the other before the Emperour Conſtantine. But how can **great.**
this be a good motiue for you M. Horn, to pronounce him
therefore a *Supreme Gouernour in all cauſes temporal and ſpi-*
rituai , ſeing it dothe not appere what thoſe cauſes were,
which the biſhops did put vp vnto him ? They might be,
and ſo it is moſt likely they were, cauſes temporal . Verily
your ſelfe confeſſeth, they were *priuat quarrels :* and ſo no
matter of faith and religiō, (of which can growe no priuat
quarrels, but cōmō cōtrouerſies) but as it may ſeme, it was
ſome priuat cōtétiō betwene neighbour ād neighbour (for
at that time euery town had bis biſhops, yea many meane
Villages alſo) concerning the limites and boundes of their
poſſeſsions, or ſuch like mattter , which is a matter plaine
temporall.   Beſide this they were not al at diſſention but
certaine , and perchaunce very fewe: how is then M. Fekenham condemned by 318. Biſhops of Nice? I ſee you wil
play ſmal game, rather then ye wil ſit out. I wil now bring
you for M. Feketham, and for the Popes ſupremacy, no ſuch
trieflinge toyes and foliſhe gheaſſes : but a ſubſtantial au- **Athanaſ.**
thour Athanaſius him ſelf, that reciteth out of Pope Iulius
epiſtle, that this famous and moſte godly ſynode decreed: **Apol,2.**
that no biſhop ſhould be depoſed , onleſſe the Pope were firſt
thereof aduertiſed: and that nothing owght to be determined
in Councel, but that he ſhould be thereof made priuye before.
But why doe I craue ayde againſt you of this Councell, **M. Horne**
ſeing your own example plainlye deſtroyeth your imagi- **cōuicted**
ned Primacy, in that Conſtantine anſwereth to theſe quar- **by his**
reling biſhops, *that it was not lawful for hī to be their Iudge?* **owne**
Which ſentence of his being ſo plaine , you more groſſlye **example**
then truely or politykely would elude, as thowgh Conſtā- **of Cōſtā-**
tin meant no ſuch matter, but politykely ſpake this becauſe **rines dos**
                    C C iij   he would **ing:s.**

he would not irritate them , or leafte by priuate quarrels the weighty caufe of the faith in hand fhould be hindred. Such gay glofes that deftroy the text, may you by your extrauagant Authority make at your pleafure . But the fentéce of Sozomene only laied forth, fhal both difcouer your baftard glofe , and open alfo your vntrue handling of his text. For Conftantine refufing to iudge of the bifhoppes complaintes, calling them firft (as Ruffinus at large reherfeth) *Goddes, and fuch as ought to iudge ouer him, not to be iudged of him, or of any men at al, but of God only* , he addeth and faieth as Sozomenus your alleaged Author reporteth . As for me , ἀνϑϱώπῳ ὄνϳι, *being a man* (which woordes you guilfully left out) *it is not lawfull to take vpon me* ⸤οιαύτην ἀκϱόασιν, fuch *iudgement* not *the iudgemēt*:as you abfolutely but vntruly turn it:For ftraight he expoūdeth what maner of iudgement it is not lawful for hī to take vpō him: adding immediatly ἱεϱίων κα⸤ηγοϱούντων κỉ κα⸤ηϛοϱουμένων *whē prieſts are parties plaintifs and defendants*, not *of fuch Prieſtes &c.* as you, now the third tyme in one fentence, moft lewdely and liyengly doe tranflate it. Thefe woordes therefore of Conftantine, thus fpoken to the Bifhoppes, were not *politikely* (as you glofe Maifter Horne) but religioufly and reuerentlye deuifed , as to whome in plaine woordes he faid : *Deus vos conſtituit Sacerdotes , & poteſtatem vobis dedit de nobis quoque iudicandi , & ideo à vobis rectè iudicamur. Vos autem non poteſtis ab hominibus iudicari* . God hath appointed you Prieftes: And hath geuen you power, to iudge ouer vs alfo : And therefore we are orderly iudged of you. But you can not be iudged of men . Here by the waye, Maifter Horne: The beft, the nobleft, and the wyfeft Emperour that euer Chriftendome had, confefleth
the

Ruffin. lib. 1. c. 2. hiſt. ſuæ eccleſiaſt.

Sozom. li. 1. cap. 17.

Three vn truthes of M Horn. in tranfla ting of one greke fentenſe. *Ruffin. lib. 1. cap. 2.*

the Bisshoppes his superioures and iudges : Shewe you
where euer any wise or good Bisshop so flatly agnised the
Emperour his superiour or Iudge in matters of Religion.

Nowe that this facte of Constantine proceded not of
policie, but of reuerence : beholde, howe this example
was interpreted afterward aboue a thousand yeares past,
both of Emperours and of Bisshops . Martianus that ver- Concil.
tuouse Emperour protested openly in the Councell of Chalcedō.
Chalcedon, that he was present there, *after the example of* Act.1.
Constantine, not to shew his power, but to confirme his faith.
And Saint Gregorie putting Mauritius the Emperoure
(who in a chafe had called him foole) in mynde of the duety he owed to Gods ministers, rippeth vp to him particularlye this verye fact of Constantine, refusing to iudge
vpon the bishopes complayntes &c. and addeth in the end Gregor.li.
as an ἐπιφώνημα, these woordes . *In qua tamen sententia pie* 4. epist.31
Domine, sibi magis ex humilitate, quàm illis aliquid præstitit
ex reuerentia impensa. In which sentence yet (my good
Lorde) Constantyne more profited him self by humilitie,
then he did the Bishopes, by the reuerence he shewed
them.

It was saieth Saint Gregorye, *Reuerentia impensa*, a reuerence shewed to the bishopes, that Constantine would
not iudge ouer their complaintes : It was *politikelye* done,
saieth. M. Horne. Such a politike prelate hath Winchester
diocese of him. Verely of that notable See with such prelates lately beautified, and now of this man so contaminated, we may say as Cicero saied of Pompey the greate his
palace possessed of Anthonie that Infamous Rybalde .
O domus antiqua, q̃ dispari Domino dominaris ? For with the In Phil.2.
                                                     like

like ſincerity doe you through the whole booke procede, ſometyme flatly belying, ſomtyme nypping their ſenten-ces, but wel nere continually concealing the circumſtan-ces and whole effect of your alleaged Authours, as we ſhal in the proceſſe ſee .

M. Horne. The.36.Diuiſion. Pag.23.b

The next day after, they aſſembled at the Emperours palayce, he com-maunded them to goe into the Councel houſe, to conſult of the matter, (the coũcel houſe vvas vvithin Themperors pallayce,trimly furniſhed vvith ſeates, aptly ordred for ſuch purpoſe,as it vvere in rovves.) They entred in,and vvay-ted vvithout any doings,til the commiug of the Emperour, vvhoſe ſeat vvas of gold, placed at the firſt beginning of the rovves:(.90.) vvho being entred and placed in his ſeate,maketh an oration vnto them,declaring the conten-tiõs ſprõg vp amõgeſt them ſelues,to be the occaſion vvherefore he called thẽ together:and the ende is(ſaith he)that this diſeaſe might be hea-led through my miniſtery. After this he maketh an earneſt exhorta-tion,mouing them to quietnes, forgiuing one an other, for Chriſt comm a-undeth(ſaith he)that vvho vvil receiue pardon at his hande, ſhal alſo for-giue his brethern. After this moſt graue exhortation to vnity,and concorde, in truth,he geueth them (.91.)leaue to conſult of the matters in hande,pre-ſcribeth vnto them a(.92.)rule,vvhereby they muſt meaſure, trie,and diſ-cuſſe theſe,and(.93.)al other ſuch diſputations, and controuerſies, in mat-ters of religion,to vvitte, Sanctiſsimi ſpiritus doctrinam præſcrip-tam,The doctrine of the moſt holy ſpirit before writen . For (ſaieth he)the bookes of the Euangeliſtes, and of the Apoſtles and alſo the Prophecies of the olde Prophetes, doe euidently teache vs of Gods meaning. VVherefore laying a ſyde al diſ-corde of enemity,let vs take the explications of our queſtiõs, out of the ſayings of the holy Ghoſt. VVhen the parties vvaxed vvarme in the diſputations,and the contention, ſomvvhat ſharpe, then the Emperour, as a vviſe moderatour,and ruler, vvoulde diſcourage none, but myldely caulmed ſuch as he ſavv ouer haſty vvith mi'de vvoordes, coolinge their heate:and commended ſuch as reaſoned deeply vvith grauity.

Stapleton.

In all this talke is naught els but a heape of vntruthes, ād
vaine gheaſſes , nothing to the principall purpoſe materiall : which will well appeare in a more open declaration
of that, which you haue patchedly and obſcurely ſhewed,
as it were, a farre of to your Reader, concealing (as your
maner is) all that any thing concerneth the Biſhops authoritie in thoſe matters. Firſt then you tell vs out of Euſebius, that Conſtantine in the Councell of Nice, *ſate in a ſeat*
of golde, placed at the firſt beginning of the rowes. But you
leaue out *Modica,* a ſmall ſeate, or as Theodoret alſo calleth
it, θϵόνϛ σμικροί Τϵ̀ν] Θ̱ ϕ̓ μέσῳ : ſitting in the middeſt in a
low ſeate : You conceale alſo that whiche Euſebius your
alleaged author in that very place addeth : *Non prius in ea*
ſedit, quàm annuiſſent Epiſcopi: He ſate not downe before the
Biſhops had geauen him leaue. For ſo importeth the word
ἐπιτρέψαι : vſed by Euſebius and Theodoret alſo. Which
declareth very well the Biſhops ſuperioritie in the Councell, where matters of faithe were to be treated. Nowe
where you adde out of Theodoret , that the Emperoure
ſhould *geue the Biſhops leaue to conſult. &c.* Theodoret in
the place alleaged hath no ſuch wordes. You imagine, by
like, the Biſhops had of the Emperoure ſuche a licence as
your Engliſh Statutes require . *That the Conuocation ſhall*
make no Eccleſiaſticall lawe without the Kings conſent. No,
No. Conſtantine demeaned not him ſelfe ſo ſtately. You
haue heard what his behauiour was, and ſhal heare yet farder, by your next vntruth, which is this. You ſay, th'Emperour *preſcribed them a rule whereby they ſhoulde meaſure,*
trye, and diſcuſſe, theſe and all other ſuch diſputations &c. But
you ſay it vntruely. For immediately after the wordes by

D D   you

Euſeb. li.
3. cap. 10.
de vita
Conſtant.
Theodor.
li. 1. c. 7.

you alleaged, to shew therby the Emperours rule and prescription. Theodoret addeth : *These things and such like he
vttered as a naturall louing child, to the Priestes, as to his Fathers.* If Children prescribe rules to their Fathers when
they geue them good counsail , then did also Constantine
here prescribe a rule to the Bishops. But if so to say, is more
then childish, consider M. Horne how like a babe ye haue
reasoned against the authority of such blessed Fathers, the
Fathers of that most holy and learned Councell.

Verely S. Ambrose, who knew, I trow, better what was
done in the Nicene Councel then M. Horne doth, and is of
somewhat more credite too , reporteth farre otherwise of
Costantines doings, then M. Horne counterfeiteth. Thus he
Ambros.
Lib. 5.
Epist. 32. saith:And I pray you M. Horne, marke his saiyng wel. *Si cō-*
ferendū de fide, saderdotum debet esse ista collatio: sicut factū est
sub Cōstantino Augustæ memoriæ principe, qui nullas leges antè
præmisit, sed liberum dedit iudiciū sacerdotibus. If conferéce
must be had of the faith, this cóference ought to be kept of
Priests: as it was done in the time of Cōstantine a Prince of
noble memory:who(whē cōtrouersy of the faith spróg vp)
did not before prescribe any lawes, but left to the Priestes
the free iudgemēt and determination. Yet saith M. Horne,
that Cōstantine *prescribed to the Bishops, a rule wherby they*
should measure, trye and discusse the controuersie in hande.
Wherin obserue diligently (gentle Reader) that S. Ambrose
is direct contrary to M. Horne, not only touching this particular fact of Constantine (the one saiyng that he prescribed before hand no lawes at all, but left to the Bishops the
triall of the controuersie free, the other auouching that he
prescribed a rule to trie and discusse the matter by) but also
touching the whole estate of the question betwene M.
Horne

Horne and M. Fekenham here. For S. Ambrofe wil haue cell.
the conference and trial of the faith to appertain to Priefts
chiefly and onely.   For thefe wordes he fpake againft the
yong Valentinian, who being feduced in his minoritie, as
our late Soueraine King Edwarde was, would haue the
matter of faith to be tried in Palaice before him and his
benche, as matters of faithe are nowe in the Parliamente
concluded.   Contrarywife M. Horne will haue the fupreme iudgement of matters of faith to reft in the Prince,
and all thinges meafured by that rule and fquare that the
Prince prefcribeth.   You fee howe the iudgement of the
Auncient Fathers, accordeth with the opinion of vpftarte
Proteftants.

   But will you knowe, M. Horne, what Conftantine intendeth in that his exhortation made to the Billhoppes ?
He findeth fault, and worthelye, with fuche as were faultye for their diuifion and diffention in Relligion, and doth
referre them to holye Scripture, that dothe euidentlye inftructe vs of Gods minde.   But (wherein your liegerde-
maine burfteth out) you fhufle in of your owne this fyllable *All*. a pretye knacke, I promife you, to fwete your
anfweare withall.   It is true, that we muft meafure and
difcuffe our controuerfies by Scripture, and neuer refolue
againft Scripture : So where there is no plaine Scripture, Traditiõs
there the Apoftolicall traditions, the decrees of Gene- are to be
rall Councelles, the authoritye of the vniuerfall Churche regarded,
make a good plea.   And thefe Nicene Fathers added vnto vvhere
the common Creede this woorde ὁμοούσιον : exprefsinge Scripture
liuely the vnitie of Chriftes Diuinitie in one fubftaunce faileth.
with the Father, though the word appere not in fcripture,
and though the Arrians would neuer receiue or allowe it.

Eutiches the Archeheretique deniyng that Chriſt had two natures, was wonte to aſke of the Catholiques: In what ſcripture lye the two natures? To whom Mamas the Catholike Biſhop anſwered, where find you *Homouſion* in the Scripture? Well ſaith Eutiches, in caſe it be not in the holy ſcripture, it is foũd in the expoſitiõ of the holy Fathers. Thẽ replied Mamas: Euẽ as *Homouſiõ* is not foũd in the ſcripture, but in the Fathers expoſitiõ and interpretatiõ: So is it with theſe wordes two natures of Chriſt, which wordes are not in Scripture, but in the Fathers. Ye may hereby perceiue, M. Horne, that ye muſt not ſequeſter and ſonder the Scripture, from the cõmon allowed expoſition of the Fathers: nor geue iudgement in all cauſes by bare ſcripture only, as ye woulde make vs beleue, but take the faith and faithfull expoſition of the Fathers withal. In like ſorte obiected the Eunomians againſt Gregory Nazianzen for the Godhead of the holy Ghoſt. πόθεν ἡμῖν ἐπεισάγεις τὸν ξένον θεὸν, τὸν ἄγραφον? *From whence bring you vs foorth this ſtraunge and vnwriten God?* But Gregory Nazianzen anſwereth them, and you withal, M. Horne. ἔνδυμα τῆς ἀσεβείας αὐτοῖς ἐστὶν ἡ φιλία τοῦ γράμματος. The loue of the letter, is a cloke to them of their wickedneſſe. Thus you ſee, M. Horne, how wel *Patriſas,* and howe like you are to your progenitours and auncetours, auncient heretiques, Arrians, Eutychians, and Eunomians. Is this the grounde, M. Horne, that moued you among other Articles propoſed to the fellowes of the new Colledge in Oxforde, to make this one alſo vnto the which they ſhoulde ſweare, or rather forſweare: *that out of holy Scripture all controuerſies might ſufficientlye be conuinced?* I wiſh here, if I ſpeake not to late, to that godly foũdation, to the which being (though vnworthy) a member

Vide Act. 1 Chalced. Concil. pa. 776. col. 1.

Gregor. Nazian. lib. 5. De Theolog.

Art 1. An. 1566. Angl. 18. Mart.

ſometime

ſometime thereof, I ought of duety to wiſh the beſt,rather
to forſake (as many,God be praiſed,haue done) the comfortable benefit of that ſocietie , then by abſolute ſubſcribing to ſuch a daungerouſe Article, a ſnare in dede againſt
many Articles of our Faith,to fall to the approuing of your
hereſies , and ſo to forſake the Catholique ſocietie of all
Chriſtendome, and of that Churche wherein our Godlye
founder (Biſhope Wicame of famous memorie) liued and
died. Thus muche by the waye. To returne to you M.
Horne , a vehement perſequutour of that yong company,
I tel you again,to make your maters more apparāt, ye haue
ſlilye ſhifted in this prety ſillable, *All.* The like part hath the
Author of your Apologie plaied with S. Hierome,turning
him to their purpoſe and yours here againſt Traditions,ſay-
ing : *Omnia ea quæ abſque teſtimonio ſcripturarum, quaſi tra-*
dita ab Apoſtolis aſſeruntur , percutiuntur gladio Dei. All
things (ſay they) which without the teſtimonies of Scriptures are holden,as deliuered frō the Apoſtles,be throughlye ſmitten doune by the ſworde of Gods worde . Where
to frame the ſentence to his and your minde , ye haue by
like authoritie,ſet in this ſyllable *All,* alſo.

The Apo
logy hath
ſhifted
this ſyl-
lable, Al,
into a
ſentēce of
S. Hierōs.

  M. Horne. The. 37. *Diuiſion.* pag. 24. b.

  VVhen they had agreed of the chiefe pointes , vvherefore they vvere aſ-
ſembled, the Emperour him ſelfe calleth foorth Aceſius a Biſhoppe at Con-
ſtantinople, of the Nouatians religion, and (.94.) examineth him openlye,
touching theſe Articles, vvhereunto the vvhole Councell had agreed and
ſubſcribed. He vvriteth his letters to the Churche at Alexandria,vvhere
the controuerſie touching the Diuinitie of Chriſt began, declaringe, that he
him ſelf together vvith the Byſhops in the Coūcel,had taken vpon him(.95.)

Euſeb.li.3
De vita
Conſtāt.
Socr.li.1.
cap.8.
Socr. li.10
cap.9.
Theod.
li.1 ca.13.
The.94.
vntruth.
For he

                DD iij   the

had but priuate talke vvith him,no open examination. The.95. Vntruthe. For
Conſtantine did not this as the Iudge ouer Doctrine,or as Supreme gouernour,but
as deſiring aboue meaſure to ſerue the church vvith the Biſhops,as he proteſteth in
the ſame ſētēce ſaiīg:ἐγὼ ὁ συνθεράπων ὑμέτερ᷍ καθ᾽ ὑπερβολὴν ἵναι χαίρων,
vvhich vvordes you nippe of from the middle of the ſentence.

the searching foorth of the truthe, and therefore assureth them, that all things
vvere diligently examined, to auoid all ambiguitie and doubtfulnes: vvherfore he exhorteth and vuilleth them all, that no man make any doubte or
delaies, but that cherefully they returne againe into the most true vvaye.
He vvriteth an other to all Bishoppes, and people vvhere so euer, vvherin he commaundeth, that no vv itinge of Arius, or monument conteyninge
Arius doctrine, be kept openly or secretly, but be burnt vnder paine of death.
After that all the matters vvire concluded, and signed vvith their handes
subscription, the Emperour dissolueth the Councell, and licenseth euery one
of them to returne home to his ovvne bishopricke, vvith this exhortation,
that they continue in vnitie of faith: that they preserue peace and concorde
amongst them selues, that from thence forth they abide no more in contenti-
Sozomen. ons: and last of all, after he had made a long oration vnto them, touching
li. 5. c. 25. these matters, he commaundeth them, that they make prayer continuallye
for him, his children, and the vvhole Empire.

Stapleton.

Socra. li. 1
cap. 10.

King Hē
ries sitting vpō
Lambert.

The. 553.
leafe
Socr. lib 1.
cap. 10.
Niceph.
li. 8. ca. 20

There is no matter heere greatly to be stayed vppon.
The matter of Acesius proueth litle your purpose. Onlesse
perchaunce, ye thinke that Constantine examined Acesius
of his faith, and heard his cause, as King Henrie did Lambert the sacramentaries cause, sitting vpon him as Supreme
head, and pronouncing by his Vicegerent Cromwell, final
sentence against him. For the whiche sentence M. Foxe
vvonderfully reueleth with the King, and reuileth him too:
which discourse if any man be desirous to see, I remit him
to M. Foxes madde Martyrologe. The talke of Constantine with Acesius the Nouatian was onely priuate, as both
Socrates and Nicephorus doe reporte it. Open examination no Writer mentioneth. It is Maister Hornes vntruthe.

His Proclamation that no man should kepe Arius books
vnder

vnder paine of deathe, dothe not iuſtifie this ſupremacie
by you imagined.   This was but an outewarde execution
of ciuile puniſhmente in the aſſiſting of the Nicene Decrees.   Nowe, touching that you tell vs, howe Conſtantine licenced the Fathers to departe, if he ſaied: Gramercy
moſte reuerend Fathers, for your great paines and trauail,
nowe may you in Gods name, reſorte to your cures and
flocke, God ſpeede you, God proſper your iourney : And
if he bare their charges too, that were poore Biſſhoppes.
as he did, in caſe he woulde not ſuffer them to depart till
all matters were throughlye and finallye diſcuſſed, What
then ? What ſupremacy maketh al this? Or how is this a-
ny thing like to the Supremacy now ſworen vnto ?

M. Horne. The. 38. Diuiſion. pag. 24. b.

*Arius counterfeiting a falſe and a feined confeſsion of beliefe, like an hy-
pocrite, pretending to the Emperour, that it vvas agreable to the faithe of
the Nicene Councel, humbly beſeching the Emperour, that he would vnit
and reſtore him to the (.96.) mother Churche, and therefore
hauing friends in the Emperours Court (as ſuche ſhall neuer vvante ſau-
tours about the beſt Princes) vvas brought into his preſence, vvhom the Emperoure him ſelfe examined diligentlye, and perceiuinge no diſagree-
ment (as he thought) from the agrement made in Nicene Councell (97.) abſolued and reſtored him againe. vvhervnto Athanaſius, vvho knevv Arius
throughly, vvould not agree, and being accuſed therfore vntoth'Emperour,
vvas charged by letters from him, that he ſhould receiue Arius, vvith theſe
threates, that if he vvould not, he vvould (.98.) depoſe them from his Biſſhoprike, and commit him to an other place. The Arrians heaped vp many
and horrible accuſations and ſlaunders vpon Athanaſius, vvhervpon the Emperour doth ſummon a Councell at Tyre, and ſendeth commaundement by his
letters to Athanaſius, that vvithout all excuſe, he ſhould appeare there, for
othervviſe he ſhould be brought vvhether he vvould or no. He vvriteth to the
Councel his letters, vvherin he declareth the cauſes vvhy he called that Councel.
He ſhevved vvhat he vvould haue and vvhat they ought to do, ãd preſcribeth
vnto thē the form ãd rule vvherby theiſhuld iudge ãd determin in that Synod.*

Athana-

Theod.
li.1 ca.14
The.96.
Vntruth.
The very
vvoordes
of Arius
falſified,
The.97.
Vntruth.
No ſuche
vvordes
in Theo-
doret, or
in any o-
ther of
the eccle-
ſiaſticall
Hiſtoriãs
Socr lib.1
cap.28.
The.98.
Vntruth.
No ſuche
thing nei
ther inSo
crates nor
in Theo-
doret, for
any mat-
ter of A-
rius.
Theod.
li.1 ca.37

*Athanasius appeared, appealed, fled to the Emperour, and declared the in-
iuries offered against him in that Councel. The Emperour tooke vpon him*

Soc.lib.1.
cap.34.
(.99.) A
heape of
vntruths
as before
in the.32.
Diuision
and third
Chapter.

*the hearing of the cause, sent his letters to the vvhole Synod, commaunding
them vvithout al excuse or delay, to appeare before him in his palaice, and
there to shevv hovv vprightly and hovve sincerely they had iudged in their
Synod, as i haue shevved(.99.) before. VVherein obserue diligently, that the
Emperor taketh vpō hi, and no fault found thervvith, to examine and iudge
of the doings of the vvhol Coūcel. Thus far of Cōstantine and his doings, in the
executiō of his ministerie, and especially in perfourming that part, vvhich he
called his best part, that is his gonernement, and rule, in Ecclesiastical mat-*

The.100.
vntruth.
Facing ād
impudēt.
generally
auouched
but notin
one par-
ticular
proued.

*ters, vvherein it is manifest, that by the practise of the Catholique Churche
for his time approued and commended by all the Catholique Priests and Bishops, in the Nicene Councell, the supreme gouernment, authority, and rule,
in (.100.) all maner causes both Ecclesiasticall and Temporall, vvere claimed and exercised by the Emperour, as to vvhom of right, suche like povver
and authority, belonged and appertained.*

Stapleton.

Beholde nowe an other Argument of M. Hornes imagined Supremacie. Arius hypocriticallye dissemblinge
his heresie, and pretending his faithe to be agreeable to
the Nicene faith, *humbly besecheth Constantine, to vnite and
restore him to the Mother Churche. And so he was absolued
and restored.* Truely here had ye hitte M. Feckenhā home

Theodor.
li.1.c.14.

in dede, had there bene any such thing in your Authour, as
in dede, there is not, nor can be, onlesse Constantine had
bene also a Priest. In dede he released him from exile, be-

Ruff.lib.1
cap.11.
Tripart.
li.3.ca.6.

ing before circumuented by a crafty Epistle of his and Euzoius together, which in wordes semed to agree with the
Nicene Councell, but in meaning farre disagreed. Yf ye
call this, vniting to the Mother Church, your Mother hath
a faire Childe, and a cunning Clercke of you: And yet were
ye much more cunning, if ye could finde any such disordi-
nate

nate and folish false phrases in any mans penne sauing your
owne. Neither can I tell in the worlde, where to find, or
where ye found this peuish hereticall fond phrase, onlesse
it were of Arius him selfe, of whome ye seme to take it .

And yet durst not he, as starke an heretik as he was, to ha-
sard so farre as ye haue done. In deede in his craftie and
subtile letter, so ambitiously and coulourably penned, that
Constantine supposed , it agreed very well with the very
definition of the Nicene Councell, in the ende thereof, he
made sute vnto Constantine to be receiued againe into the
Catholique Comunion, in these wordes, speaking for him
selfe and Euzoius his mate : *Quapropter rogamus vniri nos
per pacificam & Dei cultricem pietatem tuam matri nostræ Ecclesiæ iubeatis.* Wherefore we beseche your honour being
a peaceable Prince, and a true worshipper of God to commaund that we may be vnited to our Mother the Church.
Ye see, good Reader, if M. Horne hath any Author, who,
and of how good credite he is : euen no better then Arius
him selfe. And yet in this pointe is M. Horne worse then
he, and corrupteth and wresteth not onely the Catholique
writers, but Arius wordes too. For Arius doth not desire
Constantine to *restore him,* as M. Horne faineth, but *to geue
out his commaundemente , that he might be restored :* and by
whome was that, M. Horne, but by the Bishoppes? And
this thing Constantine him selfe well vnderstode, and therfore though glad to see them (as he thought)to haue changed their minde, yet (*not presuming* (as Sozomen writeth) *to
receiue them into the Communion of the Churche , before the
iudgement and allowance of mete men according to the Lawe
of the Churche*) he sent them to the Bishops assembled then
(for an other matter) in Councell at Hierusalem, that they

E E should

*Hist. trip.
lib. 3. ca. 6
Sozomen.
li 2. c. 27.*

M. Horn
hath no
Author
but Arius
to helpe
him.
M. Horn
wresteth
euē Arius
vvords.

*Sozom.
lib. 2. c 27*

It is pro-
ued by
Constan-
tine him-
selfe that
it vvas
the bis-
hops
part and
not his to
restore
Arius ād
other he-
retiques
to the
Churche.

shuld examine his and his companions faith: *Et clementem su-*

Trip.lib.3.
cap. 5.
Sozo. vti
supra.
Ruff.li. 1.
eccles. sua
hist.ca 11.
Trip &
Sozo. vbi
supra.
Trip li.3.
cap. o
Ruff. li. 1.
cap.11.
Theodore.
li.1.ca.14
Trip. li. 3.
ca. 10.
Socrates
b.1.ca.38.

per eis sententiam proferrent : and that they shoulde geue a merciful iudgement vpon them, yf they did truely repent. Ruffine also writeth agreable vnto this adding, *so that A-lexander the Bisshop did therto assente .* Eusebius and other dissembling Catholik bisshops, which were in hart Arians stil(as it did afterward appere)forthwith (in the Councel) receiued Arius into their communion.But when he came to Alexandria, he could not ther be receiued.The Catholike bisshop Alexander of Alexandria yet liuing, would not admit him.Then remayning there a long tyme as excommunicated, *he desired* (saieth Theodoret)*to be by some meanes restored again, and beganne to counterfeite the Catholike.* But when Alexander his bisshop and Athanasius his successor could not be so circumuented , he attempted ones again the Emperours fauour. And so by the means of Eusebius of Nicomedia an Arriã bisshop in hart, he was brought to the Courte at Constantinople , and to the Emperours speach, the secõd time after his banishmët. Where the Emperour desirous to trie him, asked Arrius, if he agreed with the Nicene Councel, vpon which request he offred to the Emperoure a supplication and a foorme of the Catholike confessiõ, pretending to sweare to that, but deceauing the prince with a contrary faith in his bosome , and swearing to the faith in his bosome. By these means th'Emperour dimissed him And therevpõ the factiõ of Eusebius wët forthwith τῆ σννᾶϑ'κ αντῷ βία, *with their accustomed violëce* (saith

Theodor.
lib.1, cap.
14.
Socrat. li.
2,cap.29.

Theodoret)*to Alexãder the B.of Cõstantinople, and required him to receiue him into Cõmunion.* The Bishop vtterly refused to do it notwithstãding the Courtiours request or Princes pleasure:*because* (saith Alexãder)*being, by a whole CoũceU*

condemns

cō demned he cā not be restored. The factiō of Eusebi⁹ threatned Alexāder, that if he would not by faire meanes restore him, they would force him therto by foule meanes, saiyng: *As against your Wil we haue made him come to the Emperours speach, so to morow against your wil, we wil make you to receiue him into your Church.* To this point therfore, the mater was now brought, that Eusebius with his faction conducted by force Arius to the Cathedrall Churche at Constantinople, there by violēce to Church him: But lo, as they were going with al their heretical band to the church to play this part, God shewed his mighty hād, euen as he did vpō the Egyptians in the read sea, specified in the old Testamēt, or vpon Iudas in the new. For in the way Arius was driuē to seke a place to ease nature: where sodainly he auoided with his excrementes his very bowels and entrails: ād in that filthy place gaue ouer his foule filthy stinking soule. A mete carpet for such a squier. And this is, loe, the mother Churche wherunto Arius was restored and vnited. For other restitution by the true Catholike Bishops, whose office it was as ye haue heard, to restore him, had he none. And nowe with this miserable and wretched ende of this Archeheretike Arius, wil I also end the doīgs of Cōstantine the great, wherin I haue so farre forth proceeded, as M. Horne hath ministred occasion. As for the Councel of Tyrus, whereof here againe mētion is reiterated, I haue spoken both in this boke, ād also against M. Iewel, as is before noted. And now may I boldly vnfold your cōclusion, M. Horne, where you say *that the Nicen bisshops agnised this kind of regimēt in the great Cōstantine* and say quite cōtrary, *they agnised no suche regimēt* which also I haue proued against you euē by your own examples of Cōstantine, and the Nicen Fathers, especially of Athanasius, present at the said Councell.

Theodor. vt supra. Euss. li. 1. eccles. hist. ca. 13. Tripart. li. 3. cap. 10. Socrat. li. 1. cap. 38.

The notable death of Arius.

The Sōnes

THE SECOND BOOKE   Anno. 350.

M. Horne. The. 39. Diuision. pag. 25. b.

The 101.
Vntruth.
Sozome
belyed.
They
made la-
ves a-
gainst the
Idolaters
but not
lavves ec-
clesiasti-
call.
Theod.
li. 2 cap. 1.
The. 202.
Vntruth.
For Con-
stantine
the great
did not
depose
Athana-
sius.
Sabell.
Platin.
The. 103.
Vntruth.
Liberius
neuer be-
came an
Arrian.
Socr. li. 2.
ca. 36. 37.

Constantines sonnes, claimed and toke vpō them, the same authority, that their Fathers had done before them : and as Zozomen (.101.) reporteth of them, did not only vpholde and mainteine, the ordinaunces made by their father Constantine, in Church matters, but did also make nevv of their ovvne as occasion serued, and the neçessitie of the time required.

Constantinus, after the death of his father, restored Athanasius (vvhom his father had (.102.) depoled) to his bishoprike againe, vvriting honourable and louing letters to the Churche of Alexandria, for his restitution.

Constantius depoled Liberius, the Bishoppe of Rome, for that he vvoulde not consent to the condemnation of Athanasius, in vvhose place Fœlix vvas chosen, vvhom also the Emperour depoled for the like cause, and restored a-gain Liberius vnto his bishoprik, vvho being moued vvith th' Emperors kind-nes (as som vvrite) or rather being ouercome vvith ambition (.103.) becam an Arrian. This Emperour depoled diuers bishops, appointing other in their places. He called a Synod at Millayn, as Socrates vvitnesseth, saiyng: The Emperour commaunded by his Edict, that there shoulde be a Synod holden at Millayn. *There came to this Councell aboue. 300. Bishoppes out of the VVest Countries. After this, he minded to call a gene-rall Councell of all the East and VVest Byshops to one place, vvhich coulde not conueniently be brought to passe, by reason of the greate distaunce of the places, and therefore he commaunded the Councell to be kept in tvvo places, at Ariminum in Italie, and at* Nicomedia *in* Bythinia.

The. 5. Chapter. *What Ecclesiasticall gouernement the Sonnes of Constantine the Great practiled.*

Stapleton.

YF Constantines Sonnes claimed the same authoritie that their Father had in caules Ecclesiasticall, then were they no supreame Iudges, no more then their Father was, who was none as I haue said and shewed. Yet saith M. Horne, *They not only mainteined their Fathers or-dinaunces in Church matters, but also made new of their owne.* But al this is but a loud and a lewd lye. Which (to be short)

shal

ſhal ſone appeare in the wordes of Zozomene (M. Hornes Author) who in the boke ād chapter quoted by M. Horne writeth thus : *The Princes alſo* (he meaneth Conſtantines Sonnes) *concurred to to the encreaſe of theſe things* (he ſpeaketh of encreaſing the Chriſtian faith) * *ſhewing their good affection to the Churches no leſſe then their Father : and honouring the Clergy, their ſeruaunts, and their domeſticals, with ſingular promotions and immunites. Both confirming their Fathers lawes, and making alſo of their owne, againſt ſuch as went about to ſacrifice, to worſhip Idols , or by any other meanes fell to the Grekes or Heathens ſuperſtitions.* Lo, M. Horne, heare what your Author ſaith. As before Cōſtantine promulged lawes againſt Idolatrie, and honored the Church of Chriſt, and the miniſters thereof, ſo did his Sonnes after him.   As for Church matters, as Conſtantine the Father , made no lawes or decrees therto apertaining, no more did his Sōnes. It is but your impudent vntruth.   Now touching the firſt aud eldeſt ſonne of Conſtantine, called alſo Conſtantine, we haue here of him as many lies as lines.   Firſt in that M. Horne ſaith, that *his Father depoſed Athanaſius* , who was depoſed by the Biſhops, and not by Conſtantine, for he baniſhed him, but depoſe him, he neither did, nor could. The ſecond, that this Conſtantine reſtored him to his biſhoprick againe : wherein he belyeth (and ſo maketh the third lye) his Author Theodoret, who ſpeaketh of none other reſtitution, but that he releaſed him from exile and baniſhmente : which ye wote is no Biſhoply, but a Princely function and office. But now we may be of good comforte.   For hauing boren out this brunt, I truſt we ſhal ſhift wel inough for all the reſidue. For now, lo, we haue an Emperour, that as far as I can ſee , tooke vppon him in dede, in many things M.

Three vn truthes of M Horns in fovver lines.
Tripart. lib.3.ca.8.

Theod. lib 2.ca 1. M.Horne now God be thāked hath foūd his ſuprē head in cōſtātius the Arriā Emperor

EE iij.   Hornes

Athanasi-
us ad soli-
tariam vi-
tam agen-
tes, vbi &
litera Ho-
sij recitan-
tur ad Có-
stantium.
Hilarius
in lib. con-
tra Con-
stantium.
vVhat li-
king the
catholiks
thē liuing
had of yt.
VVhat
Hosius
sayde to
him for
this supre
macy.
Vide Sui-
dam in
Leontio.
VVhat
Leontius
sayde to
him for
this supre
macy.

Novvel
fol. 114.

Hornes supremacy. Which may be proued by Athanasius, Hosi°, Hilarius, ād Leótius Bishops of the very same time: But praise be to God, that the same men (al notable lightes of the Catholike Church) which declared that he vsed this authority, do withal declare their great misliking thereof: ād make him (som of thē) a plain forerūner of Antichrist: as I haue before declared out of Athanasius. *Meddle not Sir Emperou* (saith Hosius) *with maters of the Church, neither commaūd vs in such things, but rather learne them at our handes: God hath betakē and cōmitted to thée th'Empire, ād to vs, hath he cōmitted Church matters.* And Leontius B. of Tripolis, at what time this Constantius being present at a Synod of Bishops was very busy in talke to set forth certain cōstitutiōs, saith boldly vnto him: *Syr I maruail with my self why that ye leauing your own, busy your self with other mēs affaires: the commō welth and warlik maters are cōmitted to your charge: the which your charge you forslow, sitting amōg the Bishops ād making lawes cōcerning maters Ecclesiastical, wherin ye haue nothīg to do.* And if this mā deposed Bishops, as ye say, then haue ye foūd a fair welfauored presidēt to groūd your primacy vpō. How wel fauored a presidēt he is, ād how worthy to be folowed, if ye list to see, M. Horn, ye may learn of M. Nowel who saw farder in this mater a great deale, then your prelatship. He hath laid forth no lesse then .13. Articles against this your supreme gouernour (M. Horne) to proue that he was for his busy gouernmēt in dede a very Antichrist. Thus you iarre ād iūble againe one agaist an other, and can neuer agree in your tales. As for that he called the Coūcel at Arie minū, ād els where, that induceth no such primacy as I haue and shal better herafter declare, namely whē I com to your own author the Card. Cusan°: In the meā sesō, ye haue ministredto me a good mater to iustify the Popes primacy. For

behold

behold Damaſus broke ād diſanulled al that was don at Ari ſtātine
minū(ſaith Theodoret)becauſe his conſent wāted thereto.

And here that Councel which the Emperour by his ſu· Theod.li.
preme gouernmēt(as M: Horn fanſieth)ſōmoned,the Pope ¹·cap· ²²·
as a Superiour gouernour to this ſupreme gouernour, quite
diſanulled, which made S. Ambroſe to ſay: *Merito Conciliū* Ambroſ.
illud exhorreo. I do for good cauſe abhorre that Councell. li 5.ep.32.
For which cauſe alſo,it is to this day of no authoritie at all.
Thus al M. Horns exāples run roūdly againſt hī,ād quite o-
uerturne his purpoſe . For why? How can poſsiblie a falſe
cauſe be truly defended ? That you ſay, *Liberius* the Pope
of Rome *became an Arriā*,is a ſlāuderous Vntruth It is your
brethrēs cōmō obiectiō,ād hath ſo oft bē ſoluted by the Ca
tholiks,that your part had bē now(bearīg your ſelf for a ler
ned Prelate)not to reſume ſuch ruſty reaſons, but to replie
againſt the Catholiks anſweres ād ſolutiōs,if ye were able.
The worſte that euer Liberius did (to make any ſuſpitiō in
him)is,that after baniſhmēt he was reſtored, and yelded to Athanaſ.
Cōſtātius . But Athanaſius ſaith expreſly,that the ſame his ad ſolut.
yelding was not to the Arriā hereſy , but *to the depoſing of* vitā agēt.
him frō his Biſhoprik.And that was al that the Emperor re- Tripart.
quired of *Liberius*, as it maye appeare by the learned and li.5.c.4.17
ſtout cōmunicatiō had betwen this *Liberius* ād the Emperor in Rome, as Theodoret at large recordeth. And to this
he was driuē *by force of tormtēs*, ſaith Athanaſius.Nowe for
hī *to become an Arriā*. is volūtarily to teache , to beleue,or
to allow the Arriā hereſie. Are thei al,trow you,Caluiniſts
in Englād which for fear of diſpleaſure, of baniſhmente, or
ofloſſe of goods,do practiſe the order ofthe Caluiniſts ſupper or Communion? As they are no right Catholiques, ſo
are they not proprely Caluiniſtes or Heretiques . They
                                                                                    are

are neither hotte nor colde. God will therefore (but if they repent) ſpue them out of his mouth. As for Liberius, S.

ᵃBaſil, and ᵇEpiphanius, S.ᶜAuguſtine, ᵈOptatus, ād S.ᵉAm-broſe doe ſpeake honourably and reuerentlye of him, and doe reken him among the rew of the Romaine Biſhoppes: which they would neuer haue done, if (as M Horne ſaith) he had bene, *become an Arrian*, It ſemeth M. Horne is of alliaunce with M. Iewel. So hard it is for him to tel a true tale. Nowe to the next.

M. Horne. The. 40. Diuiſion. Pag. 26. a.

Valentinianus *the Emperour, after the death of* Auxentius, *an Ar-rian biſhop of Millaine, calleth a Synod of biſhops at Millayn to conſult a-bout the ordering of a nevv biſhop. He preſcribeth vnto them in a graue ora-tion, in vvhat maner a man qualified ought to be, vvho ſhould take vppon him the office of a biſhop. They paſſe to the election, the people vvere di-uided, till at the laſt they all cry vvith one conſent, to haue Ambroſe, vvhom although he did refuſe, the Emperour commaunded to be baptiꝫed, and to be cōſecrate biſhop. He called an other Synod in Illirico, to apeace the diſſentiōs in Aſia and Phrigia, about certaine neceſſary Articles of the Chriſtian faith: and did not only confirme the true faith by his (.105.) royall aſſent, but made alſo many godly and ſharpe Lavves, as vvell for the maintenaunce of the truth in doctrine, as alſo (.106.) touchinge manye other cauſes, or matters Eccleſiaſticall.*

The ſixth Chapter : Of Valentinian the Emperour.

Stapleton.

VAlentinian the Emperour commeth in good time. I meane, not to proue your Primacy, M. Horne, but qnite to ouerthrowe the ſame. For this is he that made an expreſſe Lawe, that in Eccleſiaſtical matters, only Eccleſiaſticall men ſhould iudge. S. Ambroſe witneſſeth it expreſſely

expreſſely m an Epiſtle he wrote to younge Valentinian, this mans ſonne. The forme of the law was this. *In cauſa fidei vel eccleſiaſtici alicuius ordinis eum iudicare debere, qui nec munere impar ſit, nec iure diſsimilis. Hæc enim verba reſcripti ſunt, Hoc eſt ſacerdotes de ſacerdotibus voluit indicare.* That in the cauſe of faith, or of any eccleſiaſtical order, he ſhould iudge, that was neither by office vnequall, neither in right vnlike. Thoſe are the words of the Reſcript. That is, he wil haue Prieſtes to iudge ouer Prieſtes. Thus S. Ambroſe plainely and expreſſely in one ſentence qyyte ouerturneth al M. Hornes ſupremacy.

Yea ſo farre was this Emperour from al gouernment ouer Prieſtes m matters eccleſiaſtical, that euen in matters ciuil or temporal, he woulde not ſuffer prieſtes to be called to the ciuil court. For thus it foloweth immediatlye in S. Ambroſe. *Quinetiam ſi aliàs quoque argueretur epiſcopas, & moram eſſet examinanda couſa, etiam hanc voluit ad epiſcopale iudicium pertinere.* Yea farder, if a biſhop were otherwiſe accuſed, and ſome matter of behauyour or outwarde demeanor were to be examined that matter alſo he would to belong to the iudgement of Biſhops. Beholde, gentle Reader, what a ſupreme gouernor in al cauſes both ſpiritual and temporal ouer prieſts and Biſhops M. Horne hath brought forth. Verily ſuch a one, as in very ciuil cauſes refuſeth gouernment ouer them.

But this is he that *commāunded Ambroſe to be conſecrated biſhop of Millayn* (ſaieth M. Horne) *and in that election preſcribed to the biſhops in a graue oration, what a qualified man a biſhop ought to be &c.* What then M. Horne? was he therefore ſupreme gouernour in al cauſes eccleſiaſtical? Yea or in this very cauſe was he, thinke you, the ſupreme

gouernour? If you had tolde vs some parte of that *graue
oration*, somewhat therein perhaps would haue appered
either for your purpose, or against it. Now, *a graue oratiō* he
made, you say, but what that graue talke was, or wherein it
cōsisted, you tel vs not. Verily a graue oratiō it was in dede,
ād such as with the grauity thereof, vtterly ouerbeareth the
light presumption of your surmised supremacy. For this a-
mōg other thigs he saied to those bisshops grauely in dede.

Theod.lib.
4.c.5. Τοιοῦτον δ̕ ἡ οὖν &c. *Such a mā therefore do you place in this bis-
shoply throne, that we also which direct the Empire, may gladly submitte oure heads to him, and reuerence (as a medicinable
remedy) the rebukes that he shall make ouer vs: for men we
are, and must nedes falle somtyme.* So, M. Horne, woulde this
Emperour haue a bisshop qualified (and so was in dede this
Ambrose then chosen passingly qualified) that he shoulde
tel and admonish boldely the Prince of his faultes, and the
Prince should as gladly and willingly obey him, yea and
submit his head vnto hī, not be the supreme Head ouer hī:
as you most miserable clawbackes (vnworthy of al priestly
preeminēce) would force modest prices vnto. This was the
graue lessō he gaue to the bisshops (as Constantin before to
Theod.li.
1.cap.7. the Fathers of Nice) ὡς παῖς φιλοπάτωρ: *as a naturall louing
child,* τοῖς ἱερῦσιν ὡς πατράσι, *to the Priestes as to his Fathers:*
not to them as his seruauntes or subiectes in that respecte.

You say farder (but you say vntruly, to be alwaies like
your selfe) that this Emperour *confirmed the true faith* (decreed in a Synod in Illyrico) *by his royal assent*. As though
your Reader shoulde straight conceyue, that as the
Quenes Maiesty confirmeth the Actes of parliament with
her highnes royall assent, and is therefore in dede the Supreme and vndoubted Head ouer the whole parliament, so
this

this Emperour was ouer that Synod . But Theodoretus (your Author alleaged)ſaieth no ſuch thig:Only he ſaieth.

 Τὰ παρ᾽ ἐκείνων ὡς ἡγίων ἐπισκόπων κ̀ ψηφισθέντα, κ̀ κυρωθέντα τοῖς ἀμφισβητοῦσιν ἐξέπεμψε. *Thoſe thĩgs that had ben decreed and eſtabliſhed by the Biſhoppes, he ſent abrode to thoſe that doubted thereof.* Other confirmatiõ then this,is not in your Author or any otherwhere métioned . And this was plain miniſterial.execution of the decrees,no royall confirmatiõ of them.

Theod.lib. 4 cap.7.

M. Horne. The 41. Diuiſion. Pag.26.a.

Theodóſius,vvas nothing inferiour to Conſtantine the great , neither in zeale,care,or furtherance,of Chriſtes Religiõ. He bent his vvhole povver, and authoritie,to the vtter ouerthrovve of ſuperſtition , and falſe Religion, ſomevvhat crept in againe, in the times of Iulianus,and Valés,the vvicked Emperours. And for the ſure cõtinuance of Religion reſormed,he made many godly Lavves, he defended the (.107.) godly biſhop of Antioche Flauianus,againſt the biſhop of Rome and other biſhoppes of the V.Veſte, vvho did (.108.)falſely accuſe him of many crymes: and at the légthe,by his careful endeuour in Churche matters and his(.109.)Supreme authoritie therein,this moſte faytful Emperour,ſayeth Theodoretus,ſette peace and quietnes amongeſt the Biſhoppes, and in the Churches. He called a conuocation of the Biſhops,to the ende that by common conſent,al ſhould agree in vnytie of doctrine confeſſed by the Nicen councel,to reconcile the Macedonians vnto the catholique Churche,and to electe and order a Byſhop in the ſea of Cõſtantinople, vvhiche vvas than vacant. VVhen the tvvoo fyrſte pointes could not be brought to paſſe,as the Emperour vviſhed,they vvent in hande vvith the third,to conſult amongeſt them ſelues touching a fitte Biſhop for Conſtantinople. The Emperour , to vvhoſe iudgement many of the Synode conſented,thought Gregorie of Nazianzene, moſte fitte to be Biſhop : but he did(.111.)vtterly refuſe that that charge.

FF ꝯ Than

The 107. vntruth. Flauianus in that matter betvvene the Emperour ãd the biſhops of the vveſt proued a periured perſon. The 108. vntruthe mere ſlãderous. The 109. vntruth. Thereappeared no ſuch Supremacy ouer Churche matters in Theoſius.

The 110.vntruthe. Al this vvas but one Councel,though they are tolde (to make a ſhevv of Supremacy in th'emperour)as if they vvere.3.ſeueral Councels. The 111.vntruthe,For he vvas for a time the biſhop there,as ſhal appeare.

than the Emperour commaundeth them to make diligent inquisition for some godly man, that might be appointed to that roumme. But vvhen the Bishops could not agree, vppon any one, the Emperour commaundeth them to bring to him the names of al such, as euery one of them thought moste apt to be Bishop, vvriten in a paper together. He reserued to him self (saith Sozomenus) to chose vvhome he liked best. VVhen he had redde ouer once or tvvyse, the sedule of names, vvhich vvas brought vnto him, after good deliberation had vvith him self, he chose Nectarius, although as yet he vvas not christened:

The 112. vntruth. The bil shoppes might (if they had listed) most law fully haue remoued him.

and the Bishops maruailing at his iudgemēt in the choise, (.112.) could not remoue him. And so vvas Nectarius baptized, and made bishop of Constātinople. vvho proued so godly a bishop, that all men deemed this election to be made by Themperour, not vvithout some miraculous inspiration of the holy ghost. This Emperour perceiuing, the Church had ben long tyme molested, and drayvē into partes by the Arianisme, and like to be more greuously torne, in sonder vvith the heresy of Macedonius, a B. of Cōstātinople, and knovving that his supreme gouernmēt, and empire vvas grue him of God to maintene the common peace of the Church, and confirmation of the true faith, summoneth a Synode at Constantinople, in the thirde yeere of his reigne (vvhich is the second great and general councel of the sovver notable and famous œcumenical councels) and vvhen al the bishops vvhome he had cited, vvere assembled, he cometh into the councell house amongest them, he made vnto them a graue exhortation, to consulte diligently, like graue Fathers of the matters propoūded vnto them. The Macedonians depart out of the Cytie, the Catholike Fathers agree, conclude a trueth, and send the canons of their

The 113. vntruth. For not to be so cōfirmed as M.Hor. fancieth. That is, by the vvaye of Supreme gouerne ment &c.

conclusion to the Emperour (.113.) to be confirmed, vvriting vnto him in these vvords: The holy counsaile of bishops assembled at Constātinople to Theodosius Emperour, the moste reuerent obseruer of Godlines, Religion, and loue towardes God: VVe geue God thankes, who hath appointed your Emperial gouernmēt for the common tranquility of his Churches, and to establishe the sounde faith. Sithe the tyme of our assembly at Constantinople by your godly commaundement, we haue renewed cōcorde amongest our selues, and haue prescribed certaine Canōs or rules, which we haue annexed vnto this our writing: we beseche therefore your clemency to commaunde the De-

cree of

cree of the Counsaile to be stablished by the letters of your
holines, and that ye wil confirme it, and as you haue honoured the Church by the letters wherewith you called vs together: euen so, that you wil strengthen also the final conclusion
of the Decrees with your own sentence and seale.

After this he calleth an other (.114.) Councel of bishops to Constantino-
ple of vvhat Religion so euer, thinking that if they might assemble together
in his presence, and before him conferre touching the matters of Religion,
vvherein they disagreed, that they might be reconciled, and brought to vnity
of Faith. He consulteth vvith Nectarius, and sitteth dovvn in the Coun-
sel house amongest them al, and examineth those that vvere in Heresie, in
such sort, that the Heretikes vvere not onely astonied at his questions, but
also beganne to fal out amongest themselues, some liking, some misliking the
Emperours purpose. This done, he commaundeth eche sect, to declare their
faieth in vvritinge, and to bringe it vnto him: he appointeth to them a
daye, vvhereat they came as the Emperoure commaunded, and deliuered
vnto him the sourmes of their faieth in vvritinge: vvhen the Emperoure
had the sedules in his handes, he maketh an earnest praier vnto God, for
the assistace of his holy spirite, that he may discern the truth, and iudge right-
ly. And after he had redde them al, he condemneth the heresies of the Arians
and Eunomians, renting their sedules in sundre, and alovveth only, and con-
firmeth the faith of the Homousians, and so the Heretiks departed ashamed
and dasht out of countenance.

Sozom, li.
5. cap. 10.
The 114.
vntruth.
This vvas
no other,
nor no
Councel
at al.
The 115.
vntruthe
in reaso-
ning. For
al this
proueth
no vvhit
any spiri-
tual Su-
premacy
in Theo-
dosius.

The.7.Chapter: Of Theodosius the first, and his dealing in causes Ecclesiasticall.

Stapleton.

THis Theodosius had no greater care to further true
religió, then ye haue to slader and hinder it: and that
by notable lying, as it will, al other things set a parte
appere, by the heape of lyes, that in this story of this one
Emperour, ye gather here together. And first that ye call
Flauian *the godly bishop of Antioche*: For albeit, he stode
very stowtly in the defence of the Catholike faith and suf-

A heap
of lies ga-
thered
together
in the
one story
of Theo-
sius.

fred much for it , yet in that respecte for the which , he is
here by you alleaged,he was not godly. As one that came
to his bishoprike , againste the canons and contrarye to
the othe taken, that he woulde neuer take vppon him to
be bishop of Antioche, Paulinus lyuing:and ministring by
this meanes an occasiõ of a greate schisme to the Church,
which continued many yeares. And for this cause the A-
rabians,the Cyprians,the Aegiptians with Theophilus Patriarche of Alexandria,and the west Churche , with Pope

Socra. lib.
5.cap. 15.
Theo.li, 5
cap. 23.
Sozo.li.7.
cap. 11.
Vi de Amb.
epist. 78.
tripartili,
9.cap.26.
& 44.
2.
3.
Theod.lib.
5.cap.23.

Damasus,Siricius,and Anastasius,would not receiue hi into their cõmuniõ.Neither could he be setled quietly,ãd receiued as Bisshop,vntil he had recõciled hiself to the Pope,
and that his fault was by him forgeuẽ. For the which purpose he sente to Rome a solẽpne ambassade:And so it appereth . that the . 2. lyne after ye adioyne a freshe lie, that
the bishop of Rome did falsly accuse him of many crimes,who
layde to him,no lesse crimes,then al the world did beside,
which was periury,and schisme. Then as though ye would
droppe lies,or lie for the whetstone,ye adde that by his supreame authority he set peace and quietnes in the Church
for this matter,shufflig in by your supreame lyig authority
these words *supreame authority*,which neither your author
Theodoretus hath, nor any other: yea directly contrary to
the declaratiõ of Theodoretus; who in the verye chapter
by you alleaged reciteth the ambassade I speake of,which
is a good argumẽt of the Popes Supremacy:and may be added to other exãples of M.Doctor Hardings,and of myne
in my Return &c. againft M.Iewel in the matter of recõci-
liatiõ.For as fauorable as themperour was to him and for
al the Emperours supremacy,the Emperour himself commaũded hi to go to Rome,to be recõciled,he being one of
the

The
popes pri
macy pro
ued euen
by M.
Hornes
ovvne
ftorye.
Reconci
liation to
the pope.

the foure patriarches And Flauianus was fayn alfo, to defire greate
Theophilus bifhop of Alexandria to fende fome body to
Pope Damafus, to pacifie ād mollifie his anger, ād to pardō
hi: who fent Ifidorus for that purpofe. And as I haue faid,
Flauianus hi felf afterward fent Acatius and others his ambaffadours. Which Acatius pacified the fchifmes that had
cōtinued.17. yeres, and reftored, as your own author Theodoret' faith; peace to the Church, *pacē* (faith he) *Ecclefiis re-
ftituit.* Which words though Theodoretus, doth fpeake of
thēperor Theodo. yet he fpeaketh the like of Acati' which
ye guilefully apply to Theodofi' only, ād as falfely conclude
therof, that Theodofi', therfore fhould be fupreme head of
the Church. For fo by that reafon Acati' fhould alfo be fupreme head of the Church. Now foloweth M. Horns narratiō of certain coūcels holde vnder this Theodof:', fo difor
derly, fo cōfufely, fo vnperfectly, and fo lyingly hādled, as a
mā may wel wōder at it. He maketh of two coūcels kepte
at Cōftātinople three: wheras the. 1. ād. 2. is al one (being the
fecōd famoufe general coūcel) ād properly to cal a coūcell
the third is none, but rather a conference or talke. The firft
Coūcel, which he tolleth vs of, *was called* (he faith) *o electe
ād order a bifhop in the fea of Cōftantinople.* Which (in cafe
he cā proue the diftincted Councels) was don in the Coūcel general, and in the fecōde as he placeth it ād not in the
firft. As alfo the electiō ād ordinatiō of Nectari'. He faieth
that Gregory Naziāzene was neuer bifhop of Cōftātinople but did vtterly refufe it. Wheras after he had taught
there. 12. yeares, to the great edifying of the Catholikes
againft the Arians, not enioyinge the name of a Bifhop all
this while, he was at the lengthe, fette in his bifhoply fee,
by the worthy Meletius bifhop of Antioche, and by the
whole nōber of the bifhops affebled at the general cūcell.

Thowgh

4.

5.

6.

7.
Socra lib
5. cap. 6.
Theod. lib.
5 cap. 8.
Gre. Nif.
in vita
Greg. Na-
zianzen.
Nicep. lib.
12. cap. 11.

Though in dede he did not longe onioye it, but voluntarily, and much againſt this good Emperours mynde, gaue it
ouer, to auoyde a fchifme, that grewe vppon his election.
For whome Nectarius (that M. Horne ſpeaketh of) was
chofen, being at that tyme vnbaptized. And ſo chofen by
the Emperour, as M. Horne ſaieth, *that the Biſhops though
they meruailed at the Emperours iudgement, yet they coulde
not remoue him.* Wherein ye may note two vntruthes, the
one that M. Horne woulde gather Theodoſius ſupremacy by this electiõ. Of the which electiõ, or rather naminge
(for the Emperour only pricked him) I haue alredy anſwered in my Refutile againſt M. Iewel, and faid there more at
large. And the biſhoppes, with common confent of the
whole Synod, doe pronounce him and creat him biſhop,
as alſo in their letters to Pope Damaſus they profeſſe. The
other that the Biſhops *could not remoue him* Yes M. Horn
that they might, afwel by the Apoſtolical, the Nicene, and
other canons of the Churche, as by the very plaine holye
ſcripture, and by S. Paule by expreſſe wordes forbidding it,
for that he was *Neophytus*. Suerly of you that would ſeame
to be ſo zelouſe a keper of the fincere worde of God, and
ſo wel a ſcriptured man, this is nothing ſcripturelye ſpoken: And therefore this your ſayinge muſte needes make
vppe the heape. Yea and therefore they might lawfullye
haue infringed and annichilated this election: ſauing that,
they bore with this good gracioufe Emperour, that tendred Chriſtes Church and faith ſo tenderlye, euen as Melchiades before rehearſed bore with the good Conſtantin.

Here may we now adde this alſo to the heape, that ye
woulde inferre this Soueraynety in Theodoſius, becauſe
the Fathers of this general Councel deſired him to confirme

Sozom. li.
7. cap. 8.
κοινῇ ἐ-
φῳ η̃
σκινῷ δ.
Theod. lib.
5. cap. 9.
μετὰ κοι-
νῆς ὁμο-
νοίας.

Can. apoſ.
79.
Can. Nic.
2.
Laod can.
3.
Aurel 2.
can. 1.
1. Tim. 3.

firme their decrees and canons . Which is a mighty great
copioufe argumente with you throughout your booke, all
in fewe words eafie to be anfwered and auoyded. For this
kind of confirmation is not , nor euer was required, as
though their ordinaunces were voyde and fruftrate without it : as al that ye now doe, haue don, or fhal doe in your
fynodes and conuocations without the ratification of the
Quenes Maiefty. Which thig for decrees of the Churche,
ye doe not, ye haue not, nor euer fhal be able to proue. But
to this ende , were the Emperours required to confirme
Councels that the willing and towarde people might haue
the better lyking in them, and be the more allured carefully and exactly to obferue them , vpon the good lyking of
their prince: And withal that the frowarde and malignate
people , that make no great accompte of the cenfures of
the Churche, becaufe yt doth not prefently touche the body , or any temporal loffe, might for feare of ciuil and temporall punifhement, be brought the foner to keepe and obferue the . And this litle fhort, but fo true an anfwere, as ye
fhal neuer with al your cuning honeftly fhift it of, may fuffice to euacuate and emptye a great part of your boke refting in this point.

But to fhew in this place, ones for al, how emperors haue
dealed ad may deale in General Councels, either for calling
them, or for confirming them , or for their demeanour in
them, I wil put certayne points or Articles, and note thereby what the practife of the Churche hath bene in this behalfe : to thentent that the Reader maye knowe , what
it is that we defende, and what had bene your part to haue
proued, leaft walking alwaies in generalities , we fpende
words without fruit, and bring the caufe to no certaine if-

The greate VVhye and to what end the Emperours confirme the lawes of the Churche.

Howe Emperors haue and may deale in Generall Councels.

few. And this I professe to take of one of your own special
authors M. Horne, the Cardinal of Cusa, out of whō you al

leage afterwarde a longe processe, as one that made wholy for you. And in very dede he speaketh as much for the
Emperour, and for his prerogatiue in ordering of generall
Councels, as he could possibly finde by the continual practise of the Church from Constantines tyme down to his,
which was to the late Councell of Basil vnder Sigismunde
the Emperour, in the yere. 1432.

Cusanus
lib.3.c.9.
de Cōcor-
dia Catho-
lica.
Lib. 9.epi.
54.

The first poirt thē is, *that Kigs ād Prices, ought to be careful
and diligēt that Synods ād Coūcels may be had*, as the especial
aduocates of the Church, and as of greatest power to procure quiet paisible passage to Coūcels, abyding there ād re-
turnīg home againe. Exāple in an admonitiō of S. Gregory
to Theodorike the Frēche King, exhorting to see a Synod
called in his realme for the repressing of Simony.

The seconde point is, that to such Synods *Princes ought
to come with all mekenesse, reuerence and humility and with
gentle exhortations.* Examples are Riccharedus, Sisenādus,
and Chintillanus Kigs of Spayne, as we shal hereafter more
largely declare, in certain of the Toletane Councels.

The third poirt is, that as Kigs and Prices for their own
prouinces do cal prouincial Synods, so the Emperorus for
the whole corps of Christēdō do cal Gēneral Coūcels. *Nō
qp eactiuē sa exhortatorie coligere debeat.* Not that by force
or cōstraint, but by way of exhortatiō he ought to cal thē.
Examples are the Councel of Aquileia vnder S. Ambrose:
the 4. General Councell vnder Pope Leo: the sixt vnder
Agatho: the 7. vnder Adriā the first with the rest, as of eche
in their places we shal declare.

The fourth: that the Emperor *in case of a general schisme,
ought first to certifie the Pope of the necessity of a Councel and
require*

require his consent to haue it in some certain place assembled.
So did Valentiniã and Martiã the Emperours to Pope Leo
for the Chalcedon. So did Constantin the 4. to Pope Agatho for the sixt general Councel.

The fift point is, that the Pope summoneth and calleth al
general Coūcels, far otherwise thē do the Emperours. *For
the Pope as the chiefest, and as hauīg power to cōmaund ouer al
other bishops for the principality of his priesthood by the power
cōmitted to him ouer the vniuersal Church, hath to cōmaund al
faithful Christiãs, especially bishops and priests to assemble and
mete in Councel. But the Emperour exhorteth and inuiteth
bishops, but cōmaundeth the lay, to a Councel. And the Canons
do cōmaūde, that without the Authority of the bishop of Rome
no Councel cã be holdē.* Not so in the Emperor. For the Ephe-
sin cōuēticle was disanulled, because Leo his legates were
reiected, though Theodosi⁹ the yōger, did cōfirm it and allow it. So the great Coūcel of Ariminū was cōdemned, because Pope Damasus sent not thither, though Constantius
themperour summoned it and allowed it. And the greate
Coūcel of Sardica preuailed, because by Pope Iulius it was
called and allowed, though Cōstātius thē Emperor resisted
it and refused it. And thus much for the first beginninges of
the Coūcel. Now in the Coūcel it self, what is the Princes
part, ãd what the bishops, it shal appeare. Let thē the sixt
point be, that at the Councel being, the Princes office and
care ought to be, *to prouide that al tumult ãd disorder be auoyded, and to remoue such as are to be remoued* So did the iudges
in the Chalcedō Coūcel, remoue Dioscor⁹ fro the bēch, ãd
admit Theodoret, the one by pope Leo cōdēned, the other
recōciled. So when the parties waxed warm, they did their
best to brig thē to a calm. So did also Cōstāti in his own person in

greate
In epist.
preambu.
Chalc. cōa
cil. In 6.
Syn. act 1.

Cap. 15.

Tripart.
hist. lib. 4
cap. 9. &
19.

Athanas.
Apolog. 2.

Cap. 14.

son in the firſt Nicene Councel, as M. Horne hath him ſelf alleaged, and as Euſebius reporteth.

Seuenthly the Lay Magiſtrates or Princes : being placed in the Council in the roomes of Emperours and kings, *Non habent vocem Synodicam, ſed ſolum audire debent:* haue no voice as a parte of the Synod, but óly are there to heare. This practiſe is clere in al the Councels, as it ſhall appere in the particulars hereafter. The iudges therefore and Princes delegates mencioned in the Chalcedon and other Councels, are in the Councels, much after a ſorte, as the Speaker in our Parliaments. To open and ſet forth to the Councel all matters to be treated vpon. To appointe (by the aduiſe of the Councel) the next metings, to breake of the preſent ſeſsion, to promulge the Councels Sétence: and ſuch like matters as belong to more orderlye and quiet proceding in al things.

Eightly the force and Vigour of the Sentence in Coũcel dependeth only of the Biſhops, which make the Coũcel, *& non ex Imperiali commiſsione* and not of the Emperours Commiſsion, *whoſe Authority is inferiour to the Synod*, ſaieth Cuſanus. And ſo the Continuall practiſe will proue.

Ninthly the Emperour, the Princes, and their Oratours do ſubſcribe *as witneſſes of that is done :* but as iudging and determining, only the biſhops in all Councels haue ſubſcribed.

Tenthly for the ende and conſummation of all Councels, the Emperours and Princes *ought to prouide, that ſuch things as are decreed and determined by the holy Councels, may be obſerued, and by lawes and penaltyes they ought to force their ſubiects to the obſeruation thereof.* But to confirme by

waye

waye of Ecclefiaftical Authority and Supremacy, it hath greate
euer belonged only to the bifshops of Rome, as by the
continual practife of the Church it hath and fhal yet better
appeare. In this fence, and as I haue already faied, Emperours haue confirmed, and by their edictes eftablifhed the
Councels, lawes, and decrees of the Churche. And thus
you fee M. Horne particularly and plainly what we attribute to Emperours and Ciuil Princes in the calling, ordering and confirming of Councels, and what we deny moft
iuftly vnto them. If you proue that which we graunte, you
fhewe your felfe a flender fcholer, and a weake aduerfary, that will take vpon you to confute that practife, the
limites and conditions where of you knowe not, which
is altogether to fight in darkeneffe or with your owne
fhadowe. If you can proue that which we deny, lette
the truthe goe on your fide. But you neither haue in this
booke, neither fhall euer be able to proue it. To auoyde
therefore hereafter the fuperfluyte of vnfruteful talke, as
well for myne, as for the Readers eafe, in al your like obiections of Emperours calling and confirming of Councels, I wil referre you to the anfweres and diftinctions prefently made.

To returne nowe to Theodofius, and to you M. Horne,
we haue one vntruthe more to charge you withal: for that
you would eftablifhe this peerleffe and Supreme Authority in Theodofius, becaufe he hauing receiued in writinge
the faith as wel of the Catholikes, as of the Eunomians,
Arians, and other heretiks, after the reading of them, ren-
ted all the fhedules, fauing that which was deliuered by
the Catholiks, whereupon *the heretikes departed afhamed
and dafhte out of countenance*. Whome he had, as ye alfo

GG iij   write

write,before examined of their faith,and that after ſuch ſorte,
that they were not only aſtonyed,but began to fall out amōges
them ſelues,ſome lyking.ſome miſlykīg the Emperours purpoſe.
But alas good M Horne,whie are ye your ſelf,nowe as ye
ſeame to me ſo ſodenly daſhed out of countenance? Yea
and whiche is maruayle in ſo harde a metall , me thinketh
ſomwhat aſhamed to,and wonderfullye aſtonied withall.
Why man? Pluck vp your harte,and be of good cowrage.
You wil perchaunce ſay I borde with yowe, and am ſette
vpon my mery pynnes. I woulde to God the matter were
ſuche as yt myght be better lawghed at , then pitied . And

The one
of them
euer law-
hed , the
other e-
uer wepte

that it might ſerue more for *Democrytus* thē *Heraclytus*,and
yet to ſay the truth , there is cauſe and to muche for them
bothe.Perchaunce nowe ſome mā wil think I doe but ieſte
when I ſpeake of ſhame: I would God yt were or myght
ons be truelye ſayde of youe , yt were a goodly ſparcle of
grace growing.Wel I put of that to other mēs iudgement.
But that *ye are daſhed out of countenance* , yea that ye are

M.Horne
no leſſe
aſtonied
in the tel-
ling of
this ſtorie
then the
Ariās and
other he-
retiks thē
vvere
vvhē the
thing
vvas don.

wonderfully aſtonied and that euen for the ſame cauſe , and
after the ſame maner as the Arians and other heretikes thē
were,I dare ſay it,and proue yt to . For if the Arians were
*aſhamed and daſhed out of countenaunce,*vpō theſe doinges
of Theodoſius onely,how much more are yowe *aſhamed*
*and daſhed out of countenaunce,*whoſe hereſies are cōdemned,by ſo many Kings and Catholyke Emperours?Or yf ye
ſay ye are not aſhamed then muſt I replie , ô ſhameleſſe
fellowe,and more impudente then the Arians.I nowe adde , that ye are more aſtonied then the Arrians and other
heretikes with this facte of Theodoſius , and therfore full
ſlylie and wvhlye,what was the doinges of the Emperour
ye haue ouerhipped,whyche yf ye had put in,would haue
ſerued

serued, afwel againfte yowe, as yt did againfte them. And
therfore the memorie of yt fo aftonied yowe, that ye durft
not for fhame name the matter, and yet for folly coulde ye
not forbeare to patche yt in, as a fpeciall matter aduaun-
cyng your fupreamacy. For firft, as Theodofius did not allowe, the open difputations of the Arians, Macedonians,
Eunomians, whiche were verie redie to the fame, fo vf he
had bene lyuing of late, he woulde not (ad euē for the fame
caufe he difalowed the other) allowed your late weftmyn-
fter difputations: beinge more mete to leade the common
people out of the truthe, then to confirme them in truthe,
whereof we haue alredie fomwhat towched. But nowe I
praye yowe M. Horn tel vs what was the Emperours purpofe that fome heretyks lyked, fome miflyked? wherin as
yt were the dogge drinking in Nilus, as the olde peruerbe
is, for feare of ftinging ye dare not tary. Wel becaufe ye are
aftonied at the memory of yt, I wil tel it for you. The Emperor demaūded of the heads of the fecte, *whether they did
allowe and receyue, the fathers of the Churche that wrote before the diuifion beganne: Yea marye* fay they, *what elfe? We
reuerence and honour them as our mayfters: for feare* (faieth
the ftory) *leaft yf they had fayde otherwyfe, the people would
wonderfully haue mifliked theyre doings: Wel fayd.* fayeth the
Emperour. *Are ye then cōtente, for this matters cōtrouerfed
to ftād to their fayings and teftimonie? Here they beganne the
one to ftare vpon the other, and wifte nere what in the world
to anfwere: and fynally fell owt* as your felf write, *amongs thē
felues* Now let the Emperor cal the Anabaptifts, the Zwinglians, the Lutherans, and demaūde of them, the fame queftion, woulde not the matter fo fall out thinke you? Yea
hath yt not alreadye fo fallen out, and daylye fo falleth

out

greate

VVhy
M. Horne
hath lefte
out the
principal
matter of
his ovvn
ftorve.
Tanquam
canis bibēs
in Nilo.
Hovv
Theodo-
fius the
Emperor
dafhed
the here-
tikes out
of coūte-
nance.
Sociat. li-
5. cap. 10.
The hee-
retiks fell
at diuifiō
before
Theodo-
fiō, vvher-
vpon he
teareth
their fhe-
duls of
theirfaith
vvhich
they of-
fred.

out more and more againft you and your Brethern,to your
great fhame ? And thincke you, that yf Theodofius were
lyuing now , he would not deale with your Billes , as he
dealed with theirs? Woulde he not teare a fonder the fhedules,of al your falfe faithleffe faith?Yes that he would affuredly. The greauoufe remembrance of this did,fo aftone
you,that it caufed you,thus to leaue the matter it felf,that
was *by fome liked,and by fome mifliked*, and to tel a liking or
miflikinge of I can not tel what.

Ye maye
fee the ful
anfvvere
of this, in
the Con-
futation
of the
Apology
fol.31.
Cod.Om-
nis vtriuf-
que fexus.

Now how fo euer ye haue maymed the narration of the
ftorye,and making the befte ye can of the matter for your
purpofe, primacy can ye make none of it . For the doinge
of Theodofius reacheth not to the determination of anye
thing in queftion alredy not determined , but to the execution of the Nicene Councel:commaunding by expreffe
decree,that al fhould obeye the faith of Damafus Pope of
Rome,and of Peter Patriarche of Alexandria, both defenders of the Nicene Councel.

The
Popes
Primacie
proued
by the
doinges
of Theo
dofius, ad
the Cou
cels by M
Horne
alleaged.
Vide Tō. 1.
Concil. in
Concil. A-
quil. pag.
397.col.1.b

Let me now a while after al this your miferable wrefting and writhing,ad liberal lying to,deale fhortly ad fim-
ply with you:and fee whether I can pycke out any thinge
of Theodofius and thefe coucels doings for the Popes primacy. Why then? Ys it not Theodofius that referreth the
decifiō of Ecclefiaftical caufes to the Biffhops? Was it not
he,of whō S. Ambrofe faied: *Ecce quod Chriftianus cōftituit
Imperator.Noluit iniuriā facere facerdotibus. Ipfos interpretes
cōftituit facerdotes.*Behold what the Chriftiā Emperor hath
appointed . He would not doe iniury to the Prieftes . He
hath appointed the Priefts them felues to examine the matter? Was it not this Theodofius the great,M. Horne? Yes
furely it was he. Was it not Theodofius, to whome Saint
Ambrofe

Ambrofe enioyned penance, which he moft humbly obeied? Where was Theodofius Ecclefiafticall fupremacye
then? Is it not Damafus the Pope, that calleth thefe Bif: *Tripart.*
fhops affembled at Conftantinople, euen to Rome, there to *li.9.ca.30.*
aide and afsift him in keping of a Councel? What? Saied
they to him, Syr we haue nothing to doe with you, ye are ἡμᾶς, ὡς
a forrain Bifhop to vs of the Eaft? Nay nay, they confeffe οἰκεῖα μέ
that he called them as his members (thē muft he needs be the λη προςε-
head)*to the Councell at Rome.* Yea they confeffe, that by his καλέσα-
letters they came to the Councel at Conftantinople: they σθε.
declare their good wil and readines to come to Rome too: *Theod.li.5.*
but for their excufe they alleage many reafonable caufes, *cap.9.*
none of thofe that the Proteftants alleage at this day. And
finally in the name of the whole, thei fend certaine of their
Bifhops thither. Now further, doe not thefe Fathers decree at this their general Councel, that the Church of Cō- *Can.5.*
ftantinople, fhoulde be the firft and chiefe of al other after
Rome? Do they not then therin acknowledge the Popes
Primacie? It is writen, M. Horne: *Sapientis oculi in ca-* *Ecclefiaft.*
pite eius, ftultus in tenebris ambulat. The eies of a wife man *cap.2.*
are in his head alwaies opē, and in a readines to direct him
in his way: whereas the folifh man walketh in darckneffe,
being vncertaine and vnfure which way to take or to goe.
Now whether your eyes priyng and feking forth this ftory
of Theodofius were opened or fhutte, I leaue the iudgement to the indifferent Reader: But this dare I firmely a-
uouche, that thefe things whiche I haue nowe laft rehearfed, befide other, that I willingly omitte, drawe much nearer to make the Pope fupreme head of the Churche, then
anye thinge ye haue broughte foorth, for the doinges of
Theodofius, to make him Supreame Head. Which when

ye haue al fayde and done be nothing agreable to the artiꝰ cles in queſtion betwene vs, concernyng our princes regiꝰ ment. And therfore yf the matter were much ſtronger of your ſide, touching Theodoſius, yet did ye nothing touche that ye owght to touche.

M. Horne. The. 42. Diuiſion. pag. 27. b.

<table>
<tr><td>

The.116.
vntruthe.
That vvil
neuer apꝰ
peare.
The 117.
vntruthe.
Such cerꝰ
tiſication
appeareth
not in the
ſtory.
The 118.
vntruthe
Falſe trãſ
lation, as
ſhail ap-
pere.
Li.5 ca 27
The 110.
vntruthe.
No ſuch
rule, or go
uernemēt
conïeſſel
by the Bi-
ſhop of
Rome,
Luithꝰ
prand.

</td><td>

Theodoſius *left his tvvo ſonnes Emperours, of the vvhich I vvil ſay but litle: yet vvherein it may moſte (.116.) maniſeſtly appeare, that the ſupreme gouernement in cauſes Eccleſiaſtical belonged to the Emperours.*

Archadius *the Emperour, vvhen* Nectarius *the biſhop of Conſtantinople vvas dead, and ſo the ſea vacant (.117.) vvas certiſied thereof. he cauſeth* Iohn Chryſoſtome *to be called from Antioch: he commaundeth the other biſhoppes collected into a Synode, that they admoniſh Chryſoſtome of Goddes graces, and vvhat belongeth to ſuche a chardge, and that they chooſe and order him to be the biſhop of Conſtantinople.* In vvhich dooinge, *(ſaith* Theodoretus *) the Emperour declared what careful endeuour, he had about the holy (.118.) Churche matters. But this ſupreme authoritie, to care, appoint, and procure vvoorthy and good Paſtours or biſhoppes, vvhen the ſeas vvere vacant, appeareth more plainly in* Honorius *the Emperour, brother to* Archadius, *vvhome the biſhop of Rome him ſelfe in his decrees, and his Gloſars on the ſame, cõfeſſe and acknovvledge to haue the ouerſight, rule and gouernement in the elections and orderinge of biſhops, yea (119.) ouer the biſhoppe of Rome him ſelfe.*

After the death of Pope Sozimus, *vvere tvvo Popes chooſen at ones in a great Schiſme, the one* Bonifacius primus, *the other* Eulalius, *vvhereof vvhen the Emperour* Honorius, *had notice beinge at* Millayne, *he cauſed them bothe to be baniſhed Rome: But after ſeuen monethes,* Bonifacius *vvas by the Emperours cõmaundement, called againe and cõſirmed (.120.) by his authoritie in the Apoſtolicall ſea. This* Bonifacius *beinge novve ſettled in the Papacy, by humble ſuite to the Emperour, prouideth a remedie againſt*

ſuche

</td></tr>
</table>

The 110. vntruthe. He vvas then to the temporalties of the biſhoprike reſtored, but he vvas the true Pope, before.

suche mischiefes in time to come. The case vvas this, saith the Glosator, Boniface the first, did beseeche Honorius the Emperour to make
a Lawe, whereby it might appeare, what were to be done,
when twoo Popes were chosen at ones by the vndiscreetnes
of the Electours, contendinge amongest them selues. Honorius
did than constitute, that neither of those twaine shoulde be
Pope, but that in a newe Election a thirde shoulde be chosen
by common consente. *If twoo(saithe the Emperour in his Lavve made*
at the humble sute of Bonifacius)by chaunce againste righte be cho-
sen, thorough the vndiscreete contention of the Electours: wee
permitte neither of them to be Priest or Pope: but wee iudge
him to remaine in the Apostolike sea, whom the diuine iudge
mente, and the common consente dothe appointe fro amon-
gest the Clergy in a newe Election . Vppon this vvoorde, vvhere the
*Emperour saithe(*wee permitte*)the Glosar saith , and so the Emperour dothe not onely abrogate the clayme of bothe those that
be chosen in the contention, but dothe make them bothe for
that time vnable, and dothe decree an other to be take out of
the Clergie for that time. *Againe the Glosar interpretinge this (the*
diuine iudgement) *saithe:*this is the meaninge that the Emperours wil and election muste stande, the Clergy and the whole
people acceptinge with thankefull minde whome the Emperour doth choose . For the Emperours were called in those
daies holy, and their rescriptes and iudgementes Diuine . *Here*
you see by the(.121) Popes decrees and Glosars, that the Emperour had the
supreme rule and gouernement in Churche causes, and this vvas the(.122.)
continual practise of the Churche for the most parte , yea euen the bisshoppes
of Rome before they vvere ordered and consecrated, had their election ratified
and confirmed by the Emperours, their Lieutenant, or other Princes.

Dist.79.
Si duo.

Gratian.
dist.63.

The 121.
vntruthe.
Carolus
Molineus
is none of
the Popes
Glosars.
The 122.
vntruthe,
vtterly
vnproued

The. 8. Chapter. Of the Sonnes of Theodosius, Honorius and Archadius.

Stapleton.

HH ij   Now

NOwe folowe in rew Theodoſius his ſonnes: Archadius and Honorius, of whome M. Horne ſayeth he wil ſay but litle, belike, becauſe he hath ſaid to much of theyre father alredye, and more then he can iuſtifie, or for that he wil make vs a ſhorte tale, but yet a ſweete. And wherein *it ſhal moſt manifeſtly appere, that the ſupreame gouernement in cauſes eccleſiaſtical belonged to the Emperours.* Al Archadius doings here ſtande in appointinge S. Iohn Chryſoſtome to be biſhop of Conſtantinople, a moſt worthie man who dowbteth? And I woulde to God as this his firſte dealing with Chryſoſtome was to his worthy prayſe : ſo he had not by his after dealinge blotted and blemiſhed the ſame.

The eleſ
ſtion of
S. Iohn
Chryſoſto
me by Ar
chadius
maketh
him no ſu
preame
head.
Tripart.
lib. 10. c. 3.
Socrates.
lib. 6. c. 2.

As for this election, firſt Archadius did it not of his own Supreme authoritie, but the fame of Iohn Chryſoſtom being great, and after ſome debate aboute the election, *Intra modicũ tẽpus cõmuni decreto omniũ clericorũ, & laicorũ Imperator Archadius euocauit eum.* Within a litle while (ſaieth Socrates) by the common decree and agreement of all the Clergy and of al the lay, the Emperour Archadius ſent for him from Antioche to Conſtantinople, and ſo by the common decree of al eſtates (as the order of electiõ then was) he was elected biſhop, not by the Emperours ſupreme and abſolute Authoryty, as M. Horne fancyeth. The Theodoret though he tel not ſo much , yet dothe he not attribute the matter to the Emperour: as a parte of his gouuernement. Which that it might ſome waies appere, M. Horn thought good to ſpyce a litle the text with the powder of his falſe tranſlation, that yet ſo it might ſomewhat relys in the Readers cõceit for his ſurmiſed primacy. For Theodoret ſaieth not, that in this dooing, *the Emperour declared what careful endeuour*

endeuour he had aboute the holy Churche matters but περὶ τὴν
Ἰὰ θϊὰχ σπзϛϊν , the care that he had about Gods or godly matters. Which care is commendable as in all men, so in princes especially , for the greater good they are able to doe.
But such care of Gods matters emporteth no gouuernement in such matters. As neither the care of Churche matters importeth iurisdictiō : Though yet that soundeth nearer to iurisdiction then the care and zeale about godly maters.　And therefore M. Horne thought good with this litle poore helpe of false translation, a little to itche forward
his miserale and barraine cause.　And that we shoulde the
more fauourably winck at his liegerdemain, he phraseth it,
the holy Church matters. Speaking very holily and reuerently, that we might not suspect him of forgery .　Whereas
in the original text of his author, there is no worde, of eyther *Church* or *holy Church*.　Last of all, though we graunted him (which we neither will nor may , considering the
whole story, as Socrates describeth it) that Archadius him
selfe appointed Iohn Chrysostom to be Bishop, yet maketh
it not any iote to proue any Supremacie in him , eyther in
al, or in any cause ecclesiastical. Vnlesse we wil haue euery
laie patrō that preseteth his Priest to a benefice, to be suprē
heade also : or measure the matter by the greatenesse and
weight of the patrimony and liuing, and not by the weight
of reason. But now M. Horne, in an il time for your self, ād
for your supremacy, haue ye here put me in remēbrance of
this Archadius, and S. Iohn Chrysostom. Yf you would pur-
posely haue sought a meane to haue geuē your self a greate
and a shameful fall, that all that beholde you, mighte laughe
you al to skorne: ye could not haue foūd lightly any where
els a better occasion.　For this Archadius being Emperour

Theo-
dosius
Theod.
li. 5. c. 27

περὶ τὰ
θεῖα .
Circa res
diuinas.

M. Hornes
primacy
ouerthro-
wen by
his own
example.
Gorgius
Alexand.
in vita Io.
Chrysost.

of the Eaſt, as Honorius was in the Weſt, was excómunicated of Pope Innocétius for baniſhing of the ſaid S.Chry-
ſoſtom being moſt wrongfully depoſed by his enemies , by
the procurement of Archadius his wife.Now Syr I beſech
you tel me who is ſupreme head,the Emperour,or he that
excómunicateth th'Emperor, eſpecially being vnder an o-
ther Patriarche and reſidét ſo far of, as Cóſtantinoplé is fró
Rome ? The next narration ſeing it toucheth nothing, but
matters of election,requireth no great anſwere:namely ſeing M.Horne him ſelf.hath made a ſufficiét anſwer againſt
him ſelf.For if th'Emperour made a law touching th'electió
of Popes,at the Popes own deſire,belike here was no great
Supremacy:eué no more then the Pope was cótent either
to geue hi,or to ſuffer at his hand. Neither the baniſhing óf
both Popes fró Rome,eſpecially in a ſchiſm,as this was,by
M.Horne here ſpecified,cauſeth any ſpirituall iuriſdiction,
the matter it ſelfe being mere temporall , as the matter of
the election being (in this caſe) only begunne,not brought
to perfection. Beſide this , here is no preſidente of our
elections in England. For here is both the Emperors,the
Clergyes, and the peoples conſente in the Biſhoppelye e-
lection.

I woulde nowe paſſe ouer to the next matter , ſauing
M.Horne here commeth in with his Gloſatour and Gloſar
after ſuch a cunninge ſorte, lawlike , and gloſelike , that it
woulde not be to haſtely lepte ouer. Firſte he alleageth
the Gloſatour, as he calleth him , and that I am aſſured, is
meante , and ſo to be proued of him that is the common
expoſitour of the Canon Lawe , as appeareth by Maiſter
Hornes owne allegations. But that he bringeth out of
his Gloſar, I am aſſured , is not to be founde in him that he
calleth

calleth Glofatour. And fo haue we an other extraordinary
glofe by M. Horne now firſt authoriſed. But perchance ye
wil meruaile, good Reader, eſpecially ye that are exerciſed
and trauailed in the Canon Law, that M. Horne ſhuld haue
ſo deape and rare knowledge in the gloſes of the Canon
law, that perchàce this queſtion might appoſe the beſt Doctor in the arches, onles it wer M. D. Ackworth M. Horns
ſone in law, who perchàce by his fathers ſpeciall còmiſion,
though perhaps M. Horne neuer read the gloſar him ſelfe,
hath authoriſed vs a new gloſar. And now me thiketh your
eares itch to heare what gloſar this ſhuld be. It had ben wel
don for M. Horne to haue eaſed his Reader and me to in ſo
doutful a mater. But ſeing we haue foùd him out at the lègth
out he ſhall, and al the world ſhall now know him, and ſhall
know M. Horne much the better by and for him. Therfore
to be ſhort, it is *Carolus Moline⁹* a frenchman, whoſe gloſe is
as far as I can yet learn, ſcarſe ſeuen yeres old, or therabout,
ſcarſely paſt his infancy, and woulde hardly be allowed to
ſpeake, onleſſe M. Horn had biſshopped it. Wherfore I ſee
no cauſe, but that I may according to my manner, ſcore vp
this to.   But yet if M. Horne will needes haue him a Gloſar (with the which perchaunce I will not greatly ſticke,
eſpecially in that ſence , as merely we call a Gloſar in our
tongue, that is a vaine lyer) and thinke he may truely ſo
call him, I will not muche contende with him . For if he
ſkape ſcoring vppe for calling him Gloſar here , ſurely he
ſhall by no meanes ſkape for calling him the Popes Gloſar the tenth lyne immediatlye following.   For *Mollines*
us is ſo the Popes Gloſar, that he loueth the Pope , and alloweth his authoritie, euen as well as M. Horne him ſelf:
as appereth as wel by his notes adioyned to the olde intèr-
pretour

A neuve
gloſe of
the Canõ
law, now
ſirſte au-
thoriſed
by M.
Horne.

Vide editi-
onem iuris
canonici
in.4, Lug-
duni cum
gloſ.1559.

pretour of the Canon law, new and frefh fet out', as by his other workes extant in print,condemned among other inhibited bookes by the late General Councel. And whoe would haue thought that M.Horne had fuch wife , wilie, wittie, frefh fetches ? I perceiue a ragged Colte may yet proue a good Horfe.

M. Horne. The. 43. Diuifion. pag. 2 9 .b.

Sabellicus fpeakinge of the contentious entraunce of Damafus the firft into the Papacy, vvhiche vvas not vvithout great bloudfhed,as Volateranus faith , dothe note the ambition of the Prelates,to be the caufe of fuche cōtention about their atteininge of fuch roumes. For now (faieth he) the ambicious defire of honour, had by litle and litle, begon to entre into the mindes of the Bifhopes. The vvhiche vvas proued ouer true,not onely in the elections of the Bifhoppes of old Rome , but alfo in many Bifhoppes of other Cities, efpecially of nevve Rome . Thefe difeafes in the Churche minifters, and the diforders thereout fpringyng: the Emperours from time to time ftudied to cure aud refourme : vvherefore Theodofius *and* Valentinianus *vvhen they favve, the great hooting and fhoouinge at Conftantinople, about the election of a Bifhop after the death of* Sifinius *fome fpeakinge to preferre* Philippus,*other fome* Proclus,*both being minifters of that Churche,did prouide a remedy for this michiefe,to vvitte,they them felues (.123.) made a decree,that none of that Church fhould be Bifhop there,but fome ftraunger from an other Churche, and fo the Emperours fent to Antioche for* Neftorius,*vvho as yet vvas thought both for his doctrine and life,to be a fitte paftor for the flocke,and made him Bifhop of Conftantinople.*

Liberat.
cap.4.
Socr.lib.7.
cap 29.
The 123.
vntruthe
No fuch
decree ap-
pereth:
neither in
Liberatus
nor in So
crates.

Stapleton.

This man is nowe againe in hande with the Emperours ordinance concerning the election of the Bifhop of Conftantinople:but by the way,or being as he is in dede,al out of his waye and matter to , he toweheth what flaughter there was at Rome , when Damafus was made Pope , and fo rūneth backe agayne out of the way,and out of his matter:

ter : which he might ful wel haue let alone , sauing that he
would shewe his great familiaritie and affinitie with Iulian
the Pelagian. Who for lacke of good matter to iustify his
own, and to infringe the Catholik doctrine, fel to controlle
the Catholikes for their manners , and namely for this dis-
fention at the creation of Damasus. Of which cotentiō, Sabellicus, saith M. Horne, speaketh : and Volaterranus sayeth
it was not without much bloudshed. As though Sabellicus
said not also , that the matter was tried with strokes. But
where to finde or seke it in either of them , M. Horne leaueth vs to the wide worlde. But what is this, M. Horne, a-
gainst Damasus Primacie , who was also a true and a good
godly learned Bishop : whom S. Hierome for all this contention, recognised as head of the Churche, and as greate a
Clerke as he was, yet being in doubte by reason of diuerse
sectes about Antiochia in Syria, with what persons to communicate, moste humbly requireth of him to knowe, with
whom he should communicate, and with whom he should
not communicate ?

What is then your argumēt, M. Horne ? Is it this ? Damasus entred into the See of Rome by force and bloudshed:
Ergo, the Emperour at that time was Supreme gouernour
in all causes Ecclesiasticall. Verely either this is your argumēt, or els you make here none at al: but only tel forth a
story to no purpose, except it be to deface the holy Apostolik See of Rome, which in dede serueth euer your purpose
both in bookes and in pulpitts. What so euer it be you haue
in hand beside, the Pope may not be forgotten.

Now that you tel vs of *a decree made* (by th'Emperours
Theodosius and Valentinianus) *that none of the Churche of*
Constantinople should be Byshop there, but some straunger frō

M. Horne
folowerh
Iulian the
Pelagian.
Aug. lib. 6
cō. iulian.
De consti-
tuendo &
Epiʃcopo
diʃʃenʃionē
populi Ro-
mani in-
ʃultabndus
obiectas,
Volat. int
lib. 22.
pag.409.
multi mor
tales ex
viraque
parte in-
terʃecti.
Sabel. en-
nead.9.
li.9. Vi &
armis cer-
tatū, com-
petitore ʃu
perato.etc
Ad Dam.
Damasus
Primcy
recogni-
ʃed by S.
Hierom

Theo-
dofius

Liberatus
cap. 4. in
Breuiario.
Socrates
li. 7 ca. 29
Niceph.
li. 14. c. 34
35. .
The. 124.
Vntruth.
Theodof.
in thefe
doings by
you allea-
ged, vvas
vngodly.
The. 125.
vntruthe.
Vtterlie
vnpro-
ued
The. 126.
Vntruth.
For not
by his au-
thoritie.
The. 127.
Vntruth.
He gaue
no fuche
Cōmaun-
dement.
The. 128.
Vntruth
The Coū
cell refi-
fted and
refufed
the orde-
ring of.

an other Churche, you tell vs a mere vntruth : Your alleaged Authors Socrates and Liberatus fpeake no one woorde of any fuch *Decree.* The words of Liberatus (who tranflated in maner the wordes of Socrates) are th efe: *Sifinius being departed, it femed good to the Emperours, to appoint none of the Church of Conftantinople to be bifshop there, but to fend for fom ftraunger from Antioch in Syria(from whence they had a little before, Iohn Chryfoftome) and to make him Bifshop.* And this worde for worde hath alfo Socrates , but he addeth more : διὰ τοὺς κενοσπουδαςὰς ἐκ τῆ ἐκκλησίας. *Becaufe of the vaine triflers and bufy heades that were of that Churche.* Of any Decree that the Emperor fhould make, none ofthem both doe mention. But at that time only the cafe then in Con-ftantinople fo ftanding, and their luck before being fo good in Iohn Chryfoftom, who from a ftranger became their bi-fhop, it pleafed the Emperours fo to doe. And al this they did by way ofprouifion for the Church quiet, not by waye of abfolute authority or any forceable Decree, as M. Horn fableth and ouer reacheth his Authors.

M. Horne. The. 44. Diuifion. pag. 28. b.

As Conftantinus *and* Theodofius *the elder, euen fo* Theodofius *the feconde a very (.124.) godly Emperour, hauing and practifing the (.125.) fupreme gouernment in Ecclefiafticall caufes , feeinge the horrible Herefies fpronge vp, and deuidinge the Church, but fpecially by* Neftorius, *did (126) by his authoritie cal the thirde general councel at* Ephefus, *named the firft* Ephefine *souncel, geuinge ftreight (.127.) commaundement to al Bifhops whwerefoeuer , that they fhoulde not faile to appeare at the time appointed, and further vfed the fame povver and authoritie, in the ordering and gouer-ninge thereof by his (.128.) Lieutenaūt* Ioannes Comes Sacrenfis, *that other Godly Emperours had beene accuftomed to vfe before him , according to the cōtinual practife of the Churche, as it is plainely fet foorth in the booke of general Councelles.*

In this councel there happened fo greuous contention betvvixt Cyrillus

Bifshop

Biſhop of Alexandria, and Iohn Biſhop of Antioche, both beyng othervviſe godly and learned mē, that the councel vvas diuided thereby into tvvo
partes: the occaſion of this Schiſme vvas partely, that Cyrillus and certaine other vvith him had proceeded to the cōdemnation of Neſtorius, before that Ioānes vvith his cōpany could com, ād partly for that Ioānes of
Antioch ſuſpeded Cyrillus of certain Hereſies, miſdeeming that Ciril had
made the more haſte to confirme them before his comminge. He therefore
vvith his aſſociates complaineth, and laieth to Cyrilles chardge, that he did
not tary according to the commaundement of the Emperour for the comming of the Biſhops of other Prouinces, vvhich vvere called thither frō all
partes, by the cōmaundement of the Emperour: That vvhan the noble Earle
Candidianus commaunded him by vvriting, and vvithout vvriting, that
be ſhould preſume no ſuche matter, but that he and thoſe that vvere vvith
bim, ſhould abide the comming of the other Biſhops, neuer theleſſe he proceeded: that he and his company vvere the authours of diſſenſion and diſcord
in the Church: and that they had geuē the occaſion, that the rules of the Fathers, and the decrees of the Emperours vvere broken, and trodē vnder foote:
vvherefore they iudge Cyrill of Alexādria, vvith Memnō biſhop of E-
pheſus, to be depoſedfrō their biſhopriks, and Eccleſiaſtical miniſtery: and
the other their aſſociates to be excōmunicate. The vvhich their doinges they
ſigniſie to the Emperour Theodoſius by their Synodical letters, to vnder=
ſtande his pleaſure, in (.129.) allovving or diſallovvyng of their Synodicall
ades. After this came the biſhop of Romes legates, before vvhome in the coucel Cyrillus and Memnō offered vp their libelles, depoſing a conteſtation
againſte Iohn and his party to haue them cited, and render the cauſe of their
depoſition. The biſhoppe of Romes legates, vvith the conſent of the councell,
on that parte, ſendeth for Ioannes and his parties, vvho returneth this an=
ſvveare: Neither ſende you to vs, nor wee to you, bicauſe wee
looke for an anſweare * from the Prince touching you. Therfore ſaith Liberatus: Cyril and Memnon, ſeekinge to reuenge thē
ſelues, did condemne Iohn and all thoſe that ſtood with him,
who ſuffered manye diſpleaſures at Epheſus thoroughe the
pride of theſe twaine. The Emperoure ſendeth to the vvhole
Councell his anſvveare in vvritinge, on this ſorte: VVee allowe
the condemnation of Neſtorius, Cyrillus, and Memnon: the

The
Secōd
this
Lieutenāt
Iohn.
Cyril.ep.
22.Tō.4.
Liberat.
cap.6.
All this
vvas a
leude faƈt
vvhiche
neuer cā
to effeƈt,
ād vvher-
of they al
repented
after, yet
M. Horne
buildeth
vpon it.

The 129.
vntruth.
The ſtory
hathe no
ſuche
vvoords.

*So did
alvvaies
Schiſma-
tiks, ſuch
as theſe
vvere.

other actes and condemnations, whiche you haue made, we
disallowe, obseruinge the Christian faithe, and vprightnesse
which we haue receiued of our fathers ad progenitours. etc.
Certaine of the Bishops did satisfie the Emperour (.130.) whō
he commaunded to enter into the Church, and to ordeine an
other Bishop for Constantinople in the place of Nestorius.
These things thus done, the Emperour dissolued the Coūcel,
and commaunded the Bishops to depart euery man to his own
coūtrie. VVithin a while after, the Emperour perceiuing the
dissension betwixte Cyrill and Iohn to continue, whiche he
thought was not to be suffered: called Maximianus, and many other Bishoppes that were then at Constantinople, with
whome he cōsulted, how this schifm of the Churches might
be taken away. *Whose aduise had, the Emperour sent a noble man,
Aristolaus with his letters to Cyrill and Iohn, commaunding thē to come
to an agreement and vnitie betwixte them selues, otherwise he would
(.131.) depose and banish them both. Wherevpon followved a reconciliation
betwene the two bishops, and much quietnes to the Churches.*

The 13.
vntruth.
These
vvordes
nippe l of
in the
middle.
Bicause
the greate
and gene
ral coun
cel doing
all things
regularly,
hath con-
demned
Nestorius.
By vhich
appereth,
the Coū-
cel gaue
sentence
ouer the
Heretik,
not them
perour.
The.131.
vntruth,
the word
depose,
is not in
Liberat.

The 9.Chapter. Of Theodosius the Second: and of the Ephe-
sine Councell, the third Generall.
Stapleton.

HERE followeth now an other Emperour Supreme
head of the Churche as well for calling of the firste
General Councell at Ephesus, as also, for ordering
and gouerning of it by his Lieutenaunt. Yf M. Horne do or
can shew any decree or determination in matter of faithe,
or any other Ecclesiastical matter made by Theodosius or
his deputy, then were it somewhat. He sheweth no such
thing, nor can shew any such matter. Al this ordering and
gouerning, is concerning the externall and outward matters, and to see al things done quietly and orderly: and by
ciuile punishment to correct such as disobey the Councel.

All

All the which are no matters of spirituall gouernement.   Secōd
Let vs then consider the particularities.

The calling of the Ephesine Councel by this Emperour *Niceph.*
Theodosius(which yet was at the requeft of Cyrillus the *li.14.c.33*
Patriarch of Alexandria,not by the Emperours owne authoritie)M. Horne fetteth foorth in thefe words : *geuing*
ftreight commaūdement to al Bif hops wherefoeuer, that they
*fhould not faile to appeare.*As though the Emperour had fo
peremptorily cited them,and fummoned thē both,as Princes and Ciuile Magiftrates doe cite their fubiectes for ciuil
matters. Whereas the hiftory of Nicephorus by him alleaged,geueth forth no token of fuch peremptory *commā-*
*dement,*but rather of the contrary.For the Emperour in his
letters whereby he fummoned them,addeth this reafon or *Niceph.*
threat to them that would draw backe. *Qui enim vocatus* *li.14.c.34*
*non alacriter accurrit,non bonæ is confcientiæ effe apparet.*For
whofoeuer being called,hafteneth not,verely he appereth
to haue an euill confcience. In which woordes he rather
chargeth their confcience before God, then their loyal o-
bedience to him:as Iofaphat did to the Prieftes and Leuits
of the olde Law,as before hath ben fhewed.Neither vfeth *2.Paral.*
any other threat or force of commaundement to expreffe *19.*
fo much as an ynckling of that glorioufe fupremacye that
M.Horne would fo faine finde out.

Againe,*the ordering and gouerning* (as you call it) of the *Vide Cyril.*
Councell, by *Ioannes Comes the Emperours Lieutenaunte,* *Epift.22.*
was fuche as Cyrillus and al the Catholique Bifhoppes of *Tom.4.*
that Councell,complained of. Firfte ,*becaufe he made no*
true relatiō to the Emperour,what was in the Councel done.
Then becaufe he laboured to haue Iohn of Antioche with
his confederates, reduced to the Communion of the holy

Theodosius

Councel hauing broke the Canons: To the which requeft, the Councell refifted plainlye, faiyng: *It is not poſsible to force vs hereto, except both that which they haue done againſt the Canons, be diſanulled: and alſo they become humble ſuppliauntes to the Councell, as ſuche whiche haue offended.*

When Iohn the Lieutenant could not winne his purpoſe this way, by force of authority, whiche thoſe Biſhops acknowledged none at all, for any matter Synodicall to be concluded, or decreed, he went about by a ſleight to compaſſe them. He deſired them, *to geue him in writing a confeſsion of their faith: and I, ſaied he, will cauſe the other to ſubſcribe therevnto, and ſo to agree with you.* This he did (ſaieth the Councel) that after he might make his vaunte, and ſay,

Concilia-
ui eos ad
amicitiā
humanis
inter ſe of-
fenſis diſ-
ſidentes.
Nō expo-
nimus nos
contume-
lia.

I haue brought theſe biſshops to an attonement, being at variaunce among them ſelues, vpon worldly diſpleaſures. And the Councell eſpiyng this, replied againe, *they woulde not geue the world occaſion of reproche and ſhame.* And as for the cōfeſſion of their faithe which he required, they anſwered. *We be not called hither as heretikes, but we are come hither to reſtore the faith that hath bene deſpiſed, which alſo we do reſtore. And as for the Emperour, he hath no nede nowe to lerne his faith: he knoweth it wel enough, and he hath bene baptiſed in it.*

Thus we ſee the *ordering and gouerninge*, whiche M. Hornes cauſe dependeth vpon, of this Lieutenāt and Emperour too, was a mere tyrānical violēce, not ſuch as *other godly Emperours accuſtomed to vſe before him, as* M. Horne auoucheth. So did not Conſtantine in the Nicene Coūcel. Nor Theodoſius this mans Grandfather in the Councell of Aquileia. But this was ſuch a tyrannicall gouernment, that Cyrillus and the whole Synod writeth thereof thus. *We be*

Cyrill. vbi
ſuprà.

all

all in greate vexation, being kept in with the guardes of fouldi-
ars, yea hauing them by our beddes fide when we flepe: fpecially
we, faith Cyrillus. *And the whole Councell befide, is much we-*
ried and vexed, and many are dead. Many other alfo, hauing
fpent all doe now fell their neceffaries. This, lo, was the honorable gouernement of M. Hornes fupreame head. By M. Horne
force of armes to extort a cōfent. Such a gouernour would groūdeth
the great Turke be, or the Souldan, if he ruled againe. his prima-
But fuche rough paterns pleafe verye well this rough and cye vpon
rude Prelate. *Similes habent labra lactucas.* Wheras ther- the doe-
fore he calleth this Emperour Theodofius, *a verie godlie* Schifmac
Emperour, feing he calleth him not godly in this place, but tical Bif-
in refpect of his actions hereafter to be by him rehearfed, thop.
which are very lewd and naught, as it hathe and fhall yet
better appeare, it is a plaine vntruth, what fo euer he were *Donec pœ-*
in other thinges. And therefore either he fhoulde haue *nitentiā a-*
forborne fo to call him, at the leaft in this place, or fhoulde *gatis, et a-*
haue founde fome better matter for him to haue practifed *nathema-*
his Supremacie vpon. *tifetis, hæ-*

For al Maifter hornes declaration refteth in this, that he *retica ca-*
defended Iohn the Bifhoppe of Antiochia, and a fewe of *pitula quæ*
his confederates, the fautours of Neftorius, in this Coun- *à Cyrillo*
cell condemned. Whoe made Cyrillus and the refidew *Alexādri-*
of the Ephefine Fathers (two hundred in number) heretiks, *no epifco-*
and called their doings hereticall, as euidentlye appeareth *funt cōtra*
by the felfe fame Authour and chapter, that M. Horne *Euangeli-*
taketh for his helpe and ayde. But to fweete this vnfaue- *cam & ca*
ry declaration wythall, he calleth thys Ihon *a godlye man :* *tholicam*
and wandering here and there in by circumftaunces, lea- *doctrinam*
ueth owte thys, leaft the godlye Reader might fone fuf- *Liberatus.*
pecte thys Primacye, ftandynge vppon no better grounde. *cap. 6.*

Yet

Yet will M. Horne ſaye, that Theodoſius practiſed this Supremacy here. Firſt by the Earle Candidianus his De-putie, who on the Emperours behalfe inhibited Cyril and the other, that they ſhould not procede til the comming of Iohn the Patriarche of Antiochia. Then, that after the ſaid Iohn had condemned Cyril and Memnon, and depoſed the from their Biſhopriks, the Emperour confirmed Iohns ſen-tence. Thirdly that ſeing the diſſenſion betwixt Cyril and Iohn to grow more and more, comaunded them to agree, otherwiſe he would depoſe and baniſh them both. Laſt of all, that Iohn being cited to anſwere before the Popes Le-gate, would not come, but ſaid, he looked for the Princes anſwere.

But theſe things neither ſeuerally nor iointly are of any force. Firſt, Candidianus doings, as ye ſee, goe no further then to the externall moderation, diſpoſition, and order of the Councels doings. Whiche, as we haue before ſaide, is one point of the Emperours dealing in Councelles, as the Churches beſt Sonne, not as Supreme gouernour thereof. Secondarily, the Emperoure depoſed not Cyrill, ❦ the ſchiſmaticall aſſemble of Iohn and his coſociates to the nū-ber of. 34. as Liberatus writeth: and that contrary to the minde of al the reſidue, whoſe ſentence though wrongful-ly geuen, Theodoſius ſiniſtrally affected and ſeduced, doth confirme. Wherein he is no principall worker, but an exe-cutour of the ſentence. Thirdly, the Emperour threatned no depoſition or depriuation, but baniſhment only, which is no Spirituall but Ciuile puniſhment, and ſo impertinente to our matter. Therefore where you adde, *he would depoſe the* to ye are but a Gloſar. And as good a gloſar for the Pope as your brother Molineus. For Liberatus your author, hath no fuch word. Only he faieth. *He threatened to fende them both to Nicomedia in banifhment.* Laft of al , Iohn beinge fuch a mã, ãd fo vpholdẽ by the Emperour,what meruaile yf he woulde not appeare before the Popes Legat, of whõ he thought he fhould be cõdemned? There is no felõ by his good wil,that would appere at the Kings bẽch,but would refufe it,yf he might be afsifted therin. And yet it is an or- dinary ãd a lawful cowrt,that not withftãding:and fhould be,though an hundred fuch fhould refufe it.

Wel Sir: Now that ye haũe fpẽt and empted your proufs for the vpholding of Theodofius primacy,wherin ye work lyke one that taking vppon him to guyde other in the night , woulde put out the candle or torch and conducte them by a lanterne,let vs for our fyde fee,yf we can fetche any better light afwel from other,as euen from your owne Author , and from the doings of your owne councell and your owne Emperour,for the bifhops and the popes eccle fiaftical primacy . I fay then that the head and prefidẽte of this councel was Celeftinus the Pope: and in his fteade the forefayde Ciril, and not the Emperour or his deputie. Vpõ this as a certayne truthe all the ecclefiaftical writers afwel Latins as Greke,vniformely agree,yea the whole councel yt felf of Ephefus agnifeth this Cœleftine as theire prefi- dente and head,as appeareth by the nexte general councel of Chalcedo fhortly folowing , and in the Ephefin coũcels letters to the Emperour Theodofius him felf: and to the Emperour Valentinian. And leaft ye fhould thinke,the fpi- rituall men, and the councels encroched to muche vppon the Emperours iurifdiction,and did thẽ iniury,as ye , your Apologie,M.Iewel,and your other bretherne complayne, lo Themperour Marcianus , and the Emperour Iuftinian

Proufes for the Popes pri macy ta- ken out of the Ephefine Councell and M. Hornes ovvne author. *Profper in Chronic . Euang.li. 1. cap. 4.* Nicep.lib. 14.cap.34 Con.Flor. fef.5. et 8. Chal.fyn. Act 4.pa gina.874. Celeftine confefed the prefi- dente of the Ephe fine coũ cel by tvvo Em perours. Pro Mar. vide act.3 Cõc.Chal.

The
Ephe-
fine.

Pro Iufti.
edict. eius
tom.2.cō-
cil.

M Horns
primacye
deftroied
by his
ovvn:
author.

Liberatus
in breuiar.
cap.22.
tom.2.cō,
pag.119.
M.Iewels
errour:
In his Re-
ply fol.
254.
M.Horne
noteth
not the
author ād
chapter
of his de-
claration
ād vvhy?
Euag.lib.
1.cap 4.

in their open proclamations do plainly profeſſe, that Pope
Cœleſtine by his deputy Cyril, was preſident of that Coūcel. I trow M. Horne this is no lanterne light ſhut vp in a
darke dymme Horne, but good torche light, or rather the
fayre bright light of the ſonne it ſelfe.

In caſe al this will not ſerue the turne, we wil drawe
ſomwhat nearer, euen to your owne author, your owne
Emperour, yea your owne wordes to, and by them proue
our intente: and then I truſt ye wil be fully ſatisfied. Who
is he then Maiſter Horne, that writeth : *Multos in
hoc mundo reges eſſe , & non eſſe vnum , ſicut Papa eſt ſuper
Eccleſiā mundi totius.* There are many Kings in the world,
and no one King of the whole : as the Pope onely is the
gouernor ouer the Church throughout the whole world:
Surely it is your own authour Liberatus . And hereby appeareth well M . Iewels great errour, and M . Nowelles
to, affirming ſtoutely and aſſuredly, that one man can no
more haue the rule of the whole Church, thē of the whole
world. Liberat⁹ a writer about xi⁶.yers paſt, reporteth that
aſſertiō, ſpokē of a holy biſſhop to the Emperor Iuſtiniā, ād
yet accōpted therfore neither fooliſh nor wicked. You be-
gāne your narratiō with the diſſentiō of Cyrillus and Iohns,
but your memory or your truth fayled you, whē ye lefte
out the author of whō ye toke it ād the chapter. Perchaūce
ye were here aſtonied, as the heretiks were before Theodoſius. For euē in this place your author ſheweth, that Cœ-
leſtin was the preſidēt of this coūcel, by his deputy Cyrill:
to whō he gaue inſtructiōs and informatiōs by letters, how
he ſhould demeane hī ſelf with Neſtorius, and preſcribeth
him a certain order for his doings. And therfore Cyril him
ſelf, at what tyme he ſhould pronounce final ſentēce of depriuation.

priuatiō againſt Neſtorius, ſaieth he was forced therto by Cœleſtinus letters. In the geuing of which ſentēce, neither thēperor, nor his Lieutenant, had any thing to do, either in allowing or diſallowing: ād that wil I proue vnto you euē by your own ſupreme head Theodoſius writīg to Cyrillus, *vt perturbatio quæ ex cōtrouerſiis iſtis accidit, ſecūdū ecclesiaſticos canones diſſoluatur,* that the hurly burly which thē was for cōtrouerſies of religiō, might be pacified and quieted according to the ecclesiaſtical canōs. Now by the ecclesiaſtical canō the ending and determinatiō of matters ſpirituall apperteyneth to the clergy, ād not to the layty. Now alſo both to anſwere you, and to take ſome hādfaſt againſt you of ſuch things, your ſelfe haue alleaged: wil ye know M. Horne whether the doings of the erle Cādidianus thēperors deputy, reached to the diſcuſſiō or determinatiō of any matter ecclesiaſtical, or no? I ſay, no. And for my ſaing to be cōfirmed I appeale to your own ſupreame head Theodoſius, and plead for my ſelf, the very cōmiſſiō, that he gaue to Cādidianus. *Deputatus eſt Cādidianus magnificus Comes trāſire vſa ad ſanctiſſimā ſynodū veſtrā, ac in nullo quidē quæ facienda ſunt de pijs dogmatibus quæſtiones communicare. Illicitum namq̄, eſt, eũ qui nō ſit ex ordine ſanctiſſimorum epiſcoporum ecclesiaſticis immiſcere tractatibus.* I haue ſent, ſaith thēperour Theodoſius, the noble erle Candidinianus, as my deputye vnto your holye Synode, geuinge him in charge, not to medle in anye poynte towchinge queſtions to be moued abowte godlye doctryne and Religion. For yt is vnlawfull for him, whiche is not of the order of holye Biſſhoppes, to entermedle with Ecclesiaſticall matters. But yet ye ſaye, Iohn and his fellowes woulde not appeare before the Popes Legates : A true man

Coūcei.
Cyrillus gaue ſentēce agaiſt Neſtori⁹ by Celeſtin⁹.
Cyril. epi. 11. &. 12.
Tom. 4. Cyril. epi. 17.
Proued againſt M Horne by Theodoſius hiſelf that thē peror is not ſupreame head in matters ecclesiaſtical.
M. Horns owne example alſo of Candidinia⁹ turned agaiſt hi.
Cap. ſatis euidenter diſtin. 96.

The Ephe-fine.

This Iohn refufed to come be-fore the Popes Le gates and the Coū-cel by as good right, as M Horne and his fellovves refufed the Coū-cel of Trent.

Liberatus cap.6.

M.Horns fupremaꞓ cye de-ftroyed by his ovvne author and chapter.

ye are in this point. It was fo in dede, wherein his doinges were as good as yours and your felowes Proteftante bif-fhops, which being and that with a large faufe conducte, called to the late Councel of Trente, durft not, ye knewe your caufe fo good, fhewe your face in fuch an ordinarie and learned confiftory. Ye knew ye were no more able, to fhewe good caufe why ye haue depofed the Catholike Biffhoppes, then coulde your Iohn, why he depofed Cy-rillus and Memnon. And therefore he being called to geue a reckoning of thofe his doings before Pope Celeftins Le-gates, who were then prefident themfelues (for Cyrill and Memnon then both put vp their complaintes to the Popes Legats, the newly come from Rome to Cōftātinople) and before the whole Coūcel of Biffhops, durfte not appeare.

But loe now out of your own place ād chapter, an other opē proufe againft you, for the Popes, ād the ecclefiaftical primacy. For not withftāding all that euer your Emperour and fupreme head did, and for al his allowing of Iohns wyc-ked proceding: the Popes Legats and the Councell with a more Supreme Authority refumed the matter into their hāds: to whō alfo Cyrill and Memnon biffhops of Ephefus vniuftly depofed, offred their billes of cōplainte: wherevpō Iohn was cited to appere. who playd the night owlespart, not able to abyde the cleare light of the Popes authority, ād of fo honorable a Councel. And fo haue ye cōcerning this Ephefine Councel fpoken altogether, as we faye, *ad Ephe-fios*, and very poore ayde are ye like to take at this Coun-cels hands. Nay, ye are quyt ouerborē ād ouertilted there-with. As it fhall yet more at large appere to him that will

Art. 4. fo. 337, et 138

vouchefafe to reade, that I haue writen of this matter a-gainft M. Iewel, in my Returne of vntruthes.

M. Horne

M. Horne. The 45. Diuision. Pag.30.a.

Eutyches stirred vp much trouble in these daies : vvherefore he vvas cited
to appeare before Flauianus Bishop of Constantinople, and other Bishops
assembled in a Synode, to ansvveare vnto his heresies : vvho vvoulde * not
appeare but fledde vnto the Emperour Theodosius., and declareth vnto
him his griefe. The Emperour sendeth vnto the Synod vvith Eutiches, one
of his chiefe officers Florentius, vvith this mandate: Bicause wee study
carefully for the peace of Goddes Churche, and for the Catho
like Faith, and wil by Goddes grace haue the righte Faithe
kepte, whiche was sette foorth by the Nicene Councell, and
confirmed by the Fathers at Ephesus, when Nestorius was cōdemned: wee wil therefore there bee no offence committed
aboute the aforenamed Catholique Faithe, and bicause wee
knowe the honourable Florentius, to be a faithfull and an ap-
prooued man in the righte faith, wee wil that he shalbe present in your Synode, bicause the conference is of the Faithe.
He vvas there asistaunt vnto the Fathers and (.132.) examined Eutyches
openly in the Synode, (.133.) diuerse times of his faithe, and finally saide vnto
him: He that (saithe Florentius) doth not confesse in Christ tvvo
natures, doth not beleeue aright: and (.134.) so vvas Eutyches excommunicate, deposed, and condemned. Eutyches rested not here, but obteined that the Emperour did commaunde a nevv Synode to be had at Constantinople, vvherein to examine the actes of the former, vvhether that all
thinges touching the proceding against Eutyches, vvere don orderly and
rightly, or no. He appointeth besides Florentius, diuerse (.135.) other of his
nobles to be in this councel, to see the doings thereof. But vvhen Eutyches
coulde not vvin his purpose in neither of these Synodes, he procureth by friēd-
ship of the Empresse Eudoxia and others, that the Emperour should call a
Synode againe at Ephesus: to the vvhich Synode the Emperour prescribeth
a fourme of proceding. This Synode vvas a vvicked conuenticle, vvherein
the truth vvas defaced and Heresie approued, the Emperour being seduced
by Chrysaphius, one of the priuy chamber, and in most fauour vvithe
him.

*He vvas
an here-
tik I vvar-
rant you,
that
vvoulde
not ap-
peare be-
fore his
bishop,
but fled
to the
Prince.
Liberat.
cap.11.
The.132.
vntruth.
Florētius
vsed no
examina-
tion at al.
The 133.
vntruth.
He neuer
asked hī
but one
question.
The.134.
vntruth.
Not so.
that is
not by
Florētius,
but by
the Coū-
cel he
vvas cō-

K K iij The

demned, and deposed. The 135. vntruthe. Nicephorus hath no such thing.

The. 10.Chapter,of Eutyches the Archeretike.
Stapleton.

AS Eutyches that falſe monke did,ſo do ye flie frō your
ordinarie Iudges to ſuche as be no Iudges in the matter . Neither the preſence of Florētius, or any other
the Emperours deputy in the councel, maketh the Emperor, as I haue ſayd ād ſhewed before,a ſupreame head.And
in as much as the Emperor ſayth,that *becauſe the cōferēce is*
of ſayth, he woulde his deputy to be preſent : that is graunted
Diſt. 96. (whē matters of faith are debated)not only to Emperours,
Vbinam. but to al Chriſtē mē. But hereof yt may be inferred that in
Chal. Act. Coūcels aſſembled for diſciplin eccleſiaſticall , and not for
3.pa.838. faith,thēperor and his deputy haue nothīg to do:which in-
Cabil. frigeth the greateſt part of your ſupremacy. And which is
can.6. plain both by the rules , and by the practiſe of the Church
Milleuit. expreſſed in the Coūcels of Chalcedon,of Cabylon,and of
Cap. 19. Milleuitum . Now as we graunt the Emperours deputye
may be preſent in the Councell, where matters of faith
are in debate:ſo how he is preſent , and to what ende , and
that he hath no authoritye to determyne and decide the
controuerſies, we haue alredy proued by Theodoſius him
ſelfe.To ſtoppe belyke this gappe,ye imagin Florentius to
play the Iudges parte,as to *examyne Eutyches openly in the*
*Synod of his faith,*and how he belieued . Examination Florentius vſed none, but as any lay man beſide might haue
don,he demāded what he beleued: which demaunding is
not to determin,what and how he ought to belieue.Again
where you adde, *diuerſe tymes of his faith* , this is an other
vntruth.For Florentius in al that Synode neuer aſked him
but one queſtion (which you here alleage) and that after
the Synode hadde nowe condemned him . But I ſuppoſe
ye would

ye would faſten the Iudges part vpon him, becauſe he ſayd to Eutyches, he that doth not confeſſe in Chriſte two natures, doth not belieue a right. This might anie other mã haue ſayd to, and this is but a ſymple ſentence. And as ſimple as yt is, ye thought not very ſimply, but dubly and craftely, yea altogether falſly, minding to beare the ignorant reader in hãd as thoughe this had bene the final ſentence . And therfore ye ſay, and ſo was Eutyches excommunicated , depoſed , and condemned. But by whom, I pray you, Maiſter Horne ? By Florentius, or Flauianus in the Councell ? And when and howe , I praye youe ? Did not the Councell before theſe woordes of Florentius, demaunde of Eutyches his faithe ? Yea , did not they tell him ? Thou muſt confeſſe thus , and Liberatus cap. 11. curſe all doctrine contrary to this faith ? Nowe when Eutyches would not, and ſaid , as ye ſay in many thinges , he would not, becauſe the holy ſcripture hadde no ſuche matter, then did the Councel curſe him : And after this curſe Florentius ſpake the woordes by you reherſed . Afterwarde was he curſed again, and depriued of his prieſtly honour, not by Florenrius, but by his owne biſſhop Flauianus, as it is conteined in the chapter by you quoted . Yea that more is, a playn place withal of the Popes primacy to. For both Flauianus ſent this his Sétéce to Rome, and Eutyches thus códemned, cóplayned by his letters vpon Flauianus, and appealed, to Pope Leo. But Eutyches reſted not here: (ſaieth M. Horne) In dede in Eutyches we haue a paterne of you and your felowes, that wil be ruled by no lawe or order of The Popes primacy pro ued by M, Horns ovvn au thor and chapter. the Church. This Eutyches being firſt three ſeueral tymes cyted by his owne biſſhop and Patriarche Flauianus, would not appeare before him, but by the meanes of one Chryſaphius his Godde childe , a buſkyn gentleman aboute the

the Emperours preuy chamber, brought the matter to the
Prince. Then a prouincial Synode being called by the Emperour, and Eutyches condemned, he appealed from the
Emperour to Pope Leo . Being by him alſo condemned,
he woulde not yet yelde . No in the generall Councel of
Chalcedon being thriſe ſummoned by the whole Councell of 630. Biſhoppes , his pride and obſtinacy was ſuche,
that he woulde not appeare , nor being there with ful cōſent condemned, would yet yelde thereunto . And al becauſe the ij. natures of Chriſt in one perſon (which he denied) was not expreſſely found in the Scriptures . In all
theſe (except his only appealing to Rome) he ſhewed him
ſelfe as right an heretike, as any that nowe liueth. But this
is a wōderful foly, or rather madnes in you to procede on,
and to alleage farder matter of Theodoſius doinges for
calling other Councels in the mayntenance of Entyches
Leo epiſt. at Conſtantinople and Epheſus, and by and by to declare,
51. ad Pul that the ſaid ſynode of Epheſus, was a wicked conuēticle,
cheriam. as it was in dede, and as Leo calleth it, *Non iudicium, ſed la-*
trocinium. No iudgement, but a tyrannical violence, and al
thinges there done againſt *Flauianus*, afterwarde reuerſed
by Pope Leo: a moſt certain argument of his ſupremacye.
And yet ye cal your Emperour, a godly Emperour, neither
ſhewing of his repentaunce, nor of any his good doinges.
Thus ye ſee how pitefully euery way ye are caſte in your
own turne.

M. Horne. 46. Diuiſion. Pag. 30. b.

Leo the firſt, Biſhop of Rome a learned and a godly biſhop , although
not vvithout al faultes, maketh humble ſupplicatiō vnto Theodoſius the
Emperour, and vnto Pulcheria: that there might be a general
Coūcel called in Italy, to aboliſhe the wicked errour in Faith,
confirmed

confirmed by the violence of Diofcorus . The felfe fame Bifhop of Rome with many bifshops kneeling on their knees,
did moft humbly befeeche in like fort Valentinianus the emperour, that he woulde vouchefaulfe to entreate and exhorte
Theodofius the Emperour to cal an other Synode , to reuoke
thofe euil aftes and iudgementes, which Diofcorus had caufed to be don in the condemnation of Flauianus Bifshop of
Conftantinople and others . *In vvhich examples it is manifeft, that
the bifshops of Rome did (.136.) acknovvledge the fupreme gouerment , direction and authority in calling of Councels, vvhich is (. 137 .) one of the
greateft amongeft the ecclefiaftical caufes or matters , to be in the Emperours, and Princes, and not in them felues .*

ged any fuch matter, and Leo left of al other ,   The.137. vntruthe. It is no ecclefiaftical caufe at al, as the Emperours vfe it.

The
greate
Liberat.
cap.12.

The.136.
vntruth.
The
Popes ne
uer ac-
knovlea-

The. 11. Chapter. Of Pope Leo the great, and first of that name .

Stapleton.

IT is well and clerkly noted of you M . Horne, that Leo,
*being a godly and a learned biffhop was not yet without all
faults* It was wel fpied of yow, leaft men fhould think he
was borne without originall fynne (which I dowbt whether yowe wil graunt to Chriftes mother) or take him for
Chrift him felf . For who, I befeache yowe, is without all
faultes ?

But what a holy, vertuous and godly man this Leo was,
I let paffe to fpeake (though very much might be faid therin) bicaufe the good or euil life of a Pope or any other man
is not material to the doctrin which he teacheth, or to the
matter we haue now in hand. But verely for his right faith,
true doctrine, and found belefe (for the which you feme to
taxe him) I wil with ij. fhorte faynges onely of ij. generall

Coūcels ſhortly note to the Reader, both what an abſolute
doctour this Leo was, and what a malapert comptroller
you are. The Chalcedō Councell of 630. biſhops do expreſſely and plainely profeſſe their Iudgement of this bleſſed
father Leo (in their ſolemne ſubſcription) in theſe wordes.

Act. 4. pa. 871. col. 1. Tom. 1. Con.

*Nos ſummè orthodoxum eſſe ſanctiſsimum patrem noſtrum
Archiepiſcopum Leonem perfectiſsimè nouimus .* We moſt
perfitly know, that our moſt holy father Leo the Archebiſhop, is of right iudgement in religiō, in the higheſt degree.
Loe M. Horne thoſe fathers ſo many and ſo lerned with
one conſent do ſaye : Not that they thinke or beleue, but
that they *knowe* : and that not ſuperficially or ſlenderly,
but *perfectiſsimè* moſt perſytly, moſt exactly , moſt aſſuredly : And what knowe they ſo ſurely ? Forſothe that their
moſt holy father Leo is *Orthodoxus*, a right beleuer, a true
Catholike , a ſounde teacher of Gods people . And not
onely ſo, after a common or meane ſort, but *Summè Orthodoxum* : Catholike and right beleuing in the higheſt degree:
without any blotte or blemiſh in that reſpecte . After
ſuche a Sentence , ſo proteſted and pronounced, of ſuche,
ſo many, ſo lerned, and ſo auncient fathers aboue vnleuen
hundred yeres paſte , in ſuche and ſo ſolemne an aſſembly for the abſolute and vndoubted commendation of that
excellent prelat, whence crepe you, with your lewde ſurmiſe , or with what face dare you deface him ? With the

Cōcil. Cō ſtant. 5. Act. 1. pag. 74. Tom. 2. Cō cil.

like conſtāt and abſolute cōmendatiō (without any ſurmiſed exceptiō at al) in an other general Coūcel, the next after this, he is called by the cōmon voyce of the Eaſt Biſſhops, *Illuminator & Columna Ecclesiæ.* A geuer of light, and
a piller of the Churche. You come to late, M. Horne, to
blotte or to blemiſh the Reuerēt memory of ſo bleſſed, ſo

learned

lerned and so much commended a father. His light so shy-
neth that no horne can dymme it. His doctrine is so stroge,
that no surmise can weaken it. The more you kicke at
this piller, the more you breake your shinne. The more
you deface him, the greater is your owne shame.

Therefore as your glosing here was causeles̄e, so surely your meaning is graceles̄e. Verely suche as if ye had
expres̄ed it, woulde forthwith haue disgraced and quyte
ouerthrowen your false conclusion immediatly folowing,
freighted almost, with as many lies as lynes. For touching his suyte to the Emperour to haue a Councell called, you must vnderstande M. Horne, that the bare calling of Councells suche as Emperours haue vsed, is not
one of the greateste amonge Ecclesiasticall causes, nor,
to speake properlye, any matter Ecclesiasticall at all, but
a prouision by the waie of exhortation for the bishops to
meete in some conuenyent place without breache of the
ciuill order, which forbiddeth *Illicita collegia* : that is, vnlawful assemblies, as the same shoulde for such be accōpted
if thēperor had not allowed them: And not only thēperor,
but any other prince being lorde of the territory or soyle,
where the bishops woulde assemble. In dede the discussion
and determination of matters of faith in Councelles may
wel be said to belong to the great ād weighty causes of the
Church, but this belōgeth not to lay princes: and this not
withstādig, Leo is so far off frō acknowledging this supreme
gouernmēt and authority in calling of councels, that yf I be
not deceiued, ye your self do know ād belieue the cōtrary,
and therefore durst not speak what ye thought, but vnder
such dark and mystical talke. For I pray you, M. Horne,
what is the fault ye find in Leo, worthy to be thus touched

*Tit de Il-
licitis col-
legijs.*

by yow onleſſe yt be, that he moſte playnely and ſeriouſly auowcheth this ſupreame authoritie to reſte in the ſee of Rome? And then fare wel your goodlie concluſion. What other ſecrete faults, by your ſo quick prying egles eye, ye haue in him eſpied, I wot not. But your brethern of the beſt and learned ſorte, fynde, as farre as I can fynde, none other fault then this that I haue ſayde: wich is no fault at al. And therfore in your ſhrewde and vnhappie meaning, thowgh not in your expreſſe péning, yt is a verye vntruthe. Yet yf ye wel pretend ignoráce, and make men belieue ye know no ſuch thing in Leo, but that yowre cócluſion is true, and taketh place as wel in him as other biſſhops, then wil I load and preſſe you, with ſuch good and euidéte proufs, fetched no farder then from Leo him ſelf, that ye ſhall be fayne, yf ye haue any grace to acknowledge the truthe. For whether ye regarde his doings or his ſayings, both are in this pointe moſte notable.

S. Peters primacy he doth euery where confeſſe. As appereth in many of his ſermons, and in his other workes. For Leo ſaieth: *Quoniam & inter Apoſtolos, in ſimilitudine honoris fuit quædam diſcretio poteſtatis: & quum omnium par eſſet electio, vni tamé datũ eſt, vt cæteris præemineret.* Whereas all the Apoſtles were of lyke honour (he meaneth in Apoſtleſhip and prieſthood) yet was there difference of power amõgs them, and where as al were of lyke elected, yet was yt geuen to one to be peerleſſe aboue the other. Wherein he meaneth Saint Peter. Leo ſaieth, that where other Biſhops haue their ſeueral and appointed care, the

care

Proufs out of Leo for the popes primacy. See his 3 ſermon vvherehe calleth S. Pet. head of the Church. Epiſt. 82. vel aliás 84. ad Anaſtaſium cap. 11. Tom 1. cō= ſil. pag. 709.

Ad vnam Petri ſedem vnerſalis eccleſiæ cura conflueret. Ibidem.

Vt pro ſolicitudine quam vniuerſæ ecoleſiæ ex diuina inſtitutione dependimus: epiſt. 87. ad epiſcopos Aphrican.

care of the vniuerſal Church cometh to the only ſee of S.
Peter. Leo ſaith, *that euen by Gods own ordinance , he taketh
care, for the whole Churche*. And Leo ſaieth, *Vt ab ipſo quaſi
quodam capite , dona ſua velut in omne corpus diffunderet, vt
expertemſe miniſterij intelligeret eſſe diuini, qui auſus fuiſſet
a Petri ſoliditate recedere: hunc enim in conſortium indiuiduæ
vnitatis aſſumptum , id quod ipſe erat , voluit nominari, dicen-
do. Tu es Petrus & ſuper hanc Petram &c.* that from S. Peter
the Apoſtle as from the head God powreth al his gifts into
the body, and that God toke him into the felowſhip of the
indiuiſible vnity. The meaning whereof Leo him ſelf expoundeth, ſaying, *that he ſhall not be partaker of Gods miſte-
rie that departeth from Peters ſowndenes: and for that Chriſte
who is called in ſcriptures the rock, gaue the ſame name to Peter.* And here yt ſhall not be much out of the way to note,
that M. Iewel recyting this place, doth not only diſſimble
that this is writen of the godlie and learned man Leo: but
alſo fathereth yt vpon Pope Bonifacius , who writeth it
to, but as ye ſee, not originally. And moſt lyingly for *vnitatis* putteth in *trinitatis*: as though Leo ad Bonifacius ſhould
make S. Peter one of the three parſons of the bleſſed Trinitie. Being in this poynt, the popes gloſar, as good as Mo
lineus, or M. Horne him ſelfe. Whiche Molineus in this
place gloſeth apaſe, but not for the pope, but as much as he
can againſte him. And yet for this matter much better then
M. Iewel, reading aſwell here as otherwhere in the canon
lawe: *vnitatis, & non trinitatis*. This nowe by the way , to
ſhewe yow, that there be more popes gloſars, then Molineus, and withal, one of M. Iewels prety knackes, worthy
to be added for an after reckonig to ſuch as M.D.Hardig,
D.Sanders, and I haue moſt rightfully charged him with.

Leo epiſto
87.ad epiſ.
Vicuñe.
prouinciæ:
tom.2.côc.
ſel.705.
Extra de
elect.& e-
lecti poteſt
c.ſunda-
menta.
levvell
Pag.311.
A vvret-
ched cor-
ruption
made of
Pope Leo
his words
by M.
levvel.
Vide dict.
c.ſunda-
menta in.
6. & diſt.
19.ca.ita
Dominus:
in editio.
Lugd.1559

Let vs now returne to Leo, and fee whether as
in woordes he did amplifie this fupreame authority: fo in his doinges he practifed it, or no . Who
is he then, that reuerfeth the vnlawfull doinges
of Bifihoppe Hilarius at Fraunce ? Leo . Who is
he, that *calleth to a generall Councell the Bifshoppes
of Tarracone , Lufitania , Fraunce and Carthage?*
Leo . Who is it that *appointeth his deputye Poten-
tius to heare and refourme matters Ecclefiasticall in
Aphrike?* Leo . Who is he that doth appointe
Anastasius the Bifihoppe of Theffalonica, *to be his
deputye and vicegerente for matters Ecclefiasticall*
in thofe quarters ? Leo . Who is he that reftored to his bifihoprike the learned Theodoretus biffhoppe of Cyrus dwellinge farre of in the eafte,
vniuftlye depofed of Maximus his owne Patriarche, and of Diofcorus ? Leo . Who is he that
fendeth his deputy Iulian to the Emperour Marcian to remayne in his cowrte , and to fupplye
his office ; in fuch thinges as fhoulde be done, a-
gainft heretikes in thofe quarters? Leo. Who is he
that did annichilate ād reuerfe by the authority of
S.Peter the Apoftle , the doings of a nōber of Biffhoppes at Conftantinople , before the Bifihoppe
of Alexandria and other patriarches contrarye to
the canons of Nice ? Leo. Who is he that fendeth
his Legates to be prefidentes in the great Councel at

Dict.epift.87.
Dedimus literas
ad fratres & coepif-
copos Tarraco . Car-
tha. Lufitanos atque
Gallicos eifque con-
cilium Synodi ge-
neralis indiximus.
epiftola. 93 ad Tur-
biū .cap. 7.
Vicem cura noftra
proficifcenti à nobis
fratri & confacer-
doti noftro Potentio
delegantes. epiftola
87. ad epifcopos A-
phrican.
Dilectioni tuæ vi-
cem mei modera-
minis delegaui . epi-
ftol.82.
To.1.Con.pa.742.
Vicem ipfe meam cō-
tra temporis noftri
hæreticos delegaui,
atque propter eccle-
fiarum pacifque cu-
ftodiam, vt a comi-
tatu veftro non ab-
effet, exegi. epift.55.tom.1.Concil pag.674 In ipfo Leon. 57. Confenfiones Epifcoporū
fanctorū canonū apud Nicæā condita: ū regulis repugnātes, in irritū mittimus.& per au
thoritatem beati Petri Apoftoli generali prorfus definitione caffamus . Ad Pulcheriam
epift.55.Tom.1.concil.pag.672. Epiftola 47.& 49.

cel at Chalcedo?Leo.Which him felfe fignifieth in his let
ters afwel to the whole Coūcell as to thēperour Marcian.
Who is he that confirmed the Decrees of the Councel of
Chalcedo,being therto required,as wel by the whole Coū
cel,as by thēperour Marciā? Leo.Who is he that cōfirmed
Anatholius and Proterius the ij. chiefe Patriarches in the
Eafte,one of Conftantinople the other of Alexādria? Leo.
And who is he that in fummoning the Councel of Chalcedon, yelded not otherwife to the Emperours appoynt-
ment for the place , but with an exprefle exception, faying ? *The honour and right of the See of S. Peter the moft bleffed Apoftle , referued :* Leo . Wherein he expreflely fignified, that the Summoning of the Councell of right appertayned to his Apoftolike See . What faye yowe to all
this, Maifter Horne ? Howe well dothe , Pope Leo , acknowledge your fupremacy? For fhame leaue of ons thefe
lyinge conclufions.Hard yt will be I trowe,yt feameth to
be fo naturall an humour in men of your religion. But yet
nothing is hard to the willing,and to him that will hartely
feke for grace at Gods hande. The which I praye him of
his mercy fende yowe : And learne I praye you to fynde
faulte with your felf, as ye haue greate caufe , rather then
with this good vertuoufe bifhop , faultlefle I dare faye for
fuche matters,as ye take for greate faultes in him . But to
ende this matter , I muft commende yowe for one thinge,
for ye haue fcaped one fcoringe that your fellowe M. Iewell did not fcape : for writing that Leo did kneele with
other bifhops,which the wordes of his authour Liberatus
by you here truelie reherfed , do not importe.

Margin notes:

greate
Epift. 59.
& 61.
Act.3.
Chal. cōc.
Epif. 33.
40 ' 4.55
Epift.68.
Leo epift.
47.

It is in
the 477.
vntruth.
In our
Returne
Art.4.fo
lio 142.

                                    M.Horne

Mar-tianus
Nice. lib.
15.cap.12.
Leo epist.
44.

M. Horne. The. 47. Diuision. Pag. 3'. a.

Marcianus, a godly Emperour, and very studious about the Christian Religion, succeded Theodosius, vvho besides that of him selfe, he vvas much careful to suppresse al heresies, and to refourme the Churches, restoring Religion to purity vvithout error, vvas also hastened hereunto by the earnest sute of Leo bishop of Rome: vvho in diuerse and sondry epistles, declaring vnto him in moste humble vvise, the miserable state of the Church, doth beseche him, that he vvould vouchsaulfe to cal a general councel. Many other bis-shops make the same suite vnto the Emperour, and to the same ende: complai-ning vnto him, of the miserable destructiõ, and horrible disorders, in Church causes. An example and paterne of their supplications, vvherby (.138.) may ap-peare, that they acknovvledged the Emperour to be their Supreme gouer-nour, also in Ecclesiastical causes, or matters, is sette foorth in the Chalcedon councel, in the supplicatiõ of Eusebius, the bishop of Dorelaum, vnto the Emperour: vvho maketh humble supplication as he sayth, for him selfe, and for the true or right faith. we flie vnto your godlines (saith this bishop vnto the Emperour) bicause both we and the Christian faith, haue suffered much wrong against al reason: humbly cra-uing iustice, and for that Dioscorus hath doon many, and that no smal offences, both against the faith of Christ and vs: pro-strate, we beseche your clemency, that you wil cõmaund him to answere to the matters, we shal obiecte against him: (.139.) wherein we will proue him to be out of the catholike faith, defending heresies replete with impietie. VVherefore we beseche you to directe your holy and honourable commaun-dement, to the holy and vniuersal councel of the moste reli-gious Bishoppes, to examen the cause betwixt vs, and Dios-corus, and to make relation of al thinges, that are doon, to be (.140.) iudged as shal seeme good to your clemency. The Em-perour protesting that they oughte to preserue the furtheraunce of the right fayth and Christian Religion, before al other affaires of the commõ vvealth: sendeth their letters of summons to all bishoppes, commaundinge them to repaire to Nice, a citie in Bithinya: there to consulte and conclude, an vni-tie and concorde, in religion, and matters perteining thereunto, that here-after all altercation and doubtfulnesse be taken cleane avvay, and an hole-some

Act. 1.
The 138.
vntruth.
Neither
by Leo
his epistle
neither
by the bis-
shops sup-
plication
any such
thig doth
appeare.
The 139.
vntruth.
In nipping
of a clause
in the
middest,
vtterly
ouer-
throvvig
M. Horns
principal
purpose.
The 140
vntruth.
False trã-
lation.
In epist.
preamb.

ſome trueth in Religion eſtabliſhed, addinge (.141.) threates, and puniſhe-
ment to them that vvould refuſe to come at the time appointed. VVhat baſ-
ſembly vvas made at Nice of all the biſhops, and that the Emperours could
not come thither, to be preſent in the Synode perſonally, vvhich they had pro-
miſed and did much couette, they vvrite vnto the vvhole Synode, vvilling thē
to remoue from Nice vnto Chalcedon vvithout delay: vvhere they aſſembled
at the Emperours (.142.) commaundement, to the number of. 630. bi-
ſhoppes.

The.12.Chapter. Of the Emperour Martian, and
of his calling the Councel of Chalcedon.
Stapleton.

M. Horne is nowe harping againe vpon his old ſtring
of calling of Councelles : and would eſtabliſh Marcianus eccleſiaſticall primacy thereby. But eyther
his eies, his lucke, or his mater was not good, to happe vpō
no better place then he doth, which doth beare him quyte
ouer, and ſetteth forth pope Leo his primacye ſending his
ambaſſadours and vicegerents to Cōſtantinople to reforme
hereſies, and to pardon and recōcyle ſuch heretical biſhops
as were pœnitente: vnto whome he adioyneth as his delegate, euen the Biſhoppe and Patriarche of Conſtantinople. And declareth this his doings in his letters as wel to
the Emperour him ſelfe : as to Anatolius the Patriarche.
Nowe what yf pope Leo requireth a councell at the Emperours hands ? what doth this blemiſh his authority, more
thē yf the Pope now ſhuld require the Emperor, the french
and Spaniſhe kings, and other princes, as he did of late, to
ſende their biſſhops to the councel? Verely that the Emperour ſo ſhould doe, it was of all times moſte neceſſarie in
Marcian his tyme: the.3 patriarches of Alexandra, Antiochia, and Hieruſalem, with a great number of Biſhops in the

MM   Eaſt,

Chal-
cedon

The 141.
vntruthe
Marcian
vſed no
ſuch threa
tes.
Vide epiſt.
preamb.
Cōc.Chal.
Tom.1,Cō.
pag. 734.
col. 2.
The 142.
vntr. At
his exhor
ratiō, not
commaū.
dement.

Fp 42.&
44 alias
44. &
46.Tom 1
Conc. di-
cta epiſt.
42 a ibi
eſt 44.

*Generale
Concilium
ex præcep-
to Chriſtia
norũ prin-
cipũ,& ex
cōſenſu A-
poſtolicæ ſe
dis placuit
cōgregari.
Epiſt. 9.
alias 61.
ad Iuue-
nalē.Tom.
1.Concil.
pag.676.
Socra.li.1.
cap.8.
Councels
cā not be
kepte
vvithout
the con
ſent of
the Pope.
Beatiſſimi
Petri iure
atque ho-
nore ſerua
to.Ep.45.
alias. 47.
Tō.1.Cōc.
pag.663.
col.2,4.*

Eaſt, taking then the Archeheretike Eutyches part,againſt
the good and godly Catholike byſhop Flauianus , whome
Dioſcorus with his factiō murdered . Was it not then high
time to ſeke al ayde and helpe,both ſpiritual and temporal?
Or is it any diminution to the ſpirituall power , when the
temporall power doth helpe and aſſiſt it ? Or thinke yow,
would this pernicioũſe peſtilent fellow Dioſcorus, and his
faction any thing haue regarded Pope Leo his eccleſiaſtical authority,which before had ſo notoriouſly tranſgreſſed
both Gods lawes and mans lawes,onleſſe the good Emperour had ioyned his aſſiſtaunce vnto it ? And this maye be
anſwered for the calling of many other generall Councels
by the Emperours : eſpecially of the firſte ſeuen hundred
yeares after Chriſt,when the Patriarches them ſelues were
Archeheretikes , and the matters not like eaſily to be re-
dreſſed by the Churche authoritie onely. Yet neyther did
any Catholique Prince call,or could call a Councell without or againſt the Popes wil and conſent . If ye thinke not
ſo, as in dede ye doe not , then thinke you farre a wrong :
And the *godly and learned Biſhop Leo* , as you call him , is
able, if you be capable and willing toward any reformation,ſone to refourme your wrong iudgement. Who declareth expreſſelye,that euen the Councell of Chalcedo was
ſummoned, *by the commaundement of the Emperours , with
the conſent of the See Apoſtolique* . Surely it was a rule and
a Canon in the Church,aboue.12. hūdred yeares now paſt,
that no Councell could be kept (as Socrates witneſſeth) *without the authoritie of the Biſhop of Rome:* And that by a ſpeciall prerogatiue and priuilege of that See. This prerogatiue Leo alſo doth ſignify, ſpeaking of this Emperour Marcian,who called the Chalcedon Councel,but yet,ſaith he,

With-

*Without any hinderance or preiudice of S. Peters right and ho:
nour*, that is by and with his consent, being S.Peters successour, in the Apostolique See of Rome.

I meruail much, that ye frame this supremacie of Marcian by the supplication of the Bishop Eusebius, desiring the
Emperour to procure by his letters that the councel would
heare his cause against Dioscorus, which serueth rather for
the Councels primacy. The remouing also of the Councel
from Nicæa to Chalcedo, doth serue to as litle purpose. For
the cause of the trasposing was, for that Leo by his ambassadours had signified, that the Bishops would not assemble,
onlesse th'Emperour would be there personally, for feare
of seditió and tumult of Eutyches disciples. It was therfore
translated to Chalcedo, being nigh to Constantinople, that
the Emperour might be there the more comodiously. And
so that which was done by the good Emperor to assure ād
honour th'Eclesiasticall authority, ye turne it to the hinderance and derogation of it. But in the supplicatió of Eusebius which you haue put so at large in your booke, it is a
world to see how vntruly you haue dealt, partly with nipping of sentences in the midst, partly with false translation.
First you leaue out at the very begining of the Bishops sup:
plication, wherin he shortly declareth the whole effect of
his request, saiyng: *The entēt and purpose of your clemency is to
prouide for all your subiects and to helpe all that are iniurioufly
oppressed, but especially such as beare the office of Priesthod.* By
this beginning it appereth, the Bishop requested onely the
Emperours external and ciuill power for redresse and help
against iniuries. And becaufe this should not so appere, you
thought good to leaue it quite out. Againe in the processe, where the sayed Bishoppe saieth: *Prostrate we*

Vide Tom.
1. Concil.
pag.735.
&.736.

Act.1.
Cōc.Chal.
pag.741.

MM ij   beseech

*befeech your clemencie that ye will commaund Diofcorus to
anfwere to the matters we fhall obiect againft him.* It folo-
loweth which you leaue out, *the euidences of his doinges a-
gainft vs being read in this Councell,* by which words the bi*
fhop required the Conncel to be his Iudge, not the Emperor: and leaft that fhald appere you leaue it out: At the end
where the latine hath, *perferre ad fcientiam veftræ pietatis
omnia quæ geruntur,* you turne it : *to make relation of all thins
that are don,to be iudged:* where you haue put in thefe words
(*to be iudged*) of your own liyng liberality, more then your
latine hath: and al to perfuade,that the bifhoppe requefted
here the Emperoure to be the Iudge betweene Diofcorus
and him. Which(if ye had put in the whole wordes of your
Author) would haue eafely appeared nothing fo , but rather the contrarye : as by the places by you omitted , and
nowe by me expreffed , the circumfpect Reader may fone
perceiue.   Thus like as your doctrine , fo is your manner
of writing, falfe , vnperfect, and vntrue.

  Againe in all this tale, Maifter Horne, though you tell
vs at large howe the Emperoures Marcian and Valenti-

In epift.
Praamb.
Concil.
Chalced.
Tom.1.
ʾag.733.
34. &
735,col.2

nian *fente their letters of Summons to all Bifshoppes commaunding them, &c.* Yea , *adding threattes and punifh-
mentes to thofe that refufed to come at appointmente,* Yet
you tell vs nothing that the Emperoure *firfte wrote vnto
Pope Leo , and obteined his confente and Authoritye.*
And then that in his letters of Summones to al Bifhops,
certified them expreffely of the Popes pleafure, and laft of
all that the Popes Legates required the Emperours *to be
prefente perfonallye at the Councell, or els they woulde not
come there themfelues.* All this yow lette paffe. In deede
it maketh not for yow . But it fheweth againft yow and
              for

for vs , very well and plainely , that the supreme summon
and citing of the bishops to that general Councel, yea and
the Emperours owne presence there, proceded directlye
and principally from the Pope and his Legats. It declareth
well the Popes supremacy in that affaire, as we shal in many other moe pointes decypher vnto yow anon more at
large. Neyther doth the Emperour vse in his letters of Sū-
mon, the wordes of commaundemente , but saith : *Venire
digne mini.* Vouchesafe ye to come. And againe. *Adhorta-
mur.* we exhort you to come. This was the practise of Emperours (as I haue noted before out of Cusanus) by the way
of exhortation to call Councels : not by forceable cōman-
dement, by threates and punishmēt, as you vntruely report.

The.143.
Vntruth.
They wer
no rulers
suche as
M. Horne
tancieth.
Act.1.
The cause
of discord
vvas that
they tau-
ght not
*quod veri-
tas aut
doctrina
patrum
requirit,*
that
vvhiche
truth or
the Fa-
thers do-
ctrine re-
quireth.
This you
omit. For
vvhy: it
shevved
your ovn
case.
The.144.
Vntruth.
The Em-
peroure

M. Horne. The. 48. Diuision. pag. 31. b.

*The Emperour assigneth Iudges and (143.) rulers in the Sinode about.
24. of the chiefest of his Nobles and Senateurs. after al the Bishoppes and the
Iudges vvere assembled in the councell house , vvhiche vvas in S. Euphemies
Church: the Emperour Martianus, vvith Pulcheria, entreth in amongst
them, and maketh an Oration vnto the vvhole Councel, to this effecte . First
he declareth, vvhat zeale and care he hath for the maintenance and furtherance of true Religiō: Then he shevveth, that partely the vanitie, partely the
auarice of the teachers, had caused the + discorde and errour in Religion: He
addeth the cause vvherefore he chardged them vvith this trauaile : And last
of all he (.144.) prescribeth a fourme, after vvhich they must determine the
matters in controuersy. Thus done, the Iudges sate doune in their places, and
the Bishoppes arovve, some on the right hand , and others on the left hande.
And vvhan that Dioscorus vvas accused , and the Iudges vvilled him to
vse his lavvfull defence, there began to be amōgst the Bishops vvhote scholes,
vvanting some modesty, vvherefore the Iudges at the first stayed them vvith
milde vvordes. VVilling them to auoide confusion : but being earnest, they ouershot the modesty of so graue men : vvherefore the honourable*

MM iij Iudges

The Coũ-
cell of
prescri-
bed no
fourme at
al for de
terminig
of maters
in cõtro-
uersie.
The.145.
Vntruth.
notorius.
The Iud-
ges depo-
sed not
Diosco-
rus, but
the Coũ-
cell,

The aun-
svver cõ-
cerning
the Coũ-
cell of
Chalcedo

The E-
phesine
and the
Chalcedõ
Councell
shevved
in a darke
horne.

Iudges and Senate of the Laity, appointed by the Emperour, did reproue them
saying : These popular acclamations, neither becommeth Bifshoppes, neither yet helpe the parties : be ye quiet therefore,
and suffer all thinges to be reherfed and heard in order with
quietnes. VVhen the Iudges and Senate, had duely examined
the causes, they gaue (.145.) sentence to depose Dioscorus and
others : So that this their iudgement semed good to the Emperour, to whom they referred the whole matter.

*The. 13. Chapter. Of the Chalcedon Councell, and how the
Emperour with his deputies dealed therin.*

Stapleton.

WE are now in order come to the Coũcel of Chalcedo, the actes whereof being very long and tedious, the leaues in the great volume rifing to the
number of one hundred and more , M. Horne hath here
and there pried out good matter as he thinketh, to depresse
the Popes primacie withal. Wherein he so handleth himselfe, that he semeth to me for many causes neuer to haue
read the acts, but to haue taken things as they came to his
handes, miniftred by his friends, or by his Latine Maifters.
Ones, this is sure, that for some of his allegations , a man
may pore in the booke, til his eies dafel againe, and his head
ake, ere he shal find them, and in such prolixitie of the matter, when he hath found them, and well weighed them : a
man would thinke, that M. Horne had either loft his wits,
or els were him selfe a sleape , when he wrote those arguments : or els which is worst of al, that he was paft al shame
and grace. For as ye faw, good Readers, the Ephefine, so
shall ye now see the Councell of Chalcedo , by no cleare
candle or torche , but all in a darke horne . Wherein he
playeth like a falfe wilie marchaunte , that will not shewe
his

his wares,but in a darke fhoppe. But by Gods helpe I fhall
bring his naughty marchãdiſe into the bright ſhining light,
that al men may openly at the eye ſee al the leudnes of it.

And to begyn,with the firſt action of the ſaid Councel,
and to followe M. Hornes ſteppes with a litle tracing,ther
ſterteth vp at the firſt(I will ſpeake with the leaſt.)a brace
of lyes, beſyde other vaine and impertinent talke. Of hys
Iudges, whereby he woulde haue the Reader to thinke,
that theſe noble men were Iudges in the deciſion and determination of matters eccleſiaſtical,he commeth altogether to ſhort, as ye ſhal anon vnderſtande. And therefore
this ſhall be the firſt lye. The ſecond lye is that he ſaieth.
The Emperour *preſcribed a forme, after Which they muſte
determine the matters in controuerſie.*For in al the Actes of
that Councell, there appeareth no ſuch fourme or preſcription made.It is vſual with M. Horne,in euery Councel to report ſuch a preſcription. But as he hath often ſaied
it,ſo hath he not once proued it, or ſhewed it by any one
Authority,but his owne,which is a ſingular authoritye;to
lye as lewedly (allmoſt) as M. Iewell. Yet to bleare the
Readers eye, and to ſeame handſomly to furniſh his matter by ſome preſident and example, he layeth forth for his
proufe, that theſe Iudges gaue ſentence to depoſe Dioſcorus the Patriarche of Alexandria, and others.This is alltogether falſe.

For firſte they were no competent and ordinary Iudges
being mere laye men, eſpecially in cauſes eccleſiaſtical to
depoſe a Biſhoppe. Secondlye,puttyng the caſe,they had
bene lawefull and ordinarye Iudges, yet was yt no finall
and iudiciall ſentence. For a final ſentéce muſt decide and
determine the matter,by an abſolut códemnatió or abſolu-
tion:

See the.1.
ſome of
councells
the 736.
leaf and
737. col.
1. & 2.

See the
831.leaf,
col.2.

4.Cauſes
to proue
that Dioſ-
corus
vvas not
depoſed
by them,

tion : which was not done here, this pretenſed ſentence being as your ſelfe write, cõditional: *So that this their iudgment ſemed good to the Emperour, to whom they referred the whole matter*. And here by the waye falleth out an other vntruth: for the Nobles them ſelues doe not cal this ſaying

Videtur nobis iuſtã eſſe.
See the 847. leafe col. 1.

a Iudgemẽt, but ſay, yt ſemeth vnto vs iuſt. Which words by lawe importe no final iudgemẽt. Fourthly and laſte, this was no iudgemente, neither was Dioſcorus depoſed here in this action (for in the beginning of the next action, the Iudges confeſſe, that ſentence was not yet geuen vppon Dioſcorus.) but in the thirde action: and that not by theis Iudges, as ye cal them, but by Pope Leo his deputies, and the reſidew of the Biſhoppes without any referring of the matter to th'Emperor as the Iudges doe here.

Martians oration returned vpon M. Horne.

The reſt ye talk of in this place is of no weight: and yf it weyeth anie thing, yt weieth againſt you, as Marcians oration, whych tendeth to this, that in new queſtions and diſſenſions of religion, *we muſt haue a ſpeciall regard to the doctrine, teaching and writing of the former fathers and coũcels:* which rule and forme of Iudgemẽt preſcribed by him you quit left out, as a rule in dede, importing a plaine deſtructiõ of your new goſpel. Now if the making of an oration by a

See the 740 leafe col. 1.

lay man imploieth any authority, voice, or iuriſdictiõ in the Coũcell, then were many lay men (the ambaſſadours for their Princes, that made orations there, yea and found many faultes to in the Church, and deſired the reformation of them) members and Iudges of the late Councel of Trent, which is notoriouſly falſe: and ſo is that alſo that ye write of the noble men at Chalcedo. And whereas they founde faulte wyth the populare acclamations of the Biſhoppes, which of a great zele to the catholik faith cried out againſt

Dioſco-

Dioſcorus and other that depoſed the godly Biſhop Flauianus, and that they would not receiue Theodoretus, nor
heare ſuch matters as he had to propoſe, becauſe he for the
time, helde againſt Cyrillus and other Catholikes: and that
theſe noble men endeuoured to ſet an order and quietnes
among them, doth plainly ſhew, wherein theſe noble mens
office did reſt : as nothing touching the definition of anye
matter ſpiritual, but to prouide that al things might be don
with order, indifferency and quietnes. For if a man conſider, what diſorder, tumulte, crueltie, yea and murder too,
fell in the ſecond Epheſin Councell, whiche cuſtomably is
rather called a Conuenticle, and a cõſpiracy, for the maintenaunce whereof, ye make Theodoſius a very godly Emperour, and how that Dioſcorus and his cõfederats, would
not ſuffer the Catholique Biſhops Notaries, as the manner
was, to write the actes there done : but thruſted them out,
and put in Notaries of his owne at his pleaſure, howe he
came to the other notaries and brake their wrytinges and
fingers to : howe that he forced the biſhops to ſubſcribe to
a blanke : that is, in cleane paper, wherein nothyng was
writen: howe that, Dioſcorus would not ſuffer the epiſtle
of Leo the Pope ſent to the Councel to be read: and finally, howe that he ſlewe the bleſſed Biſhop Flauianus : he
that, I ſay, cõſidereth and wel weigheth the premiſſes, and
that a great numbre of thoſe ſchiſmatical biſhops were alſo
with Dioſcorus at Chalcedo, ſhal ſone perceue, what nede
there was of theſe noble mens aſſiſtance, & that they might
wel haue to doe there, thoughe not in ruling and iudging
any ſpiritual matter, yet in the indifferent ruling and direction of the Catholike Biſhopes external doings, and to ſee
that al things might procede with quietneſſe and without

M. Horns
argumẽte
for the
exclamaꝛ
tiõ retur-
ned vpon
him ſeifꞓ.
See the
74ꞓ leaſe,
cohꞓ.

See the
750.leaſe.
1.&.2.col
See the
847.leaſe
coh.1.

N N   par-

parcialitie. Which anfwere ones made, will ferue alfo for many other General Councels. But what a wicked Cham are you, M. Horne, that reueale to the common people in your vulgare bookes, the faults and diforders of your moft holy and reuerent Fathers, the Fathers of fo famous, and fo learned a Councell? Verely Conftantine the Greate, that noble Emperour, *would caft his Imperiall garment* (he faid)

Niceph.
li 8. ca. 16

to hyde a Bifshops faulte, if by chaunce he fhould fee any. And becommeth it your vocation, bearing the roume of a Bif-fhop your felf, to tel the people *of the Bifshops whot fcholes, of their want of modeftie, and of ouerfhoting them felues?* You a Bifhop of Gods Church? Nay your fprit fheweth it felfe more bucherly then Bifhoply, and as mete to carie a rake as a Rochet.

M. Horne. The. 49. Diuifion. pag. 32. a.

Act. 2.

In the next action, the Iudges and Senate after reherfall made, vvhat vvas done before, dooe propounde vnto the Synode, vvhat matters vvere novv to be confulted of, and vvilleth them to make a pure expofition of the faith, and that vvithout any finifter affection, declaring that the Emperour and they, did firmely kepe and beleue, according to the faith receiued in the Nicen Councel: vvhereunto the Bifshops alfo accorde, and faith, that noman maketh, or may attempt to make any other expofition. Certaine of the Synode defired to heare the Symbol of the Nicen Councel re-cited, which the Senate and Iudges graunted vnto them.

Stapleton.

By this alfo it may eafely be fene, wherein the duety and office of thefe Ciuil Magiftrats did ftad. *videl.* to fee the Bi-fhops requefts, of reading this booke or that booke, this e-uidence or that euidence, put in execution. And fo it ma-keth rather againft M. Horne then with him.

M. Horne.

M. Horne. *The. 50. Diuifion. Pag. 32. a.*

After that it vvas agreed vpon by the vvhole Synode, that Dioſcorus *fhould be depoſed, the Synode vvriteth vnto the Emperours* Valentinia-nus *and* Martianus, *ſaiyng in this fourme :* Grieuous diſeaſes nea-deth both a ſtroige medicine and a wife Phyſition : For this cauſe therfore, the Lord ouer al hath appointed your godlines as the beſt and chiefe Phiſition ouer the diſeaſes of the whole world, that you ſhould heale them with fitte medicines. And you moſt Chriſtian Emperours, receiuing commaundemēt frō God aboue other men , haue geuen competent diligence for the churches, framing a medicine of cōcord vnto the Biſhops (.147.) *This, thus in vvay of Preface ſaid , they declare vvhat they haue done touching* Dioſcorus, *they ſhevve the cauſe and reaſons that moued them thervnto : both that the Emperour ſhoulde conſider his vvickedneſſe, and alſo the ſinceritie of their ſentence.*

cell.
Act. 3,
630 Biſ-
ſhoppes.
(.146.)cō
feſſe the
Princes
ſupremas
cie in Ec-
cleſiaſti-
cal cauſes.
The.146,
Vntruth.
moſt ri-
diculous,
as ſhall
appeare.
The.147.
Vntruth.
In cōcea-
ling the
next ſen-
tence fo-
lovving
opening
the whol
matter.

Stapleton.

Now loe M. Fekenham muſt nedes yeld and geue ouer. For euen the whole Coūcel, to the number of. 630. Biſhops doth confeſſe (ſaith M. Horne) *the princes ſupremacy in cauſes eccleſiaſtical* (it is wel, it is not yet in al cauſes Eccleſiaſtical) And therefore this note is faſtened in the Margente , as it were with a tenpeny naile, and yet al not worth a hedleſſe pinne. For I beſeech you , Maiſter Horne , howe can this notable concluſion of yours take anye anker holde of any ſaiyngs of the Councell by you here alleaged? How farre and how deaply your ſharpe ſight can pearce, I know not. But for my part I muſt confeſſe my ſelfe ſo blind, that I can ſee no cauſe in the world why ye ſhould furniſh your margent with ſuch a iolie note.

Wel, I perceiue euery mā can not ſee through a milſtone: But yet eyther my ſight and my braine to , faileth mee, or

all

all this great prouf ſtandeth in this, that the Councell calleth the Emperours, *the beſt and chiefe phyſitions ouer the
diſſeaſes of the world, for framing a medicine of concorde to the
Biſshops*: By my trowth, it is wel and worſhipfully concluded, and ye were worthy at the leaſt, to be made a poticar
rie for your labour. Sauing that it is to be feared, if ye ſhuld
procede on the body, as ye doe nowe with the ſoule, ye
woulde kil manie a poore mans bodie, with your olde rotten drugges, as ye do now kill many a ſowle with your peſtiferous poyſoned drawght of heretical potions, they take
at your hands. But nowe to anſwere to you, and to your ſo
farre fette phiſike: I pray yow M. Horne, why doe ye cut

A Copie
of M. Ie-
wells rhe-
torike in
his Reply,
the 225,
page.

of the tayle of your owne tale? Why do ye not ſuffer the
fathers to ſpeake their whole mind? And to ruffle a litle in
M. Iewells rhetorycke, *what? were the fathers ſtayed with
the choygnecoughe, and forced to breake of theyre matter and
tale in the myddeſt? Mark well gentle reader, and thow ſhalſee
the whole Councel of. 630. biſſhops ſet to ſchole, and kept in awe,
and not ſuffred to vtter one worde more, then M. Horne will
geue them leaue*. For the next wordes that immediatly fol-

Act. 3. fol.
861. col. 1.

lowe in the ſame matter are theſe. *Pontificibus cōcordiæ me-
dicinā machinantes: vndiq́, enim nos congregantes omne com-
modaſtis auxilium, quatenus facta interimantur diſcordiæ &
paternæ fidei doctrina roboretur.* For yow (ſay the fathers to
the Emperours) aſſembling vs from all places, haue holpen
al that may be, to pacify and kil theſe diuiſions and diſſenſions, and that the fayth and doctrine of our fathers may be
ſtrenghthened. What worde is here M. Horne, that any
thing towcheth your purpoſe? Here is nothing, but that the
councel was aſſembled by their good help, which as I haue
often declared, ſerueth not your turne to make them ſupreame

preame heads . Nowe becaufe throwgh their meanes the
Councell came together , in the whiche a quietneffe was
fet in religion , the Councell calleth them phyfitions , yea
and the chiefe : as they were chiefe in dede, in refpecte of
their cyuill authoritie wherewythe they did afsifte the
Councel, and did helpe by this minifterie of theirs , not by
anie iudicial fentence, or other Ecclefiafticall acte (which
ye fhal neuer fhewe) to quiet and pacefie the greate diffenfions then raigning and raging. And fo were they phifitions in dede, but the outwarde not the inward phifitions.
The fathers were the inwarde phifitions . They made the
verye potion , for the difeafe . And becaufe we are ons
entred into the talke of phifitions, they were the very phifitions of the fowle . The fcripture faieth of the king : *re-*
gem honorificate : honour the kinge , yt faieth alfo of the
phifition: *honora medicum.* Honour the phifition . But what
fayeth yt of the priefte ? The prieftes, fayeth S. Paule, *that*
gouuerne well are worthy of double honour: againe, *obeye your*
rulers (meaninge the Ecclefiafticall rulers) *for they watche*
to geue a reckoning for your fowles . And the Ecclefiafticus
fayeth, *humble thy fowle to the prefte.* So that ye may fee M.
Horne, the prieftes to be the true and higheft phifitions,
as farre pafsing and exceding the other phyfitions , as the
fowle paffeth and excedeth the bodie : and then muft the
fpirituall primacye nedes remayne in them . And that doe
thefe Iudges here euen in this Action , expreffely protefte
and confeffe againft you. For they fay touching the point
of doctrine then in queftion. *Quod placuit reuerendo Conci-*
lio de fancta fide, ipfum nos doceat. Let the Reuerend Councel it felfe teach vs and infourme vs, what is their pleafure
touching the holy faith: You fee here, they toke no fuprem

vvhy the
fathers cal
the Em-
perours
the chiefe
Phifitiõs.

1. Pet. 2.
Ecclefiaft.
38.
1. Timo. 5.
Heb. 13.
Ecclefi. 4.

NN   iiij   gouern-

gouernemente in this caufe ecclefiaftical, in determining,
I fay, the true faith: (as you will make Princes beleue they
may and ought to doe)they yet being the Emperours deputies, but lerned humbly of the holy Councel, what their
determinarion in fuch matters was. Thus at the length
your great mighty ʒ oft, is thwyghted to a pudding pryck.
Neither fhal ye be able of al theis.630.bifhops to bring one,
that mayntained your pretenfed fupremacy. And when he
proueth yt to you good reader by theis 630.bifihops, or by
anie one of them I dare fay M. Fekeham wil take the oth,
and fo wil I to. For it is as true, as the nobles gaue fentece
to depofe Diofcorus and others. Who is not, as yet depo-

M.Horne
contrarie
to him
felf in on
leaf.

fed and that wil I proue by M.Horne him felf: who fayth,
that in this actio the whole fynode agreed, that Diofcorus
fhould be depofed: and fo ful pretely doth he cal back that
he fayd not fyftene lynes before : and proueth him felf, a-
gainft him felf, that their faying was no fentence.

M. Horne. 51.Diuifion. Pag.32 . b .

The 148.
vntruth.
There is
no fuche
muft
in all the
Councell.

*In the fourth Action, vvhen the rehearfall of al things paffed before vvas
done, the Iudges and Senate afketh if all the Bifshops agree: vvhervnto they
anfvvered yea, yea. The Synode had requefted the Iudges and the Senate, to
make fuite to the Emperour for fiue Bifshops, vvhich othervvife (.143.)muft
be depofed, as vvas Diofcorus, vvhich they did, and made this relation vnto
the Synode : That the Emperour, perceiuing the humble fuite of
the Synod, doth licence them to determine touching the fiue,
what they thought good : admonif hing them notwitftading,
to geue good hede what they did: for that they muft make an
accompt to God of their doings.*

Stapleton.

M.Horne would fayne fafte fome ecclefiafticall iudgemet, vpo thefe lay men, as the depofitio of certain bifhops:
which he fhal fynd, whe he ca fynd that they depofed Diofcorus

ofcorus.It is playn,fayth M.Horn,for the whole councell
maketh humble fuyt,to the Emperour,to licēce thē to determi-
ne towching fyue biſſhops, which otherwife Muſt be depofed,
as Diofcorus was. Ha good M.Horn,haue ye found now at
the length, *a muſt?* That is wel and in high tyme efpied out
of you,or els al theis your great doigs muſt lie in the mire.
But I belieue whē we haue al done,we ſhal fynd no muſt,
but a playn myſt,that ye lyke a wily ſhrew , haue caſt before the eies of the ſimple readers,to blind thē withall. Yf
I fay not true , thē like a true mā of your word point with
your finger,the leaf ād line wher,in al the acts of this coūcel your *muſt* lieth. I am aſſured,that neithet in the 4.actiō
wherby ye now plead,nor in the. 1. actiō,wherby ye haue
alredy pleaded(which both places ſpake of thofe fyue biſhops)is anie mutterīg in the world of your muſting.Truth
it is that in the firſt actiō,theis fenatours,thowght it reafonable,that Diofcorus ād theis fyue bifhops,being the ring-
leaders of that wycked conuenticle at Ephefus, ſhould be
depofed , but not by the way of any finall or iudiciall fentence,as ye fable . But as they thowght them worthy to
be depryued,fo neither did they depryue thē,nor thought
them felues or the Emperour mete parfons to depryue
them,but the councel. And therfore immediatly followeth
that they ſhould be put , from all theire biſhoply dignitye.
But by whome M.Horne? *A fancto Concilio :* by the holy
councell. And howe I pray yow? *fecundùm regulas.* Accordinge to the canons. Then here ſtāndeth the cafe . The
Emperoure , and not withowt caufe , was in this mynde,
that as they mighte and owghte by the Canons to haue
bene depryued , fo that execution ſhoulde haue bene
done accordinglye : for example fake , as yt was allredye

A fancto
concilio ſe
cundū re-
gulas , ab
epifcopali
dignitate
fieri alie-
nos.
Pag.831.
col.2.

done

The true
meaning
of the
place by
M. Horne
alleaged.
Anno. 25.
Hē.8.c.19.
*Sententia
veſtra per-
miſit deli-
berare de
Thalaſsio
& quæ
vobis pla-
cuerint.
Fol. 872.
col. 2.
Liberatus.
in Breuia.
cap. 17.*
ποιμέσιν
οὖτε φίλη
κλεπτι
δ'εἶ νυκ
τος ἀμεί-
νω.
*Quia con-
ſenſerant
in ſubſcri-
ptione epi-
ſtoke Leo-
nis, &c.*

done vpon Dioſcorus . And yet leauing the final determination (as otherwiſe he could not chooſe, if he would followe the Canons by his deputies alleaged) to the Biſhops.
And this is the *Licence* ye falſely ſpeake of . For proprely
licéce it was none, neither doth the latine word inforce it,
but that he permitted and ſuffered them to do therin their
pleaſure : which words doe not neceſſarilie declare his ordinary authority to let them (as the Prince may let your
Conuocation Decrees by act of Parliament) but onely the
geauing ouer and yelding to the Fathers, in that mater, frō
his owne mind and ſentence, which he thought good and
reaſonable. Thē Fathers on the other ſide, thought not beſt
to exact the rigour and extremitie of the Canons, but ſeing
theſe fiue were hartely penitent, and had ſubſcribed to the
Epiſtle of Leo, whiche before they refuſed, and for feare
of a great ſchiſme, as Liberatus noteth, that happely might
by this rigoroüſe dealing enſue, toke the milder way , and
ſuffred them to remaine in their dignitie, and in the Councell with them. See now M. Horne , if this be not rather
a miſt then a muſte, a darke miſt, I ſay, mete for theues as
Homer ſaith, and not mete, as he ſaith, nor acceptable to
the ſhepheard. How vnmete then for you M. Horne, that
taketh vpn you to be the ſhepheard and paſtor of ſo many
thouſand ſoules, that ſhould kepe your flocke, from al ſuch
hurtefull myſtes of falſe doctrine ? Yea to feed them with
thē ſame, and to make him beleue, and that by the authoritie of this honorable Councel, that ye feed them well, and
that ye muſt ſo feed them. And yet, lo, like a blind Prophet
ye haue ſaid truer then ye wiſt of: ſaiyng they muſt be depoſed as Dioſcorus was. For Dioſcor⁹ was not depoſed at
all, by thoſe whome ye fable to haue geauen ſentence.

Againe

Again fee what falleth out otherwife againft you . For yf
the lay iudges depofed in the firft action Diofcorus , they
depofed alfo thele fyue. For al cometh vnder one trade ād
courfe of woordes . And thus euery waye ye walke in a
mifte, wandring pitifully to and fro , ye can not tell why-
ther.

Dicta pa.
931 col. 2.
Videtur
nobis fe-
cundum
quod Deo

*placitum eft, iuftum effe fi placuerit diuinißimo & pijßimo Domino noftro , eidem pœna
Diofcorum reuerend. epifcopum Alexandria, & Iuuenalem reuerend. epifcopum Hierof.
& Thalafsium &c.*

M. Horne. 52. Diuifion. Pag. 32. b.

*In the fifth Action, the Iudges vvilled the Synode, to reade thofe thinges,
vvhich vvere agreed vpon touching the Faith: vvhereabout began a great
contention, one parte of them allovving , an other forte difallovving that
vvas redde amongeft them. The iudges feing the exclamations and confufion
that vvas amongeft them, appointeth a Comitty, choofing foorth of fundry
partes a certaine number to goe afide vvith the iudges, to make a refolutiõ.
VVhen they preuailed nothing, they threatened the vvhole Synode , that they
vvould fignifie thefe (. 149.) difordered clamours vnto the Emperor, vvhich
they did. The Emperour immediatly of his (. 150.) Supreme authority, appointed the order of Committies , vvhich the iudges had deuifed before : geuing
them in commandement, that going afide by them felues , they fhould cõfult
and conclude a truthe in Faith, vvith fuch plainneffe , that there might no
more doubtes arife thereof , vvhereunto al fhould agree. The Synode obeyed,
and folovved the Emperours direction, and the Committies vvith the Iudges
goeth a fide into a fecrete place, maketh conference, concludeth, and cometh
again into the Synode , and reciteth their determination . vvhereunto the
vvhole Synode gaue their confent, and fo the Iudges commaundeth, that this
their definition fhould be fhevved vnto the Emperour.*

The 149.
vntruth.
The word
diforde-
red, levv-
dely ad-
ded to
the text,
to make
coulour
of re-
proche.
The 150.
vntruth.
Not by
any his
fupreme
authority
but at the
bifshops
choife ād
pleafure,
as fhal ap-
peare.

Stapleton.

Ye fhewe nothing that either the Emperour or his deputyes made any definitiõ of the faith. Now thē yf the Fathers

thers could not agree, themperour did wel to find out some meanes by committies to bring them to agremente, which is no spiritual matter. And so ye come not nighe to that ye should haue proued by a great deale. But let vs a litle consider the maner of these Comitties, the cause and the end thereof: and we shall see M. Horne quyte ouerthrowen with his own sway, and a moste euident argument of the Popes supremacy. At the beginning of the fyfte Action a forme of the faith being openly read, all the Bisshops cried, *præter Romanos & aliquos Orientales*, beside the Romanes and some of the East: *Definitio omnibus placet*. The determination pleaseth al.

Concil. Chalced. Act.5.92. 879.col.2

Vppon this when they coulde not agree the Popes Legat stode vp, and said. *If these men agree not to the letters of the Apostolike and most blessedman Pope Leo, commaunde it that we haue them copied out that we may returne home, and there kepe a Councel.* For this loe was the cause of

The cause of the comitties made in the v. Action.

al that garboyle. Dioscorus with Eutyches were alreadye condemned: the Nestorians in like maner. And the forme of faith after a sorte was agreed vpon, but not in such sorte as in the Popes letters it was conceiued. And againſt the foorme of the Popes letters all the Bisshoppes of Aegypt, of Asia, of Illiricum, Ponthus and Thracia, very hotlye resisted, affirming that the definition was otherwise perfect enoughe. Which the Romaines and certaine of the Easte Bisshppes as earnestly denied. Herevpon the iudges to make the matter come to an agrement, made first a Committy in this sorte: *that of all the foresaide prouinces, three should be chosen, and they togeather with the Romaynes and six of the Easte Bisshoppes shoulde conferre a parte.* But this order beinge misliked, and the greater nomber of Bis-

shops

shoppes ſtil crying to haue it paſſe, as it was firſt concei-ued, not paſsing vpon the forme conceiued in the Popes letters, the iudges aſked thoſe that ſo cried, *whether they allowed the letters of Pope Leo, or no?* When they anſwered, *Yea: and that they had alreaaye ſubſcribed thereunto*, the Iudges inferred. *Lette then that be added to the definition which is in thoſe leters cõpriſed.* The Biſhops of AEgipt and other crying alwaies to the contrarye, the debate was ſi-gnified to the Emperour. The Emperour ſent back againe, *that they ſhoulde take the order of Committye appointed, or yf that liked them not, then they ſhould make an other Cõmittye by their Metropolitanes, and euerye man declare his mynde, that ſo the matter might come to an ende. But* (ſaith the Em-perour) *yf your Holynes will none of this neither, then knowe you certainelye, that you ſhall come to a Councell in the weſt partes, ſeing you will not here agree.* And this alſo was that the Popes Legates before required. And the Biſhoppes of Illyricum as excuſing them ſelues, cried. *Qui contra-dicunt, Romam ambulent.* Theſe which doe not agree, let them walke to Rome.

Had Maiſter Horne and his fellowes bene in that caſe, they woulde haue cryed: *what haue we to doe with Rome, or with that forayne Prelate, the Pope?* But the Biſ-ſhoppes and Fathers of thoſe dayes knewe a better obe-dience to the See Apoſtolike. And therefore in the ende the Popes Legates with a fewe other of the Eaſte, pre-uailed againſt al the reſte of AEgypt and Aſia, of Illyricũ, Pontus and Thracia: and endited the forme of their defini-tiõ of the faith, according to the tenour of Pope Leo his let-ters, inſerting his very words to their definitiõ. Otherwiſe

O O ij   as the

Pag.880. col.1.

Si vobis hoc nõ pla-cet, ſingu-li ſidẽ ſuã &c. Si au-tem neque hoc velit veſtra s̄-ctitas, cog noſcite quia in partibus Occidẽta-libus fieri habet ſy = nodus, cõ quòd &c.

as the Emperour and the Popes Legates before threatned, they should al haue trotted to Rome, and there haue finished the Councel. Such was the Authority and preeminence of that Apostolike See of Rome, and so wel declared in this fifte Action, out of which M. Horne concealing the whole yssue, order, and cause of the debate, thought only by a simple commyttye, to proue his Supreme Gouernement in the prince. Thow seest nowe gentle Reader, that by the prince his owne confession, by the Legates protestation, and by the ende and yssue of the whole Action, the Superiority rested in the Church of Rome, and in a Councel to be had there, in case they would not presently agree. So harde it is for Maister Horne to bring any one Authority, that maketh not directly against him, and manifestly for vs.

*It vvas because he would folovve, Doctrina Patrum. The doctrine of Fathers: vvich you leaue out.

The. 151. vntruth, in dissembling a greate part of the Sentence.

* Ergo, it vvas before defined without the emperor royal assent.

M. Horne. The. 53. Diuision. Pag. 33. a.

The Emperour cometh into the Synode place, in his owne persone, vvith Pulcheria, his nobles, and Senatours, and maketh vnto the Synode an oration, of this effect. He careth for nothing so much, as to haue all men rightly persuaded in the true Christian faith: He declareth the occasions, * vvhy he sommoned the Synode: He comaundeth that no man be so hardy, hereafter to hold opinion, or dispute, of the Christian faith, othervvyse than vvas decreed in the first Nice councel, he chargeth the therefore, that all partaking, cotentio, and couetousnes laide apart, the onely truth may appeare to a' men. He declareth his coming into the Synod, to be for none other cause, the (. 151.) to confirme the faith, and to remoue from the people in tyme to come, all dissention in Religion. And last of al, he protesteth his vvhole care, and study, that al people may be brought into an vnity, and vnisourme agreement in pure religion, by true and holy doctrine. The chief Notarie humbly asketh of the Emperour, if it vvil please him to heare their * definition redde: The Emperour vvilleth that it should be recited openly: he enquireth of them al, if euery man consented thereunto: they answere, that it is agreed vppon by al their consentes. VVhereunto they adde many acclamations, commending

the

*the vvorthines of his Emperial gouernmēt,cōcluding:*By the O worthy
Emperor, the right faith is confirmed, herefies banifhed,
peace reftored,and the Churche refourmed. *After thefe acclama=*
*tions,the Emperour doth openly declare vnto the Synode a * ftatute,vvhich*
he maketh to cut of and put avvay from thencefoorth, al maner occafion of
contention about the true faith , and holy Religion .The vvhole Synode
defireth the Emperour,to diffolue the councel,and to (.152.)geue thē leaue
to departe:vvhereunto the Emperour vvould not confent ;but (.153.) com-
maundeth that none of them depart.

cel.
* For exe
cution of
the Coū=
cel.
The 152.
vntruth.
No fuche
words in
the Actes
The 153.
vntruth,
as before

Stapleton.

Here is nothing,whervpon ye fhoulde frame any conclufion of Supremacy . Concerning Marcians oration we
haue fpoken fomwhat before:and nowe ye geue vs more
occafion , efpecially to note your true and accuftomable
faith,in the true reherfal of your Authour.For yf ye hadde
not here maimed and mangled your owne allegation , ye
had made your felf a ful anfwere, for al this your bible bable,to proue the Emperours fupremacy, for that they called or were prefent in the Councels.*We* (faieth this noble
Emperour*)are come into this prefent Councel, not to take vp-*
pon vs or to practife any power therein , but to ftrenghten and
confirm the faith,therin following the example of the religious
prince Conftantine . By which woordes he declareth,that
the Emperours authority and powre taketh no place in
the Councel,to determyn or define any thing (which neither is founde of the doings of Conftantine , or this Marcian,or of any other good Prince)but only by ciuil penalties,to confirme and ftrenghthen the decrees , as did Cō-
ftantine,and as this Emperour did alfo, as appereth by his
woordes fpoken to the Synode, in this fixt action by yow
recited. Thefe woordes of Marcian ye haue cut from the

Hovv ād
vvhye
Prices are
prefente
in Coun=
cels.

Fol. 893.
col.2.

OO iiij   refidew

Multum
quidë eſt in
itinere fa-
tigati, laʒ
boré per-
ferétes. ve-
runtamen
ſuſtinete
tres adhuc
aut qua-
tuor dies.
Et preſéti-
tibus ma-
gniſicétiſs.
noſtris in-
dicib. que.
cũque vul-
tis mouete,
competens
adepturi
ſolatium.
Nullus ve
ſtrũ ante-
quã perfe-
ɛ̃ti termini
ex omnib.
proſerãtur
à S.cõcilio
diſcedat.Fol. 894.col.r.

reſidue of the ſentence : leaſt otherwiſe it ſhould haue
by Marcian him ſelfe appeared that ye were but a gloſar, a
Popes gloſar I ſay, as your brother Mollineus is : when ye
wrote of the fiue Biſhops , that otherwiſe muſt haue bene
depoſed. Cõcerning the ſtaiyng of the Fathers, that would
haue departed, whiche ye inforce as a thing material, if ye
had not followed your accuſtomable guiſe of diſmembring
your Author, ye ſhould haue found a ſmall matter. *Ye haue*
(ſaith Marcian to the Fathers) *ben much weried by your iour-*
ney: and haue taken great paines. Yet beare you and ſtaye you for
iij.or.iiij.daies lõger: And our honorable Iudges being preſent,
moue you what matter your hart deſireth, and ye ſhal not faile of
cõuenient comfort. But let no man depart, til all things be fully
finiſhed. What leaue is there aſked here to depart, or what
cõmaundemẽt is made to ſtay and tarie? No, no, M. Horne:
Princes were not thẽ ſo Imperiall ouer Biſhops, as your diſſolute hereſies haue cauſed of late ſo.ne to be.

M. Horne. The. 54. Diuiſion. pag. 33. b.

Baſſianus, *of late the Biſſhop at* Epheſue, *complaineth vnto the Empe-*
rour, to direɛ̃ his letters to the Synod, to haue his cauſe heard. The Emperour cõmaundeth the Synod to heare the matter. *The Iudges cõ-*
maũdeth Stephanus *Biſſhop of* Epheſus, *to make anſwere vnto* Baſſianus *his complaint. After due examination had by the Iudges, openly in the*
Synod *in this cõtrouerſy, the Iudges aſked of the Synode, vvhat they iudged*
to be done. The Biſſhops adiudged Baſſianus *to be reſtored. But the Iudges*
appointed by the Emperour, vvould not (.154.) allovv that ſentence, but dee-
med neither of them both vvorthy to occupy that Biſhoprike, and that there
ſhould be a third choſen, and admitted to that ſee, to the vvhich (155) iudge-
ment the vvhole ſynode did accord. After the end of this Councel, the Empe-
rour

The. 154. Vntruthe. They neither allovved nor diſallovved any ſentence of the
Couucel, but ſhevved only their aduiſe and minde. The. 155. Vntruthe. It vvas no
iudgement at all.

rour do:b confirme the determination the of by his publique Dccree.

Stapleton.

M.Horn wil not leaue his laical iudgemét fo:(being mar
uelous propenfe and enclined that way)belike becaufe, he
is become by the Canons a lay man him felfe, throughe his
vnlaufull mariage : and therefore yet ones againe , they by
their iudgement, if we wil credit M.Horne, do reuerfe the
iudgement of the whole Synode, in the caufe of Bafsianus
and Stephanus. In dede, if M.Horne could proue, that the
whole councel had firft geuen fentéce, here had ben fomwhat for him with fome good countenaunce, to haue fette
forth and furnifhed his new primacy withal. But now neyther the whole Synode gaue yet iudgemente in the caufe,
neither was it any iudgement geuen by the laie men, more
then vvas before againſt Diofcorus. For lo, M.Horne, they
faye, *nobis videtur,* it feemeth to vs. But will ye fee it is no
fentence? Then I pray you marke well what followeth.
After they had told their minde and opinion, they adde and
faye : *But we leaue the whole matter to the Councell, to geue
what fentence, it fhall pleafe them in this matter.* Ye will
fay, yet the whole Coũcell followed the aduife of the iudges. Then it appereth it was but an aduife, no fentéce that
they gaue foorth before. Els it were maruaile, if fo fodainly they wente from their owne determination. But
will ye fee, how wifely this mater is handled of M.Horne?
Yf the firft was a refolute and a final fentéce of the whole
Coũcel, what authority had the laie men to infringe it ? Or
how cã ye fay they did infringe it, when they left afterward
the whole determinatiõ therof to the Coũcel? Thus ye fee
euery way, that the more ye ftriue ãd ftrugle in this mater,
ãd with this coũcel, the more ye mefh and intãgle your felf.

But

Act.11.pag
915.col.1
Totũ autẽ
cõcilio fan
cto relin-
quimus
quate-
nus fenten
tiam qua
in hac cau
fa fuerit
vifa, de-
promat.

In talibus
fanct. Coc.
contingit
frequẽter,
vnum ex
præfentib⁹
reuerend,
episcopis
aliquid di
cere, &
quod ab
vno dictũ
eſt, tãq̃ ab
oibus ſi-
mul dica-
tur, & fub
ſcribatur
& intelli-
gatur, hoc
ab exordio
fubfecutũ
eſt in tan-
tum vt
vno dice-
te, ſcriba-
m⁹, ſancta
Synodus
dixit.
Act.¹.pa.
791.col.2.
* the true
vnderſtã-

But perchaunce as ye fee, or may fee yf ye be not blynde, that ye are in the pytte or faſte in the myre : ſo ye fee not how to get out. And ye wil ſay, as ye ſay ãd truely to, that the Iudges aſked the Synod, what was to be don, and that they adiudged Baſsianus to be reſtored. I graunt ye Sir: ye play now the true reporter: but either ye do not, or wil not vnderſtand that wich ye reporte. For ye ſhall fynde a rule, and that euen in this Synode, that ſomtyme yt is writen (by the Notary) the Synode ſayth, when the whole Synode ſayeth not, but ſome of the Synode. And ye being ſo well trauayled by your ſelf, or your frendes in this Synode, ſhuld haue cõ-ſidered this rule, neceſſary to bring you out of the pytte of errour ye are fallen in. Wel perchaunce, as ye lack no cou-rage, ye will not ſo geue ouer, and will ſay the matter fa-reth not ſo here: and when yt is ſayd The Iudges aſked the Synode,* yt muſt be take for the whole Synode. Now you put me to my ſhifte in dede: But I truſte to ſhift whith you wel inough. What ſay ye the to Liberatus, by you oft re-hereſed, that ſayeth as I ſay, that the whole Synode did not agree, that Baſsianus ſhulde be reſtored, but parte of the Sy-node: and therfore the matter was put ouer to an other me-ting, at which metig the whole Synod vniformely agreed, that aſwel Baſsianus as Stephanus ſhulde be remoued? In caſe this anſwere wil not contente you I wil I am aſſured, yf any moſt reaſonable anſwere wil contente you, ſet you ouer to ſuch witneſſes, as your ſelf hitherto haue beſt liked and ſought all your helpe and ayde for your ſupremacy at their hands: I meane your Iudges and ſenatours the Empe-rours deputies. For wheras ye alleage the matter, as finally determined in the.11.action, the very ſame matter was re-
sumed

ding of the place by M. Horne alleaged.

fumed in the. 12. action. *Becaufe (fay they) that after our oft mouing the matter to you,and requiring, that ye woulde geue fentence concerning the biffhoprike of the holy Church of Ephefus,there is no perfytte and refolute anfwere made: Let the holy ghofpell &c.* I truft by this tyme M.Horne, ye wil wifely geue ouer this matter of Bafsianus and of all the refidewe of this Councell, that ye haue vniuftly pleaded vppon : and require of vs to belieue yow no better, then ye can fhewe caufe . Onlefle ye will haue vs vppon your bare worde to credite yowe. which I think wife men,wil not be to hafty to do, excepte ye canfhewe fome as good commifsion, as the Apoftles had.For the bringing forth whereof, we are contente to geue you a good long day. As for this councel whervpõ ye would feme your proufs fhuld refte, ye haue not fhewed yt to vs by anie good and cleare light,but as ye haue done before, the Nicen and Ephefine,very obfcurely and vnperfectly .

Glorioſiſſimi iudices dixerunt. Quoniam ſepe nobis interloquẽ tibus & poſcentibus proferri ſententiam de epiſcopatu ſancta Eccleſia in Epheſo cõ ſtituto, perfecta reſpõſio nõ eſt dæta,Venerabile &c.
Act.12 pa.916.col.1.

The. 14.Chapter. Contayning euident proufes out of the Chalcedon Councel,for the Popes and bifhops Supremacy , in caufes eccleſiaſticall.

Owe good Reader thowgh M.Horne be fufficiẽtly alredy anfwered for the folutions of his argumẽtes, as we nede not greatly to ftay here lõger, yet if we can fhew you no fayrer nor clearer light, for the illuftratiõ and confirmation of our affertion,and that euen from this councel,then M.Horne hath don for his:than for my part, I fhal yelde to M.Horne,and fo I fuppofe M.Fekenhã wil to.Wherfore following M. Horns trace and fteps we wil

Aƈ.1.pa.737.col.1.b
Paſchaſio & Lucētio
reuerēd. Epiſcopis, &
Bonifacio religioſiß.
preſbytero tenētibus
locū ſanƈtiſſ.etreue-
rendiſſ. archiepiſ.al-
mæ vrbis Roma Leo-
nis Anatolio.&c.
Aƈ.1.pa 741.co.1.a
Quia Synodū facere
auſus eſt ſine authori
tate.Romanæ ſedis :
quod nūquā ritè fa-
ƈū eſt nec fieri licuit
Rome heade of all
Churches.
Aƈ.1.p.740.co.2.c
Romam Eccleſiarū
omnium caput .
Aƈ.1.pag.741.col.
1.a.

Euag:lib.2.ca.16.
Dioſcorus cōman-
ded by Leo to ſtā:,
and not to be pla-
ced among the Biſ-
ſhoppes.
Vniuerſal Biſhop.

róne ouer the Aƈts of the ſaid Coūcel,though wōderful long and tedious,and compendiouſly gather
ſome material thing for our ſide.

Firſt then to begin with the firſt Seſsiō,it is moſt
certain,that the Popes Legates,be named and placed before al other Biſhops and Patriarchs, though
one of them was but a Prieſt and no Biſhop. Here
ſhal ye find the wicked B. of Alexandria called to
an accōpt for mainteining the doings of a Council,
whervnto the B.of Rome gaue no cōſent or autho
rity,which(as it is auouched there)was neuer lawful to do. Here ſhal ye find and heare Rome called
the Head of all Churche..Here ſhal ye find that Pope
Leo gaue cōmaundement to his Legates,that they
ſhuld not ſuffer Dioſcorꝰ to ſit among th'other Biſhops, but to ſtand as a perſon accuſed, and defendant, and ſo the Legates tolde the Senatours , and
that in caſe they wold ſuffer the mater to go other
wiſe,that they ſhould be excōmunicated:and thervpon he was cōmaunded to ſit in the middle a part
from the reſt. Here ſhall ye finde that the learned
Biſhop of Cyrus Theodoretus,depoſed by Dioſcorus and Maximus his own Patriarche,was receiued
and placed among the biſhops,becauſe Leo had reſtored him. Here ſhal ye find that nor laie men,nor
Prieſts,haue *voice in the Councel*, but *Biſhops only.*
Here it appeareth why the Ciuil Magiſtrate is preſent in the Councell : not to geaue ſentence, or to
beare

Aƈ.1.pa.742.a. Recipiens locum a Sanƈtiß. epiſcopo inclyta vrbis Romæ.
The Pope reſtoreth Theodoretus the Biſshoppe
Aƈ.1.pa.775.col.1.a. Petrus Preſbyt. dixit. Nō eſt meū ſubſcribere,epiſcoporū tātū eſt .
It appertaineth to Biſshoppes onely to ſubſcribe in Councel.

beare the greateſt ſway there in matters Eccleſiaſtical, as M. Horne imagineth : but, as it appeareth
by Theodoſius the Emperours comiſsion geuen to
the Earle Elpidius, *to ſee there be no tumulte, and in
caſe he ſee any trobleſome or tumultuous perſon, to the
hurt and hinderance of the Catholik faith, to impriſon
him, and to certifie th' Emperour of him, to ſee the maters procede orderly, to be preſent at the iudgemet geuing and to procure that the Councell ſpedily and cir-
cumſpectly proue their matters.* In this Seſsio ye ſhall
find that not only Flauianus, that godly Biſhop and
Patriarche of Conſtantinople wrongfully depoſed
by Dioſcor°, appealed to Rome, but that Eutyches
alſo that Archeheretique, iuſtlye condemned by
Flauianus, for his reliefe, pretended an appellation
made to Leo by him ſelfe.

In the ſecond Seſsion Leo his Epiſtle was read,
the Councell crieth out, *Petrus per Leonem loquu-
tus eſt*. Peter hath ſpoken out of Leos mouthe.
But of all, the thirde Seſsion is ſo freighted with
ample and plaine teſtimonies for the Eccleſiaſtical Primacy, that I muſt rather ſeke to reſtrain and
moderat them, then to amplifie or enlarge them.

In this thirde Seſsion, Pope Leo is called *the
vniuerſall Archebiſhop*, the *vniuerſall Patriarche*,
the *Biſhopee of the vniuerſall Churche*, the *Pope of
the vniuerſal Church* the *Catholike or vniuerſal Pope*.
And now muſt M. Iewel, if he be a true man of his
worde, yelde and ſubſcribe : being anſwered euen

PP ij by

Nullu fieri tumultu permittere, ſedſi que videretis coturuatio-nibus & tumultui ſtudente, ad leſione ſancta fidei, huc cu-ſtodia mancipare, & ad noſtram perferre notitiam & cauſam quide ordine proue-nire, intereſſe autem iudicio, et opera dare celere & circumſpe-ctam probationem à ſancta Synodo fieri. Act.1.pa.744.b.

VVhy laie men are preſent in Coucels.

Act.1.p.790.col.1,C, &.823.col.2.

Appeales to Rome frō Conſtātinople.

Act.2.pag.834. col.1.b.

Peter ſpeaketh in Leo.

The pope vniuer,
fal biſſhop.
M. Iewel muſte
fubfcribe.
Act.3.pag.847.col.
2.b.&c.
The popes legates
geue letece againſt
Diofcorus the Pa-
triarch of Alexan-
dria.
Leo per nos & per
præſentē Synodum,
vnà cum ˙er beatiſſ.
& ōm laude digno
beato Petro Apoſto
lo, qui eſt petra &
crepido catholicæ ec-
cleſia,& ille qui eſt
recta ſidei fundamē
tum nudauit eu˜n tā
epiſcopatus dignitate
quā etiam ab omni
ſacerdotali alienauit
miniſterio.

Our proteſtant bi-
ſhops are in the
ſame caſe as Dioſ-
corus vvas.

by the verye preciſe woordes and termes of his
owne, thoughe peuiſhlye and foliſhly propoſed,
queſtion: In this ſeſsiō the Popes Legates pronoūce
ſentence againſt Dioſcorus, the Patriarche of Alexandria, and doe, *by m̄ Authority of Leo and S. Peter* (who is called there, *the Rocke and the top clyffe
of the Catholike Churche*) *depryue him of all prieſtlye
miniſtery and biſshoply dignity, for that he communicated with Eutyches being by a Councel condemned,
for that he preſumed to excommunicate Pope Leo, and
being thriſe peremptorely ſummoned to the Councell
woulde not come*. And how are ye now M. Horne
and your felowes to be countted Biſſhoppes, that
refuſe, the authoritye of the generall Councel of
Trente, and durſt no more ſhewe your face there,
then durſte Dioſcorus at Chalcedo? And can no
better defende the depoſition of the Catholik Biſſhops in Englande, then could Dioſcorus, the depo-
ſicion of Flauianus at Epheſus? And to ſay the truth,
ye can much leſſe defende your ſelf. And where is
nowe your acte of parliament, that annichilatteh
and maketh voyde al Eccleſiaſtical Authority, ſauing of ſuch perſons as are inhabitants, within the
realme? Dioſcorus was a foole that could finde no
ſuch defence for him ſelfe : or elſe he neded not to
haue paſſed a button for the Councel of Chalcedo:
Vnleſſe happely we think we haue a ſpecial priuilege, and as we be enuironed, and as it were wal-
led vp, frō the world by the great Oceā ſea, as the
poete writeth of vs: *Et penitus toto diuiſos orbe Bri-
tānos*: ſo we may take our ſelues to be exēpted and
closed

clofed vp from the faith and religion of all Catholike people in the world. But let vs goe foorth with
owre matter: Ye fhal then find in this third fefsion,
that *the Popes Legate was prefidente of the Councell
for Leo, and fubfcribed before all other.* In this fefsion
the whole Coũcel calleth *Leo the interpretour of S.*
Peters voyce to al people. In this fefsion the whole
Coũcel fayeth *that Leo,* thẽ far of at Rome, *was pre-*
fidẽt ãd ruler of the Coũcel, as the Head is ruler of the
body. And that *theperors were prefidẽts there moft de-*
cẽtly, to adorne ãd fet forth the fame, endewaring to re-
new the building of the Church of Hierufalẽ cõcerning
matters of faith, as did Zorobabel and Iefus in the old
lawe. And this place only were fufficient, to anfwere your whole booke, and to fhew either your
ignorance or frowarde quarrelling in making fuch
a fturre and bufines, for Princes authority in Coũcels. In this fefsiõ the whole fynode faieth, *that the*
keping of the vineyard (that is of the whole Church)
was committed of God to Leo. In this fefsion the
whole Councel, thowghe Leo his Legates were
prefent, and confirmed al thinges that there paffed
towching matters of faith, doth yet neuertheleffe
pray Leo him felf alfo *to confirme their decrees.* And
here might the Author of your Apologie Maifter
Horne, if yt pleafed him, as merely haue iefted and
fcoffed againfte thefe. 630. Fathers, as he doth a-
gainft

Councell

Act. 3. pa. 858. col. 1.
b. 8;5. col. 2. b.

Pafchafius vice bea-
tiſſimi Leonis preſi-
dens fufcripſi, dict.
pag. 858.
The popes legate
prefident of the
Councel.
Act. 3. pag. 867. col.
1. b.
Vocis beati petri orbi
cõſtitutus interpres.
The councel cõfeſ-
feth Leo to be their
head and ruler.
Quibus tu quidem,
ſicut membris caput
præeras, in his qui
tuum tenebant ordi-
nem beneuolentiam
præferens. Impera-
tores verò ad or-
nandum decentiſſi-
mè præsidebant, ſi-
cut Zorozabel &
Iefus Ecclefiæ Hie-
rufalem ædificatio-
nem renouare circa
dogmata adnitẽtes.
Act. 3. in relatione
ſynodi ad Leonẽ pa.

867. col. 1. Act. 3. pag. 867. col. 2. a. *Cui vineæ cuftodia a faluatore commiſſa eft. Act. 3.*
pag. 868. col. 2. a. Rogamus igitur & tuis decretis noftrum honora iudiciũ, et ficut nos
cupidi in bonis adiecimus confonantiam; fic et firmitas tua filÿs (quod decet) adimpleat.
et mox: Omnem vobis geftorum vim inſinuauimus ad comprobationem noftræ ſinceri-
tatis et ad eorum quæ à nobis gefta funt, firmitatem et confonantiam.

gainst the Fathers of the late Coūcel at Trente, for
the clause : *salua Apostolicæ sedis authoritate* : Here
might be demaunded of these.630 . Fathers, what
thei neaded in this case,the matter being resolued
vpon by the whole Councel , yea by his own deputies to,to sende to Rome to Pope Leo , to haue
their decrees yet further cōfirmed?Here also might
be demaunded of those 630 . Fathers,whether yt

The childish toyes
of the Englishe
Apology.

were not a mere soly to think the holy ghost posted to Rome:that yf he staggered or stayed in any
matter,he might there take Councell, of an other
holy ghost better learned,with such other childish

Themperour Mar-
cian desireth Leo
to confirme the fa-
thers decrees.
Episl.5 9. & 60.

or rather Iewish toyes. Neither the Coūcel only,
but Marcian also the Emperour prayed Leo,*to cōfirme that which there was concluded of the faith*.In

The Senatours re
quire to be taught
of the fathers.

this sessiō the Senators(that ye would neades haue
to be the chief Iudges) *desire they may be taught of
the fathers of this Councel such thinges as appertayne
to the faith,as of them that should geue a reckoninge
aswel for their sowles, as for their own sowles.*

Scientes igitur quia,
& Deo ratione red-
dituri estis tam pro
animabus singuli ve-
stri,quam & pro no
stris omnibus qui &
docet s,quæ ad religio
nem pertinent, recte
desideramus. Act.3.
pag.832.col. 2. a.

Nowe where as ye catche as yt were a certaine
ankerhold of the supplication of Eusebius of Do-
rileum : consider I beseache yow his supplication
to the Councel too , and weighe them bothe with
the ballance of indifferente iudgemente . *I pray
and most humbly beseche your holines holy fathers*(saith
he) *to haue mercy on vs* . *And while the things
passed*

Eusebius the bishop besecheth the Councel he may be restored to his bishoprik.
*Et dum adhuc in memoria retinetis,qua antea inter nos & præsatum Dioscorum acta
sunt,decernite omnia que aduersus nos gesta sunt viribus carere: & nihil nobis ea mo-
numenta qua iniuste cōtra nos facta sunt nocere.Habere verò nos & sacerdotalem dignitatem &c.Quod impetrantes incessanter gratias agamus vestra sanctitati,*

paſſed betwixt Dioſcorus and me, be yt in freſh remē-
braunce , decree you all thoſe doings to be voyde , and
that thoſe things which wrongfully paſſed againſt vs,
may not be preiudicial or hurtful to vs , and that we
may be reſtored to our biſshoply dignity againe: which
yf we obtayne , we ſhall for euer geue thanks to your
holines. In this feſsion ye ſhal finde , that it was no
finall or reſolutory ſentence that the Senatours
gaue againſt Dioſcorus, but *a declaration of theire*
mynde and reſolutiō: the ful authority notwithſtanding remayning in the Biſhops *to whom* (and not to
the Senatorus) *God had geuen authority to geue ſuch*
kind of ſentēces. Further now, though I haue alredy
ſufficiētly ſhewed the inſufficiēcy and feblenes of
that your weake collection: yet becauſe ye haue ſo
honorably adorned your margēt, with no leſſe thē
630. Fathers cōfeſſing your ſupremacye, and al for
that they cal thēperor the beſt and cheif phiſition:
I wil be ſo bolde , thowgh but a poore and a ſecō-
dary phiſitiō , to ſay ſomwhat more to your great
and far fetched, neither good theological, nor good
phiſical argumente, and to returne your wiſe phiſical reaſon vpon your own head by the very ſame
fathers, and the very ſame place that your ſelfe alleage. For euen in the ſame page, it followeth, *that*
perchaunce Dioſcorus might haue obtayned pardon , of
thoſe his ſo great and exceſsiue enormities yf being as
the caſe required throughlye pænitent he had ſowght
for a medicine at the handes of the Councel . But becauſe he

piſci potuiſſet , ſi per dignam pænitentiam adiiſceret medicinam ab hoc vniuerſali
Concilio. Vide & ſequentia, Act 3.pag. 861. col. 3. C.

Act. 3. pag. 836. col. 1. A.

The authority to geue fentēce of de-poſitiō or excom-munication geuen to the biſhops by God.

Ioannes epiſcop. Ger-maniciæ ad Dioſcorū Senatus aduerſus tuā reuerentiā pro-mulgauit ſentētiam ſi hoc placuiſſet ſanc-tiſsimis epiſcopis quibus hanc inferre à Domino Deo cre-ditum eſt.

Act . 3 . pag . 846. col. 1. C.

M. Hornes mighty great phiſical note returned vpon his ovvn heade .

Et ſortè ſuper tantū ac talibus iniquita-tibus veniam adi-

cauſe he endured in obſtinacy, he was cut away by depoſition and excommunication from the Church, as a rotten and peſtiferouſe member, to ſaue and preſerue the
reſidewe of the bodie. Beholde maiſter Horne, the
fathers are nowe the phiſitions that might haue cu
red Dioſcorus (yf he had bene curable) of his diſeaſe: and notwithſtanding he was the captayne of
that myſcheuouſe couenticle at Epheſus, he might
yf he had ſowght for it accordingly, haue founde
perchaunce fauour, not at the Emperours, but at
the councels hands, and neither bene depoſed nor
excommunicated. Yea the Emperour Marciā him
ſelf cōfeſſeth, that theſe fathers founde out a remedy
for thoſe nawghtie errours. And howe I pray you?
Becauſe they made a playne and an open determination, what was to be obſerued concerning fayth and religion. Thus at the length your gay and freſh, your
mighty and notable note of.630.Fathers confeſsing
your phyſical ſupremacy is not worth one pipte
nutte. In this ſeſsion ye ſhal fynde, that this moſt famous Councell did diligently enquire vpon matters
of faith: By whoſe authority M. Horne think you?
By the Emperours? Naye. But by the authoritye
of the moſt bleſſed Leo: as the Emperours Valentinian and Marciā themſelues confeſſe. I truſte now
alſo ye wil the better belieue theſe. 630. Fathers,
ſaying to Dioſcorus, that they had the regular and
ordinary authority againſt him.   What ſay yow
nowe, for your ſelfe and your fellowes? Howe
will ye maintaine the vnlawfull depoſinge of the
Catholike Biſhoppes, and other in the realme by
                                              your

Marcian confeſſeth
the fathers to be the
phyſitions.
Tandem remedia cul
pabilis erroris inuen-
ta ſunt. & mox: Sa-
cerdotes quid ob-
ſeruari in religione
debeat, perſpicua de-
finitione docuerunt.
Act. 3. pag. 863. col.
1. c.
Theis fathers en-
quire of fayth by
Pope Leo his au-
thority.
Fidem diligenter in-
quirit authoritate
beatiſs. Leonis.
Act. 3. pag. 865. col.
2. a.
Sancta & magna ſy
nodo habente regu-
larem poteſtatem.
Act. 3. pag. 865. col.
2. a.
The Emperours by
their lavve can not
condemne them
vvhoſe belief the
councel allovveth.

by your ciuill and parliament authoritie, feing that
the Emperours Valentiniā and Marcian write,that
*thofe Bifshops can not by themperours lawe be condē-
ned, Whom the ecclefiafticalCoūcelcōmendeth for true
religiō?* Many things elfe are to be faied out of this
Seffion,but I wil breake of,and fhortly ronne ouer
the refidewe : noting this only for the .4. Seffion,
that it is there declared,that Diofcorus was depriued and excōmunicated to, by the Popes Legates
and the Councel: *the Emperours deputies,*which in
all other Seffions were prefent, *being then abfent,
and Without themperours or their knowledge.*Which
geueth a checke mate to all your fupremacy, and
to all your booke withall:yea and that with a feely
pawne of one only line.This is fo declared as I fay,
in the fourth feffion: but the fentēce paffed againft
Diofcorus in the third feffiō, Diofcorus not daring
to fhewe his face, and *requiring, that themperours
vicegerents might be there prefente :* to whome anfwere was made,*that When matters of correctiō and
reformation are in hande,*as thefe were(for Diofcorus was not condemned for herefie and matters of
fayth,but for his difobedience againft the pope,the
councel, and the canons)*neither the Iudges,nor any
laye men owght to be prefente .* Which anfwere M.
Horne,for all your heuing and fheuing, againft the
ecclefiafticall reformation,geueth an other paune
mate alfo in one fhorte fentence, to a great parte
of vour boke,and to al fuch ecclefiaftical vifitation
as is geuen to the prynce,by acte of parliament.

In the fyfte fefsiō a litle variance fell among the
Q Q fathers

*Quia non poffunt fa-
cerdotes conftitutio-
ne damnari,quos fy-
nodicum ornat fuper
conferuanda religio-
ne iudicium.*
Act.3.pag.865.b.
*Act. 4. pag. 872.
col.1.c.*
*Qui a vobis damna-
tus eft ignorāte diuo
Vertice, & nobis.*
Diofcorus condem
ned without them-
perours knowledg
or his deputies.
*Act.3.pa.837.co.1.b
Obfecro vt iudices
nunc fint præfentes.
Quando quædamre-
gulatia examinan-
tur,neque iudicesne-
que aliquos laicosin-
tereffe oportet.*
*Act.3.pag.838.col.
2.c.*
*Euag.li.2,c.16.
Niceph.li.15.cap.30.*
Lay mē ought not
to be in the coūcell
vvhen matters of
reformation are in
hande
*Propter fidem nō eft
damnatus Diofcorus.*
Act.5.pa.880.col.1.a
Diofcorus vvas not
condemned for mat
ters of fayth,

The biſhops that did not agree,be threatned to be ſent to Rome.

Act.5.p.880.col.2.a Qui contradicunt, Romam ambulent.

The fathers geue vp the ſentēce,not the Emperour or his agentes.

Act.5 pag.882. Definimus igitur.etc. Si epiſcopi fuerint,a= lienos ab epiſcopatu, & clericos à clero: ſi verò monachi aut laici fuerint,anathe- matizari.

Act.5.pag.885. Vniuerſalis Synodus diſcordiam, quæ ad- uerſus rectam & ca- tholicam fidē exorta eſt,expellifecit.&c. Act.6.pa.889.co.1.c

The forme of the Popes Legats ſub= ſcription.

Paſchaſinus epiſco- pus vice domini mei beatiſſ. atq; Apoſto= lici vniuerſalis Ec= cleſiæ Papæ vrbis Ro- mæ Leonis Synodo præſidēs ſtatui, con- ſenſi, & ſubſcripſi. Vvherein ſtandeth Marcian the Em=

Fathers for the framing of the final ſentēce: wher- vpon the Senatours ſaid,that *if they did not agree, a Councel ſhould be kept in the weſt parties* : meaning at Rome.The Biſhops of Illyricum cried(as I haue before ſhewed) *they that doe not agree , lette them trudge to Rome.* In this ſeſſion when they were all afterwards agreed, the final and reſolute ſentence of the matter in controuerſy, with a denunciation of depoſition and curſe againſt ſuche as ſhould re- pine agaiſt it,is pronoūced by the Biſhops,without any voice or cōſent of themperour,or of his agēts.

In the ſixt ſeſſion was preſent Marcian thempe- rour with the noble and vertuouſe Empreſſe Pul- cheria,to whome Aetius the Archedeacō of Con- ſtantinople declared, that nowe the diſcord lately ryſen among the people in matters of faith,was pa- cified by the holy Councell : aud then read to him their finall determination and ſentence . Vnto the which ſentence were annexed the ſubſcripions of all the Biſhops: And firſt of the Popes vicegerent, after the fourme of theſe woordes .

I Biſhop Paſchaſine Preſident of the Councell , in the ſtead of my moſt bleſſed Lord,and the Apoſtolical Pope of the vniuerſal Church,of the City of Rome, Leo,haue determined, conſented and ſubſcribed. Then followe the ſubſcriptions of his two colleages,one of them being no biſhop: after whō Anatolius the Patriarch of Conſtātinople, and ſo other Patriarches and biſ- ſhops. Marciā ſeing the full and vniforme cōſent of al theſe.630.biſhops, doth allowe and cōfirme their decree,and ſtrēgtheneth it with a ciuill and politi-

call

call punifhmét appointed againſt the trafgreſſours.
And in this properly reſteth the Princes office and
authority,in affaires eccleſiaſtical . In the ſeuéth
ſeſſion it is declared, that the election of Maximus
biſhop of Antioche was confirmed by Pope Leo.
In the tenth Actió,it ys openly auouched,*quia miſ
ſi Apoſtolici ſemper in Synodis prius loqui & cõfirmare
ſoliti ſunt .* That the Popes legates were allwayes
wonte in Councels to ſpeake firſt and to confirme
firſt. In the twelueth Actió the controuerſy about
the Biſhop of Epheſus was ended by the Councel,
not by théperours deputies , as it hath ben ſhewed.
In the.16.and laſt Seſſion,yt is ſayde,that Rome euer had the primacye:The whole councell ſayeth
to théperour,that God had prouided for thé an inuincible champion againſt all errours , meaning of
Pope Leo. In thys ſeſſion a greate parte of the fathers thowghe contrarye to the Nicene decrees ,
auaunced the patriarche of Conſtantinople,to gratifie themperour making his chiefe abode there, aboue the patriarchs of Alexandria, Antiochia, and
Hieruſalé. But the Popes Legates would not therto agree, no nor Leo him ſelfe : though the whole
Coũcel beſought him:but cõfirmed al other things
that the Coũcel had determined vpon: and cauſed
Anatoli' the patriarch of Cõſtãtinople, to ſurceaſe
frõ this his ambitious claime:and to cõfeſſe his faut.
Laſt of al in a letter of Paſchaſinus one of the Popes
Legates in that Coũcel touching the condénation
of Dioſcor',this pope Leo is expreſly called,*Caput
Vniuerſalis Eccleſia,*Head of the vniuerſall Church.

QQ ij

Many

perors cõfirmatiõ.
pag.893.col.2.4.
The Pope confirmeth the election
of the Biſhop of
Antioche.
Sanctus ac beatiſſ.
Papa Epiſcopatum
Maximi Epiſcopi
Antiochenæ Eccleſiæ
confirmauit .
Act.7.p.896.c.1.4.
Rome euer had
the primacie.
Roma ſemper habuit
primatum .
Act.10.p4.910.c.1.
Act.12.pag.916.
Act.16.pa.938.co.1.c
The Pope an inuicible champion againſt all errours.
Vnde nobis impenetrabilé in õni errore
propugnatoré Deus
prouidit Roma. Eccleſia Papam.
Act.16.p.940.c.2.4.
Act.16.p.938.c.1.c.
The Pope vvoulde
not allovve the decree of the Councel
concerninge the auauncing of the patriarch of Conſtãti.
Leo ep.59. & 61. ad
Iuuenalé & alios epi
ſcop.Chalced.Synodi.
Leo.ep 71.ad Anat.

Tom. 1.
Conc. pag.
945. Gregor. lib. 4.
epist. 38.
Cap. 14.
The. 155.
vntruth.
Nipping
of the Au
thor alle‑
ged, as
shall ap‑
peare.
Lib. c. 15.
The. 157.
vntruth.
Not to
depose,
but, vt ex‑
pelleretur
to expell
ro banish
The. 158.
vntruth
false tran‑
slation.
Consules
quid fieri
oporteret
Asking
counsel
vvhat he
shuld do.
Cap. 16
The. 159.
vntruth.
Liberatus
saith that
an other
vvas pla‑

Many other things myght be gathered for this purpose, as wel out of the Actes of this Councel as otherwhere, especially that S. Gregorie writeth that *of this holy Councell, his predecessours were called Vniuersall Bisshppes* .

M. Horne. The. 55. Diuision. Pag. 33. b.

This Synode being finished, the Emperour banished Dioscorus *into the Cytie of* Gangren. *VVhich thyng doon: The nobles of the Cytie (saith* Liberatus*) assembled together to choose one, both for life and learning, worthy of the Bishopricke: for this was*(.155.) *comaunded by the Emperours Decrees. At the length* Proterius *vvas made Bishop: against vvhom the seditious people rayed one* Timotheus Hellurus, *or* Ælurus, *vvho in conclusion, murthered* Proterius. *The catholique Bisoppes, vvhich mainteined the Chalcedon councel, made humble supplication vnto* Leo *the Emperour, both to reuenge the death of* Proterius, *and also*(.157.)*to depose* Timotheus Hellurus, *as one not Lavvfully instituted in the Bishoprike on the contrary parte, other Bishops make supplication vnto him, in the defence of* Timotheus, *and against the Chalcedon councel. VVhen* Leo *the Emperour had considered the matter of both their supplications, for good and godly considerations he wrote his letters to the Bishops of euery city, declaring both these causes, and willing them to send him*(.158.)*their aduise, vvhat vvas best to be done: from vvhom he receiued aunsvvere, that the Chalcedon Councel is to be mainteined euen vnto death: vvhereuppon the Emperour writeth to* Stila *his Lieutenaunt of* Alexandria, *that he should maintein the Chalcedon Councell.* Stila *did as the Emperour commaunded: he expelled* Timotheus Hellurus, and(.159.)*placed an other in his roume, named* Timotheus Salefacialius, *or* Albus, *vvho liued quietly all the raigne of* Leo, *and* Zeno, *the Emperours, til* Basilicus *gat the Empire, vvho restored* Timotheus *the Heretique: But vvhen* Zeno *recouered the Empire, this* Timotheus *poisoned him selfe, in vvhose place the Heretiques chose one* Peter Mogge. *After that* Zeno *the Emperour knevv of the crafty dealing of the heretiques, he wrote to his Lieutenaunt* Anthemius, *that he should depriue* Peter Mogge, *and restore* Timotheus *to the bishopricke, and further, that he should punish those, that were the authours to enstall* Peter Mogge.

Mogge. Anthemius *receiuing the Emperours mandate, did depose Peter Mogge, as one that was but a counterfayt made bißop, contrary to the lavves of the Catholique Churche,* and *restored* Timotheus Salefacialius, *vvho being restored, sent certeine of his Clergy to the Emperour to render him thankes.*

The .15. Chapter, of Leo and Zeno Emperours.

Stapleton.

THis collection ftandeth in the banifhing of Diofcorus, and in the election and depofing of bifhoppes:
Proterius was chofen *vniuerforum fententia*, by the
verdit of all the Citizens of Alexandria, as the maner of *Liberat.*
choofing then was, both before and after. The Emperours *cap. 14.*
commaundement was not the only caufe thereof, but the
cōmaundement of the Councell, for execution whereof
the Emperour gaue forth his letters, alfo. For concealing
whereof in your firft allegatiō out of Liberatus, you leaue
out the worde, *Et:* Alfo, where Liberatus faieth: *For this*
Was alfo commaunded by the Emperours edictes. The worde
Alfc, you leaue out, to make your Reader beleue, that the
onely Abfolute cōmaundement of the Emperour was the
caufe, that Proterius was ordered bifhop in the place of
Diofcorus. Whereas themperours edict came forth, partly for auoyding of tumultes, which the hereticall adherēts
of Diofcorus were likely to raife: And which they raifed
in dede, ftraight after the death of Marcian themperour,
and remouvng Proterius made Timotheus to fitte in hys
place: partly for executing the Chalcedon Councels Decree, which was that a newe bifhop fhould ftrayght way
be ordered at Alexādria in the roume of Diofcorus, whom *Act. 4.*
they had depofed. Nowe Timotheus was an open here-

QQ iij tike

tike, ſtanding againſt the Coūcel of Chalcedo, and a murtherer withall of hys lawefull biſhop Proterius, and therefore no greate accompt to be made of the Emperours doings towards hym he being no biſhop at al in dede. Nowe
where the Emperour cōmaunded an other to be put in his
place, it had bene well done, if ye had placed alſo (as your
author doth) the whole words and doings of themperour:
which was, *that Stila his deputy ſhuld ſet in ã other*. But whē
M. Horne? *when all the Biſſops had anſwered that the Councel of Chalcedo was to be maintayned euen to death: And that
the foreſayed Timotheus was vnworthy to be called either Biſſhop or Chaiſtian man*. And howe M. Horne? *Decreto popu
li*. With the conſente of the people: which kinde of chooſing Biſhops was then no newe thinge in the Churche,
but* vſed bothe before and after. As for the baniſhing of
Dioſcorus (being before depoſed of the Councell) I think
your ſelf wil confeſſe yt to be no ſpirituall matter.

M. Horne. *The*. 56. *Diuiſion. pag*. 34. *a*.

After this Timotheus, Ioannes de Talaida *vvas chooſen, vvhereof
vvhen Acatius Biſhop of Conſtantinople hearde, he being offended vvith
Iohn, for that he had not ſent vnto him ſynodical letters, to ſigniſie of his e-
lection, as the maner vvas,) he ioyned him ſelfe vvith the fautours of Peter
Mogge, and accuſed Iohn vnto the Emperour , as one not founde in Religion, nor fit for the Byſhoprike.* Peter Mogge *eſpying this oportunity , diſ-
ſembleth an vnity and recōciliation, and by his friends, vvynneth* Acatius,
vvho breaketh the matter to theperour, and perſvvadeth him to depoſe Ioānes de Talaida, *and to reſtore Peter Mogge: ſo that the ſame Peter vvold
firſt receiue and profeſſe the Henoticō, that is, the confeſſiō of the vnity in
faith, vvhich the Prince had ſet foorth, vvhereof this is the effect*. Zeno the
Emperor, to al Biſhops and people, throughout Alexādry, and
Ægipt, Lybia, and Pētapolis: For ſomuchas we know that the
right and true faith alone, is the begining, cōtinuāce, ſtrēgth,
and inuicible ſhyld of our Empire; we labour night ād day in
praier,

dict.ca.15.

Ambroſ.
li.5.Epiſt.
32.
Con.Ant.
can.16.
Con.Sard
cap.1.

Lib.ca.18.

praier,ſtudy,and with Lawes to encreaſe,the Catholik,and A-
poſtolike Church by that faith. Al people next after God, ſhal
bowe douns their neckſvnder our power. Seing therfore,that
the pure faith,doth on this wiſe preſerue vs, and the Romain
cómon wealth,many godly fatheis haue húbly beſeched vs,
to cauſe an vnitie to be had in the holy Church, that the mébers diſplaced and ſeparated through the malice of the enemie, may be coupled and knit together. *And after this, declaring*
his faith, to agree vvich the Nicen councel, and thoſe that condéned Neſto
rius,*and* Eutiches,(*he ſayth*) we curſe thoſe that thinke the con
trary. *After vvhiche curſe, declaring al the articles of his faith, he cócludeth*
vvith an earneſt exhortation vnto the vnitie of faith. The Empereur, ſaith
Liberatus,*ſuppoſing that* Ioannes de Thalaida, *had not ment rightly*
of the Chalcedó coúcel,but had dó al things ſainedly, vvrote his letters by the
perſvvaſió of Acatius,*to* Pergamius & Apolonius *his Lieutenantes,to*
(.161,) *depoſe* Iohn *,and enſtal Peter Mogge . Iohn, being thus thruſt out,*
repaired to the B.of Antioche,vvith vvhoſe letters of cómendacion,he vvét to
Síplici^o *biſhop of Rome,and deſired him to vvrite in his behalfe vnto* Aca
ti^o *biſhoppe of Conſtantinople,vvho did ſo,and vvithin a vvhile after, died,*

Stapleton.

The like drifte as before,followeth nowe alſo, and therfore the leſſe nede of any long or exquiſite anſwer. Sauing
that a few things are to be cóſidered, aſwel for the weighing of M. Hornes reaſons, as for ſuch matters, as make for
the popes primacye euen in thoſe ſtories that M . Horne
reherſeth. As, that pope Simplicius of whome M . Horne
maketh mention excommunicated Peter the Biſhop of A-
lexandria here mentioned benig an Eutychian. Again that
Acatius biſhop of Conſtantinople,here alſo recited by M.
Horne,was alſo excómunicated by pope Felix. What?ſai-
eth M.Horn,a buttó for your popes curſe. If that be a matter eccleſiaſtical,our Emperors haue curſed aſwel,as your
popes:Eué our Emperour Zeno that we are nowe in hand
withal.Say you me ſo M.Horne? Then ſhew me I beſeche
you,

The prin-
ces ſupre-
macye in
(.160,) al
cauſes.
The. 160.
vntruthe
ioyned
vvith ſo
lye. No
ſuche Su-
premacy
can be ga
thered of
the texte.
The .161.
vntiuth.
Not to
depoſe,
but, vt pel-
lerent,to]
driue out.
and to
baniſh.

.1.
Sigeb.in
Chron.
Pantal.
.2.
Iſidor, in
Falicé.
To.2.Có¢.
Sig. Pát.

you, by what authority? *For no man*(you say your selfe afterward)*hath authority to excōmunicate,but only the Church and those who receiue authority therevnto by cōmiſsion from the Churche.*Thus you say euen in this booke. Bring forth

*pag.●5.
col.2.*

then the Emperours cōmiſſion:Otherwiſe thinke not,we will crie *ſanctus ſanctus* to all ye ſhal ſay. And if you bring forth the cōmiſſion,then are you vndone,and al your primacy. For if the Emperour hath his commiſsion from the Church, then belike the Church is aboue him. Onleſſe as ye haue found a newe diuinitie,ſo ye can find a new lawe, wherby he that taketh the cōmiſſiō ſhal be aboue him that geueth it.This curſe then M.Horne was no eccleſiaſticall curſe:no more ſurely then if you ſhuld,if Maiſtres Madge

VVhat maner of curſe Zeʼno the ēperours curſe vvas.

played the ſhrewe with you, beſhrewe and curſe to, her ſhrewes heart.It was a zelouſe deteſtation of heretikes,as if a good catholike man ſhould nowe ſay,curſed be al wicked Sacramentaries. And whome I pray you did he curſe? Any,trow ye that was not accurſed before? No,but chiefly Neſtorius and Eutyches:which were before by general Coūcels excōmunicated.Yet for al that we haue our margent daſſhed with a freſh iolye note, that *the princes ſupremacy is in al cauſes.*I pray God ſend you M.Horne as much worſhip of yt,as ye had of your other late like marginall floriſhe owte of the Chalcedon Councell. Yet let vs ſee what proufes ye lay forthe:Why? ſay you:Was not Zeno required to cauſe an vnity in the church.Ye mary was he, and ſo was Conſtantine and Marcian to.Yea Marcian for that,was called the cheif phiſition to. But we neade not put you any more in remembrance hereof, leaſte ye take to muche pryde of yt. Yea but zeno ſayeth, that *after God all people ſhall bowe their neckes to his power*. It is ſo

in dede M. Horne. But onleſſe ye can proue, that he ſaied
to his ſpiritual power (which he ſaid not, nor meante not)
a good argument (the more pittye) hath quyte broken his
necke. Neither yet doth Zeno ſpeake of the neckes of any
his ſubiectes, but (as yt ſemeth) of ſuch nations as were his
enimies. And aſſuredly ſuch woordes al pagan Emperours
vſe. And yet they are not, I trowe, therefore ſupreme gouernours in al cauſes ſpiritual. Now yt would require ſome
tracte of tyme, fully to open either howe M. Horne hath
confounded, maymed, and mangled his authours narration,
or to ſhewe that theſe things euen in the true narration of
the ſtories, that he reherſeth, make fully agaiſt him, and for
the Popes primacy. For this Ioannes Talaida (ſaieth Liberatus) *appealed to Pope Simplicius euen as Athanaſius did.* Simplicius writeth to Acatius, who anſwereth : *that he did all
thus withowt the Popes cõſent, by the Emperours commaundement for the preſeruation of the vnity in the Church.* To whõ
Simplicius replied, *that he ought not to communicate with
Petrus Moggus for that he agreed to the Emperours order ãd
proclamatiõ: onleſſe he woulde embrace the decrees of the Coũcel of Chalcedo.* Thus letters going to and fro, Simplicius died
and Felix ſuccedeth : who doth both depriue him from his
biſſhoprike, and excommunicateth him, for taking part with
the ſaid Petrus Moggus. After the death of Acatius, ſuccedeth Flauianus, who woulde not ſuffer himſelfe to be enſtalled without the Popes conſent. Within ſhorte tyme,
Euphemius was Patriarche of Conſtantinople: who receiued ſynodicall letters from this Pope. Theſe and manye
other thinges elſe might here be ſaid, euen out of the chapter vpon which Maiſter Horne himſelfe pleadeth, which
we paſſe ouer.

R R But for

Zenõ

*Hoſtiũ ge-
nerationes
cõterētur.
oẽs autẽ
incurua-
bunt poſt
Deum ſuã
poteſtati
noſtra cer-
uicem.
Libe.c. 18
Gentes ho
ſtiles con-
terentur,
atq; exti-
guētur, &
oẽs colla
ſua impe-
rio ſecũdũ
Deũ no-
ſtro ſub-
mittent.
Nice. lib.
16.c. 12.
Libe.c. 18
Libe.c. 18
Nice. lib.
6.cap.15.
To.1.cõc.
pag.061.
col.2.*

But for the Princes Supremacy in caufes Ecclefiaftical, what hath M. Horne in al this diuifion? His marginal Note lyeth in thē duft. What hath he befide? He faith. *The Empe-ror by his Lieutenants depofed Iohn Talaida*, the Patriarche of Antioche. But this is vntrue . The Emperour in dede com-maunded his Lieutenants , *vt pellerent eum*: to expulfe and driue him out from his bifhoprike , but to depofe him, that is to make him now no Bifhop at all, that lay not in the Em-perours power. He did (as merely of him felfe a wife prelate faid in King Edwardes dayes, being then in the Tower for the Catholike faieth) but take awaye the Ricke , Iohn re-mayned bifhop ftil. And that with this Iohn Talaida fo it was, appereth well by Liberatus your owne Author, M. Horne. For this Iohn Talaida (faieth Liberatus) *appealinge* from the Emperours violence *to Pope Simplicius , habēs epif: copi dignitatem, remanfit Romæ* , remayned at Rome, hauing ftil the dignity of a bifhop , who alfo afterwarde had the Ricke alfo. For the Pope endewed him with the bifhoprike of Nola in Campania. Now as Emperours and Princes haue power(though not lawful) to expelle, and depriue men of the Church from their temporal dignities, and poffefsions: fo to depriue a man of the Church from his office of minifte-ry, to depofe a bifhop or a prieft frō his fpiritual Iurifdictiō and Authority(which depofition only is a caufe ecclefiafti-cal) to the Church only frō whom fuch Authority came, it belongeth. Princes depriuations, are no ecclefiaftical depo-fitions. Take this anfwere ones for al M. Horne you which vntruly reporte, that Princes depofed bifhops.

Liberatus Cap. 18.

M. Horne. The. 57. Diuifion. Pag. 35. a.
This Pope Simplicius confidering the great contentions that vvere ac-cuftomably about the election of Popes, did prouide by decree , that no Pope
fhould

*ſhould hereafter be choſen vvithout the authority of the Prince, vvhich decree,
although it be not extant, yet it is manifeſt inough , by the Epiſtle of Kinge
Odoacer put into the Actes of the thirde Synode, that* Simmachus *the
Pope did keepe at* Rome, vvherin the King doth not only auouche , the decree
of Simplicius, *but alſo addeth:* VVe maruaile, that without vs anye
thig was accepted, ſeing that whiles our Prieſt (*meaning the biſſhop of Rome Simplicius*) was on liue: nothing ought to haue bene
taken in hande without vs.

The.16.Chapter of Simplicius, Felix.3.and Symmachus Popes of Rome.

Stapleton.

IF Pope Simplicius by decree, gaue the Prince Authority
to confirme the choſen Pope, what helpeth this your ſupremacy? Nay doth it not much impayre the ſame ? For
then al the Princes Authority in this behalfe dependeth of
the Popes decree as of a Superiour lawe . And ſo he is ſubiect both to the law, and to the lawemaker . And yet this is
all that in this Diuiſion hath any maner inckling to iudace
the Prices Supremacy in any cauſe eccleſiaſtical. But yf M.
Horn would haue loked but a litle further and vpo the firſt
line of the next leafe, he mought haue found in the ſaid Sy
nod , that the ſee of Rome hath *the prieſtly primacy ouer all
the whole world.* And that *Councels muſt be confirmed by that
ſee,* with ſuch other like matter. For whereas this King O-
doacer, beſide the decree touchig the choſing of the Pope
(which as your ſelf ſay he made at the Popes requeſt) made
alſo an other concerning not alienating Church goods, the
whole Synod reiected and codemned it, for theſe. ij.cauſes
expreſſely. *Firſt* (ſaith Eulalius a biſſhop of Sicily , whoſe
ſentence (the other biſſhops ſaying the ſame) the whole Sy-

In Synod.
Rom. 3.
sub Sym-
macho.
Tom. 1.
Conc.pag.
1004.
col 2.
* in the
Nicene
councel,
Can. 4. &
6.
* Qui præ
rogatiua
beati Apo
stoli Petri
per vniuer
sum orbē
primatum
obtinens
sacerdotij,
statutis
synodalib°
consueuit
tribuere
firmitatē.

no.'e folowed) *becauſe againſt the rules of the Fathers, this Decree appereth to be made of Layemen, though religious and godlye, to whome that any authoritye was euer geuen ouer Eccleſiaſticall goods, it is not reade. Secondlye it is not declared to be confirmed with the ſubſcription of any biſhop of the Apoſtolike See. Nowe whereas, the holy Fathers * haue decreed, that if the Prieſtes of any whatſoeuer prouince (keeping a Councel within their owne lymities) ſhall attempt any thing without the authority of their Metropolitane or their biſhop, it ſhould be voyde and of none effeĉt, howe much more that which is knowen to haue bene preſumed in the See Apoſtolike, the Biſhop thereof not preſent (* which biſhop by the prerogatiue of the bleſſed Apoſtle Peter, hauing throughe the whole worlde the Primacy of prieſthood, hath bene wonte to confirme the Decrees of Councels) preſumed I ſay, of layemen, though certayn biſhops agreing vnto it (who yet could not preiudicat their Prelat of whom it is knowen they were conſecrated) is vndoubtedly voyde and of no effeĉt, neither any waye to be accompted amonge Eccleſiaſtical decrees?* Thus farre that Synod by your ſelfe alleaged M. Horne. God rewarde you for geuing vs ſuch good inſtruĉtions againſt your ſelfe. Or yf it came not of you, but of your frende, let him haue the thankes therefore. But yf it ſo falleth out againſt your willes both, yet God be prayſed, that as by ſinne he worketh ſomtime a greater amēdement, and turneth horrible temptations into a more confortable calmeneſſe then before the ſtorme came, ſo alſo by your vnhappy meaning hathe yet brought vs to a happye information of ſuch doĉtrine as vtterly ouerthroweth your hereſye.

For here you ſee M. Horne, not only the laie Magiſtrat, yea the King him ſelfe, yea though he were religiouſe and
godly

godly, vtterly excluded from all authority in caufes Ecclefiafticall (whereby your phantafticall Primacie vanifheth
cleane away) but alfo that the Pope(whome you cal a forraine power) hath the Primacy, the chiefty and fupreame
præeminence of Priefthode, not onely in Rome or the Romaine Prouince, but (faith this Synode by your felf clerckly alleaged) *per vniuerfum orbem*, throughout the whole
worlde, and then if you be a parte of the worlde, he is your
Primate too.   Thus much faith this Synode : and thereby
vtterly ouerthroweth the whole effect of the Othe, in both
thofe partes for the whiche the Catholikes refufe to fwere
vnto it.   Verely if ye goe on as you haue hitherto, you
wil furely be efpied for a preuaricatour, that is, for a double
faced Proctour, fecreatlie inftructing your clients aduerfarie, but in face proteftiñg to plead againft him.   For better inftructions, no hyred aduocate coulde haue geauen
vs, then you the Counterpleader haue miniftered vnto
vs.

M. Horne. The. 58. Diuifion. pag. 35. a.

Next after Simplicius vvas Fœlix the third *chofen, vvho after*
his confirmation, fent many letters as vvell to the Emperour, as to Acatius
Bifhoppe of Conftantinople, about the matter betvvixt Iohn *and* Peter,
but vvhen he coulde not preuaile in his fuite, he made Iohn *Bifhoppe of*
Nola *in* Campania. *One of the letters that Pope* Fœlix *vvrote vn-*
to Zenon *the Emperour about this matter, is put into the fift Synode of*
Conftantinople : *vvherein the Pope after the falutation, doth moft humblye*
befeech the Emperour, to take his humble fuite in good parte. He fhevveth
that the holy (.162.) Churche maketh this fuite, that he vvill vouchefafe
to mainteine the vnitie of the Churche, that he vvill deftroye Herefies, that
breaketh the bonde of vnitie, that he vvill expell Peter Mogge *bothe*
oute of the Citie, and alfo from Churche regiment : that he vvould not fuffer

Act. 1.

The 161.
Vntruth.
Thefe
vvordes
Apoftolike
and Ca-
tholique,
left out,

Vide Tom.
2.Cōc.pa.
13.in epiſt.
Felicis ad
Petrum.
Hæc legat
ſancta Dei
Apoſtolica
et Catho-
lica eccleſ.
vt ab ipſa
propter
prædictas
cauſas de-
poſitū ad
cōmunio-
nē nō ſuſ-
cipias, ſed
per diuia
nas apices
veſtra ſe.
renitatis
ab Antio-
chia conſi-
nio propel-
lite,pro ip-
ſo aut cō=
ſtituite v-
nū operib.
ſacerdotiū
ornantem
etc.Tom.2
Conc.Act.
1.Synod.5.
pag.19.b.

Peter being depoſed,to be admitted to the Communion of the Churche : but that by his honorable letters, he vvould baniſh him out of the bounds of Antioche. And (ſaith this Biſhop of Rome Fœlix vnto the Emperour) In his place appoint you one that ſhal beutifie the Prieſthode by his woorkes.

Stapleton.

You procede ſtill to bring authorities againſt your ſelfe. This Peter was depoſed I confeſſe : But by whome , M. Horne? Not by the Emperour, but euen by Pope Fœlix as appeareth but one leafe before the place which your ſelfe alleage.   And in caſe it was to painefull for you to turne backe a leafe or two before , yet might you haue vouchſaued to haue read the next lines before your own allegatiō. In the which Fœlix ſignifieth, that he was ſo depoſed , and therfore requeſteth th'Emperour to expel him,and to place ſome other mete man for him : whiche thing Popes doe at this day, requiring Catholike Princes to remoue hereticall Biſhops,and to place good in their roome,neither yet therfore are, or euer were Princes accompted, enacted , or intituled, *Supreme gouernours in all cauſes Eccleſiaſticall.* Your new Religion, hath inuented this newe Title. This Pope Fœlix alſo excommunicated Acatius of Conſtantinople,for bearing with this Peter Mogge,as witneſſeth Liberatus. Whereby appeareth clerely the Popes Primacie ouer the ij. chiefe Patriarches of the Eaſt Churche of Conſtantinople and Antioche . And you againe are with your owne examples cleane ouerthrowen.

M. Horne. The. 59. Diuiſion.pag. 35. b.

Anaſtaſius *the Emperour* (.163.) *depoſed* Macedonius Biſhoppe of Conſtantinople, *as one that falſified the Ghoſpels,as* Liberatus *ſaith.*

Stapleton.

The. 163. Vntruth. As before.

Stapleton.

If this Macedonius falsified the Gholpel, he was I wene,
worthy to be depoled.   But your Author vleth not this
worde *Depoled*, but he saieth , *he was expulsed* .   Whiche
might be, being, by an ordinary and an vlual courle, by the
Bishops first depoled. But becaule the matter is not cleare
on your side, and if it were, it did not greatly enforce : by
reason Anastasius him selfe was a wicked hereticall Emperour, and so no great good deduction to be made from his
doings : I let it passe.

*Liberatus
cap.19.*

M. Horne.   The. 60. Diuision.pag. 35. b.

About the election of Symachus, Platina *mentioneth vvhat great diuision and sedition arose, in so muche that the parties vvere faine to agree,
to haue a Councell holden for the determination of the matter.* And there
was a Councell appointed at Rauenna (*saith Sabellicus*) to the
end that the controuerly might be decided according to right,
before the king Theodoriche : *before vvhome , the matter vvas so
discussed, that at the last, this Pope* Symachus *vvas confirmed. Neuerthelesse this fyer vvas not thus so quite quenched, but that foure yeares after,
it blased out sorer againe.* VVhereat the king (*saith Platina*) beinge
displealed, sente Peter the Bishoppe of Altine to Rome, to
enioye the See, and bothe the other to be (.164.) depoled.
VVherevpon an other Synode vvas called of 110. *Bishops, vvherein (saith*
Sabellicus *) the Pope him selfe defended his ovvne cause so stoutlye, and cunningly, and confuted (saith* Platina *) al the obiections laid against him, that
by the verdict of them all, he vvas acquited: and all the fault laied to Laurence and Peter.*

*The 164
Vntruth.*
Platina
saieth not
so, but
*vt pulso
vtroque
sedem te-
neret.*

Stapleton.

What may be said for the doings of Princes in the election of the Clergie, and how your examples agree not with
our practile, I haue already saied somewhat : and that I say
to this too. But in the Diuision folowing, we shall saye to
this more particularlye.

Horne.

M. Horne. The. 61. Diuision. pag. 35. b.

Syma
chus.

The. 165.
Vntruth,
Slaunde-
rouse and
malitious
The.166.
Vntruth.
That coū-
cell vvill
shevve
they had
verye
small.
The.167,
Vntruth'
The King
him selfe
in the coū-
cel decla-
reth,that
not by
his com-
maunde-
ment,but
by the
Popes
letters,
this Sy-
nod vvas
sūmoned.
The 168.
Vntruth.
Not so.
But be-
cause as
the Coun-
cel prote-
sted,it per-
teined
not to
him or to
any mans
els.

But to thentent it may the better appere vvhat vvas the Kings authority about these matters, mark the fourth Romaine Synode, holden in the time of this Symachus, and about the same matter of his, vvhiche although it be mangled and confusedly set forth in the Booke of Generall Councels, bicause (as it may seeme) that they (.155.) vvould not haue the vvhole trueth of this dissention appeare : yet vvil it shevv much, that the Princes had (.166.) no small entermedling, and authority in Synodes and Churche matters. This Synode vvas summoned to be kept in Rome by the (.167.) commaundement of the most honorable Kinge Theodoriche. He declareth that many and grieuous complaintes, vvere brought vnto him againste Symachus Bis-shoppe of Rome. Symachus commeth into the Synode to answere for him selfe, geaueth thankes to the King for calling the Synode, requireth that he may be restored to suche things as he had loste by the suggestion of his enne-mies, and to his former state, and then to come to the cause, and to answere the accusers. The more parte in the Synode, thoughte this his demaunde reasonable : Decernere tamen aliquid Synodus sine regia notitia non Præsumpsit. Yet the Synode presumed not to decree any thing without the Kings knowledge. Neyther came it to passe as they vvished : for the King commaunded Symachus the Bishoppe of Rome, to answere his aduersaries before he shoulde resume any thing. And (.168.) so the King committed the vvhole debating and iudging of the ma-ter to the Synode, vvhich concludeth the sentence vvith these vvords: Vvher-fore according to the Kings will or cōmaundement, who hath committed this cause to vs, we refourme or restore vnto him (to Symachus) what right so euer he ought to haue within the Citie of Rome, or without.

Stapleton.

Here hath M. Horne an other fetch to proue Princes to haue the chief interest in maters ecclesiastical: as for the de-positions of Bishops, yea of the Pope him selfe. And first he is angry, that this mater in the boke of Councels is so man-gled and confusedly set foorth. But it is an other thorne
then

then this that pricketh him, that he will not difclofe to all
the worlde. For to faye the truthe, he feeth in his owne
confcience, that of all Councelles, the felfe fame Councell that he here alleageth, dothe fo fet foorth the Popes
Primacie, that the grieuoufe remembrance therof, caufeth
him to fpeake, he can not tel what. Verelye, if M. Horne
had ftepped foorth but one fote further, and turned his eie
vpon the next leafe, there fhould he haue found a clercklie
worke made by Eunodius in the defence of the Councell,
that he is in hand withall.   There fhould he haue founde
moft euident authorities for the Popes Supremacie vppon
all ftates temporall and fpirituall. He fhould alfo finde the
fame booke to be confirmed by. CC. and. xxx. Bifhops affembled at Rome in a Synode. Leaue of therfore, M. Horne
this complaint, and complaine of that, that grieueth you in
dede, and that is not of confufion, but of the confefsion ye
find there of all the Bifhops concerning the Ecclefiafticall
præeminence, liyng fo open and thicke, like a great block in
your way, that ye coulde not paffe ouer to thefe your allegations that you haue here patched in, but that you muft
needes ftumble and breake your fhinnes therat: which grieueth you ful fore. But let vs now fee, what good and holfome herbes, ye being fo cunning a gardener, haue gathered out of this garden, that as ye thinke lieth fo vnhâfomlie
and fluttifhly. Ye fay firft that this Councell was called by
the cōmaundement of the right honorable King Theodoriche.
Make him as honorable as ye wil. But other then an Arrian fhal ye not make of him. Yf ye knewe he was an Arrian,
your honour might haue bene better beftowed els where.
If ye knewe it not, then is your reading to fmall, I trow, to
furnifh fuch a boke as this is. And yet to fay the truthe, fmall

SS   reading

Pope Sima-
chus.
M. Horne
complai-
neth, but
dareth
not fhew
vvhere
the thorn
pricketh
him.

Tom. 1.
Conc. pa.
1009.

Martinus
Pol.
Sabellicus

reading will ferue the turne too. Ye fay he called a Councell: So he did. But how did he call it ? Forfoth with the
côfent of the Pope Symachus, though the Coûcel were called againft him. For when the Biffhops had tolde the King,
that *the Pope himfelfe ought to call Councels, by a fingular pri-*

Tom.1.
Conc.pa.
1007.col.1.

uilege due to the See of Rome, becaufe to that See, firft the me-
rite ād principality of S. Peter, ād after the authority of Coûcels,
fingulorum in Ecclefijs tradidit poteftatem, gaue power ouer
euery thing in the Churches, the Kinge made aunfweare,
that the Pope had declared his confente to it by his letters.
Yea and the Bifhops not fatiffied with the Kings fo faiyng,
required a fight of the Popes letters: which the King fhewed vnto them out of hăd. The Pope alfo him felf being prefent, licenfed the Bifhops to examine his own matter. And a
litle after: *Affectu purgationis fuæ culmen humiliat.* For defire
of purging himfelf he hūbleth his high authority or dignity.
Yet M. Horne addeth: *the Synode prefumed not to decree any*
thing without the Kings knowledge. Yf they had faied they
ought not, then had ye faid fomwhat. But prefume not, and
may not, are two things farre afonder. Though yet in one
fenfe in dede they might not, nor ought not to haue proceded with the Kings confent, or without , againft the Pope,
who hath no Iudge in this world but God only: Neither că

Nec ali-
quid ad fe
præter re=
uerentiă
de Ecclefi-
afticis ne=
gotijs per
tinere.pa.
1007.col.2

he be iudged by his inferiours. And fo thefe Bifhops told the
King to his face. And finally the King referreth the whole
mater to the Synode, and plainly protefteth, that *it was the*
Coûcels part to prefcribe what ought to be done in fo weighty a
mater. As for mee (faith the King) *I haue nothing to doe with*
Ecclefiaticall maters, but to honour and reuerence them, I cōmit
to you, to heare or not to heare this matter , as ye fhall thinke it
moft profitable, fo that the Chriftiās in the City of Rome, might
be fet

be set in peace. And to this point, so, is al M. Hornes supremacy driuen. The Bishops proceding to sentence, doe declare that Pope Symachus was not to be iudged by any man: neither bound to answere his accusers, but to be committed to Gods iudgemēt. And the reason the Coūcel geueth. *That it appertaineth not to the sheep, but to the pastour, to foresec and prouide for the snares of the Wolfe.* And thē follow the words that you reherse, which are no iudicial sentence, but only a declaration that he should be taken for the true Bishop as before. But to medle with the cause, and to discusse it iudicially, they would not, because as they said, by the Canōs thei could not. And therefore immediatly in the same sentence, that ye haue in such hast brokē of in the midle, it followeth : *We doe reserue the Whole cause to the iudgemente of God.*

Sette this to the former parte by you recited, being a parcell of the sayed sentence, as ye must needes doe, and then haue ye sponne a faire threade : your selfe prouing that thing, whiche of all things yee and your fellowes denye. That is, that the Pope can be iudged of no man. And so haue ye nowe made him the Supreame Heade of the whole Churche : and haue geauen your selfe suche a fowle fall, that all the worlde will lawghe you to scorne, to see you finde faulte with this Councell, *as mangled and confusedlye sette foorth,* whiche so plainelye and pithelye confoundeth to your greate shame and confusion, all that euer yee haue broughte, or shall in this booke bringe againste the Popes Primacye. So also it well appeareth, that if there were in the worlde nothing else to be pleaded vppon but your owne Councell and sentence, by you here mangled and confusedly alleged, M. Fekenham might vpon very good ground refuse the othe: and ye be cōpelled

S S ij   also

Vnde secūdum principalia præcepta, quæ nostræ hoc tribuunt potestati, ci quicquid ecclesiasticī intra sacrā vrbem vel foris iuris est, reformamus totamque causam Dei iudicio reseruantes, vniuersos hortamur. &c. Pa.1008. col.2.

also, if not to take the othe for the Popes Primacy, being of so squemish a conscience, yet not to refuse his authority by your owne Author and text so plainely auouched.

M. Horne. The. 62. Diuision. pag. 36, a.

The. 169.
Vntruth.
Such like
gouerne=
mente
vvas ne=
uer pra=
ctiſed by
any Ca=
tholique
Empe=
rour.
The. 170.
Vntruth.
Not by
one good
Biſhop,
or godlye
Father.
The. 171.
vntruthe.
Slaunde=
rouſe.
The. 172.
Vntruth.
Neither
in Frauce
nor in
Spaine
ſhall you
euer
ſhevv it.

As it is and ſhall be moſt manifeſtly proued and teſtified by the œcumeni= call or generall Councels, vvherin the order of Eccleſiaſticall gouernment in Chriſtes Church hath ben moſt faithfully declared, and ſhevved from time to time (as your ſelf affirme) that ſuch like gouernment as the Quenes Maie= ſtie doth claime and take vppon her in Eccleſiaſticall cauſes vvas practi= ſed (.169.) continually by the Emperours: and approued, praiſed, and high= ly commended by (.170.) thouſands of the beſt Biſshoppes and moſt godly fa= thers that haue bene in Chriſtes Churche from time to time: euen ſo ſhall I prooue by your ovvne booke of Generall Councels (.171) mangled, maimed, and ſet foorth by Papiſh Donatiſtes them ſelues, and other ſuch like Church vvriters, that this kinde, and ſuch like gouernment, as the Quenes Maie= ſtie doth vſe in Church cauſes, vvas by continuall practiſe, not in ſome one onely Church or parte of Chriſtendome (vvhereof you craue prouſe, as though not poſsible to be ſhevved) but in the notableſt Kingdomes of al Chri ſtendome, as (.172.) Fraunce and Spaine, put in vre: vvherby your vvil= full and malicious ignoraunce ſhalbe made ſo plain, that it ſhalbe palpable to them vvhoſe eyes ye haue ſo bleared, that they cannot ſee the truth.

The. 17. Chapter of Clodoueus, Childebert, Theodobert, and Gunthranus, Kings of Fraunce.

Stapleton.

MAiſter Horne nowe taketh his iourney from Rome and the Eaſt Churche (where he hath made his a= bode a greate while) to Fraunce and to Spaine: hoping there to find out his newe founde Supreamacye.

Yea

Yea he saieth: *He hath and will proue it by thowsandes of the beste Bisshops*. Vndoudtedly, as he hath already founde it out by the 318.Bisshops at Nice, by the 200.bisshops at Ephesus, and by the 630.bishops at Chalcedo: (who stande eche one in open fielde againſt him) so wil he finde it in Frāce and in Spayn also. If he had said he would haue found it in the new founde landes beyonde Spayn among the infidels there, that in dede had ben a mete place for his new founde Supremacy. Verily in any Chriſtened coūtre by hī yet named or to be named in this booke, he neither hath nor shall find any one Coūcel or bishop, Prince or Prouīce, to agnise or witneſſe this abſolute Supremacy that M. Horn so depely dreameth of. And that let the Cōference of both our labours trie: M. Hornes answer, and this Reply: As also who hath bleared the Readers eyes, M. Horne, or Maiſter Fekenham.

M. Horne. The 63. Diuiſion, pag. 36. b.

Clodoueus *about this time the firſt Chriſtian King of Fraunce, baptized by* Remigius, *and taught the Chriſtian faith: perceyuing that through the troublesome times of vvarres, the Church diſcipline had bene neglected and much corruption crepte in, doth for reformacion hereof call a nationall councel or Synode at* Aurelia, *and commaundeth the biſshoppes to aſſemble there together, to conſult of ſuch neceſſary matters as vvere fit, and as he deliuered vnto them to conſulte of. The Biſshoppes doe according as the Kinge* (.173.) *commaundeth, they aſſemble, they commende the Kings zeale, and great care for the Catholique faith, and Religion, they conclude according to the Kings minde, and doth* (.174.) *referre their decrees to the iudgement of the King, vvhome they confeſſe to haue* (.175.) *the ſuperiority, to be approued by his aſſent*. Clodoueus *also called a Synode named* Conciliū Cabiloneum, *and commaunded the biſshops to conſider if any thing vvere amiſſe in the diſcipline of the Church, and to conſulte for the reformation thereof: and this (ſaith the biſshops) he did of zeale to Religiō and true faith. Other ſouuer Synodes vvere ſummoned aftervvarde in the ſame City at*

As Clodoueus and Childebert here, so Charles the Frēch King that novv liueth called a Synod at Poyſſy by Paris of late yers. And yet is he not of his ſubiects take for the ſupremeGouernor in al cauſes Eccleſiaſtical.

Aurelia. 1. *Tom.* 1. *Conc.* pa. 1046.4. *Turonenſe* 2. *Can.* 22

Aurelian. 1. *in principio.*

ſondry tymes, by the commaundement of the King, named Childebert, moued of the loue and care, he had for the holy faith, and furtheraunce of Chriſtian Religion, to the ſame effect and purpoſe that the firſt vvas ſommoned for.

This King Childebert, *cauſed a Synode of Biſhoppes to aſſemble at Parys, and commaunded them to take order for the reformation of that Church, and alſo to declare vvhom they thought to be a proudent Paſtour, to take the care ouer the Lords flock, the Biſhop* Saphoracus, *being depoſed for his iuſt demerites.*

Stapleton.

M. Horne ſo telleth his tale here, as yf this King Clodoueus had had the Biſſhops at his commaundement to kepe Councels and conuocations at his pleaſure : yea and that *they referred their Decrees to his iudgement.* But now ſo it is in dede, that neither the Prince proceded herein by way of meare commaundememente, neither the biſſhoppes referred to him any ſuch Iudgement ouer their determinated Sentence. For proufe of the firſt : both the Biſſhoppes in this very Councel at Orleans doe ſay to the Kinge, that they haue deliberated vpon theſe matters *ſecundùm veſtræ voluntatis conſultationem* according to the cóſultation kept by your wil, and the Biſſhoppes of an other Councell holden after this at Toures in Fraunce alſo doe ſay of this Synode, *quam inuictiſsimus Rex Clodoueus fieri ſupplicauit,* which the mighty King Clodoueus made ſute to be called. But becauſe as the lawiers do note, the wil of a Prince, and the wil of a father, doe not differ from their commaundement, therefore that Councel which the King by ſuite and ſupplication obtayned to be called, is yet termed to be done *præcepto & iuſsione,* by commaundement of the Biſſhoppes themſelues at the Councell . For proufe of the ſeconde, I

bring

bring you the woordes of the Councel, which you in telling your tale, thought good to leaue out. The bishoppes
doe say vnto the Prince. *Definitione respondimus &c.* *We*
Ibidem.
haue by determining answered to the intent, that yf those thigs
which we haue decreed, be approued right also by your Iudge-
ment, the Sentence of so many bisshoppes, may confirme and
strenghthen the Authority of such a consent, as of the Kinge
and greate Stuarde to be obserued. In which wordes they referre not the Definition to his Iudgement, but doe shewe
that yf his consent doe concurre, then his Authority is confirmed by the verdite of Bishops so great and so manye.

But ye say *they confesse him to haue the superiority*: And
those wordes ye couche craftely among the rest, to make
To.1.cōci. pa.1046. col.1.
your Reader thinke, that the King had the Superiority in ap
prouing doctrine. But this is an vntruth. They cal hi in dede
Regem, ac Dominum maiorem, their Kinge or greate Stuard.
Which is in respecte of temporal things, and of his world-
M.Horne to proue his supre- macy al- leageth a bishop deposed for lesse fornica- tiō then him selfe vseth. Vide Tom. 2. Concil. pag.149. col 1. & Conc. Au- rel.5.can. 4.pag.ɪ
ly principality, not of any Superiority in allowing or disal-
lowing their Synodical decrees. And I praye you good Sir,
was Saphoracus deposed by the Kinge, or by the Bishops?
and was he as you say *deposed for his iuste demerits?* It had
bene wel done to haue tolde vs, why he deserued to be
deposed. But I suppose either ye know yt not, or else ye wil
not be knowen thereof lyke a wyly shrewe. For surelye as
farre as I can gather, yt was for that, he being a Bisshoppe
vsed the company of his wyfe which he maried before he
was priefte, contrarye to the olde canons, and a late order
taken in the Councell at Orlyans. Yf it be so, in what
case be you with your madge: pretending her to be your
lawfull wyfe, yea and that after your takinge of holye
orders.

M.Horne.

A Prince's charge.

The 176. vntruth.

Crafty cōnayauce as shal appeare.

A bishops iurisdictiō.

The 177 vntruth.

A parte of the Sētence nipped quyt of, in the middest.

M. Horne. The. 64. Diuision. pag. 37. a.

Theodobertus Kinge of Fraunce, calleth a Synode at Auerna in Fraunce, for the restoring and establishing the Church discipline. Gunthranus the King called a Synod, named Matisconēl. 2. to resourme the Ecclesiastical discipline, and to cōfirm certein orders, and ceremonies in the Church, vvhich he declareth plainly in the Edict, that he setteth foorth for that purpose. VVherein he declareth his vigilant and studious carefulnes, to haue his people trained and brought vp, vnder the feare of God, in true Religion, and godly discipline, for othervvise (saith this Christian King) I to whom God hath committed (176.) this charge, shall not escape his vengeaunce. He shevveth the bishops that their office is to (.177.) teache, cōfort, exhort, to reproue, rebuke, ond correct, by preaching the vvorde of God. He commaundeth the elders of the Church, and also others of authority, in the common vveale, to iudge and punish, that they assiste the bishops, and sharpely punishe by bodely punishement, such as vvil not amende by the rebuke and correction of the vvorde, and Church discipline. And concludeth, that he hath caused the Decrees in the Councel, touching discipline, and certein ceremonies to be defined, the vvhich he doth publishe and cōfirme, by the authority of this Edict.

Stapleton.

We haue nowe two Kings more of Fraunce: But in both these to proue your purpose, you haue nothing. King Gūtranus himself confesseth in the place by you alleaged: *that God hath committed to the Priests the office of a fatherly authoritye*: And sheweth to what ende the Princes medle withe matters of religion. that is, *that the sworde may amende such persons as the preachers worde can not amende.* And yt is worthy to be considered, that among other decrees that this Councel made, and the King confirmed, yt was ordayned, that the Laye man where so euer he mette a priest should shewe him reuerence and honour. And in case the Prieste wente a fote, and the Laye man ridde, the Laye mā should a light, and so reuerence him, as now the Christians are cōpelled

pelled to doe in Turkey to the Turks. And so I trowe this
Councel maketh not al together for your purpose and supposed Primacy. Only it maketh to encreace the nombre
of your vntruthes. For wheras you first talke of the Princes
vigilant and studiouse carefulnes, to see the people brought
vppe in true religion and godly discipline, you adde as the
Princes woordes. *Otherwise I, to whome God hath committed this charge, shall not escape his vengeaunce.* In making the
Prince to saye, *this charge*, you woulde make your Reader
thinke, the Prince acknowledged a Charge ouer true Religion &c. And therefore you put in the margin, to beutifie
your booke withal, *A princes charge*. But the Prince speaketh of no such charge, as shall anone appeare. And when
you adde to this, that the Prince *shewed the bishoppes, that
their office is to teache, &c.* there you leaue out, *absque nostra
admonitione*, without our admonishment, by which appeareth, the Bishops knew their office, though the Prince held
his peace: and that it depended not of the Princes supreme
gouernment, as you would haue folcke to think. These cou-
ple of vntruthes shal now euidently appeare by the whole
wordes of the King, as they were in order by him vttered,
which you haue confusely set out, putting the later parte
before the first, and the first laste, adding in one place, and
nipping in an other, thus to blinde and bleare your Readers
eies, whome plainly you ought to instruct. For these are the
wordes of Kinge *Guntranus* to the bishops of Mascon. *Al-* Matiscon.
thoughe without our admonition, to you (holy bishops) specially 2. Tom. 2.
belongeth the matter of preaching, yet we thinke verily you are Conc.pag.
partakeners of other mens sinnes, if you correct not with dailye 179.
*rebuking the faultes of your children, but passe them ouer in si-
lence. For neither we, to whom God hath committed the kings*
TT   *dome,*

Platina.
The 178.
vntruth.
A parte
of the Sē
tence bro
kē of pre
iudicial
The pope
is the
kinges
Ambaſſa.
dour.
the popes
humble
ſute to
thēperor,
(179.) for
the Ariā
heretiks.
The 179.
vntruthe
ſlaunde»
rous.
The 180.
vntruth,
This faďt
proueth
no ſubie»
ďtion on
the popes
parte.
The. 181.
vntruth.
The lavv
of Iuſtin⁹
vvas no
Eccleſia»
ſtical law
at al.

*dome, caṅ eſcape his vengeaunce,yf we be not hoſull of the peo-
ple ſubiect vnto vs.* In theſe wordes orderly laied out as the
Kinge ſpake them , thou ſeeſt gentle Reader , firſt that the
King talketh not of *this charge,* as M . Horn vntruly reporteth him,meaning a charge ouer religion , for the King expreſſely ſpeaketh of the charge of his kingdome: declaring,
that as he,for negligence in his charge,ſo the biſſhoppes for
negligence in their charge, ſhal both increaſe the wrath of
God. Alſo that *without his admonition* (which woordes M.
Horne nipped quyte of in the middeſt) the biſhop hath to
preache,to rebuke,to puniſh and correct the tranſgreſſours
of Gods lawe.Such patched proufes M.Horne bringeth to
pricke vp the poppet of his ſtraunge fantaſtical primacye.

M . Horne. *The*. 65. *Diuiſion*. pag.37. *b.*

After the death of Anaſtaſius *thēperor,* Iuſtin⁹ *reigned alone a right catholike Prince,vvho immediatly ſent meſſengers vnto the biſhop of
Rome,who ſhould both cōfirm the autority of the ſea, ād alſo
ſhuld prouide peace for al churches,ſo much as might be,with
which doings of thēperor,* Hormiſda *the biſhop of Rome, being moued,ſent vnto thēperour, with cōſent of* Theodoricus,
Legats(178) Martinus Penitentiarius *telleth the cauſe of this legacy
vvas,to entreate thēperor to reſtore thoſe biſhops,vvhich the vvicked* Anaſtaſius *had depoſed. This godly emperor* Iuſtinus *(ſaith Martin) did make
a lavv,that the Churchs of the heretiks,ſhould be cōſecrated to the Catholik;
religiō,but this Decree vvas made in* Iohn *the next Popes daies. The vvhich e»
dict vvhē the King* Theodoriche,*being an Arian(ſaith the ſame Martin)
and King of Italy,herd,he ſent Pope* Iohn (*ſaith* Sabellicus) *vvith others
in embaſſāge vnto thēperor,to purchaſe liberty for the Ariās.* Iuſtinus *receiued theſe Ambaſſadours honorably,ſaith* Platina, *ānd thēperor at the lēgth
ouercome vvith the humble ſuit of the Pope,vvhich vvas ſauced vvith teares,
graūted to hī and his aſſociats,that the Arians ſhuld be reſtored,and ſuffred
to liue after their orders. In this hiſtory,this is not vnvvorthy the noting,that
the Pope did not only ſhevv his obedience and (180)ſubiectiō to the godly Em
peror,but alſo that the ſecular Princes,ordeyned(181)Lavves eccleſiaſtical,
vvith the vvhich the Pope could not diſpēce, For al this buſines aroſe about the*
                                                                        decree,

decree, vvhich thēperor had made in an (182.) ecclesiastical cause or matter. If
the Popes authority in these causes, had bene aboue the Emperours, he needed
not vvith such lovvlynes, and so many tears to haue besought the Emperour
to haue reuoked his decree and edict.

The 18. Chapter. Of Iustinus thēmperour, and Iohn the Pope.

Stapleton.

NOw hath M. Horn for this turne left Fráce, and is returned to thēperours again: but so that he had ben as
good, to haue kept hí selfe in Fráce stil. For though he
decketh his margēt with, *the Pope is the Kings Ambassadour:*
and again *The Popes hūble sute for the Arriā heretiks* (which
yet is a stark lie as we shal anō declare) yet by that time the
whole tale is told (wherof this mā maketh a cōfuse narratiō)
neither he nor his cause shal winne any worship or honesty
thereby. I wil therfore opē vnto you gētle reader the whole
story, truly and faithfully, and that by his owne authors *Pla-*
tina, Sabellicus, ād Martin. This Anastasius was a wicked Em
peror, as M. Horne here cōfesseth. And yet two leaues before, he made a presidēt of his doings for deposing of bishops.
He defended Iohn the patriarch of Cōstātinople a great he
retik who by his asistāce most iniuriously ād spitefuly had-
led the Legats that Pope Hormisda sent to hí, exhorting hí
to forsake ād renoūce his heresy. The said heretik Emperor
Anastasius sent answere by the Legats to Pope Hormisda,
that it was thēperours part and office to cōmaūde , and not the
Popes, and that he must also obey thēperor. Surely a fair exáple
for your new supremacy. After the death of this Anastasius
strikē with lightníg frō heauē for his wiked heresy ād * diso
bediēce succedeth this Iustin, a right Catholik price by M.
Horns own words ād cōfesiō, who icōtinētly sent to Rome
his ambassadours, *which should shew dew reuerēce of faith to*
the see Apostolike. Or as Platina in other woords writeth:

M Horns
confuse
narratiō,

The sto-
ry trulye
and fully
opened.

Sabellic.
Plat. in
Homisd. l.
* As Pla-
tina vvel
noteth.
Qui Apo-
stolica se-
di debitā
venera-
tionē etc.
Sal el. en. 8
li. 2. pag.
454.

M.Horns
ovvn fto
ry confir-
meth the
Popes
Primacy.

qui fedis Apoſtolicæ authoritatem confirmarent. That ſhoulde
confirme the authority of the Apoſtolike See. And what
was that I pray you M.Horne, but to confirme the Popes
primacy, ſo litle ſet by before of the wicked Anaſtaſius, and
the heretical biſhop Iohn of Conſtantinople? And therefore gramercye that forſakinge Fraunce ye haue browght
vs euen to Conſtantinople, and to the Emperour there: ſending his ambaſſadour to Rome, to recogniſe the Popes moſt
highe authority. Yow tel vs yet farder, that the Pope Hormiſda ſent Legates to Iuſtinus. And there you breake of ſo-
dely. But what folowed? Forſoth immediatly it foloweth in
the very ſame ſentēce: *which Iuſtinus receiued honorably the*

Popes Legats, ſendīg forthe to mete thē, the more to honour thē
a great multitude of Mōks and of other Catholik ād worſhipful
mē, the whole clergy of Cōſtātinople, and Iohn their biſhop cō-
gratulating alſo. At whoſe coming, the Emperour thruſt out
of the City and the Churches, the ſchiſmatikes called Aca-
tiās (of their Author Acatius) whome Pope Felix had excōmunicated. Nowe goe forth, Gods bleſsing of your heart,
God ſend vs many moe ſuch aduerſaries: And to ſay the
truth, M. Iewel and your fellowes are not much worſe to
vs. But yet goe forward, for I hope we ſhal be more deaply
bound to this good Catholike Emperour anon: and to you
to, for bringing to our hād without our farder traiuail, ſuch
good and effectual matter for the Popes ſuperiority. *This*
godly Emperor made a law, ſay you, *that the Churches of here-*
tiks ſhould be cōſecrated to the Catholik Religiō. What did he
M. Horn? Happy are ye, that he is fair dead and buried many years agoe, for feare leſt if he were now liuing, your tē-
ples ād ſynagogs would be ſhortly ſhut vp, as they are nowe
in Antwerpe, and in al Flanders here, God be praiſed. But
who

who telleth this?Forsoth say you *Martin⁹ Pœnitētiarius*. But elder.
lo,how wisely this tale is told,asthough both Sabellicus ād
Platina the Authors of your narratiō did not write the like.
King Theodoricke tooke not in good parte, but euē to the
very harte, these doings of Iustine. And why M . Horne :
Becaufe(as ye fay now like a true mā)he was an Arriā. Say M.Horne
ye fo M.Horne?Doth the winde wagge on that fide now? calleth
For Theodoricus was,not two leaues before, *The moft ho-* rike now
nourable King Theodoriche,and the Supreame Head of the an Arriā,
Church of Rome to. But who faith M. Horne,that he was before he
an Arrian? Forfoth fay ye, Martin: and forfoth fay I, the calleth
matter is ones againe fitly and clerkly handeled. For not moft ho-
onely Martin, but Platina and Sabellicus , from whome ye
fetche your ftorie, write it alfo. This Theodorike fendeth
his Ambaffadours to Iuftine,yea he fendeth Pope Iohn him
felfe, *who with moft humble fuite fauced* (as you write) *with*
teares, entreateth the Emperour,that the Churches might
be reftored to the Arrians. The Pope was then belike an
Arrian him felfe. Surely the fimple Reader , can gather
none other thing by you, efpecially the fame being daffhed
in the margent to. Ye haue not done well to tell half the
tale, and to tell it fo fufpitiouflye. The caufe then of his VVhat
earneft fuite was, that otherwife Theodorike threatened, the Popes
to fhutte vppe all the Catholique Churches in Italie , and fuit vvas
vnder his dominion. Yea your Author Martinus writeth, nus the
that he menaced to kill all the Catholikes in Italy : whome Emperor.
he calleth *Chriftianos*. This was the caufe of his erneft fuite,
not for the fauour he bore to the Arriās, but for the fauour
he bore to the Catholiques and their Churches . Iuftinus
receiued thofe Ambaffadours, as you truly fay, honorably.
And as Sabellicus writeth , the Emperour was not onelye

Excepit
Iuſtinus
pontificem
venientem
multa ve=
neratione,
dimiſſuſq;
ad eius pe-
des adora-
uit.

crowned of Pope Iohn, but at his firſt coming moſt humbly
and reuerētly fel at his feet before him and honoured him.
But Iuſtinus did not ſo honorably entertaine him at Conſtantinople, but Theodorike at his returne did deale with
him as homly, caſting hī into priſon at Rauéna, where what
for hunger, what for lothſome filthines of the priſon, ſhortly after he died a Martyr. About which time or a litle after,
he ſlew the honorable Senatours, Symachus and Boetius.
Whiche thing al your three Hiſtoriographers doe write.
Where ye wil vs to note that, *not onely the Pope ſhewed his*
obediēce and ſubiectiō to the godly Emperor, but alſo that the ſe-
cular Princes ordeined lawes eccleſiaſtical, &c. Your double
note wil proue but a double vntruthe. For the Pope in this
ſupplicatiō obeied not the godly Emperour Iuſtine, but the
Arrian King Theodorike: Neither was it obedience of du-

Martinus
Pol. col. 98
Plat. in
Ioan. 1.
Niceph.
lib. 17.
cap. 9.

tie, but a ſubmiſsion of charitie: partly to qualifie the furie
of the Arrian tyrant, partely to ſaue harmeleſſe the whole
nūber of Catholikes in Italy, which by th'Emperours edict
ſhould cōſequently haue ben deſtroyed. Againe this decree
of Iuſtine was no eccleſiaſticall mater, cōcerning any alteration of religion, any depoſing of Biſhoppes, any order of
Church diſcipline or ſuch like, but ōly a decree for baniſhig
of Arrian heretikes, and of ouerthrowing their Synagogs:
which maner of decree being of denoūced heretiks, belongeth properly to the ciuile Magiſtrate, and is an external or
tēporal mater, no ſpirituall or eccleſiaſticall cauſe, namely
ſuch as we ioyne iſſue with you. King Phillip hath baniſhed
heretikes out of this land and hath cōmaunded their Syna-
gogues to be ouerthrowen. But he is not therfore taken for
Supreme gouernour in al cauſes, or in any cauſe eccleſiaſtical: Neither do or euer did his ſubiects ſwere to any ſuche
Title.   *M. Horne.*

M. Horne. The. 66. Diuision.pag. 38. a.

VVithin a vvhile after this thon, vvas Agapetus Pope, vvhome Thes odatus the King, sent on his Ambassage vnto the Emperour Iustinianus, to make a suit or treaty in his behalfe. Vvhen the Emperour had enterteined this Ambassadour vvith much honour, and graunted that he came for, touching Theodatus, *he earnestly both vvith faire vvordes and soule, assailed this Pope, to bring him to become an Eutychian: the vvhich vvhen he could not vvinne at his handes, being delighted vvith his free speache and constancy, he so liked him, that he foorthvvith (·183.) deposed* Anthemius *bishop of Constantinople, bycause he vvas an Eutychian, and placed* Menna *a Catholike man, in his roume.* Agapetus *died in his legacy, in vvhose roume vvas* Syluerius *made Pope, by the meanes, or rather, as Sabellicus saieth,* by the commaundemente of the Kynge Theodatus, the which vntil this time, was wōt tobe done by the authority of the Emperours (*saith Sabellicus*) for the reuenge whereof Iustinianus was kyndled to make warres against Theodatus. *Syluerius vvas shortly after quarrelled vvithal by the Emperesse, through the meanes of* Vigilius, *vvho sought to be in his roome, and vvas by the Emperours (184) authority deposed. The vvhich act although it vver altogether vniust, yet it declareth the autority that the Prince had ouer the Pope: vvho like a good Bishop, as he vvould not for any threates do contrary to his cōscience and office: so like an* (185) *obediēt subiect, he acknovvleged the Princes authority: being sent for, came: being accused, vvas ready vvith hublenes to haue excused and purged him self: and vvhan he could not be admitted thervnto, he suffred him selfe* (186) *obediētly to be spoiled of the Bishoplike apparaile, to be displaced out of his office, and to be clothed in a Monasticall garement.*

The same measure that Vigilius *did giue vnto* Syluerius, *he himselfe being Pope in his place, receiued shortly after, vvith an augmentation, for he vvas in like sorte vvithin a vvhile* (187) *deposed by the Emperours authority, bicause he vvould not kepe the promise vvhich he had made vnto the Empereße: and vvas in most cruell vvise dealt vvith all: vvhich cruelty vvas the rather shevved to him by the meanes and procurement (as* Sabellicus *noteth) of* Pelagius, *vvhom* Vigilius *had placed to be his Suffragan in his absence.*

The·183.
Vntruth.
For Pope
Agapetus
deposed
Anthy-
mus and
placed
Menna in
his room
not Iusti-
nian.
The·184.
Vntruth.
By vio
lence ba-
nished,
not by
authorite
deposed.
The·185.
Vntruth.
Ridicu-
louse.
The·186.
Vntruth.
As shall
appeare.
The·187.
Vntruth.
By vio-
lence he
vvas ba-
nished,
not by au
tority de
posed.
See oure
Returne.
Art.3.
pag·77·

The.

*The. 19. Chapter. Of Iustinian the Emperour, and diuerse
Popes and Bisshoppes vnder him.*

Stapleton.

ALL this ſtandeth in two pointes. Firſt, that an other
Pope, Agapetus by name, was againe ſent in Ambaſ-
ſage of Theodatus the King. But this (as Liberat' writeth) was a tyrannical force, made bothe to the Pope, and
to the whole Senat of Rome. Theſe Arrian and barbarouſe
Gothian Kings are no fit examples of gouernmente due to
godly Catholik Princes. And their vtter deſtructiō folowed
immediatly after, vnder Beliſarius Iuſtinians Captain. Such
bleſſed preſidents M. Horne hath foũd out, to build his imagined Supremacy vpon. The next point is, in the depoſing
of two Popes by the Emperour Iuſtinian, wherin we nede
by ſo much the leſſe to enlarge our aunſweare, for that M.
Horne freely and franckly of him ſelfe confeſſeth that they
were vniuſtly depoſed. Againe, that you ſay, *the Pope ſuffered him ſelf obediently to be ſpoiled, &c.* If your tale wer true,
that were you know, but an homly obedience: but now he
ſuffred not that ſpoile as you imagine, obediently: but was
brought to that point by a very craft and traine, as in Platina and Liberat' it may be ſene. This therfore may paſſe for
an other of M. Horns vntruths. So hard it is for ſuch Proteſtāt Prelats to tel a true tale. With the like truth you write,
that the Pope *like an obediẽt ſubieet, acknowleged the Princes
autority.* And why? Becauſe forſoth he ſuffred himſelf to be
cloiſtred vp by force of Beliſarius (or rather his wife) the
Emperours Captain. If ſuch patience parforce proue a ſubiection, then is the true man an obediente ſubiecte alſo to
the theefe, when he yeldeth him vppe his purſe in the high
waie to ſaue his lyfe .

Libera* us
cap. 21.

Tom. 2.
Conc. in
vita Sil-
uerij. Pla-
tina in Sil
uerio. Li-
ratus. c. 22

                                        But

But we fay if there had bene iuſte cauſe to depoſe them: yet neither themperour, nor the Councel could lawfully haue depoſed them. And becauſe good Reader, thou ſhalt haue a ſhorte and a ready proufe, and that framed to thy hand already by M. Horne, I remit thee to the fourth Roman Councell, wherevpon M. Horne lately pleaded, and to the very ſame ſentence that M. Horne did him ſelfe alleage. But yet by the way I muſt ſcore vp as an vntruth, that Iuſtinian depoſed Anthimus.. For it was not Iuſtiniā, but Pope Agapetus that gaue ſentéce of depoſitió againſt hiːnor he was not depoſed at that time, but before. In dede Iuſtiniā executed the ſentence, and thruſt him out of Conſtātinople, and baniſhed him, though thempreſſe toke part with him. For fiirſt we find, that Agapetus was deſired by a ſupplicatió of diuers of the Eaſt, to depoſe him. We haue alſo in the actes of the.5. generall Councel declared, that Agapetus did depoſe him. In caſe theſe teſtimonies wyll not ſerue, ye ſhal heare Iuſtinian him ſelfe, that ſhal tel you that it was not he, but Agapetus that depoſed Anthimus. *Quēadmodum nuper factū eſſe ſcimus circa Anthymū, qui quidē deiectus eſt de ſede huius vrbis à ſancto & glorioſa memoriæ Agapéto ſanctiſſ. Rom. Eccleſiæ pontifice.* Euen, ſaith Iuſtinian, as we knowe it happened of late to Anthimus, who was diſplaced from the ſee of this imperial citie by Agapetus of holy and glorioſe memorye, biſhop of the holy Churche of Rome. Neither was Vigilius *depoſed by the Emperous authoritye,* as M, Horne fableth, but for not yeldiug to the Eutychian Empereſſe, Iuſtinians wife, he was by a trayne brought to Conſtantinople and ſo baniſhed. And all this was done rather by the wicked Empereſſe, then by Iuſtiniā: who (as Liberatus writeth) reſtored again both Siluerius

V V (though

Iuſti-nian.
If ye will ſee more of theſe tvvo Poꝑes, ſe the cōfutatió of the Apologie. *Act.1.Cōſiāt.5.ſyn. to.2.Con. p.71.c.2.b. Definite ſāctiſſimi ipū alienū eſſe, & nudū ab ōni epiſ. dign. atq; efficacia. Ibid.p.67. col.2.a. Agapetus Anthimū cōdēnauit et oī dign. ſacerd. & officio nudauitet oī epiſcopat. & orthodoxonoïe. Iuſtin. in authent. in conſtit. cōt. Anth.*

Iuſti-
nian.

This Em
pereſſe
was ā Eu
tychian
heretike.
Such ex-
āples ōly
make for
M.Horne
The .188.
vntruth.
The wor-
des of Li
beratus
fouly mai
med in
the mid-
deſt.
The.189.
Vntruth.
not with
cōmiſsiō,
but to do
it by their
meanes,
vvithout
vvhome
(by order
of the ca-
nons) he
could ne
uer haue
done it.
The.190.
Vntruth.
Falſe trā-
ſlation.

Gaudēs ſe
&c. Being
gladde,
that him

(thoughe by the meanes of Beliſarius he was caried awaye
againe into baniſhment)and Vigilius alſo, though he dyed
by the way in Sicilia.

M. Horne. The .67. Diuiſ.on.pag. 38.b.

About this time, Epiphanius *Biſhop of Conſtantinople, as* Liberatus *ſayth,died ,in vvhoſe roume the Empreſſe placed* Anthymus. *About
vvhich time, vvas great ſtriſe betvvene* Gaianus *and* Theodoſius*, for the
biſhopricke of* Alexandria *, and vvithin tvvo monethes , ſayth* Liberatus*, the Empreſſe* Theodora *ſent* Narſes *a noble man, to enſtall* Theodoſius *, and to baniſh* Gaianus: Theodoſius *being baniſhed , the ſea
vvas vacant: vvhervnto* Paulus *(vvho came to Conſtantinople to plead his
cauſe before the Emperour, againſt certaine ſtubborne monkes) vvas appointed,*and he receiued, *ſayth Liberatus,*(.188.)authority of the Emperoure, to remoue heretiques, and to ordeine in their places
men of right faith. *This* Paulus *vvas ſhortly after accuſed of murther,
vvhervpon the Emperour ſent* Pelagius *the Popes proctour , lying at Conſtantinople,ioyning vnto him certaine other biſops(.189,)vvith commiſsion
to depoſe* Paulus *from the biſoplike office,vvhich they did: and they ordered for him* Zoilus,*whome afterward the Emperour depo-
ſed,and ordered* Apollo,*who is nowe the Biſhop of Alexandria (ſayth Liberatus). Certaine Monkes mette vvith* Pelagius *in his retourne from* Gaza(*vvher* Paulus *vvas depoſed) tovvards Conſtantinople,
bringyng certaine articles,gathered out of* Origenes *vvorkes, minding to
make ſuyte vnto the Emperour,that both* Origen *and thoſe articles,might
be condemned,vvhom* Pelagius *for malice he bare to* Theodorus *biſhop
of* Cæſarea *in* Cappadocia,*an earneſt fautor of* Origen,*did further all
that he might.*Pelagius *therfore doth earneſtly entreat themperour,that he
vvold cōmaund that to be dō vvhich the Monks ſued for: to vvit,that* Origē
*vvith thoſe articles ſhould be dāned. The vvhich ſuit themperour graūted,
being glad(.190.)to geue iudgmēt vpō ſuch matters,and ſo by his
commandmēt,the ſentēce of the great curſe aginſt* Origē,*and thoſe articles
vvere dravvē foorth in vvriting and ſubſcribed vvith their hands, and ſo ſent
to* Vigilius *the biſhop of* Rome,*to* Zoilus *biſop of* Alexādria,*Euphemius of* Antioche,*ād* Peter *biſhop of* Hieruſalē.*Theſe Biſhops receiuing this ſentēce of the curſe (.191.) pnoūced by themperours
com-

cōmaundmēt,and ſubſcribing thervnto:Origen was condēned
being dead,who before long agoe on liue was condemned.

Stapleton.

Here is a myngle mangle I can not tel wherof, and a tale
tolde of a tubbe, for any reaſon or certaine ſcope that I ſee
in it . Here haue we nowe, that themperours wife placeth
and ſetteth in biſhoppes to. For it was Theodora the Eutychian Empereſſe that placed and diſplaced the biſhops here
named : ſauynge Paulus whiche was made by Pelagius the
Popes Legate at Conſtantinople : whych thyng M. Horne
concealeth.But I meruaile by what warrant that Empreſſe
did al this. I dare ſay not by M.Knoxes and his fellowes,of
whom I haue ſpoken.And what biſhop, think you,that ſhe
ſetteth in?No better ſurely then her ſelfe: that is,Anthimus
the captaine of the heretikes of that time . But this geare
goeth handſomly in and out, all thyngs I warrante yow in
dewe order and proportion:euen in as good, as the matter
is good it ſelfe.For nowe M.Horne,after he hath declared,
that Anthimus was depoſed from his biſhoprike, is retourned to ſhewe howe he was firſt ordered and made biſhop.
We haue then a tale tolde, to no purpoſe in the worlde, of
Paulus the biſhop and a murtherer, depoſed , and well and
orderly to, I trowe by Pelagius the Popes proctour, and ſo
howe M.Horne frameth his primacy hereof,God woteth,
I wotte not in all the world . For as for Iuſtinians commiſſion to depoſe biſhops, if M.Horne meane of ſuch as Kyng
Edward gaue in England of late, it is M. Hornes commiſſion and not Iuſtinians . Neither hath hys author any ſuche
thing.But only that themperour gaue the biſhop authority,
to appoint Captaines and other of the Emperours officers,
to helpe forward the execution. Nay ſaieth M.Horne,the

VV ij wurſte

Iuſti-
nian.
ſelfe gaue
iudgemēt
&c. The
Author
thereby,
noteth
the Em-
perours
ambiti-
ouſnes.
The.191.
Vntruth,
Theſe
vvordes
pronoūced
by the Em
perors cō-
mādemēt,
are not in
Liberatus
Lib.c.20.
&. 23
Accepit
ab impera.
poteſtatē
ſuper ordi
nationem
Ducū ac
tribunorū
vt remoue
ret hæreti
cos,& pro
eis ortho-
doxos or-
dinaret.
Lib.c.23.

wurſte is behind. For Iuſtinian théperour gaue his iudgemente vppon Origenes and curſed him to. Here in dede
ſomwhat might haue bene ſayde ſauing that we haue ſayd
ſomwhat alredie of ſuche manner of curſing, and ſauinge
that M. Horne of hys great curteſie hath eaſed vs, ãd hath
made (I trowe againſte hys will, but nothing againſt hys
ſkill) a full anſwere for vs: ſaying that Origenes was long
before this tyme, yea *yet lyvinge condemned*. Thé was there
here no newe ſentéce or determinatió made by Iuſtinian,
but a confirmation of the olde: and no more matter of ſupremacie, then yf a man ſhoulde beſhrewe Luthers curſed harte for his newe broched hereſies, and curſe them
and him to : hys hereſies being manie hundred yeares before condéned, ãd curſed by many a good vertuous clerke,
and by many general and other Coũcels to. Neither did Iu

Cap.23. ſtiniã geue any ſentéce of curſe againſt Origen him ſelf, but
as Liberatꝰ ſaith, at his cõmaundemét or procurĩg the chief
Patriarchs, of Rome, of Alexãdria, of Antioch, ãd of Hieruſalé did it and ſo by the ordinary Iudges in this caſe, not by
the Emperours only or abſolut commandemét he was cõdemned. And we find in the acts of the . 5. generall Coũ-
Action.4. cell, Origen condemned with Arius, Macedonius, Euthy-
Cõ.5.Cõ-
ſtã.ca.11. ches and other.

The .102.
vntruth.
The biſ-
ſhopꝭ not
the Em-
perour
had the
chief in-
termed-

M. Horne.   The .68. Diuiſion. pag. 39. a.

VVhen Theodorus *biſhop, of Cæſarea in* Cappadocia *heard of this
condemnation, to be reuenged he laboured earneſtly vvith the Emperour, to
condemne* Theodorus Mopſueſtenus *a famous aduerſary of Origen,
the vvhich he brought to paſſe by ouermuch fraude, abuſing the Emperour to
the great ſlaunder and offence of the Church. Thus in all theſe Eccleſiaſticall
cauſes, it appereth the Emperor had the (.102.) chief entermedling, vvho although at the laſt vvas beguyled by the falſe biſhops : yet it is vvorthy the
noting by vvhom this offence in the Church came, vvhich appeareth by that,*
that

that follovveth : I beleeue that this is manifeſt to al men (*ſaith* *nian.*
Liberatus)that this offence entred into the Church,by Pelagius
the Deacō,and Theodorus the Biſshop,the which euē Theodorus him ſelfe,did openly publiſhe with clamours: crying,
that he and Pelagius were woorthy to be brente quicke , by
whome this offence entred into the worlde.

Stapleton.

M.Horne nowe will bringe vs a prety concluſion and
prove vs, becauſe biſhopes be at diſſention and abuſe the
Prince afſiſting nowe the one parte, nowe the other, that
the prince is ſupreame head. Whereof will rather very
well followe this concluſion . Experience ſheweth that
princes the more they intermedled in cauſes of rēligiō,the
more they troubled the Churche,the more they were thē
ſelues abuſed,and alſo miſuſed others:Therefore prices a-
re no mete perſons to be ſupreme heads in ſuch cauſes.
Examples hereof are plenty.

Conſtantin the great perſuaded by the Donatiſtes moſt
importunat ſuyt , waded ſo farre ouer the borders of his
owne vocatiō,that(as S.Auguſtin writeth) *à ſanctis anti-*
ſtibus veniam erat petiturus, it came to the point he ſhould
aſke pardon of the holy biſhops . The ſame Emperour by
the ſuit of the Arrians medled ſo far with biſhops matters,
that he baniſhed the moſt innocent,moſt godly, and moſt
lerned biſhop Athanaſius:whereof in his deathebed he repented,willing him by teſtament to be reſtored.

Theodoſius the firſt, perſuaded with the ſmothe toung
of Flauianus the vnlawful and periured biſhop of Antioch
did take his parte wrongefully againſt the weſt biſſhops
and the greateſt parte of Chriſtēdom:wwhereof we haue
before ſpoken.

*Euil ſuc-
ceſſe of
princes iſ
termedſ
ling i cau
ſes eccle-
ſiaſticall.*

*Auguſt.
Epiſt.166.*

*Tripar.l.3.
c.8.& 12.*

*Niceph.li.
12.c.24.*

Theodosius the seconde , defended the Ephesine conuenticle againſt Pope Leo , ſeduced by Dioſcorus and Eutyches, or rather abuſed by one of his priuy chamber Chryſaphius an Eunuche: and wynked at the murdering of holy Flauianus , whome the Chalcedon Councell calleth Martyr .

Zenon the Emperour deceyued by Acatius of Conſtãtinople , baniſhed Iohn Talayda the Catholike patriarch of Alexandria , who appealed from the Emperoure to Pope Simplicius . And nowe in like maner this Emperour Iuſtinian while he was ouer buſy in eccleſiaſtical matters, as one

that toke great delight (ſo noteth Liberatus) to geue iudgment in ſuch matters, being deceiued by Theodorus of the ſecte of Acephali , condemned Theodorus Mopſueſtenus and Ibas two moſt catholike biſhops, and highly prayſed in the Chalcedon Councel, wherof ſprong vp in the Church a moſte lamentable tragedye for the ſpace of many yeares

as all writers doe pitefully report. This ſame Iuſtinian alſo baniſhed the good biſhop of Conſtantinople Eutychius for not ſuffering him to alter Religion . But he reſtored him againe in his deathbed, as Conſtantine dyd Athanaſius. He woulde haue baniſhed alſo Anaſtaſius an other Catholyke biſhop of Antioche, becauſe he would not yeld to his hereſy of *Aphthartodocitæ.* Such examples ought rather to teach Princes not to intermedle with matters aboue their vocation (trulye as muche as the ſowle paſſeth the body) then to geue them anye preſidentes of ſupreame gouernemente , yea IN ALL CAVSES, as Mayſter Horne and hys fellowes, as long as Princes fauour them, woulde geue vnto them .

M. Horne. The. 69. Diuiſion. pag.39. a.

This

that follovveth : I beleeue that this is manifeſt to al men (*ſaith Liberatus*)that this offence entred into the Church,by Pelagius the Deacõ,and Theodorus the Biſshop,the which euẽ Theodorus him ſelfe,did openly publiſhe with clamours: crying, that he and Pelagius were woorthy to be brente quicke , by whome this offence entred into the worlde.

Stapleton .

M.Horne nowe will bringe vs a prety concluſion and prove vs, becauſe biſhopes be at diſſention and abuſe the Prince afſiſting nowe the one parte, nowe the other, that the prince is ſupreame head . Whereof will rather very well followe this concluſiõ . Experience ſheweth that princes the more they intermedled in cauſes of religiõ,the more they troubled the Churche,the more they were thẽ ſelues abuſed,and alſo miſuſed others:Therefore prices are no mete perſons to be ſupreme heads in ſuch cauſes. Examples hereof are plenty.

Euil ſuc-
ceſſe of
princes iﬔ
termed's
ling i cau
ſes eccle-
ſiaſticall.

Conſtantin the great perſuaded by the Donatiſtes moſt importunat ſuyt , waded ſo farre ouer the borders of his owne vocatiõ,that(as S.Auguſtin writeth) *à ſanctis anti-ſtibus veniam erat petiturus,* it came to the point he ſhould aſke pardon of the holy biſhops . The ſame Emperour by the ſuit of the Arrians medled ſo far with biſhops matters, that he baniſhed the moſt innocent,moſt godly, and moſt lerned biſhop Athanaſius:whereof in his deathebed he repented,willing him by teſtament to be reſtored.

Auguſt .
Epiſt.166.

Tripar.l.3.
*c.*8.*&*.12.

Theodoſius the firſt, perſuaded with the ſmothe toung of Flauianus the vnlawful and periured biſhop of Antioch did take his parte wrongefully againſt the weſt biſſhops and the greateſt parte of Chriſtẽdom:wwhereof we haue before ſpoken.

Niceph.li.
12.*c*.24.

VV iij.   Theo-

Co.Chalc.
Act ▪1▪ &
10.

Anno .530.

Theodofius the feconde , defended the Ephefine conuenticle againft Pope Leo , feduced by Diofcorus and Eutyches, or rather abufed by one of his priuy chamber Chry-
faphius an Eunuche:and wynked at the murdering of holy
Flauianus , whome the Chalcedon Councell calleth Martyr .

Lib.ca.18.

Zenon the Emperour deceyued by Acatius of Conftā-
tinople , banifhed Iohn Talayda the Catholike patriarch of
Alexandria , who appealed from the Emperoure to Pope
Simplicius . And nowe in like maner this Emperour Iuftinian while he was ouer bufy in ecclefiaftical matters, as one

Cap.23.
&.24.
Concil.
Chalc.
Act.10.in
fine.

that toke great delight(fo noteth Liberatus) to geue iudgment in fuch matters, being deceiued by Theodorus of the
fecte of Acephali , condemned Theodorus Mopfueftenus
and Ibas two moft catholike bifhops, and highly prayfed in
the Chalcedon Councel, wherof fprong vp in the Church
a mofte lamentable tragedye for the fpace of many yeares

Niceph.
lib.17.ca.
29.30.&
31.

as all writers doe pitefully report. This fame Iuftinian alfo
banifhed the good bifhop of Conftantinople Eutychius for
not fuffering him to alter Religion . But he reftored him a-
gaine in his deathbed, as Conftantine dyd Athanafius . He
woulde haue banifhed alfo Anaftafius an other Catholyke
bifhop of Antioche, becaufe he would not yeld to his herefy of *Aphthartodocitæ*.Such examples ought rather to teach
Princes not to intermedle with matters aboue their vocation (trulye as muche as the fowle paffeth the body)then to
geue them anye prefidentes of fupreame gouernemente ,
yea IN ALL CAVSES, as Mayfter Horne and hys
fellowes, as long as Princes fauour them woulde geue vnto them .

M. Horne. The. 69, Diuifion.pag.39. 4.

This

This Pelagius *as yet vvas but Suffragan or proctour for the Pope, vvho aftervvard in the abſence of Pope* Vigilius *his maiſter, crepte into his See, in the middeſt of the broiles that* Totylas *King of the Gothes made in Italye, vvhen alſo he came to Rome. In the vvhiche Hiſtorie is to be noted the Popes (.193.) ſubiection to* Totylas, *vvhome humblie on his knees he acknovvleaged , to be his Lorde , appointed thereto of God, and him ſelfe as all the reſte to be his ſeruaunte. Note alſo hovve the King ſent him Embaſſadoure, vvhat charge, and that by Othe, of his voyage, of his meſſage, and of his returne, the King ſtraightlie gaue vnto him: hovve buxomelie in all theſe things he obeyed : Hovve laſt of all tovvard the Emperour (being commaunded by him to tell his meſſage) he fell dovvne to his feet, and vvith teares bothe to him and to his Nobles, he ceaſed not to make moſte lamentable and humble ſupplication, till vvithout ſpeed, but not vvithout (.194.) reproche, he had leaue to returne home. But leaſt you ſhould take theſe things, to ſettie ſoorthe that Princes had onely their iuriſdiction ouer the Eccleſiaſticall perſonnes, and that in matters* Temporall*, and not in cauſes Eccleſiaſticall; marke vvhat is vvritten by the Hiſtorians.* Platina *amongeſt the Decrees of this Pope* Pelagius*, telleth (and the ſame vvitneſſeth* Sabellicus*)that* Narſes *the Emperours other deputie*, Ioyntelye with Pelagius did decree, that none by ambition ſhoulde be admitted to any of the holye Orders. Pelagius *moreouer vvriteth vnto* Narſes*, deſiring him of his ayed againſt all the Biſhoppes of* Liguria, Venetiæ, *and* Hiſtria, *vvhich vvould not obey him, putting their affiaunce in the authoritie of the firſt Councell of* Conſtantinople. *In vvhiche Epiſtle amongeſt other things he vvriteth on this vviſe:* Your honoure muſt remember what God wrought by you at that time, when as Totyla the tyraunt poſſeſſing Hiſtriam and Venetias : the Frenche alſo waſting all thinges, and you woulde not neuertheleſſe * ſuffer a Biſhoppe of Myllaine to be made, vntill he had ſente woorde from thence to the moſte milde Prince (*meaning the Emperour*)and had reciued anſwere againe from him by writing what ſhoulde be done, and ſo bothe he that was or-deined Biſhoppe, and he that was to be ordeined, were brought to Rauenna at the appointment of your high authoritie.

The.193.
Vntruth.
This vvas no ſubiection in eccleſiaſtical maters, but Rome being then cōquered by Totylas, Pelagius vithall the citie ſubmitted them ſelues.
The.194.
Vntruth.
Slaundeרous as ſhall appeare.
The. 195.
Vntruth.
For the Decree of Narſes vvas no ecclefiaſtical mater but an executiō of the churche Canōs made before.
* This proueth naughte els but

ritie. *Not long after*, Pelagius.2. *bycauſe he vvas choſen* Iniuſſu Principis, without the Emperours comaundement, *and could not ſend
vnto him, by reaſon the tovvne vvas beſeged, and the huge riſyng of the vvaters ſtopped the paſſage : as ſoone as he might being elected Pope, he ſent Gregory to craue the Emperours pardone, and to obtaine his good vvill*. For in
thoſe dayes (*ſayth* Platina) the Clergie did nothing in the Popes
election except the election had bene allovved by the Emperour .

that (as
Pelagius
the firſte
hath ordained)
the ſecular ſword
helped ,
when the
ſpirituall
could not
preuaile.

Sabellic.

Aeneid. 8.

lib. 4.

Cocernig
pope Pelagius ſét
Ambaſſadour to
themperour.

Stapleton.

M. Horne telleth vs a tale after his olde wonte , that is
without head or taile , to abuſe his ignorant reader with a
confuſe heape of diſordered and falſe wordes. Pelagius was
ſente by the Romans to King Totilas to entreat of peace,
and that he would for a time ceaſſe from warre , and geue
them truce . Saying that if in the meane whyle they had
no ſuccour, they would yelde the citye of Rome to him.
Pelagius coulde wynne none other anſwere at his hands,
but that they ſhould beate downe the walles , receiue his
army, and ſtand to his curteſy and mercye . Totilas being
afterward in poſſeſsion of the City and fearing warres fro
the Emperour Iuſtinian, ſent Pelagius to Iuſtinian, to trauaile with him for peace: ſending him withall worde, that
in caſe he would inuade Italye, he would deſtroye Rome,
and plucke it downe faſte to the ground . Totilas toke an
othe of Pelagius and hys other ambaſſadours to doe hys
meſſage faythfullie, and to returne againe theyre ambaſſade exployted. Pelagius moſt pitefullye and withe manie
teares layethe before Iuſtinian the miſerable ſtate and the
vtter deſtructió and deſolation of Rome impédente, onleſſe
he woulde forbeare warre with Totilas: yea he ád hys fellowes fell vpon theire knees moſt humblye beſeching him
to haue compaſsió of the citye. But in fyne Iuſtiniá would

not

not relent.Wherevpon sone after their returne,Rome was set al on fier by Totylas,and no lyuing creature , man , woman,nor childe suffered there to inhabite . Prye nowe M. Horne and pycke out here what ye can to establishe your primacye: your folye is to open to be in this matter withe many words refuted. Here is no one matter Ecclesiasticall, and that ye see wel inowghe : and therefore your selfe as faste as ye can woulde steale away from yt,and proue your matter otherwise . But Sir ye shall not so steale awaye,but beside the note of extreme folye,to busie your selfe and your Readers with that,which your self can not deny,nothing to towch spiritual matters,but that ye shal carry with you a lie or two. Els tel vs why you wil haue vs to note *the* *Popes subiection to Totylas* , seing that neither Pelagius was then Pope,Vigilius yet liuing at Cōstantinople,neither was he any other way subiect , then as to a Tyrant . For Totilas (who for his rage and crueltyes was called *Flagellum Dei,* the Scourge of God) at that tyme tooke Rome,and entred with the conquest.Pelagius did that homage to him, to obtayne mercy for his poore Cytyzens . And when Totylas seing him coming towarde him,said:*What meaneth this ō Pelagius?comest thou to me as a suppliant ?* Pelagius answered, sayinge . Yea *Sir I cōme to you , seing God hath made you my Lorde.But haue mercy,I beseche you,vpon your seruaunts,haue mercy vpon the poore Captiue Cytie.* And this lo was the subiection of Pelagius made to Totylas,which you wishe to be noted M.Horne,as though it made any thing for the Popes subiection in spiritual matters. Tel vs also whye ye write, that he *departed with reproche* . What reproche had he at Iustinians hand?Your authour Sabellicus sheweth of none. But see the mans folish wilynes.In dede Sabellicus writeth

Platina in Pelagio.1. Sabell. Aeneads,8 lib.4.

XX that

that Pelagius was noted as a fauorer of Anthimus : but then
ſaith he withall, that Pelagius did deteſt it of all thinges to
ſeme to fauour him. Wel, to ſupply this defect of his ſuperfluous liyng talk of Pelagi⁹, he brigeth forth a decree againſt
ſymony, made by Pelagius and Narſes th'Emperors deputy.
This is no mater of faith, M. Horne, no, nor no new decree
of maners, but ſuch as had bene decreed long before. And
therefore but an execution of the old Canons: which Narſes might medle withal wel inoughe. There is then to make
vp the mater yet ones againe a declaration concerning the
intereſt of the Emperour in the election of Biſhoppes and
Popes too : wherevnto at this time we nede not greatly to
ſay any thing: ſo much hath ben ſaid hereof before.

M. Horne. The. 70. Diuiſion. pag. 40. a.

The. 196.
Vntruth.
In that
Councell
there is
no ſuche
thing.
The. 197.
Vntruth.
They de-
clare that
the due
obſerua-
tiō therof
(not the
ſtrength)
depēded
vpō thos
Princes
good
lavves.

*About the time of Pelagius the firſt his Papacy, vvas there a Councel hol-
den at Tovvers in Frāce, by the licence and conſent of Arithbertus the King,
for the reformation of the Churche diſcipline, vvherein appeareth, that the
Kings authoritie vvas (.196.) neceſſarily required to confirme and ſtrengthen the diſcipline. For vvhere they decree of the maides or vviddovves, that
ſhall not be maried, vvithoute the conſente of the parentes, vvhiche is an
eſpeciall matter Eccleſiaſticall, they declare (.197.) the ſtrength thereof to
depend vpon the commaundement of the Prince.* Not onely (*ſay they*)
the Kings, Childebert and Clotharius of honourable memory,
kepte and preſerued the conſtitutiō of the lawes touching this
matter, the which nowe the King Charibert their ſucceſſour
hath confirmed or ſtrengthened by his precept.

Stapleton.

Nowe is Maiſter Horne reuolted to Fraunce againe, but
not to tarie there long.   For ſodainly he returneth againe
to Conſtantinople. His ſhort tale conſiſteth in two lyes.
Firſt when he ſaieth the *Kings authoritie vvas neceſſarily required to confirme the diſcipline of the Churche.* For that
neither

not relent.Wherevpon sone after their returne,Rome was
set al on fier by Totylas,and no lyuing creature , man , woman,nor childe suffered there to inhabite . Prye nowe M.
Horne and pycke out here what ye can to establishe your
primacye: your solye is to open to be in this matter withe
many words refuted. Here is no one matter Ecclesiastical,
and that ye see wel inowghe : and therefore your selfe as
faste as ye can woulde steale away from yt,and proue your
matter otherwise . But Sir ye shall not so steale awaye,but
beside the note of extreme folye,to busie your selfe and
your Readers with that,which your self can not deny,no-
thing to towch spiritual matters,but that ye shal carry with
you a lie or two.Els tel vs why you wil haue vs to note *the* Platina in
Popes subiection to Totylas , seing that neither Pelagius was Pelagio.1.
then Pope,Vigilius yet liuing at Cõstantinople,neither was Sabell.
he any other way subiect , then as to a Tyrant . For Totilas Aenead.8
(who for his rage and crueltyes was called *Flagellum Dei,* lib.4.
the Scourge of God) at that tyme tooke Rome,and entred
with the conquest.Pelagius did that homage to him, to obtayne mercy for his poore Cytyzens . And when Totylas
seing him coming towarde him,said:*What meaneth this ô Pe-*
lagius?comest thou to me as a suppliant ? Pelagius answered,
sayinge . Yea *Sir I cõme to you , seing God hath made you my*
Lorde.But haue mercy,I beseche you,vpon your seruaunts,haue
mercy vpon the poore Captiue Cytie. And this lo was the subiection of Pelagius made to Totylas,which you wishe to be
noted M.Horne,as though it made any thing for the Popes
subiection in spiritual matters. Tel vs also whye ye write,
that he *departed with reproche* . What reproche had he at
Iustinians hand?Your authour Sabellicus sheweth of none.
But see the mans folish wilynes.In dede Sabellicus writeth

X X   that

that Pelagius was noted as a fauorer of Anthimus : but then
faith he withall , that Pelagius did deteſt it of all thinges to
ſeme to fauour him. Wel, to ſupply this defeċt of his ſuperfluous liyng talk of Pelagi°, he brigeth forth a decree againſt
ſymony, made by Pelagius and Narſes th'Emperors deputy.
This is no mater of faith, M. Horne, no, nor no new decree
of maners, but ſuch as had bene decreed long before. And
therefore but an execution of the old Canons: which Narſes might medle withal wel inoughe. There is then to make
vp the mater yet ones againe a declaration concerning the
intereſt of the Emperour in the election of Biſhoppes and
Popes too : wherevnto at this time we nede not greatly to
ſay any thing: ſo much hath ben ſaid hereof before.

M . Horne. The. 70. Diuiſion. pag. 40. a.

*About the time of Pelagius the firſt his Papacy, vvas there a Councel hol-
den at Tovvers in Fraūce, by the licence and conſent of Arithbertus the King,
for the reformation of the Churche diſcipline , vvherein appeareth, that the
Kings authoritie vvas (. 196.) neceſſarily required to confirme and ſtrengthen the diſcipline. For vvhere they decree of the maides or vviddovves, that
ſhall not be maried , vvithoute the conſente of the parentes , vvhiche is an
eſpeciall matter Eccleſiaſticall, they declare (. 197.) the ſtrength thereof to
depend vpon the commaundement of the Prince.* Not onely (*ſay they*)
the Kings, Childebert and Clotharius of honourable memory,
kepte and preſerued the conſtitutiõ of the lawes touching this
matter , the which nowe the King Charibert their ſucceſſour
hath confirmed or ſtrengthened by his precept.

Stapleton .

Nowe is Maiſter Horne reuolted to Fraunce againe, but
not to tarie there long. For ſodainly he returneth againe
to Conſtantinople . His ſhort tale conſiſteth in two lyes.
Firſt when he ſaieth the *Kings authoritie was neceſſarily required to confirme the diſcipline of the Churche .* For that
neither

neither is in the Councell, neither can be gathered out of it. The second is, that the Coûcel *declareth that the ſtrength of their Decree, being a ſpeciall matter Eccleſiaſticall dependeth vppon the commaundemente of the Prince.* For the Councell declareth onely, that thoſe good Kings of Fraunce kept the Conſtitution of the Churche in that behalfe: and forced by lawe the due obſeruation thereof.   Like as Iouinian the Emperoure, made it death by lawe, to defile a Virgin or Nonne. Though that ſinne before, was by the Churche condemned. All this doth but multiplie woordes. It proueth nothing your imagined Supremacye. Mary if you will knowe M. Horne, what this Councell by youre ſelfe alleaged, maketh for the Popes Supremacie, I will not lette to tell it you.   The Fathers of the Councell do ſaye: *What Prieſt is he that dare be ſo bolde, as to doe contrarye to ſuche Decrees as come from the See Apoſtolique?* And a little after. *And whoſe authoritie may take place, if it be not theirs, whome the Apoſtolique See ſendeth and maketh his deputies or Referendaries? Our Fathers haue euer kept that, which their authoritie commaunded.* Thus you fight well for vs, but nothing for your ſelfe.

Tripart.
li.7.ca.4.

Conc. Tu-
rô.2 can.
21.

M. Horne. The. 71. Diuiſion. pag. 40. a.

The Emperoure Iuſtinianus calleth the Biſhoppes of all Churches vnto a Generall Councell at Conſtantinople, the vvhich is called the fifte œcumenicall Synode, to repreſſe the inſolence of certaine Heretiques, vvho taught and mainteined Hereſies and Schiſmes, to the greate diſquieting of the Churche againſte the doctrine eſtabliſhed in the foure forenamed General Councelles.   In the time of this Councell Menna, *the Biſhoppe of Conſtantinople departed out of this life, in vvhoſe roome the Emperour placed* Eutychius. *The Emperour gouerneth and directeth all things in this Councell, as the Emperours before him had done in the other Generall Synodes, as appeareth by the vvriting, vvhiche he ſente vnto the Biſhoppes, vvherein he*

Euag. li.
4. ca. 38.

Niceph. li.
17. ca. 27.

XX ij   ſerueth

shevveth, that the right belieuing godly Emperours his aunceſtours did al-
vvaies labour, to cutte of the hereſies ſprong vp in their time, by
calling together into Synode the moſt religious Biſhops, and
to preſerue the holy Church in peace: and the right faith to be
ſincerely preached and taught. *He allegeth the' xãples of* Cõſtãtinus
Magnus, Theodoſius *the elder*, Theodoſius *the yonger, and* Martianus *the Emperours: vvho (ſaith he) called the former generall Coun-*
celles, vvere preſent them ſelues in their ovvne perſonnes, did aide and helpe
the true confeſſours, and tooke great trauaile vppon them , that the righte
faithe ſhould preuaile, and be preached. Our forenamed aunceſtours
of godlie memorie (*ſaith he*) did ſtrengthen and confirme by
their lawes, thoſe things whiche were decided in euerye of
thoſe Councelles, and did expulſe the Heretiques, whiche
went about to gaineſaye the determination of the tower forenamed Generall Councelles, and to vnquiet the Churches.

Al this is
graunted,
but M.
Hornes
Primacie
neuer a
vvhitte
thereby
furdered.

He proteſteth , that from his firſt entraunce , he made theſe beginnings
and foundation of his Imperiall gouernement, to vvitte, the vnitie in faith
agreeable to the fovver Generall Councelles , amongeſt the Churche mini-
ſters, from the Eaſt to the VVeſt : the reſtraigning of ſchiſmes and contenti-
ons ſtirred vppe, by the fautours of Eutyches and Neſtorius , againſte the
Chalcedon Councell : the ſatiſſiyng of many that gainſaied the holy Chalce-
don Councell, and the expulſion of others, that perſeuered in their errours,
out of the holye Churches and Monaſteryes : To the ende that concorde and peace of the holye Churches and their Prieſtes, being firmely kepte, one, and the ſelfe ſame faithe, whiche the
fower holy Synodes did confeſſe, might be preached throughout Gods holye Churches. *He declareth hovv he had conſulted vvith*
them by his letters and meſſengers about theſe matters , and hovv they de-
clared their iudgementes vnto him by their vvritinges : not vvithſtanding
ſeeing certaine Heretiques continue in their hereſies : Therefore I haue
called you (*ſaith he*) to the royall Cittie (*meaning Conſtantinople*)
exhorting you being aſſembled togeather, to declare once a-
gaine your mindes touching theſe matters. *He ſhevveth that*
he opened theſe controuerſies to Vigilius *the Pope , at his being vvith him*
at Conſtantinople: And we aſked him (*ſaith he*)his opiniõ herein:
and

and hee, not once nor twiſe, but oftentimes in writinge , and
without writing, did curſe the three wicked articles, &c.
VVe commaũded him alſo by our Iudges, and by ſome of you,
to come vnto the Synode with you, and to debate theſe three
Articles together with you,to the ende that an agreable form
of the right faith might be ſet forth : and that we aſked bothe
of him and you in writing touching this matter : that eyther
as wicked articles, they might be condemned of all: or els , if
he thought them right, he ſhould ſhewe his minde openlye :
But he anſwered vnto vs : that he would doe ſeuerely by him
ſelfe concerning theſe three points,and deliuer it vnto vs. *He
declareth his ovvne iudgement and beliefe, to be agreeable vvith the faieth
ſet foorth in the forver Generall Councelles. He preſcribeth vnto them the
ſpeciall matters, that they ſhould debate and decide in this Synode : vvhereof
the finall ende is (ſaith he)* That the truth in euery thing may be
confirmed, and wicked opinions condemned. *And at the laſt, he
concludeth vvith an earneſt and godly exhortation, to ſeeke Gods glory only,
to declare their iudgements agreable to the holy Ghoſpell, touching the matters he propoundeth, and to doe that vvith conuenient ſpede.*Dat.3. Nonas
Maias, Conſtantinopoli.

The Emperoure
(198) cõmaũdeth
the Pope
to com to
the ſinod.
The. 198.
Vntruth.
For not
in that
ſence as
M.Horn
imagineth.vilz
to inforce
thereby a
Supreme
gouernemente.

Stapleton.

Here M.Horne,as he hath otherEmperors and Princes,
ſo would he now beare Iuſtinian in hand alſo,that he is and
ought to be the Supreme head and gouernour in all cauſes
euen Eccleſiaſtical and Spiritual. But Iuſtinian, if you will
hearken to his lawes and Conſtitutions, will tell you flatly
that ſuche a heade agreeth not with his ſhoulders . He
wil not be made ſuch a monſter at your handes. You ſhall
finde him as very a Papiſt for the Popes Supremacy,as euer
was any Emperor before him,or ſence him.For who I pray
you was it, M Horne,that by opẽ proclamatiõs ãd laws for
euer to continue enacted, *that the holy Eccleſiaſticall Canons
of the foure firſt Councels ſhall haue the ſtrength and force of*

X X iij *an*

Iuſtinians teſtimo=
nies for the Popes
primicie.
Cõſt.131.ex trãſl.hal
Sancimus, vt ſancti
eccleſiaſtici canones,
qui a ſanctis.4.Cõ-
cilijs, Niceno. Con
ſtãt.Epheſ.& Chal
cedon. expoſiti ſunt,
vicem legum obtine
ant. Prædictorum e=
nim ſanctorum Con-
ciliorũ decreta per-
inde vt ſacras ſcri-
pturas ſuſcipimus.&
canones vt leges cu
ſtodimus.   Ac pro-
pterea ſancimus, vt
ſecundum eorum
deſinitiones ſanctiſ.
veteris Ro.Papa, pri
mus oĩm ſacerd. ſit.
Sũmi põtificatus api-
cē apud Romam eſſe
nemo ē qui dubitet.
Lib.1.Cod.Iuſtin.de
ſumma Trinitate.
Ideóq; oēs ſacerdotes
vniuerſi orientalis
tractus et ſubūcere et
vnire ſedi veſt.San-
ctitatis properaui-
mus. & mox. Nec

an imperiall lawe? Was it not Iuſtinian? Who ys yt
that embraceth *the decrees of thoſe holy Councells,
euen as he doth the holy and ſacred Scriptures? And ke
peth their Canõs as he doth the imperial lawes?* Who
but Iuſtinian? Who enacted alſo, that *according to
the definitiõ of thoſe foure Councels, the Pope of Rome
ſhal be taken for the chiefe of all Prieſtes?* Iuſtinian.
Who yn an expreſſe lawe declared, *that no man
doubteth, but that the principality of the higheſt biſſhoprike reſteth in Rome?* Iuſtinian. Who declared
to Pope Iohn, *that he ſtudied and laboured, howe to
bring to ſubiection, and to an vnitye with the See of
Rome all the prieſtes of the Eaſte?* Iuſtinian. Who
tolde him, *that there ſhall be nothing moued perteï-
ning to the ſtate of the Churche, be it neuer ſo open
and certaine, but that he would ſignify it to his Holï-
neſſe, being head of all holy Churches?* Iuſtinian. Who
declared, that *in all his lawes and doings for matters
eccleſiaſtical, he followed the holy Canons made by the
Fathers?* Iuſtinian. Who publiſhed thys lawe
that, *when any matter eccleſiaſtical is moued, his laye
officers ſhould not intermedle, but ſuffer the Biſoppes
to ende yt accordyng to the Canons?* This ſelfe ſame
Iuſtinian.

What great impudency then is it for you to obtrude him this title of ſupreme gouernour, whiche
ſo many of his expreſſe lawes doe ſo euidently abhorre? What ſhame, infamy and diſhonour ſhoulde
it be for him, to accept any ſuch title, the Canons
                                      of

eñ patimur quicquã quod ad eccleſiarũ ſtatũ ptinet, quamuis manifeſtũ & indubitatũ
ſit quod mouetur, vt nõ ēt veſtra inoteſcat Sanct. quæ Caput eſt oĩm ſanctarũ eccliarũ.
Secũdũ eorũ definitiones &c. vt ſuprà cenſ.131. Sancimus ſacras ſequētes regulas &c.
conſt.5. Secundũ diuinas regulas ſancimms ſacras per omnia ſequentes regulas. conſt.6.

of the holy Catholike Church, and his owne lawes, ſtanding ſo plainly to the cõtrary? What? would
you haue him an heretike, as you are? Hath not he
yn hys Lawes pronounced hym to be an heretike, *that doth not cõmunicate in faith with the holy
Churche, eſpeciallye with the Pope of Rome and the
fowre patriarches?* Hath he not alſo in his ſaid lawes
ſhewed, *that the Pope of Rome hath the primacy ouer
all prieſtes, by the firſt fowre generall Councelles, vnto
the which the Pope and all other patriarches haue a-
greed?* Obtrude not therefore this preſumptuous
Title to this Emperour, who of al other moſt ſhun-
ned it. Bring forth M. Horne, what eccleſiaſticall
Conſtitutions and decrees you wil or can, made of
this Emperour Iuſtiniã. Al wil not ſerue your purpoſe one iote. This only of the diligent Reader being remembred, that all ſuch lawes he referred to
the Popes iudgement : that he made not one of his
owne, but followed in them all, the former Canons
and holy Fathers. Laſt of all that he enacteth expreſly, that in eccleſiaſtical matters, lay Magiſtrats
ſhall not intermeddle, but that biſhops ſhall ende al
ſuch matters according to the Canõs. Theſe three
thyngs beyng well remembred and borne awaye,
nowe tell on M. Horne, and bring what you can
of Iuſtinians Conſtitutions in eccleſiaſticall matters.

The effecte of all your Argumentes yn thys
Diuiſion, reſteth vppon thys poynte, that Iuſtinian made Lawes for matters eccleſiaſticall, which
thing I nede not further anſwer then I haue done.
Sauing

*Sequentes igitur ea
quæ ſacris deſinita
ſũt Canonib. Cõ.123.
Si eccleſiaſticũ ne-
gotiũ ſit, nullam cõ-
munionẽ habento ci-
uiles magiſtratus cũ
ea diſceptatione, ſed
religioſiſſ. epiſcopi ſe
cundã ſacros canones
negotio ſinẽ iponũto.
Conſt. 109. Hæreti-
cos & illi dixerũt, et
nos dicimus, quicũq;
mẽbrum ſanctæ Dei
catholicæ & apoſto-
licæ eccleſiæ nõ ſunt.
in qua & omnes ſan
ctiſſimi totius habi-
tati orbis patriarchæ
tam Romæ occidẽ=
talis, q̃ huius regiæ
vrbis, & Alexãdriæ
& Theopolis & Hi-
eroſolymorũ, & oẽs
ſub ijs cõſtituti epiſ=
copi vno ore Apoſto-
licam ſidẽ & tradi-
tionẽ prædicat. Qui
igitur incõtaminata
coione, in Catholica
eccleſia Dei amātiſſ.
huius ſacerdotib. nõ
participant, opt.iure
vocamus hæreticos.*

Sauing partly, that this lye of M. Hornes woulde not be o-uerpaffed: wherein he imagineth all things here fpoken to be done in the fifte generall Councell at Conftantinople: whereas a greate part of them were done in an other Coū-cel at Conftantinople vnder this Emperour, whiche M. Horne doth here vnfkilfully confoūde. Partly alfo to fhew yet ones again, that Iuftinian himfelf doth fo expounde his doinges, that M. Horne can not wel wrefte them to his pur-pofe. For Iuftinian faieth. *We following the holy fathers &c.* and fo forth: as we by many places of Iuftinian haue decla-red before. Againe fpeaking of things decreed in the Synod againft Zoaras. *Your fentence,* faieth he, *being of power by yt feife, our imperiall maieſtye hath made yt yet muche ſtronger, which doth expulfe him out of this imperial City.* Lo M. Horn the decree of the Synode is ftronge, thoughe the Emperour neuer confirme it, and where is then become your impe-rial primacye? Nowe farder you heare to what purpofe the princes afsifte: that is for the furtheraunce of the executiō. The bifhops had depofed Zoaras, but they by their power coulde not thruft him out of the City and banifhe him. This muft be don by the ciuil power, and this did Iuftinian, and by that made the Councels lawe the ftronger. And fo ye now heare of Iuftiniā himfelf, what is the meaning of that which you here and fo often alleage, that Princes ftrēghthē the lawes of the Church. And to fhew that the Supreme gouernment, which is the final Sentence and Iudgemēt re-fted in the bifhops, not in the Emperour, in the firft Actiō Theodorus the Emperours Officer, bringeth in the playn-tif Bifhops of Syria and faieth to the Synode. *Vt in his inter-pellanies, vos ipfis finem imponatis.* To the entent that you confidering thefe fupplications, maye make an ende of thē.

And

Cōſtit.42 in Nouel. Quā fen-tentiā tā-etſi per fe valẽtem, multo ta-mē adhuc valentio-rē, reddit maieſtas imperato-ria, quere gia hac vrbe ipsū expellit. Hovve thempe-rours be faid to ftrengthē the lavves of the Churche. Tom. 2. Conci!. pag. 21.

And in the fame Action the Emperour himfelf againe affirmeth,that: *As ofte as the Sentēce of the Prieftes hath depofed*
any from their holy rowmes , as vnworthy of priefthood , fo ofte
the Empire was of the fame minde,and made the fame order or
cōftitutiō with the Authority of the prieftes. Where you fee
M.Horne,that the depofing of Prieftes or Bifhoppes,pro-
ceded firft from the Authority , Sentence and Iudgement
of the Prieftes: And was afterwarde putte in execution by
the Imperial lawes. That is,to fay all fhortly . The bifhops
depofed.The Prince banifhed . For by death in thofe dayes
Princes proceded not againft the clergy thoughe depofed
and condemned in generall Councell. I might nowe goe
forwarde for any thing of weight remayning: fauinge that
your marginal note , that *the Emperour commaundeth the*
Pope to come to Councell , ftayeth me a litle , as making fome
good apparance for you . Ye fay *he commaunded the Pope,*
but yf ye had proued withall,that he had fuch authority to
commaunde, then would the matter ronne better on your
fyde:or that ye could fhewe that at this commaundemente
he came to the Councel , which ye are not able to fhewe.
But yet am I able to fhewe he came not. So that this induceth rather the Popes primacy,efpecially confidering, that
he was at Cōftātinople , euen whē the Councel was kept.
Marciā alfo fent his letters to Pope Leo to come to Chalce
do, ād yet he came not, but fent his deputies thither for hī.

Att.1.
pag.61.

In preã.
epift. Cōc.
Chalced.

M. Horne. The.72.Diuifion. Pag.41.b.

The (.199.) *Title prefixed to the firft general Councel,fummoned by the*
commandement of Iuftinian,telleth in effect generally, both the matter and
alfo who had the chief authority in the ordering thereof : for it is intituled:
The diuine ordinaunce and conftitution of Iuftinian the Em-
peror againft Anthymus,Seuer[9]*,Petrus,and Zoaras. Mennas the*

The 199.
vntruth.
There is
no fuche
Title.

Y Y   vniuer-

Iusti-nian.

The 200.
vntruth.
Flat and
open, as
it shal ap-
peare

The 201.
vntruth.
Not to
dispatche
(that
vvorde is
not in the
councel)
but *finem*
imponere,
to make
an end of
by finall
Sentence.

The price
the hig-
hest po-
tentate
next to
God(202)
in al cau-
ses.

The. 202.
vntruth.
You ouer
rech your
Author.
In al cau-
ses, is
more the
your Au-
thor said.

vniuersal Archebishop and Patriarche of Constantinople, vvas present in this Councel, vvho had adioyned vnto him, placed on his right hande, certain Bishops, coadiutours, named and (.200.) appointed by the commaundement of the Emperour, sent out of Italy from the sea of Rome. VVhen they vvere set thus in Councel, Themperour sent Theodorus one of the maisters of the Requestes, or his Secretarie, a vvise man, vnto the Synode: Bishops, Abbottes, and many other of the cleargy, vvith their billes of supplications, vvhich they had put vp vnto themperour, for redresse of certain matters Ecclesiastical. Theodorus *maketh relation vnto the Synode hereof, deliuereth the Billes of supplication to be considered on: presenteth the parties to the Synod, and shevveth that this is themperours pleasure, that they shoulde (.201.) dispatche and end these matters.* Paulus, *the Bishoppe of* Apamea, *in his bil of supplication, offred to the most godly Emperour in the name of al his,* acknowledgeth him to be the highest Potentate in the worlde next vnto God : who hath magnified his Empire, and throwē his aduersaris vnder him : becaufe he mainteineth the only and pure faith : offreth vnto God pure Leuen, that is to say, true doctrine as incense, and burneth the chaffe (*meaning false re ligiō*) with vnquencheable fier. *And after the declaratiō of their Faith talking of the Eutychian or counterfaite catholike,* He desireth themperour, to whom God hath reserued the ful authority to direct, to cut him from the Churche, and to expulse him out of his Dominions. *In like sort the religious men, and the Monasteries of Secū da* Syria, *doo offer vp a booke of supplication vnto the Emperour, beseeching him that he vvil commaund the Archebishoppe* Mennas, *president of the councel, to receiue their booke, and to (.204.) consider of it according to the Ecclesiastical Canons. The Emperour maketh a lavv and constitution, to ratifie and confirme the iudgement of the Synode against* Anthymus, *and other heretiks : vvherein also he decreeth touching many other ecclesiastical matters or causes: as,* No man to Rebaptize : to prophane the holy Communion : to cal Conuenticles : to dispute further in those matters concluded on : to publishe or set forth the Heretical
books:

God refereth to the prince the fulnes of direction in (.203.) Ecclesiastical causes. The 203. vntruthe, as before. For of Ecclesiastical causes, the Author speaketh not, but of banishiug heretiks, The 204. vntruth. False translatiō : for not, *to confidre,* but *Canonice finem accipere* to conclude &c. The 205. vntruthe, A parte of the sentence nipped of, quyte ouerthrovving M. Hornes purpose.

bookes:to communicate with them. *And so knitteth vp all, vvith* **nian.**
this conclusion. VVee haue decreed thefe thinges for the common peace of the moft holye Churches : thefe thinges haue *Tom.2.cō-*
we determined by fentence. (.205.) *cil.pa.20*
Act,1.Cō-
Stapleton. *ſtā.pa.20*

You goe on M. Horne, euer like to your felfe, and to *Prima er-*
your brother M.Iewel.For as at the firft,you beginne with *go eſt ſen-*
a great vntruthe, fo you procede on with a greate manye *tentia quæ*
moe.I meane not that ye cal the firft for the fifte, lette the *in Conſtā-*
printer beare this,but for the refidewe ye muft take it vpon *tinopoli cō-*
your own fhulders.As firft wher ye fpeake of the title:ther *tra Anthi-*
is no fuch title prefixed before the Councel: there is fuch a *mum lata*
fentence in dede. But that it is a title prefixed before the *eſt, ſecun-*
Councel, as though this ordination were made before the *da autem*
Councel, and fo fhould tel both the matters and who had *ſententia*
the cheif authority in the ordering thereof,this is no fimple *qua in*
lie.But euer ye fhoote to farre,or come to fhort home. Af- *Conſtant.*
ter thofe wordes by you reherfed yt followeth(which you *fuit cōtra*
leaue out) *ad Petrum Archiepiſcopū Hieroſolimorū* : To Peter *Seuerum*
Archebifhop of Hierufalē,to whō Iuftiniā did fend this cō- *Petrū &*
ftitutiō,not before the Coūcel,but the Coūcel beig ended. *Zoaram.*
The order of thefe fentences,as it is declared in the acts of *Tertia cō-*
the Coūcel was this. Firft there was a fentēce geuē at Cō- *ſtitutio eſt*
ftantinople againft Anthymus.Thē was there an other fen- *ordinaria.*
tence geuen there againft Seuerus,Petrus,and Zoaras.Thē *Quarta*
was the conftitutiō of Iuftinian (whereofye fpeake) made *autem a-*
and fente to the bifhop of Hierufalē,which kept there alfo a *ctio in*
Councel and condēned Anthimus.And al this was done in *Hieroſoly-*
fowre monethes.And therfore yt cā not be the true title of *mis,et hæc*
this Coūcel. And much leſſe tel the matter and who had *omnia in*
cheif authority there. But euery man is not fo cunning as *4.mēſibᵒ*
you, to make men weene, that the egge was a chycke *facta &*
ſancita
ſuerunt.

Y Y ij   before

before the henne had hatched . Yet for one thinge I here
commende you, for telling vs that the Popes Legats in this
Councel were set in the right hande of the Patriarche Me-
nas , whiche I suppose maketh somwhat for the Popes primacye. But that you adde , they were *named and appointed
by the commaundement of the Emperour,* I can not comméde
you. For it is vntruly saied. They were the Popes owne Legates and deputies , of his own naming and appointing, not
of the Emperours . For it foloweth in the same Constitution of Iustinian , touching these Legates : *Omnibus quidem ex Italica regione ab Apostolica sede nuper missis .* All
being lately sent out of Italy from the See Apostolike . In
like maner where you say , *Theodorus a Maister of the Requestes to the Emperour,* (as you call him) *deliuered to the
Synod the Billes of supplication to be considered on,* such consideration you finde not in the woordes of Theodorus : but
this you finde him say to the Synode . *Vt in his interpellan-
tes , vos ipsis finem imponatis .* To thentent that by your
meanes in these matters they may be ended and cócluded.
This the Emperours officer required of the Synode : that
they would make an ende of the complaintes layed in by
certaine Bisshoppes and Monkes . And this you conceale,
and alter cleane to a simple consideration , as thoughe the
Councel should haue considered , and then the Emperour
concluded. And therefore yet ones againe in this very Diuision, you tel vs of *a booke of supplication made by the Monasteries of Secunda Syria, to the Emperour, that Menna the
president of the Councel should receaue their booke and consider of it according to the Ecclesiastical Canons.* The woordes
of your Author are: *Quæ in ipso insita sunt Canonicè finem accipere conuenientibus ad ipsum &c.* that the contents of their
                                                                    booke

Tom. 2.
Conc. pa.
20.b.

Tom. 2.
Conc.pag.
21.col.1.

Tom. 2.
Conc. pa.
23. col. 1.

booke of ſupplication, *be ended and determined Canonically* (not conſidered only)and that *by the accorde* (not of Men- na only,whome only you name,being the biſhop of Con- ſtantinople) but, *of the moſt holy Romaines and the holy Sy- node* . Thus your falſe doctrine can not appeare(when it commeth to trial)but lodē alwaies with fardels of vntruths. But nowe I trowe we ſhall quickly leſe this aduantage.For ſtrayte ye bringe vs foorth a biſhop that calleth the Em- perour *the higheſte potentate in the worlde next vnto God, maintayning the onely and pure faith:offeringe vnto God pure leuen of true doctrine,as incenſe,and burning the chaff* (mea- ning,as ye ſay,falſe religion) *with vnquencheable fier.* And thinke you M Horne,that yf Iuſtiniā now lyued,he would take your doctrine for pure fyne flower , and not rather for ſtynking muſty chaffe or bran ? Well you haue hearde his iudgemente in parte aliedy . As for your bſhop yf he had ſayd,*in al cauſes,*as you make hī to ſay in the margin, he had ſaid wel towarde your purpoſe , but nothing towarde the truthe.And therefore ye hauing eſpied the former wordes not to come iumpe to your purpoſe ,ye vnderſhore them withe an other ſayinge of the ſaied biſhoppe , who ſpea- kinge of an heretyke , deſireth the Emperour *to whome God had reſerued the ful authority to directe , to cut him from the Church,and to expulſe him out of his dominions.*Ye are not for al this much the nearer : for wherein the good biſhop meante the full direction, he him ſelfe ſheweth:that is , *in cutting away of heretiks,and expulſing them out of his domis niōs.*And therefore your goodly marginal note that,*God re- ſerueth to the Prince the fulneſſe of direction in cauſes Eccle- ſiaſticall.*quayleth,and is not worth a ruſhe: Neither is yt to be collected by the expreſſe woordes of the biſhop: and yf

Y Y iij   yt were

nian.

yt were, ſauing for your ſhrewd meaning and miſtaking, yt were not greatly material. For it might ſtãd right wel, meaning of the ful and final directiõ, which is the executiõ. Ye now lay forth many eccleſiaſtical cõſtitutions : and among

Conſt 4ʒ. Hæc decre uimus ſan ſtorum pa trum cano nes ſequu- tʋ. Tom. 2. Cõc. pa. 62 Hæc ſentẽ tʋuimus, ſequentes ſanctorum patrũ dog mata.

other, *that no mã ſhal diſpute further in matters of religiõ ons concluded* (where are your Weſtmynſter diſputations thẽ?) and that themperour *had decreed all thoſe things by ſentence, for the common peace of the Church.* Ye ſay the truth , but not all the truth, for ye haue moſt falſly , following your accuſtomable humour, left out iij. or iiij. wordes ſtraytwaies following. *We haue* (ſaith Iuſtinian) *determined theſe things following the decrees of the holy fathers.* Which wordes doe ſet your ſelf and your primacy to, quyt beſide the ſadle . And thus, as theperours concluſion, that knitteth vp al, knitteth vp our concluſion to, for the eccleſiaſtical primacy, and vnfoldeth al your falſe concluſiõs in this your falſe boke: So, yf ye take and ioyne the very beginning of the ſaid cõſtitutiõ to the wynding vp of yt , the matter wilbe much clearer: and ſo clere that Iuſtiniãs cõſtitutiõ that your ſelf do bring

Conc. Cõ= ſtant. 5. Act. 1. To. 2. pag. 61.

forth, may ſerue for a ſufficiẽt anſwere to al your boke: cõcerning princes intermedling in cauſes Eccleſiaſtical. *We do* (ſaith Iuſtiniã) *no ſtrãge thĩg, or ſuch as theperors haue not ben accuſtomed vnto before, in makĩg this preſent Law:* (meaning

Tom. 2. Conc. Synod. 5. Act. 1. pag. 61. col. 2. a Rem non inſolitam imperio & nos facie= tes ad præſentem ve= ni uus lege. Quoties enim ſacerdotũ ſen-

againſt Anthimus , Seuerus, and Zoaras) *for as often as the biſhops by their ſentence haue depoſed and diſplaced out of their holy ſees and dignities any vnworthy parſons, as Neſtorius, Eutyches, Arius, Macedonius , and Eunomius, and certain other as naughty as they were: theperors folowing their ſentẽce ãd authority decreed the ſame: So that eccleſiaſtical ãd teporal authority cõcurring together, made one agreemẽt in right iudgmẽt.*

Euen

Euen as we know e it happened of Late touching An-
thimus , who was thruſte out of the ſee of this impe-
riall cyty by Agapetus of holy and gloriouſe memorie,
the biſhop of the moſt holy Church of olde Rome.

rium, Eutychen, Arrium, Macedonium & Eunomium, ac quoſdam alios ad iniquitatem
non minores illis:toties imperium eiuſdem ſententia & ordinationis cum ſacerdotum au
thoritate ſuit:ſicque diuina & humana pariter concurrentia,vnam conſonantiam rectis
ſententiis fecere: quemadmodum & nuper factum eſſe contra Anthymū ſcimus,qui quidē
deiectus eſt de ſede huius regiæ vrbis a ſancta & glorieſa memoria Agapeto,ſanctiſ. Ec-
cleſia antiquæ Romæ pontifice,eò quòd &c.

tentia quoſdam in-
dignos ſacerdotio de
ſacris ſedibᵒ depoſuit,
queadmodū Neſto-

M. Horne. The.73. Diuiſion. pag.42.a

Al things being thus done,by the commaundement of the Emperour, in
the firſt Action,and ſo foorth,in the ſecond,third,and fourth, after many ac-
clamations,the Preſident of the Councel Mennas,concludeth:ſaying to the
Synod:That they are not ignorāt of the zeale and minde, of the
Godly Emperour, towards the right Faithe,and that nothing
of thoſe that are moued in the Church (.206.)ought to be don
without his wil and commaundement.

Nothing
may be
don in
Churche
maters,
vvithout
the princ
ces autho
rity.

Stapleton.

Now goe ye M.Horne clerkly to worke . For yf ye can
roundly and hanſomly proue this , ye may perchance ſet a
new head vpon Iuſtinians ſhoulders:which yet woulde be
but an vgle and a monſtrouſe ſight.But this is neither clerkly,nor truely don of you, to turne *Conuenit,yt is mete,ſemely,*
or *conuenient:*into *oportet,* yt muſt or ought . I maruaile ye
bearing the ſtate of a biſhop,haue ſo litle faith and honeſty:
or dwelling ſo nighe Wincheſter ſchole,ſo litle ſight in the
grammer.Mennas had condemned Anthimus : the Biſhops
and other cryed,that forwith he ſhould cōdéne Seuerᵒ,Pe-
trus,and Zoaras:as he did a while after.To whome Mennas
anſwered,that it was mete to cōſult with themperour firſt.
which is very true: for his great zeale to the faith,ād for that
he had

The.206.
vntruthe
double
both in
the text
ād in the
margin :
ſtanding
in falſe
trāſlatiō.
Nihil eo-
rū quæ in
ſanctiſsi-
ma eccle-
ſiâ mouē-
tur cōuen-
nit fieri.
To.2.cōcil.
p.78.co.a

he hadde the exequution of the ſentence, this is
lyke your other knacke before, that Dioſcorus and
other muſt be depoſed. And ſurely I woulde haue
meruayled yf Mennas had takē Iuſtinian for the ſu
preame head who within fowre lynes after declareth the Pope to be the ſupreame head: and *that he
did followe and obeye hī in al things, and cōmunicated
With them, that did communicate With him: and cōdemned thoſe Whome he did condemne*. Who alſo
gaue Anthimus the heretik a tyme of repentance
appointed by Pope Agapetus, and proceded in Sētence againſt him, according to the preſcription of
the Pope, as Cyrillus proceded againſt Neſtorius
in the Epheſine Councel, according to the limitation of Pope Celeſtinus.

M. Horne. The. 74. Diuiſion. pag. 42. a.

*Such is the autority of Princes in matters Eccleſiaſtical, that
the Godly auncient Fathers did not only confeſſe, that nothing mo
ued in Church matters (.207.) ought to be done vvithout their au
thority, but alſo did ſubmitte thēſelues vvillingly vvith humble
obedience, to the direct on of the Godly Emperors, by their lavves
(.208.) in al matters or cauſes Eccleſiaſtical, vvhich thei vvuld
not haue done, yf they hadde thought, that Princes ought not to
haue gouerned in Eccleſiaſtical cauſes. The ſame zelous Emperour doth declare, that the authority of the Princes lavves doth
rightly diſpoſe and kepe in good order, both ſpiritual and temporal matters, and driueth avvay all iniquity: vvherefore he did
not only gather togeather as it vvere into one heape, the lavves
that he him ſelfe had made, and other Emperours before him, touching ciuil or temporal matters: but alſo manye of thoſe lavves
and conſtitutions, vvhich (.209.) his aunceſ ours had made in
Eccleſiaſtical cauſes: Yea, there vvas nothing perteyning to the
Church*

*Nos ſicut ſcit veſtra
charitas, apoſtolicā
ſedem ſequimur &
obedimus: & ipſius
communicatores, cō-
municatores habe-
mus, & condemna-
tos ab ipſa & nos
condemnamus.
Act. 4. pag. 87.*

*Cyrillus Epiſt. 10. &
11. & Cœleſt. epi. 12.
inter epiſt. Cyril.*

The 207. vntruthe.
The godly Fathers
neuer confeſſed ſo.
The 108. vntruthe.
Notorious and im-
pudent: often auou
ched, but neuer
proued.
Cod. lib. 1. tit. 17.

The 209. vntruthe.
Not vvhich his
Aunceſtours, but
vvhich the Apoſt-
les and fathers of
the Church had
made before.

Church gouernemente, vvhiche he did not prouide for, order and direct by his
lavves and Constitutions: vvherein may euidently appeare the aucthoritie
of Princes, not onely ouer the persons, but also in the causes Ecclesiasticall.
He made a common and generall lavve to all the Patriarches, touching the
ordering of Bishoppes, and all other of the Clergie, and Church Ministers:
prescribing the number of them to be suche, as the reuenues of the Churches
may vvell susteine: affirming that the care ouer the Churches, and other re-
ligious houses, perteine to his ouersight: And doth further inhibite, that the
ministers do passe foorth of one Churche to an other, vvithout the licence of
the Emperour or the Bisshoppe: the vvhich ordinaunce he gaue also to those
that vvere in Monasteries.   He (.210.) geaueth authoritie to the Patri-
arche or Bisshoppe, to refuse and reiect, although great suit by men of much
authoritie be made.   He prescribeth in vvhat sorte and to vvhat ende the
Churche goods shoulde be bestovved, and threatneth the appointed paines
to the byshoppe and the other Mynisters, if they trangresse this his Consti-
tution.

He prescribeth in vvhat sorte the Bisshoppe shall dedicate a Monastery:
he giueth rules and fourmes of examination, and triall of those that shalbe
admitted into a Monasterie, before they be professed: in vvhat sorte and or-
ders they shal liue together: He (211.) prescribeth an order and rule, vvher-
by to choose and ordeine the Abbat: He requireth in a Monasticall personne,
diuinorum eloquiorum eruditionem, & conuersationis inte-
gritatem: Learning in Gods vvoorde, and integritie of life.
And last of all, he chargeth the Archebisshoppes, Bisshoppes, and other chur-
che Ministers, vvith the publishing and obseruing of this his constitution:
Yea his Temporal officers and Iudges also, threatening to them both, that if
they doe not see this his Lavve executed and take the effecte, they shal not
escape condigne punishment.

He protesteth, that Emperours ought not to be carefull for nothing so
much, as to haue the mynisterye faithfull tovvardes God, and of honeste
behauiour tovvardes the vvorlde, vvhiche he saith, vill easely be brought
to passe, if the holy rules vvhich the Apostles gaue, and the holy Fathers
kept, and made plaine, be obserued and put in vre. Therefore, saith he,

Z Z   *vve solo-*

nian.
Nou. Cō 3.
Thempe-
rours ec-
clesiastical
Lavves.

The. 210.
Vntruth.
Not he,
but the
Canōs of
the Chur-
ch before
gaue that
autority.
He only
putteth
the mat-
ter by his
lavve in
executiō
Cōst. 5.
The .211.
vntruth.
Not he,
but the
Churche
prescri-
bed that
order and
rule.
Const. 6.

vve folovving in all things the sacred rules (meaning of the Apostles) do ordeine and decree, &c. and so maketh a constitution and lavve, touching the
qualities and conditions, that one to be chosen and ordered a Bishop ought
to haue, and prescribeth a fourme of triall and examination of the party, ve-
fore he be ordered: adding that if any be ordered a Bishop not *qualified according to this constitution, bothe he that ordereth, and he that is ordered,
shall * lose their bishoprikes. He addeth furthermore, that if he come to
his Bishoprike by giftes or revvardes, or if he be absent from his Bishoprike
aboue a time limited, vvithout the commaundement of the Emperour, that
be shall incurre the same penalties. The like orders and rules be prescribeth in the same constitution for Deacons, Diaconisses, Subdeacons, and Readers: commaunding the Patriarches, Archbishops and bishops to promul-
gate this constitution, and to see it observed vnder a paine.

He affirmeth that this hath ben an auncient Lavve, and doth by his authority, renevv and confirme the same: that no man haue priuate Chappels
in their houses, vvherein to celebrate the diuine mysteries: vvhervnto he
addeth this vvarning vnto Mennas the Archebishop that if he knevv any
suche to be, and do not forbid and reiourme that abuse, but suffer this constitution of the Emperour to be neglected and broken, he him selfe shal forsait
to the Emperour fiftie poundes of gold.

Also that the ministers kepe continuall residence on their benefices: othervvise the Bishop to place others in their roomes, and they neuer to be restored.

Stapleton.

We shall nowe haue a long rehearsall, full three leaues,
of many Ecclesiasticall Lawes, made by Iustinian the Emperour. But who would thinke that M. Horne were eyther so folishe to make suche a sturre for that no man deny-
eth, and the which nothing proueth his cause, or to reherse
suche constitutions of Iustinian, that partely ouerthroweth
his Primacy, partly displaceth him frō al bishoply and priestly office? But what shal a man saye to them that be past all
shame, and haue no regard what they say or doe preach or
write? Or how is this world bewitched, thus paciently to
suffer

Margin notes (left):

* M. Horn
is not
so qualifi
ed, for he
hath (he
saieth) a
wife Ergo
M. Horne
by his
ovvne
lavv, yea
of the
Apostles
making,
must lose
his Bis-
hoprik.
Const.57

Const.58

ſuffer, ſuch mens ſermons and bookes , yea and to
geue them high credit to? Tel me then and bluſhe
not M.Horn,whether ye be not one of them, that
for lacke of ſuch qualities, as Iuſtiniā, according to
the holie rules and Canons ye ſpake of, requireth
in a Biſhop,muſt loſe your Biſhoprik, and thoſe alſo that ordeined you? Is not this one of the qualities, *that a Biſhoppe ſhould haue no maner of wife*
when he is ordered? Yea that his wife that he had be-
fore he was ordered Prieſt or Biſhop, muſt haue bene
a virgin and no widowe at the time of mariage? Is
not this one of *the holye rules, whiche the Apoſtles*
*gaue, and the holy Fathers kept aud made plaine,*whiche Iuſtinian would haue obſerued and put in vre?
Now againe for Prieſt,Deacon,or Subdeacon that
marieth after he is ordered , doth not Iuſtinian eue
in your owne conſtitution ſay , *that he muſt forth-*
with be ſpoiled of all Eccleſiaſticall function and office,
and become a laie man? Loke nowe well aboute
you Maiſter Horne,and aboute your fellowes Proteſtante Biſſhoppes, and tell mee , if this rule take
place, whether ye can ſhewe among them all,any
one Byſhoppe? And ſo by the merueilous handy
woorke of God, yee are neither Parliamente nor
Churche Biſhops.What do ye tel me of Iuſtinians
conſtitutions touching Monkes and monaſteries,
and of the rules and fourmes that he preſcribed to
them? He ſayeth in dede , *that he hath a ſpeciall*
care to ſee the monaſticall rules and fourmes according
to the will of the holy Canones obſerued. He ſaith
that throughe the pure and deuonte prayers of religi-

Cōſt. 5.
Hoc aūt futurū eſſe
credimus, ſi ſacrarū
regularū obſeruatio
cuſtodiatur quā iuſti
laudandi et adoran-
di inſpectores et mi-
niſtri Dei tradiderūt
apoſt et ſancti patres
cuſtodierūt et expla-
narūt. Sancimus igi-
tur ſacras per oīa ſe-
quētes regulas.&c.
aut in virginitate
degens à principio,
aut vxorē habens ex
virginitate ad eam
venientē,et nō vidu-
ā,& mox: de cætero
aūt nulli permitten-
tes à poſitione legis
vxorē habenti talem
imponi ordinationē.
Ibidem.
Sacro ſtatim cadat
ordine, et deinceps
idiota ſit.

There is not a Pro-
teſtant Biſhop in
England by the cō
ſtitution that M.
Horne him ſelfe
alleageth.

ous

Hovve
vvell M.
Hornes
doctrine
agreeth
vvith Iu-
ftinias for
the mona
ftical life.
*Cis an
fvveret h
all your
proceffe,
M. Horn,
The Em,
perouret
foloveth!
the canõs
The Ca,
nõs vver
made of
Bifhops
in Coun-
cels and
Synods.
Ergo he
folovv-
eth the
Bifhops.
If he fo
lovve thē
he goeth
not be-
fore thē,
He dothe
not di-
rect them
prefcrib-
to them,
orgouern
them,but
is directed

oufe men, all thinges doe profper in the common wealth, both in peace and in warre. Yf then Iuftinian threatneth punifh-ment, as ye truely fay, both to fpirituall and temporall ma-giftrates for not publifhyng and caufyng hys Conftitutions made for religioufe men to be obferued: howe fharply and roughlye woulde he deale with you, your fellowes, and mayfters, that by your preachinges haue caufed fo manye monafteries to be fo pityfully ouerthrowen? Howe fhould yow efcape condigne punifhment, thinke you, that make no better of thefe Iuftinians, and not hys, but rather the holy Fathers, rules concernyng the monafticall life, then to call the fayde holy life *a foolifhe vowe, an horrible errour, and a monkifh fuperftition?*

M. Horne. The. 75. Diuifion. pag. 43. b.

*Vhan this Emperour vnderftood, by the complaints that vvere brought vnto him againft the Clergy, Monks and certein Bifhoppes, that their liues vvere not framed according to the holy Canons, and that many of them vvere fo ignoraunt, that they knevve not the prayer of the holy oblation and facred Baptifme: Perceiuyng further, that the occafion hereof vvas part-ly, by reafon that the Synodes vvere not kept accordinge to the order ap-pointed, partly for that the Bifhoppes, Prieftes, Deacons, and the re-fidue of the Clergy, vvere ordered, bothe vvithout due examination of the right faith, and alfo vvithout teftimony of honeft conuerfation: Prote-fting that as he is mindefull to fee the ciuil Lavves firmely kept, euen fo he ought (of duty) to be more carefull about the obferuation of the Sacred rules and diuine Lawes, and in no wife to fuffer them to be violated and broken. He renueth the conftitutions for the Cler-gy, touching Churche caufes, faing. *Folowyng therefore thofe thin-ges, that are defined in the facred Canons, we make a Pragma-ticall or mofte full and effectuall Lawe, whereby we ordeine that fo often as it fhalbe neadfull, to make a Bifhop. &c. And fo goeth forvvarde in prefcribing the forme of his election, examination, and approz*

prefcribed, and gouerned of them.

approbation. And *shutteth vp the Lavve about the ordering of a Bishop* nian.
vvith this clause: If any shalbe ordered a Bishop againſt this former appointed order, bothe he that is ordered and he alſo that
hath preſumed to order againſt this fourme, ſhal be depoſed.
He decreeth alſo by Prouiſo, vvhat order ſhall be kept, if it chaunce that
there be any occaſion or matter layd to the charge of him that is to be orde-
red, either Biſhop, Prieſt, Deacon, Clergy man, or els Abbot af any
Monaſtery. But aboue all things ſayeth he, vvee enact this to be obſer-
ued, that no man be ordered Biſhop by giftes or revvards: for both the geuer,
taker, and the broker, if he be a Church man, ſhalbe depriued of his bene-
fice, or clericall dignity, and if he be a Lay man, that either taketh re-
vvarde, or is a vvorker in the matter betvvene the partyes, vve commaund
that he pay double to be geuen to the Churche. He geueth lycence neuer=
theles, that vvhere there hath bene ſomethyng geuen, by hym that is ordered
Byſhoppe, of cuſtome, or for enſtallation, that they may take it: ſo that it
exceede not the ſomme preſcribed by hym in this Lavve. VVe commaund
therefore that the holy Archebiſhoppes, namely of the elder
Rome, of Conſtantinople, Alexandria, Theopolis, and Hieruſalem, if they haue a cuſtome to geue the Biſhoppes and Clerkes, at their ordering vnder twenty poūdes in gold: they geue
onely ſo muche as the cuſtome alloweth: But if there were
more geuen before this Lawe, wee commaunde that there
be no more geuen then twenty poundes. *And ſo he ſetteth a rate*
to all other Eccleſiaſtical perſons in their degrees, and according to the habi-
litie of their Churches, concluding thus: Surely if any preſume by any
meanes to take more than we haue appointed, either in name
of cuſtomes, or enſtallations, wee commaunde that he reſtore
threefolde ſo much to his Churche, of whom he tooke it. *He*
doth vtterly forbidde biſhoppes and Monkes, to take vpon them gardianſhip:
neuertheleſſe, he licēceth Prieſtes, Diacōs, and Subdeacōs, to take the ſame on
thē in certein caſes. He cōmaundeth tvvo Synods to be kept in euery Prouince
yerely. He preſcribeth vvhat, and in vvhat order, maters ſhalbe examined,
and diſcuſſed in them. Beſides theſe, he enioyneth, and doth commaunde all
Byſhops, and Prieſtes, to celebrate the prayers in the miniſtration of the Lor-
des ſupper, ād in baptiſm, not after a vvhiſpering or vvhyſt maner, but vvith a

ZZ iĳ   *cleare*

cleare voyce, as thereby the minds of the hearers, may be ſtirred vp vvith more deuotion in praiſyng the Lord God. He proueth by the teſtimony of S. Paul, that it ought ſo to be. He concludeth, that if the religious biſshops, neg lect any of theſe things, they ſhal not eſcape puniſhment by his order. And for the better obſeruing of this conſtitution, he commaundeth the rulers of the prouinces vnder him, if they ſe theſe things neglected, to vrge the biſshops, to cal Synods, and to accompliſh all things, vvhich he hath commaunded by this Lavv to be doon by Synods. But if the Rulers ſee not vvithſtanding, that the biſshops be ſlouthfull and ſlack to do thies things, then to ſygnify therof to him ſelf, that he may correct their negligece: for othervviſe he vvil extremely puniſh the Rulers them ſelues. Beſydes thies, ſaith this Emperour, vve for-bid and enioyne the Religious biſshops, Prieſts, Deacons, Subdeacons, Readers,

Con.133. The.212. Vntruth, Theſe la-wes ſhew no ſuche principa-lity.

and euery other Clergy man, of vvhat degre or order ſo euer he be, that they play not at the table plaies (as cardes, dyce, and ſuch like playes, vſed vpon a table) nor aſſociat or gaſe vpon the players at ſuch playes, nor to be gaſers at ay other open ſyghts: if any offend againſt this decre, vve commaund that he be prohibited from all ſacred miniſtery for the ſpace of thre years, and to be thruſt into a monaſtery. After thies Conſtitutions made for the gouerna-met of the ſecular Clergy (as you terme it) in cauſes eccleſiaſticall, the Em-perour deſcedeth to make ſtatutes, ordinaunces and rules for monaſtical per-ſons (commonly called Religious) declaryng, that there is no maner of

The price hath ſu-preame gouerne-met ouer al perſons (.212.) i al maner cauſes. The.213. Vntruth. Impudet. That ſet i the mar-gin, vvhi-ch is not i the text.

thing, which is not throughly to be ſearched by the authority of the Emperour, who hath (ſayth he) receiued from God the common gouernment and principality ouer al men. And (.212.) to ſhevv further that this principality is ouer the perſons, ſo vvell in Eccleſi-aſticall cauſes as Temporall, he preſcribeth orders and rules for them, and committeth to the Abbottes and Biſshoppes (iuriſdiction) to ſee theſe rules kepte, concludynge that ſo well the Magiſtra-tes, as Eccleſiaſticall perſonnes, oughte to keepe incorrupted all thynges whyche concerne godlyneſſe: but aboue all other the Emperour, who owghte to neglecte no manner of thyng pertaynyng to godlyneſſe. I omit many other Lavves and Conſtitu-tions, that not only this Emperour, but alſo the Emperours before him made, touchyng matters and cauſes Eccleſiaſticall, and doe remitte you vnto the Code, and the Authentikes, vvhere you may ſee that al manner of cauſes Ec-cleſi-

eleſiaſticall, vvere ouerſeene, (.214.) ordered and directed by
the Emperours, and ſo they did the dutifull ſeruice of Kyngs to
Chriſt, In that (as S. Auguſtine ſayth) they made lawes for
Chriſte.

The.214 vntruth.
That can not be
found either in the
Code, or i thanthē.
Auguſt. Epiſt. 48.

Stapleton.

All this geare runneth after one race, and alltogether ſtandeth in the execution of the ecclesiaſtical Lawes. Neither is there any thing here to be
ſtayed vpon, but for that he hath furniſhed his margent wyth hys accuſtomable note, *that the prince
hath the ſupreame gouernment ouer all perſons in all
maner cauſes.* Whiche as yt is largely and liberally
ſpoken: ſo is his text to narrowe to beare any ſuch
wide talke. Yea and rather proueth the contrary,
if he take the nexte line before with him, and ſtoppeth alſo his felowes blaſphemous railyngs, againſt
the holy monaſtical life. *The ſolitary and the cōtem-
platiue life* (ſaieth Iuſtinian) *is certeinly an holy thing,
and ſuch a thing as by her owne nature cōducteth ſoules to God: neyther is it fruitful to them only that leade
that life, but through her puritye and prayers to God
geueth a ſufficient help to other alſo. Wherefore themperours in former times, toke care of this matter, and
We alſo in our Lawes haue ſet foorth many things touching the dignity and vertue of religious men. For We
doe followe in this the holy canons and the holy fathers
Who haue drawen out certaine orders and Lawes for
theſe matters. For there is no thing that themperours
maieſty doth not throughly ſearch. Whiche hath receiued from God a common gouernment and principality
ouer*

Conſt. 133.
Solitaria vita atque
in ea contemplatio,
res planè ſacra eſt, et
quæ ſuapte natura
animas ad Deū ad-
ducat. Neque ijs tan
tum, qui eam inco=
lunt, ſed etiam om-
nibus alijs puritate
ſua & apud Deū in-
terpellatione compe
tentē de ſe vtilitatē
præbeat. Vnde & olī
cares Imperatoribus
ſtudio fuit habita,
& nos non pauca de
dignit. & honeſtate
eorū legibus cōplexi
ſumus. Sequimur enī
ſacros in hoc canones
et ſanctos patres qui
hoc cōprehēderūt le-
gibus. quādoquidē ni
hil nō peruiū ad in-
quiſitione maieſtati
exiſtit imperatoria,
quæ cōmunem in oēs
hoies moderationē
et principatum à
Deo percepit.

ouer all men . Nowe thys place as ye ſee, ſerueth expreſly
for the Churches principality, whoſe *holy Canons, and holy
Fathers themperour*, as he ſayeth, *doth followe* . By whiche
wordes appeareth , he made no one Conſtitution of hys
owne Authority . And therefore hath M. Horne craftely
ſhyfted in this worde *Authority* which is not in the Latine:
as though the Emperours Authority were the chief groūd
of theſe Conſtitutions , whereas it is but the ſeconde , and
depending only vpon former Canons and writtinges of holy Fathers . Yet hath this ioly gloſer placed in his margine
a *ſuprem gouernmēt and principality in al maner cauſes*. Which
is not to be founde any where in the text , but is a gloſe of
his owne making . Wherein me thinketh, M. Horne fareth
as certaine Melancholike paſsionated doe: whoſe imagination is ſo ſtronge, that if they begin earneſtly to imagine as
preſent, ether the ſight or voyce of any one that they excedingly either loue or feare , by force of theyr imagination,
doe talke with them ſelues , or crye out ſodenly, as though
in very deede, not in imagination only the thinge deſired
or feared, were actually preſent . Verely ſo M. Horne, beinge exceding paſsionated to finde out this *ſupreme gouernment in al cauſes* , by force of his imagination, putteth it in
his margin, as though the text told it him, whē the text talketh no ſuch matter vnto him, but is vtterly domme in that
point and huſhe. This paſsiō hath vttered it ſelf in M.Horne
not nowe onely, but many times before alſo, as the diligent
Reader may eaſely remember.

M. Horne. The.76. Diuiſion. pag. 45. a.

Arriamiru *King of Spaine,* (215) *cōmaunded tvvo Conucels to be celebrated in a Citie called* Brachara, *the one in the ſeconde yeare of his reigne,
the other the third yere, vvherein vvere certaine rules made or rather renued
touching*

touching matters of faith, touching Constitutions of the Church, and for the
dueties and diligence of the Clergie, in their offices.

VVambanus *King of Spaine* (.216.) *seeing the greate disorders in*
the Churche, not onely in the discipline, but also in the matters of Faithe,
and aboute the Administration of the Sacramentes, calleth a Synode at
Brachara, *named* Concill. Brachar. 3. *for the reformation of the er-*
rours and disorders aloute the Sacramentes and Churche discipline.

The. 20. Chapter. Of Ariamirus, Wambanus, and Richaredus, Kings of Spaine, and of Pelagius. 2. and S. Gre= gorie. 1. Popes.

Stapleton.

NO W are we gon from Fraūce and Constantinople to, and are come to Spaine, and to the Coūcels called of King Ariamirus and King Wambanus. But the Fa-thers at these Councels tell M. Horne for his first greeting and welcome, that they acknowleged the authority of the See of Rome : and therfore being some cōtrouersies in ma-ters ecclesiastical among thē, they did direct them selues by the instructiōs and admonitiōs sent frō the See Apostolike.

M. Horne. The. 77. Diuision. pag. 45. b.

About this time after the death of Pelagius. 2. the Clergy and the people e-
lected Gregory. 1. called aftervvards the great. But the custom was (*saith*
Sabellicus) *vvhich is declared in an other place,* that the Emperours
should ratify by their consent, th'electiō of him that is chosen
Pope. And to stay th'Emperors approbatiō (*saith* Platina) he sent
his messengers with his letters, to beseche th'Emperour Mauritius that he would not suffer th'electiō of the people ād Clergy to take effect in the choise of hi. &c. So much did this good
mā (*saith* Sabellicus) seking after heauely things, cōtemne earthly
and refused that honour, for the which other did contend so
ambitiously. *Put the Emperour being desirouse to plant so good a man in*
that place, vvould not condescend to his requesf, but (. 217.) *sent his Embas-*
fadours, to ratifie and confirme the election.

Hornes sēce. That is, as suprē gouernor but as the coūcel it selfe faith, as *Pijssi-mus filius noster :* Our most godlye Sonne. The. 216. Vntruth. No suche thing in the Coū-celi, nor that Vvā-banus cal-led it at al *Vide Brac.* 1. tom. 2. Conc. pag. 216. et 217 Can. 18. &. 23. The. 217. Vntruth. That is not in Sa-bellicus.

　　　a　　　　　This

Stapleton.

This authority toucheth nothing but th'electiō of the Pope wont to be confirmed by the Emperour for order and quietnes sake. And that but of custom only (for *the custom was* saith Sabellicus) not of any Supreme gouernement of the Prince in that behaulfe, as though without it, the election were not good. Yet I cōmend M. Horn that, he reherseth so much good cōmendacion of Pope Gregorie, that sent hither our Apostle S. Augustine. But I marueil how he can be so good a mā, and the religion that came frō him to England no better then superstiton and plaine Idolatrie, as M. Horne and his fellowes doe daily preach and write. And ye shall heare anon that he goeth as craftely as he can, and as farre as he durst to obscure and disgrace him.

M. Horne. The. 78. Diuision. pag. 45. b.

Richaredus *King of Spaine, rightly taught and instructed in the Christian faith, by the godly and Catholique Bisshoppe* Leander *Bishop of Hispalis, did not only bring to passe, that the whole natiō, should forsake the Arrianisme and receiue true faith, but also did carefully study how to continue his people in the true Relligion by his meanes nevvelye receiued. And* therfore commaunded all the Bishops within his Dominions to assemble together at Toletum, *in the fourth yeare of his reigne,*

The. 218. Vntruth. Falle trā- slation. instaurare formam, is not to make a nevve fourme, but to re- paire the olde.

and there to consult about staying and confirming of his people in true faith and religion of Christ by godly discipline. VVhan the Bisshoppes vvere assembled in the Conuocation house, at the Kings commaundement: the King commeth in amongest them, he maketh a short, but a pithy and most Christian oration vnto the vvhole Synode: VVherein he shevveth, that the cause vvherfore he called them together into the Synode, vvas To repaire and make a (.218.) newe fourme of Churche discipline, *by common consultation in Synode, vvhich had bene letted long time before by the heretical Arianisme,* the whiche staie and lette of the Arrian Heresies, it hath pleased God (*saith he*) to remoue and put away by my meanes. *He vvilleth them to be ioyfull and gladde, that the auncient*

cient

cient maner to make Ecclesiasticall constitutions for the vvell ordering of the Churche, is novve through Gods prouidence reduced and brought againe to the bounds of the Fathers by his honorable industrie. And last of al, he doth admonishe and exhort them before they begin their consultation, to fast and pray vnto the Almighty, that he vvill vouchsaulse to open and shevv vnto them a true order of discipline, vvhich that age knevv not, the senses of the Clergy vvere so much benummed, vvith long forgetfulnes. VVherevppon there vvas a three daies fast appointed. That done, the Synode assembleth, the King commeth in, and sitteth amongest them : he deliuereth in vvriting to be openly read amongest them the confession of his faith, in vvhich he protesteth, vvith vvhat endeuour and care, being their King, he ougat not only to studie for him self, to be rightly geuen to serue and please God vvith a right Faith in true Religion: but also to prouide for his subiects, that they be throughly instructed in the Christian faith. *He affirmeth and thereto taketh them to vvitnes, that the Lorde hath stirred him vppe, inflamed vvith the heate of Faith: both to remeue and put avvay the furious and obstinate Heresies and Schismes, and also by his vigilant endeuour and care to call and bring home againe the people vnto the confession of the true faith, and the Communion of the Catholique Churche. Furder alluding to the place of S. Paul, vvhere he saith, that through his ministery in the Ghospell, he offereth vppe the Gentils vnto God, to be an acceptable Sacrifice : he saith to the Bishops,* That he offereth by their mynisterie, this noble people, as an holy and acceptable Sacrifice to God. *And last of all vvith the rehearsall of his Faith, he declareth vnto the Bishoppes,* That as it hath pleased God by his care and industrie to winne this people to the Faith, and vnite them to the Catholique Churche : so he chardgeth them, nowe to see them stayed and confirmed by theyr diligente teaching and instructinge them in the trueth. *After this Confession vvas read, and that he him selfe, and also his Queene Badda, had confirmed and testified the same vvith their handes subscription : the vvhole Synode gaue thankes to God vvith manye and sundry acclamations, saiyng :* That the Catholique King Richaredus is to be crouned of God with an euerlasting croune, for he is the gatherer togeather of newe people in the Churche. This King truely oughte to haue the Apostolique re-

The dutiful care of a Prince about religion.

The.219.
Vntruthe.
No fuche
vvoords
in that
fentence
The.220.
Vntruth.
The Kigs
vvhole
vvordes
fouly mai
med and mangled,
as fhall appeare.
A Princes fpeciall
care for his fubiects
The.221.Vntruthe.
No fuch vvords in
the Councell.
The.222.Vntruth
It vvas not of the
Nicene Coucel, but
of the Coftantino-
ple Councell
The.223. Vntruth.
For not by autho-
rity of Supreame
gouernemente (as
M. Horne driueth
it) but only for the
execution of it in
his Dominions.
The 224.Vntruth.
Slaunderous and
blafphemous.
Lib.Epift.7.
Epift.126.
The Pope at that
time comeded the
Princes gouerne-
ment in caufes Ec-
clefiafticall,

reward, who hath perfourmed the Apoftolike office. *This done,
after the Noble men and Bifshops of Spaine, vvhom the vvorthy King had
conuerted, and brought to the amity of faithe, in the Comunion of Chriftes
Church, had alfo geuen their confefsion opely, and teftified the fame vvith fubfcription : the King vvilling the Synode to goe in hand to repaire and efta-
blifsh fome Ecclefiaftical difcipline, faith to the Synode, alluding to S. Paules
faiyng to the Ephefians to this effect :* That the care of a king ought to
ftretch forth it felf, and not to ceafe til he haue brought (.219.)
the fubiects to a full knowledge and perfect age in Chrift: and
as (220) a king ought to bend al his power and authority to repreffe the infolece of the euil, ad to nourifh the comon peace
and traquility: Eue fo ought he much more to ftudy, labour, ad
be careful, not only to bring his fubiects fro erours and
falfe religio, but alfo to fee the inftructed, taught, and
trained vp in the truth of the clere light, *and for this pur
pofe he doth there decree,* of (221) his own authority, comma-
ding the Bifshops to fee it obferued, that at euery Com-
munio time before the receit of the fame, al the peple
with a loud voice together, do recite diftictly the Sim
bol or crede, fet forth by the (222) Nice coucel. *Vhe the
Synode had cofulted about the difcipline, and had agreed vpon fuch
rules and orders, as vvas thought moft mete for that time ad churche, and the King had cofidered of them, he doth by his affent and
(223) authority, cofirme and ratify the fame, and firft fubfcribeth
to the, and then after hi al the Synod.* This zelous care and careful
ftudy of this and the other aboue named princes, prouiding, ruling,
gouerning, and by their Princely povver and authority, directing
their vvhole Clergy, in caufes or matters Ecclefiafticall, vvas neuer
difalovved, or mifliked, of the aucient Fathers, nor of the bifshops of
Rome, til novv in thefe later daies, the infactable abitio of the clergy, and the ouermuch negligece and vvatones of the Princes, vvith
the groffe ignorance of the vvhole laity, gaue your holy father (224)
the child of perditio, the ful fvvay to make perfect the myftery of ini
quity: yea, it may appere by an Epiftle that Gregorius furnamed
great, B. of Rome, vvriteth vnto this vvorthy King Richaredus,
that

that the B. of Rome did much cōmend this careful (225) gouernmēt of Princes in causes of religion. For he most highly commendeth the doings of this most Christian King. He affirmeth that he is ashamed of himselfe, and of his ovvne slacknes, vvhen he doth consider the trauail of Kings in gathering of soules to the celestiall gaine.
Yea what shal I (*saith this B. of Rome to the King*) answere at the dreadful dome when your excellēcy shal leade after your selt flocks of faithful ones, which you haue brought vnto the true faith by carefull and continuall preaching, &c. Although I haue medled and don nothing at al with you, doing this (227) altogether without me, yet am I partaker of the ioy with you. *Neither doth Gregory blame this King as one medling in Churche causes, vvherin he is not Ruler: but he praiseth God for him, that he maketh godly constitutious against the vnfaithfulnes of miscreants: and for no vvorldly respect vvilbe persvvaded to see them violated.*

Stapleton.

We are now vpon the soden returned into Spaine : But wonderful it is to consider, howe M. Horne misordereth and mistelleth his whole mater, and enforceth as wel other where, as here also by Richaredus, that whiche can not be enforced : that is, to make him a Supreme head in al causes Ecclesiasticall. Ye say M. Horne, he called a Synod *to repaire and make a newe fourme of the Churche discipline.* But I say you haue falsly translated the worde, *instaurare*, which is not to make a new thing, but to renew an olde : whiche differeth very muche. For by the example of the fiiste, Queene Marie repaired and renewed the Catholique Religiō. By the report of the second, you made in dede a new fourme of matters in King Edwardes daves, neuer vsed before in Christes Churche. You say also he remoued from

a iij   Spaine

Spaine the Arrians herefies. I graunt you : he dyd fo . But thinke you M. Horne, if he nowe liued, and were prince of our Coūtre, he would haue nothing to fay to you and your fellowes, as wel as he had to the Arrians? Nay. He and his Councell hath faid fomething to you and againft you already, as we fhall anon fee.

You fay : *he cōmaunded the Bifshops that at euery cōmunion time, before the receit of the fame , the people with a lowde voice togeather fhould recite diftinctly the Symbole or Crede fet foorth by the Nicene Councell*. It happeneth wel, that the Nicene Councell was added. I was afeard, leaft ye would haue gonne about to proue, the people to haue fong then, fome fuch Geneuical Pfalmes as now the brotherhod moft eftemeth : Wherevnto ye haue here made a pretty foundation, calling that after your Geneuical fort, *the Communion*, which the Fathers call *the body and bloud of Chrift* : and the King him felfe calleth *the cōmunicating of the body and bloud of Chrift*. Now here by the way I muft admonifh you, that it was not the Nicene Crede (as ye write) made at Conftantinople that was apointed to be reherfed of the people. The which is fuller then the Nicene, for auoiding of certain herefies: fuller I fay, as cōcerning Chrift conceiued and incarnated of the holy ghoft (which thing I cā not tel how or why your Apologie, as I haue faid, hath left out) with fome other like. This Councell then hath faid fomewhat to you for your tranflation, and muche more for your wicked and heretical meaning, to conuey from the bleffed Sacrament, the reall prefence of Chriftes very bodie.

But now M. Horne take you ād your Madge good hede, and marke you wel, whether ye and your fect be not of the Arrians generation, whiche being Prieftes, contrary to the

Canons

Tom.2.
Cōc.p.168
col.1.b.

Pag 168.
Ante cō-
muni-
cationem
Corporis
Chrifti.
Pag.169.
Secundum
formam
cōcilij Cō-
ftantinop,
Symbolū
fidei reci=
tetur.
Et mox.
Et ad chri
fti corpus
et fangui
nē prali-
bandū, pe-
ctora po-
pulorū fi-
de purifi-
cata ac-
cedant.
Deijs fym-
bolis vide
tom.2.
Concil.
pag 392.

Canons of the Church, which thei as mightely contemned
as ye do, kept company with their wiues, but yet with such
as they laufully maried, before they were ordered Priestes.
Who returning to the Catholike faith frō their Arianisme,
woulde faine haue lusked in their leacherie, as they did before being Arians. Which disorder this Coūcel reformeth.
The same Councell also cōmaundeth, *that the decrees of all*
Councels, yea and the decretall Epistles of the holye Bishops of
Rome, should remaine in their full strength . Bicause forsoth
by Arrians they had before ben violated and neglected , as
they are at this day by you and your fellowes vtterly despi-
sed and contemned. So like euer are yong heretikes to the
olde. *Vnū nôris, omnes nôris.* And this is M. Horne, one part
of the repairing, and the making (as you call it) of a newe
fourme of the Church discipline, ye spake of.   But for the
matter it selfe, ye are al in a mūmery, and dare not rub the
galde horse on the backe for feare of wincing.   Now all in
an il time haue ye put vs in remembrance of this Councel :
for *you must be Canonically punished* , and Maistres Madge
must be *solde of the Bishoppes,* and the *price must be geuen to*
the poore.   I woulde be sory shee should heare of this geare :
and to what pitifull case ye haue brought her by your own
Coūcel. Marke now your margent as fast and as solemne-
ly as ye will with the note : *The duetifull care of a Prince a-*
*boute Religion:*with the note of a *Princes speciall care for his*
subiects, and with such like. I do not enuie you such notes.
In case now, notwithstanding ye are so curstly handeled of
King Richaredus and his Councell , ye be content of your
gentle and suffering nature, to beare it al well : and wil for
al this stil goe forward to set foorth his Primacie, be it so.
What can ye say therein further ? I perceiue then ye make

The Pro=
testantes
follovve
the Arriās
in their
carnal le=
cherie.
Can.5.
Tolet.3.c.1

M.Horns
Madge
must be
sold for a
slaue by
this Coū=
cel which
M.Horne
him selfe
allegeth.
Illi vero
canonicè,
mulieres
quidē ab
Episcopis
venūden-
tur.et pre-
tiũ ipsum
pauperi=
bus irro-
getur.
Canon.5.

great

A greate
difference
betvvixt
the fub-
fcription
of them-
ptrours
ãd of the
Bifhops.
Sext.Syn.
Conft.act.
17.&.18.
Georgius
miferante
Deo,&c.
Definens,
fubfcripfi.
Subfcrip-
tio pijß.&
chrift,di-
lecti Cõft.
imperat.
Legimus
et cõfenti-
mus.act 18
Vt patet in
dict.tom 2
Concil. &
Ifidor.vi-
del. Aera.
627. Hoc
eft.an.589
Bed.t.li.1.
cap.23.in
Hift.gent.
Augl.

great and depe accompt that he fubfcribed before theCoũ-
cell,wherof I make as litle : confidering here was no newe
mater defined by him or the Fathers, but a cõfirmation and
a ratification made of the firſt foure Councels. Which the
King ftrengtheneth by all meanes he coulde , yea with the
fubfcription of his owne hande,becaufe the other Kings his
predeceſſours had ben Arians . Otherwife in the firſte.7.
Generall Councelles, I finde no fnbfcription of the Emperours, but onely in the fixte, proceding from the faid caufe
that this dothe, that is, for that his predeceſſours were heretikes, of the herefie of the Monothelites : but not proceding altogether in the fame order.For the Emperour there
fubfcribeth after al the Bifhops,faying onely : *We haue read*
*the Decree and doe confent.*But the Bifhop of Cõftantinople
faith: *I George by the mercy of God Bifshop of Conftantinople to*
my definitiue fentence,haue fubfcribed: after the fame fort o-
ther Bifhops alfo fet to their handes. And this was becaufe
the mater was there finally determined againſt the Mono-
thelites.In cafe this fubfcriptiõ wil not ferue the mater,M.
Horne hath an other helpe at hand:yea he hath S.Gregory
him felf,*that* (as he faith)*cõmendeth Richaredus for his gouern-*
mẽt in caufes Ecclefiaftical: and this is fet in the margent as a
weighty mater,with an other foorthwith as weighty , that
this Richaredus *called Councels, and gouerned Ecclefiafticall*
caufes,without any doing of Pope Gregory therin. But by your
leaue,both your notes are both fólifh and falfe.Folifh I fay,
for how fhuld Pópe Gregory be a doer with hĩ being at that
time no Pope,the coũcel being kept in the time of Pelagiʼ.2.
S.Gregories predeceſſour, in the yere.589. as it appereth by
the accõpt of Ifidorʼ liuing about that time: and S.Gregory
was made Pope in the yere.592.by the accompt of S.Bede.

　　　　　　　　　　　　　　　　　　　　　Falfe,

Falfe, I fay : for Richaredus called not Councelles, but one onely Councel: yea and falfe againe. For there was no go-uernement Ecclefiafticall in Richaredus doings. Neyther is there any fuch word in the whole Councel by M. Horn alleaged, nor any thing that may by good confequence in-duce fuch gouernement. I fay then further, ye doe mofte impudently, in going about to make your Readers belieue, that Richaredus and other Princes after him, were take for Supreme heades of the Church, till now in thefe later dai-es: and moft blafphemoufly in calling the Pope, for this ma-ter, the childe of perdition. As wel might you for this caufe haue called Gregorie fo too. Who is furnamed, as ye here write, the Great. But God wotteth , and the more pitie, not very great with you and your fellowes. Of al bookes, his writinges beare moft ful and plaine teftimonie , for the Popes fingular præeminence : whiche thing is in an other place by me largely proued, that though the matter here femeth to require fomewhat to be faid, I neede not fay any thing, but onely remit the Reader to that place where he fhal finde that S. Gregorie practifed this Supreme authori-tie, as wel in Spain, as other. where, throughout the whole Chriftened world. But what faith S. Gregorie? Forfothe that the King Richaredus *by his carefull and continuall prea-ching, brought Arrians into the true faith.* S. Gregorie faith wel. And yet you wil not (I trow) fay : The Prince himfelf preached in pulpit to the Arrians. What then? Verelye that which he did by his Clergie , and to the which he was a godly promoter, that he is faied to doe him felfe.   As to preache, to conuert heretiques, to decree this or that , and briefely to gouerne in caufes Ecclefiaftical. All which the Prince in his owne perfon or of his owne authority, neuer

See the 4. Article the 9. pag. and cer-tain folo-vving.

b   doth.

dothe. But by his furderance such things being done, he is saied sometimes (as here of Saint Gregorye) to doe them him selfe.

We might now passe to the next mater, sauing that as ye without any good occasion or bettering of your cause, bring in that Richaredus woorked these thinges without Pope Gregorie : So it may be feared, ye haue a woorse meaning, and that ye doe this altogeather craftely to ble-mishe and deface Sainte Gregorye with the ignoraunte Reader.　Els tell me to what purpose write ye, that Saint Gregorye was *ashamed of him selfe, and his owne slacknesse?* Why bringe you in these woordes of Sainte Gregorye, *What shall I aunsweare at the dreadfull doome, when youre excellencye shall lead with you flockes of faithfull ones, which ye haue broughte into the true faithe, by careful and continuall preachinges?* I muste then either to refourme your ig-norance (if ye knew it not before) or to preuent your rea-ders circumuention by your wilye handeling of the mater, like to be perchaunce miscaried : if ye knewe it before, ad-monish you and him, that this is spoken of S. Gregorye in deede, but as proceeding from a maruelouse humilitye and lowlines.

In like maner as he wrote to Sainte Auguftine oure A-poftle in the commendation of his doings, wherein yet vn-doubtedly he was a great doer him felfe many wayes, as by the Hiftorie of Bede clerely appeareth. Otherwife though Richaredus doings be moft glorioufe and worthy of perpe-tuall renoune, yet fhal S. Gregory match him or paffe him. Neither fhal he altogether be voide of his worthy comen-dation, concerning his care for the refourming of Spaine, and repreffing of herefies there, either by his authority, or

by

by his learned woorkes. Verely Platina witnesseth, that by the meanes of this Gregorie, *the Gothes returned to the vnite of the Catholike faithe.* Whiche appeareth not at that time any otherwhere, then in Spaine

Plat.in Greg. 1.

Hearken farder what Nauclerus one that you ofte reherse in this your booke, writeth of him: *Insuper Beatus Gregorius, &c. Beside this Saint Gregorie compelled the Ligurians, the Venetians, the Iberians, which had confessed their schisme, by their libell to receiue the Decrees of the Councell of Chalcedo : and so broughte them to the vnitye of the Churche. He reduced them from Idolatrye, partely by punnishmente, partlye by preaching, the Brucians, the people of Sardinia, and the husbandmenne of Campania. By the good and mightye authoritie of his writings, and by Ambassadours sente in conueniente time, he sequestred from the bodye of the Churche, the Donatiste Heretiques in Affrique, the Maniches in Sicilie, the Arrians in Spaine, the Agnoites in Alexandria. Onely the Heresie of the Neophites in Fraunce, rising by Symoniacall bribes, as it were by so manye rootes, was spreade farre and wide : againste the whiche he valiauntlye foughte, labouring mightelye againft it, to the Queene Brunechildis, and to the Frenche Kinges Theodoricus, and Theodobertus, till at the lengthe a Generall Councell beinge summoned, he obteined to haue it vtterlye banned and accurfed.* This saith Nauclerus of other Countries.

Now what nede I speake of our Realme, the matter being so notoriouse, that by his good meanes, by his studye and carefulnes, we were brought from most miserable idolatrie to the faith of Chrifte? And therefore as our Venerable Countreyman Bede writeth, we maye well and oughte

b ij   to

S. Gregorie our Apoſtle.
lib. 2. c. 1. to call him our Apoſtle. *Rectè noſtrum appellare poſſumus & debemus Apoſtolum. Quia cum, &c.* For, ſaith he, wheras he had the chiefe Biſshoprike in all the worlde, and was the chiefe Ruler of the Churches, that long before were conuerted to the faithe, he procured oure Nation, that before that time was the Idols ſlaue, to be the Church of Chriſt. So that we may well vſe that ſaiyng taken from the Apoſtle. All were it, that he were not an Apoſtle to other, yet is he our Apoſtle. We are the ſeal of his Apoſtleſship in our Lord God.* It appeareth Greg. lib. 2 cap. 36. that S. Gregorie had to doe in Ireland alſo by his Eccleſiaſtical authoritie. Thus much haue I here ſpoken of S. Gregorie, either neceſſarily, or (as I ſuppoſe) not altogether without good cauſe: Surely not without moſt deape harte griefe, to conſider how farre we are gon from the learning, vertue, and faith, whiche we nowe almoſt one thouſande yeares paſt, receiued at this Bleſſed mans handes. Which altogether, with our newe Apoſtle M. Horne heere, is nothing but *Groſſe ignorance.* And this bleſſed and true Apoſtle of our Engliſh Nation, *no better then the child of perdition.* That is, as he meaneth in dede, a plaine Antichriſte. I pray God, ones open the eyes of our Coūtrie, to ſee who is in dede the true Antichriſt, and who are his meſſengers and forerunners, thereby carefully and Chriſtianly to ſhun as well the one as the other. Chriſt is the Truth it ſelfe, as him ſelfe hath ſaid. Who then is more nere Antichriſte, then the teacher of Vntruthes? And what a huge number hath M. Horne heaped vs vppe in that, hitherto hath bene anſwered, being litle more then the third part of his boke? Yea in this very Diuiſion how doe they muſter? Some of them haue already ben touched. But now to the reſt more at large, let vs ouerrunne the Diuiſion ſhortly againe.

First

First besides his false translation, putting for repairing the order of Ecclesiasticall discipline, *to make a new fourme thereof*, as though that King altered the old Religion of his realme, and placed a newe neuer vsed before in Christes Churche, as M. Horne and his fellowes haue done in our Countrie, beside this pety sleight, and diuers other before noted, he hath so maimed and mangled the wordes of King Richardus (wherein the whole pithe of this Diuision resteth) to make some apparence of his pretensed Primacie, that it would lothe a man to see it, and weary a man to expresse it. Namely in the text where his Note standeth of a *Princes speciall care for his subiectes.* The whole woordes of the King are these : *The care of a King ought so farre to be extended and directed, vntill it be found to receiue the full measure of age and knowledge. For as in worldly things the Kings power passeth in glorie, so oughte his care to be the greater for the welth of his subiectes. But now (moste holy Priestes) we bestow not onely our diligeuce in those matters whereby oure subiectes may be gouerned and liue most peaceablye, but also by the helpe of Christe, we extend our selues to thinke of heauenly matters, and we labour to knowe how to make our people faithfull. And verely if we ought to bend all our power to order mens maners, and with Princely power to represse the insolency of the euill, if we ought to geue all ayde for the encrease of peace and quiet, muche more we ought to study, to desire and thinke vppon godly things, to looke after high matters, and to shew to our people being now brought from errour, the trueth of cleare light. For so he dothe whiche trusteth to be rewarded of God with aboundant reward. For so he dothe , which aboue that is comitted vnto him doth adde more, seing to such it is said, what so euer thou spendest more, I, when I come againe, will recom-*

M.Horns
Vntruths
laid forth.

Tom.2.
Conc.pag.
167.col.2.

Luc.10.

b iij   *pense*

*pence thee.*This is the whole and ful talke of Richaredus the king to the Councel touching his duety full care aboute religion.

Compare this, gentle Reader, with the broken and mangled narratiõ of M. horne, and thou fhalt fee to the eye his lewde pelting and pelting lewdneſſe. Thou fhalt fee, that the king protefted his care in gods matters to be (not his dew charge and vocatiõ, as a king)but an additiõ aboue that which was commytted wnto him, and to be a work of ſupererogatiõ, and that he extéded him felfe of zeale aboue that, which his duety ãd office required. Al which M. Horn left out, bycaufe he knewe it did quite ouerthrowe his purpofe.

He faieth againe of kyng Richaredus, *that he decreed in the Councel of his oẁne Authority, commaundyng the biſſhops to fee it obſeyued:* which wordes alfo he hath caufedto be printed in a diftinct lettre, as the wordes of his Author alleaged. But they are his owne wordes, and do proceede of his owne Authority, not to be found in the whole proceſſe of the Kings Oration to the Councell, or in the Coũcel it felfe. But contrariwife the Councell expreſſely faith of this Decree: *Confultu pÿſsimi & gloriofiſsimi Richaredi Regis conftituit Synodus*. The Synode hath appointed or decreed by the aduife of the moft godly and glorioufe King Richaredus. The Synode M. Horne, made that Decree by the aduife of the King. The king made it not *by his own authority commaunding.&c.* as you very Imperiouſly do talke. Againe where you faie that S. Gregory did *much commend the carefull gouernemeut of Princes in caufes of Religion*, S. Gregory fpeaketh not of any fuche gouernement at all. It is an other of your Vntruthes.

Cõcil. Toⁱ let.3. Cap 2. Tom.2. pag.169. Col. 1.

Vide Gre= gor.lib.7. epiſt.126.

Laſt

Laſt of all, where Saint Gregorie ſayeth of humilitie, as we haue before declared, to the king : *Et ſi vobiſcum nihil egimus* : Although we haue done nothing with you : You to amplifie the matter , enlardge your tranſlation with a very lying liberalitie, thus. *Although I haue medled and don nothing at all with you, doing this altogether without mee.* For theſe wordes , *medle, at all* , and *dooing this altogeather without me* , is altogeather without and beyond your Latine of Saint Gregorie.   Whome you ouerreache exceeding much : Making him not ſo muche as to meddle with the Kings doings, and that the king did altogeather without him : Which yet (if Nauclerus your common alleaged Author be true of his woorde) did verye muche with the King, and furdered many wayes the conuerting of the Arrians in Spaine to the Catholique faith.

But ſo it is. As in al your proufes you ouerreach mightely the force of your examples, côcluding *Supreme gouernmente in all cauſes,* when the Argumente procedeth of no gouernemente at all , but of execution, and ſo foorth, euen ſo in your tranſlations (wherein yet you looke ſingularlye to be credited, ſcarſe ones in tenne leaues , bringing one ſentence of Latine) you ouer reache marueilouſlye your originall Authorities.

Suche is your vntrue and falſe dealing, not onely here, but in a manner throughout your whole booke .   And nowe to ende this Seconde booke , with a flouriſhe of Maiſter Iewels Rhetorique, to ſweete your mouth at the ende Maiſter Horne , that ſo with the more courage we may proceede (after a pauſe vppon this) to the Thirde and Fourthe, let me ſpurre you a queſtion.

Nauclerus vbi ſupra:& Platina.

What

What M. Horne? Is it not possible your doctrine may stande without lyes? So many Vntruthes in so litle roome, without the shame of the worlde, without the feare of God? Where did Christe euer commaunde you to make, your Prince the supreme gouernour in all causes? *By what Commission, by what woordes?* Or if Christ did not, who euer els cōmaunded you so to do? *What lawe? What Decree, what Decretall, what Legantine, what Prouinciall? But what a wonderfull case is this?* The Supreame gouernemente of Princes in al causes Ecclesiastical, *that we must nedes* swere vnto by booke othe, yea and that *we must nedes* belieue in conscience, to be *so auncient, so vniuersal, so Catholique, so cleere, so gloriouse, can not now be founde,* neither in the olde Law, nor in the new, nor by anye one example of the first 600. yeares.

∴

THE THIRDE BOOKE: DIS-
PROVING THE PRETENSED PRACTISE OF
Ecclesiastical gouernmēt in Emperors and Kings as wel
of our own Countre of Englande, as of Fraunce and
Spayne, in these later .900 .yeres from the
tyme of Phocas to Maximilian next
predecessour to Charles the.
V. of famous me-
mory.

M. Horne. The.79.Diuision. Fol.47.b.

Next after Sabinianus *, an obscure, Pope, enemy and successour to this* Gregory *, succeded* Bonifacius. 3. *VVho although he durst not in playne dealing denie, or take from the Emperours, the authoritie and iurisdiction in the Popes election, and other Churche matters: yet he vvas the first that* (.228.) *opened the gappe thereunto: for as* Sabel. *testifieth, vvith vvhom agree all other vvriters, for the moste parte:* This Bonifacius immediatly vpon the entraunce into his Papacy, dealte with Phocas, to winne that the Church of Rome, might (.229.) be head of all other Churches, the which he hardely obteined, bicause the Grecians did chalenge that prerogatiue for Constantinople. *After he had obteyned this glorious and ambitious title, of the bloudy tyrant* Phocas, and that vvith (.230.) *no smal bribes: like vnto one that hauing a beame in his ovvn eie, vvent about to pul the mote out of his brothers, he made a decree,* that euery one should be accursed, that prepared to him selfe a way into the Papacy, or any other Ecclesia- stical dignity, with frendship or bribery. Also that the bisshops in euery city, should be chosen by the people and Clergy: and that the election should be good, so that the Prince of the City did approue the party by the chosen, ād the Pope addig his au- thority therto, had ones said, volumus & iubemus: we wil and commaunde. *But saith* Sabell, both these decrees are abolished.

The firſt Chapter. Of Phocas the Emperour, and of Bo-
nifacius the. 3. Pope.

Stapleton.

AVING nowe good reader, paſſed the firſt
ſixe hundred yeares, and hauing anſwered to
M. Hornes arguments, for ſuch proufes as he
pretendeth to ſerue him, for thinges don within thoſe. 6 oo. yeares: I am in a great doubte and
ſtaye withe my ſelfe, what order to take for the reſidewe
of myne anſwere. We haue gone ouer litle more then one
half, of that parte of M. Hornes booke, wherein he taketh
vpon him to be the challenger, and an apponente : and yf
we weighe the nomber of yeares, in the which M. Horne
taketh his large race and courſe, they yet remayne almoſte
a thowſande to thoſe that be alredy paſſed. Yf we meaſure
the leaues, almoſt the one halfe reſt behinde to the nomber
of. 42. Beſide the remnante of his booke, wherein he plaith
the defendants parte. I ſpeake thus much for this conſideration. Yf I ſhoulde largely and copiouſlye anſwere the reſidewe, as I haue begonne, and fullye vnfolde his fonde
follies, confuting euerye point, the booke woulde wexe to
bigge and huge. On the other ſyde, yf I ſhould lightlye and
breiflye paſſe yt ouer, perchaunce M . Horne woulde
bragge and ſaye he were not, no nor coulde be anſwered.

But yet bethinkinge my ſelfe well vppon the matter,
the compendiouſe waye ſeemeth to me at this tyme
beſte. Wherein I could be ſo ſhorte and compendiouſe, that
with one lyne, I ſhoulde ſufficiently diſcharge my ſelfe for
the whole anſwere, in ſaying ſhortly, but truely, that there
is not, no not one onely authority apte and fyt to cõclude
his purpoſe. I coulde alſo ſhifte him of an other waye : and
becauſe

becaufe M. Iewel with other his fellowes groundeth him
felf vppon yt, as a good and a peremptorye exception , I
might boldly fay, M. Horne, al your proufes after Gregory
come to late:your. 600.yeres are empted,fpente,and gone.

Again I might and truly,feing that his pretenfed proufes,
of the firft fixe hundred yeares are fo faint and weake, yea
feing that he is qnyte borne downe,with his own authors,
in the fame booke, chapter,leafe,and fomtyme line to,that
him felf alleageth: fay , that either it is moft likelye,that he
cannot bring any good or fubftaricial matter, for the latter
900. yeares, or whatfo euer yt be , it muft yeld and geue
place, to the Fathers of the firft fixe hundred yeares. And
with this anfwere might we,contemning and neglecting al
his long ragmans rolle,that hereafter followeth , fet vppon
him an other while,and fee how valiantly he wil defende
his owne heade . Which God wote he will full faynte-
lye doe. Well I will not be fo precife, as to let yt alone altogether , but I fhall take the meane, and as I thinke , the
moft allowable way: neither anfwering all at length , and
ftitch by ftitch with diligence, as I haue hitherto vfed, nor
leauing all , but taking fome aduifed choice. Wherefore
yf hereafter he bringe any accuftomed or ftale marchandize , yt fhall paffe: but yf any fyne frefhe,farre fought,and
farre bowght marchandize come , we will geue him the
lokinge on , and now and then cope withe him to . Goe
to then M.Horne,take your weapon in your hand againe,
and befturre your felf with yt , edglynge, or foyning with
the befte aduantage ye can.

The or=
der to be
take here
after in
anfwe=
ring the
refide we
of M.
Hornes
booke.

Ye fay then Bonifacius the thirde opened the gappe to
take away from th'Emperour the authority and Iurifdictio
of the popes election:Ye fay it,but ye doe not,nor ca proue

c ij   yt:Ye

it. Ye say that he *wonne of Phocas, that Rome might be head of all Churches*, meaning thereby, as appereth well by that which followeth, ād by M. Iewel and your other fellowes, that it was not takē so before. Whereof I haue alredy proued the contrary by the Councell of Chalcedo: by Victor, yea the Emperours Valentinian and Iustinian: and otherwise to. But this you reporte vntruly. For the Popes suyte was not, that his See might be the head of al Churches, but *that the see of S. Peter which is the head of all Churches, might be so called and take of al mē*. And the reason is added by Ado, Paulus Diaconus, Beda, Martinus, and others, *bicause the See of Constantinople, wrote her selfe at that time the Chiefe of all others*. This newe attempt, caused the Pope to make this suyt. Not that either it should be so (for so it had bene without the Emperours Autorytie) or that then it was first called so. Ye say he *wanne this gloriouse and ambitiouse title with no small brybes*. Ye say it, but ye neither proue it, nor can proue yt. And sure I am, that none of your authours ye name in the margent, sayth so. Neither do I yet see, wheruppon ye shuld grounde your self, onlesse it be vppon your straunge grammer, turning *Magna contentione*, with great contention, or with much adoe, into *no small brybes*: as ye did lately *conuenit*, into *oportet*. And for this that ye call this a gloriouse and ambitiouse tytle, obtayned by this Bonifacius: truth it is, that as this tytle was euer due to the Church of Rome, and confessed as I haue said, by Councels, Emperours and other longe before the time of this Phocas or Bonifacius, so neither this pope, nor anie other of his successours vsurped or vsed it, as a tytle. These be your manifold falshods M. Horne, lapped vp in so fewe lynes. After your lewde vntruthes, foloweth a copie of your singular witte.

For

Plat. in Lonisa. 3.

Ado is Chroni.
Beda de sex Aeta.
Martinus Polonus.
Paulus Diaconus.

Sabel. Aenea. 8. l. 6.
Platina, in Boni. 2.
Paul. Dia. de gestis Logobar. li. 4. c. 11.
Naucler.
Genr. 21.
Martinus Polon. Volateranus.

For to what ende,with what wifedome,or with what be-
nefytte of your caufe recyte you two decrees of this Bonifacius? I will geue yowe leaue to breath on the matter,
leaft vppon the foden you might be apalled with the que-
ftion.The beft anfwere,I wene,you coulde make,woulde
be to fay, that hereby appereth the Ambition of pope Bonifacius, 3. And then to proue that Ambition in him , by
thefe decrees,I thinke, it would trouble you much more.
For in the one he expreffely decreeth againft Ambition,in
the other he alloweth the confent of lay princes in a biffhops election.But it is wel,that as Sabel. faieth: *Both thefe
decrees are abolijfhed.* Wherof it will folowe,if that be true,
that if the decrees were good, and made for you , then yet
they continewed not , but were abolifhed . If they were
naught,and made againft the pope,yet the faulte was foone
amended.Thus how fo euer it fal out,you fee howe wifely
ãd to what great purpofe you haue alleaged thofe decrees.

M. Horne. The.80.Diuifion. Fol.48.a.

Novve began this matter to brue by litle and litle , firft he obteined to
(.231.)be the chiefe ouer al the Bifhops, then to couer vice vvith vertue,and
to hide his ambicion,he condemned al ambicion in labouring Spirituall pro-
mocion,and in the election of Bifhoppes,vvhere the confirmation before vvas
in the Emperours:bicaufe the Emperour gaue him an Inche,he toke an ell,
bicaufe he had giuen him a foote,he vvould thruft in the vvhole body, and
tourne the right ovvner out. For(.232.)leuing out the Emperour,he putteth
in the Princes of the Cities , from vvhome he might as eafely aftervvardes
take avvay,as for a fheuve he gaue falfely that unto them , that vvas none
of his to giue:graunting vnto them the allovvance of the election:but to him
felf the authority of ratifiyng , or infringing the fame , choofe them vvhether they vvould allovve it or no. And to fhevve vvhat authoritie he vvould
referue to him felfe , borovving of the tyrant , fpeaking in the finguler
nombre . Sic volo,fic iubeo,fo wil I,fo do I commaunde: for the
more magnificence in the plurall nombre , he princely lappeth vp all the

The 231.
vntruth,
as before.

The 232.
vntruth.
T hempe-
rour by
that de-
cree is
not left
out,

c iij   matter

* Novve
M.Horne
doth his
kinde.

Sabel.

The. 233.
vntruth.
4 popes
came be-
twene ād
25. yeres.

* It was
fo,vi,non
iure,by
force not
by right.

Fol. 38.

matter vvith volumus & iubemus , we will and commaunde: *VVhich vvordes, like the Lavve of the Medes and Perſians , that may not be reuoked,if they once paſſe through the* * *Popes holy lippes , muſt nedes ſtand, allovve or not allovve, vvho ſo liſt,vvith full authoritie the matter is quite daſhed. But thankes be to God for al this* (the decre is aboliſhed) *folovveth immediatly. For* (.233.) *ſhortly after,* Iſacius *the Emperours Lieutenant in Italy, did confirme and ratiſie the election of* Seuerinus *the firſt of that name, for ſaith* Platina. The electiō of the Pope made by the Clergie and people in thoſe daies, * was but a vaine thing, onleſſe the Emperour , or his Lieutenant had confirmed the ſame.

Stapleton.

WHeras ye ſay this Bonifacius lefte out the Emperour (who had the confirmation of them before) in his decree concernyng the election of Biſhops and put in the princes of the citie , and gaue falſlie that to them,which was none of his to geue:yf ye mark the words of the decree wel,the Emperour is not left out,but lefte in as good caſe as he was before. Onleſſe ye think the Emperour is prince of no city:or that all cities were at this tyme vnder the Emperour,wheras euen in our Europa,the Emperour had nothing to doe, in England,Fraunce,Germanie Spaine,no nor in manie places of Italie. And I muſt put you in remembraunce , that before this tyme , when Iuſtinian was Emperour,king Theodatus did confirme the electiō of pope Agapetus, as you reherſe out of Sabellicus . Neither did the pope as of him ſelf,and of newe geue anie authority to princes in election more thē they had before. But by his decree renewed the old order of electiō of biſhops. Which was wont to paſſe,by the cōſent of the clergie,prince, and people,with the popes confirmation afterward:Therefore ye ſay vntruly ſurmiſing that the decree of Bonifacius,was
in this

in this poynt immediatly abolifhed . Verely your example
of Ifacius the Emperours Lieutenāt litle ferueth your purpofe, who fhortly after, you fay, *confirmed and ratified the election of Pope Seuerinus.* For firft betwene this confirming of
Seuerinus , and the deathe of this Bonifacius, foure Popes
came betwene, and wel nere. 30. yeres. Againe as touching
this ratifieng and confirmation that Ifacius the Emperours
Lieutenāt practifed, will you fee how orderly it proceded?
Verely by mere violence , by fpoyling the treafure of the
Church of S. Iohn Lateranes. At the diftribution of which
treafure afterwarde fo orderly obtayned by the Emperour
Heraclius, the Saracens fel out with the Chriftiās, (becaufe
they had no parte thereof with the Greke and Romayn
Souldiours) forfoke the Emperours feruice , got from the
Empire Damafcus, al Aegypt, and at légth Perfia it felf, and
embraced Mahomet then lyuing and his doctrine , which
fynce hath fo plaged all Chriftendome. So well profpered
the doinges of this Ifacius: and fuch holfome examples M.
Horne hath piked out to furnifhe his imagined fupremacy
withall.

Bonifa. 4.
Theodat.
Lonifa. 5.
Honor. 1.

Sabellicus
Aenead. 8.
lib. 6. pag.
535.

M. Horne. The. 81. Diuifion. pag. 43. a

Sifenandus *the king of Spain, calleth forth of all partes of his dominions the Bifhops to a City in Spaine, called* Toletum . *The purpofe and
maner of the kynges doynges in that councel, the Bifhoppes them felues fet
forth, firft as they affirme:* They affemble together by the præcepts
and cōmaundement of the king, to confult of certaine orders
of difcipline for the Church, to refourme the abufes that wete
crept in about the Sacrámétes ād the maners of the Clergy. *The
king vvith his nobles, cōmeth into the cōncel houfe: He exhorteth thē to care
ful diligēce, that therby al errors and abufes, may be vvypt a vvay clere out of
the Churches in Spayn. They folovve the kinges (. 234.) directiō, ād agree vpō
many holfom rules. VVhē they haue cōcluded,* thei befech the kíg to cō-
tinu his regimēt, to gouern his peple with iuftice ād godlines.

And

Tol. 4.

The. 234.
vntruth.
The king
folovved
their dire
ctiō, not
they the
Kinges in
caufes ece
clefiafti-
cal.

The.235. vntruthe. Not simply agreed vpon, but fully and finally had decreed and determined. Tol. 5. Tol. 6.

Definitis itaque etc. Tol. 7.

The 236. vntruthe. By the bishops decree not by the kinges decree. *Decreto nostro sancimus.*

The.237. vntruthe. For not by his Supreme Authority, *Studio Serenissimi Regis* By the fauor and endeuour &c. Tol. 8.

* In that Othe, there vvas, I vvarrant you, no Supreme gouernmēt &c.

* By the vertu of a Canon made in Tolet. 7.

The.238. vntruthe. Not to assiste, but in al poīts to obey ād folovv the ordinaunces of the Synod.

The 239. vntruthe. No such matter in the Councel. Tol. 9. Tol. 10.

And vvhē the King had geuē his assent, to the rulers of discipline, vvhich they had (.235.) agreed vppon., they subscribed the same vvith their ovvn handes.

The like Synode Chintilianus *king of Spaine*, did conuocate at Toletum, for certain ceremonies, orders, and discipline, vvhich vvas confirmed by his precept and (.236.) decree, in the first yeere of his reigne. And an other also by the same king, and in the same place, and for the like purpose, vvas called and kept the second yere of his reigne.

Chinasuindus *King of Spaine*, no lesse careful for Church matters and Religion, than his predecessours, (.237.) appointeth his bishops to assemble at Toletum in conuocation. and there to consult for the stablishing of the faith, and Church discipline, vvhich they did.

Reccesiunthus *King of Spaine, commaunded his Bishops to assemble at Toletum, in the first yere of his reigne, and there appointed a Synode, vvherein besides the Bishops and Abbottes, there sate a great company of the noble men of Spaine. The Kinge him selfe came in amongest them, he maketh a graue and verye godlye exhortation vnto the vvhole Synode, he professed hovve careful he is, that his subiectes should be rightly instructed in the true faith, and Religion. He propoundeth the fourme of an * Othe vvhich the clergy and others of his subiectes vvere * vvonte to receiue, for the assurance of the Kings saulsty. He exhorteth them to ordeine sufficiently for the maintenance of godlines and iustice. He moueth his nobles that they vvill (.238.) assist and further the good and godly ordinaunces of the Synode. He promiseth that he vvil by his princely authority, ratifie and maineteine vvhat so euer they shal decree, to the furtherance of true Godlinesse, and Religion. The Synode maketh ordinaunces: the clergy, and nobility there assembled subscribeth them: and the Kinge confirmeth the same vvith his (.239.) royal assent and authority. He called tvve other Synodes in the same place for such like purpose, in the seuenth and eyght yeeres of his reigne.*

Vitalia-

*The 2. Chapter : Of other kinges of Spayne , and of
the Toletane Councels holden in their
raignes.*

Stapleton.

WE are yet ons againe come to Spayne : and we
haue nowe seuen councels summoned there, by
theis foure kings, that M. Horn here nameth. But
surely there is nothing, wherby to fasten this primacy vppon them. But here are manie playne and open things, that
do so blemish and spotte M. Horn, and his Madge and their
childrē with a most shamful reproche of perpetual infamy,
as theis coūcels here by him alleaged, may seme to remayne
in this his boke lyke the salt Stone, wherinto Lothes wyfe
was turned: that is, as a perpetual monumente of his shame
and dishonestie for euer. For where is the clericall crowne
that theis fathers require , in M. Hornes head ? What a
nomber of decrees appeare in theis councelles by M.
Horne rehersed againste the filthie fornication and mariage of such persons both men and wemen as had professed chastytie ? For the which *Potamius* the bishop of Bra-
carie is deposed: as was before *Saphoracus* (whome as ye
heard, M. Horne browght in for an example of his proufe)
in Fraunce . And here haue yowe , that not onlie Maistres Madge shall be a slaue , but her children to , thus in-
cestuously begotten, shall be made bond men. I praye yow
then what doe all theis Councells so muster here : onlesse
yt be to represente to vs, and to all that shall reade and see
M. Hornes boke hereafter, that he can alleage no Councells , but suche as make against him ? For beholde howe
manye thinges thefe Councells decree , of whiche M.
Horne , and his pewfelowes obserue neuer a white.

d   Els

Tol. 4. c. 4.
40.

Tol. 6. c. 6.
Tol. 8. c. 4
& 5. & 7
Tol. 9 c. 10
Tol. 10. c. 5.

Els where are the hallowed tapers to be vſed in the vigils
Tol.4.ca.2 decreed in thoſe Councels? Where is the Maſſe ſo expreſ-
Tol.7.ca.3 ly in thoſe Councells mentioned? Where is the order and
Tol.10. c.5 diſcipline decreed there againſt renegate Nonnes ? But to
let theſe things paſſe, what hath M. Horne, in al thoſe Coūcels to iuſtifie his primacy by? Verely in the firſt Councell
by him alleaged *Siſenandus* the kyng entring in to the Sy-
Tol. 4. in nod, began his talke to the biſhops, *Coram ſacerdotibus Dei*
prafat. *humi proſtratus* lyenge flat groueling on the ground before
the prieſtes of God. And in al that Councel he only exhorted the biſhoppes to make ſome decrees for reformation of
the Church. In the ſecond Councel by him alleaged, wher
he ſaieth *the Synod was confirmed by the princes commaunde-*
ment and decree, the wordes of the Councel write expreſ-
Tol.5.in ly the contrary . For the biſhops there of their concluſion
prafat. in that Synod do ſay. *Ex præcepto eius,& decreto noſtro ſanci-*
mus . This we ordaine by the kinges precept , and our decree . It is their decree M. Horne not the princes . And
Tol.6.c.2. ſo in the next Councell folowing, this Synod is called, *the*
biſhops conſtitution or decree : not the kinges . In the third
Councell by you alleaged, the biſhops confeſſe they were
Tol.6.in there aſſembled , *Regis ſalutaribus hortamentis abſque impe-*
prafat. *dimento.* by the holſome exhortations ofthe king without
let, ſignifiyng that by the kinges meanes they were quiet-
Tol.7.in ly aſſembled, and nothing els. As alſo in the next Councell
prafat. folowing they ſaie *Studio ſereniſsimi Regis &cæt.* by the endeuoure or fauoure of our moſt gratiouſe kinge . Nay in
the next Councel by you alleaged the kinge and his nobles
Tol.8.in confeſſe them ſelues ſubie ctes to the biſhops in ſuch mat-
prafat. ters. The king ſpeaking to the biſhops ſaieth . *En Reuerendi*
patres excelſiori mihi venerationis honore ſublimes, coram vo-
bis ad-

*bis aduenio &c.*Beholde Reuerend fathers,highe to me in a
more higher degree of honour,I come before you &c.And
touching his nobles(of whome,as M. Horne noteth, there
sate in the Synod a greate Company)he chargeth them,*vt* Ibidem.
nihil à consensu præsentium patrum sanctorúmque virorum a
*liorsum mentis ducant obtutum:*that in no point they should
direct their intention from the consent of the fathers and
holy men there present.In which words you see M. Horn,
his nobles were not there to gouerne,to direct,or to ouer-
rule the bishops : but rather to be gouerned directed, and
instructed of the bishoppes . And then as I saied , what is
there in all these Councells that may any waies furder this
vehement imaginatiō of your supremacy ? And how much
is there that ouerturneth the same , and establisheth the
Clergies supremacy, in such causes to them apperteyning?
For beside all this , lo what the Fathers in this very Coun- Tol.8.c.4.
cell do yet farder protest. They saie,*that Christ is the head,*
and the bishops the eyes . They say,that *they being of the hi-*
ghest doe rule by the highnes of theire order: and doe
gouerne the multitude of people , vnder their subiec- *Nam dùm secun-*
tion. And therevppon they say that Bisshoppes a- *dum Carnis assump=*
monge other their vertues , must excell in kepinge *tæ mysterium , Ec-*
of chastitye . And they further doe declare , that *clesiæ suæ fuerit dig=*
such as be faultye therein, shalbe thruste oute of *natus caput existere*
theire bisshoprikes . Yet one thinge there is , that *Christus , meritò*
semethe colowrablye to serue Maister Horne , *in membris eius in=*
that is, that the nobility also subscribeth . Which *tentio Episcoporū,of-*
should seame to imploye a voyce and a consente. *ficia peragere cerni-*
tur oculorum . Ipsi
d ij   Vnto *enim de sublimiori-*
bus, celsitudine ordinis regunt & disponunt subiectas multitudines plebium. Tol.8.ca.4.

Vnto the which our former anſwer may ſerue wel enough,
that the Biſſhops decreed and ruled, not the Nobles. Again
Vide Coc. 5 this may ſerue, that here in al theſe Councels, was no new
& Con. 8. matter of faith determined : but moſt of all this I am aſſured will ſerue, to ſay that many thinges were in thoſe Coūcels, enacted for the aſſurance and ſucceſsion of the Prince
and of other cyuill and polityke matters, to the whiche
noble men may ſubſcribe wel inowghe.

M. Horne. The. 82. Diuiſion. Fol. 45. a.

Diſtin. 63t . cap. 21.   Vitalianus *beinge choſen Pope, ſente his meſſengers vvith*
Synodicall letters (according to the cuſtome, *ſaith Gratian*)
to ſignifie vnto the Emperour of his election . In this Popes time
The. 242. vntruthe   (*ſaith the Pontificall*) *came Conſtantinus the Emperour to Rome,*
Slaunderous.   *vvhome this Pope vvith his cleargy, met ſixe myles out of the*
The. 241. vntruth.   *City, and did humbly receiue him . It is vvonderfull to conſider*
The Emperours   (*although the Hiſtorians, being Papiſtes for the moſt part,* (. 240.)
neuer had it.   *couer the matter ſo muche as may be*) *vvhat practiſes the Popes*
vſed to catche (. 241.) *from the Emperours to them ſelues, the ſu-*
The. 242. vntruthe   *periority in gouerning of Churche matters : vvhen they ſavve,*
Slaunderous and   *that by ſtovvte and braue preſumption, their ambitious appetites*
Rayling.   *could not be ſatiſſied, they turned ouer another leaſe, and coue-*
ring their (. 242.) *ambitious meaning vvith a patched cloke of*
The. 243. vntruth,   *humility and lovvlineſſe, they vvan muche of that, vvhich vvith*
He brought it not,   *pride and preſumption they had ſo often before this tyme attemp-*
but reſtored it &c.   *ted in vaine .*
As ſhal appeare.
The. 244. vntruthe   *VVith this vvily lovvlineſſe,* Donus *the next ſauing one to*
Notorious and fa-   Vitalianus, (. 243.) *brought vnder his obedience the Archebiſ-*
cing.   *ſhop of* Rauenna. *There had been an olde and* (. 244.) *continual*
The. 245. vntruthe   *diſſention betvvixt the Archebiſſhop of Rome, and the Arche-*
Their firſt ſtrife   *biſſhop of* Rauenna, *for the ſuperiority : The Rauennates ac-*
vvas not about the   *compting their ſea* (. 245.) *equall in dignity, and to ovve none*
Superiority : but   *obedience to the ſea of* Rome, *for they vvere not ſubiect there-*
about Tria capitula.   *vnto : To finiſhe this matter, and to vvinne the ſuperiority,* Do-
Pontificall.   nus *firſt*

nus firſt practiſed vvith Reparatus *the Archebiſhop of Ra-*
uenna, to geue ouer vnto him the ſuperiority, and become his o-
bedientiary, and that (as it may appeare by the ſequele) vvithout
the conſent of his Church. after the death of Reparatus, *vvhich*
vvas vvithin a vvhyle, Theodorus *a familiar friend to* Agatho *the Pope, and a ſtoute man, (vvhom (.246.)* Agatho *did ho-*
nour vvith his Legacy vnto the ſyxth general Councel at Côſtã-
tinople *) becauſe his Clergy vvoulde not vvayt on him on Chriſt-*
mas daye, ſolempnely (.247.) conducting him vnto the Churche
as the maner had been, did geue ouer the title, ãd mãde his ſea
ſubiect to the Pope for enuy ãd deſpite of his Clergy,
(ſaith Sabellicus*) vvherevvith the* Rauennates *vvere not con-*
tent, but being ouercome by the authority of the Emperour Conſtantin, *vvho much fauored* Agatho, *they bare it as patiently as*
they might. And Leo *the ſeconde, ſucceſſour to* Agatho, *made an*
ende hereof, (.248.) cauſing the Emperour Iuſtinian *to ſhevve*
great (.249.) cruelty vnto the vvhole Cyty of Rauenna, *and to*
Felix *their Biſhop, becauſe they vvould haue (.250.) recouered*
their olde liberty. And ſo this Pope Leo *by the commandement*
and povver of the Emperour Iuſtinian, *brought Rauenna vnder*
his obeiſance, as the Pontifical *reporteth. Theſe Popes through their*
feyned humility and obedience vnto the Emperours, vvhich vvas
but duty, vvan both much fauour and ayde at the Emperors hãdes,
to atchieue their purpoſe much deſired.

The 246. vntruth.
It vvas not that
Theodorus, but an
other, as ſhal ap-
peare.
The 247 vntruthe
as ſhal appeare.

The 248. vntruthe
groſſe ãd impudẽt,
as ſhal appeare.
The 249. vntruth,
It vvas becauſe thei
vvould maintayne
their olde diſobe-
dience.
The 250. vntruthe.
It vvas Conſtantin
not Iuſtinian.

The.3.Chapter: of Vitalianus, Donus *and* Leo *the.2.Biſhops*
of Rome: and howe the Church of Rauenna *was re-*
conciled to the See Apoſtolike.
Stapleton.

WHy Maiſter Horne? Put caſe the Pope ſignifieth
his election to the Emperour? Putte caſe the
Popes were ſometyme ſtowte and braue? And
ſometyme againe couered theyre ambitiouſe meaninge with a patched cloke of humilitye and lowe-
lines

lines? what yf the Churche of Rauenna after long rebellion became an obediētiarie to the apoſtolike ſee of Rome? This is the effect and contents almoſt of one whole leafe . What then I ſay ? Knitte vp I pray you,your concluſiō. *Ergo* a Prince of aRealme is ſupreame head in al cauſes eccleſiaſticall and tē-poral . Wel and clerckly knitte vp by my ſheathe. But Lorde what a ſorte of falſhods and follies are knitte vp together , in this your wiſe collection? As concerning the ſtowtnes and cloked humility of the Popes, your authours the Pontifical and Sa-bellicus write no ſuch thinge, but commend Vita-lian,Donus,Agatho,Leo,for very goodPopes, yea and for this their doing concerning the Church of Rauenna . Other writers commende theſe Popes alſo, for good and vertuouſe men . But I perceiue they are no meane or common perſons that muſt ſerue for witneſſes in your honorable conſiſtorie, your exceptions are ſo preciſe and peremptorye. Yet I beſeache you ſir, in caſe ye will reiecte all other,lette the Emperour Conſtantin himſelf ſerue the turne for this Vitalian. Who, at what tyme the biſhops of the eaſte being Monothelites , woulde not ſuffer Vitalians name to be reherſed according to the cuſtome in the Churche at Conſtantinople, did withſtande them . And why,thinke, you M. Horne? for any fayned holynes? No,no, but *propter collatam nobis charitatem ab eodem Vitaliano dum ſu-pereſſet in motione tyrannorum noſtrorum* . For his charity employed vppon vs , ſaieth the Emperour. whil he liued,in the remouing and thruſting out,of
thoſe

thofe that played the tyrants againſt vs . Why doe ye not bring forth your authours , to proue them diſſemblers and Hypocrites? but you ſhal proue this, when you proue your other ſaying, that there had ben *an old ād a cōtinual diſſenſiō* betwen theſe.ij.Churches,ād that the Rauēnates were not ſubiect to the ſee of Rome.This is wel to be proued , that they ought to haue bene ſubiect to the ſee of Rome, not onely by a common and an vniuerſal ſubiection , as to the ſee of all Churches:But as to theyre patriarchall ſee with-all.It is alſo aſwell to be proued,that in S. Gregories tyme, who died but.72.yeares before Donus was made pope,the Archebiſhops of Rauēna , acknowledged the ſuperioritie of the Church of Rome: as appereth by ſondrye epiſtles of S.Gregorie : and receyuid theire Palle from thenſe,a moſt certayne token of ſubiection : matters alſo being remoued from thenſe to the popes conſiſtory,yea the biſhop of Rauēna cōfeſsing that Rome was *the holy See that ſente to the vniuerſall Churche , her lawes ,* and prayeth S. Gregorie not onely to preſerue to the Church of Rauenua which pecu-liarly was vnder Rome, her olde priuileges: but alſo,to be-ſtowe greater priuileges vppon her . Wherein appereth your great vntruth,and ſoly withal:in that you ſaie, *there had bene an olde and continuall diſſention betwixt the Arche-biſhop of Rome and the Archebiſhop of Rauenna for the ſu perioritie .* Now you ſee the diſſenſion was not continual, nor very olde,it being ſo * late ſubiect to the See of Rome in the tyme of S.Gregory. Herein appereth alſo an other of your vntruths,where you alleadge out of the pontifical, that *Pope Leo brought Rauenna vnder his obeiſaunce.*For the pontificall ſaieth. *Reſtituta eſt Eccleſia Rauennas ſub ordina-tione Sedis Apoſtolica.*The Church of Rauenna was reſto-red or

Cōſtā-tin.5.

Vide Gre-gorium li. 2.epiſt.54 indict. 11. ad ioan. Epiſ. Ra-uen. li.4 epi. 54. ad Martianū epi.Rauē. epiſt. Io. Rauēnat. ad Grego. li.10. epi. 55. Qua vni-uerſali ec-cleſia iura ſua trāſ-mittit. Rauenna-ti eccleſia qua pecu-liariter ve ſtra eſt. * but 72. veres be-fore. Tom.2.Cō .p.279.b.

red or brought home againe vnder the ordering of the See Apoſtolike . In which wordes (if you had truly reported them) woulde eaſely haue appeared that the rebellioufe childe was then brought home again to obediéce,not that then firſt it was brought vnder ſubiection , as you vntruly and ignorantly ſurmiſe. You ſay alſo as ignorantly or as vntruly, that Theodorus the Archebiſhope of Rauenna who ſubmitted his Church to Pope Agatho , *was a familiar frēd to Agatho, and was of h m honoured with his legacie to the ſixt generall Councell of Conſtantinople* , intending thereby to make your reader thinke he did it of frendſhip or flattery, and not of duety. But your conceytes haue deceyued you. For the legat of pope Agatho in that Councel, ſo familiar a frend of his,and ſo much by him honoured,was one Theodorus, *presbyter Rauennas* , a prieſt of Rauenna : as both in

Iom.1.
Conc.pa.
277. a.&
282. b.

the life of Agatho,and in the very Councel it ſelf euidently appeareth. Neither could that prieſt be afterward the ſame biſhope that ſo ſubmitted him ſelf , for that ſubmiſsion was before the Councell, as in the life of Agatho it appeareth. So lernedly and truely, M. Horne in his talke procedeth.

　　With like truthe M. Horn telleth,that Theodorus made his ſee of Rauenna ſubiect to Rome , *bicauſe his clergy did not ſo ſolemnely conducte him to Church vpon Chriſtmas day, as the maner had been.* Would not a man here ſuppoſe,that this was a very ſolemne prelat , that for lacke of his ſolemnyty,would forſake his whole clergy? But it is not poſsible for theſe lying ſuperintendentes to tel their tales truly.The ſtory is this.*Theodorus the Archebiſhop of Rauenna* (ſaieth Nauclerus) *minding vpon Chriſtmas daye before the ſonne riſyng to ſay Maſſe in S. Apollinaris Church, was forſaken of al his clergy. And vntil it was towarde noone they came not at him:at*

Naucler.
Gener.23.
pag. 771.
Omnis
Clerus eū
deſtituit.

him:at what tyme by the meanes of the Exarchus,they brought him to Churche . The cauſe of this enmyty that the Clergy bore to him was , as Nauclerus writeth , for that he was a great almes man,and liberal of the Churche goods, and alſo very buſy to kepe his Clergy in good order . For this cauſe they hated him,and in ſo ſolemne a daye vtterly forſoke him:Which is more,I trowe M.Horne,then *not ſo ſolemnely to conducte him as the maner was* . To lacke the ordinary ſolemnity,andto be cleane deſtitute are two things. And there is a difference,you knowe,betwene ſtaring and ſtarke blinde. I thincke your ſelfe M. Horne as holy and as mortified as you be , woulde be very lothe to ſhewe your ſelf in S. Swithens Quyer at Wincheſter vpon a Chriſtmas day al alone,without any one of your Miniſters as ſeely as they are.Again where you ſay that *Leo the ſecõd made an end hereof cauſing thẽperour Iuſtinian to ſhew great cruelty &c.*This is a very groſſe lie. For Leo the ſecond was Pope only in Conſtantins time father to this Iuſtinian.2. And the cruelty that Iuſtiniã ſhewed to the whole City of Rauéna was after the death of this Leo.2.at the leſt twéty yers,vnder Cõſtãtine the Pope,at the later end of Iuſtiniãs reigne, being reſtored then from baniſhment, but yet continuinge in al his former cruelties . And as Nauclerus writeth , *he changed neuer a whit his former life,only excepted,that* (after his baniſhment)*he euer ſhewed Reuerence to the See Apoſtolike,otherwiſe then before* (his baniſhmét) *he was wont to do. And therefore hearing that Felix the biſhop of Rauenna diſobeied the Pope , he commaunded his Lieutenart in Sicilie to puniſh them:*which he did in dede very cruelly and barbarouſly . But that he did of his own accorde, *not by the cauſing (* as you ignorantly affirme) *of Leo the. 2 .* Who was

Naucler. Generat. 24.p.779

e   dead

dead at the leſt. 20. yers before, nor by the cauſing of Cōſtantine the Pope then, for ought that appeareth in the Stories. And therefore where you conclude, that *Pope Leo by
the commaundement and power of Iuſtinian brought Rauenna vnder his obeiſſance, as the Pontifical reporteth*, you belie
the Pontifical and the whole ſtorye of that tyme to to ignorantly. The Pontificall in dede ſaieth: *Percurrente diuale
iuſsione &c.*By the commaundement of the Emperour ſent
abrode, the Church of Rauenna was reſtored &c. But Iuſtinian it nameth not. It meaneth Conſtantine the Emperour
who ſtraight after the. 6. Councel ended, promulged that
edicte, Leo the.2.being then Pope. Suche a longe and tedious mater it is to open M. Hornes vntruthes.

M. Horne. The 83. Diuiſion. pag. 50. a.

      But Benedictus *the ſecōd, vvho ſucceded next to Leo the ſecond, vvēt*

The. 251.
vntruth.
Sanctitate
permotus:
moued
vvith his
holyneſſe
ſaith Pla-
tina : and
Sabellic⁹
alſo.
The. 252.
vntruth.
No lōger
then frō
Pelagius
the firſte,
and that
by his de-
cree.

in this point beyonde al his predeceſſours, for Conſtantin being moued vvith
his (. 251.) humanity, piety, and fauourablenes tovvards al mē, vvhen he ſent
to thēperour for his confirmation: thēperour ſent, ſaith Platina, a decree, that
from henceforth, loke whome the Clergy, the people, and the
Romain army, ſhould choſe to be Pope, al men, without delay, ſhould beleue him to be Chriſtes true vicar, abiding for no
confirmation by themperour, or his Lieutenant as it had been
wonte to be doen. &c. For that was wont to be allowed in
the Popes creation, that was confirmed by the Prince him ſelf
or his vicegerent in Italy.

      Here firſt of al it appereth (if this ſtory be true) hovve this intereſt of the
Prince in this Eccleſiaſtical matter thus continuing (.252.) long tyme, al-
though many vvayes aſſailed, and many attemptes made by the Popes, to
ſhake it of.vvas at the length through their flattery (vvhich their Para-
ſites cal humility) geuē vnto them of thēperours, to vvhom it apperteined.
But vvhether this ſtory be true or not, or if it vvere geuen, hovv it vvas
geuen, or hovv long the giftes toke place, or hovv it vvas taken a-
vvay and

vvay and retourned to the former right , may vvell be called into queſtion, for there is good (.253.) tokens to ſhevv , that it vvas not geuen in this ſort. For theſe tvvo Popes vvho ſat in the Papalſeat (.254.) but . 10 . mo-neths a peece or there about , vvere in (.255.) no ſuch fauour vvith Thepe-rour, as vvas their predeceſſour Agatho, vvho made great ſuit vnto thepe-rour for ſuch like things, and obteined his ſuit , but vvith a ſpeciall Prouiſo for the reſeruatiõ of this authority, ſtil to remain vnto theperors, as vvitneſ-ſeth the Pontificall and Gratian . He receiued from the Emperour letters (ſay they) accordinge to his petition , wherebye the ſomme of moeny was releaſſed that was wont to bee geuen (to the Emperour) for the Popes Conſecration : but ſo that yf there happen after his deathe anye election, the Biſshoppe electe be not conſecrated before the election be ſignified to the Emperour by the general decree (he meaneth the Synodicall letters) accordinge to the auncient cuſtome , that the orde-ringe of the Pope maye goe forwarde , by the Emperours knowledge or conſent and commaundement . The Gloſſar vp-pon Gratian noteth vppon theſe vvordes : VVhich ſumme was wont to be geuen: For euery Biſshop was wonte to geue ſomething to themperour at his election. But did not themperour cõmit Symony in releaſing this right vnder this cõdition, that his cõ-ſent ſhould be required in the election? anſweare, no: becauſe both theſe belonged to hĩ of right before, wherefore he might nowe remitte the one.

But as I ſaid, let it be true, that Conſtantin gaue ouer this iuriſdictiõ, but Volateranus addeth to this ſuſpected donatiõ, this clauſe, ſound true by ex-perience, which donatiõ (ſaith he) was not lõg after obſerued. And in dede it vvas kept ſo ſmal a vvhile, (.256.) that vvithin one yere after or litle more, vvhẽ the electors after lõg altercation , had agreed on Conon: Theodorꝰ theperors Lieutenãt (as ſaith Sabellicus) gaue his aſſent: ãd Pla-tina ſhevveth the ſame, although not ſo plainly. So that by this alſo it appea-reth, that if ſtil it appertained to theperours; Lieutenant, to geue his aſſet to the Popes electiõ, that than this gift is (.257.) either ſained of the Papiſtes (and that the rather vnder the name of Conſtantinus , to bleare there-vvith the ignorauntes eies , as though it vvere the graunt of Conſtantine

e ij the

Con-
ſtãt. 5.
The . 253.
vntruth.
No good
token cã
beſhewed
The. 154.
vntruth.
benedict²
2.ſate one
yere and.
10. Mo-
neths. Pã-
taleon.
The.255.
vntruth.
Bened.2.
vvas in as
much fa-
uour, as
Agatho,
with this
Emperer
The 256.
vntruth.
A falſe ãd
a fond il-
lation, as
ſhal ap-
peare,
The. 257.
vntruth.
Slaunde-
rous to al
Hiſtorio-
graphers:
Sabell.
Naucler.
Volater.
Platina
and the
reſt.

Con-
ſtǎt. 5.

The 258.
vntruth.

peuiſh ād
ſtarke
fooliſh.

*the great, as they doe about Images vvith (.258.) the name of the Nicene
Coŭcel) or by like the gift vvas not ſo authēically ratified, as it vvas vnadui-
ſedly promiſed: but hovv ſo euer it vvas, it helde not longe: the Pope himſelfe
ſolempnely vvith the conſent and decree of a vvhole Councell, reſigning al
the foreſaid graunt vnto the Emperours for euermore.*

The.4.Chapter.of Benedictus the.2. Pope, and Conſtan-
tine the. 5. Emperour.

Stapleton.

I Can not tel whether this matter is by M . Horne more
vntrulye , or more vnwiſelye handled . The Emperour
Conſtantin moued with the great vertue of Benedictus
the.2.gaue ouer to him , ſaith Platina , his accuſtomable
right, in the confirmation of the Popes election . Nay ſaith

Trithem.
de eccleſi.
ſcriptorib.

M. Horne, This was *through their flattery , vvhich their paraſites call humility.* Then by you Platina was the Popes flatterer. Verily ſuch a flatterer he was , that for his free ſpeaking agaiſt the Pope he was impriſoned. And it is not likely
that he which was ſo free with the Pope thē liuing, would
flatter with the Popes that were dead . You adde farder to

Proper
argumēts
not
vvorthe
the anſ
ſvvering.
The pope
ſupreame
head by
the place
M. Horn
himſelfe
bringeth
in.

proue themperour did not geue vp the Popes confirmatió.
For it is not (ſay you) any thinge likely: for Pope Agatho
could not obtain it , and it was kept but a ſmall tyme : and
the Pope him ſelf with the cóſent of a Councel not long after reſigned it: Haue ye done M. Horne? then I pray lappe
vp your as wiſe a concluſion, as before. *Ergo* the Quene of
England is the ſupreame head . But nowe what ſay you to
this M . Horne, that Conſtantin agniſed the Pope for *the
true vicar of Chriſte* ? Doth not Platina write this , whoſe
words your ſelf reherſe? Let the Popes cófirmatió weigh as
it may weigh: which maketh neither with nor againſt this

ſupre-

ſupremacy. Doe not theſe thre woords, Chriſtes true vicar, weigh down, ād beate al in peces, your ſely poore light rea ſons of your cōfirmatiō? Brought in I cā not tel how, ād al out of ceaſon, and nothīg pertaynīg to the kings of Englād. Who neuer had anie thing to intermedle, for the ratifying of the popes election. But what an extreme impudency is this? Or who but very euil him ſelfe, can ſuſpect ſo vily, and drawe al thinges to the worſte? If the pope be humble, thē he is (with M. Horne) an hypocrite and a flatterer. If he be ſtoute, he is a tyrant, ambitious, and proude. Contrary wiſe if the Emperour be cruel (as we ſhall ſee anon of Harry 4. and Friderike the firſt) then he doth but his right: If he doe his duty, as this Conſtantinnowe, Theodoſius, Valentinian, Marcian and Iuſtinian before, thē they are deceyued with flattery. Wo be to you that cal euill good, and good euill. For as before we ſayd, *Vitalianus, Donus, Agatho, Leo 2.* wer al commended of all writers, ſo is this *Benedictus 2.* highly prayſed not onely of Platina, but of Sabellicus and Volate- rane, *both for his lerning and for his holyneſſe.* And in reſpect of thoſe qualyties (ſaie they) Conſtantine ſent the decree that M. Horne is ſo greued withal. Yet al this to M. Horne is hypocriſy. And *the Hiſtorians*, he ſaieth, *were papiſtes for the moſt part.* It is true they were ſo : not only for the moſt parte, but altogeather hitherto. For what other hiſtorians, what other Councels, what other Church can you ſhewe ſynce Chriſtes tyme, then of very papiſtes? If you refuſe the papiſtes hiſtorians, vou muſt holde your peace , and let all this diſcourſe paſſe, from Conſtantine the firſt , downe to Maximiliā next predeceſſour to Charles the fyft. You muſt begynne only ſynce Luthers tyme : Which yet for very ſhame you haue clene omitted, not ſpeaking one word, of

Volater.
Anthrop.
lib. 22.
Sabel. Ae-
nead. 8.
lib. 6.
Fol. 49. a

e iij   Charles

Charles the fyfte or of Ferdinãde his brother the late moſt renowmed Emperours , or of any their gouuernement in cauſes ecclefiaſticall : whoſe examples yet you might as well haue browght , as of any other Catholike Emperour fence Conſtantines tyme, the firſt.But that in theſe , mens eyes and eares yet liuing,and knowing certeynely the con-trary , woulde haue condemned you : In the other being out of the memory of men yet liuing , you thought you might by ſuche homly ſhiftes as you haue made with pat-ched falſe and forged narrations , worke yet ſomewhat with the vnlerned Reader,which truſteth you better then heknoweth you.If this be not true,tel me the cauſe Maiſter Horne,why coming down to Maximilian Charles his next predeceſſour, and to Lewys the frenche kinge next before Frauncis the firſt , yow come not lower to Charles him ſelfe , and to kinge Frauncis of Fraunce ? Why I pray you , but for the reaſon aboue ſayed ? Well . If you had come lower , you might in dede haue founde prote-ſtant hiſtorians for your owne tothe . But nowe , coue-ting to haue a coloure of Antiquitie for your doinges , you are driuen to alleage onely papiſt hiſtorians, papiſt Coun-cells , papiſt doctours, papiſt Emperours. Brefely all your Authorities,teſtimonies and allegations, none other but of papiſtes . Yea the Scriptures them ſelues of whome haue you them, but of papiſtes ? No merueyll therefore if you are ſo continuallye by your owne Authorities beaten downe . In the meane ſeaſon, what hiſtorians , what Councels , what Doctours , haue you in any tyme of all the Churche , to ſpeake any one poore worde for your ymagined ſupremacy ? No , no , M. Horne . Either you

that

that nowe lyue are not the Churche of Chriſt, or ells
Chriſt hath had no Churche, theſe thouſand yeres and
vpwarde. Either you muſt condemne ſo many ages before you, or they muſt condemne you. Would God our
dere Countrie woulde ones conſider this one reaſon, and
worthely regarde the ſame.

To returne to you, Maiſter Horne, what moueth
you to ſaie, *that the Electours after longe altercation*
agreed on Conon, and *Theodorus the Emperours Lyeu-
tenant gaue his aſſent*, inferring thereof, that the Popes
election ſtill appertayned to the Emperours Lieutenant,
and to hys aſſent? Your tale is myngled with vntruthe,
and your conſequent hangeth looſely. For firſte altercation in the election of Conon there was none. Sabellicus your owne alleaged Author ſaieth. *In nullo vnquam Pontifice creando maior extitit Ordinum conſenſus:*
There was neuer more agreement of all degrees in the
creatyng of anye pope, then in this Conon. And as
for the Emperours Lieutenants aſſent, he addeth. *Præ-
ſtitit & Theodorus Exarchus ſuum aſſenſum.* Theodorus
alſo the Lieutenant gaue his aſſent: which he inferreth,
not as you doe, to ſhewe that the Lieutenants aſſent
was eyther of right or neceſsitie required, but to declare, that this pope without any altercation, for his ſingular vertues in dede, was choſen withe the conſent
of all men, yea of the Lieutenant him ſelfe. And thus
your whole and onely proufe fayleth, whereby you
would perſuade vs, that the decree of Conſtantine the Em
perour was ſo ſone after aboliſhed, or els not at al made,
but (as you moſt peuiſhly talk) *fayned of the Papiſt* hiſtoriās:
being yet al ſuch, as wrote before Luther was borne, and
therefore

Sabel. Ae-
nead 8.l.6

therefore by no reaſon in the worlde likely to be counter-
fayters eyther for our vauntage, or for your diſauauntage.
Els by the ſame reaſon you may reieƈt al hiſtories ād Cou̅-
cels and doƈtours to (bycauſe they al make direƈtly againſt
you and your doƈtrine, not only in this, but in al other your
hereſies) and ſay, that the papiſtes haue fayned ſtories , deuiſed Councels, forged olde doƈtours, yea and counterfay-
ted the Scriptures alſo, which I praye God, you Caluiniſtes
of England do not ones attempte to auouche, as the Swec-
feldians haue already begonne.

The. 259.
vntruth.
Not for
that cauſe
but his
cauſe he
could not
otherwiſe
haue had
the Em-
perours
ayde and
aſſiſtance.
Conſt. 6.
The. 260.
vntruth.
A falſe,
lewde, ād
malicious
ſurmiſe,
as ſhal ap
peare.
The Biſ-
ſhop of
Rome, at
the Empe
rors (261)
co̅maun
deme̅t in
Eccl. mat
ters.
Aƈt. 1.

M. Horne. The. 84. Diuiſion. Fol. 51. a.

But I returne againe to Agatho, *vvho (as I ſayde) being in great fauour
vvith Conſtantine the Emperour,* Determined (*ſaith* Platina) *to haue*
a councel to decide the errour of the Monothelites. *But (.259.)
bicauſe he coulde not him ſelfe by his ovvne authoritie, cal a general councel,
for that belo̅ged to the Emperour, vvho in that time vvas buſie in the vvarres
againſt the Saracens:* He waited (*ſaith* Platina) for the returne of the
Emperour.

This Conſtantinus *ſurnamed* Pogonatus, *about the yeere of the Lord
680, calleth the Biſhoppes out of all coaſtes vnto a general Councel: in his
letters of Sommons to* Donus (*but committed to* Agatho *Biſhop of Rome,*
Donus *beinge dead) he admoniſheth him of the contention betvvixt the ſea
of Rome and Conſtantinople, he exhorteth him to laie aſide al ſtrife , ſeruen-
cie, and malice, and to agree in the trueth vvith other , addinge this reaſon:*
For God loueth the trueth, and as Chryſoſtome ſaith : He that
wilbe the chief amongſt all , he muſt be miniſter vnto all (*by
vvhich reaſon made by the Emperour , it may ſeeme, that the pride of thoſe
tvvoo ſeates , ſtriuinge (.260.) for ſuperioritie and ſupremacie, vvas a great
nouriſhment of the Schiſme , vvhich vvas chiefly in outvvarde ſhevve only
for doƈtrine .*) He proteſteth that he vvill ſhevve him ſelfe indifferent ,
vvithout parciallitye to anye parte or faƈtion ., onely ſeekinge , as Godde
hath appointed him , to keepe the Faith that he had receiued vvholye
and vvithout blotte, He exhorteth and commaundeth the Biſhoppe of
Rome

Rome, not to be an hinderaunce , but to further this Councell vvith sending such as are fitte for such purpose. The bishop of Rome obeyeth the Emperours (.261.)commaundement. And the like letters the Emperor sendeth to George Bishop of Constantinople, and others . The Emperour sat in the councell him selfe, as President and moderatour of al that action: hauing on his right hande a great company of his Nobles, and of his Bishoppes on his lefte hand. And vvhan the holy Ghospelles vvas broughte foorth , and laide before them, as the (.262.)iudges, vvhose sentence they ought to follovve, as it vvas also vvonte to be doone in the fornamed Councels: The deputies for the bishoppe of Rome stande vppe, and speake vnto the Emperour in moste humble vvise callinge him moste benigne Lorde , affirminge , the Apostolike seat of Rome to be * subiect vnto him, *as the seruant vnto the Maister: and beseechinge him that he vvil commaunde those that tooke parte vvith the bishoppe of Constantinople , vvhich had in times paste brought in nevve kinds of speache , and erronious opinions, to shevve from vvhence they receiued, their nevve deuised Hereses. The Emperour commaundeth* Macarius Archebishoppe of Antioche , and his side to ansvveare for them selues . And after diuerse requestes made by him to the Emperour, and graunted by the Emperour vnto him , the Emperour commaundeth the Synode to state for that time.

The.261.
vntruth,
Notorio⁹
The Em-
perour
plainely
denieth
and dis-
clay meth
such Au-
thoryte
of com-
maūding
the bis-
shops.
The.262.
vntruth.
The Cou-
cell hath
no such
vvordes.
* It vvas
then true,
in Tem-
porall
matters.

The.5. Chapter . Of the sixt Generall Councell holden at Constantinople vnder Pope Agatho .

Stapleton.

MAister Horne, as he sayeth , returneth againe to A-gatho, wherin he doth wel: for this hath bene an ex-trauagant and an impertinent discourse . But he re-turneth withall to his accustomable dealing : sayinge that pope Agatho *of his owne authoritie coulde not call a councell.* Which neither his author Platina sayeth, nor anie other, nor he him self proueth . He coulde M. Horne haue cal-led a Councell, (and so he did call at Rome at this verie

f   tyme

Beda lib.
5.ca. 20.
Conc. 6.
Act. 4. pa.
306.
Conſtātin⁹
omnibus
ſanctiſsi.
vniuerſa-
lis Synodi
Apoſtolicæ
ſedis conci
liũ repræ-
ſentantib.
Ibidem .
Act. 18. fo.
409. col.
2. a.

The cauſe
vvhy
Pope Aᵃ
gatho ioy
ned with
thēperor
for the
Councell
to be had.
M. Horns
reaſons
out of the
6. General
Councell
for his
Primacy.

Tom. 2. Concil. fol. 280. col. 2. a.

tyme a great Councell of an . 125 . Biſſhoppes , our con-
treyman S. Wilfryde Archbiſſhoppe of Yorke and the A-
poſtle of Suſſex being one of them) without the Emperor,
and ſuch as this Emperour him ſelfe confeſſeth to be a general Councell . But becauſe , the ſchiſme of the Monothelites was deaply ſetled in Grece, and was faſt and depelye rooted by continuance of . 46 . yeares , not onely in
the Biſſhoppes of the chiefe ſees, as Conſtantinople , A-
lexandria, Antiochia, and others, but alſo in the Emperours
withall : full godly and wiſely , that the Councell might
be more effectuall and fruytful, he thowght good to worke
with the aduice and aſſiſtance of the Emperour: and ſo he
did: And this his godly pollicy had his proſperouſe ſucceſſe
accordingly.

   Maiſter Horne will nowe recite to vs his collections
oute of this Councell called , the . 6 . Generall Councell,
that he hath gathered, (but how well and fytlye to proue
his matter, ye ſhal anone vnderſtande) for the confirmation of his newe erected primacy . And firſt he glaunceth
at the See of Rome, ſurmiſing that becauſe the Emperour
exhorted the Pope to vnity , *the pride of Rome and of Conſtantinople ſtriuing for ſuperiority and ſupremacy was a greate
nouriſhment of the Schiſme* . This is a lewde and a falſe
ſurmiſe . For the Emperour in that place expreſſely telleth (by the reporte of the Greeke Patriarches) the cauſe
of that ſtryfe to be , *quòd verba quædam nouitatis intro-
miſſa ſunt* , that certaine newe doctrine was brought into the Churche . And will Maiſter Horne haue his vnproued ſurmiſe , to waighe downe the Emperours plaine
confeſsion?

The malice you talke of Maifter Horne, is in your felf:
It was not in Pope Agatho. The Emperour protefteth,
you fay, *to kepe the faith that he hadde receiued wholy and
without blotte*. Woulde God all Chriften Princes had
done fo. You hadde hadde then Maifter Horne, no place
in our countre to preache and fette forthe your damnable
herefies.

You fay farder: *The Bifshop of Rome obeyed the Emperours commaundement*. And this alfo you note verye fo-
lemnely in your Margin. But both your text and your margin, by your leaue, lyeth. For the Emperour in his letters
to the Pope (wherein he inuited him to this Councel) faith
plainely. *Inuitare & rogare poffumus ad omnem commenda-
tionem & vnitatem omnium Chriftianorum, necefsitatem verò inferre nullatenus volumus*. Well we may moue you and
praye you to fall to an vnity, but force you by no meanes
wil we. Where then is this forceable commaundemēt that
you imagine? You woulde faine haue the Emperours very
Imperiall, ouer Popes and Biflhoppes: You woulde, as
Auxentius the Arrian Bifhop did, *Laicis ius facerdotale
fubfternere*, bring vnder the Laye Princes foote, the Prieftly right and Authoritye. You woulde haue them, as the
Arrians perfuaded Conftantius,

Ibidem.

*Amb.li.5.
epift.32.
Suidas in
Leontio.*

  being fette to gouerne one thinge, to take vpon
them an other thing. This with your predeceffours hereticall Biflhoppes, your prelatfhip alfo would Emperours
fhoulde take vppon them. But they expreffelye refufe
fo to doe: they protefte the contrary: they abhorre fuche
lewde clawebackes. You adde farder, that in the
Councell, *the holye Gofpelles was brought forthe and layde
before them, as the iudges*. This is a flatte vntruthe.

      f ij   The

The Councel hath no fuch woordes,I meane *that the Gof-pels were Iudges.* No doubte but by the ghofpels the Coun-cel did iudge and determine the controuerfies,and had al-waies thofe holy books before thé , as alfo a Signe of the Croffe and other relikes,as Cufanus writeth . But a Iudge muft fpeake and pronounce a Sentence . Such is not the Scripture , but fuch are they that be (as the Apoftle faith) *Difpenfatores myfteriorum Chrifti ,* the difpenfours of the myfteries of Chrift , the ordered teachers of his woorde, the fucceffours of his Apoftles . But you to make folke wene,that Scripture alone were the only Iudge,as though the booke could fpeake and geue fentence it felfe,without a Teacher or Paftour, fticke not , to falfifie and miffere-porte the holy Councel,feing by true dealing you cáproue nothing .But it maketh perhaps for you,that the Popes Le-gates, cal the Emperour *moft benign Lord* ,and affirme the Apoftolike fee of Rome to be fubiecte to him.But they do not,I am affured,adde,in al fpiritual matters. And fo are ye nothing the nere to your purpofe:and as the Popes Legats cal him Lorde,fo pope Agatho calleth him his fonne .

And that which the Legates faid of the See Apoftolike, the fame Pope Agatho in his letters faied of the City of Rome,calling it *feruilem Principatus fui vrbem:* A Cyty fub-iect to his gouernement. And it may be well thought , the Legates fpake in no other fence , then did their Lorde and Maifter. But as for fuch phrafes S. Gregory fpake as hum-bly and as bafely to the Emperour Mauritius (which Cal-uin alfo hath noted) as euer any Pope before him , or after him did to any whatfoeuer Emperour . He called Mauri-tius his good Lorde , and him felfe,his vnworthy feruaunt. But yet (as I haue at large proued againft M.Iewel) he

practi-

De Con-
cord .Ca-
thol. li. 2.
cap. 6,
1, Cor. 4.

Act. 5.
fol. 301.

Act. 4. Cõ-
cil. 6. Cõ-
ftant. pag.
289 . a.
Gregor. li.
2. epi. 20.
li. 3. epi 16.
Inftit. lib.
4. cap. 11.

practifed in Ecclefiaftical caufes an vniuerfall Supremacy **cel.**
throughout all Chriftendome.

And nowe befide, that I haue faid, in as much as the
Popes.3.Legats,two being prieftes,and one but a Deacon,
be,as wel in the rcherfall of the Bifhops names, as in the
placing of the Bifhops, firft named, and do firft fpeake in
this action, I thinke I may make thereof alfo a better collection for the Popes Primacy,then you haue made againft
it. Whereas you fay the Emperour was prefident of the
Councel,I graunt you in that fenfe,as I haue before decla-
red:and that is,concerning thexternal order, moderation,
and direction of things to be done and heard quietly and
without parciality in the fynode:but not for any fupremacy in geuing fentence,againft their wils,as themperour him
felf euen now declared.

The Po-
pes Le-
gates are
firft na-
med, and
doe fpeke
firft in
the Coū-
cell.
How the
Emperor
is prefi-
dent of
the Coū-
cell,

M. Horne. The.85. Diuifion. Fol.51.b.

In the next fefsion after the felf fame order obferued,as in the firft, Pau-
*lus themperours Secretary began to put the Councel in remēbraunce of the
former daies proceding. The Emperor commaundeth the Acts of the Chalcedon Councel to be brought foorth and redde. At length vvhan a manifeft
place vvas alledged out of* Leo the Pope,*the Emperour him felf (.263.) dif-
puted vvith* Macarius *on the vnderftanding therof. The Secretary hauing
offred the bookes of the fifte Councel,the Emperour commaundeth the No
tary to reade them. The Notary began to reade, and vvithin a vvhile the
Popes Legats rifing vp, cried out* this Booke of the fifte Synode is
falfified,*and there alleaged a reafon therof,vvhervvith themperor and the
iudges being moued, began to look more narrovvly to the book,ād efpying at
the laft,that three quaternios vvas thruft into the beginning, theperour cōmaunded it fhould not be red. Note here,that the Popes Legats vvere but
(264)the plaintif parties in this Coūcel,ād not the iudges therof,the vvhich
more plainly follovveth: either parties ftryuing vppon a like corrupt place.
The Emperour cōmaunded the Synod and the Iudges(vvhich vvere Lay mē)*

Act.2.
The. 263.
vntruth.
For it
vvas no
difputa-
tiō, but a
fimple in
terroga-
tion.
The.264.
vntruth.
This doth
notproue
the plai-
tife par-
ties, as it
fhal ap-
pere.
Act.3.

to perufe

The. 265
vntruth.
The laye
Iudges
vver not
cō maun-
de I to de-
termine
any mat-
ter.
Conſt.im.
dixit. Sed
vnam ope
rationē nō
intelligis,
eum dixiſ
ſe.et mox:
& quomo
do intelli-
gis Dei vi-
rilē opera-
tionem?
fol.285.c.
2.a.act.2.

to peruſe the Synodical boks,and(.265.)to determine the matter,vvhich they did. George the Archebiſhop of Conſtantinople moſt humbly beſeecheth the Emperour that he vvil cauſe the letters vvhich Agatho the Pope,and his Synode ſent vnto the Emperour to be redde ones againe: the Emperour graunteth his requeſt.

Stapleton.

In theſe two ſeſsions ye can pyck no matter of any ſub-ſtance to helpe you withal:no, not of themperours diſpu-tation. And God wotte , this was but a ſleight and a colde diſputation,to demaunde two things of Macarius,and that by interrogation onely.I trowe ye ſhal fynde,but vj.or vij. lynes before,a better place for the popes ſupremacy:wher yt is ſayde,that pope Leo his epiſtle was taken of the Chal cedon Councel *as the foundation of the catholyke fayth,*being conformable to the confeſsion , of the bleſſed S. Peter the prince of the Apoſtles.But you bidde vs,*note here that the popes legates were but the plaintife parties in this Councel,and not the Iudges thereof.* Your reaſon is, becauſe they firſte ſpake and accuſed the forgery committed in a copie of the fifte Councel.If you had marked the practiſe of other Coũ cells before , M. Horne , you woulde not thoughe hyred thereto , haue made this Note to your Reader . For ſo is it in dede,that the popes legates, by the waie of prerogatiue in all Councells ,*ſemper prius loqui & confirmare ſoliti ſunt,* were alwaies wont to ſpeake firſt.So did they in the Chal cedon Councel firſt ſpeake againſt Dioſcorus , and remo-

ued him from the benche where other biſhops ſate , ma-king him to ſitte in the myddeſt , where the defendantes place was . And one of the popes Legates then ſo ear-neſtly ſpeakinge and requiringe to haue him remoued , the Emperours deputies ſaied vnto him . *Si iudicis obj*
tines

tines perſonam , non vt accuſator debcs proſequi . If yowe
beare the perſon of a Iudge , you ought not to pleade
as an Accuſer. In whiche wordes the Iudges did not
inferre(as . M. Horne here doth,) that the Popes Legate
was no Iudge,bicauſe he accuſed as a party plaintife , but
rather bicauſe he was a Iudge (bearinge the Popes perſon) he wiſhed him to forbeare accuſing. But the popes
Legates, as they were alwaies the Iudges to decree and
ſubſcribe before all other biſhoppes againſt hereſies , ſo
were they ready to accuſe and betraye the Demeanours
of Heretikes before all others . For why ? As in the Chalcedon Councell it is writen . *Miſſi Apoſtolici ſemper in*
Synodis prius loqui & confirmare ſoliti ſunt . The popes Legates were alwaies wonte to ſpeake formeſt in Councels,
and to confirme before all others . And by this the prerogatiue of the See Apoſtolike was expreſſed . And as in
the Chalcedon Councel the popes Legates were the firſt
that ſpake againſte Dioſcorus , and yet were alſo the firſt
that gaue ſentence againſte him (as I haue before pro -
ued) ſo in this Councell , as the popes Legates ſpake firſt
againſt the falſe and forged euidences,ſo thei were the firſt
(as we ſhal anon ſee)that condemned the forgers thereof,
Macarius with his felowes . And yet to ſpeake properly,
the popes Legates neither here nor in the matter of Dioſcorus,were parties plaintifs . For as there they onely, required to haue the ſentence of pope Leo executed , touching Dioſcorus his place in the Councell , ſo here they
only required the euidence to be tried,ſuſpecting it as forged, as it was in dede founde to be. And this they required,
not as plaintif parties , but to haue executiõ. which execution was in the ordering of the Emperour or his deputies.

For

Coũ-
cel.
Ibidẽ Act.
1.p.741.4

Act.10.
vt ſupra.

The pa-
pes Lega-
tes vvere
not plain
tif parties
either
here,or in
the Chal-
cedon
councell.

Cufanus
lib. 3. de
Concord.
Cathol. c.
17. & 18.

The. 165.
vntruth.
The con-
trary,
vvhich is
the Po-
pes pri-
macy is
ther clere
ly cõfef-
fed.

The prin
ce is Chri
ftes Vicar
in earth,
in caufes
(.267.)
Ecclefia-
fticall by
the popes
confefsiõ
Act. 1.

The. 267.
vntruth.
Not in
caufes Ec
clefiaftic
cal, but
for execu
tiõ of the
lavves ec
clefiafti-
call.

For looke what the chefe bifhops, or the whole Councel requred, that the Prince or his deputies (the Iudges) did fee executed quietly and orderly. Wherin cõfifted their whole authoritie and trauayle, as we haue before fhewed out of Cufanus. But to Iudge and determine belonged only to the bifhopes.

M. Horne. The. 84. Diuifion. pag. 52.a.

In the next fefsion the order and fourme obferued as in the firft, the Emperour commaunded firft of al Pope Agatho his letters to be redde : in the vvhich letters is manifeftly confeffed by the Pope him felfe : fo vvel the Emperours (.266.) fupreme gouernment in Ecclefiaftical caufes, as the Popes obedience and fubiection vnto him in the fame. For in the beginning, he declareth vvhat pleafure and comforte he conceyued of this, that the Emperour fought fo carefully, that the fincere Faith of Chrifte fhould preuayle in all Churches: that he vfed fuch mildenes and clemency, therein follovvyng the example of Chrifte, in admonifhyng him and his, to geue an accompte of their Faith, vvhich they preached: that being emboldened vvith thefe comfortable letters of the Emperour, he perfourmed his ready obedience in accomplifhinge the Emperous præceptes effectually. That he made inquifition for fatiffiynge of his obedience (to the Emperour) for apt men to be fent to the Councel : the vvhich thing, faith the Pope to the Emperour, the ftudious obedience of our feruice, would haue perfourmed foner, had it not beê letted, by the great circuite of the Prouince, and longe diftances of place. He protefteth that he fendeth his Legats according to the Emperours commaundement, not of any finifter meaninge, but for the obedience fake (to the Emperour) which (faith he) we owe of dutie. He maketh a confefsion of his faith, concerning the cõtrouerfie, adding the teftimonies of many auncient fathers. And he dooth proteft, that he vvith his Synod of the VVefterne Bifhoppes, beleueth that God referued the Emperour to this tyme for this purpofe. That he (the Emperour) occupyinge the place and zeale of our Lorde Iefu Chrifte him felfe here in earth, fhoulde giue iufte iudgement or fentence, on the behalfe of the Euangelicall and Apoftolicall truthe.

Stapleton.

What exceding and intolerable impudency is this, to be
ſo bolde as to bringe forthe Pope Agatho his letters, agaîſt
the Popes ſupremacy? If a man woulde purpoſely and diligently ſeke ample and large proufes for the confirmation
of the ſame, he ſhal not lightly fynde them more plentifull
and more effectual, then in this epiſtle , reade and allowed
of the whole Councel. *By the helpe (* ſaith Pope A-
gatho) *of S. Peter, this Apoſtolik Church neuer ſwerued*
frõ the truth into any errour. Whoſe authority as chief
of al the apoſtles al the Catholik Church of Chriſt, al ge-
neral Councels faithfully embracing, did alwaies follow
in all things. Whoſe apoſtolike doctrine all the reue-
rēd fathers embraced: and the heretiks, with falſe accu-
ſations, moſt ſpitefully deface and perſequute. Of like
authorities ye ſhal fynde great ſtore , aſwel in this
ſeſsion, as elſe where in * this Councell . Yea the
whole Councell confeſſe, that S . Peter was with
them by his ſucceſſour Agatho , and that S. Peter
ſpake by Agatho his mowthe . And yf this wil not
ſuffice, themperour himſelf confeſſeth the like.

By theſe and the like teſtimonies yt is cleare,
that the Emperour himſelf , toke the fathers to be
the iudges, in this controuerſie, and moſt of al the
Pope. To the which ſaying , it is nothing repugnante, that Pope Agatho, according to the Emperours Letters, did diligently and obediently as well
ſende his own deputies to the Councel , as procured that other were alſo ſent thither. Yes, ſaieth M.
Horne : *In thoſe letters is manifeſtly confeſſed by the*
Pope himſelfe, as wel the Emperours ſupreme gouern-
ment

g

Act. 4. pag. 290.
col. 2. a.
Cuius (Petri videli-
cet) adnitente præſi-
dio hæc apoſtolica e-
ius eccleſia, nūquā à
via veritatis, in qua-
libet erroris parte
deflexa eſt. Cuius au-
thoritate vtpote apo-
ſtolorum omniũ prin
cipis ſemper omnis ca
tholica Chriſti eccle-
ſia, et vniuerſales ſy-
nodi fideliter ample-
ctentes, in cunctis ſe-
quutæ ſunt. Omneſq;
venerabiles patres
apoſtolicã eius do-
ctrinam amplexi:
hæretici aũt falſis cri
minationibus ac de-
rogationũ odijs inſe-
quuti.
* Pag. 300. col. 2 . a.
& pa. 303. co. 1 a. &
pag. 304. col. 2. c.

*ment in Ecclesiasticall causes, as the Popes obedience and subie-
ction in the same* . This is largely spoken M. Horne . O
that your proufes were as clere , as your asseuerations are
bolde . Then were you in dede a ioylye writer . But M.
Iewell can tel you, that *bolde asseueration maketh no proufe*.
For howe I praye you shewe you this out of the Popes
owne letters ? You tel vs many thinges, that the Pope sent
his legates , caufed also other bishops to repayre to the
Councell, and woulde haue caufed more to come, if great
lettes had not hindered him. And all this you saie , *to per*
fourme his ready obedience, for satisfying of his obedience , the
studious obedience of his seruice , and yet ones againe, *for the*
obedience sake which he owed of duty . Here is I trowe obe*
dience on the Popes parte , enoughe and enough. But here
is not yet *in ecclesiasticall caufes :* Here is not yet *the Empe-*
rours supreme gouuernement. Here is not , *subiection in the*
same , that is, in Ecclesiasticall caufes . Then M. Horne
hath affirmed foure thinges , and proued but one . And
hath he , trowe we , proued that ? Verely as well , as he
hath proued the rest , of the whiche he hath spoken neuer
a worde . For what obedience was this that the Pope so
many times speaketh of ? Was it any other , then that at
the Emperours earnest request he sent his legates , and
summoned the bishops to the Councell? Yes, will M. Horn
saye : It was vpon the Emperours commaundement, that
he so did , and not at his simple request . Then remembre
I praye you the Emperours wordes before alleaged , in
whiche he protesteth, *that he can only inuite and praye the*
Pope to come to a Councell , and that force him he would not.
And if the Emperours owne wordes suffise not , then as
you haue brought the Pope againste him selfe , so I pray
you

you M. Horne, heare him ſpeake nowe for him ſelfe.
And that in the ſelfe ſame letters where he talketh ſo
muche of *Obedience*, which you liked in him very well. I
aſſure you M. Horne you ſhall heare him ſo ſpeake for
him ſelfe, that if he had by ſpirit of prophecy foreſene this
lewde obiection that you haue made, he coulde ſcante in
playner termes or more effectually haue anſwered you,
then nowe he hath by the waye of preuention confuted
you. For beholde what he ſaieth of the Emperours calling
him and mouing him to aſſemble this Councell. He ſaieth.

Nequaquam tam pia lateret intentio audientiũ, humanáue ſuſ- Concil. 6.
picio perterreretur, æſtimantium poteſtate nos eſſe compulſos, Conſtant.
& non plena ſerenitate ad ſatisfaciendum &c. commonitos, Act. 4. pa.
Diuales apices patefecerunt ac ſatisfaciunt, quos gratia ſpiritus 288. col.
ſancti, imperialis liguæ calamo, de puro cordis theſauro dictauit, 2. b.
Commonentis, non opprimentis, ſatisfacientis, non perterrētis,
non affligentis, ſed exhortantis, & ad ea quæ Dei ſunt ſecundũ
Deum inuitantis. Leſt any that heare hereof, ſhoulde be
ignorant of this godly intention, or the ſuſpicion of man
ſhoulde feare, thinkinge (as M. Horne here doth) that we
were forced by Authoryte, and not very gently exhorted to anſwere &cæt. the Imperiall letters haue declared and doe declare, writen and directed from his Ma-
ieſtyes pure harte, throughe the grace of the holy Ghoſte,
wherein he warneth, not oppreſſeth, he requyreth, not
threatneth, not forceth, but exhorteth, and to Godly thinges accordinge to God inuiteth. Lo M. Horn, you
are I trowe ſufficiently anſwered, if any thinge can ſuffyſe
you. The Emperour forced not the Pope by waye of
commaundement, or ſupreme gouuernement (as yowe
allwaies imagyne) but exhorted him.

g ij   He

He proceded not by waye of oppreſsion or threats, as by vertue of his allegeance or in payne of diſpleaſure, but by gentle admonitions and requeſtes. So did al the good Emperours before procede with biſhops in eccleſiaſtical matters: Conſtantin the firſt, Theodoſius the firſt and ſecond, Valentinian the firſt, Marcian, Iuſtinian, and nowe this Cõ-ſtantin the fyfte: not as with their ſubiectes or vaſſals in that reſpect, but rather as with their Fathers, their paſtours and by God appoynted Ouerſeers. The obedience then that pope Agatho ſo much and ſo ofte proteſted, proceded of his owne humylytie, not of the Emperours ſupremacy: of greate diſcretion, not of dewe ſubiection namelye in Eccleſiaſticall cauſes. For ſeinge the Emperour in his letters ſo meke, ſo gracious and ſo lowly, he could doe no leſſe (and the better man he was, the more he did) but ſhewe him ſelfe againe lowly and humble alſo. But when Emperours would tyrannically take vpon them in Church matters, there lacked not Catholike biſhops, as ſtoute and bolde then, as the pope was humble nowe. So were to Conſtantius that heretical tyran Liberius of Rome, Hoſius of Spayne, and Leontius of the Eaſt. So was to Valentinian the yonger S. Ambroſe, to Theodoſius the ſeconde, Leo the firſt, to the Emperour Anaſtaſius pope Gelaſius, to Mauritius S. Gregory. But M. Horne, if this do fayle, hath yet ready at hand an other freſhe, iolye coulorable ſhifte: that the Emperour, euen by Agathos owne confeſsion, *occupied the place and ʒele of our Lorde Ieſu Chriſte in earth, to geue iuſte iudgement and ſentence, in the behalf of the truth.* Nowe are we dryuen to the harde wal in dede. This geare ronneth roundly. And yf I ſhould nowe, thowghe truelye, interprete, and mollifie thys ſentence accordinge

to

to την διανοιαν , and the mynde of the speaker then
woulde you so vrge and presse το ρητον the bare letter,
that I shulde haue much a doe to rydde my handes of you.
But God be thanked , who hath so prouided that Agatho
him self,doth so plainely declare his owne meaninge , and
your false handling of the matter, euen in the verie nexte
sentence immediatly folowing:that al the worlde may euidently see,that for al your holy euangelical pretences,and
cloked cowlours,ye seke not the trowthe:but to trysle , to
toy,and contentiouslie to confounde all thinges.For it followeth.*That ye woulde voutchsauf* (saieth Pope Agatho to
the Emperour) *to exequute the cause of Christes fayth accor-*
ding to equitye , and the instructions of the holy fathers , and
the fyue generall Councells,and by Gods helpe to reuenge his in-
iurie,vppon such as condemne his faythe . And this saying of
Agatho M.Horne,may wel serue for a ful and a sufficiente
answere to al your boke, for princes intermedling in Coũcels,and for making lawes concernyng matters ecclesiasti-
call.You see by this place their gouuernement is no other,
but to ayde and asfiste for putting in execution the decrees
of Councels,and the holy Fathers Instructions. Wherfore
ye may put vp your ioly note wherwyth ye would seame
to furnishe and bewtifie your matter and margent here,in
your purse:and the lesse yt be sene,the better for yowe,for
any good,that euer your cause shal take by it.

Act.4.pa.
301.c.1.c.
Vt eius si-
dei causā
(sicut æq.●
tas exigit,
& sancto=
rũ patrũ
sacrarũq;
quinque
synodorũ
decreuit
istructio)
exequi dig
nemini, et
redempto-
ris iniuriā
desidei sua
contēptori
bᵒ per eius
præsidium
vlciscami·
mini.
Vide se-
quentia.
The. 268.
vntruth.
He vvas
not presi·
dent nor
Modera·
tour,
after M.
Hornes

       M.Horne. The.87.Diuision. pag. 2 b.

   In the next session,the Emperour sitteth as(268.)President ,and Mode-
ratour,accompanied vvith many of his nobles,sitting about him.On his right
hande sate Georgius *the Archebishop of Constantinople , called nevve*
Rome , and those that vvere vvith him:on the other side, vpon themperours
leste hande, sate the Legates of the Archebishop Agatho *of old Rome,these*
tvvo as(.269.)agent parties.VVhē they vver thus set,the Emperours Secre-
              g iij   tary

*tary brought foorth the Ghospels, putteth the Emperour in mind, vvhat vvas
done the sessiō before, and desireth his maiesty to cause Macarius and his
party, to bring out likevvise their testimonies, as the Legats from Agatho
of old Rome had don, for their party. The Emperour cōmaundeth, Macarius
obeith, and desireth that his books may be red: the Emperour commaundeth
they should so be.*   Stapleton.

M. Horne here noteth the sitting of the Popes Legates
on the lefte hand, and the Bishop of Constantinople on the
right hand: which either maketh nothing, for the abasing of
the Legats authority, either, that doth not so abase them, as
doth that I haue said auaunce them, that they are rehersed,
both in the naming and placing as wel in this very place, as
throughout al this Councel, before al other bishops: beside
the prerogatiues, which we haue and shal declare they had
in this Councel. And M. Horn must reméber that in the fift

Fol. 41.
col. 2.

general Councel they had the right hand: as him self cōfesseth. Neither was the Emperour President in this Councell, neither the bishops, the Agent parties, as M. Horne
here vntruly saith, but when the Sentence came to be pronounced, the Bishops alone gaue it without themperour. A

Supra lib.
2. Cap. 7.

moderatour in dede in external order and quyet to be kept,
théperour was, not only in this, but in al other Coūcels, as I
haue shewed before out of Cusan°, but not in geuíg solutiōs
to the reasons propoūded, or in geuing final sentéce in matter of doctrin, as the word Moderatour in the scholes soun-

Act. 7.
The. 270.
vntruth.
This
proueth
it not, as
shal ap-
peare.

deth, ād as M. Horn would haue it here to be vnderstāded.

M. Horne. The. 88. Diuision. pag. 52. b.

*After the shevving of the allegations on bothe sides, the Legates of old
Rome, desier the Emperour that they may knovve, yf the aduersaries agree
on the tenour of their tvvo forsaid suggestiōs. The aduersaries beseche théperor, that they might haue the copies of thē: théperor cōmaūdeth, that vvithout delay their request should be fulfilled. The books vvere brought forth and
sealed*

ſealed vvith the ſeales of the Iudges, and either of the parties. This againe
(.270.)proueth that the Popes Legats vvere none of the Iudges, but one of
the parties. And ſo in the eight, ninth, and tēth actiō, the ſame order of doing
is obſerued in like ſort, as before, in ſuch vviſe that no one in the Synode, nei-
ther the vvhole Synod, doth (.271.) any thing vvithout licence, and the di-
rection of the Emperour, the preſident and chief ruler in al thoſe cauſes.

cel.
The. 271.
vntruth.
For they
gaue Iud,
gemēt a,
gainſt the
heretike
vvithout
him,

Stapleton.

M. Horne is now harping vpon the ſame ſtringe that he
was harping vpon before, twiſe in the former leaf: that the
Popes Legats were no Iudges, but parties and plantiues. In
the one of the former places, he geueth no cauſe, but will
haue vs belieue hĩ vpō his bare word. Here ād in the other,
he geueth vs a cauſe, that nothing cōcludeth, for hĩ, but rather agaíſt hĩ. The Monothelits, to make their matter beare
ſome good coūtenāce, brought forth freſhely many authorities of Athanaſius, and other fathers on their ſide. The
Popes Legats eſpying, the chopping and chãging, the cutting and hewing, the mayming and mangling of thoſe teſtimonies, diſcried this falſhod to the Coūcel. Vpō this an exacte ſearch, cōference, and cōpariſon was made of other
bokes in théperous and patriarchs of Cōſtãtinople library,
and the extractes as wel of thoſe bookes, as of ſuch as the
Popes Legates had delyuered, were brought forth to the
Councel, to auoyde ſuſpicion of al ſiniſtrous working, ſealed with the Iudges ſeales. So that the fathers and the Legates gaue the iudgment (as yt afterward appeareth) that
the bookes were corrupted. The Iudges to their charge
tooke, that by the notarye the bookes ſhoulde be indiffe-
rentlye and vprightlye vewed and examined, and the true
teſtimonies to be browght to the Councell. I maruayle
Maiſter Horne, that this ſo good an argumente eſcaped you in the Chalcedon Councell: wherein likewiſe,
the

Mißi apo-
ftolici fem
per in fyno
dis prius lo
qui,et cō-
firmare fo
liti funt.
Chalc. fy-
no. act. 10
fo. 910. c. 1
The. 272.
vntruth.
He vvas
not the
iudge in
matters
there con
cluded, er
go not fu
preme go
uernour.
The. 273.
vntruth.
They yel
ded no
fuch thig
but refers
ued to
thē felues
the finall
Sentence
and iud •
gement.
M. Horns
poft laſt,
Act. 11. fo.
350. c. 2. c.

the Legates firſt of al beganne to ſpeake and worke againſt Dioſcorus, and cauſed hym to be diſplaced of ſytting amōg other biſhops, and to ſytte in the middeſt as a defendante. And yet they were hys Iudges, and they onelie pronoun-ced the finall ſentāce againſt hym: to the which the whole Councel condeſcended. Ye are then farre wyde M. Horn, frō the cauſe, whie the Legates ſo intermedled. The cauſe then was, not as ye either ignorantly or maliciouſlie pre-tende, for that they were parties: but for thys, *that the popes Legates were wont euer in councells to ſpeake firſt, and to cō-firme firſt* as I haue not much before largely declared. To that place for a fuller anſwer hereto I remitte the Reader.

M. Horne. The. 89. Diuiſion. pag. 53. a.

In the ende of the eleuenth Action, The Emperour aſsigneth certeine of his noble counſailours, to be the directours in the Synode, for that he vvas to bee occupied in other vveighty affaires of the cōmō vveale. Hitherto vve ſee hovv thēmperor in his ovvn perſon vvith his lay Prices alſo, vvas the (272) ſupreme gouernour, vvas the Preſident, euerſear, commaunder, ratifier, and directour, of al things done in the Councell. The Popes Legats and al the vvhole Councel, humbly yelding al theſe thinges vnto him (273.) alone. The reſidue of the actes, or any thing therein done, vvas likevvyſe his deede, by his deputies, although he him ſelfe in perſon, vvas not preſent.

Stapleton.

Whye good Sir? why make you ſuch poſt haſte? What are you ſo ſone at the ende of the. 11. action? Where is the beginning and the midle? where is the. 6. Action? Where are the. 8. the. 9. and the. 10. Action? I ſee your haſt is greate: what wil you leape ouer the hedge, ere ye come at it? And I might be ſo bolde, I woulde fayne demaund of you the cauſe of your haſty poſting. Perhaps there is ſome eye ſore here, or ſome thing that your ſtomake cā not beare. What?

Grea-

Greaueth yt you to heare, that our Lady was pure from
all maner fynne? Or doth yt appalle yowe to heare the
patriarch of Conftantinople, and al the biffhops his obedie
faries, with the biffhops that were vnder the patriarche of
Antioche, after they had heard readen the letters fent from
pope Agatho and his Councel at Rome, and aduifedly có-
fidered them, which (as I haue tolde yowe) were ftuffed
with authorities concernyng the popes primacy, to yelde
to the truth, and after. 46. yeares to forfake and abandon
their greate fchifme and falfe herefie? Doth it dafel and a-
mafe yowe to heare the patriarche of Conftantinople to
confeffe to the whole Councel, that yf the name of Pope
Vitalianus were receyued againe into theyre dypticha,
which they had raced out, that thofe which had fondred ãd
fequeftred them felues from the Catholike Churche,
woulde forthwithe returne thyther againe, whereunto
the Emperour and all the Councell by and by agreed, and
therevppon the Councell made manie gratulatorie exclamations? And is there anie other way to ftay and redreffe
thys huge fchifme in Englande or elfe where, but euen
to put in our Churche bokes the Popes name, and to imbrace againe hys Authoritie? Or doe ye take yt to the hart
M. Horne to fee here the pleadinge of Macarius the heretyke (which is alfo M. Iewells and your ordinarie faf-
fhion) as pleadinge vppon the doings of heretical Biffhops
and Emperours grounding hym felf vpon a nomber of patriarches of Conftantinople, of Antioche, and diuers other
biffhops with theyre Councells, yea vpon the Emperour
his father and his great graundfather, teachings and procla-
tnatiós, quite reiected and refufed? Or is it a corfy vnto you,
that the heretical writings of Macarius as fone as they be-

h ganne

*Caftita'é
Maria fan
ãa ab õni
cõtagioue
liberatæ et
corporis,
& animæ
& intel-
lectus.
Act.8.fo-
lio.313.
iubetemit
ti in dypti-
chis fan-
ctarũ eccle
fiarum no-
men fanc-
tæ memo-
rie Vita-
liani papæ
Romæ.
Act.8.fol.
315.
Coniectu
res whic
M Horn
hath
made this
poft haft.*

Act.11.p.
352.
Act.10.
Act.8 fol.
321.col.1.c
Sancta sy-
nodus di-
xit. Ecce
& hoc te-
ftimoniũ
fancti pa=
tris pere-
mifti. Nõ
congruit
orthodo-
xis ita cir
cumtrun-
catas fan-
ctorum pa
trum vo-
ces deflora
re:hareti
corũ poti⁹
proprium
hoc eft.
An hum-
ble and a
reafona-
ble re-
quefte to
the Ques
nes Maie-
fty ãd her
councell.

ganne to be read, were ftraight condemned of the bifhops, not looking for the Emperours pleafure therein, though he him felfe was then prefent thereat? Or is there yet anye other lurking fore priuily pynching your ftomake? Namely that ye fee to your great greef, that the fathers geue vs an affured marke to knowe yowe and M. Iewel by, what ye are, by your wretched wrefting and wrething, and miferable chopping and paring the auncient fathers writings: wherein ye are the true fchollers of thefe Monothelites, whofe practifes are difcried in the.6.the.8.the.9.the.10. and the.11.fefsions? The allegations of the Popes Legats, being founde truelie, faythfully, and femely done. I trowe it nypped yowe at the verie hearte roote, when ye reade (in cafe ye euer reade yt, and haue not trufted rather other mens eies then your owne) the Synode to fay, to that curfed and vnhappie Macarius, *that it was the property of an heretyke, to nyppe and breake of, to mangle and mayme, the fathers teftimonies*. And therevppon he being oft taken with the maner, and nowe cõfefsing the fame, was forthwith depriued, and his bifhoply attierment plucked from his backe.

And I would to God, yt might pleafe the Quenes Maiefty, and her honorable coũcel to play the Supreame heads as this good Emperour Cõftantinus and his Iudges did, and to make an indifferét fearch and vewe: whether the catholiks in their late boks, or M. Iewel. M. Horn, ãd other their fellowes, play the Macariãs or no: and thervppõ (euẽ as M. Horn fayd théperour Cõftantine did) to geue iuft iudgmét and fentence. Which is a redie and a fownde way for the quailing ãd appeafing of this huge fcifme. And without the which, books wil excefsyuely growe on eche part, and rather to encreafe of cõtentiõ, thẽ to any ful pacificatiõ. And

for

for my part the fault being fownd(as I dowbte nothing yt ɩcel.
wil be)and cōfeſſed therevppon on theyr part with an har-
ty renūciatiō,of al ſchiſme and hereſie, I would not wiſhe
theire riches to be plucked from them: but that they ſhuld
remaine in as good worldly eſtate as they now are in.This
is al the hurt I wiſh thē. But nowe M. Horn to returne to
the matter,ye ſee that this was but a poore iudgmēt, and a
poore ſelie ſupremacy, that ye geue to your Emperour ād
his nobles. Wherin in effect whil ye would ſeme to aduāce
and exalt thē,ye make theyr office not much better,thē the
regiſters and notaries office.Which office though it be honeſt and worſhipful to perchaūce,yet I dowbte whether it
be honorable:as not many yeares paſt one of your fellowes
and proteſtāt prelats ſayd to one that thowed his Regiſter.
*I tel thee:my regeſters office, is an honorable office.*Wel,let yt м. Iewel.
be honorable to:I ſuppoſe for all that,it ſhal not make hym
ſupreame heade of the Churche withall. And ſo hath M.
Hornes argument a great foyle.

M. Horne. The.90. Diuiſion. Fol.53.a.

*The biſhops and Clergy,vvhich vvere of the Prouince of Antioche,vvhan
Macarius vvas depoſed by the iudgement of the Synode,do make ſupplication vnto the Iudges, the Emperours deputies and counſailours, that they
vvilbe meanes vnto the Emperour to appoint them an other Archbiſhop in
the place of Macarius novve depoſed.*

Stapleton.

And wil ye play me the Macariā ſtyl M. Horne? Good
reader cōſider of M.Horns dealings,euē in this coūcel,that
I haue ād ſhal declare, whether M.Horn doth not altogether reſemble Macarius ſhameful practiſe in his allegatiōs.
One of your reaſons thē M.Horn,to proue Cōſtantines ſu
premacy by,is,that the Antiochians ſewed to themperour

to appoint an other Archbiſhop in the place of Macarius. The appointment of an Archbiſhop imployeth no ſupremacy : Diuerſe Kings of England haue appointed biſhops and Archebiſhops in their Realm: And yet none euer toke vpon them either the name or Authority of a Supreme Gouernour in al cauſes Eccleſiaſtical, vntil in this our miſerable tyme, heretikes by authority of Princes, to eſtabliſhe their hereſies, haue ſpoiled Gods Miniſters, and the Church of her dewe Authority and gouernement And I haue told you before M. Horne, that this Cõſtantin himſelf hath diſclaimed your ſupremacy, of ſupreame iudgement in cauſes eccleſiaſtical. Wherof alſo the very next matter, immediatꝰ lye reherſed before the thing you alleage, is a good and a ſufficient proufe.

I wil therfore demaunde a queſtion of you. Ye ſee, Macarius is depoſed, and that, as you confeſſe here your ſelfe, *by the Iudgement of the Synod.* Might now themperour kepe him ſtil ãd that laufully in his biſhoprik, if he had ſo would, or no? If ye ſay he might not, thẽ is he no Supreame Head. Except ye wil ſay, he was lawfully depoſed as an heretike: and therfore theperour could not kepe him in. This alſo as yet maketh againſt your ſupremacy. For thẽ the Iudgemẽt of the biſhops is aboue themperours power. But I wil further aſke you, whether yf Macarius had bene hartely pœnitent, and had recanted his hereſy to, themperour might thẽ haue kept him in? Now take hede ye be not brought to the ſtreights, which way ſo euer ye wind your ſelf. Yf ye ſay he may (as ye muſt, yf ye wil haue themperour Supreme Gouernour in al cauſes eccleſiaſtical) then is the whole Coũcel againſt you, vtterly denying him al hope of reſtitution, though the Iudges at theperours cõmaundemẽt, being moued

Act. 12. ſub finem.

ued

ued with mercy, propoſed this queſtiō to the Synod. Yf ye
ſay he may not: then do ye your ſelf ſpoile thēperour of his
Primacy. Thus ye perceiue euery way ye are in the bryers,
being conuicted by the very place by your ſelf propoſed.

M. Horne. The.91. Diuiſion. Fol.53.a.

The Iudges make them aunſvvere, that it vvas the Emperours pleaſure,
that they ſhould determine amongeſt them ſelues, vvhom they vvould haue,
and bring their decree vnto the Emperour. At the laſt the vvhole Synod doe
offer their definition ſubſcribed vvith their hands to the Emperour, beſechig
him to (.274.) examen and confirme the ſame. The Emperour vvithin a
vvhyle ſaith: vve haue redde this definition, and geue our conſent thereunto.
The Emperour aſked of the vvhole Synod, yf this definition be concluded by
vnifourme conſent of al the Biſhops, the Synod anſvvered: VVe al beleue
ſo, we be al of this mind, God ſend themperour manye yeares:
Thou haſt made al heretiks to flie, by thy meanes al Churches
are in peace, accurſed be al Heretiks. *In the vvhich curſe, the vvhole*
Synode curſeth Honorius Pope of Rome *vvith the great curſe, vvhome*
the Synode nameth in. 17. Action, one of the chiefeſt of theſe Heretiques,
vvho are here curſed. The Emperour proteſteth, that his zeale to con-
ſerue the Chriſtiã faith vndefiled (.275.) vvas the only cauſe of calling this
Synode. He ſhevveth vvhat vvas their partes therein, to vvyt, to weighe
conſideratly by Gods holy Scriptures, to put away al noueltye
of ſpeche or aſſertion, added to the pure Chriſtiã faith, in theſe
latter daies by ſome of wicked opiniō, and to deliuer vnto the
Church this faith moſt pure and cleane. (.276.) *They make a cō-*
mendatory oration vnto thēperor vvith much ioyfulnes declaring, that this
his fact about this Synod in procuring to his ſubiectes true godlynes, and to al the Church a quiet ſtate, was the moſt comely
thing, the moſt acceptable ſeruice, the moſt liberall oblatiō or
ſacrifice, that any Emperour might or coulde make vnto God.
And declaring the humble obedience to his precept or ſommons of the Biſhop
of Rome, vvho ſent his Legates, (.277.) being ſicke him ſelf, and of them
ſelues being preſent in their ovvne perſones, they doe moſt humbly be-

h iij   ſeche

The biſ-
ſhops pri
macy
proued
by the
ſaid place
that M.
Horn al-
leageth.
The 274.
vntruth,
wilful ãd
Notorio⁹
as ſhal ap
peare.
The. 275.
vntruthe
in leauig
out wor-
des mate-
rial.
VVherin
cōſiſteth
the office
of Biſ-
ſhops.
The. 276.
vntruth,
in nippig
of the
chiefeſt
parte of
the Sen-
tence.
The prin-
ces moſte
acceptaſ-
ble ſer-
uice to
God.

The.277.vntruth.That appeareth not in the Councell, neither vvas that the cauſe
of his abſence.

The 6.
Gene-
ral.
The. 278.
vntruth.
Ex more,
after the
maner,
left out.

feche him to fet his feale vnto their doinges, to ratifie the fame with the Emperial wryt, and to make edictes and conftitutiôs (.278.) wherewith to confirme the Actes of this Councel, that al controuerfie in tyme to come, may bee vtterly taken away. *Al vuhich the Emperour graunted vnto them,* adding his curfe, *as they had done before, fo vuel againft al the other Heretikes, as alfo againft* Honorius late Pope of Rome, a companion, fautour, and côfirmer, *(faith he)* of the others herefies in al pointes. *After this, the Emperour directeth his letters to the Synode at Rome of the VVefterne Bifshoppes, vuherein he commendeth their diligence about the confuting of the herefies. He defcribeth the miferable eftate the Churche vuas in, by meanes of the Herefies : for, faith he, the inuentours of Herefies are made the chiefe Biffhoppes, they preached vnto the people contention in fteade of peace, they fovued in the Churche forovues, cockle for vuheate, and all Church matters vuere troubled, and cleane out of order.* And becaufe thefe things vuere thus difordered, and impietye confumed Godlines, wee fette forwarde thyther, whereunto, it becommed vs to directe our goinge (*meaninge to feeke by al meanes the redreffe of thefe diforders in Churche matters*) wee labour with earneftnes for the pure faith, wee attende vppon Godlines, and wee haue our fpeciall care aboute the Ecclefiafticall ftate. *In confidera= tion vuhereof, vuee called the Bifshoppes out of farre diftaunte places to this Synode, to fette a Godly peace and Quietnes in the Churche matters &c.* To this epiftle of the Emperour, Leo the feconde Bifshoppe of Rome, maketh aunfvvere (for Agatho vvas deade) bye letters, vuhereof this is the effecte. *I geue thankes vnto the Kinge of Kinges, vuho hath beftovved on you an earthly Kingdome, in fuch vvyfe, that he hath geuen you therevvith a mind to feeke much more after heauenlye thinges.*

Your pietye is the fruite of mercy, but your authoritye is the keper of Difcipline : by that the Princes minde is ioyned to Godde : But bye this the fubiectes receyue reformation of diforders. Kinges ought to haue fo muche care to refourme and correcte naughtynes amongeft their fubiectes, as to triumphe ouer their enemies : for in fo dooinge they make their authoritye fubiecte to ferue him, bye whofe gifte and

protection

protection they reigne. VVherefore feinge that the holye
mother the Churche, which is the Body of Chrifte, enioyeth
by meanes of you her fincere and principall childe, an inuin=
cible foundnes. Therefore it is writen of you, mofte mercifull Prince, and of that fame holye Churche difperfed
throughout all the worlde, Kinges fhalbe thy nourfinge fathers, and in like forte it is writen, the honour of the Kinge
loueth iudgement: in that you fet much more by heauenly thā
by earthly thinges, and doe preferre without comparifon the
right faith, before all worldly cares: what other doe yowe
herein, than make right iudgement bonde and feruiceable
to Goddes honour and religion, and to offer vnto his diuine
Maieftye, an oblation and burnt Sacrifice, of fweete fauour
vppon the aultar of your harte? God infpire, encreafe and re-
plenifhe your princelye harte, with the light of the Catholique doctrine, whereby the clowdes of the hereticall prauity, may be driuen away. I receyued moft ioyfully the Synodical actes, with your letters of higheft authority, by the Legates your humble feruauntes, whiche were fente vnto the
Councell, from my predeceffour Agatho, at your commaundemēt. VVherfore with thankes geuinge I crie vnto the Lord:
O Lord faue our moft Chriftian Kinge, and heare him in the
day he calleth vpon thee: By whofe godly trauaile the Apoftolike godly doctrine or Religion, fhineth through the world,
and the horrible darkenes of hereticall malice is vanifhed a-
way. For through your trauaile, God afsifting the fame, that
mifchiefe which the wicked crafte of the Deuill had brought
in, is ouerthrowne: the benefit of the Chriftian Faith, that
Chrifte gaue to the faluation of man, hath wonne the ouer
hande. The holy and greate Generall Councell, whiche
of late hathe beene congregate at Conftantinople bye your
(.279.) order and precepte: wherein for the feruice and Minifterie fake that ye owe to God, you had the chiefe rule and
gouernemēt, hath in al points followed the doctrin of the Apoftles, and approued Fathers. * I doe detefte therfore and curfe
al Here-

Efai. 49.
Pfal. 98.
The 279.
vatruth.
No fuch
woordes
in the La
tin text.

The pope
accurfed
for here-
fie by the
fentence
of the em
perour,
the fynod
and the bi
fhop of
Rome.
* Here is
left out:
that the
See Apo-
ftolike,
Beati Petri
autoritate
confirmat
confir-
meth
vvith the
Authori-
tie of S.
Peter, the
6. Generall
Councell.

al Heretikes, yea Honorius alſo late Biſhop of this ſea, who laboured prophanely to betray and ſubuerte the immaculate
faith. O holy Churche, the mother of the faithfull, ariſe, put of
thy mourninge weede, and clothe thy ſelfe with ioyful apparaile, beholde thy Sonne the moſte conſtant Conſtantine, of al
Princes thy defendour, thy helper (be not afraide) hath girded
him ſelfe with the ſwoorde of Goddes woorde, wherewith
he deuideth the miſcreauntes from the Faithful: hath armed
him ſelfe in the coate armour of Faith, and for his helmet the
hope of Saluation. This newe Dauid and Conſtantine, hath
vanquiſhed the great Goliath thy boaſting enemy, the very
Prince and chieftayne of all miſchiefe and errours the Deuill:
and by his careful trauaile the righte faith hath recouered her
brightnes, and ſhineth thorough the whole worlde.

Stapleton.

In al this one leaf and an half, and more there is nothing
materiall but that may be auoyded by my former anſwere.
And as touching Pope Honorius we might yelde, that for
his owne perſon he was an heretyke, and accurſed to, by
the ſentence of themperour, the ſynode, and the biſhop of
Rome. I meane either that the pope is not the head of the
Church: or that the Quene of England is ſupreame head
there. Neither of theſe, ſhal he be able to proue by any collection that he can bringe of Honorius his hereſy while he
lyueth. Yf he ſay, I haue alredy declared out of the Councell at Rome, in the tyme of kinge Theodoricus, that the
Councel yt ſelf could not iudge the Pope: I will graunte yt
him, and will neuer ſteppe backe from yt. But then you
muſte Maiſter Horne, take of the fathers there aſſembled, the vnderſtandinge withall: that is, *onleſſe he ſwarue
and ſtraye from the fayth.* Ye will nowe happelye replie a-
gaine, and ſay: how ſhal the the pope (whom ye make the
vniuer-

Cóncer-
nig pope
Honorius
that M.
Horn ma
keth an
heretyke.
218.*patres
in* 5.*ſyno-
do Roma-
na. Niſi à
fide exor-
bitauerit,*

vniuerſall biſhop of the whole churche) direct the ſayde churche in a true and a ſownde fayth , him ſelf being an heretyke?Or howe can yt be,but the whole or the greater parte ofthe churche,ſhall with the head miſcarie alſo? Or howe ys yt true,that we heard at your handes euen nowe, that the churche ofRome was neuer caryed away with any errrour in fayth ? Or howe is yt trewe, that ye ſayd, that Peter had a pryuilege not onely for him ſelf, but for hys ſucceſſours alſo(which ye make the popes) not onely not to erre them ſelues , but alſo to confirme theire bretherne, and to remoue all errour from them ? We anſwere that in caſe the Pope by his open lawe and decree made with the conſent of his brethern in Synod or conſiſtory, promulged to be obſerued throwghe chriſtendomme , do ſet forth any hereſy, that your replies are good and effectuall. But ſuche a decree ye haue not ſhewed , nor euer ſhall ſhewe. For, from making any ſuche lawe the bleſſed hande of God doth vpholde , and euer hath vpholden, the popes for his promiſe ſake. Promiſe, I ſaye , made to S.Peter,not for his owne priuat perſon,but for the ſafegard of the church,which otherwyſe muſt nedes haue a great wracke in the fayth, ifthe Rock and head thereofſhoulde publikly decree hereſy. In caſe therefore the pope be pryuately a cloſe heretycke to him ſelf,or to other to,without any open ſetting forth or proclaiming his errour by a common lawe(as Honorius was, if he were an heretike)he is not proprely to be called an heretike as he is a Pope , nor the church ofRome can be ſaid to haue erred. Neither the other inconueniences wil enſue that ye brought foorth.

But verely what ſoeuer Honorius in his owne perſon was,yet certein it is,that the See of Rome both in his tyme

Plat. in Honor.1.
Sabel Ae-nead.8.
lib.6.
Tom.2.
Concil.in gest.Theo-dori.pag.228.

and euer after, was alwaies clere of this herefy, yea ād was a contynual perfecutor thereof. For both in the tyme of Honorius him felf, Pirrhus the patriarche of Conftanti-nople was bannifhed by the Emperour Heraclius into Afrike at the fuyte of the Churche of Rome (as Platina, Sabellicus and other do teftifie) for this herefye: and alfo in the tyme of Theodorus the Pope within three yeres or there aboute after the deceafe of Honorius, this Pirrhus came out of Afrique to Rome, recanted there his He-refye, and was by the Pope therefore reconciled: though afterward againe *ad proprium impietatis vomitum repedauit.* He retourned to the vomytte of his impietye. This Pope alfo Theodorus wrote to Paulus of Conftantinople a de-fender alfo of this herefye, warnyng and rebukinge him thereof.

Al this was before the tyme of this generall Coun-cell and of Pope Agatho. And therefore notwithftan-ding the priuate erroure of Honorius, whiche he neuer taughte or preached publiquely, but onely in letters com-ming foorth in his name after his deathe, was furmifed to be fuche, yet Pope Agatho in his letters (redde and al-lowed of the whole Councell) mofte truely fayed, that

Act.4.
Cocil.6.
Conft.pa.
291.c.1,4.
&c.

his Predeceffours kepte alwayes fownde and vnuiolated the faithe, and did alfo in this verye Herefye laboure continual-lye with the Bifshoppes of Conftantinople (Pyrrhus, Pau-lus, Petrus, and Sergius) to haue it fuppreffed and extin-guifshed.

So that as I fayed, though we graunte, that Honori-us was an Heretique for his owne priuate opinion, yet that he or his Churche euer decreed or publiquely al-lowed that Herefye, it can neuer truely be graunted.

And

And yet it seemeth verye straunge, that if Honorius were an Heretique , that Pope Agatho neyther in his letters reade in the whole Councell , where learnedly and particularlye he confuteth and recyteth all the Bif- shoppes that helde that herefye, neyther yet in the let- ters of the Romaine Synode of one hundred and fiue and twentye Bifshoppes redde alfo in the Councell na- ming againe particularlie the Bifshoppes of that herefy, in neyther of them, I faye, fhoulde ones name Honori- us . For neyther coulde he be ignoraunte therof, ney- ther coulde his diffimulation haue cloked the matter, but rather haue muche hafarded his creditte and efti- mation, both with the Emperour , and with the whole Councell.

Act. 4. pag 209. 300. & 304.

It is marueile alfo, that Zonaras a Greeke Writer, rea- koning vppe of purpofe all the Hereticall Bifhoppes con- demned in this fixt Generall Councell, nameth not yet at all Honorius the Pope of Rome.

Vide zona rā. Tom. ; pag. 74.

Farder it is verye likely, that if he were fo knowen an Heretique , Venerable Bede liuing fo fhortlye after that time , and recording in his Ecclefiafticall Hiftorie, diuerfe of this Popes letters directed to oure Countrye, fhoulde fomewhere touche this matter, or fhoulde not at the leaft fo Authenticallie recite his doinges and wri- tinges, as he dothe of other Popes before him , and after him . Verelie in his letters recorded in Sainte Bede, he commendeth highlye the bookes and woorkes of Sainte Gregory the firft his Predeceffour, in the whiche his he- refye (if he helde any fuch)is,as by other Catholique Fa- thers reiected.

Beda li. 2. hift. gētis Angl. cap. 17. 18. & 19.

i   ij   But

Art.4.
fol.112.
& 113.

But of this matter I haue also spoken against Maister Iewell: to the whiche this that I haue here saide, and that to
this may be added. The Conclusion both here and there is
that Honorius as Pope neuer decreed nor alowed this
heresie or any other, nor was not as Pope condemned.
And how it is to be vnderstanded, that the Pope may erre,
and yet the Church of Rome not erre, becaufe it is by M.

M. Raftel
in his
third boo
ke against
M. Iewel.
fol.144.
and.145.

Raftell fufficiently declared against M. Iewel, to that place
I referre also the Reader. Al things in al places must not be
said to the vnfruitfull werinesse bothe of the writer, and of
the Reader.

Wheras now M. Horne enforceth his pretensed supremacy, for that the Synode offred to the Emperoure their
definitio subscribed with their hands, beseching him *to exà*
mine and confirme the fame, marke him good Reader, and
eye him well. For in these three wordes, *subscription*, *ex-*

Tvvo le
gerdema
nes of M.
Hornes:
one mete
for a Ma
cariã, tho.
ther for a
gay gram
marian.

amination, and *confirmation*, lye couched two vntruths befides two Legerdemaines: One mete for a Macarian, the
other for a iolie fresh Grammarian. Your text M. Horne
where it maketh mention of this subscription, neither speaketh of examination, nor yet of confirmation. And as for
confirmation, we could beare it wel inough, sauing I know
ye haue a shrewd meaning, that would not well be borne
withal. And therefore for ones, we wil be so bolde to put
yowe to your prouf, and desire you to shewe in this place
any word of cõfirmation. I knowe he did confirme and ratify this councel, as yt appereth otherwher. But wyth such
a cõfirmation as the fathers could not vse: that is, banisshing
the gainsayers putting them owte of his protection. But

Act.18.
fol.409.
Col.1.c.

nowe to your examination.

Why M. Horne? After the Pope at Rome in his owne
perfon

perſon with a. 125. Biſhops,and after that his Legates with
289. Biſhops at Conſtantinople , haue reſolutely and defi-
nitiuely determined the matter againſt the Monothelites,
hang al theſe doings vpon a new examination and approbation of the Emperour, that if he like them not , then all
is daſſhed? Then haue the Fathers ſponne a faire threde.
Then haue ye now at length after long ſearching and hunting in the acts of this Synode, beatē out ſomwhat for your
purpoſe in dede. Goe on therfore M. Horne. Proue this,
and then let your Emperour,a Gods name, haue ſet oñ his
head,not only his Emperiall, but the Popes triple crowne
too.Shew your cardes then,M.Horne: *The whole Synode*
ſay you,*offereth their definitiõ ſubſcribed with their handes*
to themperor,beſeching him to examin and cõfirme the ſame.
Wel ſaid : But now in what part of the Councell lie theſe
words? In ſo notable a mater and cõcluſion as this is, why
do ye not ſend your Reader to the leafe or to the action at
leaſt ? And why is not this cõcluſion with a ioly note,daſ-
ſhed into your margēt? Surely the occaſion being ſo good,
and the mater ſo importãt,there muſt nedes be ſome greate
ſtay,that among ſo many ioly Notes, this only is omitted.
Wote ye then what it is,good Readers? Forſóth a woder-
ful ſtay in dede.For I aſſure you there are no ſuch wordes
in the Councel.He hath all this while outfaced vs with a
card of ten. There is none other, but this , that Theodore
the Deacon told th'Emperor : *that he had at hand ready the*
Coũcels definition,to be read to him at his highnes wil ãd plea-
*ſure.*Whervpon th'emperour by and by anſwered:*Let it be*
*read.*And when it was read,th'Emperour aſked the Coũcel,whether they wer al agreed to the definition thē read,
which when thei had al proteſted, by many acclamations,

Hanc defi nitionem pra mani- bus deferi mus veſtro ſerenitatis propoſito recenſen- dam. Acti.18. Fol.398. Col.2.

th'Emperour fubfcribed alfo thervnto, not examinig or tri-
yng it in any maner at al, but plainly protefting, that he was
ready to obey as wel al the former Coūcels as that, and for
their parts they fhuld anfwer before God in the laft iudgemēt, whether they had faid wel or euil. Now whether *re-
cēfendā* doth fignify to be examined, or to be recited ād reherfed, there is no more to do, M. Horne, but to call a faire
queft of Grāmarians, your owne nigh neighbours at Winchefter fchole. And if they geue fentēce for you, thē let the
Emperoure, as I haue fayed, weare the Popes threefolde
Crowne.

Act.18.
pag. 401. Now for your other Macarian practife: ye haue diffembled, as wel the Bifhops fubfcription, which was as I haue
fhewed, iudicially done, *defniendo*, the Popes Legates fub-
fcribing firft: as alfo th'Emperours, which was only *confen-
tiendo*: by confenting: and put to after all the Bifhoppes had
fubfcribed.

There is yet an other Macarian feat played here by M.
Horne worth the notyng both for a trial of his honefty ād
for the Readers edifiyng. He hath made two fpecial notes
in his margin: the one, *wherin confifteth the office of Bifhops*.
The other: *The princes moft acceptable feruice to God*. Two
good notes in dede and wel worth the noting, if thei be
vprightly noted.

The office of Bifhoppes is, as M. Horne alleageth, *to
deliuer vnto the Churche the faith of Chrifte moft pure and*
Act.18.
pag. 401.
Col.2.c. *cleane*. But how, he telleth not. His feate is quite to nippe
of the wordes immediately folowing, which are thefe.
*(Sicut prædictum eft) Quatenus fecūdum fancta & vniuerfa-
lia quinque Concilia & ftatuta fanctorum venerabilium patrū,
ita eam nos cuftodiamus vfque in mortem*. To thentent that

(as

(as we haue before faied, faieth the Fmperour) we alfo may kepe the faith , euen to deathe according to the fiue holy and generall Councels, and according to the decrees of the holy Reuerent Fathers. If you had put this claufe to the office of Bilhops, M. Horn, as the Emperour did, al England fhould haue fene that you and your fellowes were no Bilhops, who fo lightly and fo impudētly condemne the doctrine of the holy fathers, and do allowe but fower generall Councels, as your bretherne here in Antwerpe do allowe but three. But it went againft your confcience , to tell that, which fhould condemne your confcience. Likewife in the princes feruice to God, you faie : *the Emperour protefted his zeale , to conferue the Christian faith vndefiled*: but you leaue out againe, what he faieth immediatly after: *fecundùm doctrinam atque traditionem quæ tradita eft nobis tam per Euangelium, quámque per fanctos Apoftolos, & ftatuta fanctorum quinque vniuerfalium Conciliorum, fanctorúmque probabilium patrum.* According to the doctrine and tradition deliuered vnto vs afwel by the Gofpell, as by the holye Apoftles , and by the decrees of the fiue holye General Couneels, and of the holye approued fathers. If you had told this parte of the princes duetye, and had geuen the Emperour leaue to tell out his whole tale, the Reader fhoulde fone haue efpied, what damnable wretches yowe are , that perfuade Princes to profeffe the Gofpell onelye with out regarde of former Councels, and of the traditions of the holy fathers . And then your two marginal notes, either would not at al bene noted, or at leaft to your vtter fhame haue ben readen. Other your nippinges and curtallinges of your places might here be noted.

Edvvard. 6. Ann. 1. Tilet. in Confutat. Confef. Minift. Antvverp. pag 15. b. Act. 18. vt fupra.

As,

As that in the Councels requeſt to the Emperour, for ratifieng their determination with his ediƈt, you leaue out *ex more* after the maner, wherby is inſinuated a cuſtomable practiſe of Emperours (as we ſawe before in Iuſtinian) to procure by ediƈtes and proclamations the execution of Councels. As alſo in your long allegation of pope Leo his letters (which al we graunt vnto you, and you neuer the nerer) we might note at the leaſt half a doſen ſuch nippinges and manglinges of the text. But I thinck, M. Horne (all that hath ben ſaied being wel conſidered) you looke for no greate triumphe, for this fielde: But are content to blowe the retrayte. Be it ſo then.

M. Horne. The 92. Diuiſion, pag. 55. a.

Bamba *King of Spaine commaunded a Synod to be had at* Toletum *in the fourthe yeere of his reigne: the occaſion vvas this. There had beene no Synode by the ſpace of 18. yeeres before, as it is ſaide in the preface to this Councell, by meanes vvhereof the vvorde of God vvas deſpiſed, the Churche diſciplicine negleƈted, all Godly order diſtourbed, and the Churche toſte and tumbled, as a ſhippe vvithout a rovver and ſterne, (meaning a Kinge to call them togeather in Synode). By the carefull zeale of this Kinge, beyng called togeather they conſulte hovv to reſourme errores about Faithe, corrup=*

The. 280.
vntruthe
The word
cõmauded,
is not in
the text.
Aggregati
ſumᵇ. vide
tom. 2 pag.
270. col. 2.
Tol. 12.

Tol. 13.

tion of diſcipline, and other diſorders againſte godlines and Religion. And at the ende they doo geue great thankes vnto the noble and vertuous Kinge, by vvhoſe ordinaunce and carefull endeuour, they vvere (280). commaunded to this conſultation: vvho as they affirme of him, comming as a nevve repayrer of the Eccleſiaſticall diſcipline in theſe times, not onely intended to reſtore the orders of the Councelles before this time omitted, but alſo hath decreed and appointed, yeerely Synodes to bee kepte hereafter.

Eringius *kinge of Spaine commaundeth the Biſhopps and other of his Clergie, to aſſemble togeather at* Toletum *in one Synode the firſt yere of his reigne. And called another to the ſame place, the fourth yeere of his reigne: to conſulte about reformation of the Churche diſcipline. When the Biſhoppes,*

Bifhoppes, and the refidue of the Cleargy vvere affembled in their conuoca=
tion, at the commaundemente of the king: he him felfe vvith many of his no=
bilitie and counfailours, commeth in to them: he declareth the caufe vvhere-
fore he fummoned this Synode: he fhevveth the miferies the vvhole countrey
hath fufteined, and the plagues: he declareth the caufe, to be Goddes vvrathe
kindled by meanes of the contempte of Goddes vvorde and commaundement:
And he exhorteth them that they vvil vvith Godly zeale, ftudy to purge the
land from prauity, by preaching, and exercife of Godly difcipline , and that
zealoufly. He doth exhort his Nobles , that vvere there prefente , that they
alfo vvould care diligently for the futherance hereof: he deliuereth vnto the
Synode a booke , conteining the principall matter vvherof they fhould con=
fulte. And laft of all, he promifeth by his hande fubfcription, that he vvil con-
firme and ratifie vvhat the clergy and nobility fhall conclude, touching thefe
articles , for the furtherance of godlines and Church Difcipline.

Egita, *Kinge of Spayne,* (.281.) *caufed in his time alfo three Councelles* The.281.
to be hadde and celebrated at Toletum, *for the preferuation of Religion,* vntruth.
vvith the Church Difcipline in fincerity and puritie: vvho alfo confirmed and Of thefe.
ratified the fame vvith his Royal affent and authority. 3. Coūcels
or of any
ratifiing
thereof

The. 6. Chapter. Of three Kings of Spaine , and of the three
later Toletane Councels kept in their reignes.
by the
kings Au
thorite
or Royal

Stapleton.

A L M. Hornes force is now fodenly remoued from
affent in
Conftantinople to Spaine , where he now bloweth
the To=
a larme againe. But God be thanked for all this great
mes of
fighte, there is litle hurte donne . Yea after all this tof-
the Coū-
fing and turmoiling, and after all his great fturre and broile
cels there
againfte the pope and the clergy, he is vppon the foden be-
appereth
comme fuche an entiere and fo well affectioned frende to
nothing.
them, that (but I trowe vnwares, and therfore worthy the
leffe thanke) he tranfporteth the fupreame authority as
well in temporall as fpirituall matters from the king to the
clergy. For I befeache you M . Horne , are not dyuers of

k   the

the maters specified in the twelueth and thirtenth Councell at Toledo plaine Ciuile and Temporall? As concerning *the confirmation of King Ernigius royall Autho-*
ritie succeeding to Kinge Bamba being shorne a Monke?
Concerning *the release and exoneration of the people from*
certaine grieuouse payementes and exactions? Concerninge also *the goods of certaine Traytours* with such like?
Dothe not the Kinge praye the Prelates *to discusse his re-*
quests with their iudgementes? Doe not they *confirme*
his royall Authoritie with their Synodicall Decree? Doth
not the Kinge in his booke offred to the Councell saye,
that he moste humblie and deuoutlye lyeth prostrate
before their Reuerente assemblie? *Coram cætus vestri*
reuerentia humilis deuotusque prosternor? Dothe he not
desire them cócerning *his other ciuil ordináces,to put to their*
strog and helping hand? Doth he not plainly say, *that what*
so euer the holy assemblie of Bishops decreeth to be ob-
serued, is by the gift of the holy Ghoste established for
euer? Let me now, Gentle Reader, play Maister
Horne his parte, and make for me his accustomable
conclusion. The King requireth of the Clergy the
confirmation of his Decrees and ordinaunces , as
wel concerning matters of Faith and Religion , as
cócerning Ciuil maters : Ergo the Clergy hath the
Superioritye in bothe. And with this Argument, dothe
Maister Horne lappe vppe here his Spannishe matters.
Sauing that he telleth vs of three other Councels holden
at Toletum vnder Egita their King , which in all the volumes of the Councels appeare not, this vnder Eringius,
the 13. in number being the last : and therefore till he tell

VS

vs, where thofe Councelles may be founde, feing he hath
fo often belyed the knowen Hiftories, I will make no
curtefie to note this for an Vntruth alfo, this being a mater
fo vtterly vnknowen.

And nowe farewell Spaine for this time.   For Maifter
Horne hath manie other mightie, large, and farre Countries to bring vnder his conqueft and Supremacie : as wel
truely, as he hath already conquered Spaine : which will be
to lecfe the fielde and all his matter, gladde to efcape with
body and foule : with fmall triumphe, and fhame enough.
Goe to then Maifter Horne, and take your iourney when
and whither it pleafeth you.   Yow will wifhe, I trowe,
when you haue all fayed and done, that you had taryed at
home and let this greate enterprife alone.

M. Horne. The. 93. Diuifion. pag. 55. b.

Although about this time the Popes deuifed (282) horible practifes, vvher-
by to vviune them felues from vnder the ouerfight and comptrolment
of the Emperour or any other, and to haue the onely and Supreame au-
thoritye in them felues ouer all, as (.283.) they had alreadie obteined
to their Churche the Supreame Title, to be Heade of other Churches :
Yet the Emperours had not altogeather furrendred from them felues to
the Popes, their Authoritie and iurifdictions in Churche matters.   For
vvhen the Church vvas grieuouflye vexed vvith the controuerfie aboute
Images, there vvere diuerfe greate Synodes or Councelles called for
the decilinge of that troublefome matter by the Emperours : and at
the lafte, that vvhiche is called the Seuenth General or Oecumenical
Councel vvu caled and fummoned to be holden at Nice in Bythinia, by
Conftantine and Irene the Empreffe his Moother, vvho vvas the Su-
preame vvoorker and Gouernour (although but an (.284.) ignorant
and verye fuperftitious vvoman, I vvill fay no vvoorfe) in this matter.

The. 282.
Vntruth.
Horrible
and Slan-
derous.
The. 283.
Vntruth.
as before
is proued

The. 284.
Vntruth.
mere Slã-
derous.

k ij   For

The.7
Generall

For her Sonne vvas but aboute tenne yeeres olde, as Zonaras affirmeth, and she had the vvhole rule, although he bare the name. After the deathe of Paule, the Emperour appointed Tarasius the Secretary to be Patriarche at Constantinople, the people lyked vvell therof. But Tarasius the Emperours Secretarie refused the office, and vvoulde not take it vppon him, till the Emperour had promised to call a generall Councell, to

The. 285.
vntruthe
false traſ-
lation, vt
Eccleſiæ
uniantur.
To vnite
the Chur-
ches
vvhich
vvere
in a ſchiſ-
me.

quiete the (.285.) bravvles in the Churche aboute Images. The Emperour vvriteth to the Patriarche of olde Rome, and to the other Patriarches, vvilling them to sende their Legates, vnto a Councell to bee holden at Nice in Bithynia. The Biſhoppes aſſemble at Nice by the commaundement and decree of the Emperour, as they confeſſe in diuerſe places of this Councell. VVhan the Biſhoppes vvere ſette in Councell, and many Lay perſons of the nobility vvith them : and the holy Ghoſpelles vvere brought foorth, as the maner vvas (although the holy Goſpells vver not made (. 286.) Iudges in this councell, as they ought to haue been, and vvere in al the fore-

The. 286.
vntruthe
As much
in this
Councel
as in any
other.

named general Councels) Taraſius commēdeth the vigilant care and feruent zeale of the Emperours, aboute Churche matters: for ordering and pacifiyng vvherof, they haue called, ſaith he, this councell. The Emperour ſendeth vnto the Synod, certein counſailours vvith the Emperours letters patentes, to this effect. Conſtantinus and Irene, to the Biſſhoppes aſſembled in the ſecōd Nicene Synode, by Gods grace our fauour and the commaundement of our Emperiall authoritie. He ſhevveth that it apperteyneth to the emperial office, to mainteine the peace, concord, and vnity, of the vvhole Romayne Empire, but

The. 287.
Vntruthe
He ſaied
not ſo.

eſpecially to preſerue the eſtate of Gods holy Churches, vvhich allpoſſible care and councell. For this cauſe, he hath vvith paine gathered this councel together: geueth licēce alſo and liberty to euery mā vvithout al feare, to vtter his mind and iudgemēt frankely: to the end the truth may the better appeare. He ſhevveth the order he obſerued, in making Taraſius Biſhop: He

The. 288.
vntruth,
The defi-
nition of
the faithe
was made
vvithout
the Empe-
rours Au-
thority.

preſcribeth vnto the Biſhopps vvhat is their office, ād vvhat they ſhould doo: propounding vnto thē the holy Ghoſpelles, as the right and (287.) onely true rule they ſhould folovve. After this he mentioneth letters brought from the Biſhop of Rome by his Legates, the vvhiche he cōmaundeth to be opēly redde in the councel: and ſo appointeth alſo other thinges that they ſhould reade. There vvas (.288.) nothing attempted or done in this councel, vvithout the

autority

autority of the Emperours, as in all the former generall councels.
And so at the end, the vvhole Councell put vppe a supplication to the Empe-
rour, for the (.289.) ratifiyng of al their doings. The vvhiche vvhen the
Emperour had heard openly recited and read vnto them, they forthvvith al-
lovved, signed, and sealed.

The.7. Coapter. Of the.7. General Councel holden at Nice.
Stapleton.

PHY on all shamelesse impudencie. Doth it not shame
you M. Horne ones to name this. 7. Generall Councell, which doth so plainly accurse you and your fellowes, for your detestable saiyngs, writings, and doings, a-
gainst the holy Images, and against all such as call them I-
dols, as ye doe in this your booke? Yf the authority of this
Coũcel furnished with the presence of. 350. Bishops, established with the cõsente of the Pope, and the foure other
Patriarches, and euer since of all Catholike people both in
the Latine and Greke Church highly reuereced, may take
no force, I know not what law eclesiasticall may or ought
to take force. Yf you and your fellowes be no heretikes
(and it were but for this point onely) according to the rule
and prescription, before by me out of the Emperour Iustinians writings rehearsed, who is, was, or euer shall be, an
heretike? And can ye then for verye shame medle with
the Councel, yea to craue aide of this Councel to healpe
you to erect your newe Papalitie? Out vpon this your
exceding shamelesse demeanour. Yet were your impudencie, the more to be borne withal, if beside the matter
of Images, there were not also, most open and euident testimonie of the Popes Supremacie in this Synode. Certainelye as in the Councell of Chalcedo, after Pope Leos
letters were read, and in the sixt Generall Councell, after

k iij   Agathos

M. Horns
exceding
impudẽci
for alleas
ging for
hi the. 7.
Generall
Councell.
Qui vene-
randas i-
magines
idola ap-
pellant, a-
nathema.
Act.4. fol.
535. et act
7. fol. 603.
Fol.15.
M. Horn
is by this
Councell
declared
an Heres
tique.

Agathos letters were read: all the fathers receiued and allowed, and highly reuerenced the said letters, and were
directed by them, towchinge matters of fayth then being
controuersed: Euen so yt fared also here. The letters that
Pope Adrianus sent to théperour, and to the Patriarche of
Constātinople towching the Reueréd Images beinge proponed ād reade to these Fathers, they did most vniformely,
and most ioyfullie códescéde tó the cótentes of thé: And in

Act.2.   ful testimony therof, eche one set to hys hād ād subscriptiō.
The sayd Adriā writeth to Tarasius the patriarche of Cóstā
tinople, that ólesse, he had wel knowen Tarasius good syn-
cere zeale, ād catholike fayth touching Images, ād the sixe
general coūcels, *that he would neuer haue cósented to the cal*

Nequa-   *ling of any Councell.* Wherby ye see M. Horn that the Pope
quam ad   hath such a voyce negatyue, in summonyng and ratifiyng
Synodum   of Coūcels, that if he only had drawē backe, it had bene no
conuocā-   lawful Councel: According as the old Canon alleaged in
dā cósen-   the ecclesiasticall story commaundeth, *that without the*
tiremus.   *Popes Authorityte no Councel ought to be kept,* and according
Dict.act.   as for that only cause diuers coūcels were abolished, as the
2.fol.483   Antiochian in the East, and the Ariminense in the West.
Col.2.b.   And the sayed Pope Adrian saieth to Tarasius. *Vnde & ipse*
Ibidē fol.   *Beatus Petrus Apostolus Dei iussu Ecclesiam pascens nihil om-*
485.Col.1   *nino pratermisit, sed vbique principatum obtinuit & obtinet:*
Tripart.   *cui etiam & nostra beata & Apostolicæ sedi, quæ est omnium*
lib.4.   *Ecclesiarum Dei caput, velim beata vestra sanctitas ex sincera*
cap.9.   *mente & toto corde agglutinetur.* Saynte Peter feding the
Theodoret.   Churche by Gods commaundemét hath omitted nothing
lib 2.   at all, but euer hath had the principality, and nowe hath: to
cap.22.   whome and to our blessed and Apostolyke see, whiche is
the Head of all Gods Churches, I would wish your blessed

ſed holines wythe ſyncere mynd , and withall your heart
to ioyne your ſelf.The Emperour hym ſelf ſayth, that the
councel *was called by ſynodical letters ſente frō the moſt holy
patriarch. And a litle after ,by whoſe exhortatiō ād in a māner
cōmaundemēt we haue called you together*, ſaith th'Fmperour
to the biſhops. The Popes Legates are named firſt and ſubſcribe firſt: The Popes letters were read firſt of all in the
Councel:And that(Taraſius him ſelfe confeſſeth) *Prærogi-
tiua quadam.* For a certeyn prerogatiue dewe to the Pope.
Other places alſo of like agreablenes ye ſhal find here.
Theſe be the letters M.Horn,that ye ſpeak of,which as ye
ſay thꝰeror cōmaūded to be read opēly. Wherwith , that
ye dare for ſhame of th'world ones to medle,as alſo to talk
of the ſtory of Paulus ād Taraſius,I can not but moſt wonderfully maruayle at.This Paulus was patriarche of Cōſtātinople immediatly before Taraſius,and volūtarily renoū-
ced the ſame office,and became a monke, mynding to doe
ſome penāce the reſidue of his lyfe,for that he had ſet forth
the wycked doings and decrees of themperours againſt
the images . The Emperour was verye deſirous to place
Taraſius in hys roome, but he was as vnwilling to receyue that dignity.And whē the Emperour vrged ād preſſed hym vehemētly:he anſwered. *How cā I take vpon me to
be Biſhop of thys ſee, being ſondred frō the reſidew of Chriſtes
Church.ād wrapped in excōmunication.* Is not this then pretely ād gayly done of M.Horn,to take this coūcel as a trō-
pet in hys hand,to blowe and proclaime hym ſelf to all the
world an heretyke?Pleade on a paſe M.Horne, as ye haue
done, and yow ſhall purchaſe your ſelf at length great glo-
ry:as great,as euer had he that burnte the tēple of Diana,to
wyn to him ſelf a perpetuall memorye.To the which your
glorious tytle for the encreaſe and amplifying of the ſame,
let

Cuius hor
tatu &
veluti
iuſſu vos
congrega-
uimus.
ct.1.fol:
463.

Tom.2.
Conc.fol.
608.

Zonaras
Tom.3. &
Tom.2.
Concil.
fol.464.

Eccleſia à
reliquis ec
cleſiis
auulſa &
anathe-
mati ſub-
iectæ.
Zonar.
ibidem.

let your Vntruthes, which are here thicke and threefolde be alſo adioyned. That the Popes about this time deuiſed horrible practiſes,to haue to them ſelues only the ſupreme authority : that Irene Conſtantines Mother was an ignorant and a ſuperſtitious woman : that the matters in the. 7. Generall Councel were not iudged according to the Goſpelles: that there was nothing attempted or done in this Councell without the authority of the Emperour. In all this I heare very bolde aſſeuerations, but as for proufes, I finde none: And none wil be found when M.Horne hath done bis beſt, this yeare, nor the next neyther.

The.290.
Vntruth.
Ioyned
vvith a
Slāder.
The.291.
Vntruth.
Falſe trãſ
ſlation as
ſhall ap=
peare.
The.292.
Vntruth.
Capitaine
and noto
rious,ioy
ned vith
extreme
folly,and
groſſe ig=
norance.
The.293.
Vntruth.
He yel=
deth no
iuriſdicti=
on at al
in eccle=
ſiaſt.mat.
ters to
the laye
Prince,

M. Horne. The. 94. Diuiſion. pag. 57. 4.

Gregorius. 3. *ſent into Fraunce for ſuccour to Charles Martell, yelding and (.290.) ſurrendring vp vnto him, that vvhiche the Pope had ſo long ſought, by all ſubtile and miſchieuous meanes, to ſpoile the Emperoure and the Princes of. This ſame Gregory the third (ſaith Martinus Pœnitẽ=tiarius) VVhan Rome was beſieged by the king of Lombardy, ſent by ſhippe vnto Charles Martell, Pipines father, the Keyes(.291.) of S. Peters confeſsion, beſeeching him to deli=uer the Church of Rome from the Lombardes. By the keyes of S. Peters confeſsion,he meaneth (.292.) al the preheminence,dignitie, and iu=riſdiction, that the Popes claime to them ſelues (more and beſides that, vvhich al other church miniſters haue) ouer and aboue all manner perſons Eccleſiaſtical or Temporal, as geuen of Chriſt onely to S.Peter, for his con=feſsion, and ſo from him to the Popes of Rome by lineall ſucceſsion. Seinge that this Pope vvho vvas paſsingly vvell learned, both in diuine and pro=phane learning, and no leſſe godly, ſtout, and conſtant (if you vvill beleeue Platina) (.293.) yeldeth and committeth all this iuriſdiction and claime that he hath, ouer all perſons Eccleſiaſticall and Temporall, ſo vvel in cau=ſes Eccleſiaſticall as Temporall, vnto Charles Martell a laie Prince, and great Maiſter of Fraunce: it appeareth that Princes may lauſully haue the rule, gouernment, and charge, in Church matters. The heires and ſucceſ-*

ſours

ſours of this Charles Martell, did keepe theſe keyes from ruſting. They ex-
erciſed the ſame iuriſdictiō and gouernmēt in Eccleſiaſtical cauſes, that the
Emperours and Kings had don, from the tyme of Conſtātine the great, vntil
their tyme, vvhich vvas almoſt. 400. yeres. For Carolomanus (. 294.) ſonne
to King Pepin, and nephevv to Charles Martel, no leſſe Princelike than Chri-
ſtianly, exerciſed this his (. 295.) Supreme authority in Eccleſiaſtical cauſes,
and made notable reformation of the Eccleſiaſtical ſtate. He ſummoned a
Councel of his Clergy, both Biſhoppes and Prieſtes. 742. yere from the incar-
nation of Chriſt: vvherein alſo he him ſelfe ſate vvith many of his nobles and
counſailours. He ſhevveth the cauſe vvhy he called this Synode. That they
ſhould geue aduiſe (*ſaith he*) howe the Lawe of God and the
Churche religion (*meaning the order and diſcipline*) may be reſtored
againe, which in the tyme of my predeceſſours, being broken
in ſonder, fell cleane away. Alſo by what meanes the Chriſtiā
people may attaine to the ſaluation of their ſoules, and periſhe
not, being deceiued by falſe prieſtes. *He declareth vvhat ordinaun-*
ces and decrers vvere made (. 296.) by his authoriy in that Synode. VVe did
ordein Biſhops through the Cities (*ſaith he*) by the coũcel of the
Prieſts, ãd my nobles, ãd did cōſtitute Bonifaciʼto be the Archbiſshop ouer them (. 297.) VVe haue alſo decreed a Synode to
be called together euery yere, that the decrees of the Canons,
and the Lawes of the Churche, may be repaired in our preſence, and the Chriſtian Religion amended. &c. *That the mo-*
ney vvhereof the Churches haue been defrauded, be reſtored. VVe haue
degraded the falſe Prieſtes, Deacons, and Clerkes, being adulterers, and fornicatours, and haue driue them to penaũnce. *VVe*
haue vtterly forbidden, al maner hũting and haukig to the Clergy. VVe decree
alſo, that euery prieſt dvvellig in the dioceſe, be ſubiect vnto his ovvn biſshop,
and that alvvaies in Lent, he make an accõpt and ſhhevv to the biſhop the
maner ãd order of his miniſtery, touching baptiſm, the Catholik faith, praiers
and the order of Maſſes. And vvhãſoeuer the biſhop ſhal go his circuite to cõ-
firm the people, the prieſt ſhalbe ready to receiue hĩ vvith collectiõ ãd helpe of
the people. That the prieſt ſeke for nevv Chriſm alvvaies on Mãũdy thurſday
at the biſhops hãd, that the biſhop may be a vvitnes of his chaſt life, of his
faith and doctrine. VVe decree further, that no vnknovven biſhop or Prieſt,

l be ad-

The. 298.
vntruth.
For all
that Caro
lomanus
here did,
vvas don
by the
Cōmiſsiō
of Pope
Zachaa
rias.

*be admitted into the Churche miniſterye, before he be allovved bye the Sy-
node. He maketh many ſuch like, for the reformation of the Clergy, in vvhat
ſort they ſhalbe puniſhed, yf they commit vvhordome, and likevviſe againſte
ſorcery, vvitchcraft, diuinacions, incantations, and alkind of prophane ſuperſtitions. If ther vvere no more examples of any Church hiſtory, but this (298)
of Caloroman, it vvoulde ſuffice to make plaine that to the Princes authoo
ritye apperteineth, to make Lavves, and to the Clergye to geue him counſaile out of Gods vvorde, hovv to frame the diſcipline, to the edifiyng of Gods
Church.*

The. 8. Chapter: Of Charles Martell, and of the keyes of S. Peters Confeſſion.

Stapleton.

M. Horns
great
provves.

AS farre as I can ſee, al M. Hornes noble prowes and
great conqueſts haue bene and ſhal be vpon the lāde.
By the which he hath brought and will bring (yf ye
wil belieue him) vnder his newe Papacy many greate and
noble countries: yea Moſcouia and Aethiopia to. But happye yt is, that he is not yet come to the Late newe foūde
Landes : where the newe Chriſtian people doe as faſte,
and as reuerently embrace the Popes authority, as we, after we haue bene Chriſtian men nowe theſe thowſande
yeares, doe reiecte yt, and that with moſte ſhamefull vilany. But as I ſaid, I fynde no martiall actes of M Hornes,
vpon the ſea, but this onely, which is ſo notable and won-

Al the
Popes au
thoritye
fent away
by fea in
aſhippe.

derful, that this one way ſerue for all . For Lo he carieth
all the Popes authoritye awaye in a ſhippe, to Fraunce:
ſente thyt ier by the Pope him ſelfe, as him ſelfe ſaieth.
For as muche as he ſent to Carolus Martellus, *the keyes of
Saint Peters confeſſion* . So that nowe the Pope hathe,
beinge therto forced by Maiſter Horne, belyke in ſome
terri-

terrible combat vppon the feas with fending thefe keyes,
fo fpoyled him felfe of all his iurifdiction , that he hath no
more lefte,then haue all other Minifters of the Churche,
and euerye other poore felye Sir Iohn . This is Maifter
Horne , a iolye triumphante victorye , as euer I reade or
he.irde of : and thefe be as wonderfull keyes. Some great
and ftronge wonders haue I reade , done by keyes . As
in Italye , that fuche as be bytten with madde dogges haue
bene cured by the Churche doore keye of Saint Bellins
Churche : who beinge a bleffed man, died al to torne with
dogges . And this is writen of a greate learned man of
late memorie , borne aboute thofe quarters . I haue reade
alfo , of merueloufe greate miracles done by keyes , that
hadde towched the holye reliques of Saint Peter at Rome:
writen by Sainte Gregorye , our Apoftle, as a thynge
mofte certainelye and notoriouflye to him and to others
knowen. But yet Maifter Horne thefe your keyes feame
to me incomparablye to paffe all other : And for the
ftraungnes of the matter , and for my better inftruction,
I woulde full fayne be refolued at your handes but of two
dowbtes that trouble and incomber me .

Miracles done by keyes.

Cœlius Rhodigin⁹ Lect , an-tiq.lib.17, cap. 28.

Greger. li.6. epift. 23.

Firft feinge that this Pope , as Maifter Horne reciteth
out of Platina, *paffingly well learned bothe in diuine and pro-phane learninge , and no leffe godlye , ftoute, and conftante,*
hath yelded ouer to a laye Prince (by fendinge to him in a
fhippe Saint Peters keyes) all his iurifdiction and clayme,
that he hadde ouer all caufes Ecclefiafticall or temporall,
yet for all this good Maifter Horne , in this fo weightye a
matter,I woulde craue at your handes a litle of your good
helpe to fatisfie my mynde, yea and your wife difcrete rea-ders mynde to.

M.Horns merue-loufe ex-pofition of Saint Peters keyes.

For

For I hauing but a dull infight in fuch matters, for my part,
fee no great wifedome, vertue, or learning, and leffe ftout-
neffe in Gregorie for theis his doings. Your authors in this
ftorie, are here, *Martinus* and *Platina*. Yf we fhall by them
meafure his wifdome and ftowtenes, and other qualities

whithal: yt was partly, for that by his great carefulnes he
procured, that Rome being oppreffed by the kinge of Lom-
bardie, was releyued: partlie and that moft of al for that by
a councel holden at Rome almofte of one thowfande biffhops, he condemned and accurfed the wycked Emperour
of Conftantinople Leo, for defacyng againe after the 7. Generall Councel (beinge perfuaded thereto by an hereticall
monke) the holy images, as your authour Martinus in Gregories ftorie writeth: And Platina fayth, that he both excõmunicated themperour Leo, and by fentence declared him
to be no Emperour. And fo not whithftãding the keies of S.
Peter were fent away by fhippe, he referued to him felt one
of S. Peters keyes, and a litle more authoritie then ye were
ware of, yea fo much, that he hath geuen you a fore blowe
in the face whith his key, ãd declared, you ãd your fellowes,
and your great Emperour to, verie arrant heretyks. I muft

now ons again be fo bolde as to trouble your wifedome :
with an other as neceffarie a queftion, and that is: by what
authoritye ye auouche, that theis keyes were nothing elfe,

but the popes fupreame authoritie and iurifdictiõ? Your authors *Martinus* and *Platina* fay no fuch thing : No nor anie
other, that I could euer chãce vppõ. If this be your owne
newe frefhe inuention, then haue yowe a iolie pregnante
wytte, and ye haue deceyued afwel others, as the late reuerent father, M. Bayne, late bifhop of Lichfeld and Couē-
trie, his expectation, fomtime your reader in Cãbridge, that

was

was wont to call yow *quouis cornu duriorem*:that is , harder then any Horn . But I pray you good Sir is your authority inuoydable?Muſt we neads ſing *ſanctus,ſanctus,ſanctus*,to al your ſayings?and ſay of you as Pythagoras ſchollers were wont to ſay:*ipſe dixit*:ād reaſon no further?Let poore blont fellowes be ſo bold vppon yowe for ones,to heare frō you ſome better authoritye then your owne naked worde for this noble expoſition. Namely ſeing that your boke is not authoriſed,by the Quenes cōmiſsioners,as ſome others are. And thowgh yt wer,yet might we craue ſo much at your hands, ſeing that yowe auouche that, whiche(for all your prety expoſition)was not done by this Gregorie,nor could poſsible be done , onleſſe he had bene as frantycke as euer was madde Collyns ofBethelem . Nor I trowe , anie man woulde make or belieue anie ſuche fonde declarations,but ſuche as haue loſt theyr fyue wyttes . And therefore I ſay, of all your ſhameful lies, this maye be crowned for a noto-riouſe, a captavne and an Imperiall Lie.

M.Horns boke is not ſet forth by the Que-nes au-thoritye.

For wil you ſee gētle Readers, what were in dede theſe miraculous keyes that M. Horn hath with ſuch a ſtraunge Metamorphoſis turned into *al the preeminence, dignitie,and Iuriſdiction that the Pope hath aboue other Church Miniſters?* Verely not in al the xiiij.bookes ofOuides Metamorpho-ſis can there be founde,a more fabulous,more ridiculous,or more vnſauery and vnſenſible chaunge , thoughe he talke there of full many , as of men and wemen chaunged into birds,into ſtones,into beſtes,into ſtarres,and into I can not tel what , then is this one moſt ſingular and rare inuented Metamorphoſis of M.Hornes exacte deuiſe.And truly M. Horn you hauing ſuch a nūber of good verſyfiers to your neighbours,in the famousand wel ordered ſchole of Win-

VVhat vvere the keyesthat vver ſent to Char-les Martel

chefter, it fhoulde be an eternal monument of your fingular witte, if you did procure this your excellent Metamor-
phofis to be put alfo in verfes, and to be adioyned to the
other of Ouides, for the rarite and fingularneffe thereof.
Suche as I trowe all Europe, yea all the wide worlde a-
gaine will not be able to fhewe the like. Well: In the
meane feafon that the worthy memory hereof may not
vtterly be extinguifhed, I will fhortelye and rudelye fhadowe it out, leauing to more excellent wittes, and con-
ning workemen (of which you fhall not want M. Horne,
if you earneftlye procure them) to fette it forthe in his
coulours. Firft then it is to be vnderftanded gentle Readers, that bothe before the time of this Gregory. 3. and in
his time, and after his time, the toumbe, chappell or monument where S. Peters body laye in Rome, was called
of the Romayn writers *Confefsio B. Petri.* S. Peters Confef-
fion. Witneffe hereof before the time of Gregory the 3.
is the Pontificall of Damafus, as Georgius Caffander hath

Georg. Caf- noted out of Petrus Vrbeuetanus. Thus Caffander writeth
fander in vpon the worde *Confefsio. Frequens eft hæc vox in Pontifi-*
Ordine *cali Damafi. Ante Confefsionem S. Petri, de qua P. Vrb. Con-*
Romano. *fefsio, inquit, Capfa vel fepulchrum, vel potius corpus B. Petri*
conditum fub altari. This worde *Confefsio,* faieth Caffander
P. Vrb. in is often founde in the Pontificall of Damafus. Before S.
fcholÿs in Peters Confefsion. Whereof Petrus Vrbeuetanus faieth.
vitas Pōt. By S. Peters Confefsion is meante, the Cophyn or toumbe,
Damafi. or rather the body of S. Peter layed vnder the Aultar.

   This was a phrafe to expreffe that place, where the memory of S. Peter and of his moft bleffed Cōfefsiō cōfefsing
there Chrift, and dying there a glorious Martyr for Chrift
was by the bleffed Relike of his bodye there prefent, honoured

noured and contynewed. In the life of Gregory. 3. it is wri
ten of a Synod of. 93. bifhops holden in S.Peters Chappel at
Rome : *Coram facrofanEta Confefsione Sacratifsimi corporis* Tom. 2.
B. Petri refidentibus &cat . The bifhops fittinge before the Conc. pa.
holy Confefsion of the mofte bleffed body of S.Peter. And 434. col.
with the like phrafe it is writen of Zacharias his fuccef- 2. c
four, that he offred vp before the Confefsion of S. Peter Ibidē pag.
many Iewels and much treafure. Such phrafes are ryfe 445. c. 2.
in the 2.Tome of the Councels, and in the writers of thofe
ages . This beinge firfte knowen, lette vs nowe confider the allegation of M. Horne . He faieth Gregory.
3. *fent by fhippe to Charles Martell, the keyes of S. Peters
Confefsion* . His Author is *Martinus pœnitentiarius* , one of
the pœnitentiaries at Rome . The latin of Martinus is this.
*Claues ex Confefsione B.Petri Apoſtoli accipiens, direxit na-
uali itinere* . Here M. Horne hath clerkly turned : *Claues
ex Confefsione B.Petri* , The keyes of S. Peters Confefsion.
The latin of this Englifhe , were . *Claues Confefsionis* , not
Claues ex Confefsione . As if I fhould faie , *Claues ex Ecclefia
direxit* . It were not well Englifhed I trowe. *He fent the
keyes of the Churche* . But *He fent kayes from the Churche:*
Which mighte be other keyes pardie, then the Churche
keyes . And fo is it in this place . Pope Gregory the thyrd
fent to Charles Martell , *keyes from the Confefsion of S. Peter* . But not : *the keyes of S.Peters confefsion* . The keyes of
S. Peters Confefsion were *Claues Regni cælorum* the keyes
of the kingdome of heauen , whiche Chrifte gaue to Peter , and to onely Peter . And the whiche were not I
trowe materiall keyes, fuche as might be fente awaye, either by fea , or by lande . But keyes from S. Peters Confefsion were keyes from the body of S.Peter : keyes which
had

Char-
les.

had touched that holy relike, and which by that touch was made it felfe a Relike. Howe proue we this, you fay? Forfoth very plainely and euidently by a witneffe well nere a thoufande yeres olde, by one of the foure Doctours of the Churche, by our Apoftle, learned S. Gregory the

Gregorius firſt. Such keyes from S. Peters confeſsion to be ſent to de-
Secundino uoute perſons for holy Relikes, was in his tyme and longe
ſeruo Dei before his tyme an vſuall matter. S. Gregory writing to
incluſo Secundinus an Anachoret (as it feemeth) amonge other re-
lib.7. likes, as an Image of our Sauiour, of our Lady, and of S.
epiſtol. 53. Peter and Paule, and a Croſſe alſo, mentioneth alſo this
Indict.2. kinde of Relike, ſayinge. *Clauim etiam pro benedictione à ſanctiſsimo Corpore Petri Apoſtolorum principis &c.* We fende you alſo by this bearer, a keye for a benediction from the moſt holye bodye of Peter the Prince of the Apoſtles. A keye from the body, was a keye that hadde touched the body, or the place where the body was interred. And wil M. Horne nowe ſay, that S. Gregory ſent away to this poore Anchoret *his whole preeminence, dignity, and iuriſdiction &c.* Or becauſe he ſent alſo to one Theo-

Lib. 6. dorus a Phyſitian of Conſtantinople, *Clauem à ſacratiſsimo*
epiſt.25. *Petri Corpore,* a keye from the moſt holy body of S. Peter, thinketh M. Horne, that this Phyſitian had, *All the Popes preeminence and iuriſdiction* geuen him? Or becauſe in like maner he ſent to *Theotiſtas* and *Andreas,* two noble men aboute the Emperour, for a benediction of Saint Peter,

Lib. eodē. *Clauem à ſacratiſsimo eius corpore,* a keye from his moſte
epiſt.23. holye bodye, were they alſo promoted wyth *all the Popes preeminence, dignitye and Iuriſdiction,* as you affirme Charles Martell was here of Pope Gregory.3. for hauinge ſuche a Relike ſent him by ſhippe?

S. Gre-

S.Gregory saied,he sent those keyes for a Benediction,not
for a Iurisdiction.He sent it to the Anchoret, *vt per ipsum à*
maligno defenderetur,cuius signo munitum se crederet. That
by him from the deuil he might be defended,by whose token or remembrance he thoughte him selfe garded . He
sent it to Theodorus the Phisicyan , with a piece of S. Peters chayne enclosed , *vt quod illius collum ligauit ad marty-*
rum,vestrum ab omnibus peccatis soluat.that the same which
had tyed S. Peters necke to martyrdom , may lose yours
(saieth S. Gregory to the Phisitian) from all sinnes,mea-
ninge from the paynes of synnes . He sent it to the two
Noble men, *vt per quam omnipotens Deus superbientem &*
persidum hominem peremit , per eam vos (qui eum timetis
& diligitis) & prasentem salutem & aternam habere valea-
*tis.*To thentent that as by that keye God (*miraculously)
shewe a proude and wretched man , so by it you (saieth
he to them) whiche feare God and loue God , may haue
also bothe present sauegarde and euerlastinge . This was
M. Horne the popes meaninges and intentes in sendinge
to deuoute persons , to Noble men, and to princes,such relikes of keyes from the Confession , that is from the body
or chappell of S.Peter . And thus whereas M. Horne , by
his wonderfull inuentyue wytte had made a straunge metamorphosis , of a Relique from S.Peters body , into *al the*
preeminence dignitie and Iurisdictiõ of the Pope aboue other
Churche Ministers, they are nowe agayne by a happy re-
uolution, God be thanked,returned to their former shape,
and appere as they did before, in their owne natural like-
nesse . And that wythe more truthe a greate deale , then
Lucians Asse hauing trotted many yeres ouer downes and
dales , came at lengthe by eating of red roses to be Lucian

Lib. 7. epi
stol. 53.

Lib. 6. epi
stol.25.

Lib. eodē
epist. 23.

* Of this
Miracle,
Vide Greg.
loco citato

him selfe agayne as it was before, and as they saie, it was
neuer other.

But if M. Horne notwithstanding al this, wil yet vphold
his straunge metamorphosis, and delight him selfe stil therin, the rather bicause S. Gregory in al those places speaketh
but of a keye, and not of keyes, as Gregory the .3. is saied to
haue sente to Charles Martell: then lo M. Horne for your
ful satisfaction in this poynt, yet an other place of S. Gregory, wherein he sendeth euen keyes also. Writing to Co-
lumbus a bishop of Numidia, at the ende of his letters he

Lib. 2.
epist. 47.
Indict. 11.

sayeth. *Etiam Claues beati Petri in quibus de cathenis ipsius
inclusum est, tibi pro benedictione transmisi.* I haue sent you
also by this bearer the keyes of S. Peter, in which there is
of his chaynes enclosed for a benediction. Lo M. Horne
here are sent to a bishop of Numidia not the keyes from or
of S. Peters Confession (which you see are but keyes of or
from his toumbe or body) as to Charles Martell onely
were sent, but the very keyes of S. Peter him selfe. But
what? Had that bishoppe therefore all the popes preeminence and Iurisdiction sent him? Nay this notwithstan-
dinge, what Iurisdiction and supreme gouernement thys
verye pope practised ouer Numidia and all Afrike to,
bothe in these very letters partlye appereth, and more
largely it maye appeare, if you vouchesafe M. Horne to
reade that litle onely which in this matter I haue saied to

Art. 4. fol.
10. & 11.

your pewefelowe M. Iewell, in my laste Returne of vntruthes vppon his moste lyinge Replie. And here you
heare S. Gregory saie he sent him, these keyes, *pro benedictione* : For a benediction, not for a Iurisdiction. For a holy Relike : not for a supreme dignitie. For a deuoute remembraunce, not for a princelye preeminence : As you
most

fondelye and ignorantlye do pronounce . Yea and tel.
this you fo folowe and purfewe from hence forewarde ,
as the very grounde and foundation of all the Supreme
gouernement , whiche you woulde fo fayne faften vppon
princes heads , a thinge of them neuer yet fo much as defired or dreamed of.

For lo vpon this ioyly grounde you buylde and fay . *The
heyres and fucceffours of this Charles Martell , did keepe
thefe keyes from ruftinge* . Verely I thinke in dede bothe he
and his godly fucceffours, vfed that Relike and many other
deuoutely , and did not fuffer it to rufte aboute them . A
poynt for this relike,fay you.I faie : *They exercifed the fame
iurifdiction and gouernement in Ecclefiaftical caufes ,that the
Emperours and kings had done from the time of Conftantine
&cat.* Verelye and fo thinke I to . But you fee nowe
Maifter Horne , at lefte euery difcrete Reader feeth , that
from the time of Conftantin hytherto, neuer Prince but
heretikes, as Conftantius and Anaftafius wythe a fewe
fuche , gouuerned in caufes Ecclefiafticall . Namely in
al things and caufes,as you by Othe make folke to fweare,
I fhould fay,forfweare.

But as touchinge thys Charles Martell , and Carolomanus his fonne (whom you call his nephewe, and kinge
Pipins fonne) and their gouuernement in Ecclefiafticall
caufes,gouuernement they had none , nor exercifed none.
You tel vs of fuch a thinge, but you proue no fuch thinge.
The whole dealing of Gregory the.3.with Charles Martel
and of pope Zachary with Carolomannus his fonne , was
onely that they fhoulde take the Churche of Rome in to
their protection, (beinge then the mofte mighty princes in this parte of Chriftendom) feinge the Emperours

of Con-

of Conſtantinople had by hereſy (as Leo then the Iconomache) and other crueltyes, rather forſaken it and oppreſſed it, then ſuccoured it, and defended it . And therefore
of this facte of Gregory the. 3. Sabellicus a moſte diligente

Sabellicus
Aenead 8.
lib. 8.

chronicler, writeth thus . *Tum primùm Romanæ vrbis Apo-
ſtolicæq̃, ſedis tutela , quæ ad Conſtantinopolitanos principes (ſi
quid grauius accidiſſet) omnia ſua deſideria conferre conſue-
uiſſet , Gallorum eſt Regum facta* . Then began the Frenche
princes to take vpõ thẽ the protection of the Cyty of Rome
and of the See Apoſtolike, which had bene wonte (before)
to referre al their griefes to the Emperours of Conſtantinople, if any weightyer matter had befallẽ. And againe. *Suſ-
cepit nihil grauatè pientiſsimũ patrociniũ Carolus Põtificis roga-
tu* . Charles at the requeſt of the pope toke vpon him willingly that moſt charitable or godly protection. And this lo
was that which Pope Gregory by ſendig keyes frõ S. Peters
Cõfeſsiõ to Charles Martel, did ſeke ãd ſewe for at his hãds.
M. Horn ſhooteth farre wide to imagine herin al the popes
Iuriſdictiõ, dignite and preeminẽce to be ſent away by ſhip
into Frãce. And as for Carolomanus, of whoſe ſupreme gouernmẽt M. Horn fableth here ſo much, within. 4. yeres af-

Naucle-
rus Gene-
rat: 25. p.
793. co. 1.

ter this great Authoryty exerciſed, wẽt to Rome, offred hĩ
ſelfe to the pope, ãd was ſhorẽ in for a Mõke. And what or
wherin cõſiſted his Authoryty? *He ſummoned a Coũcel*, you
ſay, *and many decrees were made there by his Authoryty*. Yea
but why tel you not that pope Zacharias at the requeſt of
Bonifacius, gaue to him ãd to this Carolomanus , a ſpeciall
Cõmiſsiõ by his letters to cal this Synod, ãd to decree therin ſuch things as Bonifacius ſhould think behoueful for that
time? Why in your very narratiõ do you euẽ in the middeſt
of your allegatiõ where you talk of this Bonifacius , leaue
out

out quite, and nippe of thefe wordes: *Qui eft miſſus S. Petri.*
Who is the Popes Legat? Why deale you not trulye, and
why tell you not al? Forſoth becauſe truth is none in you,
and al maketh againſt you. In Nauclerus you may fee and
reade at large the Popes Commiſsion to Bonifacius and to
the Prince for keping this Synod, and for orderĩg the ſame. *Nauc.pa*
Yet you tell all for the Emperour, as though the Pope had *790. &*
don nothing. O wilful malice, and malicious wilfulneſſe. M. *751.*
Horne is not content to be blinde him ſelfe. He wil alſo
make his readers blid. And becauſe he loueth not the truth,
or the truth loueth not him, therfore he would his Reader
ſhould learne the falſhood and be as falſe as him ſelf is.

But againe what impudency is this, to bring Carolomanus doinges, by the which euen in your own narration, the
holy Chriſme, the maſſe, and other orders of the Churche, *Maſſe cõ-*
that ye haue aboliſhed, are confirmed? and your whordome *firmed, ãd*
with M. Madge, is puniſhed by derogation, penance, and *M. Horn*
otherwiſe euen by your own ſupreme head, Corolòmanus? *degraded*
Which did not degrade any prieſt actually him ſelf, or cau- *by Caro-*
ſed any to be degraded, by his ſupreame authoritye (as ye *loma -*
ſeame by a falſe ſenſe to inferre) but cauſed them by the or- *nus his ſu*
dinary meanes, and according to the rules and canons to *preme*
be degraded. Who alſo made him ſelfe no Churche lawes, *head.*
as M. Horn here vntruly noteth, but did al by the authority
of Pope Zacharias, who (as I haue ſaid, and as in Nauclere *Naucler*
it appeareth) gaue Commiſsion to Bonifacius the Biſſhop to *generat.*
kepe a Synod in the Dominion of this Carolomanus, in *25.pa.790*
which Synode all theſe Churche lawes were made. All
which euidently proueth the Popes Primacy at that tyme,
not the Princes.

M iij   M.Horne

M.Horne. The.95.Diuision. pag.58.a.

About this tyme vvas one Bonifacius not Pope, but as they call him the great Apoſtle of the Germanies, the like for all the vvorld to our Apo-ſtle here in Englaude, Auguſtinus Anglorum Apoſtolus : Either of them (.299.) might be called, the Popes Apoſtles, vvhoſe greate cham-pions they vvere. And euen ſuche Eccleſiaſticall matters as our Apoſtle trea-teth of, hath this Apoſtle in his Epiſtles to the Pope, as this . He aſketh his holines when fatte bakon fhould be eaten: The Pope an-fwereth,when it is wel fmoke dried or reſty,and then ſoddē. Likewiſe he aſketh whether we fhall eate Dawes, Crowes, Hares,and wilde Horſes : The Pope biddeth him to beware of them in any wiſe.Alſo he asketh him howe,if Horſes haue the falling fickeſſe, what we f hall doe to them: The Pope aunſwereth , hurle them into a ditche . He asketh what we fhall doe with Beaſtes bitten with a madde dogge , the Pope biddeth him kepe them cloſe,or hurle them into a pitte. He asketh if one Nonne may wafhe an others feete , as men may: the Pope anſwereth, yea, on Goddes name . Alſo he asketh , howe many Croſſes, and where aboutes (.300.) in his bodye , a man fhoulde make them . Theſe and a greate manye ſuche like , are the Popes and his Apoſtles , Eccleſiaſticall matters. But leauing theſe trifles , note that in thoſe Eccleſiaſticall matters , vvhich he did to anye purpoſe, the laye Princes hadde the entermedling , as appea=reth (.301.)by the Pope Zacharias Epiſtle to this Boniface . It is no marueile thoughe this Kinge Charoloman , as alſo Charles the greate, and other noble Princes , after their tyme eſtabliſhed by their authority in Sy-nodes manye ſuperſtitions , and (.302.) idolatrous obſeruaunces , as of Maſſes, Chryſmes , and ſuch like abuſes , beinge moued vvith the zeale, that all Princes ought to haue , but vvanting the pure knovvledge that good and faithfull Biſhoppes ſhould haue inſtructed them vvithal : ſeinge ſuche(.303.)blind buſſardes as this Boniface,had the teaching of them, vvho like blinde guides,ledde them in the bottomles pitte of all ſuperſtitions and falſe religion.

The

The.9. Chapter:Of S.Boniface the Apostle of Germany,
and of S.Augustin our Apostle.
Stapleton.

HEre is interlaced a lying flaunderouse patche al from
the principal matter,againft our apoftle S.Auguftyn,
and S.Boniface an Englifh man,and a bleffed Martyr
flayne in Phrifia by the infidels,commonly called the Apoftle of Germanye. But what a Ghofpel is this,that can not
come in credite,but by moft flaunderouse vilany , and that
againft S.Auguftin,whome we may thank and S . Gregory
that fent him,that we are Chriftē mē ? S. Gregory cōmen-
deth him for learned and vertuous,and fetteth forth the miracles wonderfully wrought by him in our Countre . And
think you nowM.Horn,that you with al your lewde,lying
rayling, or M . Iewel either,can ftayne and blemifhe that
bleffed mās memory? No,no:ye rather amplifie ād auaunce
his glorious renown and proue your felues moft wretched
and deteftable lyers:as I haue fufficiētly of late declared in
my Return vpō M.Iewels Reply. They nede not M.Horn
your cōmendatiō,which in fuch a perfon as ye are,were rather their difcōmendatiō. For the ill mans difcōmendation
is to a good man a very commendation:as contrary wife to
be commended of an il man, is no true prayfe , but rather a
a difgracyng and a difpraife . Therefore where ye cal thefe
bleffed mē,ād other bifhops of this tyme blīdbuffards,ād fay
that in Charles the great,ād other Princes then,lacked pure
knowledge,ye declare your felf what ye are,a very blinde
hob abowt the howfe,neither able to kepe your felf frō lying,nor yet frō cōtradictiō.For M.Horne I would to God,
either your felf , or a great fort of your fellowes Proteftāt
Biffhops,

Beda in
martyro-
logio.

Art.3.fol.
124.& fe-
quentibus.

M.Horns
contradi-
ction to
him felfe.

Charles
the great
learned
in the La-
tin and
Greeke
tonges.

bifhops, had befide his vertue, the learning of Charles the
great, being well fene afwel in the Greke as the Latin tôge.
And fee nowe how well your tale hangeth together. For
the very leafe before Gregorye the .3. was *paſſinglye well
learned, both in diuine and prophane learning, and no leſſe godlye*. And the fowrth leafe after, your felfe bringe forthe
Alcuinus an Engliſhman of greate learninge, as ye faye,
that faieth, as ye write, *that God incomparably honored and
exalted Charles the great, aboue his auncetours with wiſedome to gouerne and teache his ſubiectes with a godlye carefulnes*. Which wiſedome ſtode, as your felfe declare, in ordering matters Eccleſiaſticall. And Pope Zacharias that
ye here ſpeake of, was well alfo fene in the Greeke tonge:
Into the which he trâſlated out of Latin S. Gregories Dia-
loges. And now what a blinde buſſarde are you, that pleade
vpon this Zacharias epiſtles to Bonifacius to proue this
Charlemains ſupremacye, wherein the Popes primacy is e-
uidently and openly declared, (as I haue before ſhewed)
yf ye were of this ignorant: or what an impudent and a
malicioufe perfon are you, yf ye wittinglye and willingly
alleage that for you, which is moſt ſtrong againſt you? For

Vide Pôt.
in vita
Zachar.

De ſynodo autem
congregata apud
Francorum prouin-
ciam mediantibus
Pipino & Carolo-
mano, excellentiſſi-
mis filius noſtris iux-
ta ſyllabarum no
ſtrarum commoni-
tionem, peragête vi
ces noſtras tua ſan-

this Councel that ye grounde your felfe vpon, was
called in dede by Pipyn and Caroloman, but according as the Pope had geuen them Commiſſion
in his letters: And this Bonifacius was the Popes
Legate there: For concealing wherof, you left out:
Qui eſt miſſus S. Petri: Who is the Popes legat. And
the Princes were but ayders and afſiſters vnto him.
And Boniface proceding very well and canonically depofed the falfe, the adulteroufe, and the fchifmaticall prieſtes. Which fo yrketh M. Horne at
the

the very heart, remembring that if him selfe were wel
and canonically handeled, he should beare a muche
lower saile, then to beare either any Bisshoplye or
priestly office, that faring like a mad man, he speaketh
he wot nere what: and euen there, where with his
egle eies he findeth fault with other mens blindnes,
he sheweth him self, most blind bussard of al. For he
may as wel find fault with Moses Law , and by the
supreme authority of his new Papacy, he may laugh
to scorne Moses to, as wel as Bonifacius, and cal hi
blind bussard also, for his madd lawes *forbidding the
eating of the Camel, the Hare, the Swine, the Egle, the
Goshauke, the Crow, the Rauen, the Owle, the carmorãt,*
and such like. He might also as well make him selfe
pastime and ieste merely at the Canons of the sixth
General Councel, that he so lately spake of , *forbidding the eating of puddings and things suffocated.*And
perchaúce the questiõ of beasts bitten with madde
dogges hath more matter in it, then M. Horne doth
yet withal his Philosophy cõsider, or that some of his good
brethren in Germanye haue of late considered, fealing as it
were, the smart of this their ignorance, which *feading vpon
swines flesh, bitten of a madde dogge, waxed as madde as the
dog, and falling one vpon an other, most pitifully bitte and tore
one the others flesh.*As for the questiõ cõcerning the Nûne,
M. Horne hath no great cause to mislike.

Nowe in case Bonifacius had demaunded of Pope Zacharie , whether a lewde, lecherouse, false Fryer , might
lurke and luske in bedde with a Nunne , and then cloke
their incest vnder the name of holy wedlock, ãd that Pope
Zacharie had geuen as honourable an answere , as his late

Apo-

*titate qualiter egi-
sti cognouimus, &
omnipotenti Deo no-
stro gratias egimus,
qui eorum corda cõ-
firmauit, vt in hoc
pio opere adiutores
existerent, et omnia
optimè et canonicè
peregisti , tam de sal
sis Episcopis et for-
nicarijs et schisma-
ticis, quamque etiã
et c.*
Zacha:ad Bonifac.
Tom. 2, Concil. fol.
450. Col. 2.

Vvhy M. Horne is
so outragius agaîst
S. Bonifacius.
Leuit. 11.

Mé waxé
mad with
eating of
svvines
flesh bit-
tē vvith
a madde
dogge.
Lycosthen.
de Prodi-
gÿs. Anno.
1535 . In
VVirten-
bergési. du
catu. &c.

Apoſtle frier Luther,hath donne,aſwel by hys bokes,as by
hys damnable doings : then lo,had Bonifacius ben the true
and ſincere Apoſtle of Ieſus Chriſte . And then ſhould he
haue ben M. Hornes Idole. Neither did Bonifacius demãd
theſe matters becauſe he was ignorante, or in anye greate
doubte:but to worke more ſuerly. And the Pope in hys an
ſwere, telleth hym , that he was well ſene in all holy ſcripture. As for the queſtion how many croſſes a mã ſhould
make in his body,is not Bonifacius,but your queſtion.For
the queſtion was,of croſſes to be made, in ſaying the holy
canõ of the maſſe. The name of the which holy canon ye
can no more abyde , then the deuill the ſigne of the holie
croſſe:of whome ye haue learned,thus to mangle your allegatiõs,and to caſte away both crosſing and canõ wythal.

Tom.2.
Căcil.fol.
452.Col.2
Nã et hoc
flagitaſt
à nobis ſan
ctiſsime
frater,in
ſacri cano
nis prædicatione,
quot in lo
ſis cruces
fieri debeant.
Fol.453.
Col.2.c.

Mr. Horne. The. 96. Diuiſion. pag.58.a.

Adrianus the firſt, Pope,being muche vexed through his owne (.304.)
furious pride, by Deſiderius king of Lombardy,ſendeth to Carolus Ma
gnus,and requireth him of his ayde againſt the Lombardes , promiſing to
make him (.305.)therfore Emperour of Rome:Charles cõmeth,vãquiſheth
Deſiderius,and ſo paſſeth into Rome,who the Pope receiued vvith great
honour,geuing to him in part of recompence, the title of moſt Chriſtian
king, and further to augment his beneuolence tovvardes Charles , deſired
him to ſende for his Biſhops into Fraunce,to celebrate a Synode at Rome:
vvhere in vvere gathered together of Biſhops, Abbottes, and other Prelates,about.154. In vvhich coũcel alſo Carolus him ſelfe vvas preſent,as
ſaith Martinus.   Gratianus maketh report hereof out of the Churche
hiſtory on this vviſe.Charles after he had vanquiſhed Deſiderius,
came to Rome,ãd appointed a Synode to be holdẽ there with
Adrian the Pope.Adrian with the vvhole Synode, deliuered
vnto Charles,the right and povver to elect the Pope , and to
diſpoſe the Apoſtolique ſea.They graunted alſo vnto him,the
dignity of the anciẽt bloud of Rome.VVerby he vvas made a Patricià,and ſo capable of the emperial dignity.Furthermore he decreed
that.

The.304.
vntruth.
Slaunderous,.

The 305.
vntruth.
It appereth not
ſo in any
hiſtory
Diſ.63.

that th'Archbithops ād bithops in euery prouīce fhuld receiue their inueſtiture ofhim:ſo that none fhuld be cōſecrate, onles he were cōmēde d ād inueſtured Bishop of the Kinge.VVo ſo euer woulde doo contrary to this decree,fhould be accurſed, and except he repēted,his goodes alſoſhould be cōfiſcate.*Platina addeth*,Charles,and the Pope,the Romaines ād the Frēche ſweare the one to the other,to keepe a perpetuall amity, and that thoſe fhuld be enemies to thē both,that anoyed the one.

The 10.Chapter. Of Charlemayne,and of Adrian,and Leo Biſhops of Rome.

Stapleton.

THat Adriā was vexed by king Deſiderius throwgh hys owne furiouſe pryde,who was a very vertuouſe learned man,is nothing but your follithe furiouſe lying,as alſo that he promiſed to Charles to make hym Emperour,if he would ayde and helpe hym:No hiſtory ſaieth ſo,except M.Hornes pēne be an hiſtory. Now what doth it furder your cauſe , that thys Charles had the righte and power to electe the Pope, and the inueſturing of Bithops, ſeeing he helde yt not of hys owne right and tytle,but by a ſpeciall and a gratiouſe graunte of the Pope and hys Synod,as your ſelf alleage?Nay verely this one exāple cleerly deſtroyeth al your imagined Supremacy,and al that you ſhall bringe hereafter of the Emperours claime for the ēlectiō ād inueſturing of Bithops.For the diligēt Reader remēbrīg this,that the firſt Original ād Authority hereof ſprong not of the Imperial right or power,but of the Popes ſpecial graunte made to Charlemayn the firſt Emperour of the weſt after the traſlatiō therof,muſt alſo ſee,that al that you bring hereafter of th'Emperors claime in this behalfe,proueth no Primacy in the Prince,but rather in the Pope,from whō the Authority of that facte proceded,by which facte you would proue a primacy.

Magnitudine animi, conſilio,doctina,et ſanctitate vita,cū quo uis optimo pontifice comporari poteſt.

　　　　　ā ꝯ　　Horne

Not longe after, *harles,perceiuing the Churches to be muche moleſted
and drayvne in o partes,vvith the Hereſy of* Fœlix,*calleth a councell of al
the Biſhoppes vnder his dominions in Italy, Fraunce, and Germany , to cō-
ſulte and conclude a truthe, and to bring the Churches to an vnity therein,
as he him ſelfe affirmeth in his Epiſtle vvritten to* Elepandus *Biſhop of
Tolet, and the other Biſhoppes of Spaine* : VVee haue commaunded
(*ſayth Charles*) a Synodall councel to be had of deuout Fathers
from al the Churches thoroughout our ſigniouries, to the end
that with one accorde it might be decreed , what is to be beleued touching the opiniō we know that you haue brought
in with newe aſſertions, ſuche as the holy Catholike Church
in old time neuer heard of . Sabellicus *alſo maketh mention of this
Synode vviche vvas conuocated to Frankeforth:ad Caroli* edictum : at
the commaundement of Charles.

Stapleton .

This gere ſerueth for nothing but to proue that Carolus
called a councell: and here M . Horne ſayeth *Sabellicus alſo
maketh mention of this Synode cōuocated to Fräckford* . Your
alſo M. Horn, is altogether ſuperfluous, ſeing that ye named
no other author before, that ſpake of thys Synode , for Sabellicus is here poſte alone. Well, let it be Charles that called the Synode, but why do ye not tell vs, what was donne
there, as doth Platina , and your owne authour Sabellicus
alſo, declaring that ſuche iconomaches and image breakers
as ye are, were there cōdemned for heretyks ? why
do ye not tell vs alſo, who were cheif in that Coūcell: whiche were Theophilatius and Stephanus
Pope Adriãs Legates? And here appereth the wretched dealing of the authour of your Apologye, for
hys duble lye, aſwell in that he would by thys Synode proue, that a generall councell, maye be abo-
lifſhed

*Sabell.
Aen. 8.li.8
dãnata eſt
hæreſis de
abolendis
imaginib.*

Platina.
*Theophilatius &
Stephanus Epiſcopi
inſignes, Adriani no-
mine ſynodũ Franco
rũ Germanorumque
Epiſcoporũ habuere:
in qua, &cat.*

lifhed by a national as for faying, this Councell did abolifhe **leman.**
the Seuenth Generall Councell, whereas it confirmed the
faid Generall Councell, with a like Decree. And with this vntruth
the ftrongeft part of your Apologie lyeth in the duft. For of the En-
wheras the chiefe and principall parte of it is to deface the glih Apo-
Councel of Trent: and to fhew that by priuate authority of abouvte
one nation, the publike and cómon authority of a Generall this Sy-
Councel might be well inough abrogated : he could finde node.
no colour of proufe but this your Councel of Franckford,
which now as ye heare, dothe not infirme, but ratifie and
confirme the. 2. Nicene Councell. As made for the hono-
ring, and not for the vilaining of holy Images.

M. Horne. The. 98. Diuifion. pag. 59. a.

Carolus Magnus *calleth by his commaundemente the Bifshoppes of*
Fraunce to a Synode at Arelatum, *appointeth the Archebifshoppes of*
Arelatum *and* Narbon *to be chiefe there. They declare to the Sy-*
node affembled, that Carolus Magnus *of feruente zeale and loue to-*
vvardes Chrifte, doothe vigilauntlye care to eftablifshe good orders in
Goddes Churche : and therefore exhorte them in his name, that they
diligentlye inftructe the people vvith godlie doctrine, and exaumples
of lyfe. VVhen this Synode had confulted and agreed of fuche mat-
ters as they thoughte fitte for that time, They decree that their doinges fhoulde be prefented vnto Carolus Magnus, befeeching him, that where anye defectes are in their Decrees,
that he fupplie the fame by his wifedome. If anye thing
be otherwife then well, that he will amende it by The. 306. Vntruth.
his iudgemente. And that whiche is well, that he Not fo in the Coū-
will (.306.) ratifie, aide, and afsift by his authority. cel. But *vt eius adiu-*
torio perficiatur.
By *his commaundemente alfo vvas an other Synode cele-* That by his helpe
brated at Cabellinum, *vvherevnto he called manye Byf-* it mighte be en-
shoppes and Abbotes : vvho as they confeße in the Preface, did ded or brought to
confulte and collecte manye matters, thoughte fitte and necef- paffe. Not ratifi-
arie for that time : the vvhiche they agreed neuertheleffe to be ed by his Autho-
rityе.

The.307.Vntruth. Of allovving or diffalovvinge,the Councel fpeaketh not.

The.308.Vntruth. In mifreportinge the Councell.

Can.6.
Can.25.

The.309.Vntruth. They craued the Princes helpe, that the Canons might be put in execuatiō.

Can.45.

The.310.Vntruth. Notorious.It cōdemneth certaine abufes thereabout, it condemneth not the vfe it felfe.

The Prince is the Gouernour of the Church appointed of God(.311.)in ecclefiaftical caufes,

The.311.Vntruth. Auouched in the Margin, but not to be founde in the Texte.

allovved,and confirmed,amended,or (.307.) diffalovved. *As this Councel referreth al the Ecclefiaftical matters to the (308)iudgement, correction,difalovving or confirming,of the Prince:fo amongeft other matters this is to be noted,that it prohibiteth the couetoufneffe and cautels, vvherevvith the Clergie enriched them felues, perfuading the fimple people to geue their lands, and goods to the Churche for their foules helth. The Fathers in this Synod complaine , that the auncient Church order of exccmmunication, doing penaunce, and reconciliation,is quite out of vfe : Therefore they agree to craue the Princes (.309.) order , after vvhat forte be that doth committe a publique offence,may be punifhed by publique penaunce. This Councel alfo enueigheth againft,and(.309.) condemneth gadding on pilgrimage in Church minifters, Lay men, great men, and beggars : al vvhich abufes (faith the Synode)after* what fort they may be amended,the Princes mind muft be knowen.

The fame Charles calleth an other Councel at Maguntia. *In the beginning of their Preface to the Councel,they falute Charles:* the mofte Chriftian Emperour , the Authour of true Religiō,and maintenour of Gods holy Church. &c. Shevving vnto him,that they his mofte humble feruants are come thither according to his commaundement: that they geue Godde thankes : Quia fanctæ Ecclefiæ fuæ pium ac deuotum in feruitio fuo concefsit habere rectorem.   Becaufe he hath geauen vnto his holie Churche a gouernour godlye, and deuoute in his feruice: who in his times opening the fountaine of godlye wifdome,dothe continuallie fede Chriftes (hepe, with holye foode , and inftructeth them with Diuine knowledge,farre pafsing through his holy wifedome, in mofte deuoute endeuoure the other Kinges of the earth,&c. *And after they haue apointed in vvhat order,they diuide the ftates in the Councel: the Bifhops and fecular Priefts by them felues , the Abbottes and religious by them felues , and the Laye Nobilitie, and Iuftices by them felues,afsigning due honour,*

to euery perfon: it folovveth in their petition to the Prince, They
defire his afsiftaunce, aide and confirmation, of fuche
Articles as they haue agreed vppon, fo that he iudge
them worthy: befeeching him, to caufe that to be a-
mended, which is found worthy of amendmēt. *In like
forte did the Synode congregated at Rhemes(.312.) by Charles,*
more prifcorū Imperatorū, *as the auncient Emperours*
were wont to do, *and diuers other, vvhich he in his time called. I vvould haue you to note, befides the authority of this Noble
Prince Charles the Great, in thefe Church matters (vvhich vvas
none other, but the felfe fame, that other Princes from Conftantine the Great had and vfed)that the holy Council of* Mogūtia,
*doth acknovvledge and cōfeffe(313)in plain fpeach, him to be the ru-
ler of the Church(in thefe Ecclefiafticalcaufes)and further that in
al thefe councels, next to the cōfeffion of their faith to God, vvithout making any mention of the Pope, they pray, and commaunde
prayer to be made for the prince.*

The.312.Vutruth.
By the order of vvul-
farius Archbifshop
there: left out of
the Texte.

The.313.Vntruth.
In plaine fpeache
no fuche thing ap-
peareth.

Stapleton.

The calling of Councels either by this Carolus, or by
others as I haue oft faied, proueth no Supremacy: neither
his confirmation of the Coūcels, and fo much the leffe, for
that he did it at the Fathers defire, as your felf confeffe. But
now, Good Reader, take hede of M. Horne, for he would
flilie make the beleue, that this Charles, with his Councell
of Bifhops, fhould forbid landes and goodes to be geuen to
the Church of any man for his foules helth, and to be praied for, after his deathe, whiche is not fo. In deede the
Councell forbiddeth, that men fhal not be entifed, and perfwaded to enter into Relligion, and to geue their goods to
the Churche onely vppon couetoufnes. *Animarum etenim folatium inquirere facerdos, non lucra terrena debet.
Quoniam fideles ad res fuas dandas non funt cogēdi, nec cir-
cumueniendi. Oblatio namque fpontanea effe debet: iuxta illud
quod ait Scriptura. Voluntariè facrificabo tibi.*

Imputa-
tur qui-
bufdāfra-
trib. eo ꝙ
auariie
culpa ho-
mnibus
pfuadeant
vt abre-
nūciantes
feculo res
fuas eccle-
fiæ confe-
rant: quod
penitus ab
omniū mē
tib. eradi-
candū eft.
Can. 6, et
Can. 7

For

For a prieſt(ſaieth the Councell) ſhoulde ſeke the helth of
ſowles,and not worldly gaines , and Chriſtians are not either to be forced , or to be craftely circunuented to geue
away theyr goods.For it owght to be a willing offering accordig as yt is write:I wil willingly offer ſacrifice to thee.
and in the next canon yt is ſayde:*hoc verò quod quiſque Deo
iuſtè & rationabiliter de rebus ſuis offert , Eccleſia tenere debet.*What ſo euer any man hath offred vnto God iuſtly and

Can.39.   reaſonably,that muſte the Church kepe ſtyl.Now for prayers for the dead,ther is a ſpecial Canon made , in this Coūcell that in euery Maſſe there ſhoulde be prayer made for

Prayers
for the
dead.   ſuche as be departed owte of this worlde:And yt is declared owte of S.Auguſtyne,that thys was the gwiſe and faſſhion of the anciente Church.The lyke ſleight M . Horne
vſeth touching pilgrimage : the whiche his owne canon
highly comendeth,thowghe full wiſely and diſcreetly yt
preuenteth and reformeth ſome abuſes. Wherfore ye ſhall
heare the whole canon.I will ſhifte no worde, but ònly frō

Can.44.   Latyn into the engliſh . In the former canō the coūcel forbadde,that prieſts ſhuld goe on pilgrimage without the cōſent of their Biſhoppe to Rome or to Towres a towne in
France:where at the tombe and reliques of bleſſed S.Mar-
tyn innumerable miracles were donne and wrowght : as
amonge other Gregorius Turonenſis Biſhop there and a
faythfull reporter,not by vncerteyne heareſay,but by preſente eieſight,moſte fully declareth.The whiche holy reliques the hugonotes of late in Frāce haue with moſte vi-

Pilgrima-   lany diſhonored and conſumed . After which inhibition it
ge.   followeth.*For* ſay the Fathers,*ſome mē, which vnaduiſedlie*
Ca. 45.   *vnder the cowlour of prayer, goe in pilgrimage to Rome , to
Towres and other places,doe erre very much.There are prieſtes*
                                and

and Deacons and other of the Clergie, which liuing diſſolute-
ly thinke them ſelues to be purged of their ſinnes , and to dooe
their office, if they ones come to the foreſaid places.

There are neuertheleſſe laye menne whiche thinke they
haue freelye ſinned , or may freely ſinne , becauſe they frequente theſe places , to make their prayers in.   There be
ſome Noble men, which to ſcrape and procure mony vnder the
pretence of their pilgrimage to Rome or to Towres, oppreſſe many poore men, and that which they doe vpon couetouſneſſe only, they pretend to doe, for prayers ſake, and for the viſiting of
holy places. There are poore men which due this, for no other
intent, but to procure to them ſelues a greater occaſiō to begge.
Of this number are they, that wandering hither and thither,
faine neuertheleſſe that they goe thither : or that are ſo fooliſhe , that they thinke , they are by the bare view of holie
places, purged of their ſinnes : not conſidering that ſaying of S.
Hierome . It is not praiſe worthie to haue ſeene Hieruſalem,
but to haue liued vertuouſlie at Hieruſalem.   Of all whiche
things lette vs looke for the iudgemente of our Emperoure,
howe they maye be amended.   But thoſe who haue confeſſed
them ſelues to their parriſh Prieſtes , and haue of them taken
counſell how to doe penance, if imploying them ſelues to praier,
and almes geuing, and to the refourming of their life and maners, they deſire to goe on Pilgrimage to Rome or els where,
are of allmen to be commended for their deuotion.

The Fathers alſo deſire the Emperours healpe and aſsi-
ſtaunce, not his *Order*, as you vntruely reporte , for publique pēnaunce : Beſide, if it had pleaſed you , yee mighte
haue caſte in alſo a woorde or twoo more.   *Vt ſecundum
ordinem Canonum pro merito ſuo excommunicetur.* That
accordinge to the order of the Canons , he may according

*In eo pur-
gari ſe à
peccatis
putant, et
miniſterio
ſuo fungi
deberi, ſi.
&c.*
Note here
\ vel how
the chur-
ch of this
age, de-
creed opē
ly againſt
abuſes, ā d
vvinked
not at
them, as
Prote-
ſtantes
vvoulde
make
folke be-
leeue.
*Hieron. in
Epiſt. ad
Paulinū.
Tom. 1.*

Can. 25.

ding to his deferts be excommunicated. And now, good
Reader iudge thou, how truely, how wifely, or how to his
purpofe this gere is brought furth of M. Horne : and what
a fingular good grace this man hath, fo wel to plead againft
him felfe and his fellowes, for the Catholiques. And
nowe would I be in hande with Leo, fauing that Maifter
Hornes Marginall Note, feemeth to take me by the hand,
and to ftaie me a while: And yet we wil foorthwith fhake
him of, and defire Maifter Horne to ouerfee his text ones
againe, and to fquare his Note to his Texte, and not his
text after his peruerfe and prepofterous order, to his note.
I fay then, M. Horne, ye haue no words, nor mater in your
text to cal Carolus Magnus *Gouernour in Ecclefiaftical caufes*, and becaufe, befide your Note Marginall, ye note the
matter alfo fo faft in your text, which is not in the Fathers
text, faying: *the Fathers faye in playne fpeach, that he was
ruler of the Church in Ecclefiafticall caufes*, I wil note as faft
as you, and that is your one falfe lying in your text, and the
other in the margent. Onles ye may by fome new Grammar and like Diuinitie, proue that, *in feruitio fuo*, in his feruice, is Englifhed alfo, In ecclefiaftical matters,

    You tell vs farder M. Horne, that in this Councell of
Ments, the States were diuided. *The Bifshoppes and fecular Prieftes by them felues. The Abbottes and Religious
by them felues.* But you tell vs not, wherein euery State
was occupied and bufied in that Councell. That in deede
made not for you. The Councel then faith : *In prima tur-

in Con-
cilio Ma-
guntiaco.
Tom. 2.
Coc. p 630

ma confederunt Epifcopi, &c. In the firft rewe fate the Biffhops with their Notaries, reading and debating vppon
the holy Ghoffel, the Canons of the Church, diuers works of the
holy Fathers, and namely the Paftoral of S. Gregory : fearching*
                                  and

and determining thereby, that which belonged to holſome do-
ctrine, and to the ſtate of the Church. In the ſeconde rew ſate
the Biſshops and approued Monks, hauing before them the rule
of S. Benet, and ſeking therby to better the life of Monks to en-
creaſe their godly conuerſation. In the third rew ſate the Laye
Nobilitie and Iudges. But what to doe M. Horne ? To conclude of matters of Religiõ, as the laie Burgeſes and Gētle-
men do in our Parliamēts ? No, no : *Neg. nos, neg. Ecclesia* 1. Cor. 11.
Dei talē conſuetudinē habemus. Neither we, nor the Church
of God haue any ſuch cuſtom or maner. But there thei ſate
In mundanis legibus decertantes. &c. Debating in worldly
lawes, *ſearching out Iuſtice for the people, examininge dili-*
gently the cauſes of all that came, and determining Iuſtice by al
meanes that they could. Thus were the States in that Councel diuided, vnder that Noble Emperour Charlemain. And
what could this Note helpe you, M. Horne, or relieue you,
except it were that you would geue a preuy nippe to the
order of late Parliaments, where the laie not onely of the
Nobilitie, but euen of the Commons (whoſe ſentences in
treatie of Relligion, neuer ſence Chriſte ſuffred, were e-
uer hearde or admitted) doe talke, diſpute, yea and conclude of Religion, and that in the higheſt and moſt ſecrete
myſteries thereof, to the conſequente of a Generall alteration.

You woulde no doubte, as gladdelie as Catholiques,
haue the treatie and deciſion of ſuche matters in youre
owne handes onely (as in deede all Proteſtauntes beſide
you, Caluin, Melanchthon, the Magdeburgenſes with
the reſte doe expreſſelye teache, as I haue bothe in this
booke, and otherwhere declared) But this is the difference.

                        o ij   You

You are miſerable clawbackes, and as Caluin writeth, *to extolle the Ciuill Magiſtrate , you ſpoyle the Churche of her dewe Authoryte* . But the Catholikes thinke it not mete to flatter in Religiõ : *But to geue that, which is Ceſars, to Ceſar: and that which is Gods , to God* . Excepete we ſhoulde ſaye, that now you will haue Religion decided in parliament, and when, the Prince ſhall otherwiſe be affected, you will not haue it ſo decided: and that your Religion is *Ambula-teria*: a wandring and a walking Religion, teaching one thinge to day. and an other to morowe . As in dede very properlye and truly George the Noble duke of Saxony ſayed of the Lutheranes at Wittenberge , when yet your Religion was ſcante out of her ſwadling clowtes . *What the faythe of my neighbours of Wittenberge is now this yere, I knowe. But what it wil be the next yere, I knowe not.*

Yet you deſire M. Feckenham to note here an other thing, *beſides the Authoryty of this Noble Prince Charles the great* (for ſo you call him) *which* (you ſay) *was none other but the ſelfe ſame , that other Priuces from Cõſtãtin the great had and vſed :* which in deede is very true: for they had none, ne vſed none, as hath bene proued , and yet I mar-uayle , where is then become the priuilege of S . Peters keyes ſent to Charles Martell this mans grandefather, if he had, as you ſay, *none other but the ſelfe ſame Authoryte that other Princes from Conſtantin had.* If it was loſte ſo ſoone, then how is it true, that you ſaid before, *the heyres and ſuc-ceſſours of Charles Martell kepte theſe keyes from ruſting .* If it was not loſt , how had he no more thẽ other which had S. Peters keyes more then other had ? But now to your note. You will M. Feckenham to note , *that the holy Councel of Moguntia* (I am gladde you call it holy, for thẽ
you

you wil not, I trowe miſſelyke with the diuiſion of the States there, that I tolde you of euen now, neyther with the Rule of S.Benets Order, in that holy Coūcel ſtraightly exacted) *doth acknowleadge and cōfeſſe in plaine ſpeache him,* (that is, Charles the great) *to be the Ruler of the Churche in theſe eccleſiaſticall cauſes.* Now ſhewe theſe laſte wordes (*in theſe eccleſiaſtical cauſes*) in any parcel or place of the whol Councell, *in playne ſpeache,* as you ſay, and then M.Feckē-ham I dare ſay, wil thanke you for your Note, and for my parte I wil ſay, you are a true man of your worde. Which hitherto, I aſſure you, I haue litle cauſe to ſay, or to thinke. Your lying is almoſt comparable to M.Iewels. Mary you are not in dede as yet ſo farre in the laſhe, as he is. But if you come ones to Replying, as he hathe done, you wil be a Pinner I doubte not, as well as he, and telle your vntru-thes by the thouſandes. For aſſure your ſelfe M. Horne: as *vera veris conueniunt,* ſo an vntrue and falſe doctrine can neuer poſsiblye be maintayned, without horrible lying, and mayne numbers of vntruthes.

M. Horne. The. 99. Diuiſion. pag. 60.4.

Pope *Leo.3.as* the French *Chronicles, and* Nauclerus *vvitneſſeth, ſent foorthvvith after he vvas made Pope* Peters keyes, *the Banner of the City, and many other gifts vnto Charles: requiring him, that he vvold cauſe the people of* Rome *to become ſubiecte vnto the Pope, and that by* Othe. Charles *minding to gratify and pleaſure Pope Leo (there (.214.) vvas a cauſe vvherfore) ſente an Abbot on this buſines, and aſſured the people of* Rome *to the Pope by othe. This Leo (his ſtreight (.315.) dealinges vvith the Romayns vvas ſo hatefull vnto them) vvas brought ſhortly into much daungier of his life, but farre more of his honeſty. Cert. ine of* Rome *came to* Charles *to accuſe this Pope: Charles putteth of the examination of the mat-ter till an other time, promiſinge that he vvould. vvithin a vvhile come to* Rome *him ſelfa: vvhiche he did; after he had finiſhed his vvarres.*

The.314. vntruth. A levvde and a falſe ſurmyſe The.315.] vntruth. he was a moſt mylde ād mekemā.

e iij   **He**

Charlemai.

Sabell.

Platina.
Sabell.

The.316.vntruth.
The biſhops only
were aſked their
mindes.
The.317. vntruthe.
Charles tooke not
the anſwere in ſuch
parte.
The.318. vntruth.
Platina meaned
not ſo.

The.319.vntruth.
Sabellicus had no
ſuche meaning.

The.320.vntruth.
He tooke it not
vpon him,but vvas
required of the
Pope him ſelfe to
doe it.
The.321. Vntruthe.
Not able to be pro-
ued.
The.322.Vntruthe.
Leud ād ſlāderous.

⁎Yea:in manifold
battayles, not in
ғhat Iudgement.

He vvas honorably receiued of the Pope. The eight day after his co-
minge into Rome, he commaunded al the people, and the Cleargy
to be called togeather into S. Peters churche : appointing to here
and examine the Pope, touchynge that he vvas accuſed of, in the
opē aſſembly. Whē the Cleargy and the people, vvere aſſembled, the
Kinge examineth them of the Popes life and conuerſation: and the
vvhole company (.316.) beinge vvilled to ſay their mindes: anſvveare that the manier hathe beene, that the Popes ſhoulde be
iudged of no man, but of them ſelues. Charles being mooued vvith
ſo (.317.) ſore & greeuous an anſvveare, gaue ouer further
examination. Leo the Pope (ſaieth Platina) vvho did earneſtly deſire that kinde of iudgemēt (to geue ſentence be (318.)
meaneth in his ovvne cauſe) vvente vp into the pulpitte, and
holdinge the Goſpels in his handes, affirned by his Othe, that
he vvas guiltles of all thoſe matters vvherevvith he vvas
chardged. Whereunto Sabellicus addeth, the Popes owne
teſtimonie of him ſelfe, was ſo waighty, as if it had
beene geuen on him by other: ſo muche auaileth a
mans owne good reporte made of him ſelfe in due
ſeaſon, (.319.) for vvante of good neighbours. This matter,
if it vvere as the Popes flatterers vvrite, thus ſubtily compaſ-
ſed: although Martinus ſaith flatly, that he vvas driuen to
purge him ſelfe of certaine crimes laide to his chardge : yet not
vvithſtanding, the kinge toke (.320.) vpon him, both to
examine the matter, and to determine therein : and, as appeareth, tooke their anſvvere no leſſe (.321.) inſufficient,
than greuous : although he vvinked at it : bicauſe he looked
(.322.) for a greater pleaſure to be ſhevved him againe in con-
ſecratinge him Emperour, promiſed longe before : vvhiche
this Pope perfourmed, and ſolemply vvith great acclamations of the people, crovvned him Emperour of Rome : For
ſaithe Platina : The Pope did this to ſhewe ſome
thāke fulnes againe to him, who had well ⁎ deſerued
of the Churche.

Stapleton.

Stapleton.

This proceſſe ſtãdeth in the accuſation of Pope Leo the.
3.that certayne Romans made againſte hym to Charles,
bearing with yt ſuche a wonderfull ſtrength for the eſta-
bliſhing of the Popes Supremacy,that M. Horn may ſeme,
to play al by colluſiõ,and to betray hys owne cauſe . For
now hath he by hys owne ſtory,auaunced the Pope ſo (as *Regino in*
he did alſo before in alleaging the Roman Councell in the *chronic.*
tyme of Pope Sĩmachus)that he may be iudged of no mã. *Captũ ex-*
For all the clergie and people of Rome make anſwere to *cacauerũt,*
Charles hym ſelf,*that nõ mã cã iudge the Pope.* This writeth *eius radi-*
M.Horne owte of Platïna and Sabellicus:ãd other writers *citus ab-*
be of the ſame lykenes ãd agreablenes in writing with thẽ. *ſciderunt.*
Howe then M.Horne ? Where is now your primacy be- *Sed Deus*
come?I truſt now at the length ye wil diſcharge M. Fekẽ- *omnipotẽs*
ham frõ this othe.What ſay yow to your owne volũtarie *reddidit ei*
allegation,that no man forced yow vnto , but the mightie *viſum &*
truth:to the bewraying of your falſe cauſe and your greate *loquelam.*
folly?Yet leaſte his ſayde folly and preuarication ſhoulde *Mart. Pœ*
be to open,he will ſaye ſomwhat to yt, (becauſe he maye *nitent.*
ſeame to worke thowghe not as miraculouſly , yet as wõ-
derfully as euer did thys Leo:who,his tong being cut of by
the roote,as ſome mẽ write,could ſpeake neuertheleſſe)ãd
though his fowle lying mouthe againſt the Popes primacy
be ſtopped by his own true declaratiõ , yet wil he ſpeake,
not to any hys owne honour,as Leo did , but to hys vtter
cõfuſion ãd ſhame.Forſoth ſayeth M.Horne,Charles toke
thys anſwere *no leſſe inſufficient, then greauous.* Wel ſayde,
and in tyme M . Horne, ſauinge that yt is moſte vntrue:
ãd for the which as ye lay forthe no prouf,ſo ſhal ye neuer
be able to proue yt . And yet, if ye coulde proue yt , ye
ſhoulde dooe none other thinge then that whiche yee
do

doe fo folemnlye in the reſt of youre booke to proue that
which being proued, doth yet nothing relieue your cauſe.
And thinke you, M. Horne, that we are fo bare and naked from many good proufes, but that we may and canne
roundlie and redely difproue your fond fooliſh lye?   Yea
and by that booke, by the which your Apoſtle Caluin, and
your great Iewell of Englande, will (though not to their
great worſhip) defeate the Second Generall Councell of
Nice ? *The Churche of Rome* (faith he) *is preferred before all
other Apoſtolicall Sees, not by the Decrees of Synodes, but by
the authoritie of our Lord him felfe, faying thou art Peter*:and
fo forth. And faith farder, that he doth moſt defire to obey
the holſom exhortatiõs of Pope Adriã:and that Italy, Frãce,
and Germanie, doe in al things follow the See of Peter.
And now wot ye what, M. Horne ?   Forſoth this his anſwere proueth M.Iewell, as wel in the Apologie (or who
fo euer be the Author) as in his Replie to M. D. Harding,
to haue ouerthrowen not the Nicene Councell (wherein
this Adrians Legates bare the chiefe fway) as they did alſo
in the Councell at Frankfoorde, as I haue ſhewed, but hys
owne peeuiſh and fantaſtical imaginatiõn, that this Charles
ſhould at Frankford difalow the faid Nicene Synode. But
I trow ye be as wery and as much aſhamed ere this time,
of this counterfeit Charles booke : wherein by the fooliſh
and fond handling of the iconomache, the cauſe of the Catholike Church is cõfirmed, as your fellowes wilbe ſhortly
of this your boke : that I doubt not to all that be not fini-
ſtrallie affectioned, ſhal ferue, rather for the confirmation,
then abrogation, of the Popes Primacie. And becauſe, as I
fay, I ſuppofe ye wil your felues ſhortly difclaime this peuiſh booke, I wil fend you to Carolus him felfe , in his Ecclefiaſtical

Carol' his
teſtimoni
(oute of
Charls his
booke as
M.Cal-
uin and
M.Ievvel
fay)for
the Popes
Primacy.
Li.1.Car.
ca.6.

The fore-
faid boke
onerthro
vveth M.
Ievvel in
his Re-
ply ãd in
the Apo-
logie.

The Po-
pes Pri-
macy pro
ued by
the true
Charles.

clefiaſtical decrees, collected by Abbat Anſegiſus, whome ye authoriſe in the nexte leafe.   Where ye ſhall fynde this playne decree. *Neque præful ſummus a quoquam iudicabitur.* No man ſhall iudge the pope : whiche was alſo decreed in the tyme of the great Cõſtantyne and pope Sylueſter : yea before that tyme the lyke was ſayd in a councel of Marcelline pope and Martyre, as I haue otherwhere ſhewed.

Nowe then thowghe there was no cauſe whie Charles ſhoulde be greaued with this , that the whole Clergie and people wel lyked, and for the which there wer old aunciẽt preſidents: yet to goe forth, and to ſmothe this tale withal, and to ſhewe why Charles ſhould quietlie beare this grief, which was ſone born, being none at al: he addeth an other lie, whereof we haue alredie ſomwhat ſpoken: And that is, becauſe the Pope promiſed him longe before , to make him Emperour. Yea good M. Horn ſone ſayd of yowe, but not ſo ſone proued. For neither your authour Platina ſayth ſo, nor any other that I haue hitherto read . Phy on your wretched dealig, ãd wretched cauſe that ye maintayne , that cã not be vpholdẽ, but with the defacing ãd diſhonorĩg not only of the clergie, but of this worthy ãd (as your ſelf cal him) this Noble Price Charles withal. I would fayne procede to the next matter, but that your other vntruthes muſt or I go, be alſo diſcouered: as that yow ſay, without any prouf, yea againſt good prouf to be layd to the cõtrary, that this pope Leo *for his ſtreight dealings was hateful to the Romãs*: which your authors Sabellicus and Platina ſay not , but the quite contrary. For Platina among his other manifold and notable vertues telleth, *that he was a man, of myld nature, ſo that he loued all men , hated no man: ſlowe to wrathe, ready to take mercie and pitie of other.* And Sabellicus of this very matter

Vide Conſtitut. Caroli ex Anſegiſo collectas, impreſſas in 8. An. 1545. Pariſiis. Tom. 1. Cõcil. pa. 196

The new Ghoſpell can not ſtand but by defacing of al antiquitie .

Platin. *Homo certè mitis in geniÿ, vt omnes diligeret, neminem odio haberet, tardus ad iram, promptus ad miſericordiam.*

p   ſaieth

sayeth thus . *Coniuratorum odium in Pontificem inde ortum
ferunt,quòd illi liberius viuere assueti ,ferre nequiuissent gra-
uem Pontificis Censuram.* It is saied the hatred of such as cō-
spired against him,spronge hereof,that they accustomed to
liue more licentiously,coulde not abyde the Graue Rebukes and Censures of the pope. Nowe further, M. Horne being not able to denie , but that aswell Carolus, as all other
gaue ouer for any iudgmēt they wold or could geue agaīst
Leo,he falleth to quarellīg with Leo,for that,for the which
he owght to haue cōmēded him. The matter standing thus,

Rhegino
in chronic.
Cum nul-
lus proba
tor,aut te
stis legiti-
mus appa-
reret.

and no mā stepping forth lawfully to proue any thing agaīst
Leo,this good man, thowghe no man did or coulde force
him to yt,yet knowing his owne innocency, toke an open
othe vppon the holy ghospel, that he was gyltlesse from
suche matters,as were obiected against him. And here M.
Horne beinge pleasantly disposed sayeth (as owte of Platina) Leo *did earnestlye desire that kynde of iudgmente*: and
addeth by his owne lying liberalyte , that Platina mente,
that Leo was desirouse *to geue sentence in his owne cause.*
Wheras Platina meante that Leo,was desirouse,vppon the
assured truste , of his owne integritye , that the matter
might haue bene iudged : and so worthie of commendation , that he woulde submitte his cause to iudgemente,
where he neaded not, as Symachus and Sixtus did before,
And so are Platina his wordes , *qui id iudicium maximè ex-*

Naucle=
rius gene-
rat. 28.
Impreß.
Colonia.
1564 +.

petebat, to be vnderstanded . And perchaunce in some copies,*id*,is not sene. Nauclerus which seameth here as in many other places to followe Platina , and to reherse his
wordes,and whom M. Horne doth here also alleage,saith.
qui iudicium maximè expetebat. Whiche did moste ernest-
ly desire to be iudged . Whiche iudgement not procee-
dyng,

he did as muche as laye in him, that is, to purge lemaï.
him selfe by his othe. Nowe where Sabellicus speaketh of
this purgation in the commendation of Leo, saying, *that a
mans owne reporte much auayleth made in dewe ceason,* M.
Horn addeth this his pretie glose, *for wante of good neygh-
tours.* Yet I pray yowe good M. Horne take not the matter so greuously against Pope Leo: But remember that Leo
being pope did more then a protestant Prelate, (whom ye
knowe ful wel) of late did, being perchaunce more then a
suspition, that a wrong cocke had troden Cockerelles hen.
And yet the sayd prelat was not put to his purgation, and
much lesse him selfe offred to sweare for his owne honesty. I medle not with the iustifying of the matter one way
or other: Some men say that strypes may cause yong strip-
linges to saye, *Tonge thoue lyest*: but not truelie to the eye,
Eie thowe lyest, whiche can not lie in that, whiche is hys
obiecte. But let this goe. I saye yt, for none other cause,
but onely that ye haue not M. Horne so greate cause to
take the matter so hotte, against Leo.

 And now to make vp this matter, gentle reader, of Leo,
this Leo also sendeth Saint Peters keyes, yea and the banner
of the city to, to Charles as M. Horne telleth vs, yea *the
keyes of S. Peters cõfessiõ* as Rhegino telleth vs, and yet for
al that, he remayned Bisshop, Archebisshop, Patriarche, and
Pope to: yea and supreme head of the Church by M. Horns
owne tale to. But remembre your selfe better M. Horne.
You said euen nowe, they were sent awaye by Gregory
the .3. to Charles Martell, into Fraunce by shippe.
Howe then came the Pope by them agayne? Or howe did
the successours and heyeres of Charles Martell keepe
those keyes from rusting if his own Nephewe Charles the

The pope
did more
for his
purgatiõ
then hath
one of
our pro-
testant
prelate.

S. Peters
keyes lẽt
ons againa
to frãuce
and yet
the pope
remay-
nig pope
still.
In Chron.
Claues cõ-
cessionis
sancti Pe-
tri &
vexillum
dixerit.

greate

greate, lofte them, and was fayne to haue them againe by a newe dede of gifte? Or hath euery Pope a newe payre of keyes frō Chrift to beftowe as thei lift? Then the gift could be but for terme of life. And then where be the heyres and fucceffours of Charles Martell, which kept not you faye thofe keyes from rufting? O M. Horne. *Oportet mendacem effe memorē.* A lyar muft haue a good memory. Or wil you faye that this Pope Leo fent to Charles thefe keyes, as a

Sabellicus gifte to fignifie, that the city was at his commaundemente, as Bellifarius after he had recouered Rome from Totilas, of

Rhegino in Chron. whome we fpake of before fent the keyes of the city to Iuftinian themperour : and as fome men write euen aboute

claues ci- this time, this Charles receiued the keyes of the city of Hie-

uitatis cū rufalem, with the banner of the faid citye? Yet al this will

vexillo detulerūt. not work the great ftrāge miracle of fupremacie that your keies haue wrought.

M. Horne. The. 100. Diuifion. Fol. 61. a.

Anfegifus Abbas *gathereth together the decrees, that this Charles ăd his fon Lodouicus had made in their tymes for the reformatiō of the Churche*

* Vnder the name of holy fcriptures *caufes: Amongeſt other thefe:* The Canonicall Scriptures * onely to be redde in the Churches: For the office of Bifhops in diligēt preaching, and that onely out of the holy Scriptures: that the communion fhould be receiued three times in the yeere: The abrogatīg and taking away a great nūber of holy daies befides Sōdaies: and that childrē before ripe yeres fhould not be thruft into religious houfes: ād that no mā fhould be pfeffed a Mōk, except licence were firft afked and obteined of the King. He decreed alfo, and ftraightly commaunded that Monkes being Prieftes, fhould ftudie diligentlie, fhoulde write rightlie,

Ioan. A-nētinus. fhould teache children in their Abbaies, and in Bifhoppes houfes. That Priefts fhould efchue couetoufnes, glotony, alēhoufes or tauernes, fecular or prophane bufines, familiaritie of

women

women vnder paine of depriuation or degradation . He proui-
dedto haue, and placed fit paftours for the bifshoprikes and
cures to feede the people.He ordeined learned Scholemaifters
for the youth,and made deuout abbots to rule thofe that were
enclofed in Cloifters,faith *Nauclerus. As it is faid of Kinge* Dauid,*
that he fet in order the Priefts,Leuits,fingers and porters , and ordered all
the offices and officers required to be in the houfe of the Lorde,for the fetting
foorth of his feruice and Religion: Euen fo this noble Charles left no officer
belonging to Goddes Churche,no not fo much as the finger, porter or Sextē,
vnapointed and taught his office and duety,as Nauclerus telleth . Befides
the authority of this noble Prince in(.323.)gouernīg and directing al Church
matters,his zeale and care therfore (in fuch fort as the knovvledge of that
(.324.)fuperftitious time vvould fuffer)is plainly fhevved in an iniūctiō, that
he gaue to al eftates both of the Layty and Cleargy to this effect.I Charles,
by the grace of God King and gouernour of the Kingdome of
Fraunce, a deuout and humble maintainour,and ayder of the
Churche : To al eftates both of the Layety and the Cleargye,
wifhe faluation in Chrift.Confidering the exceeding goodnes
of God towardes vs,and our people , I thinke it very neceffary
wee rendre thankes vnto him , not onely in harte and worde,
but alfo in continual exercife,and practife of wel doing,to his
glory:to the end that he,who hath hitherto beftowed fo great
honour vpon this Kingdom, may vouchefaulfe to preferue vs
and our people with his protection . VVherfore it hath feemed
good for vs,to mooue you,ô ye paftours of Chriftes Churches,
leaders of his flocke,and the bright lightes of the worlde:that
ye wil trauaile,with vigilant care and diligent admonition to
guide Goddes people thorough the paftours of eternal life,&c.
Bringing the ftray fheepe into the foulde leaft the wolfe deuoure them,&c.Therefore they are with earneft zeale to be
admonifhed and exhorted , yea to be compelled to keepe the
felues in a fure faith,and reafonable continuaunce,vvithin ād
vnder the rules of the Fathers . In the vvhich vvorke and trauaile knovve yee right vvell , that our induftrie fhall vvorke
vvith you : For vvhich caufe alfo vve haue addreffed our mef-

1.Par.16.
* See our
anfvvere
before to
King Da-
uid. fo.48
The.323.
vntruth.
Boldly a-
uouched,
but neuer
proued.
The. 324.
vntruth.
Blafphe-
mous a-
gainft the
promifes
of Chrift
to remai
alvvaie
vvith his
Churche.
M.Horne
nameth
no Au-
thor of
this lōge
allegatiō,
leaft he
fhould be
taken in
trippes,
ād his vn-
truths be
difcoue-
red,as be-
fore.

fengers vnto you, who with you by our authority, fhal amēde
and correct thofe thinges that are to be amended. And therefore alfo haue wee added fuch Canonical conftitutions, as feemed to vs moft neceffarie. Let no man iudge this to be prefumption in vs, that we take vpon vs to amende, that is amiffe,
to cut of that is fuperfluous. For wee reade in the bookes of
Kinges, howe the holy Kinge Iofias trauailed, goinge the cir-
cuites of his Kingdome or vifitinge, correctinge and admonif hinge his people, to reduce the whole Kingdome vnto the
true Religion and Seruice of God. I fpeake not this as to make
my felf equal to him in holines: but for that we ought alwaies
to follovve the examples of the holy Kinges : and fo much as
we can, vve are bounde of necefsitie, to bring the people to
follovve vertuous life to the praife and glory of our Lorde Iefus Chrift, &c. *And anon after amongeft the rules that he prefcribeth vnto*
them this follovveth: Firft of al, that al the Bifshoppes and Prieftes,
reade diligentlie the Catholique Faith, and preache the fame
to all the people. For this is the firft precept of God the Lorde
in his Lawe : Heare ô Ifrael, &c. It belongeth to your offices
ô yee paftours and guides of Goddes Churches, to fende forth
thorough your Dioceffes, Prieftes to preache vnto the peopie,
and to fee that they preache rightly and honeftly. That ye doe
not fuffer newe things, not Canonicall, of their owne minde
forged, and not after the holy Scriptures, to be preached vnto
the people. Yea, you your owne felues preache profitable, honeft and true thinges, which doe leade vnto eternal life. And
enftructe you others alfo that they doe the fame. Firfte of all
euery preacher muft preache in general, that thei beleeue the
Father, the Sonne, and the holy Ghoft to be an omnipotent
God, &c. *And fo learuedly proceedeth through al the articles of our Faith,*
after vvhich he commeth to the conuerfation of life, &c. And wee doo
therefore more diligētlie enioine vnto you this thing, becaufe
vve knovve, that in the latter daies fhall come falfe teachers,
as the Lorde himfelfe hath forvvarned, and the Apoftle Paule
to Timothe doth vvitneffe. Therefore beloued let vs furnifhe

Our ans
fvver bes
fore to
the Con-
ftitutions
of Iufti-
nian, may
feruehere
to thefe
lavves of
Charle-
maine.
Both in
like ma-
ner pros
feffed
their obe
dience in
al fuch
matters
to the
See of
Rome.

our

our felues in harte and minde, with the knowledge of the lemaî.
truth, that we may be able to vvithſtande the aduerſaries to
trueth, and that thorough Goddes grace, Goddes vvorde
may encreafe, paſſe through and be multiplied, to the pro-
fitte of Goddes holy Churche,the Saluation of our ſoules, and
the glory of the name of our Lorde Ieſus Chriſt. Peace to the
preachers,grace to the obedient hearers,and glory to our Lord
Ieſus Chriſte.Amen.

Stapleton.

Many Lawes Ecclefiaſticall are here brought forth, fet
forth by this Charles, with his great care, that reached e-
uen to the finger,porter or ſextē:wherunto ye might adde,
that he made an order, that no man ſhould miniſter in the
Churche in his vſuall apparell: and that he him ſelfe fre- *Naucler.*
quented the Churche erlye and late,yea at night prayer to. *gener.28.*
But this addition perchaunce woulde not all the beſt haue
liked your Geneuicall miniſters. Then layeth he me forth,
an iniunction of this Charles in matters Ecclefiaſticall.
But conſider his ſtyle Maiſter Horne. What is it? Supreame Gouuernour or head of the Churche in all matters and thinges Ecclefiaſticall? No, but *a deuoute and an
humble mainteyner of the Churche*. Conſider againe the
order of his doinges Maiſter Horne, which are to fette
forthe iniunctions, to kepe the clergie within and vnder
the rules of the Fathers. But from whence trowe we,
toke Maiſter Horne all this longe allegation of Charles
his Conſtitutions? He placeth towarde the ende of his
allegation, in the margin, *Ioan.Auentinus,*out of whome
it may feme he toke that later parte. But as for the former
part thereof (whence ſo euer M.Horne hath fetched it) it
is founde

is founde in dede among the Conſtitutions of Charles ſet
forthe xx.yeres paſte.But there it is ſette though as a Cons
ſtitution of Charles , yet not as his owne proper lawe or
ſtatute,but expreſſely alleaged out of the Aphricane Coun
cell . For ſo vſed godly Princes to eſtabliſhe the Canons
ofthe Churche,with their owne Conſtitutions and lawes.
And in that Councell whence Charles toke this Conſtitus
tion , where it is ſaied that *Scriptures onely ſhoulde be reade
in the Churches* , it is added,*Vnder the name of Scriptures.*

And it is farder added. *We will alſo that in the yearly feſtes of
Martyrs, their paſsions be reade* . Which things M. Horne
here , but M. Iewell a great deale more ſhamefully quyte
omitted in his Reply to D. Cole:falſely to make folcke be-

Vide Diſt.
19,In me-
moriam,
& in de=
cretis.11.
q.1.Volu-
mus yt om
nes.
Se before
fol.48.

leue , that in the Churche only Scriptures ſhould be read.
    But what neade I nowe ſeke furder anſwere,when M.
Horne of his owne goodnes, hath anſwered hym ſelfe , as
ye haue hearde , good reader, ſufficientlie alredy ? And I
haue before noted of this Charles and of his ſubmiſsion to
biſhoppes, and namely to the biſhop of Rome ſo farre,that
no Emperour I trowe was euer a greater papiſte then he
was , or farder from this Antichriſtian ſupremacy that M.
Horne and his felowes teache . For no leſſe is it termed
to be of Athanaſius that lerned father , as I haue before
declared.

M. Horne. The.101.Diuiſion. pag.62.a.

    *This noble Prince vvas mooued to take vpon him this gouernement in ec-
cleſiaſtical matters and cauſes,not of preſumptiō,but by the vvoorde of God,
for the diſchardge of his princely duety , as he had learned the ſame both in
the examples of godly kings commended therfore of the holy ghoſt, and alſo
by the inſtructions of the beſt learned teachers of his time,vvhereof he had
greate ſtoare,and eſpecially* Alcuinus *an Engliſheman of great learninge,
vvho vvas his chiefe Scholmaiſter and teacher:vvhome,as* Martinus *tel-*
leth ,

*leth,Charles made Abbot of Tovvers. Amongst other many and notable vo-
lumes,this* Alcuinus *vvriteth one , entituled* De Fide fanctæ & indiuiduæ Trinitatis, *vvhich as moste meete for him to knovv,he dedicateth
to* Charles the Emperour. *He beginneth his epiftle dedicatory,after the falu-
tatiõ and fuperfcriptiõ,thus:*Seeinge that the Emperial dignitie ordeined of God,feemeth to be exalted for none other thinge,
thẽ to gouern and profite the people, I herfore God doth geue
vnto them that are chofen to that dignitie power and wife-
dome:Power to fuppreffe the proude,and to defend the humble againft the euil difpofed:wifdome to gouerne and teache
the fubiectes with a godly carefulnes. VVith thefe twoo giftes
O holy Emperour,Gods fauour hath honoured ãd exalted you
incomparably aboue your aunceftours of the fame name and
authoritie,&c. VVhat than? what muft your carefulnes mofte
deuoutly dedicated to God bringe forthe in the time of peace
the warres being finifhed,when as the people hafteneth to affemble togeather, at the proclamation of your commaunde-
mẽt(*he meaneth that he expreffeth aftervvard, by thi˙ affembly or cõcourfe,
the councel that vvas novve in hand affembled:as he faith,*Imperiali prę-
cepto:by the Emperours precept.)And waiteth attentiuely ᴐe
fore the throne of your grace,what you wil cõmaunde to euery perfone by your authoritie : what I fay ought you to doo?
but to determine with al dignitie iufte thinges,which beinge
ratified to fet them foorth by cõmaundement,and to geue holy admonitions,that euery man may retourne home mery and
gladde,with the precept of eternal Saluation, &c. And leaft I
fhould feeme not to helpe and further your preaching of the
Faithe,I haue directed and dedicated this booke vnto you,
thinkinge no gifte fo conuenient and woorthy to be prefented
vnto you:feeinge that al men knowe this moft plainly,that the
Prince of the people ought of necefsitie to knowe al thinges,
and to * preache thofe thinges that pleafe God:neither belongeth it to any man to knowe better or moe things , than to an
Emperour, whofe doctrine ought to profite all the fubiectes
&c. Al the faithful hath great caufe to reioyce of your godlines

* By other
not in his
ovvn per
fon. And
fo in all
the reft.

Char-lemai.

The price hath a prieftlie povver to fette forth Gods vvord.

The.325. vntruth, euer auou ched, but neuer pro u:d.

The. 326 vntruth. Slaunde-rous and a plaine contradi-ction.

feing that you haue the prieftly power(as it is mete fo to bee) in the preaching of the worde of God , perfect knowledge in the Catholique faith,and a moft holy deuotion to the faluatiõ of men . *This doctrine of* Alcuinus,*vvhich no doubte , vvas the doctrine of all the catholike and learned fathers in that time , confirmeth vvell the doinges of* Charles *and other Princes , in callinge councelles , in makinge decrees,in geuing Iniunctions to Ecclefiafticall perfons, and in rulinge and gouerninge them in (.325.) all Ecclefiafticall thinges and caufes . If the gouernement of this mofte Chriftian Prince in Ecclefiaftical matters be vvel confidered , it fhall vvell appeare , that this* Charles *the great , vvhome the Popes doo extolle as an other great* Conftantine *, and patron vnto them (as he vvas in deede , by enriching the Churche vvith great reuenues and riches) vvas no vvhit greater for his martiall and Princelike affaires in the politique gouernaunce,than for his godly ordering and difpofinge the Church caufes: although that in fome thinges he is to be borne vvith,confidering the (.326.)blindnes and fuperftition of the time.*

Stapleton.

The contents of thefe matters ftande in the highe com-mendation,of this Charles:which can not be commended inowghe,and whome the councell kepte at Mens , com-mendeth euen as M. Horne reporteth,for his godlie wife-dome in continual feadinge of Chrifts fheepe withe holie foode,and inftructinge them with diuine knowledge,farre pafsing thorowgh his holy wifdome,the other kings of the earthe. A wife man would now maruayle,to what end M. Horne hath heaped thefe and all his other prayfes of thys Emperour who truly can not be praifed to much: but the truer and greater his prayfe is,the more difcommendation to M. Horne and to his boke , beinge directe contrarie to the doings and belief of Charles,and this matter fo certayn-ly true,that Maifter Horne him felfe can not denie yt. Be-fide , here appeareth a contradiction the whiche Maister

Al Char-les com-mêdatiõ ferueth for no-thing but for M. Hornes difcõmê-dation.

ster Horne shal neuer shift away charging him before *for want of pure knowledge* : whereof yet he doth nothing else but purge him almost fowre leaues following together : *as one hauinge a priestlie power , to preache the worde of God , and hauing perfytte knowledg in the catholyke fayth.* And say-ing *that al the catholyk and learned fathers of that tyme con-firme well the doinges of Charles ,* which he him selfe dothe here impugne, for Masses, Chrisme , and other poyntes of catholyke religion . Consider these thinges , good reader well , and then iudge with indifferency, who be the blind bussardes, that M. Horne spake of.

Your note in the margent may be suffred wel inowgh, being agreable to your texte : onlesse yt be , that some-tyme good thinges be the worse for comminge to yl mens handes . The priestly power that Alcuinus meaneth re-steth in this poynte , that as the priestes in theyre Syno-des and preachinges set forthe the true fayeth , so doe good princes set forth the same by theire proclamations. For you will not I trowe say , that the Emperour him self preached in pulpyt with gown and surplesse, or with cope and Rotchet., as you poore soules are driuen full againste your willes to doe . And so for all your note and shrewde meaning , Charles is as farre of from his supremacy as euer he was before . Yea I will nowe proue, after the vsual sort of M. Hornes reasoning againft the catholikes, that bishops at thys tyme, yea in the tyme of greate Theodofius to, were supreame heads aswell in caufes temporall as spiri-tuall: *For* (by the decree of Charles, and Theodofius) *yt was Lawfull for all men in all suites to appeale to the bisshoppes , withowte anie appeale to be made from theyre sentence and decree .* But of this we haue spoken before more at large.

Naucler.
generat.
28. & 31.
q. 1.c. vo-
lumus. vbi
allegatur
liber Theo
dofij.

q ij   Yet

Yet you tel vs again here after your maner that this Charles *ruled and gouerned ecclefiasticall perfons in all Ecclefiasticall thinges and caufes .* This you conclude ftil . But this claufe, faying or affertion coulde neuer yet appeare in any text by you alleaged. And here I might ruffle with you in M . Iewels Rethorike for this claufe , *Supreme gouernment in all Ecclefiasticall thĩgs and caufes:*as he doth againft D.Harding for the bare termes of *Priuate Maffe, vniuerfal Bifshop, head of the Church,&c.*and fay to you. If Emperours and other Princes were fupreme Gouernours in dede in all Ecclefiafticall caufes,*fo allowed and taken in the whole worlde , why were thei neuer expreffely and plainely named fo? was there no man in the worlde for the fpace of a thowfaud yeres and more* from the tyme of Conftantine to Maximilian , *able to expreffe this name or Title ? It had ben the fimpler and playner dealing* for M. Horne *to haue faid . This Title can not yet be found,and fo to haue takẽ a longer daie.*And againe.*This title* of fupreme Gouernour in al Ecclefiaftical caufes *is the very thing that we deny,ãd that M. Horn hath takẽ in hãd to proue, and boldly auoucheth , that he hath already plainly fhewed it,* and yet not in one of his allegations it can be found . *As though he woulde fay , al the oɩde fathers of the Church both Greekes and Latines wanted wiordes and eloquence , and either they could not , or they durfte not call* the fupreme Gouernour *by his own peculiar name.* And again thus . *From the tyme* of Conftantine the great to this Charles , there haue ben of Chriften Emperours aboue. 30. and befide a greate nombre of Chriften Kinges in Spayne , in Fraunce , yea and ɩn our Countrye to , *for their Conftancy in faith , for their vertues and knowledge far exceeding the reft that haue ben fithence:(* at leaft wife by your Iudgements which condemne

Ievvel:in
his Reply
p1g.302.

Idem p4.
306.

Char-
demai.
Idem pag.
308.

demne thefe later ages)*The nombre of them beinge fo greate,*
their vertues fo noble,their power fo mighty,*it is merueyl*
M.Horne fhould not be able to fhew that any one of them all
in fo long tyme,was fo much as once Called Intitled,Saluted or
proclaymed,The fupreme Gouernour in al caufes EcclefiaſticaL
And laſt of al.This fupreme Gouernement,to *the which we*
muſt nedes fweare by booke othe,*fo Auncient,fo vniuerfall,*
fo Catholike,fo Glorioufe can not be founde neither in the Romain Empire,neither in al the Eaſte Church,nor in France,
nor in Spaine, nor in England , but muſt be fought out , in
broken fayinges of this and that man, *and that by conieƈture*
*only.*This I might , as I faid,in M.Iewels Rhetorike ruffle a
litell with you. But becaufe, as his chalenge it felfe (I beleue)fo farre mifliketh you , that you wifhe his tounge had
bene tyed to a pillery,when he vttered it at Paules Croſſe,
fo this his Rhetorike alfo pleafeth you,I trowe,neuer a
whitte .   Therefore not to trowble you ,I am content
to leaue it . Onelye I defire the Reader to marke , that
euer you conclude , pronounce and affirme in your owne
woordes, *Supreme Gouernement in al Ecclefiaſticall caufes,*
but in your allegations and Authorities being fo thicke,and
fo long,you can not for your life fo much as once finde it.
And fo Chriſten men are fworen to that , which neuer
fynce Chriſt was borne , was euer reade,fene,or herde of,
in any Councel or Doƈtour, Biſſhop or Father,Emperour
or Prince, Countrie or City whatfoeuer.

But to returne to you Maiſter Horne , whome I hadde
almoſte forgotten, I will note one moſte fonde contra-
diƈtion in you, and fo paſſe to the next Diuifion . You fay
this Prince Charles the greate,*is in fome thinges to be borne* Pag.63.
with , confidering the blindneſſe and fuperſtition of the tyme.

q iij   And

And yet you fay in leſſe thē twēty lines before: *This doctrine
of Alcuin* (who was this Charles his Chaplain) *was no doubt
the doctrin of al the Catholik and learned fathers in that tyme.*

Pag. eadē.

Now good ſir. If there were Catholik ād learned fathers in
that tyme, ād the doctrin of Alcuin⁹ was the doctrin of thē,
he alſo being themperors chaplaine, and dayly inſtructer in
Gods matters, why feare you in thēperor a corruptiō of the
blindnes ād ſuperſtitiō of the tyme ? Or what blindnes and
ſuperſtitiō is there in the tyme, whē Catholik ād learned fathers flouriſh in the time? Except you wil ſay, that to be Ca
tholik and learned, is alſo a blindnes ād ſuperſtitiō: ād that heretiks only do ſe or the vnlerned ōly haue the pure worſhip
of God? But ſo it is. That tyme cōdēneth this tyme. That Religiō cōdēneth yours. And therefore you muſt nedes either
cal thē blind, or cōfeſſe your ſelf blīd, which you cā not poſ-
ſibly do, becauſe you are blīd in dede. And why? Forſoth. becauſe euer, whē you looke vp toward the former ages, you
put vpō your eies a paire of ſpotted ſpectacles: ſo that al that
you ſe through thoſe ſpectacles, ſemeth alſo ſpotted, fowle,
ād euil fauored vnto you. And theſe ſpectacles are, The cō-
tempt of the Church traditiōs: A pride of your own knowledge in Gods word: A lothſomnes of auſtere ād hard life to
beare your * own croſſe with Chriſt. A preiudicat opiniō
of preferrīg Caluin, Melāchtō ād Luther before al the Catholik ād lerned fathers, for ſo you cal thē, of that age. With
ſuch like. If you wuld ones put of theſe foule ſpotted ſpectacles, M. Horn, thē wuld you neuer cal the time of Catholik
ād lerned fathers, a time of blindnes ād ſuperſtitiō, but then
would you ſe clerly, your own blindnes and ſuperſtition.
Which with al my hart, I pray God you may ones doe ere
your dye.

M. Horne. The. 102 . Diuiſion. pag. 63. a.

*Although herein Lodouic⁹ Charles his ſon, vvere ſomvvhat inferior to his
father: Yet not vvithſtādīg, he (. 327.) reſerued theſe Eccleſiaſtical cauſes to
himſelf,*

why pro-
teſtants
can not
ſee the
truthe,

* Matth.
10. & 16.
Marc. 8.
Luc .9.

The. 327.
vntruth.
He gaue
thē ouer,
as ſhal ap
peare.

hi ſelf, ãd vvith no leſſe care he ordred the ſame, although in ſome thĩgs, being
a very mild Prĩce, he vviked ãd bare ouer much vvith the (.328.) ambitiõ of
the Popes. Shortly after, vvhã as the forſaid Leo vvas departed, vvas Stephẽ
next elected Pope, ãd vvithout the cõfirmatiõ of thẽperour, tooke the Papacy
vpõ hĩ. Al the hiſtories agree, that he came ſhortly after into Fraũce to thẽ=
peror, but vvverfore, moſt of thẽ leaue vncertain. Platina thinketh to auoid
the hurley burley in the City that vvas after the death of Leo. Sabellicus
thĩketh thẽperors coronatiõ to be the cauſe. Nauclerus ſaith, he wẽt in
his own perſon vnto thẽperor Lodouik (.329.) about, or for the
Church matters, vvhich (330) proueth that thẽperour had chief authority
in ordering the Church buſines. But our Engliſh Chronicles, as * ſome vvri=
ters affirme, do plainly declare, that his cõming into Fraũce, vvas to make
an excuſe of his vnlaufull conſecration, againſt the decrees made to Char=
les by his predeceſſours, Adriã and Leo, fearing therefore the ſequele of the
matter he firſt ſent his Legats before hĩ to be a preparatiue to his purgatiõ,
and aftervvards came hĩ ſelf to craue his pardõ. And the rather to pleaſe thẽ=
peror, brought a moſt beautiful crovvn of gold for hĩ, and another for the Em=
preſſe (331) vvherof folovved, as Naucle. ſaith: Oĩa quæ petiit à pio Impera=
tore obtinuit, he obteined whatſoeuer he aſked of the godly em=
peror. Novv vvhẽ Stephẽ had diſpatched al his matters, he retourned home:
and ſhortly after, an other eccleſiaſtical cauſe happened, for vvithin a vvhile
the biſhop of Reatina died, and there vva⸳ an other choſen. And whẽ the
ſea of Reatina (ſaith Naucler⁹) was void, the Pope would not cõ=
ſecrat the elect Biſhop, onles he had firſt licẽce therto of them=
peror. The circũſtances of this ſtory, make the matter more plaine. The erle
Guido, had vvritẽ vnto Pope Stephẽ to coſecrat that biſhop: vvhõ the Cler=
gy and the people had elect: but the Pope durſt not enterprice the matter, till
he vvere certified of thẽperors pleaſure, and therupõ vvriteth agaĩ vnto Therle
the tenor vvhereof folovveth, after Gratianus report: I haue red your
letters, wherĩ you require me to cõſecrat the newly elect Biſ=
ſhop of Reatin, choſen by the cõſent of the Clergy ãd people,
leaſt the Church ſhould be long deſtitute of a propre paſtour.
I am ſory for the death of the other: but I haue deferred the
conſecratiõ of this, for that he brought not with him, thempe=
rors licence (vt mos eſt) as the maner is. I haue not ſatisfied your
mind herein, leſte that the Emperour ſhould be diſpleaſed at
my doing. Therefore I require you (for otherwiſe I ought not
to medle) to purchaſe the Emperours licẽce directed vnto me
by his

The.328.
vntruth.
Slaundes
rous.

The. 329.
vntruth.
Ad vitan⸗
das ſeditio
nes left
out in the
middeſt.

The.330.
vntruth.
It pro⸗
ueth not
any ſuch
matter.

* Theſe
ſome
vvriters
dare not
ſhevve
theirfaces
nor tell
out their
names.

The.331.
vntruth.
This
vvherof
foloweth
not out
of Nau⸗
clerus.

Diſt.63.

by his letters, *vt prisca consuetudo dictat* , as the auncient custome
doth wil, and then I will accomplishe your desier . I praie you
take not this my doing in euil parte. VVherof it is manifeste
inough (*saith Nauclerus*) that of the Emperours at that time , the
Bishops had their inuestitures : although Anto. doth glosse o-
therwise, saying that perhaps, this electe Bishoppe was belonging to the Court, who ought not to be ordered. Not only the
textes of many decrees in this distinction , doth confirme this

Dist.63. to be true, but also Gratian him self, and the glossars, do in manie places affirme, that this was the auncient custome, and cō-
stitution in the Churche, that the elections of the Bishoppes of
Rome, and of other Bishops also, should be presented to the
Emperours and Princes, before they might be confecrated.

*The. 11. Chapter: Of Lewys the first, of Steuē.1. Paschalis. 1. En-
genius.1. and Gregory the.4. Popes of Rome.*

Stapleton.

LVdouicus sonne to Charles the great , confirmed the
popes election, and had the inuestitures of bishops. Be
yt so M. Horn, if ye wil: what then? Haue you forgotten, that al that Authoryty was geuē to his father Charles
the great, by Adrian the pope, and that he helde that onely
of the Popes gifte? Agayne, many hundred yeares together
ere this tyme, Fraunce, Italie, Spayne , England and many
other contreis were vnder thempiere of Rome. Would ye
therfore inferre your argument, frō that tyme to our tyme,
and make those countries nowe subiect to the Empire, bicause they were then? Yf ye doe, litle thank shal ye haue for
your labour: And truely the argument holdeth aswel in the
one, as in the other: And when al is done, your cause of supremacie standeth as yt did before . Yet is the fyne and
clerkly handlyng of the matter by M. Horne, to be withall
confi-

conſidered:who like a wanton ſpanell , running from hyˢ game at riot , hunteth to fynde the cauſe, why Pope Ste-phen (whome the ſtories call an Angelicall and a bleſſed man)came to this Emperour into Frauce. He telleth three cauſes,out of three certaine and knowē Authours:ād then telleth vs , that Nauclerus ſayeth , he came for Churche matters, and ſo ful hādſomly concludeth thereby,that the Emperour had the chiefe Authoritie therein : which is as good an argument, as if a man would proue,the woman to whome Kyng Saule came and conſulted with for certaine his affaires, to haue bene aboue the King. Your Authour Nauclerus doth ſpecifie what theſe cauſes were : that is, to intreate themperour , for his enemies , and for the Ro-mans , that had done ſuche iniurie to Pope Leo,of whom ye haue ſpoken , and to pardon other that were in diuerſe priſons in Frauce,for the great owtragiouſe offences done againſt the Churche.The good Emperour ſatisfied hys de-ſire:ād ſo he returned to Rome,ād thoſe alſo which were baniſhed with him.Alſo he ſaieth he wēt to the Emperour *ad vitandas ſeditiones* : to auoyde the tumultes that were riſing in the Cytie,which clauſe M . Horne nipped quyte of in the middeſt of hys allegation. Belike M . Horne hym ſelf, thought not good to reſt in that argumente,and ther-fore he ſeketh a new, ād that is that the Pope came to ex-cuſe hym ſelf,of hys vnlawfull conſecratiō, done without the cōſente of thēperour: And to make his way,brought a moſt bewtiful crowne of golde,one for hym,and an other for the Empreſſe,wherof followed as Nauclerus ſaith that he obtayned, what ſo euer he asked of the godlye Empe-rour . But Maiſter Horne how your *wherof* followeth,yt would trouble a wiſeman, yea your ſelfe to tell. For to ſay

r   the

Nauclerus generat. 28. In A-reopagiti⸗ cis Hildiui ni pag. 60 He is ſo called of the Em⸗ perour Lodouike him ſelfe.

Nauclerus generat. 28.pag.58.

the truth yt can not followe. Nauclerus maketh mention, as I haue sayde what hys demaundes were, but of no suche crowne. Neither your other Authours Sabellicus and Pla-

Volat ant. tina. But as well Platina as Volaterranus sayth the Empe-
Lib.22. rour deliuered to the Pope at his returne , a weightye and a massie Crosse of golde , that he gaue to Sainte Peters Churche.

Now Syr, do so much for me againe, or rather for your selfe, to proue your selfe a true man and somwhat to better your own tale, to tel vs but one Author by name good or bad, that writeth, as ye say, côcerning the.ij. Crownes, the Pope brought with him, and of his purgatiô and pardô that he should craue of the Emperour. What M. Horne may do

The prety hereafter, good Reader, let him selfe wel consider. But I
proufes pray thee in the mean ceason consider, that he allegeth no
that M. better matter than this , that *our Englifsh Chronicles* (Bale
Horne belike, or some such honest man) and againe , *as some wri-*
vseth. *ters affirme* doe plainely saye so . Now though the cre-
ditte of our English Histories, in this case be very slender: yet ye see, good Reader, how he playeth and dallieth with you, neither daring to name any Originall Chronicler, nor any other that doth name the said Chronicler. But maketh his proufe onely vpon some sayes, and heare sayes.

The.332. M. Horne. The.103. Diuifion. pag. 64.a .
Vntruth. *Immediatlie after the death of Stephen* Paschalis.1.*vvas chofen Pope:*
No likli- *He being encouraged, by all (.332.) likelihode, by his Predeceffours like en-*
hode in *traunce, thinking to entreat the Emperour fo eafely as Stephen had done.*
the world *And boldened vvith a late made Canon by Stephen, fuffied him felfe to be*
can be ga *enftalled and confecrate vvithout the Emperours inuefturing , leaue and*
thered *authoritie: Neuerthelesbeing better aduifed (miftrufting his prefumptuous*
herof out *and difobedient fact vvould difpleafe the Emperour , as it did in deede) he*
of anye *fent by and by his Legates to the Emperour to excufe him felfe, and laieth al*
good hy- *the*
ftorie.

the fault on the people and clergy. Th'Emperour accepting this excuſe for that time warneth the people and Clergie of Rome,
that they take good hede,that they do no more offend againſt
his Maieſtie, but that hereafter they doe warely obſerue and
kepe the old orders and côſtitutions.*He calleth this attempt (.333.)*
plaine treaſon.   *This Emperour called a Coũcel at Frankeford,he be-
ſtovved ſpirituall promotions, and(.334.) inſtituted his brother* Drogo,*the
chiefe Miniſter or Biſhop at* Mettes.

   In the meane vvhile die h Pope Paſchalis,*next to vvhome follovved*
Eugenius,*but elected not vvithout contention,and liued but a vvhile:af-
ter vvhom ſucceded* Valentinus,*vvho liued in the Papacie but forty daies. Next vnto him vvas choſen* Gregorie *the fourthe ,* who was of ſo
great modeſty,*ſaith* Platina,that being elected Pope of the Clergie and people of Rome,he would not take vpon him the office, before he had his confirmation of th' Emperours Embaſſadours, whô th' Emperor had ſent to Rome for that purpoſe,
and to examin diligêtly that election.And Lodouicus th' Emperour,did not this of pride,but that he woulde not looſe the
priuileges and rightes of th'Empire.*Note al theſe things vvell, the
Pope on the one part,vvhã he vvas choſen vvithout any contentiõ,yet vvould
he not be côſecrat vvithout th' Emperors côſirmation:othervviſe he thought it
an vnmodeſt part.Th' Emperor on the other ſide,not only ſendeth his Embaſſadours to côſirm,but or euer they confirm hĩ,to examin,and diligêtly to diſcuſſe,after vvhat ſort he cam in,ãd vvhether he vver elected laufully or no.
And this he did,not of a pride(ſay thei)much leſſe of any vſurpatiõ,but becaus
he vvold not loſe or diminiſh the right herein,that belonged to the Emperial
(.335.)Maieſt.Here, ſay they,he did it of purpoſe, becauſe he vvould not loſe
his right,ãd not his only,but the right of the Empire.But leaſt it ſhuld ſeme
he did tirannouſly herein,and oppreſſed the church,or infringed her liberties,
it folovveth almoſt vvoorde for vvorde,in both theſe vvriters* Platina and
Nauclerus.*For he was a mild,merciful,and moſt gêtle Prince
of nature,and one that did alwaies mainteine the righte and
dignity of the Church. Lo hovv great clemêcy this is compted in him,
and the defence of the dignities and rightes of the Church:the vvhich aftervvardes,and novv of the Popes,is compted*the greateſt tyranny and oppreſ-
ſion*

r ij

The. 333.
Vntruth.
He dothe
not ſo cal
it,nor did
not ſo
take it.
The. 334.
Vntruth.
He vvas
firſt cho-
ſen of the
Clergye:
Vvhiche
M Horne
hath lefte
out.

The. 335.
Vntruth.
It vvas
no right,
of Empe-
rial Maie-
ſty,but of
the Apo-
ſtolik au-
thoritie.

To doe it
novv.as
this Le-
vves did

then yt is
counted
no tyran-
ny at all.

Wve
wishe the
same: for
the your
heresies
shoulde
sone haue
an ende

The. 336.
vntruthe.
False trã-
statiõ as
shal ap/
peare.
The. 337.
vntruth.
misseres
porting.
corã pro-
latam lau-
dibus effe-
runt.
The. 338.
Vntruth.
Accordig
to the rule
of S. Benet,
left out.

sion of the Churche that can be. But further to approue this deede of Lodouike, the foresaid authors recite many Canons, Decrees, and Constitutions,
that this Emperour made in Ecclesiastical causes and things: and especially
for the reformatiõ of the disordered behauiours of the Bisshops ãd Clergy. In
so much that Platina cõparing the dissolutenes of the church mẽ in his time,
crieth out * would God, O Lodouike, thou were aliue in these
our times, for now the Church wanteth thy most holy ordinaunces, and thy discipline. The selfe same Lodouicus (saith Platina) called a Councell of many Bisshoppes at Aquisgrane, to
Gods honour, and the profite of the Church dignitie. The Prelates in the Preface to this Synode, dooe declare, vvhat vvas the care and
authoritie of this godly Emperour in this Synode. They affirme that the most
Christian Emperour, had called an holy and Generall Congregation or Coũcell at Aquisgrane: He began therin throughly to hãdle the matter, vvith
vvisedom void of curiositie: he counsailed, yea vvarned the Holie Sinod assembled, vvhat vvas nedeful to be don, touchĩg certain chief Ministers of the
Churches: He vvarned thẽ further, to dravv out of the holy Canõs, and the
sayĩgs of the holy fathers, a foũrm of institutiõ for the sĩple sort of ministers,
vvherby they might the more easily learn to vvalke in their dueties vvithout
offéce. The Synod geueth God thãks, that he had preferd so holie, wise, and deuout a Prince, to haue the (.336.) charge and
ouersight of his Church, and the Churches nedefull businesse
or matters. The Synode, accordinge to the kings aduertisement, furthered also vvith his helpe othervvise, collecteth a fourme of Institution,
vvherin is cõteined at large, after vvhat sorte the Prelates oughte to fra ne
their liues, rule, or gouerne the people cõmitted to their cures, &c. This done,
they bring (337) to the Prince their fourm of Institutiõ, vvhich they had deuised. This Emperour calle I an other Councel at Ticinum in Italy for
the causes hereafter expressed. The matters or causes vvich the honorable
Emperour Ludouicus did commaunde his Bisshoppes to consider of, are
these: touching the state of his kingedome: of the conuersation of the Bishoppes, Priestes, and other Churchmen: of the doctrine and preachinge to
the people: of vvritinge out of Bookes: of restoring of Churches: of ordering the people, and hospitalles for strangers: of Monasteries both for men
and vvemen, (.338.) VVhat so euer is out of order in these forenamed states,
eyther

eyther through the negligence of the guides, or the ſlouthfulnes of the inferi- *ours,* I am (*ſaid he*) very much deſirous to know, and I coueite to amende or reſourme them, according to Goddes will, and your holy aduiſe, in ſuche ſorte that neither I be found repro-able in Gods ſight, neither you nor the people incurre Gods wrathful indignation for theſe things, how this may be ſear-ched, found out, and brought to perfection, that I commit to be entreated by you, and ſo to be declared vnto mee. The leſſer matters alſo, whiche in general touche all, but in eſpe-ciall, ſome, and nede reſourmation : I will that ye make en-quirie of them, and make relation vnto me thereof : as for ex-aumple, if the rulers in the Countries neglecte or ſell Iuſtice, if they be takers or oppreſſours of the Churches, widdowes, Orphanes, or of the poore. Yf they come to the Sermons. If they dooe reuerence and obey duelie their Prieſtes. If they preſume to take in hand any new opinions or arguments that may hurt the people. &c.

The Biſshoppes after they had conſulted vppon theſe matters, doe make *relation vnto the Emperour, vvhat they had done : ſhevving to him, that* *they had founde ſome of the Biſshoppes and chieſe Miniſters faultie, and* *humblie praye the Emperour on their behalfe, that he vvill of his goodnes* *graunt thoſe, ſome ſpace to amende their faultes.* *They complaine to the* *Emperour of Biſshops and Prieſts for lacke of* Preaching, *and that* *Noble men, and Gentlemen, come not vnto thoſe* (.339.) *fevv ſer-* *mons that bee. And ſo then recite many other enormities, as about* *Tythes, Inceſt, and ſuche like, eſpeciallie in religious perſons, vvho* *for the moſte parte are* (.340.) *cleane out of order. And to bring* *theſe to their former order and ſtate reſteth* (*ſay they*) *in your* *diſpoſition.* *Thus dothe this King take vppon him, and thus* *doe the Biſshoppes yeelde vnto him the* (.341.) *gouernemente,* *as vvell of Eccleſiaſticall, as Temporall cauſes and thinges.* On *this vviſe did Lodouicus alvvaies exerciſe him ſelfe : in ſo muche* *that for his careſull gouernemente in Churche matters he vvas* ſurnamed Pius, *the Godlie, , as his Father beforehim, vvas* *called* Magnus, *the Greate.*

The.339. Vntruth.
Of fevv Sermons no complainte is made.

The.340. Vntruth
A tale falſely told and out of order.

The.341. Vntruth.
No gouernemente at al named or yel-ded in Eccleſiaſti-cal things.

Stapleton.

The principall tenour of the matters here conteyned,
standeth in the confirmation of the Popes election, in calling councelles, and confirming lawes ecclesiastical. To all
the whiche we neade no farre fetched or newe solution,
especially seing M. Horne hym self, furthereth yt so wel,
as declaryng that all thinges were donne according to the
holy Canons, and sayinges of the holy Fathers : and that
many of theis matters towched the polityke gouernmente
of the realme. Yet let M. Fekenham now beware . For M.
Horne proueth yt high treason in the people and clergy,
for that Paschalis was made Pope wythowte themperours
consent. And so lo, at the lengthe here is some face of antiquity, for our newe actes of Parliamente. Well found out,
and lyke a good lawyer M. Horne. Yet I beseache you tel
vs, which wordes of all that you reherse imploye plaine
Ne âplius treason . I am assured there are none, onlesse yt be these.
simili ex- *that they do no more offende againste hys maiesty.* as your self
emplo im= reherse out of Sabellicus. And yf ye call thys treason , and
peratoria make no better prouf, I thinke neither good grammarian,
læderetur nor any good lawyer wil take your parte. For thowghe in
maiestas. latin *lædere maiestatem,* be somtyme taken for treason, yet
yt is not alwayes, neither can yt be englished treason , but
vpon the circumstances, which declare the acte to be treason. And how wil thys cruell exposition stande I pray you
with your owne declaration, in this leaf also: that thys Ludouicus was *a milde, mercifull, and moste gentle prince ?* Beside thys, it is not like he toke thys matter so heauely , for
that euen as Platina your authour here writeth out of *A-*
nastasius bibliothecarius, a worthy authour ád lyuing about
thys tyme, thys Emperour released to this Pope Paschalis
his right that he had in the election of Bishoppes, geuē before

fore to Charles by Adrian the Pope. And hereuppon might
I aſwell cōclude after your baſe and yet accuſtomable reaꞏ
ſoning, that the Princes of Englande ſhould haue nothing
to doe, with the election of Biſhopes. Yet, if there be no re
medy, let yt be highe treaſon to agniſe the Popes election
withowte the Emperours confirmation. What is thys to
the prince of Englonde, that hath nothing to doe therwith,
or to M. Fekēham, ſeing if al be true, yet it maketh nothing
for the Emperours ſupreamacy, or againſte the Popes ſupreamacy? The denial wherof in dede (the more pitie) is
taken for treaſon with vs, but yet thankes be to God, ſuche
kinde of treaſon, as a man maye loſe his head and take no
hurte by yt, but muche good: and that is to be a very true
and a bleſſed martyr.

*Nauclerus
generat.
28.pag.55
et diſt.63.
Ego Ludo-
uicus.*

*A new
kinde of
treaſon
wherin a
man may
looſe his
head and
take no
hurte.*

But now touching the particular doinges of this Emperour Ludouike, you tel vs *he beſtowed Spirituall promotions*
(and you tell vs but of one onely) *and inſtituted his brother
Drogo the Chiefe Miniſter or Biſhop at Mettes.* And here you
leaue oute, *Canonicam vitam agentem, clero eiuſdem Eccleſiæ conſentiente ac eligente,* he inſtituted him being a man
that lead a regular lyfe , the clergye alſo of that Churche
bothe conſenting and chooſing him. This you leaue out to
make the worlde beleue the Emperour beſtowed Spirituall promotions , of his owne ſupreme Authorytie abſolutely. And here you tel vs of *a right belonging to the Emperial maieſty,* in confirming of the Pope. And yet you forget,
that in the very leafe before you confeſſe , this *was made
by decrees of Adrian and Leo Popes to Charles,* this mans Father. And then was it not a right of Imperial Maieſty , but
a Priuilege frō the Apoſtolike Authoryte . As for the Clemency of this Prince ſo much commended , it was not as

*Nauclе-
rus.pag.
55.Gener.
28.*

Fol.63.b.

you

you imagine for any fupreme gouernment, but for his moft fatherly defending, aiding and fuccouring of the Church. Namely in that moft learned Councell holden vnder him at Aquifgrane, of which prefently you do talk very much, prying out for fom claufe that might make for your fuprem gouernmēt. And at laft, finding none, with a litle falfe tranflatiō, you make the Synode to fay of th'Emperour, that *he had the charge and ouerfight of Chriftes Church.* Which al in Latine is but this one word *Procuratorem*, A defendour, a fuccourer, a maintainour, not a Supreme Gouernour with charge and ouerfight. You adde alfo *the Synode was furthered with his helpe otherwife,* itching forth a litle and a litle, faine to finde fomewhat, and it wil not be. For all that furthering (that you fo clofely couer) was nothing els, but that to his great charges, he furnifhed the Councel with a goodly ftore of bookes, and greate plentye of the Fathers writings. Out of which they collected a fourme of inftitution, &c. Not the Emperour. Anon after you talke of Monafteries for men and wemen: but you leaue out: *Secundùm regulam S . Benedicti.* According to the Rule of S. Benet . Your vnruly Religion coulde not beare fo much as the Remēbraunce of that holy Rule. And al that you tell of the Emperors words to the Bifhops in the Coūcel of Ti cinū, the Coūcel calleth it only *Comonitoriū* an aduertifemēt or admonitiō. No charge or Comifsiō. You note to the Reader *certeyne enormytes recited in this Goūcel.* But wote you what thofe enormytes were ? Forfoth thefe. That the lay Nobilite, *quia ad electionis confortiū admittuntur, Archipræsbyteris fuis dominari præfumunt, & quos tanquā patres ve nerari debuerūt, velut fubditos cōtēnunt.* Bicaufe they are admitted to haue a part in the Electiō , they prefume to ouer rule

Tom. 2.
Conc. pag.
639.
Eius vide-
licet libe=
ralifsima
largitione
Copiā li-
brorū &c.

In Con.
Ticin. pag.
705.
pag. 706.
Col. 2.

rule their chief prieſtes. And whom they oughte to reuerence as Fathers, they contemne as ſubiects. Theſe were
the enormyties there recyted M. Horne. And do not you
defende this very enormytie, euen in this very place, ād by
this very Councel? When will you leaue to bringe Autho-
ryties againſt your ſelfe? As touching the matter of Inceſt,
the Synod requireth of the Emperour that to bringe ſuch
offenders to open penaunce, *Comitum eius auxilio fulcian-* *Ibid. Vt*
tur, they may be vpholded with the helpe of his Offycers. *publicæ*
Lo they require the Emperours helpe for execution. And *poßint pæ*
nitentiæ
yet you conclude after your maner. *Thus dothe the kinge* *ſubiugari.*
take vpō him, ād thus doe the Biſhops yelde vnto him the Go-
uernement as wel of Eccleſiaſtical as Tēporal cauſes and thin-
ges. And this you conclude a gouernement, whiche in all
your premiſſes was not ſo muche as named. Your Concluſion is alwaies full and mightye. But your proufes are
voyde and ſainte.

M. Horne. The.104. Diuiſion. pag.66,4.

Pope Leo.4. *vvriteth his humble letters vnto* Lotharius *on the behalfe* *The. 342.*
of one Colonus, *vvho vvas choſen to be Biſhop of* Reatina, *but he might* *vntruth.*
not conſecrate him vvithout the Emperours licence firſt obteined thereunto, *You take*
and therfore praieth the Emperour of his ſauour tovvardes Colonus: Vt *not the*
vvhole
veſtra licentia accepta, ibidem, Deo adiuuante, eum conſecra- *gloſe. The*
re valeamus Epiſcopum: That hauing your licence, wee may *nextlyne*
haue authority by Goddes helpe to conſecrate him Biſhoppe *maketh*
cleane
there. *Vppon this vvoorde,* Licence, *The Gloſſer noteth, the conſente* *againſt*
of the Prince to be required after the election be made. (.342.) *you.*
Nexte to Leo, *ſauinge the* (.343.) *vvoman Pope* Iohan, *vvas* Benedi- *Sabell.*
ctus.3. *choſen, vvho vvas ratified and confirmed by the Emperours autho-* *Platina.*
rity: vvho ſente his Embaſſadours to Rome for that purpoſe. This Pope is *The.343.*
commended for his greates godline: But he vvas ouer godly to liue longe in *vntruth.*
that ſea: neuertheleſſe he vvas not ſo godly as the moſte of his ſucceſſours *Pope*
Ione,
Pope
None.

s   vvere

vvere altogether vngodly, as your (.344.) ovvne vvriters make reporte. And to note this chaunge the better: Nauclerus telleth of diuers vvonders: hovv the Deuil appeared in an ugly shape, and hurled stones at men as they vvent by: set men togeather by the eares: bevvrayed theeues, and Priestes of their Lemmans, and such like: Hovv it rained bloud three daies and three nightes: Hovv great Grassehoppers vvith six vvings, and six fete, and tvvo teeth harder then any stone, couered the ground, and destroyed the fruites: not altogether vnlike those Grassehoppers, that S. Iohn noteth in his Reuelatiõ, to come frõ the bottõles pit, after the starre vvas fallen. After this folovved a great pestilence: VVhich vvonders, if they be true, be not vnvvorthy the notĩg considering the chaunge that follovved. For hitherto stil from time to time, although some Popes did priuily attempte the contrarye, yet the Emperours (.345.) alvvayes kept the confirmation of the Pope, the inuesturing of Bis-shoppes, and the ordering of many (.346.) other Ecclesiasticall matters, till the next Pope began openly to repine at the matter, and his successour after him to curse, and some of those that solovved, fell from chiding and cursing, to plaine fighting for the same. In the vvhiche combate, though vvith much a doe, at length they vvrong them selues from vnder the Em-perours (.347.) obedience: Yet alvvaies euen hitherto, Princes haue had no litle interest in Ecclesiastical causes, as hereafter shal appere.

The. 12. Chapter. Of Leo. 4. Benedictus. 3. Nicolaus. 1. Adrian. 2: Martinus. 2. Adrian. 3. and of the. 8. Generall Councell vnder Basilius the Emperour.

Stapleton.

WE goe on still with the Popes confirmation: a matter, as ye know, nedelesse, and such as might be spared, sauing that M. Horne must take a foile euen of his owne allegation and Glosar. Who, as he saith, the Princes consente, is required after the election, so

he

he addeth : *Nisi aliud suadeat scandalum, vel prascripta con-*
suetudo.   Onlesse, saith he, some offence , or a prescribed
custome moue vs to thinke otherwise. Then is M. Horne
in hand with Benedictus the. 3. nexte Pope to the woman
Pope Iohan : who was confirmed by the Emperour . But
here M.Horne, a man may doubt of this pointe, whether
this Benedictus was next to Pope Iohan. For if there was
neuer such Pope Iohan, then could not he be nexte to her.
And that it is rather a fable then a storie, for al your great
busines, your Apologie, and others, make therein, I thinke   Confutat
it hath ben already sufficiently proued. Neither nede you   Apolog.
to make so much wondering at the matter. Except ye list   fol.164.
to wonder at your selues, whiche doe place the Popes Supreme authoritie in Princes, be they men, or women: Yea
and chyldren to . And in so fewe yeares you haue had all
three.Man. Childe. And Woman. The lesse meruaile had
it bene, if in so many hundred yeres, we had had one woman pope , which yet as I sayed, is vtterly false: as it hath
bene sufficiently proued .

  But touching this confirmation of popes and inuesturing of bishops, which Adrian and Leo graunted to Charles the greate , whych Ludouicus hys sonne gaue ouer a-
gaine , which other princes coueted to haue after in their
owne handes againe, and which was denied them, Gratian
who hath collected the examples of both sydes , geueth
forth a true and an euident reason, as well why to the one
it was first graunted , as also why to the other afterwarde
it was most iustly denied. Of the fyrst he sayeth . *The ele-*   Dist.63.
ctiōs of Popes and of other bishops to be referred to Princes and
Emperours, both Custome and lawe hath taught vs, for the dis-
sensiōs of schismatiks and heretiks, against who the Church hath

ben defended oftentimes with the lawes of faithful Emperours.
The election therfore of the Clergy was presented to the Prin-
ces, to the entēt that, it being by their authority strengthened,
no heretike or schismatike should dare to gainsaie it. And also
to the end that the Princes them selues as deuout childrē shuld
agree vpon him, whom they sawe to be chosen for their Father,
that in all things they might aide and assist him. As it was in
the example of Valentinian th'Emperour, and S. Ambrose.
I, saith the Emperour, *wil be thy aide and defence, as it be-*
cometh my degree. And herevpon Pope Steuen (of whom
M. Horne talked euen now) made a Decree that without
the Emperours Legates were present, no bishops alreadie
chosen should be confecrated. And by reason of this Decree, the Bishops of Reatina coulde not be confecrated, as
M. Horne euen now alleaged. *But* (saith Gratian) *because*
the Emperours, passing sometime their bondes, would not be of
the nūber of cōsenters ād agreers to th'electiō, but wuld be the
first that shuld choose, yea ād put out to, oftētimes also falling to
be as false as heretiks, assaied to breake the vnity of the Catho-
like Church their Mother, therefore the decrees of the holie
Fathers haue proceded against them, that they should no more
medle with the election of bishops, and that whosoeuer ob-
tained any Church by their voice, should be excommunicated.
And as Ezechias toke awaye the brasen serpent, whiche
Moyses did set vp, because it was now abused: so the constitutions of our forefathers are sometime chaunged by the
Authoritie of the posteritie, when such Constitutiōs mere
positiue are abused. Then Gratian bringeth in diuers other
decrees against the Confirmatiō of Emperours, as of Gregorie the .4. pope : of Lewys the firste Charles hys sonne,
Henrie the first, and Otho the first Emperours : who all
gaue

gaue ouer by open decrees this priuilege graunted firſt of popes vpon good conſiderations, aud after repealed vpon as good by the ſame authoritie.

And thus you ſee, M. Horne, by your owne Authours, and by good reaſon (if ye haue grace to conſider it) you are ſufficiently anſwered for confirmation of Popes, and inue-ſturing of Biſhops : a common matter in your booke, and yet as you ſee nowe, a matter of no weight in the world.

After this, M. Horn is in hand with the raining of bloud three daies, and with many other wonders of this time: yea with the Deuil him ſelfe that bewrayed Prieſts Lemmans, whiche they kept in corners ſecrete, that now M. Horne and his fellowes, are not aſhamed to kepe openly, and haue learned a furder leſſon then Prieſtes of that age knew, that a Frier and a Nunne may laufully wedde : wherat the De-uill him ſelfe perchaunce doth as much wonder, as Maiſter Horne here doth wonder at the Deuils ſtraunge doings. M. Horns vvonder-which yet are not ſo ſtrange, nor ſo much to be wondered ful vviſe-at, as perchance your great wiſedom is to be wodred at, to dome. imagine that al theſe things chanced, for that th' Emperour had not as he was wonte to haue, the confirmation of the Popes election, and the ordering of maters Eccleſiaſticall.

M. Horne. The. 105. Diuiſion. pag. 66. b.

After Benedictus, *vv is* Nicolas *choſen, vvhom the Emperour him ſelfe being preſent, did confirme, as vvitneſſeth* Nauclerus : *At the ſame time, was the Emperour* Lodouicus. 2. *at* Rome, *who confir-med the Popes election. The ſame alſo ſayeth* Martin, *to the vvhich* Volateran *addeth of the Emperour and the* Pope : De communi con-ſilio ambo cuncta gerebant . *Al thinges were done by com-mon counſaile or conſent of both,* the Emperour and the Pope. *And leaſt it might be thought he meaneth not as vvel Eccleſiaſtical as Tem-*

S iij poral

poral matters: Sabellicus *maketh the matter more plaine, affirming that* the *Emperour and the Pope had secrete conference together many daies, and had consultation both touching the matters perteining to Christian Religion, and also of the state of Italye. And a litle after talkinge of* the *Pope :* The Pope decreed by the consente of Lodouicus, that from thence foorth, no Prince, no not the Emperour him selfe, should be present in the councell with the Clergye. onlesse it were when the principall pointes of faith were treated of.   *Hitherto in all these Ecclesiasticall causes, the Emperour hath the doinge, as (.348.) vvell or more than the Pope.*

But this last decree, that by the allovvance of the Emperour, the Pope made, exempteth Temporall Princes: from Ecclesiasticall matters in their councelles, though in the most principall matters Ecclesiasticall, concerning faith, it leaueth to them their (.349.) interestes.

Stapleton.

M. Horne hym self, to helpe our matters forwarde bringeth forth a decree made by the pope with th'Emperours consent, that lay princes should not be present in Coūcels, onlesse it were when the principall pointes of religion be treated of: at the which he wondreth as of a thing vnheard of. And yet he did, or mought haue found as much in the actes of the Councell of Chalcedo. Yea, he myght haue sene also that by the same decree, as well the people, as the prince might be present, and as much interest had the one thereyn, as the other. For, as the same Pope Nicolas sayed, geuynge a reason why the prince may be present, when matters of faith are debated, *Faith is common to all, and perteineth as vvell to the layitie, as to the Clergie,* yea to all Christen men without exception.

Yet all was not gone from them, sayeth M. Horne : for they had *their interestes still* (he sayeth) *in the principall matters ecclesiasticall, concerning faith.* But what intereste I praye you, tell vs? Was it to determine or defıne anye thing,

The.348. vntruth. For neuer so well as the Pope had.

The.349. vntruth. In mat ters of fayth the Empe- rours had no intere stes of go uernemēt

Act.3. fol.838.

Dist.96. vbinam.

thyng, or that all determinations were voyde and fruſtrate
without thẽ? Nay, but only that they might be preſent, eyther to keepe quiet and order, or els (as Conſtantin and
Marcian proteſted) *ad confirmandam fidem*, to ſtrenghthen
their owne faith : or laſt of all, to execute the Sentence and
determinations of biſhops. And ſo were theyr Ambaſſadours preſent, in the late General Councel at Trẽt: And the
Emperour and Kinges were wiſhed thẽ ſelues to be there.

M. Horne. The.106. Diuiſion.pag.67.a.

Martinus *the ſecõd gat into the Papacie* malis artibus by naughty
meanes *ſaith* Platina, *ãd as is noted in the margẽt, it vvas in this Popes
time, that firſt of all the creation of the Popes vvas made vvithout the Emperours authority: But this Pope died ſo ſhortely , as he came in naughtily.
After vvhõ Adriã the third, like vnto his predeceſſor, the ſecõd of that name*
(*vvho by cũning ſleight practiſed to* (.350.) *defraude the Emperour of his au-*
thority) eſpying oportunitie by reaſon, that Charles the emperour, as Sabel-
licus ſaith, vvas farre of, buſied in the vvarres, dothe promote this matter
to be decreed by the Senate and the people, and this he did immediatly after
he vvas made Biſhop, ãd perſuadeth thẽ, that they doo not hereafter vvayte
for the Emperours approbatiõ, and cõfirmation, in appointing their Biſhop,
but that they ſhould kepe to thẽ ſelues, their ovvn fredome. The vvhich thing
alſo Nicolaus *the firſte , vvith others attẽpted, but coulde not bringe it to*
paſſe, as Platina *reporteth. VVho alſo vvriteth, that the Romaynes had cõ-*
ceiued an hope of great liberty in the hauty courage of this Pope, being a Ro-
maine borne. But to their great griefe, he vvit hin a vvhile vvas takẽ frõ thẽ.

The.350.
vntruth.
ſlaunde-
rous, as
ſhall ap-
peare.

Stapleton.

M. Horne hath ſone done with Nicolaus the firſt, and is
frõ him leapẽ to Martinus the ſecõd. Betwene which two
were, yet. ij. other Popes, Adriã the ſecõd, ãd Iohn the.9.the
time alſo of their regimẽt, being more thẽ twẽty yeres: and
vnder whõ, eſpecially vnder Nicolaus the firſt, ãd Adriã the
ſecond as great matters paſſed touchinge our preſent purpoſe, as vnder any Popes els of many yeres before or after.

For

For vnder thys Nicolaus the firſte and Adrian the ſecond, the.8.general Councell was kept at Conſtantinople, vnder Baſilius then Emperour in the Eaſt partes: All which matter M. Horne, being in other Councels both General and Nationall ſo diligent a chronicler, hath vtterly drowned in ſilence. And yet he might Iwys haue found as much appa‑ rent matter for his purpoſe there, as in any other Councel hytherto mentioned. For Baſilius the Emperour called alſo this Councell, as other Emperours before him dyd, and M Horne might haue furniſhed his booke with ſome ioyly talke of this Emperour alſo made to the biſhops at the beginning of the Councell, touching his care and endeuour about eccleſiaſticall matters.

But there was a padde in the ſtrawe, I warrant you, that made M. Horne agaſt, and not ſo bold as ones to come nere it. Ignorant thereof he coulde not be, hauing ſene Cuſanus *de Concordia Catholica*, out of whom he alleageth in this his booke a large place, and that in the ſame booke, ãd but fiue chapters aboue the place, wher Cuſanus reherſeth out of this viij. Generall Councell, diuerſe and longe proceſſes, to ſhew of purpoſe how the Emperour Baſilius dealed and demeaned him ſelfe in that Coũcel. Ignorant therfore, I ſay, of this matter he could not be, nor laye for his excuſe, that the Actes of this coũcel are not commonly ſet forthe in the former Tomes of the Councelles. Except M. Horne alleage ſuch bookes and chapters as he neuer ſawe nor read, and ſo vttereth his doctrine vpon hereſaye and reporte of others. Shortly therfore to touche this General Councel alſo, ſeing that of all other in maner bothe generall and Nationall ſomewhat hath bene ſayd, ãd ſeing now this Councel is alſo ſet forth in the laſt editiõ of the TomeꞋ,

I wiꞋl

Cuſanus
lib.3.cap.
19.de Cõ-
cordia Ca
tholica.

Fol.85.ex
li.3.cap.13

In Tom.3.
fol.531.Co
lon impr.
An.præ-
ſente.

I will in fewe wordes declare both the Popes Primacy in
the Eaſt Church then to haue bene confeſſed, and the Laye
Princes Primacy in Eccleſiaſtical matters to haue ben none
at all.

Firſt, wheras Michael the Emperour of the Eaſt partes,
a man geué to al licentiouſnes and ryot, had thruſt out the
godly Biſhop Ignatius from the See of Conſtantinople, by *Zonaras lib. 3.*
the perſuaſion of Bardas, whome for inceſt that biſhop had
excommunicated, and placed in his roome one of his
Courtyars, and otherwiſe an heretike, Photius by name,
whome Pantaleon calleth Phocas, other Photinus : Nicolaus the firſt, then Pope of Rome after legacies to and fro,
excommunicated Photius, and Michael the Emperour for
not reſtoring again Ignatius to his See. There is extāt a moſt *Tom. 2.*
lerned and notable letter of this Nicolaus to Michael the *Conc. pa.*
Emperour, where lernedly and copiouſly he diſcourſeth *746.*
what obedience and reuerence Catholik Emperours haue
ſhewed to the Biſſhops of Rome, and howe none but heretikes and ſchiſmatikes haue diſobeyed the ſame. And
whereas this Emperour Michael had (as he ſaith) *Commaū-* *a. Diſt 97.*
ded the Pope to ſende his Legates to Conſtantinople aboute *Victor.*
that matter, a phraſe which you M. Horn make very much *b. In epiſt.*
of, this Pope lernedly and trulye aunſwereth him, that Ca- *praambu.*
tholike and good Emperours were not wonte to com- *Cōc. Chal.*
maunde their Biſſhoppes and Paſtours, eſpecially the Biſ- *c. Cod. de*
ſhoppes of the See Apoſtolike, but with Reuerence ex- *Sum Trin.*
horte and deſire them to ſuche thinges as they required: *dentes.*
which he proueth by the examples of ᵈ Honorius, b Va- *d. Conc. 6.*
lentinian and Marcian, c Iuſtinian, d Conſtantin the. 4. and *Conſt.*
e Conſtantin the fift in their letters to Bonifacius the firſt, *e. Conc. 7.*
to Leo the firſt, to Iohn the firſt, to Donus, and to Agatho *Nice.*

t   Popes of

Popes of Rome. In al which their letters thei vſe the words.
Petimus, hortamur, iuuitamus & rogamus, we beſeche, we
exhorte, we inuite, and deſire you: with all gentlenes and
Reuereçe, ſuch as the Apoſtle cõmaũdeth al me to ſhew to
their Ouerſeers, that watche for their ſoules, and ſhal geue
accõpte for the ſame. Alſo whereas this Emperour had by
a Councell of his Biſſhoppes baniſhed and remoued Ignatius, the Pope firſt ſente his Legates to examine the matter a freſhe, and to referre to the Pope vnto whom the See
of Conſtantinople of right appertayned : wherein the Legates paſsing their Commiſsion ouercome by flattery and
ambition in the Courte of Conſtantinople, confirmed Photius by their conſent. But the Pope not conſenting thereto, he cyted bothe Ignatius and Photius to Rome, as Iulius cyted Athanaſius, and Euſebius with his complices,
and required the Emperour Michael, that by his good
ayde and fauour they might appeare. In the ſame letter
alſo he declareth howe in dede amonge the Ethnikes, the
Emperour was alſo *ſummus Pontifex*, the highe Biſſhoppe.
But (ſaith Nicolaus) *Cùm ad verum ventum eſt eundem regem atque pontificem, vltra ſibi nec Imperator iura pontifica-
tus arripuit, nec pontifex nomen Imperatorium vſurpauit.*
When Chriſt the true King and biſhop came, then neither
the Emperour tooke any more vpon him the high biſſhops
right or Authoritye, neither the high biſſhop vſurped any
more the Imperial title. After this by the example of Conſtantin the great, calling the biſhops Gods, and not to be
iudged of any man, of Theodoſius the younger, charging
his Lieutenant Candidianus in the Epheſine Councel, not
to medle with any matter or queſtion of doctrine (as hath
before bene alleaged) and of Maximus that bleſſed Martyr
(whome

Heb.13.

Tripart.li.
4.cap.6.

Tom.2.
Conci. pa.
764.

(whom Conſtans the heretical Emperour nephew to Heraclius had put to death)he proueth that theperorus iudge- *Zonaras*
ment ouer biſhops, is not, nor ought not to be of any force. *lib. 3. pag.*
And therfore concludeth that Ignatius being depoſed by the *71.*
Emperial ſenténce only was not at al depoſed, but remained
as true biſhop as before. Thus dealed Nicolaus the firſt with
Michael the Greek Emperor, not vſurping any new authority to him ſelf, but following herein the examples of moſt
holye and auncient Biſſhoppes before him , and requiring
no more of the Emperour then his moſte godlye and Noble progenitours other Catholike Emperours hadde done.
All this coulde haue no place in Maiſter Hornes chronicle, either becauſe he hadde not reade ſo farre, or els
becauſe his ſleightes woulde haue bene to groſſe, to haue
picked hereof any coulourable matter for his imagined Supremacye.

Vnder Adrian the ſeconde nexte ſucceſſour to this *Vide San-*
Nicolaus, and vnder Baſilius the Emperour nexte to Mi- *ctiones ec-*
chael was holden at Conſtantinople aboute this matter *cleſiaſticas*
of Ignatius and Photius principallye , the .8. generall *collectas a*
Councell by the accompte of the Latines. In this Coun- *Franc. Io-*
cell the Legates of Adrian, Donatus and Stephen Biſ- *uerio. Im-*
ſhoppes and Marinus a Deacon were preſident, as in all *preſſ. Par.*
other generall Councelles before. In the firſte Action *An. 1555.*
the Popes letters to the Emperour were reade , wherein he condemneth the former Synode vnder Michael,
and willeth that all the monimentes and recordes thereof
be burnte. In the beginninge alſo of this Synode the
Emperour Baſilius, made an Oration to the Synode, de- *Cuſanus*
clarynge wythe what Zeale and loue to the vnytye *lib. 3. cap.*
of God his Churche , he hadde called them together, *19. De*

Concord,
Cathol.&
Tom.3.
Cöcil pag
539. edit.
poftr.

exhortinge them in many wordes to concorde and agreement. Confesing alfo that they , *Poteftatem Synodici iudicij
diuinitus acceperunt,* haue receyued from God (not by any
his commifsion) the power and authoryte to iudge in Synods. He addeth farder, that though he doubted not but that
they were altogether fuch as zealed the truth, and folowed
righteoufnes, yet (faieth he) to thentent that it may appeare
that our Imperial maiefty, *fecundùm datam fibi poteftatis mē-
furam, in ecclefiafticis negotijs nihil tacuiffe, eorum quæ debent
atque conueniunt* : hath not in ecclefiaftical matters, cõcea-
led any thinge of that which is dewe and conuenient , according to the meafure of power geuen vnto her , *depofci-
mus religionem veftram &c.* We befeche your religion or
godlynes to ouercome nowe al affection of partialyte and
hatred, and to refemble as much as is pofsible, the immutable , and vnchangeable nature of God , who neuer refpe-
cteth the perfon &c. In this Oratiõ of the Emperour three
things I woulde you fhould note and beare well away M.
Horne. Firft that the bifhops (by his confefsiõ) haue power
from God to iudge and determine in Coũcels. Their power
and Authoryty herein procedeth not of the Princes commifsion, as a fupreme gouernour next vnto God aboue the
bifhops in ecclefiaftical matters, but frõ God him felf, faieth
this Emperour. Secõdly that thémperours power is a limited power, not the chief, Supreme, ãd the higheft in all maner caufes ãd thinges. Thirdly howe it is limited : Forfothe
not to commaunde or prefcribe to the biffhops what they
fhall doe, decree or determine in ecclefiaftical matters, but
to exhorte them to concorde and vnyty in the fame.

In the feconde Action, diuerfe of the Photians offering
vp their libelles of repentaunce to the Synod, not to themperour

perour or his deputyes, were by the Synod with impofitiō of handes reconciled . In the third and fourthe Actions diuers letters were reade as wel of Michael and Bafilius Emperours to the Popes , Nicolaus and Adrian , as alfo of the Popes to them againe touchıng the condemnation of Photius intruded by Michael , and the reftoring agayne of Ignatius. In the fifte Action Photius was brought in , and the popes letters conteyninge his condemnation reade before him, vnto the which the whole Synod cryed. *Recipimus hæc omnia &c.* We receaue al thefe thinges, bicaufe they are agreable to reafon and to the ecclefiafticall rules and lawes. In that action alfo the Popes legates are called the prefidents of the Councell. In the fixt Action the Photians appearing agayne, and being moued as well of the whole Synod, as of the Emperour, to repentaunce, they yet perfeuered obftinately in their fchifme: Wherupon the Emperour gaue them feuen dayes of deliberation, after which time, if they were not in the meane while recōciled , he bad them appeare againe, faying . *Ventura fexta feria in fancta & vniuerfali Synodo ftate omnes,& quicquid definierit vniuerfa Synodus, fiet.* The next Friday, be you here prefent in the holy and vniuerfal Synod: ād whatfoeuer the vniuerfal Synod fhal define or cōclude, that fhal be done, where agayne you fee the Emperour iudgeth not in the matters then in hand, but the Coūcel. Yea he faieth plainely, *that the reftoring of* *Ignatius, was not his doing, or his deuife. But that longe before,* *the moft holy and moft bleffed pope Nicolaus examining the mat* *ter thouroughly, decreed by Synod, that he fhould be reftored to* *the right of his See agayne, and together with the holy Romayn* *Churche , pronounced Anathema to all fuche that fhould re-* *fifte that decree and fentence . And we knowing this before,*   *Cufanus*   *li.3.c.24.*

        ſ iij   faith

saieth the Emperour, *fearinge to haue the iudgement of the Curfe promulged: Obfecundare Synodico iudicio Romanæ eccle-fiæ neceffarium duximus,& huius rei gratia reddidimus ei pro-prium thronum*. We haue thought it neceffary to obeye the Synodicall Iudgement of the Churche of Rome, and for that caufe we haue reftored vnto him his owne See. Of fuch Authoryty was the Sentence of the Churche of Rome, with the Emperour of the Eaft Churche in thofe dayes. In the fame action he faieth yet farder. *Hoc folum noftrum eft fi voluerit quis nominare crimina. Alia verò om-nia Canonibus & his, quibus imperiũ Synodi credinũ eft, tradi-mus.* This only is our parte to do: if any man will bring forth any crimes, or make anye accufation, to fee it put vp to the Councell, &c. But all other thinges we leaue to the Ca-nons, and to them to whome the Rule of the Synode is cõ-mitted, that is to bifhoppes, as we hearde him before faie vnto them. Thus muche in that Action.

In the feuenth Action Photius appearinge agayne, Marinus one of the legates commaunded his ftaffe to be taken from him, becaufe it was a token of his bifhoplye eftate and dignyte. In this Action (as Cufanus recor- deth) Bahanis the Emperours Lieutenant had much talke withe the Photyans, *Hortatoriè*, by the waye of exhor- tation, mouinge them to vnytie and repentaunce. The onely fhifte of the Photyans was to fay, that the legates of the Patriarches there prefent, did not their commif- fion, but condemned them cõtrary to the Patriarches own willes and Iudgementes. Vpon this the Emperour offred them, that whofoeuer would ftand by that furmife, fhould by his prouifion be fent to the Patriarches them felues, as to Rome, to Antyoche, and to Hierufalem, and lerne of them

Libro. 3. c.20. Hor- tatoriè alloquitur vos Impe- rator.

of them the truthe . But they refufed to doe fo . At the
length the Emperour feing them obftinat and full of words
to no purpofe , fayed to them . *Omnes nouimus, quòd laici
eſtis , & non adduximus vos latrare , & fine ordine facere
verba.* We knowe all , that you are but laye men . And
we brought you not hither to barke, and to talke out of order . *But the Emperour (*faieth Cufanus*)called them therefore laye men, becaufe they were all ordered of Photius who
him felfe was no biſſhop:* Such are you and all your felowes M. Horne , no bifhops at all , but mere laye perfons,
ordered of none at all that was him felfe ordered . *And
whereas one of the Photians Eulapius by name, beganne to
talke with the Emperour , the legates of the See Apoſtolike
fayed . Eulapius is condemned and excommunicated of the See
Apoſtolike : and therefore the Emperour ought not to talke
with him . Then the Emperour fayed. I haue oftentimes and
much defired, that they might not perifh : And therefore I
called them hither: but if they will not returne to the Church,
whatfoeuer the Patriarches ſhall iudge of them , they ſhall ,
will they, nill they,ſtande vnto it. For no man can reiecte the
power that is geuen to them (* he meaneth the high biſſhops)
of Chriſt our God and Sauiour. Thus agayne you fee Maifter
Horne howe all the iudgement refteth in the bifhops, and
howe the fentence of the See Apoftolike preuayleth, and
howe buxomely (to vfe your owne worde) and obediently
the Emperour yeldeth thereunto, not intermedling farder
then to procure that all partes may be heard , that tumulte
may be auoided, and that the Iudges (for fo were the biffhops called in this Actiō) may quietly procede to Sétence,
and laft of al that the fame Sétence may be put in executiō,
notwithftanding the indurat malice of obftinat heretikes.

In the.8.

Iubet Im-
perator vt
loquami-
ni: fed vi-
dentes Iu-
dices con-
uicia ve-
ſtra, nec
audire vos
volunt.

In the.8.Action al the fchifmatical conuenticles of the Photians are condemned, and the recordes thereof burned. In that Action alfo diuers Imagebreakers came to the Synode, and were reconciled: That fecte alfo was againe accurfed. In the laft Action the Canons were reade, at the Popes Legates commaundement, to the number of. 27. In the . 22 . Canon it is decreed, that no fecular Prince intermedle with the election or choyfe of any Patriarche, Metropolitane, or Bifhop whatfoeuer, which alfo is inferted by Gratian into the decrees. Finally the Councel being ended, Bafilius the Emperour maketh a longe and a notable Oration to the Synod, exprefsing the dewe zeale and dewty of an Emperour in al Synodes and Councels . He auoucheth plainly, that to fecular and laye men, *Non eft datum fecundum Canonem dicendi quicquam penitus de Ecclefiafticis caufis : opus enim hoc pontificum & facerdotum eft* . It is not graunted by the Rule of the Churche to fpeake any thinge at al (in Councel) of Ecclefiafticall matters. For this is the worke, faith he, of Bifhops and Prieftes. And after, commeding the bifhops for their greate paynes and trauaile in that Councell, he fpeaketh to the laye Nobylyte then prefent thus. *De vobis autem Laicis, &c.* But as touching you that are of the lay forte, *as wel you that beare offices, as that be priuate men, I haue no more to fay vnto you, but that it is not lawfull for you by any meanes to moue talke of Ecclefiafticall matters, neither to refifte in any point againft the integrity of the Churche, or to gaynefaie the vniuerfal Synode. For to fearche and feke out thefe matters, it belongeth to Bifhops and Priefts, which beare the office of gouernours, which haue the power to fanctifie, to binde and to loofe, which haue obtayned the keyes of the Churche and of heauen. It belongeth not to vs, which ought*

Dift.63.
Nullus .

Cufanus
lib.3 c.23.

ought to be fedde, which haue nede to be sanctified, to be boūde, and to be loosed from bande. For of whatsoeuer Religion, or wisedome the laye man be, yea though he be indewed with all internal vertues, as longe as he is a lay man, he shal not cease to be called a shepe. Againe, a bishop howesoeuer vnreuerent he be, and naked of all vertue, as longe as he is a bishop, and preacheth dewlye the woorde of Truthe, he suffereth not the losse of his pastorall vocation and dignitye. What then haue we to doe, standinge yet in the roome of shepe? The Shepheardes haue the power to discusse the subtiltye of woordes, and to seke and compasse such thinges, as are aboue vs. We must therefore in feare and sincere faith harken vnto them, and reuerence their countenances, as being the Ministres of Almightye God, and bearinge his fourme, and not to seke any more then that which belongeth to our degree and vocation. Thus farre the Emperour Basilius in the ende and Conclusion of the eight generall Councell, and much more in this sense, which were here to longe to inserte. I blame you not nowe Maister Horne, that you so ouerhipped this whole Generall Councell, and the doinges of those .ij. Popes Nicolaus and Adrian. 2. You sawe perhaps or had hearde say, that it made clerely against you. And yet as I sayed before, apparently you might haue culled out broken narrations for your purpose as well out of this Generall Councell, as out of the other. 7. But seing you tooke such paynes to note themperors demeanour in the former. 7. I thought it a poynte of courtesye Maister Horne, to requytte you againe with this one generall Councell, for so manye by you alleaged, to your verye small purpose, as euery indifferent Reader seeth. Whether this be not to our purpose, I dare make your selfe Iudge. And nowe I wonder

v   what

what fhifte you will make to auoyde the Authoritye of this generall Councell, or of this Emperour Bafilius. Well. You maye at your good leafure thinke and deuife vppon it . I wil nowe returne to your text .

You faye Martinus the feconde (whome other more trulye call Marinus) *gat into the Papacy by naughtye meanes:* What maketh that to proue your Supremacye in the laye Magiftrat? *It is noted* , you faie , *in the margent of Platina that it was in this Popes tyme, that firſt of all the creation of the Popes was made without the Emperours authorityɛ.* You fhoulde haue tolde vs withall in what printe of Platina that note is founde . I haue fene Platina both of the Collen printe, and of the Venyce print fette forthe with the Notes of Onuphrius, and yet I finde no fuche Note in the margent . It is by like the Note of fome your brotherhood in fome copie printed at Bafill : And then is it of as good Authoritye, as Maifter Hornes owne booke is: which is God wote, but courfe . Whofe fo euers note it

Diſt . 63.
Cũ longe
Princeps
non aduo-
catur ad
electionẽ
faciendã,
fed ad cõ-
fenfum e-
lectioni
adhiben-
dam.

be, a falfe note it is . For as of a hundred and ten Bifhoppes of Rome, before this Marinus, fcarfe the fourthe parte of them was confirmed of the Emperours , fo the Emperours before this tyme neuer created Popes , but onelye confented to the creation or election made by the clergye, and confirmed the fame , for quyet fake , and for the preferuation of vnyty , as I haue before fhewed. Adrians decree that the people of Rome fhoulde wayte no more for the Emperours confirmation, was no defrauding of themperours right, as you vntrulye reporte, but a renewing of the olde liberties and priuileges dewe to the Churche by the order of Canons and Councels, and the whiche neuer came to the Emperours, but by the Popes
owne

owne grauntes and decrees (namelye of Adrian the firſt and Leo 3. as hath before appeared) and therefore by them agayne reuocable without iniurye done to the Prince, when the weale of the Churche ſo requyred. As it was at this tyme , the Frenche Emperours buſyed with warres againſt the Sarracens, and not ſo carefull of the Eccleſiaſticall peace (vppon reſpect whereof that Cōfirmation of the Pope was graunted them) as were theyr predeceſſours. Which negligence ſo encreaſed , that in fewe yeares after as we ſhall anon ſee , they not only lefte of the protection of the See Apoſtlolike , but loſte alſo the Empire, it being transferred to the Germains in Otho the firſt , whome alſo ſome Germayne writers (namelye Cuſanus) do accompte for the firſt Emperour of the Weſte, after the decaye and breache of the Eaſt Empire .

Cuſanus lib.3.c.3.

M. Horne. The.107 . Diuiſion. Fol.67.b.

The next Pope Stephen had an obſcure tyme, ſauing that Charles therein called a Councell at Collen, and after him Arnulphus the Emperour , other tvvo : the one at Moguntia , the other at Triburum.

The . 13 . Chapter : Of the laſte Emperours of Charlemaynes race, and of the Popes of Rome of that age .

Stapleton.

Ere folowe two Coūcels vnder Arnulphus the Emperour, the one at *Moguntia*, the other at *Triburum*. But what? Is there in that Councels nothing for you M. Horne? Why? There is in the Councell of Moguntia a

v ij   whole

whole Chapter intitled : *Quid sit proprie ministerium Regis.*
What is properly the office of a kynge . And in a Chapter
Cap.3.vi- so specially debating of your matter in hãd, could you fynd
de Tom.2. nothing that made for you? Then let vs see whether there
Concil. pa be any thing for vs . The Councell in that Chapter saieth.
gin.780. *The office of a kynge specially is , to gouerne the people of God,*
and to rule with equitie and Iustice , and to prouide that peace
and concord may be kept . And howe? In ecclesiasticall matters? We shal heare . For (saieth the Councell) *he ought be-*
fore all thinges to be a defender of the Churches (I thought
the Councel would haue said, Supreme Gouernour) *and of*
the seruants of God, of widowes , and Orphanes , And so furth.
Lo . M . Horne . The office of the prince is to defend
the Churche of God, not to gouerne it , not to alter and
chaunge the Religion , not to make Church lawes &c.
In al this chapter looke when you will, you shall not fynd
one worde for the Princes supreme Gouernement , or any
maner of Gouernement at al in matters ecclesiastical. And
yet this beinge as you say in the beginninge of this booke,
Fol.3.b. A principall parte of the Princes Royal povver,
the Councel of purpose treating in this Chapter only of the
princes office and power , it is more then maruayl that the
matter should in such depe silence so be wrapped vp, that
no worde or half worde thereof coulde appeare . Verely
in the next chapter folowinge it is commaunded and de-
Cap.4. creed, *that the Churches and things to them belonging should*
apperteyn to bishops: without any worde of the Princes supreme Gouernement in thinges of the Church.

    M . Horne . The: 108 . Diuision. Fol. 67. b.
  Of these Popes and those that follovved, as Formosus, Stephanus, Ro
manus, Benedictus, Leo, Christophorus, Sergius, *and a great com-*
                                      pany

pany more, the Hiſtorians geue but an homely teſtimonie , and Nauclerus *ſaith, that to ſatiſfie their voluptuous luſtes, they did maliciouſly malice one another, as moſt cruel Tyrantes, and he added this reaſon.* Cum non ex-tarent qui eorum vitia coercerent , bicauſe there was none to correcte and chaſten them for their euill doinges . *For ſo long as the Princes exerciſed their (351)authoritie in ouerſeing carefully the Church matters, and the myniſters, ſo vvel the Popes; as other Biſhoppes, there grevve no ſuch intollerable diſorders, neither yvere there ſuche mōſters(for ſo* Nauclerus *, termeth theſe* Popes *) that continued any ſpace: But vvere by the Princes authoritie ſuppreſſed, and therfore* Nauclerus *citeth out of* Pla-tina, and affirmeth it to be true, that the cauſe of theſe monſtrous Rebelles in the Churche vvas:* Quòd Reſp.ignauos & deſides principes ha-beat. Bicauſe the common wealthe had improſitable and ſlouthfull Princes. *Thus theſe vvriters burdeine and charge the Princes vvith the diſorders and enormities in Chriſtes Churche , vvherein they doo them vvronge, if they thought not, that it apperteined to the Princely au-ritie to * ouerſee, care , and prouide for the good order of Chriſtes Churche: and to redreſſe , puniſhe , and remoue the inordinate euilles therein.*

The. 351.
vntruth.
ſlaunde-
rouſly ſur
miſed, but
not able
by any
good Au-
thor to be
proued.
* This we
graunte:
But this
cometh
nothing
nere to
the pur-
poſe, and
ſcope pre-
fixed.

Stapleton.

M. Horne nowe ruſheth in withe a bedroll of certain naughty popes, down from Formoſus to Iohn the.13. Amōg whom I marueyl why you recken *Benedictus* , of whome Nauclerus writeth thus . *Huius Benedicti laus eſt , quòd in tam corruptis moribus grauiter & conſtanter vitam duxiſſe fe-ratur* . The commendation of this Benedictus is, that in ſo corrupt maners of men, he is ſaied to haue liued with gra-uitie and Conſtancie . And namely for his great humanitie and clemency he was choſen . But much more I merueyle that amonge ſo many badde you ſpeake neuer a worde of the good , namely of Anaſtaſius of whom it is writen. *Nihil habuit quo reprehendi poſſet.* He was a man that could

Gener.31.
pag.72.

Pag.74.

v iij   be char-

Pag. 74. be charged with nothing of Leo the 6. which *nihil tyran-nicum præ se tulit, rei diuinæ consulens,* shewed no tyranny in his behauyour, attending vpō Gods seruice. Of Steuen the Pag. 80. 7. *Whose lyfe was full of gentlenesse and Religion.* Of Leo. 7. Ibidem. and Steuen the. 8. bothe commended Popes. Of Martyn Pag. 85. the. *3. Who folowed also the gentle demeanour of Steuen.* Of Agapetus who is writen to haue ben *vir innocens & Reip.* Saxo grā. lib. 9. *Christianæ feruens amator,* An innocent man and a feruent tenderer of the Christian commō wealth. Of whom also the kyng of Denmark receyued the faith. All these good and vertuouse Popes in great affliction of wicked persons in those daies (for lacke in dede of Iustice in good Empe-rours) lyued, and ruled the Church betwen this Formosus and Iohn the. 13. or. 12. more then twenty yeres. But. M. Horne like a fowle sowe that nouseleth in the donghil and careth not for the fayre floures in the garden, nouseleth him selfe amonge the euyll bishops, and can not abyde to speake one poore worde for the good. And therefore as Mēmius obiected to Cato his nights Dronckennesse, for whom Cicero answereth, *why tellest thou not also of his dayes dycing?* he being in dede all the daye in the affayres of the Common wealth, so for the bedrol of your euyl Popes *For-* Plutar-chus in Catone V-ticensi. *mosus,* and the rest, I aske you whi you tel vs not also of A-nastasius, of Leo the. 6. and. 7. of Steuyn the. 7. and. 8. of Mar tyn the. 3. ad of Agapet⁹, but that you had rather be Mēmius thē Cicero, rather a rashe cōptroller thē a discrete reporter?

The. 352. vntruth: Sabellic⁵ falsified, as shal ap peare.

M. Horne. The. 109. Diuision. pag. 68. a.

Yea, Sabellicus *so wondereth at these tragicall examples of the Bi-shoppes of this time, and their horrible obliuion of Godly Religion, that he* (.352.) *ascribeth the good and godly moderatiō that was in the Bishops and the dutiful execution of their office, from Charles the great, til the ende of the Frenche*

Frenche Empire, vvhiche vvas an vvhole age : to be not so much of them selues, and their ovvne good vvilles, as of the avve and feare they had of the Princes, kinges, and Emperours, vvho vvere their guardians. And therfore concludeth, that it may be truely said, that this vvas the calamitie of Fraunce, Italy, and of the Churche of Rome : Quòd in ea gente desitum esset imperari: bicause there was (.353.) no king nor Em= perour to beare rule, (354.) meaning that although there vvere kinges and Emperours, yeat did they not execute their Princely office and authori= tie, in ouerseing, corietinge and reforminge the Churche matters, and her mynisters, and therefore the state vvas miserable. In this confusion vvere all thinges, but especially in the Church of Rome, till God stirred vp the vvyse and mighty Prince Otho the first, vvhose zeale, stoutnes and trauayle in reforming Religion and the disordred Churche, no tongue is able to expresse saith Nauclerus.

The.353. vntruth. Falſe trãſ/ lation. The.354, vntruth. Sab.mea neth no ſuch thig.

Stapleton.

You make Sabellicus to saie a great deale more thẽ euer he saied, or intended to say. For he. doth not certaynely af= cribe any such cause, as you pretend, but only he saieth. *Nõ immerito quis suspicaretur.* A mã may ãd not without a cause suspecte. But what M. Horne ? That Popes kept euill rule, and were geuen to al lewdenesse, bicause the Emperours did not ouersee them ? So you woulde haue folke to think, and therefore you make Sabellicus to conclude, *that this was the calamyte of Fraunce, Italy and of the Churche of Rome quòd in ea gẽte desitum esset imperari, bicause there was no kig nor Emperour to beare rule .* But false translation maketh no proufe. Knowe you not M. Horne, what *In ea gente,* doth signifie in englißh ? Or if we may not finde faulte with your grammer, why slacked your honesty so farre, as to leaue the englißh thereof quyte out ? What, was there a pad in the strawe ? Sabellicus then saieth, the cause of all that cala= myte was, bicause there was no kinge nor Emperour to

Sabell. Aenead.9. lib.1.

beare

beare rule , *in ea gente*, in that ftocke or line of Charles the
great, whofe pofterity had hitherto lineally reigned, downe
to Arnulphus the laft mentioned Emperour, and the laft in
dede (by the opinion of moft hiftorians) of Charles his li-
neal defcët. After whom in dede the Churche was in great
trouble and diforder, for the fpace of 50. or. 60. yeres . But
howe ? Did the euil Popes caufe that diforder? So woulde
M. Horne folowing here in the fteppes of baudy Bale, that
we fhould thinke . But as I haue noted before, in the com-
paffe of that . 50 . yeres , there were diuers good, and vertuous Popes , ruling the Churche more then twenty of
thofe. 50. yeres. And the caufe of al that diforder was not
the only euil life of certaine Popes, but much more, the li-
centious lewdeneffe of the Italians, and efpecially the Romans at that tyme, who in dede for lacke of Iuftice on the
Emperours partes (which is the thinge that Sabellicus cō-
plaineth of) liued enormoufly and licëtioufly, makig Kings
amonge themfelues, and not only oppreſsing one an other,
but alfo mofte vily and cruelly handlinge their biſshoppes
being good and vertuous . Of whóme Stephen the 8. a
Pope of much holynes at that very tyme , was of his Cytyzens fo fhamefully mangled and diffigured , that he was
fayne of a long tyme for very fhame to kepe within dores,
and fo liued three yeres in greate vexation and trouble.
The caufe of al this trouble in the Churche at this tyme, yf
you lifte fhortly to knowe (gentle Readers) Sabellicus a-
greing herein with the other hiftorians wil clerely tell you.
He faieth. *Quantū Francorum pietate &c. Looke howe muche
Rome and all Italy breathed (as it were) from a longe continuāce
of miferies , by the godlynes and bountifulnes of the Frenche
Princes* (Charles and his iffewe) *one whole age* (almoft a. 100..
yeres

Naucler.
generat.
32.p4.85.
Martinus
Pol.

Aenead.9.
lib.1.

yeares)ſo much fell it backe againe in to all kinde of calamytie,
by the ſpace of almoſt.60.yeres through ciuil Sedition.This cala￾
myty beganne,from the laſt yere of Adrian the.3. and ended in
the time of Iohn the.12. And will you ſee whereof ſprange
this calamytie?M.Horn imagineth,it was bicauſe the Princes did not practiſe their Eccleſiaſtical gouernement ouer
Popes.But Sabellicus a better hiſtorian then M.Horne,ad-
deth immediatly vpon his former wordes, this Cauſe.

Enimuero , præter Normannos &c . Verely beſide the Nor-
mans which waſted Fraunce (of which outrage , that great
chaunge of thinges then made in the worlde , ſemeth to me
to haue ſprounge)the Hunnes alſo people of Scythia,being bolde
vpon the troubles of Fraunce, comming downe into Slauony, did
conquer the landes of Gepides and Auari , people then in
thoſe quarters ſo called. The ouerrūning thē of forrain nations,and the Ciuill Seditions through out all Italy cauſed
this greate calamyty that the hiſtoryans of this time complaine ſo muche of . Whych the more encreaſed, for that
the Emperours of that time, Arnulphus, Conradus, Henrie the firſt , yea and Otho hym ſelfe vntyll the later ende
of hys Empire,partly would not, partly could not repreſſe
the tyrantes in Italie, and other where .

(*Ex qua*
iniuria vi-
detur
mihi orta
tāta rerū
mutatio,
quanta in
humanis
rebus fa-
cta eſt)

    In all whych hurley burleys , in all whych breaches of
good order , licentiouſnes of lyfe , and *corruption of the*
worlde, if the heads alſo them ſelues ,the chiefe biſhoppes,
ſometimes fell to diſorder and lewdeneſſe of life , yt is the
leſſe to be maruayled of him that wyll conſider the courſe
of Gods prouidence in thys worlde , who ſuffreth for the
ſinnes of the people,*vt ſicut populus ſic ſit & ſacerdos.* That
lyke as the people, ſo ſhould alſo the Prieſt be : who ſaieth
alſo in lyke enormities of the worlde : *Dabo pueros princi-*

In tā cor-
ruptis mo-
ribus N au
clerus ge-
nerat.32.
vbique
Eſai.24.

Oſe.4.

Esaie 3.
Et effœ-
minati do
minabun-
tur eis.
2. Reg. 24

pes eorum. I will geue them children for their Princes, meaning not onely children in age, but children in wisedome, children in strength, and children in vertue. Of which also expressely we reade, that *the wrath of God wexed hotte against Israëll, and stirred vppe Dauid to say to Ioab. Goe and number Israël and Iuda.* Of the which great vanitie and ouersight of that King, the plague fell vppon the people, and not vpon the King. So God plagueth the wickednesse of subiects with the sinnes of their Rulers, and geueth oftentimes to a froward flock, a curst shepheard. This consideration of Gods prouidéce in that corrupt time (not of corrupt faith (as you bable) but of corrupt maners) had more becommed a man of your vocation, M. Horne, and a Diuine, then such false ād lewde surmises as you haue vttered. Which you could neuer so haue cloked, if you had opened the whole historie and circumstaunces of the case to your Readers. But this you will neuer doe, saye we what we wil. Your ragged relligion must be patched vp with such broken cloutes of imperfecte narrations.

M. Horne. The.110. Diuision. pag.68.a.

The.355.
vntruth.
For these
parties
were not
sent to
Otho
against
Pope
Iohn, but
frō him,
and for
him.

At this time vvas Iohn.13. Pope, a man replete and loden vvith all dishonestie and villanie, against (.355.) vvhom tvvo of the chiefest amongest the Clergie (the one vvas a Cardinall saith Luithprandus, the other, maister of the Rolles) made complaint vnto Ottho, most humblie beseching him, to haue some compassion on the Church, vvhich if it vvere not spedilie resourmed, must needes come to vtter decaie. After vvhom came the Bishoppe of Millaine, and so one after an other, a great manie moe, making the same suite vnto Ottho: vvho being moued of his ovvne zeale to Gods glorie, but novv enflamed by the lamentable supplications of these Bisshoppes, Rex piissimus, saieth Luithprandus, Non quæ sua sunt, sed quæ Iesu Christi cogitans: The moste Relligious King hauinge carefull cogitations, not for his owne thinges,
but

but for Iesus Chriſtes maters, *addreſſed him ſelfe vvith all conueni-*
ent ſpeede into Italie, to refourme Rome from vvhence all the miſchiefe
ſprang. VVhen the Pope vnderſtoode of his comming, he prepared to receiue him in moſte honourable vviſe, and vvith ſuche humilitie behaued
him ſelfe tovvardes the Emperour, and ſhevved ſuche faire face of repentaunce, that the vvell meaning Emperour, thought he had meant
as he pretended, and ſvvare the Pope to obedience and loyaltie againſt
Berengarius *and* Adalbertus, *as* Luithprandus *vvriteth, and ſo*
returned into his countrie. This Luithprandus *is the more to be cre-* The.356.
dited, for that he vvas liuing a famous vvriter, and (.356.) *Deacon*
Cardinall, euen in the ſame time. The Pope immediatly againſt both
Othe *and* honeſty (.357.) *practiſed vvith* Adalbertus, *to depoſe this*
godly Emperoure, and promiſed him by Othe his aide. The reaſon
or cauſe why Iohn the Pope ſhoulde hate this moſte godlye
Emperoure, who had deliuered him out of the handes of
Adelbert his ennemie, and wherefore the Deuill ſhoulde
hate God his creatoure, ſeemeth not to be vnlike. For the
Emperoure, as we haue had good experience, vnderſtan-
deth things pertaining to God, he worketh, he loueth them,
he mainteineth with maine and mighte the Eccleſiaſticall
and Temporall matters, he decketh them with manners,
and amendeth them by lawes: but Iohn the Pope is againſt
all theſe thinges. The Emperoure ſeeketh by diuerſe vvayes to reconcile this Pope, and to bring him from his filthy life, to ſome honeſty,
and regarde of his office. VVhan by no perſuaſions he can vvinne him,
he determineth to depoſe him, and (.358.) for that purpoſe, he calleth
a Councell of the Biſshoppes of Italie, to the end he may ſeke the reſourmation, vvhich he mindeth, and ſavv to be ouermuch nedeful by their aduiſe.

Pope Iohn, (.359.) ſeeing him ſelfe to be tried by a Synode, runneth a-
vvay, vvhen al the people ſavv their Pope vvas turne avvaye from them,
they ſvvare fidelity to th'Emperor, promiſing by their Othes, that they vvould
neuer hereafter elect or make any Pope vvithout the conſent of the Emperour. VVithin three daies after, there vvas a great aſſemblie in S. Peters
Church at the requeſts of the Biſhops and people: In vvhich Councell ſate
the Emperour, vvith many Archebiſßhoppes and others: to vvhom the godly

The.356.
Vntruth:
This Lu-
ithprand,
vvas no
Cardinal,
Luithpr.
Vntruth.
The.357.
his Au-
thor ouer
reached.

The. 358.
Vntruth.
That cou
cel vvas
not called
to depoſe
him.
The.359.
vntruth.
He vVas
runne
avvay be
fore the
Synod
vvas any
thinge
tovvard:

x ij   *Emperour*

Emperor propoũdeth the cauſe of their aſſemble,exhorteth thẽto do al thigs vuith vpright iudgemẽt:ãd the Biſshops,deacõs, Clergy,ãd al the peple make ſolempne proteſtation , and obteſtatlon of their iuſt and vpright dealing in the cauſe propounded. And becauſe the chiefe matter touched the Pope that vuas runne avvay: the holy Synode ſaid, if it ſeme ſo good to the godly Emperour, let letters be ſent to the Pope, and cyte him to come and purge him ſelfe. The letters vvere directed in this ſourme: Otho by Goddes grace Emperour, with the Archebiſshops of Liguria, Tuſcia, Saxonia, and Fraũce, ſend greeting in the Lord to Iohn the Pope: VVe comming to Rome for our Seruice to God, and enquiring the cauſe of your abſence from your Church,were enformed by the Biſshops, Cardinales, Prieſtes, Deacons , and the whole people, of ſuch ſhameful doings by you, as we are aſhamed to rehearſe: whereof theſe are parte they charge you with: Murder, periurie,ſacrilege, inceſt with twaine of your owne ſiſters: that in your banquetes (which is horrible to be rehearſed) ye drinke wine in the loue of the Deuill : in your plaie at dice, you craue the helpe of Iupiter, Venus, and other Diuels: wherefore we pray you to repaier vnto vs your ſelfe. *To this, the Pope vvriteth this anſvvere.* I heare ſaye ye will make an other Pope, which if ye attempte, I excommunicate you all, that ye may haue no licence or power to order any,&c. *To this ſhort anſvvere the* Emperour,*vvith the Synode replieth,telling him that they had vvritten, to let him vnderſtand of the crimes vvherevvith he vvas charged, and that he had ſent them ſuch an* * *anſvveare as rather became the folly of a childe, then the grauitie of a Biſhop: as for the povver of binding and loſing, they ſay, he ones had as* Iudas *had, to vvhom it vvas* ſaide: Quæcunque ligaueritis ſuper terram.&c. VVhat ſo euer ye binde on earth,ſhalbe bound in Heauen,&c. *But novv he hath no more povver againſt the* Emperour *and the* Synod, *then* Iudas *had vvhen he vvent about to betraie* Chriſt *his* Maiſter.

Theſe letters vvere ſent vnto him by tvvo Cardinalles, *vvho returned, not finding him : and therfore the* Synode *procedeth to his depoſition :* They *beſeche the* Emperour *to remoue* Monſtrum illud, *that Monſter, and to place ſome vvorthy biſshop in his roome.*Tunc Imperator, placet inquit,

Such ſi M. Hornes anſvvere to M. Feckeham in a great part Tue.360. vntruth. A part of the ſentece leaſt out. The.361. vntruth. Theſe vvordes in the middeſt nipped quite of. To vvhõt the electiõ of your Biſshop be longeth. The.362. vntruth. Luithprandus ſhevveth no ſuch thinge.

quit, quod dicitis: Your requeſt pleaſeth me, ſaith the Emperour (360.) . *The Clergie and the people (ſaith* Nauclerus*)doth make
humble ſupplication vnto the Emperour, to prouide for them a vvorthy Biſhoppe : to vvhom the Emperour anſvvereth:* Chooſe you your ſelues
one, (361.) whom, hauing God before your eyes, ye may iudge
worthie, and I wil confirme him: *The Emperour had no ſooner ſpoken this (ſaith* Luithprandus*) than they all vvith one aſſent named*
Leo: *The Emperour gaue his conſent:* Et Ottho Imperator, Leonem
creat Pontificem, And Ottho the Emperoure created Leo
Pope (*as* Sabellicus *and* Platina *ſaith*) Here Luithprand. *tell ith at
large, hovve after this creation of Leo, the Emperour (.362.) diſſolued the
Synode, and vvhat miſchieſe the Monſtruous Pope Iohn vvrought after-
vvard· For by his friends in Rome, Pope Leo vvas driuen avvay. And after
this Monſter vvas deade, the Romaines elected Benedictus in his place, and
requireth the Emperoure vvho vvas than at Spolet, to confirme him:
the Emperoure vvoulde not, but compelled them to receiue Leo a-
gaine. And heere the Emperoure ſummoned againe a nevve Synode
vvherein he (.363.) ſatte him ſelfe, for the Canonicall depoſition of*
Benedictus. *notvvithſtanding this, ſayth* Nauclerus, *Leo being vveary
of the inconſtancy of the Romaines, did conſtitute by their conſent in the Synode holden at Rome, that the vvhole authority of choſing the Biſhop, ſhuld
remayne in the Emperour, at it is rehearſed in the decrees in theſe vvordes:*
Being in the Synode at Rome in the Church of the holy Sa-
uiour: lyke as Adrianus Biſhop of Rome graunted to Charles
the great, the dignity of patricianſhip, the ordering of the A-
poſtolical ſea, and the inueſturing of Biſhops: So I alſo Leo Biſhop of Rome, ſeruaunt of Goddes ſeruautes, with the coſent
of all the Cleargy and people of Rome, doo conſtitute, confirme, and corroborate, and by our Apoſtolicall authority, wee
doo graunt and geue vnto the Lorde Ottho, the firſt King of
Dutchmē, and to his ſucceſſours in this kingdome of Italy for
euer, the authoritie to elect after vs, and to ordeine the Biſhop
of (.364.) Rome: and ſo Archbiſhops, and Biſhops, that they
receiue of him, as they ought the inueſturing and conſecration (.365.) excepting thoſe, who the Emperour hath graunted

The. 363.
vntruthe
pregnant.
For nei-
ther the
Empe-
rour de-
poſed Be-
nedictus,
but Pope
Leo him
ſelfe, nei-
ther doth
Platina,
Nauclere
or Sabell:
make any
mention
of Synod
called by
the empe-
rour the-
reaboute.
Diſt. 63.
The. 364.
vntruth.
ſumæ ſe-
dis Apoſto
licæ. Of
the hi-
gheſt
Apoſtoli-
ke See:
leeft out.

to the popes and Archebiſshops: And that no man hereafter
of what dignitie or Relligiō ſo euer, haue power tó eleƈt one,
to the dignitie of Cōſules bloud, or to be biſshop of the(.366.)
Apoſtolike See, or to make any other biſshop, without th'Emperours conſent. And if any be choſen biſshop without he be
cōmēded, and inueſted by the King, that in no wiſe he be cōſecrated, vnder paine of excōmunication. *As Sabellicus noteth
this for a renovvmed matter, that the right of creatinge the Pope, vvas
novv reſtored to the Emperial dignity:euen ſo Nauclerus affirmeth, this
godly Imperour Otho, to be borne* In totius Eccleſiæ conſolatiōē,
for the conſolation of the whole Churche.

The.14.Chapter: Of Otho the firſt, Emperour: Of Iohn the.12. and Leo the.8. Popes of Romæ.

Stapleton.

THis declaration runneth all vppon the depoſition of
the naughtye Pope Iohn the.13.or as moſte men call
him, the.12.in a ſynode at Rome the Emperour Otho
being then preſent. But onleſſe M. Horne can ſhewe, that
this Emperour toke hym ſelf for ſupreame head in all cauſes eccleſiaſticall and temporall, and vtterlye renownced
all the Popes ſupreamacye, the caſe ſtandynge, that thys
Pope were a moſt wycked man (which we freelie confeſſe) and moſt vnworthy of that ſee, yet is M. Horne farre
of from iuſtifiing the matter. Wherin euē by hys owne author and ſtory, he ſhould haue bene vtterly ouerthrowen,
yf he had made therof a true and a faythfull reporte:which
ye ſhall now.heare,by vs, and that by hys owne chronographer, ſo that ye ſhall haue good cauſe to be aſtonied
to ſee the moſt ſhamefull and impudente dealing of thys
man. Firſt then he begynneth with a notoriouſe lie. For
neither thys Cardinall, whome Luithprandus calleth *Io-
hannem*, nor the Maiſter of the rolles, whome he calleth
Aronem

*Vide Nau-
cleru̅ ge-
nerat.33.
pag.89.
& sequēt.*

Aronem, nor the Bishop of Millain and others here named were sente to complayne vppon Pope Iohn,to Otho:
but sente to hym by Iohn the Pope hym self, which Iohn,
hys authour Luithprandus calleth the highe Bishop and the
vniuersall Pope,who most humbly beseacheth hym , that
he woulde vouchsaufe for the loue of God , and the holye
Apostle Petre and Paule, as he would wishe them to for-
gyue hym hys synnes,to deliuer hym and the Churche of
Rome to hym committed,from the tyrannye of Berengarius and Adelbertus. Wheruppon themperour gathered an
army and commyng to Italie with all spede, expulsed from
the Kyngdome of Italy the sayde tyrants:so,that yt seamed
euidente that he was ayded and afsisted by the moste holy
Apostles Peter and Paule, and (which is to be noted) he
was afterward anoynted and crowned Emperour of the
sayd Iohn though so vicyous a ma̅,and swore also obedie̅-
ce vnto him,as Nauclerus writeth.Farther he did not only
restore hym,those thinges wherof he was spoyled,but honored hym also with greate rewards , aswell in golde and
siluer,as in precious stones.And he toke an oth of the Pope
vpo̅ the most precious body of S.Peter,that he shuld neuer
ayde or afsist the sayd Berēgarius and Adelbert°.M.Horne
here nedelesse enforceth the credit of his author , as then
liuing, yea and auaunceth him to be *a famous writer and a
Deaco̅ Cardinal*,wheras he was,as far as my boke sheweth,
and as farre as Trithemius,and Pantaleon report of him, no
Deaco̅ Cardinal at Rome,but a deaco̅ of the church of Ti-
cinu̅ otherwise called Pauia in Italy:Onlesse perchau̅ce he
was such a Cardinal as the Cardinals are amo̅g the pety ca
no̅s of Poules in Londo̅ .With like truth ye say M.Horne,
ij.lines after,that the *pope practised with Adelbertus,to depose
thempe-*

*Summus
Pontifex
et vniuer-
salis papa.
Luithpra̅-
dus lib.6.
reru̅ per
Europam
gestarum
cap.6.
Naucler.
generat.
32.pag.85
Vide Tri-
themium.
in scrip.&
Chrono-
graph.
Pantaleo-
nis.
Luithpra̅-
di ticine̅-
sis Eccle-
siæ Leuitæ
rerum ab
Europæ
Impera-
tor.gesta-
ru̅ histo-
ria liber
1.&c.*

the Emperour, but your author fpeaketh not fo much , but
onlye that the Pope *promifed the forefayed Adelbertus to
helpe him againfte the Emperours power.* Then tell ye , in a
fmaller and diftinĉte letter , truely inough , but altogether
confufely,of Iohns doings,writing out of your author, *as
we haue good experience,*but who were that we , ye fhewe
not, nor to whome the wordes were fpoken .

*Affirmans
fe illū cō-
tra impe-
ratoris po-
tentiā ad-
iuturum.
Dict.ca.6.*

    Ye fay,that the Emperour called a Councell in Italie to
depofe him, that your authour fayeth not , but that , after
three dayes,themperour had bene at Rome , the pope and
Adelbertus being fledde from thence , there was a greate
affemblie in S. Peters Church , *rogantibus tam Romanis epifcopis quàm plebe,*at the defire as well of the Italian bifhops
as of the people:In the whiche councell were prefente befide the Bifhops many noble men. And the Pope ranne not
away,bicaufe of this Councell(as you vntruly reporte)but
iij.dayes after that he was fled with Adelbert⁹,the Coūcel
was called:and that not to depofe hym,but to call hym to
his anfwere:as appereth by the Emperours owne oratiofi.
Who after that Benedictus had reherfed dyuerfe of theis
horryble owtragies that ye fpecifie : themperour and the
councell fent for hym to pūrge hym felf.In the which letters fent by the Emperour ye diffemble many thinges and
difmember them,as the tytle of theperours letters whiche
was:*Summo Pontifici & vniuerfali papæ Iohanni Otho.&c.*
To the highe Bifhop ād the vniuerfal Pope,our Lord Iohn,
Otho,and fo forth.And by and by.*We afked the caufe of your
abfence,and why ye would not fee vs.your , and your Churches
defenfour.*And againe.*Oramus itaque paternitatem veſtram
obnixè veñire atque hijs omnibus vos purgare non difsimule-
tis.Si forte vim temerariæ multitudinis formidatis,iuramento
vobis*

*M.Horns
confufe
vvritig.*

*Cap.9.
Quod nos
Ecclefiæ
veſtræ ve-
ſtrique
defenfores
etc.*

vobis affirmamus nihil fieri præter Sanctorū Canonum ſanctio- *nem.* We moſt earneſtly pray your fatherhode, that ye do not forſlow to come and to purge your ſelfe. Yf ye feare any violéce of the rude and raſhe people, we promiſe you vpon our Othe, that nothing ſhal be done contrary to the Decrees of the holye Canons. After this, ye rehearſe the Popes ſhort anſwere, which yet as ſhort as it is, doth wonderfully trouble you, and ye dare not fully recite it. *I hea* *ſaie* (ſaith this Iohn) *ye wil make an other Pope, which if ye* *attempt, I excōmunicate you all, that ye may haue no licence* *or power to order any, or to ſaie Maſſe.*

It is true that ye ſaie afterwarde, that the Councell deſired the Emperour, that the ſaid Iohn might be remoued, and that the Emperour ſo anſwered. Yet ye leaue out part of his anſwere. And that is: *and that ſome other might* *be found who ſhould rule the holy and vniuerſall See.* Neither did they deſire of the Emperour any thing els, but his aſſiſtáce in the remouíg of him. Neither proprely to ſpeak, otherwiſe then by cóſenting and afſiſting, did th'Emperour create pope Leo. As appeareth by your author, ſaying: that al ſaied with one voice, *Leonē nobis in paſtorē eligimus, vt ſit* *ſummus & vniuerſalis Papa Romanæ eccleſiæ.* We doe electe Leo to be our paſtour, and the high and vniuerſall Pope of the Roman Churche, and doe refuſe Iohn the renegate for hys wycked behauiour. The wich thinge beinge thryſe by all cried owte, he was caried to the palace of Lateran: *Annuente imperatore* with themperours conſente, and thē to S.Peters Church, to be confecrated: and thē they ſwore they would be faythful, vnto him. And in thys election the people alſo had theyre conſente aſwell as the Emperour. And ſo can ye not make thys election to be a platte forme,

Hovv ād in vvhat ſorte the Empe⸗ rour had to doo vvith the Popes de⸗ poſition. Cap. 11.

for your elections nowe in Englande.

Your nexte vntruth in this narration is, that ye ſay, *that Luithprandus ſheweth, howe the Emperour diſſolued the Councell.* For he ſpeaketh no worde of the diſſoluing of the councell, but that he gaue licence to many of hys ſouldiers to departe: vppõ wich occaſion Pope Iohn maketh a new hurly bur-ley. And Benedictus of whome ye ſpeake, that was ſet vppe in Iohns place, after Iohns death by the Romans was thruſt owte and Leo reſtored againe. The whiche Benedictus was not depoſed by thẽ-perour, in the coũcel ye ſpeake of: Neyhter did the Emperour ſommon any Councell for his depoſi-tiõ, but only by fine force conſtrained the Romai-nes to admitte Leo, ãd to ſweare vnto him, as both Nauclere and Platina do write, of whom you take your matter: But it was the Pope hym ſelf, who gaue ſentence againſt hym, depoſed hym and de-priued hym as well from hys vſurped papacie, as from all biſhoplie and prieſtly dignity: yea and ba-niſhed him alſo from Rome. Yet at the Emperours requeſt, who *effuſis lachrymis rogauit Synodũ,* with teares requeſted the *Synode* for ſome mercye for him: the pope ſuffred him to remaine in the order of a deacon, but yet to liue in baniſhment, not at Rome. And this declaration, which ye haue ſo ſly-ly and craftely paſſed ouer, is a moſt euident argu-ment againſt your falſe aſſertion in this your boke, yea and ſheweth that it is not the Emperour, as ye imagĩ, but the clergy ãd the pope chiefly that hath the ſupreame authority in the depoſing of biſhops.

Whereſa

Whereas ye fay further, that this Leo with his Synode,
gaue to Otho the creation of the Popes, and the confecration of Archebiſhops and Biſhoppes : you belye the Decree. For it graunteth not to the Emperour the whole creation, and côfecration, but only the inueſturing of biſhops:
âd that the popes electiô ſhuld not be takê as effectual with
out themperours confent. Therefore in the middeſt of your
allegation, you nippe quite of after the worde , *Confecrati-*
on, vnde debent: From whence they ought: whereby is declared, that as the inueſturing and confirming is graunted
to the Emperour , ſo the Confecration is referred to that
order according to whiche before by the Canons it ought
to be. And therfore the Decree at the ende ſaith : *If anie*
be chofen Biſhop of the Clergie and the people, except he be cô-
mended and inueſted by the King of Italie , let him not be con-
fecrated. By which words it is euident, that both the choife
and the Confecration or ordering of Biſhops and Archebiſhops is referued to the Clergie and people. But thereto is
required the cômendation inueſturing, and côfirmation of
the Emperour: whiche, as I haue before ſhewed at large,
impaireth no iote the Popes Primacie, but rather côfirmeth
it : as a thing due to the Emperour rather , by the gifte and
confirmation Apoſtolicall , then otherwife : and due vnto
him for order and quietneſſe fake , not as any parte of his
Princelie power.

M . *Horne* The. 111. *Diuiſion. pag.* 70. *a.*

VVhen this godly Prince vvas dead, vvhileſt his ſonne Ottho . 2. vvas buſied
in the vvarres againſt the Sarazês : and after him his Son Ottho. 3. vvas yet
in nonage, the Popes began to vvaxe ſo euil, and the ſtate of Chriſtes Church
to decaie aſmuch as euer it did before: So daungerous a mater it is, to vvant
godly Princes to gouerne Gods Church, and to ouerſee the Miniſters therof.

y   ij   *Stapleton.*

Stapleton.

It is well you call Otho the firſt *a godly prince*. For then I truſt all that we haue ſo largely ſhewed concerning hys obedience to the See of Rome, yea to that Pope Iohn , ſo naughty a man as (thanked be God) neuer in our remembrance the like by many partes liued , you will M. Horne allowe for good and godly . Which if you doe, we ſhall ſoone be at a point touching this matter betwene you and M. Fekenham : and wil (I hope) recante and ſubſcribe your ſelfe . M . Iewell perhaps will beare you company . All that you adde of the euil popes in the time of Otho the. 2. and in the noneage of Otho. 3. is but a ſlaunderous lye. For

Nauclerus generat. 33.

as there were in that time ſome euill popes, ſo were there alſo right good, as Donus the. 2. and Benedictus. 7. who ruled the Church. 8. yeres. And the other were not ſo badde as M. Horne maketh them , but by the reaſon of factions were much moleſted, and traiterouſly vſed , not for wante of the princes gouernement in cauſes eccleſiaſticall , but for lacke in dede of the Princes Iuſtice in orders temporall . For to ſee external Iuſtice miniſtred is a matter temporall , not eccleſiaſticall . Which for the reaſons by M.

The. 367. vntruth. The king depoſed him not, but the Councel: and Arnulphus was reſto red by the Pope: and Gilbert depoſed agayne.

Horne alleaged ceaſed in dede for a time in Italy, the Emperours being allwaies in maner abſent . So neceſſary it was to reduce that Coūtrie to ſeueral Signories, as it now liueth in, and hath theſe many yeares in great quiet liued.

M . Horne The. 112. Diuiſion. pag. 70. b.

About this time Hugh Capet the French king, looked better to his Clergy in Fraūce, and callinge a Coūcel at Rhemes of all the Prelates of Fraūce, (. 367.) depoſed Arnulphus, vvhome Charles had made Biſhop there, and made Gilbert the Philoſopher Biſhoppe, vvhom aftervvards Otto. 2. made Archebiſhoppe of Rauenna. After Hugh , Robert his ſonne ſucceded , a Prince very vvel learned , and a diligent labourer about diuine or Churche matters, whiche is the propre parte of a righte king,

ſaith

faithe Sabellicus . VVhen Ottho.3. (surnamed for his excellent vertues in The.368.
that (.368.) vitious age , Mirabilia mundi , the maruailes of the vntruth.
worlde) herde of the great misorder in Rome, for the reformation therof Slaunde=
be came into Italy:but or euer he entred into Rome, Pope Iohn.17.died, and rous to
there fel no contention (*saith Nauclerus*) in the Popes Election, that age.
bicause the Prince (.369.) appointed by his commaundement, The.369.
Bruno to be pronunced Pope, who was called Gregory . 5 .*So* vntruth.
soone as the Emperour departed from Italy, the Romaines thrust out Gre- False trã=
gory, and placed one Placentinus *, vvhom they call Iohn.18. The Empe-* flation.
rour hearing hereof, came to Rome, hãged vp the Consul, and put out Iohns lusßit obti
eyes, and restored Gregory into his sea againe. I maruail that the histo= nuitque.
riãs (*saith* Platina) do rekẽ this Iohn amõgest the popes, which He com=
vndoubtedly was in his Papacy a theef, ãd a robber, for he en- maunded
tred not in by the dore, as ot right he should haue don. For he and ob=
came in by a factiõ, corrupting with mony ãd large gifts Cres- tayned
cétius the Cõsul, a most couetous wretch, ãd no lesse ãbitious. that his
VVherby, the sharpe iudgemẽt of the Emperour, is declared to be but vpright kynsman
iustice. So (370) that Platina *makĩg Gregory to be the true Pope, ãd to haue* shulde be
entred in by the dore, of vvhom he saith. Ottonis.3.authoritate põtifex named
creatur, he is created Pope by thẽperors autority, *and declaring* Pope.
the other that cam in vvithout thẽperors cõsent to be a theef and a robber: Platina
semeth to be of this opiniõ (although to (.371.) flatter the Popes vvithall, he The.370.
durst not so plainly open his minde) that vvithout the Pope be creat vvith the This ſo
Emperours confirmation and authority, he is but a thefe and a robber. that folo=
wethnot,
Next vnto him, *saith* Nauclerus, *vvas* Syluester *the second placed,* as it shall
by the Emperours appointment. (372.) *Vvho being a (.373.) Con-* appeare.
iurer, had solde his soule to the Diuel for this promotion . Neuertheleße he The.371.
vvas, saith he, so vvittie, so learned, and semed so holy, that he not onely Vntruth:
deceiued th' Emperor that made hĩ Pope, but al the vvorld besides. In vvhich Platina
Otho *the.Emperor remaining at Rome, did deliberate after vvhat sort, ãd* vvas no
by vvhat meanes he might reforme, not onely the Empire, but also hãde- flatterer,
ling (.374.) Ecclesiastical matters how he might reforme the but a free
Lawes of the Church, and bring thẽ into the auncient estate. vvriter.
Suche vvas the careful trauel of the Godly Princes, in gouerning not onely The.372.
in Temporall, but also in Ecclesiasticall thinges and causes. Vntruth.
False trã=
y iij   Benedictus flation.
Ex Impera
toris ſen=
tentia. Ac
cording

to the Emperours vvill. The.373. Vntruth. Slanderous. Syluester vvas
no Coniurer. The.374. vntruth. *Ecclesiastical maters,* Naucl.nameth not:

Benedictus *the ninth, solde the Papacy to Gregorye the sixt*. Syluester *the thirde, thrust in amongest them by frendship and briberye*.
To this case was the Papacy brought now (*saith Platina*) that
onely he that was most mighty in ambition and bribery, obteined this dignitie: there was no roume for good men. Hen-

The.375.
vntruth.
Sabelli-
cus falsi-
fied, as
shall ap-
peare.
The.376.
vntruth.,
Sabellicus
saith not
so.

ricus *the thyrd, surnamed* Pius, *came to Rome to thrust out these three
monsters, saith*, Sabellicus, *and to bring this to passe in better order, he*
calleth a Synod, *vvherein he* (.375.) *deposeth these three monstrous beastes,*
and dooth create Clement the second. *The vvhiche doon,* he sweareth the
Romaines, that they shall neuer after be present at the electiõ
of any Pope, onles they be (.376.) compelled thereunto by the
Emperour. *But after the Emperours departure from the citie:* Stephan
perceiuing the people to grudge somvvhat at Clementes election, despatched
him out of the vvay vvith a medicine for a Pope. Venenum illi miscuit,
he poisoned him (*saith Sabellicus,*) and immediatlye after his
death, entruded him self into the Papacy, without consent,
either of the Emperour, people or priest, ãd called him self Damasus. 2. *But vvithin a vvhile he died also. In the meane time the Romai-*
nes sent to the Emperour, besechinge him to appoint them some
good man to be their Bishop. *vvho made* Bauno Pope, *and vvas*
named Leo. 9.

The. 15. Chapter. of Hugh Capet the Frenche King: Otho. 3.
Emperour : and of Gregorie. 5. and Siluester. 2.
Popes.

Stapleton.

Plat.in
Greg.5.
Volat.lib.
22. An-
throp.

Among all other Popes M. Horne, you could not alleage any worse to your purpose, then this Gregorie
the. 5. For if we shall beleue Platina, Sabellicus, Volaterane, Carion and the other cõmon writers: it is this Gregorie that instituted the. 7. Electours in Germanie, and the
whole order and direction, with his Othe also, to the
Pope.

As

As touching Arnulphus the Bishop of Rhemes deposed by a Councel there called (as you say) by Hugh Capet the French King, and Gilbert put in his place, it is true
you saie : but you tell not all.   For afterwardes (as Nauclerus reporteth) becaufe Arnulphus coulde not be depofed, without the authoritie of the bifshop of Rome, M. Gilbert was depofed againe, and Arnulphus reftored. Wherevpon Gilbert fled to Otho, and was in a certaine time after
made Bifshop of Rauéna. This is the whole ftory M. Horn,
and this declareth the Popes authoritie , aboue youre Supreme Gouernour, Hugh Capet the French King.

Naucl.ge
nerat.34.
pag.96.

Where you adde, that King Robert fonne to Hugh Capet, *was a diligent labourer about Diuine or Church matters,*
if you had told forth, wherin, as your Author doth, faying:
Compofuit enim multas profas & hymnos. For he made manie
profes and hymnes, to be fong in the Churche , your tale
had bene to fmall purpofe : excepte to make fongs for the
Church, do proue a man Supreme Gouernour in al Church
caufes or things. And then you haue more fupreme gouernours then one, not onely in England, but in London, yea
and in the Court too, I trowe. Of Iohn the.18.and Gregorie the. 5. we fhal fay more anon.

Nauclerus
Ibidem.

But nowe whether Syluefter the.2 were a coniurer or
no, to your mater it maketh neuer a whit, and there is more
to be faid to the contrary, whiche neadeleffe we nede not
now to allege, then ye fhal perchaunce, this whole twelue
moneths wel anfwere vnto. But I woulde now faine afke
you M. Horne, who is this Siluefter? What was his name
before I pray you ? Forfoth, gentle Reader, this Siluefter is
he, by whofe electió to be B. of Rhemes, M. Horne in the
laft page, would proue the Fréch king to be Supreme head

M. Horns
incóftant
or igno-
dealing
touching
Syluefter
the.1.

of

of the Church: And then to set foorth the Kings Supremacie, he was Gilbert the Philosopher, and nowe for to depresse the Popes Supremacie, being made Pope him selfe,
by M. Hornes charme, is turned from a Philosopher to a
Coniurer. But to leaue al other coniectures, and especial-
lie that it is not likely, *that he solde* as ye say, *his soule to the
Deuill for that promotion*: seing, that by the report of your
own Author Sabellicus, it is said that he instructed in learning not only the French king, but the Emperour also, and
therfore was in some great likelihode of preferment without any Magical arte to be practised for the same, I say that
your selfe vnwarely haue aunswered your selfe, in calling
him a Philosopher. For being so verye fewe in the West
part in those daies skilful in Philosophie, and in the Mathe-
**Siluester
vvas no
cōiurer.
Theodori-
chus de
Nyem in
lib de pri-
uileg. &
Iurib.Im-
perij.In
volum. de
imper.et
ecclef.po-
test.pag.
832.impr.
Basil.An.
1566.**
maticalles, if anye were suche, the common people
tooke him by and by, for a Nigromancer and a coniurer.
And *Theodorichus de Nyem*, an Author by your selfe alle-
gead (*Page.83.a*) witnesseth the same, saying that this Syluester *was cunning in liberal Sciences, and a noble Philosopher
and Mathematical. I haue seene* (saith he) *certaine of his
bookes most suttill in Philosophie. And for his suche excellent
learning, multi Romani ipsum odio habebant, dicētes, quòd Magus esset, nec non magicam artem exerceret*. Many of the
Romaines hated him, saying that he was a Coniurer and
vsed witchcraft. Vpon such vaine rumours you also cal him
a Coniurer M. Horne, vttering therein as much good skil,
as you doe good will.

But how so euer it be, ye should not by your supreme authority, yet to the bewraying, either of your notable vn-
skilfulnesse (as not knowing the saied Sluyester, to be the
partye yee speake of immediatlye before) or of youre
notable

notable peruerſitie and yll dealing, ſo ſodenly haue turned
him from a philoſopher into a coniurer. Wherein yet if ye
will ſtryue and wrangle, to proue, that for all this gyſte,
Otho acknowledged the popes ſupreame authoritye, I remitte yowe M. Horne, and your reader, to the verie ſayde
diſtinction your ſelf alleage. Where ye ſhall fynd, that this
Otho or his grandfather, Otho the firſte, did by the vſuall
othe of themperours euer ſythens geuen, agniſe the pope
for the ſupreame head of the Church. So your owne ſtory
playnely and fullie opened, geueth againſte yowe a playne
and a full teſtimonie alſo, aſwell of your moſte vnhoneſte
and falſe dealinge in the handlinge of this ſtorie, as of your
moſt falſe, and yet moſt accuſtomable aſſertion, that the ſupremacie of all cauſes eccleſiaſticall remayned in thempe-
rous and not in the popes. And as for Sylueſter him ſelfe,
howe he repented at the ende, and what a miraculous token God gaue of his good ſtate, after his deathe, the lerned
Reader may ſee in ª Naucler ᵇ Sabell. and ᶜ Platina, as I haue
otherwhere touched it againſt M. Iewell.

    You reherſe here yet a nomber of popes in the creation
or depoſition of whome, themperour ſemed to haue ſomewhat to doe. But altogether as we haue often ſhewed,
impertinently and otherwiſe lyingly, and againſte your ſelf
alſo directly browght in, And to begin M. Horn euen with
your firſt example of Arnulphus, I pray you, where fynde
yowe in your authour that the kinge depoſed him? Your
authour ſayeth no ſuche matter, but that, the kinge did
caſt him in pryſon, beinge firſte depoſed by a ſynode of biſhops. Yet he made ye will ſay, Gilberte the philoſopher
        z   biſhop

Diſt. 63.
Tibi Do-
mino Io-
hanni pa-
pæ, ego rex
Otho &c.
In Roma
nullũ pla-
citũ aut or
dinatione
faciam de
omnibus
quæ ad te,
aut ad Ro
manos per
tinent ſine
tuo conſi-
lio, et quic
quid leter
ra S. Petri
ad noſtrã
poteſtatē
peruenerit
tibi red-
dam, &
cuicunque
&c.
a. Gen. 34.
b. Aen. 9.
lib. 2.
c. In Syl.
Artic. 4.
pag. 114.

Naucl gener. 33. Arnulphũ Rhemorũ Pontificē ſynodo epiſcoporũ habita ab vrbe deiectũ,
in vincula coniecit. Rhemis Gilbertũ Philoſophũ poſuit epiſcopum: Romani tamen pontificis edicto, Arnulphus, reuocato Gilberto reſtitutus eſt, &c.

biſſhop for him:and afterward Otho the.3.made him archbiſhop of Rauēna.Ye might haue added ād pope to,as your
authour doth,if ye had meant to deale playnly,ād eſpecially that the ſaid Gilbertᵒby pope Iohns authority,was thruſt
out,ād Arnulphus reſtored agayne(as you heard before).

    Ye doe nowe partly (as before, bely Platina,and partly
gheaſſe blindly,as thowghe Platina durſt not(to flatter the
popes withal)playnly opē his mynd:ād as thowgh he ſhuld

Platina
in Ioh.18.
Creſcentij
Romani
cōiulis po-
tētiafretᵒ
qué pecu=
nia corru-
piſſe credi-
tum eſt:et
mox. Mi-
ror ergo hi
ſtoricos Io
annē ipſũ
inter pōti-
fices nume
raſſe,cùm
viuēte ad
huc pōtifi-
ce Grego-
rio ſedem
occupaſſet.
be of this mynd,that he that cōmeth into the papacy without thēperours cōſent is but a theef,and a robber.Which is
as true as before ye made him therfore a traytour.For Platina geueth forth no ſuch mening.But ſheweth two cauſes
why this Iohn came not in by the dore . The one, that he
came in by bryberie.The other,that he vſurped the ſee beig
not as yet vacāt,Gregory whome ye write of,as yet lyuig,
ād beig the lawful pope choſen by the voice of the clergy,
and by the cōſent of thēperor,and all the people of Rome.

    After al this ye ſay,that Hérie the. 3.depoſed thre popes
(whom you cal *thre mōſtrous beſtes*, of ſuch a beaſtly ſprite
you are)ād yet you lie in ſo ſayīg.For thēperor by ſupreme
Authorite depoſed none.But only for quyetnes ſake(as Sa-
bel.writeth)*coegit ſe dignitate abdicare*.Forced thē al to depoſe thē ſelues.which by force no maruail if he did.But by
right neither he nor any mā liuing could haue depoſed any
pope.They may be induced either by reaſon or by force to
depoſe thē ſelues.Farder you ſay,this Emperour ſware the
Romās that they ſhould neuer be preſent at the popes electiō,onleſſe *they were compelled by thēperor*.It had bene wel
done if ye had told vs who writeth ſo,and withal, by what
warrāt thēperour could exclud the people frō their cōſent
which hitherto they gaue in the choſing of the popes . Sa-
belli-

bellicus your Author, writeth of no such copulsio. But that
they should not so doe, without his permissio, ād the reason
he addeh. *Vt dignitas maneret illi inoffensa, caueretur g̃, in po-*
sterum pontificibus .that pope Clement the chosen might co-
tinewe quietly, and that also for the quiet of other popes to
come he might prouide. Al which he did as a godly defendour, not as a Supreme Gouernor of the Church. Now if a
mā would ftād with you altogether ād fay ye belie Stephanus, ād certain other popes, of such as ye haue here named,
I think he should not say farre frō the truth. But yet becaufe
ye haue some authors on your side, I wil not greatly charge
your for this matter . You tel vs in thend of this procesie,
that the Emperour made Bauno pope, ād was named Leo.
9. But I tel you nowe. M. Horn, that the Emperors making
was after vnmade, ād this Bauno made pope by the Clergy
in Rome . For where as this Bauno chofen first of themperour, came out of Germany to Rome, al in his *Pontificalibus*
as alredy pope, Hugo that famoufe ād lerned Abbat of Clu
niacū, ād Hildebrād (who after was pope Gregory.7.) met
him in the way ād shewed him: *that theperor had no right to*
choofe the pope, that the fame right belonged to the Clergy and
City of Rome, that he should lay down his bishoply attyre, come
to Rome as a priuate man , and then if he were thought mete ,
by the lawfull confent of the clergie and city, to be chofen. Their
counfell he folowed, openly deteftinge his former rashnes,
that at the Emperours only choyfe he had taken vpon him
that highe office. Thus afterwarde in Rome he was lawfully chofen, there he was made pope, and named Leo.9. not
by the Emperour only, as M. Horne only telleth. And this
al hiftorians in maner do witnesse.

Sabel. Ae-
ne.9.li.2,

Vide Her-
mannum
cōtractum
in chroni-
cis.
Lambert.
Schafnab.
m hiftor.
Germa.
Othonem
Friſing .li.
6.cap. 33.

Sabell.
Aened. 9.
lib.2.
Naucler.
gener.35.
pag 120.
Platina in
Leo.9.

M.Horne

M. Horne. The.113. Diuision. Fol.71.b.

After this Leo, *vvhom Hildebrand ridde out of the vvay,* saith Benno
Cardinalis, *vvas* Victor *the seconde made Pope, by the* Emperours
authority *or priuilege. Shortly after, this Godly Emperour died being*

greatly praised, and surnamed, Pius Henricus, *for his dealing in the reformation of Church matters. This Emperour had called tvvo Councels, the one
at* Costance, *vvherein he vvas himself present, and after that another at* Mo
guntia, *vvherein both the Emperour and the Pope, sat in Syrod. This Pope*
saith Nauclerus, *came into Germany about the Church matters, and orde*

The.377.
vntruth.
Slaunderous:
Sabellic.

red al things therein (saith Abbas Vrspur.) *by the aduise and coun*
faile of themperor and other seculer Princes, and the bishops.
And as this Emperour had yet this interest in the Councels, and in the crea
tiō *of the Pope himself, so had he the placing and displacing, allovving ād dis*

The.378.
vntruth.
they adde
By the lavv
of Nicolas
the last pope before:
vvhich
you vntruly
haue left
out.

allovving, in other spiritual promotions, as at large appeareth in Naucler.
Stephē. 9. *vvas chosen Pope after that* Victor *had dronken of (.377.)* Hildebrands *cup. But this* Sthphen *liued not long: for* said Benno, *If any other
than* Hildebrand *were chosen Pope,* Gerardus Brazutus, Hildebrands *familiar friend would soone dispatche hī out of the*
way with poyson. Alexander. 2. *vvas chosen vvithout thēperors authority
or knovvledge, vvith vvhose electiō the vvhole Clergy of Lōbardy vvas much
offended, and refused to ovve vnto hī any obediēce, beseching thēperor that he
vvould geue them licēce to chose one of their ovvn: persuading him (378) that*

The.379.
vntruth.
For one
of them
vvas not
pope.

there ought none to be elect without the cōsent of the king of
Italy. *After thei had licēce, thei chose* Cadolus *the bishop of* Parma, *vvhō
al the Clergy of Lōbardy obeyed as their lauful Pope* The Cardinals (saith
Bēno) knowing wel Hildebrāds ambitiō, did win with much

The.380.
vntruth.
Slaunderous against the
vvhole
Church of
that age.

fute thēperors fauour and aide to their new elected Pope Cadol⁹: the which did fo depely perce the hart of Hildebrād, that
he becam a deadly enemy to thēperor for euer after cōtrary to
the faithful duty that he had sworn vnto hī. *Hard hold there vvas
betvvixt these tvvo (.379.) Popes so vvel vvith strokes as vvith vvoords: they
both gathered great armies, and vvith their armies came into the fielde in
their ovvn persones, and fought tvvo cruel and bloudy battailes, and so ruled
the (380) Schismatical Church vvith* Paules *svvorde,* Peters *keyes, being fast
locked frō thē both in* Christes *Churche: til thēperor sent* Otto *the Ahchebisshop of*

ſhop of Collein, geuing him ful authority, as he ſhould ſee cauſe, to ſet in order the Church matters. VVhã Otto came to Rome vvith this large commiſſion, he did ſharpely reproue Alexander at the firſt, Becauſe he had
takē vpõ him the Papacy without thēperours cõmaundement,
and cõtrary to that order, which the Law it ſelf, and the longe
cuſtome alſo hath preſcribed. VVhoſe vvords Nauclerus telleth thus:
How cõmeth this to paſſe (ſaith he) my brother Alexander, that
cõtrary to the maner of old time hitherto obſerued, and agaſſt
the law preſcribed to the Romain biſhops many yeares agoe,
thou haſt takē vpõ thee the Romain Papacy without the commaundemēt of the King, and my Lord Héry: and ſo beginniug frõ
Charles the great, he nameth many Princes, by vvhoſe authority the Popes
vvere either choſen, cõfirmed, or had their electiõ ratified: and vvhan he vvas
going forvvard in his oratiõ, Hildebrand Tharchdeacõ taketh the tale (.381.)
out of his mouth, ſaying in great heat: O Archbiſhop Otto, thēperors and
Kings, had neuer any right at al, or rule in the electiõ of the Romain Biſſhops. Tharchbiſhop gaue place to Maiſter Archedeacõ (.382.) by and by: For
Hildebrand knevv vvel inough, ſaith (.383.) Sabellicus, that Otto vvould
relent eaſely, and agree vvith him. In ſuch ſort alſo haue other godly Princes
been (.384.) beguyled, truſting ouer much popiſh Prelats vvith their embaſ-
ſages. VVithin a vvhile after vvhan thēperour heard of theſe doinges, he ſent
ſtreight to Pope Alexander, to gather together the Prelats promiſing that he
biſelf vvould come to the councel: to (.385.) ſet an order in the Church
matters, that al things might be don in his own preſence, vvho
vſed Alexander very gētly and friēdly, vvhervvith the Pope aftervvards vvas
ſo moued, and ſavv hovv he hiſelf had bē abuſed by Hildebråds inſtigatiõs a-
gaiſt ſo gētle a Prïce, that he vvas greatly ſory that he had attēptedto be pope
vvithout his aſſent. VVherupõ ſaith Béno, wha Alexãder vnderſtode,
that he was electedãd ēſtalled by fraude ãd craft of Hildebråd,
ãd other thēperois enemies, in his ſermõ to the people, he plaï-
ly declared, that he would not ſit in the Apoſtolik ſea, without
the licence and fauour of thēperour: and further ſaid openlye
iu the pulpit, that he would ſende foorthwith, his letters vnto
the Emperour for this purpoſe, ſo greatly he repented him of
his vſurpation without the Emperours authority.

z iij Hilde-

Platina.

The. 381.
vntruthe
Slaunde-
rous, as
ſhal ap-
peare.

The: 382.
vntruth.
For much
more was
ſayed, be-
fore he
gaue
place.

The. 383.
vntruth.
Sabell. fal
ſified, as
ſhal ap-
peare.

Sabellicus

The. 384.
vntruth,
mere ſlaũ
derous.

The. 385.
vntruth.
Sabellicus
falſified,
as ſhal ap-
peare.

Hilde
bráde.

The. 386
vntruth-
mereflaũ-
derous.
The. 387.
vntruth.
The cler-
gy of
Rome,
not he,
made all
the haſte,
† A lewde
lying tale
cōtrary to
al other
vvriters
Sabel. Pla-
tina, Nau-
clere, Ma-
rianᵒ, Ans
ſelmus ãd
other.
The. 388.
vntruth.
ſlaunde-
rous in
preferrig
the cõde-
ned fable
of one mã
before all
approued
hiſtories.
The . 389.
vntruth.
in cõcea-
ling: For
ſtraight
Nauclere

Hildebrande, vvho had long a vvayted and (.386.) practiſed to be Pope, impacient of any longer tariaunce, immediatly after the death of Alexander, gatte to be made Pope, and vvas called Gregory the ſeuenth, of vvhoſe e-lectiõ Abbas Vrſpurgenſ. ſaith: next to Alexander ſucceded Hildebrande, vnder whome the Romain common weale and the whole Church, was endaungered and brought in a great perill with newe errours and ſchiſmes, ſuch as haue not been heard of: who climbed vp to this high dignity without the conſent of the Prince, and therefore there be that affirme him to haue v-ſurped the Papacy, by tyranny, and not Canonically inſtituted, for which cauſe alſo many did refuſe him to be Pope . In this election, Hildebrande (.387.) made poſte haſte, for feare I.e had come ſhorte of his purpoſe. In ſo mucH that Nauclerus ſaith, before the exequies of Alexander vveı e finiſhed, the Cleargy and people that came to the buriall , cried out, that S. Peter had choſen Maiſter Archedeacon Hildebrande to be Pope, vvhereupon the Cardinalles vvent a ſide and elected Hildebrande. But Benno, vvho vvas a Cardinall at Rome the ſame tyme, * ſaith , that the ſelfe ſame euening and hovver, vvhen Alexander died , Hildebrande vvas enſtalled by his ſouldiours, vvithout the aſſent of either Prieſt or people: fearing leſt delay vvoulde breede peril: to vvhoſe election not one of the Cardinales did ſubſcribe: in ſo much that Hildebrande ſaid to an Abbot , that came ſhort to the election, brother Abbot yee haue taried ouer longe: to vvhome the Abbot anſvvered, ãd thou Hildebrãd haſt made ouer much haſt, in that theu haſt v-ſurped the Apoſtolik ſea agaïſt the Canõs, thy Maiſter the Pope being not yet buried. By vvhich poſt haſt, iportune clamours, and violēt electiõ, it is eaſie to ſee, hovv Platina and thoſe that follovv him, do no leſſe (388) lie than flatter iu prayſing this Pope, ãd ſettĩg foorth ſo comely a form of his electiõ. Naucl. proteſteth and promiſeth in the tellig of this Popes life to kepe an indifferēcy and fidelity, in the report of the Chronicles: and firſt reporteth the ſtate of the Church vnder this Pope vvord for vvord as I haue reherſed out of Abbas Vrſpurg. (.389.) and to declare his further vprightnes in the matter , he telleth vvhat he founde vvriten in a fine ſtile amongeſt the Saxon hiſtories: that the Biſhops of Fraunce moued the Prince not to ſuffer this election, vvhich vvas made vvithout his conſent , for if he did , it might vvorke to him inuche and greuous daungier: the Prince perceiuing this ſuggeſtion to
be true

*be true,sent immediatly his Embaſſadours to Rome, to demauude the cauſe vvherefore they preſumed vvithout the Kinges licence,againſt the cuſtome of their aunceſtours,to ordeine a Pope:and further to commaunde the nevve e-lected Pope,to forſake that dignity vnlaufully come by onleſſe they vvoulde make a reaſonable ſatisfaction, theſe Embaſſadours vvere honorably recei-ued,and vvhen they had declared their meſſage, the Pope himſelfe, maketh them this anſvvere:*He taketh God to witneſſe,that he neuer co-ueted this high dignity,but that he was choſen,ād thruſt vio-lently thereunto by the Romaines,who would not ſuffer him in any wiſe to refuſe it : notwithſtanding they coulde by no meanes perſwade him,to take the Papacy vpō him,ād to be cō ſecrate Pope,till he were ſurely certified,that both the Kinge and alſo the Princes of Germany,had geuen their aſſente.*Vvhē the King vvas certified of this anſvveare, he vvas contente and vvillingly gaue commaundement,that he ſhould be ordered Pope.He alſo reciteth out of* Blondus,*and other vvriters,*That the Kinge gaue his conſente vnto the Popes election,ſending the Biſshop of Verſelles, the Chauncellour of Italy,to confirme the election by his autho-rity,as the maner had bene,the which thing alſo,Platina(*ſaith be*) ſeemeth to affirme.

Aftervvardes the Emperour called a(.390.) Councell, vvhich he helde (as Sabellicus *ſaith) at* VVormes,*vvhereat vvere al the Biſshops of Frāūce and Germany,excepte the Saxons. The Churchmen of Rome ſent their epiſt-les, vvith greuous complaints againſt* Hildebrand *vnto this Councel: In* quibus Hildebrandum ambitus & periurij accerſunt,eundem-que plæraq; auarè, ſuperbeq; facere,conqueruntur:hocq; reie-cto, alium paſtorem poſtulant: VVherein they accuſe Hilde-brande,of ambition and periury,complainning that he dothe manye thinges proudly and couetouſlye,and therefore deſire, that he may be depoſed,and an other paſtour appoincted thē.

The (.391.) Fathers in this Councell make a Decree for to depoſe Hilde-brande,reciting therein many his greuous and horrible crymes, that moued them therto: And not only the Biſshops of Germany and Frāūce, but alſo the Biſshoppes of Italy, aſſembled togeather at Tici-num,a citie in Lombardy nowe called Pauia,did ſubſcribe this Decree

Decree.*This Synode beynge thus finished,the Emperour (saith Auentinus)vvrote tvvo letters ,.the one to Hildebrand,the other to the people and
priestes of Rome,vvherein he commaundeth Hildebrande, accordinge to the
Decree of the Councell , to retouine to his priuate life and estate , and the
Romaines to forsake Hildebrande , and to choose to them selues a Pastor,
accordinge to the manner of their auncestours.VVho so listeth to reade these
Epistles,and the se.litious(.392.)traiterous , and tragicall feates and practises of the Pope against the Emperour,bothe before,and especially after this
Decree,he may see them in* Orthwinus Gratius,*in Nauclerus, Auē-
tinus,Sabellicus,*and Platina.

The 392.
vntruth.
Rayling.

The.16.Chapter.Of Henry the.4.and of Gregory.7.other-
wised called Hildebrande , Pope.

Stapleton.

A man might make a shorte and a true answere withal,
to all thys long tale , and say that it is altogether extrauagante , and impertinente or rather directly concluding for the Popes Primacie . For thowghe Henrie the
fowrth, woulde not acknowledge Hildebrande , as pope,
yet he acknowledged an other,whom him self had set vp,
yea and the sayd Hildebrande to at the lengthe to be the
supreame head of Christes Church : as we shall anon de-
clare.So that nowe we might passe ouer , al these heynous
accusations againste this pope called,Gregorie the.7.as out
of your matter , sauinge that I thinke good to geue notice
to the reader,that yet neuerthelesse ye shall neuer be able
to iustifie them , as surmised and fayned by your authour
Benno and other his enimies,whom he had iustly excõmunicated ãd deposed for their naughtines,vpholdē ãd maynteyned by Hēry thēperor being him self also iustly excõmu-
nicated.Marianus Scotus lyuing about the same time,saith,
that

Marianus
Scotus
saying of
Hilde-
brande.

that this Gregory, was accufed of Héries fautours of many
falfe crymes , and maketh the councells kepte againft him
no better, then a confpiracie againft God and his vicar, pope Gregory. Owre country man william of Malmefburie
fayeth, that he had the fpryte of prophecie, and telleth as a
certayne and fure veritie, by relation of hym that heard yt
out of the mowthe of the famoufe Abbat of Cluniacum,
called Hugo , that this Hildebrand being but yet archdea-
con and the Popes Legate in Fraunce, hauing a bifhop before him whome he did wonderfully fufpecte for fymonie
committed , but yet not conuinced by fufficiente proufe,
commaunded him to pronounce for his purgation : *Gloria
patri , & filio , & fpiritui fancto* . The bifhop pronounced
rowndlie, *Gloria patri & filio* . But for his lyfe he could not
then , nor all his lyfe after , pronounce *fpiritui fancto* . This
Hugo reported further, that Hildebrand foretolde hym of
a great plague and peftilence ere yt came: and toid hym alfo of certayne of his pryuie thoughts . It pleafeth yowe to
make Platina but a lier and a flatterer, for that he taketh this
Gregory to be the true pope, and to haue bene moft wróg-
fully thruft out by the Emperour . Ye feame rather to encline to Abbas Vrfpergenfis and Nauclerus, who bothe yet
make againft you . For you fhal fynd in Abbas that Anfel-
mius bifhop of Luca a man as he writeth, of an excellent elo
quence, wytte, and Learning, and by whom God wrought
miracles, afwel in his lyfe tyme, as afterward, did euer acknowledg hi for the true pope, ād the other fuborned by the
Emperor, to be but an vfurper. And fo he wrote to the falfe pope in playne words. What fay you thē to your own au
thor Nauclerus, *that*, as ye fay , *proteftcth and promifcth in
telling this popes lyfe to kepe an indifferēcy and a fidelity in the
reporte*

a a

Lib. 3. at a
te. 6.
Confpiran
tes cōuene
rāt in vnū
aduerfus
Dominum
& aduer-
fus vica-
riū eius pa
pā Grego-
rium.
Vvilliam
of Mal-
mefbu-
ries fayīg
of the
fame.
Hildebrād
had the
gifte of
prophecy
Lib. 3. de
hift. An-
glicana.
Hilde-
brand ta-
kē for the
true pope
by the
godlie ād
Learned
bifhop
Anfelmus
Vide epift.
Anfelmi
apud Ab-
batem.

Opera Sigeberti Ar=
chiepiscopi Mogunt.
VVormaciæ couentus
indicitur. In conuetu
eum & Hugo Car-
dinalis venit, tragœ-
diã quandam apud
prīcipes de scelesta pa
pæ vita cōmentus fal-
so protulit.
Naucler.gener.36.
The crymes layde
to Hildebrand were
falsely layde to hī,
by the confesſion
of M.Hornes own
author vvhom he
maketh to be indif-
ferente.
Gener. 37.
Abbas Vrspergenſ.
Guiliel. Malmeſb.li.
3.de hiſt. Anglica.
Blondus.
Naucler, Gener.36.
Pope Hilbrand pur
geth him selfby re-
ceiuing the blesſed
Sacrament.

report of the chronicles ? Doth not he condemne as
feined and falſe forged lies, ſuch thigs as ye here alleage? doth he not, though he ſaieth Sigebertus and
ſome other write to the cōtrary, ſay that the doings
of this Gregory were honeſt, and proceded from a
zelouſe faith? The like ſay I of your Coūcels holdē
in Italy. Whoſe folly and falſhod euidently burſted
out aſwel otherwiſe, as in calling this Gregory the
diſciple of Berégari°: ād one that browght in doubt
the Catholike and apoſtolical faith, of the body and
bloud of Chriſt. This was a moſt notorieuſe lye: for
Hildebrādus beig as yet but archedeacō, and notwithſtāding the Popes Legat, as I haue ſaid, in Frāce
brought this Berégari°to a recātatiō: firſt at Towers
in Frāce, and afterward at Rome alſo, hī ſelf being
thē pope. Yea hīſef, thēperor being preſent, after he
had ſaid Maſſe, taking the body of Chriſte into his
hād, ſaid to thēperor. *Sir I haue ben accuſed of you and
your adherēts of diuerſe crymes, wherof yf I be gylty,
I pray God, after I haue receiued his body(which I en-
tēde preſently to receaue for my purgatiō)to ſtreke me
with ſodayne death* . Vpopn this this pope receaued
part of the holy hoſte, and woulde that thēperor
ſhould haue done the like for his purgation, but he
refuſed ſo to doe . And nowe take heade to your ſelf and
to your fellowes M.Horne, leaſt by your owne Councell
of Pauia , one of the moſte greauouſe and moſte horrible
crymes, falſlye layde to Pope Gregory , be not moſt truely
layde to you, and your adherents being the very true diſciple of the heretike Berégarius and mē that bring in doubte,
yea that accurſe and condemne the Catholik and Apoſtolical faith.

lical faith. Whose condemnation made by Pope Gregory, brand.
with his decree that he made againſt your côcubines, doth
I trow much more greue you, then doth this matter of thê- A conie⌐
perour, or any wronge ye pretende, by this Pope, to haue ⌐ture vvhie M.
bene done to him. Horne is

Nowe is your cloked diſſimulation alſo in the handling ſo much
of this ſtory to be conſidered, that dare not open the very offended
cauſe of all this diſſentiô betwene the pope ãd thêperor, and debrand.
the euente thereof. Which diſſention roſe, for that themperour woulde not remoue ſuch ſymoniacall Biſhoppes, The cauſe of the diſ-
as he kepte aboutê him, being excommunicated by Alex- ſention
ander the . 2 . Gregories predeceſſour. And that him ſelf betvvene
woulde not forbeare to ſell biſhopriks and other ſpirituall ror and
lyuings. Whereof Gregory, as ſone as euer he was electe, pope Hil
admoniſhed him, ſaying:*that being confirmed by themperour* debrand.
he would in no wiſe ſuffer and beare with his doïgs: and ther- Naucler,
fore willed him, either to procure that ſome other man ſhoulde gener.36.
be made Pope, or to amende thoſe things, that were amiſſe. This
notwithſtandinge, the Emperour did confirme him : but
beinge afterwarde ſeduced, by ſuch as Gregorie had excommunicated and depoſed, and irritated by the Popes
letters, being therein commaũded to purge him ſelf of ſuch
crymes as he was charged withal, conſpired againſte him,
with his adherente biſhoppes aſſembled (as ye write) at
Wormes : and declared him to be no Pope . The Pope
agayne accurſeth all that wycked conuenticle with the
Emperour, and depoſeth him from his imperiall dignitye:
diſcharging all his ſubiectes of al ſuch loyalty as they owed
by othe vnto him. Afterwarde alſo this Pope excommunicated the Emperour and al his adherentes. The ſame yere
(ſaith Nauclerus) the Princes and the greater parte of the
a a ij people,

people,beganne to alienat their minds from him:By reaſon

whereof a great dyet was kept of the Allemayn Princes at
Openham . At the whiche themperour was forced by the
princes of Germanie(which ſayd yf he wente not, and reconciled him ſelf to the pope,they would exequute the Po
pes ſentence againſte hym) to take his iorneye to the Pope , and commynge to Canoſſom where the Pope was,
he put of all his royall attiermente , and bare foted three
dayes together , in a colde and harde ſharpe wynter moſte
humblie craued pardon of the Pope: and at the length was
by the pope , from the ſentence of excommunication vppon certayne conditions abſolued . Whiche conditions
beinge by hym broken , beganne as hotte a ſturre as euer
was before:So farre forthe that thys Gregorie was forced

A iuſte
iudge mēt
of God
againſte
Henrye
the.4.

to flie from Rome , for feare of hys powre , to Salernum,
where ſhortly after he died.

　　Nowe good reader will ye ſee the iuſte iudgemente
of God : and therein withall a full anſweare to Maiſter
Hornes impertinente proceſſe ? After Gregories deathe,

Henry the
4.appe-
leth to the
pope.
Rom.pon-
tiſicē,ſan-
ctam &
vniuerſa-
lē ſedē Ro
manamap
pellamus.
In literis
ad Henri-
cum filiū.

thys Emperour was taken priſoner of hys owne ſonne,
and forced to reſigne and geue ouer all his royall and imperiall dignitye , whiche rebelled againſte hym,as he rebelled againſte hys ſpirituall father pope Gregorie . And
as faſte as he wrote letters before to depoſe Hildebrande
(as ye write)wherein neuer the leſſe he refuſed not abſo-
lutly the pope,but Hildebrāde(whō he toke not for pope)
which thīg I deſire the Reader diligently to note, ſo being
in this diſtreſſe in his letters aſwel to his ſon Henry (which
was Héry the 5.)as in his letters to the biſhops and nobility
of Germany (which letters ye deaply diſſemble) he appealeth to the pope,ād to the holy ād vniuerſal ſee of Rome.

Goe

Goe on nowe M. Horne, and tel vs hardlie, and lie one *Rogamus*
as fafte as ye wil vppon this Hildebrandus: that he poyfo- *vos per*
ned: firft Leo the. 9. then Victor the . 2. and after him Ste- *authori-*
uen the . 9. But fuerlye either ye are a great lier, or Hil- *tatē Ro.*
debrande was not his craftes maifter, for all that ye make *ecclefiæ,*
hi fo cunning in the arte of poyfonig. For where after Ste- *cui nos cō-*
phen, there were two other Popes : Benedicte the tenth, *mittimus*
and Nicolaus the. 2. and after them Alexander the . 2. ye *& honorē*
omitting thofe two, doe tell vs forthwith of Alexander *regni ne*
the 2. and howe that this Gregorye, who had longe away- *&c. Apud*
ted and practifed to be Pope, immediatly after the deathe *quē fi in-*
of Alexander gate himfelf to be made pope. And I am affu- *terpellatio*
red ye can tel vs no better reafon why he fhoulde poyfon, *veftra,nul*
the other firft thre Popes, then the other latter three. Nei- *laq; alia*
ther can ye tell vs anye probable reafon why he fhoulde *interuētio*
poyfon any one, or feke by this vngodly way to come to *ad prefens*
that fee, which as yet being but Archedeacon feameth e- *prodeffe*
uen by your tale, to haue bene of fuch creditte among the *peterit,ap*
Romans, as was lightly no other. As one that in fo weigh- *pellamus*
ty a caufe by the will and confente of the Cardinalles an- *R. p. &*
fwered to Otho themperours Ambaffadour, wifely and fo- *fanctā vni*
berly, and not as ye fable, taking the tale out of his mowthe *uerfalem*
in great heate . As yt pleafeth you alfo to fable, that the *R. fede &*
Archebifshop Otho, gaue place to M. Archedeacon by and *ecclefiam.*
by. And thervpō ful like your felf ye rufhe in againft popifhe *In literis*
prelates, as ye cal them, who haue beguyled godly Princes, *ad epifco-*
that trufted them ouermuch. Whereas Otho was fayne to *pos et prī-*
yelde to Hildebrande of fyne force of reafon, and to fuch *cipes.*
examples of the auncient Churche as he brought forthe. *Platina in*
For after the woordes by you alleaged, that Emperours or *Alexan.2.*
Kinges neuer had right in the election of Popes, he fayed *Naucler.*
gener. 36.

farder. *And if any thinge was attempted by violence, or other-*
wise then well, it was afterward by the Censures of the fathers
redressed. And so beginning (saith Nauclere) *from the firste*
Emperours, he continewed so longe, vntyll Anno (whom you
call Otto tharchbishop) *inswered, that he was satisfised.* This
was no hotte talke as you bable, but a lerned communication, sobre and discret. I pray you now further, to what end
or purpose serueth this narratiõ cõcerning Alexander the.
2. seing that your Antipope Cadolus was deposed, and thé-

Naucler.
dict. Gene.

perour fayne to craue pardõ for him: and seing the bishops
of Lombardy were reconciled to this Alexãder at.a. councel holdẽ at Mantua, the Emperour also ratifyiñg Alexanders electiõ ? Goe on M. Horne and tel vs that Platina and
others do lie (and that Benno one cõtrary to al others, and
an Author in this matter expressely condemned only saith
truth,) ãd flatter in praysing this pope, and in setting forth a
comely forme of his electiõ: which, what it was ye dare not
shewe, least yt shuld to much disgrace your vncomely ele-
ctiõs, ãd most of al your false assertiõs agaĩst the Popes Pri-

The same
vvriteth
Sabellic⁹
Aenead.9
lib.3.and
Nauclere
gener. 36.
pag.133,

macy. *Gregory,* sayth Platina, *was chosen with the cõsent of al*
good men. The wordes of the electiõ are noted to be of this sort
and tenour. We the Cardinals, the clergy, the acolites, the subdea
cõs, the priests of the Church of Rome, in the presence of the bis-
shops ãd Abbats, ãd of many other, aswell of the clergy as of the
Laytie this day beĩg the xxij. day of April in S. Peter Church, cal

The form
of Hilde.
brands e-
lection,

led ad Vincula, the yeare of our Lord God. 1072. doe elect, to be
true vicare of Christ Archdeacõ Hildebrãd: a mã of great lear-
ning, vertue, wisdome, iustice, cõstãcie, religiõ, a modest, a sober,
ãd a chast mã: one that gouerneth his houshold wel, ful of hospi-
talitie toward the poore, beĩg brought vp ãd taught, euen frõ his
yowthe to his age in the lap of his holy mother the Church: whõ

we wil

we wyl to be ruler of Ghriftes Church,euē with that authority. *with the which Peter did ones rule it by Gods cōmaundemēt.* Yf this be a comely forme,of electiō,as in dede yt is,ād as your felf terme yt,thē hath this comely forme,anſwered al your falfe and deforme argumēts made agaíft this Pope or his pri-macie.Yet to touche a fewe of your manyfolde vntruthes, which do ſo ſwarme in this your narration, I am forced to prológ a litle more my anſwer.You report as of Sabellicus, *that Hildebrande knewe wel inoughe,that Otto would relent eaſely.* But you ſhould knowe wel inoughe that Sabell.hath no ſuch words.Only he ſayth.*Facilè tenuit vt Otho ſibi aſſen* Aenead.9. *tiretur.* He obtayned eaſely,that Otho ſhoulde agree vnto lib.3. him.And that was by his lerned perſwaſiō, not by any co-uert colluſiō,as you do lewdely imagine . Againe you ſay, thēperor promiſed he wold come to the Coūcel,*to ſet an or der in Church matters,*prityng thoſe words in a latyn letter as the words of Sabel.Now ther are no ſuch words in your Author Sabellicus of thēperor.But only that he deſired the pope to cal a Councel,for ſetting of order in Church mat-ters,and that he woulde come.*Vt ſe preſente omnia fierent.* Sabell. vt that al thinges might be done in his preſence. The pithe of ſupra. your argumēt lay in thoſe words:and therfore thoſe words you falſely fathered vppon Sabellicus. You alleage a longe tale out of Benno againſte Hildebrande , as that after that Councell ended, *Alexander had perceyued he was inſtalled by fraude and crafte of Hildebrand,* but how true that tale is, it appeareth by that Alexander after thys Synode ended, Sabel. Ae-ſent Hildebrande in to Apulia withe an Armye , to re- nead. 9. couer to the Churche of Rome ſuche places as the Nor- lib. 3. mans had taken awaye, the whiche Hildebrand broughte Naucl.ge to paſſe . For had Alexander perceyued ſuche fraude nerat.36.

and

and crafte in Hildebrande as you and Benno do surmise, he woulde not I trowe so sone after haue putte him in suche truste and credite, in so weighty and important a matter. And this being reported by Sabell. Nauclerus, and other common writers, it is easy to iudge what a lyar your Ben-

In Indice
lib. inhib.

no is, and howe worthely this very booke of his *de vita Hildebrandi* is by general Councel forbidden and condemned. That which you alleage out of Abbas Vrspergensis against Hildebrand, is woorde for woorde recited in Nau-

Naucler.
gener. 36.

clerus (whome you alleage as one that *protesteth and promiseth to kepe an indifferency and fidelity in telling of this Popes life*) but he addeth immediatly: *Alij & fere omnes prorsus contrarium referunt*. Other writers and in maner al doe reporte the cleane contrary: that is, al for the commendation of Hildebrand. But this you without al indifferency or fidelity thought good to leaue out, and against in maner al writers to cleaue to one Abbat. Of whome when

Marianus
in fine sua
chronogr.
Sabell. &
Naucler.
vbi supra.

you tell that many refused this Hildebrand to be Pope, Marianus Scotus which lyued in that very age, Nauclerus, Sabellicus and Platina will tell you, that those *Many*, were none but *Simmoniaci & fornicarij*. The Simoniacal and the fornicatours, Such as by brybery creped in to Ecclesiasticall promotions, and such as being Priestes kept whores ād concubines, which you now call wyues. M. Horne, to saue your Madges poore honesty. Where you tel vs out of Nau-

Naucler.
gener. 36.
pag. 133.

clerus, *that the bishops of Fraunce moued the Prince not to suffer the election of Hildebrande &c.* You should haue done wel to haue tolde vs out of Nauclerus the cause why these bishops so did. Verily Nauclerus euen in the middest of the sentence whiche you alleage, saieth of those Bisshoppes: *Grandi scrupulo permoti ne vir vehementis & acris ingenij*

atque

atque fidei diftrictius eos pro negligentijs fuis quandoque di-
*fcuteret.*They fent to the Emperour, being fore afrayed,
left t is Hildebrand being a man of a vehement and fharpe
difpofition and faithe, woulde at length more roughly
and fharpely examine them for their negligences : Lo,
Mayfter Horne the loue of licentioufnes, and the feare
of difcipline for theyr defertes, moued thofe Frenche
Bifhoppes to fewe thus to the Emperoure againfte that.
Pope. But you will neuer tell all, becaufe (as I haue
faied and muft often faye)al maketh againft you.

You conclude with a peale of mofte flaunderous and
rayling lyes,fendyng vs to certain epiftles wherin we fhal
fynde, you faie, *the feditioufe,trayterous, and tragical feates*
and practifes of this Pope againft the Emperour &c. For in
Nauclerus,Sabellicus, Marianus Scotus, Volaterrane and
Platina,I am right fure there appeareth no fuche cancred
matter as you raue of, except fuche as they reporte vpon
falfe rumors.

But if you wil fee on the contrary parte, what a godly
ād lerned māhe was, how fharp an enemy to vice, namely to Simonye and Bauderye (for the whych he procured him felfe fo much enemytie) You may reade Maifter Horne, not only Nauclerus, Sabell, and Platina with
Volaterane, Blondus, Antoninus and other late writers,
but alfo Marianus Scotus, William of Malmesbury our
cowntreyman, Anfelmus that notable Bifhoppe of Luca,
who lyued all in the tyme of that tragedy, and you
fhall fynd him in all poyntes a moft excellent Bifhop and
a moft godly man. The French Bifhops for Simony, the
Germayn Bifhoppes for both Simony ād whoredome,the
Emperoure Henrye the fourth for his filthye lucre in fy-
                    b b   moniacal

moniacall practiſes, cauſed all the troubles of that age the moſt vertuoſe Pope, alwayes proceding againſt thoſe vices with the force of the ſpiritual ſworde. For the which at

the hower of his death he ſayed. *Dilexi iuſtitiam : & odi iniquitatem:propterea morior in exilio.* I haue loued righteouſnes:and I haue hated iniquyte. Therefore I die in bāniſhment.

M. Horne. The.114.Diuiſion.pag.74.a.

Henry the.5.came into Italy to end the cōtrouerſy and diſcorde, that vvas betvvixt him and the Pope, for this(.393.) iuriſdiction, and to make ſuch compoſitiō as might bring quietneſſe both to the Church and the Empyre:But Paſchalis the Pope did not muche lyke of his comming, as the Italian vvriters vvitneſſe. The Emperour ſendeth to the Pope, the Pope againe to him: certaine couenautes vvere aggreed vppon, and confirmed by othe, and aſſured by pledges on bothe the parties. But the Pope coulde not, or vvould not, keepe promiſe vvith the Emperour, for that his Biſhoppes did vvithſtande, and in no vviſe vvould ſtande to the agreement: vvereuppon folovved great tumult and a bluddy fray. The Emperour (.394.) ſeynge they for their partes, vvould not ſtande to the couenauntes, vvhiche vvere confyrmed ſo ſtrongly by othe, and hoſtages, as mighte be, vvould not in like vvyſe be bounde to his.Shortly after Eaſter follovving, there vvas a frendly peace concluded betvvixt the Emperour and the Pope, vvho crovvned Henry.5.Emperour,deliuering vnto him vvith his holy hande ſuche priuileges as his aunceſtours vvere vvont to enioie, and confirm d the ſame to him, neuer to be taken from him vnder the paine of the great Curſe. After this the Emperour tooke an othe of all the inhabitauntes in euerye Citye thoroughe Italy, for their faithfull obedience to him, and the faithfull keepinge of of this his prerogatiue, ad priuilege in(.395.) Eccleſiaſtical thinges or cauſes.

The.17.Chapter Of Henry the.5. Lotharius and Conra=
dus, Emperours.

Stapleton.

GO E on as I fayd M. Horne luſtely, and tell your tale truely and fully: and then as we haue had you hither, to, fo ſhall we haue yow ſtyl a very gentle and a tra-ctable aduerſay. What? Were there ſuch côtrouerſies, diſcordes and frayes betwixt the Pope and Henrie the fift? Thê belyke yt is no very probable tale, that your Apology writeth, that by the Popes procuring thys Henry toke hys Father priſoner, as it is in dede a foule and a groſſe lye. Yet at the length I perceiue there was a frendly peace côclu-ded (as ye ſay) and the Pope with hys holy hand delyuered to hym ſuche pryuileges as his auncetours were wont to enioy. I am glad M. Horne that the popé hath anye thing holy in hym. It is ſtrâge me thinketh to heare at your hâds of the Popes holy hâd: namely ſeing your authour Naucle-rus, ſpeaketh ofhys hâd only, withowt any other additiô. Eelyke there is come vppon yow ſome ſodayne deuotion rowards the Popes holines. But lo, I ſee now the cauſe of your deuotiô. The Popes hâd is holy with yow now , whê he being forced âd côſtrayned, deliuereth vppe ſuch priui-leges, as with his heart he did not deliuer: and therfore did afterward in a Coûcel of Biſhops reuoke al theſe doinges. Whiche your authour in the nexte leaf (as alſo Sabellicus at large) doth declare: and what ſturre âd buſînes the Em-perour made for it, ſwearing firſt to the Pope, that he wold vſe no violence, and that he woulde cauſe all the Biſhops of Germany, which had bene made by Simonye, to be de-poſed. Who yet afterward brake bothe partes of his Othe.

A ſovvle lye of the Apo= logie of Englâde,

Dato ſibi per manû Apoſtolici priuilegio inueſtitu-ræ eccle-ſiaſtica. Nauclerus gener.38. In Late-ranenſi conuentu. Sabell. Aenead.9 lb.4.

Toke the Pope out of Rome with him as prifoner, becaufe he would not confirme his fymoniacal Bifshops : And after long vexation of the Pope, and fpoiles of the Romaine territorie, extorted at the lengthe by fine force his confente thereto : which yet (after the Emperour being departed) he reuoked (as I faid) in a ful Councell. And this periurie and violence of this Emperour, the Italian Emperours doe witneffe alfo. Briefly al came to this conclufion that Pafchalis being dead, the Emperour fhortly after, renounced to the Pope Califtus the .2. all this inuefturing of Bifshops, and left to the clergy the free electió without the princes cófirmatió: which was al that Pafchalis grañted to this Emperour. For the grañt of Pafchalis (as it is recorded in Nauclere) referreth it felfe , to the former grauntes of his predeceffours made to Catholike Emperours. And farder he fpecifieth his graunt thus. *That he haue priuilege to geue the*

Gener.33.
Pag.183.
&.191. *ftaffe and the ring to al Bifshops and Abbats of his dominions, being firft freely chofen without violence or fymonie: and to be afterward confecrated or ordered of the bifshop to whom they belong* But al this was (as I haue faid) both reuoked of Pope Pafchalis, and geuen ouer of Henrie the fift.

M.Horns
difsēbling
of his au·
thors nar
ration. But I pray you tell me, was your holy hand fo vnluftie and heauy, that ye could or rather would not, fet in this alfo, being a parcell of your authors narration, and the finall conclufion of this great controuerfie ? Whiche as it was the troblefom to the church many yeres: fo it is troblefom alfo to your Reader, as occupiyng a greate parte of your booke, but no part of your principal mater, and yet as litle material as it is, in fine al agaift you. And therfore ye fhake the ful declaratió of the mater from your holy handes, as a man would fhake away a fnake for feare of ftinging.

M.Horne

M. Horne. The.115. Diuision. pag.74.b.

The next Emperour to Henrie, vvas Lotharius, vvho so laboured vvith the Pope to retaine the inuesturing of Ecclesiasticall persons, and besides that, he so trauailed in other Ecciesiastical causes, so (.396.) vvel as Temporal, that saith Vrspurg. Huius laus est à vindicata religione & legibus: The praise of this Prince is, in that he resourmed Religion and the Lawes.

Next to vvhom, vvas Conradus the Emperour, to vvhome the Romaines vvrote supplications, to come and chalendge his right in these matters, to reduce the fourme of the Empire, to the olde state whiche it was in, in Constantine and Iustinians daies, and to deliuer them from the (.3 7) tyranny of the Pope. To vvhom also the Pope vvrote humble supplications, to take his cause into his protection against the Magistrates of Rome, which toke vppon them to reduce the Pope, to the olde order and state of the (.398.) aunciente bishoppes of Rome.

Stapleton.

Let the Emperour Lotharius labour to retain the inuesturing of Bishops (which as ye heard, Henrie the. 5. resigned before to Calistus) let him if ye will needes vse that word, reforme the ciuil lawes and religion to: the meaning wherof is no more, but that he restored the ciuil Lawe (the vse therof being discõtinued many yeres) ãd restored Pope Innocẽtius the.2 to his See beig thrust out by an Antipope (wherof he was called *Fidelis Ecclesiæ aduocatus*, a faithfull deféder of the Church). Yet why do you vtter such grosse lyes, M. Horne telling your Reader, that the Romaines besought th'Emperor *to deliuer them frõ the tyrãny of the Pope*? Neyther Otho Fringensis, nor Nauclerus, who rehearseth his words haue any such thing. The Romaines at that time would be lusty a Gods name, and reduce their state to the old magnificence of the victorious Romaines, being proud of a litle victorie whiche they had against the Tiburtines.

And

The.396.
Vntruth.
Not so
vvel by a
greate
deale,
Otto. Frisingen.

The.397.
vntruth.
Lewd and
grosse as
shall appeere.
Naucler.

The.398.
Vntruth.
Not of
the aunci-
ent Bis-
hops, but
of the old
heathen
Priestes.

And therefore the Pope complained to the Emperour of
their tyrannie, not they of the Popes tyrannie. Yea they
thrusted out the Emperours *Præfectus*, and placed in his
roome their owne *Patricius*. And so woulde shake of as
well the Emperour, as the Pope.　Foorth then with the
storie.

Let Pope Lucius. 2. make hūble supplicatiō, to the Emperour Conradus, againſt the Magiſtrates of Rome, cōcerning the ciuil regiment of Rome, and their ſubiection to
Naucl.
gener.39.
the Pope in temporalities (for that was the matter and no
other, and yet were they faine ſhortlye after to ſubmitte
them ſelues to Eugenius. 3. the next Pope) Let all this be
as you tell it not perſpicuouſlie, but couertlie, as though
the Romaines then woulde haue bene Schiſmatiques, as
you are nowe, and denied his Authoritie in Spiritual cauſes, as you doe nowe, let all this, as I ſaie, be graunted vnto you: But then I pray you ſet your concluſion to it, that
therefore the Prince is Supreme Gouernour in all cauſes
Eccleſiaſticall, and then ſhall euery childe ſone conclude
with you, that your Concluſion, concludeth nothinge to
the purpoſe.　For all the ſtrife and contention here, was
partely about Temporall and Ciuill regiment, partely not
againſt the Popes Authoritie, abſolutelye, but againſt ſuch
or ſuche a Pope: whiche thing I woulde haue you wel to
note, Maiſter Horne, not here onelye, but in all theſe and
other quarrellings of Emperours againſte Popes.　That
they neuer repined againſte the Popes Authoritie, as the
Pope, but they repined againſt this man or that mā, whom
they woulde not agniſe for the Pope, but ſome other by
them ſelues elected.

　　　　　　　　　　　　　　　　　M. Horne.

M. Horne. The. 116. Diuifion. pag. 74. b.

Next to vvhome, follovved the Godly and zelous Emperour Frederike the firfte, vvho (.399.) feeing the horrible vices of the Romifsh Church, commaunded that no Legate of the Church of Rome, fhould be fuffered to enter into Germanie, without he were called or hyred of the Emperour: nor would fuffer that any man vnder the name of appellation, fhuld goe vnto the Court of Rome.

The·399. Vntruth. Horrible and noto rious. as fhail ap= peare.

After the death of Adrian the fovvrth, the Cardinals fell out amongeft them felues for the Election of a nevv Pope : fome fly= xinge to haue Rovvlande, other fome contendinge to haue Octa= uian a man, (faith Abbat. Vrfpur.) in all points honeft and reli- gious. Herevppon fprang an horrible fchifme and great difcord. Rouland fent his Legates to the Emperour Fredericus, 1. and de- fired him that he vvould (.400.) take vppe and end this conten- tion by his authoritie. The Emperour commaundeth them both to come vnto him at Ticinum, vvhere foorthvvith he fummo- ned a Councell to be holden about this matter, (.401.) minding to examine bothe their caufes, and by fearching to trye vvhofe caufe vvas the moft honeft. Rouland (.402.) being afrayed to haue the matter come to this triall, getteth to VVilliam of Si- cilia, the Emperours mortall ennemie, and vvithin tvvelue daies putteth on his Cope, and nameth him felfe Alexander : for he pur- pofed (belike) to make a conqueft of the matter. He alleaged his election to be good out of all doubt, and that he fent for the Em- perours aid, and not for his arbitrement : and therfore thought not good to bring his cafe into doubtfull queftion. The Emperour being offended vvith him, for that he vvould not obey his appoint- ment, fent tvvo Bifhops to cite him, to come vnto the Councell by the name of Cardinall, and not Pope : But Rouland refufed, confuting their citation vvith this Maxime or Principle, Roma- num Pontificem à nemine iudicari debere : The Pope ought not to be iudged of anye man. But vvhen thefe Legates from the Emperour came to Octauian, he ftraight vvai- es obeyed, and they brought him to Papia (.404.). Vfpurg. faith, that Rouland vvas oftentimes monifshed to come: and did

Nauclerus.

Vrfpurg.

Sabellicus.

The 400. Vntruth. Falfe tranflation. vt feditionē tolleret. That he vvoulde take avvay the fe- dition, not take vp the matter to his ovvne arbitrement.

Vfpurg. The. 401. Vntruth. He minded no fuch matter as fhall ap= peare. The. 402 Vntruth. He vvas gon to this VVilliam be- fore he vvrote to Frederike, by Nau= clerus. The 403. Vntruth. That appeareth not in Platina or Nauclerus. The. 404 vntruth. In omitting the next fentēce vvhe= rein the Popes Pri= macie ouer the Em perour is manifeft= lie declared.

contemne

The.405.
vntruth.
For he
had none
to geue
in that
behalfe.
The. 406.
vntruth.
In leuing
out that
which
foloweth
Per vrbē
equo insi=
dentē dedu
citet de
more ado=
rat which
sheweth
plainely
the Empe
rours in=
feriour-
nes, not
primacy.
The. 407
vntruth.
Rayling
ribauldry
*If the
only, thē
hovv is
the Price
gouer-
nour?
Or if the
Prince
notvvith
stādingis,
vvhi mai
not also
the Pope
bes

contemne all those monitions. The Emperour satte in the Councel, (as Radeuicus Frisingēsis, vvho vvrote his actes, vvitnesseth) ād made an oration vnto the Bishoppes, vvherein he declareth, and that by the example of
his aunceftours Constantinus, Theodosius, Iustinianus, and of later
time of Carolus Magnus, and other, that the povver and authority te
call Councelles, vvhere the Churche is troubled vvith any schismes, or other
perillous distourbance, belongeth to the Emperour: Notvvithstanding he cōmitted the defining of the cōtrouersie to theyr vvisedome, and (.405.) gaue
them thereunto authoritie. The Councell debateth the cause, and consulteth vvith men learned in the Lavve, and so concludeth, that Octa-
uians election vvas good, and adiudgeth him to be the righte Bishoppe of
Rome. VVhē they had thus tryed out the matter, Fredericus the Emperour saith Platina) Confirmat Octauianum Pontificem. Confirmed Octauian Pope. (.406.) The Emperour vvithin a vvhile after,
sente Octauianus, newv confirmed Pope, tovvardes Rome, vvho dyed in the
iourney. After vvhose death, the Emperour called an other councell at
VVirtzberge (as Auentinus vvriteth) vvherein vvere a great number of
Archebishoppes, and other Bishoppes, ād also many of the nobles and states
of the Empyre. In this Councell a statute or Decree vvas made by common
consente. That from hence fooorth none shoulde be Pope, ones
lesse he were created by the consent of the Emperour, accordinge as the custome had bene of longe and auncient time.
This vvorthy Emperour, vvhom the Chroniclers call Christianissimum,
moste Christian, for his zeale tovvardes Goddes Churche, endeuored not
vvithout great perill to him selfe and his estate, to reteine the iurisdiction
due to the Princes, and thereby to refourme the horrible disorders that vvere
grovven so highe, that they ouervvhelmed the Church, as in lyke sorte diuers
other Emperours end Kinges, bothe before and after, had attempted. but in
vayne: for the vvealthy pride, the fierce povver, and (.407.) trayterous
treachery of the Pope and his Prelates vvas so mighty, violent, and subtile, that there vvas no earthly povver able to vvithstande or matche vvith
them. And therefore Erasmus compteth the Popes of this time, and those
that folovved, to be the Vicars and successours of Iulius Cæsar, of Alexander the Great, of Crœsus the ryche, and of Xerxes the mighty: rather then of Christe, the onelye * Emperour and gouernour of the
Churche. Bernarde calleth Eugenius. 3. in his great pompe, and

pride

pride,rather the ſucceſſour of Conſtantinus *the highe Emperour,then of Peter the humble Apoſtle,* and Abbas Vrſpurg, *vvho lyued at this time, vvhen the Popes had ſpoyled the Emperour, and other Princes vvelnighe of* (.408.) *all iuriſdiction,rulinge all by theyr ovvne Decretalles,novve aboute this time ſet foorth* (.409.) *as they liſted,maketh a lamentable complainte of the horrible pryde and couetouſneſſe of the* (.410.) *vvhole clergy, and cō cludeth vvith theſe vvords:* Gaude mater noſtra Roma,&c. Reioyce O our mother Rome, bycauſe the ſcluſes of the hidden trea- ſures in the earthe are opened,that riuers ād heapes of mony maye flowe vnto thee in great abundance. Be glad of the ini- quitie of the ſonnes of mē, bicauſe mony is geuen to thee for the recompence of ſo great euilles . Be mery and iocund for diſcordes ſake, which is thy helper bicauſe ſhe is ruſhte out of the infernall pit,that plentiful rewardes of money might be heaped vpon the:thou haſt that which thou haſt alwaies thyrſted after : ſynge pleaſant balades, tor throughe mennes malitiouſneſſe,not by thyGodlineſſe,thou haſt ouercome the worlde.

The.408. and.409, vntruths bothe ſlaundeſ rours, neuer able to be proued. The.410. vntruth. For he ſpeaketh only of the clergi of Rome.

The.18.Chapter:Of Frederike Barbaroſſa,and of Alexander. the.3.

Stapleton.

MAiſter Horne good Reader,as he hath hitherto, ſo doth he ſtyll playe Cacus parte . This Cacus ſtole Hercules Oxen,and becauſe he woulde not haue them eſpied where they were by the track, he drewe thē into his caue by the tayles backward. Whiche thing Her- cules ſeing,did nothing miſtruſt they ſhoulde be there, but yet as he paſſed by with the droue of his beaſtes,the beaſts that were in the denne lackinge theyr company, beganne as the maner is to bellowe,wherby all this thefte was diſ- cried This boke of M.Hornes is the very denne of Cacus, into the which by a pretye ſleight , he conueyeth in hys ſtories and other prouſes, as a man maye ſay, by the

T.Liuius. Lib.1. Dec.1.

M.Horne playeth Cacus his parte, that ſtole Hercules Oxen.

c c   tayle

taile backewarde, that is not keeping the righte and cu-
ftomable waie and order in making true and faithfull allegations, but craftelie and peruerfely cutting and chopping
away fome parte of them : which partely lying in this his
Cacus denne, and as it were bellowing for his companie,
bewrayeth all M. Hornes flie dealings. So haue ye hitherto found it, and fo fhall ye ftill, good Reader, finde it, and
loe we haue at hande a ready proufe. Frederike. faith M.
Horne, *feing the horrible vices of the Romifh Church, commaunded that no Legate of the Church of Rome, fhould come
into Germanie, &c.*

 Firft, Maifter Horne, what *horrible vices of the Romiſſh
Churche* were thofe you fpeake of? It is verely, naughte
els, then a horrible lye of your fchifmatical mouth. The
beginning of the fentence, of the whiche you haue taken
the taile onely, is this. Adrian the.4. our Countrieman,
and Frederike the firft, were fallen at great variaunce.

Naucler.
gener.39.
pag.217. *The Pope complained* (faith Nauclerus your own Authour)
*that liuing betwene the fwordes of the Romaiues and William
of Sicilie, he was forfaken of the Emperoure, contrarye to his
great promifes, and fo vexed for the Emperours fake, that he
could not reaft at Rome. The Emperoure on the other fide,
pretended many things, and namely the crowning of William
the King of Sicilia : Iamque ad id vfque proceſſum eſt, vt Imperator nullum Rom. Ecclefiæ legatum, &c.* And now the
matter broke out fo farre, that the Emperour comaunded that
no Legate, and fo forth, as in Maifter Hornes Allegation.
You fee nowe, good Readers, it was no *horrible vices of
the Romifh Church* as this horrible lying fpirit of M. Horn
prateth, but a priuate quarrell betwene this Emperoure
and that Pope, that occafioned the Emperour to forbidde
            appel-

appellations to Rome , &c.   You fee howe this Cacus
hathe drawen Nauclerus his woordes by the tayle into
the lurkinge denne of his lying Conclafion.   And that
their fellowes nowe drawing nere to the others companie , the former ioyned with the later, haue euidentlye
betrayed the notable thefte of this lying and theeuinge
Cacus.

But Maifter Horne,fuppofing the Emperour vpon fuch
refpecte had fo done, tell vs,is the doings of this one Emperour , fo preiudiciall to our caufe , and fo authorifed a-
boue al exception or plea,that becaufe he did fo, we muft
ftraightwaies côfeffe he did wel and laufully ? Me thinke it
were reafon ye fhould proue this withal. Wel let this goe,
we wil not charge you at this time fo ftraightly. Yet this
queftiô I muft nedes afke you· Whether this was fo done
becaufe he thought the Pope or See of Rome had no authoritie,or for fome priuate grudge and quarell not againft
the See and Pope, but againft this Pope.

Yf ye will faye (as ye muft nedes faye this quarrel was
but a priuate and a perfonall quarrell, then is the ordinarie
authoritie as yet nothing acrafed hereby , but your Argumente is then muche acrafed.   Yf ye will fay, he denied, as ye now doe, all maner of authoritie of the See of
Rome, then muft I aunfwere you : It is not fo.For he was
crowned of this Pope called *Adrianus Quartus*, an Englifhe man : and fubmitted himfelfe after to Alexander the
thirde,as we fhall anon fee.   And further I muft anfwere
you, that you are the verye Cacus we fpake of, and that
thefe ftolê allegations fiom Nauclerus do bellow wanting
their companie, and doe difcrie all your theeuifh conuey-
aunce as we haue before declared.

Now next hath M. Horne found a Rouland for an Oli-
uer: a diſſenſion betwixt Roulande and Octauian for the
Papacie. For the appeaſing wherof, this Frederike called
a Councell, and at length the matter being heard, confirmed Octauian, who was called Victor the. 3. as the other
was called Alexander the.3. which name miniſtreth matter of mery paſtime to M. Horne to ſolace him ſelfe withal, as though Alexander named him ſelf ſo, for that *he pur-
poſed(belike)to make a cōqueſt of the mater.* And here is daſſhed in the margēt, to ſet forth ād beutify his narratiō withal, firſt, Vrſpergenſis, then Nauclerus, then Sabellicus, then
Platina, then Nauclerus againe, then beſide Radeuicus Fri-
ſingenſis in his text, Platina, and then Vrſpergenſis againe.
As though he tooke diſtinct and ſeuerall matter from eche

*Frederic. Octauianū
Pontificem cōfirmat,
eumque albo equo in
ſidentē per vrbē Tici-
nenſem ducit, & de
more adorat.
Platina in Alex.3.
Tunc Epiſc. ad pedes
ſe Octauiani proſter-
nūt. Imperator quo-
que id ipſum fecit, vt
ab eo indulgentiā ac-
ciperent,& ſibi obe-
dientiam facerent.
Vſpurg.
Quem Imperator in
Concilio Papā decla-
ratū adorauit, & e
quū eius de more per
vrbem deduxit.*
one. Whereas in a manner al they runne one way:
and wherof I am moſt aſſured, al againſt M. Hornes
owne Primacie:part of their teſtimonies being cut
of from eche of them, and ſo caried craftely by M.
Horn into his Cacus caue, bewraieth al M. Horns
theft. Wil ye proue the like regiment, M. Horne,
by Frederike his doings, that ye now maintaine?
Goe to then, and ſee ye proue it vs ſubſtantiallye.
He refuſed ye ſay Pope Rouland: yet he receiued
Pope Octauian, and confirmed him too, as ye ſay,
yea and ledde him about the Citie of Pauia ſitting
vppon a white Horſe, and then adored him too,
as I with Platina and Nauclerus ſaye, or as Vſpur-
genſis ſaieth, fell flatte before his feete, to receiue
pardon, and to become his obedienſarie. Al which
ye ſaye not, and therefore, I heare Hercules ſto-
len oxen bellowe out of Cacus denne.

Why

Barba
rossa.

Why Maister Horne can your eares paciently abide al
this? And is your Octauian for all this, as ye write, *a mã
in all pointes honest and relligious*? Some thing I perceiue
there was, that he is made a Saint after his death, and that
as it is said, there were many miracles done at his Tombe
in Luca, where he was buried before the Image of Nico-
demus. Can your ftomake difgeft all this Maifter Horn?
And can you fuffer your Supreme head, like a flaue to kiffe
the Popes feete, and to become the Maifter of his Horfe?
Can ye fuffer Miracles at the Popes tombe, and yet notwithftanding fhall he be *a man in all points honeft and religioufe?* How chance we haue not at the leaft for your cõfort one pretie nip,ãd to tel vs that he called hĩ felf Victor,
for that he entéded to be a victorious Cóquerer, as he was
in deede vppon your Supreame head the Emperour Frederike? Surely I maruaile why ye fhoulde fo fauourably
encline to this falfe Antipope,rather then to the true Pope
in dede, which was Rouland,who as Platina writeth, was
elected of.22.Cardinals: and your Octauian but of.3.onlye.
And therfore was he,and Frederik that mainteined hĩ, and
not Rouland,the occafion of the horrible fchifme ye fpeak
of.And this Rouland was euer ãd is takẽ for the true Pope,
yea and was fo taken at length by your Frederike alfo cõming to him to Venice, and kifsing his holy feete (for feeing ye haue made the Popes hand holye, I willbe fo bolde
to make his feete holy too) and ratifiyng and allowing him
by that humilitye, to be the Supreme heade of Chriftes
Churche. And fo at the length (for all your iefting) Alexander hath made as great a conquefte vppon your falfe
lying booke, and new fet vppe Primacie, as euer did the
great Alexander vpon King Darius.

Naucler.
gener.39.

Supra in
the.114.
Diuifion.

But

But lo,now ye and your companions, that can beare with Victors conqueste, can not beare,the matter being all one, the lyke in Alexander. Wherin I fee no reafon, but that perchaunce ye take Victor to be of your nighe coufinage, for that he was,as ye are,a great fchifmatike. And therfore thoughe Friderike did fuffer at the hands, yea and at the feete to of Victor, as he did at Alexanders, yet roreth

owte your Apologie againft hym,that he put yll fauored-ly and móftruouflie this Emperours neck vnder his feete. Whiche femeth to be but a fable of fuch as be parcial wri-ters,and wedded to theyre affectiós, to flaunder the Pope withal, as Carion and fuche other are that write yt: Al-thoughe fome catholyks perchaunce, reporte the fame as dothe Nauclerus,but with an addition.*vel vt Blondus fcri-bit,poftquàm Pontificis pedes imperator exofculatus eft, ad al-tare maius ambo principes fe amplexati & exofculati funt*. So that Nauclerus,whiche thowghe catholyke, yet muche inclinable as the Germans cómóly are to the Emperours parte,femeth rather to lyke the narration of Blondus, that théperour did no other thé the vfual honor in kyfsing the Popes feet. And if the tale of th'Apology were true(which M.Fox doth alfo with a ioly gay picture fet forth)thowgh yt make not for the commendation of the Popes modera-tion and humility,yet yt maketh for hys fupreame authori-ty. I obey fayeth the Emperour, *not to thee , but to Peter whome thow doeft fuccede*.

But to thentent that you M. Horne with the Apologie and M.Foxe who alwaies like beftly fwyne do noufell in the donge,and vente vp the worfte that may be founde againft Popes and prelates,may haue a iufte occafió(if any Charity be in you) to cómende the great moderation of
this

this Pope Alexander 3.you may remember, that this is he, to whō being in extreme misery through the oppressiō of the Almayne Army,spoyling ād wasting al aboute Rome, Emanuel then Emperour in the East, sent embassadours, promysing bothe a great hoste againft the Almayne Emperour Friderike,and also a vniō of the Grecians with the Romain Church,if he would suffer the Romain Empire,so lōge diuided(frō the time of Charlemayn)to come agayne to one heade and Empire : to whome also (being then in baniſhment)the sayde Emperour sent a seconde embaſsy, with great quantytie of mony, promysing to reduce the whole Eaſt Churche vnder the subiection of the Weſt, all Grece vnder Rome, if he woulde reſtore to the Emperour of Conſtantinople the Crowne of the Weſt Empire, from the which Frederike seemed nowe rightlye and worthely to be depriued. To all which this Pope (notwithſtanding the greate miseries he ſtode presentlye in, and was daily like to suffer through the power of this Frederike) answered . *Se nolle id in vnum coniungere, quod olim de induſtria maiores sui disiunxiſsent* . That he woulde not ioyne that into one, which his Forefathers of olde time had of purpose diuided . You will not I trowe denie M.Horne(all circumſtances duely cōsidered)but that this was a very great ād rare moderatiō of this Pope Alexāder 3. more worthy to be set forth in figures ād pictures to the poſteryty for sober and vertuous,then that facte of him whiche Mayſter Fox hath so blased oute , for prowde and haſty. Except your Charyties be suche (as verely it semeth to be) that you take more delight in vice then in vertue, and had rather heare one lewde fact of a Pope, then

Naucler. gener.39. pag.225.

Pag.226.

1.Cor.13.
Prote-
stants
lacke
true
Charyty.

then twenty good.If it be so with you, then is there no Charyte with you. For Charyte, as S. Paule describeth it, *Thinketh not euill,reioyseth not vpon iniquyte , but reioyseth with verytie.It suffreth all thinges,it beleueth all thinges , it hopeth al thinges,it beareth all thinges.*Contraryewyse,you not only thinke,but reporte alwaies the worst:you reioyse and take greate pleasure vpon the iniquytie of such as you ought most of all men to reuerence: you are sorye to haue the veryty and truthe tolde you. You suffer and beare no-thing in the Church:But for the euil life of a fewe you for-sake the Cōmunion and societie of the whole. You beleue as much as pleaseth you,and you hope accordingly. And thus muche by the way ones for all,touching your greate ambition and desire to speake euil of the Popes,and to re-porte the worste you can doe of them : which you in this booke M. Horne haue done so plentifullye and exactlye

Nō vt iu-
dicaret
eos,aut
causam se
dis Aposto
lica,sed
vt à pru-
dentibus
viris ad-
disceret,
cui electo
obedire
potius de-
beret.
Vrsperg.

throughe this whole processe, of the Princes practise in Ecclesiasticall gouernment, as if the euill life of some Popes were a direct and sufficient argument to proue all Princes Supreme Gouernours in al thinges and causes Ec-clesiasticall.

I coulde now shewe you other authorityes and places oute of your owne authours concerninge thys storye, of Friderike the first making directlie againste you, and wherein ye haue played the Cacus. As where ye wryte by the authoritie of Vrspergensis,that the Emperour sent for both theis Popes to come to hym,*mynding to examine both theyre causes*. For yt followeth by and by: *not to iudge them,or the cause of the Apostolique see: but that he might learne of wise men , to whether of them he shoulde rather obey.*

And

And is not this thinke you M. Horne, ſo craftely to cut of,
and ſteale away this ſentence from your reader, a preatye
pageant of Cacus? Namely ſeing your authour Nauclerus *Gener.39.*
writeth alſo the like? And ſeyng ye demeane your ſelfe ſo
vnhoneſtly, and vnclerkly in the principall matter, who
will nowe care for your extraordinarye and fooliſhe falſe M. Horns
excurſions, againſt the welthy pride, the fearce power, dinarye
the trayterouſe trecherie of Popes at that tyme? Or for procelſe
Eraſmus comparing the Popes to the ſucceſſours of Iu- ad lcwde
lius Cæſar? Or for Vrſpergenſis owtcries, againſt their rayling.
couetouſnes, and not againſte the Popes authoritye? As
for S. Bernarde, who, you ſay founde faulte with the
pompe and pride of Eugenius. 3. how clerely he pronounceth (that not withſtanding) for the Popes Primacy, I
referre you(to be ſhorte)to the Confutation of your lying *Confu.fol.*
Apologie. Al this impertinent rayling rhetorike, we freely 210.
leaue ouer vnto you,to rayle and rolle your ſelf therein,til
your tóg be wery againe,yfye wil,for any thíg that ſhal let
you.Only as I haue ofté ſaid, I deſire the Reader to marke,
that as wel this,as other emperors,were not at variáce with
the See Apoſtolike it ſelf,or ſet againſt the Popes Authority abſolutely,but were at variaunce,with ſuch a pope and
ſuch,and were ſet againſt this mans or that mans election,
not renouncing the Pope, but renouncing this man or that
man,as not the true and right Pope.

M. Horne. The.117. Diuiſion. pag.76.a.

*About this tyme,the King of Cicilia and Apulia, had a diſpenſation from
the Pope for money,to Inueſture Archebiſhops with ſtaffe or cro-* Otto Fri-
ſier,ringe,palle,myter, ſandalles or ſlippers:and that the Pope *gingēſis.*
might ſende into his dominions no Legate, onleſſe the kinge
ſhould ſende for him.

dd Staple-

England
land
before

Vid.de hoc
Nau.gen.
41 p.287.
& 288.

Stapleton.

Did the Kings of Sicilia procure a difpenſation as ye ſay M. Horne from the Pope to inueſture biſſhops and to receyue no Legate? Who was then the ſupreame heade I praye you, the Pope that gaue the difpenſation, or the King that procured yt? Ye ſee, good readers, howe ſauerlye and hanſomly this man, after his olde guiſe, concludeth, againſt him ſelf.

M. Horne. The. 118. Diuiſion. pag. 76. a.

Of (.411.) the doigs of the Kings of this Realme, in Ecclel. matters, before the Conqueſt looke in the bok De poteſtate Regia ſet out by the Prelats, 26 Hen. 8.

* *Polychron.*

Polychro. Fabian.
Polychro. Fabian.
The. 412. vntruthe. For al this vvas but one Councell.

The. 411. vntruthe. Fabiā ſaith not ſo: neither by the ſtory appeareth ſo.

Polychron.

Fabian. Polychron.

Our Engliſh Chronicles make report, that the Kings of this Realme, had not altogeather leaſte of their dealing in Churche matters, but continued in parte their iuriſdiction aboute Eccleſiaſticall cauſes, although not vvithout ſome trouble. * The Popes Legate came into Englande, and made a Coūcel by the aſſent of King VVilliam the Conquerour. And after that in an (.412.) other Coūcel at VVincheſter, * were put downe many Biſshops, Abbatts, and priours by the procuremēt of the King. The King gaue to Lāfranke the Archbiſshoprike of Cantorb. and on our Ladye daie the Aſſumption made him Archebiſshoppe. On whit Sonday, he gaue the Archbiſshoprike of Yorke, vnto Thomas a Canon of Bayon. VVhen Thomas ſhoulde haue bene conſecrated of Lanfranke, there fell a ſtrife betvvixt them, about the liberties of the Church of Yorke. The controuerſie being about Church matters, vvas brought and referred to the Kinges (.413.) iudgement., and Thomas by the Kinges commaundement, was faine to come to Lanfrank to be ſacred. And aftervvard, vvhen there grevve greater contention betvvixt theſe tvvayne about Churche matters, the Biſſhop of Rome remitted the matter to be determined before the Kinge, and the Biſshops of Englande, and ſo at VVindeſour before Kinge VVilliam and the Cleargy, the cauſe was treated. Alſo an other cauſe vvas meued before the King of the miſorder of Thurſtan, whome the Kinge

King had made Abbot of Glaſtonbury, by whoſe iudgement the Abbot was chaunged, and tourned to his
owne Abbay in Normandye: but the Monkes (.414.)
ſcattered aboute by the Kings heſt. After this the King
beſtowed many Biſshoprikes on his Chaplaines, *as
London, Norvviche, Cheſter, Couentry, &c*. And ruled both
temporalty and the ſpiritualty at his owne wil: *ſaithe
Polychronicon.* He tooke noman fro the Pope in his lãd,
(*he meaneth that the Kinge vvoulde ſuffer no Legate to enter
into the lande from the Pope*) but he came and pleaſed him:
he ſuffred no Coũcel made in his own coũtrey without his own leaue: Alſo he woulde nothing ſuffer in
ſuch a councel, but as he woulde aſſent. So (.415.) *that
in geuing, or tranſlating of ſpiritual promocions, in geuing his aſſent to Councels, and ſuffring nothing to paſſe vvithout his conſent, in hearing and determining Eccleſiaſticall cauſes, in reſt-
reining the Popes liberty, vvithout his ſpeciall licence, and in ruling the ſpiritualty at his ovvn vvil: King VVilliã ſheuueth plain,
that he (.416.) tooke him ſelf for the ſupreame gouernour vvithin
this Realm in al maner of cauſes, ſo vvel Eccleſiaſtical as Temporall.*

The.414.vntruth. They vvere ſpred into diuers houſes, ſaith Fabian. which you leaue out.

Polychion.

The.415 vntruthe. This, So that, ſolo vveth not, as ſhall appeare.

The.416. vntruth. He neuer toke hĩ ſelf, ior ſuch.

*The.19.Chapter: Of England before the Conqueſte, Of William
the Conquerour, Ruſus his Sonne, and Henry the
firſt, Kinges of Englande.*

Stapleton.

GOod readers, I do moſt hartely beſeche you, euen as
ye tender either the truth, or the ſaluation of your
ſowles, to haue a good and a ſpeciall regarde to M.
Hornes narration nowe following. For now at the length
is M. Horn come frõ his long and vnfruitfull wandering in
Spaine, Fraunce, Italie, Germany, and other countries, to
our own natiue contrey. Now, where as the late doings in

our Countrè are fuche, as we haue fequeftred our felues frõ the common and viuall obedience, that all other contries concerning authority in matters ecclefiafticall euer gaue, with a fingular and peerleffe preeminence to the fee of Rome, and do yet fequefter, the more pittie, our felues day-lie more and more, makinge none accompte of other good princes doings and prefidents in this behalf, and pretending partly in the acts of parliament, partly in the newe englifhe bokes, and daylie fermons, that this is no newe or ftraunge example in England, to exclude the Pope from all maner fpiritual iurifdiction to be exercifed and practifed there by hym: yt behoued our proteftants, efpeciallie M. Horne in thys his boke, that what fo euer his proufes were for other countries, yet for fome conuenient prouf of the olde pra-ctife concerning his newe primacie in Englande, to haue wrowght his matters fo fubftancially, that at leaftwife, for our owne Countre, he fhulde haue browght forth good aũ-cient and autentique matter. And wil ye nowe fee the wife and euen dealinge of thefe proteftant prelats? Where they pynne vp all our proufes, wythin vj. hundred yeares after Chrift: and what fo euer we bring after, theyr Iewell tel-leth vs ful merelie we come to late, M. Horne in this mat-ter of Supreamacie moft weightie to the poore catholiks, the deniyng thereof being more greauoufly punifhed by la wes, then anie other matter nowe lying in controuerfie betwene the catholyks and proteftantes in Englande: M. Horne I fay, for thys his owne country, which as approued Chroniclers reporte, and as him felf after alleageth, did firft of al the Romã prouinces, publiquely embrace Chriftes rel-ligion: for one thoufand yeares, ftandeth mute. And belike thinking that William Conquerour had conquered afwell

al the

Confyder the fub-ftantiall handling of the matter by M. Horn for Eng-lande.

M. Horn for the firfte thoufand yeares fhevveth no exam-ple of his primacie practifed then in Britannie Fol. 93. Col. 2.

all the olde catholyke fayth in Englande, as the Lande and people, fanſieth a duble conqueſte, one vppon the goods and bodies, the other vppon the ſowles and faythe of the Engliſhe men. But what ſhall I nowe ſay to this noble and worthie Champion? ſhall I dryue hym a litle backe, with M. Iewels peremptory challenge and tel him, that he commeth to late by almoſte fyue hundred yeares? Or ſhall I deale more freely and liberally with him, then M. Iewell doth whith vs, and bydde hym take the beſte helpe he can for hym ſelf? Verely M. Horne had nede I did ſo: And yet all will be to lytle for his purpoſe: aſwell for that after the conqueſt he hath no ſufficient prouf, for his pretenſed ſupremacy, as for that, what prouf ſo euer he bringeth, yt muſt yelde and geue place to the firſt thouſand yeares, whiche beare ful teſtimonie for the Popes primacie laufully practiſed in our realme before the conqueſt.

M. Horne begioeth his newe primacie vvith vvilliam conquerour, as hovv, h he had coquered both the lande and the fayth vvithall.

It were now a matter for to fyll a large volume withal, to runne a longe by theſe thowſand yeares, and to ſhewe what prouf we haue for the popes primacy before the conqueſt. My anſwere woulde waxe to bigge and to prolixe yf I ſhoulde ſo doe. But I will onelie putte the good reader in remembraunce of a matter or two: I muſte therefore pluck M. Horne backe from Williams conqueſt and deſire him to remember an other, and a better, and more aunciente conqueſte with al, in Britannie, then Williams was, yea aboute ix. hundred yeares before: when this Ilelande of Britanie was firſte delyuered from the tyrannicall yoke, and miſerable bondage of dyueliſh idolatrie: But by whom M. Horne? Suerlie by pope Eleutherius, to whome kinge Lucius ſente letters deſiringe hym, that by his commaundement he mighte be chriſtened. Fugatius and Damianus

Proufs fo the popes ſupremacie in Britanie before the Saxons came. Beda hiſt. Ang.lib.1. cap.4.

*Obſecrās,
vt per eiⁱ
māndatū
Chriſtiā⁹
efficeretur
King Lu
ciˢ ād the
realme
Chriſteⁱ
ned bi the
popes le⁴
gates.*

*Ireneus
li.3 ca.3.
Ad hāc e-
nim prop-
ter poten-
tiorē prin
cipalitatē
neceſſe eſt
oēm coue-
nire Eccle
ſiam , hoc
eſt,eos qui
ſunt vndi-
que fide-
les,in qua
ſemper ab
hijsqui siſt
vndiq; cō-
ſeruat aeſt
ea,qua eſt
ab apoſto
lis :traditis.Beda li.1.cap.13.Proſper inChronic.*

nus(whoſe holy reliques are thought to be now in Wales,
and whoſe holy remembraunce churches there dedicated
to God, in their name,doe to this day kepe and preſerue as
it were freſh and immortall) ſent to England by the ſayed
Eleutherius , did moſt godly and wonderfully ¦worke thys
great conqueſte . If I ſhould nowe aſke M. Horne, what
Lucius meant to ſend ſo farre for inſtructours and teachers
of the Chriſtian fayth , namely Fraunce beyng at hande :
where about thys tyme the Chriſtian Churches were adorned wyth many learned Biſhoppes and Martyrs: though
he woulde perchaunce ſeeke manie a pretye ſhyfte , to
ſhyfte awaye thys demaunde , yet ſhould he neuer make
any good and ſufficiente aunſweare , vntyll he confeſſed
the Popes primacye , to be the verie cauſe to ſend ſo farre
of. The which the bleſſed Martyr of God and great learned Biſhoppe of Lyons in Fraunce Ireneus writyng in the
tyme of our firſte Apoſtle Eleutherius doth confeſſe,wri-
tyng : *That all Churches muſte agree wyth the Churche of
Rome , for that the ſayed Churche hath the greater principalitie , and for that the traditions of the Apoſtles haue euer
bene kept there* .

   In caſe nowe the pope had nothing to doe in matters
eccleſiaſticall within this Ileland in the tyme of the olde
Britaines,why did pope Celeſtinus appoint to the Scottes,
theyr firſte Biſhop Palladius as Proſper writeth a notable
Chronicler of that age ? Why dyd he alſo ſend into thys
Ileland S . Germaine Biſhoppe of Antiſiodorum, to bryng
by the Apoſtolicall Authoritie the Britaynes from the hereſye of the Pelagians , as the ſayed Proſper witneſſeth ?

   Lett vs nowe come to the tyme of the Saxons con-
                            uerted

The Conqueſt.

uerted by S. Auguſtine : And then ſhall we fynd ſo manie, and ſo full teſtimonies both of the popes primacie , and of the princes ſubiection , as I trowe M · Horne him ſelfe , as impudent as he is, can not, nor will not denie them. Which I do ouerpaſſe, by reaſon they are readely to be foūd in our worthy coūtriemā S. Bede, lately ſet forth by me in the En-gliſh tongue, and in the Fortreſſe alſo adioyned to the ſame ſtorie, I will nowe adde this only, that from the time wher-in Beda endeth his ſtorie , to the conqueſt of the foreſaied William , there appeareth in our domeſticall ſtories a per-petuall and continuall practiſe of the ſaied primacie in this realme by the popes, as well in thoſe bookes as be extant in printe, as in other: As in *Aſſerius Meneuenſ.* that continu-eth the ſtorie from the death of Bede , to the yeare of our Lorde. 914. in Henricus Huntingtonienſis, Gulielmus Mal-mesburienſis, Alphredus Beuerlacenſis, Rogerus Houede-nus, Florilegiū, ſiue Mattheus Weſtmonaſterienſis, Chro-nica Iohānis Londonienſis, and many other yet not printed (that I haue not ſene) and which are hard to be ſene , by reaſon of the greate ſpoyle of ſuch kind of bookes of late made, in the ſuppreſſing of monaſteries and colleges . The which ſuppreſſion, and it were for nothing elſe, but for the loſſe of ſo many worthy Chroniclers, can not be to much lamented, the loſſe being incomparably greater , then the loſſe of any princes treaſure . The caſe is nowe to be pi-tyed , for that the verie Librarie of the Vniuerſitie of Ox-forde hath felt the rage of this ſpiteful ſpoile , not ſo much as one booke at this howre there remaining. This is one of the worthy fruits of your new ghoſpel M. Horne. As appe-reth alſo by the late vprores in theſe low Coūtries wher by the Gueſes , not onely the Monaſteries , but the Libraries alſo

Pope Celeſtinus practiſed his ſupre-macye in the Saxōs tyme.

The Po-pes ſupre-macie in Englande ſithence the Saxōs time. *Beda. lib.* 1 *ca.*29.*li,* 3.*ca.* 14. 22. *&* 25. *li.* 2. *c.* 4. *& 19.*

Fortreſſe. par. 2. c. 8. A cōplaīt for defa-cing of Libraries

alſo (namelye of the grey friers in Antwerpe) be
moſt ſhamefully defaced, the bookes burnt to aſhes,
and the olde monuments deſtroyed. The naming of
Oxforde, bringeth to my remembrance the noble
and worthy foūder of the vniuerſity there, I meane
Kinge Alurede. In whoſe tyme there was at Rome
a ſpecial ſchole or colledge, for Engliſh mē, priuileged ād exēpted frō al taxe ād tollages, by pope Martin the. 2. at the deſire of this King. Who ſent to him
for a gift a peece of the holy croſſe. This King beig
learned hiſelf loued entierly learned mē, eſpecially
Ioānes Scotus, that trāſlated out of the Greeke tōg
the works of Dionyſius Areopagita: whoō he vſed
moſte familiarly. This Alurede, being but yet yong,
was ſent by the Kinge Edeluulphus his father to
Rome accompanied with many noble men, where
pope Leo the. 4. did confirme him, and toke him as
his ſonne by adoption, and did alſo annoynte and
conſecrate him King of Englande. The manifolde
practiſe of the ſaid primacy continued from this
Kings tyme, euen to the tyme, and in the tyme of
bleſſed S. Edward, the immediate predeceſſour of
William, ſauing Harolde who reigned not one full
yeare. In the twenty yeare of the ſaid King Edwarde, the bleſſed man Wulſtanus, that was before a monk and prior there, was conſecrated biſſhop of Worceter. A man of ſuche notable vertue,
and ſuch auſterity of lyfe, as he reſembled the olde
vertuouſe and renowned religiouſe men. As one
that among all other his notable qualities, continued ſo in praying, ſtudiyng and faſting, that ſomtimes

tymes in foure dayes and foure nights he neuer ſlepte: and that litle reſte which he toke, was vpon a foorme in the Churche, vſing none other bolſterre, but his booke, wher-in he prayed or ſtudied. This man, I ſaye, was made biſhop, and confirmed by the popes Legats being then in the realm before the Cõqueſte. Our authour doth not write this of vncertain hereſay, but of certain knowledge, as a mã of that age, and one, that as it ſemeth, had ſene this bleſſed man, ãd talked with him.

He vvas cõfirmed by the popes le-gats be-fore the cõqueſt. Henry Hũtingto.

To diſcourſe vpon other particularities as vpon the con-tinual appeale to Rome, vpon willes, charteres, and ſuch o-ther writings ſent from Rome, to auoide tediouſnes I doe purpoſely forbeare. But I will nowe notifie to the good reader two thĩgs only. Firſt that from the tyme of the good Kinge Offa (in the yere of our Lord.760.) who gaue after the example of Inas not long before him, to the Pope as to the Vicare of S. Peter, the Peter pence, euen to the cõqueſt the payment of the ſaid Peter pence hath continued: and they were frõ tyme to tyme leuied, the Kings taking good diligent order, for the ſure paymente of the ſame. Second-ly that from the tyme of S. Auguſtine, the firſt Archebiſ-ſhop among the Saxons, both he and al other Archebiſhops euen to the conqueſt receaued their palle from Rome: an infallible token of their ſubiectiõ to the Pope, as Peters ſuc-ceſſour, vpon whoſe holy tombe, the palle is firſt layed, ãd after taken of, and ſente to the Archebiſſhop. As theſe two tokens of ſubiection cõtinued frõ tyme to time, to the con-queſte: ſo they continewed alſo without any interruption, (onleſſe it were verie ſeldome, and for a litle ſpace by rea-ſon of ſome priuate controuerſie, betwixte the Pope and the Kinge) euen from thence to our freſhe memorie, be-

Idem Hẽr. Hunting. Polid.l.4. The con-tinual pra-ctiſe of the popes Primacy in the re-alme of England before the con-queſte in payinge the Peter pence, ãd receiuing the palle.

ſide

fide many notable things otherwife in this realme fince the conqueft, continually practifed, that ferue for the declaration and confirmation of the faid primacy. Perchaunce M. Horne wil fay to me, Sir, though I fpecifie nothing before the conqueft to iuftifie the princes fupremacy, yet in the margent of my booke, I doe remitte the reader, to a booke

De pote- ftate Re- gia.

made in King Henry the. 8. days. Wherein he may fee, what doinges the Kings of England had in this realme before the conqueft, for matters Ecclefiaftical. A prety and a clerklie remiſsion in dede, to fende your reader for one thowfande of yeares together, in the which ye fhoulde haue laide out before hī, your beft and principal proufs, to feke out a book, he wotteth not where, and which, whē it is at lēgth foūd, fhal proue your matter, no more fubftātially, then ye haue done hitherto your felfe. And therefore becaufe ye worke by fignes and profers only and marginal notes, I wil remitte both you and my reader to a *marginal note alfo, for your and his ful aunfwere.

Nowe then, lette vs goe forwarde in Gods name, and fee whether Kinge William conquered, bothe the lande and the Catholike faithe all at ones. Lette vs confider yf this Kinge and the realme did not then acknowledge the Popes Supremacy, as much, and as reuerently as any Chriftian prince doth now liuīg. I fay nothing of the othe he toke the day of his coronation, promifing by othe to Aldrede Archbiffhop of Yorke that crouned hī, at S. Peters alter in Weftminfter, before the clergy, and the people, that he would defende the holye Churches and their gouernours. But tel your readers good M. Horn I befeche you, why that King William

Williã, contrary to the aunciét order, vſed euer before and ſince, was not crowned of Stigandus thẽ liuing and being Archbiſhop of Canterbury, but of the biſhop of York. Yf ye can not or wil not for very ſhame to betraie your cauſe tel you reader, then wil I do ſo much for you. Forſoth, the cauſe was, that the Pope layde to his charge, that he had not receiued his palle canonically. The ſaid Stigandus was depoſed ſhortly after in a Councell holden at Wincheſter in the preſence of. ij. Cardinals ſent frõ Pope Alexander the. 2. and that (as Fabian writeth) for thre cauſes. *The firſt for that he had holden wrõgfully the biſhoprik, whyle Robert the Archbiſhop was liuing. The ſecond for that he had receyued the palle of Benett biſhop of Rome, the fifth of that name. The third for that he occupied the ſaid Palle without licẽce and leſul authority of the court of Rome.* Your author Polychronicon writeth in the like effect. Neubrigenſis alſo newly prĩted, toucheth the depoſitiõ of this Stigãdus by the Popes Legat in Englãd, ãd reporteth that the Popes Legat Canonically depoſed him. What liking haue you now M. Horne of Kĩg Williãs ſupremacy? Happy are you with your fellowes, the proteſtãt biſhops, and your two Archbiſſhops, that the ſaid Williã is not now king. For if he were, ye ſe cauſe ſufficiẽt, why ye al ſhuld be depriued, aſwel as Stigãdꝰ. And yet ther is one other thĩg worſe thã this, and that is ſchiſme and hereſy. Who woulde euer haue thought good reader, that the Pope ſhould euer haue found M. Horne him ſelfe, ſo good a proctour, for the Papacy, againſte him ſelfe

ee ij

VV. Conquerours othe.
In addit. ad Noueoburg. M.S. promittẽs ſe velle ſanctas Dei Eccleſias, ac rectores defendere.

Idẽ Noueobur. M.S. Pallium canonicè nõ ſuſcepiſti.
Fabian. par. 7. cap. 220.
The cauſe why the Archbiſhop Stigãdus vvas depoſed.

Guil. Malmeſb. Stigandũ perperã & falſo Archiepiſcopũ, per Card. Rom. & Armenfridũ epiſcopum Sedunenſem deponi paſſus eſt.
Polychronic. lib. 7. cap. 1.

Neub. lib. 1, cap. 1.

M. Horne and his felovves are to be depoſed, yf he aloﬂvv VV. Conquerours ſupremacy.

self and his fellowes? For lo, this brasen face which shortly for this his incredible impudency, will be much more famouse, then freer Bacons brasen head, of the which the schollers of Oxforde were wonte to talke so much, doth not blushe, to tel thee, good reader, to his owne confusion of the Popes Legates, and the Councell kepte at Winchester: And al this is ye wotte wel to shewe, that Kinge William was supreme head in al causes as wel temporall as spirituall.   Then doth he pleade on foorth full lustely for the Pope : for Kinge William heareth a certayne Ecclesiasticall matter beinge in controuersie, and dependinge in the Popes cowrte betwene the Archebisshop of Yorke and the Archebisshop of Caunterbury : the which cause the Pope had remitted to be determined by the King and the bishops . Well said M. Horne, and like the Popes faithfull proctour. For hereof followeth that the Pope was the supreame head and iudge of the cause : And the Kinge the Popes Commisioner, by whose commaundemēt, the cause was sent ouer to be heard in Englād. And yet was Hubertus the Popes Legat present at the end this notwithstāding.

M. Horne would now belike make vs belieue, that King William also thrusted out Abbats and supressed Monasteries, when yt pleased him. For he telleth vs, *that by the Kīgs iudgement Abbat Thurstan was chaunged, and his monks scattered abrode :* but he had forgotte to set in also, that his authour, and others say: *that it was for slaying of certayne of his monkes, and wounding of certayne other . The monks also had hurt many of his men.* And your author of the Pollichronicō telleth, that these mōks were scattered abrode by the kigs hest, *by diuers bisshopriks and abbays:* which latter words ye leue out. As also you do in your Author Fabiā, who saith

not,

M Horns impudēcie.

Gul. Malmesb. Ex praecepto Alexandri. 11. ventilata est causa &c. Adfuit Hubertus Legatus Papa. Fabian. cap. 222. Polich. lib. 7. cap. 3. Guiliel. de Pontifi. Guil. Hūtingt.

not,*they were scattred about,*as you reporte,as though they had bene scattred our of thier coates, as of late dayes they were,but he saieth:*they were spred abrode into diuers houses through Englande :* so that they chaunged but their house, not their Religion. And so this was no spirituall matter that the kinge did,neither gaue he herein any iudgement in any spirituall caufe.

Nowe if all other argumentes and euidences fayled vs, to shewe that kinge William toke not him self for supreame gouernour in all maner caufes, as you moste vntruely and fondly auouche,we might well proue it againste yowe by the storie of Lanfranke,whome kinge William , as ye confesse,made archebishop of Canterburie.Though according to your olde manner ye dissemble aswell the depryuation of Stigandus,in whose place the king set Lanfranke,as that Lanfranke receyuid his palle from Rome, and acknowledged not the kinge,but the pope for supreame head of the Church.Which thing doth manifestly appeare, in his learned boke he wrote againste your greate graundsier Berengarius.Who,as ye doe nowe,denied then the transubstantiation and the real presence of Christes bodie in the Sacramente : and called the Churche of Rome,which had condemned his heresie,as ye vse to doe,*the Church of the mas lignante,the councell of vanitye,the see of Sathan.*To whome Lanfrancus answereth, *that there was neuer anie heretyke, anie schismatyke , anie false Christian , that before hym had so wyckedly babled againste that see.* And sayth yet farder in an other place of the sayd boke, *Quotquot a primordio Christiana Ecclesiæ, Christiani nominis dignitate gloriati sunt,etsi alii qui relicto veritatis tramite per deuia erroris incedere maluerunt, sedem tamen sancti Petri Apostoli magnificè honorarauerunt,*

ee iij

Notable places of Lanfracus for the popes primacie.
Lanfran. contra Berengar: de sacramēto Et hoc im pio ore garristi quod garrista nemo loquitur: nō hæreticus, non schismaticus. non falsus aliquis Christia= nus.fol.2.

Fol. 13.
Beati pa-
tres cócor
diter aſtru
xerūt,hæ
ricum eſſe
hoëm om-
nem,qui à
Romana
& vniuer
ſali Eccle=
ſia in fidei
doctrina
diſcordat,
in edit.Lo
nan. in 8.
An. 1551.

uerunt,nullamq̃, aduerſus eam huiuſmodi blaſphemiam, vel di-
cere,vel ſcribere præſumpſerunt . Whoſoeuer from the be-
gynning of Chriſtes Church,were honored with the name
of Chriſtē mē,though ſome forſaking the Truth,haue gone
aſtray,yet they honoured much the See of Peter , neyther
preſumed at any time either to ſpeake or to write any ſuch
blaſphemy.He ſaieth alſo,that the bleſſed Fathers doe vni-
formly affirme that mā to be an heretike , that doth diſſent
from the Romā and vniuerſal Church in matter of faith.

But what nede I lay furth to thee good Reader,Lanfrāks
learned books,or to goe from the matter we haue in hand
miniſtred to vs by M. Horne,cócerning this matter ſent to
be determined before the King?Such as haue or can get either Polychronicó or Fabiā, I would wiſh them to ſee the
very place: and thā wil they meruail,that M.Horne would
for ſhame bring in this matter agaiſt the Popes primacy:for
the confirmation wherof ye ſhal find in Lāfranks reaſoning
before the King for his right vpó the church of York ſom-
thing worth the noting for the Popes primacy. Beſide this
he writeth that Lanfrank was a man of ſingular vertue,có-
ſtancy,and grauity,whoſe helpe and coūſel for his affaires,
the King chiefly vſed.And therfore your cócluſion that ye
inferre , of ſuch premiſſes as ye haue ſpecified, which as I
haue ſhewed, do not impugne, but eſtabliſh the popes primacy,is a very fond,foliſh and falſe cócluſion. It appeareth
well both by Fabian and by Polychronicon, that he would
ſometime like a cóquerour for his owne lucre and ſafetie,
both diſplace the Engliſh prelats,as he did the Knights and
Nobles of the realme, to place his owne Normans in their
roome:and alſo haue a peece many times of his owne mind
cótrary to the preciſe order of the Canós and lawes eccleſiaſtical.

fiaftical. And this not only Fabian and Polychonicon, but before them both Williā of Malmesbury doth alſo witnes. Such faults therfore of Williā Cōquerour ād of others, that your authour and other reporte in diſcōmendation, ſerue you notwithſtāding (ſuch beggarly ſhiftes you are forced to vſe) for good argumēts ād ſubſtātial bulwarks, to build your newe ſupreamacy vpō. And nowe might I or anie wiſe mā much meruail, to cōſider how that ye haue ladē and freighted this one page of your boke with no leſſe then. 6. quotatiōs of the Polychromco, and yet not one of them ſeruing for, but rather againſte you : yea eche one ouerthrowing your purpoſe. And therfore becauſe ye would be the leſſe eſpied, as throughout your whole diſcourſe, ſo here ye neither name boke nor chapter of your authour. Beſide that it is vntrue, that ye write, as out of Polychronicon, that the popes Legates kept a Councell before which was kept at Wincheſter. For he ſpeaketh of none other but of that, where Stigādus, that we ſpake of, was degraded, and afterward kept ſtreighly in priſon by Williā Conquerour. And the Biſhops and Abbats ye ſpeake of, were not depoſed by the King, but as your ſelf write, *by the kings meanes and procuremēt.* Which was (as Fabiā reporteth) *all to the entent he might preferre Normans to the rule of the Church, as he had preferred his Knightes to the rule of the temporaltie : that he might ſtand in the more ſuertie of the lande.*

Lib. De pō
tif. Angli.

Polychr.
li.7.64.1.

Fabian.
cap. 220.

M. Horne. The. 319. Diuiſion. pag. 77. a.

In like mauer did his ſonne Vvilliam Rufus, vvho made Anſelm Biſhop of Yorke and aftervvard trāſlated him to Cantorbury. But within a while ſtrife and cōtention fel betwene him and Anſelm, for Anſelm might not cal his Synods, nor correct the biſhops but as the kīg would: the king alſo chalēged the inueſtiture of biſshops. This king alſo forbad the paying of any mony or tribut to Rome: *as ſaith Polychronicon.*

Fabian.

The

Matth. Par.
The.417.vntruthe.
He made holy
Church free fayeth
Fabyan.
Fabyan.
The.418 vntruthe.
For *the pleaſure of
the Kinge* left out.
The.419.vntruthe.
he fled not to Rome
but vvas ſente thi-
ther by the kinge.

Simeon Dunelmenſis
Hen. Huntingtonus
Roge. Hoxedenus.
Matt. Paris.
Mat. VVeſtmonaſt.

Polidorus.
Polidorus.
Nauclerus.
Abbas Vrſp.

The.420.vntruthe.
flatly belying Mar-
tinus.

Concerning VVil-
liam Rufus King.

The like inhibition made Henry the firſt, and (417.) *gaue Eccleſiaſticall promotions, as his aunceſtours had doone : vvherefore*
Anſelme fel out vvith the kinge, and vvould not conſecrate ſuche
Prelates, as he beynge a Lay man had made: but the Archebiſhop
of *Yorke* (.418.) *did conſecrate thē, and therefore* Anſelme (.419.)
*fledde the Realme. In an other councel at London, the ſpiritual
condeſcended, that the kinges officers, ſhould puniſh
Prieſtes for whoordome . The cauſe of this decreé, as it ſeemeth, vvas, that a Cardinall named* Ioannes Cremenſis, *that
came to redreſſe the matter , after he had enueighed agaynſte the
vice, vvas him ſelfe the ſame nyghte taken tardy.* In the which
councell alſo (*ſayth Polydore*) the kinge prouided many
thinges to bee enacted which ſhoulde greatly helpe
to leade a Godly and bleſſed life . *After this* the kinge
called an other Councell at Sariſbury , Sommoning
thither ſo well the chief of the Clergy, as the people,
and ſwore them vnto him , and vnto VVilliam his
ſonne. *VVhereupon* Polydorus *taketh occaſion to ſpeake of the
order of our Parliamente , though it haue a French name , yet in
deede to be a councell of the Clergy , and the Laitie, vvhereof the
Prince hath a full ratifiyng or enfringing voyce.* And not only
(*ſaith he*) this king did make Biſſhoppes and Abbottes
(*vvhich he calleth*) holy rites , Lavves of religion , and
Church ceremonies (*as other likervyſe cal it*, eccleſiaſtical
buſynes) but the Princes of euery natiō, begane euery
wher to claim this right vnto thē ſelues of namīg and
denouncing of Biſſhops, the which to this daie they
hold faſt with toothe and nayle, *Alſo* Martinus *here noteth.* Vntil this time, and frō thence (.420.) euē til our
daies , the king of Hungary maketh and inueſtureth
according to his pleaſure , Biſſhops and other Eccleſiaſtical perſons within his Dominions.

Stapleton.

Ye ſhal nowe good reader ſee a more euidente
teſtimonie of M. Hornes meruelouſe newe logike
and

and diuinity, wherof I ſpake euen now . For ys not this a
worthy and a clerkly concluſion?The wicked king Rufus
woulde not ſuffer the bleſſed and learned archbiſhop of
Caũterbury Anſelme,to cal hys Synodes and correcte the
Biſhoppes : he challenged the inueſtiture of Biſhoppes:he
woulde paye no tribute to Rome. *Ergo* the Quene of Englande is ſupreame head of the Church of Englande . The
loſenes and fondnes of thys argumente, euery childe may
ſone eſpie.By this argument he may ſet the Popes crowne
vppon the head of the wycked and heathen Prince eſpeciallie the tyrãte Licinius,with whome Euſebius cõparing
the good and Chriſtian Emperour Conſtantine cõpartner
with hym in the empire,ãd not in hys wyckednes,writeth
thus . Πρώτους γὲ Τοι τοὺς ὑπ᾽ αὐίον τῷ Θεῷ λειτουργίους,&c.

Firſt then he watched and obſerued the Prieſtes of God, that
were vnder hys gouernemente,and wheras they had nothing
offended hym,he by curiouſe and ſubtyle working , deuiſed pre-
tenſed matter to trouble and vexe them.When he could fynd
no iuſte matter to accuſe them withall, he made a proclamatiõ
*that the Biſhoppes for*no maner of matter ſhould aſſemble to-*
gether, and that yt ſhoulde not be lawfull to any of them to re-
*payre to theire neighbours Churches,*or to call any Synode, or*
place to conſulte and debate,vppon ſuche thinges , as appertey-
ned to the commoditye of the Churche.Thys was hys dryfte, by
the wich he ſowght theyre deſtruction . For either the Biſhop-
pes were in daunger to be puniſhed.yf they trãſgreſſed his law,
or yf they kepte the lawe,they broke the order and cuſtome of
the Churche.For they could not aduiſe thẽ ſelues in any weigh-
ty matters but in a Synode.And thys wicked mã hated of God
gaue thys commaundement , that he might worke quite con-
trarye to the doeinges of good Conſtantyne , whome God lo:
ued.

ff

ued.

M.Horne
like the
ſpider ãd
the flie.
The wor
thines of
Biſhop
Anſelme
Guil Mal
meſb. in
lib. de
Pontif.
Henric.
Hunting.
in Hiſtor.
Angl.
The cau-
ſes of diſ
ſenſiõ be
tvvene
King Ru-
fus and
Anſelmus
Edmerus.
de vita
Anſel.li 2
Regẽ pro
Eccleſiarũ
quæ de die
in diẽ de-
ſtruebãtur
relcuatione pro Chri
ſtianæ legis quæ in
multis violabatur
renouatione, pro di-
uerſorũ merũ qui õni

ued. For he, ſuch was his reuerẽce to God.ſuche was his ſtudie and endeuour to haue peace and agreemente , aſſembled Gods prieſts together. Th'other cõtrariwyſe wẽt about to diſſoluethoſe things that were wel ordeined and to breke peace ãd agreemẽt. Thus farre Euſebius of the heathen tyran Licinius. Ye play therfore M. Horn like a very ſpider, that gathereth nothig but poiſon out of ſweet herbes, and ſo doe you out of good chronicles . Ye are like to the flie that loueth to dwell in the horſe dong. I would to God your Reader M.Horne, would either aduiſedly weigh, what an ill King this Williã Rufus was,by the moſt agreable conſent of all writers: and what ſtrauge and wõderful tokẽs were ſene in his time, ãd how he ended his life being ſlaine by the glaũſing of an Ar-rowe,as he was a hũting: or the excellẽt learning,cõſtancy and vertue of the B.Anſelmus: and the great miracles,that God wrought by him,as wel before, as after his death , ſet foorth by the beſt Hiſtoriographers of that time: eſpecially of Henry Hũtington, Williã of Malmeſbury, and one Ed-merus. Who hath made.ij.ſpecial Treatiſes,the one cõcer-ning Anſelmus doings,with this king and kingHẽry, the o-ther cõcerning his priuat life. The which I would wiſh the gẽtle Reader,to read,to know the better the worthines of this man,and withal, the ſtate of the cõtrouerſy betwixt hĩ and the two kings:Williã Rufus,and Hẽry.Which in effect cõcerning William Rufus reſted in that the ſaid William, would not at the admonitiõ of this good man as wel leaue of other faults,as alſo the inueſturing of Biſhops,the pilling of the ſpiritualty ãd tẽporalty,and the ſelling of biſ-ſhopriks,which was bought and ſolde es plainly as o her marchandize:as M. Hornes Author Fabian, beſide others dothe declare : The beginning of the

Kings

ardine hominum quotidie nimis corrumpebantur, correctiene cæpit interpellare.

Kings difpleafure againft Bifhop Anfelme, rofe principally
for that he woulde not according to his expectation geue
him in the way of thanks, a thoufand pounds for making hi̅
Archebifhop of Cau̅terbury. And yet as naught as this king
was, he neuer denyed the Pope to be Supreme Heade or
Iudge of the Church, no nor the paiment of the tribut called Rome fhot: but for a time pretending he knew not who
was the true Pope (the church of Rome the̅ being troubled
with fchifme) and he feeming for the time to fauour rather
the falfe, then the true Pope, which was Vrbane. Whom,
this notwithftanding he acknowledged for the true Pope,
a̅d receiued Walter the Popes legat that brought the Palle
for Anfelme, and receiued Anfelme alfo into his
friendfhip. Henry of Huntington writeth, that the
king him felfe fent for the Palle, the which being
brought to Cau̅terburie, and fet vpon the Aulter,
was for the honor of S. Peter kiffed of al men moft
humblie kneeling.

We haue now fhewed how and after what faf-
fhio̅ the king forbod the tribut to be paid to Rome:
the which, I marueile why ye tell it rather out of
Polichronico̅, then Fabian, which faith it as well as
the refidue ye alleage. But not for any of his good dedes.
For defcribing the death of this Willia̅, he telleth, *that the*
day whe̅ he died, he held in his hands the three Bifhopriks of
Cau̅terbury, of Winchefter, a̅d of Salifbury, and diuers Abbeies,
of the which he let fome to farme. Alfo he reftrained the mony
that of old time was paid to Rome, called Rome fhot. Al which
is told of Fabia̅ and the other Chroniclers, to fhew what a
couetous man he was, and iniurious to the Church, not to
fhewe any practife of due and laufull Authoritie thereby.

Fdmer,
lib.2.

Edmer.
dict.lib.2.
Attamen pofthæc et
Vrbanum per VVal-
terum Albanenfem
epifcopum, qui palliu̅
à Roma Anfelmo
Cantuariam detulit
pro Papa fufcepit et
principum fuorum
co̅filio actus in ami-
cittam fuam vnum
recepit.
Henric.
Hunting.
Cap.225.

Yet this ſerueth notwithſtanding M.Hornes purpoſe very wel. What M.Horne ? Wil you haue our Princes now like to William Rufus , and his Father the Conquerour to taxe and pille both the Spiritualty and Temporalty of their realme, as they out of meaſure did ? For ſo both Polichronicon and Fabian report (which you conceal) that *notwith-ſtanding the ſtaie of this tribute to Rome, yet did this William pill and ſhaue his people with tribute, and miſuſe them with diuers other diſorders.* Or as Fabian ſaith, *He pilled the Spiritualtie and Temporalty with vnreaſonable taſkes and tributs.* Such a one you bring foorth as a worthy example of your new Supremacie, and yet can ye not faſten it vppon him neyther.

Concer-ning kíg Héry the firſt.

But much leſſe ſhal ye faſten it vpon king Henry folowing who (though he were for a time diſpleaſed with Anſelme, for that he would neyther conſecrate thoſe Biſhops , nor communicate with them whom the King had inueſtured, and becauſe the Pope had ſo commaunded, the matter yet ſtãding in controuerſie) did not flie, as ye write, but at the Kings deſire went to Rome, to ſee if he could mollifie the Pope : And afterwarde the king was perſitly reconciled to him : and the King made an ordinaunce and a decree, that from that time foreward, nor Biſhop, nor Abbat ſhould be inueſtured by the king or any other laie man, by the paſtorall ſtaffe and the ring. This writeth Henrie Archedeacon of Huntington, a writer then liuing. The like alſo Edmerius Anſelmes cõpanion in his exile writeth. And that the king was very gladde, that he had made peace and accorde with Anſelme.

Edmer.lib. 2. De vita Anſelmi.

Poſt ea omnia roga-uit Anſelmum rex, quatenus ipſemet Romam iret.

Henr. Hungt.

Rogatus à Rege per-rexit Romam.

Idẽ Héric. Hũgt. Anno. 1107. ſtatuit vt nũquã per dona-tionem baculi paſto-ralis vel ãnuli, quiſ̃q de epiſcopatu vel abbatia per regẽ vel quamlibet laicã ma-num in Anglia inue-ſtinetur.

Rex anteceſſorũ ſuo-

And

And had great hope, that he ſhould the ſoner ſub-
due Normandie. Euen as it chaunced: for he had
a notable victorie, and toke priſoners his brother
Robert and other Princes that aſsiſted Robert.
The whiche thing he certified Anſelme of by his
letters ſent to him into Englande : and all men of
thoſe daies imputed his victorie to the agreamente
made with Anſelme. Tel me nowe in good faith.
M. Horne, who was the Supreme Heade, the king
that yelded to the Pope for inueſturíg, or the Pope
that would neuer yelde to him, nor the Emperour
Henrie the.4. neither, in this matter, but did excommunicate the Emperour: and king Henry was
faine to forſake him and his doings, though he were
him ſelfe a mighty Prince and the Emperours Father in law, by Maude the Empreſſe his daughter.

*rum vſu relicto, nec
perſonas quæ in regi-
men Eccleſiarum ſu-
mebantur per ſe eli-
git, nec eas per da-
tionem virgæ paſto-
ralis quibus praficie
batur, inueſtiuit.
Edmer. lib.2. de vi-
ta Anſelmi.*

Idem.

*Omnes qui hæc ge-
ſta tũc tẽporis audie-
re, ea meritis cõcor-
diæ quã rex cũ An-
ſel. fecerat aſcripſere
Fabian. cap. 227.*

I now alſo perceiue that a Horne wil not lightly bluſh,
for if it could, ye would neuer for ſhame haue tolde your
Reader, of theſe Prieſtes that were punniſhed for whoredome, for ſauing of your own and Maiſtres Madges poore
honeſtie. And yet your whoredome infinitely excedeth
theirs. For they were puniſhed for keping company with
their concubines or their wiues whome they had laufully
maried before they were ordered. But you after Prieſthod
doe marie, which neuer was allowed, but euer condemned as wel in the Greke Churche as in the Latine. And
now decke your margent as thicke as ye will, with Fabiã,
Simeon Dunelmenſ. Rogerus Houedenus, Henricus Hun-
tingtonˢ, Matheus Pariſiēſ. Matheus Weſtmonaſteriēſ. and
Polidorus, ãd blow out, as it were out of your own horne,
your own diſhoneſty and ſhame as long as ye will: and ſee

*M. Horn
ſheweth
him ſelfe
vvorthy
to be pu-
niſhed for
vvhore-
dome by
his ovvn
ſtorie.*

what

Fabian.
Simeon Dunelmẽʃ.
& Rogerus Houed.
Rex tenuit Conciliũ
magnũ apud Lōdo=
nũ de vxoribus sacer
dotũ prohibilẽ is,&c.
Conceʃʃere namque
regi iuʃtitiã de vxo-
ribus (acerdotũ, &
improuidi habiti
ʃunt:accepit enĩ rex
pecuniam inʃinitam
de presbyteris & re-
demit eos.
Similia habet,&
Henr. Huntington.

Lib.11.
The order of the
parliamẽte abovvt
the conqueʃte.
Parliamẽtum eʃt ex
3.gradibus ʃiue gene-
ribus:ʃcilicet ex pro=
curatoribus cleri .mi
litibus cõmunitatis,
ciuibus & Burgenʃi-
bus, qui repraʃentãt
totam communita-
tem Anglia. Quia
quilibet magnatum
eʃt ibi pro propria
perʃona & non pro
alia.

what ʃupreamacy ye ʃhal buyld vpon ʃuch a fickle
and filthy foundation.Verely your owne authours
doe witneʃʃe,that this king kept a great Councel at
London, where *among alother Decrees* (ʃaieth Fabian)*one was,that prieʃtes ʃhould forgoe their wiues.*
And if the popes Legate was taken as ye write,in
whoredome(who yet, as Mattheus Weʃtmonaʃt.
writeth, was no prieʃt but a correctour of prieʃts,
and thereby excuʃed his fault) what doth that relieue your cauʃe, or wherein doth it ʃaue your ho-
neʃtie ? For the king did not puniʃh theʃe fornicatours , but by the clergies conʃent . Wherein they
were by thier raʃhe graunte ouerʃeen and circumuented For the King tooke a greate maʃʃe of money of the parʃons that were faultye , and ʃo diʃ-
miʃʃed them.Ye tell vs nowe out of Polidore, that
the parliament is in dede a Councel of the clergie
and the Layetie . If ye meane an Eccleʃiaʃticall
councell,then Polydore neither ʃaieth it,nor meaneth yt . For as he maketh the parliamente an aʃ-
ʃemble for politike matters, to the which the prelates alʃo come as Barons : ʃo for matters eccleʃiaʃticall he appointeth ʃpecialle the conuocation.
Truthe yt is,that before the conqueʃte and in William Conquerours tyme to (as appeareth by old
recordes, writen as it ʃemeth abowt the cõqueʃt)
the proctours of the clergye ʃate in the Lower
howʃe.And the ʃayde recordes do ʃhewe that the
Parliament properly ʃtandeth and conʃiʃteth in .3.
degrees : that is , of the proctours of the clergye ,
of the knightes of the ʃheere , and of the Burge-
ʃes

ſes and Citizens. For they repreſent the people and com-
minaltie of the realme. As for the noble men, biſhoppes and
other be there, for their owne perſons, and not for other :
yf we ſhal beleue the ſaid auncient records. Nowe though
theſe many yeres, for matters politike the couocation haue
had nothing to doe, yet as oft as any paiemēt is to be made,
it taketh no place by vertue of Parliamēt againſt the Clergy, onles the Clergie do cōſent. Yf this be true in mony maters, and if in auciēt time the Clergy had to do in ciuil maters
alſo (the which prerogatiue, belik, they left volūtarely, that
they might the better attend their owne ſpirituall vocatiō)
what an accōpt ought of all good reaſon to be made of the
late parliament, wherein mere Laie men haue turned vpſi-
downe the ſtate of the Catholique faythe againſte the full
mindes of the Clergie, I leaue it to euery wiſeman well
to conſider. But as I beganne to ſaye, If Polidore meaneth not the Parliamente to be a Councell of Spirituall
matters, to what purpoſe, or with what great wiſedome
haue ye alleaged him: or that he calleth the making of Biſſhops ād Abbats, holy rites, lawes of religiō, and church ceremonies : ſeing that the King gaue ouer the electing of biſhoppes, and ſeing that your Authour doth ſhew, that Anſelme rebuked the King therefore?

Nowe to thoſe matters of Englande M. Horne addeth
a greate Vntruthe of the Kyng of Hungarie, tellyng vs
out of Martinus, that the Kynge of Hungarie, *vntill this
time*, (which is the yeare of grace. 1110.) *and from thence
euen til our daies maketh ād inueſtureth according to his pleaſure, biſshops &c.* Thys I ſay is a great and flat vntruth. For
Martinus here ſaieth plainly the cōtrary, thus. *At this time
the King of Hūgary* (ſaieth Martinus) *writing many aduertiſe-
mentes*

M. Horns
vvildom
in reaſo-
ning aga-
inſt hym
ſelfe.

Polidorus
lib. 11.
admonea
bat ne ſan
ctos ritus,
neuè reli-
gionis iu-
ra, et cere
monias
verteret
pollue-
retque.

Martinus Polonus in,Pascha li.2.Re-nunciauit inuestitu-ris Epi-scoporum & altoru prælatoru.

ments to the Pope by his letters , gaue ouer the inuesturing of *Bishops and of other prelats,which vntil that time the kinges of Hungary were wonte to make.*These are the true wordes of Martinus in this place.Now what passing impudency is this of M,Hornes?That which his Author telleth for the Popes primacy,this man wresteth it to the Princes . And therefore whereas Martinus telleth only , that *vntill that time kinges of Hungary inuested the Bishops,*and addeth far-der that at the same time the kinge of Hungary gaue ouer the same into the Popes handes,M.Horne bothe lewdely concealeth that , and also of his owne,most impudentlye and shamelessely addeth,*and from thence euen til our dayes:* which Martinus not only auoucheth not , but telleth also plainely the contrarye:to witte,that,at that time the king gaue ouer al such matters.Farder to make the matter soūd more princely , you make Martinus say , that the kinge of Hungary inuested Bishops,*according to his pleasure.*Which wordes*(according to his pleasure)*are not in Martinus at al, but it is a poynt of your descant,vpō his playne,and a fitte of your owne volūtary, at your pleasure.In dede this soū-ded pleasauntly in M.Hornes eares,that by this exāple he might also goe for a Bishop , made at the Princes pleasure, and to be remoued againe at her highnes pleasure.   But you hearde before by the forme of Paschalis his graunte made to Henry the.4.that though the Prince haue the in-uesturing and confirming of Bishoppes graunted him , yet it was neuer so grāted to Princes,that their ōly pleasure suffised to make a man a true Bishop. For first,whom the Prince inuested and confirmed,he shoulde be,*libere præter violentiam& simoniam electus,* chosen freely without vio-lence or simony on the Princes part.Which great faultes, bothe

Vide Nau cleru ge-nerat.38. pag.183.

both the Emperours of Germanie, and the kinges of oure
land, such as had the inuesturing of Bishops in their owne
handes, namely Henrie the. 4. Emperoure, and William
Rufus of England, most grieuouslie and daily committed.
Secondarelye though he were inuested and confirmed of
the Prince, yet *post inuestituram Canonicè Consecratiõ. m*   Dist.63.
in Synod.
accipiant ab episcopo ad quem pertinuerint, after the inuesturing let them (saith Paschalis) be consecrated of the Bisshop to whom they belong. So likewise, Leo. 8. in his grãt
made to Otho the. 1. geuing to the Emperour the inuesturing of Bishops, addeth, *Et consecrationem vnde debent*, and
to be consecrated, where they ought to be. Which words
vnde debent, where they ought, you for the nonse lefte out
in your alleaging of this graunt made to Otho, to thentent
that your inuesturing of the Prince, being without any cõ-   Fol 70.
secration at al of your Metropolitane (him self poore man,   Fac. 1.
being no Bishop neither) might seme to be good and sufficient, and to haue example of antiquitie. For that purpose
also ye make Martinus here to say, that the king of Hungarie made Bishops according to his pleasure. But you see
nowe it is not the Princes only pleasure that maketh a Bisshop, but there must be both free election, without eyther
forcing the Clergy to a choise, or forcing the chosen to filthie bribery, and also there must follow a due consecratiõ,
which in you, and al your fellowes doe lacke. And therefore are in deede (by the waye to conclude it no true Bis-   An.26.
shoppes, neither by the lawe of the Churche, as you see,   Henric.8.
neyther yet by the lawes of the Realme, for wante of due   cap.14.
Confecration, expressely required by an Act of Parliamẽt,   An.1.
renewed in this Queenes dayes in Suffragane Bishoppes,   Elizab.
cap.1.
much more in you.

M.Horne.

Arnol dus.

The.421.
Vntruth.
not about
this time,
by 150.
yeares at
the leaſt.
The.422.
Vntruth.
They of
Armenia
neuer acʒ
knovvʒ
ledged
their
Price for
fuche.
The 423.
Vntruth.
Slãderuʒ
The.424.
vntruth,
moſt
lewde in
nipping
avvay the
vvordes
folovving
in the
ſame
ſentence.

The.425.
vntruth.
Neuer
able to
be iuſtiʒ
fied.

And here ſithen I am entred into the noting of the practiſes of other
Coũtries in this behalfe : I might not onely note the doings about (.421.) this
time of Frederike King of Cicill, and Iames the King of Spaine his brother,
in reformation of Relligion in their domĩnions, as appeareth in their Epiʒ
ſtles vvritẽ by Arnoldus de noua Villa, but alſo make a digreſſiõ to the
ſtate of other parts inChriſtẽdõ, as of the churches of Grece, of Armenia, of
Moſcouia, &c. that acknovvledged not any, but (.422.) only their Princes
to be their ſupreme gouernours in al things next to Chriſt: as eſpecially alſo to
note that moſt auncient part of Chriſtẽdom ſouthvvard in Æthiopia, con-
teiniug.62. kingdomes vnder the ruling of him vvhõ vve miſname Preſby
ter Ioannes, as vvho ſay he vver a Prieſt, and head Biſhop ouer thoſe chriʒ
ſtian Realmes, hauing ſuch a povver vvith them, as the Popes (423) vſurpatiõ hath chalẽged here in Europe, to be an head or vniuerſal Prieſt ãd king. If
vve may beleue Sabellicus, vvho ſaith that he hath both often talked vvith
the Marchaũts, that haue their trafique there, and hath alſo diuers times en
quired the matter by an interpretour of the inhabitaunts there borne, they
al ſay that his name is neyther Preſbiter Ioannes, nor Pretto
Ianes, but ſay they, his name is Gyan, that is, mightie, and
they maruaile greatly what the Italians meane, to call him by
the name of Prieſthode. But this they ſay, that al the ſuites or
requeſtes euen of their greate Biſhoppes, are brought before
the king him ſelf: and that all their benefices or Spiritual promotions be opteined at his handes (.424.) So that there beynge,
as Sabellicus telleth further, an exceadinge great nomber of chiefe Prelates or Metropolitanes, and vnder euerye one Prelate at the leaſte tvven-
ty Biſhoppes, all their ſutes and cauſes Eccleſiaſticall, beyng brought vnto
him, and he the maker of all theſe Prelates, Biſhoppes, and other Eccleſiaſticall perſons, he is called ouer them all, Clergy or Laie, in all cauſes
Eccleſiaſtical or themporall, Gyan the mightie, that is, the ſupreme
Ruler ãd Gouernour, ãd euẽ ſo hath (.425.) cõtinued ſithẽ thoſe partes vvere
firſt Chriſtened, (as they ſaye) of Thomas Dydimus, the Apoſtle,
vntill our tyme. But thys by the vvaye, novv from them to retourne to
our ovvne countrey.

The

The. 20. Chapter. Of the Armenians, and of the Aethio-
pians in Preto Ianes lande.

Stapleton.

A MAN would thinke that Maifter Horne was with fome ftraunge fpirituall meditation rauifhed, when he interlaced this digrefsion, woorthy belike depely to be côfidered, being here, I can not tel whether more impertinently, or more falfely, betwene the doings of king Henrie and king Stephen that immediatly fucceded him, full wifely wrenched and writhed in. For he is now vppon the fodaine, as a man rapt vppe and caried awaie not only into Spaine, but into Greece, Armenia, Mofcouia, yea and Aethiopia too. And then is he as fodainly in England againe.   About a foure hundred yeres paft, he was very bufie, and to bufie too, for his owne honeftie with Spaine: nowe after this long taciturnitie belike he hathe efpied out there, fome notable matter for his purpofe : And what is it thinke ye good Reader ?   Forfooth he commeth in, as it were in a Mummerie, and fendeth vs to *Arnoldus de Villa* *Noua*, and telleth vs that we fhall learne by him of the doing of Frederike king of Sicilie, and Iames king of Spain, in their Epiftles writen by the faid Arnoldus.   But what this Arnoldus was, Heretique or Catholique, what his bookes were, and where, and when they were printed, and where a man fhall finde any thing of him, he telleth vs nothing.

Your brother Gefnerus, M. Horn, in his *Bibliotheca* maketh métion of Arnold' a Phifitiô, ãd nûbreth his bokes. But of thefe epiftles there is no word: and maruel it is, that fuch

gg   ij

M. Horne
by a fpi-
ritual ra-
uifhmêt,
is fodain-
ly caried
frô Eng-
land to
Mofcouia
Aethio-
pia, &c.

a no-a notable worke fhoulde efcape hys handes. Suerlye with much a doe I fuppofe, I haue chaunced vppon hym, what in your brother Illiricus and what in your other frende Gafpar Hedio that addeth Paralipomena, to Abbas Vrfpergenfis, I haue by them fome feeling of thys your greate ghoftly rauifhmēte, ād feele at my fyngers endes that your Arnoldus (if he were no better then Illiricus maketh hym) was your owne deare brother, that is an Heretike afwell as your felf: and alfo that in the vehemencye of thys

Vide Pa- your impertinente madde meditatiō you are caried away, ralip. Vi- one hundred and fiftie yeares at the leafte, from the tyme fperg. & ye fhoulde haue orderly profequuted, and as many myles Matheum from the matter yt felf. For thys Arnoldus is noted to haue Flaccium writen lyke a blinde and a lewde lying prophete, abowte Illiricum the tyme of Clemente the fifte, which was made Pope in catalo- abowte the yeare of our Lorde. 1306. This Arnoldus then go teſtuṁ taking vppon him to be a prophete, fayeth that Antichrift veritatis. fhould come within. 34. yeres of his blinde prophefiyng.

Now here for hys part M. Horne alfo playeth the lying Imo quod prophete, and telleth vs of wonderfull epiftles that his au- deterius thour wrote, one hundred yeares before he was borne: eſt videtur Whiche epiftles though they be very highe and myfticall, nobis quod yet there femeth to be no greate poynte of herefie in thē. pro nihilo And whatfo euer reformation thefe kings wente aboute, habeant the epiftles feme to geue a playn teftimony, for the Popes Eccleſiam primacy, and to fynde faulte with certaine religioufe per- Roma- fons that they defpifed the Churche of Rome, and did di- nam, quia fallow appeales to that See. Yea where he telleth vs with dinulli ap- a greate mighty affertion, and fayeth. Quòd concluditur pellationi infallibiliter, quòd Antichriſtus apparebit in mundo ab hoc ad eam anno Domini. 1354. infra immediatè ſequentes 34. annos, that facta de- ferunt.

is

is, that it is an infallible conclusion, that Antechriste shall appeare in the world, within fowre and thyrty yeares immediatly folowing after the yeare of our Lorde .1354. He sayth withall, that within the sayde 34. the Saracyns should be destroyed, and the Iewes should be conuerted, *& iurisdictionem summi Pontificis per vniuersum orbe dilatari* : and that the authoritie of the Pope, should be spredde through owte all the worlde. Well, how so euer yt be , *Arnoldus de Villa noua* seameth not greatly to furder M. Hornes primacy. And it semeth to me that by ignoráce he taketh one Arnoldus for an other . In dede there was one Arnoldus Brixianus abowt thys tyme, códemned for an Heretik by Eugenius the 3. as S. Bernarde, Platina and Sabellicus doe write. Your Brother Bale sayeth, that he was condemned, for that he sayde the clergy might vse no temporal iurisdictió. And so thys Arnoldus might haue serued your turne for the tyme, and somwhat for the matter to after your accustomable reasoninge, if the authority of heretikes maye serue the turne. But let Arnoldus ád Spayne to goe for this tyme. for M. Horne hath other great coútries , that about this time taketh hys part: as Grecia, Armenia, Moscouia ád Aethiopia to, which acknouledge *theyre Princes only to be theyr supreame gouernours in al things next vnto God,* which ye muste belieue without any proufe: belyke becaufe yt is shewed to M. Horne in thys his Spirituall reuelation . For otherwise I am assured he shall neuer iustifie this most vntrewe saying. And though perchaunce some of thele coútreis did not at this tyme , shewe to the see of Rome suche obediéce, as they owght to haue done, especially the Greciás, ád Moscouites that followe the religió and order of the greke Church: yet neither doth M. Horne proue , nor

Bernard. Epist. Platina in Had. 4. Sabel. En. 9. lib. 9.

euer ſhall be able to proue, that the Churches of theſe coūtries gaue any ſuche authoritie to theyre princes : but that
they euer toke, for ſpirituall cauſes theyre patriarche and
other Biſhoppes for the ſupreame heades, in all matters ſpirituall . Maruayle nowe yt is, that M. Horne can not loke
vpon the Grecians and Armenians, but with one blind eye
bleared with affection to hereſie and hatred to the Pope.
Otherwyſe yf he woulde loke vppon them with the better
and indifferente eie, there were more cauſe whie he ſhould
regarde aſwell the aunciente Greeke Churche which acknowledged the Popes Supreamacye : as alſo the later acknowledging the ſame , in the generall councell at Lions:
wherof we haue ſpoken , and alſo afterward in the general
Coūcel at *Ferraria* and frō thēce trāſlated to *Florēce.* Where
alſo the Armenians were ioyned with the Roman Church.
But not then firſt.   For * three hundred yeres before that,
aboute .10. yeres before the deathe of Henry the firſt in.S.
Bernardes tyme , the Armenians ſubmitted them ſelues to
Eugenius . 3. ſending their chief Metropolitane who had
vnder him moe thē a thouſand Biſhops to the See of Rome,
who trauayling in iourney of a yere ād a halfe came to Viterbū, ſcarſe ij. dayes iourney from Rome , where the Pope
lay thē, of whō they were receyued, ād inſtructed in al ſuch
thinges as they ſought at his handes, touching the order of
the bleſſed ſacrifice, the obſeruation of feſtiuall dayes and
certayn other pointes , wherin they varyed from the reſt
of Chriſtendome, of which errours they are of*old writers
much ād ofté noted. And this their ſubmiſsiō to the Church
of Rome, fel before the tyme that M. Horne now talketh
of, affirming but falſly (as his maner is) that the people of Armenia, acknowleged none but ōly their princes to be their
ſupreme

* Anne.
1145.
Nauclerus
Generat.
39. pag.
231.
Volater.
Geograph.
lib. 10.
Otho Fri
ſing.
*Cōc. Nicen.2.
Cap.32.
Theophil.
in Ioan.19
Niceph. li.
18. cap.
52. & 53.

supreme gournours. Neither neded yow yet M. Horne to
haue loked so far. For if your enuious eie might haue abiddē
our own late time, and the late councel of Trent, ye should
haue found that the Armenians sent ambassadours to the
Pope recognising hys supreamacy, and desiring the confirmation of theyre patriarch of Antiochia. Ye should haue
founde, that Abdisa the patriarche of the Assyrians inha-
biting nygh to the famous floud of Tygris came to Rome,
with no small eyther trauell or daunger of hys life, to be
confirmed of *Pius Quartus* the last pope of blessed memorie : who also promised as well for hym selfe, as for those
that were vnder his spiritual gouernemēt, that he and they
woulde faythfully and constantly keepe suche decrees, as
should be set forth by the saied Councell of Trent.

Perchaunce ye will the lesse passe for the Armenians,
seeyng you haue on your syde, as ye saye, about thys tyme
the greate prince of the Aethiopians hauing no lesse then
62. Kingdomes vnder hys Dominion, the same country beyng the most auncient part of Christendome Southwarde.
And becau se your selfe haue forsaken your priesthodde,
(take heede I pray you, that ye haue not withall forsaken
your Christendome) ye are not contented with the Italians, and other that call hym Prieste Ihon, as thoughe he
were a prieste and head Bishoppe ouer those Christian realmes, hauing suche a power wyth them, as the popes v-
surpation (as ye terme yt) hath challenged here in Europe, to be an head or vniuersall priest or Kyng. And ye
would rather he should be called as Sabellicus telleth, the
mighty Gyan So called (as ye by a mighty lying exposition
of your own falsly declare ` becau se he is the supreme ruler
and gouernour of all causes aswel ecclesiasticall as tēporal.
But

But here firſt, ſeing ye pretend your ſelfe to be ſo good
an Antiquarie, I would gladly knowe, what monumentes
ye haue of the Aethiopical religion about this time? It had
bene mete ye had laied foorth your Authour for your diſcharge. Surely I beleue ye haue ſene none at al of ſuch antiquitie, and I dare boldly auouch, ye neither haue nor ſhal
ſee any, whereby ye may iuſtly gather, that the Aethiopiās
take their king for their Supreme head in all cauſes Eccleſiaſtical and Temporal. We haue to the contrary, the confeſsion of the Biſhop, *Raba Rago*, his kings Embaſſadour,

*Domianᵒ
àGoes de
Aethiopum moribus.
Pontiſicem Roma-
num tanquam pri-
mum Epiſcopum &
paſtorem ouiũ Chri-
ſti agnoſco.
Noſtri certè ab ex-
ordio primitiuæ Ec-
cleſiæ Rom. Pontificè
vt primum Epiſc.
agnouerũt, cui etiam
hodierno die vt Chri-
ſti Vicario paremus.
Anno. Dom. 1524.
Propterea dico ego
humiliter ad terram
flexis genibus, quòd
tu pater meus es, &
ego filius tuus.
Procul dubio ſancti-
tas veſtra Dei eſt
Vicarius.*

to the king of Portugale, that he made. 33. yeares now paſt.
ſaying that he doth acknowledge the biſhop of Rome, as
the chief biſhop and paſtour of Chriſtes ſhepe. We
haue his confeſsion, wherein he declareth, that the
Aethiopiās *euē frō the begīning of the Church did acknowlege the B. of Rome for the firſt ãd chief Biſhop:
ãd ſo at that day did obey him as Chriſtes Vicar.* What
ſpeak I of his Orators cōfeſsion? We haue the kings
own cōfeſsiō made to the Pope, wherin he calleth
hī *Caput oīū Pōtiſiuū,* the head of al biſhops: he ſaith
to the Pope, *Aequũ eſt, vt omnes obedientiã tibi præ-
ſtent, ſicuti ſancti Apoſtoli præcipiũt.* It is mete that al
men obey him, euen as th'Apoſtles commaund. He
ſaith moſt humbly kneling on the ground, that the
Pope is his Father, and he his ſonne: he ſaith again,
Your holines without al doubt is Gods Vicar. And
thinke ye now, M. Horne, that ye ſhal like a mighty
Giant, cōquer al your Readers, ãd make them ſuch
bondſlaues to your ignorāce and folly, that becauſe
Sabellicus ſayeth, he is called *Mightye Gyan,* therefore yee maye ſo mightely lye, as to conclude
thereby,

thereby, for that he hathe the collection of the Spirituall li-
uinges, that he is therfore the fupreame gouernour in all
caufes? Not fo M. Horn. But now fhal your greate falfhood
be difcouered, and lying fprite be coniured. For beholde e-
uen immediatly after the words by you alleaged out of Sabellicus *that al benefices and fpiritual promotions are obtayned*
at the Kings hands,it foloweth,I fay immediatly: *Quod Rom.*
Pontifex Regum Maiestati dederit: The which thinge the
Biffhop of Rome hath geuen to the Kings Maiefty. Which
woordes of your authour you haue moft lewdely nipped
quyte of. Such a Macariã you are, and fo lyke to M. Iewel
your pewefellowe. Neither doth he fpeake of any order of
relligion, about that age, fo many hundred yeres pafte, as ye
pretende, but of his and our late tyme. And fo thus are you
M. Horne after this your longe and fruitles iorney, wherin
as wayfaring men in longe iorneyes are wonte to doe, ye
haue gathered ftore of wonderfull lies to delight your hearers, that haue not trauayled fo far, withal: welcome home
againe from Mofcouia and Aethiopia, into Englande.

Sabel.ene.
10.lib.8.

Mat.Par.
Polychro.
The.416:
vntruthe.
Polychro
nicõ faith
no fuch
thing.
Mat.Par.
Fabian.
The.427.
vntruthe.
This for
foloweth
not here,
but of an
othermat
ter longe
after. See
Fabian.
cap.237.

M. *Horne. The.121. Diuifion. pag. 78 a.*

In *England alfo, King Stephã(.426.)referued to him felf, the inueftitures*
of the Prelats, as likewife after him did Henry the fecõd,that made Tho
mas Becket Archbifshop of Cãtorbury, who therat was fworn
to the King, and to his Lawes, and to his Sonne.

In the ninth yeere of his reigne, this king called a Parliamēt
at Northampton, where he entended reformation of many pri
uileges that the Clergy had, amongeft thefe, was one: that although one of the Clergy had committed felonie, murder, or
treafon, yet might not the King put him to death as he did the
Laye men. The which thing with many other, the kinge
thought to redreffe in the faid Parliament. Thomas Becket refifted him, but he might not preuayle againfte the king(427).

h h   For

For wel neere al the Bifshops of Englande were againft him.

In the.17.yere of his reigne,the king made a iourney into Ireland,where with great trauaile,he fubdued the Irifhe,and after with the helpe of the Primate of Armach , he refourmed the maners of the people and dwellers in that countrey, and that in thre thinges efpecially : Firft,in ruling and ordering of the Church by the Curates,ād how they fhould order their diuine Seruice,and minifter the Sacrament of matrimonie as it was in England,and other Chriftian Regions. The feconde was,how that the Lay people fhould behaue them felues towards their Curats,and in what wife they fhould pay and offer to God their tithes. The thirde was, tor making of their teftamentes.

Fabian.

The.21. Chapter.Of King Stephen,King Henry the.2. and S.Thomas of Caunterbury.

Stapleton.

MAifter Horn hath a marueloufe grace to dwel ftil in fuch matters as nothing relieue his caufe : that is in the inuefturing of biffhoppes.the which neither the Quenes Maiefty , or her graces noble progenitours in our tyme haue challenged,nor yet any other prince in England thefe many hūdred yers.Neither is it likely that King Stephen referued the inueftitures to him felf,afwel for that his immediat predeceffour King Henry,after fo long fturre about them gaue them ouer , as that the Pope had fo lately excōmunicated al fuch Princes.Polychronicō,which work ye cite, faith no fuch thing.Verily King Stephen,for a perpetual confirming of the clergies immunites, made this folemne othe,as it is recorded in Williā of Malmefbury. *Ego Stephanus Dei gratia &c.1 Stephen by the grace of God , by the affent of the clergy,and of the people, chofen to be King of England ,and confecrated thereunto of Williā the Archebifhop of Caūterbury ād Legat of the Church of Rome ,cōfirmed alfo afterrvarde*

VVilliam of Malmefbury

ward of Innocētius the bifhop of Rome, in the regard ād loue of God, I graūt the Church of God to be free, and do cōfirme the dew reuerēce vnto her. I promife I wil do nothing in the Church or in ecclefiafticalmatters by fimony, neither fuffer any thing to be fo don. I affirm ād cōfirm the Iuftice, the power and the orderīg of Ecclefiaftical perfons, and of al clerks, and their matters to be in the hāds of the bifhops. I do enact and graūt the promotiōs of the Churches with their priuilege's cōfirmed, and the cuftomes thereof after the old maner kept, to cōtinue and remayn inuiolas ted. And while fuch Churches fhal be void of their pper paftours, that both the Churches ād al the poffefsiōs therof, be ī the hād ād cuftody of the Clerks or of honeft mē, vntil fuch time, as a Pa- ftour be fubftituted according to the Canons. Thus far William of Malmefbury. Now that kīg Hēry the 2. fhuld referue the faid inueftitures to hifelf: (which your author Polichronicō faith not) and that the bleffed Saint and Martyr S. Thomas (whō ye cal Thomas Becket) was fworn to the fame: this tale verily hath no maner of apparāce or colour. This was none of the articles for the which the king ād S. Thomas cōtēded fo much: the which articles appere in the life of S. Thomas. That in dede which ye recite is one of thē: but how ye may proue your new fupremacy therby, that were hard, for the wifeft man in a coūtrey to tel: Yea much rather yt ferueth to the cōtrary, and proueth the Popes fupremacy, who dif- allowed the faid article with many other, the King alfo beīg at lēgth fain to yeld therin. The like I fay of the Kings doīgs in Irelād wherof ye write, which things, as euē by your own cōfefsiō he did by the helpe of the primat of Armach: fo Gi- raldus Cambrēfis, one that writeth of the kins doīgs ther, ād one that was fent thither by the kīg, faith he kept many coū cels ther, but by the popes wil ād cōfent. And Polidor⁹ fayth

Giraldus Cambrēfis
Ihe King kepeth Councels in Irelād by the Popes cōſent.
King Hē- ry cōque- red Irelād by the Popes confent.

hh ij   that

Polt.li.13.
In addit.
ad Neu-
bur.M.S.

King vvil
liā the cō
querour
moued
his right
firſt to
the Pope
ere he cō,
quered
England.

The doigs
of Kinge
Henry againſt S.
Thomas
declared
by M.
Foxe.

that the King obtayned the title of Irelond by the Popes autho-
ritie.Guilielmus Newburgenſis writeth much lyke of Williā Conquerour,*præmonſtrato prius Apoſtolico Papæ iure quod*
in regno Angliæ habebat,licentiaq̃, hæreditatem conquirendi
*impetrata,*that before he inuaded England, he did intimate
his right and intereſt to the Pope, and obtayned of him licence to atchiue and conquere his inheritaunce. Here perchaunce wil many of your ſecte maruaile, why ye haue
either named S. Thomas, or paſſed ouer the ſtory ſo
ſleightlye:and wil think, that ye are but a diſſembler and a
traytour to their cauſe, or at the leaſt a very faynt patrone
for thē, eſpecially ſeing M. Fox hath miniſtred you ſo much
good matter,proſequuting the matter. xj. leaues and more.
Your own frends wil ſay your allegations are but ſimple ād
colde,and in a maner altogether extrauagante, and that ye
might haue founde in M. Foxe, other maner of ſtuffe, as
a nomber of Kinge Henry the ſeconde his conſtitutions
and ordinaunces playne derogatorie to many of the Popes
Lawes: yea playne commaundemente, *that no man ſhould*
appeale to Rome,and that Peter pence ſhould be no more payed
to the Apoſtolicall ſee:or that, yf any man ſhould be founde
to bring in any interdiⷵt or curſe againſt the Realme of En-
gland, he ſhould be apprehended without delaye for a traytour,
and ſo executed.And finally,that no maner decree or cōmaun-
demente proceding from the authoꝛity of the Pope ſhould be re-
ceiued. You ſhall there finde, wil they ſay, concerning the
ſaid Thomas his parſon and doinges that he was no Martyr,but *a very rebell and traytour, and that all his contention*
ſtode not vppon matters of faith,religion,true doctrine or ſin-
cere diſcipline,but vpon worldly thinges:as poſſeſſiōs, liberties,
exemptions,ſuperiorities and ſuch like.

In dede

In deede thefe and fuche other lyke thynges we finde in
M. Foxe: but he ftorieth thefe thynges with as good fayth
and trouth, as he doth all his other. And here I would gladly for a while leaue M. Horne, and take him in hand, and
fhape him a full anfwere. But in as much as this would require a long procefle, and for that this my anfwere allready
waxeth lóg, I will forbeare the diligent and exact difcufsió
of the whole: and wil open fo much only to the vnleafned
reader, as may ferue hi for the true knowledge of the matter, and for the difcouering of M. Foxes crafty and vntrue
dealing: and withall for a full anfwere, to thefe friuoloufe
and falfe arguments producted by M.Horne.

And here firft, not S. Thomas, but the Kings ftoutnes
and fternnefle femeth to be reprehéded, that would nedes
haue an abfolute anfwere of him, and would not be contented with fo reafonable an anfwere as he made, *Saluo
ordine meo*: fauing my order. No nor afterward with this
exception, *Saluo honore Dei*, fauing the honour of God.
This modification or moderation may ferue to any indifferent man, that aduifedly confidereth the kings articles propofed to S.Thomas, fuch as might excufe him fró all ftoutnes and ftubbornes, that M.Foxe and his aduerfaries lay to
him. I intend not nowe to enter into any ferious or deape
examination of the fayd articles: but this I wil fay, that yt is
againft al the olde canons of the Church, yea and againfte
reafon to, that an Archbifhop fhulde be iudged of his fuffra-
gans, as S.Thomas was. Againe to omitte other articles,
there is one, that is quite contrarie to the Apoftolical doctrine, to the canons of Nice, and other moft auncient general councels: finallie to the catholyke doctrin of Chriftes
vniuerfal Churche, that is, for appeales to be made from the

S. Thomas can not iuftlie be accufed of ftoutnes and ftub-bournes.

Caufes vvhie S. Thomas fhuld not agree to the kings doinges.

Ca.8. de appellatio.
Si emerſerint ab Ar·
chidiacono, debēt pro
cedere ad epiſcopū: et
ad epiſ. ad archie. et
ſi Archiepiſ. deſuerit
in iuſtitia exhibēda,
poſtremò ad regē eſt
peruemendū, vt præ·
cepto ipſius in curia
Archiepiſcopi cōtro·
uerſia terminetur,
ita quod non debent
vlteri⁹ procedere abſ·
que aſſenſu regis.
In quadrilogo de vi·
ta B. Thomæ. lib. 5.
Vide dict
quadrilo·
gū lib.5.
impreſſ.pa
riſijs in 4.
An.1495.
in princi-
pio.
Vide foxū
fol. 48.

Cap.7.
Null⁹ qui
de rege te·
neat in ca
pite, vel
aliquis do
meſticorū

Archdeacō to the biſhop, frō the biſhop to the Arch
biſhop: ād in caſe ther be any defect of iuſtice there,
the matter to be browght to the king, and by his cōmaundemēt to be ended in the Archbiſhops cowrt,
without any further proceding, without the kinges
cōſent, wherby not only the popes ſupreme authority, but the authority alſo of al general coūcels, the
which are the ordinary and neceſſary remedies in
many caſes, did ſtād thē in the kig of Englād his grace
only, to be accepted, or to be reiected. M. Fox reciteth the kings cōſtitutiōs: but as he leaueth out this
ād many other, ād reherſeth but ſix of thē: ſo in thoſe
ſix he maketh thre manifeſt ād opē lies. For wher he
ſaith the ſayd decrees by him recited were cōdēned
by the Pope, ther were but thre of thē cōdēned, that
is the.1. the.3. ād the.4. The other thre the pope did
ſuffer ād tolerat. Againe what a decree was this, that none
that held of the king *in capite*, no nor any of his ſeruāts ſhuld
be excōmunicated, onleſſe the kig were firſt cōſulted? I trow
M. Horn hiſelf, ād his fellowes, neither kepe this preciſe order, nor wil allow it. Well, M. Fox full pretely leaueth out
this cōſtitutiō, what cauſe moueth him I cā not tel. Thík ye
nowe M. Fox, that for thoſe ād ſuch like, S. Thomas had not
good cauſe, to mollify the matter with *ſaluo ordine meo* , *&*
ſaluo honore Dei. ād whē that wold not be accepted, to gai-
ſay altogether, ād to appeale to the ſea of Rome? Ye wil ſay
this notwithſtāding, they were no matters of fayth or religiō, or true doctrine, and that he is therfor far frō the cauſe
and title of a martyr. In dede it was if not wiſely, yet wilily, ād like a crafty Fox done of you to ſcrape hí out of your
bleſſed kalender. For in good fayth place cā he haue none
there

there,onleſſe all your late ſtinking martyrs geue place,and
yelde.which are the deuils,ād not Gods martyrs,ād it were
for none other thig,but for the denial of the Popes ſuprea-
macy.The which ſupremacy is a neceſſary doctryne,to be
holdē of euery Chriſtiā mā (where vnuincible ignorāce is
not)vppō payn of dāmatiō, and euerlaſting ſeparatiō frō the
Catholik Church,and the mēbers of the ſame. Beſide this,
there are many take for bleſſed martyrs in the Church,that
died not for the faith or for doctrine beig thē in any cōtrouerſy,but for iuſtice ād truth ſake,and for theyr vertuouſe
dealig:as is the good mōke Telemachius,that ſeig at Rome
two ſwordplayers,the on of thē redy to deſtroy,ād kil the
other,vppō a great zeale,came to thē,and thought to haue
parted thē,ād ſo was ſlayn of thē him ſelf.wheruppō thēperour Honcrius reckoned him amōg the martyrs, ād made a
lawe,that there ſhould be no more ſuch kid of play exerciſed in Rome . The cauſe alſo of S.Iohn Chriſoſtoms troble
proceded not directly frō matter of fayth or doctryne, but
for reprouig thēpreſſe Eudoxia.I omit S.Quilliā and S.Lā-
...... both take for martyrs,and ſlayne for rebukig adultery.
And to come nearer to our own cōtrey and to S. Thomas
tyme, S.Alphegius Archbiſshop of Canterburie, a litle before the Conqueſt,that ſuffred him ſelfe to be ſlayne of the
Danes,rather then he would pille and polle his tenauntes,
to leauy an exceſſiue ſomme of money,that the Danes required for his redemption . Of whoſe vertue God ſynce
hath geuen greate teſtimonie, aſwell by diuerſe other miracles , as by preſeruinge his body ſo longe vncorrupted.
But the cheife and moſte aunciente preſidente of all in
the newe teſtamente is S.Iohn the Baptiſte, who died
for the

miniſtro-
rū eius ex
communi-
cetur &c.
niſi prius
rex &c.
A man
may be a
martyr,
though it
be for no
cauſe of
fayth or
relligion.
Niceph.li.
hiſt.eccleſ.
13.cap.1.
Telema-
chius the
martyr.
Theod.l.5
cap. 26.
Tr.l.10.c 2
Niceph.li.
13.cap.4.
cū ſequēt.
Sigeb.in
chronic.a.
697.et698.
Videelegā-
tē diſputa-
tionem au
Alphegus
ſit martyr
inter Lan-
frāc.Can-

tur. & Anſelmum poſtea Cant. Archiepiſcop. apud Edinerum lib. 1, de vita Anſelmi.
Vide Guliel.Malmeſb. de Pontif.lib.1.

VVat a testimony God hath geuē to the vvorld for S. Thomas doyngs.

In Qua-drilogo. li.2.c.16. Vox de cœlo elapfa fic conte-ftata eft. In dicto quadril. li.3.c.vlt. Nā & in loco pafsionis eius & vbi ante maius altare per-noctauit humādus, & vbi tan dem fepul-tus eft.etc.

for the lyke liberty and fredome of fpeache, as S. Quillian, and S. Lamberte did. To thefe we may fet Efaye and the other prophets of the olde teftamente: Howbeyt as I fayd in S. Thomas his caufe, is a neceffarie doctryne alfo imployed, that was either directly or indirectly blemifhed, by thefe ordinaunces of the king, concerning the Popes Supremacy. Now what madnes were yt for me, or any other to feke by words to fette forth this bleffed mans qualities and Martyrdome, when that God him felf, hath by fo wonderfull and ftraunge, yea by fo certayne and notorioufe miracles, afwell in the lyfe of his feruant as afterwarde, geuen to the worlde fuche a teftimonie for him, as all the deuills in hell, and theyre difciples in earth may rather gnafhe theyr angrie teathe, and enuie at, then by any good meanes deny and deface yt. True fhall yt be alfo, that S. Thomas heard long ere he returned into Englande, by a celeftiall and heauenlie voyce. *O Thoma, Thoma, Ecclefia mea gloriabitur in fanguine tuo.* O Thomas, Thomas, my Churche fhall glory in thy bloud. And true yt is, that was writen incontinently after hys death, that at the place of his pafsion, where he is buried, *paralitici curantur, cæci vident, furdi audiunt, loquuntur muti, claudi ambulant, euadunt febricantes, arrepti à dæmonio liberantur, & à variis morbis fanātur ægroti, blafphemi à demonio arrepti confunduntur: & quod à diebus paf trum noftrorum non eft auditum mortui furgunt.* Palfies are cured, the blinde fee, the deaffe heare, the dombe fpeake, the lame walk, the agues are healed, ād fuch as are poffeffed of the Deuill are delyuered, and diuers difeafes holpen, and blafphemers beinge taken and poffeffed of the deuill confounded: and finally (as our fayd authour, not fo muche an eare as an eie wytnes, faith) that which hath not ben heard of, in

of, in our fathers dayes, dead men are relieued a-
gaine. Thefe and manie other miracles fhewen afwell in England as out of England, were fo notable
and famoufe, that fhortly after S. Thomas his Martyrdome, not only the Erle of Flaunders, but the
Frenche King alfo came to Cantorburie in pilgrimage, to pray at this bleffed Martyrs tumbe. The
kinge of Fraunce offered there a chalice of golde,
and his graunt in writinge for a certayne quantitye
of wyne, yerely to be delyuered to the monks ther
to be merie withall at the folempnitye or feafte of
this bleffed Martyr.

The erle of Flaun-
ders ãd the Frenche
kinge came to Can-
terburie in pilgri-
mage to S. Thomas
*In quadrilogo lib.4.
cap. 4.*

*Obtulit munera, vi-
ñu videlicet et aurñ:
aureñ fcilicet calicẽ,
& vini centñ modios,
perpetuo ad natali-
tium diẽ martyris fin
gulis ãnis celebrãdũ
in lætitia.*

But what fhal we fay to kinge Henry him felfe?
what thowght he trowe ye of this bleffed mans doings and
death? This parte of the ftory of all other is mofte notable.
The king being in Normandy, and hearing that S. Thomas
was flayne toke the matter fo heuely, that for forty dayes,
kept him felf folitary in great mourning and lamentatio,
in great abftinence, fetting a fyde al the affayres of his great
ãd large dominiõs, for greif and forow: And forthwith fent
his ambaffadours to the Pope to purge him felfe of the fayd
murther. Wheruppõ certayn Legats were fent to him, before whom vpõ his othe he fayd, that he neither cõmaunded, nor willed that the Archbiffhop fhould be flayne, and
added that he was neuer fo fory for the death of his owne
father or mother. Yet did he not denie, but by vnaduifed
words, he gaue the murtherers an occafion of theyr fowle
enterprife. Wherfor he fubmitted him felf to the Legats to
enioyne him penaunce as they fhould thinke good. Then
was yt among other thinges enioyned him, that he fhould
breake and reuoke the forefayde ftatutes and ordinances,

*Polidorus.
in Hen 2.*

*Quadri-
logus.li.4.
cap. 5.*

The kigs
grief for
S. Tho-
mas.

Penaũce
enioyned
to the kig
by the po-
pes Le-
gats.

for the

for the which al this troble rofe:al the which cõditions the king by his othe promifed to obferue . This done the kings fon alfo promifed on his part , to fee thefe couenants kept. But yet fee the iufte iudgemẽt of God. As this king rebel-led againfte his fpirituall father S.Thomas,and his fpirituall mother the Churche , fo did his fonne and heire , with his two other fonnes,Richard and Iohn , rebell againfte him, confederating them felues with other the kinges fubieɗs, and with the Frenche and Scottifhe kinges . The king was browghte to this diftreffe, that he wyfte not in the world, what to faye , or what to doe:and being deftitute of mans helpe ranne to Gods helpe , and to the helpe of his bleffed martyr S.Thomas,at whofe great miracles done at Canter-bury all tne worlde did wonder . Wherefore forfaking Normandy where he was in more faftie, fayled into En-glande , and commynge towarde Canterbury , before he entred the city, puttinge of al his princely appparell , lyke a newe kinge Dauid, beinge perfequuted of his Abfolõ for hys fynnes,as Dauid wente out of the citie barefoted, fo this newe Dauid beinge barefoted, and all hys body na-ked, fauinge that he was couered withe a poore and a vile cote vppon the bare , beinge nowe hym felfe fearefull and tremblyng,whom before fo many nations feared and trem-bled , with muche fighinge and gronynge wente to the Martyrs tombe , where he continued all that daye , and the nighte followinge watchfull and faftinge : where he commended hym felfe to the bleffed martyrs prayers.Nei-ther was he deceyued of his good deuotion and expeɗa-tion : as we fhall anon declare . Before the fayde tombe , he toke difcipline with a rodde of euerie monke , and for his loue and deuotion to the martyr, he renounced the forefayd

The kĩgs
fonnes re-
bell to hĩ
theire car
nal father
as he re
belled a-
gainft his
fpirituall
father,
the pope
and S.
Thomas .

Quadrip.
hifto. vitæ
D.Thom.
lib.4.c 6
cũ fequẽt.

2.Re c.17
Iofephus
li.2.c. 12.
de Antiq.
Iudæo.
His mer-
uelous vo
luntarie
penaunce
In diɗa
quadrip.
& in Gul.
Malme; b.

foresayd yll ſtatütes and cuſtomes for euer, and onely ſayd
he woulde kepe ſuche as were reaſonable and good. *Guliel-*
mus Neuburgenſis, whome M. Foxe bringeth in to deface
and diſgrace this bleſſed martyr, yf yt might be, and yet not
daring, to tell either of other thinges, writen by other, or
that I ſhall nowe tell yowe out of the ſayde Neuburgenſis,
ſayeth, that the ſayd nighte, there was avoyce that ſayde
to a good and a bleſſed monke at Canterbury beinge a
ſleape: *haue ye not ſene (ſayeth the voyce) the kings*
great and wonderfull humilitie? Be thou aſſured, that
ſhortlye thende of his affayres ſhall declare howe well
God lyketh the ſame. My authour ſayth, that he heard
this from the mowthe of a reuerende Abbate, who
beinge the ſame tyme in Kente, hearde yt from a
credible and a faythfull reporter. The nexte mor-
ninge the kinge heard maſſe, before the tombe of
the martyr, and ſo departed. The very ſame daye
yea the very ſame howre that the king heard maſſe
there, vndoubtedly by the miraculous workinge
of God, the ſcottiſhe king without battayle ſcattered from the reſt of his Army, and afterde by litle
and litle all his enimies, aſwell beyond as by hither
the ſeas were quieted and pacified. All the which
proſperouſe fortune the kinge did aſcribe to God,
and to his glorious martyr S. Thomas, to whome
moſt certaynly, it was to be aſcribed. Let M. Foxe
nowe and his fellowes to, rayle at this bleſſed mã as
lõg as they will. Let hi ſcrape hi out of his kalēder,
ãdput in for hi heretiks, theeues, ãd traytors, ãdlet hi
nowe if he can for very ſhame, cal this man a tray

ii ij   tour,

Neuburg.lib.2.c.34.
Impr.Cap.19.M.S.
Viro reuerendiſſimo
Rogero ſcilicet Ab-
bate Bellelandenſi re
ſerēte cognoui, quod
&c.
Polidorus in Hēr.2.
Diſt. lib.4.ca.8. in
quadripart, & in
Neuburg.cap. 19.
Ipſa nãque die, eadē
etiam diei hora qua
miſſa interfuerat,
rex Scotorum captus
eſt: &c.
A merueloule victo
ry that God gaue
tne king the ſame
hovvre he heard
maſſe at Caterbury.
The king aſcribeth
his victorie to God
and S Thomas.
Rex autem totũ aſ-
criptt Domino, &
glorioſo martyri Th.
cui certiſſ. erat aſcr.

vvhat a madnes is it to make S. Thomas after so manie hundred yeares a traytour?

tour,and cause his name to be aboliſhed out of the Church boks,as yt hath bene of late yeares.Let them toſie and tur-moyle as longe , and as buſelie as they will . They ſhall but ſhewe theire extreme wyckednes and madnes , blaſphe-mouſly to cal him traytour,whom the king him ſelf(to whō the offence was don,if any were don)worſhipped as Gods holy martyr:they ſhal but ſtryue againſt the ſtreame,or ra-ther againſt God him ſelfe,that hath geuen throwgh out al the world ſuch a glorious teſtimony for him: and for the cō-firmatiō of the catholike doctrine of his Church,namely for the popes ſupreamacie.Which anſwere I will alſo to ſerue againſt M.Horn cōcerning al his allegations here touching the doings of the king with this bleſſed Martyr.

M.Horn. The. 122. Diuiſion. pag.78.b.

The.428. vntruth. Auouched,but vnproued

In Germany,ſucceded vnto Frederike, Henry, and next vnto him Philip, both of them(.428.)inueſturing Biſhops,and ſuffering no Legates frō Rome to come into Apulia,nor Sicilia,according to the aforeſaid compoſition,

The. 22.Chapter:Of Henry the.6:Philip,and Otho the. 4. Emperours.

Stapleton.

Ann.1230. Abb. Vrſp. in vita Henr.5. Gul.Tirius de bell ſac. li.1.ca.13. Otho Friſ. li.7.ca.16. Radulph. Piſanus in vita Ca-lixti. 2.

THat Henry and his brother Philip did inueſture biſ-ſhops,yt is not likely , and the matter woulde be bet-ter proued,then by your bare worde.Namelie ſeinge that Henrie the.5.made a full concluſion with Calixtus the ſecond(as we haue before ſhewed)that the clergie ſhould haue the election of theyre biſhops . By the which agrea-ment the contention that had continued about a fiftie yea-res for that matter was pacified. And wheras ye refer your ſelf to the aforeſayd cōpoſition,that they woulde ſuffer no Legats to come into Apulia and Sicilia,the pope is muche bound

bounde to you,for therby ye proue his supremacy:As from
whom that Composition by way of dispensatiõ proceded,
as your self before auouched,and as in Nauclerus it wel appeareth.

M.Horne. The.123. Diuision. pag.78. b.

*Next to vvhame succeded Otto ,surnamed of the Clergie the defen-
dour of Iustice for vvher as the maner of Princes vvas (saith Abbas
Vrspurgens.)cheerfully and readily to geue benefices or Churches,to those that did fiist aske them,he woulde not so doe:but
he gaue all the benefices that fel,as wel Ecclesiastical as Secular ; to those with whome he was acquainted &c. This Emperour came into Italy,claymed and(.429.)recouered al the right of the Em-
roo that the Pope(430.)vsurped vnder the name of S. Peters Patrimonie,
and called a(.431.)Synode at Norinberge about this matter, ãd
touching the(.432.)Popes authority.*

288.
Nauclerus
The. 429.
vntruthe.
ThisOtho
recouered
it not,but
lost the
Empire
him selfe.
The. 430.
vntruthe
slaunde-
rous. It
vvas no
vsurpatiõ
but lavv-
ful poses-
sion.
The , 431,
and . 432,
as shall ap
peare.

Stapleton.

Ye haue not as I said wonne so much creditte , being so
often taken in open lies,that we may truste you vpon your
worde . Tell vs therefore I pray you what chronicler calleth this Otho the defendour of iustice,and then tel vs , by
what good logike your *for* wil followe.For methinke yt is
but a selie slender *for* to say , he was defendour of iustice,
for that he bestowed spiritual lyuings vpon none but suche
as he knewe. Onlesse ye did proue withall that he knewe
none but honest men . But will you see what Nauclerus
your owne Author writeth hereof? He saith of this Otho:
*This man was praysed of many religious persons and of the
clergy, for a defendour of Iustice: When yet he was altogether
a dissembler: Nam omnia beneficia tam Ecclesiastica quàm se-
cularia, familiaribus suis quos secum ex Saxonia & Anglia
duxerat, contulit.* For he bestowed all promotions as well

ii iij   eccle-

Platina in
Inno.3.
Vide Nau
cler. gene.
41.p.274.
5.6 &.7.
Conuentū
principum
sua partis
celebrauit
Norimber
ga.

Ecclesiastical as temporall vppon his nere acquaintaunce such as he brought with him out of Saxony and out of Englande. Lo M. Horne, this *(For he bestowed)* which you brig to proue a supreme gouerment, Nauclerus reporteth to proue a partial regiment. That he telleth to his shame, you drawe it to his honour. Again what patrone of Iustice call you him, that wrongfully toke frō the Church of Rome her olde and rightful possessions, and was therfore excommunicated and deposed, of Innocētius.3. and Frederik.2. made Emperour in his place. And that, notwithstanding the diet of Otho his faction, holden at Norimberg : which you vn truly cal a Synod. Neither was it there debated of the Popes Authority in Ecclesiastical matters (which is our present matter) but only whether the Pope migt depose the Emperour: which is not now any part of our matter in hande.

M.Horne. The.124. Diuision. pag. 78.b.

Polych.
Fabian.

The. 432.
vntruthe.
No suche
vvoordes
in Fabian.

In England as Henry his father had doone before him: so folovved Kinge Richard in geuing Ecclesiastical promotions, in calling coūcels, and ordering other Ecclesiastical matters: yea. euen in his absence, being in Syria, by one that represented his person therin the B. of Ely, who called and made a councel at westminster, as the kigs procurator, and the Popes Legat, ād(.432.) spake by the Kings povver. But in this matter, kig Iohn did more then any of his predecessours, vvhich purchased him much hatred vvith the Pope and his Monkes.

The .23. Chapter: Of King Richarde the first, and King Iohn , Kings of England.
Stapleton.

NOw M. Horne is returned from Appulia, Sicilia, Germany, and Italy into Englād againe. And why thinke you? Forsoth to proue him self like a good and a faithfull proctour to the Pope, that the Pope was the supreame head of head of the Churche of England. Elfe let him wifely fhewe why he telleth, that the bifhop of Elie was *the Popes Legate?* But chiefly why he bringeth in, or is not afhamed to lay forth for his fupremacy Kinge Iohn : and to fay *that he did more in this matter than any of his predeceffours?* Ye fay truthe M. Horne, he did in dede, and being excommunicated of the Pope, for his miforder and outragious doinges againft the Churche, and the whole lande interdicted, he gaue ouer to the Pope, his crowne and kingdome : and receiued it againe at the Popes handes. And becaufe this matter fhoulde not be kepte in filence (which wifedome perchaunce and policie to, woulde haue had fo kepte) Maifter Foxe blafeth out the matter at large, and laieth forth before all men, the copie of the letter obligatorie concerning the yeldinge vp of the crowne into the Popes handes, and of certayne money yearelye to be paide. I will not, nor neede not trauayle in the curioufe triall, and examination of the circumftances of the caufe : but this only wil I fay to M. Foxe and to you M. Horne, that yf ye proceede on as ye beginne, ye are worthy to haue a rewarde at the Popes hande : either for that ye are but a diffembling counterfeyte proteftante, and the Popes pryuie frende : or yf ye be angrie with that, fo wife and fkylfull a reafoner, that ye fpeake ye wotte nere what : And while ye go about to fet the Popes crowne on the Quenes head, ye take her crowne and fette yt on the Popes head. So that it litle ferueth you to tel vs, that Kinge Iohn *vnchafed him much hatred with the Pope and the Monks.* Ye might haue put in, and with all the nobilitye and commons to, yea mofte of all, with God and good men to. But this is your, and your fellowes trade, efpeciallie Maifter Foxes in

the fet-

Acts and monuments fol. 65.

the fetting forth of this Kinges ftorie, to lye extremely, to bring thereby the clergie into hatred and enuie : as in thys

A greate vntruthe of M. Fox côcernîge the poyfoning of kîg Iohn.
ftorie among other thinges he hath done, touching the poifoning of this King by a monke of Swinftead abbey. And perchaunce ye M. Horne meante fome like matter, when ye fpeake of the monks that hated him. But becaufe I can not certainly lay this to you , I wil let you goe for a while, and be a litle in hand with M. Fox, and opé vnto thee (good Reader) that thou mayft the better vnderftande his fubftátial dealing and handling of ftories, and the better beware of his gay glorioufe painted lies, what is the common confent of our beft chroniclers in this point.

     Firft then, this is a manifeft lie, that ye fay M . Foxe , *the*
An other vntruthe, for the chroni cles doe not commonly fay fo.
chroniclers mofte agree in this , that he was poyfoned by the monke at Swinftead. Which thing I could eafely proue , by reciting fpecially, what euery authour writeth concerning the maner of his death: But M. Foxe himfelf hath, we thank him, prouided that we neade not trauayle fo farre: for lo, he bringeth in *Polidorus,* faying he died of forowe and heuines of harte: *Radulphus Niger,* faying he died, of furfeting in the
M. Foxe him felfe vnwares côfuteth his own fable of the poyfoning of kîg Iohn.
night: *Roger Houeden,* faying he died of a bluddie flixe: *Matheus Parifienfis,* faying that by heuines of minde, he fel into a feruente agewe , at the abbey of Swinftead , which he encreafed with furfeting, and nawghty diet: by eating peaches and drinkinge of newe Cifer, or fydar. Then adde ye farder Maifter Foxe that fome faye he died of a colde fweate : fome of eatinge apples : fome of eating peares: and fome of eating plummes. So haue ye here good reader , fowre chroniclers by name , and at the leaft fowre other vnnamed, that make no mention of any poyfon. Now could I bring the Polichronicon , and Fabian which reci-

tinge

ting the fayed Polychronicon, faieth that the King died of
the fluxe. Here alfo could I bring in, that thofe that write
of his poyfoning, write very diuerfly nothing agreing with
your authour in the kind of poyfon. And alfo that they re-
hearfe it rather as a common tale, then for any aſſured ftorie or truthe. Many other thinges could I bring in, but
what needeth yt, when we haue by hys owne tale ſtore
ynoughe of witneſſes agaynſt him? Yet will I adde one
more, but fuch a one, as ought to be to M. Foxe in ſteade
of a greate forte: that one I fay, of whome by all that I can
iudge (for he hath not vouchfafed ones to name him) M.
Foxe hath taken all his declaration, concerning the election of Stephen Langton, and of all the greate bufines that
iffued thereof : yea the writyng obligatorie, touching the
refigning of the crowne into the Popes handes. Whiche
lyeth in our authour worde for worde, as M. Foxe hath
tranflated it.

This our authour fheweth, that as the Kyng was going
northwarde, the grounde opened and fwallowed vp hys
cartes and caryage, that yt coulde neuer be recouered.
Wherevppon the Kyng fell into a greate griefe and hea-
uineſſe, and fetched many fighes from the very bottome
of hys harte. And beyng at Swinftead furfeated with peaches and other fruite, and there fell ficke. And fo beynge
ficke departed, and being not able to continue on horfe-
backe, came in an horfelytter to Leadforde caftle : and afterwarde to Newemarket, where perceiuyng him felfe to
be paſte all cure and remedie, he fente for the Abbatte of
Crokeftone that was fkylfull in phyficke, of whome he
was confeſſed, and receiued the Sacrament of the holye
Euchariftia. And by and by he endeth this ſtorie of King

kk

The Au-
thour of
vvhome
M. Foxe
taketh the
refidue of
his ſtorie
cōcernig
Kīg Iohn
maketh
againſt
him.
Ex Chro-
nic. Ioan.
Lōdinēſis.

Iohn,

Iohn, saying that because this king was hated of many, partly for the death of his nephewe Arthur, partly for his adultrie, partly for hys tyranny , partlye for the tribute , by the whiche he browght England into a perpetuall bondage, partly for the warres that hys doinges sturred vppe, he was scarslie worthie to be bemoned and lamented for , of anye man. Here haue we now M . Foxe fyue authors by name, and more aunciente thē your Caxtō, and of an other iudgemente, towching this kinges death , then your Caxton is: beside fowre some sayes at the leaste.

M. Foxes grounde of poysoninge kinge Iohn stādeth vpō a lyīng boke hauing no name of the auctour.
And now let vs weighe with a word or two the creditte of this yowr owne Authour . I passe ouer , that ye call yt the chronicle of William Caxton, he being neither the maker, neither the translatour, sauing he hath adioyned out of Polichronicō the description of Englande and Irelande, of Treuisa his translation, and added as they say, certayn other thinges to his vnknowen Author. Belyke ye thowght to wynne some credite to your authour clothing hym with the name of this Caxton, a man of late remembraunce, because he hath no name of his owne . And so a mete worke for you, in the darke to lurke and lie withall , and in dede

Vvhat a lying boke this fructus tēporū is that M. Fox grou deth him selfe vppon.
vnworthy to haue the name of the chronicles of England, or to be called *Fructus temporum:* being as vnfruytful as any booke that was made many a. 100. yeres. Onlesse we may call him beinge barrē of al good truthe and choise of good matter, fitte for a story of any credit or fruytful, being only fruytful ād plētiful of wōderful vntruths, and opē lewde lies. I report me (for his truth to his fable of the xxxiij. Daughters of king Diocletiā king of Syria, that after they had slain their husbands, stole away by shippe into our Ilelād of Britannie whiche was then vnhabited and vnpeopled, and afterward

terwarde beinge conceyued by deuilles browght forth gy-
antes whiche inhabited the lande, vntill the commynge of
Brute that flewe them. And that our Ilelande was called *Parte.1.*
Albion of the eldeft dawghter Albine: as afterward Britã·
nie by the name of the forefayd Brute. Againe of king Ar∫
thure, that being not able to kepe the poffefsiõ of his owne
realme from the Saxons, caried an armie of one hundred
thoufande and more into farre countries, hauing vnder his
conducte a nomber of kinges, and there flewe the Emperour of Rome, ãd difcomfited his huge army, wherin were
aboue.5.or.6. hundred thoufande armed men. Make now
M.Foxe the citezens of Rochefter beleue, that in the olde
tyme, by the prayer of S. Auguftyne, theyre forefathers *Parte.5.*
were borne with tayles: or any wife man to belieue, that
king Ethelbertus ioyning with his frend Elfride the king of
Northumberlãd(who yet was an heathen, the other being
chriftened)leuied an army, and fet vppõ the Britaines, becaufe they would not receyue and obey the fayd S. Auguftine. Make vs, if you can beleue this, with the vaine fabler
Galfride(a fadde Author with your felowe Iewel) againft *Vide præ-*
the approued hiftory of venerable Bede, and of all other *fationem*
fence his time. Make vs, I fay, M.Fox, by any good or pro- *Guilielm.*
bable demõftratiõ, belieue this and an hundred fuche other *Nevvbri-*
fables, for the which your *Fructus temporum*, is vnfruitfull *genfis de*
to his wife ãd difcrete reader: and then tel vs and fpare not, *Galfrido*
of this mõk of Swiftead. Otherwife he wer a very fwynef- *impreff.*
head that would be lightly and rafhly perfwaded, by fuche
fwynifh fables. Paynt ãd picture thẽ as faft ãd fayre as ye wil
to make fooles fayn withal: I fay not this becaufe I wil excufe hym, or any other yll monke, of theyre nawghty doinges. I do require but cõuenient proufe namely of you M.

kk ij   Foxe

Foxe,and your fellowes, that are ſo preciſe with the Catholikes for their proufes. And when ye haue al proued,ye
proue nothing to the purpoſe. For the ill doings of ſome
naughty packes,can neither deface the truth of the Catholique doctrine, nor yet ſpotte the honeſtie of other not cóſenting. And as there is no likelihode the King to be after
this ſort poiſoned : ſo is it more incredible,that this Monke
had Maſſes continually ſonge for his ſoule:and of all, moſt
incredible, that it ſhoulde be confirmed by their generall
Chapter. No, no,M. Foxe, thinke not to carie awaye the
matter ſo. Thinke not that al that reade your foolish,lewd
lying Martyrologe will ſtraightwaies without further tryall and examination, take all for the Goſpell. And ſee how
God hath prouided againſt your falſe lying fable a good and
a conuenient remedie for them that will not willingly be
caried away lyke fooles and beaſtes , for the diſcredite of
this your fable . For ſeeing that your ſelfe hath here moſt
impudently added that which is not at all in your authour,
that is, concerning the confirmation of the generall chapter : who will hereafter credite you or regarde your writinges : or who wyll not thinke , that your vnnamed and
vnfruitfull authour hath either vpon to light credite ſet in
this fable in his vnfruitfull booke, or by like impudencie as
ye haue fayned the generall chapters confirmation , hath
fained it, or taken of ſome that fained it, this whole foolish
fond fable ? Goe nowe on M. Horne : pleade on , as you
haue begonne , and bring moe ſuch examples, I pray you.

An other
great vn-
vntruth.
of M.
Foxes:
for his
authour
hath no
vvord of
this con-
firmatió.
See thys
boke
prynted
by vvin-
kin de
word.
1502.

M. Horne. The. 125. Diuiſion. pag.79.4.

In this vvhile The French King helde a Councell at Ceno-
mannia in Turon. *And after him* King Lewes did celebrate a ſolemne Coúcel at Paris,vvherat was preſent the Popes legates.
Stapleton.

Stapleton.

Plead on I fay M.Horn, ãd tel your reader that king Lewes was fupreme head, becaufe in a coũcell that he kept at
Parys *the Popes legat was prefent.* Wherby it rather followeth that it was kepte, by the Popes fupreame authority,
not by the kinges.

M. Horne The.126. Diuifion. pag.79.a.

In vvhiche time vvas Frederike the.2. Emperour, out of doubt, *faith*   The.433.
Auentinus, an other Charles the great, and without all contro-   vntruth
nerfie moft profitable for the Chriftiã cõmon wealth: vvhiche   mere
not only helde the priuileges aforefaid in Apulia *and* Sicilia *, but in all*   Slaunde-
his dominions, and about this matter,(.433.)*tamed diuers Popes , called*   rous.
and kepte diuerfe Coũcelles, afvvel by his Sonnes, as by him felfe: and ordei-   The. 434
ned certain(.434.) *Eccfefiaftical lavves againft diuerfe Heretiques, cõdẽ-*   vntruthe.
ninge their herefies and appointing hovv they fhould be ordered: ordeining   Not eccle,
likevvife many priuileges for Ecclefiaftcall perfonnes.   fiafticall
   Lavves
   as fhall
   appeare.

The.24.Chapter. Of Frederike the.2. Emperour of that name.

THE more and the deaper ye praife this Frederik, the
more and the deaper ye mefhe and wrappe your felf
in your owne fhame and greauous cõdemnatiõ. And
muche are we the catholikes bownden to the infpeakable
goodnes of God, that whereas ye and your fellowes moft
prefumptuouflye and obftinatelye, either reiecte all fuche
proufes and demonftrations as the catholikes lay for them
againft you, or moft fryuoloufly goe about to fruftrat and
elude thẽ, hath now fo entangled yow with yower owne
allegatiõ, your owne Emperour, by yow fo highlie cõmẽ-
ded, that whereas ye fay, *he tamed dyuers Popes* we fay, he
neuer fo tamed Pope, as he was tamed him felf of the Pope,
and as he tameth you, and maketh you not fo much a tame
foole , as that fo folifhlye and fondlye fet vppe your newe

M.Horne
telleth of
lavves
made by
the Em=
perour
hovv he=
retikes
fhould be
ordered,
but the
order he
fhevveth
not.

Papacy by his authority:but a very mad and an horrible heretike. I pray thee now Good Reader, geue a good and an
attentiue eare. Did then this Emperour, as ye fay Maifter
Horne, and therein truely, make lawes (though not truely Ecclefiafticall Lawes)againfte diuerfe Heretiques,con-
demning the herefies, and appointing howe they fhoulde
be ordered? If ye had tolde your Reader , the names of
the Heretiques, or their herefies, and the manner appointed howe they fhoulde be ordered , yee might haue eafed
mee offome labour, but to your owne little eafe or contentation : as proclaiming your felfe by expreffe woordes
as ye doe neuertheleffe couertlie lurking in this youre Cacus denne, an open and a notorioufe, for a number ofmoft

The He=
retikes
that Fre=
derike cō
demned,
vvere cō=
demned
before
in the
great ge=
neral coū=
cell at
Lions:

wretched and damnable errours, and a moft wretched heretique.   And here firft though I haue graunted you,that
he made lawes againfte Heretiques: yet will I not graunt
you,that they were(as ye terme thē) Ecclefiafticall lawes.
For fuche (proprely to fpeake) are made of Ecclefiaftical
perfons,in whome the Authoritie of allowing or condemning for matters Ecclefiafticall refteth.   Thefe Lawes of
Frederike were rather exequutorie of the Lawes Ecclefiafticall, then lawes mere Ecclefiaftical.   For the Heretiques and herefies by Frederike condemned, were before
condemned by the Bifhoppes and Popes,efpeciallye by the
great learned Bifhoppe Innocentius the third, in the mofte
famoufe Generall Councell kepte at Lateran in Rome.

An.1215.
Platina
In Innoc.
tertio.
In Chro=
nographia

At the whiche befide the Pope, were prefent , the Patriarches of Conftantinople and Hierufalem, three fcore and
tenne Metropolitane,and foure hundred other Bifhoppes,
12.Abbattes,and. 800. Priours conuentuals : in the whole,
as your brother Pantaleō writeth,a thoufād ād.300.Prelats:
with

with the Ambaſſadours of both the Emperours, as
wel of the Weſt, as of the Eaſt : Yea as alſo of the
Kings of Hieruſalem, Frauce, Spaine, England, Cy-
prus and other Countries. In this Councell were
condemned a nūber of heretikes, calling thē ſelues
Catharos, Patarenos, Pauperes de Lugduno, Paſſaginos,
Toſſepinos, Arnoldiſtas, Speroniſtas, and with other
ſtrauge names. There was alſo cōdemned the wicked *Almaricus: Whoſe mind the Father of lies had ſo*
blinded, that his doctrine Was to be counted not here-
tical only, but madde alſo ād furious. This coucel was
kept, this Fredericus being Emperour, who in this
point folowing th'Emperours Iuſtinian ād Charles
the Great (and ſo far I graunt it true, that ye ſay he
was an other Charles the Great) as thei before had
done, cōfirmed the lawes Eccleſiaſtical, with ciuil
ād politike ordinauces. And as they cōdemned the
heretiks, firſt by the Church condemned: ſo dothe
Fredericus to : as *Patarenos, Speroniſtas, Leoniſtas,*
Arrianiſtas, Circuciſos, Paſſaginos, Ioſeppinos, Carrace-
ſes, Albaneſes, Franciſcos, Banaroles, Comiſtas, Walde-
ſes, Burgaros, Comillos, Barrinos, Ottoleuos, & de aqua
nigra. and finally, *omnes hæreticos vtriuſq, ſexus:* All
heretiks of both kind, as well men as womē. Yet is
there great differēce, betwene the foreſaid Eccleſiaſtical, ād Emperial lawes. The Eccleſiaſtical perſons, after long ād mature cōſideration and examination of opiniōs and doctrine of the foreſaid perſons, do find their doctrine, a falſe and an heretical
doctrine, and therfor do cōdemne thē as heretiks:
they do curſe and excōmunicate them, and if they
be

Vide Decret. Grego.
tit. de heretic. c. ex-
communicamus. 2.

A raſcal rablement
of monſtruous he-
retiques names.

Ioan. Gerſ. part. 4.
Ibidē titulo de ſum-
ma Trinit. cap. 2.
Reprobamus etiam
& cōdemnamus per
uerſiſſimum dogma
impij Almarici, cu-
ius mētem pater mē-
dacij ſic excæcauit vt
eius doctrina, nō tam
haretica, quàm inſa-
na ſit cenſenda.
Vide epiſtolas Petri
de vineis Cancella-
rij Frederic. 2. li. 1.
ca. 25. 26. et. 27.
Et nouell. Fred. in-
ſertas Cod. Iuſtinia.

The difference be-
tvvene the lavves
of Frederike and
the Councell.
Dict. cap. 2. de ſum-
ma trinitate. Et c.
excommunicamus.
1. & 2. de haretic.

be perfons Ecclefiafticall, doe depriue and degrade them, and fo leaue them to the fecular power. The faid Councel ordeineth, that none fhal preach without the Popes or the Bifhoppes licence, and that all fecular officers fhall take an othe to doe their endeuour to purge their countrie of heretikes, and if nede be, to be compelled thereto by excommunication. And that all fufpect perfons fhall purge them felues, at the difcretion of their ordinarie vnder paine of excommunication, in the which if they wilfully continue one yeare, then to be taken for heretikes. Thefe and many other things the Councell ordeined in this behalfe.   The which decrees the Emperour Frederike confirmeth by his Emperial edict, adding perpetual infamie, exile, banifhmet, death, and the difheryting of their heires : and that he fhal not be take for any officer or Magiftrat, ad that al his iudge-mets and fenteces fhal be void that wil not take the othe a-forefaid. He comaudeth the houfes of heretiks and of their fautours and abettours to be plucked downe, neuer to be builded againe.   He declareth them to be inteftable: that is, neither able to make teftament of their owne nor to be capable of any benefit, out of any other mans teftimonie: and that to the fecond generation, they fhal beare no pu-blike office. And this is the manner, M. Horne, of the orde-ring of Heretiks, that ye fpeake of, appointed by your new fupreme Head the Emperour Frederike.   And fo yee fee withal how you and your fellowes were to be ordered, if he now liued. What ? Me thinke ye beginne, M. Horne, to waxe angrie and to chaufe with me, for telling you of fuch a rablement of ftraunge monftruoufe heretical names: And that ye haue nothing to doe with thefe heretiques, be-ing fuche as ye neuer heard of, no, not fo muche as their

The ma
ner hovv
heretikes
fhould be
ordered,
fet forthe
as vvell
out of the
forefaide
Councell,
as out of
Frederike
his lawes.
Dift.c.25.
cu feque-
tibus.

names,

names before. Wel, for the names, I wil not perchaunce
fticke with you, but for the wicked opinions, that they
mainteined, they are of nearer coufinage to you, then yee
were ware of, when ye wrote of Fredericus *Ecclefiafticall*
lawes againft heretikes, Ergo, heretikes they were by your
owne fentence. Wherevnto I adioyne:Ergo, you are an
heretique, as vpholding a number of their erronious opinions: for the which they were condemned as well by Frederike, as by the forefaid general Councel.

And firft to beginne with Almaricus, Did not his errors
ftand in the refufing of Images, Aulters, the inuocation of
Saintes, the tranfubftantiation of the holy Euchariftia, euē
as your brother Pantaleon writeth, faying (which is maruaile) that he was burned at Paris for teaching of errours?
A man may thinke they were errours in deede, that Pantaleon will ones confeffe to be errours. For the other a-
forefaide, he taketh not for errours, but for true doctrine.
What errours were they then? One was, that if Adam
and Eue had continued in ftate of grace, they fhould neuer
haue had children by any carnal copulatiō, but otherwife:
Yea that there fhould haue bene no difference betwen the
Male and the Female kinde. Secondly, he faied, that the
bleffed Saintes in heauen doe not fee the effence of God.
Whiche errour he learned of *Petrus Abailardus*, againfte
whome S. Barnarde writeth: and of *Arnoldus Brixienfis*,
of whome as I fuppofe, *Arnoldifta*, of whom we fpake of,
be called. Thirdly, he faid, that the bodie of Chrift is no
otherwife in the Sacramente of the Aulter, then in other
bread, and all other things. Fourthly he faid, there was
no hell. Fifthly, he denyed the refurrection of the flefh.
And yet is this Almaricus a worthy Bifhoppe, and an holy

II Martyr

Almari≀
cus is M.
Foxes ho
ly Mar≀
tyr.

Vide Foxū
fol.70.

Articles
of the cō≀
uocation
offered of
late to the
parliamēt

Martyr, in Maifter Foxes madde Martyrologe.   Neither
can he finde any matter why he was condemned, but for
teaching and holding againfte Images, whiche if it were
true, as it is falfe, yet were he but a ftarke ftinking Martyr.

I will nowe vnfolde and rippevppe the herefies of fome
other condemned by Frederike, that Maifter Horne may
fee his own iudgement, geuen againft him and his fellowes
(efpecially againft their hereticall Articles agreed vppon
in their Schifmaticall Conuocation, and nowe after fower
yeares, offered to the Parliament to be confirmed and ratified) geauen, I faie, not onely by the mofte famoufe Generall Councell aforefaied, but alfo by his owne Supreme
Head, the Emperour Frederike, and by his owne wordes
and confefsion.   And here it fhall be fufficient to fet before yow, the *Waldenfes* onely.   For as a good fellowe
ones faid, whiche had prouided a feaft furnifhed with manye difshes, to his friend maruailing at fuche plentie, but
all was but fwines flefhe, which he had by his iolie cokerie
dreffed in fuche diuerfitie : So all this rafcall rablement of
thefe huge monftruous names and fectes, are in effecte nothing but the fwinifh fecte of the Waldenfes: otherwife
called the poore brethren of Lyons, taking there, their originall of one *Waldo*, their vnlearned and blinde prefump-
tuoufe guide.   Whiche had in diuerfe Countries diuerfe
names, whereof fome ye haue heard : and were common-
lie called in England, as appeareth by our Actes of Parliamente and Chronicles, and in fome other Countries alfo,
Lollardes.   Wil ye then knowe, what their Relligion and
order was in Churche matters?   I remitte the Latine and
learned Reader to Aeneas Syluius, and to Paulus Aemilius:
                                                                                    and

and the Englifh Reader to Maifter Foxe him felfe. Who
at large to decke and beutifie his holy Canonifation fetteth
their errours and herefies foorth to his Reader. And to
be fhort, there fhal ye find, that our holy Englifh Cõuocatiõ
borowed their damnable Articles, whereof we haue fpoken, of them, and the whole order befide, of this their gaie
Gofpelling Church.

Of this fecte fprang among other, the *Albanenfes*, whiche otherwife are called *Albigenfes*, of the people called
Albij in the Countie of Tholous in Fraunce, the whiche
we haue before rehearfed. Nowe the *Arnoldiftæ* can
not be the fchollers and difciples of *Arnoldus de Villa noua*,
being at this time and long after vnborne, and fo it feemeth
that they are fo called of *Arnoldus Brixienfis*, and withal,
that as well Maifter Horne, as his Maifter *Illiricus* (from
whome he fetched thefe Epiftles of *Arnoldus de Villa noua*) are out of the waye. Maifter Horne for imagining this
Arnoldus to haue liued, aboute the time of King Henrie
the firft. And Illiricus for imagining *Arnoldiftas*, to be
named of *Arnoldus de Villa noua*, and to be condemned
before he was borne. Him felfe confefsing, that he liued aboute fuche time as we before haue declared. Maifter
Foxe alfo as greate an Antiquarie as he is, as farre as I can
learne, confoundeth thefe two Arnoldus : and maketh a
great fturre for the auauncing of his newe Ghofpel of this
Arnoldus de villa noua, being a falfe lying Prophet, as I haue
before fhewed you. And yt may be proued both by him
and by *Illyricu*, that he was an Heretique, if he mainteyned fuche errours as they fpecifie : whereof nothing doth
appeare in the forefaied Epiftles.

in hiftoria
Bohemiæ
ca.35.P.
Aemil.li.
6.Hift.
Franc.
Fol.42.
cũ fequẽt.
All our
nevve
Gofpell
fpringeth
from the
foolifhe
fond Frier
Vvaldo,
and his
fect con-
demned
by the
forefaide
Councell
and by
Frederik,
of vvhõ
the Ar-
noldifts
are called.
vide cata-
logum Il-
lirici.pag.
465.*et in*
appendice
pag.15.
impreff.
argentin.
1562.

Il ij   And

And therfore I suppose, yf any of them both mainteyned thefe errours, yt was this *Arnoldus Brixienfis*. Who for theis errours of the Waldenfes (as
it may feme) with his difciples is excommunicated
by the generall councel, as I tolde you before. Now
for the other fecte of the *Albanenfes* or *Albigenfes*, fpringinge of the loynes of the holye brother
Waldo, befide the comon and vfuall errours, of the
Waldenfes, they condened matrimony, and lyued lyke
brute beaftes in moft filthie and beaftlie bytchery.
Who not withftanding multiplied in fuch fort, and
fo defperatly fuffred al kind of punifhmet, and death
to, for the maynteyning of theire herefies, that
they were fet vpon and deftroyed with an armie.
And yet are they precioufe martyrs with M. Foxe,
though him felf confeffe, that the chroniclers make
them no better the Turkes and infidelles: and wold
fayne (for the honefty of his new ghofpell and hys
newe canonifation) that men fhoulde thinke yt
were not fo, contrary to all the Chroniclers vpon
his owne bare woorde, as one that doth not, nor
euer fhalbe able to fhewe any thinge worthye of
any credite, to the contrarye. The defperate rage
of theis wilde wodde *Waldenfes* was fuche, as I
haue fayde, that they did not fhune, but rather co-
uitte deathe, to make theyre fecte in the eies of the
worlde more commendable, (as M. Foxes holye
martyrs haue of late donne in Englande, and els
where) and for this caufe bothe the councell and
themperour calleth them *Patarenos*.   For they fo
called them felues, as in the olde tyme the Meffa-
lian

Arnoldus Brixenfis
Vide de hoc Arnoldo.
*Plat.in Adriane.*4.
Sabel. Aenea. 8.li.9
*Bernard. epi.*195.

The horrible errors
of the Albigenfes.

*Paulus Aemilius. li.
6. hift. Franc.
Ecclefiam noftram
catum infernorum
vocitabant, matrimo
nia damnabat, pro-
mifcuos concubitus,
eofque nefarios fan-
ctos ducebant.*

M. Foxe vvolde
fayn haue vs beleue
theis Albigenfes
to be martyrs.
Frid. Dict. epift. 27.
*Patarenorum com-
plices & qui vt alios
à pœna poffint exime
re, de fe velut impro-
uidi non formidant.*
vvhy thefe heretiks
called them felues
Patarenos.
*Epiphanius. li.3.
Tom. 2. Heref. 8.*

lian heretikes called them felues, for the like caufe *Marty-*
*riamos,*as men glorying, that for their feƈe and herefie had
fuffred martyrdomme. Now let Mayfter foxe make an accompte of hys holy martyrs,and fee howe manie he canne
fynde,that haue not maynteyned the fayd errours,of thefe
Albigenfes, *Paterans*, or *Waldenfes*: and he fhall fynde his
holie cataloge altogether voyde and empted. So that the
olde martyrs may take theyre olde place in the Kalender
againe.

And becaufe Mayfter Foxe doth fo highlie efteme
thefe men: and fo lightlye regardeth what fo euer either
the forfayde mofte famous and lerned councell, or the
late councell of Trente hathe fayde or donne againfte
the doƈrine of his holye Martyrs: and wyll not belieue
the catholikes, when they truelye call them furioufe and
madde martyrs, let him at the leafte belieue this Emperour Friderike, a newe greate Charles, as Mayfter Horne
fayeth,and let hym in fewe wordes, heare a rownde and
a full anfwere to all his vglie and madde martyrologe. He
then fpeaking of the feƈ of the folifhe frontyke and wood
Waldo fayeth: *In exēplum martyrũ qui pro fide catholica &c.*
They call them felues(fayeth Fridericus) as thowghe they
followed the example of the Martyrs,which died for the
catholike fayth, *Paterans,as men prompte and redie to fuffer*
death:howbeit thefe wretched Paterans,hauing no holie belief
of the eternall deitie, in this theyre owne wickednes offende
three together.that is,God,theyre neighbour,and them felues.
God I faye, whiles they do not knowe the faythe, that they
fhoulde haue in God, nor his counfayle. They deceyue theire
neighbours, whiles vnder the pretēce of fpirituall and ghoftly
feadinge,they feade them with pleafaunt wicked herefie.

the fe-
cond.

μαρ]υρια
νοὺς ἑαυ-
]οὺς ἐφω
νόμαζεν,
ὅθεν διὰ
τοὺς ὑπὲρ
τῆν ἡδὼ-
λων μαρ-
]υρήσαν-
τας.

Vide Petrũ
de vinea
Lib.1.
Epift.26.
A fhort
anfvvere
to all M.
Foxes
madde
martyro-
log,by
thempe-
rour fride
ryke M.
Hornes
fupreame
head.

But they are most cruell to them selues, whiles, beside the losse of theire sowles, as men making no accompte of lyfe, but rashelye seeking death, take a pleasure to bring theyr bodies to most payneful death, the which they might by true knowledge, and by a sownde and strong faythe auoyde, and whiche is a most greauouse thing to be spoken, they that remayne a lyue be no-thing afrayde by theyre example. We can not staye and re-frayne our selues, but that we must plucke owte our sworde, and take worthie vengeance vppon suche: being enemies to God, to them selues, and to other: persequuting them, so muche the more earnestly, by how muche the more, they are

Rome
the head
of all
churches
by Fride-
ricus cō-
fesion
againste
the Pa-
terans.

iudged to spread abrode and to practise their wycked superstition nighe to Rome which is the head of all Churches. Thus farre Friderike the Emperour.

Let nowe Mayster Foxe take this as a fytte ād worthie condemnation of al his stinking martyrs. And take you this also Mayster Horne, and digeste yt well: and then tel me at your good leasure, when ye are better aduised, what ye haue wōne by this your supreame head, or by what colour, ye can make hym Supreame Head that confesseth *the Church of Rome to be the Head of al Churches:* who also fealt the practise of the Popes Supreamacy aswel by excommunicatiō as by depryuation frō his empire, that followed the

sayde excommunicatiō: the electours proceding to a new election at the Popes commaundemente. As for Frideryke hym self for matters spirituall he acknowledged the Popes Supreamacy as ve haue heard, and as yt appeareth *in Petrus de vinea* his Chāceler, that wrote his epistles, though he thowght the Pope did but vsurpe vppon certaine possessions, which Friderike (notwithstāding his former othe made to the contrarie) did afterwarde challenge. The mat-

ter

ter of S.Peters patrimony, I will not medle withall, as not
greatly neceſſarye for our purpoſe : the which when the
Church of Rome lacked , yet did not the Pope lacke his
Supreamacie,neither ſhould lacke the ſayde Supreamacie,
thowghe he ſhould lacke the ſayde patrimony hereafter,
or though his Biſhoppricke were not indewed with one
foote of land. For it is no worldly power or temporal preeminence,that hath ſett vp the Popes primacy,or that the
Popes primacy confiſteth in , but it is a Supreme Authorytie ouer all Chriſtes flocke , ſuch as to his predeceſſour
S.Peter,Chriſt him ſelfe gaue here on the earthe , ſuch as
by generall Councels is confirmed and acknowledged,and
ſuch as the continuall practiſe from age to age without in-
termiſsion dothe inuincibly cõuince. And for this Supreme
gouernment ouer Chriſtes flocke in Spiritual matters neither this Friderike,neither any other Chriſtian Emperour
whatſoeuer (except it were Conſtantius the Arrian)euer
ſtriued or contended for with the Biſhoppes of Rome.
To conclude therefore , this onlye for this time I ſaye,
that your dealing with this Emperour, Mayſter Horne,is
to intolerable , thus to miſuſe your readers, and not to
be asſhamed ſo confidently to alleage this Emperour, for
the confirmation of your newe ſupreamacie.Now,thinck
yow that Auentinus a man of our age , and as farre as I
can iudge a Lutheran , and moſt certaynelie verie muche
affectionated to thēperours againſt the Popes , is of ſuche
credite , that becauſe he ſayeth yt , therefore we muſte
belieue him : that this Friderike was an other Charles
the greate, and moſte profitable for the Chriſtian common wealthe? Howbeit let this alſo paſſe. For the praiſe
or diſpraiſe of this Emperoure to oure principall matter,

which

which is, whether the Quene be ſupreame head and Iudge of al cauſes eccleſiaſtical, is but impertinent. And therfore we ſhall now procede to the reſidue.

Fabian.
The. 435.
Vntruth.
Captaine
and no-
torious.
Polidore
ſaith the
clean cō-
trary.
The. 436.
and. 437.
Vntruth.
For it
vvas a
tenth, no
tribute, ād
it vvas
graunted,
not deni-
ed.

In whiche time Henrie the. 3. king of Englande held a ſolemne Councell, in the whiche bothe by the ſentence of the King and of the Princes, not a fewe priuilegies, were (.435.) taken awaie from the order of Prieſthode, at vvhat time the Popes Legate required a (.436.) tribute of all the Glergie, but it was (.437.) denyed him. Robert Groſthead (vvhome yee call Saint Robert) wrote vnto the Pope, a ſharpe Epiſtle, becauſe he grieued the Church of England with taſkes and paiementes againſt reaſon: of whiche when he ſawe no redreſſe, he with other Prelates of the lād, cōplained vnto the King, of the waſt of the goodes and patrimonie of the Churche, by the Popes neare kinſemen and other alient Biſshops, whom the king auoided out of the Realme. To vvhome alſo the Emperour Frederike vvrote, that it vvas a ſhame for him to ſuffer any longer his Realme to be oppreſſed vvith the Popes tyrannie.

The. 25. Chapter. Of King Henrie the third.

Stapleton.

Concer-
ning Kig
Henrie
the. 3.

KING Henry the. 3. toke away many priuileges from the order of Prieſthode, the clergie denied a tribute to the Popes Legate, Roberte groſtheade writeth, ſharply againſt the Popes exactions, Frederike the Emperour writeth to the King, that he ſhoulde not ſuffer his Realme to be oppreſſed with the Popes tyrannie. Ergo, M. Fekēham muſt take an othe that the Quene is Supreme Head. Yf theſe and ſuch like arguments conclude, Maiſter Horne, then may you be bolde to blowe your Horne, and triumphantly to reioyce like a Conquerour.

M. Hornes
imperti-
nent Ar-
guments.

Bu

But nowe what if the matter of your argumentation be as yll, or worse then the forme of yt? Ye ought to proue that in this kings dayes the lyke regimente was for matters Ecclesiasticall as is nowe, and that the kinge toke vppon him all supreamacy Ecclesiasticall. The contrarie whereof is so euidente, by all our Chroniclers, and by the authours your selfe alleage, and otherwise in this shorte declaration of king Henry the.3. ye do so friuolously trifle, and excedingly lie, as ye haue done and will doe in the reste, that I muste, beside all other matters by me before rehersed cocerning the Donatists, saye of you, as S. Augustine sayd of them. He sayd of the Donatistes, that in theyr reasoning with the catholykes before Marcellinus. *Nimium patienter pertulit homines per inania vagantes, & tam multa superflua dicentes, & ad eadem toties conficta redeuntes, vt gesta tatis voluminibus onerata pene omnes pigeret euoluere, &c.* He suffred with ouer much patience, those felowes wandring about trifles, and so full of superfluous talke, and returning so ofte to the selfe same matters fayned and forged, that the Acts of that coferece, were so lode with such huge volumes, that it would wery any ma to reade the ouer, ad by the reading to know, how the matter was debated. Yea their extraordinary vagaries were so thick ad so many, that Marcellinus was fayn *(as Fraciscus Balduin' noteth)* almost 600. times by his sentece interlocutory to cut of their friuolous elusios. We haue nowe nead of such an other Marcellinus, to be styckler an arbitrer betwen you and M. Fekenha.

Againe the sayd S. Augustine sayd of the Donatistes (as Baldwine noteth) that he did meruaile if the Donatists had any bloud in their body, that being so often taken in manifeste and open lies, yet neuer blushed. I say then to you M.

m m Horne

M.Horne seketh by matters, leauig the principall as the Donatistes did.

August. co tra Dona. post collat. cap. 34. Tom. 7. In Collat. Carth. Conc. Dicebat se mirari Donatistas habere in corpore sanguine, qui nunquam erubescerent toties in manifesto mendatio deprehensi.

Horne that this kinge was not the fupreame head but the pope, who practifed his fupremacy in this kinges dayes, as much as any pope hath done in this realme in our tyme, or fithen this king Henries tyme. Was not the Priour of Canterbury depofed by the Pope? Were not a number of the clergy that helde with the Barons againfte the kinge depryued of their Ecclefiafticall lyuinges, and fayne to fend to Rome for their abfolution? Was not the Archbifhop of Canterburies election annichilated and fruftrated by the pope? Did not the Archbifhop of Canterbury Edmond goe to Rome for the difpatche of his Ecclefiafticall affayres? Were not S. Hewe of Lincolne and the forefayd S. Edmonde, S. Richarde bifhop of Chichefter, and S. Thomas of Canterbury by the popes authority tranflated in this kings tyme? Was not the kinge hym felfe with Pandulphus the popes Legate prefente at the fayd tranflation at Canterbury? Did not Octobonus the popes legate make certayne conftitutions ecclefiafticall, which are euery where to be had in prynt? Did not the king hym felfe procure the Popes curfe vppon the Barons that rebelled againfte hym? Was not the Pope the Iudge in controuerfy depéding betwene the kinge and the Archbifhop of Canterbury? Did not the kinge hym felfe procure to be abfolued and difcharged of his othe by the Pope, as fupreame Iudge in matters fpirituall? Did not this kinge fend his bifhops to the greate councell holden at Laterane wherof we haue fpoken, afwell as other princes did? Did not this kinge helpe with his money the Pope againfte themperour Frederike, thowghe he were allied vnto him? And fhall all this fuperiority quayle onely for fuch bare and friuoloufe matter, as you laye forth? But what yf yt be not only friuoloufe. M.

Horne,

In addit.
ad Neub.
M.S. Polichronic.
Fabian.

Polichr. et
Io Lond.
Polichro.
In addit.
ad Neub.
M.S. &
Polichr.

vvherein
the pope
practifed
his fupremacy in
Englād in
kings Hē
ries time.
Polidor.
lib. 16.

Horne,but ſtarke falſe?I maruayle ſuerly yf this kinge toke away anie priueleges from the Clergy . Why M.Horne? What kinge was yt thinke yow , that gaue the priuileges for the clergy and the commõs,yea and the nobylity to,cõteyned in *magna charta*,but this kinge?Who cauſed the biſhops of this realme beinge arayed in theyr *Pontiſicalibus* ſolemly to accurſe,in Weſtmynſter hall(the king him ſelfe and his nobility being preſent)the infringers of the ſame,but this king Héry the.3.?Who gaue vnto the Church of Poules in Londõ,ſuch priuileges as the city of Londõ had,and leaſt the citie of London ſhould take any domage therby,gaue to the city out of his checker an yearely rente of ſeué pounds euer ſyns vſually payd,but this kíg Héry?

Lo M.Horn: you heare of great priuileges gratiouſly graunted and geuen to the clergy.But what priuileges,or when any were taken away from thẽ I can not yet fynd.No, ſayth M.Horn,can ye not fynd it?Why,doe ye not then take a litle paynes,to reade my authour Polidor to whome I doe remit my reader?Yes M.Horn that paynes haue I taken, and that ſhall ye full well vnderſtand.I wil reherſe your own allegation in your authours own words. *Nowe was* (ſaieth he) *the.1226. yeare of our Lorde God , and the.9. yeare of kinges Henries raigne come. In the whiche yeare,there was an aſſemble of nobility . In this aſſemble by the conſente of the kinge and the nobilitie manie liberties and priuileges were geuen to the order of prieſthod , and to the commons, and many ordinances were made which the kings that followed,did ſo allowe,that a good part of the Law,is ga-*
mm ij   *thered*

Magna Charta.

Priuileges graũted to Poules Churche in London by the kinge.
Polidorus lib. 16. Pro ſua pietate & gratia irrogauit Paulino collegio ſacerdotũ,ea omnia liberalis priuilegia.quibus ciuitas Lõdinéſ. vteretur,frueretur, qua ne indedãnũ vllũ faceret,dedit ex ſuolẽ bras ſeptẽ , quas etiã nũc vicecomites vrbani ex arbitrio regio,quot annis capiũt Polidorus lib.16. Iam adeꝛat annus ſalutis humana.1226. & nonus,cũ regnare cepit Héricus:quo an no cõciliũ pꝛicipũ eſt habitũ:in eo concilio de regis pariterac pꝛĩ cipũ ſentẽtia,nõ parũ multa priuilegia ordini ſacerdotali,atq; reliquo populo irroga

ta ſunt multaq; leges, quas reges qui ſequuti ſunt ita approbarunt,vt inde bona pars iuꝛ ris collecta ſit,quemadmodũ in eo extat libello qui inſcribitꝛ magna Charta, & altera vulgo de Foriſta,id eſt,deſerarũ ſaltibus.

thered thereof: *as appeareth in the great Charter, and in the Charter of the Foreſte* . Howe ſay yow M. Horne, is there

any more bludde left in your body, then was in the Donatiſts, of whom S. Auguſtin complayneth? what a Macarian
pageante haue ye here played? What? Thinke yow, as Cyr-
ces turned Vlyſſes companie into hoggs , that ye maye ſo
enchaunte all your readers, by this your ſupreame lying ſupreamacy, that they ſhall be ſo ſwiniſhe , as to beleue yow
in this poynte , or in any other beinge here taken with the
maner, and as the ciuilians ſay γ᾽ ἀυτοφώρῳ? What colourable ſhifte can ye nowe pretende, to ſaue your poore honeſty? Is not this the very place , that your ſelfe tranſlate out
of Polidorus? Doth yt not ſay the quite contrary to that, for
the which ye alleage yt? The matter is ſo opē, that I wil refuſe no arbitrers, no, not your owne proteſtante fellowes.

  It is beſide the matter of the ſtory wherin your own author cōdemneth you, a law matter: Cal me therfore a queſt
of Lawiers. Let thē tel you, whether Héry the. 3. in this cō-

cel, toke away the Charter, or made and graūted the Charter . Yf perchaunce ye wil appeale from thē to the Grammarians, and ſay that *irrogare priuilegia*, is to take away priuileges (which in dede is your extreme miſerable refuge a-
gainſt al truth and the words, and meaning of your author)
I am cōtent ye choſe à queſt of thē: neither therin wil I vſe

any peremptory challenge, but am content to ſtand to the
iudgment of your nigh neighbours in the famous ſchole of
Wicheſter, or if ye wil, of M. Cooper the dictionary maker,
better acquaynted with theſe matters, thē perchaūce your
ſelf are. But ſee M. Horn how as accordīg to the old ſayīg:
vnum malū non venit ſolum. So with yow *vnum mendacium
non venit ſolum* . But that as thowgh there were a game
                                                    ſetta

set vp for lying, ye adde for the with an other lie. Ye saye *there was a tribute demaunded of all the clergy by the Legate: but yt was denied him.* Your author saith, he demaunded the tenth of the clergie, to mainteyne warre against the Saracens: and yt was sone graunted him. Your authour reciteth also, after the minde of some writers, that in a conuocation, Ottho the Popes Legate, demaunded a certayne yerelye paymente, which was denied him, but he doth improue those that so write. And so withal it is not a single but a double, or rather a treble vntruth, that ye write concerning this tribute. For this demaunde yf yt were made, was not made, *at that tyme* (as you say) when that Councel, that ye call the solemne Councel was holdē and wherin the great Charter was graunted, and where, as ye most falsly say, yt was disanulled, but in a conuocation at an other tyme. Now putting the case there were any such payment denied, doth that spoile the pope of his supremacy? By as good reason ye may conclude, yf any thing be denied the King, that he demaundeth in the parliament, that therefore he is no King. This former answere may serue you also for that ye alleage concerning Robert groshead : sauing that I may adde this withall, that he were a very Groshead in dede, that would belieue you, either when ye say to M. Fekenham (*whome ye call S. Robert*) seing M. Fekenham speaketh no woorde of this Robert, no more then he doth of Robyn goodfellowe: or that this story should make against the Popes primacie, seing that your owne authour Fabian saith, that this Robert being accursed of the Pope Innocentius, appealed from his courte to Christes owne cowrte. A manifeste argument of the popes supremacy. As for Frederyk the Emperours episte to Kinge Henry: what so euer he writeth

M. Horne alleageth
Friderikes epistle,
but litle for his
own ease, if it vver
fully executed to=
vvards himself.

against the Pope, ye would be loth I suppose, it shuld take place in Englãd. For then farewel your good-ly Manours, as Walthã, Farnhã ãd such other. Nei-ther were your gẽtleman Vssher like to ride before you barehead, but both he and you to goe a foote,

Io. Lond. in Chroni.

or rather your self to go barefoted al alone.

Iste Fridericus in proposito habuit ecclesiam ad supremam paupertatem redigere. Vide apud eũdem: partem epist. eius ad Henric. 3.

M. Horne. The. 128. Diuision. pag. 79. a.

Antoninꝰ.

Levves the Frenche King, called S. Levves, vvho as Antoninus saith, was so instructed, euen from his infancy, in all the wisedom of diuine and good orders, that there was not found his like, that kept the law of the high God, &c. made a lawe against those that blasphemed the name of the Lorde: adioyning a penalty of a whote yron to be printed in the transgressours forehead.

Append.
Math. Pa-
risiens.

Also in the yere of the Lorde. 1228. He made a Law against the Popes fraudes, concerning the preuentions and reseruations of the reuenues, and dignities Ecclesiastical, complayning that the Pope had pulled from him, the collations of all Spirituall promotions: ordeining that from hence foorth the election of Bisshops, Prelates and al other whatsoeuer, should be free, for=cible, ãd effectual to the electors Patrones ãd collatours of thẽ. Also the same yere he set forth an other Law agaíst Simony: cõ

Fabian.

plainíg of the bieyng ãd sellíg of ecclesiastical dignities. He made also certain godly Lavves against vvhoredome aud Fornicatiõ. Laste of all

Append.
Math. Pa-
risiens.

in the yeere of the Lorde. 1268. he set foorth the Lavve, commonly called Pragmatica Sanctio, vvherein in amongest other Ecclesiastical matters against the Popes pollinges he saith thus: Item, in no case we wil that exactions or greuous burdens of money, being laide on the Churche of our Kingdome by the Courte of Rome, where-by our Kingedome is miserably impouerished, be leuied or ga=thered: nor any hereafter to be layed, excepte only for a rea-

sonable

fonable,godly and mofte vrgent caufe of necefsity, that can
not be auoided:ãd that the fame be don by our expreffe (.438.)
biddinge,and commaundement of our own accord.(439.)

The.26.Chapter: Of S. Lewys the French King . Of Manfred, and Charles King of Sicilia and Apulia.

Stapleton.

Lewes his Lawe , againft thofe that blafphemed the
name of God,maketh not him fupreame head of the
Churche. Ye mowght haue put in , as your authour
doth,thofe alfo, that blafpheme the name of his bleffed mo-
ther.But the mention of this woulde haue greaued fome of
your feƈ that haue compared our Ladie to a faffron bagge,
making her no better then other women . And what yf
you or your confederats had liued then , that fay,it is Idolatrie to pray to her,and to praye her , to pray for vs to her
fonne Iefu Chrifte: fhoulde not ye haue had, fuppofe you,
great caufe to feare the printe of the hotte yron , ye fpeake
of? As for the collations of fpiritual promotions, this Lewys beftowed none but fuch as his predeceffours by efpecial licences and priuileges had graunted vnto them frõ the
biffhops of Rome . And that as I haue ofte faid, proueth no
fuperiority of gouernemẽt in Ecclefiaftical matters,except
by the fame reafon you wil make euery Patrone of a benefice to be fupreme gouernour in all Ecclefiafticall matters
to his owne Vicar and Curate . The embarringe of Exa-
ƈions from the Courte of Rome , is nothing derogatorye
from the Spiritual power or Iurifdiƈtion of the Churche of
Rome.For they are not vtterly embarred, but the exceffe
of thẽ is denied:ãd in any reafonable,godly,or vrgent caufe
of necefsity they are graunted, as your felfe alleage . But
to bet-

Frãce:
The. 438.
and 439.
vntruths.
One in
falfe trãf-
lating,the
other in
vnfaith-
ful nip-
ping.

Antoninus
part.3.tit.
19.cap.9.
Nomẽ do-
mini vel
Virginis
gloriofe.

to better a litle your badde caufe , you haue with a double
vntruthe ended your allegation.For where the King faieth,
*Nifi de fpontaneo expreffo cōfenfu noftro,*not without our vo-
luntary and expreffe confent , you turne it , *by our expreffe
bidding and commaundement,*and that it might feme to hāge
of the Kings pleafure only , you leaue out, *& ipfarum Ecs
clefiarum regni noftri:*and of the Churches of our kingdom.

But what nede we lefe more time in making more ample
anfwer , feing it is mofte certaine, that this Kinge and his
realme acknowleadged the Popes Supremacye , as muche
then as euer fince euen to this daye? For where was your
newe great Charles Friderike the feconde depofed from
his Empire,by Pope Innocentius the fourth , but at Lyons
in Fraunce ? And in whofe Kinges dayes , but of this Lewys? Who defended many yeares together the Popes of
Rome, Innocentius the.4. Alexander the. 4 . Vrbanus the.
4.and Clement the. 4. againfte the Emperour Frederike
(who therefore by treafon went about to deftroye him)but
this Kings Lewys? Who warred him felfe in perfon a-
gainfte the Sarracens at Thunys , at Clement the Popes
requeft,but this Lewys ? Who alfo before that,making his
voyage into the holy lāde againft the Souldā tooke benediction and abfolution of Pope Innocentius the.4. lying thē
at the Abbye of Cluny in Fraunce , but this Lewys? And
did not the fayed Clement make by his Authoritye.Charles
this Lewys his brother , King of Sicilia and Apulia? And
wil you make vs nowe beleue M . Horne,that this Kinge
was fuche a Supreme Gouernour , as you imagine Princes
ought to be,or that in his tyme the Popes Supremacy was
accompted a forrayne power in Fraunce,as it is with you
in Englande ? No , No ,M. Horne . Seeke what age and
what

*Annales
de France.
Fabian.
Nauclere.*

what Countre you wil, you ſhal neuer finde it while you Frãce.
liue.

Conradus, Conradinus and Manfredus, (.440.) ſtil kepte the
priuilege of the foreſaide Eccleſiaſtical matters in Sicilia and Apulia. Shortly
after this tyme Charles the King of Sicilia and Apulia, had (.441.) al or
moſt of the dooing in the elelection and making of diuerſe Popes, as of Mar-
tyn.4. Celeſtyn.5. Boniface.8.&c.

The 440. vntruthe. For they loſt them. The 441. vntruthe, as ſhal apeare.

Stapleton.

To theſe matters of Sicilie I haue already more then ones
anſwered, and doe now ſay again, that this priuilege conſi-
ſted only in inueſturing of biſhops graunted by Alexander
the.3. and after reclaymed by Innocentius the.3. Whereby
it wel appereth, that this allegation maketh rather with the
Popes Primacy, then againſt it: but moſt of all in this place.
For Pope Alexander the . 4 . declared this Manfredus the
Romain Churches enemy, as he was in dede, and a traytour
alſo both to Conradus, his brother, and to Conradinus his
nephewe, both inheritours to that kingdome, both whome
he went about to poyſon. By reaſon of which outrages, he
was as I ſaid denounced enemy to the Church of Rome by
Alexander the.4. and ſhortly after, Charles Kinge Lewys
his brother, was made King of Sicilie by Clemens the.4.
paying to the Pope a tribute, and holding of him by faithe
and homage . Such Supreme heads were your Conradus,
Conradinus and Manfredus .

As for Charles (who only by the Popes Authority came
to that dignity, as I haue ſaid) it is not true, that he (as you
ſay, had all or moſt of the doing, in the election, or making of
diuerſe Popes. For the Cardinalls only had the whole doing.
Truth it is, that a ſtrief and contention riſing amonge the
Cardinals, for the election, and many of them being encli-

Naucler gener. 41. pag. 288. Vide chronicon additum ad P. Aemil. hiſtoriã. Plat. in Nicolao.4 Cardinales ad cõcordiã & electionẽ pontificis adhortatus eſt. Idẽ in Caleſtino.5. Inſtante Carolo Rege, & Latino Cardinale pontifex creatur.

ned to

ned to ſerue Charles expeċtation, they elected thoſe which he beſt liked of. But what can all this make to proue the Prince Supreme Gouernour in al eccleſiaſtical cauſes? yea or in any eccleſiaſtical cauſe at al? Prices euē now adaies find ſome like fauour ſometimes at the electiō of Popes. But thīk you therfore thei are takē of their ſubiects for Supreme Gouernors &c? You may be aſhamed M. Horne, that your reaſons be no better.

Naucler.
gener. 42.
pag. 313. et
314. Idē
gener. 43.

M. Horne. The. 130. Diuiſion. pag. 79. b.

Edvvard the firſt, King of Englande, about this time made the Statute of Northampton: So that after that time, noman ſhould geue, neither ſel, nor bequeath, neither chaūge, neither bye title, aſsign lāds, tenemēts, neither rētes to no mā of Religiō, without the Kīgs leaue: which aċte, ſence that tyme, hath bē more ſtraightly enaċted and deuiſed wīth many additiōs, thereunto augmēted or annexed. The which Law, *ſaith Polidore,* he made (.442.) bicauſe he was *Religionis ſtudioſiſsiᵐᵒ, &c.* moſt ſtudiouſe of Religion, and moſt ſharpe enemie to the inſolency of the Prieſts.

Polych.
Fabian.
Polyd.

The 442.
vntruthe.
Polidore
faith not
ſo.

The. 27. Chapter. Of King Edvvard the firſt, of Englande.
Stapleton.

Leaue ones Maiſter Horne to proue that, wherein no man doth ſtande with you: and proue vs, that either Kinge Edwarde by this facte was the Supreame Head of the Churche: or that the Popes Primacie, was not aſwel acknowledged in Englād in thoſe dayes, as it hath ben in our dayes. None of your marginal Authours, auouch any ſuch thinge. Neither ſhall ye euer be able to proue it. Your authours, and many other, haue plentiful matter to the contrarye, eſpecially the Chronicle of Iohannes Londonenſis, which ſemeth to haue liued aboute that tyme: and ſeemeth amonge all other, to haue written of him verie exaċtlye. Lette vs ſee then whether Kinge Edwarde
tooke

Concerning Kīg Edvvard the firſt.

Polid.
Polychro.
Fabian.

tooke him ſelfe, or the Pope for the Supreame Head of the
Churche. This King after his Fathers death returning from
the holie Lande, in his iourney viſited Pope Gregorie the
tenthe , and obteyned of him an excommunication a-
gainſt one *Guido de monte forti,* for a ſlawghter he had committed . Two yeares after was the famouſe Councell holden at Lions, at the which was preſent the Emperour Michael Paleoiogus , of whome we haue ſomewhat ſpoken.
And trowe ye Maiſter Horne , that at ſuche tyme as the
Grecians, which had longe renounced the Popes authority, returned to their olde obedience againe, that the realm
of Englande withdrewe it ſelfe from the olde and accuſtomable obedience ? Or trowe ye that the true and worthye
Biſſhops of England refuſed that Councell, as ye and your
fellowes, counterfeite and parliament biſſhops only , haue
of late refuſed the Councel of Trente? No, no. Our authour
ſheweth by a verſe commonly then vſed , that it was frequented of all ſorte . And the additions to Newburgenſis
(which endeth his ſtorie , as the ſaid Iohn doth with this
King) ſaith, that *plures epiſcopi couenerunt de vniuerſis terris,*
de Anglia ibidem aderant archiepiſcopi Cantuar. & Ebor. et cæ-
teri epiſcopi Angliæ ferè vniuerſi, there came thither manye
biſſhops from al quarters: and from Englãd the Archbiſſhops
of Canterburie and Yorke, and in a maner all the other biſſhops of the realme. In this Kinges tyme, the Pope did infringe and annichilate the electiõ of the Kings Chauncelour being Biſſhop of Bathe and Welles , choſen by the
monks: and placed in the Archebiſſhoprike of Caunterbury
Iohn Pecham . In this Kings tyme the yere of our Lorde.
1294. the prior of Caunterburie was cited to Rome , and
in the yeare. 1298. appeale was made to the Pope , for a

Io. Lond.
An, 1272.

Gregorius
denus col-
ligit omne
genus.
Ioan. Lõd.
An, 1272.
& 1274.
Neuba. in
addi. M.S.
dict. anno.
1274.
Io. Lond.
1278.
Idẽ Anno.
1294. &
1298.

controuerfie towching the election of a newe Biſſhop of
Elie. Thre yeres after the biſhop of Cheſter was conſtray-
ned to appeare perſonally at Rome, and to anſwere to certayne crymes wherewith he was charged. Wythin two
yeares after, was there an other appeale after the death of
the Biſſhoppe of London, towching the election of the
newe Biſſhoppe. Yea the authority of the Pope was in
highe eſtimation, not onely for ſpirituall, but euen for
temporal matters alſo. The Kinges mother profeſſed her
ſelfe a religiouſe woman, whoſe dowrie notwithſtandinge
was reſerued vnto her, and confirmed by the Pope. For
the greate and weightye matters, and affaires ſtanding in
controuerfie and contention betwene this King Edward,
and the Frenche Kinge, the Pope was made arbiter and
vmpier, who made an agreament and an arbitrimente:
which being ſente vnder his ſeale, was reade in open parliamente at Weſtmynſter, and was well liked of all. The
Kinge and the nobility ſendeth in the yeare of our Lorde.
1300. letters to the Pope ſealed with an hundred ſeales,
declaring the right of the crowne of England vpon Scot-
lad: and they deſire the Pope to defende their right, and that
he would not geue a light eare to the falſe ſuggeſtiõs of the
Scots. There are extant at this day, the letters of Iohn Ba-
liole and other Scots agniſing the ſaid ſuperiority, ſent to this
Kinge Edwarde. In the foreſaide yeare . 1 3 0 0 . the
Kinge confirmed the great Charter, and the Charter of
the Foreſt, and the Archebiſſhoppe of Caunterburie with
the other Biſſhoppes pronounced a ſolemne curſe vpon al
ſuche as would breake the ſayd liberties. This Kinge was
encombred with diuerſe and longe warres, aſwell with
Fraunce as Scotlande, and therefore was fayne to charge
the

Idē Anno
1301 . &
1303.

Idem An.
1286.

See in
vvhat eſti
mation
the Popes
doinges
were with
the Kinge
and the
realme e,
uen for
temporal
matters.
Idem An.
1298.
Idem An.
1300 .
Vide Neu.
in addit.
M.S. anno
1291.
Idē Io. Lõ-
dinen.

the clergy and laity with many payments. But in as much, as Pope Bonifacius conſideringe the wonderfull and into-lerable exactions daylie layed vppon the clergy, of theyre princes, had ordeyned in the councell at Lions, that from thence forth the clergy ſhuld pay no tribute or taxe, with-out the knowledge and conſente of the ſee of Rome, Ro-bert Archbiſhop of Canterbury, being demaunded a tribute for him ſelf and his clergie, ſtode in the matter not without his great buſines and trouble. And at the length vpon ap-pellation the matter came to the Popes hearing. The kinge had afterwarde by the Popes conſente dyuerſe payments of the clergy.

Many other thinges could I lay forth for the popes pri-macy practiſed at this tyme in Englande. And is nowe M. Horn, one onely Acte of Parliament, made againſt Mort-maine, of ſuch force with yow, that it is able to plucke frō the Pope his triple Crowne, and ſet yt vppon the kynges head? Yf Mortmaine had bene ſo ſtraightly ſene vnto, ſome hundred yeares before, ye ſhould haue fownde your reue-newes, I ſuppoſe, very ſlender and poore. But ye beinge as good a Lawier as ye be, either diuine, or Chronicler, think belyke your ſelf to be out of the gōneſhotte, ād that Mort-maine reacheth onely to men of relligion. And yt ſemeth, ſo he and his mate may be wel prouided for, M. Horne for-ceth litle, howe litle other haue, and whether they haue ought or nought. Suerly M. Horn it ſemeth to me ſtraunge that you being a man of the Churche, and knowinge that the Clergy hath vppon the great truſte that good mē haue had of their vpprightnes and vertue, bene endewed with great poſſeſsions (which in dede ſhould be and commonly haue bene imployed vppō the nedy according to the mynd

Pol.li. 17.
Vide 6.lib.
decret. li.
3.ca. 3.de
immunit.
Ecclef.
Idē Ioan.
an. 1296.
Idem an.
1296.1297
& 1300.
Idem an.
1300. Neu.
in addit.
M. S. an.
1291. &
1292.
M. Horns
extraua-
gante ar-
gument.
Cōcernig
Mort-
maine.

of the doners)fhuld fynd fault, with Mortmaine , and with
that, which good and well difpofed men haue voluntarily
offered to the Church , to be well and charitably beſtowed . But I perceyue why ye are an enemy to Mortmaine.
For nowe haue you and your Madge lyue catle of your
owne , for the which you haue more care to prouide,then
for any Mortmaine for your ſucceſſours in the fee.

But as I was about to tell yow , ye muſt vnderſtande,
that the ſtatute of Mortmaine doth not reache to religious
men onely , but to biſſhops and other fpirituall men,yea to
lay men alſo : And was made afwell for the commodity of
fpiritualty as temporalty : to faue afwell to the one , as to
thother theire wardes , eſchetes , and other commodities
that by mortifying of Lands , are wont to followe . Well,
as litle vnderſtandinge as maiſter Horne hath of Mortmaine , and as farre as yt is from his principall matter , yet
will he , tell vs alſo out of Polidore a caufe of this Lawe of
Mortmaine : And then as he is wont, he telleth vs a caufe
fantaſied of him felfe. Trueth it is, that Polidore fayeth,that
the kinge made this Lawe to repreſſe the riot and exceſſe
of the Clergy , but Polidore was a ſtraunger , and
vnſkilful in the Lawes of our realme : and therfore
he did not fully vnderſtand the matter, thinking (as
M. Horn doth) that Mortmaine touched the clergy only : and yet he fayth it not precifely,but (*vt
fertur*) as yt is fayd . It is true alſo , that , he fayeth
this kinge was moſte ſtudioufe of relligion , but
that he fayeth this in refpecte of Mortmaine , can
not be induced , and is nothinge but M. Hornes
vayne gheaſſe, and lewde vntruth.

The ſta-
tute of
mort-
maine
doth not
touch re-
ligioufe
mē only.

Polidor.
Prudentia ſumma,
religionis ſtudiofiſsi-
mus, inſolentiæ facer-
dotū inimicus acer-
rimus, quam ex opi-
bus tum primis pro-
ficifci putabat: quā-
obrem legem ad ma-
num mortuam per-
petuaſſe fertur,vt ita
eorū luxuries coer-
ceretur.

M. Horne. The. 131. Diuiſion. pag.80. 4
At this time Philip le Beau the Frēch rig, begā his reign, brought
vp in

vp in the studie of diuinity, vnder Aegidius the Romain diuine, by (.423.)
vvhose admonitions and also of other diuines, the Kinge beinge instructed in
his duety aboue al other thinges, endeuoured him selfe about the reformation
of Religion, and ordering of Ecclesiastical matters. VVheruppō looking to the
state of the Cleargy, he (.424.) deposed a certain Bishop for Heresie, ād gaue
his Bishoprik to an other, and besides, claymed the inuestiture of al other Bishops in his dominions: and calling Councelles at home in his ovvne Realm,
woulde suffer none of his Cleargy to goo to the Popes (.425.)
Councelles. He caused the Popes (.426.) Bulles to be burned.
He cōmaunded the Popes (.427.) Legates to auoyde his realm.
He commaunded, that no money should be caried out of the
Realme to the Pope. He sette foorth a Law, that no mā shuld
goo to Rome out of his kingdom. He called a Coūcel at Paris,
and caused to be gathered thither all the Prelates and Barons
of Fraunce: to iustifie his doinges. He shewed vnto thē why he
tooke vppō hi to cal a Coūcel. He enueighed against the Pope
for heresie, Symonie, Homicide, Pride, Ambitiō. &c. ād that of
right he ought therfore to be deposed. He demaundeth of the
Coūcel, vnto whom they be lawfully sworne, ād of whō they
haue receiued their dignities? They al answere, that they are
al the beneficiaries of hi alone, ād that mindful of their Faith,
and the Kiges estate, they would suffer death, for his glory, power and saulfegard. Theruppō he setteth foorth a pragmaticall
sanctiō or forceable law to diminishe the dignity of the Pope.
Many other Ecclesiastical Lavves he made, agaīst the Ievves, agaīst the Tē-
plars, agaīst adultery. &c. He (.428.) made also Clemēt the fifth Pope, and
svvor hi to certain cōditiōs before hand: by vvhose importune meanes also, the
General coūcel of Viēna vvas holde. In which Coūcel he laboured to
haue Pope Boniface cōdēned for an Heretique, affirminge that
he would proue hi so. But the matter vvas (.429.) takē vp, ād to satisfie
the king, it was decreed, that all the processes of Bonifacius a-
gainst the kíg, were vniust, and the kinges doinges in any poīt
agaīst the Pope shuld not be preiudicial to hí, or to his heyers.

Pau. Aem.
The 423.
vntruth;
he gaue
him no
admoni-
tiō to re-
forme re-
ligion.
Anton.
Naucler.
Blond.
The. 424.
vntruth.
He depo-
sed him
not, but
depriued
hi of his
tēporal-
ties, and
that vn-
iustly.
Aemilius.
Naucler.
The. 425.
426. and
427. vn-
truthes.
by arte of
multipli-
cation, as
shall ap-
peare.
Platina.
Naucler.
The *Antonin.*

Sabell. Naucler. Sabellic. Aemyl. Appēd. Vrspurg. Antonin. Naucler. Antonin.
The.428. vntruth. He made him not, but made intercesion to haue him made.
The.429. vntruth. It vvas not taken vp, but decreed playne against the kinge.

The.28.Chapter :of Philip le Beau the
Frenche kinge.

Stapleton.

Concerning Philip the Frenche kinge, A man would thincke, that nowe at length M. Horne had fownde fome good and effectuall matter, for his newe primacy. He layeth on fuche lode againfte the Pope afwell in his texte, as in his ioly ranck and rewe of his marginall authours, that nowe at the leaft M. Fekenham muft yelde ãd fubfcribe. But yet for al this M. Horne I muft be playne with yow and tell yow, that if ye had fhewed your reader the whole and entiere ftory, out of any one of all your owne authours, for all ye haue fo clerkly and cun

M. Horns ioly rank ningly ordered and placed them: with *Paulus Aemilius*, thẽ with *Antoninus, Nauclerus, Blondus,* then with *Platina,* and after this with *Nauclerus, Antoninus, Sabellicus,* and forwith with *Nauclerus* againe, with *Sabellicus,* with *A Emilius :* and after al this with *Appendix Vrfpergenfis* , and eftfone with *Antoninus, Nauclerus,* and finallie with *Antoninus* againe, the whole primacy, fhuld (as it dothe in dede notwithftanding) haue remayned with the Pope, and not with your Philippe le Beau, make him as beau, and as faire as ye cã. Your fouldiers be very thicke and warlyk placed, but they ftryk neuer a ftroke for yowe, but that that is all againfte yowe. Neither wil I here (for it nedeth not) intermedle with the iuftice of the caufe of either fide: Let the fault light, where it fhuld light: and let this Bonifacius be as badde as ye make

Paul. AEmilius.li.8 him (thowghe your authour Paulus Aemilius a moft worthy Chronicler, by the common verdit of all learned writers) and auauncing Fraunce as highe as he may, with the faufgarde of trueth and veritie, thinketh rather the epiftles writen betwene the kinge and the Pope, wherin eche one
chargeth

chargeth the other with many faultes to be counterfeite, then true and autenthicall . For thefe matters I wil not at this tyme towche you : but for your notable , and yet accuftomable infidelity in the wretched and miferable mangling and mayming of your owne authors I muft nedes fay fomwhat vnto you. Ye doe the in this reporte of ftories, as your felf and your copanions do, and as your aucetours the old heretikes were wot to do in alleging of fcripture ad the Fathers:that is, in chopping and paring of what it pleafeth you,*and as ye are cutte of your felues from the Churche: fo dif membre you alfo your authours allegations*,euen as S. Cyprian many yeres fytheoe, hath defcribed and painted you forth. Firfte then is there any one of al your authors , that(as ye mofte wyckedly doe)goeth abowt by this ftory , either to make this king Supreame Heade of the frenche Church,or to deface and difanul the Popes Primacie? No truely: On lefe perchaunce yt be the authour, that added to Vrfpergefis, I meane your owne deare brother Gafpar Hedio, his addition afwell agreeing , for matters of fayth , with hys firfte authour Vrfpergenfis, as the legges and loynes of an horfe, wil agree with the head, fhoulders and vpper part of a mans bodie. Yea, befide his herefy, he is to yong to be alleaged for authour authentical. To be fhorte, the dealing of this kinge, proueth nothing the lyke regiment that nowe is in our realme (which is your peculiar matter , and the only matter M.Fekeham refteth vppon)and fo for al your great fturre,with burning the Popes Bulles and commauding the Popes Legates to auoyd the realme, ye goe fayre and farre fro the matter. For where you fay,*he wold fuffer none of his clergy to goe to the Popes councels*, that was but of one only Councell called againft him felf . Item where you fay, *he*

o o

Le beau.

M. Horne choppeth and pareth the auctours by hym alleaged, *Cypria: de fimplicit Prela. fiue de vnitate Ecclefiae.* Corruptores euangelij atque interpretes falfi extrema ponunt & & fuperio ra prate= reunt, partim memores, & partim fubdole corrupentes: vt ipfi ab Ecclefia fcifi funt. ita capituli vnias fententia fcindunt.

Vide Nau-
cler, gene-
rat. 44.
pag. 361.
P. Aemil.
lib. 8.
Comemo-
rat Boni-
facij in se,
Fraciam-
que noui
exempli,
decretum:
sed eu põ-
tificem
maximã
non esse,
eaque de
re cogno-
scenda sa-
crosanctã
sede n suo
antistite
tunc vi-
duam ap-
pellare.
Nancler,
gener. 44.
Diuersis
sententijs
elegerunt
Episc.
Bur. re-
ge inter-
cedente.

He *caused the Popes bulles to be burned,* first not he, but *Fami-liares Regis*, the Kings frendes and courtiars did it, and yet it was but one bulle neither, and that of the kingss owne excommunication. Againe, where you saie, *he commaun-ded the Popes Legates to auoide the realme*: It was but one Legate, about that one matter that he so commaunded. With these many vntruthes by the Arte of Multiplication, you entre your plea. Touching the matter it selfe, the Kings grudge, was but a priuate and a personall grudge and enmitie, against Bonifacius: no lasting or perpetual renun-tiation of the whole Papal authoritie, as it is euident by the discourse of al your owne Authors. And therefore Boni-facius being dead, who accursed the King, and interdited the Realme, bothe he and the Realme were released from curse and interdiction by Benedictus, successour to this Bo-nifacius. Yea Bonifacius yet liuing, this King most plainly agnised the authoritie of the See of Rome, appealing from this Bonifacius, whom he toke not for the right Pope, but an vsurper, and an intruder, to the See Apostolical, vacant (as he thought) and to the next successour. Ye heare Mai-ster Horne, notwithstanding the greate enmitie betwene the King and Pope Bonifacius, that he appealeth to the See of Rome, being as he thought vacant: and that he is, as I haue said, absolued from the sentence of excommunicati-on by Bonifacius his successour, whiche altogether ye o-mitte. But yet ye tell vs of Pope Clement the fift, made as ye say, pope by this King. But here you ouerreache your Authour, and water him with your olde lying glose. Nau-clerus neither saieth, nor could truely saye, that the king made him pope, but saith *he was made Pope by his intercessió*: Neither your Authour Antoninus saieth it. Ye saye, he
swore

swore this pope to certaine condicions. Why doe ye not beaū.

name thē M. Horne? Forsoth because in the naming of thē,

the fourme, state, and condition of this your new primacy

in your faire Phillip woulde be full ilfauoredly acrased and

defourmed. Among other there were these three : *Prima*

est, vt me perfectè reconcilies Ecclesiæ sacrosanctæ, relaxando

& veniā dando de adiutorio dato in captura Bonifacij Papæ : Se-

cundum est, vt censuras excommunicationis amoueas contra me

& meos sequaces prolatas. Tertium est, quòd mihi concedas

omnes decimas regni per quinquennium in reparationem ex-

pensarum multarum in bello inito contra Flandrenses. First,

that ye will perfectly reconcile me to the Churche : and

release and forgeue me, for that by my meanes Pope Boni-

face was taken prisoner. Secondly that you wil reuoke the

sentence of excommunication, geuen against mee and my

confederates. Thirdly, that you will graunte me for fiue

yeres the tenth of al my realme, to relieue me for the great

charges and expences, defraied in my warres against the

Flemmings. These conditions the king required the Pope

to assure him of by Othe. Then would M. Horne faine haue

Pope Boniface taken for an heretique, and saieth that King

Phillip would haue had it so declared by the Councell hol-

den at Vienna. *But the matter was taken vp,* M. Horne saith,

and to satisfie the King, it was declared, that Pope Bonifacius

doings should not be preiudiciall to him and his heires. And

why haue ye M. Horne either wilily omitted, the matters

for the which the pope was cōditionated withal: or haue so

fondly told vs against your self, of this Councell at Vienna?

Why, but to cōfirme the popes primacy, ād to declare your

selfe alsō a lyer in saying the matter was taken vp, &c. For

the Coūcel assembled of. 300. Bishops, beside other prelats,

would in no wise agree to the kings request, but declared

Antoninus
in historia
part. 3.
tit. 21. c. 1
M. Horns
ovvne
story pro
ueth most
fully the
Popes su
premacy.
Naucler.
gener. 44.
Contrariū
declarauit
scilicet ip-
sam fuisse
catholicū
& indubi-
tatū pona
tificem.
Ant. par. 3
tit. 21. c. 3.
Cōcilium
nullo mo-
do cōsen-
tire voluit
sed cōtra-
riū decla-
rauit, scia
licet ipsū
fuisse
catholicū,
& indu-
bitatū pō-
tificem.

the cōtrary: to wit, that Bonifacius was a catholike, and an vndoubted Bishop: as your owne authours Antoninus and Nauclerus specifie. Yea Nauclere addeth. *Quo rex cogebatur contentus esse.* With the which determination of the Councel, the kinge was constrayned to be contented. At the coronation of the foresayde Clement were presente,

Ant.part.
3.tit.21.
ca.1.Nau
clerus dict
gener. 44
Paul.
Aemilius.
Naucler.
volum.3.
pag.361.
Blond.
Celebraue
rat pro
unciale
Conci-
lium &c.
Ad sedem
Apostolicā
in se mitto
rē aquio-
remque
appella-
uerat.
Ant.part.
3 tit.2.c.
8.ß.20.
Naucler.
gener.44.
not only this Philip the Frenche king, but the king of Arragone, and as some write, the kinge of Englande also. Yet hath M. Horn one other prouf, to proue Philip head of the Churche, for that he deposed a Bishop for heresye, and for that he claymed the inuestiture of Bishoppes. As for the inuestitures let them goe for this time: we haue sayd inough, I suppose, of that matter. And as for deposing of a Bishope, he deposed him not but vnder pretence of heresy (saieth Nauclere)he depriued him of all his temporaltyes, and of his Bishopricke. But why doe ye not M. Horne recite the whole sentēce of your authors Antoninus and Nauclerus? For as for Blondus, writing nothing of this mater, that is of of the deposing of any Bishop, or of the claimīg of the inuestitures, for the which you seeme to alleage him, ye doe but blindly allege, and may blot hī out again: sauing that ye may truly put in, that in the Councel which king Philip called in Frāce he appealed (as I haue told you) to th'Apostolik See of Rome. But why do ye not, as I sayd, shew the whole ād entiere sentēce of your authours, fully to adorne your primacy withal? whiche is, that he toke a certayne Bishoppe, laying to hys charge that he was a Paterā heretik, spoyling hym of his Bishopryke and of al his goods: ād that he spoyled also and robbed the Bishopprykes beinge vacante, and that he would haue had the inuestitures of the Bishoppes. Now if it were so, that king Philip deposed a Bishop for heresie,

refie, yet fhuld you M. Horne of al mē take fmalleft reliefe therby. For yf Philip your fupreme head were now lyuing, and you vnder his dominiō, he might alfo depriue you and your fellowes for herefie: being as I haue before fhewed, very Paterās. And now you that make fo litle of Generall coūcels, ād ftay your felf and your religiō vpō the iudgmēts of lay princes, haue heard your cōdēnation not only frō the notable General Coūcel at Liōs, but frō your new Charles the Emperour Frederike, and from your faire King Phillip.

M. Horne
declared
ones agai
an here
tik by his
ovvne
King
Phillip.

This, this, Good Reader, is the very handie woorke of God, that thefe men fhould be caft in their owne turne, and geue fentence againft them felues. And as hotte, as erneft, and as wilie as they are, in the firft enterprife of their matters, yet in the purfuit of their vngratious purpofe, to caufe them to declare to all the worlde their fmall circumfpecti- on, prouidence, and leffe faith and honefty. Many other things might be here brought, for furder aunfweare to M. Horne, as that he faieth that this King by the Councell of Aegidius the Romaine Diuine, went about *the reformation* (as M. Horne calleth it) *of matters Ecclefiaftical,* and that Paulus Aemilius fhould be his Authour therein, which is a double vntruth. For neither is it true, that Aegidius was any counfailer or aider to refourme the Churche, or rather defourme it, after the order of M. Hornes Relligion : nor Aemilius faith it. Againe, Sabellicus is eyther twife placed in M. Hornes Margent wrōg, or he alleageth Sabellicus al- together wrōgfully. But this may goe for a fmall ouerfight.

M. Horne Ihe. 132. Diuifion. pag. 80. b.
About the time of this Councel at Vienna, *the famous fcholman* Duran- dus *fetteth forth a booke: vvherin as he reckeneth vppe diuerfe great enor- mities in Churche matters : fo for the reformation of them, he alvvaies ioy- neth the King and fecular Princes, and the Prelates ; and to this purpofe*

citeth

citeth the fourme of the auncient Councelles and many times enueigheth against and complaineth vppon the vsurped (.430.) authority of the Romaine Bishop , vvarning men to bevvare , hovv they yeelde vnto him : and prescribeth a rule for the Princes and the Prelats to refourme all these enormities, not by custome vvere it neuer so auncient , but by the vvord of God.

The .430. vntruth.
For not in spiritual matters, which is nowe the Question.

Stapleton.

Answere me M.Horne directly, and precisely, whether Durandus, in any worke of his, taketh the laye prince for the head of the Church. If ye saye, he doth not : to what purpose doe ye alleage him ? Yf ye say he doth , then his bokes shal sone conuince you. And what boke is it I praye you, that ye speake of? Why do ye not name yt ? Whie doe you tel vs of a boke, no man can tel what ? The boke there is intituled *de modo concilij celebrãdi*, which he made at the commaundemente of the foresayde Clemente . Wherein thowghe he spake many thinges for the reformation of the cowrte of Rome , yet that aswell in that boke, as in all his other he taketh the Pope for the supreame head of the whole Churche , is so notoriouse , that a man maye iudge, all your care is to saye something againste the Pope, without any care howe or what ye saye. And that ye fare much like a madde dogge that runneth foorth , and snatcheth at all that euer commeth nigh him .

Vide eundē librum titul.2.& 27.& alibi passim.

And to geue you one place for all M. Horne , that you maye no longer stagger in thys matter , behold what thys *famouse Scholeman* (as you call him) *Durandus* saieth of the Popes primacie. *Illius prælatus Papa &c.* The prelate of the whole Church is called *Papa, that is to say, the father of Fathers: vniuersal, because he beareth the principal rule ouer the whole Church: Apostolicall , because he occupieth the roome of the Prince of the Apostles: chief Bishoppe, because he is the*

Durandus de diuinis officijs lib. 2.cap.1. Num.17.

Head

Head of al Bishops &c. Lo M. Horne what a ioly Authour you haue alleaged againft M.Fekeham. Verely fuch an aduerfary were worth at al tymes not only the hearing, but alfo the hyring.But alas what tole is ther fo weak, that you poore foules in fuch a defperat çaufe, will refufe to ftrike withal?You muft fay fomwhat.It ftãdeth vpõ your honors: and whē al is faid,it were for your honefties better vnfaid.

M. Horne The. 133. Diuifion. pag. 80. b.

About this time alfo the Emperour Henry the.7 .came into Italy vvith great povver to reduce the Empyre to the olde eftate and glorie ofthe auncient Emperours in(431.)this behalfe. And on the day of his coronation at Rome, according to the maner of other Romaine Emperours,he fet forth a Lawe, or newe authentique of the moft high Tѓinity,and the Catholique faith.

Stapleton.

What matter is this M.Horne, to enforce M. Fekēham to denie the popes primacy?Wil you neuer leaue your trifling and friuolous dealing? If ye wil fay any thing to your purpofe,ye muft fhewe,that he toke not the pope,but him felfe onely and his fucceffours for fupreame heades of the Church,and that in al things and caufes,which ye fhal neuer be able to doe while ye liue,neither in this, nor in any other Emperour,King or prince what fo euer.

M. Horne. The .134. Diuifion. pag 80.b.

Nexte to Henry.7 .vvas Levves.4. Emperour: vvho had no leffe but rather greater conflictes vvith the Popes in his time(.432.)about the reformatiõ of abufes, thã any had before hѓ:the Pope novv claiming for an(433) Ecclefiaftical matter, the confirming of the Emperour, as before the Emperours vvere vvonte to confirme the Popes. About vvhiche queftion, the Emperour fent and called many learned Clerkes in(.434.)Diuinitie, in the Ciuil and Canõ Lavve,from Italy,Fraunce,Germany,Paris, and Bononia, vvhich al anfvvered, that the(435)Popes attēpts were erroneous, and derogating from the fimplicity of the Chriftian religion.

VVherypon

The. 431.
vntruth.
For not
in the behalfe of
ecclefiaftical gouernement.

The. 432.
vntruth.
The conflict vvas
farre otherwife,
as fhall
appeare.

The. 433.
vntruth,
as fhall
appere.

The. 434.
vntruth.
Poets,not
diuines.

The. 435.
vntruth.
No fuch
thing in
his Author.

The.436.
Vntruth.
For he
did it
De facto,
not De
iure.

The.437.
Vntruth
None of
his Mar-
ginal Au-
thors fay
fo.

The.438.
Vntruth.
In cõcea-
ling his
Authours
meaning.

The.439.
Vntruth.
Nauclere
belied, ãd
falfified,
as fhall
appeare.

The.440
Vntruth.
It vvas
not the
firft that
vvas laid
&c.

The 441.
and.442.
Vntruths
Pope Cle-
mẽt tvvife
flatly be-
lyed as
fhall ap-
peare.

VVhereuppon the Emperour vvilled them to fearch out the matter diligently, and to difpute vppon it, and to gather into bookes their mindes therein,
vvhich diuerfe did, as Marfilius Patauinus, Ockam, Dantes, Pe-
trarche, &c. By vvhom vvhen the Emperour vnderftoode the Popes
vfurpation, he came to Rome, called a Councell, and (.436.) depofed the
Pope, and placed an other in his roome: In vvhich Councel, the Romaines
defired to haue their olde order in the Popes election ratified by the Emperour,
to be renevved. This Emperour called alfo a very great Coun-
cell at Frankeforth, where befides ihe Spirituall and Secular
princes of Germanie, the King of (.437.) Englande, and the
King of Beame, were prefent, where by the greater and founder parte, the Popes aforefaied vfurpation was abolifhed.
VVhich fentence the Emperoure confirmed, and publifhed vvriting thereof,
that his authoritie dependeth not of the pope, but of God immediatly, and that it is a vaine thing that is wonte to be fayed,
the pope hath no fuperiour (.438.) The Actes of this (.439.) Cou-
cell againft the Popes-proceffe vvere ratified by the Emperour, as appeareth
by his letters patentes therevppon, beginning thus. Lodouike the fourth,
by the grace of God, &c. To all patriarches, Archebifshoppes,
Bifshops, and prieftes, &c. And ending thus. VVherfore by the
Councell and confent of the prelates and princes, &c. VVe
denounce and determine, that al fuch proceffes be of no force
or moment, and ftraightly charge and commaund to all that
liue in our Empire, of what eftate or condition fo euer they
be, that they prefume not to obferue the faied fentences and
curfes of the popes interdiction, &c. An other Councell he called
aftervvards at the fame place, about the fame matter: becaufe Pope Clemẽt
called it herefie, To faie that the Emperour had authoritie to depofe the pope, which herefie as principall, he laid (.440.) firft
to the Emperours charg. Item (.441.) that the Emperour affirmed, that Chrift and his Apoftles were but poore. Item, the.3.
herefie, that he made and depofed Bifshops. Item that he neglected the Popes interdightmẽt, &c. Itẽ that he (.442) ioyned
certaine in mariage in degrees forbidden (he meaneth forbidden by
the Popes lavves) and deuorceth them that were maried in the

face

face of the Church. *VVhiche in deede vvas nothing els, but that a mangeſt other Eccleſiaſticall lavves that the Emperour ſet forth, vvere ſome for mariages and deuorcements contrary to the Popes decrees.*

The. 29. Chapter. Of Lewys the. 4. Emperour.

Stapleton.

WE haue neede Maiſter Horne of a newe Iudge Marcelline, that maie by his interlocutorie ſentence, bring you, as he did the Donatiſtes from your wilde wide wandering, home againe to your matter. Let it be (for the time if ye will needes ſo haue it) that the Emperours Authoritie dothe not depende of the Pope, yea and that Pope Iohn the. 22. was alſo for his owne priuate perſon an Heretique. And then I beſeeche you adde your wiſe concluſion. Ergo Maiſter Feckenham muſt take a corporall Othe, that the Queene is Supreme Heade of the Churche of England.

M. Horns imperti nent Ar guments.

Now on the other ſide, if we can proue againſte you, that euen this your owne Supreame Head, Lewys, for ſpirituall and Eccleſiaſticall matters, agniſed the Popes and the Generall Councelles Authoritie, to be Superiour to the Authoritie of the Emperoure and of all other Princes, and that they all muſt be obediente and ſubmitte them ſelues thereunto, then ſhal Maiſter Fekenham conclude with you an other manner of Ergo, and that is, that ye and your confederates, are no Biſhoppes, as made contrarye to the lawes and ordinaunces of the Pope, and as well of the late Generall Councel at Trent, as of other General Councels: yea that ye are no good Chriſtians, but plaine Heretiques, for refuſing the Pope and the ſaid Generall Councelles authoritie. For the proufe of our aſſertion, that this Empe-

P P

rour

rour,albeit he ſtode againſt the Pope, auouching him ſelfe
for a true and a ful Emperour,thowghe he were not côfir-
med by the Pope(which was the very ſtate of the original
controuerſie betwixt hym and the Pope) and thowghe he
procured Pope Iohn(as much as lay in hym) to be depoſed,
ãd placed an other in his roume,belieued yet(this notwithſtanding) that the Pope for ſpiritual and fayth matters was
the Head of the Church(which thing is the ôly matter ſtãding in debate betwene you ãd M.Feckêhã) for prouf I ſay
of this we wil not ſtray farre of, but fetche yt,only of your
owne authours here named:who côfeſſe that he appealed,
to the very ſame Pope Iohñ,yt enformed,when he
ſhould be afterwarde better enformed: and withall
to a general councel. But what nede we ſeke ayde
at Antoninus and Nauclerus hands,when we haue
yt,ſo redy at your own hãds?For your ſelf ſay,that
he placed an other Pope in Iohns ſtead.Ergo he acknowledged a Pope ſtil: ãd as your authour ſaieth,
vt verũ Chriſti vicarium,as the true vicar of Chriſt.
Neither did your Emperour diminiſhe or blemiſhe
the Popes authority in any poynte,ſauing that he
ſayd he might appeale frô hym to the general coũcel,and that theperour was not inferiour or ſubiect
to hym for temporal iuriſdictiô.But with you ãd your bãd,
neither Pope,nor general coũcell taketh place. Now thê,
that ye are caſt eué by your own emperour,we might wel
let goe the reſidewe of your ſuperfluous talke , ſauing that
yt is worth the marking to ſee your true,honeſt, and wiſe
hãdling of it.Your firſt ouerſight ãd vntruth thê is,that ye
write,that the Pope claimed the côfirmatiô of theperour
as an eccleſiaſtical matter.In dede he claimed the ſame,ãd
ſo right wel he might do:as no new thing by him inuêted,
but

Antoniñ⁹ part.3.tit.
21.cap.5.ff.8.
Appellauit ad ipſum
Papã malè informa
tũ,benè informandũ
et etiã ad côciliũ ge-
nerale.Nauclerus
Gener 45.
Naucler. ibidem.
     Platina.
Creatus itaq; Pſeu-
dopontifex ac Nico
laus.5.appellatus ab
imperato-
re & ijs
qui cũ eo
aderant,
vt verus
Chriſti vi-
carius cô-
ſalutatur.
Naucler.
ibidem.

but browght to him frō hād to hād, frō fucceſſor, to fucceffour, by the race and cōtinuance of many hundred yeares.
And yet if we ſpeak properly, yt is no matter ecclefiaſtical
no more thē the patrimony ot S. Peter, cōfiſting in tēporall
lāds was a matter ecclefiaſtical, and yet bothe dewe to the
Pope. The one by the gyſte of dyuerſe good princes : the
other, either by preſcriptiō of time owt of mind, or by ſpecial order takē by the popes at ſuch time, as the pope made
Charles the great, Emperour of the Weſt: or whē he trāſlated thēpire into Germany, and ordeined. 7. Princes there
to haue the electiō of th'Emperor, or for ſome other good
reaſon, that yf nede be, may be yet further alleaged ād better enforced, thē that al your wytte and cōning ſhall euer
be able, wel to auoyd. Nay ſay ye, thēperour had great lerned mē on his ſyde, experte in diuinity, and in the ciuil and
canō law. But whē ye come to nōber thē, ye fynd none, but
the Poetes *Dātes*, and *Petrarcha*, Ockā the ſcholeman, and
the great heretike, *Marſilius Patauinus*. And ſhal theſe men
M. Horne coūternayle, or ouerweighe the practiſe of the
church euer ſynce vſed to the cōtrary, and cōfirmed by the
great cōſente of the catholyke writers, and dyuerſe general councelles withal ? Ye write as out of Antoninus, or
Marius, in a ſeueral and latin letter that *the Popes attemptes*
were erroneous, and derogating from the ſimplicity of the Chri-
ſtiā religiō. But ſuch wordes I fynd as yet in neither of thē,
nor in any other of your authours, here named. And your
authour Antoninus ſaieth, that in this point both Dātes ād
Ockam with other do erre: and that the monarchy of the
Empire is ſubiect to the Church euē in matters temporal.
And wheras your ſecte wil haue no meane place, for any
Chriſtians, but heauen or hell, your Dantes (as Antoninus

telleth)

Cōcernīg
the cōfir-
matiō of
thēperer
by the
Pope.

M. Horne
proueth
his nevv
primacie
by poets.
M. Hor-
nes ovvn
authour
cōdēneth
his vvyt-
neſſes.
Volater. in
Anthropo-
logia.

Antoni.
part. 3. ti-
tul 21. ca.
5. ſſ. 2.

telleth)hath fownde a meane place,befide heauen and hel,
for Socrates,Ariftotle,Cicero,Homere and fuche lyke.
Suerly Dantes,for his other opinion towching theperours
fubiection is counted not muche better then an heretyke.
As for *Marfilius Patauinus* , he hath bene afwell long agoe,
as alfo of late,largely and learnedly anfwered . But as for
thefe writers,*Marfilius Patauinus,Ockam , Dantes , and Pe-*
trarche,with diuerfe others,part of whom your brethern
of Bafil haue patched vp togeather,in a greate volume , as
they laboure al to proue the Emperour aboue the Pope in
temporal iurifdiction and gouernemet,wherin yet they er-
red(as we haue faid)fo none of the al doe labour to proue
the Emperour fupreme gouernour in fpirituall and ecclefiaftical caufes,(as you the firft founders of this herefy do
fay and fweare to,)but do leaue that to the Bifhoppes, yea
and fome of them to the Pope to.And therefore al were it
true,that they wrote in the fauoure of Lewys the. 4 .then
Emperour yet were you neuer the nerer of your purpofe
by one iote. This is M.Horne,your owne proper and fingular herefy of England to make the Prince fupreme gouernour in caufes ecclefiaftical.You only are *Laicocephali,*
that is fuch as make the lay Magiftrates, your heads in fpirituall matters.

    Ye adde then more force to your matter by a great cou-
cel kepte at Franckford, wherat the king of Beame and of
Englande alfo were prefente, of which wyth other things
is fet forth by a fpecial ad a latin letter,as the precife words
of *Marius* or of the additio adioyned to Vrfpergenfis . But
neither they, nor anye other of your marginall authours
fpeake of the king of Englad.And when ye haue al don,ad
who fo euer was there, yt was but a fchifmatical conuenticle

Bartolus in lege prima ff. de requi- rendis reis.
Marfilius Patani- nus.
Vide Hie- rarchiam Pighij.
De Iurif- dict.Im per.& ec- clefiaft.
Bafil.im- pref. Anno 1566.
The pro- per here- fy of En- glande.

ticle,and yet muche better,then your late conuocations.
Yf the articles of your fayde conuocations had comme to
theire handes,no dowbte they had bene condemned, for a
greate parte of them,for moſt blaſphemous hereſies. Wel:
The Emperour ſaith (ſay you) that his authority depēdeth not of
the Pope,but of God immediatly,and that it is a vayne thinge,
that is wonte to be ſayde , the Pope hath no ſuperiour : yf ye
could proue this Emperour an Euangeliſt,or this Coũcel a
lawfull Generall Councel, we would geue ſome eare to
you. And yf themperours authority depende ſo immediatly
of God,ſhewe vs goddes commaundement,geuē rather to
the Germans,then to the Frenche or Engliſh mē, to choſe
an Emperour. Moſt of the other princes Chriſtiã in Europa
holde by ſucceſsion,and not by electiõ. And yf ye cã ſhew
vs any other cauſe of the diuerſity,but the Popes only ordinance,then ſhal ye quite your ſelf lyke a clerke. Yf ye cã
not ſhewe other cauſe,then ſhal ye neuer be able to ſhewe
vs good cauſe,why the Pope ſhould not clayme the cõfirmation.   Yet is yt,ſayeth M.Horne,*a vayne thing to ſay the*
Pope hath no ſuperiour: but yt is more vainelye and fondlye
done of you M.Horn,to the deſcrying of your falſe dealing
and to the deſtruction of your Primacy,to bring foorth this
ſaying.For your ſayd councel recogniſeth the Pope , as ſuperiour in all cauſes eccleſiaſtical. And where yt ſayeth, yt
hath a ſuperiour,why do ye not tel vs,as your authours do,
who is his ſuperiour? Is it the Emperour wene you,or any
temporal Prince,as ye wold make your vnlearned reader
belieue?No,no.Your councel meante,and ſo both your au
thours plainely declare , that it was the generall councell,
to the which themperour had appealed. Where you adde,
the Actes of this Councell were *ratified by the Emperours*

M.Horne
leaueth
owte of
his au-
thours
vvordes.
Vide dict.
Paralip.
& Nau-
cler.pag.
384.*&*
385.*vo-*
lum.3.

letters patents, and do bring in thervpon as the Emperours letters againſt the Popes proceſſes, you beguile your Reader, and belie your Author Nauclerus. For thoſe letters patents, this Emperour gaue forth, not as ratifiyng the Actes of that Councel (as you ſay) but *De concilio quorundā fratrū Minorum ſub ſigillo ſuo:* vpō the aduiſe of certaine Minorits, vnder his owne ſeale. And againe : *vocata ſolenni curia:* At the keping of a ſolemne Courte. Of the Acts of that Councel, Nauclere ſpeaketh not in this place, neither reporteth theſe leters pattēts to haue proceded therof. Thus of Princes Courtes, ye make great Councels, and of the aduiſe of certai Friers, you frame to your Reader the cōſent of many biſhoppes. By ſuche pelting ſhiftes, a barren cauſe muſt be relieued.

But now are ye yet againe in hand with an other Councel at Frankford by this Emperour: and with certaine hereſies that Pope Clement laid to this Emperours charge. It would make a wiſe man to wonder, to conſider, to what end ād purpoſe this ſtuffe is here ſo thruſt in. Neither cauſe can I as yet coniecture any, vnleſſe I ſhoulde impute it, to Maiſtres folie, or to dame hereſie, or to both : or to the ſpeciall ordinaunce of God, that ſuffreth this man for the malice he beareth to the Catholike Church to wexe ſo blind,

An heape of Vnς truths.
Naucler.
ybi vt ſuς pra.
Paralip.
Vrſpergen.

that he ſpeaketh, he wotteth not what, and ſeeth not, whē he ſpeaketh moſte againſt him ſelfe , nor the matter that he would gladly defend. For beſide as many lies as be almoſte lines (as that he telleth of an hereſie firſt laid to the Emperours charge, which was not the firſt, as ye ſhal vnderſtand anon: Item, that the Pope ſayed he was an heretike , becauſe he ſaid Chriſt ād his Apoſtles were poore, wherin he doth excedingly lie vpon pope Clement: Item that th'Emperour

perour set forth lawes Ecclesiasticall, concerning mariages
and deuorceméts, which his Authours say not, nor is otherwise true) beside all this he declareth his Emperour to be a
very heretike, and him selfe also, or at the least to be but a
very foolish fond man.

I wil therfore for the better vnderstáding of the mater, first
rehearse you his authors wordes, and then adde to it some
further declaratió mete for the purpose. *The first heresy* (saith
Nauclerus) *was that the Emperour affirmed, that the Decree
made by Pope Iohn the.22.touching the pouerty of Christ ād his
Apostles, was heretical, swearing that he beleued the contrarie.
He auouched moreouer that it appertained to the Emperour, to
make or depose Popes. Furthermore being cited to answere in a
cause of heresie, and being accursed for his cótumacy, he hath có-
tinued almost these tēne yeres in the said curse. He retained also in his cópany, one Iohn of Landenio an Archeheretik. He maketh bisshops, he breaketh the interdict, and doth expel thē out
of their benefices that wil not breake it. He seuereth matrimo-
nies, cótracted in the face of the Church: and ioyneth persons together in the degrees forbiddē. He meaneth perchaunce* (sayeth
Nauclere) *that he maried his sonne Lewys to the Coūtes of Ty-
roles, her husbād Iohn, the king of Beames son, yet liuing: saying
that he was impotēt ād furder, (hee was maried to this Lewys
being within the degrees prohibited. Clemēt addeth beside, that
he hath set vp an Idole in the Churche, and an Antipope, and
hath de facto, deposed the Pope.* These are Nauclere, M. Horn
his authors precise words: the which I pray thee good reader to conferre with M. Hornes glose, and then shal ye see
the mans honesty and fidelity in reporting his Authors.

This Emperor then was not accópted an heretik, becaufe
he said Christ ād his Apostles wer poore, neither is this códemned

Naucler.
gener.45.
pag.390.
Prima
hæresis. Ip
se enī (in-
quit Cle-
mens) as-
seruit de-
terminat.
de pauper
tate Chri-
sti et apo-
stolorū per
Ioan.22.
factā, esse
hæreticā:
et iurauit
se credere
contrariū.
Item asse-
ruit. &c.
M. Horns
Emperor
is an he-
retike.
Vide ex-
trauagan
tē Io.22.
cū inter
de verb.
signif.

demned for herefie, by the forefaid Iohn the. 22. but to fay
Chrift and his Apoftles had nothing in cómon or in priuat,
which was the herefie of thofe that are called *Fratricelli*,
or *Pauperes de Lugduno:* moft chieflie of al men fet forth by
a Frier called *Michaël de Cefena,* and our Countriman Frier
Ockam, ãd *Marfilius Patauinus,* and by this your Emperour
Lewes of Bauarie and by *Petrus de Corbario* the Antipope,
that ye fay was placed in pope Iohns roome : who
keping a Conuenticle in Italie, condemned pope
Iohn for an Heretique, as your Author Marius declareth: So that this faction in this wife on euerie
fide banded, grew to a very great fchifme. And
many fo fondly and obftinately dwelt in this opini-
nion, that they died as obftinately and wretchedly
for it. And yet thefe men as I haue faied, are not
onely holy brethren, but holye Martyrs too, with
Maifter Foxe. And nowe good Maifter Horne,
tell vs your iudgement in the matter. Is it Herefie,
or is it no herefie , to defende this opinion obftinatlie? If ye
fay it is herefie then doe ye confeffe your newe Heade of
the Church, with his newe Idole and Antipope, an Heretique : and doe fhew your felfe a greate flaunderoufe lyer
againft pope Iohn : and a very fonde madde man , thus to
fight againft your felfe, and your owne caufe. If ye doe
ftoutelie denie this to be herefie, as yee feeme, by the order of your declaration to denie it, as well as the reft, then
fhewe you your felfe no fimple Schifmatique , nor fimple
Heretique, and fo ye are at the leaft meffhed here in foure
herefies.

      To fet fome faft footing in the difcufsió of thefe matters,
and feriouflye to weigh and examine euery thing, woulde
afke

Vide hifto-
riam Ant.
part.3.
tit.21.c.5.
ß.1.

Is Concilie in Italia
habito Io.22.hareti-
cũ declarauerat, de-
fendens Iefum eiuf-
que difcipulos adeo
pauperes fuiffe, vt ni
hil neq; in cõi, neque
priuatim habuiffent.
Quod in Cõcil. Ane-
monẽfi refutatũ eft.
Io. Marius de fchifm.
et Cõcil. part.2.c.21

Cardinal.
Flor. in
Clement.
exiui. ſ-
proinde
de verb.
fignif.
Madde
Martyrs.

aſke ſome larger talke, thē we may now (vnleſſe we would be to to tedíouſe to our reader) wel ſpare. But yet for the two principal matters, ſeing you make ſo light of Pope Iohn and the Churches Authoritie, I will conuince you, and ſufficientlye to, I hope: and by ſuche a witneſſe as your owne Emperour, of all other men in the worlde did moſt eſteme and reuerence, yea and kiſſed his fote to. Perchaūce Maiſter Horne ye longe to heare of this man? Truelye he is none other, but your Emperours dearling, and idole the Antipope. I meane Petrus de Corbario. Who at lēgth, (called no doubt thereto by the ſpeciall grace of God,) better aduiſing him ſelfe of his doings, and weighing them better with him ſelfe, after mature and ſeriouſe diſcuſsing of them, in fyne founde him ſelfe no Pope, but a miſerable and a wretched intruder, in the ſea of S. Peter: and a damnable diſturber of the peace and vnitye of Chriſtes Churche, and to ſay all at ones, a greauouſe ſchiſmatike, and an heynouſe heretike. Wherefore fynding the worme of conſcience, bytinge and gnawing his harte, he fell to greate ſorowe and lamentation, and forthwith being then at a citie in Italy called Piſa, before the Archebiſſhoppe of the ſaid citye, and the Biſſhoppe of Luke, and manye other honorable perſons aſwell of the clergy as of the laity, voluntarilie and willinglye, ſhewed howe penitente he was for his greauouſe enormities, and before them and certayne notaries, for a full teſtimonie of his true repentance, gaue ouer his vſurped primacie, and plainely confeſſed, that he hadde bene a ſchiſmatike and an heretike: and he did put him ſelfe into the handes and mercie of the right Pope Iohn the.22. And wrote vnto him reſident then at Auinion in Fraunce, his moſte humble ſubmiſsion: in

The repē٫ tance of the Antis pope ſette vp agaiſt Pope Iohn.

qq　　　　the

the which he declareth, that as him selfe was but an vsurper of the Apoſtolique See: So your Lewys of Bauarie,
was no lawfull Emperour, but an vsurper. He declareth
further that both he and the said Lewes, mainteyned diuers hereſies, and namely two of theſe that ye here ſpecify,
concerning the pouertie of Chriſt, and the making and
the depoſinge of the Pope. The which he doth by ſpeciall woordes freelie and voluntarilie, forſake, renounce,
and abiure. And promiſeth that he woulde euer after belieue, as the ſayde Iohn, and the holie Churche of Rome
belieued. Wil ye nowe ſee good Reader the wonderfull
workinge of God, that hath brought to Maiſter Horne
his owne Pope, to condemne him and his newe Heade
of the Churche Lewys, for Arrante heretikes? Yea to
make a ſhorte aunſwere to all Maiſter Hornes booke, and
to call yt hereſie, that Maiſter Horne doth ſo ſtowtlie defende, in ſaying that the Emperour ſhoulde be aboue the
Pope, and to haue authority to make or depoſe the Pope?
And thus ye heare, (Maiſter Horne) that contrary to your
ſaying Pope Iohn neither was depoſed, nor coulde be depoſed by your Emperour. I meruayle nowe ſeing that
it is a true and ſoｙnde doctrine by your newe heades tea-
chinge, that Chriſte and the Apoſtles hadde nothinge of
theire own, that your and your fellowes conſciences (who
pretende that ye woulde haue the Churche that nowe is,
reformed to the paterne of the primityue and Apoſtolicall
Churche) are ſo large, that ye are nothing pinched at cõſcience, in keping your godly and great poſſeſsions.

Specialiter cognoſco, me tenere & credere quod ad Imperato-rem non pertinet, deponere nec inſti-tuere Pa-pã, prout &c.

Vide Ro-bertũ Ar-bor 〈…〉em Epiſcopum impreſſum Pariſiis in 8. Anno. 1546.

The

Maiſter Hornes Emperour, and him ſelfe declared an heretike by his ovvne
Antipope. All Maiſter Hornes booke ſhortlie confuted by the ſayde Antipope.

*The 30. Chapter: Of Gods Iudgement vpon such Emperours,
as seme most to haue practised M. Horns Primacy.*

Stapleton.

BVT nowe M. Horne, sith we are come by course of
tymes and ages to the last Emperour, that notoriously
rebelled against the Apostolike See of Rome (for since
this Lewys the. 4. they haue al ben obedient Childrē to that
See, especially in al causes spiritual or Ecclesiasticall, euē to
the right Catholike Emperour Maximilian that now reig-
neth)I wil put you brefely in minde, to what ends al these
disobedient Emperours came. Trusting that this consideration of Gods iudgement shal be neither to you bearing your
self for a bishop in Gods Church vnpleasant, neither for me
(my vocation considered) vnmete, neither to the Christian
Reader vnfruteful.

To be short therfore, Costātius the Arriā Emperor which
banished Pope Liberius, ād plaied in dede the part of your su
preme gouernour, died obscurely and miserably whiles he
persecuted Iulyan his own Cousen.

Valens an other Arriā Emperor, and playing Rex ouer al
Catholik Bishops in the East, being ouercome in field of the
Gothes, was burned to ashes in a poore cotage, with diuers
of his nobles about him, which was neuer read of any Christian Emperour sence, or before.

Valentinian the yonger who called his bisshop, S. Ambrose to appeare before his consistory, and there to answer
in matters of faith, his end was to be kylled of his own seruants, and shamefully hanged.

Anastasius the Eutychian Emperour, and excommunicated of Pope Gelasius, was stroken to deathe with
fyre from heauen, and Mauritius an vnmerciful persecuter

Ammiā
Marcel.li.
22.

Idē lib. 3t.

Hierony.
ad Helio-
dorū. To. 1.
Ambr. lib.
5. epist. 32.
Eutropius
lib. 3.

of blessed

of bleſſed Pope Gregory, and a buſy Prince ouer his Biſhops
ſeing firſt his wife and children murdred before his face,
was murdered at laſt him ſelfe of a baſe Souldiare Phocas.

Blondus.
li.3.decad
1.Paulus
Diaconus
lib.18.
Zonaras
Tomo.3.
Zonaras
Ibidem.
Conſtans nephewe to Heraclius, baniſhed the moſt holy Pope Martinus: but ſeing him ſelfe for that and ſuch like
wicked dedes (ſaith Zonaras) hatefull to his ſubiectes, he
left Conſtantinople, and liued in Sicilia, where at a bathing
he was ſlayne. Michael, ſonne to Theophilus, a notorious
enemy to the See Apoſtolike, namely to Nicolaus the firſt,
going drunke to bed, was miſerably ſlayne by his beds ſyde,
forſaken of al his freds. And thus much of the Greke Emperours and of the Eaſt Church, only Valentinian excepted.

Nauslerus
volum.3.
Generat.
37.pag.171.
&.173.
The firſt of al the Germain Emperours that notoriouſly
diſobeyed the See of Rome, and that was therefore by the
Pope excommunicated openly, was Henry the. 4. whome
Gregory the ſeueth (otherwiſe called Hildebrad) excomunicated. His end was, as it hath before ben declared, that being firſt depoſed of his own ſon, after much reſiſtance, and
miſery, appealig, but to late, to the See of Rome, ſeing hiſelf
forſaken almoſt of al the ſtates of the Empire, in affliction
and extreme perſecution died.

Idem. Ge-
nerat.40.
pag.251.
Sabellicus
Aenead.9.
lib.5.
Friderik the firſt called *Barbaroſſa*, a man that many yeres
perſecued the Church of Rome, ad therfore worthely excomunicated of Alexader. 3. to who alſo he was forced at
legth to ſubmit himſelf, though againſt his wil, afterward in
Cicilia, being ſtrong and mery, ſodenly bathing him ſelfe in
a ryuer he was loſte.

Naucler.
Gene. 41.
pag.271.
Philip an Emperour made againſt the conſent of Pope
Innocetius. 3. and a perſecuter therefore of the Pope, in the
towne of Bromberge repoſing him ſelfe after diner in his
pryuey chamber, was ſlayne of the Countie Palatyne.

Otho

The:

Otho the fourth depofed and excommunicated of the Pope 4.
for his enormious cruelties and iniuries cōmitted in many *Pag.275.*
places of Italy, was of Philipe the French king affaulted in *& 280.*
thefe lowe countries, and put to flight, and fhortly after in *Sabell. Ae-*
Saxony died as a priuat man. *9.lib.6.*

Frederike the fecond, a prince brought vp in the Court *Nauc.Ge-*
of Rome, and fet in the Empire by the procuremēt of pope *nera. 4 2.*
Innocentius the. 3. became yet afterwarde a moft cruel ād *pag. 309.*
tyránical perfecutor not only of that See, but of al the Cler *Sab. Aen-*
gy vnder his dominions. This man being excommunicated *9. lib.6.*
of Innocentius.4. was poyfoned in Apulia as fome write,
or ftrangled, as other write, by his baftarde fonne Manfredus. Not onely this Emperour him felfe, but al his ftocke
after him perifhed, by violent deathes or imprifonmēt. His *Naucler.*
fonne and Heyr Conradus being excommunicated alfo of *pag. 313.*
Innocentius. 4. for the great outrages and oppreſions by
him commytted againft the Church, by the meanes alfo of
the fayd Manfredus, was poyfoned in Apulia.

This Manfredus commyng by thefe trayterouſe meanes *Idē.Gen.*
to the kyngdomes of Apulia and Sicilia, and afflictinge the *42.p.320.*
Churche of Rome, as his father and brother had done, was
excommunicated by Alexander the.4. and after of Charles
the Frenche kynges broother, whome Vrbanus the fourth
made kyng of Sicilia and Apulia, he was vanquifhed and *Sabel. Ae.*
flayn in the fyeld. Conradinus fonne to Conradus, and clay- *9.lib.7.*
ming after, his fathers Titles, was of this Charles alfo van- *Naucler.*
quifhed and put to death. *pag.323.*

Entius likewife an other fonne of Friderike the. 2. and
one that had longe and many yeres in his fathers warres, *Naucler.*
done great myfchief to the See of Rome, was at length take *pag.324.*
in battayle of the Bononyans, and committed to perpetual *dict.Gen.*
42.

prifon. Thus al the ftock of this Frederike the. 2. who had fo greuoufly perfecuted the Church of Rome, was in few yers vtterly extinguifhed. Which thing al hiftoriãs do worthely note, though fome more fharply them other : yet al herein agreing, that for their defertes God plaged thẽ fo notorioufly in this worlde.

Naucl. Gener. 45. pag. 379. 588. et 393. Lewys the fourth, the laft Emperour by maifter Horne alleaged, being excõmunicated twife of the See of Rome, firft of Iohn the. 22. and after of Clement the. 6. vnder whõ and in whofe fauour thofe poetes and oratours, *Petrarcha and Dantes, Marfilius*, and Ockam the fcholeman wrote againft the Popes temporalties, as he was a hunting, was taken with a foden palfey, fel from his horfe, and died.

Such endes had they in this life, that moft practifed the fupreme gouernement by M. Horn here defended. And his beft exãples and proufes, to proue his ftrange primacy, haue bene drawen from the doyngs of thefe forenamed Emperours. And verely like as in the old lawe, Saul, Achab, Iorã, Ochozias, Ioas, Amafias, Ozias, and Achas, kynges of Iuda and Ifrael died al by violent and miferable deathes, for difo-

1. Reg. 31. 3. Reg. 22 4. Reg. 9. 2. Paral. 24. 25. 26 beying the prophetes and prieftes of God, Samuel, Elias, Elizeus, Micheas ãd Efaie, ãd as their fuch deathes were manifeft argumentes of Gods indignation, and recounted for fuche in holy fcripture: fo thefe forenamed Emperours, ãd princes in Chriftes Church Conftantius, Mauritius, Valés, Anaftafius, Conftans, Michael, Henry the fourth, Friderike Barbaroffa, Philip, Otho. 4. Friderike the fecond, Cõradus, Conradinus, Manfredus, ãd Lewys the. 4. hauing fuch violent and miferable endes, vppon their notorious difobedience to Chriftes vicaires in earth, the bifhoppes of the See Apoftolike Liberius, Gelafius, S. Gregory the firfte, Martinus the firfte, Nicolaus the firfte, Gregory the. 7.

Alexan-

Alexander. 3. Innocentius the.3.and.4. Alexander the. 4.
Iohn the.22.and Clement the.6.are vnto vs profeſsing the
faith of this Church, vndoubted argumentes of Gods iuſte
indignation and plage in their behalfes,and may well ſerue
for holſome preſidentes to other Chriſten princes , not to
attempt the like. But nowe to returne to M. Horne, and to
treade, as he leadeth vs, haue out of Germany, into France,
an other while.

M. Horne. The. 135. Diuiſion. pag. 81. b.

In Fraunce king Charles (.443.) denied the Pope the tenthes of his Cler-
gie. But Philip de Valois that follovved , reformed and tooke avvay many
late vpſtart Eccleſiaſticall abuſes in the Clergy, and Prelates in his Realme:
of the vvhich, diuerſe complaints being made vnto the kinge, he called a coū-
ſel at Paris , and ſummoned thither the biſhops , as appeareth by his letters
vvherein he complaineth, that they haue enchroched from him and
his officers a great many of rightes: bringing in their noueltie
not due, and vnwonted grieues vnder the pretence of Eccleſiaſticall cauſes: whereby they haue broken the concorde of the
Clergy and the Laity, and therfore willing to prouide ſo much
as he can by Goddes help, an healthful remedy: He requireth,
and neuertheleſſe commaundeth them to appeare before him
at Parys perſonally. &c. The Prelates appearing at the day aſ-
ſigned, before the kinge in his Palayce , Archebiſhoppes, Biſſhoppes, and making reuerence to the kinges maieſtie, being
ſet down with his councel , and certein Barons aſsiſting him,
a certeine knight of the kinges councell, ſpake publykely for
the kinge in the preſence of them al, taking for his theme this
texte. Geue that vnto Cæſar that belongeth to Cæſar, and that
vnto God that is due vnto God. &c.

The kinges admonition being made, a great many complaintes vvere put
vp vnto the king by his nobles and officers, againſte the Clergies vſurpation,
in medling vvith contractes of mariages, in their priuileges of Clerkes : In
citations to their Courtes , in their excommunications, in vvilles , and
hereditamentes, in calling of prouinciall councells , in making ſynodall Dea-
crees, ād ſtatutes, in medling vvith realties, in peremptory vvrites, in examina-
tions of

Aemylius.
The.443.
vntruth.
He graū-
ted them.
Pet. Ber-
tran.

tions of mens beleues, in enioyning of money penaunces, In shauing of childrē, and vnlauful persons making them Clerkes, in whoordome and fornicatiou, in vvyddovves goodes, in bloudshead in the Churcheyarde, in inuentories, &c. and in a great many mo matters, vvhich ye call Spirituall or Ecclesiasticall causes: the Frenche kinge prouing (.444.) them to be (as in deede they vvere

The.444. vntruth. For the Frenche kinge ne sayed no proued no such matter.

no other) but temporall: neuerthelesse not standinge much about the name, nor taking them al avvay, from their iurisdiction, he onely saied, he vvould reforme them. Neuerthelesse, for certeine daies there was much disputing to and fro, whether they belonged to the kinge to reforme or no, till the king by his foresaid procuratour gaue thē the kinges determinat aunswere, declaring vnto them, howe that they ought not to be troubled, bicause the kinges intentiō was, to keepe those rightes and customes of the Churche, and Prelates which were good ād resonable, but by reason of their

The.445. vntruth. For this vvas not the Cōclu siō, as shal appeare. Aemylius. The.446 vntruth.

faultes, the iudgement which were good and reasonable, apperteined not vnto them to determine, but to the kíg. Bicause the Decree, Nouit &c. saieth, that the kinge of Fraunce in matters de Facto, hath not his superiour &c. VVhereupon hee cōcluded, that the kinge woulde heare all the informatiōs: And those Customes of the whiche he should be fully enfourmed, that they were good and reasonable, he woulde make only to bee obserued.

P. Aemy lius men cioneth no suche lavve. but plainely the con trary. The.447 vntruth. Not ther fore, P. Ae mylius fovvly abused.

In (.445.) cōclusiō the Prelats made such importune labour, that the forsaid attourney aūswered thē for the kinge, that if the Prelates thē selues would amende those thinges, that were to be amended and corrected, the king would abide till the feaste of the Natiuity next to come: within the saide terme, he woulde innouate nothing: but if within the sayde terme, the Prelates had not amended those thinges that were to be amended and corrected, that then the king would put to such remedy, as shuld be acceptable to God and the people. VVhich in conclusion the kinge vvas faine to do, by a sharpe and seuere (.446.) Lavv, vvhan he savve hovv the Prelates dallied him of, vvith faire vvordes, and (.447.) therefore be him selfe, Composuit rem sacerdotum, did set in order the matters of the Priestes.

The

*The .31.Chapter.Of Charles the .4.and Philip de Valois
sixt of that name, kinges of Fraunce.*
Stapleton.

WEll fisht, and caught a frogge. All this lóg
tale is tolde for *Composuit rem sacerdotum.*
But to touche the particulars, what wise
reason is this, or what reason at al is it, to make the
Quene of England supreame head of the Church,
because Charles the French king denied the pope
the tenthes of the Clergy? Verely his authour saith,
the king did empayre his estimation, that men had
of his vertue before by this very fact of his. Yea and
yet he sayth withall, that afterwarde he did códescéde to the popes request. Now what meaneth M.
Horn, to alleage that for prouf of dewe gouuerne-
mét, which his authors report, for prouf of vndewe
regiment? Meaneth he that al the worlde shoulde
laugh him to skorne? That which foloweth of Peter
Bertrád, and eftson of Paulus Aemilius, is M. Horns
own: making thé, to speake not theire myndes, but
what liketh him, tellig vs first an obscure, dark, false
tale, out of the sayd Bertrád: but I trust we shall drawe him
out into the fayre open light, and pluck fró him Petrus Bertrand and Paulus Aemilius with whose visour, he woulde
fayne couer the vgly face of his impudente and shamelesse
lies . Why M. Horn? hath not the Clergy to doe with matters of contracts of mariage, excommunications, wills, and
with the examination of mens beliefes, with making synodical decrees, and such like matters? Wherfor thé do ye not
shake of from you the intermedlinge with these matters?
Wel I perceiue saying ád doing are two things: and neither

rr   shall

P. A Emilius li. 8. in
Carolo Pulchro.
Carolus Rex & vir-
tutis & clementiæ
laudé, fructumq; ad
eum dié tulit, exin
aduersourmore, quòd
sacri in Ludouicú Ba
uarú belli noíe deci-
mas de sacerdotibus
Fràcispetenti pótific.
Max. Iohàni cú pri-
mum denegasset, pa-
ctione deinde expug-
natus, concessisset vt
in parté ipse veniret,
&cat.

shall Ludouicus the Emperour, though he affirmed that the Clergy should followe Christ and his Apostles in pouerty, make yowe to disclaime your goodly landes and patrimony : nor Philip Valesius the Frenche kinge make yowe to disclaime your iurisdiction. The gaine is to sweet.

Perhaps ye will answere, that I strayne yowe to farre, and

that ye do not deny, but that the Clergy may vse the iurifdiction of the forefayd matters, but not as Church or ecclefiafticall matters, but as playne temporall matters, for the Frenche kinge proued they were fo in dede. Neyther the king proued yt, nor your authour fayth yt, nor any other. The fhameleffe dealinge of this man is fuche, that he femeth to feke nothing elfe, but to ouerwhelme the worlde with wordes, litle regardinge to fpeake, not only great and many vntruthes, but euen fuch as without further triall and ftrayning hym no more, but with his owne authours, are incontinently opened and defcried. To anfwere fully, and at large to all his endleffe and importune babling, afwelhere as otherwhere would be to to tedioufe a thinge. And for this matter, in as muche as Petrus Bertrand is in prynte, I will fend the learned reader, that is defiroufe, to fee the deapth of thys matter, to the originall booke : and will nowe touche fo much onely, as fhalbe fufficiente for the vnlettered reader, to fee and confider M.Hornes vnfaythfull and wretched dealing.

Petrus Cunerius being one of the kings priuie councell proponed to the Clergy before the king, and the nobilitie. 76. articles : and wente about to proue, that the prelates and the Clergy, for fo many poynts had vfurped vppon the kinges iurifdiction, He auowched alfo, that temporall and

rall and fpirituall things, are diuided and fondred, and that
the one appertayned to the kinge onely, the other to the
cleargy onely. The archbifhop of Sans, anfwered to this
Petrus, and proued by the olde and the newe teftamēt, by
the cyuil and canon Lawe, and by the cuftome of Fraunce
tyme out of mynd vfed, and by feuerall graunts and pri∫
uileges, receiued from the kings predeceffiours, that fpirituall and temporall iurifdiction were not fo precifelie diftincted, but that one perfon might occupie both. After
him the fame daye feuenight, in the prefence of the king
ftode vppe Petrus Bertrandus a Bifhoppe of the people
in Fraunce then called Hedui, who are nowe Burgoni-
ons, and enforced the fame matter, addinge a full aunfwere, afwell to the decree *Nouit*, alleaged here by M.
Horne out of the fayd *Petrus Cunerius*, as vnto all his.
76. articles. A greate nomber of the fayde articles,
towche matters playne and mere temporall, and yet
fuche as the clergy did and might medle withall, partly by Lawe, partly by fpeciall priuilege, and partly by
cuftome. There were certayne faults and abufes fownd
in the prelates officers, the whiche the prelates anfwe- *Petr. Ber-*
red, *that yf they had knowen them before, they woulde not* *trandus.*
haue fuffred them: and promifed to forfee for the tyme to
come, for the earnefte amendinge and redrefsinge of them.
For the redrefsing whereof the kinge gaue them a tyme vn-
till Chriftmas folowinge. Nowe M. Horne would make thee
belieue, good reader, that becaufe the prelats dalied and
things were not refourmed accordingly, the kinge by a
fharpe and a feuere lawe dyd amende and correcte them.
But this is your owne Lawe, good maifter Horne, and
no Lawe at all of Kynge Philippe : made by yowe,

I say, with as good authoritie and truthe , as the damnable articles were made, in your late conuocation . Howe so euer yt be, here is nothinge amended but abuses: which to be amended no good man will I wene be angrie withall. But what say yow nowe maister Horne to the whole ecclesiasticall iurisdiction that the Frenche clergie practised ? What became of yt ? Did the king take yt away , or no ? Whie are ye tounge tyed M. Horne to tell the truth, that so freelie and liberally, yea and lewdly to , lie againste the truth? Wel : seing that ye can not wynne yt at Maister Hornes hands good reader, ye shal heare it otherwise. The

Petrus Bertrandus. effecte and finall resolution then of this debate was , that the kinge made answere to the forsayd bishop of Sans, demaunding his resolute answere, in the behalfe of the whole clergy: *that the prelates shoulde feare nothinge , and that they shoulde not lose one iote in his tyme : but that he woulde defende them in theire righte and custumes : neither woulde he geue to other an example to impugne the Churche . Whereuppon the Bisshoppe in the name of the whole clergie gaue*

M. Horns shamelesse Dealinges *to the kinge moste humble thankes* . Howe saye yowe good reader, hath this man any more shame then hath a very Horne? And dareth he to looke hereafter any honest man in the face?

Yet he wil say that Paulus Aemilius sayth, that the King *was fayne to make this sharp and seuere Lawe.* Why? Ca Paulus Aemylius, tell better what was done, then your other authour Bertrande , being presente and playing the chiefe parte in this play, and setting yt forth to the world , to your perpetual ignominie, with his own penne? Wel: tel vs then, what Paulus sayeth . Marie saye yowe , Paulus reporteth that *composuit rem sacerdotum* : he did set in order the matters

ters

ters of the Prieſtes . But who ſpeaketh of your ſharpe and
ſeuere Lawe? Wil not *cõponere rem ſacerdotũ*:agree with al
that I haue told out of Bertrand himſelf? Is now *cõponere rẽ
ſacerdotũ*:to be englifhed, to make a ſharpe and a ſeuere
law? Suerly this is a prety expoſitiõ, ãd a tryme tricke of your
new grãmer. Your Authour Aemilius vſeth his word *cõpoſuit,valdè, aptè,& compoſitè*,very aptly and fytlie. But you M.
Horne with your gaye and freſhe interpretation doe nothing elſe, but *Lectori fallacias componere*,deceyue and be
guyle your reader, or to ſpeake more fytely to our purpoſe,ye doe nothing elſe but *Legem Philippi nomine componere*.counterfeyte a lawe in Philippes name:whereof your
authour Aemilius ſpeaketh nothing . For Aemilius declaring a notable victory that this King had ouer his enemies,
ſaith:that the victory obteyned,and after that he had made
his prayers and geuen thankes therefore to God and to his
bleſſed Martyres,*cõpoſuit rem Sacerdotum*: he ſet in order
the Prieſtes matters.Then doth he ſhortly ſpecifie,that the
foreſaide *Petrus Cunerius* complained vpon the clergy for
the hearing of many matters,that appertayned to the kiges
ſecular cowrte : and that the foreſaid *Bertrandus* made him
anſwere, declaring amonge other thinges,that their beſte
Kinges in Fraunce,the moſt floriſhing and the moſt notable were euer the greateſte patrons and defenders of the
clergies liberties : and that the other that impugned the
ſame,came to a miſerable and wretched ende.He ſaith further,that the Kings anſwere being from day to day proló-
ged,the ſaid Bertrandus with a nomber of the prelates vpõ
S.Thomas of Canterburies day , went to the Kinge, ad-
moniſhig him that S.Thomas in the defence of the Church
liberties vppon that daye , ſpente his bloud and lyfe. The

Paul⁹ Ae-
milius.
Lib.8. in
Philip. 6.
Valeſio.ſup
plicationi-
bus ac gra
tijs numi-
ni ac ſan-
ctis mar-
tyribus ha
bitis rem
ſacerdotũ
compoſuit.
Prætores
regij &c.
The mat-
ter truely
declared
out of P.
Æmilius
M.Horns
authour.

P. Aemi-
lius dict.
lib. 8.
Tum Rex,
iura, in-
quit, eccle-
ſiarū auxe
rim pottus
quàm im
minuta ve
lĩ Gratias
vniuerſi e-
gere, Rex
Catholici
nomē pro-
meruit.

King at the length anſwered *that he wuld rather encreaſe,*
than impayre the Churches right. Wherevpon all rendred vnto him thankes: and the Kinge purchaſed himſelfe thereby the
name of a Catholike King. Ye heare, goodreader, an other
maner of expoſition of *compoſuit remſacerdotium,* by the authour him ſelf, then is M.Hornes gaye lying gloſe made in
his theewiſh Cacus denne. And therfore with theſe words,
wherewith Aemilius beginneth his narration, M. Horne
endeth the narration, to putte ſome countenance vpon his
falſe and counterfeite Lawe. The clergy then enioyed ſtill
their liberties and iuriſdiction, which ordinarilye they had
before, either by Law, or by cuſtome and priuilege, though
as I ſaid many cauſes were but temporall. Al the which tēporal cauſes, the ſaid *Petrus Cunerius,* by the way of cōſul-
tation only and reaſoning, declared by ſome coulorable arguments, to belong to the Kings cowrte onely. But for *ex-*
cōmunicatiōs, ſynodical decrees, examinatiōs of mēs beliefes, ād
ſuch like he maketh thē not as ye bable tēporal matters, nor
abridgeth the clergies iuriſdiction therein, but onely reproueth certayne abuſes therin committed, for the which and
for the other the clergy promiſed a reformation.

Let vs nowe ſee your policie, ād to what benefit of your
cauſe ye doe ſo lie? Imagyne (yf ye wil) that al were true, ād
for ones we will take you for Philip the French King: and
your Law made in your Cacus denne, to be in as good force
as yf yt had ben made in open parliament in France. What
M.Horns
imperti-
nent argu
ments,
iſſue ioyne you thereof? what due and ordinate conſequēt
is this: the Frenche King maketh a ſeuere lawe againſt the
clergie, vſurping his iuriſdiction: *Ergo* the Pope is no Pope:
or, *ergo* the King of England, is the Pope of Englande? A-
gayne, yf al are temporal matters, howe ſtandeth yt with
your

your doctrine, especially of this booke, that ye and your fellowes, shoulde busie your selfe therewith? Neither will yt ease you to say, that ye doe yt by the Princes commissió: for Cunerius, vppon whome ye grounde all this your talke dryueth his reason to this ende, that spirituall men be not capable of temporall iurisdiction, and therefore this commission will not serue you. And yf ye holde by commission, take heade your commission be well and substancially made. But of this commission, we shal haue more occasion to speake hereafter.

M. Horne loke vvel to your cómilsió.

M. Horne. The. 136. Diuision. pag. 82. b.

In England at this tyme many abuses about Ecclesiasticall causes, vvere refourmed (although the Pope and his Clergie, did earnestly (.448.) mainteine them) by Kinge Edvvard the. 3. vvho vvrote his (.449.) letters to the Pope, admonishing him to leaue of his disordered doings, and vvhan that vvould not serue, he redressed them by act of parliament, and (as Nauclerus saith) he commaunded that from thence forth, no body should (.450.) bring into the Realme any kind of the Popes letters, vnder the paine of drowning, and expelled al persones out of his Kingdome, that were by the Pope promoted to any benefice.

Paral. Prsp.
Fabian.　Caxton.
Polyd.　Nauclerus
The. 448. vntruth Slaunderous.
The. 449. vntruth. For those letters proue the Popes Supremacy.
The. 450. vntruth. Nauclere falsly reported.

The. 32. Chapter: Of Edward the. 3. King of England.

Stapleton.

THis argument also is right sutely to the precedent, as resting vpó the reformig of abuses, in matters Ecclesiastical. But I pray you tel vs no more M. Horn of reformig of abuses, if you wil ani way furder your preset cause, except

Cócernig King Edvvarde the. 3.

you.

you tell vs withal, and proue it to, that in such reformation,
the whole clergy, and the temporalty, tooke the Kinge and
not the Pope to be the supreame head Gouernour, and di-
recter thereof, and of al other Ecclesiastical causes also. Verily your own authors shewe playnely the cotrary. And the
Popes authority was at this tyme take to be of such weight

Polid.li.19 and force, that the great league made betwe our Kig ad the
Frech King was cofirmed by the Pope. Ye wil perhapps replie and say, the Popes whole Authority was abolished, a
commaundement being geuen vpon paine of drowninge,
no man shoulde bring into the realme any kinde of letters
from the Pope. Ye wil tel vs also, of certaine letters, that
the Kinge sent to the Pope admonisshing him, to leaue his
disordered doings: and when that woulde not serue, he redressed them by acte of Parliament. Why doe ye not M.
Horne laye forth the tenour of those letters, which as yet
I finde not in any of your marginall authours? Belyke there
lieth some thing hidde that ye woulde be loth your reader
should knowe, least yt bewray your weake and feble argumente, as yt doth in dede. Neither that only, but directlye
proueth the Popes primacy. Did this Kinge, wene you M.
Horne, cal the Pope Antichrist as ye doe? Or wrote he him
self supreame head of the Churche of England? Or did he
abolishe the popes authority in England? Harken then I
pray you, euen to the beginning of his letters. *Sanctissimo*
in Christo Patri Domino Clementi diuina prouidentia sacrosan-
cta Romana ac vniuersalis Ecclesia summo pontifici, Edwardus
eadem gratia rex Francorum & Angliæ, & dux Hiberniæ de-
uota pedum oscula beatorum. To the most holy father in Christ
the Lorde Clement by Gods prouidence the high bisshop
of the holy and vniuersall Churche of Rome, Edward by
the

the fame grace King of Fraunce and England, and Duke
of Ireland, offereth deuoutly to kiffe his holy feete . He *Penſata*
calleth the Pope, *Succeſſorem Apoſtolorum Principis*, the *etiā deuo-*
fucceffour of the prince of the Apoſtles : he defireth the *tionis plea*
pope to confider *the great deuotion and obedience, that the* *nitudine,*
King, the Cleargie, and the people had ſhewed hitherto to the *m° noſtr a*
Sea of Rome.He faieth,*vt nos & noſtri, qui perſonam veſtrā* *regia &*
ſanctiſſ. & ſanctam Rom.Eccleſiam dominari cupimus , vt de- *clerus a^c*
bemus,&c. that he and all his, did defire euen as their dutie *populus*
was, that his holy perſon and the holy Churche of Rome, *dicti regni*
might gouerne and rule. *preſtite-*

Now M.Horne vnleffe vppon fome fodayne and newe *rūt hacte-*
deuotiō ye intende to haue the pope beare rule in England *nus in obe*
againe, and will alfo offer your felfe, yf neede be, to kyffe *dientia*
the Popes fote to,wich thing this great and mighty Prince *dicte ſe-*
was not afhamed to fay, tell vs no more for fhame of *dis.*
thefe letters. Neither tel vs of diforders reformed nowe almoft two hundred yeares agoe : to make thereby an vn-
feafonable and fonde argumente to abolifhe all the Popes
authority in our Dayes. The effecte then of thofe letters
were , to pray,and that moft humbly , the Pope, that he
woulde not by referuations , collations, and prouifions
of Archbifhoprykes, Bifhoprykes, Abbeis, Priories, and
other dignities and benefices, beftowe any ecclefiafticall
lyuinges in Englande vppon ftraungers and aliens. The *Anno 25.*
whych thyng hath bene euer fynce ftraitly fene to , and *& 38.*
there were two Actes of parliament made in this Kinges
dayes,agaynſt the fayed prouifions. And yet did the popes
ordinarie and laufull authoritie in matters and caufes ecclefiafticall remayne whole and entiere as before . Neyther doe I fynde, nor take it to be true, that fuche perfons

as were promoted by the Pope, were expelled the realme.
Nor did the ftatute take place againfte fuche, as had taken
before the enacting of the fame, corporal poffefsion. As for
Nauclere, it is no maruell yf he being a ftraunger doth not
write fo exactely of our matters. And no doubte he is deceiued in writinge, that the kinge forbad any letters to be
browght from the Pope. But what fay I, he is deceiued?
Nay, you, that fhould knowe Englifhe matters better then
he, efpecially fuch as by penne ye fet abrode into the face
of the worlde, are deceiued, and not Nauclerus. Yea rather
ye haue wilfully peruerted *Nauclerus* and drawen his fen‑
tence, as Cacus did Hercules oxen, backwarde into your
Cacus denne: and to beguile and deceiue your fimple rea-

Naucler.
Gener. 46.
pag. 397. a
Omnes in
regno fuo
per papā
promotos
ad benefi-
cia expu‑
lit, & fub
pena fub-
merfionis
pracepit
ne quis
inibi lite‑
ras Apofto
licas exe=
queretur,
quafcunq;
&c.

der, and to bring him, into a fooles paradife, therin fond‑
ly to reioyce with you, as thoughe this King abolifhed all
the Popes authority and Iurifdiction. For thoughe Naucle‑
rus his wordes be general, yet they may be wel vnderftanded and reftrayned to fuche letters as conteyned any fuche
collatiō or prouifion inhibited by the ftatute. But you, leaft
this fhoulde be efpied, haue altered the forme and order of
your authours wordes, placing that firfte, that he placed
lafte. As before cōtrariewife, ye placed in Paulus Aemilius
that lafte, whiche he placed firfte. Then haue ye falfly trā-
flated your authour to wrye him to your wrōgful purpofe.
He expelled (fayeth Nauclerus) *all perfons promoted to any*
benefice in his realme by the Pope, commaundinge vnder
payne of drowning, that no man fhoulde exequute there, the
Popes letters what fo euer they were. Your authour fpeaketh
not of *bringinge letters, into the Realme :* (thofe are your
owne wordes falfly fathered vpon him :) but of exequutiō.
And therefore the generall wordes following (what fo
euer)

euer) are to be reſtrayned to the exequution of the Popes letters, contrarie to the order taken, againſt the ſayde prouiſions, and of none other. Whiche ſtatute doth no more take away the Popes eccleſiaſtical and ordinary authoritie, then this kinges royall authority was taken away, becauſe the Parliament vppon reaſonable cauſes denied him a certaine paymente that he there demaunded. And yet yf I ſhoulde followe your vayne and humour in your newe rhetoryke, I might thereby aſwell inferre, that the people toke him for no king as you by as good argumentes inferre the aboliſhing of the Popes authority. Nowe as towching theis prouiſiõs, they were not altogether aboliſhed againſt the Popes will. For this matter, was lõg in debate betwene the Pope and the king, and at lengthe yt was agreed by the Pope, that he woulde not practiſe anye more ſuche prouiſions. And on the kinges parte, it was agreed, that Archbiſhoppes and Biſhops ſhould be choſen by the Chapter of the cathedral Church without any interruption or impedimente of the king. As appeareth aſwell in the ſayde epiſtle ſente by the king to the Pope as by our chroniclers.

Polidor.
an. Edouar.3. 50.
The chronicles of Englande prited in flete ſtret 1502. withowt the authours name.
The additions of Caxtõ to polichro. Cap.4.

Polid.
The ſaide Chronicles printed in flet ſtrete.

M. Horne. The.137. Diuiſion. pag. 82.b.

Next to Lewes was Charles the .4. choſen Emperour, who helde a councel at Mentze with the Prelates and Princes, in the yere of the Lorde 1359. wherein he much reproued the Popes Legate for his diſorders, and cõmaunded the Archbiſhop of Mentze to reforme his Clergy, and the diſorders amongeſt them, for otherwiſe he would ſee to it him ſelfe. (.451.) The Popes Legate ſeing how the Emperor tooke vpon him, gate him to his ſhippe, and ſaylled to Colayn as one that fledde away. With (.452.) which doynges, the Emperour became very famouſe, for he was a man of great workes. VVho did lyghten the kingdõme of Boheme, bothe with the ſetting foorth of Religion, and with the diſcipline of Lawes, and good manners.

The.451. vntruth. For leauing out, how he wold ſee vnto it. The.452. vntruth. None of his Authors ſay ſo.

ss ij   The

The.33. Chapter.Of Charles the.4. Emperour. And of Nilus
the Bishop of Thessalonica.

Stapleton.

THis man runneth on his race ftil, to proue the Emperour Charles the. 4. alfo the Supreame heade of the
Churche, becaufe he reproued the Popes Legat, and
other of the Clergy for diforders. Goe ones to the matter,
M. Horne, and proue to M. Feckenham, that Charles toke
either him felfe to be head of the Church, or the Pope not
to be the Head. Was not this Charles crouned by Pope
Innocentius his Legate? Did not this Charles geaue the
vfuall othe that Emperours make to the Pope? And did
he not at the Popes commaundemente voide out of Italie,
ftraight after his coronation? If ye denie it, ye fhal finde it
in your owne Authour *Nauclerus. Yf ye graunt it, being
the principal, why do ye fo trifle in other things, that touch
not the principal matter ftanding in variance betwene you
and M.Fekenham? Thefe are but fonde floorifhes of your
rude rhetorique. And I may refemble your doings well to
a dead fnake: whofe taile and hinder partes, the head being
cut of, and the fnake flaine, do notwithftanding for a while
moue and fturre, yea and make a refemblance of life. Euen
fo, the head of your ferpentine and poifoned argumentatio
againft the Popes primacy, being at al times by the true and
faithful declaration of the faied Primacie, againft your falfe
arguing, as it were with a fharp fworde cut of: yet make ye
by telling vs of reformation, and fuch bie matters a counte-
naũce and refemblaũce of fome truth, or as it were of fome
life in your matter ye take in hãd to proue. And truly your
bie matters to, are cõmonly brought in very malitioufly, ignorãtly, erroneoufly, ãd foolifhly, as wel otherwhere, as euẽ
here

Gener.46.
pag.401.a

M.Horns
doings re
fembled
to a dead
fnake.

here alſo.For to leaue then other things, what folly is it for you to proue by this ſtorie the like regiment in this Empe-rours time,as is now in England (for if ye proue not this,ye proue nothing to the purpoſe)confeſsing your ſelfe,that the Popes Legat was preſent in the Coũcel with th'Emperor? And wel ye wot ye haue no Popes Legate in your cõuoca-tion.But what was the diſorder M.Horn,in the Popes Le-gate ? Becauſe he will not tell it you, good Reader, ye ſhal now heare it at my hands. *Sir* , ſaith the Emperour to the Legate, *the Pope hath ſent you into Germanie , where you ga-ther a great maſſe of mony,but reformation in the Clergie ye make none.* At which words the Legat being gilty to him-ſelf,went away.Now what inferre you hereof,M. Horne ? Do not theſe words neceſſarily import the Popes Primacy in Germany ? And that the reformation of the Clergy was at the Popes ordering,not at the Emperours ? Is not there-fore M.Feckenhã much boũd vnto you,that he hath of you ſo tractable and gentle an Aduerſarie ?

But the Archebiſhop of Mentz alſo(you ſay)is commãu-ded to reforme his Clergy.I ãſwere.If ye had told the cauſe withal,ye had ſurely deformed al your Geneuical Clergie. The occaſiõ was,for that one *Cuno* a Canon of his Church, there preſẽt, wẽt in a cap or hood,more lay like ãd ſouldior like,then Prieſtlik.What think you thẽ,this Emperor would haue ſaid to your brother *Smidelinus* the paſtor of Gepping, that preached openly before a great aſſemblie of the nobi-litie in Germany,in his Maiſters liuery girded with a wod-knife by his ſide ? Or to the late Caluiniſt Miniſters in Ant-werp,of whõ ſome preached in clokes and rapiers by their ſides? What likĩg would he haue had in your bretherns late booke made in the defence of their Geneuical apparrel, ãd

Naucler.
dict.gen.
46.& pa-
ral.Vrſp.
D.Legate,
papa miſit
vos ad Ger
maniam
in qua
magnam
pecuniam
corraditis
ſed in cle-
ro nihil re
formatis.
The popes
Primacie
proued
by the
place M.
Horn al-
leageth.
Vide Nau-
cler.p.401
col.1.gen.
46.
Staphil.in
Apologia
abſoluta
fol.77.
Surius in
comment.
breui rerũ
geſt.fo.216

for

for the vnfoldig of the Popes attierment, as they cal it? And
therfore the Quenes moſt excellēt Ma. hath don very wel
her ſelfe to ſee to theſe diſorders, as ye ſaid thēmperor would
ſee to it himſelfe. He ſaid ſo in dede. But how? To doe it by

*Naucler.
gener.46.
pag.403.*
his authority? No. But *cōmaunding the Archbiſhop to ſee to
the reformatiō of his Clergy in their apparrell, their ſhoes, their
heare, and other wiſe.* And withal he ſaid, *yf the diſordered*

*Quos cum
voluntate
Papa in
honeſtos
cōuerte-
mus vſus.*
*perſons would not redreſſe their abuſes, then ſhould they leeſe
the profites and iſſues of their beneficies: the which the Emperour would employ with the Popes cōſent to better vſes.* And
ſo haue you of your accuſtomable liberalitie and goodnes,
broughte to our hande one Argumente more for the Popes

The Po-
pes Pri-
macy yet
ons again
proued by
M. Horns
ovvne
ſtorie,
In paral.
Vrſperg.
ſuperiority. This hath your Author Nauclerus. And as for
your brother Gaſpar Hedio, though he rehearſe al the reſidue, word by word, in a manner, out of Nauclerus, yet theſe
three poore wordes, *cū volūtate Papæ,* weighed ſo heauie a-
gainſt your new primacy, that he could not carrie thē with
him. And you to be ſure, tell vs that the Emperour ſaide *he
would ſee to it hī ſelf.* But how he would ſee to it, that would
you not your Reader ſhould ſee, leaſt he ſhould ſee withal,

The falſe-
hoode of
Gaſpar
Hedio.
not your Charles, but the Popes primacie. This your diſſimulation is badde inough. But whē ye adde, with the which
doings th'Emperour became very famouſe: I ſuppoſe your
vnhoneſt dealing throughout all your booke practiſed, will
make you famous to, and yet to your no great cōmendatiō,
but to your great ſhame and infamy. Your Authors ſay not,
nor can wel ſay, he was famouſe for theſe doings. And then
come ye in as wiſely, with your, *for he was a wiſe man,* &c.
Nauclerus ſaith in dede, he was a renouned Emperour, not
for the cauſes by you aboue rehearſed: but for ſome other
that he afterward reciteth; and nothing ſeruing your, *with
the*

fourth

the *Which doings*,&c. The doings that made this Charles the 4. so famous (if ye list to know, M. Horn) were that with his greate charges and bountifulnes he erected the Vniuersitye of *Praga* in Boheme, that he founded manye Monasteries, that he brought the bodie of S. *Vitus* to *Praga*, and such like: Which you had as litle lust to recite, as you haue to follow. Only you say he was *famouse for setting forth of Religion*. A man woulde thinke that knewe you, that he was a setter foorth of your religion forsoth. But if you had tolde vs (as your Author telleth you) that he builded Monasteries, and translated Saints bodies: Euery child should haue sene, that this *setting forth of Religion* in Charles, was no such suprem gouernment as you should proue to M. Fekenham, but was (to say al in few words) a setting forth of Papistrie. See you not, M. Horne, what a faire thread you haue sponne?

Naucler. gener. 46. pag. 403.

M. Horne. The. 138. Diuision. pag. 83. a.

*At this time vvrot *Nilus the Bisshop of* Thessalonica, *declaring the (.453.) only cause of the diuision betvvene the Greke and the Latine Churche to be, for that the Pope vvould not suffer free and General Councels to be called by the Emperours, according to the aũcient custome: and that his authority is not by the lavve of God, but by the positiue Lavves of Princes, graunted only, because that than Rome vvas the greatest Citie in the vvorld, and hath no prerogatiue of Christ or Peter, more then any other Bisshoprique.*

*Nilus vvas a Schismatik of late yeares, of as good Authoritie as Frier Luther.

The. 453. Vntruth. Nil' faith no suche thing.

Stapleton.

A faire plea surely, for one Schismatique to plead vppon the Authority of an other Schismatike. As if you would say M. Horne: Aske my fellow, if I be a theefe. For both the Author Nilus, and the first setter forth therof, Flaccus Illyricus, are knowen and notorious, the one a Schismatike, the other an Heretik. And therfore what so euer ye here bring oute of Nilus bookes, it weigheth no more, then if yowe brought Illyricus him selfe, or Luther his Maister.

Concernĩg Nilus.

And

Leo Epi-
stola 84.
Sicut præ-
deceffores
mei præde
ceffóribus
tuis, ita
etiam ego
dilectioni
tuæ, prio-
rū fequu-
tus exem-
plum vicē
mei mode
raminis
delegaui,
vt curam
quam vni
uerfis ec-
clefiis prin
cipaliter
ex diuina
inftitutio-
ne debe-
mus &c.
adiuua-
res, & lō-
ginquis ab
Apoftolica
fede proui
cijs, præ-
fentiam,
quodāmo-
do noftræ
vifitatio-
nis impē-
deres.

And to faye the truth, it is nothing but an heape of vn-truthes: not only on your Authours parte, but on youres alfo, ouerreaching him fhamefully, as I fhall anon declare. But as for your authour, if he would haue confidered no more but his owne predeceffours the Archbiffhoppes of Theffalonica, he fhould haue found, that they almoft one thoufand yeares before, had an other and a better iudge-ment of the Popes authoritie: and were at that time the popes Legates for the Eafte partes: as well appeareth by Pope Leo his epiftles, to Anaftafius Bifhop there. And that the Pope had the principal charge of al churches, by Gods owne ordinaunce: contrary to the faying of your fchifma-tical authour of fo late yeres. And yet as bad as he is, he doth litle relieue yow. For he graūteth the Pope to be Pa-triarche of the Wefte Churche. And fo is he, (thowgh he were not the Chiefe abfolutelye) yet our patriarche and cheif Bifhop: and therfore cheiflie to be confulted in all greate and weighty ecclefiaftical affayres. Againe though he be badde inoughe, yet is he the worfe for coming into your fingers. For where you make him to fay, *the only caufe of diuifion betwene the Greke and the latine Churche was, for that the Pope wil not fuffer free ād general Coūcelles to be cal-led by the Emperours &c.* There is no fuche thinge in Nilus (I haue of purpofe perufed him ouer neither in the Greke nor in the Tranflation of Flaccus Illiricus. It is your own Captayne and Notorious vntruth.

M. Horne. The. 139. Diuifion. pag. 83. a.

Kinge Richarde the. 2. called a Councel at VVeftminfter (faieth Polydore) wherein it was thought good to the Kinge and the Princes for the weale of his realme of Englande, if a parte of the Popes authority were bounded within the limites of the Occean

Occean fea,*(he meaneth that it vvere driuen out of the Ifle of Britaine)*
(.454.) wherefore it was decreed,that hereafter it fhoulde be
lawfull to no man,to trie*(.455.)* any caufe before the Bifhop
of Rome:nor that any man be publikly pronoûced wicked or
enemy of Religion, that is to wit,as the cômon people terme
it,be excômunicate by his authority: nor that if any mã haue
any fuch cômaûdemêt frô him,they execute the fame.The pe
nalty ordeined to thofe that violate this lawe,was,that lofing
all his goodes,he fhoulde be cafte into perpetual pryfon.

*The.34.　Chapter : Of Richarde the feconde, Kinge of
Englande.*

Stapleton.

HEre lo,M.Horn at lêgth ftrayneth vs very fore . For
nowe all fuytes to Rome are quite cut of.　Neither
can the Pope fend any excommunication into En-
glande.What may we then fay to helpe our felues?Shall I
lette the matter goe,and let yt fhifte for yt felfe as yt may,
and reafon againfte the man and not the matter,and tel M.
Horne, leaft he waxe to proude and wanton,for this great
triumphaunte and victorioufe argumête,that yf a man that
is excommunicated , is (as he expoundeth yt)　a wycked
man,and a enemie of religion,that him felf and his fellowes
had neade to loke wel abowt them, beinge accurfed , not
only by many Popes(which now M.　Horne careth not a
rufhe for)but by many national and general coûcelles alfo?
Or fhal I tel him that,fuyte to Rome for excommunicatiô,
is but one braunche or arme of the Popes authority ? And
that the refidewe of his authority ftoode in ftrengthe and
force ftyll?And fo that he proueth not the lyke regimente
that nowe is, in the which, the whole papall authoritye
is vtterly bannifhed? Or fhall I fay, that God punifhed the

The.454
vntruth.
A fentêce
left out
quite in
the mid-
deft ope-
ning the
vvhole
matter.
The.455.
vntruth.
Falfe tran
flation.

tt　　　　king

kinge for his attempte,and as he toke away the Popes authority:ſo he loſte all his owne very ſhortly after:and loſte bothe crowne and kingdome miſerably? Or ſhall I ſay this lawe died with the kinge,and was neuer after vntill our dayes put in vre?Or ſhall i ſay that,thowghe all the Popes authoritie were banniſhed by this ſtatute out of England, M.Hornes newe ſupreamacy will not therof followe, but

Vide.c. Itẽ quia &c. Nullus de Hæretic. in conſtit. prouicial.

that the ſupreamacy in matters eccleſiaſticall , remayned in the Biſhoppes, eſpecially in Thomas Arondell Archbiſhop of Canterbury,who kepte councelles and ſynodes:and determined matters eccleſiaſticall without the kinges cõſente therunto, by whoſe prouincial conſtitution Mayſter Horne and his fellowes are declared excommunicate parſons and heretikes for the hereticall doctrine , that he and

An appeale againſt M.Horne to a queſt of tẽporal lawyers.

they maynteyne contrarie to the catholike faith? Or ſhall I yet ones againe appeale not to Rome , (leaſte M . Horne charge me with a terrible premunire) but euẽ to ſome domeſticall Iudge, and I greatly paſſe not,yf yt be to a queſt, of lawyers of his beſt frendes , to be tried by them, yf they can fynde any ſuche lawe in the Statutes of oure

An other to a queſt of grammarians.

Realme?   Againe ſhall I appeale to an other Queſte, euen of his owne nighe neighbours in Wincheſter ſchole, to be tried by them,yf I falſly accuſe M.Horne,of a moſte

The.3. to queſte of logitioners.

vntruth and falſe tranſlation? Or ſhal I appeale to his deare frendes the Logitioners at Oxford or Cambridge , and be tried by them,yf I ſay not true, ſaying now and auouching to M.Hornes owne face , that his owne allegation out of Polidore, directly proueth the Popes Primacie, and eſpecially the cuſtomable and ordinarye ſuytes to Rome? I will then holde my ſelf at this ſtay: and I will ioyne with him for theſe three poyntes.

First

First then I auouche, that there is no suche presidente to
be shewed among the statutes of our realme: and further
that neuer any suche was made in the tyme of this kinge.
Secondly I affirme, that M. Horne hathe either of deape
and grosse ignorance, or of cankered malice, maymed or
mangled his authours narration, and depraued and peruerted his manifeste meaning, by a false and counterfeite translation. The wordes of Polidore are these. *Concilium habi-* Poli.li.20
tum est ad Westmonasterium: eo in Concilio regi pariter atq;
principibus visum est è republica sua Anglicana fore, si pars
aliqua imperij Romani Pontificis Oceano terminaretur, quod
multi quotidie vexarentur ob causas qnas Romæ non facilè co-
gnosci posse putabant. Quapropter sancitum est, vt nulli mor-
talium deinceps liceret pro quauis causa agere apud Romanum
Pontificem, vt quispiam in Anglia eius authoritate, impius
religionisq; hostis publicè declararetur, hoc est, excommunica-
retur, quemadmodum vulgò dicitur: néue exequi tale manda-
tum, si quod ab illo haberet. Sincerely translated thus they
stande. A Councel (sayeth he) was called at Westmynster,
wherin yt was thowght good to the king and his Princes,
for theire common weale in Englande, yf a parte of the
Popes authority were bounded within the lymytes of the ∗These
Occean sea: ∗ *because many were dayly troubled and vexed* vvordes,
for causes, which they thowght, coulde not be well hearde at because,
Rome. Wherfore yt was decreed, that yt should be lawfull M. Horne
for no man to sue to the Pope ∗ for euery cause, to haue quite left
any man in Englande by his authority publikely pronoun- out.
ced a wicked man and an enemie of religion: that is (as the ∗Pro qua-
people commonly terme yt) to be excommunicated. And uis causa.
that, if any man haue auy suche commaundement, he doe
not exequute yt.

The

The ſtatute then doth not embarre, as ye moſt ſhamefully pretend, all ſuites to Rome, nor all excommunications,
from the Pope : but only that it ſhould not be lawfull to ſue
to Rome, and procure excommunications, indifferently as
wel in temporal as in ſpiritual matters : as it ſeemeth many
did then. And this doth nothing acraſe the Popes ordinarie authoritie. Now that this is the meaning, your Authour
him ſelfe ſufficiently declareth. Firſt when he ſpeaketh but
of a parte of the Popes authoritie : then when he ſheweth
that men ſued to Rome for ſuche cauſes, as were thought
could not be heard there : which muſt nedes be temporall
cauſes. And therefore ye ouerhipped one whole line and

M. Horne
omitteth
a vvhole
line that
openeth
the whol
matter
againſte
him.
more, in your tranſlation, thinking by this ſleight ſo craftely
to conueie into your theeuiſh Cacus denne, this ſentence,
that no man ſhould eſpie you. And for this purpoſe where
your Authour writeth, *pro quauis cauſa agere*, that is, to ſue
for euery cauſe, Ye tranſlate, *to trie any cauſe*. As though it
were al one to ſay. I forbidde you to ſue to Rome for euery cauſe, and to ſaie: I forbidde you to ſue to Rome for any
cauſe. And as though your Authour Polidore had write:
pro quacunque cauſa agere, to trie any cauſe at al. The ſtatute therefore doth not cut of al ſuites, but ſome ſuites: that
is, for ſuche matters as were temporal, or thought ſo to be.
Wherevppô it wil followe, that for all ſpiritual matters the
Popes iuriſdiction remained vntouched and nothing blemiſhed. For theſe woordes of the ſtatute, that men ſhoulde
not ſue in euerie cauſe to Rome, imploye ſome cauſes, for
the whiche they might ſue to Rome. And ſo for all your
gaie Grammar and rufiling Rhetorique, the Popes authoritie is confirmed by this ſtatute, whiche ye bring againſte
it. And this King Richard confirmed it, and was redie to
main-

teine it not by words only, but by the fworde alfo. And
therefore caufed to be gathered fiftene thoufand fotemen,
and two thoufand horfemen, and fent them out of the realme to defende Pope Vrbane againft his ennemie and Antipope Clement. You on the other fide, in this your victorioufe booke, haue brought a iolie forte of fouldiers to the
field, to fight againft the Pope, but when all is well feene
and examined, ye doe nothing but mufter lies together a-
gainft the Pope, as he did men, to fight for the Pope. A farre
of, and vppon the fodaine, an vnfkilfull man would thinke,
ye had a iolie and a well fette armie: but lette him come
nigh and make a good view, and then he fhal finde nothing
but a forte of fcar crowes pricked vppe in mans apparell.

King Ri-
chardes
armie ga-
thered for
the defẽce
of the
Pope:
Poli.dict.
lib.20.
M.Horns
armye a-
gainft the
Pope.

M. Horne The. 140. Diuifion. pag. 83.4.

The Churche of Rome at this time vvas marueilouflie torne in funder
vvith an horrible Schifme, vvhiche continued about fortie yeares, hauing
at ones three heades, calling them felues Popes, euerie one of them in mofte
defpitefull vvife, calling the other Antichrifte, Schifmatiqne, Heretique,
tyraunt, thiefe, traitour, the fonne of perdition, fovver of Cockle, the child
of Beliall,&c. Diuerfe learnedmen of that time inueighed againfte them
all three, as Henricus de Hafsia, Ioan. Gerfon, Theodorych Ny-
em, Secretarie before this, to Pope Boniface, *vvho proueth at lardge by*
(.456.) good reafons, by the vvoorde of God, and by the Popes Decrees, that
the refourmation of thefe horrible diforders in the Churche, belong to the
Emperour, and the Secular Princes. Sigifmunde the noble Emperour, vn-
derftanding his duetie herein, amongeft other his notable Actes, called a
Councell togeather at Conftantia, and brought againe to vnitie the Churche deuided in three partes: whiche Councell
(faithe Nauclerus*)* beganne by the Emperours cõmaundemente
and induftrye, in the yeare. 1414. *To the vvhiche Councel came*
Pope Iohn *before th'emperors cõming, thinking to haue* (457) *outfaced the*
Councell vvith his pretenfed authoritie, till the Emperoure came: vvho
tẽ iiij   geuing

De fchif.
lib.3.ca.7
The.456.
Vntruth.
touching
Theodo-
rich
Nyem,as
fhall ap-
peare.
Pius Pa.2.
Platina.
Sabel.

The.457.
Vntruth.
Slaunde-
rous.

geauing to all men in the Councel free libertie to speake their mindes, a great companie of horrible vices, were laied ftraight way to his chardge To the vvhich vvhen he vvas not able to anfvvere he vvas (.458.) depofed, and the other tvvo Popes alfo, and an other (459) chofen chieflie by the Emperons meanes, called Martin the fifte.

After thefe things finifhed, they entred into communication of a reformati-on bothe of the Clergie and the Laitie, to vvhiche purpofe the Emperour had deuifed a booke of Conftitutions, and alfo vvilled certaine learned Fathers there, but fpecially the Bifshoppe of Camera, a Cardinall there prefente, to deuife vvhat faultes they could finde, and hovve they fhoulde be redreßed, not fparing any degree, neyther of the Prelates, nor of the Princes them felues. VVhiche the Bifshoppe did, and compiled a little booke or Libell entituled: A Libell for reformation of the Churche gathered togeather by Peter de Aliaco, &c. And offered to the Chur-che rulers, gathered togeather in Conftaunce Councel, by the commaundemente of the Emperoure Sigifmunde. &cet. In this * Libell of refourmation, after he hathe touched the notable enormi-ties in the Pope, in the Courte of Rome, in the Cardinalles, in the Prelates, in Religious perfonnes, and in Prieftes: in exactions, in Canons, and De-cretalles, in collations of benefices, in faftings, in the Diuine Seruice, in Pi-ctures, in making feftiuall daies, in making Sainctes, in reading theyr le-gendes in the Churche, in hallovving Temples, in vvoorfhipping Reli-ques, in calling Councelles, in making Relligious fouldiours, in refourming Vniuerfities, in ftudying liberal Sciences, and knovvledge of the tongues, in repairing Libraries, and in promoting the learned: After all thefe thinges, being (.460.) Ecclefiafticall matters or caufes, he concludeth vvith the dueties of Princes for the looking to the reformation of thefe matters, or any other that needeth amendement. The fixth (faieth he) and the laft confideration fhall be of the refourminge of the ftate of the Laie Chriftians, and chieflie the Princes, of whofe manners dependeth the behauiour of the people, &cet. Let them fee alfo, that they repell all euill cuftomes contrarie to the lawe of God, and the lawe of man in their fubiectes, by the Coun-cell of Diuines and other wife men. Alfo lette them fee, that they pul vppe by the rootes, and deftroy more diligently then

they

they haue done, Magicall Artes and other fuperftitions condemned by the lawe of God, and all errours and herefies contrarie to the Faith.   Item that they watche and care earneftly
for the exalting of the Faith , and the honour of Goddes feruice, and the refourming of the Churche,that they labour and
trauaile diligentiy for the reformation of althofe things which
are mentioned afore,or here folowing, or anye other thinges
profitable,& cæt. *VVhen this booke vvas thus compiled, it* was offered vppe to the Councel (*faith Orthvvinus*) that the moft Chriftian Emperour Sigifmunde had called togeather,not fo much
for the agreemente of the Churche, as for hope of a generall
reformation of their manners : hoping verelye , that the Prelates woulde put to their helping handes , but the Romaine
craft beguiling the Germaine fimplicitie: the new made pope
featly flouted the vvell meaning Emperoure , faying that he
vvoulde thinke on this matter at laifure, & cæt.   Thus vvas
Sigifmunde the Emperour mifufed, vvhiche othervvife might
feeme to haue bene borne to haue reftored Chriftianitie to the
vvorlde againe.   *The fruftrating of this refourmation, vvas on the o-
ther fide, no leffe grieuoufe vnto the Frenche Kinge , that bothe before the
time of the Councell, and in the Councell vvhile, had greatly trauailed in
taking avvay the Popes exactions, and other Ecclefiafticall abufes , vvhervvith his Realme vvas vvonderfully oppreffed : as appeareth in the Oration that the Frenche Kings Embaffadours made in this Councell, vvritten
by* Nicol.de Clemangijs,*and fet forth in* Othvvynus Gratius *far-
dell of notable things.*

After this Councell , vvas an other holden at Bafil, *vvhither came the
Princes of* Spaine,Fraunce,Hungary,*and* Germany:*vvhiche dooinges of the
Princes made pope* Eugenius *fo to feare,that he (.461.)thought to tranflat
the Councel to* Bononia.*But the Emperour and other princes , and
the prelates whiche vvere at* Bafill, *not onlye not obeyed him,
but tvvife or thrife admonifhed him to come thither . This pope
vvas in this Councel(.462.)depofed in the.34.feffio. Of this Councel,the Em-
petour* Sigifmode *vvas the chiefe,and protector, and in his abfence appointed
the Duke of* Bauaria *in his roome,   He caufed the* Bohemes *to come to this
Councell*

Naucler.
The.461.
Vntruth,
He tran-
flated the
Councell
in deede,
not only
thoughte
fo to do.
The.461.
Vntruth:
For he
cõtinued
Pope af-
ter that
Councell,
as long as
he liued.

And whan he hearde of thofe matters in Religion, which were generally agreed vppon, he allowed them, and commaunded them to be obferued.

The.35.Chapter.Of Sigifmund and Friderike the.3.Emperours.

Stapleton.

MAifter Horne, for goddes fake remember your felf, and what ye haue taken in hande, to proue to M. Fekenhã, that is, that the Quene of Englãde owght to be fupreame head of the Churche of Englande, and not the Pope. Remẽber I pray you how weighty this is to M. Fekenham, as for the which, befide this his longe imprifonment, he ftandeth in daunger of loffe of lyfe alfo. Goe ones rowndly to your matter and bringe him fome fytte and có uenient proufe to perfwade him withal. Ye rũne on a thre leaues following, with the doinges of the Emperours Si gifmonde, Friderike, and Maximilian, and then at length after all your bufie rufle and greate turmoyle againfte the Pope, ye come to kinge Henry the .8. and to our owne dayes. Nowe howe litle the doinges of thefe Emperours proue their fupreamacie in all caufes ecclefiaftical, euerie childe may fee. And to beginne with Sigifmond : we heare of you, that in the tyme of the great and mayne fchifme, he called a councell at Conftantia, where three Popes were depofed, and that thẽ Martine the.5.was(*cheiflie by the Em perors meanes*)chofen. We heare of a booke of reformatió offred to themperour, for the abufes of fome matters ec clefiaftical. But in al that boke there is not one word either againft the Catholike faythe, or for M. Hornes herefies. Onely he reherfeth vp certayne abufes, which he woulde haue amended.

M. Hor nes to im pertinẽte proufes for fo weighty a matter.

Cõcernĩg thempe rour Sigif mundus.

And

And as for our matter nowe in hande, he sayth expreslely
*that the Church of Rome beareth the Principalyte or chief rule
in Christes Church: deriued principally from Gods ordinaunce,
and secondarely from the Coūcels.* What doth this relieue you
M. Horne? We heare farder, that themperour and other
princes would not suffer the pope to trāslate the Councell
of Basile to an other place: and finally that the pope Eugenius was deposed in the foresayd Councell at Basile. But
what serueth all this for your purpose? Yea what shameles
impudencie is this for yow, thus to vaunte your selfe, vppō
the doings of these two councels, that cōdemne your great
Apostle Wiccliffe for an horrible heretyke, and so consequently al your Geneuical doctrine now practised in England? And ye must remember, that not themperour, but the
Councel deposed these popes, that is, the bishops. You doe
synde theire sentence definityue, in the. 34. Sesion of the
Councel of Basill by your selfe alleaged. But for the sentēce
definitiue of themperour, for theis depositions, or any matter of religion, ye shall not fynd. *Ergo* the bishops were the
heads, and not themperour. And so are ye nothing the nearer for the deposition of Eugenius. Who yet, this depositiō
notwithstanding, continued pope still (as M. Iewell him
selfe witnesseth against you M. Horne) and the duke of Sa
uoye (of whome ye make mention in your nexte argumēt)
elected in Eugenius his place, by the sayde councell, was
favne to renounce his papacy, as your selfe confesse. And
notwithstanding so many and so great princes, that ye name
withstode the translation of yt, yet was the councell of Basill translated to *Ferraria* first, and thē to *Florence*: where the
greke Emperour and the Grecians were reconciled to the
vnity of the Church, and among other things, acknowled-
v v ged

Vide Petrū
de Altaco:
impres. Ba
sill. i. 18.
an. 1551.

M. Horns
gospel cō
demned
in the cou
cel at Cō-
stantia by
him allea
ged.
Tom. 4.
Concil. pa.
104. Edit.
vlt.

Cōcernīg
the prete-
sed depo-
sition of
pope Eu-
genius.
Iewvel, in
his Reply
pag. 289. c

ged the Popes Primacy. So that ye haue nowe loſt all your
goodly ſchiſmaticall argumentes that ye haue in this your
book brought out of Nilus and otherwiſe for the Grecians
rebellion againſt the ſayd primacy. But what doe you tell
vs here of Theodorike Nyem, and of his greate and large
proufes, that the reformation of the Church belonged to
the Emperours? In dede proue he would ſuch a matter. But
as for him, bothe his maner of writing is ſo courſe, and his
proufs ſo weake, that you were aſhamed to bring any one
of thē into the face of the opē Court. And in very dede, it is
but a great vntruth of yours ſo to reporte of him. Namely
out of that booke and Chapter which you alleage. For ther
he bringeth neither good reaſon, nor any parte of the word
of God(both which you auouche him to bring, and that at
large) but only one ſentence of a decree, and the exáple of
king Theodorike, in the matter of pope Symachus : which
mattѳr(as I haue before proued) maketh expreſſely for the
popes primacy. Such a diſcrete writer you haue picked out
to help forward ſo badde a matter. But to let this mā paſſe,
I will nowe aſke yow whether thѳperour toke pope Mar‑
tinus for the head of the whole Church, or no? Yf ye ſay he
did, as the force of truth will cōpell you, then to what ende
haue ye ſo buſied your ſelf with the doings of this Empe‑
rour? Yf ye ſay he did not, thē wil I ſend you to your owne
authour Nauclerus of whom ye ſhall heare, that not thѳm‑
perour, but the Cardinals elected Martinus: and that thѳm‑
perour as ſone as he was elected, fell flatte and proſtrate
before him, and with much reuerence kiſſed his feete. Now
againe if as ye ſay, *he allowed, and commaunded ſuch thinges*
as the councell agreed vppon in matters of relligion to be obſer‑
ued(this agreemēt being as it was in dede againſt your new
religion**)**

Vide Theo‑
dorichū de
Nyem No‑
rimberg.
impr. An.
1532.
De ſchiſ.
lib.3 ca.7.

Naucl. Ge‑
ner. 48.
pag. 442.
Ante pōti‑
ficē proſtra
tus cum
ſumma ve
neratione
eius pedes
oſculatus
eſt.

religiõ)what doe ye, but blowe your own cõdemnatiõ, making it as ſtrong as may be againſt your own ſelf? How Em
perours haue cõfirmed councels, I haue oftē declared. This
therfore I let paſſe, as a ſtale argumēt, according to promiſe.

But now let me be ſo bold, as ones to appoſe you M. Horn.
Who was (I pray you) at this tyme, ſupreame head of the
Church in England? Did king Henrie the. 5. take him ſelſe
(trowe ye) to be this head? I ſuppoſe ye dare not ſay it for
ſhame. And if ye dare, thē dare I be ſo bold to tel you, it is a
moſt notoriouſe lie: and withall that in caſe it were ſo, yet
did he euē about the ſame time that Wiccleff and his ſchollers were cõdemned in the Coūcell of Cõſtantia, cõdemne
thē as faſt by act of parliament in Englād. And it was (I may
ſay to you) high time. For your good bretherne had cõſpi-
red to adnulle, deſtroy, and ſubuert not only the Chriſtian
fayth, ād the law of God, ād holy Church within the realm:
but alſo to deſtroy the kīg, ād al maner of eſtats of the realm
aſwel ſpiritual as tēporal: ād all maner of pollicy, and finally
the lawes of the lād. As it is more at large cõpriſed in an act
of parliamēt, made at that time. In the which it was ordeyned, ād eſtabliſhed, that: *firſt the Chauncelor, Treaſorer, Iuſtices*
of the one bench ād of the other, iuſtices of peace, Sherifs, mayors
baylifs of cities ād townes, ād all other officers hauing the gouer-
nance of people, or that at any tyme afterward ſhulde haue the
ſayd gouernaunce, ſhuld take an othe in taking of their charge
to put theire whole power and diligence to put out, ceaſe ād de-
ſtroy al maner of errours and hereſies, cõmonly then called Lol-
lardries, within the place where they exerciſed theire offices.
And thus neither abrode, nor at home, can ve fynde any
good matter, for the defence of your newe primacy, and
your damnable hereſies.

v v ij   M.Horne

Anno.2.
Henr.5.
cap.7.

The ſta-
tute made
againſt he-
reſies in
the tyme
of kinge
Henry
the.5.

After the death of Sigifmonde, Frederike the Emperour caufed the Duke of Sauoy, that vvas made Pope, to renounce his Papacy, and commaunded by his Decree, the Prelates gathered at Bafill, to diffolue the Councell by a certaine daie. This Emperour called a Coūcell at Mentze, to make an ende, and vtterly to take away the Schifme of the Church, and to deliuer it from more greuous daungers. *He vvriteth to the Frenche Kinge thereof, declaring hovv* this Schifme did fo oppreffe his minde, and feruētly follicite him, that as well for his loue to Religion, as for his office called of God, to be the * chiefe aduocate of the Churche, he did not onely runne with diligence to fuccour it, but ftirred vp al kinges and Princes, that with a pure finceritie, delighted in the name of Chrifte, to runne with him in this fo neceffary and healthfull a worke, and to this purpofe, *he declareth hovve,* he hath appointed to all his princes and prelates an affembly at Mentze, whereat he entendeth to be perfonally prefent, and therefore defireth the Frenche kinge alfo to bee there in his ovvne perfone, or at the leaft that he vvoulde fende his Oratours thither, inftructed diftinctly vvith all vvaies and meanes, by the vvhiche the Churche might be quiet from the calamities ready to fall on her. *Pope Eugenius fent to the Frenche king, to defire him to take a vvay his (.464.) pragmaticall Lavve. To vvhom the king anfvvered, that he vvould haue it kept inuiolatly. Then the Pope defidered the king neither to admitte Bafill coūcel, nor yet the coūcel at Mētze, that vvas called: to the vvhich the kīg anfvvered, that he vvold take aduife.*

Stapleton.

Here is fmall or no matter for M. Hornes newe Primacie, and that he here reherfeth maketh rather agaynft him, then with him. For though M Horne fayed in the laft argument, that pope Eugenius was depofed, yet is he nowe pope ftyll, and thother fet in his place, faine to geue ouer: And though the princes would not obeye Eugenius, for the diffoluing of the Councell of Bafile: yet nowe it is diffolued

folued by the Emperour Friderike alfo. And what anfwere
fo euer the French King made to Eugenius, touching the
fayed Bafile Councell, the Councell is no further allowed
in the Catholike Church, then Eugenius and his fucceffour
Nicolaus did allowe the fame. And (as ye fhewe your felfe)
themperour Friderike faieth, that by his office he was called of God, to be *the chiefe Aduocate of the Church*. He
faieth not, the chiefe head of the Church, the which honour he did attribute, not to him felfe, but to the Pope only,
of whome he was crowned, as his predeceffours were.
Thefe alfo are but ftale wares, and much woren. And for
fuch I let them paffe. As for the Frenche King and hys
pragmatical fanction, which Charles his predeceffour had
made, and whiche he at the requefte of Pope Eugenius,
would not reuoke: it contained no fuch matter, as you M.
Horne doe attribute to princes nowe, neyther was that
gouernement like to that which you nowe defend. This
pragmaticall fanction ftode moft about monye matters: It
denied to the Court of Rome, the great payements which
went out of Fraunce, about Referuations, collations, ex-
pectations, and comendoes of bifhoprickes, prebendes and
benefices. Great and long contention there was betwene
certaine Kings of Fraunce, as Charles the.vij. and the .viij.
Loys .xj. and.xij. Frauncis the firft, and certaine Popes, as
this Eugenius, Pius.2.Sixtus.4.Innocentius.8.Alexander.6. *Lib.5.c.2.*
Iulius the.2.and Leo the.10. as Duarenus a vehement wri- *facr.ecclef.*
ter for the French Kings aduantage mencioneth. *minift.*

But notwythftanding all thefe matters, the Popes fupreme Authoritie in matters of Fayth and ecclefiafticall
Iurifdiction was not denied. For witneffe hereof I bring
you the wordes of the Court of Paris, vttered among the

v v iij   Articles

Fride-
rike.
Vide Dua-
renum.
de facris
ecclef. mi-
nift. lib. 5.
cap. 12. &
in append.
pro libert.
ecclef. Ga.
defenf.

Articles which they propofed to the King, about this matter, as Duarenus him felfe recordeth them. In the number.
19. thus they fay. *Ante omnia proteftatur Curia &c*. Before
all thinges the Court protefteth, *that it mindeth not to dero-
gat any thing from the holyneffe, dignity, honour, and Authority of the Pope and the holy Apoftolike See. But rather it is ready to fhewe and exhibit, all honour, reuerence and obedience,
that euery godly and faithfull perfon ought to fhewe to the chief
Paftour of the Churche. And yf any thing fall out, worthy of
amendement, it refufeth not to fubmitte them felues to the determination of the Church, which can not erre. C. A recta. 24.
q. 1.* By which allegatiõ they protefte to meane the Church
of Rome. For fo in that place we reade out of the Auncièt
decretal epiftle of Pope Luci°. 1. How thē do you proue M.
Horn by this exãple *the like gouernement in the Church caufes,* as you now attribute to the Q. Mai. and as you take vpõ
you here to proue? Graũte M. Horn to the See Apoftolike
now, as the Court of Paris graũted thē, and thē looke howe
and with what confcience you may take the Othe, which

Par. Vrfp.
The: 465.
vntruthe.
His Au-
thor mē-
cioneth
no Eccle-
fiafticall
Conftituti-
o 1s
The 466.
vntruthe.
Æneas
Syl. neuer
faid fo.

now you defend, or by what reafon you cã moue M. Fekē-
hã thereunto. I would haue you ones brig fome exãple, that
made not playn againft you, and your whole booke.

M. *Horne. The. 142. Diuifion. pag. 85. a.*

Pius the *feconde, fent his Legate the Cardinal of* Cufa, *into the countreis of Sigifmond Duke of* Auftria, *which Legate,* when he woulde
haue ordeined certain (. 465.) Ecclefiaftical conftitutions according to the Popes Law e. Sigifmonde the Duke, would not
fuffer that fuch a cuftome fhould come into Germany.

Æneas Syluius, *who after he vvas made Pope, vvas called* Pius the
*feconde, vvas of this minde before he vvas Pope, that fecular Princes might
cal councels, yea, (. 466.) maugre the Popes head, and therefore commendeth that deuife of Charles the Frenche king* which (*faith he*) is both a
fault

fault and a fhort way to ftil this mifchiefe. *He meaneth to take a-*
vvay the Schiſme, and to reſtore vnity to the Churche. Of the ſame (.467.)
minde alſo vvas his Cardinal de Cuſa, as appeareth in his booke, De Cō-
cordia Catholica, ſaying: By that which is a forefaide, it is gathered, that the holy Emperours alwaies, made the Synodical cō-
gregations of vniuerfal councels of the whole Churche: and
euen fo I my felfe, hauing fought throughly the Actes of al the
vniuerfal councels, euen til the eight councel incluſiue, celebrated in the time of Bafil, I haue found it to be true: and fo alfo in the fame eight Synod in the fift Act therof, we reade, that
the moſt reuerende prieſt Elias and Syncellus, of the trone of
Hierufalem in the hearinge of al, fpake thus: Knowe you that
in the tymes paſt, they were the Emperours, which gathered
together Synods frō out of the whole vvorld, ād they collected
their deputies, to the difpofing of fuch maner caufes: VVhofe
fteps therfore our Emperor folovving, being alfo a worfhipper
of God, hath made this vniuerfal Synod. Thus faid he there, ād
I haue alfo redde in the litle gloffe of Anaftafius (the library-
keper of the Apoftolical fea, who tranflated the fame Synode
out of Greke) vpon the fame, faying: that the Emperours were
vvont to gather vniuerfal Synodes from al the vvorld, &c.

Epiſt. 54.
ad Cæcel.
Imperat.
The 467.
vntruthe.
Cuſanus
vvas of a
far other
minde as
thei ap-
peare.

Li.3.ca.13

Par. Vrſp.
Cū veniſſet
ad ecclesiā
ſuā Brixi-
enſem in
alpib° deq;
illa diſpo-
nere volu-
iſſet pro
veteri pon-
tiſicū iure,
non paſſus
eſt Sigiſ-
mundus
dux Au-
ſtriæ, vt ea
in Germa-
niā tende-
retur con-
ſuetudo,
quòd Ro-
mani Car-
dinales eccleſias Germaniæ haberent in commendis.

The.36. Chapter. Of Aeneas Syluius, who was after, Pope
Pius.2. and of Cardinal Cufanus.

Stapleton.

YOu run ſtil at riot M. Horne, bringing in your matters
extraordinarely and impertinently, and yet adioyned
with one lye befide. For your autor fpeketh not of the
ordeining of any ecclefiafticall conſtitution, by the Popes
Legat, but that themperor would not fuffer him to receiue
the profits of the Church he had in commendo, neither any
fuch cuſtome to be brought into Germanye. Ye are then
in hande ones agayne that Princes maye call Councelles.
But when ye tell vs this owte of AEneas Syluius, and
tell vs

tell vs withall, that before he was pope, he was of that
minde, that secular princes might call Councelles : if he
were not also of that minde being pope, why tell you this
tale againft your felfe ? Had you read M. Horne that notable letter of Recantation, which this Aeneas Syluius in
his riper yeares and later dayes(after the example of S.Au-
guftin retracting in like maner diuers thinges) fent to the
Vniuerfytie of Collen,fette forth fewe yeres paft in diuers
editions,you woulde not for very fhame (if any fhame be
in you)ones haue mentioned the teftimony of this man. In
that Bulle of retractatió(forfeing as he fayth him felf the obiection that woulde be made) he retracteth and reuoketh
this errour which in his youthe at the Councel at Bafill he
had lerned,that the Coũcel was aboue the Pope.In which
he declareth at large by what meanes,by whofe aduife and
counfell, he was firft perfuaded fo to thinke, howe alfo he
was agayne brought backe from that errour, and amonge
other meanes by the perfuafion of that moft lerned Cardinall *Iulianus fancti Angeli,* who firfte at Bafill was for the
Councell againft pope Eugenius,but after (as after him all
other)reconciled him felfe to the pope,was his legate in the
Councell of Florence, (where moft lernedly he confuted
the Grekes,and reduced them al(only Marcus of Ephefus
excepted)to the Catholike doctrine of the holy Ghofte,
and to the vnyte of the Romain Church) and laft of al ferued him in embaffy againft the Turk. He proueth by Scripture,by natural Reafon, by Authorytie of the Doctours,
that Peter and his fuccefsours are the Supreme Vicairs of
Chrift,that the Church to whome Chrift gaue his * peace,
muft of necefsytie haue that kinde of regiment,by which
peace may moft be mayntained and preferued,which only
is the

*Bulla rea-
tractatio-
nũ Pij. 2.
Venetijs
an. 1564.
vnà cum
Cardillo.
Louanij.
an. 65.
Parif. an.
eodem.*

*Pacẽ meã
do vobis,
Pacem re-
linquo vo-
bis.*

is the ſtate of Monarchy , where one Heade gouerneth the
whole body, and laſt, by S. Hierom, and S. Bernard that the
biſhop of Rome S. Peters Succeſſour, is that one Head. After al which he cócludeth. *Hæc nos de Romani Pontificis Authoritate & poteſtate ſentimus, cui & cögregare Concilia gene-
ralia & diſſoluere datum eſt: qui etſi filius eſt propter regenera-
tionem, propter dignitatē tamen pater habetur: & ſicut propter
regenerationis cauſam venerari debet Eccleſiam tanquam Ma-
trem, ita & propter prælationis cauſam præeſt ei vt paſtor gregi, princeps populo, Rector familiæ* . This is our Iudgement of
the Authoritye and power of the Biſhop of Rome . To
whome it belongeth both to ſummon general Councelles,
and to diſſolue them . Who though he be a childe of the
Churche for his regeneration and newe birthe therein (by
baptiſme) yet he is for his dignity and office her Father.
And as he ought to Reuerence the Churche as his Mother, becauſe he was borne of her: ſo he ruleth the Church
alſo, as a Paſtour the flocke , as a Prince his people , and as
a maiſter his family becauſe he is made the Ruler of her. A-
gain in his very laſt words of that retractatió thus he ſpeaketh to the Vniuerſity of Collé. *Hæc noſtra ſenteutia eſt filij.
Hæc credimus & profitemur: hæc iam ſenes & in Apoſtolatus
apice conſtituti pro veritate aſſerimus: ſi quæ vel vobis vel aliis
conſcripſimus aliquando, quæ huic doctrinæ repugnent, illa tanquam erronea & iuuenilis animi parum penſata iudicia reuoca-
mus atq, omnino reſpuimus.* This is (my ſonnes) our Iudgemét.
This we beleue and profeſſe. This we now affirm in our old
age, ád placed in the Apoſtolik top. If at any tyme we haue
writen any thing either to you or to any other, contrary to
this doctrin, al thoſe things we now reuoke and vtterly re-
peale for erroneous, and light opiniós of youthely affectió.

X x   Lo M.

Cuſan.

Neq; vn=
quã ſacros
imbuimus
ordines,ni-
ſi poſt veri-
tatẽ cogni
tã Baſiliẽſi
cœcitate
relicta.

Lo M.Horn. For your Aeneas:we anſwere you with Pius: for your younge, vnkilful and leſſe aduiſed, we anſwere you by the old, the more lerned, and the better aduiſed: for your priuat and lay mã (for he had yet takē no holy orders when he returned to the obediēce of Pope Engenius) we anſwer you with the Biſhop ãd the chief of al Biſhops. You muſt re-mẽbre M.Horne, that alwaies: δ̔ἑυτεραι φροντίδες σοφώτεραι.

Next to Aeneas Syluiᵒ cometh the *Cardin.de Cuſa*, one that maketh as much for M.Horn as a rope doth for a theſe. Haue you ſene M. Horn that Cardinals book, which you allege *de Cõcordia Catholica?* If not, thē beſhrew your frend that told you of hī? If yes, thē tel vs I pray you, how like you him, ãd

Cuſanᵒ de
Concordia
Cath.li.2.
Cap.4.

his cõcluſiõs in that work? How like you his cõcluſiõ in the. 2.book, proued by the clere practiſe of the Chalcedõ ãd the Epheſin Coũcel, *fidẽ Romanæ Eccleſiæ in nulla Synodo vniuer-ſali retractari poſſe?* That the faith of the Church of Rome cã be reuoked in no vniuerſal Synod or Councel generall? For thē what wretches are you, and how cõtrary to the Fa-thers of the firſt general Coũcels, and of the firſt. 400.yers, which haue in your pelting priuat conuocations reuoked and cõdẽned in ſo many and waighty points the faith of the Church of Rome? How like you, that he telleth how in the old firſt general Coũcels, not only the holy ghoſpels, but al-

Cap.6.

ſo *lignũ S.Crucis & aliæ reliquia*, a piece of wod of the holy Croſſe, ãd other relikes were layed forth in the midle? How

Cap.9.

like you that he ſaith. *Eccleſiaſtici Canones nõ poſſunt niſi per eccleſiaſticã cõgregationẽ (quæ Synodus vel cœtus dicitur) ſtatui?* Canõs or rules touchĩg Church matters cãnot be determi-ned but by ã eccleſiaſtical aſsẽbly, which is called a Synod or cõpany, no doubt but of eccleſiaſtical perſons? For if this be true (as Cuſanᵒ ther by the practiſe ãd Canõs of the Church

proueth

proueth ir moſt true)thē hath Cuſanus vtterly ouerthrowē
your new primacy,ād in one lyne geuē you an other pawne
mate to your whole boke. For here lo are plainly excluded
al Prīces ād other laye magiſtrats whatſoeuer, who are par-
dy no eccleſiaſtical perſons. How like you that he pronoū-
ceth aſſuredly and cōſtātly,ſaying. *Papā eſſe rectorē nauiculæ* Cap. 13.
S. Petri & vniuerſalis Eccleſiæ,nemo etiā dubitat . That the
Pope is the ruler of S.Peters ſhip,ād of the vniuerſal Church
no mā verely doubteth. But how ſay you M.Horn?doubte
you, or doubt you not?How like you again where he affirmeth ād proueth the ſame ſubſtātially,as whē he ſaith.*Et ve* Cap.15.
rūeſt &c. And true it is that no iudgemēt of any Synod is auaile-
*able,wher the autority of the See Apoſtolik cōcurreth not?*wher
be thē your Lōdō conuocatiōs?But how proueth he this?the
reaſon he geueth. *Quia ſemper appellari poteſt &c . Bicauſe it*
may alwaies be appeled frō the Iudgmēt of that Synod to the See
Apoſtolik.So we reade (ſaith he) of the Patriarches of Cōſtātino-
ple,Flauianus,Ignatius,ād other:ſo of Athanaſius,of Alexādria
*and other We reade that thei appealed(*frō Synods of Biſhops)
*to the See Apoſtolik.*So alſo Chryſoſtome frō a Synod of the
Aegyptiā biſhops appealed to Innocētiᵘthe Pope.So Theodoretus frō the Epheſin cōuenticle ād his owne Patriarche
Maximᵘ of Antioch,appealed to Pope Leo,as I haue other
wher agaīſt M.Iewel declared:How like you this doctrin
of Cuſanᵘ M.Horn?As alſo wher he ſaith again expreſſely. Cap.eodē.
Fateor de cōſtitutionibus fidē tāgētibus verū eſſe , quòd ſi Sedis
Apoſtolicæ Autoritas nō interueniat,rata nō ſint,imò & ipſiᵒ Pō
tificis cōſenſus interuenire debet,cū ſit princeps in epiſcopatu fi-
*dei.*I confeſſe it is true of Conſtitutions concerninge faith,
that yf the Authoritie of the See Apoſtolike doe wante,
they are of no valewe , yea the conſent of the Pope him
ſelfe ought to concurre in ſuch caſe , becauſe he beareth
xx ij the

Cuſan
Vide pre-
ambulares
Epiſtol.
Cōc.Cha.
Tom. 1.
pag. 733.

the chiefe rule, in the biſhoply charge of fayth. Which laſt
wordes Cuſanus had lerned of the Emperours Valentinian
and Marcian in their letters to pope Leo, aboue a. xi. hundred yers paſt. How like you now M. Horn, tel me of good
felowſhip, this Cardinal of Cuſa, out of whom ſo ſadly you
alleage ſuch a longe proceſſe? Howe ſo euer you like it, it
is of vs, and of euery diligent Reader, very well to be liked,
and diligétly to be noted: I meane theſe teſtimonies of Cuſanus, not bicauſe he ſayeth it, but bicauſe he proueth it
ſo by the olde practiſe of the primitiue Churche. But eſpecially it is to be noted, that this Cuſanus writinge this
booke *De Concordia Catholica*, about the time of the Councell of Baſill, and writinge it expreſſely not for the pope,
but againſte the pope, for the Authorytie of the Councell

Cardillus
diſput.1.
fol.19.
Decanus
Sancti Flo
rini.Con-
fluentia .
Lib. 2. ca.
vltimo.
Nihil de
meis con-
ceptibus
adeo firmū
aſſero, qui
peritiorib⁹
dicam po-
tius ac-
quieſcen
dum.

aboue the pope, and for the Authoryte of the Emperour as
muche as he coulde, yet by the very force of the truthe,
which in dede lernedly and paynefully he ſerched out, he
was conſtrained to ſay and conclude for the popes Authorytie, as we haue before recited largely and amply, though
not in dede ſo fully and abſolutely, as bothe he and Aeneas
Syluius afterwarde did, by reuokinge their former errours,
in their riper ages. For this Cuſanꝰ whē he wrote this, was
not yet Cardinall, but only the deane of a Church in Coue-
léce. And in all his poſitions where he ſpeaketh againſt the
Commō opiniō of lerned mē touching the popes primacie,
aboue the general Councel (for otherwiſe he neuer denied
it) he ſubmitteth him ſelf to better iudgement, and ſpeaketh
vnder correction. Nowe to drawe nerer to your allegatiō
M. Horne, concerning the Emperours Authorytie in calling of Councels, if you take Cuſanus with his whole meaning therein, you ſhall find ſmall reliefe for your deſperat
cauſe.

cauſe. If you admitte not his whole meaning, nor will not
tary his tale out, M. Iewel wil tel you M. Horne: that is no
good maner. And he will tell you of a lawe that ſayeth.
It is againſte reaſon that one man ſhoulde in parte allowe Ievvel in
his reply.
Art. 4.
pag. 296.
the will of the dead, (ſo farre forthe as it maketh for him)
and in parte ouerthrowe it, where it ſemeth to make againſt
him. Lette vs then heare the whole meaninge of Cuſanus, concerninge the Authorytie that Emperours haue in
callinge, aſsiſtinge and confirming of Councelles, euen in
that booke where he ſayeth all he can for the Emperours.
Verely maiſter Horne in all that booke he neuer calleth
the Emperour ſupreame gouernour in all matters, no not
in any matter Eccleſiaſticall. He ſayeth the Emperour is
truly called *Aduocatus vniuerſalis Eccleſiæ*, the Aduocat Cuſanus
de Cō. Cæ.
lib. 3, c. 7.
or proteƈtour of the vniuerſall Churche. And wherein,
he declareth out of the. 8. Generall Councel. *For*, ſayth he,
as the Authoryte to define and determine thoſe thinges that
belonge to the right and vniuerſall faythe of Chriſte is com-
mitted of God to Prieſtes : ſo to gouerne, to confirme, and to
preſerue thoſe thinges that are of God by the Prieſtes orday-
ned, it is committed to the holy Empire. And this he graunteth to the Emperour onely, not to other ſeuerall princes and kinges, bicauſe he ſpeaketh onely herein of matters touchinge the vniuerſall faith of the Church. Wherein alſo he ſo farre preferreth the pope before the Emperour, that he ſayeth. *Si papa qui in Epiſcopatu fidei princi-*
patum gerit, eleƈtum in fide errare inueniret, declarare poſſet, Ibidem.
eum non eſſe Imperatorem. If the pope who beareth the prin Chalc.
cipalytie in the biſhoply charge of Fayth, ſhould finde the
Emperour eleƈted, to erre in the fayth, he might pronoūce Aƈt. 3. fol.
838.
him no Emperor. In the next chapter he proueth very wel

out of the Chalcedon Councell, the Councells of Milleuitum and of Cabylon, that in matters properly ecclesiasticall
belonging to bishops and clerckes, Emperours and princes
ought not to intermedle . Nowe touching the intermedling of Emperours and princes with Councelles , firste he
sheweth by the examples of Riccharedus Chintillanus and
Sysenandus kinges of Spayne in . iij. feuerall Councelles of
Toletum (which alfo we haue before shewed) with what
mekenes, reuerence and humilite princes ought to come to

Councells. And wheras in many Synodes , matters alfo of
the common welthe were debated , he declareth by the
practife of Aunciente time; that *In Synodicis congregationi-*

bus &c. In Synodall assemblyes (of particular prouinces *) the*
office of the kinge is to mete there, to exhorte and to strengthē
to obey and to execute the ecclesiastical cōstitutions, such as be-
longe to fayth or to the worshipping of God. But in such cōstitu-
tions as belonge to the publike state (of the common welthe)
he must together with the bishops define and determine. In all
which he ouerthroweth clerely your position M. Horne,
as you fee. And here after this in the next chapter immedi-

atly foloweth the place by you alleaged: *By that which is a-*
foresayd it is gathered, that Emperors made alwayes the Synodal
congregations of vniuersall Councels of the whole worlde &c.
For this he speaketh only of General Councels, adding immediatly in the fame fentence, which fentence you quyte
cutte of from the ende: *Locales verò nunquam eos legitur col-*
legisse . But prouinciall Synodes it is neuer read that Emperours called . And in the nexte Sentence he concludeth
howe he called the generall Councelles . *Non quòd coa-*
ctiuè fed exhortatiuè, colligere debeat. Not that the Emperour
should cal or gather thofe Councels by the way of force or

commaun-

cōmaundement but by the way of exhortation and aduiſe. And this he exemplifieth very well by the Councell of A-quileia whereat S. Ambroſe was preſent . Vnto the which the biſhops were ſo called by the Emperours Gratian, Valé-tinian, and Theodoſius (as in their epiſtle the Councel agni-ſeth) *vt epiſcopis honorificentia reſeruata, nemo deeſſet volens, nemo cogeretur inuitus:* that dewe reueréce beig reſerued to the biſhops, none was abſent that liſted to come, nor none was forced that liſted not to come. Nowe the reaſon why the Emperour may cal only General Councels, none pro-uinciall, Cuſanus addeth. *For* (ſaieth he) *When any generall daungers of fayth do occurre, or any other thing that vniuerſally troubleth the Church of Chriſt, then ought the Emperour him ſelf to attende, as a preſeruer both of the fayth and of the peace: and thē he ought firſt of all to ſignifie to the biſhop of Rome the neceſſyte of a Councel: and requyre his conſent for aſſembling a Councell in ſome certayne place. As the Emperours Martiā and Valentinian did to pope Leo for the Chalcedō Councell. Inuitā-tes atq; rogantes:* Inuitinge him and deſiringe him. As Con-ſtantin the. 4. did to pope Agatho for the. 6. general Coun-cell at Conſtantinople, writing thus vnto him . *Adhorta-mur veſtram paternam Beatitudinem,* We exhorte your fa-therly bleſſednes, vſinge all wordes of gentle intreaty, and none of forceable commaundemente as we haue before largely declared . To be ſhort, Cuſanus concludeth al this Imperiall callinge of Councelles in theſe wordes. *Iſta ſunt &c.at.Theſe are the thinges that belonge to the Emperour, tou-chinge the beginninge of a Councell , that is , to aſſemble it With exhortation , and With ſauegarde , With all liberty, With good cuſtody , all partialytie taken away, and all neceſſyte of commaundement.*

Tom.1.
Conc.pag.
395.

In præāb.
Cōc. Cha.
pa.733.
In epiſt ad
Agathonē

Lib.3.ca.
14.iu fine.

Nowe

Nowe if you wil knowe, what difference there is betwene the calling of the Pope, and the calling of the Emperour, to a Councel, Cuſanus declareth that alſo ſhortly by the pra-ctiſe of the firſt Councels thus. *Papa vt primus &c. The Pope*

Cap. 15. *calleth a General Councell* (for of ſuch he ſpeaketh) *as the chief, and as hauing a power to commaunde, through the principality of his prieſthood ouer all biſhops, touching that aſſembly which concerneth the vniuerſal ſtate of the Church, in the which he beareth the chiefe charge. By the which power committed vnto him, he may commaund the faithful to aſſemble, chiefly al prieſtes ſubiect vnto him. But the Emperour exhorteth or counſelleth the Biſhops, and commaundeth the Laye.* Thus much your own Authour Cuſanus (M. Horne) concerning the Emperours Authority in calling of Councels. I ſuppoſe if you take his whole meaning, your cauſe wil be but weakely relieued by him. And I think you wiſhe nowe, you had neuer alleaged him.

M. Horne The. 143. Diuiſion. pag. 85 b.

Next vnto Frederike vvas Maximilian Emperour, to vvhome the Princes of Germany put vp certaine greuaunces in Eccleſiaſticall matters, that anoied the Empire, in number 10. Againſt Bulles, Priuileges, Electiōs, reſeruatiōs, expectatiues, Annates, vnfit paſtours, pardōs, tythes, ād the ſpiritual courtes &c. beſeching hi, to haue ſome redreſſe herin. VVho being moued vvith the admonitions, aduiſementes and exhortations of the learned Clergy, and the godly Princes, at the length called a Councel at Triers and Colayn, for the redreſſe of theſe and other enormities, in the yeere of the Lord: 1512. vvhich vvas the fourth yeere of the moſte renoumed King of Englād,

Para. Vrſp. *King Henry the eight.* In this Councel amongeſt other thinges becauſe there was a ſuſpicion of a Schiſme breedinge, and of greauaunces in the Churche, it vvas neceſſarily decreed, that the Emperour and Princes electours, vvith other Princes and ſtates of the Empire, ſhould looke about them, and vvel cōſult by fult by what means, thefe greeues might be taken away moft commodiouflie, and the Schifme remoued, and euill thinges reformed to edification. It was decreed alfo againft blafphemours, to paie either a fomme of money limited, or to fuffer death. And that all men fhould knowe this decree, it was thought good to the Princes, and ftates of the Empire, that al Preachers and perfones, fhould at all high feaftes preache vnto the people thereof faithfully. *This being done, Maximilian fette forth a decree for the taking avvaie of the forefaied Ecclefiaftical greuaunces:* Orth. Grat. * *vvherein he declareth, that though of clemencie he haue fuffered the Pope and the Clergie herein, as did his Father Frederik:* Yet not withftanding fith that by his liberality, the worfhippe and feruice of God hath fallen to decaie, it apperteineth vnto his dutie, whom God hath chofen vnto the Emperial Throne of Rome, that amongeft all other mofte great bufineffes of peace and warres, that he alfo looke aboute him vigilantlie, that the Church perifhe not, that Regilion decaie not, that the worfhippe of the feruice of God, be not diminifhed &c. *In confideration vvhereof, he prouideth, that a man hauing in any Citie a Cañonfhip or Vicarfhippe, enioy not any prebende of an other Church in the fame Citie, &c. Making other decrees againfte fuinge in the Ecclefiaficall Courtes for benefices, for defence of Lay mens Patronages, for penfions againft bulles, and cloked Symonie &c.*

The 468. vntruthe The Emperor did not conclude to haue that cõuéticle

After this, the (.468.) *Emperour and Levvys the French King, concluded togeather to call a (.469.) generall Councell at Pife: to the vvhich alfo agreed a great part of the Popes Cardinals. Many (faith (.470.) Sabellicus)* began to abhorre the Popes Courts, faying, that al things were defiled with filthy lucre, with monftruous and wicked luftes, with poifonings, Sacrilegies, murders, and Symoniacal faiers, and that Pope Iulius him felfe vvas a Symoniake, a dronkarde, a beafte, a worldling, and vnworthelye occupied the place, to the deftruction of Chriftendome, and that there was no remedie, but a General Councel to be called, to helpe thefe mifchiefes, to the which his Cardinalles accordng to his othe, defired him, but they could not obteine it of him.

The 469. vntruth. It vvas a priuate conuenticle, no generall Councel. The 470. vntruth. No fuch thing to be found in Sabellicus.

Maxi-

Maximilian the Emperour, being the Authour of it, with Lewes the Frenche King (becaufe the hiftories doe beare recorde, that in times paft the Emperours of Rome had wont to appoint Councels) they appoint a Coũcell to be holdẽ at Pyfe.

The.37. Chapter. Of Maximilian the Emperour : Great Grant father to Maximilian the Emperour which now liueth.

Stapleton.

THough Maximilian the Emperour redreffed certaine grieuaunces, that the Churches of Germanie fuffred through paiements to the Romaine Court, as did the French Kings about the fame time , yet did he not thereby challenge the Popes Supremacy, but moft reuerétly obeied the fame, as did (this notwithftanding) the French Kings alfo, as I haue before declared. Which (to omitte al other arguments) appeareth wel by his demeanour, at his later daies, in the firft ftarting vppe of your Apoftle, I fhoulde faye Apoftata Martin Luther : and alfo by the proteftation of his nexte fucceffour Charles the fift of famous memorie, protefting openlye at his firft dyet holden in Germanie at Wormes, that he woulde followe the approued Relligion of his mofte Noble Progenitours of the houfe of Auftria, of whome this Maximilian was his Graundfather. Whofe Relligion and deuotion to the See of Rome from time to time, his nephew Charles in that affemblye extolleth and fetteth forthe as a moft honourable and worthy example. Whiche in him howe great it was, if nothing els, yet your deape filence in this place, of fo noble an Emperour , vnder whome fuche importante concurrents befell geaue vs well to vnderftande. For had there bene in him the leaft inckling

Vide Pontanũ lib.2 Rerũ memorab. pag.52.

inkling in the worlde of any inclining to your factious sect, he shoulde not thus haue escaped the famouse Chronicle of this your infamouse Libell. And yet verely as wel you might haue broughte him, and Ferdinand his brother, yea and our late Gratiouse Soueraigne Queene Marie too, for example of gouernemente in Ecclesiasticall causes, as you haue broughte Maximilian his predecessour, and a number of other Emperours before.

As for the Generall Councell, that you saye Maximilian and Lewys the Frenche King, called at Pyse, it was neuer taken for anye Generall Councell, nor Councell at all, but a schismaticall assemblie procured against Pope Iulius by a fewe Cardinalles, whome he had depriued of their Ecclesiasticall honour. And it was called onely by the meanes of the Frenche King in despite of Pope Iulius, for making league with the Venetians, and for mouing Genua to rebelle againste him. As for Maximilian, he doubted in dede a while (being for the said league offended with the Pope) *Pietro* whiche waie to take, but seeinge the matter growe to a *Messia in* Schisme, he rased that Conuenticle, being remoued from *vita di* Pise to Millaine, and agreed with Pope Iulius. By whom *Massimi-* also, and by Leo the.10. his successoure, this Conuenticle *liano.* was dissanulled in a Generall Councell holden at Laterane in Rome. To the whiche Councell at length, as wel the Schismaticall Cardinalles, as all other Princes, condescended. And thus euer, if there be any thing defectuouse or faulty, that you make much of, and that maketh for you: but if the faulte be refourmed, and thinges done orderlye, that you will none of, for that is against you.

As for that you tell vs out of Sabellicus, *That many beganne to abhorre the Popes Courtes,*&c. not telling vs withal, where in Sabellicus that fhould appere, his workes being fo large, it femeth to be a manifeſt Vntruth. For neither in his Aenead. 11. lib. 2. where by the courſe of time it ſhoulde be found, neither in *Rebus Venetis,* nor anye otherwhere can I yet finde it. And therefore vntill you tell vs , where that ſhamefull accuſation was layed in , and by whome, we doe iuſtlie aunſwere you, that it fauoureth ſhrewdly of a lie.

And yet if all were true, what proue you els, but that then the Pope was an euill man, and his Courte licentiouſly or-dered? Whereof if you inferre, M. Horne, that therfore the Prince in England muſt be Supreame Gouernour, then on the contrarie fide we may reaſon thus. The Pope that now liueth, is a man of miraculouſe holineſſe, of excellente learning, and no waies reprehenſible : His Court alſo is di-ligently reſourmed , and moſte godly ordered (as all that now know Rome, can and do witneſſe). Ergo the Quenes Maieſtie now, nor no other Prince, can or ought to be ſu-preme Gouernour in al cauſes Eccleſiaſticall.

M. Horne. The. 144. Diuiſion. pag. 86 b.

The 471. vntruth. For not aboute Churche maters, but about maters of the court of Rome.

Maximilian the Emperour, Levves the French Kinke , and other Prin-ces beyonde the ſeas , vvere not more carefully bent , and moued by theyr learned men to reſourme by their authoritie the abuſes about (.471.) Church matters, then vvas King Henrie the eight, at the ſame time King of Eng-land, of moſt famous memorie, vvho follovving the humble ſuits and petiti-ons of his learned Clergie, agreeing thereupon by vniſourme conſent in their Conuocation, toke vppon him that authoritie and gouernment in all matters or cauſes Eccleſiaſticall, vvhich they aſſured him to belong vnto his eſtate, both by the vvoord of God, and by the auncient Lavves of the Churche: and therefore promiſed, in verbo ſacerdotij, *by their prieſthoode, not to*
doe

doe any thing in their Councell without his assent, &c.   And this Clergie
vvas not onely of Diuines, but also of the vvisest, most expert and best learned in the Ciuil and Canon Lavves, that vvas than or hath bene sence , as
D. Tonstall Bishoppe of Duresme, D. Stokesley Bishop of London, D. Gardiner Bishop of Vvynton, D. Thirlebie Bishoppe of VVestminster, and after of Norvvich, and your old Maister D. Bonner, vvho succeded Stokesley,
in the See of Lodon, and many others: by vvhose aduise and consent there vvas
at that time also a learned booke made and published, De vera differen-
tia Regiæ potestatis & Ecclesiasticæ, vvhiche I doubte not , but yee
haue sene long (uthen. Neither vvas this a (.472.) nevv deuise of theirs to
please the King vvithal, or their opiniō only, but it vvas ād is the iudgemēt of
the most lerned (473) Ciuiliās and Canonists, that vvhē the Clergy are
faulty or negligēt, it appertaineth to th'Emperor to cal general
councelles for the reformation of the Churche causes, as Philippus Decius a famous Lavvyer affirmeth. And the Glossator vppon this
Canon Principes, affirmeth, that the princes haue iurisdiction in
diuers sortes within the Churche ouer the Cleargy, when they
be stubbourne, ambitious, subuerters of the faith, falsaries,
makers of Schismes, contemners of excommunication : yea
also wherein so euer, the Ecclesiasticall povver faileth or is to
vveake, as in this Decree, He meaneth vvhere the povver of the Church
by the vvorde of doctrine preuaileth not, therein must the Princes authority
and iurisdiction take order, for that is the plaine prouiso in the decree. The
vvordes of the decree are as follovv, The seculer princes haue (.474.)
oftentimes vvithin the Church the highest authority, that they
may fence bv that power, the Ecclesiastical discipline. But with
in the Church the povver (of princes) should not be necessary,
sauing that, that thing vvhich the priests are not able to do, by
the vvorde of doctrine, the povver (of the prince) may *commaund, or obteine that, by the terrour of discipline : The heauenlie kingdome dothe oftentimes preuaile or goe forvvarde
by the earthlie Kingdome, that those which being vvithin the
Churche, dooe againste the faithe and discipline, maye be
broughte vnder by the rigoure of princes : and that the povver of the princes, may lay vppon the neckes of the proude,

yy iiij   that

The 472. vntruth. It vvas a mere nou-elty.

The 473. vntruth. No Ciui-lians nor Canoni-stes are of the iudge-ment, vvhiche M. Horne here de-fendeth. Const. 151 23. q 5. The 474 Vntruth. False trā-slation. Nonnun-quā som-times.

*There is diuerse readinges imperet or impetret.

that same discipline,whiche the profite of the Churche is not
hable to exercise:and that he bestowe the force of his authoritie,whereby to deserue wooreship . Let the Princes of the
worlde wel knowe,that they of duety shall rendre an accópt
to God for the Churche,VVhiche they haue taken of Chriſte
to preserue. For vvether the peace and discipline of the
Churche be encreased by faithfull princes,or it be loosed: He
doth exacte of them an accompt , VVho hath deliuered his
Churche to be committed to their povver.

The Prin
ces shall
geue an
accompt
to God,
for the
Ghurch,
and the
discipline
thereof

The. 38.Chapter. Of kinge Henry the.8 .our late Soueraigne.

Stapleton.

Cócernig
the do=
inges of
king Hé=
ry.the. 8.

WE are at lengthe , by the course of tyme which
M.Horne hath prosequuted , deuolued to owre
owne dayes,and to the doinges of kinge Henry
the eight for the confirmation whereof,he hath fetched frō
all partes of the world so long,so many,and yet al impertinente argumentes . Belyke nowe for his farewell , and to
make vs vppe a plausible conclusion , he will loke more
narrowly , and more substancially to the handling of his
proufes,and wil perhappe lyke a good oratour in the win -
ding vp of his matter leaue in the readers heartes by some
good and effectuall probation,a vehemente impressiō and
perswasion of his surmised primacie.He hathe perchaunce
reserued the beste dishe to the last, and lyke a good expert
captaine,will set his strongeste reasons and authorities,

The order
of M.
Hornes
proufes.

tanquam triarios milites,in the rearwarde. And so suerlye
yt semeth he will doe in making vp his matters with fyue
authorities that is , of one Diuine , and fowre Lawyers.
The diuine being a Spaniard:and of his lawyers thre being
straungers,two Italians,and one frenche man, all being ciuilians

uillians of late tyme: The fourth being our contryman and
a temporall lawyer of our realme. For the Diuine and our
countriman the lawyer, he stiꝛketh not to breake his araye
and course of tyme, the one lyuing aboute. 900. yeares, the
other fowre hundred yeares sythence . Let vs then cōsider
his proufes, and whether he doth not, according to his accustomable wonte rather featly floute hym, then bring his
reader, any matter to the purpose.

You will nowe proue to vs M. Horne, that king Henrie
was taken and called the Supreame Head of the Churche
of England, and that lawfully.   And whie so, I pray you ?
Mary say ye because the conuocation promised hym by
theire priesthod they woulde doe nothing in theire councelles withowte his consente . Why M. Horne, take you
this promise to be of so great weight ? Dothe the consideration and estimation of priesthod weighe so deaply with
you nowe? Ye wil not be of this mynde long. For ere ye
haue done, ye wil tell M. Fekenham, that there was none
of them al priestes: and that there is but one onely prieste
which is Christe.   Yet will ye say, a promise they made.
Truthe yt is: but vnlesse ye can proue the promise honeste
and lawful (which we vtterly deny) then this promise will
not relieue you. And, this is but one braunche of the vnlawfull supreamacie that king Henry practised : therefore
thowghe this doinge were tolerable and probable to , yet
vnlesse ye went to a further proufe, ye shall wynne litle at
M. Fekenhams handes. I am content to passe ouer the residewe of his vsurped supreamacie for this tyme I demaūd
of you then, what one thing ye haue hitherto browght for
to perswade any reasonable man, for this one pointe : that
is, that the Bishoppes can determyne nothing in theire synodes

Cōcernig
the cōuo-
cations
promisse,
to make
no cōsti-
tution
without
the kings
consente.
Fol. 95.

M.Horn
hath not
proued in
all his
boke that
such con=
sent is ne=
cessarie.

nodes to be forcible, vnlesse the Prince agree also to yt?
Suerlye no one thing. That Bishoppes voluntarely desired
their good and catholyke Princes to ioyne with them, yea
and submitted sometimes the iudgmente of theire doinges,
of theire great humility, to some notable Princes, ye haue
shewed: and withall that in some cafes yt is conueniente
so to be donne. But ye can full ill wynde vp your conclusion vppon this. Which ye forseeing, did shewe vs a tricke
of your newe rhetorike and fyne grammer, turning *conuenit* into *oportet*: making yt is conueniente, and yt muste be
so, all one. Ye will belyke take better handfaste nowe: But
wil ye now see his sure handfaste good Reader? Suerly the
first is not very faft, as whe he telleth vs owt of Decius, ad

M.Horns
Samplõs
post vvil
fall on
his ovvn
heade.

owt of the glofe of the Canõ law, that princes may cal coũcels, and that in some cafes they haue iurifdictiõ in Church
matters: wherin we haue alredy fayde inowgh. And how
slenderly and loofely this geare hangeth with his affertion,
yt is opẽ to the eye. I trow he fticketh fafter to his diuine,
thẽ to his lawyer, and therefore he bringeth in Ifidorus extraordinary. 900. yeares almoft owt of his race and courfe.
Here, here (as yt femeth) is his anker hold, and for this caufe
afwell the whole allegation is here producted, as alfo one
peace of the fame, fet in the firft page of his whole boke, as
a fure marke to direct the reader by: and as yt were a Sampfons pofte for M. Horne, to buyld his boke vppõ. But take
good head M. Horne yt be not a true Sampfons pofte, and
that it bring not the whole howfe vpon your own head,

as yt doth in dede. Wherunto good reader, feing M. Horne
hath chofen this as a notable allegation to be eied on, fetting the fame in two notable places, I woulde wifhe thee
alfo to geue a good eye thereunto, and to fee, if it can anye
way pofsible make for him.

I fay

I say then M.Horne, that this allegatiō goeth no further,
then that the Prince, by his cyuill and worldlye power
shoulde afsiste and maynteyne the Churche and her doctrine. And that this allegation directly and rowndly proueth the contrarye of that, for the whiche ye doe alleage yt, that is, that yt proueth the ecclefiaft call authoritie, and not the cyuill, to be cheif and principall, in caufes ecclefiafticall. And that in effecte the whole tendeth to nothing elfe but that, as I fayde, the Princes
shoulde defend the Churche. I will not ftande here in rip-
ping vp of wordes with you, or in the diuerfity of reading,
and that fome old copies haue : *who hath committed his
Churche to be defended of theire power:* and that your (*hath
deliuered to be committed*) feameth to ftande in your tranflation vnhanfomly. I will faye nothing, that *credere* and
committere : is all one in Latin. Let this goe, I finde no
faulte with you, for tranflation, but for yl application. Yf ye
had brought this authority to proue, that the prince fhould
defende the Churche (for the whiche ende and refpecte it
was writen) I woulde fay nothing to you. But when ye
will bleare our eies and make vs fo blinde, that we fhoulde
imagine, by this faying of Ifidore, that the king is Supreame
Head of the Churche, or that his affente is neceffarie to
the Synodes of Bifhops and coūcelles, I wil fay to you, that
the cōtrary, wil be much better gathered of this allegatiō.
The very firfte wordes wōderfully acrafe your newe primacy, and fomwhat alfo your honefty, peruerfly trāflating,
nōnunquā: which is, *fomtime*, or now and thē, into *oftētimes*.
But let yt be, for *nonnunquam, fepe:* let them oftētymes haue
the higheft authoritye in the Churche. Vnleffe they haue
yt ftyll, they cannot be called the Supreame Heades in all

z z   caufes

Vide deftru
ctorū vi-
tiorum im
prefs. No-
rinberg.
1496.part.
6.cap. 40.
Qui eorū
poteftati
fuam Ec-
clefiam
tradidit
defenden-
dam.

23.q.5.c.
Principes.
Principes
feculi non-
nunquam
intra Ec-
clefiam po-
teftati-
adeptæ cul
mina te-
nent.

Vt per ean
dē potesta
tem eccle-
siasticam
disciplinā
muniant.
Cæterū in
tra eccle-
siam pote-
states ne=
cessaria
non essent
nisi vt
quod non
preualent
sacerdotes
efficere per
doctrina
sermonē,
potestas
hoc impe-
ret per di-
scipline
terrorem.
Et mox.
Vt qui in-
tra ecclesi
am positi
cōtra fidē
& discipli
nā agunt,
rigore prin
cipum cō-
terantur.

causes ecclesiastical. And so theis very words make a good argumēt againste your primacy. But now M. Horne, what is the cause, whie they haue this high authority either somtimes, or oftétimes? Isidore straytwayes sheweth the cause: *that they may* (as your self tranflate *)sence by theire power the ecclefiastical difcipline.* Ye heare thē the scope, and final purpose of this allegation, for Princes authority in matters ecclesiasticall, that is to defende the Churche. And therefore as I sayde, yt is more sutely, to reade, *tradidit defendendam,* then *tradidit cōmittendā.* And for this cause the Emperours call them selues not *capita Ecclesiæ,* not the heades of the Churche, *sed aduocatos Ecclesiæ,* but the aduocates of the Churche, as your self tel of themperour Friderike. Goe we now forth with Isidorus: But first I aske of you M. Horne, that make the Princes to be heades of the Churche, and to haue so muche to doe, in matters ecclesiasticall, that the Bishops can decree nothing that shoulde be auaylable withowt theyre special ratification (for the setting forth of the which doctrine ye are content, for this tyme that priestes shalbe priestes, and may sweare by their priesthod, and not by theire aldermanship or eldership) whether suche authority in Princes be absolutelie necessarie to the Churche or no? Yf ye say no, thē conclud you against your self ād your whole boke. Yf ye say yea, then conclude you against the truthe, and againste your authour, who sayeth, *that suche authority of Princes in the Church is not necessarie, but for to punishe those that contemne the worde of doctrine, the fayth, and discipline of the Churche.* Of whome haue we receiued M. Horne the worde of doctrine, the faythe and discipline of the Churche? Of the Apostles, and theire successours the Bishoppes, or of the Princes? I suppose ye will not saie of

Princes.

Princes. Then muft ye graunt that for thefe matters the primacy refteth in the clergy, of whom the Princes the felues,
haue receiued theire faith: ad to whom in matters of faith,
and for the difcipline of the Churche they muft alfo obey:
and as cafe requireth, fet forth the doctrine of worde wyth
theire temporal fworde. Whiche if they do not, but fuffer
throwghe theire flacknes, the faythe and difciplyne of the
Churche to be loofed, *God, who hath committed his Churche* M. Horns
to be defended by theire power wil exacte an accompte of the, booke in
as your authour Ifidore writeth and your felf do allege. So anfwe-
that now we fee euen by your own allegatio in whom the redby his
fuperiority of Churche matters, remayneth : that is, in the gation.
clergy: And that Princes are not the heades but the ayders,
afsifters, and aduocates of the Churche with theire teporal
authority. And to this ende, all that euer ye haue browght
in this your boke cocerning the intermedling of Princes in
church affaires, ca only be referred. And this your own allegatio is afwel a fufficiet anfwere to al your argumets hitherto laid furth for the princes fupremacy, as a good iufti-
fication of the Clergies primacy.

Wherfore if you harken but to your owne allegation,
and will ftande to the fame as you wil your Readers to do,
placing it (as I haue faid) in the fore fronte of your booke,
you muft nedes ftand alfo to the next parcell folowing making clerely for the Clergies fuperioritie in Ecclefiafticall *Ifidorus.*
caufes. Thefe words I mean, that *withi the Church the power*
(of Prices) fhuld not be neceffary faying that, that thing, which
the Priefts are not able to do by the word of doctrine, the power
(of the price) may comaud by terror of difcipline. And I doubt
nothing, but that we are able wel and furely to proue as wel
by his other bookes, as by his gathering of all the Councels

together, into one volume yet extāt, that Iſidorus thought of the Popes Primacy then, as Catholiques doe now. For an euident proufe wherof, behold what this Auncient and learned Biſhop Iſidorus writeth.   He ſaith : *Synodorum congregandarum authoritas Apoſtolicæ ſedi commiſſa eſt. Neque vllam Synodū generalem ratam eſſe credimus aut legimus, quæ non fuerit eius authoritate congregata vel fulcita. Hoc Authoritas teſtatur Canonica, hoc Eccleſiaſtica hiſtoria comprobat , hoc Sanƈti Patres confirmant .* The Authoritie of aſſembling Coūcelles, is committed to the See Apoſtolike. Neither doe we beleue or reade any Geaneral Councell to be ratified, whiche was not either aſſembled or confirmed with her Authoritie. This to be ſo, the Authoritie of Canons doth witneſſe. This the eccleſiaſtical hiſtory proueth. This the holie Fathers confirme.   Lo you ſee. M. Horne, what the iudgement of Iſidorus was aboue.900.yeres paſt, howe iumpe it agreeth with the aſſertion of Catholiques now, and how direƈtly it ouerthroweth yours. This therfore being ſo ſure a Principle on our parte , and ſo clerelie proued : bethinke your ſelfe now, M. Horne, how your new Primacie wil be proued by this allegation.

   Touching that you ſaie, *This Clergie (in King Henries daies) was not only of Diuines, but alſo of the wiſeſt, moſt expert, and beſt learned in the Ciuil and Canon Lawes, that was or hath ben ſence, as D. Tonſtal, D. Stokeſley, D. Gardiner, D. Thirlbie, and D. Bonner,* by the euident falſehood whiche you praƈtiſe in alleaging theſe witneſſes, a man may iudge with what fidelitie you haue handled the reſt , throughout your whole booke.   Who is ignoraunte , that not one of theſe Reuerent Fathers did ſincerely thinke that to be true, which you here impute vnto them? For whereas
                                                                        all

Iſidorus in præfat. Cōciliorū.

Trip.li.4. cap.9. &.19.

all vpright iudgement fhoulde come of a mans owne free choife, not ftained or fpotted either with the hope of priuate lucre and honoure, or with the feare of great lofle, the one of thofe two things which of all other, moft forceably carieth men away, from profefsing their owne confcience, did ftoppe thofe men from faying and vttering that, which otherwife they would moft gladly haue vttered : fithens as they were put in hope of al promotion, if they agreed with the Kings will (of which they made, I iudge, the lefle accompte) fo difagreeing from the fame, they were certaine to loofe bothe goods and life, and alfo their good name, in the fhew of the worlde, as who fhoulde haue bene put to deathe by the name of Traitours, whiche is the thing that all true fubiectes doe chieflie abhorre.   Yet you knowe in fuche forte fuffered a great many, notable both for learning and vertue, as D. Fifher Bifhoppe of Rochefter, Syr Thomas More, a great number of the Carthufians, befide diuerfe other of all eftates.   You knowe alfo, the matter, then was not fo fifted and tryed by learning, as it hath bene fince. And we know, they were the fecrete fnakes of your adders broode, that induced the King to that minde, not any of the Doctours here by you named, who all againfte their willes, condefcended therevnto.

Howe then are they broughte foorthe for witnefles of your herefies, who for feare of deathe faied as you doe, and that no longer then the forefaid impedimente laie in theyr waye?   For when the ftate of the worlde was otherwife that without feare of deathe they might vtter their minde freely : who knoweth not, that all they who liued to fee thofe daies of freedome, in all theire woordes and deedes, protefted that the Pope, and not the King, was head of the

Churche vnder Chrift ? Neuer hearde you (M. Horne)
that when your owne brethren , being arryued before D.
Gardiner the Bifhope of Winchefter, and then Chauncelour of England, had faied, they lerned theyr difobedience

vnto the Pope, out of his booke, *De vera obedientia , &c.*
then he aunfwered that if they had bene good Scholers,
they would haue folowed theyr Maifter in his befte, and
not in his worfte doeinges . Againe, if they had erred
through his Authority, whē he was not fo wel learned and
grounded , they fhould much more repēt and recāt through
his Authority , being nowe better lerned through longer
ftudie , and better grounded through longer experience.
And this Doctour Gardiner , when he was mofte of your
fide , in this one matter , yet he was fo fufpected of the
Kinge for fecrete conference with the Pope, by letters to be fent by a ftraunger in the tyme of his embaf-
fye on this fide of the Seas, that (as Mafter Foxe repor-

Actes and
monu-
mentes.
pag. 824.
col.1.
& 816. teth) for this verie caufe, *Kinge Henrie in all Generall*
Pardons graunted after that tyme , dyd euermore excepte,
all treafons committed beyonde the Seas , whiche was meant
for the Bifhoppes caufe: This ys that Doctour Gardiner
who at Paules Croffe , in a mofte Honorable and full Audience, witneffed not onely his owne repentaunce for
his former naughty doings,but alfo that King Henry fought
diuerfe tymes to haue reconciled hym felfe againe , to
the See of Rome , as who knewe, that he had vnlaw-
fully departed from the vnytie thereof, and had made
hym felfe the Supreme Heade of the Churche of Englande , altogether vniuftly.

This is that Doctour Gardiner,who lying in his deathe-
bedde, caufed the Pafsion of Chrifte to be readen vnto
him

hym, and when he hearde it readen, that Peter after the denying of his Maifter, went out and wepte bitterlie, he caufyng the Reader to ftaye, wept him felfe full bitterlie, and faied: *Ego exiui, fed non dum fleui amarè*: I haue gone out, but as yet, I haue not wepte bytterlie. And is nowe Doctour Gardiner a fitte witneffe for your fecular Supremacy M. Horne?

Marcellinus the Pope being afearde of deathe dyd facrifice vnto Idolles: And the fame Marcellinus repenting his vniufte feare, dyd afterwarde facrifice his owne bodie and foule for the loue of Chrifte, fuffring Martyrdome for his fake. Will you nowe proue Idolles to be better then Chrifte, by the facte of Marcellinus? Or fhall not the laft iudgemente ftande rather then the firft? What meane you then to alleage the iudgementes of Doctour Gardiner, Doctour Thirlbey, Doctour Tonftall, and Doctour Bonner, fith you knowe that all thofe chaunged their mindes vppon better aduife? Or whie died Doctour Tonftalle, in prifonne? Or why lye the other learned godly Bifshops yet in prifonne, if they are of your nfinde? But if you knowe that they diffente vtterly from you, and yet doe pretende to bring their Authoritie for you, this fact declareth, that you are not only a fond wrangler, but alfo a wicked falfarie: and that you knowe as well Saint Auguftine, whome you alleaged before fo largelye, and all the Councels and princes with al other Authours by you producted, are none otherwife of your minde, then are Doctour Thirlebie, and Doctour Bonner, whome you fo impudentlie make to fpeake as Proctours in your caufe, albeit they are readie to fhedde their bloude againft this your opinion.

Once

Tom. 1.
Concil. in
vita Mar-
cellini.

Once in maner the whole clergy of the Realme sinned most greuously, by preferring the secular and earthly kingdome, before the Magistrates of the heauély kingdome. But that sinne of theirs al those now abhor, and haue before abhorred, to whó God gaue grace to see the filthines and the absurdty thereof.　　And surelye vntil the rest bothe of the clergy and of the layety, do hartely repét for that most filthy and absurd dede, wherein they withdrewe the Supremacy from S. Peters successours, and gaue it to the successours of Iulius Cæsar, vntill I say they repent for it, and refourme that minde of theirs, as much as lyeth in thé, they cã neuer be made partakers of the kingedome of heauen: But only they shal inherit the kingdome of the earth, in whose Supremacy they put their cófidence. You Mayster Horn, haue in dede great cause to make much of this earthly Supremacy.　　For had not the clergy and temporalty geuen that to kinge Henry. 8. you and your heresies coulde haue had no place now in the throne of that Bishopprike, which was ordayned not for Robert and his Madge, but for chast prelates, and suche as shoulde preferre the soule before the body, the kingdome of heauen before the kingdome of the earthe, Peter before Nero, Christ before Antichrist. For so I doubte not to say, with the greate Clerke, and most holy Bishop Athanasius , that a Christian kinge or Emperour,

See before. fol. 97.

setting him selfe aboue bishops, the officers of Christ, in matters of the faythe , is a very Antichrist. Which Antichristian facte in dede hathe bene the first gate and entry for all those heresies to enter, which the Prince him selfe then most abhorred, and against the which bothe he had lately before made a lerned booke , and did publishe after (but in vayne) for a stay thereof, the six Articles. In vayne, I say,

I fay : for the order of dewe gouernement ones taken a-
way, the knotte of vnity ones vndone, the heade being cut
of, howe coulde it otherwife be, but falfe doctrine fhould
take place, a feparation from the corps of Chriftendome
fhoulde enfewe, and our Countrie a parte of the body fall
to decaie in fuche matters, as belonged to the Heade, to
order, direct and refourme ? This horrible finne Maifter
Horne woulde make a vertue. But all ages, all Councels,
all Princes, yea the holy Scriptures are directly againft him,
and doe al witneffe for the Pope and Bifhoppes againft the
Prince and lay Magiftrat, that to them not to thefe, belongeth by right, by reafon, by practife, the Supreme and
chiefe gouernement in al caufes and matters mere Ecclefiaftical and fpiritual.

M. Horne. The. 145. Diuifion. pag. 87. 4.

To this (. 475.) *effect alfo vvriteth* Petrus Ferrarienfis, *a
notable learned man in the Lavves, faying:* Thou ignorāt mā,
thou oughteft to know that the Empire (*the Emperour*)
ones in tymes paft, had both the fwoordes, to witte,
both the Temporal and Spiritual, in fo much that the
Emperours then beftowed (. 476.) al the ecclefiaftical
benefices through the (477) whole world, and more,
they did choofe the Pope, as it is in *C. Adrianus* Dift. 63.
And the fame Petrus *in an other place, faith thus:* Marke after
what forte and how many vvaies thofe Clergymen,
do fnare the Lay, and enlarge their ovvne iurifdiction:
but alas miferable Emperours and fecular princes,
which doe fuffer this and other things: you both make
your felues fclaues to the Bifhoppes, and ye fee the
vvorlde vfurped by the infinit vvaies, and yet ye ftudy
not for remedy, becaufe ye geue no heed to vvifedom
and knovvleadge.

*In form. lib. quo agi-
tur ex fubft. in verbo
ex fuo corpore.*

The. 475. vntruth,
For this Petrus
vvriteh for the Po-
pes Supremacy, not
for the Princes in
Ecclefiaftical mat-
ters.

The. 476 vntruth?
Not poffible, to be
true.

The. 477. vntruth.
Falfe tranflation, as
fhal appeare.

*In form. refponf. con.
ad verb. tanquam
publ. ex com.* n. 10.

a a a   *Stapleton*

Ferra-
rienſis.

YF your law be not better thē your diuinity, we neade
not much to feare our matter: And ſo much the leſſe,
yf that be true, that a good mery fellowe, and vnto
you not vnknowen, reading your boke of late ſayd, that he
durſt lay a good wager, that yf ye were vppon the ſodayne
well appoſed, ye were not able to reade the quotations, by
your ſelfe in the margent alleaged out of this Petrus : and
withal, that ye neuer readde that, which ye alleage out of
Quintinus, or yf ye did, ye do not vnderſtande yt, or at the
leaſte ye doe moſt wickedly peruerte yt. But let this goe,
as merely ſpoken : for thoughe ye neuer read the authour,
nor can redely at the firſt (perchaunce) reade your owne
quotations, the whole matter being by ſome of your frēds
and neareſte affinity brought ripe and ready to your hand,
we ſhal be wel cōtēt frō whēce ſo euer yt come, ſo it come
at length to any purpoſe and effeĉt, whereof I for my parte
haue litle hope. For what if in the old tyme the Emperours
confirmed popes ? What if the cleargy vſurpe and intrude
in many thinges vppon the ſeculer princes iuriſdiĉtion ? Yf
ye may herof make a ſequele, that either the king of Englād
is ſupreame head of the Church: or that, the vnlawful promiſſe made by the biſſhops by their prieſthod (which ye
eſteme as much as yf they had ſworne by Robin hode his
bowe) doth bynde them, as a lawfull promiſſe, I will ſay, ye
are ſodenly become a notable lawyer, and worthy to be re-
tayned of councell in greate affayres . I am aſſured of one
thinge, that howe ſo euer ye lyke him in this poynte, yet
for other poynts of this his boke, that you alleage, you like
him neuer adeale: As, for the inuocation of Saints: yea for
the Popes Primacie, by the which he ſayth: *A periured mīn*
(which

M. Horns
imperti
nēt argu-
ments.

Practica
Iohānis Pe
tri Fer. In
forma in=
ter. fiend.
cum reo,
cōuento in
aĉt. ʒcali.

which otherwife is reiected) *may be by the Popes difpenfa-* rienſis.
tion admitted to beare Wytnes:and that a clerke irregular can
not be abfolued, but by the Pope . Which followeth the very *In forma*
place by yowe alleaged, with many fuch lyke, not making *iurameti*
very much to your lykinge . Nowe what yf I fhould fay *teſtium.*
vnto yowe, that you and your authour to , yf he fayth fo, *Numeri 7.*
fay vntruely, affirminge the Emperour to haue both the *In forma*
temporall and fpirituall fworde ? And what if I fhould fay *refponfi rei*
that thereis no more truth in that affertion, than in the o- *couenti ad*
ther, that he beſtowed all the benefices through the whole *verbū tā-*
worlde ? For your chapter *Adrianus* , that you alleage, *quam pub*
fpeaketh of the Emperour Charles the great who was not *lice excō-*
Emperour of the whole worlde, nor of halfe Europa nei- *municatū*
ther , and therfore he coulde not beſtowe the benefices *nu nero.11*
of the whole worlde. Yf ye wil fay, that your authour faith
truly , and ye haue tranſlated truely , for the text is *per fin-* *Dict. cap.*
gulas prouincias:I graunt yowe it is fo : but yet is it vnſkil- *Adrianus*
fully and ignorantly tranſlated: for ye fhoulde haue fayed, *diſt.63.*
through out euery prouince , or contrey fubiect to the Romā
empire. For the Romans did call all countries , that they
had conquered (Italie excepted) prouinces , and the people *Prouinciales* . I fay nothing nowe, that this chapter rather enforceth then deſtroyeth the popes primacy . For
Charles had neither authority to beſtowe the Eccleſiaſticall benefices, nor to choofe the Pope : but as he beinge
a mere ſtraunger before, toke thempire at the popes hand,
fo did he take alfo this fpeciall priuilege and preroga-
tyue.

M.Horne. *The.146.Diuifion. pag.87.b.*

Like as Petrus Ferrarienfis *attributeth bothe the ſwordes,*
that is, both the ſpirituall and the temporall iurifdiction to the Emperour:
aaa ij   So.

So (.478.) Io. Quintinus Heduus *a famous professour of the lavv in Paris , and one that attributeth so much to the Pope as may be, and much more than ought to be, saith that:* In solo Prin cipe omnis est potestas: in the Prince (.479.) alone is al power, *and thereto* (480.) *auoucheth this saying of* Specu- lator, De iurisdict. omnium iudicum: Quod quicquid est in regno, id esse intelligitur de iurisdictione Regis: that whatsoeuer is in a kingdome , that is vnderstan- ded, to be vnder the iurisdiction of the kinge. *To vvhich* (.481.) *purpose he citeth an auncient learned one in the Lavve vvhose name vvas* Lotharius, *vvho, saith he, did say:* That the Prince is the fountaine or welspring of all iurisdictiō *and protesteth also him selfe to be of the* (.482.) *same mind.*

The. 39. Chapter. Solutions to Argumentes taken out of Quintinus Heduus, a Doctour of Parys.

Stapleton.

LET vs nowe take heede : for M. Horne wonderfully lassheth on , with *Io. Quintinus Heduus*, and runneth his race with him two full leaues together . And yet for all this sturre, and heapinge Lawe vppon Lawe, we might graunt him, all that euer he bringeth yn , without any pre- iudice of our cause: and would so do in dede, sauing that the handling of the matter by M. Horne is such as requireth of vs a special specification. Neither can I tell, of all the disho- nest and shamefull pageantes that he hath hitherto played,

whether there be any comparable to this . I can not tell whether his folly or his impudency be the greater: but that bothe excede, I am right well assured. And yet I trowe he owght not to beare all the blame, but may parte stake with his collectour , who hath abused his ignorance , as hym selfe doth abuse his readers ignorance. The answere would

growe

growe longe and bigge , yf I fhould fully as the cafe requireth , rippe vp,and open all thinges,and then at large confute them , which at this tyme I intende not : but in vfinge
as muche breuity as I may, to lay before thee good reader,
and to difcipher the fafhion and maner of his dealinge.
Wherein euen as Medea, fleinge from her naturall father,
and runninge away with a ftraunger,with whome fhe fell
in loue:her father purfuing her,and fhe fearing to be taken,
flewe her yong brother fcattering his limmes in the way,
therby to ftay,what with forowe,and what with long fee-
king for his fonnes body, her fathers iourney: euen fo M.
Horne running away from the catholyke Church his mother,with dame herefie , with whofe filthy loue he is rauif-
fhed,to ftay the reader that woulde trace him, and his herefyes , for the authours he alleageth , doth fo miferably
teare them in peces , and difmember them , that yt would
pity any good Chriftian mans harte to fee yt , as muche
as yt pitied kinge Oëta father to Medea to fee that miferable and lamentable fight:and very bufie will yt be for him
to finde out the whole corps of the fentences , fo wretchedly cutte and hewed by M.Horne: and here and there
in thefe two leaues fo miferably difperfed. We wil notwithftanding trace hi as we may.The the better to vnderftad his
firft allegatiõ,ye fhal vnderftãd that ther is a kind of Iurifdictiõ which is called of the Ciuiliãs *merũ imperiũ* that is, power oflyfe ãd death:which whether it refteth in the price
only, or in other inferiour magiftrates,the Lawyers do not
al agree . Lotharius fetled al in the prince : to that opinion
Quintinus alfo inclineth . But then maketh Quintinus an
obiection. *Whie* fayeth he , *Howe is yt true,that the prince*
onelye hath this mere empire or iurifdiction , feinge that we

M.Horn
for his
wretched
handling
of Quin-
tinus cõ-
pared to
Medea.

VVhat
vvas the
opiniõ of
Lothariꝰ,
of whom
M. Horn
fpeaketh,
and hovv
it is to be
vnderftã-
ded.

aaa iij   *affirme*

Quasi Principum nomine pontifices nõ intelligantur. Dist. 35. c. 4.

Nos bonorum ciuilium duntaxat extra Ecclesiam populariumque dignitatum regem tenere fastigiũ intelligimus &c.

* Eduardi.3. An.15. cap. 3. Clerkes peeres of the lande.

affirme, the Churche to haue yt also? Whereunto he answereth, that vnder the name of Princes, are cõteyned the highe Priestes : from the which our Actes of parliament doe not all disagree, calling Bisshoppes the *Peeres of the realme. *When we say, saieth he, with Lotharius, that the Kinge is the fountayne of all iurisdiction, we meane as Lotharius doth, not of the Churche, but of the ciuill magistrates, vnder the Kinge.* The said Quintinus saieth, *Gladium pontifex vtrũq; gestat, exercet alterum Rex solus, quem pontifex etiam desertus a suis, in hostes licitè stringit.* The Pope hath both the swordes, that is, both temporall and spiritual iurisdiction, yet the King alone, vseth the one of thé, that is the téporal: the which the Pope may notwithstãding, yf he be forsakē of his own, vse also. But as I was about to tel you out of Quitinus, he saith: *Probauimus Ecclesiam Deo militantem se noluisse temerè negotijs secularibus implicare, temporalemq; iurisdictionem principibus sponte reliquisse, tamq; libenter, tamq; animo prompto & facili, vt regũ propria videatur. Idcirco scriptum est à Speculatore, quòd quicquid est in regno, id esse intelligitur de iurisdictione regis.* We haue proued, that the militant Church doth not but vpõ good cause intermedle with seculer affaires: yea rather geueth ouer to Princes the temporall iurisdiction so gladly and so willinglye, that yt seemeth to appertayne to the Princes onely. And therefore Speculatour writeth, that what so euer is in a Kingdome, that is vnderstanded to be of the Kinges iurisdiction. And for this some were persuaded, that the spirituall and temporall iurisdiction stode so contrarie one to the other, that one man might not exercise both. But Quintinus hiself misliketh

VVhy Speculator saith, al that is in the realm to be of the Kings iurisdictiõ

Ecclesia vtrũq; gladiũ tenet, vtramque pariter habet in risdictionẽ.

liketh this opinion, and faith, euen in the faid place, where he fpeaketh of Speculator, that the Church only, ad not the Princes feculer, hath both fwordes, and both iurifdictions. And vpon this occafion he doth vehemently inueighe againft Petrus de Cugnerio of whome we haue fpoke, that did fo ftifflye ftand againft the Frech clergy for their teporall iurifdictio: and prouoked the King Philip Valefius, as much as in him laye, to plucke it away fro the clergie. He calleth him a mifhapen parfon in body, a moft wicked ma, and to fay al in one, a very knaue. And thoughe his name were then terrible, and thowgh he would feeme for his great wifedome to carrie al the realme vpo his fhulders, yet was he euer after, but a lawghing ftock to me: and becaufe he durft not for fhame after this great challege, fhew hifelf abrode, as he was wont to do, for M. Peter de Cugnerio, he was called in their tong *M. Pierre de Coynet*: as a ma would fay, M. Peter that lurketh in corners.

But wil ye now heare M. Horne this your own authour Quintinus how he expoudeth *copofuit re facerdotum*, that is, how the King fet in order the matters of the priefts? Wil ye heare alfo, what fharpe Law he made againft the, as you auouch that he did? He faith of the king. *Pronuciauit Ecclefia, & feuda, & teporalia quae, bena propria fibi poffidere poffe. at q, in illa iurifdictione habere* He gaue fentece and pronouced, that the Church might poffeffe fealtes and other temporal things, ad haue iurifdictio therein. So much for our firft entrauce into Quitinus. Wherin befide the fhame that ye muft take, for your worfhipful glofe vpo *copofuit re facerdotu*, firft ye fee, that he improueth *Ferrariefis* ad fuchlike, as attribute
to the

Nouimus virumq; gladium foli Ecclefia datum, hoc eft, ecclefia pontificem habere ius & poteftatem in fpiritualia fimul & in omnia temporalia, atq; ex ijs decernere & ftatuere ex caufa poffe, cuius decretis ftandum.

Gibere deformem. Flagitiosiffim° quidam & poftea: tam infenfo nebulone.

Quintin° declareth M. Horn to be a lier in the ftory of kig Philip va lefius be fore re herfed.

Menf. Sep. 1. *An* 1329 fyue flat vntruths of M. Horn in leffe then 15. lynes.

to the Emperour the spiritual and temporal sworde. Then
that he is of a quyte contrarie mynde, to that, that ye
woulde by a sentence here and there yll fauouredlie, and
disorderly patched in, enforce vpon, as thowgh he should
thinke, that al iurisdictiō should come of the Prince. Thirdly it is vntrue that he auoucheth Speculatours saying : He
auoucheth as ye haue hearde the contrary. Fowrthly it is
vntrue, that he bringeth in Lotharius, to confirme that,
which Speculatour said. For he intreateth of Lotharius, before he alleageth Speculator, and doth not alleage Lotharius for that purpose ye speake of. Fiftly and last, Lotharius
is not as ye pretende of this mynde, that all iurisdiction cometh of the secular Prince. For Lotharius meaneth not of
the clergies iurisdiction, which cometh not of the Prince,
but of the iurisdiction of Laye men, which all together dependeth of the Prince.

The. 483.
vntruthe.
In that
place he
proueth
the cler-
gies po-
vver, not
the Prices
in ecclesia
stical mat-
ters.

M. Horne. The. 147. Diuision. pag. 87. b.

*And vvriting of the Kings povver in Eccle.(.483.)matters or causes, he
citeth this Canon* Quando vult Deus *foorth of the decrees, vvhereuppon
he as it vvere commenteth saying,* Thus is the reason vvherefore, it
is leaful for the Prince, some vvhiles to determine those things
vvhich concerne the Church, least the honesty of the mother
*(he meaneth the Church)*should in any thing be violated, or least
her tranquilly should be troubled, specially of them, to vvhom
she is committed*(meaning the Church Ministers)*.

*Duabus
regulis cō-
cludā: pri-
or est sem-
per in fidei*

Stapleton.

Leaue ones M. Horne, this peuishe pinching and paring, this miserable mayming and marring of your authours.
Your author M. Horne, geueth two rules: the first for the
autho-

*& peccati materia, ius Ecclesiasticum attendendum est, & in foro ciuili, tumque cessat
omne iuris imperatorÿ mandatum & aboletur.*

authority and matters of the Church saying that, *in matter
of fayth and synne, the lawe of the Church is euer to be obserued,
and therto all princes lawes must yelde* : whiche rule he proueth at large. And thus yow see your owne authour standeth agaift you, for one of the cheif matters of your booke,
wheri ye wil, in al matters to be determined by the Church,
that the princes cõsent is to be had. The 2. rule, is touching
the prince: wherin he sayth, *that it apperteyneth to the kings
and princes of the worlde, to desire that the Church theyr mother, of whome they are spiritually born, be in their tyme in rest
and quietnes. And this is the reason*, and so forth as your self
reherse. What can ye gather of this, that is sayde, that
somtyme the princes may determine of thinges touchinge
the Church: seyng as ye haue heard before, this determination toucheth not fayth or synne, nor can be vsed of them
generally, but sometymes for the quietnes of the Church?

c. Quãdo
vult Deᵒ.
23.q.4.

M. Horn. The. 148. Diuision. pag. 87. b.

If there be any other thing, this chiefly is an Ecclesiasticall
matter, namely to call or conuocate Councelles (*saith Quintinus*) But this is the opinion, *saith he*, of many learned men, that
the Emperour may conuocate a general Councel, so often, and
for any cause, whan the pope and the Cardinalles be noted of
any suspiciõ, and doo forslowe ãd ceasse, either for lacke of skil:
or peraduenture of some euil meaning, or of both, or els whan
there is any schisme. Cõstãtinus, *saith he*, called the first Nicene
coũcel, the other * three general Coũceis, Gratianus, Theodosius, and Martianus themperours called by their edict. Iustinianus called the fifte general coũcel at Cõstantinople: themperor Cõstãtine. 4. did cõuocat the sixt general Coũcel agaift the
Monothelytes. The authority of the kig Theodorike cõmaunded the Bishops ãd priestes forth of diuers prouices to assemble
together at Rome, for the purgatiõ of Pope Symachus the first.
Carolus Magnus, as it is in our histories, cõmaũded fiue Coũ-

† Howve
farre all
this is
true, it
hath at
large ben
shevved
in the se-
cõd book

cels to be celebrated for the Ecclefiaftical ftate, to wit,

The 484.vntruth.
His Author fpea-
keth not of tvvo
Councels,

Moguntinum, Remenfe, Cabilonenfe, Arelatenfe, and Turonenfe. The Pope calleth the Bifhops to Rome, or to fome other place: the King dooth forbidde them to go, or he commaundeth them to come to his Court

The king is to be obeied in (485.) Ec
clefiafticall caufes,
and not the Pope.'
The. 485. vntruthe.
Quitinus auouched
no fuche thinge.
The. 486. vntruth.
That is meant in
feudis & regalibus:
which you haue
quyte left, out of
Quintinus.

or (.484.) Councell: the Biffhoppes mufte obey the kinges precept, not onely in this cafe, but in any other matter what fo euer befides finne : for he that dooth not obferue his bounden fidelitie to the kinge: whe-ther he be a Biffhoppe, Prieft, or Deacon, is to be throwne foorth of his degree or place. *For the proufe vvhereof he citeth many Canons out of the decrees, and conclu-deth thus:* to be briefe, this is mine opinion: whan the kinge calleth together the Prelates to a Councell, and to reforme the ftate of the Church, they are bounde to obey, yea although the Pope (.486.) forbidde it.

Stapleton.

This is our olde matter of calling of Coũcels by princes: wherin you fee you authour maketh no general or abfolut rule as you doe, but for certayne tymes and confiderations: for the which I will not greatly ftande with yowe, feinge that your authour confeffeth that which we moft ftand for, and ye ftande moft againft: that the prince in fuch coũcels, hath not the fuperiority, but the cleargy. For he faith: *I vvil*

Intereffe
tamẽ volo
reges tan-
tũ & non
praeffe, ta
libus facer
dotum cõ-
uentibus.

that princes be prefent at fuch Councelles, but not prefident. And therfor Quintinus wil not be aduocat, for the bifhops, that by their priefthod promifed, that they woulde enacte nothing in their fynodes without the kings confente. Yet haue ye one prety knacke more in Quintinus to proue the king fupreame head, and not the pope. For if the kinge on the one fyde, and the pope on the other fide call the bif-fhops to a Councell, the Biffhoppes mufte obey the kinge, and not the pope: *and not onely in this thinge, but in all*
other

other thinges whatſoeuer *beſide ſynne*. Happie is it, that
ye haue putte in, *beſide ſynne*: for this putteth you quite
beſide your cuſhion, as they ſay, and beſide your matter
and purpoſe. For this is ſynne, yea and one of the moſte
horrible kindes of ſynne, that is a ſchiſme, for any prince or
anie other to holde a councell, contrary to the councell
ſummoned by a lawfull Pope. Such neuer had anie good
ſucceſſe as the eccleſiaſticall ſtories euery where reporte.
And as Aarons rodde deuoured the roddes of Iamnes and
Mambres, and other ſorcerers in Aegipte : and as his rodde
onely among all the roddes of the ſchiſmaticall and mur-
muringe people of Iſraell, did geue forth yong ſlippes, and
braunches: and for a memoriall was reſerued in the tabernacle: Euen ſo, thoſe councells, that the pope gathered or
allowed, haue deuoured and aboliſhed all other vnlawful
and ſchiſmaticall conuenticles. They onely floriſh, and be
in eſtimation, and are and ſhalbe for euer preſerued in the
tabernacle of Chriſtes Catholyke Churhe.

Num.17.

*Al ſchiſ-
maticall
coūcels ar
fayne at
the lēgth
to yelde
to the po-
pes coū-
cells.*

I will not walke in the largfelde of this matter that here
lieth open: The Frenche kinges doinges onely, whereof ye
talke, ſhall be a ſufficiente confirmation for our ſide, and
ſuch ſtories onely as your ſelf haue browght forth for the
ſtrēgthnīg as ye thought, of your purpoſe: As the coūcel of
Rhemes that the kīg Hugo Capet aſſembled depoſing ther,
as ye write, the biſhop Arnulphus. What was the iſſue M.
Horn? Did not Benedictus the.7.ſummone an other coūcel
euē in the very ſame city, ād reſtored Arnulph⁹ again? Was
not al, that your ſayre kīg Philip attēpted agaīſt the pope Bo
nifaci⁹ in his coūcels in Frāce brought to naught by a coūcel
ſūmoned by the Pope as we haue before declared? we haue
alſo ſhewed how that the Laterā councell aboliſhed the Pi-

*Fol. 70.
Io. Mari⁹
de ſchiſin.
& concil.
differ.par.
2.cap.6.*

bbb ij   ſane

fane conuenticle, that Lewes the Frenche king, and others maynteyned as your felf write. Wherfore yf your authour had thus writen, neither his tyme is fo auncient, nor his authoritie fo great, but that a man might haue fayde, that he was wonderfully deceyued. But it is not he, but you that with your falfe fleight and craftie coueiance deceyue your readers. Your authour fpeaketh not, of two councells, the one fummoned by the pope, the other by the king: but fpea keth of bifhops, that held by fealty and homage lands of the king. And then fayth, that *quoad feuda & regalia:* concernig

Idē Quin-
tinus, Ari
ftocrat.fo.
135.Parif.
1552.
Quatenus
ad feuda
& rega-
lia per-
tinet, per
glofam ca.
reprehen-
fibile.23.
qu. 8.

theis fealties and royalties, the king is aboue the bifhops, as he is aboue all his other vaffals. And therfore if the pope on the one fide, fend for a bifhoppe, and the kinge on the other fide, fend for him: concerning his fealty and homage matters, he ought to goe to the king: otherwife he fhoulde rather obey the pope the the king, as appereth (fayth Quintine) in the glofe, to the which he referreth hym felf. Theis wordes *feuda and regalia,* haue ye fliely flipt ouer, as though Quintinus had auouched the bifhops fubiectiō in Ecclefiaftical matters. You could not otherwife haue decked your margent, with your gay and frefhe lying note: *that the king is to be obeyed in Ecclefiaftical caufes, and not the Pope.* And fo are ye now fodainly become fo fpiritual and fo good an ecclefiaftical man, that *feuda and regalia:* are become matters ecclefiaftical. Which is as true, as ye may be rightfully called an ecclefiaftical man, hauing a Madge of your owne to kepe your back warme in the cold winter nightes: and by as good reafon ye may cal her an ecclefiaftical woman to.

M. Horne
leaueth
out that
vvhich
ferueth
for the
opening
of the
vvhole
matter.

M. *Horn. The.* 149. *Diuifion. pag.* 88. *a.*

The people doth amende or reforme the negligence of the Paftour *Can. vlt. dift.* 65. Ergo, the Prince alfo may do the fame.

If the

If the Bifshop wil not,or doe forflovve to heare and to decide
the controuerfies of his Cleargy : the Bifshop being flowe or
tarying ouer longe , nothing dooth hinder or ftay (faith the
Canon)to afke *Epifcopale Iudicium*,the bifshoply iudgement of
the Emperour. If it happen that the Priefts be not diligent a-
bout the Aultar offices:if concerning the temple , neglecting
the Sacrifices,they haften into kings palayces,runne to wraft-
linge places,doe prophane them felues in brothelles houfes,
and yf they conuert that which the faithful haue offred,to
the pleafures of them felues,and of theirs:wherefore fhal not
the Princes, whome the Catholique Faith hath begotten , and taught in the bofome of the Church,cal
againe,and take vpon thē felues the care of this matter? *and fo proueth at large by many examples out of the Hifto-*
ries,and the Lavves,that this care and charge in Ecclefiafticall
(.487.)matters and caufes belongeth to the Princes , vnto the
vvhich examples,he addeth this: In our Fathers tyme (*faith*
he)Kinge Lewes . 11.made a conftitution,that Archebifshoppes,Bifshops,Abbottes,and who fo euer hadde
dignities in the Church,or had the cure of other benefices, fhould within fiue monethes ,reforte to their
Churches,and fhould not remoue any more frō théfe,
diligently there labouring in diuine matters, and facrifices for the faulfty of the king and his kingdome,
and that vnder a great paine of lofing all their goods
and lands.Here Quintinus *doth greuoufly complain of the*
*diffolute and mofte * corrupt maners of the Cleargy , vvhereto he*
addeth,faying: VVherefore than f hould not Princes cōpell this lewde idle kinde of men to do their dueties?

The.487. vntruth.
This chardge is
not in Ecclefiafti-
cal matters,but a-
boute Ecclefiafti-
cal perfons in tem-
poral matters,as
for external order
to be kept, and in
execution of the
ChurchCanons ,
requiringe the Pri-
ces ayde &c.

*VVho more cor-
rupt,then your
nevve Clergy now
of handycraft Mi-
nifters?

Stapleton.

May the people M.Horne amende and reforme the negligence of the paftour? And that by the Popes Lawe to?
Then belyke the headleffe people of Germany , and your

M.Horns
impertia
nent alle-
gations.

headleffe

headleſſe bretherne that of late haue made ſuch ruffle , in
theſe lowe countres here, ſhal finde ſome good defence for
their doings, to ſaue the reaſt from the gybet or from the
ſacke, which haue not yet paſſed that way . Then may yt
ſeme a ſmal matter that the laye people haue by a late Acte
of parliamente transformed and altered the olde relligion
againſt the minde of all the Biſhops and the whole conuocation. But your authour ſaieth . *Ecclesiæ nihil est licentius,*
Democratia. There is in the worlde , nothing more perni-
ciouſe to the Church of God, then is ſuch vnbrideled liber-

Dist . 62.
Docendus. tie of the people, which *must be taught and not followed*: as he
alleageth out of Pope Celeſtin, ãd that but two diſtinctiõs,
before that diſtinction, which your ſelf alleage . And what
great reformation is it M. Horn, that your diſtinction ſpeaketh of ? Suerly none other, but that, *yf it chaunce all the biſ-*

Dist. 65.
Si forte. *ſhops of one contrie to die, ſauing one, and yf he be negligent in*
procuring the electiõ and ſubstitutiõ of ſome other in their pla-
ces, that the people may goe to the biſshops of the contrey next
adioyning, and cauſe them to ordeine ſome new biſshops . We
are alſo content, that yf the biſhops or others be negligent,
the prince may compell them to doe their dewty. But then
loke wel to your ſelf. For who is more *negligent about the*
Aultars, and worthy to be puniſhed therfore, thē they that

Howe
handſome-
ly M. Hl.
pleadeth
againſt
him ſelfe . throwe downe Aultars? Who *neglect the ſacrifices* but yow
that deny the ſacrifice and the preſence of Chriſt in the Sacramēt? Who be thoſe but you and your fellowes, that *cõ-*
uerte to the pleaſures of thē ſelues and theires, that which the
faithful hath offred to Chriſt in laying out the Church goods
vpõ your ſelf, which ſhould haue no parte of thē, being become by your mariage a laye man: and in the mainteyninge
ãd purchaſing for your vnlawful wyues childrē? Now who
                                                                be thei

be they that prophane the selues in brothel howses,let the
old constitutions of the Churche tel vs. A man would-litle
think,that ye would euer haue pleaded so agaīst your own
self.But what can you bring,(I would fayne know,)that is
not against you,in so badde a cause?

M. Horne. The. 150. Diuision. pag. 88. b.

If you delight in antiquites (saith he)no man doth doubt,but
that in the primatiue Church,the Princes did iudge both of the
Ecclesiasticall persones and causes:and did oftentimes make
good Lawes for the trueth against falsehood.Arcadius ād Honorius religious Princes doe(.488.) depose a troublesome Bisshop both from his Bishoprik,sea,and name.The.13.first titles
of the first booke of Iustiniās Code,collected out of the Cōstitutiōs of diuers Emperours,doe plainly intreate and iudge of
those things which appertain to the Bishoply cure. For what
perteineth more to the office of a Bishop,than Faith? the Baptism?then the high Trinity?than the conuersation of Mōkes?
the ordeining of Clergymen and Bishops?and than many like
lawes,which doubtles doe concerne our Religiō,ād Church.
But the Nouel Constitutions of themperour Iustinian are full
of such Lavves. And least peraduenture some man might suspect,that this vvas tyranny, or the oppression of the Churche,
Iohn the Pope doth salute this Emperor,the most Clemēt Son
learned in the Ecclesiastical disciplines,and the most Christiā
amōgest Princes. Epist.inter claras. De summa Trin. C. Childebertus
the King of Frāce,did(.489.)exact of Pelagius.2.the cōfession
of his faith and religion:the which the Pope both speedely ād
willingly did perfourme C. Sat agendum. 25.q.1. V.Vhan I was in
Calabria, saith Quintinus, by chaunce I founde a fragment of a
certain booke in Lombardye letters,hauinge this inscription:
Capitula Caroli. Then followeth an epistle beginning thus : I
Charles by the grace of God,and of his mercy ,the Kinge and
gouernour of the kingdom of Fraunce,a deuout defendour of
Goddes holy Churche , and humble healper thereof.

To al the

L. Quicū-
que:de E-
pis.et Cler.
The. 488.
vntruthe.
The place
alleaged
shevveth
of no bis-
shops de-
posed by
these Em-
perours.

The. 489.
vntruthe.
The King
did not
exact any
thing.

To al the orders of the Ecclefiaftical power, or the dignities of the fecular power: greeting: *And fo reciteth all thofe Ecclefiafticall Lavves and conftitutions, vvhich I haue vvriten before in Charles the great.* To al which (faith *Quintinus*) as it were in maner of a conclufiō, are thefe woordes put to: I will compell al men to liue accordinge to the Canons and rules of the Fathers. Lewes the Emperour, this Charles Sonne, kept a Synode wherein he forbadde all Churchmen, fumptuoufnes or exceffe in apparaile, vanities of Ievvels, and ouermuch pompe. Anno Chrifti. 830. He alfo fet forth a booke, touching the maner and order of liuing for the Churchmen. I doubt not, (faith *Quintinus*) but the Church fhould vfe, and fhould be bounde to fuch lawes.

The. 490. vntruth. He meaneth not fo, but fuch as being made in former Canons, the Princes confirm ād promulge by their lavves alfo.

(*meaning, as Princes* (.490.) *make in Ecclefiaftical matters*) Pope Leo. 3. (*faith he*) being accufed by Campulus and Pafchalis, did purge himfelt before Charles the great, being at Rome, and as yet not Emperour. *Can. Auditū. 2.q.4.* Leo. 4. offereth him felfe to be rēfourmed or amended, if he haue done any thing amiffe by the iudgement of Lewes the Frenche Kinge, being Emperour. *Can. Nos ft incompetenter. 2.q.7.*

The. 491. vntruth. For concealinge, vvho commaunded him, vvhich vvas the Pope him felfe.

Menna whom Gregory the great calleth mofte reuerende brother and fellow Bifhop, beíg now already purged before Gregory, is (.491.) cōmaunded a frefhe to purge himfelf of the crime obiected, before Bruchinīld the Queene of Fraunce *Ca. Menna. 2.q.4.* In which queftion alfo it is

The. 492. vntruth. This is not in Quitinus. printed at Lyons, An 1549.

red, that Pope Sixtus. 3. did purge himfelfe before the Emperour Valentinian. *Can. Mandaftis.* So (.492.) alfo Iohn. 22. Bifshop of Rome was compelled by meanes of the Diuines of Paris, to recante before the Frenche King Philippe, not vvithout triumphe, the vvhich Io.

The Pope an (493) heretik compelled to recante before the French King. The. 493. vntruthe Slaunderous.

Gerfon telleth in a Sermon. *De Pafc. The Popes Herefy vvas, that* he thought, the Chriftian Soules not to be receiued into glory before the refurrection of the Bodies. Crefconius a noble man in Sicilia, had authoritie or povver geuen him of Pelagius the Pope, ouer the
Bifshops

Bifhoppes in that Prouince, oppreſsing the Cleargie with ve
xations. Can. illud. 10. q. 3. The whiche Canon of the law, the
Gloſſar doth interprete to be writé to a ſecular Prince, in Ca.
Clericũ nullus. 11. q. 5. The Abbottes, Biſhoppes, and the Popes
them ſelues, in ſome time paſte, were choſen by the Kinges
prouiſion. Cap. Adrianus. 63. diſt. And in the ſame Canõ. Hinc
eſt etiam. 16. q. 1. Gregorius wrote vnto the Dukes Rodolph,
and Bertulph, that they ſhoude in no wiſe receiue prieſtes
defiled with whoredome or Symony, but that they ſhould forbidde thẽ frõ the holy Miniſteries. § Verum. 32. diſt. in whiche
place the interpretours doo note, that Laimen ſometimes may
ſuſpende Cleargymen from their office, by the Popes cõmaũn-
dement: yea alſo they may excõmunicate, whiche is worthy
of memory. *Hytherto Quintinus a learned lavvier and a great main*
teinour of the Popes iuriſdiction, hath declared his opinion, and that agrea-
ble to the Popes ovvne Lavves, that Princes may take vppon them to go-
uerne in Eccleſiaſtical (.495.) matters or cauſes.

Stapleton.

All this proceſſe following tendeth to proue, that princes haue a gouernemente in cauſes and matters eccleſiaſtical. We might perchaũnce ſtande with M. Horne for
the worde gouernemente, which I ſuppoſe can not be iuſtified by any thing he ſhall bringe forthe, but we wil not.
For we nede not greatly ſticke with him for the terme, we
wil rather conſider the thing yt ſelf. Firſt then ye enter M.
Horne with an vntruth, or two. For properly to ſpeake,
neither were any princes, that you here reheiſe, iudges in
cauſes eccleſiaſtical, thowgh they had therein a certain intermedling: neither dothe the lawe ye ſpeake of, tel of any
Biſhoppes depoſed by the Emperours *Arcadius* and *Ho-*
norius: but this, onely that if any Biſhop be depoſed by his
fellowe Biſhoppes, aſſembled together in councell, howe
he ſhalbe ordered, yf he be fownde afterwarde to attempte

any

the 494.
vntruth.
greate,
in falſe
reaſonig.
For none
of al theſe
examples
do proue
the popes
Primacy.
The 495.
vt. truth.
That hath
not bene
proued,
out of
Quintin⁹
in ſuch
ſece as the
Acte at-
tributeth
to the
Prince.
L. quicun
que de E-
piſcopis
et clericis.
Quicũque
reſidetibus
ſacerdotĩ-
bus, fuerit
epiſcopali
loco & no
mine de-
truſus, ſi
aliquid
cõtra quie
tẽ publicã
moliri&c.

Quin-
tinus.
Dicta ep.
inter cla
ras de sū-
ma Trini-
nitate.
Vt nō ve-
stra inno-
tescat san-
ctitati,
quia ca-
put est
omnium
sanctarum
ecclesiarū.
Dict.ca.
Sat agēdū
2 j.q.1.
Sat agēstū
est, vt pro
auferendo
suspicionis
scandalo.
Cōsidēter
à nobis po
stulauit
(vtdecuit)
quatenus.
&c.
Dict.c.
Nos si in-
competen-
ter.2.q.7.
& ibi in
glos.

anie thing againſt the common wealth. Concerning the
doeinges of the Emperour Iuſtinian in matters eccleſiaſticall: we haue ſpoken at large alredie. And if he were, as
ye terme him moſte Chriſtian amongeſt princes, and learned in the eccleſiaſtical diſciplines: why doe you not belieue him calling Pope Iohn, that ye here ſpeake of, *heade
of the Churche*, and that in the verie place by you alleaged?
What gouernance in matters eccleſiaſticall, I praye you
was it in Kinge Childebertus, if Pope Pelagius, to auoyde
ſlaunder, and ſuſpicion, that he ſhould not thinke wel of the
Chalcedon Councell, ſent to the ſaied King at his requeſte
the tenoure of his faythe and beliefe? Therefore you doe
abuſe your Reader, and abuſe alſo the woorde., *exacte:*
whiche ſignifieth to conſtraine or compel. And that dyd
not the Kinge, but only dyd require or demaunde. Touching the Emperour Charles, it is. I ſuppoſe ſufficiently anſwered alredye. And if nothing were anſwered, that
youre ſelfe nowe alleage maie ſerue for a good anſwere.
For he maketh no newe rules or Conſtitutions in Churche matters, but eſtabliſſheth and reneweth the olde,
and ſaieth: *He wil compell all men to lyue according to the
rules and Canons of the Fathers.* Neither doothe he call
him ſelfe heade or Gouernoure of the Churche, but *a deuoute defender, and an humble helper.* But when he ſpeaketh of his worldlie kingdome, he calleth him ſelfe, *the gó-
uernour of the kingdome of Fraunce* We nede now anſwere
no further for Lewys the Emperour, Charles the great his
ſonne, then we haue already anſwered: neither touching
Leo the.3. Yf ye ſay, that the Emperour was iudge in the
cauſe of Leo the 4. I graunt you, but not by any ordinarie
authoritie, but becauſe he ſubmitted him ſelfe and his cauſe

to the Emperours iudgemét, as it appereth by his own text
and the glofe.   And it is a rule of the Ciuill Lawe, that yf
any man of higher Authority, wil fubmit him felfe and his
caufe to his inferior, that in fuch a cafe he may be his iudge.

But now at length, it femeth you haue found a laie perfon, yea a woman, head of the Churche: and that a reuerend Bifhop was cómaunded to purge him felf before her.
Whie doe ye not tel vs alfo who cómaunded him?
It was not Brunichildis the Frenche Queene, but
Pope Gregorie that cómaunded him. And when, I
pray you? Surely when he had purged him felf before at Rome, before Pope Gregory. And why was
he, I pray you, fent to the Queene?   Surely for no
great nede, but for to caufe his innocencie, to be
more euidently and clerely knowen. Here by the
waie, I woulde afke M. Horne, what authoritie
Gregorie had to call this French Bifhop to Rome?
Hath he not trow ye, by his owne example, proued the Popes Primacy? And hath he not done the
like in the matter of Pope Sixtus? Verely his text
faieth: *that the Councell which the Emperour Valen-*
tinian commaunded to be holden, and before the whi-
che the Pope Sixtus purged him felfe, was affembled
by the faied Pope Sixtus authoritie, and that he nea-
ded not to haue made his purgation, but made it vo-
luntarilye to auoyde fufpition, not binding his fuccef-
fours to followe this exaumple, but to be free and at
their owne libertie.   But this matter I leaue to be
handeld more at large by Maifter Dorman againft
Maifter Nowell, who maketh (to his feming) gaie
fporte therewith.

ccc ij   Then

Heduus.

Lib.14.
Eft recep-
tum, &c.
ff. de iurif-
dic. omniú
iudicum.

Caufa.2.queft.4.
cap. Mennam.

Reuerti illum, pur-
gatum abfolutúque
permifimus.

Vide marginalé glo-
fam ibidem.

Dict.c.mandaftis.
ibidem.

Quod audiens Valé-
tinianus Augustus
noftra authoritate
Synodum congregari
iufsit: & mox Li-
cet euadere aliter
fatis potuiffem, fufpi
tionem tamen fugiés
coram omribus me
purgaui. Sed non
alijs qui noluerint,
aut fponte hoc non
elegerint, faciendi
formam dans.

*In exem-
plar. Lug-
dun. An,
1549. in
volum. 14.*

A groffe
errour of
M. Iewel
pag 275.

Then followeth in M. Horne the recantation of Pope
Iohn wherof his Author Quintinus fpeaketh neuer a word,
and yet is it here placed in the midle of Quintinus matters,
and in a diftinct letter. And this patche as it difclofeth the
groffe errour of the Englifh Apologie, and of M. Iewell in
his Replie imputing to this Pope, *that he denied the immortalitie of fowles* : fo it proueth nothing in the world the laye
Princes primacie, no nor any herefie in Pope Iohn neither.
For if he mainteined any fuch errour, it was before he was
Pope. And in cafe he thought fo after he was auaunced
to the See Apoftolicall (which can not be proued) yet he
did not cōmaūd yt to be publikly beleued, by any definitiue
fentence or open decree. And therfore as gaily as ye haue
garnifhed your margent : with *the Pope an Heretique compelled to recant before the French King,* neither you, nor your
Apologie, nor M. Iewel, fhall take any greate woorfhippe
thereby : but you muft all three (if M. Iewell and the Authour of the Apologie be two) recante, as well as he, and
beare him companie. The Apologie and M. Iewel, for flaū-
dering him with a wrong and a farre more grieuous error,
then he euer helde. You, as well for reporting this out of
Quintinus (who faieth it not) as for your impertinent and
foolifh plea, pleading thereby for your new fecular primacie. Which wil as well follow of this ftorie, as it is true
that Pope Iohn denied the immortalitie of foules. The refidue that followeth, partly we haue anfwered, as touching
Cap. Adrianus. 63. Diftinct. Partly it may be anfwered in few
wordes : and that is, that it maketh al directly for the Popes
Primacie, as from whom the laie men that M. Horne fpeaketh of, had al their authority, as appereth by his own exāples. If he would haue proued any thing cōcludingly for his
purpofe,

purpofe,he fhould haue concluded,that the Pope tooke his
authoritie of the laie men. Now prouing the contrarye him
felfe, he miniftreth good matter againft him felfe.

M. Horne. The.151.Diuifion. pag. 89 b.

Befydes thefe Lavviers, this vvas the common opinion of the chiefeft vvri-
ters of the common Lavv of this realme,as appeareth(.496.) by Braughtonin
thefe vvoordes : Sunt & fub rege &c. Vnder the King are bothe
free men and bondemen,and they be fubiect to his power and
are all vnder him,and he is a certaine thing or creature that is
vnder none but onely vnder God. *And againe in the Chapiter the*
title vvhereof is this. Rex non habet parem, &c. The King hath
no peere or equall in his Kingdome : The King *(faith he)*in his
Kingdom hath no equall, for fo might he lofe his precepte or
authoritie of commaunding,fithe that an equall hathe no rule
or commaundement ouer his equall : as for the King himfelfe
ought not to be vnder man,but vnder God,and vnder the law,
becaufe the Law maketh a King. Let the King therefore attribute that vnto the Lawe,that the Lawe attributeth vnto him,
to wit, dominion and power. For he is not a King in whom
will and not the law doth rule, and that he ought to be vnder
the Law, Cùm fit Dei Vicarius, fith he is the Vicare of God,
it appeareth euidently by the likenes of Iefu Chrifte, whofe
vicegerent he is in earth : *and vvithin a litle after he concludeth thus:*
Igitur non debet maior effe eo in regno fuo (.497.) Therfore
there ought to be none greater then he in his kingdome.

Braughtö
lib. 1. cap.
de Papa.
Archiepif-
copis & a-
lijs prælat.
The 496.
vntruth.
The con-
trary ap-
peareth
plainely
by Brau-
ghton,as
it fhalbe
declared.
The 487.
vntruth.
A parte of
the fen-
tence ope
ning,and
anfvver-
ing the
vvhole
obiection
nipped
quite of.

The.40.Chapter. Concerning Braughton, Maifter
Hornes laft Authour.

Stapleton.

HAppie is it, that M. Horne writeth in Englifh, and to
Englifh men, and not in Latine. For furelye as oure
Countrie hath fhutte out the Popes authoritie , yea
and

ād al maner of ecclefiaftical authority, that it fhal not paſſe
the Ocean ſea towarde it: So may al other nations muche
better exclude the authority of a temporall lawyer of our
realme that it paſſe not the ſayde Ocean ſea toward them.
But becauſe our Chriſtian belief(the more pity)is become
of late nothing elſe but a Parliamēt matter, and a matter of
commō lawe: and ſeing we haue eſtraunged our ſelf from
the olde cōmon catholike faith into a late vpſtart, and into
a priuate and national fayth of our owne, and yet for ſome
colour wil pretend, it was at leaſt the aunciente faythe of
this realme, I wil make none exceptiō againſte M. Hornes
plea, but wil ioyne iſſue, and cope with him euen with our
own lawe, and with his owne authour. And that M Horne
fhall not ſay I deale with him hardly and pinchingly, but
freely and liberally : I do here offer to be tried, not by the
Pope (for feare of a premunire) but by the Iudges of the
kinges benche: and by al other the Quenes May . Iudges,
yea by all the lawyers of the realme to, that by the cōmon
lawe of the realme in Braughtonstime the king was not taken for the head of the Churche, but the Pope. And if M.
Horne may proue the contrary to my aſſertiō, by Braughton , then dare I offerre in M. Fekenhams name, that he
fhal take the othe: and if he wil not, I, for my ſelf dare promiſe ſo much, ād wil performe it: and fhalbe cōntēte withal , that M. Horne for this his highe inuentiō, fhal be made
ſergeant of the quoif alſo. Why ſaieth Mayſter Horn, what
meane you to ſay ſo? Do not I plainly alleage by Braughton his wordes , *that the kinge is vnder none , but onely vn-*
der God? That the kinge hath no peere or equall? That there
ought to be none greater in his kingdome then the kinge?
Yea to conclude, *that he is the Vicar of God?* Are not theſe

Braughtons wordes? Do I mifreherfe them, fayeth Mayfter Horne? And what will ye haue then more, will he
faie? Forfoth Mayfter Horne we loke for, but three litle
wordes more that is,that ye proue vs owt of Brawghton,
that the kinge is the greateft in his realme, and the Vicar of
all, not in matters cyuill, which we willinglye graunte
you, but for matters ecclefiafticall. Wherof ye haue not
yet owte of Braughton browght fo much as one worde.
And fo haue you for all this ioly fetche,fetched in nothing
to your purpofe, but haue fifhed all this while in Braughton all in vayne.   Yet is there one thing more we loke
for, that is,to haue an honefter man, and of better, and
more vppright dealing and confcience, then ye are of, to
reporte Braughton And then we haue fome hope, that as
you can proue nothing by him,for your new primacie: So
fhall we proue euen by your owne authour, that by the
common lawe of the realme, the Pope was then the cheif
head of all Chriftes Churche. And me thincke, thowghe
in your texte there is nothing but the duskifhe, darke,
hornelight of an vnfaythfull and blinde allegation, that
yet in your margent,there appereth a gliftering day ftarre,
and that the fonne is at hande to open and difclofe to the
worlde by the bright beames and moft cleare light of the
catholyque faythe, fhyning in youre owne Authoure,ei-
ther your exceding malice, or your moft palpable groffe,
and darke ignorance. Wherewith for your defertes and
fpitiful heart to the catholyke faith, God hath plagued you
no leffe then he did the Aegiptians. Why M. Horne? Hath
Braughtō thē a Title *de Papa, Archiepifcopis,& alijs prelatis:*
of the Pope, Archbifhops and other prelats What? Is there
nothing in him but a bare and naked title? What fayeth
Braugh-

Hovv
vvret-
chedlie
M.Horne
alleageth
braung-
ton.

Braughton in his text ? Doth he fay that the Pope hath nothing to doe, but in his owne diocefe, and no more than o-
ther Bilhoppes haue? Doth he fay, that he is not the head,
and the fuperiour of al other Bilhopes? Or doth he fay, as
ye faie, that all Ecclefiafticall iurifdiction commeth from
the King only? Or doth he fay, that the Kinge is aboue the
the Pope, and head of the Churche him felfe ? Wel . Ye
haue feene the ftarre light in the margent : Nowe fhall ye
see alfo, to the vtter deftruction of your newe primacie,
and to your great difhoneftie, for this your deteftable dealing, the bright daye light. Ye tel vs out of Braughton, that
al , *afwel freemen as bondmen , are fubiecte to the Kinge his*
power. You tel vs , *the King hath no Peere:* what of all this?
Tel me withall for what the title of the Pope and Arche-
bilhope ferueth? Verely it ferueth to direct vs to your own
confufion and fhame. Ye tolde vs euen in the other page of
this leafe, that Kinge Childebertus exacted of Pope Pelagius the confefsion of his faith, whiche he voluntarily offered. But fuerly the cōfefsiō of this matter, wil not come frō
you freely and voluntarily, but it muft be exacted from you,
and brought from you by the verie violence of the mofte
ftronge and forcible truth . Let vs then heare Braughtons
owne wordes. He faieth: *There is a difference and diftinctiō*
betwen perfon and perfon. For fome there are, that be in excel-
lencie and prelacie, and be rulers aboue other. As in fpirituall
matters and thofe that appertaine to priefthood, our Lorde the
Pope, and vnder him Archebifhopes , and Bifhopes , and other
inferiour Prelates . In temporall matters alfo Emperours,
Kinges , and Princes, for fuche thinges as apperteine to the
kingdom: and vnder them Dukes, Erles, Barons and fuch other.
    Againe he writeth thus in an other place : *Sunt enim*
                                       caufæ

ght̃o.

Eodē libro

cauſe ſpirituales &c . There are, ſaieth he, ſpiritual cauſes, *in
the which the ſeculer iugde hath no cognition, neither can put
them to execution, becauſe he hath no puniſhement for them.
For in theſe cauſes , the iudgement apperteyneth to the eccleſiaſtical iudges who hath the gouernance and defence of prieſthoode. There be alſo Secular cauſes , the knowledge and
iudgemente whereof apperteyneth to Kinges and Princes,
who defende the Kingdome , and with the whiche the Clergie ſhoulde not intermedle: ſeeing that the iuriſdictions of them
are ſondred and diſtincted: vnleſſe yt be when one ſworde
muſte helpe the other .* I truſte by this Maiſter Horne ye
doe, or may vnderſtand, what is meante, when Braughton
calleth the Kinge , the Vicar of God : and ſaieth , there
ought to be none greater then the Kinge in his kingdome.
Whiche rule woulde haue bene playner, if ye had added
the three woordes following : *In exhibitione iuris .* That
is, in miniſtring of euerie man ryght and iuſtice : whiche is
altogether miniſtred in mere prophane and ciuill matters
vnder and by the Kinges Authoritie, and whiche woordes
are by you nipped quite of verie miniſterlyke. We will
yet adde the third Authoritie out of Braughton, becauſe it
doeth not onely make againſte this newe vpſtarte Supremacie, but aunſwereth alſo as well to the olde Cugnerius,
as to our newe Cugnerius (M . Horne) his fonde argumentes againſt the ſpirituall iuriſction.

*Ergo non
debet ma-
ior eſſe in
regno ſuo
in exhibi-
tione iuris.*

　　Braughton then after that he hath ſhewed , that there is
one iuriſdiction , that is called ordinarie , and an other of
delegates, and holding by commiſsion, and that as well in
the temporall as ſpirituall Courte: and that theſe two iuriſdictions be diſtincted, and that the Iudges of eche ſorte,
ſhoulde take heed , that they doe not intrude vppon the

Libro 4.

　　　　　　　　　ddd　　　　other

Matters apperteiz
ning to
the fpiriz
tual iurifz
diction.

other: he telleth vs of fome particularities, of matters apperteyning to the Churche Iurifdiction. Firft that none of
the clergy may be called before a fecular iudge, for anie
matter towching the ecclefiafticall courte, or for any fpirituall matter, or fuche as be annexed and coherent. As
when penance is to be enioyned for any finne or trefpafe,
wherin the ecclefiaftical Iudge hath the cognitiō, and not
the kinge: for it doth not apperteine to the king or to the
temporall Iudge to enioyne penaunce. Neither can they
iudge of matters coherent and annexed to fpiritual things:
as of tithes and fuche other: as, concerning mouables be-
quethed in a mans teftament, nor in a caufe of matrimony.
Nor if a mā promife mony for mariage as (he faith) he hath
before declared. For in altheis things the clerke may bring
the caufe frō the tēporal to the ecclefiaftical Iudge. And fo
haue we found M. Horne by the common lawe in Braughtons time the Popes fupreamacy in Englande, and not that
onely, but alfo, that afwel Braughton as Quintinus be hard
againft you and your Petrus Cugnerius for the minifhing
and defacing of the fpiritual iurifdiction: and for your vntruth in auowching that the medling with contractes of
mariages, enioyning of penaūce, and fuche like, are nothing
but temporal matters perteining to the kinges iurifdiction.
And thus in fine, to be fhorte, where your proufes fhould
be ftrongeft, there are they moft acrafed and feble: ād your
fowre lawyers, with your Diuine, proue nothing to your
purpofe, but al againft yt.

Braughz
ton and
Quintin⁹
be againft
Petrus
Cugneriz
us that
M. Horne
before al-
leaged,
Prius
fol.82.

The.498.
vntruth.
You haue
proued
nothing
leffe.

M. Horne. The.152.Diuifion.pag.90.4.

Thus haue I fufficiently (.498.) proued, that the Emperours and Kinges,
ought, haue, and may claime, and take vpon thē fuche gouernement, in Spiritual and Ecclefiaftical caufes and matters, as the Queenes Maieftye novv
dooth.

doothe. In confirmation vvhereof I haue bene more large, than othervvife I vvoulde, but that the proufe hereof doeth reproue, and fully aunſvveare the principall matter of your vvhole booke: and therefore I maie vſe more briefneſſe in that vvhiche follovveth. I haue made proufe vnto you, (ſufficient to remoue (.499.) your ignorance, both of the matter, and the vvaie vvherby to knovve, confeſſed by you in your Minor Propoſition. And this haue I done by the ſelfeſame meanes, that you require in your iſſue. I haue made proufe of the Supreame gouernment in Eccleſiaſtical cauſes, to belong vnto Kings and Princes, by the expreſſe (.500.) cōmaundement of God, vvhere he did firſt deſcribe and ſet foorth, the duety and office of Kings. I haue made the ſame more plaine and manifeſt, by the (.501.) examples of the moſte holy gouernours amongeſt Goddes people, as Moyſes, Ioſua, Dauid, Salomon, Ioſaphat, Ezechias, Ioſias, the Kinge of Niniue, Darius, and Nabugodonoſor: vvho expreſte this to be the true meaning of God his commaundemente, by theyr practiſe hereof, ſo hyghly commended euen by the holy Ghoſt: vvhervnto I haue added certaine prophecies, forthe of Dauid and Eſaie: vvherby it is manifeſtly proued, that the holy ghoſt doth loke for, exact, and challenge, this ſeruice and (.502.) Supreme gouernment in church cauſes, at princes handes. I haue declared that the Catholike church of Chriſt, did accept, and repute theſe hiſtories of the old Teſtamēt, to be figures and prophecies, of the like gouernmēt and ſeruice, to be required of the Kinges, in the time of the nevve Teſtamēt: I haue cōfirmed the ſame by the manifeſt Scriptures, of the (.503.) nevve Teſtamēt: VVherevnto I haue adioygned the teſtimonies of (.504.) auncient Doctours, vvith certain exāples of moſt godly emperors, vvho being ſo taught by the moſt Catholik Fathers of Chriſts church, did rightly iudge, that the vigilāt care, euerſight, ād ordering of church cauſes, vvas the chiefeſt and beſt part of their miniſtery, and ſeruice vnto the Lord. I haue ſhevved plainly, by the order of ſupreame gouernmēt in church cauſes, practiſed, ſet forth, and allovved, in the greateſt and beſt Coūcels, both (.505.) General and Nationall: that the ſame order of Gouernement, hath bene claimed and put in vre by the Emperours, and allovved, and much commended by the vvhole number of the Catholike Biſhops.

ddd ij I haue

The 499. vntruthe. You haue proued nothing ſufficient to ſatiſfie M. Feckeham, or anie meane man.

The 500. Vntruthe. you haue ſhewed no ſuch commaundement.

The 501. vntruthe. None of your examples haue ſerued your turne.

The 502. vntruthe. Your prophecies haue proued no ſuch Supreme Gouernment.

The 503. vntruhe. No Scripture of the nevve Teſtament hath proued the like gouernment &c.

The 504. vntruthe. Your Auncient Doctours ſtand plaine againſte you.

The 505. vntruthe. The practiſe of all Councelles bothe Generall and Nationall hath vvitneſſed the popes, not the Princes Primacy.

The 506:
vntruth,
Ye haue
not pro-
ued the
like go-
uernemēt
by any
one king
or prince.
The.507.
Vntruth
Partiall
thei could
not be for
your part,
being the
aduersari,
vvas not
thē extāt.
The. 508.
Vntruth.
No Ca-
tholique
denieth,
but the
Pope can
lie and
fvvear to,
as bad as
any other
The.509.
Vntruth.
Most im-
pudent.
Thei haue
all depo-
sed ō our
side clene
againste
you, and
do yet to
this daie,
some of
thē stand

I haue made plaine proufe hereof, by the continuall practise of the (506.) like Ecclesiastical gouernment, claimed and vsed by the kinges and Princes, euen vntil the time that you your selfe did allovve, confesse, and preache the same many yeares togeather : All vvhiche to your more contentation here-in, I haue proued by those Hystoriographers, that vvrote not onely before the time of Martine Luther, least ye might suspecte them of partialitie a-gainst you : but also suche in dede, as vvere for the moste parte (.507.) par-tiall on your side, or rather vvholie addicte and mancipate to your holy Fa-ther : as Platina, Nauclerus, Abbas Vrspurgensis, Sabellicus, Ae-neas Syluius, Volateranus, Fabian, Polychronicon, Petrus Ber-trandus, Benno Cardinalis, Durandus, Paulus Aemilius, Mar-tinus Pœnitentiarius, Pontificale, Damasus, Polydorus Virgili-us, &c. all your friendes, and vvhome you may truste, I vvarraunte you, on their vvoorde, being the Popes svvorne Vassalles, his Chapplaines, his Cardinalles, his Chamberlaines, his Secretaries, his Librarie keepers, his Penitentiaries, his Legates, his Peterpence gatherers, his svvorne Monkes and Abbottes, as vvell as you, and some of them Popes them selues, vvhich, your friendes saie, can (.508.) neyther lie, nor erre from the truth. And besides all these, the fovver pointes of your issue, according to your re-queste, proued at large, for the better reducing of you from vvilfull and ma-licious ignoraunce, to knovve and acknovvlege the inuincible trueth hereof: I haue added to your petition, a fift pointe, vvhiche you tearme a vvoorke of Supererogation. For, to confirme my proufes vvithall, I haue produ-cted for vvitnesses, your best learned, although othervvise Papishe, Ciui-lian and Canon lavvyers, vvho haue deposed directlie on my (.509.) side againste you : Namely Doctour Tunstall, D. Stokesley, D. Gardiner, D. Bon-ner, D. Thirlbie, D. Decius, the Glossaries vppon the Lavv, D. Petrus Fer-rariensis, D. Io. Quintinus : to vvhome I mighte adde the Ciuilians and Canonistes that vvere in or tovvard the Arches in the last ende of King Henrie, and all the time of King Edvvarde, vvith all the Doctours and Proctours of or tovvardes the Arches at (.510.) this time. VVherefore you vvill novv, I trust, yealde herein, and recken your selfe vvell satisfied, take vppon you the knovvledge hereof, and to be readie to testifie the same vppon a booke othe, for so haue you promised.

The

against you. The.510.vntruth.Slaunderous to the learned of the Arches

*The conclusion of the three bookes going before, with a
briefe recapitulatiō of that which hath bene saied.*

Stapleton.

NOwe doth M. Horne blow out of his iolye Horne,
a glorioufe and triumphant blafte, to fignifie to all
the world, what a renowned cōquefte he hath made
vppon poore M. Fekenham. He fetteth forth his army to
the vewe of the worlde, wherby he fayeth he hath obteyned this famoufe victorie: furnifhed with a number of moft
holie gouernours amongeft Gods people, before the comming of Chrift, as Moyfes, Iofue, Dauid, the king of Niniue,
Darius, and Nabuchodonofor: furnifhed with the manifeft
fcriptures of the newe teftamente, and the examples of the
moft godly Emperours, with generall and nationall councelles, with the cōtinuall practife of the Churche, with the
Popes fworne vaffales, his chaplaines, his cardinalles, his
chamberlaines, his fecretaries, his librarie kepers, his penitentiaries, his legates, his peterpence gatherers, his fworne
monks and Abbattes, yea to confirme vp his proufes withal, with the teftimony of Doctour Gardiner, D. Tonftal, D.
Bonner, and D. Thirlbie. And therfore he trufteth that M.
Fekenham will nowe at length, yelde and recken hym felf
wel fatisfied, and take the othe of the fupremacy.

This is a Royall and a Triumphante conquefte in deede,
Mayfter Horne, if it be as you vaunte. But yet, I would
muche foner beleue yt, yf I hearde any indifferent man
befides your felf, fay as much. For thowghe, as I heare fay,
you coulde handle your clubbe, your buckler, and your
wafter wel and cuningly, whē ye were in Cābridge, wherof ye wil not fticke, as yt is reported, now and thē to talke,
when ye are difpofed to bragge of your yowthly partes

there played, yet to fay the truth, in this combate with M.Fekenham I fee no fuch manlines in you. Neither haue ye plaied fo clofely, but that a man may eafely reache you a rappe vppon the head, armes, or fhoulders, and caufe you there to cratche and claw with your fingers, where it ytcheth not. Yea ye are beaten quite out of the field, with your owne proufes and weapons.

And as for M. Fekhenhá ye haue not faftened vpon him as much as one blow. What fpeak I of a blowe? No not fo much as a good phillip. And therfore wheras ye fo brauely bragge, and fo triumphaütlie vaunt, that all is yours, when in dede ye haue loft al, I thinke good to put you in remembraunce of the great wife man that Atheneus writeth of: Lib.12. who as often as any fhip came to the haué with marchandize, would runne thither with al hafte, and welcome the mariners with great ioye and gratulation, reioycing excedinglie and thanking God that had fent home his Marchádize, fo fauflie, and fo profperouflie. For the poore man (fuch was his wifedome) being owner of no part, thought al to be his. I fay, it fareth euen fo with you, M. Horne. Of al the good Emperours, Kings, Fathers and Councelles by you rehearfed, crie you as much and as long as ye will, that they are al yours, yet there is not fo much as one, yours. Ye haue not brought fo muche as one authority directly or indirectly cócluding your purpofe. Els fhew me, but one of al the forefaid Authors that faieth that the Pope hath no authoritie either in England or in other countries out of Italie. Shew me one that faith either in plain words, or in equiualent, that the Prince is Supreme head in al caufes ecclefiafticall. Yea fhewe me one, that auoucheth the Prince to be the Supreme gonernour in any one caufe mere ecclefiaftical

aftical. And thinke you now in the folding vp of your conclufion, to perfwade your Readers, that yee haue them all on your fide? Or blufh you not to vaunte, that you haue proued your affertion, euen by thofe that your felfe côfeffe were wholy addicted and mancipated to the Pope? And what can more euidently defcrie and betraie your exceeding follie, and paffing impudencie, then dothe this mofte ftrange and monftrous Paradoxe? But who woulde haue thought, that of all men in the worlde, your Rhethorique would ferue you to bring in the moft Reuerend Fathers in God by you named, as good motiues to perfwade M. Fekenham to take this othe, which for the refufing of the very fame othe, were thruft out of their Bifhopricks, and caft into prifon, where yet they remaine, fuch as yet liue? This point of rhetorical perfwafion, neither Demofthenes, nor Cicero (I trow) could euer attaine vnto.

See M. Hornes maruey-lous Rhe-terique.

Seing then all your Rhetorike confifteth in lying, and your triumphant conclufiô is folded vp with a browne dofen of feueral vntruthes, allowing you thirteen to the dofen, I wil affay M. Horne with more truthe and fimplicitie, brefely to vnfolde, for the Readers better remembraunce, and for your comfort, the contentes of thefe three bookes, wherin you haue plaied the Opponêt, and haue laied forth the beft euidêces that you could, for proufe of your ftrauge and vnheard paradoxe of Princes Supreme Gouernmêt in al ecclefiaftical caufes. I haue therfore not only difproued your proufes al along frô the firft to the lafte, but I haue alfo proued the contrary, that to prieftes, not to princes appertaineth the chiefe gouernemêt in caufes Ecclefiaftical. In the firft boke, your fcripture of the Deuteronom, côman deth the king to take of the priefts, not only the boke of the

Cap.8,

Lawe,

lawe, but alſo the expoſition thereof. To your examples of
Cap.9.10. Moyſes, of Ioſue, of Dauid, of Salomõ, of Ioſaphat, of Eze-
11. 12-13. chias and of Ioſias, I haue ſo anſwered, that it hath euidẽt-
14.&15. ly appeared the Supreme gouernement in ſpiritual matters
to haue reſted in the highe Biſhops, Prieſtes, and Prophetes: not in them: Moyſes only excepted, who was a Prieſt
alſo, not only a Prince of the people. Your idle obiections
out of S. Auguſtin, and of the Donatiſtes examples, haue
nothing relieued you, but only haue bene occaſiõ to make
opẽ your extreme folly, and to reuele your couſinage with
olde heretikes to al the worlde. Your Emanuel hath vtterly ſhamed you: and your diſorderly talke of Cõſtantin hath
nothing furdered you. Your textes of the newe Teſtamẽt,
haue bene to to fondly and fooliſhly alleged, to ſet vp that
kinde of gouernemẽt which Chriſt and the Apoſtles neuer
ſpake word of. Laſt of all wheras you blindely vttered, the
ſtate of the Queſtion, as one that loued darkenes and ſhũ-
ned the light, where only Truthe is to be founde: I haue
opened the ſame more particulariy, and diſcouered withal
your double Vntruth aboute the tenour of the Othe. Thus
muche in the firſte booke, beſide many priuat matters betwene M. Feckenham and you: wherein you haue bene
taken in manifeſt forgeryes, lyes and ſlaunders. Beſides alſo
a Note of your bretherneſ obediẽce to their Supreme Go-
Cap. 3. uernours as well in other Countres as iñ theſe lowe Coũ-
Fol.16.b. tres, here, and of their late good rule kept, of which I ſuppoſe, bothe you and your cauſe ſhall take ſmall reliefe and
leſſe honeſty.

In the ſecond booke I haue not only diſproued all your
pretenſed proufes of Princes ſupreme gouerment in al cauſes eccleſiaſticall, but I haue in them all directtly proued
the

the popes primacy withall. I haue I fay fhewed the practife of the former. 600. yeres, namely from Conſtantin the great downe to Phocas, to ſtande clerely for the popes primacy, I haue fhewed that Conſtantin in all his dealinges in the Nicene Councell againſt the Donatiſtes, in the matter of Athanaſius, with the Arrian biſhoppes, and with Arrius him felfe, neuer practiſed this Supreme Gouuernement, which you fo fondly vpholde: but in al matters Eccleſiaſticall yelded the gouuernement thereof vnto Biſhops.

I haue fhewed, that the Sonnes of Conſtantin the greate practiſed no Supreme gouernement at al in any eccleſiaſtical cauſe, much leſſe in al cauſes.

Your next example Valentinian the elder, is fo farre frō al gouernement of the lay prince in Eccleſiaſticall cauſes, that he decreed the plaine contrary, yea and made it lawful in ciuill matters to appeale to the biſhoply Iudgement.

Theodoſi⁹ the great hath bene proued to be no fitte ex- ample of your lay ſupremacy in cauſes eccleſiaſtical: But in his exāple the Popes Primacy is clerly proued, namely by a Recōciliation made of Flauianus the intruded patriarche of Antioche to pope Damaſus, ād alſo by the letters of the Ge neral Councell holden at Cōſtantinople vnder this Theodoſius. In that place alſo I haue fhewed by ten ſeueral articles, what and howe farre Emperours may and haue dealed in General Councelles.

In the examples of Archadius and Honorius, ſonnes to this Theodoſius, as their pretēded Primacy is proued to be none, ſo the primacy of Innocentius, thē pope, is clerly pro- ued, as one that for the iniuſt depoſitiō of Iohn Chriſoſtom excōmunicated themperor Archadius, the vpholder therof. Alſo of Damaſus then pope, by the ſuyte of S. Hierom,

e e e   made

made vnto him.

Cap.9. fo, 127.&·fe. In the example of Theodofius the fecōd, and the practife of the Ephefine Coūcel the third General, M. Hornes purpofe is ouerthrowē, and the popes primacy is by clere practife teftified, as well by the faied Councell, as alfo by M. Horns owne Authours, Liberatus and Cyrillus.

Cap. 10. The doinges in the caufe of Eutyches, brought forth, by M. Horne to proue the princes Supreme gouernment in al Ecclefiafticall caufes, do proue clerely the popes primacy, euen in the very Author and chapter by maifter Horne alleaged.

Cap. 11. Pope Leo ftrayned by M. Horn to fpeake fomewhat for the Princes Supremacy in matters Ecclefiaftical, hath fpoken and done fo much to proue the primacy of the See of Rome, that if M. Horn wil ftand to his owne Author, he is vtterly confounded and forced to agnife the popes primacy without all maner of doubte.

Cap. 12. By the example alfo of Martian the Emperour, for calling of the Chalcedon Councell, nextly alleaged, M. Horns purpofe is no whit furdered, but Pope Leo his primacy euidently proued.

Cap. 13. By the Actes alfo of the fayd Councell, the popes and the bifhops Supreme Iurifdiction in al ecclefiaftical matters to be treated, examined, iudged and defined, throughe out the whole Councel appeareth, and M. Hornes purpofe remayneth vtterly vnproued.

Cap. 14. I haue farder out of the fayd Chalcedon Councell, being the fourthe Generall, and fo one of the foure allowed in our Countre by Acte of parliament in the reigne of the Elizab. An.1. Queenes Mai. prefent, gathered euident and fundry argumentes for proufe of the Popes and bifhops Supremacy in

caufes

caufes ecclefiafticall. And here I require M. Horne, or any mans els whatfoeuer to fhewe, howe it is pofsible without manifefte contradiction, to allowe the Authorytie of this fourthe Generall Councel, and to bannifhe the Popes Authorytie, which this whole Councel agnifed, or to geue to the Prince Supreme Authorytie in al ecclefiaftical caufes, the fame by this Councel refting in the bifhops only, not in the Prince at all.

It hath confequently ben fhewed againft M. Horne, that *Cap. 15.* his exáples of Leo and Zeno Emperours haue proued nothing leffe then his imagined Supremacy.

His next examples of three popes Simplicius, Felix. 3. and *Cap. 16.* Symachus, haue al proued fo manifeft teftimonies for their owne Supremacy, euen out of the bookes and places by M. Horne alleaged, that in this matter he femeth a plaine preuaricatour, and one fecretly defending the caufe, which he feemeth openly to impugne.

Nowe in Fraunce M. Horne, your lucke hath bene no *Cap. 17.* better, then before in the Eaft Church and in Italy it was. Your arguments in this behalfe haue bene to to pelting and miferable. But the bifhops Iurifdiction in all thofe matters hath bene as euident.

Your ftory of Iuftinus the elder (nextly by you alleaged, *Cap. 18.* but confufedly and out of meafure mangled) being wholy layed forthe, hath plainely proued the popes Supremacy, and nothing at al the princes.

Iuftinian your next exaample, and largely by you profe- *Cap. 19.* cuted, hath neuer a whit proued your matter, but for the Popes abfolute Supremacy hath diuerfe waies pronounced, not onelye in his behauyour in the fifte Generall

Fol, 171.

Fol 174.

Councell, but in his Edictes and Constitutions, which you for your selfe so thicke haue alleaged . In that place also I haue noted by diuerse exáples, what euil successe Churche matters haue had, whé Princes most intermedled Ther also by the way a Councell in Fraunce by M. Horne alleaged, hath openly pronounced for the popes vniuersall Supremacy.

Cap.20.

Your last examples taken out of Spayne haue nothinge relieued your badde cause, but haue geuen euidét witnesse for the Bishops Supremacy in ecclesiastical causes. And thus farre haue you waded in the first. 600. yeres after Christe, without any one prouf for your newe Laicall Supremacy. But for the popes and Bishops Supremacy in matters of the Church, the Cótinual practise of that first age and that in al Countres hath clerely pronounced , as hath bene at large shewed.

In the third book, as the race you runne is the longer, ád triple to that ye ranne in before, so is our cause the stróger, and yours the febler, or rather the wretcheder , that in the cópasse of.900.yeres, that of so many Emperors, kings and princes, of so many Coũcels both General and National, of so diuerse parts of the Christened worlde, al the East part, Italy, Fraunce, Spayne, Germany, and our own Countre of Englád, yea of the Moscouites, Armeniás and Aethyopiás to, of all these I say not one Prince, Councel or Coũtre maketh for you, and not one prince, Councell, or Countre maketh against vs, but all haue agnised the popes primacy, and not one in the worlde of so many hundred yeres, haue agnised or so muche as hearde of, muche lesse sworen vnto, the Princes Supreme Gouuernement in all Ecclesiasticall causes.

Your

Your firſt proufe belyeth flatly the See of Rome , and *Cap.* 1. proueth nothing by any doing of Phocas the Emperour,the Supremacy that you woulde proue.

The Kinges of Spayne and the Toletane Councelles *Cap.* 2. haue made nothinge for you,but haue clerely confounded you, not only in the principal matters in hande , but alſo in diuers other matters by your lewde hereſies denied.

Your patched proufes and ſwarming vntruthes in your *Cap.* 3. next narratiō touching certain Popes of Rome, and of the Churche of Rauéna, haue diſcouered the miſerable weke-neſſe of your badde cauſe , and nothing relieued yowe: the Popes Primacy by your owne examples notwithſtan-ding eſtabliſhed.

Your fonde ſurmiſe againſt the Decree of Conſtantin. *Cap.* 4. 5.Emperour, for the prerogatiue of the See Apoſtolike, as it nothing furdered your matter in hande,yf it had not bene made , ſo it ſhewed wel the miſery of your cauſe , that to make your paradoxe to beare ſome credit,you were fayne to diſcredit al the Hiſtoriās and writers of that matter,cal-ling them Pàpiſtes,the Popes Paraſites,and fayners of that which they wrote .

The practiſe of Eccleſiaſticall gouernement vſed in the *Cap.* 5. ſixt general Councel,next by you alleaged,cōfirmeth both in word and dede the Popes Primacy and the Biſſhops Su-preme iuriſdiction in matters Eccleſiaſticall , and geueth forth no maner inckling of your imagined Supremacy . In which only matter beſide twenty vntruthes by you vtte-red there about, you are as much confounded as in any o-ther Councell or Countre before , notwithſtanding your great obiection of Pope Honorius , to the which I haue there ſufficiently aunſwered.

e e e iij   Your

Cap.6.   Your talke of the three Kings of Spayne next enſewing, and of the three Toletane Councells kept in their reignes, doth ſo litle diſproue the Supreme iuriſdiction of Biſſhops in Eccleſiaſtical cauſes, that it maketh them Supreme iudges euen in ciuil cauſes. So wide you are euer from prouing your purpoſe.

Cap.7.   The.7. General Councel by you ſhortly noted, doth amply and abundantly confirme the Popes Primacy , and nothing in the worlde helpeth your purpoſe.

Cap. 8.   Charles Martel ād Carolomanus his ſonne exerciſed no whit of your imagined Supremacy, but haue cōfeſſed both clerely the Popes Primacy, by their doings, euē in the matters by your ſelf treated. Your moſt ignorant and ridiculous expoſition made of the keyes of S . Peters Confeſsion ſent to this Charles, and your extreme ſonde argument deducted thereof, hath vtterly ſhamed you , yf any ſhame be in you.

Cap.9.   Your ſlaunderous reproches againſt S . Auguſtine our Apoſtle , and S. Boniface the Apoſtle of Germany, and holye Martyr, haue redounded to your owne ſhame and follye , your cauſe thereby nothing in the worlde furdered: No, yf yt had bene all true , which you hadde reported of them.

Cap.10.   Charlemayne for all his callinge of Councelles, confirmynge of the ſame , and publiſhinge of Churche Lawes, practiſed not yet anye like Gouuernement in Eccleſiaſticall cauſes, as you haue defended , no nor anye Gouuernement at all , but was lead and gouerned him ſelfe in all ſuche thinges of the Fathers and Biſſhoppes then liuing, eſpeciallye of the See of Rome . The whole Order alſo of

the

the Councelles by you alleaged, hath plainelye condemned the prophane maner of determinyng caufes Ecclefiafticall nowe vfed by mere laye men, at the warrant of
fuche as yowe are. But for the Popes Primacye none
more clere then this Charlemaine, bothe in his doinges, *Vide fol.*
as in the caufe of Pope Leo the. 3. and in his fayinges, as *240.b. &*
in the booke fo much by you and your fellowes alleaged, *244.b. Itē*
and in the decrees it appeareth. *fol. 48.*

Lewys the firft, fonne to this Charlemayne practifed *Cap. 11.*
no parte of your Supremacye, but the Popes at that tyme,
hadde as full vfe thereof, as any Popes before or fithens,
the confirmation of the Pope, before elected and chofen,
notwithftandinge, of the which matter in that place I *Cap. 12.*
haue aunfwered you fufficientlye. There alfo you haue
Maifter Horne out of the Notable Epiftle of Nicolaus. 1.
to Michael the Emperour, and by the practife of the. 8.
Generall Councell at large declared vnto you, both the
Popes Primacye in all Spirituall matters, and the Emperour or Princes fubiection in the fame, by the Confefsion of
the Emperour himfelfe Bafilius of Conftantinople prefent
in that Councel.

Arnulphus his example hathe nothinge holpen yowe: *Cap. 13.*
The bedroll of certaine euill Popes by yow browght in,
onelye declareth your malice to Gods Vicares, and fur-
dereth nothinge your badde caufe. Your furmife adioyned of the caufe of the calamities at that tyme, hathe argued your greate folye, and ignorance of the ftories, except we fhall fay, that malice made you blinde.

Otho the firft fhewed fuch obedièce to the See of Rome, *Cap. 14.*
yea to the naughty Pope Iohn the. 12 that he is no fit exaple
for the

for the like gouernement in Princes as you maintayne, but for the like obedience to the See Apoftolike, as Catholike Princes and Emperours haue alwaies ſhewed, you coulde not haue brought a more notable or excellent example: ãd that proued out of the Authours by your felfe alleaged.

Cap. 15.   Hugh Capet the Frenche King, and Otho the. 3. Empe-rour haue euen in the matters by your felfe treated, bene proued obediēt and fubiect to the See Apoftolike, without any colour of the like gouernement as you woud faften v-pon them.

Cap. 16.   Your great matter of Henry the. 4. and Pope Hildebrãd hath concluded flatte againſt you, with a great number of your lewde vṇtruthes in that behalfe difcouered and con-futed. The Popes Primacy, in no matter more, abundantly and clerely proued.

Cap. 17.   The matter of inuefturing biſhops (your chief matter to proue the Princes Supremacy in al Ecclefiafticall caufes) in Henry. 5. Lotharius and Conradus, Emperours, hath pro-ued your purpofe no deale at al, namely Henry. 5. refigning vp all fuch pretenfed right to pope Calixtus the. 2. But in al thefe matters, how beaftly you haue belyed the ftories, I haue I truft, fufficiently declared.

Cap. 18.   Frederike Barbaroffa fpeaketh no woorde for your bar-barous paradoxe: he obeyed no lefſe then other Emperors the See of Rome, vea and at the laft fubmitted himfelfe to the Pope, whõ before he perfecuted, not as true Pope, but as he thought, an intruded Pope. He neuer made queſtion whether he ought to obeye the See Apoftolike, or no, but only he doubted who was the true elected Pope, and tooke parte with the worfte fide. The queſtion nowe in our dayes is farre vnlike: And fo are your proufes M. Horne farre and
extreme

extreme wide from the purpofe in hande.

Nowe for matters of our owne Countre, and for Eccle- *Cap. 19.*
fiafticall gouernement practifed therin, you are fo ouertaken as in no Countre more. It hath well appered, by that I
haue at large fayd, and proued, that longe and many yeres
before the Conquefte (at which time you onely beginne
your courfe) as well in Brytannie before the Saxons coming, as in England (after of thē it was fo called) the Popes
Primacy was clerely confeffed and practifed, euen as it is
at this day amonge the Catholikes euery where. As for the
gouernement of William the Conquerour, of William Rufus his fonne, and of kinge Henry the firft, it hath bene proued fo farre vnlike to that which you pretende of right to
appertayne to the Crowne of Englande, yea to all princes whatfoeuer, that the Popes Supreme gouernement
in fpirituall matters, is by their examples, yea euen by
the teftimony of your owne Authours, fo expreffely
proued, and fo ftrongely eftablifhed, that a man may
well wonder, what wytte, honeftie or difcretion you
had, ones to touche the remembraunce of them for proufe
of fo badde a caufe. Your patched adiuncte of the kinges
of Hungary, hath appeared a greate vntruth on your part,
and nothing for your purpofe : except lies can proue your
purpofe.

That which foloweth of the Armenians and of the *Cap. 20.*
AEthyopians, proueth alfo mofte euidently the Popes
Supremacy in thofe Countries : but proueth no whit
your fingular paradoxicall primacy. Verely fo fingular,
that in no one parte of the vniuerfall worlde it can be
founde.

The doinges of King Stephen and kinge Henry the .2. *Cap. 21.*

fff   haue

haue proued the popes Supremacy in our Cositre, but that kinde of Supremacy as you imagine, they make no proufe of in the worlde. The Martyrdome of. S. Thomas by the way also is defended againſt your ād M.Foxes lewed lying about that matter.

Cap 22.

Henry the. 6. Philip, and Otho the. 4. Emperors of Rome, haue bene no fitte examples for the like gouernement now in England: and your ſely argumentes in that behalfe haue bene to to childiſh and feble.

Cap. 23.

Your proufes of kinge Richard the firſte, and of kinge Iohn haue appeared mere ridiculous. Onely by occaſion therof, the lewed lying of M.Foxe hath bene partly diſcouered, touchinge kinge Iohn. Your matters of Fraunce about that time haue proued the popes primacy, not the Princes.

Cap. 24.

By the diſcourſe of Friderike the. 2. his doinges, as your principall cauſe hath taken a great foyle, ſo a mayne number of other your hereſies, by your own Authours and your owne Supreme head condemned, haue geué a great cracke to al your Religion beſide.

Cap. 25.

The time of kinge Henry the. 3. condemneth alltogether the primacy in your booke defended, and pronounceth clerely for the Popes Supremacy, by ſundry and open practiſes, as Appeales to Rome, depoſitions of prelates by the pope, makinge of Eccleſiaſticall lawes by his Legate, and ſuch other. And for your parte in that place, you haue vttered your greate ignorance euen in the latin tongue.

Cap. 26.

At that time alſo S. Lewys the Frenche kinge agniſed no leſſe the popes primacy in Fraunce: and therefore can be no fitte example of ſuch Supreme gouernement, as by

as by Othe M. Feckenham is required to fweare vnto.
The like alfo appeareth by the ftate of Apulia and Sicilia in
thofe dayes.

As for kinge Edwarde the firfte, kinge of England , the *Cap.27.*
Popes primacy in his time was fo well agnifed in the realm
of England, that euen in temporal matters his Authorytie
tooke place . Your fonde furmife of the Statute of Morte-
mayne, hath exemplified your lewde lying , and encreafed
the number of your maniefolde vntruthes : It hath not exemplified your pretended primacy, neither any thinge furdered you, for proufe of your matter.

Philip le Beau, as beau and fayre as he was , yet hath he *Cap. 28.*
bene nor fayre nor fytte example for the Supremacy that
fo much ye feeke for, and can not yet finde . His doinges
haue nothinge derogated from the popes Supremacy . But
he, as his progenitours , liued and dyed in the obedience of
the See Apoftolike in all Spirituall and Ecclefiafticall
matters. Durandus your owne Author hath cleane ouerthrowen you: and your great Councel of Vienna, yea your
owne fayre Philippe hath pronounced you an Heretyke.

Lewys of Bauary , as much as you bable of him, *Cap.29.*
hath nothinge relieued you : Neither yet his poetes Pe-
trarche and Dantes : All that greate ftrife was aboute
the popes temporall primacy , not of his fpirituall fupe-
riorytie, which neuer yet kinge Chriftened denied , vntill
thefe late dayes in our owne Countre , by the meanes of
fuch Apoftatas as you are.

You haue hearde alfo in that place M. Horne by the e- *Cap. 30.*
numeratio of al fuch Emperours, that notorioufly haue re-

belled againft the See Apoftolike, what Gods Iudgement hath bene ouer them, and to what euill endes they came through Gods vengeaunce.

Cap. 31. Philip of Valoys, for all your *Compofuit rem facerdotum*, yet maketh he nothing for your purpofe, but both in your owne very matter he concluded againfte you, and otherwife with mere fpirituall Iurifdictions, he neuer intermedled, nor claymed the vfe thereof from the Spirituall Magiftrate. Your owne Authours, and witneffes, Paulus Aemylius and Petrus Bertrandus haue depofed againfte you, and your owne kinge Philippe hath condemned you.

Cap. 32. & 34. Kinge Edwarde the. 3. and Richarde the. 2. of England, for al that you reporte of them, out of Nauclere and Polidore, haue notwithftandinge pronounced clerely for the Popes Primacy: and declared withall bothe you and your felowes, to be no true members of the Churche, that they liued in, but to be plaine Apoftatas and fchifmatikes from the fame.

Cap. 33. 35. 36. & 38. In like maner Charles the. 4. Sigifmunde, Friderike the. 3. and Maximilian the firft, al moft Catholike Emperours haue taken great wronge at your handes, being made to fay and doe, that which they neuer fayd ne did : Yea and for the which, if they liued agayne, they woulde order you, as they did the Huffyttes, and Wicleffiftes your progenitours in their dayes.

Cap. 37. Aeneas Syluius and Cufanus, your two efpecial Authors haue fo pronounced againft you, that no man I trowe, except he had a face of horne, woulde for very fhame haue brought the into the open Courte. But (as the prouerbe is) looke howe you haue brewed, fo muft you bake.

But

But what shall I say to your last witnesses, the Catho- *Cap. 39.*
like Bisshoppes and Doctours of our owne Countre, to D. *& 40.*
Quintinus of Paris, and Petrus of Ferraria, last of all to Philippus Decius the lawier, and Brawghton our Countreman? what extreme vncourtesy, I may wel say impudency,
hath it bene on your part, so violently and desperatly to
drawe them to the barre, where you were right sure, to be
condemned by their verdicte, but that you thought you
might frame their tales for them, and that no man woulde
comptrol your extreme lying, of the which in my Preface
I will say more? Thus you haue it truly and shortly repeted vnto you M. Horne, both what you haue not done,
and what I haue done. I require you before all the
worlde (yf you intende to Replye,)to answer
to euery particular as I haue done, and
so to proue your selfe an
honest man.

fff iij   THE

THE FOVRTH BOOKE: CON-
TEYNING A FVL CONFVTATION OF
M. Hornes anſweres, made to M. Fekenhams
Reaſons, for not taking the Othe of
the Supremacye.

✿✿✿

The. 153. Diuiſion. pag. 94.b.

M. Fekenham.

The ſeconde chief point is, that I muſt vpon a booke othe, not only teſtifie, but alſo declare in my cõſcience, that the Queenes Highneſſe, is the only Supreame gouernour of this realme, aſwel in all Spiritual or Eccleſiaſticall things or cauſes, as Temporall. But vpon a booke othe to make any ſuch declaration in conſcience, it may not poſſible be vvithout periury, before that a mans cõſcience be perſwaded thereunto: therefore (my conſcience being not as yet perſuaded thereunto) I can not preſently vvithout moſt plaine and manifeſt periury, receiue this Othe.

M. Horne.

As there is no difference in matter betvvixt theſe tvvo Propoſitions, I Teſtifie in conſcience, and I Declare in conſcience, although to ſeeme ſubtile, you (.511.) vvould haue the ſimple conceiue, by vvay of amplification much diuerſitie: Euen ſo this vvhich ye call the Second chiefe point, varieth (.512.) no vvhitte in matter from the firſt, and therefore my former anſvveare ſerueth to them both, if ye vvil needes make tvvo in ſhevv, of that in very dede is but one.

The ſecõd point.

The. 511. vntruthe. M. Fekenham maketh not this difference, but a farre diuerſe, as ſhal appeare. The. 512. vntruthe. It varieth very muche.

The.

*The first Chapter:Conteyning M.Fekenhams first reason,taken
out of the Actes of the Apostles: And by the way
of King Lucius.*

Stapleton.

ITHERTO hath M.Horne,twéty ful leaues
and more enlarged his proufs touchig the cófirmatió of his newe ecclesiastical superiority.
Hitherto he hath assaide with al force to beate
down to the ground the Popes Primacy, which
yet notwithstáding al this terrible assaulte standeth as ftróg
and as sure as euer it did before.Yea I.truft ftróger ád-furer
with al those,that but indifferétly haue perufed ád waighed
our two former labours.Now the an other while M. Horn M.Horne
wil playe the lusty defendát:wherin he seemeth to make as novv be-
light of al M.Fekenhás arguments,and to take thé to be of gineth to
no more ftrength thé is the weight of a fether.But feing he play the
hath alredy také fo many foyles,and fo many woundes,ahd parte.
femeth with his own weapons,to haue by rafhe hardines
wel beaten himfelfe , in fetting vpon his aduerfarie : hard
will yt be for him,to beare of fuch blowes ,as his aduerfary wil beftowe vpó him.Neither thinke good reader , that
he fhall euer foyle other mens reafons that can not found-
ly or fothly confirme his owne.Yet let vs trie howe he wil
fhifte for him felf.And now fee, howe euen at the firft entraunce , he playeth fowle playe and wrangleth . For M.
Fekenham doth not make difference betwixte *to teftifie in
confcience*, and *to declare in confcience* , as Maifter Horne
fayeth , he dothe : but betwixte to take an othe that the
Queenes Maiefty is fupreame Heade in all caufes , and to
declare the fame in confcience,which are two things.For a
man maye and many doe (the more pity) take an othe for
feare,

feare loue, or rewarde, quyte contrary to their côscience.
And that we nede not to feke farre for an example, euen
in this matter of Supremacy, which we nowe are in hande
withal.

Though therefore a mã may be perfwaded as many (the
more pitie) are, through pretence of obedience, through
feare of difpleafure, or through the loue of worldly promotions, riches, or pleafure, to take the othe : yet to declare
the fame in confcience no man can pofsibly (as Maifter
Fekenham moft trulye reafoneth) without manifeft periury, except his confcience be perfuaded thereunto. Now
to perfuade the confcience, requireth either a foden reuelation, or miraculoufe infpiration from God (which is not
to be prefumed without fome euident figne thereof) or
els a traƌ of time, to be inftruƌed, informed and taught that
which we neuer lerned before. M. Fekenham therefore ãd
ãl fuch as feare God, who haue lerned in the ghofpell to
forfake father and mother, wyfe and children, goods and
landes and al that in this worlde is dere, for Chriftes fake,
that is, for euery truth concerning Chriftian Religion, fuch
I fay neither being infpired from God by foden reuelation,
neither by any of your preachings, or writings being yet
informed or inftruƌed, can not pofsibly though a thoufand aƌs of parliament fhould commaund it, declare in their
confcience, declare I fay in their very confcience and hart
thought, that they beleue verely fuch fupreme gouernement in the Prince, as the aƌ expreffeth and intêdeth . Mê
may be perfwaded to take the othe, which is an externall
faƌ, by external refpeƌs of force, feare, or fraylty: but perfwaded to declare the othe in his confcience, no man can
be without an internall perfuafion of hart and minde : Cô-

trary

trary to this internall perſwaſion and conſent (whiche no
power of Princes, no force of acts, no law or ſtatut worldly can euer make) who ſo euer declareth externallye by
booke othe, and worde of mouth, that he ſo thinketh, he
incurreth manifeſtly the horrible crime of periurie, ád that
of double periurie: which God wil neuer ſuffer vnreuéged
without hartie repétance. To this moſt ſtróg and inuincible
reaſó, M. Horn anſwereth not a word, but maketh his Reader beleue that M. Fekenham putteth a difference betwen
teſtiſiyng in cóſcience, and declaring in cóſcience. Which
he doth not, but thus. Betwene *teſtiſyng by boke othe*, and
declaring in conſcience, he putteth a true difference, as we
haue ſaid largely. Now how well M. Horne hath pleaded
to perſwade M. Fekenhams conſcience, thou feeſt good
Reader, ifthou haue diligétly read and cóferred his proufes,
and our confutation. I doubt not, but many Catholike men
wil be perſwaded (in conſcience at leaſt) neuer to take the
othe, whiche you ſo ſingularlie contrarie to all Chriſtendome beſide, doe defende.

M. Fekenham.

And for the perſuaſion of my conſcience in this mat-
ter, I ſhall againe ioyne this iſſue with your L . That yf
your L. or any other learned man of this whole Realme,
ſhalbe able to proue, that our Sauiour Chriſt in his Gho-
ſpel and Teſtament, did committe the ſupreme gouerne-
mét of al ſpiritual and eccleſiaſtical cauſes in his Church,
not vnto his Apoſtles, being Biſhops and Prieſts, but to
Emperours and Empreſſes, Kings and Quenes, being for
the whole time of Chriſtes abode here vpó the earth, Ido-

latours

cōstātine the firste Empe- rour that did ioign his sword to the mainte- nance of God his vvoord. Act,2.

latours and Infideles, and so continued for the space of .300. yeres after the aßension of Christ: Constantine the Emperour being the very first Christian Kinge, that we reade of: when your L. shalbe hable to proue this, either by sentence or halfe sentence, woorde or halfe woorde of Christes Ghospel and last Testament: Then I shal yelde in this seconde pointe, aud with moste humble thankes, thinke my selfe well satisfied in conscience. And when your L. shalbe hable to proue, that these woordes spoken of the Apostle Paule at Miletum, vnto the Bishoppes of Ephesus: Attendite vobis & vniuerso gregi, in quo posuit vos Spiritus Sanctus Episcopos regere Ecclesiā Dei, quam acquisiuit sanguine suo: Take hede therefore vnto your selues, and vnto the whole flock of Christ, wherof the holy Ghost hath appoincted or made you Bishops, to gouerne and rule the Church of God, whiche he hath purchased with his bloud. VVhan your L. shalbe hable to proue, that these words do not make ful and perfect declaration, that the holy Ghost had so appoincted al spiritual gouern- ment of Christes flocke vnto Bishops and Priestes: But that kings, Quenes or princes may haue some part of spiri- tual gouernmēt with them, or rather take the supremacy and chiefe part of spiritual gouernmēt from them: I shall then yeelde, and thinke my self in conscience wel satisfied, touching the saiyng of S. Paule.

M. Horne. The. 154. Diuision. pag. 9 b.

That our Sauiour Christe hath committed, the Supreame gouernmēt in all Spirituall or Ecclesiasticall causes, to the Magistrates and Princes, is al-is alreadie proued, by perfect vvordes add vvhole (.513.) sentences of Chriftes Ghospell, and last Teftament : and therfore if your ftaie bitherto, hathe bene of confcience vnperfuaded through vvante of knovvledge , and not of peruerfe opinion, mainteined vvith the vaine defire of glorie and reputation, you muft nedes yelde, and be vvell fatiffied in confcience. You auouche this (.514.) Argument as inuincible, The Emperours and Empreffes, Kings, and Queenes, vvere for the vvhole time of Chriftes aboade here vppon the earth, idolatours, and infidels, and fo continued by the fpace of .300. yeares after the Affention of Chrifte : Conftantinus the Emperour being the very firft Chriftian King that vve reade of : Ergo, our Sauiour Chrifte did not committe the Supreme gouernemente in Spirituall or Ecclefiafticalcaufes to Emperours , Kings, and Princes. This Argument holdeth good, neither in matter, nor yet in fourme. There vvas in the time of Chriftes abode here vppon earth, if vve may beleue Eufebius, and Nicephorus the Ecclefiaftical hiftorians, a King in Edeffa, vvhofe name vvas Agbarus. This King beleued in Chrift, as Eufebius reporteth, although as yet vveakelie. In his Epiftle vvhich he vvrote vnto Chrift, he faluteth Chrift, to be Iefus the good Sauiour : he thinketh by the miraculoufe vvorkes vvhich he hath heard done by Chrift, that he is either God him felf, or els Gods fonne: and he offereth vnto Chrift fuch fruits of thankefulnes, as fo yong and tender a faith might for the time, bring forth. And Chrift in his refcript vnto Agbarus, affirmeth that he vvas no infidel, or idolatour, faying: Beatus es quòd in me credidifti, cùm nõ videris me: Agbare thou art bleffed, becaufe thou haft beleüed in me, whẽ thou haft not fene me. Befides this your ovvn felf, haue affirmed oftẽtimes, ãd fo doth your *Popifsh tales declare, that the. iij. vvife me, that came forth of the Eaft, to vvorfhip the nevv borne King of the Ievves, vvere Kings, and lie beried in the great doom at Collain, as the Colonifts make mẽ to beleue. called yet amõgft the vulgar Papifts, the three Kings of Collain. If there be any crediitte to be geuen to the narration of Eufebius and Nicephorus touching Agbarus King of Edeffa , and to the cõmonly receiued opiniõ of your Popifsh church, cõcerning the three Kings of Colain, thefe foure, vvere Kings in the time of Chriftes abode here in earth, and yet not Idolatours nor infidels, all the vvhole time of Chriftes aboade here; but faithfull vvoorfhippers of Chrifte : VVhereby the former parte of the matter in the Antecedent of your Argument is difproued, Neither is that true , vvhiche you put in the feconde parte ,that the Emperours and Kings

continued

Side notes:

The.513. Vntruth. Not one fentence hath ben broughte to proue that.

The.514. Vntruth. M.Fekã hã auoucheth it not for fuche, as it fhal appeare.

* A Proteftaticall flaunder.

continued Idolatours for the space of. 300. yeares after Chriſtes Aſſentiō: For although for the moſt parte, during that ſpace, they vvere ſuch, yet vvas there in that time ſome Godly Princes that vvere othervviſe geue. Euſebius in his Eccleſiaſticall Hiſtory, maketh mention of one Philippus, a moſte Chriſtian Emperour, of vvhom, and his ſonne alſo, being Emperour vvith him, Abbas Vrſpurgenſis vvitneſſeth, that they vvere the firſt of al the Romaine Emperours, that became Chriſtians, vvho alſo declared by theyr (.515.) deedes and vvorkes (as Abbas ſaieth) that they had in them the feare of God, and the moſt perfect Chriſtian faith. Conſtantinus alſo the Emperour, Father to Conſtantine the greate, did moſte diligently of all others, ſeeke after Gods fauour, as Euſebius vvriteth of him. He did prouide by his gouernment, that his ſubiectes did not only enioye greate peace and quietnes, but alſo a pleaſant conuerſation in holines and deuotion towardes God: Idolatours and diſſemblers in Religion, he baniſhed out of his Courte: and ſuch as confeſſed Gods truth, he reteined and iugded moſt worthy to be about an Emperour, commaunding ſuch to haue the guarde, both of his perſon and dominion. He ſerued and worſhipped the only true God. He condemned the multitude of Gods that the wicked had. He fortified his houſe with the praiers of holy and faithful men, and he did ſo conſecrat his Court and Palaice, vnto the ſeruice of God, that his houſholde companie, was a congregation or Church of God within his palaice, hauing Gods myniſters, and what ſoeuer is requiſit for a Chriſtian congregation. Polidorus in his Hiſtorie of Englande, affirmeth alſo of this Emperour, that he ſtudied aboue al other thinges to encreaſe the Chriſtian Religion, vvho after his death vvas rekened in the nūber of ſaincts. To theſe ſevve adde Lucius a king of our ovvn country, vvho although he vvas not in might cōparable to Cōſtantine the mighty Emperor, yet in zeale tovvardes God, in aboliſhing idolatry and falſe religion, in vvinning and dravving his ſubiects by al meanes to the Chriſtiā faith, in mainteining ād defending the ſincere Chriſtianity to the vttermoſt of his povver, he vvas equall vvith Conſtātine, and in this pointe did excel him, that he longe before Conſtantine brake the Iſe, gaue the onſette, and ſhapt a patern for Conſtantine to follovv, vvhereby to vvorke that in other parts, vvhich he had achieued vvithin his ovvn dominiō.

This

Li.6.c.34

The 515. vntruth. In diſſembling vvhat deſdes and vvorkes thoſe vvere.

Li. 1. de vit. Conſt.

Lib.1.

This noble king, of very loue to true Religion(.516.) *as* Pólido-
re *teſtiſied of him,* Procured him ſelfe and his ſubiectes to be baptiſed, cauſed his natiõ to be the firſt of al other prouinces, that
receiued the Goſpell publiquely, did drawe his people to the
knowledge of the true God, baniſhed at ones al maner of prophane worſhipping of Goddes, and cõmaunded it to be leaſt.
Cõuerted the tẽples of the Idolatours, to be Churches for the
Chriſtiás. And to be ſhort, he emploied and did beſtowe al his
ſeruice and power moſte willingly to the furtherauce and encreaſe of the Chriſtiã Religiõ, whiche he pláted moſt ſincerely throughout his countrey: and ſo leſte it at his death , *almoſte
an hũdreth yeres before Conſtantine vvas Emperour: and therefore vntruely
ſayed of you, that Conſtantine vvas the very firſt Chriſtian king, that ioyned
his ſvvorde to the maintenaunce of Gods vvorde. Sithe this king* Lucius, *ſo
longe before Conſtantine, did not only theſe thinges, that Polidore aſcribeth
vnto him, but alſo did thẽ of his ovvn authority, vvithout any (.517.) knovvledge or conſent of the Pope.* Nor Eleutherius *then Biſhop of Rome , to
vvhome aftervvardes king* Lucius *did vvrite, to ſee ſome of Cæſars*
and the Romaine Lawes ; *vvas any thing offended vvith the kinges
doinges, but greatly (.518.) commending him therein, councelled him not to
ſtand vppon the Romain lavves, vvhiche, ſaith the Pope, might be reprehen-
ded: but as he began vvithout them, ſo to go on , and dravv Lavves (. 519.)
alonely out of the Scripture, vvhich aftervvardes more at large , the Saxon
kinges, as, (520.) Iune and Aluredus did.*

The epiſtle of Pope Eleutherius *to king* Luci⁹ *is, as follovveth,* Petiſtis
à nobis &c. You haue deſired of vs, that the Romayne Lawes,
ãd the Lawes of Cæſar, might be ſent ouer to you, the which
ye would haue vſed in (your) kingdome of Brytanny . VVe
may at al times reproue the Romaine Lawes, and the Lawes
of Cæſar, the lawe of God we can not . For ye haue receyued
of late (by the diuine mercy) in your kingdome of Brytany, the
Lawe and faithe of Chriſt. Ye haue with you in *(your)* kingdome, both the old and newe teſtament: take out of them the
Lawe (by the grace of God) through the councell of your
kingdome, and by it (through Gods ſufferaunce) ſhall ye rule

ggg iij (your)

The 516.
vntruth.
Polidor⁹
text vily
mangled,
as ſhall
appeare.

The 517.
vntruth,
of al other
moſt no-
torious,
and cõtra-
ryto al hi
ſtorians
vvhatſoa
euer.

The. 518.
vntruth.
The epi-
ſtle folos
wing re-
porteth
no ſuche
thinge.

The. 519.
vntruth.
No ſuch
thinge in
the pope⁹
pretenſed
letters.

The. 520.
vntruth.
Kinge
Iune, nes
uer drew
out ſuche
lavves.

(*your*) kingdome of Britanie, for you are the Vicar of God in (*your*) kingdom, according to the Prophet King: The earth is the Lordes, and all that therein is, the compaſſe of the world, and they that dwell therein. And againe, according to the Prophet king: Thou haſt loued righteoſnes, and hated iniquitie, wherefore God, euen thy God, hath anointed thee with the oile of gladnes aboue thy fellowes. And againe according to the Prophet Kinge : geue the Kinge thy iudgement O God, and thy righteouſnes vnto the Kinges Sonne. For it is not : geue the iugement and righteouſnes of Cæſar, for the Chriſtian nations and people of (*your*) kingdome, are the kinges ſonnes, which dwel and confiſte in your kingdome, vnder your protection and peace, according to the Goſpel, euen as the henne gathereth together her chickes vnder her winges. The nations indede of the kingdom of Britany, and people are yours, ād whom being diuided, you ought to gather together, to concorde and peace, and to the faith, and to the Lawe of Chriſt, and to the holy Church, to reuoke, cheriſhe, mainteine protect, rule, and alwaies defende them, both from the iniurious perſons and malicious, and from his enemies. VVoe be to the kingdome whoſe King is a child, and whoſe Princes banquet early, a King I name not for his ſmal and tender age, but for follie and wickednes, and madnes, according to the Prophet King: bloudthirſty and deceitfull men, ſhall not liue out halfe theyr daies. By banqueting, we vnderſtand glotonie, through glotonie riotouſnes, through riotouſnes al filthie and euil thinges, according to Kinge Salomon : wiſdome ſhal not enter into a frowarde ſoule, nor dwell in the body, that is ſubdued vnto ſinne. A kinge is named of ruling, and not of a kingedome, ſo longe as thou ruleſt well, thou ſhalt be king, which vnleſſe thou doe, the name of a Kinge ſhall not conſiſt in thee, and thou ſhalt leſe the name of a King, which God forbid. Almighty God geue vnto you, ſo to rule your kingdom of Britanie, that ye may reigne with him for euer, whoſe Vicar ye are in the kingdom aforeſaid, VVho with the Father &c.

Stapleton.

Stapleton.

M. Fekenham will nowe shewe three causes, why he can not be perswaded in cõscience to take the othe. The first is, for that Christe appointed to his Apostles and theyr successours being bishoppes and priestes, the supreamacie of spiritual gouernmente, and not to Princes, being in Christes time, and so cõtinuing idolators and infidels, to the time of Cõstantin the great. He proueth his assertiõ by S. Paule: speaking thus to the clergy. Take hede therfore vnto your selues, and vnto the whole flock of Christ, wherof the holy ghost hath apoīted or made you bishops, to gouern ād rule the church of God, which he had purchased with his own bloud. Here againe M. Horne wrágleth with M. Fekenhā, ād wresteth his saying, yea and belieth him to, as though he should *auouche as an inuincible argumēt*, that which he speaketh of the infidel Princes : whiche is not his principall argumente, but incidently browght in, the pithe of the argumente resting in the authority of S. Paule before specified. And therefore thowgh Abgarus with the three Magi, that came to honour Christes byrth, with the Emperour Philippus, and king Lucius were Christened, yet is M. Fekenhãs argumente framed vppon the authority of S. Paules words litle acrased or febled : vnlesse M. Horn cã proue (which he doth not, nor cã not) that these, and other Christiã princes before Cõstantine had the supremacy of al causes ecclesiasticall. For the kind and maner of their gouernment in spirituall matters M. Horne alleageth nothing : and to say the truthe nothing can be alleaged. And verie litle also wyll be founde for any matter ecclesiasticall, that maye seeme to towche theyr personnes. And yet that lytle that we fynde in stories maketh altogether, aswell againste some

other

Three causes that staye M. Fekēham, frõ taking the Other

The first. *Attendite vobis & vniuerso gregi, in quo posuit vos spiritus sanctus episcopos regere ecclesiã Dei, quam acquisiuit sanguine suo.*

M. Horn imagineth that to be M. Fekenhams principal argument that is not.

Chriftes
Image
fent to
Abgarus.

Niceph.
l.17.c.16

Vide Me=
taphraft.

Of the
firft Chri
ftiã Em=
perour.
Philip.

Hovve
corruptly
ãd vvret-
chedly M.
Horne
handleth
the ftorie
of them=
perour
Philip.

Eufeb. lib.
6.cap.25.
hiftor.ec-
clefiaft.
Abbas Vr-
fpergen.

other part of M. Hornes new relligion as againft this new
Supremacie. As Chriftes Image printed in a lynen clothe,
by Chriftes owne hande and fent to this Abgarus: by the
which many yeares afterward the Citie of Edeffa was mi-
raculouflie preferued being befieged by Chofroes the king
of the Perfians. Which Image alfo was afterward brought
to Conftantinople with much reuerence and honour, and
thereby many great miracles wrought, as the Emperour of
Conftantinople Conftantine doth write, who was prefent
when the Image was brought thither.

That litle alfo that we haue recorded, in ftories of the
Emperour Philip and his fonne, maketh altogether againft
your new religion, and efpeciallie againft your new primacie: which is the matter that prefentlye we haue to deale
withal. Shewe your Reader, I befeeche you, M. Horne,
what was that wherein *by their woorkes and dedes they declared* (as you fay) *that they had in them the feare of God,
and the moft Chriftian faith.* Come on good M. Horne,
and declare vs this. Surely, good Reader, there was neuer
beare that came to the ftake with worfe will, then Maifter
Horne wil come nigh this point. For if he come ones nigh
to it, he fhal forthwith declare him felfe, void and empty of
the Catholike faith, for the denying of the Popes and clergies Supremacie (wel to be proued euen by this ftory) and
void alfo of al feare of God, for the wretched hewing and
mangling of his Authour, and for leauing out that, for the
which they are commended, *for their faith and fear of God.*
The caufe then, whie Eufebius, and after him Vrfpurgenfis,
fo writeth, is, for that *this Philip and his fonne, being in the
Churche vppon Eafter eue, and minding to be prefent at the
Sacrifice, and to communicate: Fabian the Pope woulde not*
                                                                    fuffer

suffer them vnleſſe they would firſt confeſſe theyr faultes, and
ſtande amonge the penytentes. Whereunto they obeyed moſt
gladly, declaring (euen as M. Horne writeth) *by theyr dedes*
and workes that they had in them the feare of God, and the
moſt perfeĉt Chriſtian faith. Where is now in youM Horne
the feare of God? Yea where is your Chriſtiā faith? Beſides
confeſsion of ſinnes and a place of penitentes, this ſtorie
hath alſo a teſtimonie of the ſacrifice of the Churche, and
of the Popes and Clergies Supreamacie ouer the Frince,
which you ſo ſtoutlie denie, making the Prince *Supreme in* The cauſe
al cauſes without exception.   And therefore without all that mo ̅
faith, and feare of God, ye haue ſtollen away all this, and ued M.
conueied it from the ſight of your Reader, into your darke Horne ſo
Cacus denne. The like pageant, yea and excedingly much this ſtory
worſe, plaie you with the ſtorie of our moſt noble, and firſt
Chriſtian King Lucius.   For here ye doe not onely by a
ſlie ſluttiſh ſilence, diſſemble the doings of Pope Eleuthe- *Beda li.1.*
rius, as ye did before of Pope Fabian, but impudentelye a- *eccleſ.hiſt,*
uouche, that King Lucius *did all thoſe things mentioned by* *ca. 4. mi-*
Polidore, of whiche the Chriſtening of his whole Nation is *ſit ad eum*
the chiefe, and ſo conſequentlye, that he was Chriſtened *Britānorū*
without any knowledge or conſent of Pope Eleutherius. Bring *Rex epiſto*
foorth, M. Horne, but one Authour in Greke, Latine, or *lam obſe-*
Engliſh, good or badd, new or old, Catholike or Heretike, *crans,vt*
(vnleſſe perchaunce you may ſhew ſome one of your late *per eius*
brethren, that write ſo, and yet after long ſearch I can find *mandatū*
none ſuch, that writeth as ye write: and then am I content *efficeretut*
though this be of al other a moſt euident, and a notoriouſe *chriſtian⁹.*
lie, to remitte it you at our next reckoning, whiche yet for *Idē pror-*
the better keping of your accōpt, I muſt not now let paſſe *ſus Damæ*
vnſcored. I neuer before readde it, no I neuer readde any *tificali.*

li h h   Chronicler

Kinge

Galf. Mo
numetes.
Epiſtolas
Eleuthe-
rio Papæ
direxit, p:
tens vt ab
eo chriſtia
nitatem
reciperet.
Li.1.ca.4.
Galfr. Mo
num. &c.
Aſſerius
Meueueſ.
in annali-
bus Angl.

Cēt.t.de ſcript.Brit.
Eluanũ & Meduinũ
ad Eleutheriũ Ro.
Pontificē miſit , cum
quibus ille ſuos lega-
tos remiſit Fugatiũ
ac Damianũ,qui no-
uis ritib. ac ſolēni e-
piſcoporũ diſpoſitione
eā formarēt Eccleſiā.
Graftō in the abrid
gemēt of the chro-
nicles of England.
Naucler-gener.6.
Sabel.enead.7.li.5.
Io.Laz.in epit. hiſt.
vniuerſ. Ado iu Chro.
Tom.1.Concil pag.
191.edit. vlt.

chronicler newe or olde , vnleſſe yt be ſome of your late
bretherne, or ſuch Catholikes as write but very cōpēdiou-
ſly, and as yt were abridgmētes of thinges, which doth not
expreſſely write that king Lucius ſent to Rome to Pope
Eleutherius, that he might be by his aduice and authority
Chriſtened: but the negatiue thereof I neuer as I ſay read,
nor ſhal I trowe fynde any ſo madde , and ſo maliciouſe a
writer, as ye are, to write yt againe. I referre you for our
owne countremen, to Beda. Who writeth, *that king Lucius*
wrote an epiſtle to pope Eleutherius, that by his commaunde-
ment he might be chriſtened. I referre you, to our Britiſhe
chronicler, tranſlated by Geffrie of Monmoth : and to one
other of our owne contrey, that wrote abowt.700.yeares
ſithens in lyke effect. I referre me to Héry of Hungtingtō,
to William of Malmesbury, to *Alphredus Beuerlacenſis* , to
Iohannes Londonenſis, to Polychronicō, to the chronicles
of Englande, that M. Foxe calleth Caxtons chronicles. And to a number of other of our owne cōtry,
which partly I haue ſene, partly I haue not ſene.

And to come to our owne time, to Bale your cheif
antiquary: and to Grafton writing thus. *This Lucy*
ſent louing letters to Eleutherius thē Biſhop of Rome,
deſiring him to ſende ſome deuoute and learned man,
by whoſe inſtruction both he and his people might be
tawghte the faith and religion of Chriſt. It were now
ſuperfluouſe, to ouerlade my anſwere or the Reader, with the external and Latin writers: as *Naucle-*
rus, Sabellicus , Platina , Iohannes Laziardus , Ab-
bas Vrſpergenſis, Ado, but eſpecially *Damaſus in vita*
Eleutherij: ād a nūber of the like, which agree with
our own chronicles. Some perchaunce wil thinke,

that

that Mayfter Horne would neuer be fo impudent, as to us.
gainfay all theis wryters and chroniclers, and that as he
fetcheth all his narration towching Lucius owte of Poli-
dorus:fo he hath at the leafte for this pointe Polidorus on
his fide. Yf it were fo , though yt were a foolifh and a fond
fhifte,yet were yt fomwhat colourable,to fhifte from him
felf, fo notable a lie. But Polidorus writeth conformably to
all other . And as yt is true that Mayfter Horne boro-
weth all the refidewe of Polidorus : fo mofte wretched-
lie he difmembreth from the refidewe of Poli- *Polidorus lib.2.*
dorus narration , all that towcheth Pope Eleu- *Ifte anno falutis hu-*
therius. *Lucius (fayeth Polidore) in the yeare of* *manæ 182.regni vero*
our Lorde.182. and the yeare of his reigne.13.of verie *13.vera religionis a-*
true loue to religion ,fent letters to Eleutherius the *more ductus cū Eleu-*
Pope to procure that he and his people might be made *therio Romano Pon-*
Chriftians. Fugatius and Damianus men of fingular *tifice egit, vt fe ac*
vertue were fente thither: which did baptife the *fuos ad Chriftianorū*
kinge with al his courte , and people. All this hath *numerū cœlefti fonte*
M . Horne broken and cutte of from the myddle *perfufos adiungeret.*
of the fentence , and thereby hath mangled and *Mißi funt eò Fuga-*
torne the fame as miferablie , as euer did Medea *tius ac Damianus*
her chylde , for that he well fawe , yt made no- *viri pietate fingulari*
tablye for the Popes primacy. Whiche you fhall *hij rege cum tota do-*
well perceyue, yf you doe deaplye confider the *mo populoq; vniuer-*
caufe, that moued the Kynge to fende fo farre as *fo baptifarunt,fubla-*
to Rome. *toque &c.*

    A man woulde at the firfte fight thinke the
doinges of the king very ftraunge,namely confidering that abowt this time liued in Fraunce the great
clearke and Bifhoppe Ireneus with many other famoufe men , whofe ayde he might haue craued

for his neceſſary inſtruction in the Chriſtian faith. Neither did he lacke at home, of his owne ſubiectes that could well (as yt ſemeth) haue ſerued his turne.   And yet no doubte, this good kinge had a good and ſubſtantial grow+ nde for his doinges. It is then to be cóſidered, that anon after the death of Chriſte and ſo euer after vntil Lucius time, there were amonge the Chriſtiáns, a number of heretikes, whiche as they bore the name of Chriſtians, ſo by theyre hereſies they loſte the benefitte of their Chriſtédome: as the Simonians (the ſchollers of Simon Magus) Menandrians, the Saturninians, the Baſilidians, the Nicolaites, the heretikes called *Gnoſtici*, for the excellent knowledge they pretended to haue aboue other mē: the Cherinthians, the Cerdoniás, the Phrygians, the Moṅtaniſtes, the Marcionites with diuerſe other. Eche ſecte contending theire owne falſe faith

Niceph. li. *4.6.19.* to be the true, and the onely Chriſtian faith : yea manie of them were taken for Prophetes, as *Montanus* and others. Many ſuffred death for Chriſte with thoſe that were catholike, and that with great pacience . Among them was a

Idem li.3. *cap.36.* prieſt called *Metrodorus* a Marcionite. Of the which ſecte euen in Lucius time, a great number ſuffred in the perſecution raiſed againſt the Chriſtians . Whereof the ſecte cra-

Euſeb. li. *5.cap.16.* ked very muche, and made thereof a great argument, that they were in the true faith: and a muche better argumēte, then doth Mayſter Foxe for his madde martyrs, that died moſte wilfullie for playne and open hereſie . Lucius then vnderſtáding of this, had good cauſe to be careful by whom he receiued his Chriſtendome, leaſt chauncing vppó ſome falſe ſhrew, and taking him for his inſtructour, he might rather chaunge one errour, for an other, then put yt cleane away: and for an Idolatour become a falſe Chriſtian . The

wante

wante of this good choyfe of Inftructours, was the caufe
why Valens the Emperour became an Arrian and fuche
an horrible bloudfucker of the catholikes. This alfo was the
caufe that the Gothes ãd Vãdales, were Arriãs. Who moft
cruelly afflicted and martyred thowfandes of Chriftians.
What was then the furefte way for Lucius to auoyde this
daunger. Dowbtles the very fame that he toke, that is , to
fend to the Churche of Rome, which neuer erred in faith,
and which *was the principal Churche, and with the which al
other Churches mufte agree, by reafon of the cheif principalitie
of that Churche,* as Ireneus that bleffed bifhop and Martyr
wrote, euen in the tyme of this Lucius ? This principalitie I
fay hath fo troubled M. Horne, that he durft not truely reporte his owne authour, yea fo amafed him, that falling fo-
dély in a rage, hath framed vs fuche an open and malicioufe
lie, that who fo euer wil hereafter trufte him, is well worthie to be beguiled.

And wil ye, yet fee an other as greate a madnes of this
man? As he mofte fhamefully denieth theis doinges of Lucius with Pope Eleutherius, againfte the vniforme côfente
of al hiftoriographers, fo hath he fownde letters of Lucius,
with Eleutherius anfwere , wherof no one of al the fore- côcernĩg
fayde chroniclers maketh mention, nor any other, that I cã Pope
yet lerne of, containinge matter altogether vnprobable Eleuthe-
and vnlikely, and therefore mete , after this fowrtene hun- rius let-
dred yeares nowe at length to come owte of Trophonius king
and Cacus blĩnde denne, and be fet in M. Hornes boke as a Lucius.
notable matter of antiquity to furnifh and bewtify his new
fupremacie withal. He layeth vs forth an epiftle of Eleutherius: but out of what authour he hath taken yt, or in
what library we fhal fynde yt, he will not tell vs. The beft

Kinge

Author,I wene, that he can alleage for it , wil be some recordes of parchement in the Guild Halle. But then M.Ie-
wel wil answere you for me, M. Horne : *A Calues skinne
is no sufficient warrant of truth. Lies haue bene writen in letters of golde.* Wel, make the best of it, and iustifie it as you
may. As our cause can take no preiudice by it : So you shal
take much shame by it, if not for the matter it selfe , yet at
the least for three or foure pretie lies that you adioyne, to
companie this notable Epistle. For first , there was neuer
any Saxon king that made any notable Lawes called Iune.
There was one called Inas, and he in dede with king Aluredus or Alphredus, ordeined many Lawes, but that they
shoulde be suche Scripture lawes as Maister Horne saieth,
drawen alonely out of the Scripture , it is Mayster Hornes
vaine dreame. And in case they had so great regarde to
scripture onely, and measured and squared their lawes and
doings by scripture, belike M.Horne will beginne to haue
some better liking of Religious men, and of the Popes Primacye also. For it was this king Inas, that * gaue the Peter
pence first to Rome , and renouncing his Realme went to
Rome and professed him self a Monke. Both which things
vndoubtedly, by M.Horn, he must nedes find in Scripture.
It is this Alphredus, that was anointed and crowned King
at Rome, as we haue told before, and therfor is called the
Popes sonne adoptiue. Now wheras ye bring this Epistle
to proue, that the king was christened without the Popes
cosent, ad that the Pope was nothing offeded with the kigs
doings, but greatly comended him therin : neither the one
nor the other, can be proued by this Epistle. This is a mete
and couenient glose for such a worthy epistle: In the which
also there is no probability in the world. For as other Coutries, that were subdued by the Romans, especially such as

were

Ievvell.
pag 86. in
his reply.

*Naucle-
rus put at
hunc fuisse
Edeluul-
phum Al-
phredi pa-
trem, Ge-
nerat. 29.
pag.61.
Alibi vo-
cat eum
Adulphu.
Gener.41.
pag. 280
Henricus
Hunting .
Asserius
Meneues.
Pol. li. 4.
Pag. 89.

were reduced into a forme of a Prouince, and had their rulers and Lieutenaūts frō Rome (as Britain had) receiued the
Romaine and Ciuil Law, so is it to be thought of Britaine.
And Polidorus writeth, that Agricola (th'Emperor Vespasi-
ans deputie) gaue to the Britaines certain Romane lawes ād
orders, to be vsed and practised by them. Neither is it likely,
but that before this time, there was some copie of the Romaine lawes in Britain, the yōg Noble men of the Realme
being much geuē to be eloquēt in the Romain tong, wherin Agricola did prefer thē before the Galles or French mē,
and being brought vp in Rome: especially Coilus, king Lucius father spēding al his youth there: So that Lucius had no
nede to send to Pope Eleutherius for Cæsars lawes. And if
he had nede, it is more likely he would haue sente to some
other then to Eleutherius, who with other blessed Popes
at that time, medled (God wot) litle with Cæsars Ciuill lawes, or with any other lawes of Pagan Princes. But of al o-
ther things, Eleutherus answer is most vnlikely. For who
would think him so vnwise and so vnskilfull, that he would
appoint the old and the new Testament only as sufficiēt to
gouern and rule a cōmon welth by? Which thīg was neuer
yet practised in any Christiā coūtry, nor cā possibly be practised: the old law, being al in a manner abolished, and the
new Testament cōsisting of such principles of the Christiā
faith as be immutable, ād not variable: wheras politik lawes
haue ben, are, and euer shalbe and so must be, according to
many incidents alterable and variable.

   This epistle then, be it true, or be it a counterfait doth as
yet serue M. Horne to no great purpose: but for any thing
we haue brought out of this Epistle, M. Horne perchance
wil not him self greatly passe of it. There is an other priuie
treasure

Lib. 2.
Dedit le-
ges et Ro-
mana qua
dam insti-
tuta vtē⸗
da intro⸗
duxit.
Vide Cor⸗
nel. tacit.
in vita
Agricola.

treafure hiddē here , for the which,I fuppofe this Epiftle is chiefly brought forth,and that is to proue euē by the Pope Eleutherius him felf,that the King and not the Pope is the fupreme heade in al caufes Ecclefiafticall. For Eleutherius faith,that Lucius was *Vicare of God in his Kingdome.* This, this is the marke that M.Horne al this while hathe fhot at: this is the caufe,that this Epiftle, that hath fo many hūdred yeares lyen dead, is now reuiued by M. Horne.   Yea for this claufe,this Epiftle was folemply alleaged in open parliament againft the Popes Primacie. And feeing that your new Diuinitie now,is nothing but Englifh and Parliament Diuinitie : I will remitte you ones againe , M. Horne, to your owne Braughton , who vfeth the fame woordes. Which muft nedes be (as by him appeareth,) taken , that the King is Gods Vicare in his Kingdome,that is, in the tē-porall adminiftration of Ciuile, and not for Spirituall mat-ters.And therfore,this Epiftle doth as wel ferue M.Horne to proue the Princes Primacie by,as it ferueth M.Iewel to proue that the feruice muft be in theEnglifh tongue:which is as true as that other where he faith, that Lucius *fente to Rome to Eleutherius, for his aduice touching the ordering of his Church.* Wherein if M. Iewell meane , that he fent to Rome before he was Chriftened,then haue ye one witnes more againft you. But if he meaneth, as it femeth he doth, by his difcourfe of thefe letters that you fpecifie , parte wherof he alfo reciteth, and among other things, that the King is Gods Vicare : then is he alfo deceiued.For in thefe letters king Lucius doth not afke his aduife in any Church matters,but requireth only to haue Cæfars lawes fent him, appeareth by the tenour and purport of the faid Epiftle. So that I perceiue, this Epiftle is an Inftrument to fet forth
the

How and vvherein King Lucius vvas Gods Vicare.

In his Replie fol.19. This Epi-ftle,be it a true or a falfe epi-ftle, ney-ther ma-keth for M.Horne nor for M.Ievvel

the new Ghospel many wayes: but for such a Ghospel such
a proue is very mete.

We will therfore nowe passe forth to the residewe of
your answere, where you goe about to disproue M. Fekenham, saying that Constantine the great was the first Christiã king. The force and weight of his argument (as I sayd)
doth not stande vppon this, whether there were any Christian kings before Constantinus the great. This is but a by
matter, and yet ye dwell vppon it, and handle the matter
seriously, as thoughe all lay in the duste, if there were
any kinge Christened before Constantine. But herein ye
do but trifle with M. Fekenham: who saieth not simply or
absolutely that Constantin was the first Christiã king, but
the *firste that ioyned his sworde to the maintenance of Goddes
worde*: as in making sharpe Lawes againste Idolatours and
heretikes: and in making sharpe warre againft Maxentius
and Licinius, that persecuted the Christians, which thinges
are not read of any king before him. Againe if there were
anie other Christian princes, they were very fewe, and of
small dominion and rule. As Abgarus, who seameth by his
own lettres to Christ, to haue ben lorde, but of one small
and obscure towne: As the .3. wise mé that are called kings,
to auauce the honour of Christes natiuitie, and are thought
to haue ben either kings or Lordes *in Arabia minore*. which
may perchaunce be called kings, aswel as those were called
in holy scripture, which did scorne and checke holy Iob.
Yf there were any of greater renowne and dominion, as
king Lucius, Philip themperour, Constantius, Constantinus
father, yet becaufe either they did not ioyne theyr sworde
to the mayntenaunce of Gods word, or for that their successours were paynims and Infidells: as it chaunced to the

*Concer͛
ning M.
Fekenhãs
saying that
Cõstãtin
the great
vvas the
first Chri-
stiã king.*

*Niceph li.
2. cap. 7.
Mihi verò
oppidum
quoddam
est modicũ
quide, nec
admodum
celebre: v-
triq; tamẽ
nostrũ per
cõmodum.
Tobiæ. 4.
Sicut bea-
to Iob, in-
sultabant
reges.*

iii   sayd

sayd Lucius and Philip , there is the leſſe accompt made of thē. How ſo euer it be, M. Fekēhā ought not to be reprehēded in this, hauīg good authors that wrote ſo before him: namely Euſebius, Lactantius, and S. Ambroſe, who all cal Cōſtantinus the firſt Emperor that from the beginning of the world was chriſtened. Which thing belike they write , for the cauſes, by vs reherſed, or ſome lyke. Yea he hath S. Auguſtin to cōfeſſe ſo much as he did, as M. Horn him ſelf wil anon tel vs. But yet ſee good reader the wiſe and polityke handling of the matter by M. Horn. He goeth about to diſproue M. Fekenham , for ſavinge there were no Chriſtian princes in Chriſtes tyme, and for his relief, brīgeth me forth Abgarus and the thre wiſe men, but ſo as he ſemeth to take it, but for a fable. And therfore he ſayth, *yf we may belieue Euſebius and Nicephorus:* againe, *yf there be any creditte to be geuen to the popiſh Church concerning the 3 kings:* and doth nothing vnderſtād, that the more he defaceth their kingdoms, the more he defaceth his own anſwere, and ſtrengtheneth his aduerſaries argument.

Solus æuo vniuerſo regenitus imperator atq; ſacris initiatus eſt in Chriſto.
Lib. 4. De vita Cōſt. ex tranſl. Ioan. Porteſij. Lact. de falſa relig. cap. 1. Amb. de obitu Theodoſij.
Aug. ep. 50

M. Horn. The. 155. Diuiſion. pag. 94. b.

Thus it is made maniſeſt, that bothe your argument faileth in truthe of (.521.) matter, and you your ſelf vvere beguiled through ignorāce, by (.522.) vvante of readinʒ. But put the caſe that your antecedent vvere true, yet is it a faulty fallax made à dicto ſecundùm quid, ad ſimpliciter, and the conſequent follovveth not, for that there is more conteined in the concluſion, than the antecedent doth comprehende, vvhich is ſuch an euiʼlfauoured forme of argument, that youge ſtudentes in the ſcholes vvoulde be aſhamed therof. The Donatiſtes made the like obiectiō againſt the catholique fathers, vvherto S. Auguſtine maketh auſvvere. The ſtate of the Apoſtles time , is otherwiſe to be thought of, than this time, all thinges muſte be doon in their time: In the Apoſtles time, this prophecy was yet in fulfillīg : wherfore dothe Heathē rage, ād the people muſe vpō vaine thinges? The kinges of the earth ſet them ſelues, and the

The. 521. vntruthe.
It is true in matter, as hath bene proued.
The 522. vntruthe, mere ſlaūderous.
Epiſt. 50.

Pſalm. 2.

the Princes confult together againſt the Lorde and his Chriſt. As yet that was not in hande which is ſpoken a litle after in the ſame pſalme:and nowe ye kings vnderſtand,be learned ye Iudges on the earth, ſerue the Lorde in feare , and ioy in him with reuereͨe.Therfore ſeing that as yet in the Apoſtles time, kinges ſerued not the Lorde,but ſtill did deuiſe vaine thinges againſt God and his Chriſt,that al the foreſayinges of the Pro· phete might be fulfilled, than truely impieties coulde not be inhibited by prices Lawes,but rather be mainteyned.For ſuch was the order of the times , that both the Iewes fhoulde kill the preachers of Chriſt,thinking to doo God good ſeruice ther-in,as Chriſt had forfpoken:and alſo the gentiles fhoulde rage againſt the Chriſtians,that the martyrs might winne the victo﹣ry thorough pacience. But after that this began to be fulfilled which is writen:And al the kinges of the earth fhal woorfhip *Pſalm.72.* him, and al the nations fhal ſerue him : what man,onleſſe he be not wel in his wittes,wil ſay that Kinges ought not to haue a ſpecial regarde for the Church of Chriſt,and al manner god-lines amongeſt their fubieͨtes?

Stapleton.

We haue declared,that M. Fekenham his ſaying of Cõ-ſtantinus the great,and the firſt Chriſtian king may be born in a right good ſenſe,ãd alſo that he ſpeaketh therein agrea-ble to moſt auncient and lerned writers.And if he were de-ceyued,as ye write, *by ignorance and want of reading*(which is of your part a mere ſlãderous lye)the pyth yet of his ar-gument ſtanding vppon the ſaying of S. Paule , is nothinge therby blemiſhed.And of al men you may worſe lay igno-rance to his charge,that haue vttered in this very parte and parcel of your anſwere not only ſo much groſſe ignorance, but ſo exceding and cãkred malice,eſpecially in the ſtory of king Lucius. And here alſo yet ones againe to compare M. Fekenham with the Donatiſts for framing an argument frõ

M. Fekē﹣hams arͬ gument falſely cõ pared vvith the Donatiſts argumēt.

iii ij   the

the vſe and exáples of the Apoſtles, and of the primitiue Churche: wherein beſide your malice, you bewraye your owne vnſkilfulnes. For this redoundeth altogether vppon you, and your owne fellowes. For wherein reſteth all your eloquence againſt the Catholike Churche , but that it is not conformable nowe to Chriſtes, and the Apoſtles tyme, and to the primitiue Churche ? Namely touching inuocation of Saints, ſuffrages for the dead: touching adoratiõ and eleuation of the bleſſed Euchariſtia, the minglinge of water and wyne, receyuing vnder one kinde, ſole receyuing, and a number of the like?   Yea and before that any Prince woulde ſay or doe for you, you coulde M. Horne with your fellowes play the Donatiſts in dede, and inueigh againſt the téporalties of Biſhops, agaíſt their lordely trayne and reuenewes, becauſe forſoth the Apoſtles were poore, and vſed no ſuch ioylyte. But nowe who more ioyly then M. Horne himſelfe, or who more lordely then your Lord-

In his firſt Reproufe. Fol.74.b. & 75.a. Marke good reader that to reaſon from the order of the Apoſtles to our time, is novve vvith M. Horne an ill fauoured forme of arguïg.

ſhips are? Again what is more vſual with M. Nowel (a man, I trowe, of a rare Spirit) then to make this tyme the tyme of the primityue Churche : that we be the Phariſees , and they forſoth the Apoſtles . That nowe we may not preſcribe with Antiquity , Traditions, or Conſent of our Elders, againſt them, becauſe the Scribes and Phariſees , preſcribed ſo againſt Chriſt and his Apoſtles . What then? Is Luther their Meſsias , and Caluin their Paule ? But to returne to our matter : Though already the Catholiks haue ſufficiently anſwered to al theſe reaſons, yet now haue we gotten at your hands an anſwere , for this and all the like: that to argue frõ the Apoſtles tyme, to our tyme, *is a fallax à dicto ſecundũ quid ad ſimpliciter: that it is an yl fauored forme of argumente , that yonge ſtudientes in the ſcholes woulde be*

aſha-

afshamed of: and to be fhorte, that it is a reafon of the Donatiftes aunfwered and confuted by S. Auguftine. It is alredy M. Horne fufficiently by vs declared ; that the Donatiftes caufe, and S. Auguftines aunfwere to them hath
no maner affinity with M. Fekenham his reafon. They
denied, that princes had any thing at al to doe in matters of
the Churche, or in punifhing thofe that breake the Ecclefiafticall lawes. M. Fekenham denieth not, but that Princes may lawfully punifhe heretikes by lawes : He confeffeth alfo, that Princes may wel and commendably medle as
minifters, ayders, and as afsifters by their temporal fworde,
for the furderance and mayntenance of Ecclefiaftical matters, but not to rule and prefcribe, as the chief gouernours
of all caufes Ecclefiaftical: I muft tel you againe M. Horne:
There is great difference betwene ftaring and ftarke blind.
And as bufie as ye are now again with the Donatifts, ye lacked a litle falt of difcretiō in alleaging of this place of S. Au- M. Feken-
guftine. For this confirmeth M. Fekenhams former faying,   hams fay-
that in Chriftes ād the Apoftoles tyme ther were nō Chri-   ing cōfir-
ftian Princes. *In the Apoftles tyme*, faith S. Auguftine, as your med by
felf report his words, *Kings ferued not the Lorde, but did de-* M. Horns
uife vayne things, againft God and his Chrift*. And here might   ovvn al-
                                                              legation.
a man now, that would follow your vayne and humour, encounter with S. Auguftine, and obiect vnto him, King Abgarus, and the thre Kings, that came to honour Chriftes natiuity, ād fuch other. But though they had ben greater Kīgs
thē they were, and that there had ben fome few other lords
or Kings to, that did ferue Chrift: yet would no wife man
for the caufe by me before reherfed, quarrell with S. Auguftine. For a general rule, is not by one exception or two,
notably blemifhed or impayred. Such kinde of phrafes are
                              iij iiij   to be

Vt defcri-
beretur v-
niuerfus
orbis.
Luc. 1.
Murmura
uit omnis
congrega-
tio filioru̅
Ifrael.
Exo.c.16.
to be fou̅de afwel otherwhere, as in holy fcripture. As whe̅ it faith, *that the whole worlde was defcribed by the Emperor Auguftus.* And yet is it wel knowen, that he had nothing to doe, with a great part of the worlde. It is writen alfo, *that all the people of Ifrael did murmure :* and yet all did not murmure. Such kinde of phrafes are verefied of the grea-ter, or the more notable parte.

M. Horne. The. 156. Diuifion. pag. 95. 4.

You frame an other reafon vpon S. Paules vvords vnto the bifhops of E-phefus : vvhereby to proue, that al gouernement in fpiritual or ecclefiafti-cal caufes, belo̅geth to Bifshops and Priefts, and not to Princes, and Ciuil Ma-giftrats, thus you argue: The holy ghoft appointed al fpiritual gouernement of Chriftes flocke vnto Bifshops and Priefts, as the vvords fpoke̅ by S. Paule, doe make full and perfect declaration: Ergo, Kings, Queenes, and Princes, may not claime or take vpon the̅ any part of Spiritual gouernement, much leſſe

The.523.
vntruthe.
It is a
goodargu
ment, no
Sophifti-
catio̅ at al.
take the fupremacy, and chief part of fpiritual gouernement from them. For anfvveare, I deny this argument, for it is a naughty and deceiptful (.523.) *So-phiftication, called,* Fallacia æquiuocationis. *There is equiuocatio̅ in this* vvord (Priefts) *and fo in thefe vvords* to gouerne a̅d rule the Church of God. *This vvorde* Prieft, *hath diuers fignificatio̅s vvhich are to be obſer-ued: leaft the fimple readers be confirmed or brought into errour thorough the equiuocatio̅ therein. The Scripture fpeaketh of a priefthood after the order of Aaron: after vvhich order you vvil not co̅feſſe Apoftles, and the Bifshops their*

Heb. 7.
fucceſſours to be Priefts, an other kind of Priefthod is, after the other of Mel-chifedech, and Chrift only vvithout any fucceſſour in that priefthood, vvas the alone Prieft of that order. The third kind is an holy and princely Prieft-hod, of the vvhich order not only the Apoftles and their true fucceſſours, but alfo Kings, Queenes, Princes and al maner of faithful Chriftians are Priefts. There is in common opinion amongeft the Papifts, a fourth kind, vvhich is a

The.524.
vntruthe.
A plaine
herefy.
The.525.
vntruthe.
*maſſinge and facrificig priefthod: after vvhich order, Chriftes Apoftles a̅d the true myniſters of his Church vvere (*524.*) neuer priefts: for that order belo̅-geth only to the Apoftolical Clergy of the Romifhe Antichrift. If your mea-ning therefore be, that Chrift left any kinde of gouernement or rule of his Church to Bifshops and Priefts, after this popifhe order, your opinio̅ is (.525.) hereticall*

hereticall, and your assertion vtterly false. Therefore vvhere I shal after vvardes in my speaking cal the ministers of Christes Church, Prieltes, I geue you to vnderstand, that I doe therein but follovv the vsuall and accustomed kinde of speache vvhich is (.526.) improper although in longe vse. Likevvise to gouerne and rule the Church of God: is of tvvo kindes and sortes, the one is by the supreme authority and povver of the (.527.) svvorde, to guide, care, prouide, direct and ayde Gods Church, to further, mainteine and setfoorth the true Religion, vnity and quietnes of Gods Churche: and to ouersee, visit, refourme, restraine, amende and correcte all maner persons, vvith al maner errours, superstitions, heresies, schismes, abuses, offences, contemptes and enormities in or about Gods Church. Which gouernement and rule apperteineth onely to Kings, Queenes, and Princes, and not to the Apostles, Bisshops and Prieltes: vvhereof S. Paule speaketh nothing at al in this sentence by you alledged to the Bisshops of Ephesus. The other sorte is to feede the flocke of Christ vvith the Spiritual foode of Gods vvord, vvhich is the (.528.) only rule and gouernement that belongeth to the Apostles, Bisshops and Ministers of Christes Churche, and of none other maner rule speaketh S. Paule to the Bisshoppes of Ephesus, vvhich he maketh most plaine both by the expresse vvords of the sentence auouched, and also by the vvhole circumstance of the same place. The vvord that S. Paule vseth, doth proprely signify to feede, as the sheapeherd feedeth his sheepe, and by a figuratiue speach to guide, gouerne or rule: and therefore if you vvould haue dealt (529) plainly, and haue vttered S. Paules meaning according to his propre speache, vvhere you say, To gouerne and rule, doubling the vvoordes as it vvere to amplifie the matter, that the truth might lesse appeare, you ought to haue said, to feede the Church of God. for that is the Apostles (530) propre saying, and so the old translateur of Chrysostome doth translate it vppon the Epistle to the Ephesians, and also expounding this same place of the Acts of the Apostles, vt pascatis Ecclesiã, to feede the Church. S. Peter making the like exhortation, to this of S. Paule, to the Bisshops dispersed, vseth that selfsame vvord, saying:

Pascite

It is a Catholike and and vniuersall opinion of the Churche.

The .526. vntruth. Notorious, as it shal appere out of S. Augustine.

The. 527. vntruthe, The povver of the svvorde ruled the Ievves Synogoge, not Christes Churche.

The. 528. vntruthe. Not that only, but also to correcte, to rebuke, and to refourme.

The. 529. vntruthe. He dealt plainely, and translated truly.

The. 530. vntruthe. For ποιμαίνειν, the Apostles vvorde, signifieth as properly to rule as to feede.

Cap. 4.
Act. 24.

*Pafcite,quantum in vobis eft,gregem Chrifti:*Feede fo muche as you may,the flocke of Chrift. *Chrift him felfe alfo tea-ching Peter,and all other Bifhops, vvhat manner of rule and go-uernement,as properly geuen them by Gods vvoorde, they fhould haue in the Church,doth expreffe it,vvith the felfe fame vvoorde, faying:*Pafce agnos meos,feede my Lambes. *To rule and gouerne the L-houfehold faithfully and prudently, Chrift expoun-deth to be nothing els in general, than to geue meate vnto his fa-mily in due feafon.Neither did our fauiour Chrift geue(.531.)other povver,authority or commifsion vnto his Apoftles , and fo to all other Bifhops as properly belonging and onely to the Bifhoply of-fice , then this:*As my Father fente me,fo I fende you,re-ceiue the holy ghoft,whofe finnes yee remit, they are remitted,whofe finnes yee retaine,they are reteined, goo therefore,and teache all nations,Baptizing them in the name of the Father , and of the Sonne , and of the holy Ghoft:teachinge them to obferue al thinges, that I haue commaunded you.*So that the Bifhoply rule ãd gouernement of Gods Church,cõfifteth(.532.)in thefe three points, to feade the Church vvith Goddes vvoorde,to minifter Chriftes Sa-cramentes,and to binde and lofe:al vvhich three partes, Chrift cõ-prehendeth vnder this one faying:*to geue meat to the Lords family in due feafon. And S. Paule in thefe vvoords,*to feed the Churche of God.*The circumftaunce of the fentece vvhich you alledged foorth of the Actes,doth alfo fhevve in the example of Paule him felfe,vvho vvas inferiour to none of the Apoftles, and Church myniſters in any point, that he claimed or tooke vppõ him none other rule or gouernement , than(.533.) of feedinge Goddes Church vvith the fpirituall foode of the Ghofpell.He fetteth foorth the execution of his ovvne office, and by that example moueth the Bifhoppes of*Ephefus to the like,faynge : I haue ferued the Lorde with all humblenes of minde : I haue leaft no-thinge vndoone,that might be profitable to you : but I haue declared and taught you openly and priuely the repentaunce and faith in God,and Iefus Chrifte . I re-ceyued

Ioan. 21.

Math. 24.

The.531. vntruthe. For he gaue in o-ther places other povver and Autho ryte: Namely in his lafte Supper, Luc.22.and alfo af-ter his Afcenfion by the holy Ghoft inftructing them and their fucceffors for euer . Ioan. 14. &.16.

Math. 28.

The.532. vntruthe. It confifteth not in thefe.3.points only, but in many moe:) as hath bene fhe-vved.

The.533.vntruthe. For S.Paule befide, excõmunicated of-fenders,as.1.Tim.1. ordeined bifhops, as Tite and Timo-thee, made orders in the Churche. 1.Cor.11.&cæt.

eeyued an office of miniſtery from the Lorde Ieſus, to teſtifie the ghoſpel of Gods grace, and to preache the Kingdome of God, I haue hidden nothing of Gods councel from you. Take heede therefore to your ſelues, and to Chriſtes flocke (*as I haue done*) whereof the holy Ghoſt hath appointed you Biſshoppes (*as he did me*) to feede the Church of God (*as you knovv and ſee that I haue done*). *This that you cal to gouerne and rule, vvas vvith Paule* to * ſerue with lowlines, to myniſter with watchefulnes: to preache, teache and teſtifie the Ghoſpel, and the kingdome of God publikely and priuately, and to ſhevv, to the flocke al the Councel of God, touching their ſaluation, keepinge nothinge thereof from them. *To gouerne the Churche of God after this ſorte belōgeth to the only office of Biſhops and Church miniſters, and not to Kinges, Quenes and Princes: vvho (.534.) may not, neither doo, clayme or take vpō them, this kjnd of ſpiritual gouernement and rule, or any part thereof vvith the biſshops, neither do they take the ſupremacy and chief part of this ſpiritual gouernement from the Church miniſters. As contrary vviſe the Church miniſters, ought not to claime and take vpon them the ſupremacy of gouernement, as the (.535.) Papiſtes of longe tyme haue done frō Kinges, Queenes, and Princes.*

* As though humilitie and gouernement could not ſtande together, ād agre both in one perſon.
The.534. vntruthe, for by vou they may take al vpō them, ergo this alſo.
The. 535. vntruthe, mere ſlaūderous.

Stapleton.

M. Horn hath hitherto (good reader) proceded altogether hiſtorically, aſwel in brigig forth his poore ſely proufs againſt M. Fekenham, as in his firſt aunſwere to M. Fekenham, by the ſtory of King Lucius and others: but nowe will he ſhewe you a copie of his high diuinitye, and of his greate diuine knowledge, in the ſoluting of theologicall argumentes.

M. Fekenham proueth by S. Paule, that they are Biſshops and Prieſtes, and not the Princes that gouerne Chriſtes Church. Nay ſaieth M. Horne here, this is a naughty, a duble and a deceitful ſophiſtication: in the worde prieſt, ād in the worde to gouerne: and he is angrie with M. Fekenham for

Concerning this vvorde, Prieſt.

kkk   ham for

ham for the terme of priestes,and wil nedes haue ministers
placed for them. But how chaunceth yt M.Horne, that ye
put not in also,for bishops,superintendēts?Shal the inferiour
clergy change their papistical name,and wil you reserue to
your self stil the name of Bishops,becaufe it is more lorde-
lyke?It is a wonderful thing to cōfider the practife of thefe
proteftants:To make a way to their new diuinity.they firft
began to alter the vfual names, chaunging confefsion into
knowledge,penance into repentance, Church into cōgregation,Image into idole,with many fuch like. So to make a
way,to induce men to belieue that Order is no Sacrament,
and that there is no facrifice in the Church,they could not,
nor cā abide the name of priefts.Tyndal was much trobled
in the framing of fome other word for it.Firft he tranflated
for priefts,*feniours*:but his folly being therein wel efpied,he
tráflated afterward for *feniours,elders.*Which word(elder)
doth no more fignify a prieft,thē it fignifieth an elderftycke.
M.Horn though he be wel cōtēted with the word elders,
as ye fhal hereafter vnderftand, yet here he wil haue them
called Minifters:and geueth vs plainely to vnderftand,that
though he vfe the vnproper terme of prieftes,yet he meaneth minifters,as though euery Prieft be not a Minifter(although euery Minifter be not a prieft)and fo very ofté called in the holy fcripture. As wher it fpeaketh of thofe which
do facrifice in the clergy,it calleth thē indifferétly prieftes
or minifters And therefore Moyfes faith, of the fonnes of
Aarō that were priefts: *Quādo appropinquāt altari, vt mini-
ftrēt in fanctuario.*Whē thei draw nere to the aulter to minifter in the fanctuary. Ioel calleth the priefts, *ministers of
the aulters.*In Hieremy God faith, *that priefts are his mini-
nifters.*S.Paule faith,*Omnis quidē facerdos prafto est quotidie
mini-*

Exod. 28.
Ioelis. 1.
*Viulate Mi-
niftri alta-
ris.*
Hiere. 33.
Sacerdotes
Miniftri
mei.

miniſtrãs, & eaſdē ſemper offerēs hoſtias, euery prieſt is redy *Heb.10.*
dayly to miniſter, euer offering the ſame hoſts . And in the
new teſtament, where it is writen, *miniſtrantibus illis, & ie-*
iunantibus, as they miniſtred to our Lord and faſted, the ſaid *Act.13.*
word, (λειτουργόιωῖων) may wel be traſlated, *as they made ſa-* λειτουρ-
criſice: according to Eraſmus his iudegmēt. Yf thē miniſters γόιωτωρ
ſerue the aulter aſwel as prieſts, what hath M. Horn gained, αὐτῶ
by the ſhiſting of the word prieſts into miniſters?Suerly this τῶ κυρίω
is a wōderful ſhiſting ghoſpel, that cā not ſtād but by ſhiſtig:
ād that muſt nedes ſhyſt away this word prieſt, which hath
ben vſually frequēted ād cōtinued, not only amōg vs in Englād, ſythēce the time we were firſt chriſtened, but amōg o-
ther natiōs, as Dutchmē, high Almaines, Frēchmē, Italiãs, ād
Spaniards, as it appeareth vnto thē that be ſkilfull in theſe
tonges. But to cal the Miniſters of Chriſtes Church, by the
name of Prieſtes, is *a kinde of ſpeache* (ſaith M . Horne) *im-*
propre, though longe in vſe: and for ſuch he proteſteth to vſe
it, as oft as he vſeth the word, Prieſt, in that ſence. The proper prieſthods he auoucheth to be only thre . Of Aaron: of
Melchiſedech: ād of that other Order, which is cōmō to all
Chriſtiãs, mē ād wemē. But ô Lord, what a blid buſſard hath
malice and pride made you M. Horn? Think you it an opiniō among the cōmon Papiſts only (as you ſay) to auouche
a fourth kind of ſacrificing prieſthod? What think you then
of S. Auguſtin that lerned Father of Chriſtes Church? Was
he a Papiſt to? Or was he one alſo of the Apoſtolical clergy
of the Romiſh Antichriſt? Harkē I pray you what his iudge-
mēt is herein. He ſaith, that in the Apoc.20. ād in S. Peter (1. *Augu lib.*
Pet.2.) where the princely prieſthod cōmō to al Chriſtē mē *20. de Ci-*
is ſpoken of: *Nō vtiq, de ſolis epiſcopis & presbyteris dictū eſt,* *uitate Dei*
qui propriè iā vocātur in Eccleſia ſacerdotes, ſed ſicut oēs &c. *cap. 10.*

kkk ij   It is

It is ſpoken not of Biſſhops and Prieſts alone, which nowe in the Church are properly called Prieſts: but as we call al (the faithful)Chriſtians, becauſe of the myſtical ointment, ſo we cal al the faithful Prieſts, becauſe they are the members of one Prieſt, that is, Chriſte. Here you ſee M. Horn, that it is an opiniō not only among the cōmon Papiſts, but with S. Auguſtin alſo that ther are yet in the Church, beſide that Pricely Prieſthod that you ſpake of, biſhops ād prieſts, ād that properly ſo called. And dareth your impudēt mouth, auouche that kinde of ſpeache impropre, which S. Auguſtin auoucheth to be properly ſo called, and that in the Church of Chriſt to? Goe M. Horne, and tel your frendes this tale. For your fréd, I aſſure you, he had nede to be, more then his owne, which wil beleue you in this moſt impudēt and moſt vnchriſtian aſſertion . A prieſthood there is M. Horn, and that a proper prieſthod of biſhops and prieſts in the Church of Chriſt, beſide that of Aarō in the old law, or of Melchiſedech in Chriſtes only perſon, or of this pricely prieſthood cōmō to al Chriſtiās: who are no more properly prieſts, thē thei are Princes, and whoſe cōmō prieſthod no more excludeth the proper prieſthod of Biſhops and prieſts in the Church, thē doth their kingdō (for kings in like maner al Chriſtiās are called in the places of holy Scripture laſtly noted) exclude the proper kingdō, of Emperours, kings, and other Princes. To cōfute yet farder this Antichriſtiā ſolutiō and to proue that this propre prieſthod is a ſacrificig prieſthod, wuld require ſome cōueniēt tract of tyme, ād more thē we cā cōueniétly now ſpare for auoiding of tediouſnes. But what nede we ſeke farre, for a ſolutiō, or tarry long therin, ſeing as cūning as M. Horne is, hiſelf hath in his own ſolutiō proued the ſacrifice of the maſſe ? For to goe no farder M.

Horne

Horn,then your owne chapter and allegatiõ,I reaſon thus. Chriſte contineweth a prieſte accordinge to the order of Melchiſedech for euer:the ſacrifice of which order he ſhewed in his laſt Supper . *Ergo* there is and euer ſhall be that ſacrifice of our true Meſchiſedech , which he offred in his laſte Supper , whiche is the ſacrifice of the maſſe in the Church . *Ergo* it is vntrue,that Chriſte hath no miniſteriall prieſthood or Sacrifice in the Churche.For as Chriſt offered in his laſt ſupper his owne body:ſo all prieſts do offer, and ſhall offer for euer the ſame body in the holy maſſe. And for this cauſe is Chriſt called a prieſte for euer , in the chapter by yowe reherſed,and in the pſalmes.I bringe not, M.Horne,this argument,nor frame yt, of my ſelf:it is Oecumenius(M.Horne) an aũcient and a notable Greciã that ſo writeth,and therin vttereth not his owne mynde onely, but the mind of Chryſoſtomus, ãd other fathers,yea and of the whole Greke Church.Here perhaps M. Horn wil take ſome holde,and anſwere that M.Iewel hath anſwered ſufficiently to Oecumenius in his Reply to M. D. Hardinge. What kinde of anſwere it is and howe ſubſtantiall, it will wel appere,when the Reioynder ſhal come to this Article touching the ſacrifice . And yet I ſuppoſe men that be not to much and to ſiniſtrally wedded to their owne fantaſies, may ſee good cauſe,by ſuch other anſweres as are made to part of his reply,what to iudge of the whole. In the meane ceaſon mark good reader,what kind of anſwere he maketh to rydde him ſelf from this authority of Oecumenius. I wil omitte al other,ãd touche one poynt onely of his anſwere, whereby thou mayſt haue a taſte of the whole. Firſt then I pray you cal to remembraunce,what a ſcoffing and wondringe he maketh at the name and authority of Leontius,

Hebr.7.
Oecumenius ſen-tence of the ſayd ſacrifice. *Sacerdos in æternũ.* *Pſal.19.* *Tu es ſacerdos in æternũ ſecundũ ordinẽ Melchiſedech.* conſider M. Iewels anſ-ſwere to the ſayed Oecumenius.

M. Iewels hypocritall diſsimulation.

k k k   iij   alleaged

alleaged by M.D.Harding with: *what is this Leontius that
wrote this ſtory?or who euer hearde of his name before ?* with

In his re-
ply ſo 75.
much other gay glorious rhetorike.But who is it M.Iewell
but Leontius that ye ſo hardly reaſon againſt for *adorate ſca*

Ievvell
fol.503,
Vid.2. Còc.
Nicenum,
actio. 4.
Non. 1.vt
in levvell.
pag. 517.
bellū pedū eius,adore ye the footſtole of his feat? Now how
cãye make ſuch meruel at him,and demaūd whē he was,ād
what he was:ſeing your ſelf impugne him amõg other that
be alleged in the 2.Nicene Coūcel. Namely ſeing in the very ſame leaf, wherin is conteyned the argument ye do impugne,it appereth alſo,what he was,and whē he was: that
is,ſuch a notable father ād learned biſhop,out of your quarrelling exceptiõ of your. 600.yeares, that he hath eſcaped,
and is aboue all your ſolemne and peremptory challenges.
Truely good reader this is a ſtraunge metamorphoſis and a
ſodaine rauiſhmēt of M.Iewel . For as much as he wõdreth
at Leõtius name in his Reply againſt priuate maſſe, as hardly, and as ſtoutly as he reſoneth againſte him in his reply a-
gainſt the adoration of Saynts Images : yet he is fallen into
ſo great familiarity and lyking with him , that in his Reply
againſt the ſacrifice,to deface Oecumenius , he is content
to authoriſe him for a good and a ſufficient writer.And becauſe Oecumenius telleth vs,*that Chriſt is and ſhall be ſacrificed by the prieſtes , and his holy body to the worldes ende*

Fol.580.
Nos Chri
ſtiani pro-
pemodum
quid ſit
ara, &
quid ſit vi
ctima,neſ-
cimus.
*ſhalbe offred vp in the holy maſſe.*M.Iewel to auoyd this,ſaith:
*what ſacrifice or aulter meaneth,we being Chriſtian people, in
a manner can not tell.*which are the words of the ſayd Leõ-
tius.But yet according to M.Iewells old wonte falſly tranſlated,and moſt falſly and impudētly applied to that,which
the authour neuer ment.And that this holy handling of the
matter may not lightly be eſpied,he alleageth the.2.Nicene
councell, beinge very long and tediouſe:and neither leafe

nor

nor actiõ of it named, neither dareth ons for ſhame to name
Leontius the authour of the ſentence. Nowe Leõtius doth
not meane of the aultar that Chriſtian men vſe to the honour of God, or of the ſacrifice of Chriſtes bleſſed body
(which is the matter that Oecumenius proueth, and ought
to be diſproued by M. Iewel) but of the aultars dedicated
to the deuills, and of the deteſtable ſacrifice that
the infidells did make thervppon, as ye ſhal vnderſtande by his owne wordes. *Theis Iewes* (ſayth Leõtius) *may be aſſhamed, that worſhipping theire owne
kinges, and the kinges of other people, do ſcorne and
ſkoffe at vs Chriſtians, as though we were Idolatours.
For we in euery city and countrie euery day and houre
do ſtande armed againſt idolls: we ſing Pſalmes againſt
idoles, we make our prayers againſt them. And then
howe can they for ſhame call vs idolatours? where are
nowe the oxen, the ſheepe, yea theire owne children,
that the Iewes were wonte to offer in ſacrifice to their
Idoles? Where are the ſmoking ſacrifices? where are the
aulters, and the ſheding of bloudde? Suerly we Chriſtians can not in a manner tell, what is an aulter, or
what is the ſacrifice* (of beaſts) for that is properly *victima*, and of that Leontius ſpeaketh. Thus writeth
this aunciente learned biſihoppe about a thowſand
yeares paſte, againſte the Iewes, that called Chriſtian men Idolatours, for worſhippinge of images.
And the lyke anſwere we catholyks may make a-
gainſt theis our newe Iewes. And ſo at the length
Leontius, that M. Iewell hath ſo wondred at, hath
confuted with his ſhort anſwere al his, and M. Cal-
fields, and ſuch other theirblaſphemous talk againſt
                                                      the

*Nicena. 2. ſynodi
Act. 4. fol. 517.
col. 2. Pudore ſuf-
fundantur Iudęi
qui proprios réges et
alienos adorãtes, nos
Chriſtianos tãquam
idololatras irrident.
Nos aũt Chriſtiañi,
oĩbus in ciuitatib. &
regionib. indies et in
horas ſingulas cõtra
idola ſta nus armati
cõtra idola pſallim⁹,
cõtra idola & preces
fundim⁹. Et qua tã-
dem fronte Iudæi nos
vocant idololatras?
Vbi nunc ſunt quæ
olim ab iſtis oblata
ſunt idolis boũ, ouiũ
& filiorum quoq; vi
ctimæ? vbi ſacrificio-
rũ fumi? vbi aræ et
perfuſiões ſanguinũ?
Nos verò Chriſtiani
propemodum quid ſit
ara, quid ſit victima
ignoramus.*

the catholyks for worſhiping of the image of Chriſt ãd his
Sayntes:and hath bewrayed M.Iewels abhominable ſhifte
made to anſwer Oecumenius,vnder the viſour of this coulorable authority.And nowe may al men as much wóder at
M.Iewells doinges,as he doth at Leontius name:And I am
deceyued if euer there were any poore owle ſo gaſed and
wondered at of the byrdes,as men wil hereafter wonder at
M.Iewel,for theis wretched and miſerable ſhifts. Thus thẽ
the argument of Oecumenius(M.Horne)contrary to your
Antichriſtian blaſphemy againſte the ſacrifice of the maſſe

M.Horn, denying
the ſacrifice , ma-
keth a playne vvay
for Antichriſte.

Daniel, 12.
Quum ablatum fue-
rit iuge ſacrificium.
Aug. de ciuit. Dei.
lib.20.ca.23.&.29.
Proſper de diuinis
pro.niſſ. & prædict.
dimid.temp.cap.13.
Hier. in dict.cap.12.
Primaſ.in apoc.li.3.
cap. 11.
Greg.l 32.
in Iob.14.

ſtandeth vntouched and vnblemiſhed, for any thĩg
that M.Iewel hath or cã ſay,or any other of al your
ſect.The ſacrificing prieſthod M. Horn for al your
ſpite ſhal cõtinewe,and ſhal not vttterly fayle vntil
the time of Antichriſt.Thẽ ſhal it fayl in dede for thre
years ãd an half,according to the prophecy of Daniel,ãd the ſayings of the fathers, namely of S.Au-
guſtin,Proſper,Primaſius,S.Hierõ,and S.Gregory.
Wherfor it is not the Pope,but your ſelf M.Horn,
that with this your ful vnchriſtiã doctrin, ãd deueliſh diuinity , in ſoluting M. Fekenhams argument,
prepareth a redy way for Antichriſt.

An an-
ſvvere to
M.Horne
for M.Fe-
kẽhãs ttã-
ſlating of
the vvord
ποιμαινειν
Paſcere
vel regere.

There is nowe an other equiuocatiõ eſpied by M.Horn
in the worde to gouerne and rule : and that *there are two
kindes of ſorts to gouerne and to rule the Churche of Cod , the
one by the ſupreame authority and power of the ſworde,belõging
onely to princes:the other by feading the flocke, with the word
of God,by miniſtring Sacraments,and by bynding and loſing,be-
longing only to biſſhops and Church miniſters . Which kinde of
ſpirituall gouernment,princes may not neither doe claime.* And
therfor M.Horn ſayth that M.Fekenhã did not deale plaĩly
in tran-

in tranſlating to gouerne and rule the Church , for that S.
Paules worde doth properly ſignifie to fead, as the ſheep-
heard feadeth his ſheepe : neither doth yt ſignifie to gouerne and rule but by a figuratiue ſpeache. By this reaſon
M. Horne might aſwell proue, that Agamemnon was no
king , nor ruler , whome Homer calleth ποιμένα, a paſtour
or ſhepheard:or Dauid to be no kinge or ruler, whome the
ſcripture ſo calleth alſo.   *Thou ſhalt*, ſaieth the ſcripture,
feade my people of Iſrael , thou ſhalt be captaine ouer Iſrael.
Againe: *whome I haue cōmaunded to feade my people.* And in
an other place . *He fead thē in the innocēcy of his heart* with
many like phraſes occurrent in the ſcripture. M. Fekēham
therfore dealt plainely, when he tranſlated to gouerne and
rule:euē as Eraſmus doth trāſlate it out of the Greke which
hath, *regere,& non paſcere :*that is, to rule, and not to feade.
And your brother Edmūde Beke that tranſlated the Bible,
printed at Londō in the yere.1549. though he turne biſhops
into ouerſeers, and church into cōgregation, yet he tranſla-
teth theſe words here, ποιμαίνειν, &c. *to rule the cōgregatiō.*
By likelihod M. Horne thīketh, that there is no true rule or
gouernmēt but where the ſword beareth rule: wherein he
thīketh as wel, and reaſoneth as ſubſtācially, as doth M. Iewell, auouching that S. Peter was not head of the Church,
becauſe he toke vp his lodgīg with a poore tāner. Ye think
to groſly ād baſely M. Horn of the Churches autority. The
Church hath his rule ād gouermēt, yea his ſword to, which
may aſwel and as truely be verefied in the Church regimēt
as in the cyuill regimente. Yea the Church regimente
is incomparably the higher, and by ſo much as the excellēcy of the ſoule is aboue the body . Neither doth this word
ποιμαίνειν, that is to fede, as the ſheepherd feadeth his ſhepe,

Pa-
ſtours.

2.Reg.5.
*Tu paſces
populum
meū Iſra-
el:& tu
eris dux
ſuper Iſra
el. Cui
præcepi vt
paſceret
populum
meū ca.7.
Pſalm.77
pauit eos
in innocē-
tia cordis
ſui.*

So dothe
alſo the
Engliſhe
trāſlation
of the
nevv te-
ſtament
prīted at
zurich.
An.1550.
In his
Replie.
pag.239.

The fhe‑
pherdes
office reſ‑
ſembleth
moſt pro‑
perly the
Biſhopes
Office.

Geneſ.31.

derogate anie thing of the Eccleſiaſtical dignity, but rather
doth encreaſe and amplifie it . The paſtorall office of the
feelde ſhepperd, doth moſt liuely ſignifie, ſet out , and ex‑
preſſe to vs the office, the greatnes, and the excellency of
this paſtorall charge. The Eccleſiaſticall paſtour hauing as
great an accõpt to make to his Maiſter Chriſt, for hys ſpiri‑
tual flocke, that is, the ſoules of the peple cõmitted to him,
as hath the feeld ſhepherde for his ſheepe. This is the ſpiri‑
tual Iacob watching carefully day and night , both in colde
and heate vppõ his flocke, that muſt make good to his mai‑
ſter what ſo euer by theſte is imbeciled, or by wild beaſtes
deuowred. The ſhepeherd M. Horne doth not onely feede
his ſheepe, and carefully choſeth owte ſuche grownde and
paſtour, as is moſte conueniente and holſome for them: but
beſides that, ſondreth the whole and ſownde, from the in‑
fected and rottē: he greaceth and tarreth them, he byndeth,
he cutteth them, he hath a ſtaf with a hooke to draw thē
in when they ſtray: he hath a ſtaf to beat away the wolfe:
he hath a folde to cloſe and ſhutte them vp ſaufe from the
incurſiõs of the woulf, ãd other rauening beaſts. And what
doth all this, but reſemble and expreſſe vnto vs the paſto‑
rall office of Biſhops and prelates ? Who owght to tell the
people what is good and bad, what is trueth , what is falſ‑
hod, what is hereſye , what is Catholyke fayth but theſe
paſtours? Where was then thys leſſon of late , when laye
men only by acte of parliamente toke vpon them to teache
the whole clergye ? Did not then leſſe men , then kinges,
Quenes, and Princes (who may not, you ſay nowe, clayme
or take vpon them this kinde of ſpiritual gouernement and
rule, to fede the Churche with Goddes worde) take vpon
thē to fede all the realme with ſuch doctrine as it pleaſed
the

the parliament to allowe, the parliament I ſay of lay men onely, not one Biſhop amonge them, you being neither by the lawe of God (which no realme cã alter) neither yet by the lawe of the realme any Biſhoppes at all : but onely the Quenes Commiſsioners, in matters of the Churche ? And what can be more vnſeamely and more vnnatural, thẽ thus the ſheepe to feade the ſheepherd , and not the ſhepheard to fede the ſhepe? O what times, o what mãners are theſe?

To proceede , what higher Authoritye can there be in the world, thẽ by baptiſme to make a Chriſtian ſowle? thẽ by pronuncing the ſolempe wordes appointed by Chriſte to cauſe to be preſente the body and bloudde of Chriſte ? And that ſame to miniſter to the deuoute and wel diſpoſed people when ſo euer they call for yt? What rule and regimente is comparable to the rule and regimente of the ec-cleſiaſtical ſhepherde, in the taking or excluding any out of his ſpiritual folde: that is, in binding and loſing , in forge-uing or retaininge of ſynnes, in making owte excommuni-cation, or in the releaſing of the ſame vppon dewe repen-taunce? Herken, herken good M. Horne , what that noble prelate Chryſoſtomus writeth of this gouernment. *Etenim qui terram incolunt. &c.* There is (ſayeth Chriſoſtomus)a power geuẽ to them that dwell and be cõuerſante in the earth, to diſpẽſe and diſpoſe heauẽly thinges, Which power God Would not geue neither to angelles nor archangelles . For yt Was not ſpoken to them, What ſo euer ye binde in earthe ſhalbe bownde in heauẽ: and What ſo euer ye loſe in earth ſhalbe loſed in hea-uen. The Worldly Princes haue alſo an authority to binde : but only touching the body: but theſe bondes of the prieſtes bynde the ſowle alſo, and do reache euen as farre as heauen. So that What ſo euer the prieſtes do benethe (in the worlde)the ſame

Chryſo-ſtoms ſai-yngs tou-ching the ſpirituall gouerne-ment.

Lib. 3. de dignitate Sacerdotij

lll ij God

*God doth ratifie aboue (*in heauen) *and the Lord doth confirme
his seruants sentence.* And he saith anon after. *If the kinge
doth honour any of his subiectes, so farre, that he geueth him authoritie to imprison, or release out of prison whom he wil, this
fellowe shalbe counted most fortunable, and a most happy man.
But the priest, hath receiued from God a much greater power:
and by so muche the greater, as heauen excelleth the earth, or
the soule the bodie.* And by and by. *It is a madnes (*saieth he)
*to despise this principalitie, without the whiche we can not be
partakers of our saluation, or of such good thinges as are promised vs. For if no man can enter into the kingdome of heauen,*

Vide. li. 6.

*unlesse he be regenerated by water and the holy Ghoste: and he
that doth not eate the fleashe of our Lorde and drinke his bloud*

Porrò illū
ipsū opor-
tet tantò
oibs rebus
illis p̄stare
p̄ quib. in-
tercedit,
quātò par
ē vt subdi-
tos præfe-
ctus excellat. Cū aūt
ille & spiritum San-
ctū inuocauerit, sa-
crificiūque illud hor-
rore ac reuerētia plē
nissimū perfecerit,
cōmuni omniū ma-
nibus assidue pertra-
ctato, quære ex te,
& cæt.

*is berefte of euerlasting lyfe: and all these thinges are not done,
but by theyr holy handes, I saie by the handes of the Priestes:
Howe maie it be, that without theyr helpe, a man maie either
shunne hell fier, or obtaine the rewarde of the croune reserued
in heauen?* Againe he writeth, *that the priest is the ambassadour from al the worlde to desire God to be merciful, not only for
the sinnes of the lyuing, but for the dead also* . And anon after
speaking of the sacrifice of the Masse, that you denie, and
shewing what excellencie in vertue the Bishope or priest
ought to haue aboue other: he saieth, *that he must in
al things excel other for whō he maketh this intercessiō
to God, so far as it is mete that the ruler passe and ex-
ced the subiect. For* (sayth he) *whē the priest hath called for the holy Ghost, ād hath made the sacrifice, which
we ought most to reuerence, and to tremble and feare
at, handling continually our common Lord: I demaund
among what states shal we place him? How great integrity shal we loke for at his handes? How great holines
and*

*and deuotiõ? Cõſider what thoſe hãdes ought to be, that ſhal mi-
niſter ſuch things? Cõſider what tong he ought to haue, that ſhal
ſpeak ſuch words: Cõſider finally that his ſoule ought to be of all
other moſt pure ãd holy, that ſhal receiue ſo great, ãd ſo worthy
a ſpirit.* At that time (he meaneth of the cõſecratiõ of the bleſſed ſacrifice) *the angels are preſent with the prieſt, and al the
orders of the heauẽly powers do make a ſhoute : the place that is
nigh to the alter, is for the honor of him, that is ſacrificed, reple-
niſhed with the companies of angels. Which a man may wel beleue, by reaſon of ſo great a ſacrifice as is then made.*

Thus muche haue I ſhewed you M. Horne owt of that
moſt learned light of the Greeke Church, Ioannes Chriſoſtomus, aſwell to cauſe you to vnderſtand your deteſtable
hereſie againſte the prieſthod of the newe teſtamente, as
that the prieſtes haue a dignity, and a ſingular excellẽt regimente, aboue ſecular Princes . They haue their ſpirituall
ſword, that two edged ſword I ſay, that cutteth both bodie
and ſoule, and by excõmunication (if the party repent not)
caſteth both into the deape dongeon of hel. And ſhall all
this be counted no rule nor regiment M. Horne , being in
dede the cheif and the principal regimẽt of al other? It is, yt
is M. Horn the higheſt gouernmẽt of al other, and of greateſt charge, and importance. And muche better may yt be
ſaid to this euãgelical paſtour, that was ſayd to Agamẽnon.

Οὐ χρὴ παννύχιον εὑδ᾽ ἓν βχληφόρον ἄνδ᾽ρχ
ὦ λαοίτ᾽ἐπίτετράφαται, κὴ τόσσα μέμηλεν.
*It is not mete for him , all the night longe to ſlepe.
that hath ſo muche people, and ſuche a charge to kepe.*

Yea, ye are forced your ſelf M. Horn to cõfeſſe yt a ſpiritual gouernmẽt and rule. Wherby of neceſsity followeth
the ouerturning and ouerthrowĩg of your lay ſupremacie.

Iliad, β.

Locus al-
tari vici-
nus in illa
us honore,
q̃ imola-
tur ange-
lorũ cho-
ris plenus.
eſt. Id
quod cre-
dere abũ-
de licet vel
ex tanto
illo ſacri-
ficio quod
tũ peragi-
tur.

For thefe being the chiefmatters or things Ecclefiafticall,
as your felfe can not denie,and the Prince hauing nothing
to doe with them, as you alfo confeffe, it can not be poffible, that the Prince fhould haue the Supremacy in al caufes or things Ecclefiaftical. And fo neither M.Fekenham
nor any man els may take this othe for feare of euident and
open periurie. And of all madnes, this is a madnes, and a
moft open contradiction to remoue thefe things from the
Prince, as ye do, and yet to attribute to him without anie
exception the fupremacy *in al things or caufes Ecclefiaftical*
Yea and to vrge men by othe to confeffe the fame. Which
kind of arguing is as wife as if a man woulde affirme, God
to be the maker of al things,the geuer of all things,the pre-
feruer of al things, and yet by and by to faye : God can not
geue the effect of grace to externall Sacramentes, God can
not preferue his owne bleffed Mother from al actual or o-
riginal finne. Whereof will followe, that God in dede is
not omnipotent or almightie : thofe things being taken a-
waie from him, wherein chieflie his almightie power confifteth. For in fuch miraculous operations, furmounting
farre al power of men, God moft proprelie fheweth himfelfe a God. As in fuch actes and caufes Ecclefiaftical(as
binding and loofing, preaching the worde, miniftring the
Sacraméts,&c.) confifteth fpecially and moft proprely the
rule and gouernement Ecclefiaftical. We nede not therfore wraftle with you herein any farther, M. Horne, feing
you can fo preatily geue your felfe a notable fall.

Yet one thing would I faine knowe more of you, M.
Horne, if I may be fo bolde, and learne, what you meane
nowe at the length to come in *with the fupreme Authority
and power of the fworde.* What meane you, I fay, to define
vnto

The
Princes
fupremat
cy ouers
throwen
by that
that M.
Morne
him felfe
grauteth.

vnto vs, *the one kinde and ſorte of gouerning the Churche of God,* in theſe wordes: *by the ſupremē Authoritie and power of the ſword to guide, care, prouidc, direct and ayde Gods Church, &c?* In all your booke hithei to, of ſuch ſupreme Authoritie and power of the ſworde, you neuer ſpake worde. Howe chaunceth it then, the ſworde commeth in nowe? Doth the ſupreme gouernement of the Churche of God conſiſte in the power of the ſworde? Then howe was the Church of God gouerned.300. yeres and more before the time of Conſtantine the Emperour, who was the very firſt (as hath bene ſhewed) that by the power of the ſworde, I ſaie, by the power of the ſworde, guided, cared, prouided, directed and aided Gods Churche? Did the Churche of Chriſt want a Supreme gouernour all thoſe.300. yeres and more?   Againe, doe the Lawes of the Church take force by the power of the ſword? You with M. Nowell, and with the Acte of Parliament, do take away from the clergie the power and Authoritie to make Churche Lawes, and Conſtitutions: and you ſay and ſwere to, that no Conuocation or Councel of Biſhops, ſhal or may haue force or Authoritie to decree any Coſtitution Eccleſiaſtical, without the Princes conſent, licence, and ſupreame authoritie. For this purpoſe alſo you haue alleaged the practiſe of ſo many Coūcels both General and National, to make proufe that by the ſupreame Authoritie of Emperours and Kings, Canons and lawes of the Churche haue bene enacted and decreed, not by the Biſhops and Councels it ſelfe. Wherin how ſhamefully you haue miſreported the whole practiſe of the Churche, I haue ſufficiently ſhewed in the ſeconde and third Bookes. But in all your ſo long proceſſe you neuer yet openlie ſaid, that by the power of the ſword ſuche

Canons

Canons and Lawes tooke place. And come you nowe
to saye, that all this proceded of the power of the sworde?
Where is then nowe become the libertie of the Ghospell,
that your graundsir Luther, and all your protestant progenitors of Germany do in al their writings so much extolle,
maintaine, and defende against the Secular swoorde of
Ciuill Magistrates? Againe you M. Horne, that doe
force the Scholers of Oxforde to sweare by booke Othe,
that Scripture onelye is sufficiente to conuince euerye
trueth, and to destroye all heresies, you that will beleue
nothing, but that as plaine Scripture auoucheth vnto you,
tell vs, I praye you, where finde you in all Scripture, that
the Supreame Authoritie to gouerne the Churche of
God, is by the power of the swoorde? What? Did
not the Apostles gouerne the Churche of Christe all the
time of their abode here in earth? And when or where I
pray you, vsed they the power of the Sword? Or because
they vsed not that power, wer they not therfore the suprē
Gouernours? Had they not a power and iurisdiction Ecclesiasticall? Saint Augustine affirmeth: *Doctores Eccle-*

*siarum Apostoli omnia faciebant : & præcipiebant qua fierent,
& corripiebant si non fierent, & orabant vt fierent.* The
teachers of the Churches, the Apostles did al things. They
cōmaunded things to be done, they rebuked and vsed discipline yf things were not done. And they prayed, that
things might be done. This declareth that a gouernmēt and
iurisdictiō thei vsed beside the bare preaching of the word.
But this gouernement (saith M. Horne) was not by the power of the sword, which belōgeth only to Kings and Princes. Lerne now then M. Horne, that the Church of Christ
hath a power aboue the sword, ād that as the Iewish Syna-
gogue

gogue was ruled with the fworde, the tranfgreffours of the *fword.*
lawe being punifhed by death, fo the Churche of Chrift is
ruled by the Spiritual keies committed to the Apoftles and
their fucceffours, and the tranfgreffours of the Churche
lawes are punifhed with the fpiritual fworde of that iurifdiction. S. Auguftine faith: *Phinces the Prieft flew the ad-* *De fide &*
ulterers with the fword: which truely was fignified to be done *operibus*
in this time with degradations and excommunicatïons, when *Cap. 2.*
as in the Church difcipline, the vifible fworde fhould ceafe. *Cùm in Ec*
Lo, M. Horne. The vifible fword is no part of the Church *plïna vifi-*
difcipline nowe. It was among the Iewes a greate part of *bilisfuerat*
their difcipline. Marke that it was no parte of the Chur- *gladius*
che difcipline. I doe not denie, as the Donatiftes did, *ceffaturus*
that becaufe in the Apoftles time, Princes vfed not the
fwoorde vppon Heretiques, and difobediente Chriftians
therefore they fhould not now vfe it. But I faie the Princes
fworde is no parte of the Churche difcipline. I fay with S.
Auguftine, this vifible fword in the Church difcipline cea-
feth. If the Prince vfe the fworde, it is no Ecclefiafticall
gouernement, nor it is not the fupreme gouernment. The
Bifhop hath a farre fuperiour gouernment, and a more terrible fworde to ftrike withall. Of the whiche S. Auguftine *Decorrep.*
faith: *Ipfa quæ damnatio nominatur, quam fecit epifcopale Iu-* *& gratia*
dicium, qua pœna in Ecclefia nulla maior eft, poteft.&c. That *Cap. 15.*
punifhment which is called condemnation, which is made
by the iudgement of the Bifhoppe, then the whyche
punyfhment there ys in the Churche no greater, may yet
(yf yt pleafe God) turne to a holefome correption.
And agayne of the Churche difcipline he fayeth, where
by the Churche (not by anie Prince) the ftubborne and
difobedyent offender ys pronounced an Ethnicke and a
m m m publi-

fword.
Contra ad
uerfar.
legis &
propheta-
rum.lib.1.
Cap.17.
publicayne, *Grauius eft, quàn fi gladio feriretur, fi flammis abfumeretur, fi feris fubrigeretur.* This is a more greeuous punifhment, then if he were ftryken with the fword, then if he were fpent vp in flames of fyere, then if he were rent with wilde beaftes. You fee then the Church hath a greater power to punifhe withall, then the princes fworde. And to proue vnto you euidently, that the Princes fworde can be no part of Ecclefiaftical or Spiritual gouernement, I will wifhe you to marke but this one reafon. The Churches power, iurifdiction, and gouernement, extendeth to the foule, ouerfeeth, guideth, and ruleth the foule of man, not the bodie or any thing appertaining to the bodie. But the Princes fwoorde can not reache to the foule of man. Ergo the Princes fworde can not be any fitte meane to gouerne as the Churche doothe, or to beare the Supreme gouernment in Church matters. The Maior or firft Propofition is clere and confeffed not onely of al Diuines, but of all Chriftian men that know what the Churche and the foule meaneth. The Minor is alfo cleare, if by nothing els, yet by this onélye place of the Ghofpell where

oure Sauiour faith : *Feare not them that kill the bodie, & poft hæc non habent amplius quid faciant :* and then haue no more to doe. As muche to faie : whofe fwoorde can not reache to the foule. Or as an other Euangelift writeth : *Whiche can not kill the foule..* And what is more repug-

naunt to reafon, then to teache, that the Prince his fword whyche can not hurte the foule, fhoulde be the fupreame Gouernoure of the Churche, all whofe power is ouer the foule? Whereof I reafon thus. The Prince can not punnifhe the foule of man : Ergo he hathe no iurifdiction ouer it. Item he can not relieue it, or releafe it, being

being in the boundes and diftreſſe eyther of infidelitie, or of ſinne : Ergo he can not be the ſupreame guider, and gouernour of it. Onely the Biſshoppes and Prieſts, doe pu-
niſhe the ſoule by excommunication and binding of ſinnes.
Onely the Biſshoppes and Prieſtes (I ſaie Maiſter Horne,
thoſe that are *proprelie called Prieſtes*) can releaſe, abſolue,
and make free the ſoule of man from the boundes and fet-
ters.of infidelitie and ſinne : Ergo they onelye haue the
true and proper gouernmĕt ouer the ſoul:If ouer the ſoule,
Ergo in al Spiritual or Eccleſiaſtical cauſes which al tende
to the ſoule helth and to the only gouernment of the ſame.

I graunt for preſeruation of externall quiet, vnitie and
peace in the Church, the Princes ſword walketh and puni-
ſheth the body of mĕ in the church. But this is no Church
diſciplin(*in the which* as S.Auſtine teacheth *the viſible ſword*
ceaſeth)this is no Churche gouernemente , deſcribed vnto
vs in the Ghoſpell, and practiſed of the Churche Miniſters of all ages and times.   But this is a Ciuill gouernemente, aiding, not gouerning the Churche in times of extreme frowardeneſſe and obſtinacie of Heretiques and
miſſebeleuers.   This dothe (as all other worldlye things
doe) ſerue the Churche of God, as the bodie ſerueth the
ſoule, for execution of Churche lawes , for repreſſing of
ſchiſmes and ſeditions, and for the maintenaunce alſo of
dewe obedience in thoſe men , whoſe frailtie or malice is
ſuche, that they more feare the temporall ſwoorde, then
the ſpirituall, and are moued more with externall damma-
ges, then with Eccleſiaſticall cenſures , briefelie ſuche as
feare more the torment of the bodie, then the loſſe of their
ſoules.

And ſtandeth it nowe with your truthe and honeſty to

ſay,that the ſupreme gouernment of the Church, ſtandeth
in the power of the ſworde? But why(as I ſayed before)
ſay you it now at the length,which before you neuer ſaied,
but rather ſo extolled the princes ſupreme gouernement,
that you made him an accurſer of heretikes, a maker of
Churchlawes and conſtitutions a principal confirmer of al
Councelles, yea and a preacher of Gods wordes to? And
neuer ſpake worde of the ſword, but couertly concealed
that pointe vntill nowe? Why M. Horne,but becauſe the
euidence of holy Scripture alleaged by M. Feckenham forced you thereunto? The place I ſay of the Actes, where
S.Paule confeſſeth,that the Biſhopes and prieſtes (*properly
ſo called*, M· Horne, as S. Auguſtine telleth you) were appoynted of the holy Ghoſt to feede and to rule the church,
forced you to this plaine diſtinction, and to graunt nowe
which you neuer graunted before, a certaine rule and gouernement to Biſhoppes and prieſtes, which princes haue
nothing to doe withall, plaine contradictorie to your former aſſertions, and to the Othe which you defende, attri-
butyng ſupreme gouernement to the Princes in all maner
cauſes eccleſiaſtical or ſpiritual without exception. This
alſo forced you to limit the Princes gouernemēt with the
power of the ſworde,which in Churche'matters (as hath
bene proued)is nowe no power at all (though among the
Iewes it were)and which alſo, if it were a power, is not
yet the ſupreme power,ſeing the Biſhops and Prieſts haue
a farre greater and higher power to exerciſe and to practiſe vpon the ſoules of men, ouer which the Church properly,chiefly and only ruleth and gouerneth,not ouer the
body,otherwiſe thē the neceſſary cōiunctiō of both impli-
eth the one with th'other.Gods name be bliſſed.The truth
hath

hath forced you to open your owne falfhood, and the ab- fword.
furditie of your affertion, which you would fo fayne haue See the
concealed. The truthe alfo hathe driuē you to graunte that force of
rule and gouernement nowe to Bifhoppes and Prieftes, truthe.
which hitherto in your booke , and which alfo by the tenour of the Othe by you defended , is attributed to the
Prince only, and cleane taken away from the Bifhops and
Prieftes: Yea and to auouch, that Princes neyther may, nor
doo clayme any fuch rule vpon thē, when yet by you and
by the Othe, they bothe may and ought to claime no leffe
then all together, without any exception or limitation in
the worlde.   Wherefore (as I fayed before) we nede to
wreftle no farder with you, feing you can fo roundly geue
your felfe fo notable a falle, and caft your felfe fo properly
in your owne turne. And to auoide tedioufnes, I am dryuen here to breake of, defyrous otherwife to open diuerfe
your other and greate abfurdities in thys Diuifion. Nowe
fome of them I will note in your margin among your manyfolde vntruthes , and content my felfe at thys prefent ,
with that which hath bene fayed .

The. 157. Diuifion. pag. 97. a.

M. Fekenham.

*And when your L. fhalbe hable to prooue, that thefe
woordes of the Apoftle Paule , and by him written in his
Epiftle vnto the Hebrewes:* Obedite præpofitis veftris, & Heb. 13.
fnbiacete eis: ipfi enim peruigilāt, quafi rationē pro animabus veftris reddituri, vt cū gaudio hoc faciāt, et nō gemētes.
Doe ye obey your fpirituall gouernours, and fubmit your felues
vnto them, for they watche, as men which muft geue accompt
for your foules: that they may doe it with ioye & not with griefe.

                    m m m   iij   VVhan

VVhan your L. ſhalbe hable to proue, that theſe wordes were not writen of the Apoſtle Paule, aſwel for al Chriſtian Emperours, Kings and Queenes, as for the inferiour ſort of people, thã ſhal I in like maner yelde touching that text of Paule, and thinke my ſelfe very wel ſatisfied.

M. Horne.

No man hath or doth denie, that the Church miniſters hath to gouerne the flocke by preaching, and feeding vvith the vvorde, vvhich is the rule or gouernement, that Paule ſpeaketh of in this place alſo: vvhereto all princes are and ought to be ſubiecte and obedient. For this ſubiection and obedience, to the vvorde of the Ghoſpel, taught and preached by the Biſhoppes, ſitting in Chriſtes chaire, vvhich is the vvhole (.536.) rule and gouernement they haue or ought to claime, as propre to theyr calling, is commaunded ſo vvell to princes, as to the inferiour ſorte of the people, as you ſay truely, although your cauſe is no deale holpen, nor my aſſertion any (.537.) vvhis proued thereby.

The .2. Chapter, Of M. Fekenhams ſecond reaſon, for not taking the Othe: grounded vpon S. Paule Heb. 13.

Stapleton.

THE ſeconde authority that M. Fekenham bringeth is out of S. Paule *Obey your* (ſpiritual) *gouernours, and ſubmitte your ſelues vnto them, for they watche as men, that muſte geue an accompt for your ſoules.* In which wordes th'Apoſtle, as he teacheth the ſhepe to obey, ſo he techeth the paſtours *vigilare & clauum ac gubernacula tenere,* ſaieth Theodoretus, to watch and to rule the ſterne. For anſwere to this, M. Horne is yet ones againe reuolted to his feding, and woulde fayne feade vs forth with a foliſhe flie flawe, as thowghe this were meante no further, then that ſpirituall men may feade the people and Prince to, with the
worde

worde of God:wherunto all afwell the Princes as people are bownde to obey.*And this,*he faieth,*is the whole rule and gouernmente that they can properly clayme .* Nay Mayfter Horne, not fo , let them haue fome more gouernemente , and at the leafte , fo muche as your felf graunted them euen in the lafte leafe before :that is,to minifter Sacramentes, and to bynde and lofe. Will ye fo fone abridge your late liberalitie? What yf the people Mayfter Horne, or the Prince either will fet light by the preachers worde, and will amende neuer a deale the more , for all his preaching,but wexeth worfe and worfe, efpecially in opē and notorioufe faultes?Is there no further remedy,but to fuffer al thinges to runne on ?Ys the Bifhop thinke you now excufed?Why had then Ely fuch a greauoufe punifhment for his vnruly children?He tolde them theire faultes,he tolde them that all the people fpake yll of them. But yet both he and his had a terrible punifhmente,*quòd non corripuerit eos.* Becaufe he did not rebuke thē:yet did he rebuke thē . But for that he did not rebuke them fo vehemently and fo earneftly as he fhoulde haue done : and as S.Hierome fayeth, *coercuit & corripuit eos,fed lenitate feu manfuetudine paternali,nō feueritate & authoritate Pontificali.* He did correcte and rebuke thē,but mekely and gently as fathers are wōte, not feuerely,nor with fuch autority as he being the bifhop fhould haue done.Then yf gentle or fharpe words wil not ferue,the euāgelical paftour muft take the ftaf in his hand, and breake the obftinat and ftubborne hart with a terrible blowe of excōmunication , he muft fequefter this fcabbed fhepe frō the refidue of the flock.For as S.Auguftin faieth, *An nō ptinet ad diligentiā paftoralē,ēt illas oues quæetc.à grege aberrauerint,fi refiftere voluerint,flagellorū terrorib.vel etiā doloribus reuocare ?*

I. Reg .2.

Vide Dionyfium. 1.reg.2.

Auguftin. epift.50.

Doth

Dothe it not appertaine to the paſtoral diligence, to call backe ſuch ſheepe, as doe goe aſtraie, and if they reſiſt, to call them backe with terroure of the rodde , yea and with ſtripes too ? And this is the rodde S. Paule ſpeaketh of, and threateneth the Corinthians withall. This is the rod with the which he beat the fornicatour there. This rodde many biſhops vſed againſt Princes and Emperours. This rodde Marcians Father being a Biſhoppe , vſed againſt his owne ſonne for deflouring a Virgin. To this ſpirituall Authoritie the offéder, what ſo euer he be, prince or other, is ſubiect : and therfor this proueth euidently the Eccleſiaſticall Supremacy to reſt in the Clergy, ād not in the Prince, which muſt obey as well as the other. And therefore it is not true that ye ſaye, that M. Fekenhams cauſe is no deale holpen by this place, nor your aſſertion any thing improued.

1. Cor. 4. & 5.

Epiphan. hareſ. 42. li. 1. tom. 3

But let vs ſteppe one ſteppe farder with you M. Horne, vpō the groūd of your preſent liberalytye, leſt as you haue begonne, you pinche vs yet farder, and take away all together from Biſhops and Prieſtes. *Subiection,* you ſay, *and obedience to the Word of God taught and preached by the Biſhops &c. is commaūded ſo Wel to Princes, as to the inferiour ſort of the people.* If ſo M. Horne, howe did a lay parliament vtterly diſobey the doctrine of all their Biſhoppes, and enacte a new contrary to theirs ? What obediéce was there in that parliament, ſo expreſſely required here by S. Paule , and ſo dewe euen of Princes them ſelues, as you confeſſe, to their Biſhoppes ? Will you ſay the Biſhoppes then preached not Gods worde? And who ſhal iudge that? Shal a lay parliament iudge it? Is that the obedience dewe to Biſhoppes? In caſe al the Biſhops of a realme erred, is there not a generall Councell to be ſought vnto? Are there not other Biſhops

of

of other Coūtries to be coūteled? Is not al the Church one ſtours.
body ? In matters of faithe ſhal we ſeuer our ſelues frō our
Fathers ād Brethern (the whole corps of Chriſtédome beſide) by the vertue of an Acte paſſed by lay mē onely? No
biſhops, no Clerke admitted to ſpeake, and ſay his minde?
O lamentable caſe. God forgeue our dere Countre this
moſt haynouſe treſpaſſe . Then the which I feare our Realme committed not a more greuous (except the firſt
breache in Kinge Henries dayes) theſe many hundred
yeares.

Yet one ſteppe farder . The Prince muſt obey and be
fedde at the Biſhoppes hande : you confeſſe. What is that?
Is it not, he muſt learne howe to beleue, and howe to ſerue
God? Is it not the paſtorall office, as S Auguſtin teacheth, *Auguſtin.*
to open the ſpringes that are hidden , and to geue pure and *de verbis*
founde water to the thirſty ſhepe ? Is not the ſhepeheardes *Dom.ſec.*
office, *to ſtrenghthen that is weake , to heale that is ſicke,* *Ioā.ſerm.*
to binde that is broken, to bringe home againe that is caſte *34.*
away to ſeke that is loſte, and ſo forthe, as the Prophet Eze- *Ezech.34*
chiel, deſcribeth? And what is all this, but to teache, to correct, to inſtructe, to refourme and amende all ſuch thinges
as are amiſſe, either in faithe or in good life ? If ſo, then in
caſe the realme went a ſtray, ſhoulde not they redreſſe vs,
which were paſtours and ſhepheards in Chriſtes Church?
If our owne ſhepheards did amiſſe , was there in all Chriſtendom no true Biſhoppes beſide, no faithfull paſtour, no *In lib.de*
right ſhepeheard? Verely S. Auguſtine teacheth at large, *paſtoribus*
that it is not poſsible, that the ſhepheards ſhoulde miſſe of *Cap.10.*
the true doctrine. What ſoeuer their life or maners be. But *1. & 13.*
put the caſe ſo, that we may come to an iſſewe. Muſt then
the Prince fede vs , alter our Religion, ſett vp a newe,

ſtop the ſhepheards mouthes, plaie the ſhepheard him ſelf.
Is this, M. Horne, the obedience that you teach Princes to
ſhew to their ſhepheards? God forgeue them that herein
haue offended, and God (in whoſe hands the harts of Princes are) inſpire with his bleſſed grace the noble hart of our
moſt gracious Souerain the Quenes Maieſty, that her highnes may ſee and conſider this horrible and deadly inconuenience to the which your moſt wicked and blaſphemouſe
doctrine hath induced her grace. You are the woulfe, M.
Horne. And therfore no marueile if you procure to tie the
ſhepheard faſt, and to mouſell the dogges.

The .158. Diuiſion. Pag. 97. b.

M. Fekenham.

1. Cor. 14. *And when your L. ſhall be able to proue, that theſe*
wordes of Paule: Mulieres in Eccleſijs taceant, &c. **Let**
the wemen kepe ſilence in the Churche: for it is not permitted
vnto them there to ſpeake: but let them liue vnder obedience,
like as the Law of God appointeth the, and if they be deſirous
to learne any thing, let them aſke their huſbands at home, for it
is a ſhameful and rebukeful thing, for a woman to ſpeake in the
Church of Chriſt. *VVhen your L. ſhalbe able to proue, that*
theſe wordes of Paule, were not as wel ſpoken of Quenes,
Ducheſſes, and of noble VVomen, as of the meane and in-
feriour ſorte of VVomen: like as theſe wordes of almigh-
tie God, ſpoken in the plague and puniſhment firſt vnto
our mother Eue for her offence: and ſecondarily by her
vnto al women without exception. vidz. Multiplicabo æ-
Gen. 3. rumnas, &c. **I ſhal encreaſe thy dolours, ſorowes and concei-**
uings, and in paine and trauaile, thou ſhalt bring forth thy chil-
dren,

ozen, & thou ſhalt liue vnder the authozity & power of thy huſ-
bãd and he ſhal haue the gouernment and dominion ouer thee.

*VVhan your L. ſhall be able to proue, anye exception to
be made eyther in theſe woordes ſpoken in the olde lawe,
by the mouth of God: eyther in the wordes before ſpoken
of the Apoſtle Paule in the newe: than I ſhall in like mã-
ner yeelde, and with moſt humble thankes, thinke my
ſelfe very well ſatiſſied in conſcience, not onely touching
all the afore alleaged teſtimonies, but alſo in this ſeconde
chiefe pointe.*

M. Horne.

*I doe graunte the vvoordes of the holie Scriptures in bothe theſe places
to be ſpoken to al ſtates of vvomen vvithout exception. But what make
they for your purpoſe, hovve doe they conclude and confirme your cauſe?
VVomen muſte be ſilent in the Churche, and are not permitted to ſpeake:
That is, as your ovvne Doctour* Nicolaus de Lyra *expoundeth it,* women muſte not teache and preache the doctrine in
the Churche, neyther diſpute openlye: *Therefore
our Sauiour Chriſte dyd not committe to Kinges, Queenes,
and Princes, the Authoritie to haue and take vppon them
(.538.) anye part of gouernement in Eccleſiaſticall cauſes.
As (.539.) though a younge Nouice of your Munkiſhe ordre
ſhoulde haue argued: Nunnes muſte keepe ſilence, and maye
not ſpeake in the Cloyſture, nor yet at Dynner, tyme in the fray-
trie: therefore your deceyuer the Pope dyd not committe Authoritie to his Prouincialles, Abbottes, Priores, and Prioreſſes,
to haue and take vppon them the gouernement vnder hym ſelfe
in Munkiſhe and Nunniſhe cauſes and matters? VVhat man
vvoulde haue thought Maiſter Feckēham to haue had ſo (.540.)
little conſideration, although vnlearned, as to vouche the ſilence of vvomen in the Churche, for a reaſon to improue the
Authoritie of Princes in Churche cauſes?*

The .538. vntruthe.
M Feckenham rea-
ſoneth not ſo. But
thus. Therefore
vvomen can not
take vppon them
the Supreame go-
uernement in all
cauſes &c.

The .539. vntruthe.
The argument is
nothing like.
The .540 vntruthe.
This argument is
made vvith good
and greate conſi-
deration, as I ſhall
appeare.

nnn ij   The

THE FOVRTH BOOKE

The. 3. Chapter. Of M. Fekenhams third reason taken out of
S. Paule also. 1. Cor. 14.

Stapleton.

MAifter Feckenham his thirde reafon is, that women *are not permitted to fpeake in the Church*, and therefore they can not be the heads of the Church. To this M. Horn anfwereth: firft that this place of S. Paul muft be vnderftanded of teaching, preaching, and difputing: and that therfore it wil not follow thereof, that they may not take vpō thē any gouernment in Ecclefiaftical caufes. And then being merily difpofed, he faith this Argumēt is much like, as if a yong Nouice fhuld reafon thus. Nūnes muft kepe filēce in the Cloifture: therfore the Priorefles haue not the gouernment in Nūnifh caufes and matters. Cōcerning the firft part of his anfwere, I fay that the argument is good ād fufficiēt. For if teaching, preaching, and difputing in matters of religiō, be caufes and matters ecclefiaftical: and if womē be imbarred frō this, then is there a fufficiēt caufe, why M. Fekenham may not take this othe, that a woman is fupreme head in al caufes fpiritual ād ecclefiaftical: Namely to erect and enact a new and proper religiō throughout her realme by the vertue of her own proper and fupreme gouernmēt. For to this end, M. Horn, is the othe tēdred. It is to euidēt. It can not be diffembled. Againe, the faid place of S. Paul is of the order and māner of expoūding of fcripture, as it appeareth by the text. If then S. Paul forbiddeth a woman to expoūd fcripture : how can a woman take vpon her, to be the chief iudge of al thofe that expoūd the fcripture? I mean in that very office of expoūding Scripture, in decreeig, determining, and enacting, what religion, what beliefe, what doctrine fhal take place. And fuch fhee muft nedes be, if fhe

be

be a fupreme head. Suche do you and your fellowes make her.Such authority you M.Horn,throughout all this boke, attribute to your new fupreme heads,Emperours and Kigs by you alleaged.You make them to preache,to teache and to prefcribe to the Bifhops in their Coucels,what and how they fhal do in their ecclefiafticall matters.If then by you a fupreme Gouerner in ecclefiafical maters, muft be fo qua-lified,as to be prefent in Councels of Bifhops, to prefcribe rules for the Bifhops to follow,to determine what they fhal do,and to cofirme by royal aflet the decrees of bifhops,yea and to make them felues,decrees and coftitutions ecclefia-ftical,but a woman by S.Paule,may not ones fpeake in the Church,that is,in the Cogregatio or aflembly of the faith-ful,and by you a woma may not preache,teach,or difpute: vndoubtedly both by S.Paul,and by your own cofefsion,a woma can not be a fupreme Gouernour, fuch as the Othe forceth me to fwere. I fay,fupreme gouernour in al eccle-fiaftical caufes. No nor in fo many caufes by a great deale, as you pretend in this your booke other Kings and Princes to haue practifed fupreme gouernmet in.Cofider now,M. Horne,how it may ftad with S.Paules doctrine,that a wo-man may be a fupreme gouerner in al ecclefiaftical caufes: namely fuch as you in this boke,would make your Reader beleue,that al Emperours,Kings and Princes hitherto haue bene.   Now put the cafe(as we faw it viij.yeres paft)that in a doubtful matter of doctrine and religion to be tried by fcripture,the whole number of bifhops agree vpo fome de-terminate and refolute expofition with their Clergie, and would by an Ecclefiaftical law of Couocation or Councel fet forth the fame? Al their refolutio and determination is not worth a rufh by your Othe and by your maner of talke

nnn   iij   in

in this booke,if the Prince doe not allowe and côfirme the
same. And how this wil ftâd with S.Paul in this chapter,tel
vs I pray you: presupposing (as the ftatute requireth) that
the Princes allowing though she be a woman,is neceffary.
And now are ye come to th's point,and driuê therto by the
force of this place,to fay:that the place doth not proue,but
a womã may haue fome gouernmêt in ecclefiastical caufes:
As though the Queftiõ were now of fome gouernmêt only,and not of Supreme and abfolute Gouernment in al maner thinges and caufes ecclefiastical.If therefore this place
do proue,that a womã hath not the Supreme and abfolute
gouernement in all caufes ecclefiasticall,but that in fome,
and them the chiefeft, she muft holde her peace, as yt doth
euidêtly,and ye can not denie yt:then is M.Fekenham free
frô taking the othe of the fupremacy,and then hath S.Paule
vtteily confuted that Othe,and your whole booke withal.

This I fay alfo,as by the way,that yf this chapter muft be
taken,for teaching,preaching and difputing,as M . Horne
faith and truely,that M.Iewell went far wide frô S. Paules
meaning, when he applied yt to the cômon feruice of the
Church,whereof it is no more meat,thê of the cômõ talke
in tauernes. As for M Hornes fecôd mery mad obieêiõ,no
mã is fo mad to make fuch an argumêt but hifelf. And therfore he may as long,and as iolily as he wil,triûph with him
felf in his own folly. Yet I would wish M.Horne to fpeake
wel of Nunnes , were it but for his grandfir Luthers fake,
and the heauêly coniunêiõ of him and a Nonne together:
Which vnhappy côiunêion of that Vulcã and Venus, en-
gêdred the vnhappy brood of M.Horn ãd his felowes. But
that this folish fond argumêt is nothing like to M. Fekenhãs
argumente,yt may eafely be proceiued , by that we haue
alredy and fufficiently fayde.
                                                    M.

The third chiefe point is ,that I muſt not only ſweare
vpon the Enaugeliſts, that no foraine perſonne , ſtate or
potentate, hath or ought to haue any power or authoritie.
Eccleſiaſtical or Spiritual within this Realme : but alſo
by vertue of the ſame Othe, I muſt renounce all forraine
power and authorities, which for a Chriſtian man to doe,
is directly againſt theſe two Articles of our Crede: Credo
ſanctā ecclefiā Catholicā: I do beleue the holy catholik hurch.
Credo Sanctorū cōmunioné: I do beleue the cōmuniō of ſaints.
And that there is a participatiō and cōmunion amongeſt
al the beleuers of Chriſtes Church, which of the Apoſtle
Paule are called Sainets. Adiuro vos per Dominū vt lega-
tur hæc Epiſtola omnibus ſanctis fratribus. *And herin I do*
ioyne this iſſue with your L. that whā your L. ſhalbe able
to proue by Scripture, Doctor, General Coūcell, or by the
cōtinual practiſe of any one Church, or part of al Chriſtē-
dome , that by the firſt Article, I beleue the holy Catholik
Church, *is meant only that there is a Catholike Church of*
Chriſt, and not ſo that by the ſame article euery Chriſtiā
man is bound to be ſubiect and obedient to the Catholike
Church, like as euery member ought to haue obediēce vn-
to the whole myſtical bodie of Chriſt. And further when
you ſhall be hable to proue by the ſecond Article: I dooe
beleue the Communion of Saints , *is not ſo meante , that a*
Chriſtian man oughte to beleue ſuch attonement, ſuchs
a parti-

*a participation and communion, to be amongeſt al belee-
uers and members of Chriſtes Catholike Churche in doctrine, in faith, in Religion, and Sacramentes, but that
it is laufull for vs of this Realme therein to diſſent from
the Catholike Churche of Chriſte diſperſed in all other
Realmes: and that by a corporal Othe it is laufull for vs
to renounce, and refuſe to haue communion with the Catholike Church ſo diſperſed, bycauſe it is a forrayne authoritie and power out of this Realme: when ſoeuer your
L. ſhalbe hable to proue this by Scripture, Doctour, Generall Councell: or yet by continuall practiſe of any one
Church, or parte of al Chriſtendome : Than ſhal I in lyke
manner, yelde in this third point, and with moſt humble
thankes, ſhal thinke my ſelfe very well ſatisfied therein.*

M. Horne.

The. 541.
vntruth.
It contei-
neth an
argumēt,
that M.
Horne
ſhal neuer
aſſoyle.

The 542.
vntruth.
Slaunde-
rous and
iniurious

This thirde chiefe pointe is (.541.) nothing els, but *a misshapened
lumpe of wordes*: conteining firſte an argument grounded vppon a kinde
of Oppoſition, that no wiſe or learned man euer redde of, but is newelie
forged and hammered out of your owne braine: Then, an iſſue, to haue
me prooue that thinge, vvhiche being rightly vnderſtanded, no Chriſtian
doth doubte of, or will denie. And laſte of all, an huge heape of flatte
and manifeſte (.542.) Lyes againſte the whole Realme, to ſet a good
face vppon an euill fauoured cauſe, vvhich can finde no helpe or eaſe by
plaine and ſimple truthe. The weightie burden, that you are loden vvith
and can not beare, is that you muſt by Othe renounce all foreine povver
and authoritie : the cauſe that maketh you fainte and feeble, is, that it is
directly againſte two Artiles of our Creede : So that your feeble reaſon is
grounded after your ſimple ſkill vppon the place, ab oppoſitis & pug-
nantibus. Before I aunſwere to the argument, I will put the Reader

in remembraunce of the diuision vvhiche you make, chopping and chaunginge one (.543.) Article in tvvaine, to make some shevve of an heinous matter. Surely it vvere ouermuche detestable, if you vvere moued to svveare but against one article of our Creede, as yee vvere neuer moued by me, either to or fro, to svveare anie thinge at all. There be three symboles or Creedes, vvhiche haue bene allovved and receaued of Christes Catholique Churche. The symbole of the Apostles, of the Nicer Councell, and of Athanasius. The Apostolicall is so called, bycause it vvas collected (as some saye) by the tvvelue Apostles, and therefore conteineth (as the commonly receiued opinion is in Christes Churche) according to the number of the tvvelue Apostles, but tvvelue Articles, vvhiche are called in the vsuall speache of the Catholique Christians, the tvvelue Articles of our Creede or beliefe. If this, I beleue the communion of sainctes, be a seuerall Article from this, I beleue the holy Catholique Churche, as you doe phantasie, then there muste needes be at the leaste thirtene Articles of the Creede, contrarie to the (.544.) vniuersally receiued opinion of the Catholique Churche. You vvere vvonte to staye your selfe muche vpon the custome of the Catholike Churche, and vvoulde vrge stiflie although not so trulie the vniuersallie receiued opinion of the Catholique Churche, as a matter that might not bee reiected, or denied: and hovve chaunceth it novve, that you are become suche a chaungeling, that cleane (.545.) contrarie to the vse of the Catholike Church, vvhiche acknovvledged but tvvelue, you vvil make thirtene Articles of the Creede at the leaste? Besides this, the Catholike Church in the tyme of Cyprian and Augustine, and before also, dyd not reken or iudge these to be tvvo seuerall articles, but did coumpte them one article, concluding these vvordes, the communion of Sainctes, in this sentence, I beleue a Catholique Churche of Christe, reciting the Symbole vvithout rehearsall or mentioning, the communion of Sainctes, as it is plainely sette foorth by S. Cyprian and Augustine, in theyr expositions of the Apostolicall Creede. The matter meant by the communion of Sainctes, is vttered in these vvordes: I beleue the holy Catholike Churche of Christe. VVhereunto hath bene added sence these auncient Fathers tymes, as it maie seme by the vvaie of explication, communiou of Sainctes, to expresse in plainesse of speche, that Christes Catholique Churche,

ooo is nothing

The.543. vntruth. For they are 2.diuers articles, not one. Clemes in compend. de fide.

The.544. vntruth. The commō opiniō of lernedmē rekoneth more thē 12. Articles.

The.545. vntruth. As before

is nothing els, but a felovvfhip, and comunion of faithful ones, vvhich are fain-ctes. Novv let vs fee bovv to fvveare, as this third chiefe point of the Othe fet-teth forth, is directly againft this article of our Creede, I beleue the holy Catholike Church, the communion of Sainctes. All true fubiectes ought and muft renounce and forfake all foraine iurifdictions , povvers, fu-periorinie, preheminéces, and authorities of euery foraine Prince, and prelate, ftate, or potentat. This is the propofitio of that part of the Othe: to the vvhich adioyne this propofition, all true fubiectes ought and muft beleue, an holy Catholike church of Chrift, the comunion of fainctes. Efpy novv vvhat oppofition is bet vvixt thefe tvvo propofitions , that they may not both matche together, and be verified in one true and faithful fubiect. The one, fay you, is directly againft the other. Then fay I, there is a direct oppofitio and re-pugnancy bet vvixt them, by due examination vve fhal find out the oppofitio. Trie the partes of thefe propofitios feuerally vvithout the verbe that coupleth them together, and you fhal not find any oppofion, either cotrary relatiue, priuatiue, or difparat: ioyne them together vvith the verbe that coupleth, ad being propofitions, they are not one againft the other cotrary, fubcotra ry, fubalterne, nor (546) cotradictory, ad therfore vntruly, ad not leffe vnfkilfully babled of you , that the one is directly againft the other, vvhen a yong fcholer that hath red but the rudiméts of his Logik, could haue fene and iudged, that ther is in the no oppofitio or repugnancy at al. To renouce ad forfake (.547.) Antichrift and his church by othe or knovvlege and to beleue in Chrift and rightfully by al maner of vvaies, ftandeth neither directly xor in directly one againft the other, but are matched together and agreeth iupe one vvith the other. Surely your eyes vver not matches, neither vvere your vvittes at home, vvhe you fpied out this repugnancy , if you had not publifhed this learned peece of vvorke, your friendes fi ould neuer haue knovvren, vvhat an huge heape of coning and knouledge , is hidde in that litle head of yours. The demaud in your iffue is eafely proued by the defcriptio or definitio of Chriftes true Cathclike church. The catholike Church of Chrift, is a multitud, fociety, and comunio of fainctes and faithful ones, that haue ben, fhalbe, and are novv one liue in the earth , hovve and vvherfoeuer they be diuided and difperfed in time and place, the vvhich multitude of faintes, haue a participatioin comunio amogft thefelues of al good things, geue, grauted, and grovvig fro god through Chrift, of fpirit, faith, facraméts, praier, remiffio of fyns, and heauelyblife: and

The. 546.
vntruth.
They are
plainecō-
tradicto-
ry one to
an other,
as fhal ap
peare.

The.547.
vntruth.
ioyned
vvith im
piety. The
catholike
Churche,
that you
by othe
renoūce,
is the
Church of
Chrifte,
not of
antichrift

The defi
nition of
the catho
lique
Churche*
vnperfect
as fhall
appeare

are vnited to Chriſt their head by faith, and faſtened together amōgſt theſel-
ues, as mēbers of one body vvith the bōd of loue. To this catholike Churche,
euery Chriſtian man is bounde to bee ſubiect and obedient as a member
ought, and may be ſubiect and obedient to the body.

And vve due teache and cōfeſſe in this Church ſuch an attonemēt, participatiō, and cōmunion, among all the members in doctrine, faith, Religiō, and
Sacramēts, that neither this, nor any other Realme, may lauſully diſſent frō
this Church, or renoūce and refuſe to haue cōmunion therevvith, as God be
praiſed vve of this realme do novve ſhevve our ſelues by al Chriſtiā meanes,
neuer more at any time, to (.548.) agree and cōſent in the vnity of this Ca=
tholike Church, in neceſſary doctrine, right faith, true Religiō, and the right
vſe of Chriſtes Sacramentes. The foule (.549.) lies that you heape
together, vvherevvith ſhamefully to deſoyle your ovvne neaſt and
natiue coūtry, neadeth none other cōfutatiō, thā only to make the
plaine to be ſeen and iudged of al mē, that the Realme may be ſory, that euer it neſtled ſo vnnatural and filthy a byrde, and your
friendes aſhamed of ſo malicious and impudent a Liar. This is a
levvde (.550.) Lie, that this Realme diſſenteth frō the Catholike
Church in the forenamed poits. This is a (.551.) ſhameful Lie, that
by corporall othe or any other vvaies, vve renoūnce and refuſe to
haue cōmunion vvith the Catholike Church oſ Chriſte. And this
is a monſterous (.552.) Lye that the catholike Church is a foraine
authority ād povver out of this Realm. VVho vvas euer ſo madde,
as ones to thinke, or ſo doltiſh as to ſpeake any thing againſte the
Catholike Church, but ſpecially to forſake it, and that bicauſe it is
a foraine povver and authority. The Othe maketh no mention in
any one vvorde of the Catholique Church, it ſpeaketh of (.553.) a
foraigne-Prince, Prelate, and Potētate, and ſo of the foraigne Povver and authority of ſuche a foraigne ſtate. Vvherevpon M. Fekenhā cōcludeth as it vvere by Reuelatiō, in a Mōkiſhe dreame,
vvithout rime or reaſon, that therfore the catholike Church is for-
ſakē, as though there vvere no differēce betvvixt a foraine Prince,
or prelate and the Catholiqu: Churche: or that the Catholique
Church might be called a foreine Povver, or a forine authority to a
Chriſtiā Realm. This is ſuch a nevv kind of Diuinity is vvas neuer
heard or redde of in any vvriter, no not in the Legēd of Goldē Lies.

The.548. vntruth.
You haue no agree
ment, conſent, or
vnite of doctrine
amōge your ſelues.
The.549. vntruth
mere ſlanderous.
The.550. vntruth.
M. Fekēhā ſaied not
ſo of the Realme.
The.551. vntruth. It
is right true that in
effect you do ſo, as
it ſhall appeare.
The.552. vntruth.
For M. Fekenham
ſaied not, that it is
ſo, but that by Othe
you make it ſo,
vvhich is true, as it
ſhal be proued.
The.553. vntruth.
Notorious. The
Othe ſpeaketh of
Euery foraine Pre-
late, not of a foraine
prelat. You are
novv aſhamed
your ſelfe of the
Othe, M. Horne,

ooo ij   The

*The.4.Chapter,defending M. Feckenhams thirde chiefe poynt,
and prouing euidently,that the Othe deſtroyeth two Articles of our Crede. And by occaſion,of the proteſtantes diſſenſion in theſe lowe Countres here.*

Stapleton.

TH E effect of M.Fekenhams third poynt, reſteth in
this,that he cānot vouchſafe to take the othe,for that
it is againſt two articles of the faith: *I belieue the holy
cathol, ke Church* and *I belieue the cōmuniō of Saints*.For the
which argumēt M.Horn ſetteth vpō him with great force
both of diuinity and logike.He maruaileth, that M.Fekēhā
cōtrary to th'opiniō vniuerſally receiued of al the catholik
Church maketh of xij.xiij. articles of the crede:making the
cōmunion of ſaints an article of the faith , which was none
in the time of S.Cypriā and S.Auguſtine. Then like a luſtie
logicioner he auoucheth,that there is no way any cōtra-
dictiō to the catholike faith,in taking an othe , for the renouncing of al foraine power . Laſt of al he ſetteth forth a
definitiō of the catholike church.Suerly M.Fekenham had
nede beware now leaſt M.Horne proue him an heretike,
for he can not be farre frō hereſy,that mainteineth an opiniō cōtrary to the vniuerſal church.But becauſe ye charge
him ſo hardly M.Horne,we muſte ſee wel to the matter,
and we muſte cōſider ſomwhat exactly,whether there be
no more articles then xij.to be belieued. And here though
ye beare the countenance of a great Biſhop , I muſt be ſo
bold to bring you to your cathechiſme,and to ſeuer euery
thing into his owne proper kinde. The firſt article then is,
I beιieue in God.The.2.*I belieue in God the Father*,The.3 *that
he is omnipotente*:The.4.*that he is the creatour of heauē and
earth:*

*earth:*The.5.*I beliewe in Iesus Christ:*The.6 *I beliewe he was
coceiued of the holy ghost* The.7.*That he was borne of the virgin Marie:*The.8.*That he suffred vnder Pontius Pilatus : and
the.*9 *that he desceded into hell.*The.10.*that he rose fro death
the.*3.*day.*The.11.*that he asceded into heauen:*and the.12 *that
he shall come to iudge the quicke and the dead:*Here haue ye
alredie twelue articles : the denial of any one of the being
ope heresie. And the immediatly haue we yet certaine articles more. As:*I beliewe in the holy ghost,I beliewe the catholike church, the comunio of saints,the forgiuenes of sinnes, the
resurrectio of the flesche,and the life euerlasting.*Denie me,yf
ye dare M.Horne any one ofthese to be an article of our
faith coteined by expresse words in the comon crede.I say
nothig here of many other articles that ye are aswel bound
to belieue as these. As that Christe is consubstantial to the
Father,that he hath two natures,and two willes, and that
the holy Ghost procedeth from the Father and the sonne,
with such like.The opinio of many learned me in the churche is, M.Horne, that there be fowrtene articles of the
faith,wherin aswel the diuines as the canonistes do como-
ly agree. And to omitte other coutries, the bishops of En-
glad in their sinodes haue determined ad take order by di-
nerse costitutions prouincial, that aswel the articles of the
faith accordig to this nuber,as the.10.comaudemets should
be quarterly expounded, and declared to the people by
theire curates in the vulgar tong.Truth yt is, that they are
commonly called the.12.articles of the faith, not becaufe
they are precisely but xij. But becaufe yt is thowght that
the Apostles before they were disperfed abrode in the
worlde to preache, made eche one a parcel of the comon
crede.And for that caufe,they are vfually called the.12.ar-

ticles

*In hoc co-
muniter
cocordant
Iheologi
& cano-
niste.
Gull.Lin-
vvood in
cotit.pro-
uinc. de
summa
trinit.ca.
1. §.item
alij.
D.Thom.
2.2.q.1.
Arti.8.
Host.&
Io.And.in
rub.de
sum.tri-
nitate.
Ruffinus
i symbolo.*

ticles.Or for that they be reducible to.12. principal articles,
to the which fome do reduce thē,or to.14..as they are vſually reduced in the Schooles. In this fort the Article of the
cōmunion of Saints,may be cōprehended in the Article of
the holy Catholike Church.Vnder the whiche as ye fay,S.
Cypriã and S.Auftine do cōprehend it.Yet in this point ye
are deceiued,that ye fuppofe the expofitiō of the Crede to
be made by S.Cyprian.For it is not his expofitiō,but Ruffinus or fome others:as the thing it felf fheweth moft euidēt-
lie. Touching the.2. point,we feare nothing your Logike,
nor your high cūning : wherby ye tel vs of an *oppofitiō contrary,relatiue,priuatiue,and difparatiue : and of Propofitions*

M.Horne
depra»
ueth M.
Fekenhãs
argumēt.

*cōtrary, fubcōtrary, fubalterne,and cōtradictory.*Leſſe Logike
might haue ſerued,M.Horne: for ye do not foile M. Fekēhams,but your own Argument.And then is it an eafy matter for a man,framing an argument of his own,to frame alfo what folution it pleafeth him.   But let vs take M. Fekenhams true argument,and we fhal find a plaine contradi-
ctory(which is the extremeft of al oppofitiōs) betwen the
tenour of the Othe,and betwen this Article of our Crede,
that M Fekenham here toucheth. *This is (*you fay your felf
here M.Horne*)the propofitiō of that part of the othe. Al true
fubiects ought and muft forfake al foraine iurifdictiōs,powers,
fuperioritie , præeminences and authorities of euery foraine
Prince,and Prelate,ftate or Potentate.*The propofitiō of M.

The othe
cōtrarye
to an Ar»
ticle of
our crede

Fekenhã,is,that *to beleue the holy CatholikChurch,*is as much
to fay as *to be fubiect and obediēt to the Catholik Church.* But
the Catholik Church cōprehēdeth al the corps of Chriftēdom,as wel without the realme as within the realme,fub-
iect and obediēt to one head the Pope of Rome. And this
Pope of Rome is to you a foraine Prelate , Power and Potentate,

tentate, as your self doth afterward expoūd it: Ergo by vertue of the oth, you force al the Quenes subiects to renoūce
and forsake al the corps of Chriftēdom without the realm:
which is, as I haue said, the extreme cōtradictory to this, Al
true subiects ought and muſt beleue, obey, and be subiect to
the whole corps of Chriftendom, as well without the Realme as within.

You anſwer. *The Othe maketh no mētion in any one word
of the Catholike Church.* But I replie: In that you exclude al
foraine power and authoritie, you exclude also the Catholik Church, which is no leſſe forain to you, thē is the Pope,
to whom that Church is subiect, as the body to the head.

You saye, the Othe *ſpeaketh of a foraine Prince, Prelate,
and Potentate, and ſo of the foraine power and authority of ſuch
a foraine ſtate.* but I replie: Firſt that you belye the Othe.
For the Othe ſpeaketh, not, *of a forraine Prince, Prelate
and Potentate,* but *of euery foraine Prince, Prelate and potentate,* as but the ſecond leafe before, your ſelfe deſcribeth
this part of the Othe. And ſo expreſly you renounce, as al
Princes ſo all Prelates of Chriſtes Churche, whiche is the
whole Catholike Church. And ſo the Othe is plaine contradictory to this Article : *I beleue the Catholique Churche.*

Secondarily, I replie, that the foraine authoritie of ſuch
a foraine ſtate is (in your ſenſe) the whole Churches authoritie ſubiect to the Pope of Rome. And ſo ones again, by
the report of your Oth in renoūcing al forain autority, you
renoūce al the Churches authority without the realme of
Englād: as much to ſay, you renoūce to beleue ād obey the
Catholikchurch. And as much to ſay, you proteſt by oth, to
beleue and obey, only the church within the realm of England, Cōfider now, good Reader, whether this third part of
the

the oth, be not mere cōtradictory in effect, to this article of
our Crede, *I beleue the Catholike Church*: suppoſing that we
muſt not onely beleue, but alſo obey and be ſubiect to the
Catholike Church. Which is the Argumēt that M. Fekenham propoſeth, and is the demaund in M. Fekenhams iſſue.
To the which M Horne anſwereth neuer a whit. But frameth a nother oppoſition ſuch as in deede might well become a dremer in his dreme. Againe, betwen this Article

An other
contradi-
ction be-
tvvē the
Othe, and
an article
of our
Creede,

of our Crede: *I beleue the Cōmunio of Saints* (ād your othe)
*I renōuce al foraine iuriſdictiōs, power, ſuperiority, praeminēce,
of euery foraine Prince and Prelate* : is a plaine and extreme
cōtradiction. For as to renōuce euery forain Prince, bindeth
al the ſubiects of Englād, to obey ōly the prince of that lād,
and no prince out of the lād, in al tēporal cauſes ād things :
which part of the Othe no Papiſt in England euer refuſed
to take (and which for my part, M. Barlow of Chicheſter
can beare me witneſſe, I refuſed not, but expreſſie offered
my ſelf to take, at what time vpō refuſal of the other part,
he depriued me (as much as laie in him) of my prebend in
that church, ſo to renōuce euery forain Prelate (as the othe
expreſly ſpeaketh) bindeth al the ſubiects of England to o-
bey only the Prelates of that lād, and not to obey any Prelate without the land what ſoeuer he be, in any ſpiritual or
Eccleſiaſticall cauſe. Which is as euery man may ſee, the
extreme cōtradictory to this Article of our Crede, *I beleue
the Cōmunion of Saints*. Wherby is ment, as M Fekenhā reaſoneth (and M. Horne denieth not, nor can with any ſhame
deny) that euery Chriſtian man ought to beleue a perfecte
attonement, participation, and cōmunion to be emongſt al
beleuers and members of Chriſtes Catholike Churche in
doctrine, in faith, in religion, and ſacraments.

He

He confeſſeth alſo, that it is not lauful for vs of the realm of England therin to diſſent, from the Catholik Church of Chriſt diſperſed in al other Realms. This is a moſt true and inuincible oppoſition betwene the Othe and the article or parte of our Crede: moſt truly and learnedly ſet forth by M. Feck. lewdly diſſembled ãd no whit anſwered by M. Horn.

Now though you and your felowes M. Horne, wil ſeme to expound by the authority *of euery foraine Prelate*, the authority of the Pope only, yet who ſeeth not, what an heape of abſurdities doo folow therof?

VVat it is to re-noũce the authoriue of euery forray n prelate.

For firſt, is the Pope *euery forain Prelate?* or yſhe be not, why ſweare you againſt *euery forain Prelate?*

1.

Secondly is *euery forain Prelate*, the Pope? then haue we I trowe more Popes then one.

2.

Thirdly, why ſhould yow rather meane by a forain Prelate the B. of Rome in Italy, then the B. of Millayn in Lombardy, the B. of Toledo in Spain, the B. of Liſbona in Portugal, the B. of Parys in Fraunce, the B. of Ments in Germany, or any other biſhope in theſe lowe Countries here, in Sicily, in Polonia, in Pruſsia, or any other where, without the Realm of Englãd? Or what is ther in the B. of Rome, to make hĩ forain, which is not alſo in al the forenamed biſhops, yea, ĩ al catholik biſhops beſide thoſe of the realm of Englãd?

3.

Fourthly, when you *renounce euery forain Prelat*, You doe plainly renoũce al Prelates whatſoeuer without the realm of Englãd: and ſo you renoũce al ſociety, cõmuniõ ãd Feloſhyp of ſaints, that is of faithful folk in the Church of Chriſt.

4.

Fiftly albeit the othe, had expreſly named or entended to renoũce the pope only, yet in ſo doing they had renoũced al Catholik biſhops beſide. And that not only, becauſe al Catholike biſſhoppes are ſubiect to the Pope, as to their head

ppp (wherby

(whereby renoũcing the Head, you renoũce alſo the bodye vnder that Head) but alſo, becauſe the faith, the doctrin, ãd the religiõ of the Pope of Rome is no other, thẽ the faith do ctrin ãd religiõ of al other Catholik biſhops. Neither is the faith of other Catholik biſhops any other faith, thẽ the Pops faith is. Therfor who renoũceth by othe the Pope of Rome for a forain Prelat, and his faith ãd doctrine for forain, he re- noũceth alſo by othe, the faith and doctrine of al other Ca- tholik biſhops without the Realme of England for forain.

6. Sixtly in renoũcing, *all power and Authority of euery forayn Prelat*, you renoũce the Lutherã and Sacramẽtary Superin- tẽdents, of Geneua, of Zurich, of Baſil, of Wittẽberg and of al other proteſtãt prelats without the realm of Englãd, no leſſe then the Catholike biſhopes in Germany, or any other where. And ſo ſtãd you poſt alone in matters of religiõ, noe to be informed, inſtructed, or corrected in any doubtefull matter, or peril of ſchiſme. As though you had a warrãt frõ the holy Ghoſt, neither to faile in the faith, nor at any time to haue Prices that may fayle. For al this you annex ãd vnite to the Crown of Englãd for euer. Seuẽthly ãd laſt in exclu-

7. dig ãd renoũcing euery forain Prelat, *ãd al power*, *Authority ãd Iuriſdictiõ of euery forain Prelat*, you exclude ãd renoũce the whol body of the Church without the realm, which cõ ſiſteth moſt pperly ãd moſt effectually of the biſhops ãd pre lats the heads therof. And as in tẽporal Iuriſdictiõ, the othe bindeth al the ſubiects of the Realm of Englãd to obey the only kings and Quenes of that Realm (which we doe grãt alſo moſt gladly) ſo that if al princes in the worlde, woulde ioyne together ãd cõclude a kind of regimẽt, appoint lawes ãd enact ſtatutes for the better ordering ãd directing of the cõmon wealth, the ſubiects of Englãd by vertue of this othe are boũd to renoũce al ſuch power, except our own price

would

would allow thē and cōdefcēd thervnto (which thing is rea
fonable enough, for al coūtries nede not to be gouerned in
external maters after one fort, nor at al times a like, the ftate
therof beig chāgeable ād mutable) euē fo in fpiritual or Ecclefiaftical Iurifdictiō, the othe fo expreffely renounceth al
power ād Autority of forain prelats, that if al prelats ād bifhops of the world befide, wolde mete together or otherwife agrei one truth, order, or law ecclefiaftical (which hath
oftē ben don and may alwaies be done in general Coūcels)
the fubiects of Englād are boūd vnder pain of periury ād of
a præmunire to renoūce al fuch orders, lawes, ād decrees or
cōcluded Truthes: which is fhortly to fay, to renounce and
forfweare al obediēce to the General Councels, that is, the
whole corps of Chriftendome reprefented therin, except it
fhal pleafe the price ād prelats of our Coūtre to agre to the
fame. Which is to make our price, ād our prelats either as fu
periours to al other prices ād Coūtries, or at the left as alie-
nats ād ftrāgers frō the whole body of Chriftendō befide, as
though we had a proper Chrift, a proper Ghofpell, ād looked for a proper heauē, in the which other chriftened Natiōs fhould find no place. And what is this els, but by booke
Othe flatly to renoūce the Catholik Church, ād the cōmuniō of Saints, both which in our Crede we profeffe to beleue? Thefe be (M. Horn) the horrible abfurdities that doth
neceffarily folow of this part of the Othe: And wheras M.
Horn fayth, *it were ouer much deteftable if M. Fecknam were
moued to fweare, but againft one article of our Crede*, M. Horn
mufte nedes confeffe this othe to be ouer muche deteftable, whereby not onely M. Fekenham, but many other are
moued and forced to fweare againfte an efpeciall article
of our Crede: to wit, Againft our obedience to the Catholyke Churche. The effecte of the Othe, and the fence of

that Article, being cleane contrary one to the other. The which, that it may to the vnlerned Reader more plainely appeare, in this Table following I haue opened the whole contrariety.

THE TABLE

The Article of our Crede.

I beleue the Catholike Churche.

Hereof ariseth this proposition, as M. Fekenham by a similitude setteth it forth, and M. Horn alloweth it. fol. 100. b.

All Englishmen being Christians ought to admitte, and receyue, professe, and obey the Authority of the Catholike Church, that is, of the bishops of all Christendome (of whome the greatest part are forayne prelats to our Realme) in matters of faith and doctrine touching the same.

The contrary hereof is.

No Englishmen though Christians, may admitte, professe or obey any Authority of any forain prelat without the Realme of England.

The tenour of one parte of the Othe, as M. Horne reporteth it: pag. 99. b.

All true subiectes ought and muste renounce and forsake all forraine iurisdictions, powers, superiority, preeminences and Authorities of euery forayn prince and prelat, state or potentat.

The equiualent of this part of the Othe is.

No true subiect of England (though Christian) ought or may admitte and receyue any forraine Authority, power or Iurisdiction, of any forayne prelat.

Thus then, the equiualent proposition of the Othe, matcheth iumpe with the contrary of the Article, and standeth cleane opposite to the equiualent of the Article. Thus.

The

The equiualēt pro-
pofition of the Arti-
cle of our Crede, is.

Al Englifhmen be-
ing Chriftiās ought to
admit and receiue the
autority of forain pre-
lats,(the moſt part of
Chriſtēdome being to
vs foraine)in matters
of faith and Doctrine
touching the fame by
them authoriſed.

Contrary.

The equiualent of
the Othe,is.

No Englifhmen
thoughe Chriftians
ought or may admitte
and receyue any fo-
rayne Authoritye of
any forayne prelat.

CONTRADICTORY.

CONTRA-DICTORY.

Subalterne.

Subalterne.

Some Englifhmen
being Chriftiās ought
to admitte and recey-
ue the Authoritye of
forayne prēlats &c.

Subcontrary.

Some Englifhmen
being Chriftiās ought
not to receiue and ad-
mit , but to renounce
and forfake al forayne
authority of al forayn
prelats &c.

By this it appeareth, that the equiualent of the Othe is
cleane contrary to the plaine fence of the Article of Our
Crede , fette forthe by M . Fekenham in the fimilitude of
the members and the body : and in the fame fimilitude cō-
feffed of M. Horne for good. By this alfo it appereth , that
a true fubiect taking the Othe (meaning as he fweareth,

p p p iij   which

which if he doe not , he forſweareth himſelfe) and a true Chriſtian profeſsing his Crede can not poſsibly ſtande together , but are direct contrarye one to the other. The one profeſsig obediéce to the body of the Church (côſiſtig for the moſt and chiefeſt parte of forayne Biſſhoppes) as euery member muſt obey the whole body: the other renoū-cing flatly all Authoritye of all forayne prelates, as in dede no member of that Catholike body , but as a ſchiſmaticall parte cutte off from the whole . Then will it to our greate confuſion of vs be verified which S. Auguſtine ſaieth . *Tur-*

Confeſ.lib. 3. Cap. 8. *pis omnis pars eſt , ſuo vniuerſo non congruens.* Filthye and ſhamefull is that parte, which agreeth not with his whole. And which is not only ſhamefull , but moſt pernicious and daungerous of all , what place ſhall then all General Councelles haue with vs? *Quorum eſt in Eccleſia ſaluberrima Au-*

Epiſt. 118. ad Ianua. *thoritas:* whoſe Authority in the Church is moſt holeſome, ſaieth S. Auguſtin?

Verilye the Chriſten inhabitants of our Countre , more then a thouſande yeres paſte had learned an other leſſon. For whereas the Pelagian heretikes hadde infected the

Beda . lib. 1. Cap. 17. Brittaynes with their peſtiferous hereſie , the Brittayneſ them ſelues being (as venerable Bede recordeth) neither willing to receaue their lewde doctrine, neither able to refute theire wyly and wicked perſuaſions : deuiſed this holſome Councell to ſeke for ayde of the Biſſhoppes of Fráce, againſt their ſpirituall enemies wherevpó two learned biſſhops of France *Germanus* and *Lupus* were ſent into Brittanie, to redreſſe and repreſſe thoſe hereſies. If thoſe Catholike Brittanies had taken ſuch an othe, as M. Horn here doth iuſtifie: they ſhould I trow haue incurred periurie or treaſon, to ſeke redreſſe in matters of religion at the handes
of thoſe

of thofe foraine Biffhoppes.

Likewife when Melitus the firft Biffhoppe of London
trauailed out of Englande to Rome, to counfell Pope
Boniface of matters touching the direction of the Englifhe
Churche: when alfo the Clergy of Scotlande, being troubled with the Pelagian herefie and fchifmaticall obferuation of Eafter, fent to Rome for redreffe, Maifter Horne
muft be driuen to fay, either that thofe Biffhoppes committed periurie and treafon againft their Princes, or els
that in thofe dayes no fuch othe was tendred, nor no fuch
regiment practifed on Princes partes, as this othe commaundeth.

Farder, if it be neceffarie, reafonable, or requifite, that
*all true fubiectes muft renounce the Iurifdiction and Autho-
ritye of euery forain prelate*: Howe farre was S. Auguftine
ouerfene, which fo often tymes, fo earneftlye, and fo expreffely chargeth the Donatiftes, with the Authoritie,
power and iurifdiction of forain prelates beyond the feas
out of Afrike? He faieth of them, touching the accufation
of Cecilianus their Biffhoppe, *Quem primò vtique apud col-*
legas tranfmarinos conuincere debuerant. They ought firft
of all to haue conuinced him before his fellowe Biffhops
beyond the feas. He faith farder, that in cafe Cecilian
hadde bene gyltye, they ought not therefore to feparate
themfelues from the Churches beyonde the feas, of E-
phefus, of Smirna, of Laodicea, and of other Countreis.
He faith, *the whole Churche of Chrift is but one bodye*: And
they that feparate them felues from that bodye, *vt eorum*
cōmunio non fit cū toto, quacūq, diffunditur, fed in aliqua parte
feparata inueniatur, manifeftum eft, eos non effe in Ecclefia Ca-
tholica, fo that they cōmunicate not with the whole (body)
wher-

Bed.lib.2.
cap.4.
Idem lib.
eodem ca.
19.

Epift.48.
ad Vincen-
tium.
Côt.Dona.
poft colla-
tionē.ca. 4

Lib. de v-
nitat. Ec-
clefia.c.4

wherfoeuer it be fpred abroad, but be foūd to be feparated in fome parte therof, it is manifeft, that they be not in the Catholike Churche.

I fay nowe M. Horne: yf by vertue of this othe euerye true fubiect muft renounce euery foraine prelate: then did S. Auguftine much wronge to the Donatiftes, to require them to conuince their aduerfarie before the Bifhops beyond the feas, which doth import an Authority of al thofe forain bifhops ouer the Africans alone: thē was he to blame to charge them with feparatiō frō forain prelates of Ephefus, Smirna, and Laodicea, and other Countreis. Laft of all, then was he farre wyde to pronounce them for mē cleane out of the Catholike Churche, which feuered them felues from the fociety of any part thereof. Then alfo might the Donatift (had he learned fo far furth his leffon as you haue) both eafied him felf of much trauell out of Afrike into Italy and Fraunce, and alfo might fone haue ftopped S. Auguftines mouth, faying: What haue we to doe with forain prelates beyond the feas, what nede we care for their Authority, iurifdiction, fociety, and communion? We are true fubiectes of Afrik. We renounce al foraine power, Iurifdiction and Authoritye.

And truely I fee no caufe, but with as good reafon and confcience, al fubiects of all realmes may and ought to renounce by othe the power and Authoritie of al forain prelats or bifhops out of their land and Countre, as we of Englād muft ād ought fo to do out of ours. Which if it be ones graunted, enacted and agreed vpō in al other realmes, as it is in oures: what ende wil there be of fchifmes and diffenfion in the Church? What hope of vnytie can be cōceyued? Or howe can euer vnytie be long maintayned? What communion,

nion,what fociety,what felowfhippe can there be amonge Othe.
Chriften people?What Authorytie fhall general Councels
haue,which confifte in maner altogether in forayn prelates
and bifhops,if this othe be accompted good?In the firft,fe-
cond,third,fourth,fyft,fixt,feuenth and eigth general Cou- *Act.4.*
cell of Chriftendom we reade not of any one Braityne or *pag.304.*
Englifh bifhop to haue ben prefent there.In the 6. general *&.306.To.*
Councels pope Agatho côfeffed that Theodorus the Arch- *2.Concil.*
bifhop of Caunterbury was called thither,and long looked
for.But for his great charge at home, in thofe beginnings of
the Englifh Church he came not. Wilfrid of Yorke was at
Rome,but not at Conftantinople where that general Coucel was holden. What thê?fhal our Church of England renounce the Authoryte of al thofe general Councels as the
Authorytie of foraine prelats by vertu of this Othe? What
can be more deteftable or abhomynable ? But they which
conceyued and endyted firfte this thirde parte of the Othe,
of renouncing all Authoryte of euery forain prelat , had they
not(trow you M.Horn) a directe ey to general Councels,
and did they not by that claufe clofely difburden and difcharge the whole realme of al obedience to general Cou-
celles,namely to the general Coûcel of Trent that thê was
affembled? And if they intended not fo much, fee you not
then,howe vnaduifedly,howe daungeroufly,and to howe
great a preiudice that part of the Othe was conceyued and
endyted? Agayne yf fo much was not intended,howe cometh it to paffe,that in the iniunctions where the Othe is
drawen (as much as may be)to a gentle expofition,this part
is not fo interpreted,as it might not feme to exclude the
Authority of general Councels: then the which there is in
the Churche no higher or more Supreme Authoritye,ex-

cept

cepte the Pope him felfe, that is the vndoubted Heade thereof.

M Feken-
hā declered, By this that hath ben faid appereth M. Horne, how falf-ly and flaunderoutly you charge M. Fekenhā with thre fe-ueral lies *lewde, fhameful, ād moftrous.* For firſt it is no lewde lie, but a foule and lewde herefy of yours, that you haue e-rected a new faith, a new Religion, and a new vfe of Sacra-ments, not only to al the Church throughout the worlde before your daies, but alfo frō your felow proteſtāts the Lu-therās, the Ofiādrins ād the Anabaptiſts. If you take this for a flaūder, clere your felf of your horrible herefies ād fchifms in the table of Staphylus. It is no fhameful lie, but a fhameful and worfe then a deteſtable cafe, that by this corporall othe you haue forced many a foule to renoūce and refufe in effect, though not in plain words (the deuil hifelf would not be fo bolde, at leſt at the beginning) thefe two Articles or points of our faith, *I beleue the Catholik Church*, and, *I be-leue the Comunion of Saints.* It is no mōſtrous lie, but a moſt monſtrous and pytiful cafe that, you by othe renoūcing *the power and Authority of euery forain prelat* in plaine Englifhe, haue made the Catholik Church which cōfiſteth of al fo-rain prelats and biffhops out of England, not of Englifh bif-fhops onely, in plaine Englifhe a mere foraine power and Authority out of Englande. For yf euery foraine prelat be renounced, is not all power and Authority of the Church which dependeth only of Prelates and Biffhops, açcomp-ted alfo forayne, and for very forayne renounced? It is fo. It is fo, Maifter Horne. The Othe runneth largely and ex-preffely. You can not, you may not, you fhal not (God ge-uing vs his grace) bleare our eyes with vayn talke, or make vs to fay we fee not, that which we fee, we heare, we

feele

feele, we vnderstande. You sawe, you sawe your self M. Horne, that the woordes of the Othe being taken as they lie *verbatim* (as you say they must) did expressely renounce the Catholike Churche. And therefore (Marke wel gentle Reader) You M. Horne thinking and labouring to remoue this opinion from the Reader (for though you thinke in very dede, that nor Churche nor prelat, but only the expresse liuely worde of God muste be heard and obeyed, yet yow dare not as yet for very shame to expresse that detestable minde of yours, the lusty braue Chalenge of Maister Iewel offering to yeld to any one sentence or any one old doctor withdrawing you perhaps not a litle therfro) do tel hi that *the Othe maketh no mention in any one worde of the Catholike Church, but it speaketh* (say you) *of a forain Prince and Prelate &c.* Wherein to auoyde the manifest absurditye, you flatly belye the Othe. For the Othe speaketh not (M. Horne) *of a forain Prince and Prelate &c.* But the Othe expressly saith, *of euery forain Prince and Prelat &c.* Now whē it renoūceth the power *of euery forain Prelat,* it renounceth the power of al Catholik Bishops without the realm of England, which al are *forain Prelats* to the realm of England, whereupon in dede M. Fekenham cōcludeth, not *as it were by reuelation in a Monkishe dream without ryme or reason* (as that grosse head of yours most vilely rayleth against such a sobre and discrete prelate) but with good reason and plaine euidence, that *therefore the Catholik Church is by Othe renoū-ced.* Not *as though there were no difference betwene a foraine Prince or Prelat, and the Catholike Church* (as you ful peuishly make Maister Fekenham to reason) but bycause there is no difference betwene *euery foraine Prelate* (as the Othe speaketh) and the Catholike Churche.

Seing

Seing(as I haue often faid)the Catholyk Church confifteth *of euery forayn Prelate*,without the realme of Englâd,much more then of al the prelates within the realme of Englâd. Yea though euery foraine prelate without the realme of England,may and haue in many General councells prefcribed ouer al the bifhoppes of England, yet all the Bifhoppes of England nether haue or may at any tyme prefcribe ouer *euery foraine Prelate* without the realme of England . This othe therfore excludeth plainely the Authority of the Catholike Church , and fighteth directiy againft all good reafon and order.

M.Horns definitiō of the Churche. M.Horns Church cōpared to the fchifma-tical tem ple of Sa maria. Iofephus de bello Iu daico li.7. ca 30. & de Antiq. lib.11. ca. vltimo. Ioan. 4. Deut.12. &.2.pa-ral. 7. Iofephus antiq li.11. cap. vlt.

Now the definitiō or defcriptiō of the catholik Church, fuch as ye bring,is much lyke to a fhooe,that ferueth euery fote:or to a Welfhmans hofe, that ferueth euery legge. *Simon Magus, Marcion, Hebion, Manicheus, Photinus, Arrius, Neftorius* and al other fects that euer were , will graunt to this your definition,and wil therby challenge the Church to their fect only,as ye do to yours . But herein your fynagoge refembleth the faulfe and fchifmatical téple that Onias made in Aegypte:and Sanaballites in Samaria in the mount of Garizim,wherof the ghofpel of S.Iohn fpeaketh,though yt doth not fo exprefly name it. And though God had fpecially appointed the temple of Hierufalé to be his true and holy temple,and would al facrifices to be offred there: yet the Samaritanes toke their temple to be the true and the only temple where God would be honored in : And fayed that all offerings and facrifices fhould be made ther,and not at Hierufalem.*The Iewes* (fayth Iofephus) *when they had vi-lawfully maried , when they had tranfgreffed and violated the Sabbot day,or eaten meates,or don other things,contrary to the Lawe, fearing punifhment for the fame, would fly to the Samaritanes,*

*ritanes,and to the falſe biſhop there,and complaine to him,that they were wrongfully vexed,at Hieruſalem,*and ſo did ioyne with the ſayd ſchiſmaticall factiõ at the temple of Garizim. And,*there was(*ſayth Ioſephus*)continuall ſtrief,and conten-* *tion betwene the Iewes and the Samaritanes,eche parte with* *much ſturre and buſines,preferring and auauncing their owne* *temple* , yea the matter went ſo farre, and the Samaritanes waxed ſo hotte and feruent at the length,that they offered them ſelues to die in the quarrell and defence of theire hill and temple.And this controuerſy,burſting out at Alexãdria into a ſedition,was tried (by the commõ conſent of both parties) by the kinge Ptolomeus Philomitor . *Eche of them* *making this offer,that,that party ſhuld ſuffer death,whoſe proufs* *ſhuld be founde defectyue and inſufficiente :* the iſſewe of the whole contention was,that the king pronounced and gaue ſentence for the Iewes:*bicauſe they proued the continual ſuc-* *ceſsion of their biſhops at Hieruſalem from the beginning,and* *that the kings of Aſia had euer honored , and with great re-* *wardes enriched that temple as Gods true temple.*Wheruppon the proctours of the Samaritanes were by the kinges com-maundement put to death, whome notwithſtãding the Sa-maritans toke for as bleſſed martyrs, as M.Foxe taketh,any of his ragged rablement in his new holy martyrologe.This ſchiſmatical ſynagog is the very patern of your Church M. Horne. Sentence hath bene geuen againſt your ſynagoge, by many good and catholike kings,by many general coun-cells.And yt is a moſt euident,yea and a blaſphemous lie a-gainſt the Sáints in heauẽ,to ſay as ye doe,*that al the Saints* *and faythful Chriſtiãs,that be or hath bene,are of your Church.* What ſo euer viſour ye put vppon your Church,when we ones come to the cheif poynte,to knowe the Church by,

qqq iiij   and

Lib.12.
ca.1. Ant.

Idẽ lib.13.
ca.6. Ant.

and by the which the temple of Hierufalem was iuftified:
I meane the continuall fuccefsion without any interruptiõ
of bifhops in the fea of Rome, and in al other openly knowen to be catholik Churches,maynteyning that faith, that
ye namely in this boke impugne:then it wil eafely appeare,
what your Church is,and howe vnperfytte your definition
is , that lacketh one infallible marke,whereby ye may fone
diffeuer the falfe from the true Church,to wytte,the knowẽ
fuccefsion of bifhops from age to age , in all places of the
Chriftened worlde,al which the worde , *Catholike*,impor-
teth:and the which therfore you haue omitted,bicaufe you
are not in dede of the Catholik Churche:and bicaufe thofe
markes,of vniuerfalyte,of Antiquite,and of a knowen fuccefsion doe vtterly wante, in that you call your Churche.
Els if you haue thofe markes,and we haue not , procure , I
pray you M.Horne,that fome one of your brethern(I prouoke them al in this matter) doe anfwere, if he can,to the
Fortreffe of our firft fayth,by me fet forth,and annexed to the
hiftory of venerable Bede.Let any one of them al difproue
the reafons there brought,out of the Pfalmes,the prophets,
and of the Ghofpel,if he cã,wherby it is clerly proued,that
that Church only(which you cal papiftry muft be the true
Church of Chrift . I fpeake not this, vpon any confidence
of my owne doinges,which I doe fincerely acknowleadge
to be very fimple and bafe,but vpon the confidence of the
caufe : which I doe affuredly knowe in this pointe to be fo
ftronge,that al the heretical affaultes you fhal make againft
it,fhall neuer be able to fhake it . Thus of that.

Now,wheras the Catholik Church requireth, as M.Fek.
fheweth *a cõmunion of Saynts,in one doctrine,one fayth of Sa-*
*craments and other things:*the lack of this cõmuniõ and par-
ticipa-

ticipatiō of this one fayth doth bewray what your Church is:which fore fayne would ye falue, but with howe euidēt and howe notorious a lye,ye force not.For what pafsig ād fhameful impudécy is it for vou,to vaunt your felf and your newe Ghofpel to be at an attonement and agreemēt in religion:feing that it is fo euidēt to al the world, that the Lutherans and the Zuinghians be at the daggers povnte with their hot cōtentiō in the facramétary matter. If the Church nowe of England be Catholike , then is the Saxonicall and Germanical Church hereticall. As contrary wife if Luthers Church be catholik,then is your Church heretical . Howe can ye bragg as ye doe,that *you nowe agree and confent in the vnyte of this Catholyk fayth in necessary doctrine* at home fo much,you fay , as *neuer at any time more*,feinge that fo late one of your owne proteftant bifhops,in opē parliamēt ftood againft your boke of articles lately fet forth as agreed vpō in your cōuocation?And feing the fayd boke, offred vp to be confirmed by parliament was reiected?

But what a perpetual fhame is it to you M.Horn, and all your holy brotherhood,that yet to this howre the tragedy of your horrible diffenfion lafteth,euen in the firft foundation of your ragged Ghofpell in thefe lowe Countries here of Brabant and Flaundres ? If you know not the cafe, I will fhortly certify you the newes. In the towne of Antwerpe your brethren the Sacramentaries of Geneua had theire churches fairly built . The Lutherans alfo had theire churches.This was euident to the eye.Our owne countremen the marchants ther can beare me witneffe . Is this an agreement M.Horne,that you muft eche haue your Churches a parte,your feuerall preachers , your parted congregations? that one mufte be called the Martiniftes Church

Nevves out of Flaūdres for M. Horn and his brethern.

of Mar-

(of Martin Luther so called) the other must be called the
Caluinists Church, of Caluin of Geneua? But forth. It came
to the point in Antwerpe, that the Caluinistes tooke armes
against their Prince, the .xiij. of Marche last being thursday.
A worthy monyment of their holy profession. For wil you
knowe the cause why ? Forsoth because the same daye in
the forenoone, certain of their brethern to the number of
200. and vpward were slayne in the fielde beside a number
drowned in the ryuer , and taken aliue , nigh to Antwerpe
by a power of the Lady Regent, which said brethern with
a great number more had made a profession (which also
for certain dayes they had put in practise) to range aboute
the Countrie, and to ease al Churches and Churchmen of
their goods, mary yet of conscience , not iniuring any laye
man. The quicke iustice done vpon such open robbers and
theues, the holy brethern of your sect not abyding, foresee-
ing that yf such pageants were longe played , their partes
were like to followe, moued them immediatly as I said to
take armes against their Prince in Antwerpe, to require the
kays of the gates , the Churches of the Catholikes to be
disposed at their pleasure, the expulsion of al religious persons and priests &c . All which things were graunted vnto
them by the gouernor of the town, vpon a dayes deliberation, that al thinges might be done quietly : And they thus
for the space of .ij. nightes and one day ruled al the roste in
Antwerpe. What outrages in that small season they committed, namely vpon the poore grey friers, whose knowen
vertues irked them most aboue al other orders , I let passe.
The Saterday being the .xv. of Marche in the morning, whē
your brethern the Sacramétaries M. Horn, contynuing stil
in Armes, ād gapíg hourely for the satisfying of their gredy
appe-

appetite, thought prefently to become Lordes of fo riche a towne, they fawe fodenly in Armes, brauely and ftrongly appointed againft them, not only the Catholike marchãts, Italians, Spanyardes, Portugalles, Burgunyons ãd Antwerpians them felues, but alfo they fawe M. Horne to their great greefe the very Martiniftes or Lutherans (betwene whom and you, you pretend allwaies fuch agreement) in Armes alfo againft them. And that morning lo M. Horne was the laft ioyful houre that your Sacramẽtary brethern fawe in that towne. For immediatly finding themfelues to weake, they were faine to yeld vp the artillery which vppon the foden two dayes before they had feafoned vpon, and in ftede of their beggarly and trayterous crie of which all Antwerpe before did ring, in ftede I fay of *Viue le Geus,* to crye, full fore againft their hartes: *Viue le Roy.* God faue the kinge. From that day forewarde your brethern went backewarde. Valẽcene the firft and chief rebelling towne wythin ix. dayes after was taken. The preachers within xiiij. dayes after that, bothe Sacramentary and Lutheran haue voyded the towne, yea the whole countre. God be praifed. But this I tell you M. Horne, that you may note, howe the Lutheranes them felues ftode in Armes againft the Caluiniftes: Proteftants againft Proteftants, yea in the quarell of proteftanticall prowes.

    In like maner, in the yere. 1561. in Aprill, the Senat of Francford being Lutherãs, banifhed out of their towne the renegat Caluiniftes of Fraunce. In the fame yere, the inhabitans of Breme being Caluiniftes draue out the Lutherãs.

Vide Fran cifcũ Phi- lippũ, & Surium.

    If all this will not ferue to proue a clere and playne diffenfiõ in matters of religiõ againft you, thẽ behold an other argumẽt inuincible M. Horne. Your brethern the Sacra-

mentaries

Lu-
ther,
and
Calui.

mentaries in Antwerp haue publiſhed in print a Confeſsiō
of their falſe faith. The Lutherans or Martiniſts haue printed alſo an other of theirs. Both are cōfuted by the Catholike Doctors of this Vniuerſity. The firſt by *Frãciſcus Son-*
nius B. of Hartoghenbuſch. The other by *Iudocus Tiletanus,*
a learned profeſſour of Diuinitie here. The Lutherans pretend to be called by the Magiſtrates of Antwerp. The Caluiniſts for lacke of ſuch authority, haue printed their Confeſsiō *Cũ gratia & priuilegio Altiſsimi.* With grace and priuilege of the higheſt. And this lo, was I trow a more *Speci-*
al Priuilege, then M. Iewels was, though he prited his Replie to, *With Special Priuilege.* But ſuch *Priuileges of the hig-*
heſt, euery raſcal heretik can pretend, no leſſe then the Sacramentaries. And this is a high Diuinitie, the publiſhing
wherof paſſeth al Princes Priuileges, and muſt be ſet from
the higheſt him ſelf. Bilike theſe mē would ſeme to be cal-

Galat, I.

led as S. Paul was, *Nō ab hominibus, neq̃ per hominē , ſed per*
Ieſum Chriſtũ, Not of men, nor by man, but by Ieſus Chriſt,
euen with a voice frō heauen. O peuiſh pride and moſt ſod
preſumption. But to the matter.

The Lutherans or Martiniſte Miniſters of Antwerpe in
their Confeſsion haue one whole Chapter *Contra errorem*
Sacramentariorum : Againſt the errour of the Sacramentaries. It is the ſeuententh in number. In that Chapter they
proue the Reall preſence, and the Conſecration of the
Myſteries, and they labour to cōfute the ſond obiectiōs of
the Sacramentaries (vſed alſo very ſadly of M. Iewel in his

In Cōfut.
Miniſtro-
rum Ant-
vverp. fol.
92. & .93.

Replie) againſt the Reall preſence, touching the tropicall
ſence of Chriſtes wordes (whiche they denie vtterly) and
touching the aſſenſion of Chriſte into heauen, which they
proue (though by an other errour of their owne, as Tiletanus

nus at large declareth) that the fame article maketh nothig against the Real or Corporal prefence of Chrift in the Sacrament.

Briefely the Lutherans do thus pronounce of your Brethern the Sacramentaries Communion M. Horne, which you doe make fo holy a matter. The Lutheran Minifters of Antwerp in their printed Confefsion, fay thus : *Caluiftarum Letturgia nõ vno facrilegio vitiat e, cõtaminataq̃, eft, eoq̃ (proh dolor) pafsim innumeras animas æterno exitio inuoluit.* The Cõmunion of the Caluinifts is defiled and contaminated with diuers Sacrilegies: ãd therfore (alas) it enwrappeth euerywhere infinit nũbers of foules into eternal damnatiõ. Lo, M. Horne, what agreemẽt in Religion there is betwen you Proteftaunts. Your holy Cõmunion of England is cõ= demned for facrilegious, and damnable of your owne brethren the fcholers of Martin Luther, whom your Apology commendeth *for a moft excellent man, and one fent of God to lighten his Church.* All that frequente your holie Communion, Maifter Horne, are damned, faie the Lutherans of Antwerpe.

Vide Tiletani præfat. ad Senatũ Antwerp.

Bragge no more, Maifter Horne, of your agreement. Your horrible diffention gliftereth fo cleere, cryeth fo lowd, and bluftereth fo great, that as long as we haue eyes to fee, eares to heare, and hands to fele, we can not choofe but behold it in the face, we muft nedes heare the voice of it, and our fenfes muft of necefsitie palpablie feele it. And the fight, the voyce and the fenfe therof, cõuinceth vnto vs with an vnuincible Argument, that your whole Religion is a cleere herefie, as proceeding from the Deuill the fpirit of diffention, not from God, who is the God of vnity, peace and concorde.

1. Cor. 14.

The

The fourth and laſt point is, that I muſt ſwere to the obſeruatiō of this othe, not only to the Quenes highnes ād our ſoueraign Lady that now is, but alſo vnto her heyers and ſucceſſours Kings and Queenes of this Realme. And bicauſe euery Chriſtian man ought to be carefull to auoid periurie therein, I would right gladly knowe, that if any her highnes ſucceſſours ſhould by the refuſall of the ſaid title of Supremacie, bind her ſubiects by the like ſtatute lawe vnto the cleane contrarie (experience whereof was of late made here in this Realme, that it is yet freſhe in the memories of all men) In this caſe I would right gladly knowe, what authoritie is able to diſpence againe with this Othe. And if there be none at all, then the ſubiectes of this Realme in this caſe are bounde, and that by booke Othe, to liue in a continuall diſobedience to the lawes of their ſoueraigne Lord or Ladie, King or Quene: the caſe wherof is very lamentable. And chriſtian charity would, that it ſhoulde be foreſeene and prouided for. And for mine owne parte (being further touched herein, then I haue yet expreſſed) my very truſt and hope is, that the charity of this our newe refourmed Churche here in this realme, ſhal not be found ſo colde and ſhorte, as in prouiding ſo ſharpe lawes and paines of death to force men to take this othe, of the Quenes Highnes Supreamacie, but
that

that it will prouide alfo fuch meanes and wayes , wherby the fubieﬆs may receiue the fame with fafe cōfcience, and without al periurie. And in fo doing, I ﬆhal moﬆ willing-ly fubmit my felfe, and receiue alfo that part of the Othe. And ﬆhall further therevpon fet foorth the Quenes high-nes Supremacie with al Titles and Prerogatiues , bothe by penne and worde of mouth, and that with as defirous harte and glad will, as any fubieﬆ that is this day liuing in her highneﬆe Realme. So that of the premiﬆes ye may well vnderﬆande, that there is in mee no other caufe of ﬆaie, touching the later part of this Othe, then very con-fcience. And that I would before right gladly know (tou= ching thefe forenamed points) how I might fweare vnto them, and not committe periurie therein .

M. Horne.

As euerie Chriﬆian man ought to be carefull to auoide Periurie both in this and al other matters : euen fo wife men may well knovve, vvhat you meane by the conditionall cafe ye put , of the refufall by her highneﬆe Succef-fours of this Title: vvhereto the holy Ghoﬆe maketh you this plaine anfvver: Spes Hypocritæ peribit: The Hypocrites hope ﬆhall perifhe. *You fprinkle this doubtfull cafe, vvith a pouder of late experience , vvhiche feafoneth your mater,* De faﬆo, non de Iure . *For it is not lavvfull for any Chriﬆian prince to refufe (.554.) this Supremacie, vvhich is the beﬆe parte of his princely Miniﬆery, and feruice vnto God . Neither may he more binde his fubieﬆes by lavve to become fvvoren to the Pope and Poperye, than to the (.555.) greate Iurke and turkerie. For that the Pope is a more peril-lous (.556.) ennemie vnto Chriﬆ , than the turke: and Popery much more Idolatrous, then turkery. And therefore there is no humaine Authoritie, that can difpence vvith the violation of this lavvfull Othe , made of duety vnto the Chriﬆian Princes.*

ⲅⲅⲅ   iij   This

The. 554.
vntruth.
It is not
lauful for
any Price
to take it.
The. 555.
vntruth.
Horible
and Pro-
teﬆante
lyke.
The. 556.
vntruth.
Extreme
ﬆlaunde-
rous, as al
the world
knoweth
yea M.
Horne
him felf.

This is a lamētable cafe I graūt, that fubiectes fhould liue in cōtinual difoo
bediēce to the lavves of the prince, vvhether it happē for that the lavves be fo
vngodly, that a chriftian fubiect may not vrith good cōfciēce obey thē (expe-
rience vvherof vvas of late made here in this Realme.) Or for that the ftub-
borneffe of the fubiect mainteined vvith a vvicked , and yet a vaine hope.
be fo ftiffe, that vvilfully he liueth in a cōtinual difobediēce to the Godly lavve

The. 557. *of his foueragine, vvherof experience is made novv at this time in you, and*
vntruth. *a ferve others of your (.557.) confpiracie There is good cause, vvhie ye fhould*
The com *haue your very truft ād hope (as you faie ye haue, hovv vngratioufely foeuerye*
panie of *thik) affured of thecharity ofourchurch nevvly reformed after the rule of gods*
catholy- *vvord, vvherat ye Popifh * fvvine grunte and groine. For you, in your ovvne*
kes is no *felf, haue perfect experiēce, that the fupreme gouernour vnder Chrift of this*
cōfpiracy. *realm folovving the exāple of her heauēly father, doth boūtifully, of her good-*
* modeftia *nes, vvith much more patiēce, and lōg fufferig allure yʲu to dutiful repētāce.*
veftra (M *And hath further prouided fundry meanes and vvaies, vvherby to remoue your*
Horne) *vvilful ignorance, and to endue you vvith fufficient knovvledge of the truthe,*
not a fit *hovv ye might vvith falfe confcience receiue this dutifull Othe of a true fub-*
omnibus *iecte, vvithout all periurie.*
hominibus

The 5. Chapter. Of M. Fekenhams fourth chiefe point.

Stapleton.

IN this Diuifiō you lie and raile blafphemoufly and horribly, euē as if Sathā had presētly entred into you, and prō-
pted vnto you at your backe, both fuch cācred matter as
your poifoned hart hath cōceiued, ād alfo fuch foul termes,
as your fpritifh pen hath endited. M. Fekenhā demaūded of
you a very reafonable demaund, that is, in cafe he or other
fhould now take this new found Othe, and that it fhould fo
chaūce, that any of the Princes fucceffours fhould bind his
fubiects by the like ftatute law, to the cleane cōtrary, how
they might be difpenfed withal. To this, you M. Horne, in
ftede of fome good reafō, fal to deteftable railing: and ye fay
that the 2.oth muft in no wife be geuē, for that *the Pope is a*
more perillous enemy vnto Chrift, then the Turke, and Poperie
is more idolatrous, then Turkery. Of the which blafphemoufe
answere

anſwere (yſyt be true)yt muſt by a neceſſary conſequente follow,that not only al the catholik princes that now liue, but that all the other that either liued in Englande ſence it was firſt chriſtened by S . Auguſtin our Apoſtle , or elſe where in chriſtēdome for this. 15. hundred yeares,with all their people,be and haue bene idolatours,and worſe then Turkes.For by Popery M.Horne meaneth the Popes religiō:which is none other now,thē yt was whē Englād was firſt chriſtened , as appeareth by the hiſtorye of Venerable Bede ād by the Fortreſſe ānexed therevnto.Yea thē it was 15.hundred yeares paſte.Al the which time all Chriſtiā and catholik natiōs,were euer ioyned with the ſea of Rome in one faith and religiō.A heauy and a ſorowful thing yt is to heare out of the mowth of one that beareth him ſelf for a prelat of the ſee of Wincheſter,ſuch ſpitiful words for the which he may be ful wel a prelat of the Alcoran. How be yt as horible as this talke is , yt is no vnwonte talke to the beſt of this new goſpelling generatiō. For euē the Apoſtle of thē Luther maketh more accompt of the Turke, then of many Chriſtiā princes:ād for a while he both preached ād wrote,that yt was not lawful for Chriſtians to kepe anye warre with him . Namely that *to warre againſt the Turkes, was to reſiſt God,viſitīg our iniquites bythē.*It is one of his Articles that he defendeth againſt the Church of Rome. And yt is writen that the Turk hearing of theis his doinges, and into what diuiſiō he had brought Chriſtēdom,liked it very well:and enquiring of his age, when he heard he was fifty yeres old, I would,ꝗ the Turke he were yonger,the tyme ſhoulde perhaps ones come , when Luther ſhoulde fynde me his good Lord: which whē Luther heard of, he bleſſed him ſelfe and ſaied: God ſaue me from ſuch a good Lorde.

Yea

The Turke is muche bovvnde to M. Horn ād, to his M. Luther and other his fellovves. Art.34. Vide Roſenſ. Vide dubitantium Lindain pag.322. ex Malto Tom.3 in loc.Com. pag. 195.

Yea euen to this day Luther hath many schollers that de-
horteth Chriſtian mē to reſiſte the Turkes, eſpecially *Claudius Monerius* one of the late holie martyrs of this newe
ghoſpelling Church: who miſliketh all the Chriſtian mens

*Vide Cri-
ſpinum in
biſtoria
pſeudos
martyrū
lib.5.in
Claudio
Monerio.*
defence, that they make to withſtād the Turke, and ſaieth,
*that the knightes of the Rhodes are nothing but a graf that
the heauenly Father neuer graffed, and therefore owght to be
plucked vp by the roote.* Let no man nowe merueill, yf the
Turkes proſper ſo againſte the Chriſtiās, ſeing that he hath
ſuche frendes at home here amonge our ſelues. Wherof
you M. Horne are not one of the leaſt, but a very Goliath,
and much worſe then he, ſo deſperatly and ſo arrogantlie
defying and reuiling the hoſt of the liuing God, that is the
whole catholike churche, much more vilanouſly and tray-
terouſly, than the ſayd wicked Philiſtian did. For he was a
ſworen and profeſſed enemy to the people of God: and
therefore therein he did but his kinde. But you profeſsing
your ſelfe not only a friēd, but alſo a Captaine of the Chriſtian army, (the place that you occupie, conſidered), do
beare thereunto, a deueliſh and a Philiſtian harte, as your
Turkiſh, not Chriſtian penne hath vttered . And yet yf ye
had proued any thing all this while in your anſwere, to the
derogation of the Popes authority, or of the religion, that
he mainteineth, mens eares woulde leſſe haue glowed, to
heare you talke ſo Turkiſhlie. We haue in dede great bra-
uery in talke, and horrible woordes, withowt any ſubſtantiall proufe of the matter ye take in hande. Yea, ye are rather ouerborne and beaten downe with a number of your
owne allegations and authorities.   As for the place of Iob
ye alleage, that the hypocrites hope ſhall periſhe, doth no
more touche M. Fekenham and his fellowes , then yt did
touche

touche the blessed man Iob. Baldad did vntruely charge him with yt, and ye doe as baldly, and as vntruely charge nowe the catholikes therwith. The Cat holiks haue almost one thousand of yeres quietly possessed and enioyed their faith in our realme that ye peuishely and prowdly call Popery. The religion that ye professe hath not as yet, continewed there vnder anie one Prince tenne yeares together. Miracles ye worke none, though many woders ye worke, for your procedinges are altogether to be wondered at. Neither the lyfe of your sect is so vertuouse, nor the learning so greate, that either wyse men, and suche as haue the feare of God in them, may sodenly be drawen from theire aunciente Catholike faith: or that ye may so binde Princes nowe lyuing and all theire successours, by suche a Turkish answere to a reasonable demaunde, as they may not in any wise mainteyne that faith, that notoriously and commonly was mainteyned in Englande almost a thousande yeares, ere ye were borne. M. Feckenhas most reasonable demaud therfore remayneth vnanswered, and the foule absurdyte, which he obiecteth vnauoyded, appereth well (as it is in dede) by your silence vnauoydable.

The. 161. Diuision. pag. 102.4.
M. Fekenham.

Here foloweth the Resolutions of the areforesayde Scruples, made by my L. Bishop of VVinchester.

For a resolute answere to all the saide Scruples, ex-
pressed in the forenamed poinctes, his L. sayde, that he
did muche lamente, that the right meaninge of the Othe,
had not beene in season opened and declared vnto me,

whan

whan the onely lacke of the right vnderstanding thereof,
hath bene the cause of such staies and distourbance of cōscience. VVhereas the Q. Maiesties meaning in that Othe,
is farre otherwise, thā the expresse words are, as they lie
verbatim, like as it doth well appeare by her Highnes
interpretatiō made thereof in the Iniunctiōs. There vnto
my obiectiō was, that vndoutedly her Highnes did fully
meane and mind to claim and take al spiritual gonernmēt
vpō her: for besides the expres wordes of the Othe, whervnto al mē be bound to swere verbatim as they lie, without al chaunge and alteratiō making of any word or sense
thereof, her Highnes (in the interpretation set foorth in
her Iniūctiōs) doth by very playn words, claime the same
spiritual gouernmēt here in this realme of the Church of
England, that her highnes father Kinge Henry, and her
brother king Edwarde did enioye and claime before her:
in the which iniunctiōs, aud in the late acte of Parleamēt
also her highnes doth claime no more spiritual gouernmēt
nor no lesse, but so much in euery point, as they had without all exception. For answere his L. did still continue in
the deniall thereof, and that her Highnes meaning was
not to take so much of Spiritual authority and power vppon her, as they did: with affirmation, that he did moste
certainly and assuredly know her highnes minde therein.
Then for some issue to be had of this matter, seeing that
the meaning of the Othe, is not as the expresse words doe
purporte.

purport: And feing that his L. did fo well vnderftand her Highnes meaning therein, and thereby the very righte fence therof, I befought him, that his L. would take fome paines for truthes fake to penne the fame: wherevpon his L. did penne and write the interpretatiō of the faid Othe as hereafter foiloweth. I. A. B. do vtterly teftifie and declare in my cōfcience, that the Q. Highnes is the only Supreme gouernor of this Realm, and of al other her Highnes dominiōs and countries, aswel in al fpiritual or ecclefiaftical things or caufes, as tēporal. That is, to haue the foneraingtie and rule ouer al manner perfons, borne within her Realmes, dominions and coūtries, of what eftate either Ecclefiaftical or tēporal fo euer they be. And to haue authority and power to vifit the Ecclefiaftical eftate, and perfons, to refourme, order, and correct the fame : and all maner errours, herefies, fchifmes, abufes, offenfes, cōtemptes, and enormities. Yet neuertheles in no wife meaning, that the Kings and Queenes of this Realme, poffeſſours of this crowne, may challenge authoritie or power of minifterie of diuine offices, as to preache the worde of God, to minifter Sacramentes or rytes of the Churche appointed by Chrifte to the office of Churche minifters, to excommunicate, or to binde, or loofe. Of the whiche fower pointes, three belong onely to the Ecclefiaftical minifters, the fourthe is cōmon to them with the congregation, namely to excōmunicate. And that no forain Prince,

sss ij   Perfone,

Perſon,Prelat,State or Potẽtate, hath or ought to haue any iuriſdiction,Power, Superioritie, preheminence, or authority eccleſiaſtical or Spiritual, within this realme. And therefore I doe vtterly renounce al foraine iuriſdictions,powers, ſuperiorities, preheminences,and authorities : That is,as no Secular or Laie Prince,other than the King or Quenes poſſeſſours of the Croune of this Realme, of what Title or dignitie ſo euer they be , hathe or oughte to haue, anye Authoritie,ſoueraigntie, or power , ouer this Realme , ouer the Prince or Subiectes thereof. Euen ſo no manner of foraine Prelate or perſon Eccleſiaſtical, of what title , name , ſo euer they be, neither the See of Rome, neither any other See, hathe or ought to haue, vſe, enioye, or exerciſe, any maner of power,iuriſdiction,authority, ſuperioritie,preheminence, or priuilege ſpiritual or eccleſiaſtical within this realme, or within any the Quenes highnes dominions or Coũtries. And therefore,al ſuche foraine power vtterly is to be renoũced,and I do pmiſe,&c.vt ſequitur in forma iuraméti.

M. Horne.

The.558.
Vntruth.
Shamful.
For they
are your
very own
as it ſhall
appeare,

Theſe that ye terme Reſolutions,are none of (.558.) mine, they are like him that forged them, falſe, feined, and malitious. They be your owne , eyther ye could not, or ye vvere aſhamed to adioyne my anſvvere to your ſeely obiections, and therfore ye feygned mee to vtter for reſolutions , your owne peuiſh cauillations. This report is falſe, that I ſhould affirme thē Queenes Maieſties meaning in that Othe to be farre othervviſe then the expreſſe vvords are as they lie verbatim. This my conſtant aſſertion,that her highnes
minde

mind and meaning is, to take so much, and no more of spiritual authoritie and povver vpon her, than King Henry, and king Edvvard enioyed and did iustly claime, you vntruely seygne to be your obiectiō. And that I should affirme of most certaine and sure knovvledge, her Maiesties mind, or the very right sence of the Othe, to be othervvise thā it is plainly set forth, is a malicious sclander, vvherof I vvil setche no better profe, then the testimony of your mouth. Ye cōfesse that the interpretatiō folovving, vvas pēned and vvritē by me, to declare the very right sence and meaning of the Othe, vvherein ye haue acquited me, and cōdēned your self, of a manifest vntruth. For the right sence and meaning declared in the interpretatiō that I made, and you haue set forth, doth (.559.) plainly shevve the cleane contrary, if you marke it vvel, to al that you here set forth in my name, vnder the title of my resolutions to your scruples. Furthermore, in the preface to your fornamed points, ye haue declared by vvord and vvriting, that I did require you presently to svveare and by othe to acknovvledge her highnes to be the only supreme gouernour in al spiritual or ecclesiastical things or causes. If this be true, that you haue said, it is manifest by your ovvn cōsession, that I declared her maisties meaning in that Othe, to be none othervvise than the expresse vvords are, as they lye verbatim. For vvhen I shevve her meaning to be, that ye should acknovvledge in her highnes, the only supremacy, I do declare plainly, that she meaneth to exclude, * al other men frō hauig any supremacy: for this exclusiue, only, cā not haue any other sense or meaning. And vvhā I add this supremacy to be in al spiritual causes or things, I shevve an vniuersal cōprehension to be meant vvithout exception. For if ye * except or take avvay any thing, it is not al. And you your self tooke my meaning to be thus. For ye chalēge me in your second chefe point, and cal for profe hereof at my hand, vvhich ye vvould not do, if it vvere not mine assertion and meaning. For vvhy should I be driuē to proue that vvhich I affirme not, or meant not. Besides these in your vvhole trauaile folovving, ye labour to improue this (as you saie) mine assertion, to vvit, that al spiritual iurisdiction dependeth vpon the positiue lavv of Princes: If this be mine assertion, as ye affirme it is, and therfore bend al your force to improue it, ye vvittnes vvith me (.560.) against your selfe, that I declared her maiesties meanīg, vvas to take neither more nor lesse authoritie, and iurisdictiō, vnto her selfe, than king Hērie and King Edvvarde had, for they had no more thā al. And if her Maiestie take any lesse, she hath not al. Touching therefore these false, seined, and slanderous

Marginal notes:
The.559. Vntruth. your interpretatiō agreeth vvith your resolutiōs, the interpretation exceptig certaine iurisdictiōn in causes Ecclesiasticall from the Prince, vvhereof doth follow, that (as the resolutions reporte) the Othe must not be taken, as it lieth verbatim.
*So al general coūcelles are excluded.
*VVhy thē do ye exclude out of the Oth preachig, Ministrig of sacramēts bindig, ād losing. etc The. 560. vntruth.

Not against him selfe. For first you saied so: but in your resolutiōs, and interpretation of the Othe you saie the cōtrary. And so in both places you are truly charged.

derous refolutions, as they are by you moſtē vntruly forged: euen ſo, vvhether this bee likely, that in a yeres ſpace vvel nigh, I vvould not in all our daily cōference, make (.561.) one reaſon or argumēt, out of the Scriptures or other authority, in the maintenaunce of mine aſſertion : and to reſolue you in the ſame, I referre to the iudgemēt of all the Papiſtes in the Realme, that knovv both me and you. Againe, though ye doo denie that I ſo did, and therefore do report none, there bee many both vvorſhipjul ād of good credit, yea and ſome of your ovvn deer friendes alſo, that are vvitneſſes of our talke, and can tell vvhat reaſons I haue made vnto you, bothe out of the Scriptures, and other authorities and proofes out of the Churche hiſtories , ſuche as ye coulde not auoide, but vvere forced to (.562.) yelde vnto. And vvhether I ſhould ſo doo or not, I might referre me vnto the teſtimonie of your ovvn mouthe, both thā and ſithē ſpoken to diuerſe, that can vvitneſſe the ſame, that ye affirmed this (although vntrulie) that you neuer found anie, that ſo much ouerpreſſed you, as I did, vvhich your ſaing, although moſt vntrue, yet it ſhovveth , that ſomevvhat I ſaied to confirme mine aſſertion, and to confute yours.

The .561. vntruth. M. Fekēham deʒ nieth it not, in any his vvordes aboue reʒ herſed.

The .562. vntruth. M. Fekēhā neuer yelded to any your proofes, reaſons, or Au- thorites.

The ſixt Chapter, concerning the Reſolutions that M. Horne gaue to M. Fekenham, to the .4. forenamed poyntes.

Stapleton.

THIS proceſſe following ſtandeth vppon certain re- ſolutions of M Hornes, as M. Fekēhā ſaieth. But M. Horne denieth thē. And therefore being *quæſtio faĉti* as they cal yt, and the doubte reſtinge vpon priuate talke, that paſſed betwene them: I cā geue no certaine iudgmēt: but muſt referre yt, ro the diſcrete conſideratiō of the in- differēt reader. Yet ſo muche as I know, I wil ſay, and that is, that I vnderſtande by ſuche as haue had at ſeueral times cōmunicatiō with the ſayde M. Fekenhā and emong other thinges, of this conference, heard M. Fekenhā ſay, that tou- ching theis reſolutions, he hath thē of M. Daniel, thē ſecre- tary to M. Horne, his hand writing, redie to be ſhewed at all tymes If yt be ſo, yt is likely, that M. Daniel can and wil

teſtifie

teſtifie the truth, in caſe he ſhoulde be required : of whoſe
hand writing M Fekenhā ſaieth he hath alſo certaine other
thinges copied out. But yet becauſe, the euent of things to
come are vncertaine, let vs imagine an vnlikely caſe, that
is, that M. Daniel wil deny theſe forſaied writings to be of
his hād: and that thē M. Horne will much moi e ſharply and
vehemētly crie out againſt theſe reſolutions, then he doth
now, that they are none of his, *but lyke to him that forged
them, falſe, feyned and malicioufe*, with much other like matter that he laieth forth for his defence nowe . Suerly then
though M. Fekenham were lyke to haue therbye no great
preiudice in the principal matter, (for whether theſe reſolutions be true or falſe, the principal point is neither greatly bettered, nor much hindred by them) yet ſhould M. Fekenhā perchaunce greatly impayre his honeſty and good
name therby. Let vs thē as I ſaid, thinck vpō the worſt, and
whether that M. Fekenham as he hath, (as ye haue heard,)
much good defence for the principall pointe, ſo he may in
this diſtreſſe, fynde any good reliefe, for the defending and
ſauing vpright of his honeſty . Ye wil perchaūce good reader now thinck, that M. Fekenhā is in a very hard ād ſtrayt
caſe: and that yt were a great difficulty to find any apparāt
or honeſt help for him. And yet for al this ther is good and
great helpe at hāde. For I wil be ſo bolde my ſelf for ones,
to take vppō my ſelf to make a ſufficient proufe, that theſe
reſolutions are not M. Fekenhams, but M . Hornes owne.
And yf his ſecretary will not ſerue, I wil bring forth one
other witnes that ſhalbe ſomwhat nerer him, and that M.
Horne can not, nor ſhall, for all the ſhiftes that euer he
ſhall make, refuſe : and that is Mayſter Horne him ſelfe,
and no worſe man. For thoughe I be not very priuie and
certaine

certaine what paſſed betwixt M. Horne and M.Fekēham
at Waltham:yet of the contentes of this his printed anſwere to M Fekenham I am aſſured, and ſo conſequentlie
that theſe are his reſolutions, confeſſed more then ones
or twiſe,by his owne mowthe and penne.

Conſider therfore good reader,the ſtate of the queſtion
touching theis reſolutions.Is yt any other, then that as M.
Fekenham auowcheth,M.Horne tolde him,for a reſolute
anſwere,*that the Quenes Mai. meaning in the othe is farre
otherwiſe,then the expreſſe wordes are in the ſtatute,as they
lie verbatim? And that thinges are therefore with ſome gentle vnderſtanding to be interpreted,and mollified? And therfore,that thoughe the wordes of the ſtatute be general and preciſe, that ſhe onely is the ſupreame gouernour of the realme
aſwell in all ſpiritual or eccleſiaſticall thinges or cauſes,as temporall: Yet in no wiſe the meaning is that the kinges or Quenes may challēge authority or power of miniſterie of diuine offices,as to preache the worde of God, to miniſter Sacramētes,
to excommunicate,to bynde or loſe?* To this effect come M.
Hornes reſolutions in the interpretatiō of the Othe, made
by him at M.Feckenhams requeſt as M. Fekenham ſaieth.
But M.Horne doth flatly denie, that euer he made anie
ſuche moderation or mollification, and laieth forth manie
reaſons to perſwade the Reader, that M. Fekenham hath
ſlaundered him. He ſaieth *the right ſenſe of the othe,is none
other then yt is plainely ſet forth.*he ſaith:*that the ſupremacie
is onely in the Quenes highnes:for this excluſiue(onely)cā not
haue any other ſenſe,or meaning.* He ſaith moreouer, *when I
adde this ſupreamacie to be in all ſpiritual cauſes or thinges, I
ſhewe an vniuerſal comprehenſion to be meante withowt exception,for yſ ye excepte or take away any thinge,yt is not all.*

Are

Are not theis your owne words M.Horne?do not then so
generall and peremptory wordes of the statute , especially
your precise exposition adioyned thervnto, expresly geue
vnto the Quenes Mai.not only a simple and parted authority,but the cheifest,the principaleste, and a general or vniuersal authority in al thinges and causes whatsoeuer , as to
preach,to minister the sacraments , and to lose and bynde,
aswell as in other matters ? Is it not euident, that theis are
things spiritual and ecclesiastical.Do ye not attribute *without exception* , as we haue declared , by your owne words
the supremacy to the Quene in al causes and thinges spirituall?How then can it be possible , but that by a necessary
consequent, ye doe also attribute , to her the supremacy in
the causes Ecclesiastical before rehersed?And think yowe
then M.Horne,that M.Fekenhã and his fellowes may take
the othe with sauf conscience?And think you, that though
the pope had no authority in the realme,the Quenes Mai.
might haue so large and ample authority,the holy scripture
being so playn to the contrary?Is it not likely therfore,that
in your conference with M.Fekenham , ye did forsee this
mischief,and therfor(though ye deny it here so stifly) that
ye gaue him in dede such resolutions as be here specified?
Suerly it is a thig most probable.For ye make the very same
resolutions to hym euen in this your answere also.For doe
ye not expressely say a fewe leaues before , that *princes* Fol.96.
neither do,nor may claime to preache the word of God , to mi- &.97.
nister the Sacramentes,or to bynde and lose ? Do ye not say,
that this is *a spirituall gouernement and rule , belonging onely* Fol.107.
to the bishops and Church rulers? Do ye not confesse within &.108.
4. leaues followinge the lyke ? And that *Bisshoppes haue*
the spirituall Iurisdistion ouer theire flocke , by the expresse

worde of God : and that thereby Princes haue not all maner of fpiritual gouerment? Is not this agreable to the refolutiôs that M.Fekenham faith he receyued at your handes? Again M.Fenkenham addeth, that in your faid refolutions, ye faye that the authority to excommunicate is not properly perteyning to Princes, but apperteyneth to the whole côgregation afwell as to them. Doe ye not confeffe, I pray you, the fame twife in your anfwere immediatly following after this? Why fay you then, that thefe refolutiôs are feyned by M.Fekenham? Why fhould any man thinke that M. Fekêham fhould falfly charge you with thefe refolutiôs in priuat conference, that your felf in your own book, doe fo plainly and openly auouche ? Why fhould not men thinke alfo fuch other things as ye here charge M . Fekenham withall to be vntrue, feing that ye doe fo falfly accufe M.Feken.for framing refolutions, in your name, that are your own in very dede? Or why fhould any man truft you in thefe greate and weighty matters, which ye hâdle, that ye fpeake, ye câ not tel what, burfting out into fuch open and fowle contradictions, as yt would aftone any wife man to confider them: attributing to the Quenes Maie. the fupremacy in al fpiritual caufes or things without exception, and yet your felf, excepting diuerfe things fpiritual, and geuing the fupremacy of them to the cleargy? I woulde fayne know of you that fo lately ruffled fo frefhly with your oppofitiô contrary, relatyue, priuatiue, and difparatyue, and with your propofitions contrary, fubcontrary, fubalterne and côtradictory: yf a man man may fynd a more fowle contradiction thê this I now laye before you out of your own booke.

*Fol.*105. 107.

A contradiction irrecôcileable in M. Horne.

You fay firft fol.104. b.in fine.

When I adde this fupremacy to be in all fpiritual caufes , or
thinges

things, I shewe an vniuersall comprehensiō without exception
For yf ye except or take away any thing, it is not all.

Hereof, ariseth this vniuersal affirmatiue.

Al spiritual causes without exceptiō are vnder the supreme
Gouuerment of Princes.

Item you say: fol 96.b.

To feede the Church with Gods worde, to minister Christes
Sacramētes, and to bind and lose (fol. 97.a.) Kings, Queenes, ād
Princes may not, neither doe clayme or take vpon thē, this kind
of spiritual gouernement, and rule, or any part thereof &c.

Hereof ariseth this particular negatiue.

Some spiritual causes are not vnder the Supreme Gouerne-
ment of Princes.

Now let vs cōsider, in what kind of opposition, these
your two propositions do repugne. Thus stande the oppositions.

All spirituall causes without exceptiō are vnder the Supreme Gouernemēt of Prínces.	Contrary.	No spiritual causes at all are vnder the Supreme gouerment of Princes.
Subal-terne.	CONTRA-DICTORY. CONTRA-DICTORY.	Subal-terne.
Some spiritual causes are vnder the Supreme gouerment of Princes.		Some spiritual causes are not vnder the supreme gouernement of Princes.

Subcontrary.

By this it appereth, that your two propositions do stāde in the
extremest kind of al oppositions: which is: Contradiction.

And

And though this be a poore fely, and an infufficient fhifte,
to make fuch refolutions, yet is it the befte ye may nowe
fynde to qualifie and mitigate the general words of the fta·
tute. Which in dede are fo general and peremptorie, that
they may in no wife be borne without fome qualification.
Which is nowe fo notorioufe, that there is a qualification
made in the Quenes Maie. iniunctions, that men fhould not
take the general claufe fo largely, as to collect thereby, that
the Kings or Quenes of our realm may challege authority
ad power of minifterie in the diuine offices in the Church.
Which doth agree with your refolutions : and therefore
there is no caufe in the worlde, why ye fhould deny them
to be yours, and fay that they be falfly and flaunderouflye
fayned vpo you by M.Fekeha:vttering his owne peuifh ca-
uillatios, as ye fay vnder the name of your refolutios.Nowe
though this be a neceffary interpretatio and moderatio, yet
this doth not take away the fcruple that remaineth, ftaying
M. Fekenha and other to, in taking the faid othe : for that

Note. this interpretatio, is not made by acte of parliament, as the
ftatute was. Neither doth the Acte or Statute referre it felf
to any fuch Iniunctions to be made, for the qualificatio or
reftrayning of any thinge in the Acte or in any braunche
thereof cotayned, no more then it doth to M.Horns book.
Neither hath any Iniunction by the lawe of our Realme any
force to reftrain, weake or mollifie the rigour or generality
of an Acte of parliamet. And in cafe it had, yet ther remain
many other as great fcruples.Namely, that fwearing to all
caufes, the pricipal caufes are excepted, and fo he that fweareth forfweareth, and befide, that al ecclefiaftical authority, afwel of the fea of Rome, as of al general coucels, is euidetly aboliflhed, by the faid ftatut. And in as much as gene-
nerall

ral Coũcels, do beare ãd reprefent the parfon of the whole
Church, wherof the Pope is head, no Chriftiã mã ought to
receyue fuch othe, imploying the denial of the authority of
the Pope the head, and of the whole body of the Churche
befide.

The . 162. Diuifion . pag. 104.. b.

M. Fekenham .

*Hereunto I did make this obiection following. Thefe
woordes of the firft part of the othe, I. A. B. doe vtterly teftifie and declare (in my confcience) that the Q. Highnes
is the only fupreme gouernour of this Realme, as well in
all Spiritual or Ecclefiafticall thinges or caufes, as Temporal (befides the particulars expreffed in your L. interpretation made thereof) they doe by expreffe woordes of
the acte geue vnto the Queenes highnes, al maner of iurifdictions, priuileges, and preeminences in any wife touchinge and concerninge any Spirituall or Ecclefiafticall iurifdiction within the Realme, with an expreffe
debarre, and flat denial made of al Spiritual iurifdiction
vnto the Biffhops therof, to be exercifed ouer their flocks
and cures, without her highnes Special commiffion to be
graunted thereunto: They hauing by the expreffe worde*
of God, commiffion of Spiritual gouernement ouer them.
Commiffion to lofe and bind their finnes. Commiffion to
fhut and open the gates of heauen to them. Commiffion to
geue vnto them the holy ghoft by the impofition of their
handes. And they hauing by the expreffe woorde of God
fuch a daungerous cure and charge ouer their foules, that

Act. 20.
Ioan. 20.
Math. 16.
Act. 8.

ttt iij   God

God hath threatned to require the bloud of such as shall
perishe at their handes. Notwithstanding, these and many such other like comissions graunted vnto them for the
more better discharge of their cure, and that by the mouth
of God they may not exercise any iurisdictiō ouer thē, they
may not visit thē, they may not reforme thē, they may not
order nor correct them, without a further comission frō
ỹ Q. highnes. Suerly my good L. these thinges are so strāge
vnto me, and so contrary to al that I haue rede, that I am
not hable to satiffie my consciēce therin. Your L. aunswer
vvas, that for as much as al Spiritual iurisdictiō, and authority to make Lawes and to iudge the people in courtes
Ecclesiastical, to visit thē, to reforme thē, to order ād correct thē, doth depēd only vpō the positiue Lawes of Kings
and Princes, ād not vpō the Law of God, therfore neither
did the Apostles of Christ, neither the Bishops and their
successours may exercise any iurisdictiō vpō the people of
God, iudge thē, visit thē, refourme, order ād correct them
without authority and comissiō of the King and Prince.

Heb.13.
Ezech.

M. Horne.

It is very true, that after ye had quarelled muche in sondry thinges touching vvoordes and termes expressed in the Act of Parliament, and in the interpretation of the Othe : Yee did neuertheleffe finally agree in the vvhole
matter thereof, finding onely doubt in one point of mine assertiō, namely touching iurisdiction Spirituall or Ecclesiastical, al vvhich you affirmed, contrary to mine assertion, to be committed by Christe to Bishops and priestes, as
proprely apperteyning to their office and calling vvithout further commission
or authority from Princes or any other povver. The distinction that I made
of Ec-

of Ecclesiastical iurisdiction, I vvil first repete, and than put mine answveare to your argumentes. Spiritual Iurisdiction is diuided into tvvo sortes. the one is called Cohibytiue, *the other not* Cohibityue. *That vvhich is called not Cohibityue, is that iurisdiction or povver that is exercised and vvoorketh in the invvarde and (.563.) secrete courte of conscience: that is (.564.) the preaching of the Ghospell, mmistration of the Sacrameies, and the absoluing and reteininge of sinnes by the vvoorde of God in the publique mynistery. This therfore they call not Cohibityue, bicause in the Court of conscience, no man is bound or levvied vnvvillingly or against his vvill. To exercise this kind of Iurisdictio, neither Kinges nor ciuill Magistrates, neither any other persone may challendge or take vppon him, onlesse he be lavvfully called thereunto. Iurisdiction Cohibityue hath (.565.) tvvo partes, the one consisteth in the exercise of excommunication, and circumstaunces thereunto required by Christes institution: the vvhich povver or Iurisdiction belongeth to the Church onely, and (.566.) not to the Prince, Bishoppe or Priest: for no man hath authority to excommunicate, but onely the Churche, and those vvho receiue authority thereunto by commission from the Church. The other kinde of Cohibitiue iurisdiction is a povver or authority, that consisteth and is exercised , in foro caularum, in the courte of caules, and apperteineth ad externum & publicum forum, to the externall and publike Courte, and is defined to be, saith* Antonius, *an authority or povver to declare the Lavv, geue sentence and to iudge in all controuersies (pertayninge to the Courte) vvhat is euery mans righte, and in summe, to doo those thinges that iustice dooth require accordinge to the Lavves.* Ioannes Quintinus *defineth Iurisdiction, to the same effect, but openeth the nature therof more plainely, saying,* Iurisdictiō is an office and authority, to declare the Law, that is, to admynister iustice and equity, and to gouern the peo ple with right ād Lawes. whā I name an office (saith he) I meane that iurisdictiō hath in it selfe a necessity to declare the Lawe: for office is that which euery man is bound to doo: to declare the lawe, is, to exercise iudgementes, wherevppon commeth iurisdiction (he meaneth, that iurisdiction hath the name and is so called of exercising iudgementes) iudgementes are exercised onelye
of them

of thē that haue iurifdictiō, that is, power to iudge. Iurifdiction confifteth only in the contentions or debating of matters in Courte or iudgements. This authority to iudge dooth difcende nowe from the (.567.)
Prince alone, in whome only is all power. By vertue
of (.568.) this iurifdiction (faith *Antonius*) the Churche
minifters accordinge to theire offices rightly enioyned vnto them, may lawfully vifite, enquire of mens
manners, punifhe the faulty, fend foorth apparitours
or fommoners, cyte the fturdy and ftubborne, repreffe
their malepartnes, call and fommon meete perfonnes
to the Synode prouinciall or generall, confirme the
matters decreed in the Synode or Coūcell(.569.) pardone faultes, chaunge or mitigate the penaūce enioyned for confeffed faultes, condemne Heretiques and
their writinges, examine all mens writinges who fo
euer, before they be fet foorth or publifhed, and after
due examination, iudge whether they conteyne founde or peftilent doctrin, ordeine Decrees, Lawes, ceremonies and rytes,
conftitute Bifshoppes and other Church minifters, alfo depofe
degrade, make them irreguler and vnhable to haue holy orders, determine illegitimation in perfonnes for maryage, beftowe Ecclefiafticall benefices, and exact tythes and annates.
*Thefe and many other thinges may be lavvfully doone by thofe that haue the
povver of this Cohybitiue Iurifdiction,* which is not (.faith he.) properly
fignified by the name of the keyes: for although it may be named (in fome refpect) a Church key: yet it differeth very much
from the keyes of the firft Courte, that is, of the Courte of Confcience. For the vfe of thofe keyes, that are occupied in the
Courte of confcience, belongeth onely to the Euangelicall
Prieftes. But this Iurifdiction may lawfully be exercifed of
thofe that are not minifters of the woorde and Sacramentes,
and are not Prieftes. *As the tvvo former partes of Ecclefiaftical iurifai-
ction haue their vertue, povver, and inftitution of Chrifte immediatly, euen
fo this third part, vvhich is fated to confift in foro caufarum, vvith thofe
thinges*

The.567. vntruthe.
Quintinus fpeaketh
there of temporall
Iurifdiction, not of
Ecclefiafticall.
The.568 vntruthe.
Antonius falfified.
He fpeaketh not of
this Iurifdiction, that
is, of that vvhich
cometh from the
prince onely.
The.569. vntruthe.
A great deale left
out in the midle.
plainly confutinge
M. Horns purpofe,

things vvhich may be vfed or exercifed by vertu thereof, doth depende vpon the (.570.) pofitiue Lavves of Chriftian Magiftrats, or vvhere, fuch vvanteth vpõ the pofitiue rules and orders of that Church, vvhere fuch orders muft be practifed: and not immediatly vpon the Lavve of God.

The. 7. Chapter. Howe M. Horne reftraineth the Othe to one kinde of iurifdiction, thereby to auoide M. Fekenhams vnuincible Argument taken out of Gods woorde.

Stapleton.

AMonge other obiections that M. Fekenham made againft the fupremacy in the conference at Waltham, this was one. That Biſhops had their warrante and commiſsion for their exercife of their fpiritual function and office by the expreſſe woorde of God: therefore he could not with quiet confcience allowe the othe, that geueth the Prince fupremacy in all caufes fpiritual, with al priuileges, and preheminences in any wife touching any fpirituall iurifdiction. He miſliketh, that Biſhops hauing fuch commiſsion by Gods worde, may not vifite and reforme their cures without a further cõmiſsiõ from the Queenes highnes. M. Horne thinketh to wipe al this away with a diftinction borowed, as he faith, of one Ioánes Antonius Delphinus. If any Catholik (good reader) fhould haue brought a teftimony out of this Author againft M. Horne, yt fhould haue ben with great contempte refufed and reiected by and by. But now feing M. Horne himfelf hath authorifed him: I truft he wil allowe him to be alleaged for our fide alfo. And then fhall M. Horne take fmall cõfort of any diftinction, to be found in him: being one that auoucheth the popes fupremacy, as much as any man, yea aboue al generall Councelles.

vvv   Yet

The. 570.
vntruthe.
Yourown
Author,
Antonius
calleth
this Opinion Impiũ
errorẽ; a
vvicked
errour,

An anſ
ſvvere to
Io. Anto.
Delphin⁹.
Io. Anthoⁿius Delde poteſtã
ẽcclef. Venet. 1552.
in. 8.

Yet M. Horne thinketh so to bewytche his reader, as yt were with certayne magical incantations, that he shoulde beleue this Anthony to be of his opinion. We wil therfore for the better disclosing of M. Hornes iuggling, gather so much out of Anthonius, as we must necessarily do, for the illustratiō of this matter. This Anthonius diuideth (as other scholemen doe) al authority Ecclesiastical, into the power of order, and into the power of iurisdictiō. The first power as he declareth, doth reste in the interpreting of the sacred Scripture, in the consecrating of the body and bloudde of Christ, in ministring of Sacraments, in geuing holy orders, and beside other things in coupling of parsons together by mariage sacramētally. The power of iurisdictiō he definetħ as M. Morn doth, and doth diuide it into *Cohibityue*, ād *Not Cohibityue*: as M. Horn doth. But for the residewe, M. Horn plaieth the Medea, as he did before with Quintin'. And besides maketh such expositions, as neither his authour hath, nor otherwise are true. And as skilful a Logician as he pretendeth him self: he neither followeth the order of his author, not yet the true order and trade of the rules of Logik: that is, first to define, and thē to diuide. But peruerteth and confoundeth, aswel the order as the truth of al things. Wel we wil walke also a litle disorderly, to trace M. Horn in his own steppes. *The iurisdiction not cohibityue* (saith M. Horn) *is that iurisdiction or power, that is exercised, and worketh in the inward and secrete court of consciēce, that is, the preaching of the Ghospel, ministratiō of the Sacraments, and the absoluing or reteyning of syns by the word of God in the publique ministery.* This sayth M. Horn, but not his authour: who referreth to the not cohibityue Iurisdiction, only absolutiō in the secret Court of conscience, Who saith also, that *preaching and expounding*

Tvvo povvers in the Churche: the firste of order or of the keyes: the second of iurisdiction.

Fol. 105. a.

Lib. 2. pa. 76.

Lib. 2. pa. 36. b. & 37. a.

pounding of holy scripture, with the ministratiō of sacraments is no part of iurisdictiō ecclesiastical, but belōgeth to the keies of order. Neither doth your authour call preaching and mini-string of Sacramens, the secret cowrt of conscience, nor he cā iustly do it: being a thing openly done, sene, and hearde: but he so calleth priuate confession only (becaufe it is done priuatly and secretly, betwene the party and the consef-for). And this no man doth vnwillingly: for though a man may by commaundement of his bishop be al-lotted to a certaynē parish and curate : yet vnlesse he do submitte him self to his parrochial priest, and open vnto him his synnes, he can neuer be losed by him. To confesse the which priuy and secrete faults he can not be forced, but by his owne conscience. And vnlesse he cōfesse thē, he can not be absolued. To this cōfession then it appertayneth, that is sayd: *no mā is bownd or losed vnwillingly* (which you for the tēder loue ye beare to priuat confession do altogether dissemble) and not to preaching or ministring of Sacramēts, as ye seeme to say. Which preaching and ministring of Sacraments doe not appertayne to the, not cohibityue iurisdiction, as abso-lutiō doth, but to the power or kaye of order, which (pro-perly to speak) is no Iurisdictiō at al. The which as M. Horn doth confound: so doth he imagine of his owne fantasticall braine, *that the iurisdiction cohibitiue hath two parts: the one standing in excommunicatiō, belonging neither to king, nor bishoppe, but to such as haue commission from the Church : the other in hearing of causes in the external and publyke cowrte.* All this is but an heape of follies and lies. For first, his Au-thour, doth not so diuide cohibityue iurisdiction : as yt doth euidently appeare in hym, and we shall anon more plainly open it. Againe is not excommuuication geuen and

Io. Anth.
Delph. lib.
2. pag.
76. b.

Quamuis prælati su-perioris voluntate quis parochiali sacer-doti subijciatur, ta-mē nisi ipse vltrı sub ijciat seipsū: nūquam poterit absolui á pec-catis. In secretissimo enī foro cōsciētiæ ne-mo absoluitur inuit.

pronounced in publike and external cowrt vppon the hearing of caufes there? Why do ye then feuer, and difmember
excommunication from the hearing of caufes ecclefiaftical?
Now that excommunication fhould neither properly apperteine to the prince, nor to bifhops, but to the whole
Churche and congregation, is a fonde, folifh and frantyk imagination of M. Horne, as euen alfo his Author Antonius in
this very booke largely proueth. And as it is not farre from
herefy: fo perchaunce it is not farre from a premunire.

What meane you Maifter Horne by this Churche? The
whole Churche can not affemble together. And if you
meane a generall councell, whiche in dede reprefenteth
the whole Churche: when fhall we haue any man excommunicated? For of fuche councells very fewe, fyth
the Chriftiã fayth was firft receaued, haue bene affembled.
And yet as fewe as they are, diuerfe of them haue alredy
excõmunicated fuch herefies as ye mainteyn. Yf ye meane
of the particular Church where the party fhall be denounced excommunicate, then muft we haue both men, womẽ,
and children folemply fummoned to affemble when any
excommunication is made. For they be afwel parts of the
Church, as the wifeft and the eldeft parfon of the parrifhe.
And as euery part of your anfwere in this point imployeth
a great folly: fo the greateft of all is, to fee yowe after this
fort to handle your matters, that ye haue now by this your
wife reafon fruftrated and made voyde al the excommunications, that haue bene made any day this. 8. yeares, and
more either by your felfe, yowre officers, or by the arches,
or any other Ecclefiafticall cowrte in Englande. And
nowe may the poore honefte and catholyke woman of
Winchefter, that vppon falfe excommunication (if your

owne

M. Horne in daüger of a premunire.

M. Horns doctrine maketh fruftrate al the excõmuni- cations made in England theis 8. yeares.

owne doctrine be true)hath bene kepte so many yeares in
the Marshalsea, goe home and serue yowe with a write
vppon an action of false inprisonment : either else shewe
vs good M.Horne your commiſsion, to excommunicate,
that you haue receiued from the Church or congregation.
Commiſsion ye haue none from the Quenes highnes:(for
as you say,she hath no such power her self) from the congregation you haue none:(from the which two you deriue
all cohibityue iurisdiction) and from the Pope, ye neither
haue,nor wil haue any.From whence fetche ye then your
cohibityue iurisdiction to excommunicate ? Now as I sayd
take ye hede, leaste to your greate folly be annexed also a
daungerouse premunire.

   As for M.Fekenham,if he deny this and other Ecclesiastical iurisdiction to depende vppon the prince onely, he
doth constantly,and agreably to him self,and to a catholike
mā: but you neither agree with the catholik,nor with your
statute Law, nor with your owne self. The catholiks say,
that this iurisdictiō cometh not originally from the prince,
but being in the Church, when fewe or no princes were
christened:the princes when they first receiued the fayth,
finding this iurisdiction in the Church, so lefte yt, and did
rather encrease and amplify it, thē in any part diminish the
same. The statute sayth,that the prince is supreame head in
al causes ecclesiastical:by the statute also all iurisdictiō ecclesiastical is vnited and annexed to the crowne of the re-
alm.Ye say,the statute must be takē as the words lye *Verba-*
*tim,*without any exception.What then in the worlde,may
be thought more contrarie or repugnante, either to the
wordes of the statute or your own,then when ye say. *For*
Nomā hath Authoritie to excommunicat but onely the Church?

An other
irrecōci-
liable cō-
tradictiō
in M.
Horne.

vvv iiij   Which

Which is to fay : *This power of excommunication belongeth to the Church only, and not to the Prince*, adding alfo, as a reafon: the prince hath no authority to excommunicate? Is not this alfo a manifeft derogatió and impayring of the prerogatiue royal touching matters Ecclefiaftical, to imbarre the Prince al authority of excommunication? May not M. Fekenham here returne wel vpon you, your own wordes?

Fol.3 co.2. *What fauftie meane ye to her perfon, when ye bereue the fame, of a principall parte of her royal power? What quietnes fike you to her parfon, when ye goe aboute to bring the fubiectes to a mifliking of her royall power : which is a preparation of rebellion againft her parfon?* Nowe what cofonage this opinion, yf ye obftinately mainteyne it, hath with herefie, the holy 1.Cor. 15. fcripture may witneffe . What commiffion had S.Paule of the Churche, when he excommunicated the fowle fornicatour at Corinthe? What is the rodde that he threatneth 1.Cor.4. the Corinthians withal, but this excómunication? By what commiffion of the Church did he either excommunicate 1.Tim.1. 1.Cor. 6. Himeneus, and Alexander, or denounce Anathema to him that loued not our Lord Iefus Chrift? What commiffió had S.Peter , when Ananias and Saphira by him excommunica-ted died forthwith? What commiffió had al the Bifhops fy-thens, namely Innocentius the Pope, that excommunicated themperour Arcadius? And S.Ambrofe that excommunica-ted the Emperor Theodofius ? with a thowfand other, that denounced excommunication without any fuch falfe imagined commiffion?

Actorũ. 5.
Nicephor.
lib.13.cap.
34.
Idẽ lib.12.
Cap. 41.

After your diuifió, fantaftically by you framed, ye come to the definitió of Cohibitiue iurifdictió: wherin ye do not fo much miffe of your authors words, as of his opé meanig, comprehending vnder this general definition afwell excó-muni-

munication,as any other matter.Neither are you contente
to tel vs Delphinus definition,but of vour large liberalitye,
you adde,an other neadlesse out of Quintinus:but so, that
after your wont,ye infarse of your own, *that all authoritye
to iudge difcedeth from the prince alone.*Which thing Quintinus saith not of Ecclesiastical,but of temporal iurisdictio,
as we haue declared before.And therefore, when ye infer
by vertue of this iurisdiction, faith Anthonius,the Church mi-   See hovv
*nisters,&c.*meanig by the iurisdictio coming fro the Prince   M Horne
only,ye lewdly lie,afwel vpo Anthonius,as Quintinus.For   playeth
neither of them faith so,but both the quite cotrary. Wher-   the Cacus
of doth follow , that al that,which ye reherse immediatlie   to take af
as out of Quitinus nothing furthereth your pretensed su-   vvay the
premacy.And in case yt did,as ye haue hitherto playde the   authority
peuishe and theuishe Cacus with your authours,to blemish   munica-
the Popes:so now play you the like pageant to ble-   tion from
mish the Prices iurisdictio.For in the midle of your   the Price.
own allegatio,ye haue pared away certain words,   *Ide lib. 2.pag.84.*
touching the forefaid excomunication.In your au-   *Determinata in co-*
thor M.Horn after these words,*to confirme matters*   *cilio confirmare.ex-*
*determined,in the fynod or councel,*followeth,*to ex-*   *comunicare, excom-*
comunicat,and to reconcile to the Church excomunicat   *municatos,cu vt de-*
parsons duely repenting,to referue cases, and to releafe   *cet refipifcunt eccle-*
cafes referued,to geue pardos , to change and mitigate,   *fie reconciliare,cafus*
referuare,referuatos
ad fo forth,as in your allegatio is cotained.After this   *cafus relaxare, dare*
ye fay,that this cohibitiue iurisdictio may be exer-   *indulgentias , penas*
cifed by fuch as are no priefts.I graut you:but what   *qua pro peccatis in-*
is that for your purpofe ? For as your Authour fayeth fo,   *fligunur,comutare.*
euen fo he fayeth, that at the leafte he mufte haue the
clericall tonfure or crowne , without the which, though
he were a religioufe profeffed man , he could not exercife
                                                         this

this iuriſdiction. And this is a good and a ſufficient argument (if you will ſtande to your own Author Anthonius Delphinus) why neither you, nor your fellowes may lawfully practiſe any ſpirituall iuriſdiction. Farder the very next Chapter in this Antonius, of whom M. Horne hath alleaged ſo much, conſiſteth only in prouing, that this ſeconde Cohibytiue Iuriſdiction is in the Churche, by Gods ordonaunce, not by the Commiſſion of Emperours. And this he proueth expreſſely againſt ſuch as M. Horne himſelfe is. I meane againſt the ſcholers of Luther, againſt the preſent proteſtants of our daies: calling their opinion and M. Hornes aſſertion here: *Impium errorem.* A wicked errour. And thought Maiſter Horne to proue by the ſame Antonius in the next Chapter before, that the ſecond Cohibytiue iuriſdiction depended of Princes Commiſſion, which in the Chapter following he doth of ſette purpoſe confute? O what is Impudency, yf this be not?

M. Horne. The. 163. Diuiſion. pag. 106.

You tooke vpon you to proue, that this (. 571.) ſeconde kinde of Cohibitiue Iuriſdiction vvith the appurtenances thereof: as I haue reherſed, vv is appointed by the expreſſe vvord of God immediatlie to Biſshoppes and Prieſtes, vvithout further commiſſion of Princes or other povver, vvhich I denied.

Novve lette vs conſider the force of your proufes, and ſee hovve thei cõ-clude your cauſe. Fiſt yee ſaie, that the woordes of the firſt parte of the Othe, doe by expreſſe woordes of the Acte, geue vnto the Q. highnes all maner of iuriſdictions, priuileges and preeminences in any wiſe touching and concerning any Spiritual or Eccleſiaſtical iuriſdiction within the realme, with an expreſſe debarre and flat denial made of al Spiritual iuriſdiction
vnto

vnto the Biſhops therof to be exerciſed ouer their flockes and cures without her highnes ſpecial commiſsion,to be graunted therevnto:they hauing by the expreſſe word of God,commiſſion of ſpiritual gouernment ouer them.*Your (.572.) euil dealing vvith the vvordes of the Acte of the Othe,expreſſeth an vnkindely meaning to the Prince and the ſtate:for that either the Acte or the Othe debarreth or denieth expreſſely or couuertly the to Biſhops of this realme to exerciſe ouer theyr flockes and cures , vvithout her highnes ſpecial commiſsion graunted thereto, any ſpirituall iuriſdiction aſsigned to a Biſhoppe by the vvorde of God,is altogether (.573.) vntrue . The Statute geueth,or rather reſtoreth to the Prince Iuriſdiction and Authority to enquire after vvhat ſorte,the Eccleſiaſticall ſtate and perſonnes behaue them ſelues in their cures and chardges , to reſourme and corecte the diſorders , negligencies , and enormities riſinge amongeſte them to the hinderaunce of theyr Office in theyr cures and chardges , and in ſumme to order and prouide , that they doe execute theyr Office accordinge to theyr calling in theyr cures and chardges . This is not to debarre or denie the the exerciſe of theyr office vvithout a ſpecial licece.Neither do the(.574.)expreſſe vvords of the ſtatut geue to the prince al manner of iuriſdictiōs in ſuch abſolute vviſe, as you report,in any wiſe,and any ſpiritual iuriſdictiō within the realme.For theſe termes,all maner,in any wiſe, and any ſpiritual iuriſdiction,vvhich you enforce ſo much,are not found in the gift or reſtitutition of ſpiritual iuriſdictiō made by the acte vnto the Prince : but in that part vvhere the acte geueth aftervvard povver and authority to the Prince to execute the Iuriſdictiō,novv * vnited and annexed to the Croune,by mete delegats,to be aſsigned,named,ād authoriſed by cōmiſsiō or letterspatents vnder the great Seale of england. If ye vvil hereof infer, that bycauſe the princes haue by vertue of the acte,full povver and authority to name,aſsigne,and authoriſe any perſon vvhom they ſhal thinke mete to exerciſe,vſe,occupy,and exequute vnder the,al maner of iuriſdictions,priuileges and prebeminences in any vviſe,touching or concerning any ſpiritual or eccleſiaſtical iuriſdictiō vvith—*

The.572.vntruthe. Sclaunderous. M. Fekenhā reported the effecte of the Othe truely.

The. 573.vntruthe. For that is moſte true, as it ſhal appeare.

The.574. vntruth. The expreſſe wordes of the Statute doe geue to the prince,povver to Anthoriſe men to vſe all maner of iuriſdictions,as it is here reported,abſolutely. Ergo it geueth to the Prince the iuriſdictiōs alſo

* Marke: If this iuriſdiction be vnited to the croun which the Prince in al maner doth aſsigne, name, ād authoriſe other to execute, why ſaied you before, that the Statute gaue not to the prince all maner of iuriſdictions?

The.575. vntruthe. It is no Sophistica-tiō at al: you proue no such thing.

The. 576. vntruth. For they are not re-strained in any part of the Acte.

The.577. vntruthe. This limitatiō vvēt before, it is not ad-ded after those ge-neral vvordes here noted. See the Acte it selfe. Againe it is in effecte,no limita-tion at all, as shall appeare.

The. 578. vntruthe. These words make no limitatiou of ec-clesiastical iurisdic-tion authorised by the prince,neither doe appertayne therevnto.

The. 579.vntruthe. This is a false addi-tion not expressed in the Acte,but ra-ther denyed by the generality thereof.

in theyr dominions or countries: Therfore al maner iurisdictiō is in the prince to be exercised,vsed,occupied,and executed by them, for othervvise you vvil say,the princes cannot geue ād cōmit to others, that vvhich they haue not receiued and is not in thē selues. Your argument is easely answvered in fevv vvords:it is a foule (.575.) Sophisticatiō,à secundū quid ad simpliciter. These vvords of the act,al maner,in any vvise,are(.576.)restrained and bou-ded,vvithin the limites of the gift:vvhere you of purpose, to beguile the simple vvithal, do let thē runne at large, and set them forth as mere and simple vniuersalles vvithout any limites at al. The Acte geueth or restoreth to the prince iurisdictions,priuileges,superiori-ties,and prebeminencies,spirituall and ecclesiastical,but it(.577.) addeth this limitation suche as by any spirituall or ecclesiasti-cal povver or authority hath heretofore ben,or may lawfully be ex-ercised or vsed: And for that these vvords (as by any spiritual or ecclesiastical power or authority hath heretofore ben, or laufully be exercised and vsed) may be maliciously stret-ched by avvrāgling Papist,and might seme to som, that haue good meaning also,to geue ouer large a scope, the mater or obiect vvher in,or vvhere about,those spiritual or ecclesiastical iurisdictiōs, pri-uileges,superiorities,and prebeminēces,are exercised, vsed and doe consist,is limited ād added in these (.578.)expresse vvords(for the visitation of the ecclesiastical state and persōs,and for reformatiō,order and correction of the same,and of al maner errors,heresies,schismes,abuses,offences,contē-ptes,and enormities)vvhich vvords of limitatiō in the gift,as they geue not to the prince,the exercise of that iurisdiction that cō-sisteth and vvorketh in the invvarde and secrete court of cōscience, by the preaching of the vvord and ministration of the Sacramentes, vvhich belōgeth only and alone to the Bishops,neither do they au-thorise the prince to vse that iurisdiction that belongeth properly to the vvhole church:euē so do they geue rightly vnto the prince to ex-ercise al maner iurisdictions,priuileges,superiorities, and preemi-nences in any vvise touching,and cōcerning any spiritual or ecclesia-stical iurisdictiō,(.579.) cōteined vnder the second kind of cohibitiue

tiue iurisdictiō:for that may the Prince lawfully exercise and vse,
and doth not belōg vnto the Bishops,othervvise then by(.580.)cō-
mission,and authority of positiue Lavves, This limitatiō of iurisdiction set forth by expresse vvords in the Act,you knovv right vvel:
ye vvere also at sundrie times put in mind thereof,and you vvere
vvel assured,that your alleaging the vvords of the Act so darkly,
cōsusedly,and(.581.)vntruly,could neuer further your cause amōgest the vvise:and yet vvould you nedes publish them in this sort
to the people,vvherby at the least,to make both the Prince and the
lavv odious vnto the simple subiects.The Bishops haue by the expres vvord of God,cōmissiox of spiritual gouernmet ouer their flock
that is,to fede the flock of Christ,cōmitted to their charge, vvith
Gods holy vvord,as I haue declared before. They haue cōmission to
absolue the saithfully penitēt,and to retaine or bind the impenitēt:
that is,to(.582.) declare and assure both the one and the other,by
the vvord of the Ghospel,of Gods iudgemēt tovvard thē. VVhat vvil
ye infer herof? VVil ye cōclude therfore,they haue al maner of Spiri
tual gouernmēt or iurisdictiō ouer thē? Yōg Logiciās knovv this is
an*yl cōsequēt,that cōcludeth vpōone or diuers particulars affirma
tiuely an vniuersall. Thus(583.) ye argue, Bishops by the expres
vvord of God,haue cōmission to preach to their cures,to remit or re
tein sinnes:Ergo,they haue cōmission by the expres vvord of God,to
Sēmon Coūcels,or Synods general or prouincial,to visit:that is,iu
dicially sitting in iudgemēt,to enquire of mēs maners,and sorinsi-
cally to punish or correct and to decide the cōtrouersies amōgst the
people:touching contracts of matrimony,vvhordom,tythes,sclaun-
ders,&c. And to ordeine Decrees, Lavves, Ceremonies, Rites,
&c. If this conclusion follovv consequently vpon your antecedent,
thē doth it ouerthrovv the doctrin of your Romish diuinity,vvhich
grauteth not to the Bishops imediatly from God this povver,vvithout a special commission from the Pope in vvhom only,as the*Papists say,is sulnes of
iurisdictiō and povver. But if this conclusion follovv not consequetly vpō the
ātcedēt,as a mā more thē half blind may plainly see it doth not:thē haue ye
concluded(584)not big at al by Christes diuinity that may further the matter ye haue taken in bande to proue. You falsly reporte the scriptures in this
that you saie:the Bishops haue cōmission by the expres vvord of God to geue
vnto their flockes aud cures,the holy Ghoste by imposition of their handes.

x x x ij

The.580. vntruthe.
To say so,is impius
error.A vvicked er-
rour,by Antonius
Delphinus M.Hors
nes Authour.
The.581. vntruthe.
Sclaunderous. The
vvords of the Acte
vvere by M.Feken-
ham plainely and
truely sette forth.
The.582.vntruth.
Ioyned vvith an
heresie, as I shall ap-
peare.
*Such an euel cōse-
quēt you haue vsed
throughout your
booke,of certaine
dealings cōcluding
supre gouernment
in al causes,
The.583. Vntruthe.
M Fekenham ar-
gueth not so.
*Thē S.Bernardis a
Papist who saith so
Epist.238. Solus ipse
Rom. Pont. plenitu-
diℏē habet potestatū.
The 584. Vntruthe.
For M.Fek. therby
cōcludeth that by
such cōmissiō beig
giuē to bi-
shops ime-
diatly
sōdiod in
som spiri-
tuall cau-
ses,the
Princes au-
thorising
for al ma-
ner of spi-
For

For the place vvhich ye quote for that purpose, expreßeth no such commißion, neither (.585.) any other place of the holy scriptures. The Bißhoppes haue so daungerous a cure and chardge ouer the soules committed vnto them, that God vvill require the bloud of those that perißhe (thorough their negligence) at their handes: and therfore hath geuen them sufficient commißion for the discharge of their cures. It vvere therefore an * horrible absurdity, if they might not exercise any Iurisdiction ouer them: if they might not visit, refourme, order and correct them, by that commißio vvithout a further commißion from the Q.highnes. But doo yee not perceiue, vvhich the most simple may see, vvhereof also yee often vvere admonißhed by me, your vvarbling sleight, and Sophisticall quarellinge in equiuocation of vvordes and termes? As there are tvvo (.585.) sortes of Iurisdictio vvhereof the one not Cohibitiue, properly belongeth to the Bißhoppe vvhich he may and ought to exercise ouer his flocke, vvithout any other commißion than of Christ: so to visit, refourme, order and correct, are of tvvo sortes: the one a * Scripturely visitacion, reformation and correction by the onely vvorde of God, vvhich the Bißhopppes may and ought to exercise in time, and out of time, vvith all poßible vvatchefulnes and diligence vvithout any further *commißion. The other kinde of visitation, reformation and correction, is Forinsecall or court-ly, vvhiche I comprehende vnder the seconde kinde of Cohibitiue Iurisdiction, and this the Bißhoppe may not exercise vvithout a further commißion from the Prince. VVerefore it is ouer foule an absurdity in you to inferre, that the Bißhops may not exercise any Iurisdictio, visitacio, reformatio or correctio, bicause they may not vse this Forinsecal, or courtly vvithout the Princes commißion.

The.585.vntruth, ioyned vvith an heresy.

*Here M.Horne cōdēneth the doinges in kinge Edwardes daies, and now also for an horrible absurdite, as shall appeare.

The.585 vntruthe, Vnproued as before.

†A nevv terme for a nevv doctrine.

¶This is againste the Acte. For no Iurisdiction vvhatsoeuer can be vsed, or exercised in Englãde vvithout the Princes speciall commißion.

Stapleton.

M. Horne after that he hath bene so bolde with Delphinus, to frame his argumentes and wreste then at his owne pleasure: he is as bold with M. Fekenhams arguments also. M. Feckenham argueth thus. Spiritual gouernment is geuē to Bishops by Gods speciall worde, namely to loose and

bynde

bynde,to ſhutte vppe heauen gates, and to geue the holie
ghoſte.Ergo the Prince is not the ſupreame gouernour in
all cauſes ſpiritual according to the wordes of the ſtatute:
Ergo all maner ſpirituall iuriſdictió is not to be authoriſed
of the Prince , as the Acte expreſſely and moſt generallie
auoucheth:Ergo yt is not true,that they may not viſite or
reforme theire flocke withowt the Princes commiſsion.
This argumentes being good and ſownd,M.Horne leapeth
me in and ſaieth:*that M . Fekenham toke vppon him to proue*
the ſecond kind of cohibitiue iuriſdiction to be,by the expreſſe
worde of God immediatly appointed to biſhoppes and prieſtes,
without further commiſsion of Princes. And this argument
he doth more ſolély repete againe in the.2.leaſe following
and goeth about to ſoile yt,being his own, and not M.Fe-
kenhás argument.For thinke you M. Horne , that M . Fekenham hath or will allowe your firſt and ſeconde cohibitiue iuriſdiction?His examples are of the power of order,
or of the keies:and of that,that you cal the firſt Cohibitiue
iuriſdiction.Why then do you ſo falſly charge him,leauing
out the firſt two , and the verie principall partes? Let vs
nowe heare what ye ſay further to him.

  You accuſe his euill dealing with the words of the acte,
expreſsig an vnkindly meaning to the prince and the ſtate.
Yea ſay,*that thoughe the ſtatute doth geue,or rather reſtore*
to the Prince, all maner of iuriſdictions, or preheminences
towching any Eccleſiaſticall iuriſdiction: yet the wordes muſt
not be taken ſo generallie , but muſt be referred and limited
to , and with other wordes of the ſayde ſtatute , that is,for the
viſitation ,reformation , and correction of the eccleſiaſticall
ſtate,and of all maner of errours and hereſies.

  By the which wordes of limitation the Prince as you

x x x iij   inferre

Marginal notes:
Act.20.
Ioan.20.
Math.26.
Act.8.

M.Horne frameth argumẽts of his ovvn ãd thẽ laieth thẽ forth as M.Fe-kenhãs ar gumẽtes.

M.Horne taketh vpõ him to re-ſtrayn the gene-ral vvor-des of the ſtatute to take avvay from the Prince the Auto-rity of ex cõmuni-cation.

inferre of it, *is as well reftrained from doing any thing in the publike minifterie, by preaching or miniftring Sacraments: as from that iurifdiction that ftandeth in excommunication, and hath onelie thereby the fecond kinde of cohibitiue Iurifdiction.* Surelie here is a marueiloufe and a woderfull interpretatio. M. Horne vrgeth M. Fekenha to fwere, that he beleueth in confcience, that the Prince is *Supreme Gouernour in all caufes Ecclefiaftical.* He addeth as ye haue heard, *that thofe wordes muft be take without limitatio or exceptio* : and yet him felfe excepteth the chief things or caufes ecclefiaftical. Wherby a man may much better coclude and fwere to the cotrary: that is, that the Prince is not Supreme Gouernour in al Spiritual caufes. Surelie to imagine, and to defende the Prince to be fupreme ruler in al caufes, ad yet to abridge his authoritie in fo many caufes, is much like, as if one fhould fay and affirme of fome man, that he is a king : but yet he is able to comaund no man to prifon, for any offence: he is a king, but if ther be any warre, he can comaund no man to ferue him: he is a king, but yet if there be any bufineffe, ftur, or diforder in the people, he neither can punifh the, nor make out any decree or proclamatio againft his rebels. Of the which premiffes (they being true) it wil follow, that in deede he is no king. But furely, M. Horne me thinke (as I haue faid) that ye aduenture very far and dagerously, whe in the other part touching iurifdiction, ye reftraine and limit the ftatute that *geueth the authorifing of al maner of iurifdictio to the Prince, yea anexeth, and vniteth the fame to the Croune:* to the fecod cohibitiue oly. And what kind of vifitatio or reformatio fhal the Prince make by his ecclefiastical authority , if you take away the authority to excomunicat, which al ecclefiastical vifiters haue, ad euer had: and which alfo expreffly belogeth

to

See the abfurdity of M. Horne in expou ding the Othe.

to the fecōd kind of cohibitiue iurifdictiō, which you make
to depēd of only princes, by your own author Antoni⁹,as I
haue before fhewed. Cōfider M. Horn whether M. Fekēhā
may not iuftly fay to you, *that you deal very yl with the words
of the act, and you expres an vnkidly meaning to the Prince ād
the ftate.* Wel:if there be no remedy, but that by your interpretation directe contrary to all reafon and the manifefte
wordes of the ftatute, the ftatute it felfe may be fo eluded:
and that ye may by your owne abfolute authority fpoile
your fupreame head of one cheif pointe and power ecclefiaftical, yea of the very cohibitiue Iurifdictiō, which you
woulde feme to graūte him with this your pretie and newly coyned. diftinctiop, which princelike ye woulde haue to
be as yt were good and currāt mony: I meane of your two
kindes of cohibitiue iurifdiction, which I fuppofe fhall neither be founde in any good Diuine, nor in any boke of the
temporall lawe in all Englande, yet woulde I fayne heare
from you of fome good and conuenient proufe, whie the
feconde cohibitiue, as ye call yt, remayneth in the prince
onely, more then the firft. Or why if that remaine, excommunicatiō being a part thereof remaineth not in the Prince
alfo? I would know farder whē euer this iurifdictiō was takē away frō the Prices, that it muft now be reftored again.
Verely that which they neuer had, could neuer be takē a-
way And muchleffe can it be reftored thē, which by no
right euer belonged to thē. For fhew M. Horne, yf you can
with al your ftudy and cōferēce with your frendes but one
exāple of any Catholik Prince, either in Englād, or in al the
world befide, that gaue the bifhops any cōmifsiō, for the fecōd cohibitiue iurifdictiō: as ye call it fpecified in thofe exāples that your felf reherfe cut of Antonius. I wil geue you
                                                    one

Edvvard.6.Dei grat.
&c.Reuered. Thoma
Cant. Archiepisc.etc.
Quandoquidē omnis
& iuris diūēli autho
ritas,atque etiā iuris
dictio omnimoda, tā
illa qua Ecclesiastica
dicitur, q̃ secularis,à
regia potestate velut
à supremo cap.&c.
Dat.7.die,mēs.Feb.
An. 1546. & Regni
noſtri primo.

Ibidem.
Ad ordinādū igitur
quoscūque intra dio
cœsin tuā Cātuar. ac
ad omnes etiā sacros
& presbyterarios or
dines ǫmouēdū prā
sentatosque etiam ad
beneficia ecclef.&c.

Ibidem.
Per praeſentes ad no
ſtrū duntaxat bene-
placitū duraturas cū
cuiuslibet cōgrua &
Ecclesiaſtica coertio-
niū potestate.

Per literas datas,4.
Maÿ. An. 1547. ad
eundē Tho.Cantur.
Per alias liter.datas
dict 4.Maii,
An.1548. 28.Iunÿ.
Acts and Monu-
mentes Fol.771.

one whole twelue moneths, M. Horne, to bring
foorth but one such example. I neuer read,I neuer
heard of any suche commiſsion. Onely in the late
daies of king Edward the sixt his time, I finde such
commiſsions, by the whiche al Archbiſhops, Biſſhops,and other Ecclesiaſticall perſons did then exerciſe all their Ecclesiaſticall iuriſdiction. There I
finde,though vntruely, that all iuriſdiction as well
Secular as Spirituall, ſprang from the King as Supreme head of all men. By the said commiſsion a-
mong other things the Biſhops tooke their authoritie,not only to heare Ecelesiaſtical causes iudicially, but euen to geue holye orders alſo : as appeareth by the tenour of the same. They receiued alſo
by vertue of the commiſsion all manner of power
Ecclesiaſtical:and al this no longer then during the
Kings pleaſure. And therefore within three moneths afterward,all Biſhops and Archbiſhops were
inhibited to exerciſe any Ecclesiaſticall iuriſdictiō,
vntil the viſitation appointed by the king were ended. There was alſo an other inhibition made, that
no Biſhoppe nor anye other Ecclesiaſticall perſon
ſhould preache any ſermon, vntil ſuch time as they
were ſpecially thereto licenſed by the king. And
haue you not read or heard,M. Horne, that in the
ſecond yeare of king Edwarde the.6. letters were
ſent from the L. Protectour to the Biſhop of Wincheſter, D.Gardiner,*commaunding him in the kings
behalfe,and charging him by the authority of the same,
to abſteine in his ſermon from treating of any matter
in controuerſy cōcerning the Sacramēt of the Aulter,*
and

and the Maſſe, and only to beſtowe his ſpeache in the experte explication of the articles preſcribed vnto him, &c? Knowe you not,that two yeres after that the ſaid Biſhop being examined before the kings Commiſsioners at Lambeth, the tenth article there layed againſt him was, *that being by the King commaunded and inhibited to treate of any mater in controuerſie concerning the Maſſe,or the Sacrament of the Aulter, did contrary to the ſaied commaundement and inhibition declare diuers his iudgementes and opinions in the ſame?* And that in his final pretended depriuation ,made at Lambeth the 14. of Februarie,this(as it is there called) diſobedience againſt the kinges cōmaundement,is expreſſly layed againſt him? Did not the king here take vppon him the very firſte cohibitiue iuriſdiction, as you cal it? Dyd he not abridge Chriſtes commiſsion,geuen immediatly to Biſhopes,and limitte the exerciſe thereof to his owne pleaſure and commaundement?

Againe were there not iniunctions geuen by the ſayed king Edwarde, to the Biſhope of London D. Bonner, *with Articles thereto annexed for him to preache vpon?* And dyd not his great examination and depriuation enſewe thereof? Looke in your felowe Foxe, and you ſhall finde the whole ſet out at large. If therefore by the Othe now tendred,*the Queenes highnes meaning is, to take vpon her,ſo much and no more of ſpiritual authority and power,then king Henry and king Edwarde enioyed and did iuſtly claime,for they had no more the all,* which you auouche to be your conſtant aſſertion, and the true meaning of the Othe,ſee you not,that by the othe euen the Authoritie of preaching Gods word , which Authority and commiſsiō Biſhops haue immediatly from God, dependeth yet of a furder commiſsion from the Prince,

yyy which

which you cal *an horrible abſurditie*? See you not alſo, that the Biſhopes had al maner of eccleſiaſtical puniſhment geuen them by the princes commiſsion, without any ſuche commiſsion made as you imagine touching excommunication?

Thus haue you taken awaye the very Scripturely viſitation, Reformation, and Correction, (as you call it) from the Biſhoppes and from theyr commiſsion geuen to them by the woorde of God, and haue made it to depende vppon a further commiſsion of the Queenes Hyghnes pleaſure: For that by letters patentes ſhee maye and hath inhibited for a ſeaſon the Biſhoppes of her realme to preache the worde of God, as her brother kinge Edwarde before did. And this you call M. Horne, *An horrible abſurditie*, as it is in dede moſte horrible: and yet ſuch as you ſee by vertue of the Othe our Princes bothe may and haue practiſed. Woe to them that induced good Godly Princes

therevnto. For in dede hereof hath proceded the whole alteration of religion in our country. And hereof it followeth, that religion in our countrie ſhal neuer be ſetled, or of long continuaunce, excepte Princes alwaies of one minde and Iudgement doe Raygne. Hereof it followeth, that we ſhall neuer ioyne in Faithe and Doctrine with other chriſtened Realmes and with the whole vniuerſal Church except our happe be, to haue a prince ſo affected, as other Chriſten princes are. Hereof it followeth, that though our Prince be Catholike, yet thys Authorytie ſtandinge, our Faythe is not Authoryſed by Gods worde and the church, but by Gods woorde and the Prince, that ys, by Gods woorde ſo expounded and preached, as the prince ſhall commaunde and preſcribe it.

Briefly

Briefely hereoffoloweth,that the faith ofEngland is no faith at al builded vpon the authority of God and his Mini-sters,who haue charge of our soules,but is an obediéce on-ly ofa temporal law,and an opinion chaungeable and alte-rable according to the lawes of the Realme.

These are in dede moste horrible absurdities , and moste dyrecte againste the vnitie of the Churche, whiche aboue all thinges ought to be tendred , and without the whiche there is no saluation . This destroyeth the obedience of faithe,and setteth vp onely a philosophicall perswasion of matters ofReligion.This cleane defaceth alltrue Religion, and induceth in place therof a ciuil policie.To côclude,this maketh a plaine and directe waye to al heresies.For ifeuer (which God forbidde)any Prince of our land should be af-fected to any heresie,as of Arrianisme, or any suchlike,the supreme Authority of the prince remaining as the Othe graunteth, and as king Edward practised, should not al the Bishops either be forced to preache that heresy, or to leese their bishopriks,other placed in their romes which to please the Prince,ād to climbe to honor, would be quick enough to farder the procedings ? Any man of mean côsideration may see these inconueniences, and many moe then these, which ofpurpose I leaue to speake of.   To returne there-fore to you, M.Horne,whether you and your fellow Bis-shops haue special cômission from the Quenes Ma. for the exercise ofyour iurisdictiô,I know not:But I am most cre-dibly informed ye haue none. And as for excômunicatiô,ye wil haue none ofher:neyther wil ye acknowlege any such authority in her. And therfore ye had nede to looke wel to your self,and what answere ye will make, if ye be ones cal-led to an accompt,either for this kind of doctrine,so dero-gatory to the statutes,and the Quenes M.prerogatiue,that

The Othe.

Take hede M Horne of periurie.

ye would feme to maintaine:either for the practife of your iurifdiction without any fufficient Commifsion. Remem=ber now among other things, M. Horne, whether this dea-ling be agreable to your Othe, by the which ye promifed, that to your power ye would afsift and defend al iurifdicti-ons, priuilegies, preheminences, and authorities, graunted or belonging to the Quenes Highnes, her heires or fuccef-fours : or vnited and annexed to the imperiall Crowne of the realme. Ye may thinke vpon this at your good leafure. Remember alfo how you wil ftand to this your faying:*that the expreffe woordes of the Statute doe not geue to the Prince all maner of iurifdictions.* The Acte faith fo expreffelie in thefe wordes. *And that your Highnes, &c. fhall haue fulpo-wer and authoritie by vertue of this Act, &c. to afsigne, name, and authorife, when and as often as, &c. And for fuche and fo long time as it fhal pleafe your Highnes, &c. fuche perfons, &c. as your Maieftie &c. fhal thinke meete to exercife, vfe, occu-pie, &c. all maner of iurifdictions, priuileges, and præeminen-ces, in any wife touching or concerning any Spirituall or Eccle-fiafticall inrifdiction within thefe your Realmes, &c. and to vifite, refourme, redreffe, order, correct, and amend all fuche errours, herefies, fchifmes, abufes, offences, contempts, and enor-mities whatfoeuer, which by any maner Spiritual or Ecclefia-ftical power, authoritie or iurifdiction, can or may lawfully be refourmed, ordered, redreffed, &c.* Here in thefe woordes you fee, M. Horne : *ful power and authoritie* is geuen to the Prince, to authorife any man at his or her pleafure to exe-cute or exercife *A L manner of IVRISDICTIONS : in any wife concerning any SPIRITVAL IVRISDIC-TION :* Item to redreffe and correct all enormities what-foeuer, which *by any maner Spiritual or Ecclefiafical power,*
AVTHO-

AVTHORITIE or iurisdiction, can or may lawfully be redressed and corrected. Here, M. Horne, is no exception
of cohibitiue, or not cohibitiue Iurisdiction. Dare you then
to restraine the Act of Parliament, to the only second kind
of Cohibitiue Iurisdiction, a kinde of Iurisdiction by your
selfe inuented? But marke howe you haue confounded
your selfe. You denie these generall tearmes to be found in
the gift of Sp'ritual Iurisdiction made by the Act: But, you
say, it is afterward found. And where afterward? Forsoth
say you, *In that part where the Act afterward geueth power
to the Prince to execute the Iurisdiction, NOW VNITED
and annexed to the CROWNE, by mete delegates to be assig-
ned, &c.* Marke wel what you haue said. You auouch the
same iurisdiction which is by the Prince to be asigned, and
authorised in all maner, &c. as before you haue heard, the
same so Generall and vniuersall Iurisdiction, I saye, you a-
uouche to be *vnited and annexed to the Crowne.* If that, so
generall Iurisdiction (as hath ben saied) be vnited vnto the
Crowne, whie denie you, *that the expresse words of the Statute doe geue to the Prince all maner of Iurisdictions.* Are
you not contrary to your selfe? The Prince hath power to
execute all maner Iurisdiction by meete delegates by him
asigned by your owne confesion, and the plaine woordes
of the Act. The same Iurisdiction so by the Prince to be executed, is vnited to the Crowne, you say: Ergo all maner
of Iurisdictions are vnited to the Crowne: you saye. It
is vnited to the Crowne: Ergo it is geuen to the Prince.
Thus by your owne wordes you are confounded, and proued vntruely and wrongfully to reproue M Fekenham for
missereporting the Othe in that thing, which bothe the Tenour of the Othe hath, and your own confesion agniseth.

THE FOVRTH BOOKE

You thinke this general gifte may be auoyded by the limitation,that you ſay,is added.But you report the Othe vn-
truly.That limitation is not added to theſe general wordes:
For it goeth before theſe general words in a former braͤche
of this Statute.And your ſelfe confeſſe , that theſe general
wordes are ſette after the gifte or reſtitutiõ of ſpiritual Iuriſdiction made to the Prince,in the which that limitation
as you ſay,is foũde.And how caͤ thẽ,I pray you,that which
weͤt before be a limitation of that which came after ? Who
ſeeth not your extreme foly herein,and the miſerable ſhifts
that you are driuen vnto?

Now,you cõfeſsing the ſame general and vniuerſall Iuriſdictiõ of which by vertue of th'Acte,the Prince hath the
aſsigning aͤd authoriſing, to be vnited to the crown,which
is to be in the Prince, and reprouing M . Feckenham for ſo
ſaying,doe find fault alſo with his reaſon,why he ſhould ſo
ſay,and do cal his reaſon or argumẽt *a ſout ſophiſticatiõ.* His
reaſon,as your ſelf reporteth it,is this.Princes haue not thẽ
ſelues al maner of eccleſiaſticall Iuriſdictiõs: ergo they can
not geue and cõmit the ſame to others.That they haue not
al maner of Iuriſdictiõs your ſelf denieth:for they haue ſaie
you only the forinſecal and Courtly Iuriſdiction,or as you
call it the ſecõd cohibitiue Iuriſdictiõ:and not any ſpiritual
Iuriſdictiõ touching the ſecret Courte of Cõſcience. Thus
the Antecedẽt you graunt,being forced therto by the Scriptures by M.Feckenhaͤ alleaged . Why deny you then the
Cõſequent?You pretend for your denial,a limitation to be
made in the Acte of thoſe generall wordes,*al maner,in any
wiſe* and *any ſpiritual Iuriſdiction:* but that is now found to
be but a fable,by reaſon that this limitatiõ goeth before in
an other braunche of the Acte,and theſe generall wordes
doe

do folow afterward, as your felf alfo confeffe . But to make
a limitatiō, before the thing to be limited is fpokē of, is agaīft
al order and courfe of writing, or reafon. Yet you vrge this
to your Reader, againe and again: faying: *that the matter or
chieēt wherin or wherabout thefe fpiritual Iurifdiēiōs* (to be
by the Prince afsigned) *are exercifed, is limited ād added in
thefe expreffe wordes (for the vifitation &c.*) which wordes
are not added to the general gifte of afsigning and authorifing all maner &c. For they goe before that generall gifte,
neither do or cā they limit that generality going (as I haue
oft faid) before it. I defire the Reader for better trial hereof
to cōfider and perufe the Aēt it felf. Thus thē this limitatiō
that you pretēd being but a mere forged and fained matter,
the argumēt of M Feckenhā ftādeth fure: and you your felf
worthy of fmal thanke, euen at their hādes which deuifed
that braunche of the Aēte, for reftrayning and limiting the
general power and Iurifdiēiō geuē to the prince, to the only forinfecal and Courtly Iurifdiēiō, which you cal the fecond kinde of cohibitiue Iurifdiēiō. You fee by that which
hath bene faied, the Aēte geueth to the prince al together
without exception.   This fhifte therefore failing you, you
frame to M. Fecknā fuch an argumēt, as he neuer made, but
fuch as you haue in dede throughout your booke ful many
made: I meane *vpō one or diuers particulars to cōclud affirmatiuely an vniuerfal:* which you fay, *is an euil confequent* . For
what other haue al your proufes or cōclufiōs ben through
out your booke hitherto, thē thefe? Suche a prince called a
Councell: or inueftured Bifhoppes, or depofed Bifhoppes,
or made conftitutions ecclefiafticall: ergo fuch and fuche
a prince were the fupreme Gouernours in al ecclefiaftical
caufes: I fay not, you haue proued they did fo , abfolutely
by their own Pricely authority: You haue miffed in al your
proufes

proufes as well appereth to any indifferent Reader and
peruser of bothe our writinges: But I saie, in case you had
proued your Antecedēts good, was not this allwaies your
Consequent? I say vpon one or diuers particulars to conclude affirmatiuely an vniuersal? For what one Emperour
or Prince amonge so many, so longe a succefsion, and in so
diuers countres, haue you brought forthe, by whose example by sufficiente enumeration of all partes, you might lo-
giquely and reasonably cōclude the affirmatiue vniuersal,
that is, *the Supreme gouernement in al spiritual or ecclesiastical thinges or causes.* You haue not M. Horne, brought any
one suche. Shewe but one, and I will allowe you in all.
And come you nowe to charge M. Fekenham with thys
foule and euil consequent? What? Thought you so by preuention to blame M. Fekenhā, that you might escape therby the blame your selfe? or thought you we shoulde haue
forgotten to charge you herewith, excepte your selfe by
charging an other, had put vs in minde thereof? Vpon this
imagined Conclusion of M. Feckenhams you induce a di-
lemma, that whether the Conclusion folow or not folow,
yet he shal alwaies remayne in some absurdite. But we say,
that as he neuer made that consequent, so also that it foloweth not. Then say you. *If the Conclusion folowe not cōsequēt-
ly vpon the Antecedent, than haue ye concluded nothing at
al by Christes diuinity, that may further the matter ye haue
taken in hande to proue.* To the which I answere: That M.
Feckenham hereby fully cōcludeth his principall purpose.

For, Commifsion of Spiritual gouernement being geuen
(as he reasoneth, and you exprefly cōfefse) to Bishops immediatly from God, by Christ him selfe true God, not only in some, but euen in the principall spirituall causes, as to
fede

fede the Church with true doctrine, to preache the worde, to bind and loofe, to minifter the Sacraments, it foloweth euidetly, that the Prince is not the Supreme Gouernour in al Spiritual caufes: And that the Acte hath wrongfully geuen to the Prince the ful authorifing *for al maner of fpiritual caufes in any wife concerning any Spirituall or Ecclefiafticall iurifdiction to be vfed and exercifed by perfons, when and as often, and for fuch and fo long time as it fhal pleafe the Prince to authorife them*: It foloweth, I faye, that the Acte hath wrongfully geuen al this to the Princes authorifing, feeing that God him felfe hath already geauen it to the Apoftles and their fucceffours, Bifhops and Prieftes in his Churche, without any comifsion or authorifatio for any prince of the earth whatfoeuer. *God hath* (your felf fay, M. Horn) *gené to the Bifshops fufficiét comifsion for the difcharge of their cures: It were therfore* (you fay) *an horrible abfurdity, if they might not exercife any iurifdictio ouer thé, by that comifsio, without a furder comifsion fro the Quenes highnes.* But bothe by the practife in king Edwardes daies (at what time by the Kings letters patets, bifhops had a fpecial comifsio to minifter the Sacraments, and to preach the word, fro the Prince, and at the Princes pleafure, as it hath before ben declared) ad alfo by the plaine Act in the Quenes M. daies now reigning, bifhops can not exercife, vfe, or execute any Spiritualiurifdiction, without the Authorifing, naming, and afsigning of the Prince, yea and that no oftener, nor no longer, then it fhall pleafe the Prince to Authorife them (fo that beeing a Bifhoppe to dave, to morowe (by the Acte) he fhall be none, if it pleafe the Prince to diffauthorife him, or difcharge him) *Ergo*, by Maifter Hornes own confefsion and plaine conftante affertion, bothe in King Edwardes dayes

ZZ Z   and

and now in the Acte, *an horrible abfurdity*, is committed.
You haue faied M. Horne a great deale more againft the
Acte, then euer M. Feckenham faied. Beare therefore with
him and vs I pray you, yf to auoide fuch *an horrible abfur-*
dity, bothe he and we refufe the Othe of this acte.   Some
reafon, I perceiue, M. Sampfon and D. Humfrey of Oxford
had, when they refufed this othe, being tendred vnto them
by a Commifsion. They faw it was in dede a moft horrible
abfurdity, fo to weakē Gods authority, that it muft yet not
of congruite, but of necefsite and by force of lawe be bol-
ftered as of it felfe infufficient, with the Princes authorifing and letters patents. They fawe it was a great impiety,
that bifhops and Paftours by Gods lawe ordayned to fuche
offices, fhould no oftener exercife their offices, nor no lenger remaine in the faied offices, then it fhould pleafe the
Prince for the time to Authorife them and allowe them.
Therefore thefe men them felues, no doubte true fubiectes
to the Quenes highnes, and well willers to her Maieft.
Perfon, refufed yet this Othe, as is aboue faied.

But what a conclufion is this M. Horne, how fowle an
abfurdity is it, to take the Othe of fupreme gouernemente
in al fpiritual thinges or caufes, in which Othe alfo you fay,
nothing may be excepted: for if you except any, it is not al(thefe
are your owne wordes) and yet to make nowe a limitatiō
and to except fo many and fo principall caufes ecclefiafticall, in the which (as you fay alfo) the Prince hath no gouernement at all, but only the Bifhops, as hauing fufficient
commifsion herein from God him felfe? Whereas if there
were in dede any limitation by the Acte expreffed or intēded, (as there is not in dede any at all in the Authorifing
of mete perfons to execute all maner of fpirituall Iurifdictions

ctions) it were yet open and manifest periury to sweare to a supreme gouernement in all causes without exception. What yf you, and your felowes intende not, or meane not al maner spirituall causes? Can this excuse them which sweare to all, from manifest periury? How many haue receyued the Othe, which neuer vnderstode worde of any suche limitatiō? If you meane in dede a limitatiō M. Horne, procure thē that the limitation be put to the Othe expressly, that men may sweare to no more then is intended. Els if you intangle mens soules in open periury, vnder a couert limitation, assure your selfe, you and al other the procurers hereof shal answer full derely to God for all the soules that hereby haue perished. And assure your self, that, as the holy ghost infallibly threatneth, *he wil come, as a quicke witnesse against al periured and forsworen persons*. Neither yet doth the limitatiō, excuse thē frō periury, which sweare Princes to be supreme gouernors in some spirituall causes, who are in dede no gouernours at al in such causes, nor euer had by the lawe of God, any spiritual charge or Iurisdictiō cōmitted vnto them. But yet if this limitation were annexed, the periury were the lesse, and the dealing were more playne, though not therfore good. In the meane while you which force men to sweare to al ecclesiastical causes, and yet will except so many ecclesiastical causes, how vnreasonably ād how absurdely do you write? But of these your contradictory assertions I haue before spoken. *Malach. 3*

If I should here aske M. Horne, what Authorite the parliament had, to geue to the Prince, all or any Iurisdiction at all in matters mere spiritual, that parliament especially consisting only of the lay, the bishops and the whole Conuocation withstanding that gifte with al their power, I be-

leue it would trouble him or any wise man els to geue any
good reason therefore, the obediéce of a Chriſté má to the
Catholike Church(which al Chriſtians in their Crede doe
profeſſe)preſuppoſed. If I ſhould farder aſke M. Horn again
how he cã goe for a biſhop, and write him ſelfe (as he dothe
in his booke)the B. of Wincheſter, being called to that functiõ only by the letters patents of the Prince, without due

2. Tim. 1. Cõſecration, or impoſition of handes by any Biſhop or biſſhops liuing, which impoſitiõ of hãdes S. Paule euidētly practiſed vpõ Timothe, ãd the vniuerſal Church hath alwaies
vſed, as the only ãd proper meanes to order a biſhop of the
Churche, I am wel aſſured, neither he nor al his fellowes,
being all vnordered prelats ſhall euer be able to make any
ſufficient or reaſonable anſwer, (anſwering as Chriſtiã Catholike mē)whereby it may appeare, that they may goe for
right biſhops of Chriſtes Church:but that thei muſt remain
as they were before, or mere lay men, or ſimple prieſtes.

Laſt of al take you yourſelf in dede M. Horn for a biſhop?
If ſo, thē may you preache the word, miniſter the ſacramēts,
bind ãd loſe, vpõ the cõmiſsiõ geuē vou by God in holy ſcripture, without any furder cõmiſsiõ of the prince. If you may
ſo do, thē put the caſe, the Q Mai.that now is, or any other
king or Qaeene of England hereafter ſhould forbid you to
preach the word, to miniſter the ſacraments, or to execute
any other part of the biſhoply functiõ, and by cõmiſsiõ appoint ſome other to that functiõ? Wil you obey, or wil you
not? If yea, thē do vou forſake your duty and charge cõmitted vnto you by God. If not, thē by vertue of this Act, you
incurre the penalty therof. To this queſtiõ anſwer M. Horn
if you be able:and make, if you cã, Chriſts cõmiſsiõ, the holy
Scriptures and this Act to agree both together, that the keping

ping of the one, import not the breach of thother. But this
ſhal you neuer be able to do while you liue, ſtǎding to that,
which in this your booke you haue cǒfeſſed. Thus you ſee
euery way, how in your own ſayings you are intrapped, o-
uertakě, and cǒfounded. And ſo muſt it nedes fal out with e-
uery mǎ that with any truth or ȵbability, laboreth to maintain an vntruth or abſurdity. As for your forged and preſūp-
tuous limitatiǒ vpǒ the words of th'Act, and abridgǐg of the
Q̨ Ma. autoriti therin expreſſed, I leaue that mater furder to
be cǒſidered by the graue wiſdom of the moſt Honorables.

Here remain yet ſome vntruthes by you auouched, that
would be cǒfuted, which becauſe the anſwer alredy waxeth prolixe and long, I wil but touch. The holy Goſpel ſaith,
Whoſe ſyns ye retain ſhalbe retained: whoſe ſyns ye loſe in earth,
their ſyns ſhalbe looſed in heauě. Cǒtrary to the plaine words
of the goſpel you wil haue no actual bindǐg or loſing by the
prieſt in dede, but *a declaratiǒ ǎd an aſſurǎce,* that they are loſed, or boūd: cǒtrary I ſay not only to the words of the goſpel, but alſo to the doctrin, ǎd practiſe of the vniuerſal Church: wher the prieſt hath euer ſaid to the penitět: *Ego abſoluo*
te &c. I abſolue thee: ǎd ſaieth not, I declare and aſſure thee
that thou art abſolued. This is a plaine hereſy, not much vnlike to the Nouatiǎs, whǒ S. Ambroſe cǒfuteth : ſauing that
their hereſy is not ſo large as is yours. For they, but in certain crimes denied power of loſing in the church, referring
that power in ſuch caſes ǒly to God. You deny to be in the
church any power at al, either of bindǐg or of loſing, referring al the power to God only, ǎd not cǒſidering how God
is to be praiſed, *qui talě poteſtatě dedit hoïb.* Who gaue ſuch
power to men. Which the cǒmon Iewes had yet the grace
to cǒſider in the high Biſhop ǎd chief prieſt, Chriſt Ieſus our
Sauiour.   An

Vide Am-
broſ. de
Pœnitent.
lib. I. c. 2.

Math. 9.

An other of your hereticall vntruthes in this place alſo is, that you denie the ſacramente of confirmation: and that the holie ghoſte is not geuen by the impoſition of the Biſ-

Math 9.
Luce. 24. ſhoppes hands. We reade in S Luke, that Chriſte at his aſcenſion, promiſed the holy ghoſt to them, which was per-

Act. 19. formed vppon whitſonday. And what was that but their confirmatio? We reade, that S. Paule after he had baptized certain parſons (in the which baptiſme no doubte they re-ceiued the holy ghoſte) he put his handes vppon them, and they thereby receiued the holy ghoſte. And this was their

Act. 8. confirmation. The like is written in the place here by M. Fe kenham alleaged, of the Apoſtles Peter and Iohn, that put theire handes vppon thoſe that before were baptized, by Philip the Deacon, and they thervppon receiued the holy ghoſte. The which did in the primitiue Churche worke in the Chriſtians with inuiſible grace and viſible miracles, at the time of their confirmatio: as yt now worketh by inui-ſible grace onely, with a ſtrengthening and confirming of

Vide caput
Spiritus
ſanctus, et
cap. de ijs
verò & c.
vt Epiſ=
copi de
conſecra-
tione. the ghoſtly and ſpiritual giftes before receiued: wherof the Sacrament hath his name. And therfore the Biſhoppes cō-miſsion for geuing, by the impoſition of theire handes, the holy ghoſte, may be iuſtified aſwell by the former autho-rities of ſcripture, as by the authority, practiſe, and doctrine of the Churche, that belieueth, that the holy ghoſte is geuē for the encreaſe of al ſpiritual ſtrength in confirmation.

The. 164. Diuiſion. pag. 109. a.

M. Fekenham.

Wherevnto I do adioyne this obiectiō following. Firſt for the time of the old lawe, whiche as Paule ſaide was a very figure of the new, Moſes, Aaron, Eleazarus, being Prieſtes

Priests,they had by the very expreße worde of God, this Othe.
iurisdiction ouer the people of God,as to sit in iudgement Exod.24.
vpon them, and that not only in Ecclesiasticall, but also Exod.29.
in Politike and ciuill matters and causes: they did visite Num.17.
*them,they did refourme them,they did order,correct, ãd
puniſh them,so oft as cauſe required,and without al commiſsion of any ciuill Magistrate, Gouernour, Kinge or
Prince.   Besides that for the whole time of the olde
Lawe, there was an expreſſe Law made,where by allCi-
uillMagiſtrats and Iudges were cõmaunded in al doubtfull matters, to repaire to the Biſshops and Prieſts , and
to ſtaie vppon their determinations and iudgemẽts,with-
out declining on the righte hande or the leſte.And if that
any mã ſhould diſobey the determinatiõ once geuen of the
Prieſt,*Morietur homo ille: *like as it appeareth. Deut.17.*

M.Horne.

This adiũct vvil not ſerue your turn, for it is not poſsible to ſtretch it vvith- The.587.
out burſting,to ioyn with that you muſt conclude. You begin , to ioyne your Vntruth.
vvorke together vvith a ſaying of S. Paule,vvhich he(.587.)neuer ſaid,you For S.
ſhould haue noted the place vvhere S.Paul ſaith,that the old Lavv vvas a Paul ſaith
very figure of the nevv.There is no ſuch ſaying : S. Paule ſaith to the Heb. ſo,as ſhall
that the Lavv hath the ſhadovv of good things to come, &c. The.588.
vvhere he ſpeaketh not (.;88.)generally of the vvhole Lavv, but of the cere- vntruth.
monialpart and Sacrifices,vvhich vvere ſhadovves of Chriſt and his Sacri- That is
fice,ãd not of the Biſshops iuriſdictiõ after Chriſt,vnder theLavv of the Go- ſpokẽ of
ſpel.Thus aptly alſo do your allegatiõs out of thold teſtamẽt ſerue your purpoſe: S.Paule
for one of the three,to wit.29 of Exod.hath no woorde of this iuriſdiction : generally
only it ſheweth the manner of conſecrating the Prieſt , and the ceremonies of the
therabout.In the.24.of Exodus it is ſaide, that vvhen Moſes vvente vvhole:
vp into the Mount, he ſaid vnto the Elders ; Tary vs here vntil lawe.

vve

Lyra.

we retonrne vnto you. Beholde Aaron and Hur, are here with you: if any mã haue ought to doe, let him come vnto them, *that is, if any mater of cõtrouerſie ariſe in mine abſence, let Aaron and Hur, haue the hearing and deciding of it, as I ſhould haue , if i vvere preſent . By this place Aaron had no authority geuen vnto him, but for a time in the abſence of Moyſes, by commiſſion from Moſes, the chiefe ruler and gouernour of Gods people , and that not alone, but hauing Hur one of the Elders, an Auncient and a vviſe man iorned in commiſsion vvith him . This allegation maketh directly (.589.) againſt your concluſion: for it ſhevveth that Aaron had this Authoritie but by commiſsion from Moyſes the Prince of the people . In the thirde place,* Num. 27. *vvhere God ſhevved vnto Moſes, that Ioſue ſhoulde gouerne the people after him, it is ſaied : that* Ioſue ſhould ſtand before Eleazar the Prieſt, who ſhal aſke Councel for him by the iud- gement of Vrim before the Lord, and at his word they ſhal go out and in, both he and the people of Iſraell: *that is, vvhan Ioſue ſtandeth in doubt vvhat to do for the better gouernment of the people, either in the time of peace or vvarr, he ſhal vnderſtand Gods vvil therin by the high Prieſt, to vvhom the Lord vvil miraculouſly declare his vvil and pleaſure by the light or ſhining of the* Vrim *and* Thumim, *and according to Gods vvil ſhevved in the* Vrim, *to the high prieſt, and by him to Ioſue , he muſt direct and order his goeing in and out: Ergo, ſay you . The Biſhoppes and Prieſtes novve in the tyme of the Ghoſpell , haue Iuriſdiction by the expreſſe vvord of God , to keepe Courtes, to call Councels , to make Lavves , and forinſe- callie to viſite, reſourme, order , and correcte their flockes and cures. The moſte ſimple can iudge of this (.590.) ſequele . After like ſorte it is vvriten* Deut. 17. *That vvhan hard and doubtful caſes come before the iudges or in- feriour Magiſtrates , vvhich cannot eaſely be tried or founde out by them: than the inferiour Magiſtrates ſhall goe to the highe Prieſte, and to the chiefe iudge at Hieruſalem for the tyme beinge , vvhoe ſhallſhevve vvhat is to be doone : vvhoſe ſentence and iudgement muſte not be diſobeyed , vnder the pains of death . Doe you not aptly conclude , thinke you , that the Bi- ſhopes in the time of the Ghoſpell ought to haue this Courtly iuriſdiction . by- cauſe the high Prieſt, and the (.591.) Temporall iudge, did determine doubt- full caſes in the time of the olde teſtament ? For the Prieſt alone did not de- termine al cauſes, as you ſeeme to alleage the texe,*

The. 589. vntruth. It maketh not a whit aga- inſt M Fe- kenhams cõcluſion Aaron the being not yet Prieſt at all.

The. 590. vntruth. For the ſequele is good, as it ſhal ap- peare. The. 591. vntruth. The vvoorde temporall lewlely added to holy ſcripture.

The

The.8.Chapter:Conteyning a Confutation of M. Hornes
answer to the Obiections of M.Fekenham layed
out of the olde lawe .

Stapleton.

IF a mã that hathan aduerſary and ſuch as he wil and muſt
fight withall, may firſt by ſome prety deuice fynde the
meanes, that his aduerſarie may be caſte in priſon, and
when he ſhal come to the combate,may appointe him alſo
his weapon,or by a ſleight conueye awaye his aduerſaries
good weapon, and in ſteade thereof, geue him ſome feble,
weake,and rotten ſtaff to fight with , then may this crafty
falſe ſouldier,ſone be a conquerour.It ſeameth now to me,
that M.Horne,that pretendeth him ſelf to be the prelate of
the honourable order of the Garter, doth much diſhonour
him ſelf,and ſheweth to great cowardnes, offering M.Fe-
kenham in this combat,to much wrong:firſt procuring by
ſiniſter accuſations,that he was reſtrayned of his liberty,ãd
then afterward in this his anſwere,geuing M.Fekenhã by a
prety legerdemaine as it were a poore ſlender and weke
weapon,for his inuaſiue armure: who otherwiſe had prouided for himſelf very wel:I meane of ſuch argumẽts as M.
Fekenham hath made,which M.Horne taketh vpon him to
ſoile and confute:after what ſorte ye haue partly ſene,and
ſhal forthwith haue further experience.M.Fekenham then
argueth after this ſorte.In the olde Law which,as S.Paule
ſaith,is a very figure of the new, Moyſes, Aaron,and Eleazarus,being prieſts had the chiet iudgment of matters Eccleſiaſtical without any commiſsion from the cyuill magi-
ſtrat:Again, al aſwel cyuill magiſtrates and iudges as other
were commaunded vpon payne of death,to obey the determination of the prieſt in doubtful matters.*Ergo* the laye

M.Horne
vſeth no
faire play
vvith his
aduerſary.

aaaa   Prince

Prince is not the fupreme head or iudge in al fpiritual and ecclefiaftical caufes. *Ergo*, the biffhops may vifite and correct their flock without any commifsio of the Prince. This is good reader M.Fekenham his good and ftronge inuafiue weapon. Ye fhal now fee, howe M. Horne doth flilie and craftely imbecile ad fteale away this armure from him, and geueth him as it were a bulrufh in his hand, and then fteppeth forth, like a new Goliath againft litle Dauid. And firft, ye may note what a profounde diuine he is, that maketh yt a ftraunge thing to heare that S. Paule fhould take the old Teftament for *a very figure of the newe*. And yet this is fo

Tha: the old teftament is a figure of the newe. Heb. 10.

fure, and fo founde a principle, and fo eafie to be proued by all the new Teftament : and fo throughly and conformably confeffed, as well of the Catholiks as proteftants, that I meruaile what Maifter Horne meaneth thus to wrangle. Nay, faith Maifter Horne, yet S. Paule faith not fo: he faith in dede, that *the lawe, hath the fhadowe of good thinges to come :* but that perteyneth onelye to Chriftes facrifice, whereof the olde lawes facrifices were fhadowes, and not to the biffhops iurifdiction vnder the ghofpel. Why Maifter Horne, is there none other place in S.Paule, that may ferue

1. Cor. 9. Non obliz gabis os bo ui triturā= ti. nũquid de bobus cu ra eft Deo? nā propter nos vtique fcriptum eft.

M.Fekenhams turne think you, but this? You know M.Fekenham quoted not this place which you alleage, nor any other, but being a matter fo knowen and côfeffed, left it vnquoted. Therefore if S.Paule fay fo, either here, or other-where, M.Fekenhãs faying ftandeth for true. What fay you then to S.Paul, that faith, that which was writen in the old law, *thou fhalt not muffel the mouthe of the oxe that treadeth out the corne, to haue bene writen for vs:* and therby proueth, that the laye men fhould temporally relieue their fpirituall paftours? Doth he not here take the old law for a very figure of gure of the new? Again doth not S. Paule fay, *that Agar ād the mount of Sina did reprefent the olde Lawe, and Ifmael the Iewifhe Synogoge: as Sara and Hierufalem doe reprefente the ghofpell, and Ifaac the Churche of Chrifte? Which is our mother* : as Saint Paule there faieth. Doth not S. Paule there bidde the Church of the Gentiles, that was before Chrift barren and idolatroufe to reioyce, for that fhe fhould paffe the Iewes and the Synagoge in all vertue, and in number of people? And doth not he further fay, that as Ifmaell perfequuted Ifaac: fo fhould the falfe Iewes, the infidelles and heretikes perfequute the true Churche of Chrifte? And who is this Ifmael, yf ye be not? that doe not onelye perfequute the Catholiques, but vilanouflye flaunder the whole Churche as Turkifhe and idolatroufe, and as voyde and barren of al true relligion? Doth not the faid S. Paule write alfo, *that our Fathers were all vnderneath a clowde, and, that all paffed the fea, and that all were baptized by Moyfes in the clowde, and in the fea,* and that *thei all did eate one fpirituall meate?* Doth not he alfo playnelye faye, that *thefe thinges chaunced to them in a figure?* Here, here is the figure Maifter Horn, not of the carnall facrifices only, fignifying the facrifice of Chrifte: but of two of our greateft Sacramentes, yea and yf there be no moe in number then ye and your fellowes faye, of all our facraments. Here S. Paule faieth plainely, that thofe thinges that chaunced to the Ifraelites pafsing the read fea, and eating Manna, were fhadowes and figures for vs: that is, the read fea of our baptifme: the Manna and the water that flowed out of the Rocke, of our Manna: that is, of the bodye and bloudde of Chrift that the Chriftians receaue in the blefsed *Euchariftia*. As S. Ambrofe, S. Auguftine and the other

Ad Galath. 4.

1. Cor. 10.
Hæc in figura facta funt noftri, & mox. Hæc oia cō tigerunt illis in figura.

Fathers

fathers do moſte fully and amply declare. Here might I by
this figure inferre many things againſt your deteſtable doctrine and blaſphemy blowen out againſte our heauenly
Manna, in the forſayd ſacrament: but we will not goe from
our matter. Many like places of S. Paule I do here omitte,
which may iuſtifie M. Fekenhams ſayinge, of the which it
pleaſeth yow to pycke out that one, that ſeemeth to yowe
weakeſt, and yet it is as ſtrong or ſtronger thē any other.
For though S. Paule doth ſpeake in that place, of the ſacrifice of Chriſt, that was ſhadowed by the carnal ſacrifices of
the Iewes, and goeth about to proue, that by the ſacrifice
of the Lawe ſynne was not taken away, but by the only ſacrifice of Chriſt: yet the reaſon that he layeth forth for the
maintenaunce of his aſſertion, can not be reſtrayned to the
carnal ſacrifices only, but is a general rule to argue from the
olde Teſtamente to the newe : that is, that the old Teſtamente was but a ſhadowe : the newe teſtament is the
very expres image of the celeſticall and heauenly thinges.
And therfor Dionyſius Areopagita, Gregory Nazianzene
and others ſay, that the Church of Chriſt, ſtādeth as it were
in the midle betwene the ſtate of the ſinagog of the Iewes,
and the ſtate that ſhal be in heauen: wheruppon it will follow that as thoſe thinges, that be done in the Church preſently, are a figure of thoſe things that we ſhall ſee in heauen (as S. Paule calling our preſent ſtate (*in enigmate*) teacheth) ſo thoſe things that chaunced in the ſinagog were a
figure of thoſe thigs, that now are don in Chriſtes Church.
And as our preſent ſtate, walking by fayth, is yet but *in ani-*
gmate, in a darke repreſentation, but afterward we ſhall ſee
the glory of God *facie ad faciem*, face to face, as S. Paule teacheth: ſo the ſtate of the olde lawe was accordinge to the

Apoſtle

Ad. He.10.
Vmbrā enī
babens lex
futurorū
bonorū, nō
ipſam ima
ginem re-
rum.
Greg. Na-
zianz. in
orat. De S.
Paſcha.
Paſcha le-
gale figu
ra figura
erat. &c.
1. Cor 13.
Adhuc in
ænigmate
Illic facie
ad faciem.

Apoftle alfo, *Pædagogia ad Chriftū,*an Introdnctiō to Chrift, and as Gregory Nazianzen calleth it,*Vallum quoddam inter Deum & idola medium,* a certayne trenche or walle fet in-differently betwene God and Idols, fo as we fhould paffe from that to God,as from the fampler to the veritie,frō the figure to the thinge,and frō the fhadowe to the body.And therfore among other things frequented in the Church,the ecclefiaftical *Hierarchia,*or fupreamacy,as it is a lyuely,and an expreffe image of one God,in heauē,aboue fo many and infinite nombers of holy fpirits:fo no doubt, it hath his fha-dowe in the olde teftament . And what other was he that M.Fekenhā here fpeaketh of,but the high prieft M. Horn? And was not he the fupreme iudge of all matters ecclefia-ftical?In al which caufes lay there not an appeale , from all other prieftes iudegments in doubtful cafes ,to him keping his refidence in Hierufalem : euen as the courfe of all ap-peales , in fuche matters runneth nowe from all partes to the pope,remayning in Rome?This is euident by the place that maifter Fekenham citeth: where yt ys writen, that *yf any man ftubbornelye and proudely difobeyed the prieftes com-maundement ,that he fhoulde by the commaundement of the Iudge be putte to death .* The practife of this fupreme iudge in caufes Ecclefiafticall may be eafely iuftified , by many examples of the olde teftament, namely by the doinges of the good kinge Iofaphat : who in the ftate of the lawe be-inge the figure , renewed thofe thinges infringed and bro-ken then by the idolatroufe and hereticall Iewes, the true image whereof, fo longe kepte and reuerenced amonge the Chriftians,is nowe broken by yowe and fuche as yow are . *This Iofaphat placed at Hierufalem the leuites and priefts and the chiefe of the famylyes of Ifraell to heare fuche caufes*

In orat.de S.Pafcha. diaτὲί-Χιᵒμα.

Deut. 17. Qui autē fuperbierit nolens obe dire facer-dotis im-perio,ex decreto Iu dicis mo-rietur ho-mo ille.

2.Par.19.

aaaa iij   as fhould

as should be deuolued thither from all other quarters, tou-
ching any question of the Lawe of God (concerning matters of
beliefe *) touching commaundements (* pertayning to the precepts moral *) touching ceremonies, and touching iustifications,*
that is, iudicial precepts, geuen for the keping and obseruation of Iustice . In all theis the Leuites, and priests, and the

Amarias chief of the familyes were the Iudges : *Amarias the highe*
aūt sacer- *priest being chiefe ouer them al in theis and such other matters*
dos & pō- *pertayning to God and to religion .* Thus lo at length ye see
tifex ve= the shadowe and figure Maister Horne, in the olde lawe
ster in his mete together, not onely for the sacrifice of Christe , but
que ad for the highe and chiefe prieste also, that should be amonge
Deūperti- the Christians aboue all other states spirituall or temporall
nēt præsi- in all the worlde . Neither can ye nowe, either deny this
debit. plaine and euident figure , or deny, that there is any good
sequele of argumente to be deriued from the figure of the
olde Lawe, to the newe testament. And verely (to leaue
all other things that may be thereto iustly sayed) you of
all men can leste disallowe this kinde of colleetion and arguing , whiche to iustifie your newe Laical primacy haue
vsed the sayed argument your selfe . Neither doe I buylde
so muche vppon the figure , nor make so greate accompte
of yt, as I doe of the drifte and force of very reason , that

There is a muste dryue vs to condescende to the order of the Church,
greater and doth extorte our confession in this poynte . Whiche
necessity reason is, that God loueth his Churche , aswell as he did
to haue the Iewes Synagoge , and hath as louingly , as plentifully,
one high and as effeetually prouided for the good gouernement of
prieste a- the same , as he dyd for the synagoge . And therefore to
monȝthe the same , as he dyd for the synagoge . And therefore to
Chriſtiãs pacifie Diuisions , schismes, and heresies, he hath pro-
thē the le uided vs one spirituall Cowrte, to decide , and vtterly to
vves had.
deter-

determyn al controuerfies, rifing vppon matters of religion, as he prouided for the Iewes. And fo much the more, amonge Chriftians then among the Iewes, for that the Chriftians, beinge of fo many and diuers nations, tongues, wyttes, manners, and fafſhions, many cōtrouerfies for fayth and religion, and of more weight and moment, will alfo arife and fpringe vppe, then euer rofe amonge the Iewes beinge but one onely Nation. Efpecially the Apoftle foretellinge vs, that herefies muft arife. And yf there be not one certayne iudg appoynted, to whome all nations muft indifferently obeye, yt mufte neades be, that Chriftendome fhall contynewe in a continuall broyle and ruffle of fects and herefies? Which alfo haue in our tyme fo terribly and hugely encreafed, by nothinge more, then that we geue no eare to this one iudge: and that we do not, as our forefathers haue done, ftaye our felues, and depende vppon this the higheft cowrte of all Chriftendome. Ye fee nowe good reader both the figure, and the reafon of the figure: what fayeth nowe M. Horne to it? Full pretely I warrante yow: and that is, that Maifter Fekenham doth not aptly conclude, that *the biſhoppes in the tyme of the Ghofpell owght to haue iurifdiction by the expreffe woorde of God, to kepe cowrts, to call Councells, to make Lawes, to vifite, and to reforme &c. becaufe the highe prieft, and the temporall iudge, did determyne doubtfull cafes, in the tyme of the olde teftament: for the prieft alone did not determyne all caufes, as M. Fekenham feameth to alleage the text.* Here may yow playnelie fee, that Maifter Fekenham can not vfe his owne armure, but fuch onely as Maifter Horne wil graunt him. For neither M. Fekenham fpeaketh *of the temporall iudge,* nor his texte, be it Latin, Greke or Hebrewe. They all

1. Cor. 12.

M. Horne fetteth forth his ovvn argumēts as thoughe they vvere M. Fekenhams.

all fpeake of a iudge, but nothing is there to fignifie this woorde *temporall*. This woorde is fhamefully infarfed by Maifter Horne, to vpholde his temporall fupremacye, by this place moft greauoufly battered. The iudge and the high Prieft is al one, as doth appere by the letter, and by the doing of Kinge Iofaphat, which was conformable to the cōmaundement of Moyfes, where as Amarias is appointed the chief for fpiritual matters, as Zabadias was for thofe thinges that perteyned to the Kinges office. Which may be wel vnderftanded for the bodilie punifhment of thofe that difobeyed the high prieft, and to put them to death, yf the cafe required, according to the Lawe. And in that fenfe yt may be taken perchaunce for a temporal Iudge. This notwithftanding yt agreeth well enowghe, with the high prieft to. For that diuerfe tymes afwell before there were any Kings as afterward, the high prieft had the cheif regiment, both temporal and Ecclefiafticall: but though he had not euer the temporal, yet had he euer the Ecclefiaticall fupremacy: And therefore it is writen of the Prophete Malachie, that *the lipps of the prieftes fhall preferue knowledg, and they fhall feke the lawe at his mowthe.* And it is here writen, who fo euer *difobeyeth the prieft, fhal die.* He faith not, who fo euer diofobeyeth the temporal Iudge. For the high Prieft is the Iudge: al one perfon, and not two. And fo S. Cyprian with the other fathers taketh place. When I fpeake of the high prieft, I exclude not other of the clergy, with whome the Pope, in all graue and weighty caufes vfeth to confult, and of congruence ought fo to do, and fo it was in the old Law. Neither M. Fekenham, as ye charge him, faith fo, but layeth forth the text as it is, faying, that he

that

1. *Reg*. 4.

1. *Mach*. 14

Mala. 2.

Deute. 17.

Cypr. lib. 1. *epift*. 3.
Quibus honor tātus de Dei dignatione conceditur, vt quifquis facerdoti eius, & ad tempus hic iudicanti non obtēperaret, ftatim necaretur.

that difobeyeth the prieft, fhall die for it . Nowe the highe
prieft being this authorifed, and Mofes, Aaron, and Eleazarus being fuccefsiuely the highe prieftes, it muft nedes follow, that they had the chiefe fuperiority for matters ecclefiaftical, neding no further authority, then that they had by
the expreffe woorde of God , for the executing of theire
office, whether it were in geuinge fentence , and making
decrees Ecclefiafticall , or in vifiting and reforming the
priefts, and Leuites that were vnderneth them: which if ye
can fhewe they did not , nor coulde do , but by the ciuill
magiftrates authority , we fhall then geue you fome eare.
But ye proue it not, nor euer fhall be able to proue this paradoxe . And therfore we paffe not , whether it be true or
no , that in the. 29. of *Exodus* , there is neuer a worde of
iurifdiction. It is fufficiente, that Maifter Fekenham proue
Aaron to haue bene the highe priefte , as he was in dede,
and fo yt appeareth there. Where nowe ye would returne
againft M. Fekenham the. 24. of *Exodus* , ye haue forgotten your felfe . For at that tyme Aaron was not yet made
highe prieft, but afterward he was fo made, as appereth in
the 3. chapter after: *Videlicet cap. 28.* And therfore he might
haue a commifsion to heare caufes in Mofes abfence well
inowgh: Mofes being then both the prince , and the highe
prieft alfo, ãd he, as is fayd, being yet no prieft at al. For your
anfwere to the.3. place by M. Fekenhã alleaged, we might
paffe it, fauing that by your cõming in with *Vrim* and *Thu-*
nim you haue much holpen M. Fekenhã his argument, and
cut your felf with your Thunim quite ouer the thume. For
though theis outward miraculoufe fignes, do not nowe appeare in our high prieft, yet the thing that was fignified by
Vrim ãd *Thunim* fet in the breftplate of the high prieft, that

Vide Exod.
24.&.28.

ís,light and perfectiõ,as fome expoũd it,or as our cõmõ trãf-
latiõ hath, doctrin ãd verity:remaine now in our high prieft
afwel as they did thẽ remaine in the high prieft of the olde
Tẽ ftamẽt,yea and much more . And therfore the true doctrine is to be fetched at the high priefts or bifihops hands,
in al doubts and perplexities of religiõ,ãd fo cõfequently all
lawes,decrees,and ordinaũces, made for the obferuatiõ of
his fentẽce and determinatiõ,are to be obferued. To what
purpofe were it for priefts to declare ãd determin the truth,
if they might not by fome forcible Lawe cõpel men to the
keping of the fame,which is nowe chiefly practifed in the
Church by excõmunicatiõs,as appereth by general , and by
other Coũcels?The like hereof the Iewes had in thrufting
the difobediẽt ãd rebellious perfons out of the Synagõge.

Io.cap. 9,
& . 12.

Now to imagine fuch an vnprobable and an vnlikely paradoxe,that bifhops hauing cõmifsiõ frõ God to fede the peõ-
ple;to teache them,and inftruct them, and hauing a charge
of their foules,for the which they fhall make to God an accompt,may not vifite and reforme their flock by examina-
tions,iudgements and trialles forinfecal,alfo by excommunication,depriuation,or fuch like ecclefiaftical punifhmẽts,
without a new commifsion frõm the Prince, and to bringe
nor reafon,nor authority,nor Scripture,nor Doctour , nor
coũcel,nor exãple in Chriftes Church at any time practifed
for the cõfirmatiõ of yt,but only a decree of laye men,con-
trary to their own Paftours and bifhops : it is fuch a kind of
perfuafiõ,as wel may be forceable,to the hãd ãd the mouth,
to extort frõ thẽ an outward cõfent for feare of difpleafure,
but to the hart and cõfciẽce of a Chriftẽ mã profefsing obediẽce to Chrift and his dere Spoufe the Church ãd perfourming the fame,it fhal neuer be able to perce vnto.As for the
Sequele

Sequele of M.Feckéhás argumēt,whereof you say,*the moſt*
ſimple cā iudge,as though it were but a ſimple ſequele,to infer vpō the Biſhops authority in the old law,the Iuriſdictiōs
ofthe biſhops in the new Teſtament, or vpon the example
of Eleazar to inferre forinſecall, as you call it, iuriſdiction
in biſhoppes,it appereth by that hath ben ſaid,both that the
deductiō frō the old law to the new is right good and ſuch
as your ſelf moſt plētifully haue vſed in the firſt part of your
book:yea ſo far,that you charge M.Fekn.(though vntruly)
for a Donatiſt,for ſeeming to auoid ſuch kind of prouf: and
alſo it appereth that a vaine thing it were for biſhops now
(after the example of Eleazarus) to haue the directing, feeding,and ordering of Gods people,ifthei had not withal po
wer and authority to cal back ſuch as goe a ſtray, to puniſh
the offenders,to viſit their cures,to rēfourme diſorders, to
make lawes for order to be kept &c.in vain I ſay,ſeing that
the one without the other neither was at any tyme auaylable,neither can by any reaſon poſsibly be auailable.

M . *Fekenham.* The . 165 . *Diuiſion.* pag . 110.4.

The ſeconde,in the newe Teſtament : like as our Sa-
uiour Chriſte did committe and leaue the whole Spiri-
tual gouernement,of his people and Churche vnto his A-
poſtles,and to the Biſßhoppes and Prieſtes , and the ſuc-
ceſſours of thē:So they did practiſe al Spirituall gouern-
ment ouer them,they did execute and geue iudgement in
the Churche of Chriſte: they did refourme , order , and
correcte all diſorder therein , and that without all com-
miſßion,ayde,or authority of any Temporall Magiſtrat,
King,or Prince,for the ſpace of three hundreth yeres in

bbbb ij   the pri-

THE FOVRTH BOOKE

Lib. 1. hist.
Tripa c. 9.

the primatiue Churche of Christe, vnto the time of Con-
stantine, he being the first Christian Kinge and Empe-
rour, which did ioyne his sworde to the maintenaunce of
Gods worde.

M Horne.

Like as the Apostles had in commission povver from Christe our Sauiour,
to vvhome al povver vvas geuen both in heauen and in earth: so faithfully
they cxecuted the authority and charge committed vnto them, not seeking
their ovvne honour by vsurpation, but the glory of Christ by the abasing them
selues euen vnto the death. Their commission regestred by S. Mathevv appea-
reth in these vvordes. Goe and teache al the nations, baptizing
them in the name of the father, and of the sonne, and
of the holy ghost, teaching them to kepe all things,
which I haue commaunded you. *Hovv faithfully they*
exercised this authority according to the commission, S. Luke
shevveth in his Chronicle, called the Actes of the Apostles, and set-
teth forth one notable example hereof, in Paules oration, made to
the Elders of Ephesus, called to Miletum: He taketh them
to witnesse, that he kept nothing backe from them,
that might be for their profit, but shewed them al the
councel of God. *It is much (592) maruail that Paul shevved*
al Gods councel vnto them, and yet made no mention of any Fo-
rinsecal, iurisdiction as geuen them by the commission of Gods
vvorde. The godly Bishops that succeded the Apostles for manye
yeres after, follovved the doctrine and examples of the Apostles,
yet (592.) neuer exercising iurisdiction Forinsecal, neither iudging,
reforming, ordering, or correcting, othervvise than bye preaching,
publikely or priuately, vvithout especial consent and commission
of their Churches, during the time, thei had no Christian Prince or
Magistrate. Constãtinus, *as I haue said, vvas not the first Chri-*
stian King: But he vvas the very first Emperour, as your ovvne
vvriters doe vvitnesse, that (.594.) gaue Bishops authority to
iudge and exercise iurisdiction, ouer their Clergy, and that gaue to
the Bishop of Rome povver and (.595.) authority ouer other Bis-
shops, as

The 592 vntruthe.
No maruail at all.
For all Gods Coun-
cel that Paule she-
wed, is not expres-
sly mentioned in
the Scripture. It is
a most fond colle-
ction.

The 593. vntruthe.
The Apostles ex-
ercised such iuris-
diction vvithout
any commission,
but from God.

The 594. vntruthe.
The bishops exer-
cised al kind of Iu-
risdiction ecclesiast.
before Constantine
vvas borne.

The 595. vntruthe.
Constantin gaue to
the Pope no suche
Authority, but fur-
dered the executiõ
thereof.

shops,as iudges haue the King ouer the n,and that gaue to him
povver and iurisdiction ouer al other Churches,if that Donation
be not forged vvhich Gratian *citeth. And* Petrus Bertrandus
a Bishop, a Cardinal,and one of your best learned in the Canon
and Ciuil lavves,in his treatise De origine iurisdictionum,
affirmeth. that Theodosius *and* Carolus Magn⁹,did(596)
graunt vnto the Churche al iudgementes.For the proufe
vvhereof,he auoucheth diuerse decrees,and(.597.)addeth, That
such grauntes were afterwards abrogated.

Dist.86.

The.596. vntruthe.
For this graūt tous
ched not the eccle=
siastical ordinarye
iurisdiction of Bis=
shops.

The.597.vntruthe.
Bertrandus affir-
meth the plain cō=
trary.

The.9.Chapter:Of Spirituall Iurisdiction exercised by bis-
shops vvithout Princes commissions,and be-
fore Constantines time.

Stapleton.

MAister Fekenham bringeth now forth certain auto-
rities of the new testament,for the iustifying of his
purpose,as that Christ committed to his Apostles, Act.20.
and to their successours the whole spiritual gouernement,
and that they did practise and exercise the same.300. yeres
together without any maner of commission from Princes,
euē to the tyme of Cōstantin the great.M.Horn thinketh
it a sufficient answere with stoute asseueration voyde of al
maner of probation,to auouche that they had a commissiō,
he dareth not say now of their Princes(being al, or almoste
al infidels)but of their Churches. Yea well and sone saide
M.Horne:but yf ye would withall haue layde before your
reader,but one authour old or new,good or badde(vnlesse
perchaunce ye may bring some of your own fellowes)and
but one example for these.300.yeres, we would the better
haue born with you.Now ye tel vs the Apostles did preach
and baptise, and other such extraordinary matters,leauing
the thing vnproued,wherein lieth al the question betwene

bbbb iij   you and

yow and M. Feckenham. Your affertion is altogeather incredible, and a very peeuiſhe fantaſticall imagination, that no man of the clergy or Laiety theſe 300.yeres was excōmunicated, for any manner of offence, no prieſt was forbydde to miniſter the Sacraments, or depoſed for his defaults, by his biſhoppe,but by a ſpeciall commiſsion of the prince, or whole Churche. Ye may aſwel pul downe the towre of London M. Horne with your litle finger, as ye ſhall be able to proue this fonde aſſertion. But yet before Cōſtantinus the great his time,ye think your ſelf cock ſure. Let vs then ſee howe ſure ye are,euen of this your onely example.Verely I ſuppoſe,that no man lyuinge, vnleſſe he hath a braſen face,would for ſhame of the worlde thus demeane him ſelf,in ſo graue and weighty matters, and lnck ſo many Lies together, as lynes, as you doe in this your falſe narration that nowe followeth. *Conſtantine*, you ſay, *was the very firſt emperor,that gaue biſhops authority to iudge and exerciſe iuriſdiction ouer theire clergy*. What Emperour then,I beſeche you, graunted to the Apoſtles authority,to make ſuche Lawes, and conſtitutions Eccleſiaſticall as be nowe extante,which haue in them diuers paynes and penalties, as excommunication, and depriuation againſt the trāſgreſſours? By what Emperours or other lay mans warrant,did the biſhops kepe ſo many Councelles, as we fynd they kepte, before this Conſtantines tyme?Namely the 2. Synods kept againſt Paulus Samoſatenus in Antioche, the Councel of Carthage in Afrike vnder S.Cyprian,the Coūcells of Gangra againſt Euſtachius, of Ancyra againſte the Manichees,of Neoceſarea againſt the Archōtici,the Coūcels alſo vnder Victor the pope at Rome,vnder *Narciſſus* at Hieruſalē,vnder *Palmas* in Pontus,vnder *Ireneus* in Fraūce, vnder

M. Horns
aſſertion
incredible.

*Vide conſt.
Apoſtol.
Clementis
in Tom.1.
Cōcil.vlt.
editionis.*

*Euſ.ecclehiſt.li.5.c.
23.lib.7.
cap.26.&
28.lib. 6.
cap.43.Socra.lib.2.
cap. 43.
Niceph li.
4.cap.22.*

vnder *Bacchylus* at Corinthe , vnder *Fabianus* alſo and *Cornelius* at Rome, and diuers other biſhops in other Coūtres, all before the dayes of the firſt Coūcel of Nice vnder Cōſtantin, al without any Cōmiſſiō frō Princes of this worlde, al groūded vpō their own ſupreme gouernmēt and Iuriſdictiō geue vnto thē by th'expres word of God. What warrāt had they for the eccleſiaſticall decrees by thē there ordeyned? By what princes or lay mans cōmiſſion, were Valentinus, Paulus Samoſatenus, ād the whole rablemēt of forenamed heretiks cōdēned ād excōmunicated? By what cōmiſſiō did the bleſſed biſſhop of Antiochia, ād martyr Babylas, forbid thēperour, that he ſhould not enter into the Church amōg the Chriſtiās? If the biſhops had nothing to du , but to preach and miniſter Sacramēts, and no iuriſdictiō in hearīg of cauſes, before the time of this Conſtantine, what did the biſhops of Alexandria with a ſolēne iudgmēt ſeate, appointed withī the Church ther for the biſhops of that ſea? What warrāt had Pope Victor, for th'excōmunicating of the blaſphemous heretike Theodot'? Yea what authority had he to excōmunicat the biſhops of Aſia ſo far frō hī? What warrāt had *Fabianus* the pope, of whom we haue ſpokē to appoint thēperor as we haue ſayd, to ſtād amōg the penitēts as a parſon excōmunicated ? By what commiſſiō made the bleſſed Pope ād martyr Antherus certaine lawes eccleſiaſtical, and among, other touchīg the tranſlations of biſhops ?

But here M. Iewell will helpe yowe at a pinche like a truſty frende, and with a newe ſhi te wil pleade vppon the ſtate inficial, denyīng vtterly the old decretal epiſtles , and among other this : and will ſtand vppon no foggy or falſe ground, as he ſaieth M.D. Harding doth , but ſet his faſt foting vppon a ſure and an infallible reaſon, againſt Antherus epiſtle making mention of the biſhoppes Felix, and Euſebius

that

Euſe.li.4. ca.11.& li 7.ca.26. Chryſo in orat cōtra gent. quod vnus ſit Deus. Euſe.eccl. hiſt. li.7. cap.26. Euſeb.lib. 5.cap.28. Idē. & eodē lib cap. 25.

Euſeb.lib. 6.cap. 25. Vide decr. epiſt. Antheri.

Ievvel in his reply. pag.223.

that were not borne al the time Antherus lyued. But what
ifthey were borne before him, where is all this your great
holde then? YfI ſhould alleage Sabellicus, though he be a
very good Chronicler, and well allowed, or any other Latin man, to make this epiſtle authenticall, perchaunce ye
would cry out againſt him and ſay that he were partiall, ād
a papiſt to. I wil therfore prouide you a Grecian, and a late
Grecian to, whom ye ſhal haue no cauſe to refuſe as ſuſpected, and that is Nicephorus, by whom it may wel appeare
that the Grecians toke this Decree for authentical. In him
alſo, ſhal ye find expreſſe mention of the ſayd Euſebius and
Felix. Ye ſhall alſo there find a notable place of the authority of the ſea of Rome that ye impugne, that ſuch tranſlations muſt be authoriſed by the popes aſſent and confirmation. Seing then Nicephorus is no papiſt, why ye call him
one of our owne writers I knowe not, being no Latin mā,
but a Grecian, and infected alſo with theire ſchiſme: and
yet notwithſtanding in all other things catholyke, and full
againſt your newe hereſies. And for that reſpect I am content to take him for one of our writers. And now woulde
I ſee, what vantage ye can take at his hande, for the prouf of
your fowle falſe paradoxe. Yf ye will proue any thinge for
the relief of your paradoxe, ye muſt proue, that no Chriſtian biſſhops vnder the Roman empyre, had authority to
iudge or exerciſe any iuriſdictiō ouer theyr clergy, but ſuch
as they had by commiſsiō and graunt from Cōſtantinus. Let
vs then heare Nicephorus him ſelf, that euery mā may ſee,
that ye can not poſsible ſtretche him without burſting, to
ioyne with that, which you ought to conclude. *Qua verò*
imperator Conſtantinus obſeruantia erga profeſsionem fidei no-
ſtræ fuerit, abunde illud quoque teſtatur, quòd clericos omnes
conſti-

Vide Sab.
Aenead.7.
lib.7.

Niceph.li.
14.c.39.

Niceph li.
7.cap 46.

constitutione lata immunes libero∫g̃ e∫∫e permi∫it:iudiciumg̃ &
iuri∫dictionem in eos Epi∫copis ∫i quidem ciuilium iudicum cog-
nitionē declinare vellēt,mādauit : & quod epi∫copi iudica∫∫ent,
id robur & authoritatem∫ententiæ omnino habere debere de-
creuit.Firma quoque & immutabilia e∫∫e voluit, quæ in ∫ynodis
con∫tituta e∫∫ent , & quæ ab epi∫copis iudicata forent, vt ea à
magi∫tratibus rempublicam admini∫trantibus,militarique quæ
∫ub cis e∫∫ent manu exequutioni mandarentur, atg̃ ad rem col-
*lata perficerentur con∫tituit.*This thing al∫o (∫aieth Nicephorus) doth abundantly te∫tifie , what honour and reuerence
he did beare toward our faith , that he ordeyned by a lawe
of his making,that all , that were of the Clergie ∫houlde be
free and exempted frō paying tribute: and that in ca∫e they
would refu∫e the iudgement of the temporall magi∫trates,
that the Bi∫hops ∫hould haue the iuri∫dictiō vpon them,and
geue ∫entence in the cau∫e . And that the ∫ayed epi∫copall
iudgement ∫hould haue ful ∫trength and authority . He ordeined al∫o , that tho∫e thinges that were decreed in a ∫y-
node of Bi∫hopes,∫hould ∫tande ∫tronge and immutable,and
that the bi∫hoply iudgement,∫hould be put in execution by
his ciuil magi∫trates , with the helpe of ∫uche ∫ouldiers, as
they had vnderneath them.Stretche this nowe M. Horne,
to your conclu∫ion,if ye can without bur∫ting.

 We haue here a Lawe of Con∫tantine,that tho∫e that be
of the Clergie , may choo∫e whether they wil an∫were for
any matter,what ∫o euer it be before a laie man.They may
if they wil cau∫e the matter to be deuolued to the Bi∫hop:
but here is neuer a word of Eccle∫ia∫tical matters. In ∫uch
Con∫tãtine geueth the bi∫hops no iuri∫diction, for they had
it before. Neither is there here any one woorde, that the
Bi∫hoppes ∫hould neither ∫ummon Councelles , nor make

VVhat
maner of
iuri∫dicti-
on Cō∫tan
tin gaue
to the
Bi∫hopes.

cccc   eccle-

ecclesiastical Lawes without the Princes consent. Here is a plaine ordinaunce that the lay Magistrates shal see, that the Synodical Decrees shall be put in execution. Wherby contrary to the conclusion that ye mainteine through out this your answere, it well appeareth, that the Princes part is onely to see, that the Ecclesiasticall decrees made by the Bishops be kept and put in vre, and not to haue any necessarie consente, in the allowing, or dissallowing of them.

Which appeareth also most euidently in Eusebius writing *Euseb. li.4* of this Constantine in this sort: *Quæ ab Episcopis in publicis* *cap.27.* *conuentibus editæ erant regulæ, sua consignabat & confirma-* *De vita* *bat authoritate:* He signed and confirmed with his Autho- *Constant.* ritie, suche Canons or rules, as the Bisshoppes in their assemblies had decreed. But how? As though without his royall assente, the Canons shoulde haue beene voide, and of no Authoritie, as you woulde make folke beleue? No, but (as the same Eusebius writeth in the same place) *Ne reliquarum gentiū principibus liceret, quæ ab eis decreta essent, abrogare:* to the intent that it should not be lawful for Princes of other Nations to abrogate or refuse the Bishops Decrees. And the reason he addeth immediatly: *Cuiusuis enim Iudicis sententiæ Sacerdotū Dei Iudiciū anteponendū esse.* For the Emperour estemed that the iudgemēt and determination of the Priests of God, was to be preferred before the Sentence of any other what so euer Iudge. This man there-

fore M. Horn (to tel you it ones again) can be no fitte exāple of the like gouernment now by you mainteined in the Quenes highnes person, and al other the inheritours of the Realme of England.

Now as Constantine did set the Clergie at their liberty, whether they would answere in any secular court: So the

noble

noble Emperour Theodofius fet as wel al the Laitie as the Clergie, at the like libertie, and ordeined,
that the plaintife in any caufe, any time before the
fentence, might breake of, from his ordinary Iudge,
and bring the matter whether the defendāt would
or no, to the Epifcopal audience. The which ordinaunce, the Great Charles about. 400. yeares after
renewed to be inuiolably obferued of all his fubiectes, as wel the Romaines and the Frenchemen, as
the Almanes, the Bauarians, the Saxons, the Turin-
giās, the Frifons, the Galles, the Britanes, the Lom-
bards, the Gafcons, the Beneuentanes, the Gothes,
and the Spaniards.

As ye do with Conftantinus Magnus, fo doe ye
with Theodofius Magnus, and with Carolus Magnus conftitutions: bringing them forth out of your
blind Cacus denne, to dafel and bleare the Readers
withal: as though the Bifhops helde their ordinarie
iurifdiction Ecclefiafticall, by thefe decrees onely,
which do nothing thervnto appertaine, but fhew a
marueiloufe priuilege geuen to them to heare and
determine alfo all tēporall matters brought before
thē. And if thefe graunts wer afterward abrogated,
yet was that no abrogatiō to the iurifdictiō, that is
proprely the ecclefiaftical iurifdictiō: and your author doth not fay, that fuch graūts wer afterwards
abrogated, but doth reafon againft them that faide
they were abrogated   Neither is his booke entitu
led *De origine iurifdictionū* but *de iurifdictione Ecclefiaftica*. And was this Petrus Bertrandus then as
you fay, *a Bifhop, a Cardinal, and one of our beft learned men in the Canon and Ciuil Lawes?*

cccc ij   Sure-

Vide. c. quicūque etc.
volumus. ii. q.
*Quicūque litem ha-
bens fiue petitor fue-
rit (alias fiue reus)
vel di curfis tempo-
rum curriculis, fiue
cum negotium pero-
ratur, fiue cum iam
cœperit promi fentē
tia: fi iudiciū elege-
rit facrofanctæ fedis
antiftitis ilico fine
aliqua dubitatione,
etiam fi pars alia
refragatur, ad epif-
coporum iudicium,
cum fermone liti-
gantium dirigatur.*
*Petrus Bertrandus
in libello de iurifdi-
ctione ecclefiaftica.
Sed dices quòd ifta
lex eft abrogata vt
videtur tangere glo-
fa ibidem, fed hoc
non valet, quia li-
cet ifta lex non fue=
rit in corpore iuris
redacta, tamen pro-
pter hoc nō eft abro-
gata. imò. &c
cōfider hovv hādã
fomly M. Horn ala
leageth Bertrādus.
Vide, Horne. fol. 82.*

Suerly then may your Petrus Cugnerius, thoughe ye a-
uáce him as a worthy knight, go hide his head in a corner.
For againſte him and his foliſhe fonde arguing againſte the
ecclefiaſtical liberty is all his booke writen, as I haue before declared.

Wherfore all this your tale that the biſhops held their
iuriſdiction ouer theire clergy by Conſtantine his ghifte, is
as true, as your other adiuncte: that he gaue the Biſhops of
Rome power and authority ouer other Biſhoppes and ouer
al churches. He might well as he did in dede, reuerently
agniſe, and by his Imperial authoritie confirme and corroborate the vſual authoritie of the Popes holines : but that
the original of this authority, as ye imagine, came frō him,
ys a great vntruth. For euen before his time, and after, not
onely the Chriſtians, but the verie infidelles, ſuche as were
acquainted with the maners and faſhions of the Chriſtians
did wel knowe, that the Biſhop of Rome was counted the
cheif biſhop amonge them al. And for this cauſe Ammia-
nus Marcellin⁹an heathniſh cronicler writeth, that though
Athanaſius the good biſhop were by a councell of Arrian
biſhoppes condemned, yet that notwithſtanding, Conſtā-
tius fonne to this Conſtantinus, and an Arrian, and his plain
open enemie, was erneſtlie in hande with Pope Liberius
alfo to confirme their fentence, and was by him baniſhed,
becauſe he would not condeſcende to theperours requeſt.
Againe before the time of this Conſtantinus, Paulus Samo-
fatenus biſhop of Antiochia being depriued by a councell
of biſhoppes, and an other appointed by the fayde councel
in his ſtede, kepte ſtil poſſeſsion, nothing regarding either
the fentence of depriuation or of excommunication. The
Emperour Aurelianus being certified of this matter gaue
com-

Confider
how hā-
fomly M.
Horne
alleageth
Bertran-
dus.

Vide Horn
Fol. 82.

The Po-
pes au-
thoritie
that M.
Horne
denieth,
confeſſed
by infi-
delles.

Ammian.
Marc. re-
rũ Rom.
lib 15.
Eufeb. lib.
7. c. 26.

commaundement, that he whome fo euer the bifhoppe of
Rome, with the bifhops of Italie fhould acknowledge for
the bifhop of Antiochia, fhould be taken and accepted for
the true bifhop. And fo was Paulus by this Emperours cõmaundement, though he were a very infidell, thrufte out, *Vide libel-*
and an other fet in. What proufe haue ye now, M.Horne, *lũ eius ad-*
that the Pope hath his authoritie from Conftantine? Sure- *tunctũ ea*
ly Gentle Reader, none other but the Donation of Con- *piftolis*
ftantine, whiche he him felfe doth not beleeue to be true: *Leonis 1.*
and therefore dothe qualifie it with thefe woordes, *if it be* *impreß.*
not forged. *Col. in*
　Whiche being fo, why doeth your wifedome then, M. *fo.cap.13,*
Horne alleage it? Neither wil I here, though Leo the 9. *Auguftin.*
doth conftantly teftifie, that he fawe and had him felfe the *Stenchus*
originall of this donation laide by Conftãtinus owne hand *Eugubin.*
vpon the bodie of S. Peter, though Eugubinus anfwereth
to all Laurence Valla his obieĉions againfte this *In Nomocanõ, Pho-*
donation: yea though Balfamon a Grecian, and an *tij. titulo.8.*
open ennemie to the Pope, alleageth this Donati- *Diftinĉt.96.c.*
on as authentical: I wil not yet, I fay, refolue any *Conftantinus.*
thing for the one, or the other fide: I will take it *Quoniam vbi prin-*
as I find it, and take you withall, as I find you, and *cipatus Sacerdotum*
that is a plaine open lyar. For howfoeuer the Do- *& Chriftianæ reli-*
nation be, the Pope toke not his Supremacy of this *gionis caput ab im-*
Donation, but had it before, of an higher Empe- *peratore cœlefti con-*
rour, and that is, of Chrifte him felfe. Whiche the *ftitutum eft, iuftum*
forefaid donatiõ doth alfo openly teftify, but not in *non eft, vt illic im-*
the.86.as ye falfly quote it, but in the.96.diftinĉtiõ. *perator terrenus ha-*
beat poteftatem.

　M.Fckenham.　The.'66.Diuifion. Pag.111.a.

At the firft Councel holden at Hierufalem, for the re-
formation of the controuerfy that was than at Antioche,
　　　　　　cccc iij　　touching

touching Circumcifion , and the obferuation of Mofes
Lawe, decree was made there by the Apoftles and Prie-
ftes, vnto the beleuers at Antioche, that they fhould ab-
fteine from thefe fowre chiefe and neceffary thinges, viz.

Act. 15. ab immolatis fimulachrorum, à fanguine & fuffocato, à for-
nicatione, à quib. cuftodiétes vos, bene agetis. *The whiche*
firft councell was there affembled by the Apoftles of
Chrift. The Decrees and Lawes, were made there by thē:
The cōtrouerfy at Antioche, was by them reformed; or-
dered, and correɛted without all commiffion of any tem-
poral Magiftrate, King, or Prince.

M. Horne.

God be thanked , that S. Luke maketh to vs a fufficient report of this
councell, vvho maketh no mention of any (.598.) Prieft there prefent, as you
vntruely report, onles ye vvill thinke he meant the order of Prieftes , vvhan
he named the faɛtion of the Pharifees. Whether the Apoftles called this coūcel or not: or that the Congregation being affembled together in their ordinary fort, for praier, preaching, and breaking of bread, Paulus and Barnabas, vvith the others, fent to Hierufalem , did declare the caufe of their
meffage before the vvhole Churche, vvhich is more likely, I vvil not determine, bicaufe S. Luke maketh no mention thereof . But if it be true, that ye
affirme, that the Apoftles called or affembled this Councel, then vvas it not
the authoritie or Aɛte of one Apoftle alone. Befides this , if the Apoftles called this councel, they called the Laytie fo vvel as the Clergy to the councell:
yea, as may feeme probable, mo of the Laytie than of the Clergy. The decrees
vvere not made by the Apoftles (.599.) alone, as you falfely feyne . For S.
Luke faieth, the decree vvas made by the Apoftles , Elders, and the (.600.)
vvhole Congregation. The Apoftles, I grauut, as vvas mofte couenient vvith
the Elders had the debating, arguing and difcuffing of the queftiō in cōtrouerfie. They declared out of the holy Scriptures, vvhat vvas the truthe: And
I doubt not but they declared to the Church, vvhat they thought moft cou-
uenient

The. 598.
vntruth.
For the
Apoftles
and the
Elders,
named of
S. Luke
vvere
prieftes.
The. 599.
vntruth.
M. Feckē-
hā faied
not of the
Apoftles
alone, but
by the
Apoftles
and prie-
ftes,
which is
true.
The. 600.
vntruth.
S. Luke
faieth no
fuch thig
of the
vvhole
congre-
gation.

uenient to be determined: But the determination and decree, vvas by the common consent, both of the Apostles, Elders, and (.601.) people. Therfore this controuersy vvas reformed, ordered, and corrected , not by the authority of the Apostles alone , vvithout the Elders , neither they togeather did it. vvithout the assent of the Churche, and so this allegation maketh no (.602.) deale for your purpose, but rather cleane against it.

The.601. vntruthe.
The people had not to doe vvith determination of it.
The.602. vntruthe.
For it proueth, Iurisdiction in the clergy, and povver to make ecclesiasticall lawes, vvithout consmission from the Prince.
Act. 15.
Concerning the decree of the Apostlesmade at Hierusalem.

Stapleton.

There followeth now an other reason out of the newe testamente, browght forth by M. Fekenham . The effecte wherof is, that the Apostles and other priestes, both assembled in councel, and reformed wrong opinions among the Christians, setting abrode theire decrees without any conmission of any ciuill magistrate: which is quite contrary to the absurde opinion mainteined by M. Horne: who is faine therefore to wince hither ãd thither, and wotteth not well where to rest him self for a resolute answere. First he quarrelleth with the worde, Priestes, and to no purpose: the argumente remaining sownde and whole, be they to be called Priestes, or be they to be called Elders. For though before the worde, Ministers, did like M. Horne well , yet the worde Elders liketh him here better . Priestes he is assured there were none among the Apostles, in this councel, vnlesse they were the Pharisees . And so with his pleasante pharisaicall myrthe, he maketh the Apostles them selues Pharisees. For Priestes it is certain they were, as I haue declared before. Nowe for the worde πρεσβύτερ⊙, (which word the Latin and our tonge, and almost al other tongues in Europa , namelie the Frenche , the Italian , the Spaynishe, the highe and lowe Dutche , yea and all other as farre

farre as I can yet learne , doe expreſſe by a like worde deriued from the Greke) though yt ſignifie an elder in age ,
by the proper ſignificatiō of the Greke word, yet in ſcripture it ſignifieth that office and dignitie in a man that we
cal Prieſthod : that is , ſuch an Elder as is a Prieſt withall.
And yet not alwaies to be ſo called for his age, as appereth
by Timothee who was but yong. Truth it is, that this word
in Greke πρεσβύτερ☾, ſometime ſignifieth the inferior in
dignitie, and him that is vnder the Biſhoppe, and ſometime
the Biſhop . As ſometime this woorde *Apoſtolus*, ſignifieth
none of the.xij. Apoſtles , but a Biſhop : and ſo is the one
and the other confounded in Scripture.

  Whereof Theodoretus is an vndoubted witneſſe. For
thus he writeth : *Eoſdem olim vocabant preſbyteros & Epiſ-*
copos, eos autem qui nunc vocantur Epiſcopi, nominabant Apo-
ſtolos. Procedente autem tempore nomen quidem Apoſtolorum
reliquerunt ijs qui verè erant Apoſtoli: Epiſcopatus autē appel-
lationem impoſuerunt ijs, qui olim appellabantur Apoſtoli. Ita
Philippenſium Apoſtolus erat Epaphroditus, Ita Cretenſiū Ti-
tus, Aſianorum Timotheus. In the old time (he meaneth the
Primitiue Church , as with the like terme Chryſoſtō doth)
men called Prieſts and Biſhops all one. But thoſe whiche
are now called Biſhops, they called Apoſtles. Afterward
in proceſſe of time , they lefte the names of Apoſtles, to
thoſe which were in dede Apoſtles. And biſhops they called thoſe, whiche in olde time were called Apoſtles. So
Epaphroditus was the Apoſtle of the Philippenſes, ſo Titus
of the people of Creta, and Timothe of the Aſians. Thus
then, thoſe which were in dede Biſhops, being in the Apoſtles time called Prieſtes , verely in this place alſo of the
Actes, by theſe wordes Prieſts, may very wel be taken not
only

Theodoret.
in commē-
tar. in epi.
1. Tim. 3.
& Phil. 2.

Hom. 36.
in 1. cor. 4

only fimple Priefts, but euen thofe that were Bifhops too·
And then hath M. Horne loft al the grace of his Pharifaical
iefting. But now is the man in a great mufe with him felfe,
whether he may graunt to M. Fekenham, that this Councell was called by the Apoftles : though of his modeftie
(which is here to be wondered at,it fheweth it felfe fo fel.
dome) he wil not determine the matter.　And then doth
he ful fadlie imagine, as a thing mofte likely,that the Apoftles Paulus and Barnabas came to Hierufalem iump at that
time, that the Apoftles and the congregation were affembled already together to common prayer. And by as good
likelyhood they made pofte hafte to prefent them ere the
congregation brake vppe, leaft they fhould haue loft their
iourny for lacke of authority in the Apoftles to cal a Coūcel : or tarrie at leaft vntill the next time, that they affembled for praier. And whie, I pray you, might they not as
wel call a Councel, as affemble together for other caufes ?
And whie do you fo fondly ground your likelineffe vppon
that, which hathe no likelihood ?　And why doe ye thus
wrangle, feing S. Luke him felfe fheweth plainly the caufe
of their meeting? *Conuenerunt q̃, Apoftoli & feniores vide-*　Act.15.
re de verbo hoc. The Apoftles and the Priefts affembled together to confider of this matter. Then haue we an other
fnarling, that this was not the acte of one Apoftle alone.
Neither dothe the Pope alone (for that belike is the matter
ye fo clofely fhote at) make any decree, but either by a coūcel, or with the aduife of his Cardinales and others.Which
in all weighty matters no doubt he dothe, though he after
al, as the head, geue the Sentence. At length yet M. Horn
taking a better hart vnto him felfe,goeth roundlye to the
matter,and refolueth vs,that this Decree was made not by

　　　　　　　　dddd　　　　　　　　the

the Apoſtles only, and the prieſtes, but by the whole Congregatiō ther preſent, as S. Luke faieth. Then is there good
cauſe to beleue him, M. Horne. I heare you ſay, that Saint
Luke ſaith, *the decree was made by the Apoſtles, Elders, and
the whole Congregation.* But as yet I heare not S. Luke ſay

Aɛ̃. 15. so, nor euer ſhal hear him ſo ſaie. S. Luke ſaith, firſt, *that the
Apoſtles and Prieſts gathered them ſelues togeather to conſult
vpon the matter.* He ſaith, that S. Peter ſpake firſt his mind,

Ibidē. 14. and S. Iames, being Biſhop there, confirmed his ſayings.
S. Luke alſo calleth theſe decrees, *the decrees of the Apoſtles and Prieſts,* ſpeaking no worde of the whole congregation. And when the contention for keping Moſes Law
waxed hotte at Antiochia, the Churche there ſent Paulus
and Barnabas and others to Hieruſalē, but not to the whole

Ibidem. 2. congregation, but *to the Apoſtles and Prieſts.* Truth it is,
that it appeareth alſo in S. Luke, that by cōmon conſent of
the Apoſtles of the Prieſts, and of the whole congregatiō,
Iudas and Barſabas were elected to accompanie S. Paul and
Barnabas in their iourny to Antiochia, ād to preſent to the
Chriſtians there, the Deerees of the Councel: but that the
decree was made by the whole cōgregation, that doth not
appeare: but only that they did, as meete it was, reuerently
conſent, imbrace, and receiue it : as the Catholike Princes
and al their people that be Catholik, do allow, imbrace, and
reuerēce the late Synod holden at Trent, where were preſent the Ambaſſadours of al the ſaid Catholike Princes, and
yet had they there no abſolute voice or conſent, touching
the definition of the queſtions there debated and determined. Nay, not the laie men onely, but the very Prieſts them
ſelues, haue no neceſſary cōſent, which ſtandeth in the Bi ‧
ſhops only, as the whole practiſe of the church ſheweth frō
the

the Apostles time. Therfore in the fourth General Coûcell *To. 1. Côc.*
of Chalcedô the Bishops cryed. *Synodus Episcoporum est, non* *Act. 1. p. 4.*
clericorum. A Synod or Councel consisteth of Bishops , not *745. vel*
of the (inferiour)clergy. And againe in the same Councel: *postr. edit.*
Petrus a priest protested no lesse, saying: *Non est meum sub-* *tom. 3.*
scribere, Episcoporum tantùm est . It is not my parte to sub- *pag. 19.*
Act. 1. p. 4.
scribe, it belôgeth only to Bishops. Thus subscriptiô, (wher-
775. &
in necessary consent is expressed)is confessed to pertayne *pag. 47.*
to bishops only, not to Priests. And therfore yt is very like- *Tom. 2.*
ly, that theis that you call *Elders* , were not single priestes, *edit. postr.*
but bishops also. Wherein as I will not côtende, so though
yt were true, that the whole côgregatiô gaue their voice,
yet the supremacy in the sayed and other matters remayned not in them, but in the Apostles as may wel appere by
this very place, to him that wil but reade and consider the
text of S. Luke.

M. *Fekenham.* The. 167. Diuision. pag. 111. b.

The Apostles also hearing at Hierusalem , that Sa- *Act. 8.*
maria had receiued the woord of God, they did sende Pe-
ter and Iohn, to visite thê to confirme them in faithe, and
that they might receiue the holy Ghost by the imposition
of their handes. Paule and Barnabas did agree betwixt
them selues, to visite al those Cities and bretheren, which
they had côuerted to the faithe. The woordes of the Scri- *Act. 15.*
pture are these: Dixit ad Barnabam Paulus, reuertentes, vi-
sitemus fratres per vniuersas Ciuitates, in quibus prædica-
uimus verbum Domini, quomodo se habeant . *In the*
which visitation , the Apostle Paule : Electo Sila per-
ambulabat Syriam & Ciliciam, confirmans Ecclesias, præ-
cipiens custodire præcepta Apostolorum & Seniorum.

By the whiche wordes it right well appeareth, howe the Apostles and Priestes at Hierusalem, ouer and besides the Ghospell whiche they taught, they did make certaine Decrees, Lawes, and ordinaunces, the whiche the Apostle Paule in his visitation, gaue commaundement to the Syrians, and Silicias, to obserue and keepe. VVhat Lawes and orders did the Apostle make and appoint vnto the Corinthians, that men should neither pray nor preache in the Churche with their heades couered? VVhat reformation and order did he make and appoint vnto them, for the more honourable receiuing of the Sacrament, and that partly by writing, and partly by woorde of mouthe, saying: Cætera, cùm venero, disponam, and in his seconde Epistle to the Thessalonians, he saith, Fratres state, & tenete traditiones quas didicistis, siue per sermonem, siue per Epistolam nostram. VVhat orders and Decrees did the Apostle Paule make, touching praiyng and preaching vnto the people in tongues vnknowen, and that all women shoulde keepe silence in the Churche and Congregation? These and many suche other like Lawes, orders, and Decrees, were made for the reformation of the people in the Churche of Christ, by Christes Apostles, by Bishops and priestes, as the successours of them, and that without all commission of any Temporal Magistrate, Emperour, King, or Prince, Constātinus being the first Christian Emperour, like as I haue saide.

2. Cor. 11.

2. Cor. 13.

M. Horne

M. Horne.

Your vvhole drifte in this parte is , to proue that Bishoppes and Priestes may visite, geue the holy Ghoste, by the imposition of their handes: and make lavves orders, and decrees to their flockes and cures, Your proufe consisteth in the example of the Apostles , and this is your argument : The Apostles visited, gaue the holy Ghost , and made Lavves, orders , and decrees , vnto their flockes and cures, Ergo, *Bishoppes and Priestes , haue authoritie and may make Lavves , visit and geue the holy Ghost to their flockes and cures. The insufficiency of this consequent, doth easely appeare : to those that doo consider the state and condicion of the Apostleship , and compare thervvith the office of a Bishop or Priest . The Apostles did , might , and could doo, many thinges that Bishoppes and Priestes, neither may, nor can do. The matter is more plaine than that needeth any proufe. But as the sequele faileth in forme, so let vs consider the matter, vvherupon ye grounde the sequele, that your frindes may see vvhat foule shiftes ye are driuen to make, for the maintenauce of an vniust claime. That the Apostles did visite their cures and flockes, you proue by tvvo places of the Actes: in the first place , ye (.603.) feine the Scriptures to say, that it saieth not: for in the eight of the Actes, there is no mencio made of any visitatio: the other place speaketh only of a (.604.) Scripturely visitatio, and nothing at al of your Forinsecall or Canon Lavve visitation. The Canon Lavves visitation, is to be exercised by a great number of such persons, as the Scripture (.605.) knovveth not. And the matter vvherabout that visitation is occupied for the moste parte, is directlye (.606.) againste the Scriptures . The personnes that may lavvfullye visite in youre Canon Lavve visitation, are* Popes , Legates from the side : Legates sent and borne , Legates and messengers of the Apostolik sea, Patriarches, Archebishoppes, Bishoppes, Archdeacons , Deanes , Archepriestes , Abbottes , and other inferiour personnes hauing iurisdiction. All Archebishoppes whiche are Legates borne , haue authority to visit their prouinces by double right, to wit, by right Legatine, and by right Metropolitane, ad so they may visit twyse in the yere. All these visitours muste beginne their visitation with a solemne Masse of the holy ghost. The Bishoppe and euery ordinary visitour , must beginne his visitation at his Cathedrall

The.603.
vntruth.
For the
scriptures
report so
much in
effect.
The.604.
vntruth.
The actes
speake of
no such
visitatio.
The.605.
vntruth,
as it shall
appeare.
The.606.
vntruth,
slaunde-
rous bold-
ly auou-
ched, but
no vvay
proued.

Church

Churche and Chapter. He muſt come into the Church where he viſiteth, and firſt kneele downe and pray deuoutlv, chieflie directing his eies and mind to the place wherein the honourable ſacramēt of Chriſtes Body is hiddē and kepte. *The matters of the Canō Lavve viſitatiō are in parte theſe.* The viſitour ought to view diligētly, whether the place wher the Sacramēt is kept, be cleane, wel garniſhed and cloſe, for the Euchariſt, and the holy Chryſme ought to be kept ſhut vnder locke and key. He muſt ſee, that there be great lightes of waxe to geue light in that place, Thē muſt he viſit the place of the holy reliquies, ād of Baptiſme. And ſearch diligētly what māner of place it is, ād whether it be kepte ſhut. Beſides this he muſte viſit the Aultars and litle Chappelles, and muſt with his eies viewe the whole Church whether it be cleāly and cleane. Thē he muſt viſit the veſſelles and Churche veſtymentes, whether they be cleane, and kepte in a cleane place, as they ought to be, and whether the veſtimētes be ouermuche worne and brokē, and in caſe the viſitour ſhal finde ſuche veſtimētes vncleane, rēte, and cōſumed with occupying, he muſte burne thē in the fire, and cauſe the aſhes to be buried in ſome place, whereby ther is no paſſage. But in any wiſe let him not ſuffer (ſaith Socius) purſes or ſuch like thinges to worldly vſe to be made of the copes or tunicles. Laſt of al, let him ſuruey the houſes and poſſeſsions belonging to the Churche. The Biſhop dooth viſit alſo, to biſhop enfantes, and to cōſecrate or hallow Churches. The viſitour alſo ſhall enquire and examine, whether any mā knowe or beleeue, or that the fame is, that the Sexten, the Treaſurer, or the Veſture keeper, hath well and ſaufly kepte, the veſſels, veſtimentes, and other thinges or ornamentes of the Churche, as Maſſe bookes, Grayles, Antiphoners, Legendes, and other thinges appointed to diuine Seruice, and whether any thing moueable, or vnmoueable, be diminiſhed, and by whome, wherefore, whan, and after what ſorte, whether they be diligently preſent at the Dirigees for the dead. And whether the veſture keeper or Sexten, keepe warelie

and

cleanly the Churche, the Eucharift, the Reliques, the Fount, the Churchyardes, and fuche other things. And he fhal examine the Prieftes in the countrie in faying of their Maffes. But lette euerye Vifitour vnderftande (*faith mine Authour*) that fame the greateft queftion or controuerfie which was betwixt three rurall Perfonnes or Prieftes: vvherof tvvo of them ftroue about the vvoordes of Confecration, the one affirming, that the vvordes are to be pronounced thus: Hoc eft corpus meus: the other, Hoc eft corpus(*I thinke he fhould haue faid* corpum)meum. Thefe tvvo chofe a thirde Priefte, vvho vvas taken to be better learned, to be arbitour, and to decide this high queftion: vvhofe anfvvere vvas, that he him felfe ftoode euer doubtfull in this queftion: and therfore in fteede of thefe vvordes of confecration, did alvvaies vfe to faye one Pater nofter. Furthermore the Vifitour muft enquire, vvhether the laity make their confefsion once in the yeare, and receiue the Eucharifte at Eafter. And vvhether they be flovve, or denie to paie their tythes and fruites. The Archebifshoppe muft in vifiting any of his Suffraganes, exactly enquire and examine the Canons and Clerkes of the Cathedrall Churche, vvhether they knovv, beleue, or that the fame is, that the Bifshop hath couered or borne vvith fome mens faultes for money, or other temporall commoditie. *Can you finde in the Scriptures any one of thefe Vifitours, or anie one of thefe vveightie matters enquired of, by* Peter, Iohn, Paule, Sylas, Barnabas, *or by any of the Apoftles in their Vifitations, vvhich vvere Scripturely vifitations? No furely, it is not pofsible: For thefe Idolatrous (.607.) vanities, are manifeftlie repugnaunt to the Holie Scriptures. Amongeft all the rable of thefe Canon Lavve vifitours, ye can not finde in the Scriptures, not fo muche as the bare Title of (.608.) one of them, onelefe it be of a Bifshoppe: vvhiche name applied to the man, as the Scriptures defcribeth the man, that is called to that office, can no (.609.)more agree vvith a Cannon Lavve Bifshoppe, then vvith the Ciuill Lavve Bifshoppe, vvhofe office vvas, as it is fette foorthe in the Digeftes, to haue the rule and ouerfighte of all maner of victualles in the Citties, as it vvere the chiefe Clerke of the markets. As the matter of the Apoftles vifitations*

ftandeth

The.607.
Vntruth.
flāderous
as before.
The.608.
Vntruth.
The titles
of diuerfe
of the are
tobe foūd
there.
The.609.
Vntruth.
The Bifshops of
the Canō
lavve, are
fuch as
the Scripture defcribeth.
Lib.50.
Tit.4. De
muner. &
honor.

standeth directly (.610.) against the greatest parte of the matter whereabout your Popissh or Canon Lavve visitation is exercised : Euen so the holy Scripture that you auouche, for the geuing of the holie Ghoste, maketh (.611.) nothing at all to proue your purpose. For Saint Luke in that place speaketh (.612.) not of an ordinarie povver, that shoulde remaine in the ministers of the Churche for euer, but of a speciall gifte to vvorke miracles, and to geue that povver to others, vvhiche shoulde continue but for the time vvhiles Christes Churche vvas to be erected, and the vvoord to be founded through the vvorlde : And therefore Chrysostome saieth : That this gift pertained onely to the Apostles. For (saieth he) the Conuertes in Samaria had receiued before Peter and Iohn came, the spirit of Remission of Sinnes : But the spirite of Myracles, that is, the gift of tongues, healing, prophecing, and suche like, vvhich are the giftes of the holie Ghoste, and therefore are called the Holie Ghoste, they had not as yet receiued. There vvere many that by the povver of Goddes Spirite coulde vvoorke miracles.but to geaue this povver to others, none coulde doe but the Apostles. For that vvas propre and onelye in them. Marke novve the sequele of your allegation for preufe of your purpose : Thus (.613.) you argue : the Apostles gaue by the imposition of their handes, to the Samaritanes, the giftes of Healing, Prophecying, of Tongues, &c. Therefore euerye Bisshop and Priest hath povver to geue the same gifts to their flocks and cures. There vvas neuer none so blind or so ignorantly brought vp in your cures, belonging to the Abbey of VVestminster, but that did vvel perceiue, that neither your Bisshops, Abbottes, or Priests, had or could doe any such feate. They like Apes, imitated the outvvarde signe or ceremonie.but the invvard grace they vvanted.

Stapleton.

The.610. Vntruth. Euer repered, but neuer proued.

The.611 Vntruthe. For it proueth an ordinarie power in bishops aboute the Sacrament of confirmation, vvhich they exercised vvithout any commission from the Prince.

The 612. Vntruthe. For he speaketh bothe of the ordinarie vse of that Sacrament, and of the extraordinarie gift of Miracles,

The 613. Vntruthe. For M. Fekenham argueth not so. It is your ovvne Argument.

In this parte M. Fekenham prosequureth his proufe out of the newe Testamente, alleaging for his purpose manye places thereof. As of Peter and Iohn *that went into Samaria to vi-*

to vifite the Chriftians there, to confirme them in fayth, and to geue them the holy Ghofte by the impofition of their hands. Of Paulus and Barnabas that vifited many contries, *commaunding the Chriftians there to kepe the commaundements of the Apoftles and priefts:* with certaine orders and lawes made by S.Paule. But al this M.Horn thinketh may be wiped away with one general anfwer of an infufficiét confequécy: for that the Apoftles did and could do many things that bifhops and priefts neither may, nor can doe nowe: I wil not ftriue with you M. Horne what the Apoftles did in other thinges, but yf they practifed any iurifdiction in makinge of Lawes, in vifiting, in reforming without the cómifsió of any Laicall authority: then is M. Fekenhás argument good and fufficient. Thé haue we the practife of the Apoftles and primatiue Church againft this your newe Paradoxe. Thé hath M. Fekéhá wrapped you vp alfo ád mefhed you in a fowle contradiction, as one that affirmeth the quite contrary dyuerfe tymes before.

Vide fol. 105.col.1. in princip. & fol.110. col. 2, in fine.

And yet becaufe ye fhal not carry ád fteale away the matter fo, but be more fully anfwered, I fay ther was an ordinary, ád ther was alfo an extraordinary authority in the Apoftles. The ordinary authority of the Apoftles (in the which we are now) remaineth at this day ád fhal remain for euer in the Church, in the bifhops their fucceffours. The extraordinary authority either died with thé, or at left cá not be vfually pleaded vpó. The lyke argumét as ye make here, againft the authority ád iurifdictió of bifhops, M.Iewel ád your fellowes make againft the Pope , that thoughe S. Peter were head of the whole Church and was affured by the promiffe of Chrift that *prayed for him , that his fayth fhulde not fayle,* yet can not al his fucceffours the Popes challenge the fame

Double authority in the Apoftles, ordinary and extra ordinary.

Luc.22l. M Ievvel in his reply agaift M.D.Har ding.

eeee being

being a special prerogatiue gratiously geué to him. But here
we muft vnderftād, that Peter was priuileged, for his owne
perfon, and he was priuileged alfo, in refpect, of the cōmon
weale of the whole Church. And therfore yf we refpect S.
Peters perfon, the persō of his fucceffor is not fo priuileged,
but he may fal and erre in his own priuat opiniō and iudgemēt. But if we refpect the whole Church, whereof he hath
the rule then we fay he can not erre in any decree or order
that he fhal publikely make for any matter of faith: Leaft by
this his opē errour the whole Church fal alfo into the fame.
The prouidēce of God (which a Diuine fhuld alwaies haue
an eie vnto) fuffreth not fuch an incōueniéce in his Church.

Again, the Apoftles had perfonal priuileges of more ample grace, thē their fucceffours haue. And therfore by theis
wordes, *what fo euer, ye fhall bynde vppon the earth &c.* And
by thofe other, *as my father fent me, fo I fend you :* they had
authority eche of them to preach throughout the whole
world and in whatfoeuer part therof: ād in this refpect they
were equal with S. Peter : but their fucceffours at Alexandria, Antiochia, ād Ephefus do not fuccede to thē, nor inioy
this extraordinary powre of preaching ād teachīg through
out the world, ād euery part therof, but the ordinary ōly ād
vfual power within their own Dioceffe or Patriarchfhip.
The faid extraordinary authority remaynīg with the popes
only as the fucceffours of S. Peter: who was head of the A-
poftles (not in the Apoftlefhip for in that all the Apoftles
were equall) but in bifhoply Iurifdiction. After lyke fort the
Apoftles had a certain peerleffe authority to fpeak in diuers
tongs, to prophecy, to reuiue the dead, to heale the ficke, to
caft out diuels, and to do many other miracles. This power
doth not defcéd to al their fucceffours ordinately, but now
and thē to fome certain, to whō it pleafeth God, to difpēce
thefe

thefe graciouſe gifts vnto. As he hath don to many a bleſſed biſhop ſyth the apoſtles time, ãd to many other euen in our daies, as to the bleſſed Fathers of the ſociety of Ieſus, in cõuerting the newe found Indiãs frõ paganiſme to the faith of Chriſt, and as alſo to our holy Father the Pope that nowe liueth (as we are moſt certainly informed) God hath abundãtly geuē this heauēly gift of workĩg miracles. But we are out of this caſe: we reaſō of an vſual ãd ordinary power that the apoſtles ſucceſſors muſt nedes haue, and haue as wel as they, for the neceſſary gouernement of his Churche. As to preach to the flocke of Chriſt, to gouern ãd to direct thē, by good orders ãd lawes, to reform the offendours, to excõmunicat the diſobedient to improue, rebuke, or exhort with al lõg ſuffering, ãd good doctrin, to viſit thē, to correct the vnquiet, to cōfort the feble mĩded, to forbeare ãd receiue the weak, ãd to haue a cōtinual paciēce in al mē: By impoſition of hãds to geue holy orders in the ſacramēt of cōfirmatiõ (as Peter and Iohn the apoſtles did when they viſited Samaria) with many other things belõging ordinarily to all biſſhops. Nay ſaith M. Horne, *ther is no mentiõ made of viſitatiõ in the eight of the Actes.* What ſhal we trifle cõcerning the word viſitatiõ, if it be not ther, in caſe the thĩg it ſelf be there? Verely if the very word haue any force with you M. Horne, you haue it plain in the next allegatiõ of M. Fekenhã out of the.15. of the Actes: where S. Paule ſaid to Barnabas, *Let vs viſite our brethern, &cæt.* But I pray you tell vs, why were Peter and Iohn ſent into Samaria, but to confirme the Samaritanes, and to geue the Sacramente of confirmation to thoſe that were latelie baptized? This Sacrament of Confirmation is one of the principall thynges, the whiche the Biſſhoppes do vſe in their viſitation. Here

Matt. 28.
Marc. 16.
Act. 20.
Math. 18.
Act. 16.
2. Tim. 4.
1. Theſſ. 5.
1. Tim. 5.

Act. 8.

Act. 15.

M.Horne runneth to his olde ſhiſt yet ons againe, and ſaith here was no ſacrament geuen, neither any holy Ghoſt at al. *But the ſpirite of miracles, as the giſte of tonges, of healing, prophecying, and ſuch like, which are the gifts of the holy ghoſt, and therefore called the holy Ghoſt.* And then doth M.Horne ieſte at this ſequele. *The Apoſtles gaue theſe giftes. Ergo euery prieſt and biſhop may geue them nowe.* And then he addeth for his pleaſure, *that there was neuer any monke in the Abbay of Weſtminſter ſo ignorantly brought vp, but knewe wel inough, that the biſhops could do no ſuch feate.* Truth it is, that they receiued the holy Ghoſt, and theſe outwarde giftes

The holy ghoſt is geuen in confirmation. withal at their confirmation. And as the Apoſtles only by the impoſition of handes gaue theſe giftes, as ye confeſſe: ſo Confirmation to this day perteineth to the biſhops only, that repreſente the Apoſtles. Nowe that confirmation is

Hiero. cont. Lucifer. Si hoc loco quæras, qui in Eccleſia baptizatus, niſi per manus epiſcopi non accipiat ſpiritum ſanctum: diſce hanc obſeruatione ex caau=thoritate deſcendere, quod poſt aſcenſum Domini ſpirit° S. ad Apoſtolos deſcendit, & multis in locis idē factitatū reperimus. Auguſt. Contra literas Petiliani. lib. 2, Cap. 104.

no ſacrament, or that the holy ghoſt is not thereby geuen, neither Chryſoſtomus whome ye recite, nor any other auncient authour auoucheth. And that thoſe that were baptized were afterward cōfirmed by the biſhop, ād receiued the holy Ghoſt, when there were no viſible ſignes, S. Hierome plainely teſtifieth. And S. Auguſtine confeſſeth, it is a Sacrament, as Baptiſme is. Of this holy Ghoſt that is geuen without any outward miracles, ſpeaketh M.Fekenham, and no one worde of miracles. Wherefore this miſſhapen argument that ye bring forth, is yours, and not his. To the ouerthrowe of ot the which foliſhe fonde argument I aunſwere, that there was neuer none ſo blinde or ignorantly brought vp in the monaſtery of Weſtminſter, that could not well perceyue, that this is a very il fauored kind

red kinde of reaſoning, and ſuch as was neuer vſed amonge
the Catholikes.

As for his anſwere to M. Fekēham touching the ſecond
allegation, out of the . 15. of the Actes, is ſuch as is mete for
ſuch a ghoſpelling prelate: that is, to leaue reaſoning, and to
fal to rayling, and ſo to elude his Readers expectation, and
the argument: that he is not, nor euer ſhalbe able to anſwere.
Yet like a cunning Diuine and a verie ſkilfull viſitour, he
teacheth vs, that there are two viſitations, the one a ſcripturely, the other a forinſecall or a canon lawe viſitation.
Then haue we a longe leſſon out of one *Socius*, he ſhoulde
haue ſayde *Socinus*, what perſons may viſite, and what
matters they owght to enquire vppon in their viſitation.
And in effecte he doth nothing elſe in all this his extrauagant declaration, but mocke, and mowe: and like the di-
uelles Iacke anapes potteth at the good rites, cuſtomes
and vſages of the Catholike Churche, and at the bleſſed ſacrament to. And ſolaceth him ſelfe pleaſantly, and maketh
ioly ſporte at poore Sir Iohn lacke Latin: that could not
tell whether he ſhould ſay *Corpum meum*, or *Corpus meus*.
At length he concludeth full ſolemnelie, that neither the
perſons that exerciſe the canonicall viſitation, nor the
matters there enquired of, can be founde in ſcripture, no
not the bare title of any of theſe viſitours, vnleſſe it be a
Biſſhoppe. And yet theſe canon Lawe Biſſhoppes, he will
not haue called biſſhoppes neither: vnleſſe it be, for that
they may be ciuill Lawe Biſſhops: that is aſmuche to ſay,
as clerkes of the market. Howe thinke you good readers?
Is not Maiſter Fekenham his argument grounded vpon the
plaine ſcriptures and doinges of S. Paule, which did *viſite*
the Chriſtians, and commaunded them to kepe the Lawes and

M. Horns extraordinary rayling proceſſe.

Li. 50. tit. 4. de mu-neribus & honoribus.

Act. 15.

ordinaunces that the Apostles had made, without any laical commiſsion, very ſcripturely and prelatelyke of this greate ſcriptured man ſoluted? Thinke you, that this man hath any reuerence to God, any regard either to his matter, or to his Reader? Or thinke you, that this man lacketh not as much witte, as he doth vertue, learning, religion, and true deuotion, that with his malice to putte out one eie of the Catholikes, putteth out both his owne eies? and that can tell no faulte of the Catholikes, but that the ſame redoundeth double or treble againſt him ſelf and his affinitie? *Amonge all the rable* (as M. Horne termeth them) *of the canon Lawe viſitours, he can not finde as much as the bare title of any of them in ſcripture*. Seing this man is ſo preciſe and peremptory in his termes, we wil ſee whether we can finde any of them either in expreſſe termes, or at the leaſt

2. Cor. 5.
Ephes. 6.

in equiualent. In dede this worde *Papa* is not founde there, but his equiualent *Pater* is founde there. Legates we fynde ſtore, though not with ſuch preciſe termes as ye adioyne, as ſpeaking of Legates ſent and borne. The woorde Patriarche is ofte in ſcripture: Biſſhoppes we fynde, Deacons we fynde, prieſts we fynde. Therefore this is but a groſſe and a rude Rhetorike, to fynde faulte with the name of Archebiſſhop, Archedeacon, and Archprieſt, which ſignifieth no more then the chiefe of the biſſhoppes, deacons or Prieſtes. But in caſe you wil no better beare with Legates borne, and Archebiſſhops, you ſhal quite beare away both the audience, and the Arches, and the Courte of prerogatiue, and the Archbiſſhoprik withal of Canterbury. As for Deanes, who are called in Latin *Decani*, yea and Abbats to, for *Abba and Abbas* is al one, we finde in ſcripture. And I pray you what perſons be the chief viſitours nowe in England,

gland,but such as beare the names , that ye say , can not be
found in scripture,as Archbisshops, Bisshops, Archdeacons,
and Deanes?And you M.Horn that haue ben such a solēne
visitour,first for the Quenes M.and then in your own pretensed Diocese,and in the Vniuersity of Oxford,think you
that a man may synd your name or the name, of your visi-
tourship in any place of the Bible?And yf we may not find
it there,then by your own rule,when ye come next in visitatiō to Oxford,the schollers may synd some prety exceptiō against you.Thus you see good readers,I am fain to play
the child,with this childishe Prelate. Let vs now leaue the
names and goe to the matter of your visitatiō that ye kepe
now a dayes. Shall we find nothing there but scripturely
matters ? I pray you tel me then good M . Horne,in what
scripture ye find it,I will not say,that a monke , a nunne, a
priest or bishop may marie (for I am sure scripture is against
it, cōdēning the frailest kind of womē for maryīg after their
vowe,but in what scripture find you it , that (in case their
mariage be lawful)*the priest or deacō shal not marie, without
the aduice or allowance had vpō good examination by the bisshop of the same diocesse , and two Iustices of the peace of the
saide shere?* And that *the mariages of Bisshoppes must be allowed by the Metropolitane , and the Queenes highnes commissioners?* Why ? Are ye, that should be the Fathers of the
realm now come to this point , that for lacke of your discretion, ye must be made wardes and haue your gardons?
They that be vnder their fathers rule, by ciuill Lawe can
not marrye withowt their Fathers consent : but by the
same Lawe a Bisshoppe is fortwith exempted and acquited from all iurisdiction, that his Father hadde before vppon him . But ye contrarie wise are brought vnder the iurifdiction

vvhether
their vifi-
tations
novve are
al scriptu-
rely.
1.Tim.5.
Habentes
damnatio-
nem quia
primam f-
dē irritam
fecerunt.
See the in
iunctions

rifdiction of euery meane gentleman:and abridged of that
liberty of mariage,that euery poore plowghman hath.And
yet is this (as abfurde as yt is) an Iniunction belonging to
your newe Laicall vifitation . It were a matter for a iufte
volume,yf I fhould here profequute your other fcripturely
matters,that ye haue fette forth in your vifitations : efpecially in your late vifitation by your deare Chaunceler and
fonne exercifed at the Newe Colledge in Oxforde : who
propofed there to be fubfcribed a rablemente of blafpe-
moufe and hereticall articles , a number of them beinge as
fcripturely matters, as this propofition, is either fcripture-

Falfe Lati
in maifter
Horns ar
ticles pro
pofed to
be fubfcri
bed in his
vifitation
at Oxford

lyke or grammarlyke : *Regina eft vnicus & fupremus gubernator regni in caufis Ecclefiafticis & temporalibus.*But of this
your clerkely grāmar we haue had much experiéce in this
your anfwere.Amende:Amēde for fhame your barbaroufe
Latin, and put in *vnica & fuprema gubernatrix ,*if ye will
nedes maintayn the propofitiō:which yet doth not fo much
contrary the rules of grammar,as it doth the rules of Chriftian religiō. And beare with poore Sir Iohn , and his *corpus
meus,*which is as good Latin (Sir Robert) as your *Regina
gubernator vnicus, &cat.* And be not fo harde as ye are in
your iniunctions,to exclude from all cure or fpirituall function , fuche as of late Dayes were made prieftes otherwife vtterly vnlearned as ye fay , *but that they coulde reade
to fay mattins and maffe.*For yf ye be fo ftraite laced to your
minifters,ye are lyke to leaue but a fewe : and to haue the
moft parte of your cures vnfurnifhed, and ferue the parifh
Churches yourfelfe . For a greate parte,yea and a notable
number of your minifters can not reade Latin. And therfore M.Nowell, beinge in his laft booke againft M. Dorman,in the fame vayne that you here are M.Horn, and fett

in a

in a pelting chafe, with an inuincible place out of S. Ambrofe, ruffling in his lufty rhetorike, againft poore Sir Iohns,
as you do here, durft not yet to cal thē *Sir Iohn lacke latins*, Nouvell
but ful prouidently called thē, *Sir Iohn lacke lerning*. Bicaufe fol 80.
forfothe he fawe full wel, that his felowe Miniftres were fac. 2.
Sir Iohn lacke latins, as well as poore prieftes. Mary yet perhaps in his conceyt, they lacked not lerninge, bicaufe they
can reade in the Englifh bible. Therefore he thought it the
fureft to call ignorant prieftes, *Sir Iohn lacke lerninge*, not
Sir Iohn lacke latins. This point of wifedome you may M.
Horne lerne hereafter of M. Nowel, to faue the honefty
of your Sir Iohn lacke latins, fwarming nowe as thicke
in England as euer they did before. Yea fuch preachers
fyll the moft parte of your pulpittes, and the eares and
hearts of the people with much herefie, and fetteth them A mini-
at a lewde licentioufe liberty to fpeake what they will, ftrig prea
and do what they lifte. And here it commeth to my mind, cher that
that was credibly tolde me touching one of theis your mi- could not
niftring preachers, that not many yeares fythens came to a read his
parifh within the Dioceffe of Winchefter to preach: And licēce geē
being demaunded his Licence did exhibite it, but beinge uen him
required before the people to reade yt, could not: wher- to prēach
vppon the people fell into fuch a lawghter, that our preacher had no great lufte, to fhewe his cunning there, but
full flily fhronke away from them, and ftole away with
his clerkly fermon that he thought to haue made there. See what
And wherein I pray you refteth a greate parte of your clerkly
newe clergy, but in butchers, Cookes, Catchpoules, and and god-
Coblers, Diers, and Dawbers, fellons carrying their marke ly curats,
in theire hande in fteade of a fhauen crowne, fiffher men, in Eng-
gunners, harpers, Innekepers, Merchauntes and Mari- land.

ffff   ners,

Matt. 4. ners, Netmakers, potters, potycaries, and porters of Be-
linſgate, pynners, pedlers, ruffling ruffins, ſadlers, ſheermen,
and ſhepherds, tanners, tilers, tinckers, trumpeters, weauers,
whery men &cæt. Demaunde of theis freſh clerks M. Horn
at your next viſitation, whether it muſt be read *corpus meum*, or *corpus meus*, And ſee, whether any of them can reſolue his felowes better, then the prieſt, you ſpeake of did,
that being him ſelf doutful, vſed (as you ſay) his *Pater noſter*,
in ſtede of the words of conſecration. Wil they not trowe
you, make anſwer, as a Miniſter in M. Iewels dyoceſe did?
who in a viſitatiõ being appoſed for trial of his latin tõgue,
what caſe was *Decenter*, anſwered, that he thanked God
highly, that he had neuer learned that Romiſh ãd Papiſticall
latin tongue? But what Latin ſhal a mã loke for at ſuch mẽs
hands? yea or what honeſty either? To deſcribe the diſſolut
and naughty viciouſe lyfe, of your miniſters, would fill vp a
booke of a good quãtity, ãd the hearers eares with to much
lothſomnes. I coulde here rippe vppe a number of deteſtable partes, and ſome of them playde in your pretenſed
Dioceſe: eſpecially of William Webbe the trumpetour and
miniſter of Otterborne nighe to Wincheſter: who hauing
a Ghoſpelling yokemate of his owne, tawghte a yonge
mayden in the Churche to ſinge the holy Geneuical pſalmes, and as he corrupted her ſowle with wicked hereſy,
ſo he defyled her body with ſuche lewde lechery, that he
was faine to flee the pariſh for ſhame. And yet as I here ſay
he is become at London an holy miniſter againe. I wil forbeare to lade your honeſt eares (good reader) with any
moe ſuch diſhoneſt and ſluttiſh ſtories, wherof we haue, the
more pity, to much plenty. Theis ãd ſuch like are the wicked king Hieroboams miniſters, the which falling from the
true

The trũ petour miniſter at Otterborne.

true Church of Hierufalem into idolatry, as you and your fellowes are fallen into herefy (which is alfo in fcripture called idolatrie) *made the loweft of the people, and fuch as were not of the tribe of Leuie peculiarlie and onelye by God appointed, his priefts.* Was not, I befeache yow M. Horne, the diforder of theis and other, both in theire lyuinge and preaching fuche, that the Quenes Maiefty of her gracioufe goodnes, caufed a number of Licences geuen them to preach, to be called in againe? For all that ye haue fo ofte vifited, get yow out ones agayne in vifitation M. Horne and amend your owne people, and your owne felfe principallie, accordinge to the rules of the holy fcripture, and then call your vifitation a fcripturely vifitation, and the other among the Catholyks nothing but a forinfecall and a canonicall vifitation. Suerly yt is a merueloufe Ghofpell, that ye haue of late broched, which befides mofte deteftable herefies, importeth fuch a breach and diffolution of all honeft and vertuoufe lyuing, that your owne Apoftle Luther was fayne to call vppon the Duke of Saxony, to make vifitation vppon vifitation for reformation. And fayne to crye out, that his newe Ghofpellinge children were worfe then euer they were vnder the pope: yea tenne tymes worfe then the Sodomites. Therefore talke as holily as ye will, of your fcripturely vifitations, the truthe ys, they are as dyrecte contrary to fcripture, as darcknes ys to lighte, and they are the very nurferies of all herefyes and licentioufe lyuing. And fhortly, but withall truely to conclude, how fcripturely they are, I fay ye cã no better iuftify your vifitations and other your doings by fcripture, the the deuil him felf could iuftifie his allegation: bringing forth fcripture, not to the poore fimple and vn-

ffff ij   lettered

Margin notes:
3.Reg.12. Fecit pro-phana in excelfis,et facerdotes de extremis populi quino erãt de filijs Leui.

Luth. fu-per poftil. 1.Domin. aduentus.

In vvhat fenfe a mã may call their vifitations in England fcripture-ly vifitations or preachigs

Matt. 4. lettered people as you doe, but to Chriſt him ſelf: willing him to caſt him ſelf down frõ the pinacle of the téple, with *ſcriptum eſt enim,*for it is writen:ſayth the deuill. And what is the ſcope of all your doynges and preachinges to the people,but *mitte te deorſum?*Caſt thy ſelf headlong downe from the highe towre of the lyghtſome catholyke ſayth into the lowe darke Dongeon , of all deueliſhe hereſie ? From the highe mounte of a vertuouſe and an auſtere lyfe , in to the lowe vale of all licentiouſe and diſſolute behauiour? What is all your preaching, but downe, downe, downe with holy bread , holy water , with all the holy ceremonies in baptiſme , and in the other ſacramentes , with faſtinge , with nighte prayer , with all prayer to be made for owre fathers or frendes ſowles , or to the bleſ-ſed Virgin Mary,and to all other Hallowes , with al Aul-

O deteſta ble im⸗ piety. ters , with maſſe , yea and with the bleſſed body of Chriſt in the Sacramente : which hath bene moſte vilanouſly defiled not onely by blaſphemous bokes and ſermons , but

The er⸗ ror agaiſt the reall preſence of Chriſt in the ſa⸗ cramẽt,is for any lavve made to the cõtra⸗ ry to be taken for hereſie as it vvas vvont to be. moſt wickedly taken from the aulter , and moſte horribly yea and that in our moſt famouſe Vniuerſity, conculced with the wicked feete of one of your Ghoſpellinge prea-chers ? And by what warrant , ye may ſette forth in your ſo ſcripturely viſitations this your hereticall doctrine a-gainſt the reall preſence of Chriſtes body in the Sacramẽt I knowe not . The playne and open wordes of ſcripture lye manifeſtly againſte yow with,*hoc eſt corpus meum:*Ge-nerall Councells haue determined againſte yow : Priuate councels, and amongs other our conſtitutions prouinciall, determine againſt yow : and remaine yet in force,euen by the lawes of the Realm,being by no Act of parliamẽt taken away . But contrary wiſe ſuche as vnreuerently ſpeake a-
gainſt

gainſt it, are by Acte of parliament adiudged to impriſon-
mēt,and to a fine to be made at the Princes pleaſure.Brief-
ly the faith of the whole Churche ſtādeth againſt you. Yea
M.Cheney one of your owne proteſtant Biſſhcps in open
parliament of late dayes ſtode againſt you.Your ſynodicall
and heretical articles,by the which ye would haue this,and
other hereſies confirmed,are reiected.Yea Luther him ſelf
full ſolemply proclaymeth you all heretiks.How can yt thē
be,that your and your fellowes viſitations,in the which ye
haue ſet forth ſuch a falſe doctrin repugnāt to al theſe,ſhalbe
yet called a ſcripturely viſitation?No,no M . Horne,for all
your pecocks tayle gliſtering with goodly and ſcripturely
talke,we perceyue your filthie hereſie wel inough , when
we loke vpon your fowle feete . Awaye , away with theſe
painted woordes,wherwith men wil not alwaies be made
fooles : nor will take your viſitations to be ſcripturely, as is
this , that ye here alleage, made by the bleſſed Apoſtles.
Which thing though I cā not,nor wil deny:yet yf I ſhould
take vpon me the euāgelical perſon of M.Iewel,or of your
Apoſtle Martin Luther,or your owne either,methinke the
Gētils might aſwel haue found fault with the Apoſtles decree made and ſet forth by them afterward in their viſitatiōs:
as your ſaid Apoſtle doth againſt the Councel of Trent and
others,or as ye doe againſt the bleſſed biſhop and Martyr
Bonifacius , for whome we haue alredy anſwered . They
might haue ſaid:ye reſtraine our Euangelicall liberty , and
yet ye bring not one woord of ſcripture to confirme your
decree withall . For though S.Iames brought forth a teſtimony out of the Prophet Amos, yet yt toucheth nothinge
the matter there concluded.   Then might they haue ſaid,
why Syrs, what meane you , will ye haue vs to be Iewiſhe

An.1 . Ed.
6.cap.1. &
An.1.Eli.
cap.1.

A man
may fynd
as good
matter aſ
gainſt the
decrees of
the Apo-
ſtles as Lu
ther ſyn-
deth aſ
gainſt the
generall
Coūcells,

againe, in forbearing of puddings and thinges ftrangled? Why doe ye forbidde vs to eate of fuch meates, as are of-fered to the idolles? We doe wel knowe, that they are no Goddes, and the meate is neuer a whit the worfe : and our Maifter Chrift hath taught vs, that it is not that, that entreth by the mouth, but that, that goeth from the mouth that cō-tamineth and defileth the man. This and much more out of the principles of Luthers ghofpell they might haue faide to the Apoftles: and as truely as Luther and your fellowes alleage thefe and the like thinges, againft the Lawes of the Churche, againft vnwriten verities, againft fafting daies, and otherwife. Or as ye alleage the like to deface our holy vertuoufe countremā Bonifacius and Auguftinus. But it is high tyme to breake of our fcripturely vifitatis, and to fet vpon other matters.

Prius fo.58

M. Horne. the . 158. Diuifion. pag .114. 4.

Touching the thirde part of your prouſe, vvhereby yee conclude, that bi∫= ∫hops and Priefts make Lavves, orders, and decrees, to their flocks and cures, becaufe the Apoftles ſo did, as you ſay: although I neede make none other anſvvere, then to deny your argumēt, vvhich you can by no arte (.6 4.) main-teyne, the inſufficiency vvhereof is manifeſt ; to thoſe that haue but a little ſkil, either in Logike or Diuinity: Yet I vvil briefly cōſider the places, vvher-vpon you grounde this miſhapen ſequele, that the vnſkilful may ſee, hovve little they make for your purpoſe . After that S. Paule had founded the Churche of Corinthe, and had brought them to Chriſt through the prea-chinge of the Ghofpell, there ſprange vp amongeſt them in his abſence many vices and offences, contrary to the Doctrine he had taught, and the Godly ad-monitions, that he had geuen vnto them: vvherefore being aduertiſed there-of, he vvrote his Epiſtle vnto that Churche, vvherein he reproueth their faultes, partely in general, and partely in ſpecial: And in the ende of the tenth Chapiter, concludeth vvith this Generall admonition, that All thigs be done without offence, and to the Glory of God . In the.xi. Chapiter, he reproueth certeine faultes in eſpecial, cōmitted by them in their

publique

The. 614.
Vntrutne.
The argu-
ment is
right
good, as it
hath in
the for-
mer diui-
fion ap-
peared.

publique aſſemblies, and Churche meetinges, contrary to this generall admonition, and contrary to that he had taught them in ſpeciall, touchinge their
honeſt and comely behauiour in their publique praier, preaching, and com-
municating in Chriſtes Sacramentes, vvhich of all other thinges ought chief=
ly to be ſo done, as thereby God may be glorified, and al offences eſchued. To
this ende S. Paule had taught the Corinthes, that in theſe publique and holy exerciſes, it is moſt ſeemely, that men prophecy and pray bare headed: Cō-
traryvviſe vvomen, not vvithout their heades couered. Many obſerued
this comelyneſſe in prayer and propheciyng, as Paule had taught them: O=
thers contentiouſly did vvithſtande and gaineſay the ſame, as an order that
Paule had deuiſed, and brought in of his ovvne deuiſe, beſides
Gods vvoorde, as you alſo (.615.) Imagine that Paule made
this order beſides the Goſpel, of his ovvne authority, vvherevvith
to binde the Corinthes. To aunſvvere both the contentious Phi-
loſophers, than amongeſt the Corinthes, and the ſuperſtitious Papiſtes, novve in (.616.) lyke ſorte moleſtinge the Chriſtians, S.
Paule proueth, that this comelynes is grounded vppon Gods or=
dinaunce, and not a Lavve nevvely deuiſed of his ovvne authoritie beſides the Goſpell. This is his proufe, the man by
Goddes ordinaunce hath the ſuperioritye, and the vvoman muſt
be in ſubiection. God hath appointed for them both, ſignes and
tokens of this dominion and ſubiection, He hath ordeyned, that
man in token of ſuperioritie, ſhoulde haue hi head vncouered:
as contraryvviſe the vvoman, in token of ſubiection, to haue her
head couered.

The. 615. vntruthe.
For M. Fekenham
ſaid not the matters
done at Corinthe
to haue bene done
beſide the Ghoſpel,
but the decrees of
the Apoſtles ſo to
haue bene done.

The. 616. vntruthe,
for neither the Co-
rinthes nor the Ca-
tholikes novv, obſ
iſted in like ſorte.

Therefore, if man laye avvay that ſigne and token of dominiō
vvhich God hath ordeined for him to vſe, and taketh vpon him the ſigne
and badge of ſubiection, he diſhonoureth God his head, and breaketh his ordinance. And ſo the vvomā if ſhee leaue of the couerture of her head vvhich
God had geuen to her, to be vvorne as a token and badge of her ſubiection,
and taketh vpon her the ſigne of ſuperiority, ſhe diſhonoreth her head, and
breaketh Gods ordinaūce. S. Paule addeth an other reaſon, vvherby he pro=
ueth, that this vvas no Lavv made by him to the Corinthes. Nature, ſaith he,
hath taught you this comely order. If this vvere a Lavve and Decree of nature, it vvas not S. Paules deuiſe beſides Gods vvoorde. S. Ambroſe vppon
this

The.617. vntruthe.
S. Ambrofe faith
not: of Gods lavve:
but *fecundum legem*,
according to the
lavve: and he mea-
neth the old law Le
uit.19. not the lavv
of the Gofpell.
The.618. vntruthe.
It vvas S.Paules
lavv, though Gods
lavve alfo, as fhall
appeare.

The.619.vntruthe.
If you meane the
vvriten gofpel, as
you feme to doe,
ãd as you muft do,
if you reafon vvel.

The. 620.
vntruthe.
For they
are bothe
Gods or-
dinaunces
and S.
Paules to,
as fhal ap-
peare.

this place faith,that S.Paule fpake thefe woordes,accor-
ding to (.617.)Gods Lawe,which forbiddeth(*faith he*)
the man to weare his heare.Chryfoftome *affirmeth this
to be an ordinaunce of nature.*But,faith he,whan I fpeake of
nature,I meane of God,who is the authour of nature.
*So that it is manifeft by S.Paules ovvn proufes in defence of that
he had taught,and by the vvitneſſe of S.Ambrofe and Chryfoftom,
that the man to be bareheaded,and the vvoman couered, vvas
(.618.)not a Lavve,order and decree, made by S. Paule to the
Corinthes,as you vntruly fable,but Gods ordinaunce,made plain,
fet forth,and taught by him,that all thinges might be don in the
Churche in comely order,to Gods glory.Of like forte vvas the reformation and order.vvhereof you fpeake about the more vvorthy
receiuing the Lordes Supper. The Apoftle maketh thereaboute no
nevve Lavve,order,or decree,befides (.619.)the Ghofpell,but reproueth the Corinthians, for that they did not about the receipte
thereof,obferue the lavve of the Gofpell : He blameth them in general,that their Churche aſſemblies vvere not to the encreafe,but
rather to the decreafe of vertue in thē felues: He reproueth thē that in ſtead of
brothlery loue,vnity,and concorde,there vvas Contempte,Schifme,and dif-
fenſion amongeſt them : He rebuketh them ,for that they made that Supper
Priuate,vvhich the Lorde him felfe had made,and inſtituted to be commō:
He reprehendeth them for Drunkenneſſe,and that vvith the contempte of the
poore: And he fharpely fhaketh them vp,for that they abufe the Church,con-
temning the right vfe thereof. Is not this Chriſtes Lavve , that the people
fhould encreafe in vertue ? Is not this Chriſtes commaundement , that the
Chriſtians fhould liue in brotherly loue , vnitye , and concorde ? Is not this
Chriſtes Inſtitution,that his Supper fhould be cōmon,and not Pryuat?Doth
not Chriſtes lavv condēne Drunkerdes,and contempte of the poore? And is not
this Gods decree, that his houfe fhould not be prophaned or abufed ? If thefe
be Gods ordinances,as you can not deny them to be,than are they (.620.)not
Paules lavves,orders,or decrees,neither by vvriting or vvorde of mouthe:
othervvife than that Paule vvas Gods mouth and fcribe, to vtter , not his
ovvne lavves befides the Ghofpell, but Gods ordinaunces comprehended
vvithin his Ghofpell . So that vvhether being prefente, he taught them by
vvorde,*

*vvorde, or being abfent by vvriting, he neither vvritte nor fpake, other then he had * receiued of the Lord. He promifed, fay you, to difpofe other things at his comming. It is true, but not othervvife then he did thefe aboue mentioned. He exhorteth, fay you, the Theffalonias, to abide in the traditions, vvhich they had learned by vvoorde or by vvriting. Yee fay truth : but he dothe not therby binde them to this, as to a lavve, order, or decree, made by him, befides the Ghofpell : but hee montfheth them, as S. Ambrofe expoundeth his meaning, To ftand faft, continue, and perfeuere in the tradition of the Gofpell. So that the traditions he fpeaketh of, are not other then the Doctrine of the (.621.) Ghofpel.*

I maruaile not, that ye (.622.) mifreporte Sainte Paule, faying that he made orders and decrees, touching praying and preaching vnto the people in tongues vnknovven, and that all vvemen fhould keepe filence in the Churche and congregation, for it may feeme, yee neuer readde the place, but tooke it, as you heard it reported. If you had readde the place, you might haue feene vvith your ovrne eyes, that S. Paule fpeaketh no vvhitte of that matter in the thirteenth, as yee vntruely auouche: and in the fourtenth you fhould haue perceiued, that he in plaine fpeach proueth you a lyar: For that he (.623.) denieth that thefe vvere his orders or decrees, affirming them to be the Lords commaundementes. and fo dothe Theophilact. Glofs. ordinar. and Lyra vvitneffe alfo vvith Paule, teftifying that thefe vvere his vvords and meaning. Thefe places thus rightly confidered, it may eafilie appeare vnto the mofte vnfkilful, hovv litle (.624.) your purpofe is holpen by them, and that thefe groundes doe faile you : So that your vvhole fhift being fifted, is founde naughie, bothe in matter and fourme.

M. Horne.

Three other places remaine of M.Fekenhās allegatiō.The firft, but the.3.in order, that men fhould pray and prophecy

(that

2. Thef. 2.
Concer-
ning cer-
taine de-
crees and
orders
made by
S. Paule
alleaged
by M. Fe
kenham.

(that is, preache or expounde fcripture) theire heades vncouered: and that the womē fhould pray with their heades
couered. The fecond is of fuch orders as the Apoſtle Paule
ordeyned touching the holy Sacrament of the Euchariſtia.
The thirde, that he ordeined manie thinges afwell by writing, as withowt writing, and in all this feaking for no cō-
miſsion at any lay mans hand. To the two firſt M. Horne
faieth, that they were no lawes of Paules made by his authority befides the ghofpel to binde the Corinthians as M.
Fekēham imagineth, but they were Gods own ordinaūce.
For God had fo ordeined to fignifie the fuperiority in the
man and fubiection in the woman: and yt was the very law
of nature. And for the .2. point he did ordein no new thing,
but did fet forth onely Gods owne lawes: and that is, that
his fupper fhould be common, and not priuate. In condemning alfo according to Gods lawe drunckerds, and the cō-
tempte of the poore and fuch as againſt Gods decree prophaned or abufed his houfe. And S. Paule him felf denieth,
that theis were his orders or decrees, but faieth they were
the Lords commaundements. And to the thirde he faieth,
that whether S. Paule taught by writing or by worde, he
taught nothing, but that he receiued of the Lorde: neither
for any promife he made to difpofe things at his comming,
did he difpofe any thing otherwife then he receiuid of the
Lorde. For al this your folemne anfwere, ye haue foluted
M. Fekenhams argumente neuer a whit: which doth not
contende in this place, whether this ordinaunce may be
called properly Paules or Gods ordināce, or whether they
were befide the ghofpel or no, or what kinde of traditions
they were that Paule taught. The argumēt reſteth in this,
that theis lawes, orders, and decrees, were fet forth, publifhed

lifhed and diuulged,yea put in execution by vifitatiõs, and
otherwife without any warrãt of ciuil price. Neither doth
M.Fekenhã fay,that theis ordinaunces were made *befides
the ghofpel,and deliuered to the Corinthians*,as ye fay *he imagineth*.Your felf M.Horne doe but dreame this : for thofe
words of M.Fekenhã,*of decrees made befide the gofpel* are re
ferred to the lawes made by the Apoftles in their fynod,
not to the orders apointed to the Corinthiãs. And to thofe
decrees of the Apoftles you haue anfwered neuer a word,
but with a fhorte vntrue anfwere,of a fcripturelike and an
vnfcripturelyke vifitation,and a longe bible bable againfte
the order of fuch vifitation as the Catholik Church vfeth,
you haue trained your Reader with idle talke, nothing to
the purpofe.By a like craft ye make yt the thirde pointe in
M.Fekenham that,which he fpeaketh of lawes and orders
made by the Apoftles, where yt was his fecond allegation
as yet by you vnanfwered,but altogether vnder the vifour
of a fcripturely vifitation,diffembled.For there ye fawe ful
wel ye were fo mette withall,and fo ftrained, that ye had
no fterting hole, vnleffe ye.woulde fay , that yt was Gods
lawe in the newe teftament,that Chriftian mẽ fhould eate
neither puddigs,nor any thing ftrãgled: which ye thought
belike to be a great incõuenience, andtherfore ful clofely,
and in greate huckermucker,ye paffed yt ouer.   And yet
might ye haue frefhely reafonedthe matter therto, yf your
ftomacke would haue ferued you with telling vs:*vifum eft
fpiritui fancto & nobis* Ir femeth to the holy Ghoft and to
vs.And is not this Gods lawe thẽ alfo good M.Horne?This
geare I perceiue your weake ftomacke could not wel di-
geft.For yf yt could,and you withal could digeft orderlie,
plainely,and truely any good anfweare , ye fhould haue at

length

M.Horne
being not
able to
anfvvere
M.Fckẽ
hãs 2.al-
legation,
diffem-
bleth it
altoge-
ther.

length anſwered your ſelfe:and ſhoulde haue founde yt as
true,that the ordináces cócerning the head couered or vncouered,and cócerning the bleſſed Sacramẽt,be ãd may as
wel be called the ordináces or cómaundemẽts of S.Paule,
as the other are called *præcepta Apoſtolorũ*: the cómaundemẽts of the Apoſtles.And what ſhould we reaſon longe in
this matter,ſeing that S.Paule him ſelfe calleth theis *præce-*
pta mea my precepts,or cómaundements? And *ſicut tradidi*
vobis as I haue deliuered vnto you?And doth not S. Paule
ſay plainely, that *he.ordayned to the Churches of Galatia Col-*
lets or gatheringes of Almes *to be made euery Sonday?* And
ſaieth he not of him ſelfe,that *he gaue precepts to the Theſſa-*
lonians?Which yet he writeth not in his epiſtles,but referreth thẽ to their former knowledge of deliuered doctrine
by word of mouthe. Otherwiſe yf ye wil ſo preciſely vrge
the matter,we muſt now no lóger cal the old law,the law
of Moſes:we muſt no lóger name the prophecies of Hieremie,Ezechiel,or Daniel:no more the ghoſpel of S.Math.S.
Luke,S.Mark,or S. Iohn.we muſt no lóger ſay,*the ſword of*
*God and of Gedeõ:*nor *the people beliued God and his ſeruante*
*Moſes.*But, God be thãked,theſe things wil ſtande together
wel inough with a good cóſtructió,and by a diuers relatió.
Neither are they more cótrary,thẽ whẽ Chriſt ſaid : *my do-*
ctrine,is not my doctrine: *but my Fathers that ſent me.*Yf we
cóſider the pricipal author of theſe lawes,thẽ are thei Gods
ordináces,ãd not Pauls or the Apoſtles:by whoſe graciouſe
inſpiratió ãd ſuggeſtió they wer made.S.Paule ãd the Apoſtles were but miniſters: ãd in that reſpect they may be called their lawes:euen as the miniſters by their miniſtery do
truly forgeue and remitte ſinne. We muſt yet further cóſider here two things.The firſt,that ſome lawes there be of
the Churche,that are properly called Gods lawes:as theſe

that

Act.15.&
16.

1.Cor. 11.

1.Cor.16.
1.Theſſ.4
Scitis quæ
præcepta
dederim
vobis.

Iudic.7.
gladius
domini &
Gedeonis.
Credide-
rũt domi-
no,et ſer-
uo eius
Moſi.
Ioan.7.

A diſtin-
ctió to be
noted, of
God his
lavves,
and the
Churches
lavves.

that the Apoſtles ſet forth in holy ſcripture, which Chriſt e
him ſelfe taught thē:as concerning baptiſme, the holy Euchariſtia,and ſome other thinges . Some other lawes there
are that the Apoſtles ſet forth,but not ſuche as they receiued atChriſtes own hāds,and by his mouth,but by his holy
ſpirite after his aſcenſion : whiche are for that cauſe called
Chriſtes ād Gods lawes:as for that the Apoſtles had al their
authority to make ſuche lawes of him,they are called alſo
the lawes of the Apoſtles.Namely theſe that were made in
the firſt coūcel at Hieruſalē,the which M . Fekenhā alleageth for his purpoſe. And betwixt theſe two,ther is a great
differēce.For Chriſt gaue by him ſelfe fewe precepts , and
and of thoſe matters onely that were neceſſary for our ſal-
natiō:And therfore they may by no humaine authority be
infrīged or aboliſhed.But the precepts of the Apoſtles touching the gouernaūce of the Churche, though no man cā
by priuate authority breake thē,yet may they,and are,ma-
ny of thē,by the authority of the Church aboliſhed. Namely ſuch as were made for certain and ſpecial reſpectes,and
not to cōtinewe for euer but for a time. As was the decree
of the Apoſtles made at Hieruſalem touching the eating of
puddinges and thinges ſtrangeled.   So we ſee the Sabboth
day turned into the ſonday.So we ſee, that though Chriſt
celebrated his holy maundy of the bleſſed Euchariſtia at
night and gaue yt to his diſciples after ſupper , and in both
kindes,yet the Church vſeth it faſting,and for lay mē vnder
one kinde.For thoughe Chriſte cōmaunded vs to receiue,
which no man can diſpenſe withall , yet *for the maner and*
faſhion(ſaieth S.Auguſtin)*he cōmaūded nothing,but reſerued*
that honour to the Apoſtles,by who he intēded to directe the
*Churches.*Who therfore alſo toke order for yt,eſpecially S.

gggg iij   Paule

(marginal notes:) A differē/ce be/tvvene the Apo/ſtles ordi/nances, and thoſe that pro/perly are called Gods or-dinances.

Auguſt. 118.ad Ia-nuar.Et ideo non præcepit quo dein-ceps ordi= nē ſume-retur,vt Apoſtolis per quos Eccleſias diſpoſitu-rus erat, ſeruaret hunc ho-norem.

Ibidem. Vnde intel ligi datur (quia multū erat, vt in epiſtola to tum illum agendi or dinē inſinuaret, quē vniuerſa per orbem ſeruat Eccleſia) ab ipſo ordinatum eſſe, quod nulla morum diuerſitate variatur.

M Feken ham ſpea keth of one thig, and M H reaſoneth agaiſt an other thing.

Paule among the Corinthians according as he promiſed. *I wil diſpoſe other things when I come.* Which is the place M. Fekenham groundeth him ſelf vpō againſt you. And thereupon S. Auguſtine thinketh, *that whiche is vniformely and generally vſed throughout Chriſtendome, touching the order in the adminiſtration of this Sacrament, to haue ben ordeined by S. Paule, which he could not ſo conueniently preſcribe and appoint in his Epiſtle.* So that ye ſee, that though it be true, theſe orders and lawes may be called Gods ordināces and lawes, yet they are and may alſo well be called, the lawes and ordinaunces of the Apoſtles. And thus M. Fekenhams Argument ſtandeth as before, in his ful force euery way. And all your talke concerning the Lords ſupper, is quite from the purpoſe. You tell vs, that all was Gods Law that S. Paule appointed in the ſaide Epiſtle to the Corinthians. Which if it were ſo, yet ye reaſon not againſt M. Fekenham, who ſpeaketh not of thoſe things that he tooke order for in his Epiſtle, but of thoſe things that he toke order for at his comming. Whereof he ſaid : *Cætera cùm venero, diſponam.* Other things I wil ſet in order when I come. Which as they were done without writing (as many things alſo that he deliuered by tradition to the Theſſalonians, as M. Fekenham rehearſeth out of S. Paule) ſo were they done againſt your fond concluſion, that is, without any other warrant of any lay perſons. Neither is the ordinaunce of praying and preaching, the head vncouered, proprely Gods law: for then had it bene indiſpenſable : And then had you and your fellowes, that preache with your cappe on your heades, nede to thinke vpon ſome good anſweare, for the violating of Gods Law. And wemen come to the Church to be maried with their heads open, whiche might not be ſuffred,

fuffred, if it were directly againſt Gods law. And though
S Paul geueth this reaſon of ſuperioritie, and ſubection, becauſe (as it ſeemeth) it was a cuſtome or maner proper to
the Iewes , yet both among the Romaines and other Gentils, in S. Paules time, and alſo throughout al Chriſtendome
at this daie, the opening and diſcouering of the heade, is a
token of ſubiection , and of duetifull honour to our Magiſtrates and other Superiours.

Wherefore, if we conſider the Scripture well , we ſhall
finde, that S. Paule and the Apoſtles gaue many precepts in
their Epiſtles, of which in the written Goſpell , nothing is
mentioned or ordeined. And ſo your Lutheran Concluſion wil appeare ſtarke falſe and dangerouſe, where you ſay:
That Paul gaue not his owne lawes beſide the Ghoſpel, but Gods
ordinaunces comprehended within his Ghoſpell. And againe,
That Paule whether being preſent, he taught them by worde,
or being abſent, by writing, he neither wrote nor ſpake other
then he had receiued of the Lorde. And laſt of al, *So that the*
traditions that Paule ſpeaketh of, are not other then the Doc-
trine of the Ghoſpell. This is, M. Horne (as I ſaid) a Lutheran
and a dangerous concluſion. For by this rule you woulde
fruſtrate al the lawes of the Church (as Luther your Grád-
ſir did) which are not expreſſely comprehended in the wriǂ
ten Ghoſpell.   For this beeing put, that the very Apoſtles
made no lawes or ordinaũces, but ſuch as they foũd before
recorded in the Goſpel, then (ſay you) by what authoritie
can the Prelates of the Churche at any time hereafter take
vpon them to make ſuch lawes, as are not expreſſed in the
Goſpel? To mete therfore with this wicked ſequele, ãd to
detect your lewd cõcluſion, I wil ſhortly touch a few moe
exãples of ſuch lawes and ordinaunces as th'Apoſtles made
and

Vide Hep-
tacolõ.L.
Campeſtri
cõtra Lu-
ther. Apo=
logiam.
An. 1523.

and not recorded, made, or ordeined otherwise in the Gof-
1.Cor.5. pel. Firſt, S. Paule to the Corinthes, forbiddeth them to eate
with drockards, with robbers, with fornicatours , with the
couetous, ād with idolators. In the Gofpel no ſuch reſtrait
appereth. Nay rather we ſee there Chriſt him ſelf, did eate
Lu.5.&.7 with publicans and ſinners. Again to the Galathiās he cry-
eth out: *Behold I Paul ſay vnto you: If ye be circūcided, Chriſt*
Gal 5. *profiteth you nothing.* What Gofpel teacheth Paul ſo to ſay ?
What Gofpel doth cōdemne circūcifion? Nay rather, ſaith
Mat.5. not Chriſt in the Gofpel, *I came not to vndoe the lawe, but to*
Philip.3. *fulfil it?* And yet not here only, but to the Philippéſes moſt
Coloſſ.2. earneſtly he chargeth them to caſt of the yoke of the law.
1.Tim.3. The like he doth to the Coloſsiās, teaching thē to make no
Tit.2. more accōpt of their *Neomeniæ* and *Sabbata.* Nowe for the
precept that S. Paul geueth to Timothe, *that a Biſhop ſhould*
be the man of one wife: What Gofpel preſcribeth it, or com-
maūdeth it ? To Titus alſo, the lawes that he geueth to yóg
wemen, to widowes, ād to old wemē? Are not al theſe and
many more (which for breuities ſake I omit) mere cōſtituti-
ons and lawes of th'Apoſtls, without any word made therof in the Gofpel ? And what els intēded Chriſt, I pray you,
M. Horne , when he ſaied to his Apoſtles a litle before his
Ioan.16. Paſsion, *I haue many things yet to ſay vnto you: but you are not*
&.14. *able to beare them now. Howbeit when the Spirit of Truth ſhall*
come, he will teache you all Trueth, then that by the ſpirite of
Truth, the holy Ghoſt, they ſhould learne and teache many
Truthes, which in the Ghoſpell (where onely the doctrine
and doings of Chriſt are recorded) they had not learned?
And this holy Spirit he promiſed ſhould remaine not with
them only for their abode here in earth, but with the Chur
che for euer.

To

To gene vs to vnderstand, that as they, so their Successours in the Churche from tyme to tyme should be taught of the holy ghost, and teache vs againe al maner of Truthe. Wherof vnuincibly foloweth, not only that they taught and doe teache many moe things then Christ in the ghospel taught, but also that those their doctrines and teachinges (as proceding from the holy Ghost the Spirit of Truth) are infallible, found and right holsome, and of vs therefore vndoubtedly to be obeyed and beleued. Wherby is ouerthrowe M. Horn your most damnable and wicked conclusion, affirming the Apostles to haue made no lawes of their own besides the ghospel, but only such as were Gods ordinaunces comprehended in the ghospel. For nowe we see both by exaples of their doings, and by vnuicible reason out of the ghospel, that they made lawes of their own besides the ghospel, ad might both lawfully and assuredly so do, they being alwaies propted of the holy Ghost therein, and their lawes therfore being not theirs only, but bearing also the force and value of Gods lawes, so farre, as is before declared. Farder by this it appereth, that as the Apostles the, so their successours now and alwaies heretofore had and haue full and sufficient authority to make ecclesiasticall lawes or decrees ouer al their flocks from Christ himself without any iote of Commissio fro the laye Prince, or any other lay Magistrat. And so your principall conclusion goeth ones again flatte down to the grounde.

The.169.Diuision. pag.116.b.
M.Fekenham.

The which noble Emperour Constantinus, for the repression of the Arians errours and heresies, he did at the request of Syluester then Bishop of Rome, cal the firste

b b b b   Councel

Councell at Nice: where he had, to the Bißhops there af-
fembled thefe woordes: Cùm vos Deus Sacerdotes confti-
tuerit, poteftatem tradidit iudicandi de nobis. Et ideo nos à
vobis rectè iudicamur. Vos autem, cùm nobis à Deo, dij dati fitis, ab hominibus iudicari non poteftis. &c. Valētinianus
Imperator cùm ille rogatus effet ab Epifcopis Hellefponti
Bythiniæ, vt intereffet confilio, refpondit : Mihi quidem
cùm vnus de populo fim, fas non eft talia perfcrutari, verum
facerdotes quibus hæc cura eft, apud femetipfos congregen-
tur, vbi voluerit. Theodofio Imperatori Ambrofius ingref-
fu intra cancellos templi interdixit, inquies: Interiora ô Imperator facerdotibus folis patent. &c. Cui egit ob id gratias
Imperator, afferens fe didiciffe difcrimen inter Imperatorem & Sacerdotem.

Libro. 10.
Hiſt. Eccl.
cap . 2.

Lib. 7, hiſt.
Trip. ca. 12

Theod. li.
5. hiſt. Ec-
clef. ca. 18.

M. Horne.

It is manifeſt, that Conſtantin called the firſt Nicene Councel,
but very vnlikely, that he did it at the requeſt of Syluefter, be-
cauſe this Council vvas (. 625.) not in the time of Syluefter, but
vvhiles Iulius *vvas bifshop of Rome, vvho by reaſon of his great*
age could not be there preſent in his ovvne perſon, and therfore ſent
in his ſtede Vitus *and* Vincentius, *as the Eccleſiaſtical hiſto-*
ries report, and Epiphanius *affirmeth, that Conſtantine called*
this Councel at the earneſt ſute of Alexander *Bifshop of Alex-*
andria, vvhereto Ruffinus *addeth, many other of the Cleargy*
alſo. But if it be true as ye ſay, that theperour called the Councel at
the requeſt of the Pope, than both thoſe Papiſtes are (626) Liars,
vvhich affirme that the Pope called this Councel, and your cauſe
by your ovvn confeſsion is much hindred: for if the Emperour cal-
led the Councel, and that at the requeſt of Syluefter the Pope, as
yee ſay; or at the earneſt ſuite of Alexander, *and other godlye*
Bifshops, as Epiphanius *and* Ruffinus *affirme : It appeareth*
plainly, that both the Pope and the other Catholik Biſhops, did
therby acknovvledge the (. 627.) ſupreame povver and authorities
to ſome

The. 625. vntruthe.
It vvas in the time
of Syluefter, as ſhal
appeare.
Nicep. lib. 8. ca. 14.
Sozom. lib. 1. ca. 17.
Lib. 2. to. 2, He. 68.
Lib. 1. cap. 1.

The. 626. vntruthe
ſlaunderous . For
both ſtad vvel to-
gether, as ſhall ap-
peare.

The. 627. vntruthe.
As it ſhall appeare
out of Cuſanus M.
Hornes ovvn Au-
thor.

to ſommon and cal Councels, vvhich is a (.628.) principal parte of your purpoſe, and of the Eccleſiaſtical iuriſdiction cohibitiue, to be in themperour, and not in them ſelues: for othervviſe they might, ãd vvould haue don it, by vertue of their ovvn office, vvithout any ſuit made to the Emperour, to execute that vvhich belonged vnto them ſelues. Ihemperour refuſed to iudge the quarreling accuſations of the biſhops aſſembled at the Nicen Councel, one quarreling and accuſing an other, and referred the iudgement of them to Chriſt, This vvas his modeſty, Policy, and prudent foreſight, leaſt by ſifting thoſe priuat quarrels, he might haue hindred the common cauſe, as I haue ſaid before, and is plainly to be (.629.) gathered of Ruffinus and Nicephorus, and (.630.) not for that he thought his authority might not ſtretche ſo farre, as to iudge the Prieſts and their matters, as ye vvould haue it to ſeme: for as he him ſelf proteſteth, this aboue all other things, to be the chief ſcope and ende of his Emperial authority, namely that the Catholik Church be preſerued in vnity of faith, ſincerity of loue, cõcord in godly Religiõ, and that the diſeaſes therein, as Schiſmes, Hereſies, &c. might be healed by his miniſtery: euen ſo forſoke he no occaſion or meane, vvhereby to vvork forth this effect of his miniſtery and office, vvhether it vvere at ſome tyme by relenting and remitting ſomvvhat of his autority, or by exerciſing the ſame to the vtmoſt, in al matters, and ouer al perſones. He thought it the beſt for this tyme by (.631.) relenting to beare vvith the vveakenes of thoſe fathers, thereby the better to encourage thẽ to ſtãd faſt, and ioyntly againſt the cõmon enemy, for the furtherance of the truth. But aftervvad, vvhan the Coũcel or Synod vvas aſſembled at Tyre by his cõmaũdemet, ãd that Athanaſius had made cõplaint vnto him, of the vniuſt dealing of that councel to deface the truth, themperour did exerciſe the ful authority of his miniſtery, and called al the Biſhops vnto hĩ, to this end, that he by his (.632.) ſupreme authority, might examine their doĩgs, ãd iudge of the vvhole Coũcel, vvhether thei had iudged vprightly, ãd dealt ſincerely, or not. This he did at the ſuite of the moſt godly biſhop Athanaſi⁹, vvho vvold not haue attributed this (.633.) authority to the Emperour, if it had not apperteined to his iuriſdiction

bbbb ij   *to haue*

The.628.vntruthe. It is no part of eccleſiaſtical Iuriſdiſtion, as the Emperour doth it.

The.629.vntruthe. No ſuch thing can be gathered of thoſe Authours. The.630. vntruthe. For if he thought not ſo, as he ſaied, it vvas no Policy, but a ſinne. Lib.1.cap.2. Lib.8.cap.16. Euſeb. lib.3. De vita Conſtant.

The.631.vntruthe. He relented nothig but ſhevved his due Reuerence.

Sozom.lib.1.cap.4. The 632.vutruthe. Facing, as hath before ben ſhevved in the.2.booke cap.3. The.633 vntruthe. Athanaſius attributed no ſuch Authority, to the Emperour, but of all mẽ, denied it moſt vnto him. See before.fol.94. and ſo forth.

to haue iudged the bishops and their doinges: neither vvould the Catholique Fathers of that tyme, haue suffered this and many other such like doinges of this most Christiā Emperour, to haue passed vvithout some admonition or misliking, if they had not acknovvledged the authority in him to be lavvful. He commaunded the Bishops euery vvhere, to asseble at his appointmēt, vvher, and vvhā he vvould. He sharply reproueth Alexāder Bishop of Alexādria, and Arius, for the contention stirred vp by them. He (634) iudged Cecilianus Bishop of Carthage, to be lavvfully cōsecrated, and ordered, and condemned the Donatistes . And these Bishoppes assembled at the Nicen Councell by his commaundement, of vvhom ye speake, acknovvledged the Emperour to haue authority to iudge them and their causes, (.635.) or els they had doone folishly, to offer their billes of complaint vnto him , vvhome they thought had no authority or might not iudge and determine thē. But in case it vvere true, that the Prince might not iudge the Priestes nor their causes, vvhat conclude you thereof? You can not conclude your purpose, for this is no more a good consequent: Constantinus vvould nor could lavvfully iudge the Priestes assembled at Nicen Councel: Ergo, (.636.) Bishoppes and Priests may cal councels, make Lavves, orders, and decrees, to their flocke and cures, and exercise al maner iurisdiction cohibitiue, Then this, Yorke standeth but .iij. myles from Pocklington, Ergo, your pocket is ful of plummes.

The .634. vntruthe. The Pope and the Bishoppes Iudged it, not the' mperor, but vvith their leaue. See before Fol, 92.

The .635. vntruthe. this or els, foloweth not. Many are som tymes called to iudge betvvene parties, vvho yet haue no Authoritye ouer the parties.

The .636. vntruthe. This Erg, is your ovvne, not M . Fes kenhams.

The .10. Chapter. Conteyning a defence of three exāples brought forth by M. Fekenham, touching three Emperours, Constantin the greate, Valentian the first, and Theodosius the firste.

Stapleton.

Although that, which M. Fekēhā hath alredy layd forth out of holy scripture, be sufficiēt to shew ād proue, that the superiority in al causes ecclesiastical, doth not rest in laye

in laye princes, but in the spiritual rulers, yet will he nowe
adde and adioyne therunto, such a forcible argument, that
shall beate downe to the ground M. Hornes newe Laicall
supremacy. M. Horne with al his witte and cunning goeth
about to auaunce his new supremacy, and to depresse and
abolish the other, as contrary to scriptures, and iniuriouse
to the Emperours, and princes. Nowe to stoppe his lyinge
mouth M. Fekenham bringeth forth thre of the worthiest
Emperours that euer were, and al thre lyuing when Christian religion most florished, that by plaine wordes confesse
the cleargies superiority in this behalf: that is, Constantine
the great, Valentinian the first, and Theodosius the great.
This Constantine at the request of Siluester the pope called
the first general councell, at Nice, where diuerse bisshops
being at contention for certain matters, offered their complaints to him. To whom Constantine answered, *that where
as God had made them priests, he had geuen them authority to
iudge ouer him. And therefore they might well be his iudges.
But ye* (sayth he) *may be iudged of no man.* Good Lorde, how
farre discrepant is the iudgment of this our noble contry mã
(as our Chroniclers cal him) and most worthy Emperour
from the iudgement of M. Horn and his felowes? He dis-
claimeth flatly this newe superiority: Yet you nowe after
one thousand and almost thre hũdred yeares, by preaching
and writing, yea by premunire, and the sword do maintaine
the same. This answere presseth M. Horne very sore, and
therefore, he seketh euery corner to hide his head in, and
yet he can fynd no good or quiet resting place. And firste
he would fain take some holde in a by matter, which is, that
Constantin did not cal the councel at Siluester his request:
because the councell was not in the tyme of Siluester, but

(marginal notes:) Constantine acknowledgeth the cleargies superiority.

Ex. Ruff. lib. 10. eccles. hist. cap. 2.

hh hh iij   of Iu-

of Iulius. I deny your argument M. Horne. For it muſt neades be, that the biſhops, reparing to Nice frō al quarters of
Chriſtendome, ſhould haue a conuenient time to come thither: And Nicephorus writeth, that the ſame Councel dured three yeares and more. And then may it wel ſtand, that
Syluſter died either after the ſummoning, and before the
full aſſemble of the biſhops, or at leaſt before the end, that
ſo ſome part of it might falle in the time of Iulius, notwithſtanding that Marcus came betwene, who ſate in the See
litle more then two yeres. Neither doth your authours by
yowe cited, deny that it was called at Syluſters requeſte,
nor any other of the auncièt writers, that euer I read. But I
ſay further vnto you, that as Conſtantine did cal it at his requeſt, ſo did he him ſelf cal this councell: the one by his ſpiritual, the other by his tēporal authority: which in all good
princes tyme, doth euer ſerue the other. The one (as your
own Author Cuſanus teacheth) by force of Authority and
cōmaundement ouer al biſhops, ouer whom he is the head:
The other by way of exhortation, of temporall ayde and
ſuccour, as I haue before at large recited his wordes. But to
leaue Cuſanus, for proufe that Syluſter called this
Councel, I am able to bring againſt you, at the leaſt
two or rather thre hundred witneſſes, ād the worſt
of them ſhall be a biſhop, and ſo aūcient withal, that
none of thē liued this. 800. yeres. Perchaūce ye thīk
that I do but ieſt with you: No truely M. Horne, I
meane plaine fayth, without any figure of rhetorike, or ſuch lying figures as ye are wel acquainted
withal. Herken you thē, what the ſixt general coūcel (wher were preſent about. 300. biſhops) ſaith to
theire Emperour Conſtantine beinge then preſent
there.

Li. 8. c. 26.

Li. 3. c. 15.

Vide fo. 118

Synodus ſexta ī ſer-
mone acclamatorio
ad Imperatorem.
Act. 18. fo. 403. co. 1.
Arrius diuiſor atque
partitor Trinitatis
inſurgebat, & conti-
nuò Cōſtantinus ſem
per Auguſtus, & Sil
ueſter laudabilis, ma
gnam atque inſignē
in Nicæa Synodum
congregabant.

there. *Arrius* (say they) *which diuided, and sundred the Trinity, arose and by and by themperor Constantine and the prayse worthy Syluester, did assemble at Nice a great and a notable Synod.* See M. Horn. Where ye wil not suffer M. Fekenhã, saying Constantine called the councel at the request of Syluester, ye must nowe be content to suffer him, whẽ he telleth you, that he did cal it him self also. Beside the vndoubted testimony of these so many and Auncient Fathers, we haue the witnesse of Chroniclers, as of Eusebiꝰ, Damasus, Isidorus, Photius, Platina, Regino, Pantaleon, and diuers other. And so withal is your secõd shift, shifted away: wherby'ye would make your reader beiue, that the pope ãd the other bishops did acknowledg Cõstantins supremacy, in calling of Coũcels, being as ye say, the principal part of iurisdictiõ Ecclesiastical cohibitiue. For as this is vntrue, that the bare calling of a councel is any such principal part, as we haue before declared: so it is vntrue also, that ye say, that the pope called not this councell. Theis strings being very weake, and therefore sone broken as ye see, he setteth out the thirde, and that is weakest and wurst of al. And all this stringe hangeth vppon a foolishe synnefull ciuylity and policy, that Maister Horne imagineth full fondly in this worthy prince Constantine. As thowghe he spake those wordes, for his *modesty* onely, and for *a policie* and *a prudent forsighte: least by siftinge those priuate quarells, he mighte haue hindred the common cause: and not for that he thoughte his authority mighte not stretche so farre as to iudge the priests. And therefore thoughe he politykely relented at this time, yet afterwarde at the councel at Tyrus he shewed hym selfe as supreame Iudge in causes Ecclesiasticall.*

It is

Eusebius. in Chron.
Damas. in Pontif. Isidorus tom. 1. Cõcil. in
præfat. Nic. Cõc. Platina in Siluestro. Rheg̃ino in Chron. Pantaleõ in Chronograph.
Photius Patriarch.
Cõst. de 7. Conc.
Oecum. ad Michaelẽ Bulg. Principem.

Vide fol. 118. lib. 1.

Maledi-
cta glosa
quæ de-
ftruit tex-
tum,

It is wont to be fayed M. Horne , curfed is that glofe that deftroyeth the text. Suerly ye are very imprudently ouer-fene in this your anfwere? For all this is but a peuifhe and a wretched policy:wherewith you difhonour this noble mo-narch. And ye haue forgotten the rules afwell of diuinity as of policy. For as it is policy , fomtyme to diffemble a truth, fo to tel an vntruthe,is at all time a fynne , yea though the truth be offenfiue to no man , but officiable and profitable to many. As S. Auguftin doth at large difcourfe the matter.

Aug. ad
Confentiū
de mãda-
tio Tom. 4

Now if the Emperour be the prieftsiudge:then doth Con-ftantins faying conteyne a plaine lye. Seing that before he expreffely confeffed them *to be his Iudges*, and fayd farder, *that they coulde be iudged of no man* . We leaue this politie therfore and prudent forfight, to your generatiõ, as vnmete either for Conftantine, or for any other a much meaner ca-

The po-
licy of
our newe
euangeli-
cal fchole

tholyke man. This kynd of policy a man may fynd in great ftore in M. Iewels Reply, and in this your anfwere . This is the very practife of your newe Euangelicall fchole . You feme to be perfuaded, to make no accompt of lying, fo that your lewde caufe may be furdered . But thoughe you be naught your felues, you muft not fo iudge of others. Verely Conftantin fpake as he thought and the very truth. And he confeffed as plainely, *that they were his iudges*: As you fawe before in his own wordes. For he fayd to the bifhops plain-ly. *That they could be iudged of no man.* Neither is it to be ga-

Ruffinus.
li. 1. ca. 2.
Nice. li. 8.
cap. 16.

thered by Ruffinus and Nicephorus, as ye pretende, that he thought not fo as he fpake , or fpake thofe wordes , for that only, that the cõmon caufe fhould not be hindered, which mighte and fhould haue gonne forward, though he had not fpoken theis words . In dede he burned their bills of com-plaints, and fo cut away their priuat quarelling, leaft it fhuld

haue

haue ben any hinderance to the principal matter, that was
then to be difcuffed and debated vpon. And in cafe the có-
plaintes had bene fuch, as Conftantin might haue heard and
determined, he might haue referued them vntil the ende of
the Coūcel: and then haue heard thē without any preiudice
or ftay of the common matters . Now what kinde of matters thefe were, for the which the Biffhops did contende,
it doth not appeare. Yf they were tēporall, then whether
Conftantine might heare them, or might not , yt maketh
nothing for his Ecclefiaftical fupremacy. Yf they were fpiritual matters, then are we fure , he might not heare, as the
chiefe and principall iudge . Priuate quarrels they were as
your felf confeffe, and therefore by all likelyhood of temporal matters: wherein for all that, themperor thought him
felf nō mete or cōueniēt iudge, vpon priefts . And that well
appereth to be his minde, by that we haue faid before, that
he made a law, wherby al priefts conuented before any tēporal iudge, might refufe him, and require the matter to be
hearde of the bifhop. But of this matter fee our anfwere before in the Second booke.   *Cap.4.fo.*
    103.et.104.

    Ye are now bufie again with the Coūcel of Tyrus, with
Cæcilianus, and fuch other matters, to proue Cōftantin the
fupreame head. Whervnto feing we haue * alredy fufficiētly anfwered, we wil not encomber the Reader again with
thē in this place: And neade fo much the leffe, that ye feme
to faynte and geue ouer your holde, and your fond glofe a-
gainft the plaine text: and by putting the cafe it were true,
which is true in dede: feke yet an other corner to crepe in,
and fay that though Cōftantin would not or could not lawfully iudge the Priefts, yet it will not followe , that bifhops
may cal Councels, make lawes, and exercife al maner of iu-

* Lib . 2.
cap.2. &
3.fol.90.&
fequentib.
Item. fol.
94.et feq.

          rifdiction

rifdictió cohibitiue. Ye fay truly M.Horn, it wil not follow in dede. Neither M.Fekenham driueth any fuch reafon. It is fufficient, that they may exercife any cohibitiue iurifdiction without the princes commiffion, which you haue hitherto denied: affirming, that they can not do it without the Princes warrant: nor the Prince him felf. touching the firft cohibitiue iurifdiction, as ye haue diuided it. But yf they be iudges, thē muft it nedes follow, that they haue fome iurifdiction cohibitiue. For as the lawe faith. *Iurifdictio fine modica correctione nulla eft.* Iurifdiction without fome compulfion is no iurifdictió. Againe yf Cóftátinus were not the fupreme iudge, nor could be: thē are not other Emperours or Princes, iudges any thing more, then he was, ād fo hath M. F. by this iuftified his affertion. This argument therfore, that ye miflike, is not M.Fekenhās, but your owne. Who fhal let you to like or miflike your owne reafons at your pleafure. And therefore, for aunfwere to this your peuifhe argumēt, I fay, yt followeth no better, thē yf a man fhould fay. York ftādeth but thre myles frō Pocklingtō: *Ergo* your pocket is ful of plūmes. And fo haue you ful wifely ftopped not M.F. but your own mouth with an hādful of your own plūmes. If Priefts be iudges, they haue not therby al maner of iurifdictió cohitiue: for thē fhould they haue al tēporal iurifdiction afwel as fpiritual. But yet for fuch caufes as they be lawfull iudges in, they may make lawes and orders iudicially, and may haue, yea and muft haue all ecclefiaftical iurifdiction, for the execution of their iudgement.

De officio eius, cui mandata eft Iurifdictio : Mādatam.

The. 637. vntruth. For that hiftorie maketh

Of the like fourme alfo are the confequents, that ye make vpon the hiftories of the Emperours Valentinian and Theodofius. And as you cā not faften your purpofe by any good fequele vpō thefe hiftories, fo that hiftory that ye alledge of Valentinian, maketh much (.637.) again your purpofe. Firft

it is

it is vncertein and may be doubted, vvhether this anſvvere that ye affirm to
be Valentinians, vvere his or Valens the Emperours vvords. for as Sozomenus one of the Tripartit Eccleſiaſtical hiſtorians, affirmeth this ſuite
to be made by Catholik Biſshops of Helleſpontus and Bithynia, vnto
Valentinian, and that this vvas his anſvvere to their petition. Lue ſo Socrates an other of the ſame tripartit hiſtorians affirmeth, that this ſuit vvas
made by the Macedonians, vnto Valens the Emperour, vvho graunted
the their petition, the rather ſuppoſing, that the matter ſhould haue ben determined in that Coūcel, after the minds of Eudoxi⁹ and Acatius. And it
is not from the purpoſe to note vvhich of theſe Emperours cauſed this Coūcel to be called, for the one of tl̄ē. Valentinian vvas a Catholik Emperour,
the other Valés, an Arian. Secōdly you do (.638.) falſely report the ſtory, for
the Biſshops of Helleſpōt⁹ and Bithynia, did not make ſuite vnto Thēperour Valentinian, that he would be preſent in the coūcel: but
by their meſſenger, did humbly beſeche him, that he would commaūde
al the Biſshops, as Nicephorus reporteth it, or that he vvould ſuffer and
geue leaue vnto the biſshops to haue a Synod or Councell, vvhich
they held after licence obteined at Lampſacum, as Socrates
and Sozomenus, the Tripartite Hiſtoriãs, make relatiō. Thirdly, the Emperour doth (.639.) not ſimply refuſe or deny the ſearch
and diligent enquyrie of theſe matters, as things nothing apperteining to his office, or not lavvſull for him to enquire of: as yee
vvould haue it ſeeme, but excuſeth him ſelfe by his earneſt buſines and vvant of leyſure, ſaying, It is not lawful. (.640.)
(meaning that his leiſure, from the vvaighty matters of the
common vveale, and iuſt oportunitie, vvoulde not eaſely vovve
ſuffer him) to trauaile in thoſe cauſes; and therefore reſerreth
the exacte ſifting of thoſe thinges to them, vvhoſe offices and
charge, vvas properlye to be occupied in thoſe matters. That
this is the true purporte of his vvords in his right ſenſe and
meaning appereth plainly by the (.641.) due circumſtances
ſette ſooth in the ſtorye; and alſo by Nicephorus an Eccleſia-
ſticali hiſtorian, vvho rightly vnderſtode his meaning, and reporteth it in theſe vvords: Mihi negotijs occupato, & reip.
curis diſtento res eiuſmodi inquirere, non facile eſt.

much for
M.Feck.
purpoſe,
as ſhall
appeare.
Lib.6.
cap.7.
Lib.4.
cap.2.
The.638.
vntruthe
ſlaunde-
rous.M.
Fekenhā
repor-
teth the
ſtory tru-
ly.

The.639.vntruthe.
He doth ſimply de-
ny it, as ſhall ape-
peare.

The.640.vntruth.
He meant not ſo, as
it plainly appereth
by Sozomenus,
Paulus Diac.and
Caſſiodore.

The.641.vntruthe.
by the Circumſtā-
ces no ſuch thing
appereth.

Lib.11.cap.3.

It is no light or eafy matter for me, that am nowe occupied with bufineffes, and filled fo ful as I may be, with the cares of the common weale, to enquire or fearche fuch matters. *Laſt of al, vvhether tl.e Catholique Biſshops of* Helefpontus *and* Bithynia *, required the Emperours preſence in the Councel, as ye affirme, or they required thervvith his labour and trauaile in the debating or ſearching the truthe of matter, vvhich may ſeeme at the firſt by the bare vvordes of his aunſvvere:*

The.642. vntruth.
They acknovvled-
ged not thereby a-
ny ſuch Iuriſdictiō,
but they craued his
ayde and aſſiſtance
for quyet and or-
der ſake.

The.643. vntruth.
M·Fekenham ſaith
not, they required
theperourto deale
in debating ſuch
matters, but only
to be preſent.

or they deſired onely licence of him and permiſſion to aſſemble togeather in Synode or Councell, to determine and decree vvith the truth, againſt the Arianiſmes, vvhich the moſt and beſt part of the Hiſtorians agree vnto. Their ſute and humble petition, maketh plainly againſt your preſumpteous aſſertion, in that they acknovvledged (.642.) thereby the iuriſdictiō to call Councels, to be in the Emperour, and not in Biſshops or Prieſts, vvithout ſpeciall leaue, licence, and commiſſion from the Prince. For if the povver and iuriſdiction to cal Councels, had ben in them ſelues vvithout the Emperours commiſſion, vvhat neaded them to haue craued licence of the Emperour? And if it had not bene lavvfull for the Emperour to haue ben preſent in the Councel, and to haue dealte in the diligent ſearche and debating of matters in Religion, then theſe Catholique Biſshoppes did vvickedly, vvho as you (.643.) ſay, moued him therevnto.

Stapleton.

A cōfuta-
tion of M.
Horns an
ſvvere to
Valenti-
niās ſtory

Hiſt. trip.
li.7,c.12.

The next ſtory is, of Valentinian themperour, whom the Catholiks required, that he would vouchſauf to be preſent among them in their Councel. Who made them anſwere, *that it was not lawful for him being a lay man, to ſearch out ſuch matters. But ye that are prieſts* (ſaith he) *and that haue the care of theſe matters, may at your pleaſure aſſemble your ſelfe where ye will.* To this allegatiõ Maiſter Horne aunſwereth.

Firſt, that it is not certaine, whether the ſuyte was made to Valentinian, or to Valens his brother, which was an Arrian.

Secon-

Secondly he faith, that M. Fekenhã doth falſly reporte the ſtory : for that the biſhops did not make ſuyte to him to be preſente, but that he would commaund the biſhops, as Nicephorus reporteth it, or ſuffer, or geue leaue to the biſhops to haue a ſynode, as Socrates and Sozomenus make relatiõ.

Nicephor. lib.11.c.3.

Thirdly that themperour doth not ſimply denie, that the ſearch of theis matters apperteyne to his office, but excuſeth him ſelf, by his earneſt buſines and want of leaſure : as Nicephorus, who rightly vnderſtode his meaning, reporteth. Laſt of all, what ſo euer the ſuyt was, they acknowledged the iuriſdiſtion to cal Councells to be in the Emperour : or elſe what neaded they to haue craued licence of the Emperour?

Your firſte, and ſecond ſolution M. Horne, though they were true, wil litle relieue yow. And yet aſwel in the one, as in the other M. Fekenham reporteth no more then the very wordes of his Authour, that wrote the Tripartite hiſtory. Firſt that the catholyks ſent to Valentinian, and not the Macedonians to Valens. This ſaith the Tripartite alleaged by M. Fekenham: this ſayth Sozomenus: this ſayth Paulus Diaconus, this ſaith Nicephorus with others. As for Socrates, though he write otherwiſe, yet his credit is the leſſe, both for that he is knowen, to haue miſſereported other things, namely about the matters of Athanaſius and Arrius, contrary to all other writers, and alſo for that he is noted of ignorance by Euagrius an other Eccleſiaſticall writer, about the ſtory of the Epheſine Coũcel: So litle cauſe you had to charge M. Fekenham of miſreporting, your ſelf forſaking the conſent of ſo many, to folowe one againſt all the reſt, when M. Fekenham folowed the conſent of the moſt and the beſt writers.

Trip.li.7. cap.12. Sozo. lib. 6.cap.7. Pau.Dia. in addit: ad Eutro pium. Niceph.li. 11 cap.13. Euagrius lib.1.ca.5. ϳ κỳ Σω κρατης αϛυοκῷς, ιϛερως ιϛορησα

Tripart.ca.12.li.7.
Vt dignaretur ad do-
gmatis emendatione
intereſſe. Paul.Diac.
quatenus dignaretur
ad dogmatis emēda-
tionem intereſſe.

Paul.Diaconus.
Mihi cum ſubiecto po
pulo de huiuſmodi ne
gotijs curioſè agere
fas nō eſt.vt ergo vi-
detur vobis ſacerdo-
tibus,facite.

Tripart.lib.7.ca.12.
Mihi cū vnus de po-
pulo ſim,fas non eſt.
&c.

Sozom li.6. cap.7.
ἐμοὶ μεῖα λαοῦ τε
ῖαχμένῳ ὀυ θέμις
ῖοιαῦτα πολυπρχ=
μονεῖν , οἱδε ἱερέις
διςῖουῖ8 μέλει,καθ̓
ἑαυτοὺς ὅπῃ βού-
λονῖαι σωϊτωέςῃ.

As for the ſecond point,the ſayd tripartite hath
euen as M. Fekenham doth alleage it , and ſo hath
Paulus Diaconus to:that is,*that yt would pleaſe hym*
to be preſent ,that wronge opiniōs might be reformed.
For the.3.point alſo M.Fekenhā ſwarueth nothing
from thē ſayd tripartite . Nay ſayth M.Horne, the
dewe circumſtance ſet forth in the ſtory , and Nicephorus who rightly vnderſtode the Emperours
meaning declare,*that when he ſayd it was not Law:*
full for him, he meant:it was no lighte or eaſie matter
for him being occupied with buſines and care of the cō-
men welth,to ſearch ſuch matters. But howe proue
you,that Nicephorus a very late writer ſhould vnderſtand his meaning better,then Paulus Diaconus
that lyued at leaſt ſowre hundred yeares before Ni
cephorus,that writeth thus ? *It is not lawfull for me,*
and my people curiouſly to medle with ſuche matters.
Wherfore doe ye that are prieſts,as ye ſhal thinke good.
Why ſhould we thinke,that Nicephorus ſhould be
more priuy of themperors right meaning, then was
Epiphanius the tranſlatour of the Tripartite , writinge at leaſt. 600. veares before Nicephorus was
born?Yea why ſhuld we thik that Nicephor⁹ ſhuld
ſee more deaply the meanig of thēperor, thē the o-
riginal authour him ſelf Sozomene,that liued about
the ſaid Emperours time?Who writeth,that thēperour Valētiniā anſwered. *It is not lauful for me,being*
a lay mā,to be curiouſe in the ſearchīg of theis matters.
Let the biſhops,to whoſe charge theis matters apper-
tain,aſſéble thē ſelues,at what place they liſt. Neither
cā the circūſtāce of the ſtory of Valētiniā as ye imagine,

gine, leade a mã to your sense. For whether we cõsider this answere, or the answer he made at the electiõ of S. Ambrose, we shal fynd al to be of one sort. *Chose ye*, saith thẽperour to the bishops, *such a bishop, for Millane, to whõ we that gouern the empire, may sincerly submit our head: ãd whose admonitiõs we, whẽ by any fraylty, as mẽ are wont, we trespasse, may of necessity recieue as of the physitions medecine.* And whẽ the bisshops would haue sette ouer the choise and the appointment of the newe bisshop to him, because he was a wise and a godly Prince: Nay sayth he: *This enterprise or worke passeth our vocation or degree. For ye that are indewed with the grace of God, and shyne brightlie with that light, may much better make this election.* The Emperour also vnderstanding, that S. Ambrose was chosen, sayd: *I thanke thee my Lord God, that it hath pleased thee, to commit mens sowles, to him* (meaning S. Ambrose) *to whõ I cõmitted mens bodies*. For before S. Ambrose was chosen bisshop of Millane, he was the gouernour of those quarters vnder the Emperour. But to put the matter out of doubt, let vs harken to S. Ambrose, and to that, that he sayeth of this Emperour. This Emperours sonne the yonge Valentinian sent for S. Ambrose to come to his consistory: ãd there to reason and dispute before him, ãd other as Iudges, against the Arrian bishop Auxencius. To whome S. Ambrose answered: *Sir: your father did not onely say it in wordes, but ordeyned by a law, that in matters touching fayth, or ecclesiastical order, he ought to be iudg, that is neither vnequal in office, nor vnlike in right. For theis are the words of his rescript or Law: that is, that priests should be iudges vpon priestes. Yea if a priest*

were

Eutrop.
Cui & nos qui gubernam⁹ imperiũ, sincerè capita nostra submittamus, & eius monita dũ tanquam homines deliquerim⁹ necessariò veluti curantis medicamenta suscipiamus.

Tripart. li. 7. ca. 8.
Theodor. li. 4. ca. 6.
μεῖζον ἢ καθ᾽ ἡμᾶς τὸ ἐγχείρημα.

Eutropius ibidem.
Gratias tibi ago Domine, quia huic viro ego quidẽ commisi corpora, tu autem animas.

Ambros. lib. 5. epistola. 32.

were otherwise accused, and that he were to be examined of his manners and lyfe, he would that the bishops should be iudges. Wherfore his owne lawe may best serue, for the interpretation of his answere made to the bishops of *Hellespontus.* And this with the other premisses declare euidently, themperours meaning, and that he thought it did not properly belong to him, but to the bishops, to intermedle with the affayres Ecclesiasticall.

Neither doth Nicephorus any thing hinder our purpose. For that, that he saith, wil wel stand with Sozomenus. And it is probable the Emperour sayd both. And as yt is in holy scripture, that one place supplieth the defect of the other: so is it also in chroniclers. And that perchaunce ye sawe your self, and therfore ye runne to your accustomable reason, as yt were to your Bulwork, *that the princes had authority to call councels, and not the bishops: for else* (say you) *what neaded them to haue craued Licence of themperour?* Wherein I answer, they neaded his ayde for oportunyte of time and place. And as at all tymes the bishops haue wrought in calling of Councels with the princes assistace, so at this time, (the Arrians and other heretiks bearing such a sway in the worlde) yt was great wisedome, to attempte no councell without notice geuen to the prince, and his consente had thereunto. Namely considering what persequutions the Catholikes of late had suffred vnder the Arrian Emperour Constantius, and that theire decrees could not be effectually executed against rebellioufe heretyks, who cotemned excommunication, and al other Ecclesiasticall iurisdiction, neither they them selues coulde safely and quietly assemble together, without the speciall ayde of the Prince.

M. Horne

M. *Horne. The. 171. Diuision.pag.119.a.*

Although yee (.644.) vntruely reporte the storie of Theodosi-
us the Emperour, and Ambrose the Bisshoppe of Millaine, yet can
you not by any meanes vvrast it, to serue your purpose (.645.)
any vvhitte at all. For if it vvere true, that Ambrose forbadde
Theodosius *the Emperour the entraunce into the Chauncell: or*
that the Emperour had said to him, that he had learned the dif-
ference betvvixt an Emperour and a Priest, yet can you not con-
clude thereof: therefore Bishops and Priests haue povver and au-
thoritie to make Lavves, Orders, and Decrees to their flockes
and cures, and to exercise the seconde kinde of Cohibitiue iurisdi-
ction ouer them. Theodosius, *as the Author vvriteth, came into*
the Chauncell to offer his oblation, vvhereat S. Ambrose found no
fault: But vvhen he staid there still to receiue the holy Mysteries,
S. *Ambrose sent him vvord to go foorth and abide vvith the other*
of the Church, for that place vvas only for the Priests: For vvhich
monition the Emperoure vvas retourned to Constantinople, and
came on a time into the invvarde place or Chauncell to offer his
oblation, and vvent foorth againe so sone as he had offred, Ne-
ctarius the Bishop demaunded of him, vvherefore he taried not
still vvithin, meaning to receiue the holy mysteries: To vvhome
the Emperour maketh ansvvere, saying: I haue scarsely learned
the difference betvvixt an Emperour and a Priest.

The.644.vntruth.
The storie is by M.
Fekenham truelye
reported.

The.645.Vntruth.
It serueth the pur-
pose many vvaies,
as shall appeare.

Theod. lib. 5. c. 18.

Marke here, Gentle
Reader, hovve M.
Horne telleth only
the Storie, and so
stealeth avvaye
vvithout any e ans
vveare in the
vvorlde.

Stapleton.

The third story is of th'Emperour Theodosius the Great,
whome S. Ambrose forbadde to enter into the Chauncell,
saying: *The inner partes of the Church, ô Emperour, lie open*
for Priests only, &c. whome the Emperour thanked for this
admonition, saying: that he had now learned a difference
betwixt an Emperour and a Priest. First M. Horne findeth
this faulte with Maister Fekenham, that he vntruely reporteth the Storie of Theodosius: then in case this were a true
reporte, that it can not be by any meanes wrested to serue

A confu-
tation of
M. Horns
ansvvere
to the sto
ry of The
odosius.

Theod.
lib. 5. c. 18.

kkkk   M. Feken-

M. Fekenhams purpofe any whit at all. For if it were true, yet could he not conclude, that becaufe S. Ambrofe forbad Theodofius thentrance into the Chauncel, that Bifhopes haue power to make Lawes and decrees, to theyr flockes and cure, and to exercife the feconde cohibitiue iurifdiction. I nowe perceyue, that Horace faying is true.

Breuis effe laboro : Obfcurus fio.

Whiles men feke breuitie, they fal into obfcuritie.

So perchaunce M. Horne might haue faied, and truelie to M. Fekenham. But that he faieth, that M. Fekenham maketh a mifreporte of the ftorie, that he fayeth verie plainely, but as falfely. And therefore both to fupplie this defecte, and fhape M. Horne a plaine and a ful anfwere, I wil a litle more open this ftorie.

The people at Theffalonica in a fedition and an vprore flewe certaine of the magiftrates, wherevppon. Theodofius, though otherwife a good and a verie temperate man in al his doinges, being entred into a great rage and choler, commaunded the people of that Citie to be deftroyed by his armie : which in a furioufnes without anie confideration flewe fuche as by chaunce they firfte mette withal: were they Citizens, ftraungers, or foreners, were they giltie, or were they vngiltie. After a certaine tyme it chaunced, that this Emperour came to Millane, and being there, after hys cuftome repayring to the Churche, S. Ambrofe mette hym, and forbadde him to enter: mofte vehementlie reprouing hym for the fayed fhawghter : afking, howe he coulde finde in his confcience, eyher to lyfte vp hys handes to God, defiled with fuche a foule murther, or with the fame to receyue the holie bodie of Chrifte, or to receyue with hys mouthe the precioufe bloude of Chrifte, by whofe

The ftory of Theodofius, the Emperour and S. Ambrofe, opened.

Niceph. li. 12. cap. 40 & 41.

Theod. lib. 5. cap. 18.

whofe furioufe and ragnge commaundemente fo muche
bloude had bene fhedde? Wherefore he woulde, that the
Emperour fhoulde turne home againe, and that he fhoulde
pacientlie fuffer the bonde, the which God had with his
heauenly fentence allowed, meaning this fentence of ex
communication. The Emperour as one browght vppe in
Goddes Lawes, obeyed hym, and with weapinge teares
departed : where he continued eight monethes, and neuer
came all thys while to the Churche, nor receyued the
facramente of Chriftes bodie. The folemne feaft of Chri-
ftmaffe being nowe come, he was in great heuines
and foroweto confider that euery poore begger
might goe to the Churche, and he onelie was
fhutte owte. And full bitterlie complayned and
moned with him felfe, that he was excluded,
not onelie from the Churche, but from heauen
alfo. For he did well remember, that Chrifte fayde
plainlie. that what fo euer was bownde in earthe
of Goddes Prieftes, fhoulde be bownde alfo in
heauen.

At lengthe after he had fent Ruffinus a noble
man, to entreat with S. Ambrofe, he went him felf,
neither yet would prefume to enter, vntill S. Ambrofe had abfolued him, and lofed his bodes: which
he did moft humbly and penitently craue at his
handes, offering hym felfe to receyue fuche farder penaunce, as S. Ambrofe fhoulde enioyne
hym. Wherevpon S. Ambrofe enioyned him (for
his penaunce) to make a Lawe, that fuche capi
tall fentences and iudgmentes as fhoulde feame to
be made extraordinarilye, and contrarye to the

Of the penaunce of this Empe⸗ rour en⸗ ioyned him by S. Am⸗ brofe.

*Mihi porro non mea
dò id tangere licet,
verum etiam cœlum
ipfum claufum eft.
Neque enim diuini
illius oraculi non me-
mini quod difertis
verbis ftatuit: qua-
cunque a facerdoti-
bus Dei ligata fue-
rint in terris, ea etiã
in cœlis certa effe
ligata.*

*Te autem oro, vt
vincula mea foluas.*

Et mox

*Tuæ vero, ò vir diui-
ne id eft operæ, indi-
care mihi & tempe-
rare facra medicina
remedia.*

common order and cuſtome of themperours, ſhould not be put in execution, til.30.dayes after the ſentēce. That in this meane while, the Prince might, yf nede were, better aduiſe him ſelfe, either for the moderation or the aboliſhing of his cōmaundement. Which law was preſently made and ſubſcribed with Theodoſius handes, and doth at this day re-

Vide Cod. Theod, li. 9.tit. 40 lib.:3 In Cod. Iu-ſin.lib.9. tit. de pœ-nis: Si vindicari.

main to be ſene in the Code. The Emperour being at lēgth reconciled, and ſuffered to enter into the church, went vp into the chauncel to offer, and there remained, willinge to receiue the Sacramēt of Chriſtes bodie, as the Emperours were wonte to doe. But S. Ambroſe ſent to him a deacō to warne him to depart into the body of the churche: for that the inwarde temple was a place for the prieſtes only. And thervpon he departed, and thanked S Ambroſe. And comming afterwarde to Conſtantinople, when he had done his offeringe in the chauncell, woulde not tarrie,

Niceph.li 12.ca.41. Vix aliquando tandō (inquit) quod diſcri= mē ſit inter impera-torem & ſacrorum antiſtitem, cognoui: vix veritatis doĉto-rem inueni.

but departed into the body of the Church: though Nectarius the Patriarche there were not contente with yt and willed him to remaine ſtill: to whome he anſwered. I haue ſcarſly nowe at length learned the difference betwixte an Emperour, and a prieſt. By this ſtory, firſt ye vnderſtande, what a cauillor, and what a quarreller M. Horne is : to charge M. Fekenham with the vntrue reporte of this ſtory. For as for the firſt, truth yt is. S Ambroſe did not fynde faulte, that he ſhoulde enter into the chancel, nei-

Μόſις ἐφη βαſι-λέως κỳ ἱερέως ἐ-ſι∂ἄχθην ∂ιαφο-ρὰν, μόſις ἔυρον ἀ-ληθείας ∂ι∂ἄσκα-λον.

ther M . Fekenham ſaieth ſo . But ſayinge , he forbadde him to enter , and addinge no more but theſe wordes , the inwarde partes , be for the Prieſtes, & cætera this & cætera. declareth, that M Fekenhā meante not of the bare ingreſſe, but of the ingreſſe

and

and tarying withall, accordinge to the ftory: to the which
he doth referre him felfe with this *& cætera*. And therfore
as there is no caufe, why he fhoulde vntruely reporte yt,
making nothing for his purpofe, nor againfte you: fo con-
fideringe the maner of his vtterance, yt is truely reported. and ye Mayfter Horne fhewe your felfe but a wrangler. For the .2. poynte, though in dede Theodoretus faieth
as you reherfe μογις, that is, fcarfly, or hardlye : yet the leauing owte of thofe two fyllables, is not any way beneficial
to M. Fekenham, or preiudiciall to your caufe, or worthie
to be noted for any vntruth. For yt is very true, that Theodofius had learned a difference betwixt themperour and
the prieftes, thoughe fcarflye and hardlye, and in longe
time.

Nowe we haue proued M. Fekenham an honefte man,
and cleared him, we geue you warninge to fee to your
felf, and that you prouide afwel for your felfe and your honefty, which ye fhall neuer doe. Remēber I pray you, what *Vide fu-*
aduantage, or what great honefty ye toke before, for the al - *pra fol.*
leaging of Theodofius doings. Take hede I fay, leaft his fto- 119. b. &.
ry yet ones againe put you to as much fhame. I wil not tar- 120. a.
ry vppon other incidente though great matters.   As that The ftory
this ftory geueth a fure recorde and teftimony againfte dofius
your fynagoges, or rather Barnes (.1.) afwell for the pluc- makech
king downe of the chauncell, and makinge no difference manie
betwene the Prieftes and the lay mens place (.2.) as alfo for ʃointes
taking away the oblation and prefence of the bleffed bo- of M.
die and bloudd of Chrifte, teftified by this ftory . ·In the doctrine.
which oblation, the cheife office of the Priefte remaineth : and for the which, as being one principall caufe,   ·1·
in the auncient and primitiue Churche the Churches   ·2·
kkkk iiij   were

were not barnes or cockpittes, as yours are now, but somely and orderlie diſtinĉted, with the Chauncel to the Prieſtes onlie : and with the bodie of the Churche, peculiarlie appointed to the people. This I ſay, I wil now leaue largelie to diſcourſe vppon (.3.) and alſo that this Storie deſtroyeth your other hereſie, that Prieſts do not remit ſinnes, but declare onely ſinnes to be remitted. For Theodoſius confeſ-ſed, that by the ſentence of this Biſhoppe, he was excluded not only from the Church, but from heauen alſo. I wil now diſcourſe only, whether this ſtorie be aptly brought foorth (.4.) for M. Fekenhams purpoſe, which ye denie.   But he that doth not ſee moſt euidentlie, that this Storie proueth S. Ambroſe, for cauſes Eccleſiaſtical to haue bene the head of the Church of Millaine, and not the Emperour, he will neuer ſee any truth, as long as he liueth, and is like to him that in a faire ſunny daie ſtoppeth his eyes with his handes at midnoone, and then crieth out that they are fooles, that ſaie it is daie lighte.   No, no, euery man may eaſely ſee by this Storie, that the tenour of your othe can not poſſi-blie be iuſtified : whereby men are vrged to ſwere, that the Prince is ſupreme head not in one or two, but *in A L cauſes or things ECCLES IASTICAL*. Surely an vntrue and an horrible propoſition. The which S. Ambroſe, if he now liued, rather then he woulde confeſſe, he woulde be diſmembred with wilde horſes. This is to open, and to euident an abſurditie, and though ye will not, or dare not confeſſe it with plaine wordes, yet as we haue declared, it may be wel gathered your ſelfe doe not like it. And therfore ye craftelie wind your ſelfe from that, as much as ye may poſſiblie, and finde many ſtarting holes : as in the former leafe, *That out of Conſtantinus Storie it may not be gathered, that Biſhops*

3.

4.

M. Horns
ſtarting
holes,
vvhen he
is preſſed
mere.

Biſhops

Bifshoppes haue all manner of Cohibitiue Iurifdiction. And here : *that it can not be proued by this Storie of Theodofius, that they haue the feconde Cohibitiue Iurifdiction.* But in cafe out of bothe it may be gathered (as it is in deede neceffarilie gathered) that the Prince is not fupreame Heade in all matters Ecclefiaftical: then is Maifter Fekenham free from taking the Othe, as being fuch, as neither he, nor any good man may with fafe confcience receiue.

Now further, what if of this Storie, it fhalbe proued moft euidently, that Bifhops haue not only the.2.Cohibitiue, but the firft Cohibitiue too, as ye call it ?   And that it is fo , I fette faft footing, and ioyne iffue with you.   And firft, for your firft Cohibitiue Iurifdiction, as ye call it , in which by you is comprehended excomunication, whiche ye fee here practifed without any Princes commifsion, yea vppon the Prince him felfe.   And as no man euer read or hearde, that S. Ambrofe had any other commifsion , either from Prince or from his Churche, to excommunicate Theodofius, and that as it is not likely , that the whole Church and Congregation of Millaine woulde agree to the excomunication of the Emperour : or that they had any fuch authoritie : So a man may doubte, whether there were any one laie man or Prieft, that was of fuch courage as herein to ioyne with S. Ambrofe in fo dägerous, but yet a worthy enterprife. Surely S. Ambrofe had none other cömifsion, then all other Bifhops then, or fithens haue had.   None other, I fay, then he had, when he excomunicated a feruant of the Erle Stillico, for forging of falfe letters. Which excömunication wrought fo wöderoufly, that he waxed mad, and was poffeffed of the Diuel, that began al to teare him. None other then he had, when he excömunicated alfo Maximus the tyrät: not without

5.

Paulinus in vita Ambrosȷ̃.

Ibidem.

Niceph.li.12.cap.41
Vinculum quod Deus
cœlitus sub calculo
comprobauit, suscipe.

Ambros lib.5.epistola
28.ad ipsum Theodo-
sium. Ita me Deus ab
omnibus tribulatio-
nibus liberat, quia
non ab homine neque
per hominem, sed a-
pertè mihi interd·ctu
aduerti: Dum enim
essem sollicitus, ipsa
nocte qua proficisci
parabam, venisse qui-
dem visus es, sed mi-
hi sacrificium offerre
non licuit.

Officiorum lib.2 ca.
27.Sic Episcopi affe-
ctus boni est, vt optet
sanare infirmos, ser-
pentia auferre vulne-
ra: adurere aliqua
non abscindere,postre
mò quod sanari non
po est,cum dolore
abscindere.

out great daunger of his life. None other I say, then that, that he receiued of God, when he was made Bishope. This iurisdiction then did S. Ambrose exercise by his supreame Ecclesiasticall authoritie, vppon the higest Monarche of al the world. This did he by his episcopal office, and yet not without a plaine celestiall reuelation to encourage hym therto, and to confirme him, as him selfe declareth. Herein his doinges were agreable to his teachinges. For he taught with all other Catholikes, that this excommunication perteyneth to the Bishopes ãd not to the multitud. *The Bishops office is* (sayth he) *if it may be to heale canckered and foystered soores, and if that may not be, to cut the perniciouse and rotten partes quite of.* It is then a most true principle, that Bishops neede to looke for none other warrant to excõmunicate any man, that deserueth excõmunication: no nor the Prince neither, putting the case as ye falsely do, that he is the head of the Church. And therfore either you muste take from him thys vnnatural and monstrouse head, by which ye sette two heades vpon one bodie, or ye muste graunte him authoritie to excommunicat to.

Maruell it is to me, if this your preaching and teaching be so true and sure as ye make it, that the learned men about Theodosius could not espie it. O that ye had bene at his elbowe to haue enspired him whith a litle of your newe diuinitie: ye might haue wonderfullie eased his woful harte, and perchance if you might haue proued your doctrine, haue worne for your labour the Popes triple croune

by

by Theodoſius good helpe·, for ſuche good ſeruice in ſo
greate diſtreſſe. What a ſort of dolts had Theodoſius being
ſo mighty a Prince about him: that none of them could tell
him, that he neded not to paſſe a butte for S. Ambroſes ex-
comunicatio, vnleſſe he ſaw yt withal ſealed by the whole
congregation ? Yf Theodoſius had learned this leſſon he
would haue ſhifted wel inough for him ſelfe, nor neded not
to haue pined away ſo many moneths with cotinual mourning and lamentatio . But ſuerly yf ye had tolde him ſo M.
Horne, he would haue take you as ye are, that is , for a lier,
and an heretike. He was as I haue ſayed, brought vp in the
knowledge of Gods law, ad knew ſul wel, that he was laufully excommunicated, by S. Ambroſe . The whiche he did
muche feare, pronounced not by a Biſhop onely, that hath
therto ordinary, but (ſuch was his deuotio and his life ſo co-
formable to Gods lawes) of other that had none authority
at al. And therefore being on a time excommunicated, of a
froward mok, hauing none authority therto: he would neither eat, nor drink vntil he wer aſſoiled of him: yea though
th'Archbiſhop him ſelf of Coſtatinople offred to aſſoil him.

Niceph. li.
14. cap. 3.
Adeò reli-
gioſus
Theodoſius
fuit, vt ã-
que ſuam
accuratiſ-
ſimè ad
diuinas
leges cõ-
poſuit·

We will now come to the 2. cohibitiue, as ye cal yt, and
to the authority of making lawes and decrees, euidently to
be proued by this ſtory. For from whenſe commeth this
order and maner to diſtincte the chauncell from the bodie
of the Churche, and to place the prieſtes in the one , and
the laity in the other : but from the Biſhops, without any
commiſsion of the Prince or people ? The which order
and lawe ye ſee, that S Ambroſe appointed to the Prince
hym ſelfe: which he euer afterward kepte, thoughe before
he vſed the cotrary . Againe doth not S. Ambroſe preſcribe
to Theodoſius for his penaunce , a certain lawe and order

to be

to be set forth by him, by his proclamation? Thirdly is it not a Law made of the Bishops and councel without any commission of Princes or people , that *a sentence ones geuen , or order taken in matters Ecclesiastical,none of the Clergy should appeale vpon paine of depriuation to any ciuile Prince ?* And that we go not from the storie and time of Theodosius and S. Ambrose : did not S. Ambrose with the whole Councell kept at Aquileia depose Palladius, for that he, among other things, would haue had certaine noble men to haue ben associate to sitte in iudgement with the Bishops in the time of Theodosius ? Of the which I haue spoken more largely in my Returne,&c. against M. Iewell.

Thus ye perceiue good Reader , how aptly and fitly M. Fekenham hath accommodated to his purpose , the stories of these three Emperours, and to what poore shifts Maister Horne is driuen for the maintenance of his euill cause,that he hath taken in hand to defend. Thus you see also,how to this storie of S. Ambrose and Theodosius M. Horne hathe answered no one word, but making a short recitall thereof, stealeth faire away, without any answere at all.

M. *Fekenham*. The. 172. *Diuision. pag*. 119.*a*.

M.Iohn Caluine,intreating of the Histories betwixte these Emperors Valetinian,Theodosius,and S.Ambrose, after a log processe wherin be maketh good prouf,that all spiritual iurisdictio doth appertain vnto the Church,and not vnto the Empire, he hath these woordes folowing: Qui vt magistratum ornet,Ecclesiam spoliant hac potestate,non modo falsa interpretatione Christi sententiā corrumpunt,sed sanctos omnes Episcopos, qui tam multi à tempore Apostolorum extiterunt,non leuiter damnant.Quod hono-

rem

Marginal notes:
Cōc. Mi-leuit.c.19

Th. 1.cōc. in concil. Aquil.

Art. 4. fol. 108.

Cal.Insti-tut.cap.8.

rem officiū́que Magiſtratus falſo prætextu ſibi vſurpauerit.
How they do ſpoil the Church of that authozity, therby to adozn
tempozal Magiſtrates, not onely by cozrupting Chziſt his ap=
pointment and meaning therin: But alſo they lightly cōdemne
and ſet at naught al thoſe holy Biſhops, which in ſo great num=
ber haue continued frō the time of the Apoſtles hitherto, which
honour and office of Spiritual gouernmēt they haue (ſaith Iohn
Caluin) vſurped and taken vpon them by a falſe pzetext and title
made therof. *And againe Iohn Caluin ſaith :* Qui in initio tan- Cal.in.7.
topere extulerunt Henricum regem Angliæ, certe fuerunt ca. Amos.
homines incōſiderati. Dederūt illi ſummā omniū poteſtatē.
Et hoc me ſemper grauiter vulnerauit, erant enim blaſphe-
mi, cum vocarent ipſum ſummū caput Eccleſiæ ſub Chriſto.
They which in the beginning did ſo much extoll Henry King of
England, and which did geue vnto him the higheſt authozitie in
the Church, they were men which lacked circumſpection, and of
ſmall conſideration: which thing (ſaith Iohn Caluin) did at all
times offend me very much, foz they did commit blaſphemie, and
were blaſphemers, when they did cal him the ſupzeame Head of
the Churche.

M. Horne.

The collectour of your common places did (.646.) beguile The 646. Vntruth,
you, vvhiche you vvoulde haue perceiued, if you hadde readde M.Fekenham vvas
MaiſterCaluine vvith your ovvne eyes. He entreateth(.647.) not beguiled, but
you.
not in that place of the Hiſtories betvvixte the Empeours Va- The 647.vntruth.
lentinianus, Theodoſius, and Sainte Ambroſe. He He doth entreate, as
confuteth the opinion of ſuch as thinke the Iuriſdiction that Chriſt ſhall appeare.
gaue vnto his Church, to be but for a time, vvhileſt the Magiſtrats The.648. Vntruth.
excōmunicatiō be=
vvere as yet ynfaithfull, and proueth that the Iuriſdiction of the longeth to the Biſ=
Church, vvas geuen ofChriſt to remaine til his ſecond cōming, and ſhoppe by Chriſtes
belongeth only to the Church, and not to the Prince (.648.) Biſhop, cōmiſſion without
ani furder cōmiſſiō
or Prieſt, vvithout ſpecial cōmiſſion frō the Churche. The vvhiche frō the Church, as it
Eccleſiaſtical Iuriſdiction, * I comprehended vnder the firſt kind of hath before bene
cohibitiue Iuriſdictiō. You do M. Caluin not double, but quadruple, declared.

*you do ſo in dede,
but none els beſide
you.

llll ij   yea

yea much more vvrong about the cuting of his sentence, for as ye haue vntruely reported the circumstance of his sentence, so haue you hackte from the beginning thereof one material vvorde, part of it you haue obscurely tanslated, the other part falsly, and by altering his vvords and sense, ye haue belied him, slaundered the auncient Bishopes, and haue auouched M. Caluin (if those vvere his vvordes and meaning, vvhich you in your translation Father vppon him) directly against your selfe: vvhich you meant not, for ye thought (as I suppose) you had so cunningly handeled him, that he should haue scrued your turne. If this your euil dealing vvith M. Caluin, proceeded of ignoraunce, for that his Latine vvas to fine for your grosse vnderstanding, ye are somevvhat to be borne vvithall: but if you haue thus dealt of purpose, than your malice is ouer great, ye shevve your selfe shameles to deale so vnhonestly, and that in the sight of al men. After that M. Caluin hath proued, that our sauiour Christ gaue the discipline of excommunication vnto the Church, to be exercised continually by the same: to the censure vvhereof all estates ought to submitte the selues, for if he be an Emperour, he is vvithin , or vnder, and not aboue the Church, He concludeth vvith this sentece: Quare illi qui vt Magistratum ornent &c. *VVherefore they which to adorne the Magistrate, doe spoile the Church of this power (to exercise the discipline of excommunicatio) do not only corrupt Christs sentece with a false interpretation: but doe also, not lightly condemne al the holy Bishopes, which were so many from the Apostles time : for so much as they (al the holy Bishopes) haue vsurped to them selues the honour and office of the (ciuil) Magistrate vnder a false pretense or colour. The first vvord of the sentence vvhich knitteth the same, as a conclusion to that, that goeth before, ye haue lefte out. Hovve darkely ye haue translated the first parte of the periode , may appeare by conference of your translation vvith the Authours vvordes. The laste parte ye haue falsely translated, tourning the Coniunction into a Pronoune relatiue, and translating this vvord* Magistratus *(vvherby Caluin meaueth the ciu l Magistrat) by these vvordes, spiritual gouernement, and so haue cleane altered both the vvordes and (.649.) sense of M. Caluin, and yet shame not to belie him, saying (Iohn Caluin saieth) vvhich he saieth (.650.) not. But it is M. Fekenham that saieth, and so belieth Caluin, and (.651.) slaundereth the auncient Bishopes, as though they (for to them this, they, hath relation) had*

taken

The. 649.
vntruth.
The sence
is not altered.
The. 650.
vntruth.
For he
saieth it
by the
vvay of
an obiection
The. 651.
vntruth.
M. Fekenham slaundereth
not the
Fathers.

taken vpon them the office of the Magistrate : as they had done in dede, if al manner correction and iudgement had belonged to the Magistrate, and none at al to the Church, by vvhose commission they exercised this iurisdiction. If this vvere M. Caluines saying, as ye translate him, that they (all the holie Bishops from the Apostles time) haue vsurped and taken vpon them the honour and office of Spiritual gouernement, by a false pretext and title made thereof, then haue you alleaged M. Caluin against yourselfe, for this sentence, if it vvere true (. 652.) ouerthrovveth your purpose, nothing more.

The. 652. vntruth. It ouer-throweth not M. Fekenhãs purpose, but côfir-meth it.

The. 11. Chapter. How Iohn Caluine alleaged by M. Fekenham, plainly condemneth M. Horns assertion.

Stapleton.

IN al this Diuision, M. Horne, you continue like to your self, false and vntrue. For first where you tel M. Fekenhã that the collector of his cômon places beguiled him, whi-che he shuld haue perceiued, if he had read Caluin with his own eyes : I answer he was not deceiued by his collector, but you are deceiued by your Collector. For Caluin entrea-ting of Iurisdictiô Ecclesiasticall in the same Chap-ter, in which the words recited by M. Fekenhã are côteined, allegeth out of S. Ambrose his Epistle to the Emperour Valentinian, that the foresaid Em-perour Valentinian enacted by plaine Lawe as we haue shewed, that in matters of Faith, Bishoppes shoulde be Iudges.   And in the said Chapter, and in the next also, Caluine sheweth that S. Ambrose would not suffer Theodosius to cômunicate with other. True it is therefore that (as M. Fekenhã saith) Caluine in that place intreateth of these Histories betwixt S. Ambrose, and the Emperours Theodosi-us and Valentiniã: and you for denying it, haue en-creased the huge nûber of your notorious vntruths.

Vide Cal-ui institut. editas in folio. Anno 1551. li. 4. cap. 11. fol. 451.

Cap. 11. fol. 447. Sed accidit sæpenu-mero vt sit negligen-tior magistratus imò nõ nunqua forte vt sit ipsemet castigandus: quòd & Theodosio Cæsari contigit.

Cap. 12. fol. 454. Sic Theodosius ab Ambrosio ob eadem Thassolanica perpetra tam iure communio-nis priuatus, &c.

Goe we now to the allegation yt selfe. M. Horne complaineth, that the firſt worde of the ſentence which knitteth the ſame as a concluſion to that that goeth before, is
quite laſte out by M. Fekenham. And yet when all is done,
yt is but a poore *Quare*, that is, wherefore : which may be
lefte owte withowte any preiudice of the ſentence in the
worlde: and being put in, neither helpeth M. Fekēham, nor
hindereth M. Horne. Reade then good reader thus: *Wherfore they that do ſpoyle*, and ſo forth. And then make an ac-
cōpte what is won or what is loſt by additiō or ſubtraction
of this *Quare*. Yet is the firſt part of the periode (ſaieth M.
Horne) darkely trāſlated. In dede the firſt word, *How*, how
it commeth in, I know not, and yt ſemeth to be a litle ouerſight of the author or ſome faulte of the ſcribe eaſie to be
remedied, and is to be tranſlated, thus: *they that do ſpoyle. &c.*
and afterward , *doe not onely corrupte, but do alſo not lightly
condemne*, and ſo forth: the ſenſe alwaies notwithſtanding
comminge to one. And as for the coniunction turned into
a pronoune: yf ye reade *damnant quòd honorem &c*. which
is but a ſmal alteration: the matter is ſone amended. And al
this is litle or nothing preiudiciall to the whole ſentence.
But I perceiue for lacke of ſubſtancial anſwere, ye are driuen thus to rippe vp ſyllables and to hunte after termes. As
for the tranſlating of the worde *Magiſtratus*, (whereby ye
ſay Caluin meaneth the ciuill magiſtrate) into the worde
ſpiritual gouernmente: whereby Mayſter Fekenham (as ye
ſay) hath altered the wordes and ſenſe of Caluin , for the
wordes which is a matter but of ſmall weight, I will not
greatly ſticke with you: but for the altering of the ſenſe, I
fynde litle or none alteratiō. For ſeing that Caluin doth anſwere thē, that mainteined al iuriſdictiō and puniſhment to

apper-

In the En-
gliſh trā-
ſlation,
fol. 402.

appertaine to the ciuil magiſtrate, and none to the church,
and bringeth in for an abſurdity againſt thē, that they that
ſo thinke, muſte condéne al the holy Biſhops, for taking vp≠
pon them the office and honour of a Magiſtrate, by a falſe
pretexte and title, in as muche as this honour and office,
that olde Biſhoppes toke vppon them, was the authority of
excōmunicatiō, which is one pricipal power of ſpiritual go≠
uernmēt, there cā be no notable or preiudicial alteratiō of
the ſenſe it ſelf, which euery way cōmeth to one iſſue. And
therfore yt is true inough, that Iohn Caluin ſayth as by way
of an obiećtion, that which M.Fekenhā auoweth him to
ſay: And there is no lie therin at al, as ye imagine: Neither
are *the Fathers ſlaūdered by M.Fekenham,* as ye cauil: but yf
any ſlaunder be in this pointe, Caluin is the Father of the
ſlaūder, whoſe words or the very ſenſe of thē M.Fekenham
reporteth.   And for the ſame cauſe they do nothing *ouer-*
throwe M.Fekenhams purpoſe, being not originallye of hym
propoſed, but owt of Caluin as an abſurdity againſt certain,
that doe challége al iuriſdićtiō to the ciuill Magiſtrate. And
therfore you in attributing theſe wordes to M.Fekenhā, as
his peculiar wordes, play with him as your Apology doth
with Cardinall Hoſius: imputing to him the hereſy of the
Swenkefeldians, that he reciteth not by his own words, but
by their own words. I ſay thē theſe wordes make nothing
againſt M.Fekenham, but plainely againſt the othe, that ye
mainteine, and againſt your aćte of parliaméte, that vniteth
al iuriſdićtion eccleſiaſticall to the Croune, and againſt M.
Horne that mainteineth the ſaide ſtatute. Againſt whome
now I make this argument borrowed of his own Apoſtle
Iohn Caluin. *They, which to honour the Magiſtrat, do ſpoile the*
Church of this power (meaning of excommunication) *do not*
                                                              onely

See
Hoſius
In his
booke,
Of the ex≠
pres vvord
of God.
Foll. 47.
M. Caluis
ſentence
alleaged
by M.Fe≠
kenham
condem≠
neth our
aćte of
parlia≠
ment.
In the en≠
gliſh trā≠
ſlation.
Fol. 402.
pag.1.

only with false expositiō corrupt the sentēce of Chriſt;but alſo do not ſclēderly cōdēne ſo many holy Biſhops,which haue ben frō the time of the Apoſtles:that they haue by falſe pretēce vſurped the honour and office of the Magiſtrate.But our actes of parliamēt geue al maner of eccleſiaſtical power and iuriſdictiō to the Prince.Ergo,our lawes condēne al the holy Fathers ād biſhops:and do falſly interprete Chriſtes ſentence.What part of this argumēt cā ye deny?The maior is your Apoſtle Caluins,euē according to your own engliſh Trāſlatiō,ſene and allowed according to the order appointed in the Quenes Maieſties Iniunctions ſo that you cā by no meanes quarell againſt it . The minor is notoriouſe by the very tenour of the othe,to the which ſo many haue ſwore , or rather forſworen.Wherefore the concluſion muſt nedes followe.

The parliamente geueth to the prince the Supreme Gouernmēt in al eccleſiaſtical cauſes,and the authoriſing of al maner eccleſiaſtical iuriſdictiō.You and your Maſter Caluin,do reſtrain this generality:For excōmunicatiō you ſay, belōgeth neither to Prince nor Biſhops,but to the church.Now ſeing you haue for this your opiniō no better authour,then Iohn Caluin one of the archeheretiks of our time,whether his authority,though it be very large ād ample with you,ād your brethern,wil ſerue for the interpretatiō of the ſtatute, in the kings benche,I referre that, to other that haue to do therin.On the other ſide,ſure I am yt wil not ſerue,whē ye come before the eccleſiaſtical bench of Chriſtes catholike church,nor of the Lutherā Churche,no nor ſerue your M. Caluin neither. And this his and your interpretation,doth plainely condemne the late lawes of our realm,and geueth M. Fekenham and all other a good and ſufficient occaſion to refuſe the othe appointed by the ſtatute,as cōdēning ſo many holy Biſhops for exerciſing that iuriſdiction, that appertey-

Printed in Londō An.1561.

M.Caluin and M. Horn cō= demne aſwel old holy Bi= ſhops,as the late acte of parlia= mente.

perteined not to thē, but to the Prince. To the Prince I fay,
by you M. Horne, who doe geue to the Prince al maner of
iurifdictiō coteined in the fecond kind of cohibitiue iurifdictiō, in the which fecond kind excōmunication is exprefly
coteined by your own Author Antoni⁹ Delphinus: though
you in reciting his wordes, haue nipped quite away frō the
middeft the wordes expreffing the fame, to beguile therby See fol.
.448.
your Reader, and to make him beleue, that Antonius was
your Author herein. It is not then M. Fekeham, but your
Maifter Ihon Caluin, and your felf alfo, that condēne al the
holy bifhops, yea S. Paule and the other Apoftles to, which
exercifed this iurifdictiō and al other iurifdiction in ecclefiaftical matters, without any warrant frō the Prince, or the
Church. Namely the bleffed bifhop S. Ambrofe for excommunicating of Theodofius. And fo al your falfe accufations
wherwith ye charge M. Fekēhā, redoūd truly vpō yourfelf.

Wher you fay, that *Caluins Latin was to fine for M. Fekenhams groffe vnderftāding.* what a fine Latin mā your felf are, Fol.480.
I referre the Reader to this your owne booke, and to your
articles lately fet forth at Oxford. The places I haue before
fpecified, and therfore nedeleffe here to be recited againe. The 653.

vntruth.
M. Horne. The. 173. Diuifion.pag.120 b.
And againe Iohn Caluin vvriting vpō Amos the Prophet, is by you alleged For it ferueth mus
to (.653.) as litle purpofe: For be it that thei vvhich attributed to King Hēry chz more
of famous memorie, fo much authoritie (vvhich greeued Caluin) vvere mē not for our
vvel aduifed in fo doing, and that thei vvere blafphemous, that called him the purpofe,
fupreme head of the church (ye knovv vvho they vvere that firft gaue to him as fhall
that title and authority) yet your (.654.) cōclufiō follovveth not herof. There- appeare.
fore Bifhops and priefts haue authority to make lavves, orders, ā. decrees, &c. The.654.
to their flockes and cures no more thā of his former faying. Chrift gaue to his vntruch.
Church this auhoritie to excōmunicat, to bind and to loovfe. Therfore Bifhops This is
and Priefles maie make lavves, orders, and decrees, to theyr flockes and cures. not M.
Fekenhās
mmmm   Stapleton cōclufion

Stapleton.

Caluin faith in plain words, *It is blafphemy to cal the Price of Englãd fupreme head of the Church.* He faith alfo, *They that fo much extolled King Henry at the beginning, foothely they wanted dew cõfideratiõ.* This is your fecond and better Apoftle M. Horn, that hath brought your firft Apoftle Luther almoft out of conceyte. This is he M. Horn, whofe bookes the facramentaries, efteme as the fecond ghofpel. This is he M. Horne, that beareth fuch a fway in your congregation and conuocation now, that ye direct al your procedings by his Geneuical inftructions and examples. This is he, whofe inftitutions againft Chrift, and the true diuine religion, are in fuch price with you, that there be few of your proteftãte fellowe Bifhops that wil admit any man, to any cure, that hath not reade them, or wil not promife to reade them. The Catholiks deny your new fupremacy : the Lutherans alfo deny it: Caluin calleth it blafphemous. Howe can then any Catholike man perfuade his confcience to take this othe?

M. Horne is not a ble to an-fwere to M. Feck. touching Caluin that faith it is blaf-phemy to cal the Prince head of the Chur-che.

And what fay you now at length to this authority M. Horne? Mary faith he : *I fay, that though it be true, yet it will no more followe thereof that Bifhops may make lawes, orders, and decrees, then of his former faying : that Chrift gaue to the Churche authority to excommunicate, to binde, and to lofe.* In dede ye fay truthe for the one, it is but a flender argu-mente: The Ciuil Magiftrate is heade of the Churche : *Er-go*, Bifhoppes may make Lawes : and Maifter Fekenham was neuer yet fo yll aduifed and fo ouerfene, as to frame fuch madde argumentes. This argumente cometh frefh and newe hammered out of your owne forge. But for the other parte, if a man woulde reafon thus, Bifhoppes haue power to binde and to loofe : *Ergo* they haue power to make

make lawes , orders and decrees &c . he fhould not reafon amifle:feing that by the iudgement of the learned, vnder the power of binding and loofing , the power of making lawes is contayned . Which alfo very reafon forceth . For who haue more fkill to make lawes and orders
for directing of mens confciences, then fuch whofe whole
ftudy and office confifteth in inftructing and refourming
mens confciences? But Maifter Fekenham doth not reafon fo , but thus . It is blafphemy to call the Prince heade
of the Church : *Ergo* Maifter Fekenham can not with faufe
confcience take the othe of the fupremacy , and that the
Prince is the fupreme head. Againe the Prince hath no authority or iurifdiction to binde or lofe , or to excommunicate: *Ergo*, M. Fekenham can not be perfuaded to fwere to
that ftatute that annexeth and vniteth al iurifdiction to the
Prince, and to fwere that the Prince is fupreme gouernour
in all caufes Ecclefiaftical. Thefe be no childifh matters M.
Horne. Leaue of this your fonde and childifhe dealings, and
make vs a directe anfwere to the arguments as M . Fekenham propofeth them to you : and foyle them well and fufficiently , and then finde faulte with him , yf ye wil, for refufing the othe . But then am I fure , ye wil not be ouer
haftie vpon him , but wyll geue him a breathing tyme for
this feue yeres at the leaft, and for your life to. For as long
as your name is Robert Horne ye fhall neuer be able to
foyle them . Neither thinke you , that in matters of fuche
importance, wife men and fuch as haue the feare of God
before their eies, wil be carried away from the Catholike
faith with fuch kind of aunfweres.

The words of Iohn Caluin, be manifeft, and can not be a-
uoided. He faith. *Erāt blafphemi, cū vocarēt ipfum Sūmū capat*

*Ecclesiæ sub Christo.*They were blasphemous,whē they cal-

Calui: in
Amos c.7.
fol. 292. led him(he meaneth kinge Henry.8.) the Supreme head of the Church vnder Chriſt. And who were thoſe that Caluin calleth here blaſphemous? You would M. Horne your Reader ſhould thinke,that he meaned the Papiſtes, for you referre that matter to M.Fekenhams knowledge,ſaying to him,*You knowe who they were,&c.*as though they were of M.Fekenhams friendes,that is to ſay, Catholikes , as he by Gods grace is. And ſo ful wiſely bableth M.Nowel in hys

Fol. 127. ſecond Reproufe againſt M.Dorman.But that Caluin mea-neth herein plainely and out of all doubte the Proteſtants and his owne dere brethern,it is moſt euidēt by his wordes immediatly folowing,which are theſe.*Hoc certè fuit nimiũ: ſed tamen ſepultum hoc maneat ; quia peccârunt inconſiderato zelo.*Suerly this was to much. But let it lie buried , for that they offended by inconſiderate zele.Tel me nowe of good felowſhip M.Horne,were they M.Feckenhams frendes,or youres,were they Catholikes,or Proteſtants , that Caluin here ſo gently excuſeth,wiſhing the matter to be forgotté, and attributing it rather to want of dewe conſideration, and to zele,then to willfull malice, or ſinnefull ignoraunce? Euidēt it is he ſpake of his brethern proteſtants of Englād, and for their ſakes he wiſheth the matter might be forgot-ten.With the like paſsion of pity, in his commentaries vpō S.Paule to the Corinthians,whē he cometh to theſe words alleaged there of the Apoſtle.*Hoc eſt corpus meum* : This is my body , remembring the ioyly concent of his bretherne about that matter, he ſaith . *Non recenſebo infælices pugnas,*

Caluiu: in
cōment.in
1.Cor. 11. *quæ de ſenſu iſtorum verborum,Eccleſiam noſtro tempore exer-cuerunt.Vtinam potius liceat perpetua obliuione eorum memo-riam obruere.* I will not reaken vp , the vnhappy combats,
that

that haue exercifed the Church in our time, about the fenfe
of thefe words. I would rather they might ones vtterly be
forgotten. And by and by he reiecteth the opinion of Caroloftadius, calling it *infulfum comentum*, a doltifh deuife. I
fay then of Caluin: the bemoning of the matter, betrayeth
his meaning. It is not his maner perdy, to bemone the Papiftes. Proteftants then nedes muft they be, whome Caluin
there calleth blafphemous.

But here note good Reader what fhiftes thefe fellowes
haue, when they are preffed to fee the truthe. M. Nowell
laieth al the fault to falfe reporters, and as Caluin pitied him
and his felowes for inconfiderat zele, fo he pitieth Caluin
againe for incôfiderat beleuing of falfe reporters. But what **Fol.127.**
a foolifh pitie this was, on M. Nowells part, and how vnfa-
uerly he foluteth this obiection, I leaue it to M. Dorman,
who will I doubt not, fufficiently difcouer his exceding foly herein. Thus then M. Nowell. But what fhifte hath M.
Horne? Forfothe full wilely and clofely he ftealeth cleane
away, from the matter it felf, framing to M. Feckenham an
argumente, whiche the bafeft Logicioner of a hundred
woulde be afhamed lo vtter. And thus with folie on the
one fide, and crafte on the other fide, willfulnes ouerco-
meth, herefie contineweth, and the obiection is vnanfwered.

Yet to preffe it a litle more, for fuch as haue eies, and fhut
thê not againft the light, you fhal vnderftâd, that Iohn Caluin was offended not only with his brethern of Englâd, but
alfo with thofe of Germany, yea and of his own neighbors
about him, for attributing to Princes the fpirituall gouernemêt, which M. Horn auoucheth, to be *the principall parte of* **Fol.14.**
the Princes royall power. In the booke and leafe before no-

Caluin vbi
supra.

ted he faith. *Sed interea funt homines inconfiderati, qui faciu̅t illos nimis fpirituales. Et hoc vitium pafsim regnat in Germania. In his etiam regionibus nimium graffatur. Et nunc fentimus quales fructus nafcantur, ex illa radice, quòd fcilicet principes et quicunque potiuntur imperio, putent fe ita fpirituales effe, vt nullum fit amplius Ecclefiafticum Regimen. Et hoc facrilegium apud eos graffatur, quia non poffunt metiri fuum officium certis & legitimis finibus: fed non putant poffe fe regnare, nifi abolea̅t omnem Ecclefiæ authoritate̅, & fint fummi iudices tam in doc trina, quàm in toto fpirituali regimine.* But in the meane while there are vnaduifed perfons, which doe make the̅ (he meaneth Lay Princes) to fpirituall. And this ouerfight rayneth moft in Germany. In thefe Countres alfo it procedeth ouermuch. And nowe we feele what fruytes fpringe vp of that roote: verely, that Princes and al fuch as do beare rule, think the̅ felues nowe fo fpirituall, that there is no more any Ecclefiaftical gouerneme̅t. And this facrilege taketh place among the̅, bicaufe they can not meafure their office, within certayn and lawful boundes. But are perfuaded, that their kingdome is nothinge, except they abolifh all Authority of the Church, and become them felues the Supreme Iudges, as wel in doctrine, as in al kinde of Spirituall gouernement. Hitherto Iohn Caluin.

Fol.106.b

Fol.4. b.
& .5.a.

If M. Feckenham or any Catholike fubiecte of England had faid or write̅ fo much, you would haue charged him M. Horn *with an vnkind meaning to the Prince a̅d to the State,* yea and fay, *that he bereueth and fpoljeth the Prince of the principall part of her royall power.* But now that Caluin faith it, a man by you not onely eftemed, but authorifed alfo fo farre as is aboue fayd, what faye you to it M. Horne, or what can you poffybly deuife to fay? He calleth yt plaine facrilege

ſacrilege, that princes can not meaſure and limit their power, but that they muſt become the ſupreme Iudges in all
Eccleſiaſticall gouernement. And doe not you M. Horne
defend, that princes not onely may, but oughte alſo to be
the Supreme Gouernours in all Eccleſiaſticall cauſes?
All, I ſay, nay you ſay your ſelfe, *without exception*. For Fol. 104. *a*
if (ſay you) *ye excepte or take away any thinge, yt ys not all.*

    You thē M. Horn that auouch ſo ſternly, that the Prince
muſt haue al ſupreme gouernement, in matters Eccleſiaſticall, anſwer to your Maiſter, to your Apoſtle, and to your
Idoll Iohn Caluin of Geneua, and ſatisfie his complaynte,
complayning and lamenting, that Princes wil be *the Supreme
Iudges, as well in doctrine, as in all kinde of Spirituall gouernement.* Anſwer to the zelous Lutherans, and the famous ly-
ers of Magdeburge: who in their preface vpon the 7. Cen-
tury, complaine alſo ful bitterly, that the lay Magiſtrats wil
be *heads of the Church,* wil *determine doctrine, and appoynte* In preſat.
to the Miniſters of God what they ſhall preache and teache, and Centur. 7.
what forme of Religion they ſhall folowe. And is not all your
preaching and teaching, and the whole forme and maner
of all your Religion nowe in England, enacted, eſtabliſhed
and ſet vp by acte of parliament, by the lay magiſtrats only, An. 1. *Eliz*
the Miniſters of God, all the biſhops and the inferiour clergy in the Conuocation howſe vtterly, but in vayne, reclay-
ming againſt it?

    Speake, ſpeake Maiſter Morne: Is not all that you
doe in matters of Religion, obtruded to Prieſtes and
Miniſters by force of the temporall Lawe? Aunſwere
then to Caluines complaynte. Aunſwere to your bretherne of Germanie. Yea, aunſwere to Philippe Melanchthon the piller and ankerhold of the ciuill Lutherans,
                        who

Melanch-
thō in exa
mine ordi-
nandorū.
Luth.con-
tra articu
los Louan.
Tom. 2.

who faith alfo, that in the Interim made in Germany, *Po-*
teſtas politica extra metas egreſſa eſt. The Ciuil power paſſed
her boundes: and addeth. *Non ſunt confundendæ funĉtiones.*
The funĉtions of both Magiſtrats are not to be cōfounded.
Yea anſwer to Luther him felfe the great grādſir of al your
pedegree. He faith plainly. *Non eſt Regum aut Principum e-*
tiam veram doĉtrinam confirmare, fed ei ſubȳci & feruire . It
belongeth not to Kings or Princes, fo much as to confirme
the true doĉtrine , but to be fnbieĉte and to obeye it. See
you not here, howe farre Luther is frō geuing the fupreme
gouernemēt in al Ecclefiaftical caufes to Princes? Anſwere
then to thefe M. Horne . Thefe are no Papiſtes. They are
your own dere brethern : Or yf they are not , defye them,
that we way knowe, of what feĉte and company you are.
What? wil you in matters of Religiō ſtand poſt alone? Wil
you fo rent and teare a fonder the whole Coate of Chriſt,
the vnity of his dere fpoufe the Church , that you alone of
England, contrary, not only to al the Catholik Church, but
alfo contrary, to the chief M. of Geneua Iohn Caluin, contrary to the Chief Maiſters of the Zelous Lutherans Illiricus and his felowes, contrrary to the Chief M. of the Ciuil
Lutherans Philip Melanchton, yea and contrary to the father of thē al Martin Luther, briefly cōtrary to al fortes and
feĉtes of Proteſtants, you wil alone, you only, I fay, and a-
lone, defende this moſt Barbarous Paradoxe, of Princes fupreme gouernement in al Ecclefiaſticall caufes, all, as you
fay without exception ? Sirs. If you lyſt fo to ſtand alone
againſt all, and by Othe to hale men to your fingular Paradoxe, not only to fay with you, but alfo to fwere that they
think fo in confcience, gette you alfo a Heauen alone , get
you a God alone , get you a Paradife alone . Vndoubtedly
and

and as verely as God is God, feing in the eternal bliſſe, of all
other felicities peace ād loue muſt nedes be one, either you
in this world muſt drawe to a peace and loue with al other
Chriſtians, or you muſt not looke to haue part of that bliſſe
with other Chriſtiās, except you alone think, you may exclude al other: and that all the worlde is blinde, you onelye
feing the light, and that all ſhall goe to hell, you only to
heauen.

O M. Horne. Theſe abſurdites be to groſſe and palpable. If any Chriſtianity be in men, yea in your felfe, you and
thei muſt nedes fee it. If you fee it, ſhut not your eies againſt
it. Be not like the ſtone harted Iewes, that feing would not
fee, and hearing would not heare the Sauiour and light of
the worlde.

To conclude: Mark and beare away theſe. ij. points on-
ly. Firſt, that in this ſo weighty a matter, to the which on-   **1.**
ly of al matters in controuerſy, men are forced to fweare
by booke othe, you are contrary not only to al the Catholike Churche, but alſo euē to al maner of proteſtants whatfoeuer, be they Caluiniſtes, Zelous Lutherās, or Ciuil Lutheranes : and therefore you defende herein a proper and
fingular hereſy of your owne. Next, conſider and thinke   **2.**
vpon it wel M. Horne, that before the dayes of Kinge Hēry the.8. there was neuer King or Prince whatfoeuer, not
only in our own Countre of England, but alſo in no other
place or countre of the world, that at any tyme either practiſed the gouernement, or vſed ſuch a Title, or required
of his fubiects ſuch an Othe, as you defende.

And is it not great maruail, that in the courfe of ſo many
hundred yeres fence that Princes haue ben chriſtened, and
in the compaſſe of ſo many Countres, lands, and dominions,

no one Emperour, Kinge, or Prince can be fhewed, to haue
vfed, or practifed the like gouernement by you fo forceably maintayned? Yea, to touche you nerer, is it not a great
wonder, that wheras a long tyme before the daies of King
Henry the. 8. there was a ftatute made, called *Praerogatiuæ*
Regis, contayning the prerogatiues, priuileges and preeminences due to the Kings Royall perfon and to the Crowne
of the Realm, that I fay in that ftatute fo efpecially and diftinctly comprifing them, no maner worde fhould appeare
of his fupreme Gouernement in all Ecclefiafticall caufes,
which you M. Horn do auouche *to be a principal part of the*
Princes Royall power? If it be as you fay, *a principal part of the*
Princes Royal power, how chaūceth it, that fo principal a part
was not fo much as touched in fo fpecial a ftatut of the Prices prerogatiues and preemineces? Shal we think for your
fake that the whole Realm was at that tyme fo iniurious to
the King ād the Crown, as to defraude ād fpoyle the Prince
of the principal part of his Royal power? Or that the King
himfelf that then was of fo fmal courage, that he would diffemble and winke thereat, or laft of al, that none of all the
pofterity fence would ones in fo long a time cōplaine therof? Againe at what time King Héry the. 8. had by Acte of
parliament this Title of Supreme head of the Church graūted vnto him, howe chaunceth it, that none then in al the
Realme was found, to challenge by the faied Statut of *Prae-*
rogatiuæ Regis, this *principal part* (as you cal it) *of the Princes*
royal power, or at the left, if no plain challége could be made
thereof, to make yet fome propable deductiō of fome parcel or braunche of the faid Statut, that to the King of olde
time fuch right appertayned? Or if it neuer before appertayned, how can it be a principal part of the Princes Royal
power?

power? What? wāted al other Princes before our dayes the principal part of their royal power? And was there no abſolut Prince in the Realm of Englād before the daies of King Henry the.8. We wil not M. Horne, be ſo iniurious to the Noble Progenitours of the Quenes Maie. as to ſay or think they were not abſolut and moſt Royal Princes. They were ſo, and by their Noble Actes as wel abrode as at home, ſhewed thē ſelues to be ſo. They wāted no part of their Royal power, and yet this Title or prerogatiue they neuer had.

This hath ben your own deuiſe. And why ? Forſothe to erect your new Religiō by Authority of the Prince, which you knewe by the Churches Authority could neuer haue ben erected. And ſo to prouide for one particular caſe, you haue made it M. Horn a general rule, that al Princes ought and muſt be Supreme gouernours in al eccleſiaſtical cauſes. Which if it be ſo , then why is not Kinge Philip here, and King Charles in Fraunce ſuch Supreme Gouernours ? Or if they be , with what conſcience, doe your bretherne the Guets here, ād the Huguenots there diſobey their Supreme Gouuernours, yea and take armes againſt their Princes Religion? VVhy the Othe vvas deſuiſed.

What? Be you proteſtants brethern in Chriſt, and yet in Religion be you not bretherne ? Or if you be bretherne in religiō alſo, how doth one brother make his Prince ſupreme Gouernour in al Eccleſiaſtical cauſes without any exceptiō or qualificatiō of the Princes perſon, and the other brother deny his Prince to be ſuch Supreme gouernour, yea ād by armes goeth about to exterminat his Princes lawes in matters eccleſiaſtical? Solute al thoſe doubtes, and auoid al theſe abſurdities M. Horn, and then require vs to geue eare to your booke, and to ſweare to your Othe. Note the Abſurdity.

M. Fekenham

Athan. in epist.ad so litariam vitam a- gentes.

Hosius Episcopus Cordubensis, qui Synodo Nicenæ primæ interfuit, sic habet, sicut testatur D. Athanasius aduersus
Constantium Imp. Si istud est iudicium Episcoporum, quid
commune cum eo habet Imperator? Sin contrà, ista minis
Cæsaris conflantur, quid opus est hominibus titulo Episcopis? Quando à condito æuo auditum? quando iudicium Ecclesiæ authoritatem suam ab Imperatore accepit? aut quando vnquam pro iudicio agnitum? Plurimæ antehac Synodi
fuerunt, multa iudicia Ecclesiæ habita sunt. Sed neque patres istiusmodi res principi persuadere conati sunt, nec princeps se in rebus Ecclesiasticis curiosum præbuit : nunc autem nouum quoddam spectaculum ab Ariana heresi editur.
Conuenerunt enim Hæretici & Constantius Imperator, vt
ille quidem sub prætextu Episcoporum, sua potestate aduersus eos quos vult vtatur.

M. Horne.

As it is very true, that Hosius *Bißhoppe of* Corduba *in* Spaine, *vvas in
the first councel of* Nice, *so is it as vntrue, that these be his vvoordes, vvhich
you haue cited in his name, for they be the saiynges of* Athanasius, *and not
of* Hosius. *VVherein ye haue done* Athanasius *threefolde vvronge, first to
attribute his vvritinges to an other , then also to cause him therein to beare*

The. 655. *vntruth,* Athana- sius beas reth no vvitnes againft him selfe but agaiſt you.

*false vvitnesse (.655.) against him self, and thirdly , in that ye haue left out
the first vvoorde of his sentence , vvhich is a materiall vvvorde , and bringeth in this his saying, as a reason of that vvhich goeth before.* Athanasius
*findeth him self greeued, that both he and many other Godly Bißhops for the
truth it selfe, suffered much cruelty, and vvere vvrongfully condemned , not
according to the order of the Ecclesiastical iudgement, but by the cruel threates of the Emperour* Constantius *beinge an Arrian and a fierce maintei-
nour of the Arianisme. VVho notvvithstanding subtilly couered his ungodly
dealing vnder the pretense of a iudgment or sentence past by Bißhops in Sy-*

node or

node or conuocation,vvhich he called Epifcopale iudicium, a Bifshoply iudgement. *But fayth Athauafius,* Conſtantius can not fo hide
him felfe,feeing that there is at hand that can plainly bewray
his wilines. for if this be the iudgement of Biſshoppes, what
hath the Emperour to doo therew ith?But if on the cótrary fide
thefe things be brought to paffe through Cæfars threates,what
neadeth men,that haue but the name of Bifshoopes,&c. *There
are tvvo thinges neceſſarily to be confidered , for to vnderſtande rightly the
true meaning of* Athanaſius *in this place by you alledged:firſt vvhat vvas
required to that vvhich he calleth the iudgement belonging to Biſshoppes,or
the Biſshoply iudgement . Than vvhat vvas the dooinges of* Conſtantius,
pretending a iudgement of Biſhoppes . Liberius *the Biſshop of* Rome *, as*
Athanaſius *reporteth in this fame Epiſtle requireth in a Synod eccleſiaſtical,*
that it be free from feare,farre fromthe palaice,where neither
the Emperour is prefent,neither the Earle or Capitaine thru-
ſteth in him felfe,nor yeat the Iudge dooth threaten. *He meaneth, that it be free from feare, threates , and vvithout
this,that the Emperour or Rulers, do li nitte or* * *prefcribe to the
Biſshops vvhat they fhould iudge.This appeareth more plainly by
S.* Ambrofe,*vvho alfo fpeaketh of the lyke matter , yea vnder the
fame* Prince, *fayinge:*Cóſtantinus fet foorth no Lawes before hande,but gaue free iudgmét to the Prieſtes,The
felfe fame alfo did Cóſtantius(*in the begining of his regime*)
but that which he wel begó,was otherwife ended.For
the Bifhops at the firſt had writté the fincere faith, but when as
certaine mé vvil iudge of the faith vvithin the Palaice,*he meaneth after the opinió of the Courtiers and* * *prefcription of the Prince,other-
vvife it vvas not vnlavvful to iudge of matters,concerning faith vvithin the
Princes Palaice.the Prince alfo beynge prefent , for the firſte Nicen councell
vvas holdé vvithin the Emperours Palayce,ád he him felf vvas prefent a-
mógeſt thé:*They brought this to paffe, that thofe iudgements of
the Bifhops vvere chaúged by Circumfcriptions. *Then is required in a Synode(faith he)that* the only feare of God,and the inſtitu-
tions ofthe Apoſtles,doo fuffice to al thinges . Next, that the
right faith be approued , and Herefies, vvith the mainteiners

* Marke that M. Horne mifliketh novv,that Empe rours fhuld prefcri be to bifshops. Yet his exáples before tended mofte to proue they did fo: ád the Othe impor teth,that Princes may prefcribe &c.

* Then Sį Ambrofe meaneth againſt you,as Aⁱ thanafiuſ did be fore,

thereof,be caſt out of the coūcel,and than to iudge of the perſones that are accuſed of any faulte. *So that the Biſshoply ſeſsion or
iudgement,muſt haue freedome,muſt iudge by the only vvoorde of God,muſt
haue the Biſshops that doo iudge to be of the right faith, and muſt firſt examine the Religion and faith of the partie accuſed,and then his faith.*Conſtantius,*vvho not vvithſtanding that he did pretēde a biſsoply iudgmēt vſed
none of theſe obſeruances,but the cleane cōtrary, for as* Athanaſius *cōplay-
neth in this Epiſtle , themperour vvrought* all togeather vvith treates,
menaſsing the Biſshops,other to ſubſcribe againſt Athanaſius,
or to departe from their Churches:*VVho ſo gaynſaid the ſubſcription,*
receiued to revvarde,either death or exile.He without any p-
ſuaſiō vvith reaſons cōpelleth al mē by force ād violence,in ſo
much as many Biſshops afterwards excuſed them ſelues , that
they did not ſubſcribe of their own volūtary, but vvere cōpelled by force. VVhereas(*ſaith he*)the faith is not to be ſet foorth
vvith ſvvoordes or dartes,or by vvarrelike force,but by coūſai-
ling and perſuading.*He in the ſteade of Gods vvord,vſed his ovvn vvil,
appointing and preſcribing vvhat ſhuld be determined,anſvvering the godly
biſshops,vvho obiected againſt his vnorderly doings,* the Eccleſiaſtical Canō,
at quod ego volo pro Canone ſit. Let my vvil ſtand for the Ca-
nō:Pretending a iudgmēt of Biſshops,he doth vvhat ſo euer liketh him ſelf. *VVhereas* Hoſius *ſaith,cyted by* Athanaſius *in this Epiſtle:*Themperour ought to learne theſe things of the Biſshops,
and not to cōmaūd or teache thē vvhat to iudge in this kind of
iudgmēt,*for the Prince ſhuld not ſhevve him ſelf ſo buſy or curious in Eccleſiaſtical things,that his vvil ād pleaſure ſhuld rule or guyde thē,in ſteade
of Gods vvoord,and the godly Canōs of the fathers.*Cōſtātius vvould haue
no other biſshops but Ariās,*vvhich vvere no biſshops in deede,as* Athanaſius
ſaith,and much leſſe apt to iudge of the matter,touchīg a principal article of
our faith,or of the faithful biſshop Athanaſi°:*and takīg his hereſy as an vn
doubted truth,that might not be called into queſtiō,he ſought by al meanes,
to haue* Athanaſi° *cōdēned,and al biſshops to refuſe his cōmuniō,and to cōmunicate vvith the Arians.Theſe diſorderly dealīgs of thēperour,* Athanaſi°
cōdēneth,*as directly agaiſt the order of Eccleſiaſtical ſeſsiō or Synode,hovv ſo
euer he pretēded vnder the colour of the biſshoply iudgemēt,to abuſe his ovvn
povver*

povver and authority after his ovvne luſte againſt vvhom he vvoulde. You
vvould haue it ſeeme to the ignoraũt, that Athanaſius mynd in this place
vvere to denie, that Princes ſhould (.656.) medle or deale in Eccleſiaſticall
thinges or cauſes, vvhich is farre frõ his meaning: for he him ſelf vvith ma
ny other godly biſshops, as I haue ſhevved before, did acknovvledge the Princes authority herein, and in this ſame epiſtle he him ſelf cõfeſſeth this Emperours authority to cal coũcels, and citeth Hoſius alſo, vvho enclineth to that
purpoſe, both of them confeſſing, that Conſtans and Conſtantinus Thẽ-
perours, did cal al the biſshops to the councel, vvhich he calleth Sardiceſe
conſilium: about the accuſations and crimes laid in againſt Athanaſius.
And Theodoretus affirmeth, that this Emperour Cõſtantius called a
Synode at Millaine about ſuch like matter, at vvhoſe calling the faithful biſhops aſſembled, parentes regio edicto, obeying the Kinges Summons: vvhich they vvould not haue done, if it had beene * vnlavvful for
him to haue had any dooings about councelles. But vvhen he abuſed his authority in the councel, as though his povver had beene abſolute, vvithout limites or boundes, vvilling them, yea compelling them, to doo after his vvill
againſt good conſciencience, they vvould not obey him. Quin etiam palam
preſentem regem coarguebãt impij & iniuſti imperij, but did
openly reproue the King for his wicked and vniuſt rule or cõmaundement: vvherby is manifeſt, that Athanaſius, ſpeaketh (.657.)
not againſt the Princes authority in Eccleſiaſtical matters, but againſt his ti-
ranny, and the abuſing of that authority, vvhich God hath geuẽ him, vvhervvith to myniſter vnto Gods vvil, and not to rule after his ovvne luſte: they
commende the authority, but they reproue the diſorderly abuſe thereof. Novv
let vs ſee hovv this ſaying of Athanaſius helpeth your cauſe. Conſtantius
the Emperour dealt vnorderly and after his ovvne luſt againſt Athanaſius
and others, pretending neuertheleſſe the iudgement of Biſshops, vvhich Atha
naſius miſliketh, as is plaine in this place auouched: Ergo, Biſshoppes and
Prieſtes may make lavves, decrees, orders, and exerciſe the ſecond kind of Cohibitiue Iuriſdiction ouer their flockes and cures, vvithout commiſſion from
the Prince or other authority: I doubt not but yee ſee ſuch faulte in this ſequele that yee (.658.) are, or at leaſt ye ought, to be aſhamed therof.
The,

ſticall cauſes. The. 658. vntruthe. It is your ovvne ſequele, not M. Fekenhams,

*The. 12. Chap. Conteyning a Confutation of M. Hornes anfwer,
made to the woordes of Athanafius.*

Stapleton.

HEre is nowe one other allegation by M. Fekenham propofed out of Athanafius. Hofius the Bifhop of Corduba (faith M. Fekenham) who was prefent at the firft Nicene Councel, hath thefe wordes, as Athanafius writing againft the Emperour Conftantius doth teftifie. *Yf this be a iudgement of Bifhops, what hath the Emperour to do therewith? But one the contrary parte, yf thefe thinges be wrought by the threates and menaces of Emperour: what neade is there of anye men befides, to beare the Bare Title of Bifhoppes? When from the beginning of the worlde hath it bene heard of, that the iudgement of the Churche toke his authority of the Emperour? Or when hath this at any tyme bene agnifed for a iudgement? Many fynodes haue ben before this tyme: many Councels hath the Church holden: but the tyme is yet to come, that either the fathers went about to perfuade the Prince any fuch matter, or the Prince fhewed him felfe to be curioufe in matters of the Churche. But nowe we haue a fpectacle neuer fene before: brought in by Arrius herefye. The heretikes and the Emperour Conftantius are affembled, that he may vnder the colour and title of Bifhops, vfe his power, againft whome it pleafeth him.* M. Horne to this allegation aunfwereth, that M. Fekenham doth Athanafius threfolde wronge. &c.

Athana-
fius in E-
pift. ad fo-
litariā vi-
tam agē-
tes.

Athan. in
epift. ad fo
lit. vitam
agentes.

To the firft wronge I replie, that putting the cafe that thefe are not Hofius his words, but Athanafius: M. Fekenhams matter is nothing thereby hindered, but rather furthered: confidering the excellent authority, that Athanafius hath and euer had in the Churche. And Hofius hath

euen

euen in the said epiſtle of Athanaſius, and but one leaf before, a much like ſentence, proceding of a couragious and a
godly boldenes. *Medle not you Syr Emperour* (ſaieth he to the
forſayed Conſtantius) *with matters Eccleſiaſtical, neither*
commaund vs in this parte, but rather learne theſe thinges of vs.
God hath committed to you the Empire, and to vs thoſe things
that appertaine to the Churche. And therefore, euen as he
that maligneth and ſpiteth your Empire, doeth contrarie Gods
ordinance: ſo take ye head, leaſt ye in medling with matters of
the Church, doe not runne into ſome greate offence. Whereas
(for the ſecond wrong done to Athanaſius) you ſay, that M.
Fekenham hath lefte one material word out of Athanaſius,
ye haue turned that worde, to one halfe hundred wordes,
with a nedeleſſe declaration the ſpace of one whole leafe
at the leaſt. And yet you neuer come nigh the matter. Beſide (ſuch is your wiſedome) ye alleage in this your extraordinarie gloſe an epiſtle of S. Ambroſe, which doth ſo cōfirme M. Fekenhams preſent allegation, and is ſo agreable
to Athanaſius, ād ſo diſagreable to the cheife principle of al
this your boke, that I maruel that euer ye would ones name
it, vnleſſe ye neuer read it your ſelf, but truſted the
collector of your cōmon places. For the law of Valentinian, whereof we ſpake before, is in that epiſtle, to the yong Valentian. *Whē euer heard you* (ſayth
he) *that in a cauſe of faith lay mē gaue iudgment vpon*
a Biſhoppe? If we will peruſe and ouerloke, either
the order of holie write, or the Auncient tyme: who
is there that will denie, that in matter of Faythe,
I ſaie, ſaieth S. Ambroſe, *in matter of faieth, but*
that the Biſhoppes are wonte to iudge vppon the Em-
perours, and not the Emperours vppon the Biſhoppes?

Atb. in
dict. epiſt.
ad ſolit.

Quādo au
diſti clemē
tiſſ. impe-
rat. in cauſa fidei lai-
cos de Epiſcopo iudi-
caſſe?   Et mox.
Certè ſi vel ſcriptu-
rarum ſeriem diui-
narum, vel vetera
tempora retracte-
mus, quis eſt qui ab-
nuat in cauſa fidei,
in cauſa inquā fidei,
Epiſcopos ſolere de
imperatoribus, non
imperatores, de Epi-
ſcopis iudicare?

oooo   He

He faith againe afterward : *If there be any conference to be had touching the faith, it muſt be had emong the Prieſtes.* And how this doctrine of S . Ambroſe which is the doctrine of the catholike Church, and moſt conformable to the ſaying of Athanaſius, agreeth either with your late acte of parliament, wherby the catholik biſhops were depoſed, or with the doctrine of your boke, euery man may ſee. Yea S. Ambroſe ſaieth yet farder, that the Emperour Valétiniã, whoſe ſonne (being enduced thereto by the Arrian biſhop Auxétius) woulde nedes call the biſhop before his benche, and Iudge ouer him, made an expreſſe lawe, that: *In matter of faithe , or of any eccleſiaſtical order, he ſhould iudge, that were neither by office vnequal, neither by right vnlike.* That is as S. Ambroſe him ſelfe expoundeth it . *Sacerdotes de Sacerdotibus voluit iudicare.* He woulde haue Prieſtes to iudge ouer Prieſtes. And not only in matters eccleſiaſtical or of faithe, but ſaieth S. Ambroſe: *Si aliâs argueretur Epiſcopus, & morũ eſſet examinanda canſa, etiã hanc voluit ad Epiſcopale iudiciũ pertinere.* If otherwiſe alſo a Biſhop were accuſed, and a queſtion touching maners were to be examined, this queſtion alſo that Emperour woulde haue to belonge to the trial and Iudgement of Biſhops. Here you haue, that yt belongeth not to Princes to be iudges vppon prieſts either in matters of faith, either in matters touching liuing and maners: which doth vtterly deſtroy al your new primacy, and your late acte of Parliament, depoſing the right Biſhoppes, as I haue ſaide. And we are wel contente that councelles ſhoulde be free from al feare, and that Princes ſhoulde not appointe or preſcribe to Biſhops, howe they ſhould judge, as ye declare owt of Athanaſius and S. Ambroſe. Let this be as muche material as ye wil to a biſhoply iudgméte. But

I pray

Et poſtea.
Si conferēdum eſt de fide, ſacerdotum debet eſſe iſta collatio .

Ambroſ. lib. 5. epi. 32. Ibidem.

I pray you, is there nothing elſe, that Athanaſius ſaieth is material to the ſame? Yes truely. One of theſe materiall thinges was, that this Councel was made voyde and annichilated, for that Iulius the Pope did not conſent to yt, as the canons of the Churche require: *Which commaunde, that neither councel be kepte, nor Biſhoppes condemned withowte the Authoritie of the Biſhoppe of Rome.* And therefore Iulius did rebuke the Arrians, *that they did not firſt of all require his aduice, which they knewe was the Cuſtome they ſhoulde, and take their definitiō from Rome.* This Pope alſo did reſtore Athanaſius againe to his Biſhopprike, as your author Athanaſius hym ſelfe declareth out of the ſayde Iulius epiſtle to the Arrians. See Mayſter Horne what a materiall thing ye haue lefte out, ſo materiall I ſay, that it maketh all your ſynodes, and all your depriuations of the Catholyke Biſhoppes voyde: as were the doinges of the Arrians againſte Athanaſius. Nowe as you haue lefte out theſe materiall thinges: ſo haue ye browght foorth no materiall thing in the worlde to auoyde Athanaſius authority. And therefore for lacke of ſounde and ſufficient anſwere, ye are driué to make peuiſh argumentes of your own, and then to father them vppon M. Fekenham ſaying to him. *I doubt not, but that ye ſee ſuche faulte in your fonde ſequele, that ye are, or at the leaſt wiſe owght to be, aſhamed thereof.*

But the Sequele of M. Feckenhã is this. He ſaith to you with Athanaſius: *whē was yt heard from the creatiō of the world, that the iudgmēte of the Church ſhoulde*

VVhat materiall thing M. Horne hath lefte out touching this ſtory of the depoſition of Athanaſius.

Socrat. lib. 2. cap. 8. & 17.

Sozom. lib. 3. cap. 8. 10. & 11.

Trip. lib. 4. cap. 9. 15. & 19.

Athanaſ. in Apolog. 2. contra Arrianos. Oportuit ſecundum canonem, & non iſto modo iudicium fieri: oportuit ſcribere nobis omnibus, vt ita ab omnibus quod iuſtum eſſet decerneretur, & mox. An ignari eſtis hanc conſuetudinem eſſe vt primum nobis ſcribatur, vt hinc quod iuſtum eſt, definiri poſsit? Quapropter ſi iſtuc huiuſmodi ſuſpitio in epiſcopum concepta fuerit, id huc ad noſtram Eccleſiam reſerri oportuit.

*should take his authority of the Prince?When was this agnised for a iudgement?*And so forth   Yf the Prince be supreame head in al causes ecclesiastical,if al iurisdictiō ecclesiastical, be vnited and annexed to the crowne:yf the synodical decrees of Bishoppes be nothing worth withowt the kinges expresse consente: yf catholike Bishops be deposed by the Princes commissiō:yf lay men only may alter the olde auncient religiō(al which things with other like are now done and practised in Englande) thē doth the Church iudgmēt in Englande, take his authority of the prince and lay mē. And then may we wel,and ful pitifully cry out , *whē was there any suche thinge frō the creatiō of the worlde heard of before?* This this,is M.Fekenhams argument M. Horne: this is his iuste and godly scruple that staieth him, that he rūneth not headlong to the deuill , in taking an vnlawful othe,against his conscience: settled vpō no light,but vppon the weighty growndes,of holy scripture, of general coūcels, of the holy and blessed fathers,finally of the custome and belief of the whole catholike Churche:and namely among all other of this authority brought out of Athanasius: who also in an other place saieth , *that the Arrians assembles coulde not be called synodes, wherin the Emperours deputy was president.*

Wherefore it is a most opē an impudent lye that ye say, that M Fekēham causeth Athanasius to beare false witnes against him self:how proue you this,good Syr ? *By this,* say you,*that yt is euident by Athanasius and Hosius to,that Princes haue to medle and deale in causes or thinges ecclesiasticall, namely in calling of councelles ,for by this Constantius and his brother Constans the Sardicense councel was summoned* . A worthie solution perdy for you, and a wonderfull contradictiō for Athanasius.Ye shew vs,that they called this coū-

Marke M.Fekēs hams ine uitable ar gument.

Athanas. apol. 2. cōtra Arari. Qua fronte cōuentū synodi appellare audēt, cui Comes prasedit?

cell:

cel:but that there was any thing ſpokē or done in that coūcell by Athanaſius (who was there preſent) or other , that
ſhould cauſe Athanaſius to be cōtrary to him ſelf, ye ſhew
nothing.Shal I thē anſwere you,as M.Iewel anſwereth M.
D.Harding,naming this councel,but referring the Reader
to the conncel it ſelf?*This coūcel*, ſaith M.Iewell *is brought*
in,al in a mummery,ſaying nothing. And then he addeth:*yet*
foraſmuche as theſe men thincke yt good policy to huddle vppe
theire matters in the darke,it wil not be amiſſe,to rippe them
abrode,and bring thē forth to light. And yet for all this great
brauery and bragge,he leaueth the matter of this coūcel as
he fowndyt,and ſpeaketh no more of yt,one way or other.
Me think M.Horne , that you treade much after his ſteps.
Ye name the coūcel,but ye tel vs not one materiall worde
for your purpoſe out of it.I wil thérfore furniſhe that, that
lacketh in M.Iewel and you:eſpecially ſeing the matter is
ſuche as toucheth the depoſing of Athanaſius, that is, our
preſent matter,and withal,al this your preſent Treatiſe and
anſwere to M.Fekenham.

I ſay thē firſt:the conditiōs that ye require in a Biſhoplie
iudgmēt were here exactly obſerued.This coūcel was farre
ād free frō al feare,farre frō the pallace. Here were preſent
no Coūties with ſouldiars as it was wōt to be in the Arriās
ſynodes,to extort the cōſent of the Biſhops. Whervpō the
Arriā biſhops,who were called to this coūcel,ād came thither in great nūber,ſeing this,and ſeing Athanaſius preſent
(whom they had vniuſtly depoſed)yea and ready to āſwer
thē,and to diſproue their wrōgful doings,and finding their
own cōſciencs withal gilty,had no more hart to abide the
triall of this free Synode , then you and your other Proteſtante bretherne had to appeare in the Councell of Trent.

In his re-
plie.Fol.
240.

A prettie
mummery
of M Ie-
vveland
M. Horn
concer-
ning the
Sardicēſe
councell.

Ath.in
dict.epi-
ſtol.ad ſo-
lit. vitam
agentes.

o o o o iij   And

Theodor.
li.2.ca.8.
Niceph.
li.9.c.12.
Id quod
Conſtans
ſic petierat
Conſtãtius
aũtē aſſen
ſerat.

And therfore ful pretely ſhronke and ſtole awaie. The order of this Councel was a verie Synodicall and an Epiſco-
pal iudgemẽt. Neither Emperour was preſent, nor anie deputie for him, that I haue yet read of, though at the requeſt
of Conſtans the Catholike Emperour, and by the aſſent of
Conſtantius the Arrian, that councel was aſſembled. Neither was there either in the tyme of the councel, or afterwarde the councel being ended, anie conſent or confirmation required of the Emperour: and yet were there a greate
number of Biſhopes excommunicated and depoſed to. The
ſentence of Pope Iulius, which, in a councel at Rome a litle
before, reſtored Athanaſius and other Biſhopes by the Arrians in the Eaſte vniuſtly thruſte out, was exequuted. Ma-

Vide epiſt.
Concil.
Sard. in
Theodor.
li.2.ca.8.
Tripart.
li.4.c.24
Athanaſ.
in epiſt. ad
ſolit. vitã
agentes.
Cano.4.5
7.8.& 13.

nie lawes, orders, and decrees touching matters eccleſiaſtical were in this councel ordeined. Namely for depoſing of
Biſhopes, and placing others in theyr romes, in all which yt
was decreed, *that if a Biſhope depoſed by his fellowe Biſhoppes
at home* (for Princes depoſed none in thoſe daies, though
baniſh and expell they did) *would appeale to the Biſhoppe of
Rome, that then the Biſhops who had depoſed the partie appealing ſhould ſend informations to the Pope, and that if he thought
good, the mater ſhould be tried a freſhe: otherwiſe the former
iudgement to take effect.* For final deciſion alſo of ſuch appel-
latiõs made to Rome, it was in this general councel decreed,
that the Pope might, *either appoint cõmiſsioners to ſit vpõ the
matter, in the Court from whence the appeale came, or if he
thought ſo meete, to ſend legates from his owne Conſiſtory to decide the mater.* In lyke manner it was there decreed, *that Biſhopes ſhould not haunte the Emperours palaice,* excepte for
certaine godly ſuites there mentioned, or *inuited thither of
the Emperour himſelfe.* Alſo of Biſhopes not to be made, but
ſuch

ſuch as had continewed in the inferiour orders, certayne
yeres,&c. it was in that councel decreed. All which and diuers other eccleſiaſticall maters that councel determined,
without any ſuperiour Authoritie from the prince.

And ſo to conclude, this one Councel that ye bring in,
but in a mummerie, your falſe viſor being taken from your
face, openeth what ye are, and anſwereth fully al this your
booke: as wel for the principal mater, that the Pope ys the
ſupreame head, and that Biſhopes maie appeal to him from
all quarters, as that the Prince hath no neceſſarie voyce in
Councelles. Againe, that as wel the firſt as the ſecond cohibitiue iuriſdiction (as you diuide them) belongeth to the
Biſhopes.

This coū-
cel vvas
holden,
An.350.

Laſte of al your greate principle, that you and your M.
Caluin ſo ſtronglye builde vppon, that no excommunication ought to be made without the conſente of the congregation, where the partie that is or ſhalbe excommunicated
dwelleth, is vtterly deſtroied For *Theodorus*, *Narciſſus*, *Acha*
tius, *Stephanus*, *Vrſacius*, *Valens*, *Menaphontes*, and *Georgius*,
Arrian Biſhopes, were in this councel depoſed, and excommunicated, without anie conſent or foreknowledge of the
congregation where they dwelled. And as this was done in
this councel againſt theſe men: So was the like done in o-
ther councelles againſt many other heretikes. Wherefore
this is a moſt abſurde propoſition of Caluin, that M. Horne
his ſcholler ſo hardly maintaineth. The ſtorie of this coūcel
is at large declared by Athanaſius hym ſelf, and moſt ſtrongly confirmeth that his former ſaying, that it is no Councell
of Biſhopes which hath his authoritie of the Prince. Neither can M. Horne make light of this Councel as well for
the foreſaid cauſe, as for that it was populouſe and frequented

M. Horne
and Cal-
uins opi-
nion con-
futed by
the pra-
ctiſe of
Sardicēſe
Councel.
Vide Atha-
naſ, ibidē.

Cano, 21. Omnis sy-nodus di-xit:vniuer sa quæ con stituta sūt Catholica ecclesia in vniuerso orbe diffu sa custo-diat.

ted by a greate number of Bishoppes of thyrtie and fyue Prouinces there present, of the whiche our *Britannia* was one, and as well Catholike for fayth, as auncient for tyme, and suche a one as theyr Decrees bynde the whole Churche. And the whole Synode sayeth: *Let all the Catholike Churche dispersed through out the worlde, keepe and obserue all that we haue ordeyned.* And thus muche haue I sayed, to fyll vp your emptie boxe of the Sardi-cense Councell, that you and M. Iewell playe the iolie mummers withal.

The, 175. Diuision. pag. 123, a.

M. Fekenham.

Hier, 1.

Allmightie God saieth by his Prophete Hieremie, which was bothe a Prophete and a Prieste. Ecce dedi verba mea in ore tuo : Ecce cōstitui te super gētes & super regna, vt euellas & destruas,& disperdas,& dissipes,& ædifi-

Greg. Na-zian, de Hier. dict. oratioe 18. ad subdi-tos timore perculsos, & impera tore irasen tem.

ces,&plātes.Gregorius Nziāzenus sermone de dictis Hiere-miæ ad Iulianum Imperatorem : putas ne patimini vt verū vobiscum agam, suscipitis ne libertatem verbi, & libenter accipitis, quod lex Christi sacerdotali vos nostræ subiecit potestati,atque iustis tribunalibus subdit? Dedit enim nobis potestatem, dedit principatum multò perfectiorem princi-patibus vestris,aut nunquid iustum videtur, si cedat spiritus carni,si àterrenis cœlestia superentur, si diuinis præferantur humana? Sed patienter quæso accipite libertatem nostram. Scio te ouem esse gregis mei, scio te intra sacra altaria cum veneratione subijci manibus sacerdotis, &c.

Ezech, 34

And by this Prophete Ezechiel almighty God saieth: Væ Pastoribus Israel, quod infirmū fuit, non consolidastis, quod

quod ægrotū, non sanastis:quod confractum non alligastis:
quod abiectum,non reduxistis:quod perierat,non quæsistis.
*Into the whiche maledictions and curses , the Bishoppes
and Priestes muste needes incurre, if they haue no Iurisdiction ouer theyr flocke , if they maie not visite them,
if they may not resourme them , if they maie not order
and correcte them, at all tymes as they shal see cause.*

Chrysostomus Homil. 5. de verbis Esaiæ , vbi Sacerdotem astruit esse medium inter Deum & Hominem , nul-
lumque honorem in terris illius honori posse conferri.

*Chrysost.
Hom. 5.de
verb. Esa.*

*And therefore here to conclude this my obiection
vnto your L. answeare, I shall here finishe the same, saying with the blessed Martyr Ignatius , S Iohn the Euangelistes disciple.* Quòd nemo præter Episcopum aliquid
agat eorum quæ ad Ecclesiam pertinent . *And so to adioyne herevnto the sayinge of S. Augustine, who in spea-
kinge* Contra Iulianum, ait de Doctoribus Ecclesiæ: quod
credunt, credo : quod tenent, teneo: quod docent,
doceo: quod prædicant, prædico : istis cede, & mihi cedes. &c.

*Ign. epist.
7 ad
Smyrnēs.*

M. Horne

In all this parte there is not (.659.) one sentence , that can
be dravven by any force to helpe your cause . It suffised you, to
heape vp a sorte of testimonies togeather , to make a shevve,
allthough nothing to the purpose . Yea the vvoordes spoken to
the Prophete Hieremie maketh plainely (.660.) againste you.
For they shevve, that the ministers in Gods Churche , haue authoritie to plucke vp by the rootes , and to destroie euilles and
the kingedome of Satan, to plante good thinges, and

*The· 659. vntruth.
Most impudent,
as shall appeare.*

*The. 660. vntruth.
After the same ma∞
ner, as before.*

to edifie the Churche, *as the glose interlined hath it*, or all maner wicked and falfe doctrine, and what so euer the heauenly Father hath not planted, *as the glose ordinary expoundeth it*. But the meanes *vvhereby this iurifdiction and authority is exercifed*, is (.661.) limited and appointed *in thefe vvordes*: Beholde I haue put my woordes in thy mouthe, *faithe God to Hieremy. So that other iurifdiction ouer people and kingdomes, than the preachinge of Goddes vvorde Hieremy had not.* Hieremyes mouth is touched, *faieth the glose ordinary*, and the Lordes woordes are geuen (*to him*) that he fhoulde receiue boldenes to preache. *Of this boldenes to preache the vvoorde of God, fpeaketh* Gregory Nazianzen *.in the place by you alledged. After he had comforted his hearers, he tourneth his fpeache to the Princes, and fuche as vvere in authority*, mufte we fpare you (*faithe he*)bicaufe of your power, as though we feared, or were afhamed of the liberty geue vs of Chrifte? Chriftes lawe hath made you fubiect to my power, and to my iudgement feate. *He fpeaketh of a fpirituall fubiection by faith, and obediece to the minifter, exhortinge, comfortinge, and edifiing to eternall life by the vvoorde of God. And he addeth more expreffely, vvhat maner of rule or empire he challengeth, namely fuche as bringeth the flea fhe to be fubiect to the fpirite, fuche as maketh earthly thinges fubiect to Heauenly. And the fubiection he requireth is none other, than fuch as the fpirituall fheepe oyveth to the fpiritual paftour, vvhofe rule and fubiection Chrifte vttereth in this fentence:* My fheepe heare my voice and follow me. *I knovv faith* Nazianzene *to the Emperour*, that thou arte a fheepe of my flocke; *and therevpon he concludeth that he muft, boldely preache the vvoorde to the Emperour, and that he on the other fide is fubiect therto and ought to obey. And* *this is the propre Iurifdiction that belongeth to the Bifhoppes and Priefes, the vvhiche if they exercife vvith all poffible diligence and faithfulnes, they fhal efcape the curfes that the Prophete Ezechiel menaffeth: As cotraryvvife if they vfe neuer fo princely your popifh, or rather pompous Canon Lavve iurifdiction, vvhiche confifteth in* Courtly confiftories, *and Forinfecal iudgemets, farre difagreing fro the right iurifdiction of true and Chriftianlike Prelates, they fhal not in the ende efcape the deferued maledictios, and curfes threatned to fuch by the Prophet Ezechiel.*

The.661. vntruth. The Iurifdiction of church Minifters is not limited in thefe vvordes.

Ioan. 10.

*This is fo in dede but not this only: †Be not your Cofiftories Courtly and pompous M. Horne? Remebre your felf, I pray you.

The.

*The.13.Chapter.Of M.Feckenhams laste Authorities al-
leaged out of holy Scripture, and out of certaine doctours, for proufe of the Bishoppes Iurisdiction in matters Ecclesiastical.*

Stapleton.

THIS parte of M.Fekenhams obiectió (being the very laſt, conteineth vj. authorities: two také out of the
holy ſcripture, fowre out of the holy Fathers, Gregory Nazianzene, Chryſoſtom, Ignatius and S.Auguſtine.
But in al this ſaieth M.Horne, there is no one ſentéce, that
may be drawé by any force to helpe M.Fekenhá his cauſe.
This is a ſhorte and a bolde aſſeueration M. Horne : let vs
then ſee by the examinatió and diſcuſsing of your anſwere,
whether that M.Fekenhams allegation be no ſtronger thé
ye imagine. Thus ſaith thé God to the Prophete Hieremie. *Hiere.c.1.*
*Beholde, I haue put my wordes in thy mowth:beholde this day
haue I ſet thee, ouer the natiós and ouer kingdoms to plucke vp,
to roote out, to deſtroy, and to throwe downe, to builde, and to
pláte.* And Ezechiel the prophet crieth out. *Wo be vnto the
ſhepherdes of Iſraell. The weake haue ye not ſtrengthened, the
ſicke haue ye not healed, neither haue ye bownde vp the broké,* *Ezech.*
nor brought againe that which was driué away: neither haue ye 34·
ſowght that which was loſt. Gregorie Naziangene ſpeaketh
vnto the Emperor in this ſort. *Wil ye ſuffer me to deale truely
with you? Wil ye receiue the liberty of Gods word, wil ye gladly
take yt, that Godds lawe doth ſubiecte you to our prieſtlie power,
ãd to our lawful iudgmét ſeates? For certaily God hath geué vnto
vs a power he hath geué vs a pricipality, much more perfect thé
is yours. Or doth it ſeme to agree with iuſtice, that the ſpirite
ſhould yelde to the fleſhe, that earthly things ſhoulde ouercome*

PPPP ij   *heauenly*

heauenly thinges, and that worldly thinges shoulbe be prefer-
red to godly thinges? I knowe that ye are a shepe of my flocke : I
know that at the holy aulters, ye do submitte your self vnder the
Priestes handes with reuerence. Thefe three authorities M.
Horne would remoue out of the way with one fimple folution: that neither Hieremie, nor Ezechiel, nor Gregorie
Nazianzene fpake of any other iurifdiction, then of boldlie
preaching Gods worde, to the which the Emperour is fubiecte and owght to obey. And this is the proper iurifdictio
that belongeth to Bifhoppes, which yf they diligetly exercife, they neade not feare Ezechiel his curfes.

But ô Lorde God, what maner of anfwere is this? Namelie for one that taketh vppon him, to be him felfe a paftour and a prelate of the Churche? Is there no other M.
Horne but preaching prelacy in Chrifte Churche? It is to
be wifhed, that men woulde geue fo good, and fo attetiue
eare to theire fpiritual paftours, that by theire earneft preaching they woulde reforme them felues. But what yf after
many and erneft admonitiôs, the party be neuer a whit the
better, but rather endured, either to continewe his vitioufe
liuing, or his peftilent and vngodly teaching? Shal not the
paftour procede to excommunication? Or yf the party be
a fpiritual man, to depofition and depriuatiô? Or thinke ye,
that all men do améde by wordes onely? Or thinke ye, that
the paftour is excufed, yf he procede no farther? No, no M.
Horne, your doctrine is infenfible, abfurde and moft repugnant to al the examples and practifes that we fynde in the
Church frô Chriftes time to our owne, that I euer read or
heard of and moft euidetly côfouded by our prophete Hieremie. In whofe wordes we haue a liuely patterne of the
bifhoplie office, practifed by S. Paule and the Apoftles, by

generall

general and national councelles:and by an infinite number of holy learned and auncient Biſhoppes: by S. Paule in the Corinthian, and in Alexāder and Himeneus, of whome we haue ſpoken before. *I would to God,* ſaieth S. Paule, *they that diſquiet you, were quite cutte of.* Heare M. Horne, what he ſaieth of this authority. *Arma militiæ noſtræ non carnalia ſunt, ſed potentia Dei ad deſtructionem munitionum, conſilia deſtruentes, & omnē altitudinem extollentem ſe aduerſus ſciē-tiam Dei, et in captiuitatem redigentes omnem intellectum in obſequium Chriſti, & in promptu habentes vlciſci omnem ino-bedientiā.* The weapons of our warfare (ſaieth he) are not carnal, but mighty throughe God, to caſte downe holdes, caſting downe the imaginatiōs and euery highe thing, that is exalted againſt the knowledge of God, and bringing into captiuity euery thowght to the obedience of Chriſte: and hauing redie vengeance againſte al diſobedience. You ſee how conformable S. Paules ſaying is to the ſaying of the prophete. Whoſe ſayinges ye cā not by any good interpre-tation reſtraine to preaching onely. Whiche thing as yt is euident in S. Paule, may alſo be gathered out of the words of Hieremie. For immediatly after the wordes alleaged by M. Fekenham, theſe wordes followe. *After this, the worde of the Lorde came vnto me, ſaying: Hieremie, What ſeeſt thou? And I ſayd, I ſee a rod of an almond tree* as Theodoſio tran-ſlateth, or as the 70. haue *I ſee a ſtaf made of a nutte tree:* or as our common tranſlation hathe, *I ſee a waking rodde.* This is the paſtoral rod or ſtaf M. Horne, that prelates doe, and haue euer vſed in excommunicating and depoſing perſons incorrigible. This is the rod that S. Paule threatned the Co-rinthians withal. *What?* Saieth he, *Wil ye that I ſhal come vnto you with a rodde, or in loue, and in the ſpirite of meekenes?*

1. Cor. 4.
& . 5.
Galath. 5.
Vtinā ab-
ſcindātur
qui vos
contur-
bant.
2. Cor. 10.

Hierem. 1.

1. Cor. 4.
Quid vul-
tis? in vir-
ga veniam
ad vos, an
in chari-
tate &
ſpiritu
manſuē-
tudinis?

The barke of the almon is bitter, but the fruite is moſt pleaſante. So the paſtoral rodde, though for the time it ſeemeth
paineful and greauouſe, yet to them, that thereby amende
them ſelues, it bringeth afterwarde great comforte . And
therefore it is writen : *Thy rodde and thy ſtaffe haue confor-*
ted me. And S. Paule ſaieth, he excommunicated the fornicatour at Corinth, *to the deſtruction of the fleſhe , that the*
ſprite might be ſaued in the daie of our Lord Ieſus. Which benefitte they ſhal enioye, that, by this paſtoral rodde, maie be
brought to true penance, and to the earneſt amendment of
theyr wickednes. As contrarie wiſe they, that by this rodde
wil not be reformed, but remain ſtil with Pharao wiful, obſtinat, and hard hearted, ſhal really feale that, that the Prophet Hieremy ſawe by a viſion, incontinently after he had
ſeene the rod: that is, *a ſething pot,* prepared to boyle them
in hel, that neither by preaching, nor by paſtoral ſtaffe will
fal to earneſt repentance. And not they only , but ſuch Paſtours alſo, as either for negligence or feare forſlowe to do
theyr dewtie: whether it be in the exerciſing of the paſtoral word, or els of the paſtoral ſworde: and ſuche chiefly as
take awaie from them, and deny them theyr paſtoral ſword.
Which hereſie tendeth to the vtter deſtruction of al eccle-
ſticall power and diſcipline : which power is (as all other
things of the newe teſtament are) verie plainely ſhadowed,
by the old Teſtament: Namely by theſe wordes of God ſpoken by Hieremy, repreſentinge the parſon of the Chriſtian
Paſtour: expreſſed, as yt were , by the office of an huſbandman or gardiner : or as Ezechiell expreſſeth his dutie, by the office of a Shepherde . As the huſbandman
doeth not onelie donge and fatte hys grounde : as the gardiner doeth not onelie water hys garden , but bothe of
them

Pſalm 22
Virga tua
& baculus
tuus, ipſa
me cõſola-
ra ſunt.
1. Cor. 5.
In interi-
tũ carnis,
vt ſpiritus
ſaluus ſit
in die Do-
mini no-
ſtri Ieſu
Chriſti.
Hierem. 1.
Ollam ſuc
cẽſam ego
video.

them rooteth out vnprofitable herbes , weedes , and
rootes: And as the ſhepherd doth not only bring his flocke
to good and holſome paſtours, but hath his tarre, to tarre
them, his ſtaffe to beate awaye the rauenouſe beaſtes
and birdes , his knyfe to launce them , and his place to ſea-
uer and ſhutte vp the infected from the ſownd and whole:
Euen ſo it is not inough for the ſpiritual gardiner, as it were
by Gods worde to water the harde ſtonie hartes of the
ſinners, and with the ſame as it were to fatte the leane and
barren harte of man:but he muſt alſo, when the caſe ſo requireth, weed out of Chriſtes gardē, the wilful, and the obſtinat : as it were brambles, briers, and thiſtles choking the
good groūd, and plāte in their place other good graffes. And
muſt not only with his tōge, as it were with his barkīg dog,
but with hys paſtorall ſtaffe alſo dryue awaye the wolfe
from the flocke: partly by excommunication, partly by depriuation. And he muſt in this part remember, that Chriſte
had his whip alſo, to whip and ſcourge thē out of the tēple
that prophaned the ſame . The ſpiritual paſtour hath beſide
preaching, authority alſo to bind and loſe the ſinnes of hys
flocke:ſo that if he loſe thē, Chriſt loſeth them:if he bindeth
them, Chriſt alſo bindeth thē. Of this and of the like authority meaneth Gregory Naziāzene, ād not of bare preaching.
This is the power that he ſpeketh of, this is the lauful iudgemēt ſeat of the church, this is a pricipality aboue al worldly
princes power. Theſe ſo ample words go further M. Horne,
then preaching, vnleſſe men preache alſo, with theyr hands
aſwel as with their mouthes. For Naziāzen writeth, *that the*
Emperor with reuerēce ſubmitteth himſelf vnder the Prieſtes
hands at the holy alters. What? Are aulters holy? What an holie deede haue ye then and your fellowes done M. Horne,
that

that haue throwen doune all aulters , whiche haue conti-
Contra gentiles quod vnus Deus.
nued euen fithens we were firft chriftened? And by hauing
ofthe which Chryfoftomus proueth, that our Ilelande of
Britanie had receiued Chrifte and his Ghofpell ? Where＇
vppon it wil followe, that in taking away ofthem, ye haue
taken away Chriftes fayth withall: as in dede ye haue for a
great parte of the fame: as appeareth by your dayly doinges
and your wicked articles in your Synagoge of late vnlaw-
fully agreed vppon: efpecially touchimg the reall prefence
of Chriftes body in the Sacrament. For the vnblouddy offering ofthe which to our ineftimable comforte the aulters,
do ferue in Chriftes Catholike Church. To the receiuyng
wherof no man can be admitted but by the fpiritual Paftor,
no not the Emperor him felfe, whom as wel as the pooreft
man, he may exclude from the fame, if he thinke it expe-
dient. As appeareth by the ftorie of the Emperour Theodofius, by vs reherfed : which is the thing that Naziāzene
alfo doth here though obfcurely fignifie: as alfo abfolution
to be receyued by the handes ofthe fpiritual Paftour . To
enioye the which the greateft Prince in the world fubmitteth his head vnder the paftors hands, as appeareth by our
Pro Amb. vide Ni- ceph.li.12 ca.41.Pro Aug.hom. 49.ex.50. homilijs. Tom.10.
authour here , and by other auncient Fathers, namely S.
Ambrofe and S. Auguftin. Wherefore ye do very fondly to
make this great and high iudgemēt feate nothig but prechig.
And yet if it were fo, M. Fekēhams allegation taketh place,
and is fufficient to acquite and difcharge him from the othe.
For what pricipality fo euer it be, that our author fpeaketh
of, affured we are it is an ecclefiaftical authority or principality. We are again afwel affured, as it here appereth, and
ye grauntit alfo , that this power excelleth any temporall
principality. Ergo, we may infer , that the prince is not fupreme head in al caufes or things ecclefiaftical.

M.Horne

Chryſoſtome in the homily by you cited condemning the pre-
ſumptuouſnes of the King Ozias, in enterpriſing to offer incenſe,
vvhich belonged by Gods commaundement only to the Prieſt, doth
compare the obiect or matter of both their Miniſteries togeather,
affirming, that the Prieſtly dignity reſpecting the matter vvhereabout it is exerciſed, vvhich is heauenly and ſpiritual, doth farre
exceede the other, for the * matter thereof is but earthly and outvvarde. His vvordes maketh his meaning plaine: The kingly
thron (ſaith he) hath the adminiſtratiõ of earthly thigs.
and hath not beyonde this power, any further authority. But the throne of the Prieſt is placed in heauē, ãd
he hath authority to pronounce of heauēly buſineſſes,
who ſaith theſe thinges? the King of heauen him ſelf:
what ſo euer ye lowſe on earth, ſhalbe lowſed in heauen alſo, what may be compared with this honour?
Heauen taketh of the earth principal authority to
iudge. For the iudge ſitteth in the earthe: the Lorde
(Chriſte) followeth the ſeruaunt, and what ſo euer this
(ſeruaunt) iudgeth in the inferiour (partes) that ſame he
(Chriſt) approueth in Heauen. Therefore the Prieſt ſtãdeth a meane or mediatour betwixt God and mans
nature, bringing vnto vs the benefites that come from
thenſe (from Heauen) &c. Theſe vvoordes of Chryſoſtome if
they haue not an * indifferent interpretour, that vvil make his
vvordes by iuſte circumſtaunce to ſerue his meaning, and not to
bind his meaning to his bare vvords, vvil make Heauē to (.662.)
receiue authority of the earth: vvil proue Chriſt to be inferiour to
the Prieſt, and the Prieſt to haue the mediation betvvixt God and
man by meanes vvhereof vve may receiue the Graces that cum
meth from Heauen, vvhich mediation belongeth (.667.) ouely to
Chriſte.

* If the matter of the Princely Miniſtery is but earthly and outvvard, as you here confeſſe, hovve can the Prince haue ſupreme gouernement in matters heauenly and ſpiritual, as the principal matter of his royal povver?

†VVhy ſlippe you ſo then avvay M. Horne, and geue your ſelfe no indifferent interpretation vpon his vvordes?

The .662. vntruthe, For his vvords import no ſuch incõueniençe, as ſhall appeare.

The .667. vntruth, For ſo much mediation belongeth alſo to the Prieſt through Chriſt.

Stapleton.

I commend you M. Horn: This is one of the ho-
neſteſt

qqqq

nefteft partes that you haue plaied in al your anfwere. You haue truely fet forth Chryfoftomes words and at large for the former part: I would haue wiffhed that ye fhould haue fet in alfo thre or foure lines more that immediatly doe follow: wel I wil fupply the refidewe, leaft ye waxe to proude of this litle praife. *Therefore the Prieft,* faith Chryfoftomus, *ftandeth a meane or a mediatour betwixt God and mās nature, bringing to vs the benefits that come frō thence (frō heauē) and cayring our petitions thither, reconciling our Lord when he is angrie to both natures, and deliuering vs, when we offend oute of his hands. And therfore God hath fubiected the Kinges head*

So S. Paul reafoneth Heb. 7.

vnder the Priefts hāds, teachīg vs, that this Prīce (the Prieft) is greater then he. For why? that, that is the inferiour taketh bleſſing of that which is the better. So far Chryfoftomus. As ye began liberally and freely, in fupplying the former parte of the fentēce of Chryfoftomus : So I meruel, that ye breake of fo fone, and went not through with it. But yet I haue the leſſe meruel, cōfidering that this was not don by chāce or cafualty, but of a fet, and a fhrewde wily purpofe. For yf ye had fet out at large the whole as we haue don, ye had deftroyed your own peking glofe wherwith ye glofed Gregory Nazianzene. For Chryfoftom writing how the King fubmitteth his head to the prieft, euen as Gregory did, and that the prieftes authority is aboue the kigs authority, meaneth of an other matter thē preachīg, as it euidētly appereth by his words: ād fo may he ferue againft your folifh deuice for a good interpretour, of Gregory Naziāzene. Whom as I may wel take for a good interpretour: So I meruel, what he fhal be, that ye wil take for an indifferēt intetpretor of Chry, foftomes fentēce. For by your iudgemēt an indifferēt interpretor nedēs muft we haue, to make his words and his meanig agree: ād yet your felf ftele clofe away without any furder an-

der anſwer, or any interpretatiõ at all geuen, differét or indifferét. The ſentéce as Chryſoſt. vttereth it, your weke ſto-
mack cã in no wiſe digeſt. And al the world hitherto this. xi.
hõdred yeres ãd more, God be thãked, hath digeſted it wel
inough tyl now of late your new Apoſtles Luther ãd Caluí,
cã neither abide Chryſoſtõ, that ſaith, ãd moſt truly, *that the*
prieſt is a mediatour betwen God ãd vs, nor Chriſt hiſelf, who
ſaith to the prieſt: *whoſe ſyns ye bind vpõ earth, ſhalbe boũd in*
heauẽ alſo. Here we muſt nedes haue theſe new Apoſtles as
indifferét interpretors, againſt Chryſoſtõ and Chriſt hi ſelf:
leſt that Chriſtes office, to whõ this mediatiõ belõgeth only, be takẽ away, by the prieſt, yea leſt Chriſt be made inferiour to the prieſt. Suerly if there were ſuch daũger in the
matter, it were high time to loke wel vpõ Chryſoſtom: neither if this ſurmiſe were true, ſhuld he be called by my iudgmét any more the goldẽ mouth Chryſoſtom. But (God be
thãked) there is much more feare then neadeth. Yea al this
is but an hipocritical feare and ſanĉtimony, ſuch as the wicked Kíg of Iſrael pretéded, whẽ he tore and cut his apparel
reading the King of Siria his letters, that ſent to him Naamã,
that he might be cured of his Leproſy. But the Prophet He
liſeus was neuer a whit offended with thoſe letters. And as
Heliſeus was a mediatour betwẽ God ãd Naamã for the cu
ring of his bodily leproſy: ſo is the prieſt a mediator betwẽ
God ãd his people for the curĩg of their ſpiritual leproſy in
their ſoule: without any preiudice or blemiſh to Chriſtes me
diatiõ. For Chriſt is the only mediatour, as both God ãd mã,
that is, as a meritoriꝰ and effeĉtuall mediation , valuable
through it ſelf: the prieſt or prophet is mediator as mã only:
that is, as a miniſter ãd meanes õly inſtrumétal, not effeĉtual:
called ãd choſen to ſuch office by Graçe eſpecial, not of hĩ
ſelfe, but through his commiſsiõ only effeĉtual or valuable.

Matt. 16.

4. Reg. 5.

Hovve
Chriſt ãd
hovv the
Prieſt is
a media-
tour.

And

And fo is Mofes, fo are others alfo , called in fcripture mediatours. I would now knowe of this fcrupuloufe confcienfed man concerninge the other poynt , whether , in cafe a prince did appoint any one man in his realme, to geue out his pardon in his name to fuch as were offendours, and that no man fhoulde ones loke to enioy any pardon, but hauing recourfe to this his deputy : I fay I woulde knowe , whether by thys the prince fhoulde be counted inferiour to his fubiecte.

But what meane I, to defende that renowmed auncient Father and his golden mouth, againft the foolifh blaft of fo lewde an horners mouth ? What nede I feeke any defence for the wordes alleaged by M. Fekenham , when that , M. Horne is quite ouerblowen with his owne blaft: telling vs by his own allegation, yea truely, and out of the faid Chryfoftome, that *the king hath the adminiftratiō of earthly things, and befide this power hath no further authority.* The matter alfo of his Miniftery , fayth M. Horne , is but earthly and outwarde. *Ergo* fay I for M. Fekenham, the kinge is not fupreame head in all caufes Ecclefiafticall, or fpiritual. What fay I in all caufes ? Nay not in one caufe mere fpirituall or Ecclefiafticall : as hauing nothing to doe in any fuch , but in worldly and earthly caufes only. And thus ye fee, howe wel theis two fathers, Gregory Nazianzene, ād Iohn Chryfoftome the two greate pillers of the Greke Church , may be eafely drawen without any great force, to helpe M. Fekenhams caufe.

Here nowe by the way, may be noted, that M. Horne, for al his great reading, and for all the want of reading that he fyndeth in M. Fekenham, hath wonderfully ouerfhotte him felfe , and hath by his ouerfight loft a ioly triumphante

matter

matter that he might haue had, to haue triumphed vppon
M. Fekēham. He might haue fayd, I pray you M. Fekēham:
was Iulian the wicked Apoſtata a ſheepe of Chriſtes flock,
being a renegate, a panyme, and a moſt cruel perſequutour
of the Chriſtians? VVhat? Did he ſhewe any reuerēce to the
holy aulters? Did he reuerently ſubmit his head vnder the
prieſtes hands? This and much like rhetorik might M. Horn
yf either his readinge, or his remembraunce woulde haue
ſerued, haue here vttered againſt M. Fekenham. And to ſay
the truth M. Horn, I muſt yelde and confeſſe, that ye haue
founde one companion now, yea one Emperour I ſay, that
neither reuerenced aulters, nor the prieſtes hands, no more
then ye doe now. And therfore in dede lo, this obiectiō, yf
it had cōme in time, would haue dreſſed M. Fekenham. But
I truſt, ſeing the faulte is found and amended to your hand,
that ye wil fynd no great matter againſt him: neither could
greatly before, being as it ſemeth his ſcribes fault, putting in
Iulianum, for *Valentem*.

The. 177. Diuiſion. fol. 125. 4.

Novv ſith in al theſe obiectiens hitherto, ye haue brought foorthe (.668.)
nothinge at al, that eyther made not againſt your ſelfe, or that maketh any
vvhitte for you, it is more then time yee dravve to Concluſion, and becauſe no
good Concluſion, can follovve of euil premiſſes, yee vvere dryuen to conclude,
and finiſbe vp your obiection vvith the like patchinge, vvreſting and (.669.)
falſifying your Autbours, as ye did before: and therefore in the Concluſiō, like
to him, that hauing no right to any, claymed all, to obteine ſomevvhat at the
leaſt: Euen ſo you, to proeue that your Biſsbops, and prieſtes haue al iuriſdi-
ction Eccleſiaſtical, alleage a peece of a ſentence out of Ignatius, *vvhich*
barely by it ſelſ recited, gee·ieth not onely all that vnto the Biſbboppe, but all
tbinges belonging to the Church beſides, and that no man may do any thing,
not ſo much as tol a bell to ſeruice, or ſvveepe the Church, but only the Biſbop
muſt dooe all (.670.) alone. VVhich concluſion ſome of your complices vvould
ſo litle allovve, as thoſe vvbom yee vvuld ouerburden, and yee your ſelſ might

go play

qqqq iij

The. 668.
vntruth.
moſt im-
pudent, as
by that
hath bene
ſayd, vvel
appereth.
The. 669.
vntruth.
Slaunde-
rous.

The. 670.
vntruth.
Ridicu-
lous.

go play you, as one that had naught to dao, in any thinge perteining to the Church. But to helpe the matter, and to make Ignatius vvords plain vvithout abfurditie, you muſte take vvith you the reſidue of the ſentence that follovveth, vvhich yee leaue out, of The Sacrament of Thankeſgeuing, *and* (.671.) Celebrating the Diuine Seruice, *and then it ſhall eaſely appeare, that* Ignatius *talketh of ſuch doigs of a biſhop, as in deede declare his functiō and office, ād yet jurthereth no vvhit the Cōcluſiō of your obiectiō.*

Stapleton.

The concluſiō of M. Fekenhams obiections being knitte vp with a ſentence of Ignatius, that is, that no man ſhoulde doe any thing in matters eccleſiaſtical without the biſhops conſent: M. Horne anſwereh, that he is fayne to finiſh vppe his concluſion *with patching, vvreſting, and falſifying his Authors.* He ſayth, that M. Fekenham *is like tvvone, that hauing no right to any, claimeth al, to obtayne ſomwhat at the leaſt* and being ſet in his mery mode, he returneth Ignatius ſentence by the which M. Fekenham would challenge as he ſaith al iuriſdiction to biſhops, ſo pretely and pleaſantly vpon him, *that himſelfe might goe play, as one that had nothing to doe in any thing perteyning to the Church, no not ſo much as to tol a bel to ſeruice, or ſweepe the Church but that the biſhoppe muſt do yt all alone.* And then ſadly falling to a graue expoſition of Ignatius, and to take away all abſurdity, he byddeth M. Fekenham to take the reſidew of the ſentence with him, that he lefte out, *of the Sacrament of thanks geuinge, and celebrating the diuine ſeruice*: and then he ſayth it ſhall eaſely appeare, that Ignatius furthereth nothing M. Fekenhams cōcluſion. I like yt well M. Horn, that you, ſuch a feate mynſer and miniſher, ſuch a Macarian parer and pincher of your Authours ſentences, and narrations throughe owt your whole booke, do nowe cal for the whole ſentence of Ignatius at M. Fekenhams hands. Your requeſt is ſo reaſonable, that it may not be denied you. Nay you muſt nedes haue it,

and

and your reader to, and it were for no more, but to fhewe
him of your good gracioufe dealing: who euen there, where
you fynd faulte with M. Fekenham, for not taking the refidewe of the fentence with him, do your felf fondly abufe
your reader and Ignatius withall, not daringe ons to recite
the whole fentence following. For if you had, you fhould
haue ftopped therwith your owne fowle blafphemoufe
mouth, againft *the maſsing and facrificing prieſthod*, as you Prius f. 95
call it. And your reader fhuld haue fene, that you might afwel cal Ignatius *one of the Apoſtolical clergie of the Romiſh*
Antichriſt, for this pointe, as thofe that you commonly call
papifts. And feing you charge (but moft vntruly) M. Fekenham, *for patching, wreſting, and falſifying*, to furnifhe vp his
conclufion withall, let vs fee howe worfhipfully and howe
fowndly you conclude your owne anfwere. M. Fekenham
telleth you of a general rule, out of Ignatius, recitinge his
wordes truly, though fhortly. You leauing out that which
Ignatius fayth in dede, bring vs forth that which he fayeth In the
preface.
fol. 5. in
this booke
not. For feing you fet forth your interpretation with a diftinct letter, theis wordes muft be taken, as your authours
wordes, and not as your owne, according to your promife
made at the beginning. Nowe there are no fuch wordes in
the Latin tranflation, as you reherfe, as the formall wordes
of Ignatius. In dede he nameth *Euchariſtia*, but the worde
Sacrament he hath not, neither theis wordes *celebrating the*
diuine feruice. Neither do you truly expreffe the Greke fentence. We graunt you neuerthelefle, that it is a facramét of
thäks geuing: but now we fpeake not whether it may be fo
called, but whether your author fo calleth it. Againe I afke
you, what is the thíg ther that is fo excellét ád thäks worthy,
that the whole is called * *a thäks geuíg?* Suerly it is fo called,
becaufe

Ἐκείνη
βεβαία
εὐχαρι-
ςία ἡ ζεῖο-
ζωἡ ὑπὸ
τὸν ἐ-
πιςκο-
πον οὖσα:
ἢ ὦ ἂν
αὐτὸς ἐα-
πιτρέψῃ.
* Εὐχα-
ριςία.

becaufe there is prefent in the faid bleſſed Sacrament ; the real body and bloud of Chriſt, left to his Churche to be offred for a remembraunce of his death: and to be moſt reuerently to our great and ſpiritual comfort receiued, as ofte as we are therevnto godly diſpoſed , and worthely prepared. This is the pretiouſe diſhe that Chriſt feadeth his Churche withall.

Plutarch, in M. Antonio,
It is writen, that Cleopatra the Quene of Aegyt exceded in ſumptuouſe feaſting, and that ſhe put an excellente pearle, and refolued it with vineger, and then dranke it vp. There be that do valew the price of the faid pearle at fiftie thouſande poundes of our money . But it is an other maner of diſhe, and of much higher price that Chriſt hath left vs, for this oure ſpiritual banket , euen his owne moſt preciouſe and bleſſed body : the fame I fay that died vpon the Croſſe for vs . Great cauſe haue we then to render moſt humbly to our graciouſe good Lorde our moſte bounden and dewtifull thankes for ſuch a feaſte. And moſt iuſt cauſe haue we M. Horne, to curſe your M. Caluin , and all your ſacramentary ſect, and your late damnable articles, that like moſt wicked ſtewardes haue coueyed away this beſt diſhe, and do feede Gods people , with a peece of bare bread, in

Vide Theodoret. im-patibilis Dial.3. Eucharistias & ob-lationes non admit-tunt, quod non con-fiteantur, Euchari-stiam eſſe carnem ſeruatoris noſtri Ie-ſu Chriſti, quæ pro peccatis noſtris paſ-
ſtede of Chriſtes moſt precious body, bereuing Chriſtes Churche of this moſt comfortable meate. But herein ye followe your fathers Caluin, Zwinglius, Wicleff, Berengarius, and ſuch other that the deuil ſturred vp againſt this bleſſed Sacrament: yea anon after the Apoſtles time , and in the time of Ignatiꝰ. For he doth write of ſuch heretiks as would not (by the report alſo of Theodoretus) admitte, the Euchariſtia, and the ſacrifice: for that they did not confeſſe

fesse the Eucharistia to be the flesh of our Sauiour Iesu Christe, *sa est, quã*
the which did suffer, for our sinnes, and which the father by his *puter sua*
goodnes did resuscitate.*See M. Horn the cause why we may *benigni-*
wel call this Sacrament, the Sacrament of Euchariſtia, that *tate suſci-*
is, of thanks geuing, becauſe there is preſente the body of *tauit.*
Chriſt, and offered to. The body of Chriſt being really preſent in the ſacrament, and the oblation that the Church maketh of the ſame, ye can not abide M. Horne. Ignatius in
this place by M. Fekenham recited, maketh expreſſe mention of the maſſe, and of this oblation, and as it were expounding the wordes by M.Fekenham reherſed, ſayth, *that*
yt is not lawfull neither to offer, nor to make ſacrifice, *Propterea non licet*
*nor to celebrate maſſe without the biſhop.*The like he *ſine epiſcopo neq; of-*
ſpeaketh other where:*doe nothing,*ſayth he to He- *ferre, neq; ſacrificiũ*
ron the Deacon, *without the biſhoppes, for they are* *immolare, neq; miſ-*
prieſts: they do baptiſe, they do offerre ſacrifice, they *ſas celebrare.*
gyue holy orders, they put their hands vppon men, thou
doeſt miniſter to them, as S.Stephen did at Hieruſalem *Ad Heronem.*
*to Iames, and to the prieſts.*But M.Horne full true- *Nihil ſine epiſcopis*
ly, and full lyke hym ſelfe, telleth vs a tale of the *agas, Sacerdotes eni*
Sacramente of thankes geuinge, and celebratinge the *ſunt, tu verò miniſter*
*diuine ſeruice:*and then, that this place doth not one *ſacerdotũ, illi bapti-*
whitte further M.Fekenhams concluſion. But as we *zant, ſacra faciunt,*
haue concluded you euen by Ignatius hym ſelfe a *ordinãt, manus impo*
duble heretike, both for the ſpoyling vs of the pre- *nunt, tu verò eis mi-*
ſence of Chriſtes body, and of the oblation of the *niſtras, vt Hieroſoly-*
ſame:ſo ſhal we conclude you a lier, in that you de- *mis S. Stephanus Ia-*
ny, that this place maketh any thinge for M.Feken- *cobo, & præsbyteris.*
ham. For lo:thus he argueth.
                                                    M.Fekenhams ar-
  The prieſts them ſelues in matters Eccleſiaſtical, gument deducted
ſhuld do nothing belonging to their office without out of Ignatius.
                   rrrr   the

the will and confent of the bifhops. *Ergo* much leffe the lay men or prince, which are no fpirituall men, fhould medle in matters Ecclefiaftical, efpecially they fhuld not change the olde religion, they fhuld not abolifh the bleffed Sacraméts, the prince fhoulde not call him felfe fupreame head of the Church, the parliament fhould not annexe all fpiritual iurifdiction to the crowne at leaft without the confent of the bifhops. What fay I without the confent? Nay againft the full and conformable affent of all the catholyk bifhops, and the whole conuocation, offering theire moft humble petition, and fupplication to the parliament, that there might be no fuch alteratió. And yet the parliamét Law of one realm for the alteration of relligion, yf al the bifhops had confented, were not a fufficient difcharge in confcience. When ye can wel foyle this argument M. Horn, then I fuppofe ye fhall fynd M. Fekenham fomwhat conformable to your requeft, in the taking of the othe.

Againe M. Fekenhá prayeth you, to take the whole fentence with you: and to take the paines but to reade vj. or vij. lynes further, and to confider what you fhal fynd there. That is: *that no man is more honorable in the Church, then the bifhop, and that we muft honour him firfte, and the king after him.* Of the which fort of fentences his epiftles are ful, directly impugning your newe pretenfed fupremacy. And now ye neade nothing to feare that, which ye tell vs for a great incóueinence, that if Ignatius fentéce be not wel and wifely weighed, the bifhop muft both toll the bell to feruice, and fweepe the Church allone. This is but a poore office for a bifhop, and al this highe fetche neded nothing, fauing that, after this your long and paineful trauayle také to confute fo clerkly, theis fewe obiectiós of M. Feké. ye thought

good

to refresh ād quické your weary sprites, with this your mery sportig. And yet take ye hede, that it turne not vpó your
self M. Horne in very good erneft. For of this once I am affured, that if ye meafure the matter by the old canōs of the
aūciēt Church, you that mainteyn fo many heynoufe herefies, if you may haue any office at al in the Church, you cā
haue no better, thē to toll the bel to feruice, ād fweepe the
Church, or fuche like. And yet I doubt, whether you may
haue as much as that office, beig for theis your herefies with
bel, boke, ād cādel accurfed, ād by the Church befome, that
is, by the fentéce of excómunication fo cleane fweeped out
of the Church, that as I fayd, I doubt whether by the olde
canōs ye may medle with the bafeft office of al perteyning
to the Church. And yet for any yl wil I beare to your perfon, in cafe ye were a good ād a catholike mā, I could for my
part be cótent, that ye enioyed your bifhoprike ftil, ād that
as amply as did any of the moft Catholik prelats before you.

M. Horne. The. 178. Diuifion.pag.125.b.

So that your Conclufion being yet as infufficient as the reft, you are faine
to adioyne an other peece thereunto: VVherein although yee fhevve hovve euil
a ioygner you bee, to adioyne thofe tvvo peeces of fentences togeather in one
Conclufion, that are of cleane fundry matters, yet in one poynt yee haue made
them both agree, that as yee vvrefted the one, fo ye not only vvreft, but flatly The. 672.
(.672.) falfifie the other, and yet neither of thē both ftand you in any fteade vntruth.
to helpe your obiection, much leffe to conclude the fame. For firft, hovv dooth as fhal ap
this follovve: S. Auguftine faith (fay you) of the Doctours of the peare.
Church: That they beleeue, I beleeue: that they holde, I holde:
that they teache, I teache: that they preache, I preache: yeelde The. 673.
to them, and thou fhalt yelde to me (.673.) Ergo, *Bifshoppes and* vntruth.
Prieftes haue povver aud authority to make lavves, orders, and Decrees, and This is
to vfe all cohibitiue iurifdiction ouer their flockes and cures. Novve if your not M Fe
freendes, that haue beleeued hitherto as you beleeue, haue helde, as kenhams
you holde, taught as you teache, preached as you preache, and belee- your own

rrrr ij uinge

ning the vpright dealing and conscience, that you pretende, haue yelded vnto you herein, do but a litle examine your (.674.) false dealing vvith those Fathers, vvhom you vvould seeme so vvholy to follovve, I thinke they vvould no longer beleeue you, holde vvith you, nor yelde vnto you, but suspect you as a deepe dissembler, or rather abhorre you, as an open sclaunderer and belyer, not only of me, but of the anciēt Fathers themselues. For first I vvould learne of you, vvhere S. Augustine hath those vvoords, in at his sixe bookes against Iulian, Istis cede, & mihi cedes, if he haue them, shevve vvhere: if he haue them not, then hovve ye follovve S. Augustine? Hovv dare you impudētly say, ye preache and teache that he did, vvhen ye manifestlye (.675.) mangle, alter, peruert, and corrupt the saying that he did teache. In dede for fashions sake ye cite a peece of S. Augustins sentence, that they beleue I beleue, &c. but for that vvhich follovveth: istis cede, & me non cædes: yelde to thē, and thou shalt not strike or whippe me: you (.676.) haue put in these vvordes, istis cede, & mihi non cedes, yelde to them, and thou shalt yelde to me: and yet this corrupting of the sentence maketh it serue no vvhit the more for your purpose, but vttereth your falshood: that belike vvil not spare to corrupt that vvhich maketh flat against you, that thus vse to corrupt this, vvhich maketh neither to nor fro vvith you, nor against me. But as S. Augustine vvriting in the same matter against Iulian, a Disciple of Pelagius, an (.677.) Englsh Monke, dealing vvith S. Augustine, as ye haue lon vvith me, said to Iuliā: so say, I to you. Ye feine me to say that I say not, to conclud that I cōclude not, to graunte that I graunte not, and you cōclude to your self that vvhich I deny, &c. In dede you haue laboured more to finde out those reasons vvhich ye might better vtter against your selfe, than against me. But in such a cause ye should not neede to take such peines, yf you had any shame in you. S. Augustin in these bookes against (678) Iuliā, as in his other against the (679) Donatistes, (as I haue declared before) did attribute vnto themperours and Princes, the Bishops and Priestes, such Ecclesiasticall Iurisdiction as I haue don. Of the same minde that he vvas herein,

vvere

The.674. vntruth. Slaunderous.

The.675. vntruthe. Most impudent ād outragiously slaūderous, at it shal appeare.

The.676. vntruth. All copies haue those vvordes. M. Fekēham hath not put them in.

The.677. vntruth. Pelagius vvas no Englishe Monke.

Lib.3.

Lib.5.

The.678 and. 679. vntruthes. For S. Augustine in the saied bookes is plain for the Popes Primacy, not for the Princes.

rrere also (680) thofe Fathers, that he cyteth. VVherfore you vvil novv I truſt,
according to your promiſe, yelde and relente: If not to me for ſtubborne hart:
yeat according to your concluſion to S Auguſtine, and the auncient Fathers,
to beleue herein that they beleue, tó hold that they hold, to teache that they
teache, to preache that they preache, aud no more to vvringe, maime, ſlaū-
der and belie them. And than both I and all other faithfull Chriſtians vvill
both better beleeue you, and geue God thankes for you.

Stapleton.

M. Fekenham concluding his obiections with Ignatius
adioyneth a general proteſtation of his faith taken out of
bleſſed S. Auguſtin his bookes againſt the heretike Iulianus.
Thus. *That they beleeue, I beleeue: that they hold, I hold: that*
they teache, I teache: that they preache, I preach: yeld to thē and
thow ſhalt yelde to me . Here doth M . Horne ſo reuell a-
gainſt M . Fekenhā, as he hath not don the like in all his anfwere . Firſt he denieth, that of this place of S . Auguſtine
may any good ſequele be gathered, that Biſhops may make
lawes, or vſe al cohibitiue iuriſdiction. Then as hauing now
M. Fekenham in ſuch a fowle euident faulte, as by no pretext maye be couered, he thinketh that for this falſe dealing, his owne frendes wil take him, for a deape diſſembler,
yea rather will abhorre him as an open ſlaunderer and belier of the fathers, as a manifeſt mangler, alterer, peruerter,
and corrupter of S. Auguſtine . For in ſtede of *iſtis cede, &*
me non cædes, yelde to them , and thou ſhalt ſtrike or whip
me, he hath put in: *iſtis cede, & mihi cedes.* Yelde to them,
and thow ſhalt yelde to me . And then ſaith further , that
belike M. Fekenham will not ſticke to corrupte that which
maketh flatte againſt him , that thus vſeth to corrupt that,
which maketh neither to nor fro, with him ſelf, nor againſt
him ſelfe. After this he rolleth in S . Auguſtines ſentences,

　and

and layth them forth againſt M.Fekēhā,for this his euil dealing with him, as S . Auguſtin doth againſt Pelagius a Brit-
tayn monke. Finally as though now the battel were wōne,
and a ful conqueſt made vpon poore M.Fekenham,he calleth vpon him to yelde and relente . Mary ſir this is a terrible blaſte in dede blowen out of Maiſter Hornes mouth
for his farewell: This is ſuch a bluſtering tempeſt ſturred vp
by our newe Aeolus, that (as it ſeemeth) M . Fekenham
muſt nedes be ouerblowen with the vehemency of yt.But
we will yet ſeeke out , and ſee the very foundation , and
the original cauſe of all this broyle . By al likelihodde M.
Fekenham hath founde ſome good apparance of great aduantage in corrupting theſe wordes of S.Auguſtin . For no
man lightly is ſo doltiſh, to vſe ſuch foule and ſluttiſh ſhifts,
without ſome cōfort and hope to further his matter by.Ac-
cording to the old ſaying *Cui bono.*Nay ſaith M.Horn: The
corrupting of the ſentence ſerueth no whit the more for
M.Fekenhās purpoſe.No doth it not M.Horne?and would
M.Fekenhā deale ſo fondly by opē falſhod to ſtaine his honeſty ād for *whippe me* ,trāſlate, *yelde to me* , without any be
nefit of his cauſe?Suerly thē were he worthy(aſwel as I loue
him)to be twiſe whipped,once for falſhod,ād ons more for
folly.Therefore this your accuſation euē by your own tale,
and by *Cui bono,* is vtterly incredible.

And yet yf he had ſo falſly and ſo foliſhly demeaned him
ſelf,ſeing it toucheth no part of the ſubſtance of the queſtiō
that lieth betwixt you ād him : you playe with him yf not a
foliſh,yet to vehemēt an oratour : ād haue ſauced your ora-
tory with ouer much gal ād egernes.And for al your blow-
ing and bluſtering , your great hil bringeth forth nothing,
but a poore Aeſops mouſe .

Yet ſay

Yet fay you, this is a naughty part of him, fo manifeftly to
mãgle and to corrupt S. Auguftin. Perchaunce good reader
thou doft now looke for an anſwer, and how M. Fekēham
may faue his honefty, agaíft this mighty accufatiõ. And fuerly what anſwer I may beft make, I can not redely tel : but
this will I tell you in the meane feaſon, that ſuch as vſe to
play their part very wel otherwiſe, yet ſomtimes at the very laft caft, for ſome foliſh diſorder they are hiſſed and clap-
ped out by the multitude. With what ſhoting thē, ãd clap-
ping ought this waynſcot faced mã, to be driuen, as it were
frõ this ftage, that hauíg throughout his book plaied ſo many foule ãd vilanouſe parts, for his *Valete* ãd *Plaudite*, plaieth
as euill or a worſe part, then he hath plaied in all the reſidewe of his booke?

There be no moe examples of S. Auguftins works printed, that I haue fene, but four : the firft printed at Baſil, the
fecõd and third at Paris, the fourth at Liõs : ãd al theſe haue
iftis cede, & mihi cedes. Yeld to them, and thou ſhalt yeld to
me. Only the later editiõ of Paris readeth in the text as M.
F. readeth, but putteth in the margent, as a diuerſe reading,
& me non cades, as M. Horne ful peuiſhly and wretchedly
would make folke beleue it ſhould only be read. What deteftable impudency thē is this, for M. Horn, to crie out vpõ
M. F. being a poore priſoner, after this outragiouſe ſort, and
for the allegatiõ of this place, ſo fternely ãd fiercely to vaũt,
ſaying: *How dare ye impudētly ſay, ye preache ãd teache that he
did, whē ye manifeftly mangle, alter, peruerte, and corrupt the
ſaying that he did teache?* And to aſke of him where Saint
Auguftine hath theſe woordes in all his ſixe bookes a-
gainft Iulian, *iftis cede, & mihi cedes?* The truth is, thoughe
as I ſayde, all theſe copyes haue theſe woordes in this
order,

An. 1528.
in ſol.
An. 1541.
& . 1555.
in ſol.
An. 1563.
in 8.
Lib primo
cont. Iul.
Cap. 2. *in*
medio ca-
pitis, tom.
7.

order, yet by forgetfulnes M. Fekenham hath not set in the
booke. And wil ye see, howe wel the matter is amended by
M. Horne? After all this ruffling and blustering he him self,
hauing al copies against him, nameth not, either any of theis
sixe bokes, or any place, where any boke of S. Augustines
should be printed, that shoulde haue any such text of suche
tenour as he doth alleage. And yet doth M. Horne (as ye
haue hearde) as though it were right true, yea and a synne
against the holy Ghost, all to reuile M. Fekenham: and leaueth not there: but that, which S. Augustine most truely obiected to Pelagius, doth he most vntruely obiect against M.
Fekenham: euen as truely, as that the sayd Pelagius was an
Englilh monke, who was dead and buried, before the Saxons entred Britanny. For Pelagius died in the time (at the
least of *Theodosius* the seconde) and the Saxons entred the
realme in the tyme of Marcianus, as witnesseth S. Bede.
And before Britanny was commonly called England, Pela-

Beda. li. 1.
cap. 15.
Polid. li. 3.

gius was dead at the lest one hundred yeres. But before it
was christened, more then a hundred and a halfe.

But nowe concerninge the matter yt selfe, whether the
Councels, the fathers, both olde and newe that you M. Horn
haue alleaged, and especially S. Augustine may not truely
say to you, that he said to Pelagius: I referre it to the indifferent reader. Suerly there is none of them al (as may easely
appeare to the diligent reader) but may iustly say to you.
M. Horne, *ye fayne me to say that, I say not: to conclude, that I*

Aug. li. 3.
cotra Iul.

conclude not: to graunt that I graunte not : and you conclude to
your self that, which, I denie: Againe. In dede ye haue laboured
more to fynd owt those reasons, which ye might better vtter a-

Lib. 5.

gainst your self, than against me. But in such a case ye shuld not
nede to take suche paynes yf yow had shame in you. Whether I
say

ſay truely or no in this, I referre thee, good Reader, to my
whole anſwere, and thoſe that wil ſee it cōpendiouſly proued, to my preface, and to the Concluſion of the thirde
booke.

And here woulde I faine breake of my confutation of
M. Hornes anſwere, to S. Auguſtines teſtimony, ſauing that
he doth otherwiſe ſo excedingly belie S. Auguſtine here,
that I may in no wiſe altogether paſſe ouer this ſhameleſſe
demeanure. You ſay then M. Horne, *that S. Auguſtin aſwel
in his bookes againſt Iulian, as in his bookes againſt the Donatiſtes, is of your minde towching the eccleſiaſtical ſupremacy in
Princes*, as ye ſay ye haue declared. And *that the Fathers
whome S. Auguſtine citeth agaiuſt Iuliā, are of the ſame minde
alſo.* Shewe me then good M. Horne, but one authority out
of S. Auguſtine, or any one of the Fathers, whome he reherſeth, which are *Cyprianus, Ireneus, Baſilius, Hilarius, Am-
broſius, Hieronymus,* and Pope *Innocentius* with others, eyther that the Pope hath not the ſuperiority in matters Eccleſiaſtical, or that Princes haue the ſame. All that hitherto
ye haue browght out of S. Auguſtine, with whoſe ſayinges
ye haue filled vp ſome leaues, reacheth no farther, thē that
Princes may by their lawes puniſhe ſuche, as be diſobediēte
to the Churche lawes : for the whiche thing no man doth
contende with you. But we woulde fayne ſee you ones
drawe to the queſtion yt ſelfe, and to ſhewe ſome open
place of S. Auguſtine, either for the Princes or againſte
the Popes ſupremacy: wherin ſeing ye haue done nothing,
we wil aſſay what we can ſay for the Popes primacy by S.
Auguſtine.

To auoyde tedioufnes we will reherſe but a fewe teſtimonies, and ſuche onely, as we haue taken out of his bokes

Lib. 1. cō-
tra Iulia-
num.

Places
out of S.
Augu-
ſtine for
the popes
primacy.

S S S S   againſt

Quis nescit, illum Apostolatus principatum cuilibet Episcopatui praferenda? De Bapt. contra Do nat. lib. 2. cap. 1. Epistola. 165. Numerate vel ab ipsa sede Petri: ipsa est petra, quam non vincunt superba inferorum porta. In Psalm. contra partem Donati. Epistola. 157. ad Optatum. Ab Innocentio & Sozimo toto orbe Christiano danati. Epistola. 90. 91. 92. & 93. Dicta epistola. 91. Patres non humana sed diuina decreuere sententia, vt quicquid de disiunctis, remotisque prouincijs ageretur, non prius ducerent finiedum, nisi ad huius sedis notitiam perueniret, vbi tota huius authoritate, iusta qua fuerit pronunciatio firmaretur.

againste the saide Donatistes, and Pelagians. Who is it then M. Horne, but S. Augustine that writinge againste the Donatistes, saith *that the principality of S. Peters Apostleship is to be preferred, before any other bishoprike?* Who is it but S. Augustine, that vseth to bringe againste the Donatistes, the authority of the sea of Rome as a singular and a principal authoritye? Who ys yt but S. Augustine, that writinge againste the saide Donatistes sayeth, *the sea of Peter, is the rocke that the proude gates of hel do not ouercome?* Let vs now come a litle to the Pelagians.

Their capitain Pelagius, and an other archeheretike of theire secte called *Calestius, were condened by Pope Innocentius and Sozimus, throwgh out al the Christian world.* They were also condemned in Aphrike by the bishops there. Yet S. Augustine writeth not, that they were condened by the through out al the world, as he doth of the said two Popes: because the sentence of the Aphricane Bishoppes bounde the Aphricanes onely: the Popes sentence bounde the whole worlde. And therfore the sayed Bishoppes, after they had condemned those heretikes, *desired Pope Innocentius to confirme their sentence:* which thing Innocentius did, as appereth by his answere to the foresaide Bishoppes, yet extant in S. Augustines works. Which letters geue a verie ample testimony for the Popes supreamacye: and sheweth amóg other things, *that yt was a rule kepte throwgh out al the worlde, that in graue and weighty matters ecclesiastical, and for the determinatió of mat*

ters

ters of faith, nothing was wont to be done without the Popes consent and authority. Againe S. Augustine writing against the saide Pelagiās, sendeth his boks to Pope Bonifacius, *to examine and amende thē*, *yf any thing misliked him:* and saieth: *that the saide Bonifacius had the preeminēce in the pastoral watchtowre.* S. Augustine also in this boke against Iulian the Pelagian, numbring vp a number of holy and aunciéte Bishoppes, as *Ireneus, Cyprianus, Hilarius,* and others, saieth: *that Pope Innocentius though he were later in time, yet was he before them, for his place and dignity.* He doth vrge, and presse very muche the saide Iulian with the authority of the Apostolicall sea and of the sayde Innocentius. Yea and that for an heresy, that your Apostle Caluin, and our good new bretherne in Englande, both in theire preachinges and teachinges do mainteine: that is , *that children thoughe they be not baptised, shall yet that notwithstanding enioy the euerlastinge life.* These testimonies do fully declare S. Augustines minde, touching the Popes Supremacy , quite repugnante to the doctrine of this your booke. . Wherby yt appereth, that ye litle regarde , howe and after what sorte , ye doe alleadge hym : and that ye doe not alleadge him, for any good matter ye fynde in him, but onely to make an owtwarde shewe and aparance , to the vnlearned and vnskilful people, to beguile them wyth smothe talke, and fayre wordes.

Et Epistola.93.
Diligenter ergo et congruè Apostolico consulitis honori, honori inquā, illius, quem præter illa quæ sunt extrinseca, solicitudo manet omniū Ecclesiarum, super anxijs rebus quæ sit tenenda sententia, antiqua scilicet regulæ formam sequuti, quam toto semper ab orbe mecū nostis esse seruatam.
August.contra .2. Epist.Pelag.lib.1. cap.1. Quāuis ipse in eo præmineas celsiore fastigio speculæ pastoralis.
Hæc ergo ad tuam potissimum dirigere sanctitatem non tam discenda quàm examinanda, & num forsan aliquid displicuerit emendanda constitui.
Lib.1. Et si posterior tempore prior loco. August.dict.lib.1.

THE FOVRTH BOOKE

M.Fekenham.

After long expectation, and many promises, his L. final answeare to the sayd obiections, was as hereafter foloweth.For as much as I doo perceiue, that you are not to be resolued in this matter,I shal here stay and procede no further with you in the same: and like as you haue bene,so you shalbe vnto me most hartely welcome:You shal lacke nothinge that is in my house to pleasure you: And from hencefoorth I shal leaue to haue any further talke or conference with you in these controuersies of Religion. And for all such talke and wryting as hath passed already betwene vs,I shal perfourme this my promise,both first and last made vnto you, that you shalbe well assured, not to suffer any hurte or dammage thereby.

M.Horne.

You deliuered this obiection vnto me in vvritinge, betvvixt Easter and Vhitsontyde, about the ende of Aprill:vvithin tvvo daies folovving,vvhen I had redde the same,I tould you,that in the collection of your common places, you vvere much abused,for that you had mistaken thē,and obserued no iuste circumstances of the authorities, vvhereby to haue knovven the authours meaning : And so vvee continued in debatinge and reasoning , from time to time,about this matter of Iurisdiction,and others,vntil the beginning of September folovving,before vvhich time, your obstinacy grevve so much , that I vvas forced,through your vnorderly behauiour,to restreigne you of your licētious talke,aud sequester you from conference vvith any, hauinge so muche before abused your self,and especially in mine absence, and I vvas the rather moued so to doo, for that I perceiued al that I did,vvas but in vaine:as at diuerse times and often , I repeated that vnto you , obstinatelie bente to the contrarie, meaninge by such stoutenesse to recouer your credite, vvhiche

through

through your inconstancy vvas so empaired amongest your friendes. I sayd, at your first comming, and many times after, you beinge sente by the Honourable Councel, that you vvere vvelcome, vvhich by good prouse, although vtterly vvithout any your good deserte, yee founde true. I did say, that I vvould leaue to haue any further talke or conserēce vvith you, touching matters of Religiō, or any other: but you shuld haue shevved the time and place, vvhere, and vvhen these vvoordes vvere spoken: I spake them the Sonday at after diner, vvhen in your gallorie, I did reprooue you of your disorders, and therefore restraigned you of suche libertie, as before yee had enioyed. The promise made vnto you, not to vtter that vvhich yee should say by vvaie of reasoning, in prieudize of the Q. Maiesties Lavves, I haue hitherto, and yet doo firmelie keepe to you, as you can not iustlie chardge me vvith the contrarie, in anis particuler pointe, aud so you haue susteined no hurte or domage therebie.

M. Fekenham.

The perfourming of his promise was as hereafter foloweth. First there was a rumour spersed abroade very shortly after by his seruantes, that I had subscribed to certaine articles, tenne in number.

Second, there was by his seruantes a further rumour raised, of my recantation, time and place appointed therof to be at the Parishe Church of VValtham, where his L. did then manure and abide.

Thirdely, his L. did at his open table, and in the præsence of many, chardge me with the change of my Religion nine times, and beinge putte in further remembrance by one M. Denny who was a Sogener with him, his L. saied, that I had altered and chaunged my Religiō, not onely nine times, but nineteene times, and that I was of no Religion.

Fourth, his L. did permitte the saied M. Denny at his open table to to much to abuse me. Where the saied M. Dennie did openly and before manie, chardge me with these three crimes following. First, with incontinencie of life, thus saying: That if I had not as many children, as he, he did knowe, that I had deserued to haue so manie. Second, with glottonie, affirming that I was an Epicure. Third and last, with hypocrisie, and that I was a greate dissembler and an hypocrite. The saied M. Dennie being a man to me wholly vnknowen. His L. did shewe him self openly to be so well pleased with these his slaunderouse wordes, that he ministred iust occasion for me to thinke, that his L. had procured the saied M. Dennie thereunto.

Fifth, by so much the more I had good cause to thinke so, for that his L. did immediatly therevpon, viz. within one houre after, in fortifiyng the saied talke, commaunde me to close imprisonment.

Sixth and last, after that he had kept me sixe weekes in close imprisonment, by his L. complaint I am nowe at this present prisoner in the Tower, much contrary to his promise before made.

The premisses being true (lyke as they are all moste true) being to openly commited, and before to many witnesses to be denied: your Honour may easily iudge, with what wisedome, discretion, and charitie I haue bene vsed, I being a poore man, the Q. Maiesties prisonner, and to

his L. committed (I dare boldly affirme) to be well vfed.
It was very ftraunge to me, to fee fuche behauiour openly
fhewed at the table of fuch a man. Surely for mine owne
parte, I was neuer fo vfed, neither openly nor priuately
at any mans table before in my whole life. My humble
fute therefore vnto your Honour is, that proufe and trial
may be had of my trueth herein, and what my deferuings
hath bene for the whole time of mine abode there. In due
fearch and examination hereof I doubt not but there fhal
fall out matter betwixt vs, either of much fimplicitie and
trueth, or els of greate crafte and falfehood: either of ho-
neft, vertuoufe and godly, or els difhoneft, vitioufe and
vngodly vfage: and either of much light, learning, and
knowledge, or els of very groffe ignoraunce, and palpable
darkeneffe: let it fall and light on the whiche fide it fhall
happe, vppon the triall and examination made, I doubt
not, but that your Honour fhall haue a full fhewe and a
fufficient proufe made, of euery thing that hath paffed
betweene vs. There may be deniall made for a fhifte and
fome fhort time: but for any long time it may not pofsibly
endure, euery thing being fo openly committed and done,
fo diuerfe and manie beyng of knowledge and witneffe
thereof.

M. Horne

To *this challenge of promife breache, in thefe fyxe pointes: Truely I*
knovve not *of any rumour fpredde of you, by any of my feruauntes, or other-*
vvife

wife that yee fubfcribed to any Articles, ne yet euer herde any thing hereof, before I favve the fame reporte in your booke publifhed: And if any fuche rumour vvere fpredde by any my feruauntes or other, you fhoulde haue named him, that he might receiue condigne punifhment therefore.

Seconde, as to the further rumour of your Recantation, I fay likevvife I vnderftoode nothinge but by your ovvne reporte in your booke, and therfore referring the Authour to be punifhed accordingly, I thinke the punifhment ought to light vppon your felfe.

Thirdly, as to my chardge of your changinge in Religion. ix. times, yee. xix. times, I faide fo, and that (.681.) truely vppon proufe of your vnconftât affirming and denying, not fo fevve times, as I had good experience oft in you, and can haue vvitnes in the fame.

The. 681.
vntruth,
most eui-
dent and
Slaunde-
rous.

Fourthly, touching your abufing by M. Denny, yee mifreporte the Gentleman, as to any thinge that euer vvas fpoken before me. But if any fuche vvere, it vvas as I herde fay at my retourne home (for I vvas abroade in preachinge vvhan fuche fcoffinge talke vvas betvvixte you) by occafion of fome talke miniftred on your parte to M. Denny, partely by vvay of merie talke betvvixt you tvvaine, and partly fturred vp by your vnfeemely vvords, and yet none of all thefe in my hearinge. But in the laft daie, vvhan I reftraigned your liberty, you did fo much before me at my table prouoke the faide gentleman by calling him Epicure, for that he fafted not as ye faied, that I, fearing leaft M. Denny like a younge man fhoulde geue fome euill vvordes againe, vvilled him to fay nothing, for that I my felfe vvoulde anfvveare the matter for him: Mine anfvveare vvas, that I meruailed vvhy you vvould cal him Epicure: for if you fo thought, becaufe he did eate fleafhe, and neuer fifhe, I faied, he might (.682.) fo vvel faft, vvith fleafhe, as vvith fifhe: but if it vvere for that he vfed not abftinency, I faied in that M. Denny did more then you: for vvhere you had euerie daie in the vveeke your (.683.) three meales, fridaie and other, the gentleman vvas contented three daies in a vveeke, vvith one meale a daie, and neuer did eate aboue tvvo. And as it is vntrue, that either M. Denny vvas a man to you vtterly vnknovhen, beinge conuerfant togeather in one houfe a quarter of a yeere before, and in famil ar company, yea fought many times by you to play at the bovvles, to vvalke in the parke, and to be mery togeather : fo is it alfo vntrue, that I hearde you fo abufed as I coulde or did like therein,

The. 682.
vntruth.
Ioined
vvith a
groffe er-
rour.
The. 683.
vntruthe
flaunde-
rous, as al
that
know M.
Feckenhã
can vvit-
neffe.

and

and so vntruely doe you surmise, that I shoulde procure M . Denny, *by any meanes to abuse you, as yee malitiousely conceiue of me.*

Fiftely, *as to the restrainte of your liberty, vvhiche you cal close imprisonment, to haue ben for these talkes betvvixt* M. Denny *and you , vvithin one hovvre after:* You knovve right vvel, *that your restrainte vvas not vppon that occasion, but vppon your seemelie behauiour aboute other matters, vvhereof ye make no mention , least you shoulde haue prooued your self a* Lier. *After I had in fevve vvoordes calmed the storme that seemed vvoulde arise betvvixt* M.Dennie *and you, I entred into talke vvith you in matters of* Religion, *as I vvas vvont to doo dailie before. The talke vvas of venial and mortal sinne: you haue not forgottē the occasion, I am sure: for if you haue in your remembraunce the Monkish (.684.) Iebusites , you cal them Iesuites, you may remember, that a crosse that came from them, gaue the occasion of the talke in that matter. I proued that no (.685.) sinne is so venial as it could be remitted by any ceremonie: yea, there is no sinne but the same (.686.) of it selfe is mortal, and yet venial to be purged by the merites of Christe onelie: and that al sinnes, vvere they neuer so mortal , vvere neuerthelesse venial, sauing al only the sinne againste the holy Ghoste, vvhiche is irremissible. For this my saying, and other pointes vvhich I condēned , ye sel into such a rage, that ye not onely railed against the Bishop of Sarisburie, saying: he vvas vtterlie vnlearned, and that he should neuer be hable to ansvvere* M . Hardinges *booke, but also openly called me almoste in plaine termes Heretique, and said,* my doctrine vvhiche I preached (yet ye vvould neuer heare me) *was erroneous, filthy, and blasphemous: so filthely your blasphemous mouth, coulde raile against (.687.) Gods truthe. VVherupon, I, to staie yoū, saied alonely that those vvere vnmann. rlie vvordes to be spoken at mine ovvne table: and therfore vvould as thā say no more opēly vnto you there, but tolde you that after dinner I vvoulde shevve you more of my minde, betvvixt you and me. And so shortly after dinner, I came vp to you and there calling you into the Gallory of my house, adioining to your chamber, I put you in remēbraunce of that vvhiche I had before oftentimes admonished you of your outragious talke in mine absence, vsed oftentimes opēly at my table, vvhereof I had sondrie times geuē you vvarning for that the same might breede peril to your selfe, blame to me, and offence to others. And bicause I foūd stil the cōtinuāce of that your misorder: yea, to be muche more vehenēt many times in*

The.648.
vntruth.
slaunde-
rous and
Ievvish:
The.685.
vntruth.
heretical:
The.686.
vntruth,
in like
maner
plaine he
reticall.

The. 687.
vntruth.
Your do-
ctrine
hath no
affynite
vvith
Gods
truthe.

tttt   mine

mine abſence than in my preſence: Therefore I vvilled you thenceforth to abſteine from conferring vvith anie man in any vviſe at all, addinge that you
ſhould haue to your chamber, al things neceſſary, and vvhat meate you vvold
competently appoint for your ovvne diet, vvhich ye had accordinglie. And
although I did reſtraine you from comming to mie table, or to goe ſo much
at large as you had doon: yet had you no other keper than you had before,
vvhich vvas your ovvn man: you had a faire Gallory adioyning to your chā-
ber, opening to mie parke, your ſeruaũt a chamber by him ſelf, next to yours,
ye had Leades faire and large, on the vvhich ye might vvalke, and haue pro-
ſpect both ouer the Parkes, Gardeins, and Orchardes. And therevvith thriſe
in the vveake at the leaſt, vvhiles I laie at VValtham, vvith one by me appointed, you vvalked abroade into the Parkes, Garden, and Orchard: and
this you call your cloſe empriſonment. Sixthly, touching my complaint to the moſt honourable of you, vvherby you vvere remitted

The. 688. vntruthe.
M. Fekenham hath
in no point belyed
you in his ſhedule
ſpread abrode, but
vvil ſtand to al that
is cōteyned therin.

priſoner againe to the Tovver, vvhat the ſame vvas, their ho-
nours can vvel declare, if their pleaſure ſo be: beinge ſuer that I
haue not broken promiſe vvith you hitherto, in vttering your opiniõ againſt the Lavves of the Realm, as I haue before ſaid, vvhich
ye ſhevved at anie time in the priuate conference. And ſo ye haue
not anie cauſe to challenge me in that behalfe.

To conclude, by the premiſſes it maie appeare to the honourable
as by a taſt, vvhat ſinceritie there is in you. Againe, that this your

The. 689. vntruthe.
The Catholike faith
is no errour.

quarelling and (.688.) belying me by ſpreading this booke, vvas
and is chieflie, to recouer your credit vvith thoſe of your faction:
vvho as I haue ſaied, had conceiued doubt of your reuolt,
and to confirme them in their grounded (.689.) errour, and herevvith to bringe me and other ſuche as I am, into obloquie and

The. 690. vntruthe
ſlaunderous. Nei-
ther M. Fekenham.
Nor other Catho-
likes doe impugne
the Quenes Lavv-
full Authority, but
onely ſuche as is
novve proued to
be vnlavvfully

hatred. And laſtlie, to impugne and barke againſt the Q. Maieſties
(.690.) Lavvfull and due authoritie, vvhich you and your complices dailie labour to ſubuert: vvhich matter I referre to be further conſidered, by the graue vviſdome of the moſte honourable.

FINIS.

attributed to her Hignes, by ſuch as you are.

The.14.Chapter,of certaine priuate matters betwene M.Feke-
ham and M.Horne. And of certaine especial heresies
auouched by M.Horne, wherby to conclude, he
concludeth himselfe a plaine heretike.

Stapleton.

THis being the laſt parte of all, ſtandeth moſte vppon
mutuall accuſations : M.Fekenham ſynding him ſelfe
greaued, that he ſhould be miſſuſed at M.Hornes table, and there to be noted of incontinencie, gluttonie, and
hypocriſie : that rumours ſhould be ſpread abrode by M.
Hornes ſeruantes of his ſubſcription and recantation : and
finally that contrary to M. Hornes promiſe made to hym,
that he ſhould ſuffer no domage or hurte for any wordes
paſſed betwixt them , he was firſt reſtrained of his libertie
accuſtomable by M.Horne, and kepte there cloſe priſoner
vj. wekes : and afterward by his procuremeut remitted to
the Towre.

M.Horne on the other ſide denieth, that euer he was
priuie to any ſuch rumour, and complayneth as faſt vppon
M.Fekenham, and his diſorder, as calling M.Deny Epicure
at his owne table, and for openly calling him ſelf almoſt in
plaine termes heretike. He putteth M.Fekēham in remembraunce of certaine talke paſſed betwene them : *as that*
a man may faſt aſwell with fleſhe, as with fiſhe: of mortall and
deadly ſynne, and other matters. As for the reſtraynte of his
liberty, he ſayth it came vppon his owne diſorder : and that
in cōplayning vpon him to the Councell, he brake no promiſſe with him. Theſe matters then being ſuch as priuately
paſſed betwene them , I beinge one that neither was then
preſent, nor yet ſithence fully vnderſtanding any certainty
of them, muſt leaue this to M. Fekenhams owne defence,

when the time fhal ferue. Sauing that fo muche , I can fay, that I haue bene credibly enformed, that M. Fekēham doth deny, as wel that he mifufed M. Deny, as fuch other things as M. Horne chargeth him withal, and is ready to ftand to, and to iuftifie al fuch things as are conteined in this his fhedule if he may be fuffred: And fuerly among other things, to them that knewe his order and diet, either before his comming to prifon, either in the towre, when he had the liberty of the fame , wheras I am credibly enformed , he neuer made three meales, it can not feme credible and likely, that he fhuld at Waltham as M. Horne faith, make three meales, afwel friday as other daies.

One thing I am fure of M. Horn, he toke no part of your flefhly breakfafts and fuppers, that ye haue had in good ftore in your houfe vppon the fridaies and other fafting daies. Which example to be fhewed in your houfe , being a man of fuch vocation and countenaunce , againft the Lawes of the Church and the realme, how it may be allowed, I leaue it to the confideration of others. For I fuppofe neither your felf, nor Maiftres Madge, with al your other flefhly company , are fallen into fuche weaknes , feblenes and confumption , nor are of fo timeroufe and fcrupuloufe a confcience , that either ye neade , or will tarrie for a Licence: I wil not fay to be fought at Rome, but nearer hand, at London .

And what neade this prelate of any other Licence, that can fo pretely licence him felfe to faft with flefh afwell as with fifhe? *For a man may* (faieth he *) faft afwell with flefhe as with fifhe.* Wel fpoken, and like a good Turk or Iewe : For at a good Chriftians mouth I neuer heard that rule, nor euer reade it before. In the primitiue Church men fafted in great

numbers,

numbers, both from fiſh and fleſhe: but this prelate leaſt the
generation of his ſpirituall children, ſhould be to much hindered, by eating cold fiſh, hath found a new diuinity, wherby we may faſte with a fatte pigge or capon vppon good
friidaie, leaſt for fayntnes we fal vnder the croſſe as Chriſt
did. I ſay, this is a new diuinity. For from the Apoſtles time
hitherto Lent hath euer bene faſted, aſwel in our realme, as
in al Chriſtendom beſide. Wherof nowe almoſt xiij. hundred yeares ſithence, our moſt noble countreman and Emperour Conſtantinus, geueth vs a full godly teſtimony, aſ-
wel for our *Ileland of Britany*, as for *Rome, all Italie, AEgypt,*   *Euſ.l.3.de*
Fraunce, Lybia, all Grece, al the countries called Aſiana and Pō-   *vita Cōſt.*
tica Regio, Cilicia, and for al the Churches of the Eaſt, Weſt,
South, and North: And this lent faſt was frō fleſh at the leſt,
as it appeareth euidently, both by Epiphanius aboue xj. hū-   *Li.3.Tom.*
dred yers paſt, and by a Councel of Laodicea, holdē about   *2. hæreſ.*
that time. Yea they were counted plaine heretiks, that cō-   *75. Laod.*
temned the Lente and other faſtinge daies: As the Aerians,   *Can.50.*
Iouinians, and ſuch other.   *Hier.con-*
     tra Iouin-
 And nowe haue we a ſubtile inſoluble, *that there is no*   *Epiph.vbi*
ſynne, but that the ſame of it ſelfe is mortal ſynne, and yet there   *ſupra.*
is no mortall ſynne, but that the ſame is veniall. For he ſaieth,
he proued to M. Fekenham, that there is no ſynne ſo venial, as
it could be remitted by any ceremonie, yea there is no ſinne, but
the ſame of it ſelf is mortal, and yet veniall, to be purged by the
merites of Chriſt onely: and that al ſynnes, were they neuer ſo
mortal, were neuertheleſſe venial, ſauing al only the ſyn againſt
the holy Ghoſt, which is irremiſſible. Suerly this is a notable cōcluſion to lap vp your worthy boke withal. Wherin for al
your ſubtelty, are as many errours and hereſies, as are lines.
And would God ye would haue ſhewed as withall, what
t.t t t iij   godly

godly Father ye haue for your Authour , in thefe your abfurde and falfe propofitionis.   Well , well,as muche as ye
crake,that ye proued this gere to M.Feckenham,I muſt tel
you,ye haue not yet proued nor euer ſhal proue yt as long

M.Horne
is aſha,
med to
ſhevve
his do,
ctour.
VViclef.li.
3.cap.1.
trialog.
Solũ pecca
tũ finalis
impœnitē.
tiæ,quod
eſt peccas
tum in
ſpiritum
ſanctum ,
propriè eſt
mortale.

as ye liue.And ye dare not for ſhame,ſhewe the authour of
your doctrine : who is no better then the Archeheretyke
Wiclef. Who ſayeth there is no ſynne properly to be called mortal,but the lacke of finall repentance, which is the
ſinne againſt the holy Ghoſt. Or yf ye haue any better authour,we woulde gladly ſee him:and would gladly at your
good leaſure better vnderſtand,how ye could either rydde
your ſelfe from many fowle errours, or from a fowle contradiction,in thefe your ſo fewe lines.

For firſt where you ſay , that no *ſinne is ſo venial, as it
coulde be remitted by any ceremony:*yf you vnderſtode what
venial ſinne were,a man of your vocatiõ would be aſhamed
ſo to ſay. And therfore I wil firſt open your ſecond errour
vpon the which this former is grounded. Which is this.
*There is(*you ſay)*no ſinne,but the ſame of it ſelfe is mortal,and
yet venial,to be purged by the merites of Chriſte onely.* Is this
your diuinitie M.Biſhop ? Nowe forſothe a worthy diuine
you ſhewe your ſelfe , and more mete to be a pariſh clarke
in Kingy ſtrete in Wincheſter,then a biſhop of that famous
See.For how ſay you M.Horne?Is euery mortal ſinne alſo
venial?And is euery ſinne of it ſelfe mortal?Let vs then ſee

D.Thomas
1.2.q .72.
Art.5.

Mortall
ſynne.

what is mortal ſinne,and what is venial.Mortal ſinne is cõmitted,whē we doe any thing againſt Gods law, or againſt
the loue we owe to him, or to our neighbour for his ſake,
with an auerſiõ or turning away frõ God him ſelfe. Which
Acte forſaking the euerlaſting goodnes and cõuerting our
ſelues to the vnlauful vſe of his tēporal creatures,is a deadly ſinne

ly fynne, that is fuch as deferueth by the law and iuftice of
God, euerlafting death. Of fuch mortal fynnes excluding
from the kingdome of God, you haue in S. Paule diuerfe
enumerations,bothe to the Corinthians, and to the Gala-
thians: which howe they may be made venial you fhal neuer fhewe:but howe they may be made no finnes at al that
is,howe they may be vtterly forgotten and forgeuen, yt is
eafy to fhewe:forfothe by the merites of Chriftes pafsion,
as a meritoribus caufe:by the mercy and Iuftice of God, as
by a formal and efficient caufe, our own repétaunce going
before according to the facrament of penaunce with al the
partes thereof, as by a neceffary difpofition of the matter
apte to receiue this effecte, which is Reconciliation with
God after our falle.   Veniall fynne is a difordinat affection
or pafsion difordering our dewe loue to God and our dew
obedience to his lawe,either by frailty of light motiós and
incitations (againft the which we fight not fo ftrongly as
we fhoulde,neither watche fo warely as we ought) or by
natural infirmity of the olde corrupted Adam, or by excu-
fable ignoráce of the particular factes, in al which we forfake not God,nor our loue to him and to our neighbour,
but are for the time rather letted and hindered, then auer-
ted or remoued from our loue and duty to God.This fynne
is called venial or pardonable,for that the Acte thereof excludeth vs not from the kingdome of heauen, neither maketh vs deadly guilty in Gods fight. And the reafon is,be-
caufe fuch motions of frailty, and fuch light negligences
(without the which this life is not lead) are but a fmode-
ring heate of the olde fyre of originall finne cleane quenched in the water of baptim:Quenched I fay,for any gylti-
neffe thereof to remayne,but not quenched vtterly for the

1.Cor.6.
Galat. 5.

*Vide Con-
cil. Tridēt.
Seß.6.ca.
7.& Sef-
fion.14.
cap.3.*

Veniall
fynne.

operation

operation and working thereof. The olde Adam worketh ſtill in vs, and rebelleth againſt the ſpirite (notwithſtanding he was drowned in Baptiſme) but the ſpirite of the newe man in Chriſt reſiſteth, and fighteth daily againſt him. In which fight and combat the beſt men are ſometime venially ouercomed, though not deadly, as moſt men are.

This is the clere doctrine of S. Auguſtin, and of al the learned Fathers by him alleaged in his ſecōd Booke againſt Iuliā the Pelagiā: Of S. Ambroſe, S. Cypriā, S. Chryſoſtome, S. Hierom, Gregorie Naziāzene S. Hilarie, S. Baſil, S. Ireneus, with certain other, by him, as I ſaied, alleaged againſt Iuliā the Pelagiā. And to be ſhort with you herein M. Horn, behold one direct ād clere ſentēce of S. Auſtin, cōformable to al thoſe holy Fathers ād Doctours, in which he ſhortly and clerely cōfuteth your moſt ignorāt cōfuſiō of venial ſinne ād of mortal: ſaying that *euery ſinne of it ſelf is mortal.* For after he had alleged al the forenamed doctours, ād laſt of al in this place S. Ambroſe, cōcerning the remnāts of original ſin in vs, which by your doctrine ād Melāchthōs, is deadly and mortal ſinne, thus he cōcludeth him ſelf. *Ecce quantā nos pugnā etc. Behold what a greate fight or cōbat, this valiaūt ſouldiar of Chriſt, ād faithful doctor of his Church* (he meneth S. Amb.) *ſheweth vs to haue with ſinnes allready dead ād ſlayne:* (he meneth original ſinne in baptiſm) *for howe is* (that) *ſin dead ſeing that it worketh many things in vs, whē we ſtriue againſt it? What many things are theſe, but fond and hurtful deſires which draw the conſenters vnto them into deſtruction: Which yet to ſuffer and not to yeld vnto, is a combat, a conflict and a battail? Nowe betwene whom is this battail but betwene good and euill: not betwen nature and nature* (as the Manichees imagined) *but betwene nature and ſynne: (ſynne, I ſaye, already dead, but yet to be buried, that is, wholily to be healed.*

Lib.2.cō-
tra Iul.
Pelag. To.
7.Fol.213
a. in Fol.
Pariſ.
Anno. 55.

Howe

Howe then ſay we, this ſinne is dead in baptiſme (as alſo this mã
ſayth, S. Ambroſe) and howe do we yet confeſſe, that it dwelleth
in our membres, and worketh in vs many deſires , we ſtriuing
ſtill againſt it (as alſo this Ambroſe confeſſeth) but bicauſe this
ſinne in reſpect of the gyltyneſſe thereof, wherein (before baptiſme) we were faſt tyed, is dead, and yet beinge dead rebelleth,
vntyl by perfect buryal it be quite healed. And yet this ſinne is
not nowe (after baptiſme) in ſuch ſorte called ſinne , as that it
made vs guilty (before God) but bicauſe by the gyltineſſe of A-
dam it was made (ſynne) and bicauſe alſo by rebelling it dra-
weth vs to ſin , except the grace of God by Ieſus Chriſt our Lord
do helpe vs, that this dead ſinne do not ſo rebelle , that by ouer-
coming vs it waxe againe alyue, and reigne (in our mortal body). In this battail fighting and toyling, as longe as this life is a
tentation vpon the earthe,* we are not therefore in ſinne, becauſe this which in ſuche ſorte is called ſynne , worketh in our
membres, contrarying the lawe of (our) minde , as longe as we
conſent not vnto it in the vnlawfull deſires and motions of it.
For as touching our ſelues, we ſhould remaine, alwaies without
ſinne (vntill this euill were (vtterly) healed) if we did neuer
conſent to the euill. But in ſuch thinges as by the rebellion of
this euill, we are ouercomed in, though not deadly, but venially,
yet ouercomed, in ſuch thinges I ſay, we contract or gette that
wherby we muſt daily ſay: Lorde forgeue vs our treſpaſſes . As
(for example) maried folke, when for pleaſure only they excede
the meaſure neceſſary for generation. As alſo continent and
chaſte perſons, when they ſtay in ſuch thoughtes with ſome de-
lectation, not yet determining the wicked deede, * or bearinge
(the wicked dede) of him that doth determine it , but not a-
uerting ſo diligently as they ought the intention of their minde
from ſuche thoughtes , nor yet riddinge them ſelues ſo ſoone

*Nõ idee
ſine pecca-
to non ſu-
mus.

Sed in qui-
bus ab illo
rebellãte,
etſi nõ læ-
taliter, ſed
venialt-
ter, tamen
vincimur,
in his cõ-
trahimus,
vnde quo-
tidie dica-
mus. Di-
mitte no-
bis debita
noſtra.
* ve ge-
rentes de-
cernentis.

ʋ ʋ ʋ ʋ   from

from the thoughtes (being ones fallē into them) *as they ought.* Thus farre S. Auguſtin. Theſe two exáples he geueth of ve-nial ſinne. And for theſe veniall ſinnes we muſte ſay daily (ſaith he) *Lord forgeue vs our Treſpaſſes.* Accordig to this do-ctrine he teacheth in an other place, wher he writeth thus. *The ſonnes of God as longe as they liue in this mortal life, they fight with their mortalite. And though it be truly ſaied of thē: As many as are lead with the Spirit of God, thoſe are the ſonnes of God, yet they are ſo ſtirred with the Spirit of God and doe ſo profit to Godward as the ſonnes of God, that yet as the ſonnes of mē, eſpecially by reaſon of their corruptible bodie moleſting thē, they falle back to thē ſelues ward, with certain humain motiōs, and therefore do ſinne. There is a great difference, as we haue largely ſaied. For though euery Crime* (by which terme he cal-leth mortal ſinne) *be a ſinne, yet euery ſinne is not a Crime.* As much to ſay, euery venial ſinne is not mortall or deadly. *Therefore we ſay in dede, that the life of holie men, as long as they liue in this mortalite, maie be founde without Crime,* or deadly ſinne. *But* (venial) *ſinne if we ſaie we haue not, we de-ceaue our ſelues* (as the holy Apoſtle ſaieth) *and Truthe is not in vs.* Here againe S. Auguſtin maketh a clere differēce be-twene the crime or deadly ſinne, which maketh vs the ſon-nes of wrath, ād betwene the venial ſinne, with the which we continewe yet the ſonnes of God: and the which holie mē in this life neuer lacke. But God forbidde that holy men ſhoulde neuer lacke deadly and mortal ſinne : which vpon M. Hornes doctrine (*that euerie ſynne of it ſelfe is mortall*) muſt nedes folow. No. No M. Horne, your lewd ſpirit and the holy Spirit of the lerned fathers are farre wide a ſonder.

This you learned of Melanchthon, and he of Luther, the very ſynke of all your filthie hereſies . But howe lear-

nedly

In Enchi-
ridio cap.
64.
Rom.8.

Sap. 9.
Crimen.
Peccatū.

1.Ioan, 1.

nedly and pithely this fonde and lewde doctrine of Melanchthon, Luthers, and youres was confuted by Doctour Eckius, in the open disputation betwene him and Melanchthon at Wormes, you may M . Horne (for you make no deinty, I thinke, to reade heresye bookes) see and reade to your greate cōfusion euen in the very workes of Melanchthon printed at Wittenberge . Anno. 1564. Where also you shall finde a Notable place of S . Augustine corrupted first by Luther, and then by Melanchthon, so clerely detected and pressed of Doctor Eckius, that Melanchthon was fayne in that honourable Assembly openly to recante, and to say. *Quod ad me attinet, agnosco male citatum esse.* As for my owne part, I confesse it was wrōgfully alleaged. The place was this. Where S . Augustine wrote : *That Concupiscence was taken away by baptisme , non vt non sit , sed vt non imputetur,*not that yt shoulde be no more in man after baptism, but that after baptisme it should no more be imputed vnto vs, yf by deliberat consent we yelded not thereto: Luther ād Melāchton mad S. Augustin to say:*That sinne was takē away by baptism, not that it cōtinewed not stil in mā, but that it should no more be imputed to mā.* By which feate ād sleight, by turning Cōcupiscēce into sin, they proued both their Imputatiue righteousnes, as that mā was neuer iuste , good, and holy, but only was accepted for such, though he remained stil a sinner ād had sin alwaies in him , and also that the same sinne was in him a deadly and mortall sinne. Which is the thinge that M Horne here affirmeth, auouching that *euery sinne of yt selfe is mortal.*

Which (to make an ende hereof shortly) is as much to say, as euery sicknesse infirmitie or disease is of it self death. For as the body liueth by the soule , so the soule liueth by

Tom 4. in Actis vvormaciensibus. Fol. 650 & sequent. Pag. 656. in fine.

vvvv ij   God.

God.As the body dieth , when the foule is feparated from it,fo the foule dieth, when God is gone from it .   Which matter S.Auguftin moft excellently handleth in his notable worke *de Ciuitate Dei* . As therefore not euery difordered affection of the body killeth it out ofhande,but the body is longe and much vexed with defeafes and infirmites before it dye,yea and as longe as the defeafe reacheth not to the harte or roote of vital humour where hence the life fpringeth,as longe as that principle of life is whole and founde, the body liueth and dieth not:fo not euery couerfion ofthe foule to the creatures,bredeth a feparation of the foule frō the Creatour:but the foule fighteth againfte the flefhe,and though in that fight it take a blowe , yea and a wounde to now and thē,yet the fowle recouereth it felfe and yeldeth not wholy to the flefhe,or to any other creature, but cleaueth ftil to God his Creatour , loueth him ftil, kepeth his lawe,and fo falleth not deadly , neyther fynneth mortally, vntyll it geue ouer to vice,and forfaketh God. Which euil men doe,without any fight or combat at al. But good men eithernot at al,or very feldom and after great fight:and the are they no more good men or the childrē of God, but are nowe become the children of wrathe , fo to perifh euerlaftingly,except they repente.This is a greate and a clere diftinction betwene mortal finne and venial fynne.

Now where you adde,that though euery fynne be of yt felfe mortal, yet *it is alfo venial to be purged by the merites of Chrift only*,yf you take venial for pardonable or remifsible,we graūte,euery fynne be it neuer fo mortall,is in fuch a fenfe venial the fynne againft the holy Ghofte , which is finall impenitēce,alonely excepted.But yfyou take venial, as it is an oppofite to mortal ,as M. Fekenhā tokeit,whē he

auou◦

Lib.13.
Cap.23.
& 24.
Lib.14.
Cap. 4.
& 9.

auouched that by a godly ceremony venial fynnes may be remitted, and as you muft take it, yf you wil cõtrary M. Fekenhams affertion, then are you in an other foule errour. For as the venial fynne is not mortal (as I haue proued) fo neither is any mortal fynne venial, as longe as it is mortall. This confounding of degrees in fynne, to make all mortall, is a Stoical and Barbarous paradoxe, opening the gate to al diffoluteneffe and licentioufneffe: not only cõtrary to truth and lerning, but cõtrary to good life and good maners. And it femeth to agree iumpe with Luthers paradoxe, wherein he taught and defended, *That a good worke, be it neuer fo wel done, is according to the mercy of God a venial finne and according to the Iudgemẽt of God a mortal finne*. Which ftraunge paradoxe of that fonde fryer beinge lernedly and pithely confuted of our learned and holie countreman the bleffed Bifhoppe of Rochefter Doctour Fyfher, I remitte the lerned Readers to that place: where alfo they fhall fynde this diftinction of mortall and veniall finne, clerely profecuted againfte the wicked doctrine of Luther there, and againft the peuifhe affertion of M. Horne here.

Roffenfis cõtra Articul. Lutheri. Art. 31. & 32. Vide & Cõcil. Trident. Seff. 6. Can. 25.

Where you adde, *by the merites of Chrifte onely*, yf you meane as by the principal effect, and by the vertue wherof only all other workes of men are auaylable and meritorious, I graũt you fay wel. But yf you fay mortal fynne is purged by the merites of Chrift only, excluding by the worde only, al repentance, contrition of harte, confefsion of the mouthe, and fatisfaction of our owne partes to our ability, I note it for an other foule errour and wicked herefye of Luther your grandfir, whereby to extolle the merites of Chrift, you doe ful peuifhly exclude al worke of mã, which yet the Scriptures expreffely require to concurre with the

merites

merits of Chriſt, not as of thē ſelues ſimply auailable, but as by the merit of Chriſtes paſsiõ, auaylable: ãd as the workes of the holy Ghoſt, geuē vnto vs by Charity poured into our harts, good ãd meritorious. Remēbre M. Horn what Chriſt ſaid to the Phariſees. *Oportebat iſta facere, & illa nõ intermittere.* You ought to doe theſe thigs, ãd notte omit the other things. Put altogether M. Horne. Chriſtes merites purchaſe heauē to mankind: It is moſt true. And yet it purchaſeth not heauē to the Infidell, to the Iewe, to the heretike, or to the wicked Chriſtiã. But õly to ſuch as haue *faith that worketh by charity*, which charity cõprehēdeth al maner of good works.

You affirme beſide againſt M. Fekenham *that no veniall ſinne can be remitted by any ceremony.* For a ſhort anſwer to this point (bicauſe largely this matter is treated by M. Allen in his laſt booke of the power of prieſthod &c.) heare what S. Auguſtin ſayth in his Enchiridio, within few chapters after the wordes laſtly recited, where he made a diſtinction betwene *crimen* and *peccatum.* Thus he ſaith. *De quotidianis autem breuibus leuibúſque peccatis, ſine quibus hæc vita non ducitur, quotidiana oratio fidelium ſatisfacit.* As cõcerning the daily, ſhort, and light ſinnes, without the which no man liueth, the daily prayer of the faithefull doth ſatisfye. By the daily prayer he meaneth the *Pater noſter*, as in the ſame chapter he expoundeth him ſelf. Againe in the next chapter he teacheth, that by all kindes of almes dedes (vnder almes dedes comprehending al good workes) ſuch venial ſins are forgeuē: Thõ he ſaith after a lõg enumeratiõ of good works. *Multa itaq, genera ſunt eleemoſynarũ, quæ cũ facim̃, adiuuamur vt dimittãtur nobis noſtra peccata.* There are therfore many kinds of almes dedes, which whē we doe, we are holpē to haue our ſins forgeuē vnto vs. Nowe why are the ſaying of our daily prayer, ãd the doïg of almes dedes, thought of this
lerned

Rom 5.

Luca. 11.

Galat. 5.

In Enchiridio c. 71. Delet omnino hæc oratio minima & quotidia-na peccata.

Cap. 72.

lerned Father to redeme thefe fmaller finnes, but bicaufe as
firch fins are not cōmitted with a total auerfiō frō God the
creatour(for fo were they mortal, not venial but by a fraile
cōuerfiō to the creature, fo again euery good motiō to God
ward again, expreffed by fome fuch vertuous act, redemeth *D. Thomas*
in the fight of God the former declinig frō God . This Re- *par. 3. q.*
uerēt motiō to Godward as it is expreffed by S. Auguftin *87. Art. 3.*
here for exāples fake, in fayig the Pater nofter, and in doing
of almes dedes, fo by the Iudgmēt of the Church, which no
true Chriftē man ought to myftruft, the fame is alfo expreffed, in kneeling, in knockig the breft, in kifsing of holy reliks,
or in any holy ceremony, don for the honour of God ād of
his Saīts, which redoūdeth to hī, for whofe fake they are ho
nored. By this M. Horn you may fhortly vnderftād, in what
fenfe the Catholiks affirme, that by a holy ceremony venial fins may be takē away. And thus the Croffe that came frō
the Iefuites to M. Feken came in a good howre. As by the
occafiō wherof, you haue difcouered vnto you fome of your
lurking herefies, ād the Catholike faith is fomwhat opened
(more perhaps thē you wold it wer)to al fuch as haue grace
to harkē thervnto.   Your farder affertiō that al mortal fyns
are alfo venial, faue ōly the fyn agaift the holy Ghoft, is the
new fcoured herefy of Wiclef, as is before touched. But fee
you not , that when ye faye there is no mortall finne , but
the finne againft the holy Ghofte , howe contrary you are
to your felfe, faying that al finnes are mortal, and yet againe
affirming there is no mortal finne at all, but one? Whereby
ye go very nere to the Pelagians herefie, taking away originall finne. For if there be no mortall finne, but the finne
againft the holy Ghofte (that is, lacke of repentance , as
Wicleff declareth) then did not Adam cōmitte any mortal
                                                           finne:

Vide Aug.
cotra Iul.
per totum.

finne:for he died penitently. And then, if he comitted no deadly finne in the tranfgreffion of Gods comaundement: he could not transfunde originall finne that fhould kill his pofteritie, which was a braunche of the Pelagian herefie.

Neither wil it helpe you to fay,that there is no fynne, fauing lacke of repentaunce , but is purged by the merits of Chrift. For the queftion is not , when we fpeake of veniall and mortall fynne, howe it may be taken away or forgeuen,but what payne and penalty eche of his owne nature deferueth.Venial fynne deferueth no other payne,then temporal paine. Mortal finne deferueth euerlafting paine.

But here is no place , exactly to difcuffe thefe matters. And I haue faied this onely,to fhew,what a fort of errours and herefies ye wrap vp with the clofing of your boke:and that if it were but for theis only, M.Fekenham might haue called you , and that iuftly in plaine termes (without any almoft)an heretike. As for M.Iewel, if M.Fekenham faid(as ye fay he fayd)that he fhould neuer be able to anfwere M. Doctour Hardings boke,he faid nothing but truth : which doth well appere to any indifferent Reader, by the labours of thofe that haue confuted already the ftronger, the greater,and the more important partes of his Reply : and haue alredy difcried about one thowfand of manifeft errours and lies in him . To what number then , thinke you, will they mufter, if a whole confutation of all the remnant fhould come forthe ?

Here would nowe fomewhat be faied to your anfwere, concerning the rumour of M.Fekenhams fubfcription and recantation:and I fuppofe if I knewe the whole circuftance of the matter,I might eafely confute al your anfwere therin.And yet as ftraunge as ye make your felf to that rumour

or anie

or any knowledge therof, a man may wel gather, and go no
further then your owne booke, that your selfe miniſtred
great occaſion of ſuche rumours: as telling him ſo often in
your anſwere, *of the feare of reuolte that his frendes had in*
him: with the whiche alſo you ende your anſwere. In tel- Fol. 2.
ling of him, *that he ſemed to be reſolucd, and in a maner fully* Fol. 130.
ſatisfied at your hands. And that *ye made relation thereof to*
certaine honourable perſons: and finally, that your ſelfe do Fol. 128.
plainely here confeſſe, that ye ſayed, *that M. Feken-*
ham had chaunged his Religion nine tymes, yea nintene ty-
mes. But theſe matters I will leaue: as alſo your vnkinde
and vngentle dealing with him: and your complaintes
againſte him, contrary to your promiſſe: and will nowe
onely put your Reader in remembramce, of the Ieſuites,
whome ye call *monkiſhe Iebuſites*, and pray him withall
well to conſider the order and trade of theire lyues, and
doctrine, yea the glorioufe iſſewe that hath and daylie
doth followe thereof, comparing them with the doinges
and doctrine of you and your fellowes. And then I doubte
not, but he will thinke, that this is nothing but vile and
wicked rayling in you, to call them Iebuſites, and that in The Ie-
compariſon to you, and your ghoſpelling bretherne, they ſuites.
may be counted lyuing angells. Yf the profeſſion of a religiouſe and a monaſtical life deſerue in them this contume-
ly and reproche at your handes, then may ye call S. Baſil,
S. Hierome, S. Auguſtine, S. Chryſoſtome, S. Gregory our
Apoſtle, with Ruffinus, Epiphanius, Paulinus, Caſsianus,
and a nūber of other auncient and godly Fathers Iebuſites to. And ſee ye not M. Horne, howe this your blaſphemie doth not redounde to thoſe Fathers onely, but euen
to our Sauiour Chriſte Ieſus him ſelfe, whoſe name they
beare,

See more
of this in
the For٤
treffe an﹐
nexed to
Vener,
Bede. Fol.
73. & feq.
beare , and whofe fteppes they moft diligently and moft
erneftly do followe, afwel by a vertuoufe auftere lyfe, as by
paineful preaching? Which their trauaile our Sauiour Iefus
hath fo profpered and bleffed, that your newe Apoftle Luther hath not brought fo many Chriftian foules by his poyfoned herefie to deftruction and damnation in Europa : as
they haue brought Panyms, Mores, ād Turks many a thoufand mile from Europa , from Paganifme to the catholike
faith, from the which we haue departed and runne awaye
hedlong.

Mark the
proui﹣
dence of
God.
Neither can I either to much thinke vpon , or to much,
prayfe the wonderfull prouidence of God in this behalfe.
For euen as a thoufand yeares fithence, the Chriftian Empire, and faith beganne to decay in Afia and Afrike by curfed Mahomete, caufed the decayed faith, againe to fpringe
and take roote in the weft parte of the worlde : as namely
among vs in England, and afterward among the Germans,
the Bulgarians, the Polonians, the Hungarians, the Danes,
Parte.1.
Cap.16.
fol.71.
& fequen.
the Prufsians, the Lituanians, and among a number of other
nations, as I haue in the Fortreffe annexed to the hiftory
of Bede declared : fo nowe in the latter daies the Empire
of Conftantinople becomming Turkifhe, and in our daies a
great part of our owne Europa, being (the more pity) caried
away with errours and herefies, God hath of his wonderful
mercy and goodnes, in mans remembrance, opened and re-
ueled to vs, as it were a newe world, of the which neither
by writing nor otherwife, we euer heard any thing before.
And which is a caufe of deper and more ample thankes, he
hath by his prouidence fo ordeyned, that the fayd coūtries
befide in Afia and Aphꞌica are become of plaine and open
Idolatours, of Mores and Sarazens, very good Chriftians: ād
that

that cheifly by the great helpe and trauaile, of thefe bleſſed
and vertuouſe Iefuites, whom you ſo lewdly cal Iebuſites.
By whom alſo God hath ſhewed ſuch wonders and miracles, as the hearing or reading of them, were to any good
Chriſtian heart of al things moſt comfortable. And ſuerly if
a man would deaply and throughly weigh and conſider the
greatnes of this benefite, he might wel doubt, whether after the creation of the world and the redemption of mankind by the paſsion of Chriſt, there be any one benefitte or
worke of God, more wonderful then this: or whether there
be anie one ſtate or vocation in Chriſtes Church, after the
Apoſtles, more worthie laude and prayſe then theſe, that
you ſo vilanouſly call Iebuſites. So filthely your blaſphemous mouth can raile againſt Gods truth. No no, M. Horn,
theſe be no Iebuſites. The Iebuſites be the curſed ſede of
Cham, curſed of Noe their father for diſhonouring of him. *Geneſ.9.*
Ye, ye are the Iebuſites, that the celeſtiall father with his
owne mouth, hath curſed for making his Spowſe your mother an idolatrouſe ſtrompet and harlet. Whome the bleſſed Ieſuites, as good graciouſe children, honour and reuerence. Who worthely beare that name alſo, theire workes
being correſpondent to theire name, which doth ſignifie a
Sauiour.   For they, by their preaching haue ſaued, and
brought from damnation many an hundred thouſand of
ſoules, to the euerlaſting bliſſe of heauen, the which God of
his goodnes and mercie graunt vnto vs.   Amen.

F I N I S.

Laus Deo, qui dedit velle,
& dedit perficere.

A TABLE OF THE PRINCIPAL
MATTERS AND PERSONS IN THIS
booke debated, or otherwise contayned . The
figure noteth the leafe. a. and. b. the
first and second side.
(?¿?)

THE TABLE.

 Cons

THE TABLE.

THE TABLE.

yyyy   Mar‑

THE TABLE.

THE TABLE.

THE TABLE.

THE TABLE.

Faultes escaped in the Printing.

Leaf	Syde	Lyne	Faulte	Correction.
15.	1.	In the Margent	Aene.Pius	Aeneas Syluius.
32.	1.	In the Margent	vvordes	vvardes
40.	2.	1.	The.9.	The.8.
,	2.	In the Margent	Pſal.98.	Auguſt.in Pſal.98.
68.	2.	25.	the	for the
75.	2.	2.	Emanuel	Andronicus.
105.	1.	32. In the Margent put:		An.25.Hen.8.cap.19.
109.	2.	27.	σ ωκἤδ'κ	σ ωκἤδ'κ
149	2.	31. In the Margent.	Vniuerſal Biſhop.	Put it out.
152.	1.	1.	yt	yet

* Special, lie to be correcſted *

Leaf	Syde	Lyne	Faulte	Correction.
194.	1.	19.	neither	though
		20.	vvith diligence	Yet not vvith ſuch diligēce
206.	1.	24.	ἑτέρɑς ἐδ'ιχτιϱδν,	ἑτέροις ἐπιχτιϱεῖν,

The vvhole ſentence in ſome Copies is quite leaſt vnprinted, vvhich is this,
ἑτέρɑ δ'ιἐπτιν]ɑχϑἐν]ɑς, ἑτέροις ἐπιχτιϱεῖν.

Leaf	Syde	Lyne	Faulte	Correction.
227	2.	In the Margent.	Romano	Miſſa Romana.
232.	1.	In the Margent	Beda in marty rologio.	In martyrologio Beda, ſeu in additionibus ad idem.
234.	1.	In the margent.	To the allegation, ſet.	Platina in Adriano.1.
241.	1.	31. In the Margēt	dixerit:	direxit.
246	1.	23.	his	this
262	1.	5.	buſyed	being buſyed
282.	2.	7.	Emperours	vvriters.
249	2.	In the margent.	Guil. Hunting.	Henr.Hungtingt.
303	1.	In the margent.	Epiſt.	Epiſt.195.
310.	1.	31. In the Margēt	aſcrib.	aſcribendum.
321.	1.	27.	an	and.
355.	1.	In the margent.	c.2.	cap.12.
Ibidem		In the margent.	487.	497.
429	2.	8.	not	contrary not.
380.	1.	In the toppe of the page	1550.	1150.
	2.	In the margent.	mandatio.	mendacio.